Catharina Day

IRELAND

'The purples of the mountains melt into
chessboards of cornfields, in which the
stooks stand like golden pieces. Houses are
whitewashed, glens are deep and the coastline
is made ragged by the force of the Atlantic,
with sandy bays and rocky cliffs.'

CADOGANguides

Contents

About the author

Catharina Day comes from a long-established Irish family. She was born in Kenya but moved to County Donegal as a small child. She attended school in Ireland, and then went to university in England. She was married in County Donegal, and visits frequently with her husband and four children from her home in Scotland. She has compiled an anthology of Irish literature. (Acknowledgements can be found after the Index.)

About the updater

Amy Corzine grew up in Texas. Thirty years ago she went to Ireland to study its folklore, after discovering that it was the source of many of the fairytales she loved as a child. Subsequently she studied theatre in London, where she now works as an editor and writer. She is author of Cadogan's forthcoming publication, *Take the Kids: Ireland*.

Cadogan Guides
Network House, 1 Ariel Way, London W12 7SL
cadoganguides@morrispub.co.uk
www.cadoganguides.com

The Globe Pequot Press
246 Goose Lane, PO Box 480, Guilford,
Connecticut 06437–0480

Copyright © Catharina Day 1990, 1993, 1995,
1998, 2002
Updated by Amy Corzine 2002

Cover and photo essay design by Kicca Tommasi
Book design by Andrew Barker
Cover photographs: © Alex Robinson
Maps © Cadogan Guides, drawn by Map Creation
Ltd. Based on Ordnance Survey Ireland Permit
No. 7517 © Ordnance Survey Ireland and
Government of Ireland
Editorial Director: Vicki Ingle
Series Editor: Christine Stroyan
Editor: Joss Waterfall
Editorial Assistance: Georgina Palffy, Nick Rider,
Linda McQueen, Tori Perrot
Art direction: Jodi Louw
Designer: Tracey Ridgewell
Indexing: Isobel McLean
Production: Book Production Services

Printed in Italy by Legoprint
A catalogue record for this book is available
from the British Library
ISBN 1-86011-865-8

Ireland
a photo essay

by Alex Robinson

01

Aran Islands, Co. Galway

Giant's Causeway, Co. Antrim

dry stone wall, the Burren, Co. Clare

Gougane Barra, Co. Cork

Kenmare, Co. Kerry

bar life, Dublin

potter's workshop, Co. Cork

Atlantic Drive, Co. Mayo

Connemara, Co. Galway

Republican and Loyalist murals, Belfast

graveyard, Co. Mayo

Lough Doo, Co. Mayo

boat maintenance, Kinvarra, Co. Galway

Dingle Peninsula, Co. Kerry

Ring of Kerry

clochans, Co. Kerry

Rock of Cashel, Co. Tipperary

Kenmare, Co. Kerry

Crown Liquor Saloon, Belfast

Clonmacnoise, Co. Offaly

Georgian door, Dublin

City Hall, Dublin

Birr Castle Gardens, Co. Offaly

Ballybunion, Co. Kerry

About the photographer
Alex Robinson has taken pictures for various broadsheets and broadcasters, travelling in Asia, Latin America, Europe and Australia. He now lives between the UK and Rio.

Introduction

Ireland is the perfect place to take a holiday. This lovely island has physical and spiritual qualities that are seldom found in the Western World. The pace of life is relaxing, the scenery beautiful and varied, with the sea never far from sight. Dublin, the capital, is cultured, attractive and easy to explore. The people of the country are easy to meet and invariably courteous and friendly. The climate is good and, though it's often damp, when the sunshine comes in soft shards it intensifies the already beautiful colours of the landscape. Forget sun culture and all its paraphernalia; travel with stout shoes and a warm jersey.

There is no such thing as a tiresome, hot journey in Ireland. Country roads are usually empty, and traffic jams are still an exception in most places. Some visitors bent on 'doing' Ireland get from one end of the country to the other in a day's drive, but this is not the way to travel at all. If you rush, the charm of the country and the people will pass you by, and the Irish do not approve of rushing.

Whatever direction you decide to go in, it is possible to stay in tranquil country houses, where the proportions and furnishings of the rooms are redolent of a more gracious age. Not only is the food delicious – fresh seafood, local meats, game and vegetables – you can also taste well-chosen wines and, of course, decent whiskey and beer. You will find the owners and staff of these places keen to help with any request you have, whether it's finding the origins of your great-granny, or directing you to the best fishing, golf, beaches, crafts and sites of historical interest.

It is so easy to travel in a country where you can explain your needs in English, and find yourself understood. Dry archaeological and historical facts suddenly become much more fascinating when you can ask for the local version of events, and hear for yourself the wonderful stories that make up history. Hearing the sound of spoken Irish is another pleasure that's in store. You'll discover a race who can express themselves with great character, humour and precision.

When you're in Ireland, it is certain that the irritations and annoyances which can accompany one through everyday life will disappear, and your desires for a good day's walking in the mountains, a spot of fishing or a good read before a warm fire will be become realities. However, it is important not to stick rigidly to a plan and become irritated when it has to be delayed, for nothing in Ireland can be planned right down to the last detail. Sometimes information can only be found out on the spot, since opening times, timetables and other schedules tend to be more subject to change than in other countries.

Ireland remains largely agricultural, with relatively few areas of industrial development. There are few huge motorways, endless suburbs, belching factories, marching powerlines, and little of the ugly side-effects of industry. Hopefully, the Irish will ensure things stay that way. Its population is relatively small, at about five million, and the Six Counties which form part of the United Kingdom make up 1,556,000 of that total. The differences between the Six Counties, colloquially referred to as 'the North', and the Republic of Ireland, 'the South', are explored in the 'History' section later in the guide, and will become apparent as you read the chapter on each county.

For years there has been a commonly held misconception that it was dangerous to travel in the North. Violence was confined to very small areas and no tourist has even been harmed by the Troubles within Ireland. Sensible, unprejudiced travellers will soon discover that, with the exception of a few well-known areas, the North is a quiet, unspoilt and attractive region. If your sympathy for the ordinary people of the province and your admiration for their courage and forbearance has been stirred by their problems, one of the most positive things you can do is visit the province itself.

Both North and South share a fascinating past; as Yeats wrote, 'Behind all Irish history hangs a great tapestry even Christianity had to accept, and be itself pictured there.' The Irish race has a long memory and a poetic imagination, which gives each hill, lough and pile of stones a background or story. The history of Ireland has been turbulent, and its telling fraught with prejudice and misunderstandings. But it is fascinating to approach it through its literary tradition. Ireland had its Golden Age of learning roughly between the 6th and 11th centuries; Frank O'Connor described it as the civilization of 'the little monasteries'. Monks transcribed the Celtic oral culture, wrote poetry and honoured God during the Dark Ages, when the rest of the Continent was in the hands of the Barbarians.

Ireland also had a strict bardic tradition, according to which members of the poets' guild had to study for up to 12 years before they were qualified. From that disciplined environment came mature poetry as evocative and delicate as poetry from China: stirring epics such as *The Tain*, which chronicles the wars of a heroic race, and moving love laments. Most of us can only read these poems in translation from the Gaelic, but luckily the translators, often present-day Irish poets, bring them close to us. From the 18th century, the ability of the Irish to express themselves in the language of the Saxon is apparent from the works of Jonathan Swift through to W. B. Yeats and the marvellous poets of today, such as Seamus Heaney. Poetry, theatre and the novel have continued to thrive since the heady days of Ireland's cultural renaissance and the uprising against the British in 1916; arts and music festivals flourish throughout the country today. Go if you can to the Abbey Theatre in Dublin or the Druid Theatre in Galway to see a play by Sean O'Casey or Brian Friel. Arts and music festivals flourish throughout the country.

Modern Ireland conjures up a romantic idyll of whitewashed cottages set against a mountain landscape, and in places, this is still possible to find. But much has changed; many technological companies have been attracted to the country's highly educated young population, and have brought wealth, prosperity and transformation to the land. As a traveller in Ireland you will be able to enjoy all the conveniences of modern-day Europe and still lose yourself in its wilderness and beauty.

By the end of your holiday, you may feel tuned in to the country and its people to the point where that famous saying can be aired yet again: that (the English) are more Irish than the Irish themselves: *Ipsis Hibernis hiberniores*.

A Note on Names

You will find that there are occasions when place names vary in spelling from those in this guide book. This is because different translations from the Gaelic exist, and there is no completely standardized map to follow. Bartholomews, Ordnance Survey, the RAC and the AA produce very good and detailed maps.

The Gaeltacht

This is the name given to several areas in Ireland where (Irish) Gaelic is spoken as the everyday language. These areas are mainly in the West, in Counties Donegal, Mayo, Galway and Kerry. You can expect all the signposts to be in Irish.

A Guide to the Guide

After a brief **Introduction** to this island and its people, and a selection of the Best of Ireland, there is a **History** from pagan times, which outlines the main events and problems that constitute the complex Ireland of today. This is followed by a brief résumé of the **religious** background and a selection of the country's most famous saints. Next are features on the **Old Gods and Heroes**, and ancient sites and early architecture in **From Stone Circles to Castles**. The next section, **Topics**, gives brief insights into notable features of Ireland and Irish life. These include some fascinating pieces on the Fairy People and Historic Houses and Gardens, and useful information for genealogists in 'Trace your Ancestors'. Then there is a comprehensive and important **Travel** section followed by the **Practical A–Z**. This is packed with information that will help you get the best from your visit, including advice on where to stay and eat, sports and leisure activities.

The 32 counties are divided into the provinces of **Munster**, **Connacht**, **Ulster** and **Leinster**, with Belfast and Dublin featuring separately from the rest of the counties. This constitutes a gazetteer of the whole country with lots of local history and anecdotal knowledge together with descriptions and details of the places of interest. Full, practical lists of transport facilities, tourist information centres and festivals are given at the beginning of each county section in grey boxes. Where counties are divided into smaller areas, then the listings for shopping and leisure activities, places to stay and eat and entertainment are found in grey boxes near to each area's heading (e.g. 'The Ards Peninsula' in County Antrim).

At the end of the book there is an essay on **Language**; a **Glossary** of archaeological, architectural and associated terms; a brief **Chronology**; a recommended **Further Reading** list; and a comprehensive **Index**.

Chapter Divisions

80 km
50 miles

N

Atlantic

Ocean

North Channel

Derry

NORTHERN

IRELAND

Belfast

Donegal

13
ULSTER

Sligo

Irish

Sea

12
CONNACHT

R E P U B L I C

Galway

Dublin

14
LEINSTER

O F

Wicklow

I R E L A N D

Limerick

11
MUNSTER

Wexford

Waterford

St. George's Channel

Cork

Celtic

Sea

The Best of Ireland

Art galleries: The Glebe Gallery, Co. Donegal; National Gallery, Dublin; Crawford
Gallery, Cork; Chester Beatty, Dublin.

Beaches: There are many beautiful, unspoilt strands; in particular, Portsalon,
Co. Donegal; Magilligan, Co. Londonderry; Keel, Achill Island, Co. Mayo; Inch, Co. Kerry;
Streedagh, Co. Sligo; Ballyconneely, Co. Galway; White Strand and Spanish Point,
Co. Clare; White Park Bay, Co. Antrim.

Carved high crosses: Moone, Co. Kildare; Cardonagh, Co. Donegal.

Castles: Carrickfergus and Dunluce Castles, Co. Antrim; Parke's Castle, Co. Leitrim;
Cahir Castle, Co. Tipperary; Trim Castle, Co. Meath; Doe Castle, Co. Donegal.

Craft Shops: Ballycasey Workshops, Co. Tipperary; Nicholas Mosse Pottery,
Bennetsbridge, Co. Kilkenny; Craft Park, Roundstone, Co. Galway.

Equestrian events: Dublin Horse Show; Ulster Harp National; Galway Races.

Festivals: Wexford Opera Festival; Kilkenny Arts Week; Galway Film Festival;
Galway Oyster Festival; Belfast Arts Festival; Dublin Drama Festival;
Feis na nGleann, Co. Antrim; Music Festival in Great Irish Houses; Willie Clancy
Summer School, Co. Clare, Puck Fair, Co. Kerry; Boley Fair, South Down.

Fine houses: Castletown, Co. Kildare; Bantry Bay House, Co. Cork; Castle Coole,
Co. Fermanagh.

Folk parks: Cultra Park, Co. Down; Bunratty, Co. Clare; Ulster American Folk Park,
Co. Tyrone.

Gardens: Birr Castle, Co. Offaly; Mountstewart, Co. Down; Annestown, Co. Cork;
Glenveagh, Co. Donegal.

Golf courses: Bundoran; the Royal County Down, Newcastle; Royal Portrush;
Portmarnock; Lahinch; Ballybunion; Killarney; Galway City; Rosses Point;
Portsalon, Co. Donegal.

Landscapes: Most of the coastal and mountain stretches of Connacht, especially
between Westport and Clifden; views from the top of Croagh Patrick; and Achill
Island. Wild bog between Mulrany and Bangor Erris; coastal and mountain stretches
in Co. Donegal, especially from Lough Salt and from the top of Muckish Mountain.
The Antrim Coast, the Burren, Bantry Bay, Knockmealdown Mountains, the Ring of
Kerry, the Sperrin Mountains.

Museums: Ulster; National Museum, Dublin.

Pubs: Dick Macks, Dingle; Mary Anne's, Castletownshend; Crown Liquor Saloon,
Belfast; The Stag's Head, Dublin; Rita's, Portsalon; Moran's on the Weir, Clarinbridge;
Rotterdam Bar, Belfast.

Round towers: Glendalough, Co. Wicklow; Devenish Island, Co. Fermanagh;
Ardmore, Co. Waterford.

Ruined friaries and churches: Cong, Co. Mayo; Killaloe, Co. Clare; Dysert O'Dea,
Co. Clare; Clonfert Cathedral, Co. Galway; Moyne, Co. Mayo.

Unusual activities: Seaweed baths, Enniscrone; Sham Fight, Scarva; hurling matches
anywhere in Ireland; Donegal Motor Rally; Puck Fair, Killorgin; Lammas Fair,
Ballycastle; visit to Doon Well, Co. Donegal; Lough Derg Gourmet Ride.

History

I found in Munster, unfettered of any
Kings and queens, and poets a many –
Poets well skilled in music and measure,
Prosperous doings, mirth and pleasure.
I found in Connaught the just, redundance
Of riches, milk in lavish abundance;
Hospitality, vigour, fame,
In Cruachan's land of heroic name
I found in Ulster, from hill to glen,
Hardy warriors, resolute men;
Beauty that bloomed when youth was gone,
And strength transmitted from sire to son.
I found in Leinster the smooth and sleek,
From Dublin to Slewmargy's peak;
Flourishing pastures, valour, health,
Long-living worthies, commerce, wealth.

from *Prince Alfrid's Itinerary*
(version by James Clarence Mangan)

If you happen to fall into conversation with an Irishman in a bar, the subjects of religion and politics are bound to arise. With luck you'll have a cool glass of Guinness in your hand, for discussions on Ireland are inevitably emotional. The Irish are good talkers and have very long memories, so it's worth having some idea of their history.

Many of Ireland's troubles have stemmed from her geographical situation; too far from Britain to be assimilated, too near to be allowed to be separate. Queen Elizabeth I poured troops into the country because she appreciated the strategic importance of Ireland to her enemies. Over the centuries Ireland has been offered help in her fight for independence, but it was never disinterested help; whoever paid for arms and fighting men in Ireland wanted to further their own military, political, religious or ideological cause. France in the late 18th century supplied arms to Ireland to distract England from other policies; and in Northern Ireland the IRA were supplied with some guns by foreign powers. Most recently, over 30 years of European Union (EU) membership has paid dividends for Ireland. The economic disparity with the UK has narrowed considerably, and Ireland has gained in self-confidence in a union where the centre of power is not London, but Brussels. The shared economics of EU membership are helping to undermine political and religious differences.

General History

Pre-Celtic Ireland

The hills and river valleys are scattered with ancient monuments dating from the Stone, Bronze and Iron Ages. Most of them have some kind of religious significance, and they have been swathed in romance and heroism by the Celtic story-tellers or *shanachies* in the cottages and castles. Unfortunately only a few of these traditional oracles survive today as 'memory men'.

The earliest record of man in Ireland is dated to between 8,700 and 8,600 years ago, as deduced from fragments found at a camp in **Mount Sandel** near Coleraine. The people of this time lived a nomadic life, hunting and trapping; they could not move around very easily as the countryside was covered by forest, interrupted only by lakes and rivers. They used *curragh* boats, similar to the ones used today by fishermen in the west of Ireland, and built lake-dwellings, or *crannógs*. No one is sure where these people came from but they had the island to themselves for 3,000 years. Then came **Neolithic** man, who was perhaps the **Fir Bolg** of Celtic mythology: at this stage everything is very vague. These people were farmers and gradually spread over the whole of Ireland, clearing the forest as best they could with their stone tools. They evidently practised burial rites, for they built chambered tombs of a very sophisticated quality, decorated with spirals and lozenge shapes. For example, the Great Burial Chamber at Newgrange in the Boyne Valley, which dates from 2500 BC, has a chamber large enough to contain thousands of cremated bodies. These people must have been very well organized, with the energy and wealth to spare for such an ambitious project – similar in its way to the pyramids, and a thousand years older.

Around 2000 BC yet another race appeared, who were skilled miners and metal-workers. They were called the **Beaker People**, or the **Tuatha Dé Danaan**, as they are known in legend. They opened up copper mines and started to trade with Brittany, the Baltic and the Iberian Peninsula. They had different beliefs about burial: their dead were buried singly in graves lined with stone slabs and covered with a capstone. Other peoples with different burial habits and funeral rituals also arrived at this time, though it is not clear in what order they arrived, or to what extent they intermingled. They are named after objects associated with their culture, hence we have Bowl Food Vessel People, Urn People and Vase Food Vessel People. There are a thousand chambered graves, ring-shaped cairns, standing stones, rows and circles of stones left from these times, concentrated in the Boyne Valley; they hint at various rituals and, it has been suggested, at observations of the stars. They are often called 'fairy stones', and the chambered graves have been nicknamed 'Dermot and Grania's bed'.

The Celts

The first arrival of the Celts cannot be precisely dated; a few may have come as early as 900 BC, though the main waves of Celtic invaders occurred between 700 BC and 400 BC. These people had iron weapons and defeated the Beakers, whose legendary magical powers were no defence against the new metal. Known as the **Celts** or **Gaels**, the new invaders had spread from southern Germany, across France, and as far south as Spain. Today everybody in Ireland has pride in the 'Celtic' past: epic tales sing the praises of men and women who were capable of heroic and superhuman deeds, and their beautiful gold jewellery is carefully preserved as proof of their achievements. The Celts brought to Ireland a highly organized social structure, and the La Tène style of decoration (its predominant motif is a spiral or a whorl). Ireland was divided into different clans with three classes: the **free**, who were warriors and owned land and cattle; the **professionals**, such as the jurists, Druids, musicians, story-tellers and poets, who could move freely between the petty kingdoms; and, finally, the **slaves**. Every clan had a petty king, who was under the authority of a high king at Tara, Co. Meath.

The Gaels made use of many of the customs and mythology that had existed before their arrival, so their 'Celtic' civilization represented a unique mix. They were also very fortunate, for although they were probably displaced themselves by the expanding **Roman Empire**, once they got to Ireland they were protected to some extent by England, which acted as a buffer state. The Romans never extended their ambitions to conquering Ireland, so the Gaels were able to develop their traditions, unlike Celts elsewhere in Europe. They spent most of their time raiding their neighbours for cattle and women, who were used as live currency. In their religion, the human head was all-important as a symbol of divinity and supernatural power – even when severed from the body it would still retain its power. Warriors used to take the heads of slain enemies and display them in front of their houses. The Gaels also believed firmly in an afterlife, and would lend each other money to be repaid in the next world.

The Arrival of Christianity

Christianity was brought to Ireland in the 5th century AD by **St Patrick**, and quickly became accepted by the kings. **Cormac MacArt**, who ruled in Tara about a century and a half before St Patrick arrived, had already seen the light and told his court of Druids and nobles that the gods they worshipped were only craven wood. The Druids put a curse on him and soon afterwards he choked to death on a salmon bone; just before he died he ordered that he was not to be buried in the tomb of Brugh (Newgrange) but on the sunny east point by the River Rosnaree. When St Patrick lit a fire which signalled the end of Druid worship, legend has it that he was looking down from the Hill of Slane on to Rosnaree. The Christians skilfully reconciled their practices and beliefs with those of the pagans; a famous saying of St Columba was, 'Christ is my Druid'. The early Christians seem to have been very ascetic, building their monasteries in wild and inaccessible places. You can still see their hive-shaped dwellings on **Skellig Michael**, a windswept rocky island off the Kerry coast. The Irish monasteries became renowned for their scholarship throughout Europe, which was submerged in the Dark Ages, and produced beautiful manuscripts like the famous *Book of Kells*.

The Viking Invasion

The tranquillity of Ireland, 'land of saints and scholars', was brutally interrupted by the arrival of the **Vikings** or **Norsemen**. They were able to penetrate right into Ireland through their skilful use of the rivers and lakes. They struck for the first time in 795, but this was only the start of a 300-year struggle. Much treasure from the palaces and monasteries was plundered, for the buildings had no defences, so the monks built round towers in which to store their precious things at the first sign of trouble. Eventually the Norsemen began to settle down; they founded the first city-ports – Dublin, Wexford and Waterford – and started to trade with the Gaels. Military alliances were made between Celts and Vikings whenever it helped a particular native king in the continuous struggle for the high kingship. After a short period of relative calm another wave of Norsemen invaded and the plundering began again; but **Brian Boru**, who had usurped the high kingship from the O'Connors, defeated the Vikings at Clontarf in 1014 and broke their power permanently. Unfortunately for the Gaelic people, Brian Boru was murdered by some Vikings in his tent just after the victory at Clontarf. Havoc and in-fighting became a familiar pattern, as the high kingship was fought for by the O'Briens, the O'Loughlins (or O'Loghlens) and the O'Connors. The Gaelic warriors wasted themselves and their people, because no single leader seemed strong enough to rule without opposition. The next invaders saw that their opportunity lay in the disunity of the Irish.

The Norman Invasion and Consolidation

In the mid-12th century the Pope gave his blessing to an expedition of **Anglo-Normans** sent by **Henry II** to Ireland. The Normans were actually invited over by the King of Leinster, **Dermot MacMurragh**, who had made a bitter enemy of **Tiernan O'Rourke** of Breffni by running off with his wife, Devorgilla. He also backed the wrong horse in the high kingship stakes, and the united efforts of the High King Rory O'Connor and O'Rourke brought about a huge reduction in MacMurragh's kingdom. So he approached Henry II, offering his oath of fealty in exchange for an invasion force of men with names like Fitzhenry, Carew, Fitzgerald and Barry – names you still see in Irish villages. The Normans were adventurers and good warriors: in 1169 several Norman nobles decided to try their luck in Ireland, and found it easy to grab huge tracts of land for themselves. The Gaels had faced so few attacks from outside their country that they were unprepared for battle – yet although their weapons were inferior, they had the advantages of greater numbers and a deep knowledge of the countryside. The Normans had a well-equipped cavalry who rode protected by a screen of archers. Once they had launched a successful attack, they consolidated their position by building moats, castles and walled towns. **Strongbow**, one of the most powerful of the Norman invaders, married MacMurragh's daughter and became his heir, but his successes and those of the other Norman barons worried Henry II. In 1171 Henry arrived in Ireland with 4,000 men and two objectives: to secure the submission of the Irish leaders and to impose his authority on his own barons. He achieved both aims, but the Gaelic lords still went on fighting. In fact, the coming of the Normans began a military struggle which was to continue over four centuries.

The Bruce Invasion

In 1314 **Robert Bruce of Scotland** decisively defeated English forces at Bannockburn, and was in a position to try and fulfil his dream of a united Celtic kingdom by putting his brother **Edward** on the throne in Ireland. At first his invasion was successful, but he left a trail of destruction behind him. The year 1316 was marked by famine and disease exacerbated by the war. His dream brought economic and social disaster to Ireland, and when Edward Bruce was defeated and killed at Dundalk, few of his allies mourned his death. The Normans' control fluctuated within an area surrounding Dublin known as the Pale, and they became rather independent of their English over-lord; in some cases, such as the de Burgos (Burkes), they became more Irish than the

Irish. In the north and west the Gaelic lords continued to hold their territories. To do so they imported Scottish mercenary soldiers, called **gallowglasses**, who prolonged the life of the independent Gaelic kingdoms for more than two centuries after the defeat of Edward Bruce.

The Nine Years' War: Elizabethan Conquest and Settlement

Ever since the Norman invasion, Ireland had been ruined by continual fighting. By the late 16th century, **Queen Elizabeth I** was determined to bring the Irish more firmly under English control, especially the Ulster lords who had so far maintained almost total independence. Elizabeth took over the Irish policy of her father which had never been fully implemented; her government decided that all the Gaelic lords must surrender their lands to the Crown, whereupon they would be regranted immediately. At this time Ulster, today the stronghold of Protestantism, was the most Gaelic and Catholic part of Ireland, and it was from here that the great **Hugh O'Neill** and **Red Hugh O'Donnell** launched a last-ditch struggle against Elizabeth. Initial successes bolstered the rebels' morale. Elizabeth, recognizing the gravity of the situation, sent over her talented favourite soldier, the Earl of Essex. Most of his troops died from disease and guerrilla attacks, and with no reinforcements he had little alternative other than to make a truce with O'Neill. Disgrace and execution were his reward. In February 1600 Lord Mountjoy arrived in Ireland with 20,000 troops. Risings at Munster were crushed, and with them the aspirations of Connacht and Leinster. The Gaelic chiefs were ruthless in their allegiances. They had hailed O'Neill as Prince of Ireland but now, anticipating defeat, they deserted him. O'Neill's hopes were raised by the long-promised arrival of Spanish troops at Kinsale in 1601, but they only numbered 4,000. When they did do battle against Mountjoy, the Irish were left confused when the Spaniards failed to sally out as arranged.

The Flight of the Earls

O'Neill returned to Ulster on 23 March 1603 and made his submission to Mountjoy, only to learn in Dublin later that Queen Elizabeth had died the very next day. He is said to have wept with rage. Amongst all the nobles, only he might have been able to unite the Irish and beat Elizabeth. O'Neill had his titles and lands returned to him, but the Dublin government, greedy for his property, began to bait him. It took his land at the slightest excuse and forbade him to practise Catholicism; abandoning hope and his followers, he sailed to Europe. This 'Flight of the Earls' took place on 14 September 1607, from the wild and beautiful shores of the Swilly. It symbolizes the end of Gaelic leadership and a new period of complete domination by the English. The Irish lords took themselves off to the courts of France and Spain or into the foreign armies. They had spent most of their energies warring among themselves, and at the last moment deserted their country, and left the Irish peasants with no leadership.

The Confederation, Cromwell and the Stuarts

By the 1640s, Ireland was ready for rebellion again – there were plenty of grievances. **James I**, a staunch Protestant, dispossessed many Gaelic and old English families in

Ireland because they would not give up Catholicism, and he began the '**plantation**' of the most vehemently Catholic province, Ulster, with Protestant settlers. Previous plantations had not worked because of inclement weather, but James knew the Scots could skip about the bogs as well as the Irish. When **Charles Stuart** came to the throne, many Catholic families hoped that they might be given some religious freedom and retain their estates, but nothing was legally confirmed. In 1633 **Black Tom**, the Earl of Strafford, arrived with the intention of making Ireland a source of profit rather than loss to the king. In his zeal to do so he succeeded in alienating every element in Irish society. His enemies amongst the Puritans in Ireland and England put pressure on the king to recall him and he was eventually executed. English politics became dominated by the dissension between the Roundheads and the Cavaliers and the hopeless Irish took note. Their maxim was 'England's difficulty is Ireland's opportunity'. Charles attempted to deal with the growing unrest in Ireland by giving everybody what they wanted, but he no longer had enough power to see that his laws were carried out. The Gaelic Irish decided to take a chance and rebel; many of them came back from the Continental armies hoping to win back their old lands. In October 1641 a small Gaelic force took over the whole of Ulster and there were widespread uprisings in Leinster. In Ulster, the Gaelic people had been burning for revenge and the new planted families suffered terribly. This cruel treatment has never been forgotten by Ulster Protestants.

The Dublin government was worse than useless at controlling the rebels, who continued to be successful. While the government waited for reinforcements from England, they managed to antagonize the old English, because they made the mistake of presuming that they would be disloyal to the Crown, and so viewed them with suspicion. The old English families decided to throw in their lot with the rebels since they were already considered traitors, but on one condition: a declaration of loyalty from the Gaelic leaders to the (Catholic) English crown, which was now seriously threatened by the Puritans.

The Confederation of Kilkenny

By February 1642 most of Ireland was in rebel hands. The rebels established a provisional government at **Kilkenny**, and Charles began to negotiate with them, hoping to gain their support against the Puritans. Things were too good to last. The destructive factors that have ruined many Irish uprisings, before and since, came into play: personal jealousy and religion. The old English were loyal to the king and wanted a swift end to the war; the Gaelic Irish were only interested in retrieving their long-lost lands and were ready to fight to the bitter end. This disunity was exacerbated by the rivalry between the Gaelic commander, **Owen Roe O'Neill**, and the commander of the old English army, **Thomas Preston**. In October 1645 the Papal Nuncio arrived and the unity of the Confederates was further split: he and O'Neill took an intransigent stand over the position of the Catholic Church, to which Charles I could not agree.

The rebels won a magnificent victory over the Puritan General Munro at Benburb, but O'Neill did not follow it up. The confederates, torn by disunity and rivalry, let opportunities slip past and they lost the initiative. Eventually they did decide to support the king and end their Kilkenny government, but by this time Charles I had been beheaded and his son had fled into exile. The Royalists were defeated at Rathmines in 1649 and the way was left clear for the Puritan leader, **Cromwell**, who landed in Dublin soon after. Cromwell came to Ireland determined to break the Royalists, break the Gaelic Irish, and to avenge the events of 1641 in Ulster. He started his campaign with the **Siege of Drogheda**, and there are the most gruesome accounts of his methods. When his troops burst into the town they put Royalists, women, children and priests to the sword; in all, 3,552 dead were counted while Cromwell only lost 64 men. Catholics curse Cromwell to this day. The same butchery marked the taking of Wexford. Not surprisingly, he managed to break the spirit of resistance by such methods and there were widespread defections from the Royalists' side. Owen Roe O'Neill might have been able to rally the Irish but he died suddenly. Cromwell's campaign only lasted seven months, but he took all the towns except Galway and Waterford. These he left to his lieutenants.

By 1652 the whole country was subdued, and Cromwell encouraged all the Irish fighting men to leave by granting them amnesty if they fled overseas. The alternative to exile was, for many families, something that turned out to be even worse: compulsory removal to Connacht and County Clare. Some families had been neutral during all the years of fighting, but that was never taken into account. Cromwell was determined that anyone suspect should go 'to Hell or Connacht'. The government had lots of land to play around with after that. First of all they paid off 'the adventurers', men who had lent them money back in 1642. Next, the Roundhead soldiers, who had not been paid their salaries for years, were granted Irish land instead. In this manner, the Cromwellian Settlement parcelled out even more land to speculators, foreigners and rogues.

Stuart and Orange

After the **Restoration of the Monarchy** in 1660, the Catholics in Ireland hoped for toleration and rewards for their loyalty to the Stuart cause. They felt threatened by the fast-expanding Protestant community, but Charles did not restore many Catholic estates because he had to keep in with the ex-Cromwellian supporters, although Catholics were given a limited amount of toleration. However, with the succession of Charles' brother **James II**, who was a Catholic, in 1685 things began to brighten up. In Ireland, the Catholic Earl of Tyrconnell became commander of the army and, later, chief governor. By 1688 Roman Catholics were dominant in the army, the administration, the judiciary and the town corporations, and by the end of the year Protestant power in Ireland was seriously weakened. James frightened all those Protestants in England who had benefited from Catholic estates. They began to panic when he introduced sweeping acts of toleration for all religions. His attempts to re-establish the Catholic Church alienated the country to such an extent that the Protestant aristocracy eventually invited **William of Orange** over to England in November 1688 to relieve his father-in-law of his throne. James fled to France but soon left for Ireland, a natural base for the launch of his counter-attack. By the date of his arrival in March 1689, only Enniskillen and Londonderry were in Protestant hands.

The Siege of Londonderry and Battle of the Boyne

The subjugation of the Protestant city of Londonderry was James' first aim. In a famous incident celebrated in Orange songs, a group of apprentice boys shut the city gates to the Jacobite (English Catholic) army; and so began the famous **Siege of Londonderry**. The townspeople proved unbreakable, even though food supplies ran very low and they were reduced to eating rats and mice, and chewing old bits of leather. Many died of starvation during the 15 weeks of the siege, but just as they were about to give in, the food ship *Mountjoy* forced its way through a great boom built across the Foyle. This military and psychological victory was of enormous significance in the campaign. When William himself arrived at Carrickfergus in June 1690, James confronted him at the Boyne. William of Orange had an army of about 36,000, comprised of English, Scots, Dutch, Danes, Germans and Huguenots (French Protestants), against James' army of about 25,000, made up of Irish and French. William triumphed, and James deserted the battlefield and left Ireland with haste.

In the **Battle of the Boyne** James seems to have completely lost his nerve. The Jacobite forces had to retreat west of the Shannon to Limerick, and William promptly laid siege to it. So weak were its walls that it is said they could be breached with roasted apples. The Catholic defence of Limerick was as heroic as that of Londonderry. Patrick Sarsfield slipped out with a few followers, intercepted William's siege train and destroyed it. William then gave up and left for England leaving Ginkel in charge. The next year the French King Louis XIV sent over supplies and men to fuel the Jacobite cause, hoping to divert William in Ireland for a little longer. The Jacobite leader St Ruth, who landed with them, proved a disaster for the Irish; Sarsfield would have been a better choice. Ginkel took Athlone and Aughrim in June and July of 1691, after two battles that gave rise to stories of Jacobite courage, which have inspired patriot poets and musicians. The last hope of the Catholic Irish was now Limerick.

The Treaty of Limerick

Sarsfield skilfully gathered together what Jacobite troops were left and got them back to Limerick. (St Ruth had been killed by a cannonball and, rather typically, had appointed no second-in-command.) Ginkel tried to storm the town from both sides, but still Limerick held out and he began to negotiate with Sarsfield. Honourable terms were made for the Jacobites, and Sarsfield signed the famous **Treaty of Limerick** in October 1691. The next day a French fleet arrived and anchored off the Shannon estuary, but Sarsfield stood by the Treaty, which seemed to guarantee quite a lot: Catholics were to have the same rights as they had had under Charles II and any Catholic estates which had been registered in 1662 were to be handed back; Catholics were to be allowed free access to the bar, bench, army and parliament; and Sarsfield was to be given a safe passage to the Continent with his troops. But the Treaty was not honoured, except for the last clause which got all the fighting men out of the country. This was one of the dirtiest tricks the English played; to be fair to William of Orange he wanted the treaty to be enforced, but being new and unsure of his support he complied with the treachery. Eleven thousand Irish Jacobites sailed away to join the French army, forming the Irish Brigade. Over the years many came to join them from Ireland, and were remembered in their native land as the **Wild Geese**.

The Orange/Stuart war still lives vividly in the imagination of the people today. The Siege of Londonderry has become a sign of Protestant determination: 'no surrender 1690' is scrawled, usually in bright red paint, on the walls and street corners of Loyalist areas in Northern Ireland. The Battle of the Boyne is remembered in a similar way.

The Penal Laws

The defeat of the Catholic cause was followed by more confiscation of land, and the **Penal Laws**. A bargain had been struck with the Protestant 'planters' who were allowed to keep a monopoly of political power and most of the land, in return for acting as a British garrison to keep the peace and prevent the Catholics from gaining any power. To do this they passed a series of degrading laws, which briefly were as follows: no Catholic could purchase freehold land; any son of a Catholic, turning Protestant, could turn his parents off their estate; families who stayed Catholic had their property equally parcelled out amongst all the children, so that any large estates soon became uneconomic holdings; all the Catholics were made to pay a tithe towards the upkeep of the Anglican Church; all priests were banished; no Catholic schools were allowed and spies were set amongst the peasants to report on 'hedge schools', a form of quite sophisticated schooling that had sprung up (priests on the run taught at these schools and celebrated Mass); a Catholic could not hold a commission in the army, enter a profession or even own a horse worth more than £5. These anti-religious laws had the opposite effect to that intended – Catholicism took on a new lease of life in Ireland. In addition, **economic laws** were introduced that put heavy taxes on anything that Ireland produced – cloth, wool, glass and cattle – so that she could not compete with England. The trading regulations were particularly disadvantageous to the non-conformist Ulster Protestants, and many of them left.

Gradually however, things began to relax. The Catholics had been well and truly squashed. The Protestants began to build themselves grand and beautiful houses, leaving the damp and draughty tower houses to decay. Irish squires were famous for their hard drinking; the expression 'plastered' comes from the story of a guest who was so well wined and dined at a neighbour's housewarming party that he fell asleep against a newly plastered wall. He woke up next morning to find that his scalp and hair had hardened into the wall.

As the 18th century progressed, however, there were signs of aggression amongst the peasantry; agrarian secret societies were formed with names like the **White Boys, Hearts of Oak**, and the **Molly Maguires**. They were very brutal and meted out rough justice to tenants and landlords alike. If any peasant paid rent to an unfair landlord, he was likely to be intimidated or have his farm burnt down. In Ulster, peasant movements were dominated by sectarian land disputes. The Catholics were called the **Defenders** and the Protestant groups the **Peep-O'Day Boys**. In the 1770s the Penal Laws were relaxed a little; Catholics were allowed to bid for land, and they incensed the Protestants by bidding higher. After a particularly bad fight between the two sides which the Protestants won, the **Orange Order** was founded in 1795. A typical oath of one of the early clubs was, 'To the glorious, pious and immortal memory of the great and good King William, not forgetting Oliver Cromwell, who assisted in redeeming us from popery, slavery, arbitrary power, brass money and wooden shoes.'

The **American War of Independence** broke out in 1775 and Ireland found itself undefended. There were fears of an invasion by France or Spain and a general feeling that there ought to be some sort of defence force. The **Volunteers** were organized with officers from the Protestant landowning class; but as the fears of invasion receded they turned their considerable muscle to the cause of political reform, and Britain began to fear that they might follow the example of the American colonies. Irish Protestants and Catholics alike watched the war with approval, particularly since many of the rebel Americans were of Ulster/Scots blood. The landowners had their own parliament in Dublin, but all important matters were dealt with by London. A group of influential landowners began to think that Ireland would be much better off with an independent Irish parliament. In 1783, the British Government, influenced by the eloquence of the great speaker **Henry Grattan**, acknowledged the right of Ireland to be bound only by laws made by the King and the Irish parliament. Trade, industry and agriculture began to flourish, and the worst of the Penal Laws were repealed or relaxed.

Grattan's Parliament

Grattan's Parliament was really an oligarchy of landowners, but at least they understood the problems of the economy and tried to bring a more liberal spirit into dealings with Catholics and dissenters. Grattan wanted complete Catholic emancipation, but for that the Irish had to wait. Trinity College was made accessible to those of all religious persuasions, though Catholics were forbidden by their bishops to go there. The great Catholic Seminary at Maynooth was founded and endowed with money and land from the Protestant aristocrats, who were worried that the priests educated at Douai might bring back with them some of those frightening ideas of liberty and equality floating around France. Dissenters were given equal rights with the Established Church at this time.

Dublin was now a handsome Georgian city, a centre for the arts, science and society. To pay for all this pleasure landowners began to sublet their estates to land-hungry tenants. In the early 1790s fear and anger swept through Europe in the form of the French Revolution, and the governments of Europe, whether Catholic or Protestant, drew nearer together in mutual fear. Many who at first were delighted with the revolution in France became disgusted with the brutality of its methods. The Irish government disbanded the Volunteers and got together a militia and part-time force of yeomanry. It was nervous of a French invasion and increasingly of a middle-class organization, the 'United Irishmen', who were sick of a government that only spoke for a tiny proportion of the population.

Wolfe Tone and the United Irishmen

The aim of the United Irishmen was to throw open the Irish parliament to all Irishmen, irrespective of their rank or religion. Many United Irishmen were from

Ulster non-conformist backgrounds. Initially the movement was to be non-violent, but when war broke out between England and France, all radical societies were forced to go underground. No liberal ideas could be tolerated during the war effort. **Wolfe Tone** was a Dublin lawyer and a prominent United Irishman; he crossed over to France to try and persuade the French Directory to help.

The Protestant Wind

Wolfe Tone succeeded brilliantly in arguing a case for French intervention and, on the night of 16 December 1796, the last great French invasion force to set sail for the British Isles slipped past the British squadron blockading the port of Brest, anchoring off Bantry Bay five days later. They waited for one clear, calm day for the frigate carrying the Commander-in-Chief to arrive; then the wind changed and blew from the east, remembered in all the songs as a 'Protestant Wind'. The fleet endured the storm for three days, then the ships cut cable and headed back for France. Only Wolfe Tone and his ship, *The Indomitable*, remained and, as Tone put it, 'England had not such an escape since the Armada'.

Meanwhile, in the Irish countryside, increasingly brutal attempts were made by the militia and the yeomanry to stamp out sedition. In Ulster, where the United Irishmen were strong, efforts were made to set the United Irishmen against the Orangemen, many of whom had joined the yeomanry. This continual pressure forced the society to plan rebellion. However, government spies had infiltrated its ranks, and two months before the proposed date many of the leaders were arrested. By this time many Irish peasants had joined the United Irishmen, inspired by the heady doctrine of Tom Paine's *Rights of Man*. The increased power of the Irish parliament had not meant more freedom for them – on the contrary the heretics and alien landlords now seemed to have more power to persecute them in the forms of tithes and taxes. Yet the Gaelic-speaking peasants had little in common with the middle-class agitators either, and their anger was even more explosive.

The 1798 Rebellion

In May 1798 the rebellion broke out. The United Irish leaders had planned a rebellion believing that they could count on an army of over 250,000. However, the absence of leadership and careful planning resulted in local uprisings with no central support; even those which achieved some success were quickly crushed. In Ulster there were two main risings, under **McCracken** and **Munro.** The risings both enjoyed brief success, during which time the rebels treated any Loyalist prisoners well – a marked contrast to what had happened in other counties. However, the sectarian battles between the Peep-O'Day Boys had already soured the trust of the Catholics, and many of them did not turn up to help the mixed bunch of United Irishmen. Poor Wolfe Tone and others who had started the society with such hopes for affectionate brotherhood saw their ideals drowned in a sea of blood.

Nugent, the commander of the government forces in Ulster, decided to appeal to the rebels who had property to lose, especially those in the rich eastern counties, and he proclaimed a general amnesty if the County Antrim rebels gave up their arms. The rebels of County Down did not get off so humanely: when they had been routed and shot down they were left unburied in the streets for the pigs to eat. McCracken and Munro were executed.

The Races of Castlebar

As the war between France and England became more embittered, Wolfe Tone succeeded in raising another invasion force. On 22 August 1798, the French **General Humbert** arrived in Killala Bay with 1,000 men and more arms for the rebels, although most of them had dispersed. Humbert captured Ballina and routed 6,000 loyalist troops in a charge called the 'Races of Castlebar'. But there were not enough rebels and Humbert had to accept honourable terms of surrender in September. Only a few weeks later, another French expedition arrived with Tone on board and entered Lough Swilly. It was overcome by some British frigates and Wolfe Tone was captured. He appeared before a court martial wearing a French uniform and carrying a cockade. The only favour he asked was the right to be shot, which was refused, whereupon he cut his own throat with a penknife and lingered in agony for seven days.

In the space of three weeks 30,000 people, mostly peasants armed with pitchforks and pikes, women and children, were ruthlessly cut down or shot. The rebellion of 1798 was one of the most tragic and violent events in Irish history, horrifying people to such an extent that they desperately began to search for ways of bringing about change in a non-violent way. Ideas of political and religious equality were totally discredited, as a result of the deaths and destruction of property. The British Government found that an independent parliament was an embarrassment to them, especially since the 'Protestant garrison' had not been able to put down the peasant rising without their help.

The Union

William Pitt ('Pitt the Younger'), the British Prime Minister, decided that union between Great Britain and Ireland was the only answer. First he had to bribe the Protestants to give up their power; many earldoms date from this time. Then the **Act of Union** was passed, with promises of Catholic emancipation for the majority. Pitt really did want to give them equality, for he saw that it was a necessary move if he wished to make Ireland relatively content.

Unfortunately Pitt was pushed out of government, and **King George III** lent his considerable influence to those opposed to Catholic emancipation: he claimed that the idea of it drove him mad. The Union did not solve any problems, as the Catholics felt bitterly let down and the temporary Home Rule of Grattan's Parliament was looked back to as an example. Irreconcilable nationalism was still alive and kicking. Union with England was disadvantageous to Ireland in the areas of industry and trade, and many poorer Protestants were discontented – although from now on the Ulster non-conformists supported the Union, for many had been disillusioned by the vengeance exacted on Protestants by the Catholic peasantry. The terms of the 1801 Act were never thought of as final in Ireland, although the English failed to understand this.

The Liberator: Daniel O'Connell

Catholics still could not sit in parliament or hold important state offices or senior judicial, military or civil service posts. Finally, they found a champion among themselves: a Catholic lawyer called **Daniel O'Connell** who believed that 'no political change is worth the shedding of a single drop of human blood'. O'Connell founded the **Catholic Association** which, amongst other things, represented the interests of the tenant farmers. Association membership was a penny a month and brought in a huge fighting fund. Most important of all, the Catholic priests supported him, and soon there were branches of the association everywhere. A turning point for Irish history and the fortunes of Daniel O'Connell came with the Clare election in 1828, when the association showed its strength. O'Connell had an overwhelming victory against the government candidate when all the 40-shilling freeholders (the Catholic electorate) voted for him. The whole country was aflame: they wanted Daniel at Westminster. **Wellington**, the Prime Minister of the day, was forced to give in, and the **Emancipation Bill** was passed in April 1829. But this was not a gesture of conciliation, for at the same time he raised the voting qualification from 40 shillings to a massive £10. Protestant fears had been raised by the power of such a mass movement, for tenant farmers had dared to vote in opposition to their landlords, even though voting was public. To English Catholics Daniel was also a 'Liberator'.

For 12 years O'Connell supported the Whig Government and built up a well-disciplined Irish party whose co-operation was essential to any government majority. He was then able to press for some very necessary reforms, and when the viceroy and his secretary were sympathetic, much was achieved. However, with the return of the Conservatives in 1840, O'Connell decided it was time to launch another popular agitation campaign, this time for the repeal of the Union. His mass-meetings became 'monster meetings', each attended by well over 100,000 people. The government refused to listen on this issue; British public opinion was firmly against it and in Ulster there was a distinct lack of enthusiasm. Daniel O'Connell arranged to have one of his biggest meetings yet, at Clontarf, where Brian Boru had defeated the Vikings. The Government banned it and O'Connell, unwilling to risk violence, called it off. He himself was arrested for conspiracy and sentenced by just the sort of packed jury he had been trying to abolish. Luckily for him, the House of Lords was less frightened and more just; they set aside his sentence. But by then O'Connell's influence had begun to fade, and some Irish began to look to violence to achieve their aims.

The Young Irelanders

Within the Repeal Association was a group of young men who called themselves the **Young Irelanders**. They had founded *The Nation* newspaper to help O'Connell, but they soon began to move in a different direction. They believed that culturally and historically Ireland was independent of England and fed their enthusiasm on the painful memories of 1798, composing heroic poetry which they set to old ballad tunes. They were useless at practical politics and did not have the support of the clergy. In 1848 they responded to the spontaneous and romantic uprisings in Europe with one of their own. It was a dismal failure and alienated many people who had been in favour of the Repeal of the Union. The Nationalist movement was not to become respectable again until 1870.

The Great Hunger

The diet of an ordinary Irishman consisted of six pounds of potatoes and a pint of milk a day, and he lived in miserable conditions. The Cromwellian and Williamite plantations, together with the effect of the Penal Laws, left the Catholics with only five per cent of the land. Except in the North, where a thriving linen industry had grown up, people had to make their living from farming. Absentee landlords became more of a problem after the Union, their agents greedier and their rent demands even higher. From 1845–49 the **potato blight** struck, with tragic results.

The population of Ireland, as in the rest of Europe, had begun to rise quickly in the late 18th century, perhaps because the potato could feed large families on small plots of land. The most deprived and populated area of Ireland was the west, where the potato was the only crop that would grow; it alone sustained the fragile equilibrium of large families on tiny holdings. The scene was set for agricultural and social catastrophe. As the blighted potatoes rotted in the ground, people ate cabbage, wild vegetables, turnips and even grass, but these could not supply more than a few meals. Gradually, thousands of people began to die of starvation, typhus fever, relapsing fever and dysentery. Even so, corn and cattle were still leaving the country; nothing was done that might interfere with the principle of free trade and private enterprise. The government's attitude was rigid, though they did allow maize in, a crop nobody had any vested interest in. Food distribution centres were set up and some relief work was paid for by the government. But this was not very sensible sort of work, mostly digging holes only to fill them in again: something constructive like laying a network of railway lines might have interfered with private enterprise. Out of a population of eight and a half million, a million died and another million emigrated.

Emigration

The Irish had been emigrating for years, first to escape persecution by fleeing to the Continent and then as seasonal labour for the English harvests. The Ulster Scots had set the first pattern of emigration to America. They had found that Ireland was not the promised land, after being lured over there by grants of land and low rents. Bad harvests, religious discrimination and high rents sent them off at the rate of 4,000 a year. Not many Catholics followed, for there were still restrictions on Catholic emigration. Many Irish went to Australia as convicts or free settlers. But the heaviest years of emigration were just after the famine, especially to the USA. People travelled under appalling conditions in boats called 'coffin ships'. It took six to eight weeks to get to America in those overcrowded and disease-ridden conditions. By 1847 nearly a quarter of a million were emigrating annually.

Irish priests followed their flocks out to America and Australia and founded churches wherever they were needed, so a distinct Irish Catholic Church grew up. Such an influx of starving, diseased Irish Catholics was quite another thing to the steady flow of a few thousand Ulster Scots, and initially a lot of people were prejudiced against them. Most of the emigrants left Ireland loathing the British in Ireland. Their children grew up with the same hatred, and sometimes became more anti-British than the Irish left in Ireland. This bitterness was soon transformed into political activity, aided by the Young Irelanders who had fled to America. Many of the emigrants had come from the west where the Gaelic language and culture survived relatively undisturbed. The rest of Ireland, especially the east, was quite anglicized and became more so with the development of education and transport.

America and Irish Politics

In 1858, **James Stephens** founded a secret movement in Ireland called the **Irish Republican Brotherhood** (IRB). Shortly afterwards, he and **John O'Mahony**, a comrade from the uprising of 1848 who had fled to America, reorganized the Irish Catholics in America into a twin movement called the **Fenian Brotherhood**. The Fenians called themselves after the legendary Fianna Warriors and were dedicated to the principle of Republicanism. Because of the need for secrecy, the IRB was generally known at this time under the name of the Fenians, the American part of the organization, which was able to function openly. In Ireland, aided by money from America, the Fenians started up a newspaper, *The Irish People*, which was aimed at the urban worker. When the American Civil War was over many Irish-American soldiers came over to help the Fenians in Ireland, although their military operations were always dismal failures. But Fenianism remained a potent force. The unfortunate execution of Allen, Larkin and O'Brien in England in 1867, who became known as the Manchester Martyrs, became further powerful propaganda for the Fenian cause. **John Devoy** in America and **Michael Davitt** of the **Irish Land League** were imaginative enough to see that violence was not the only way to fight high rents. They made a loose alliance with **Charles Stewart Parnell**, the leader of the **Irish Party** in the House of Commons. John Devoy was head of the **Clan-na-Gael**, an organization which cloaked Fenianism. In America, through the Fenians, Parnell was able to collect money for the land agitators. John Devoy gave money and moral support to the revolutionaries in their fight for independence. The Clan created good propaganda for the Nationalists and, between the death of Parnell and the rise of **Sinn Féin** (the new Nationalist party), did everything it could to drive a wedge between the USA and England, and to keep the States neutral during the First World War. It even acted as an intermediary between Germany and the IRB, who were negotiating for guns.

The Irish-Americans played such an important part in Irish politics that it is worth jumping forward in time for a moment to recount subsequent events. In 1918 **Eamon de Valera**, born in America, was elected by Sinn Féin as head of a provisional government. He came to America with high hopes during the War of Independence in Ireland. He wanted two things: political recognition from the government for the Dáil Eireann – the Irish parliament set up in Dublin in 1919 – and money. He failed in his first aim: he was rebuffed by President Wilson, himself of Ulster Scots blood, and very proud of it too. However, De Valera got plenty of money, $6 million, in the form of a loan, but he fell out with Devoy. He founded a rival organization called the **American Association for the Recognition of the Irish Republic** (AARIA). When Ireland split over the solution of partition and there was a civil war, the Republicans, who rejected the partition, were supported by the AARIA, whilst the Free Staters had Devoy and Clan-na-Gael behind them. The leading spirit of the AARIA was **Joseph McGarrity**, who later broke with De Valera when he began to act against the IRA. His group and their successors have continued to give financial support to the IRA during the present troubles in Northern Ireland.

Now to return to the efforts of the British government to forestall the repeal of the Union and the efforts of various organizations to bring it about.

Tenants' Rights and the Land War

The British Government was blamed by many in Ireland for the tragic extent of the famine, but the government was blind to the lessons it should have taught them. The famine had only intensified the land war and the 1829 Act simply enabled the impoverished landlords to sell their estates, which the peasants had no money to buy. So the speculators moved in, seized opportunities for further evictions and increased the rents. Tenant resistance smouldered, stimulated by the horrors of the famine. Michael Davitt organized the resistance into the **National Land League**, with the support of Parnell, the leader of the Irish Party in the House of Commons. In the ensuing **Land War** (1879–82), a new word was added to the English language – 'boycott'. The peasants decided not to help an evicting landlord with his crops and he had to import some loyal Orangemen from Ulster to gather in the harvest. The offending landlord was a Captain Boycott. The tenants wanted the same rights that tenants had in Ulster and fair rent, fixity of tenure and freedom to sell at the market value. They also wanted a more even distribution of the land – at that time three per cent of the population owned 95 per cent of the land.

Behind all the agitation at this time, and all the obstruction the Irish Party caused in parliament, was a desire for the repeal of the Union. But the politicians saw the problem as religion, over-population, famine, anything but nationalism. It did not enter English heads that the Irish might not want to be part of Britain – with the Union, in their eyes, Irishmen were on an equal footing with the rest of Great Britain; they were part of the Empire. The Union was also a security against foreign attack and had to stay. Only one man said anything sensible on the subject and he was not listened to. **J. S. Mill** said that England was the worst qualified to govern the Irish, because English traditions were not applicable in Ireland. England was firmly *laissez-faire* in her economic policies, but Ireland needed economic interference from the government. This the English politicians had resolutely refused to do during and after the famine. **Gladstone** and other Liberals were aware of the discontent. They tried to take the sting out of Irish nationalism by dealing with the problems individually, believing that then the nationalist grievance would disappear.

Killing Home Rule with Kindness

One of the first things to be dealt with was religion, for it could not be kept out of politics. The Protestant Ascendancy still monopolized powerful positions, despite Catholic emancipation. There may have been no legal barriers any more, but there were unofficial ones. The Anglican Church of Ireland remained the Established Church until 1869, and until then the Irish peasants had to pay tithes to it. The Catholic hierarchy wanted state-supported Catholic education, but the government tried to have inter-denominational schools and universities. This never satisfied the Catholic Church and consequently, much later on, it supported the illegal nationalist organizations. Unfortunately the government was unwilling to establish the Catholic Church in Ireland as they would have had problems with the Protestants in Ulster, so although the Catholic Church had consolidated its position, it was not conciliated.

The distress of the peasant farmers had, by this time, become identified with nationalism, so the government set out to solve the economic problems, thinking that this would shatter the nationalists. But they acted too late. Only in 1881 were the demands of the tenants met. Large amounts of money were made available to tenants to buy up their holdings and, by 1916, 64 per cent of the population owned land. (Many of these new owners had the same surnames as those dispossessed back in the 17th century.) But Britain was remembered not for these Land Acts, generous as they were, but for the Coercion and Crime Acts which the minister for Ireland, **Balfour**, brought in to try and control the unrest and anarchy which existed in some parts of the country. The **Land Purchase Acts** took away the individual oppressor and left only the government against whom to focus discontent. The peasants had been given more independence and the landlords were virtually destroyed, therefore the Union became even more precarious. The Nationalists could not be bought off.

Home Rule for Ireland?

Parnell forced the government to listen, often holding a balance of power in the House of Commons, and for a while he managed to rally the whole Nationalist movement behind his aggressive leadership. The bait of universal suffrage was enough for the Fenians to try and overthrow the Union from within the system. The **Secret Ballot Act** in 1872 made this even more attractive than abortive rebellions. But the **Home Rule League** did not succeed, even though Gladstone and the Liberals, who were in Opposition at that time, had promised to support it. Parnell's aggressive tactics alienated many Englishmen and his Protestant origins upset some of the Catholic hierarchy, who thought he should have concentrated a little more on pushing the Catholic university they wanted. Also, his affair with Kitty O'Shea and involvement in a divorce case shocked many Victorians and non-conformists in the Liberal Party. They demanded that Parnell should be dropped from the leadership of the Irish Party, and when the Catholic hierarchy heard this, they also began to openly scold 'the named adulterer' and turned their congregations against him.

Another reason for the failure of the Home Rule Bill was that the predominantly Protestant and industrial North of Ireland had no wish at all to join the South. The North thought that it would be overtaxed to subsidize the relatively backward, agrarian South, and the Protestants were frightened of being swamped by the Catholics. Their fear produced in them a siege mentality; Parnell's divorce case was like a gift from heaven and gave the Protestants a reprieve. English opinion was still against Home Rule and it was only because the Irish Party had made a deal with the

Liberals that there was any hope of their succeeding. With the fall of Parnell, the Irish Party split and lost much of its importance.

Parnell's fall in 1891 and the failure of the 1893 Home Rule Bill initiated a resurgence of revolutionary nationalism. The younger generation was shocked by the way the Catholic Church within Ireland condemned Parnell over the O'Shea case. And, as the moral authority of the Church was cast aside, so was one of the barriers to violence. Parnell's failure to work things out through Parliament seemed to indicate that only violence would work. Young people started to join the Irish Republican Brotherhood, and even the Church began to show more sympathy, because at least nationalism was preferable to the atheistic socialism that was creeping into Dublin.

Gaelic Cultural Renaissance

There was a new mood in Ireland at the end of the 19th century. The people were proud of being Irish and of their cultural achievements. Unfortunately only 14 per cent of the population spoke the Gaelic language (the famine and emigration that followed had seriously weakened its hold); English was taught in schools, knowledge of it led to better jobs and opportunities, and Irish music and poetry were neglected except by a few intellectuals. However, it was in the stories of Ireland's past greatness, her legends and customs, that many diverse groups found a common ground. In 1884 the **Gaelic Athletic Association** started to revive the national game, hurling. In 1893 the **Gaelic League** was formed. Its president was **Douglas Hyde**, who campaigned successfully for the return of Gaelic lessons to schools and Gaelic as a qualification for entry to the new universities. He never wanted the League to be a sectarian or political force, but it did provide a link between the conservative Catholic Church and the Fenians and Irish Nationalists. 'The Holy Island of St Patrick' developed an ideal: that of the Catholic, devout, temperate, clean-living Irishman. The Gaelic League and the Gaelic Athletic Association were used by the IRB as sounding boards or recruiting grounds for membership.

The Liberals returned to power in 1906 and things began to look brighter for Home Rule. In 1910 **John Redmond** led the Irish Party and held the balance of power between the Liberals and the Conservatives. In 1914 Asquith's **Home Rule Bill** was passed, although it was suspended for the duration of the First World War. But six years later Ireland was in the middle of a war of independence and the initiative had passed from the British into the hands of the revolutionary nationalists. This happened because the British Government had left Home Rule too late; the time lag between when it was passed and when it actually might be implemented gave the Irish public time to criticize it and see its limitations. The nationalists began to despair of ever finding a parliamentary solution, for the British could now not force the North into Home Rule and were shutting their eyes to the gun-running which had been going on since the formation of the Ulster Volunteers (*see* below).

The Irish people were rather lukewarm about organizations like the IRB and its associated, new **Sinn Féin** Party, founded by Arthur Griffith. In fact, military recruitment, relative prosperity, and the nominal achievement of Home Rule brought Ireland and the rest of Britain closer together during the War. The IRB's military council wanted to do something to stem the fragmentation of their movement. An event on Easter Monday in 1916 meant all was 'changed utterly'. (W.B. Yeats).

Easter Rebellion 1916

Plans for a national rising with German support were made. The support did not arrive but, despite the confusion, the IRB leaders were determined the rising should go ahead in Dublin. It happened very quickly – suddenly the tricolour of a new Irish Republic was flying from the General Post Office in Dublin. Two thousand Irish Nationalist volunteers, led by **Patrick Pearse** of the IRB, stood against the reinforcements sent from England and then surrendered about a week later. People were horrified at first by the waste of life, but then the British played into the hands of Patrick Pearse. All 14 leaders were executed after secret trials. The timing of the uprising was no coincidence. Pearse and the others wanted it to be a blood sacrifice in order to breathe new life into the nationalist cause.

The executions happened before there could be any backbiting as to why the whole thing had been a muddle. Suddenly they were dead, and pity for them grew into open sympathy for what they had been trying to achieve. The Catholic Church was trapped in the emotional wave which advocated revolution. The party that gained from this swing was **Sinn Féin**; it was pledged to non-violent nationalism and was the public front of the IRB. John Redmond, the leader of the Irish Party at Westminster, had urged everybody to forget their differences with England and fight the common enemy, Germany, but the Irish Nationalists, who were negotiating with the Germans, saw things in a very different light. Many Irishmen did go and fight for Britain: some 200,000 men enlisted, but the feeling grew that Redmond was prepared to compromise over Home Rule and shelve it until it suited the British. Sinn Féin, under the influence of American-born Eamon de Valera, set out to mobilize popular support through propaganda and electioneering.

When conscription was extended to Ireland in 1918, even more people decided that Sinn Féin was the only party which could speak for them. It won all the Irish seats bar six. Redmond's party was finished. The only problem was that 44 of the Sinn Féin members were in English jails; those that were not met in Mansion House and set up their own Dáil Eireann. Eamon de Valera made an audacious escape from Lincoln prison and was elected the first President of the Irish Republic in 1919. The Irish Volunteers became the **Irish Republican Army**, and war was declared on Britain.

The North

Meanwhile in the North a leader had been found to defend the Union in Dublin-born **Edward Carson**. He was a leading barrister in London (he cross-examined Oscar Wilde in that notorious lawsuit), and was openly supported by the Conservatives in England. In 1912, as the Home Rule was being discussed in Parliament, a solemn **Covenant of Resistance to Home Rule** was signed by hundreds of thousands of Northern Unionists. The **Ulster Volunteers** were formed, and pledged to use all means possible to not come under an Irish parliament in Dublin. After the Easter rising of 1916, Carson was assured by **Lloyd George** that the six northeastern counties could be permanently excluded from the Home Rule Bill of 1914. When the **War of Independence** broke out in the South, the British offered them partition with their own parliament whilst remaining within Britain. Today they still feel their ties are with a liberal Britain, not the Catholic South. (Remember that, until very recently, in the Republic there was no divorce, limited contraception, mixed marriages were discouraged and the Welfare State is still comparatively undeveloped.)

The War of Independence

The British Government had been caught out by the Dáil's Declaration of Independence. The British were busy trying to negotiate a peace treaty at Versailles and the Americans made it clear that they sympathized with the Irish. Ammunition raids, bombing, burning and shooting began in Ireland, mainly against the Irish Constabulary. The British Government waited until the Versailles Conference had come to an end and then fought back. The **Black and Tans** were sent over to reinforce the police, and Lloyd George tried to play it down as a police situation. Their methods were notoriously brutal and it seemed that their reprisals were more vicious than the IRA incidents that had provoked them. It became a war of retaliation. **Michael Collins** was in charge of military affairs for the IRA; he waged a vicious, well-thought-out campaign against the Black and Tans. By July 1921 a truce was declared because the British public wanted to reach a compromise. In October an Irish delegation, which included Griffith and Collins, went to London to negotiate with Lloyd George. They signed a treaty which approved the setting up of an Irish Free State with Dominion status, similar to Canada. The British were mainly concerned with the security aspect and they made two stipulations; that all Irish legislators should take an oath of allegiance to the Crown and that the British Navy could use certain Irish ports.

Civil War

The Republicans (or anti-treaty side) in the Dáil were furious. They regarded it as a sell-out. They did not like the oath, or the acceptance of a divided Ireland. Michael Collins saw it as a chance for 'freedom to achieve freedom' and when it came to the debate on it in the Dáil, the majority voted in favour of the treaty. De Valera was against the treaty and, as head of the Dáil, he resigned; **Arthur Griffith** succeeded him. In June, when the country accepted the treaty, civil war began. The split in the Dáil had produced a corresponding split in the IRA; part of it broke away and began violent raids into the North. The remainder of the IRA was reorganized by Michael Collins into the Free State Army. When he was assassinated, a man just as talented took over, **Kevin O'Higgins**. This period is remembered as the **War of Brothers**, and it was bitter and destructive. Men who had fought together against the Black and Tans now shot each other down. Finally, the Republicans were ready to sue for peace. De Valera, who had not actively taken part in the fighting but had supported the Republicans, now ordered a cease-fire. The bitterness and horror of the Civil War has coloured attitudes to this very day. The differences between the two main parties, **Fine Gael** (pro-treaty) and **Fianna Fáil** (anti-treaty), are historical rather than political, although perhaps in foreign policy Fianna Fáil has taken a more anti-British line. Fine

Gael held power for the first 10 years and successfully concentrated on building the 26-county state into something credible and strong. In 1926 De Valera broke with Sinn Féin because they still saw the Dáil and the government in power as usurpers, as bad as the British, and refused to take up their seats. De Valera, the master pragmatist, founded his own party, the Fianna Fáil; the new state wanted a change, and in 1932 he formed a government. He soon made it clear that Ireland was not going to keep the oath of allegiance or continue to pay the land annuities (the repayment of money lent to help tenants pay for their farms).

De Valera

In 1937 De Valera drew up a new **Constitution** which named the state Eire, or Ireland. It declared Ireland a Republic in all but name and seemed a direct challenge to the Northern Ireland Government. Article 5 went like this: 'It is the right of the Parliament Government established by the Constitution to exercise jurisdiction over the whole of Ireland, its Islands and territorial seas'. Article 44.1.2. recognized 'the special position of the Holy Catholic, Apostolic Roman Church as the guardian of the Faith professed by the great majority of its citizens'. De Valera would not go so far as to 'establish' it, as the Church of Ireland had once been, and as the Catholic hierarchy wanted. (This article was removed from the Constitution in the 1970s). Both parties had trouble with extremists in the 1930s; Fine Gael had to expel General O'Duffy of the Fascist Blue Shirt Movement, and Fianna Fáil were embarrassed by their erstwhile allies in the IRA. De Valera dealt with the situation by setting up a military tribunal and declaring the IRA an illegal organization in 1936. The IRA did not die but went underground and continued to enjoy a curious relationship with the government and the public. When it got too noisy it was stamped on; but the IRA continued to be regarded nervously and with respect for its ideals, and its members' intransigence seemed to be in line with Ireland's dead patriots. In 1939 Eire declared itself neutral during the Second World War, which further isolated it from the rest of the British Isles. In 1949, Costello's Interparty Government finally inaugurated a Republic and broke Commonwealth ties. Relations between the North and the South remained cool until the tentative *rapprochement* in 1965 between Lemass (the Taoiseach of Eire) and O'Neill (the Prime Minister of Northern Ireland.) But relations cooled again rapidly as the Troubles (1968–1970) began and two members of Taoiseach Lynch's Fianna Fáil ministry were implicated in gun-running for the IRA.

Northern Ireland

The North Today

It is very difficult to be impartial about the Troubles in Northern Ireland – they have been tragic and frightening. With the ceasefire holding at the time of writing, the interparty Assembly elections in June 1998 have provided a structure of government on which to try and build a stable society, so there is hope for the future, albeit a very cautious one. The basic reason for the start of the Troubles is that the Catholic minority in the North did badly with the division of Ireland in the 1920s, and once the Northern Ireland State was set up they were treated as second-class citizens. The series of events that lead up to the present situation is discussed in more detail below. Before you read on, you may find it useful to look at the glossary of Northern Irish political parties and terms at the end of this chapter.

Discontent Amongst Ulster Catholics, 1921–69

The Ulster Protestants made up two-thirds of the population of Northern Ireland, and the Catholics, the rest. Under the leadership of Edward Carson and James Craig the Ulster Protestants had managed to wrest their bit of Ulster from the rest of Ireland, and preserve the Union with Britain. They repudiated the idea of a Catholic, Gaelic Republic of Ireland, and held themselves aloof from events in the Free State, (later the Republic). No attempt was made to woo the Catholic Nationalists, perhaps because the Protestant leaders, ever-anxious about being turfed out of the Union with Britain and into the Republic of Ireland, directed all their energies into preserving the Union. The **Government of Ireland Act** in 1920 gave Westminster supreme authority over Northern Ireland, which was run internally from a separate Parliament at Stormont Castle. The **Ireland Act** of 1949 enshrined the constitutional guarantee that gave the Stormont Parliament the right to decide whether Northern Ireland would remain in the UK or not.

All Catholics were regarded as supporters of the **IRA**, an organization which was indeed a real menace to this shaky state. It was seen as imperative that Catholics should never be allowed into positions of power and influence. **Sir Basil Brooke** (1888–1973) was typical of the type of blinkered cabinet minister who ran the government for years. He, along with **James Craig** (1871–1940), first Prime Minister of Northern Ireland, encouraged Protestants to employ only Protestants, for he, like others, believed that the Catholics were 'out to destroy Ulster with all their power and might'. He became Prime Minister in 1943 and played an active role in linking the Orange Order, of which he was a leading member, with the government of the time. Protestant businesses tended to employ Protestants and Catholics employed Catholics. There were few mixed housing areas or marriages. The Catholic priests fiercely defended their right to run Catholic schools – as they still do.

Government went on at a mainly local level through county and town councils. The Loyalists ensured that they always had a majority on the councils through the use of **gerrymandering**. The local voting system also favoured Protestants, who were often wealthier, for the franchise was only granted to house-owners or tenants, and the number of votes allocated to each person could be as high as six, depending on the value of their property. Because the Protestant rulers controlled housing schemes and jobs, the working-class Protestants were given the lion's share of any existing housing or jobs. Northern Ireland had a much lower standard of living than the rest of the UK, and any advantages were eagerly grasped by these workers, who displayed little feeling of worker solidarity with their fellow Catholics. They never could escape from their religious prejudices to unite against the capitalists, although the ruling class had feared their alliance during the 1922 riots over unemployment.

The Catholics themselves were ambiguous about the State; in the 1920s most of them were Republicans, and they never gave up hope that the Dublin Government might do something about this situation. Many believed that the Six Counties could not survive and, in the beginning, Nationalist Republican representatives refused to sit at Stormont. On the other hand, others had watched with horror the bloodshed and bitterness that resulted from the Civil War in the Irish Free State. After being educated, many of the bright ones emigrated rather than fight the system. The IRA attempted over the next 50 years to mount a campaign in the North but gained little support; a big campaign in 1956–62 that killed 19 people failed miserably. The local Catholics did not back them, and the **B Specials** (Protestant-dominated special police force) zealously pursued the culprits – often at the expense of law-abiding Catholics, who were left resentful and disgruntled. For the time being the Protestant Unionists were able to dominate Catholic Nationalists in elections in a proportion of about four to one. This gave them a feeling of security, which was also bolstered by the gratitude of the British government for their loyalty and help during the Second World War, when the North of Ireland had been a vital bulwark for the rest of the UK.

The Civil Rights Movement – British Troops Move In

Yet things had to change. As young, educated Catholics and Protestants grew up, they began to agitate about the obvious injustices, and the **Civil Rights Association** was formed in 1967. Unfortunately, the marches that drew attention to their aims also attracted men of violence on both sides and, as the marches turned into riots, the Protestant Loyalists, including the **Royal Ulster Constabulary** (RUC) and B Specials, seemed to be in league with the Protestant mobs against the Catholics. At this point the discredited IRA failed to seize their opportunity to woo the Catholics, who were both confused and frightened.

The Catholics initially welcomed the British troops, who were brought in to keep the peace in August 1969 after the Loyalists and police beat up Civil Rights marchers at Burntollet, and later the inhabitants of the Bogside in Londonderry. At that time **Terence O'Neill** had taken over from Lord Brookborough as Prime Minister at Stormont. Although of the same Unionist Ascendancy stock, he realized that something must be done to placate the Nationalists. The few liberal gestures that he made towards the Catholics and the Republic opened up a Pandora's box of fury and opposition amongst the Protestant Unionists, the most extreme of whom found a leader in the **Reverend Ian Paisley**. The reforms O'Neill planned over housing and local government had come too late, and he was swept away by the Protestant backlash when he called a General Election in April 1969. The brutality with which the police had broken up the Civil Rights marches had stirred support for the IRA, and the Summer Marching Season was marked by even more violence.

The IRA Exploit Events

The IRA organized itself to exploit the situation. It split into two after an internal struggle, and the murders and bombings that dominated events after this time are mainly the work of the Provisional IRA, best-known today as the IRA. The British Army lost the confidence of the Catholic community it had come to protect through heavy-handed enforcement of security measures. Besides, the IRA posed as the natural guardians of the Catholics, so there were cheers amongst the Catholic Nationalists when the IRA killed the first British soldier in October 1970. The IRA aimed to break down law and order; to them any method was legitimate, and any member of the army or police a legitimate target.

The Stormont Government hastened to pass some much-needed reforms between 1969 and 1972. The RUC was overhauled, and the B Specials abolished. A new part-time security force was set up within the British Army, called the **Ulster Defence Regiment (UDR)**. In 1971 a new Housing Executive was set up to allocate houses fairly, irrespective of religious beliefs. The IRA conducted a destructive bombing campaign in the cities – innocent civilians were killed or injured and buildings destroyed. British soldiers responded to rioting in the Bogside in January 1972 by killing 13 people on what has become known as **Bloody Sunday**. A cycle of violence begetting violence began to spiral, and society divided along even more sectarian lines than before. The legacy of hatred, psychological distress and bitterness that has built from this time is terrible to contemplate.

UK Attempts to Solve the Problem

In 1972 the Stormont Government and Parliament were suspended by the British Government, which had always retained full powers of sovereignty over it, and Direct Rule from Westminster was imposed. The head of government was a **Secretary of State for Northern Ireland**, appointed by the Prime Minister of the UK and a member of the British Cabinet. The Secretary governed through ministers and civil servants. Members of Parliament from the constituencies of Northern Ireland, elected from various parties, sat in Westminster, where they tried to bring Northern Irish issues to the attention of the House. **Internment** was introduced in August 1971, and large numbers of terrorist suspects were imprisoned without trial. This hardened Catholic opinion against British justice, and the practice was gradually phased out after a couple of years. Subsequently, the **Diplock System of Criminal Courts** was introduced, which means alleged terrorists are tried by judges who sit alone without juries. It was justified by the amount of intimidation to which the jury could be subjected. Various power-sharing initiatives between the largely Protestant Unionist parties and the Catholic and Nationalist SDLP did not get off the ground, so Direct Rule continued. The suspension of the Stormont Parliament removed the constitutional guarantee of the 1949 Act but it was renewed in the 1973 **Constitution Act**, which established the principle that any change in the status of Northern Ireland would have to have majority consent.

The Sunningdale Agreement

In December 1973 the leaders of the Northern Irish parties, a new Executive, and Ministers from the United Kingdom and, for the first time, the Republic of Ireland, met at Sunningdale in England. They agreed to set up a **Council of Ireland** to work for co-operation between Northern Ireland and the Republic. The Agreement provided for a new type of Executive in Northern Ireland, in which power was to be shared as far as possible between representatives of the two communities in a joint govern-ment. It was the dawn of a new hope for the province, but the Unionist masses and the Republican terrorists did not want this new co-operation to work. Faced with a general strike called by the Ulster Workers' Council, which paralysed the province, the government did not use the army to break the strike, but allowed intimidation by 'Loyalist' paramilitary organizations to win the day. The Unionist members of the Executive resigned, and Direct Rule had to be resumed. Many people believe that if the Sunningdale Agreement had been implemented, much suffering could have been avoided, and Ireland might be a more stable place today.

The Victims of the Troubles

The province suffered sectarian killings, bombings, and the powerful propaganda of the hunger strike campaign by IRA prisoners in the early 1980s. The economy was struggling and well-educated members of society, both Protestant and Catholic, left in droves. However, since the first cease-fire in 1994, things have improved, the economy has picked up and foreign investors are looking again at Northern Ireland. The Ulster people have suffered the gradual erosion of their society through violence, intimidation, and the subtler psychological effects that violence induces. On the positive side, the spirit and bravery of the Ulster people remains unbroken, and manufacturing businesses continue to thrive and to compete in international markets. But the statistics in such a small population are grim. Between 1969 and 1994, 3,168 people lost their lives and around 3,300 people have been injured and maimed, of whom around 2,200 have been civilians. Feelings of despair, fear and outrage in both communities led to extreme attitudes in the 1980s. The Reverend Ian Paisley and his colleagues had a huge following, whilst support for Sinn Féin increased considerably at the expense of the constitutional nationalists in the SDLP.

The Anglo-Irish Agreement

In 1985, after initial efforts by **Garrett Fitzgerald**, the Fine Gael Prime Minister of the Republic, and **Margaret Thatcher**, the British Prime Minister, the **New Ireland Forum** met in Dublin. It was agreed that Northern Ireland would remain in the United Kingdom as long as the majority so desired, but that the Dublin Government should have an institutionalized consultative status in relation to Northern Irish affairs.

The effect of the Agreement was largely positive, although gradual. Both governments made progress in the complicated area of extradition and cross-border security, especially after the general revulsion in the Republic against the IRA bomb attack in Enniskillen in 1987. The British Government grasped the nettle of injustice over the conviction of the 'Guildford Four' and the 'Birmingham Six', prisoners unjustly convicted of bombings in mainland Britain. The re-opening of these cases and the subsequent acquittal of these prisoners dissipated much bad feeling in the Republic of Ireland, where there is great scepticism about British justice in relation to the Irish. One of the most important achievements of the Agreement was that the Irish Government formally accepted 'the principle of consent' by the people of Northern

Ireland. Any change in the Constitution Act of 1973 had to have majority consent. The Unionists were not mollified by this, for it was enshrined in the Constitution of the Republic that the Irish Republic claimed the whole island, and this claim had not been given up. The Agreement made the world realize that the 'Brits out' solution would mean forcibly transferring a million-strong Protestant population into a united Ireland that did not really want them, and the probability of bloody civil war.

The strength of the emotional link between the rest of the UK and the Northern Irish has changed since the beginning of the century. The Union was no longer regarded as a cause in itself; many English, Welsh and Scots know little about the North of Ireland, and questioned the lives lost and money spent maintaining the Union. The Unionists understood this very clearly and felt increasingly threatened. The Nationalists had not rejected the IRA, who continued to work for the destruction of the six-county state through murder and bombing campaigns in Ulster. On mainland Britain and Europe, the IRA followed a campaign of bombing 'soft' British military targets, and assassinating British politicians and industrialists in order to turn British public opinion against the Union with Northern Ireland.

1990–93

Inter-party talks began in Northern Ireland and, before they broke down, some progress was made in defining the three complicated relationships between the North and the UK, the North and the Republic, and the Republic and the UK. This meant there was a set of negotiating mechanisms for the peace process to be furthered. British policy continued to try and find the middle ground between opposing parties in the North, and it was hoped that the politics of the extremists would wither away. In 1992 and 1993, the IRA carried out bombing attacks in the financial heart of London and elsewhere. One such attack in a shopping centre in Warrington killed two children; there was worldwide revulsion, and a peace movement was launched in Dublin. The IRA could continue their campaign of violence indefinitely, but there were signs that key elements in the IRA wanted to try and change things through political action. In April 1993, **John Hume** of the SDLP started a dialogue with **Gerry Adams** of Sinn Féin. Both the British and the Irish Governments reacted furiously to this but popular nationalist support for the dialogue, in both the North and South, forced the governments to rethink their policy. The British Prime Minister, **John Major** and his Irish counterpart, **Albert Reynolds**, began a new policy of trying to draw the extremists into the political process and to aim at all-party talks for a lasting constitutional settlement which would bring peace. In October 1993, the IRA planted a bomb in a Belfast fish and chip shop killing ten people; a terrible revenge was exacted by extremist loyalists who shot 14 people in a public house in Greysteel. Both acts horrified the people of Northern Ireland.

The Downing Street Declaration

On the 15th December 1993, the Irish and British Prime Ministers presented a **Joint Declaration** which successfully managed to address the competing claims of the Nationalists and the Unionists. The British Government declared in the document that Britain 'had no selfish strategic or economic interest in Northern Ireland' and recognized the right of the people of Ireland, North and South, to self-determination. Both governments affirmed that the status of Northern Ireland could only be changed with the consent of 'a great number of its people'. In the event of an overall political settlement, the Irish Government declared it would drop its claim to the Six Counties contained in articles 2 and 3 of the Irish Constitution. The Irish Government would establish a forum for peace and reconciliation at some later date. Both governments offered a place at the negotiating table to the extremists on both sides if they renounced violence.

Cease-fire

After a disappointing reaction to the Declaration and prevarication for several months, the IRA eventually announced 'a complete cessation of military operations' on 31st August 1994. In the following weeks the extremist Unionist forces of the UFF, the UVF and the Red Hand of Ulster announced a cease-fire, conditional upon the IRA's continuing cease-fire. This cease-fire brought great opportunities for eventual peace, and the people of the North became increasingly convinced that they must find politicians who were prepared to find new ways of setting their differences. An end to the day-to-day killing was a huge relief to everybody who lived there. Unfortunately, the main protagonists still disagreed over major issues such as the release of prisoners, the withdrawal of the British Army, decommissioning of arms amongst terrorist groups, the future of community policing in Northern Ireland, and the role of the Southern Irish Government in the future of the province.

The British and Irish Governments produced two important framework documents in 1995. These sought to provide a basis for discussion in a **Northern Irish Forum** with elected delegates from all the different parties. The framework documents proposed a new assembly elected by proportional representation, a new relationship between North and South and between all the countries surrounding the Irish Sea. However, the discussions met stalemate over the **decommissioning of arms**. The IRA and Sinn Féin wanted the British Army to withdraw first and all political prisoners to be released before they gave up any of their weapons. The Unionists wanted the IRA to give up their arms first as a sign of their good intentions. In February 1996, the IRA declared their part in the cease-fire over with a bomb attack on Canary Wharf in London, which killed two people. The talks continued without Sinn Féin, little progress was made, and things looked very gloomy.

In the UK, the Conservative Government under John Major was replaced in May 1997 by a Labour Government with a huge majority. The new Prime Minister, **Tony Blair**, was no longer reliant on the Unionist vote in the House of Commons which gave him a freer hand all round. The Official Unionists, under the leadership of **David Trimble**, were breaking out of their reactionary 'Ulster Says No' mould, and it seemed as if the influence of Ian Paisley and his DUP was on the wane.

In the British elections, Sinn Féin's **Gerry Adams** and **Martin McGuinness** were voted into Westminster, although they did not take up their seats. In the Irish Republic, a general election brought a victory for Fianna Fáil, and their leader, **Bertie Ahern**, said he was willing to talk to Sinn Féin about a new cease-fire. The new Northern Ireland Secretary of State, **Mo Mowlam**, also promised to admit Sinn Féin to the talks if they called a new cease-fire. The American senator **George Mitchell**, who had been given the delicate task of brokering all-party talks, suggested that the talks on the decommissioning of arms should take place at the same time, but separately, as the talks on the future of the province.

Sectarian tension was heightened in the mid-1990s when Orange marchers insisted on taking their traditional routes, which often lay in Catholic areas. In July 1997, at Drumcree in Portadown, violence flared up and spread throughout the province when an Orange Order march was forced down the Garvaghy Road, centre of the local Nationalist community, on its way from Drumcree Church. The reaction within the community was intense in the face of what they saw as sectarian intimidation. The head of the Orange Order Lodges decided to cancel and reroute some of the potentially violent 12th July marches. Tension in the province was running high after events at Drumcree, but this gesture from the Orange Order helped. Horrible sectarian murders added to the tension, but the restoration of the IRA's cease-fire in August improved matters considerably. In September 1997 the leaders of Sinn Féin joined the all-party talks. The Official Unionist Party dropped its demand that the decommissioning issue must be settled before any negotiations could begin. Instead, an independent commission on illegal arms decommissioning was set up.

At last, negotiations between all the concerned parties could begin; both the Irish and British Prime Ministers emphasised that there was now a clear agenda and timescale, and that the talks must not get lost in prevarication. The talks consisted of three interlocking and interdependent strands: the internal settlement of the province; North-South relations; and Anglo-Irish relations.

On 11 April 1998, after many vicissitudes, the world was told that there had been an historic agreement. The **Good Friday Agreement** mapped out radical new arrangements for a devolved Ulster Assembly, a council of ministers linking Northern Ireland and the Republic, and limited cross-border bodies who would work things through together. A new Council of the Islands would be set up which would link all the devolved assemblies in the UK, and in Dublin and London. The Irish Government promised to amend Articles 2 and 3 of its Constitution which lay claim to the Six Counties. In return, the British Government stated that it would replace the Government of Ireland Act.

The people of Ireland from both sides of the border voted their approval of the Agreement in a **Referendum** in May 1998. However, the slow progress towards implementation of the terms of the Agreement is frustrating and has suffered some discouraging setbacks. Many Unionists are against the Agreement, and their vote is split, as was very apparent in the Assembly elections in June 1998 and the United Kingdom elections in June 2001. The new Assembly requires representatives to classify themselves as either Unionist, Nationalist or 'Other'. Certain legislation requires the consent of all three groups. The various Unionist parties make up the largest group in the Assembly. The SDLP is the dominant Nationalist Party, followed by Sinn Féin. The principal 'other' party is the Alliance, who polled badly.

David **Trimble** of the UUP was appointed the Assembly's First Minister with **Seamus Mallon** of the SDLP as his deputy, with executive authority in the hands of twelve ministers who, along with 98 others, make up the **Northern Ireland Assembly**. The Assembly decides on the internal affairs of state, while security, justice, and taxation remain the province of the Secretary of State and government in Westminster. One of the Assembly's initial tasks has been to decide on the areas of cross-border co-operation between the North and South. Slowly, new structures and organizations have been created to fulfil strand one of the Good Friday Agreement. The Unionists are aware that over the next 25 years or so, the population will become more balanced, and thus their negotiating position will weaken. The Nationalists too, are weary of the Troubles, and have seen their status within the province improve significantly over the years, while Sinn Féin and other Republican groups are experiencing the many dividends of joining the democratic process. Although, as yet, they have not given up their arms, which is the cause of the current stalemate.

There are major problems ahead over the question of arms still held by the IRA and Loyalist terrorist groups, and the resolution of the Drumcree parades issue, which each year is banned by the cross-party Parades Commission, set up to arbitrate over contraversial parades. The future of community policing in Northern Ireland is also problematic. The IRA has been policing Catholic West Belfast for many years, to protect their own financial empire, and to control lawless youths. Historically, there has always been Catholic hostility towards the RUC and few Catholic recruits into the force because of their fear of the IRA. In order to make the RUC more attractive to Nationalists it is in the process of reform. In July 2001, its name was changed to the **Police Service of Northern Ireland**, and the uniform and oath of allegiance altered. This reform of the RUC is necessary if the rule of law is to be reimposed on criminal activities and extortion rackets run by terrorist groups. Punishment beatings and sectarian beatings have not ceased. The **Omagh bombing** on August 15th 1998 was the most horrific in terms of civilian massacre with 28 people killed and hundreds injured. This was perpetrated by the **Real IRA**, a splinter group of the Provisional IRA which has emerged since the Sinn Féin leadership agreed to the ceasefire and the Good Friday Agreement.

Since then, the people of Northern Ireland have benefited hugely from the devolution of government, both Nationalists and Unionists. But unfortunately, a worrying polarization has been highlighted by the 2001 British elections: Nationalists and Unionists are even more deeply divided than before the Good Friday Agreement. Sinn Féin and Ian Paisley's DUP have increased their votes and MPs at the expense of the more moderate parties. Under John Reid as Secretary of State, the Belfast Agreement is still afloat at the time of writing, despite the institutions having been suspended and re-established twice. The IRA have made steps towards decommissioning, but the middle ground in politics is shrinking as the months go by.

Devolution could however emerge from this crisis stronger than ever. Despite the frustrating set-backs, the cease-fire and the Agreement are still felt to have been the irrevocable beginnings of a new phase; newspapers have reported a massive influx of returning Ulster folk and others from the British Isles into Northern Ireland. Their votes will have a significant effect on future voting patterns.

The Republic Today

The Irish Republic has a titular Head of State, a **President** who is elected for seven years by the vote of the people. The President is empowered on the recommendation of the Dáil to appoint the Prime Minister (**Taoiseach**, pronounced 'tee-shookh'), sign laws and invoke the judgement of the Supreme Court on the legality of Bills. S/he is also supreme commander of the armed forces. The Irish Parliament consists of the President and two Houses: the Dáil and the Senate. The Dáil is made up of 166 members (TDs) elected by adult suffrage through proportional representation. The Senate is made up of 60 members: 11 are nominated by the Taoiseach; 49 are elected by the Dáil and county councils from panels representative of the universities, labour, industry, education and social services. The average length of an Irish government is three years.

In the 1970s and 1980s each Irish government had to face unemployment, growing emigration and a huge national debt. In 1988, incomes measured by GDP per head were just 63 per cent of those in the UK. However, by 1998, the Republic had overtaken the UK, and today its GDP is one of the healthiest in the European Union. The forecast for the future is that the Republic's economy could grow annually by over four per cent a year, despite the downturn in the world economy. European investment in technology, food processing, pharmaceuticals and the marketing industries has benefited Ireland enormously. This is partly because of its young, well-educated population and skilled workforce. Emigration has almost halted. In fact, growing numbers of economic refugees, particularly from Eastern Europe, are entering the country, causing a worrying upsurge in racism. On the positive side, a recent US survey of 22 countries found that Ireland was overall top for feelings of national pride. The Republic is a major supporter of the EU and has been famously described as 'Europe's best pupil'. Ireland has done very well economically from EU funding, and it is now becoming a net contributor to the EU after years of being a net recipient. The Irish people voted against the Nice Treaty in June 2001, which was designed to integrate 12 countries from Eastern Europe into the EU. This was in direct opposition to what the Irish political establishment wanted; obviously a gulf has arisen between the Government and the voters. Ireland has however adopted the Euro along with most other EU countries.

The principle of neutrality so long adhered to in foreign affairs is no longer certain. Developments within the EU may see a watering down of Irish neutrality, as they include a commitment by all members to a common security policy and involvement in the 60,000-strong Rapid Reaction Force. The traditional lines of Irish parties are also changing from the pro- and anti-treaty (of 1921) stances. **Mary Robinson**, when Head of State (1990–97), brought a new flexibility and dynamism into politics here. Her policies have continued with the election of **Mary McAleese** in 1998.

In the spring of 2001, Ireland escaped the Foot and Mouth epidemic which ravaged mainland Britain, with only a few cases. The whole country united to prevent the disease getting a foothold and disinfectant footmats were everywhere, which was a great boost psychologically, as everybody was seen to be doing their bit to stop the disease in its tracks. Cultural and sporting events were cancelled, and the crisis had passed by the summer.

Irish Political Parties

The origins of the two major Irish political parties, Fianna Fáil and Fine Gael, hark back to the violent differences between those against the Free State Treaty and those for it in the turbulent 1920s.

Fianna Fáil: has established itself as the dominant ruling party.

Fine Gael: the second largest party in the country. It is close to other Christian Democrat parties in Europe, and has strong European inclinations.

The Labour Party: has found it difficult to gain popular support as people have tended to be very conservative and voted as their family do – either Fine Gael or Fianna Fáil. This is changing as Labour has increased its power base in the last 15 years in Dublin and Cork, and formed coalition governments either with Fianna Fáil or Fine Gael.

Sinn Féin: the political arm of the Provisional IRA (which is a banned organization) but does not command much support in the Republic. However, in the mid-1980s Sinn Féin dropped its absenteeist policy, and has for the first time accepted the seat it won in the last general election (the last time it won a seat was in 1957 and the last time a Sinn Féin member took up a seat was in 1922).

Other Parties in the Dáil

The Democratic Left: formed in 1992 after a split in the Worker's Party. The Worker's Party suffered from the split and has no seats in the Dáil. Originall formed by a breakaway group from the Republican Movement. Between 1977 and 1982 it was known as Sinn Féin, the Worker's Party.

The Progressive Democrats: founded in 1985 by former members of Fianna Fáil after a split in that party. It is currently in a coalition partnership with Fianna Fáil.

The Green Party: allied to Greens in 28 other countries.

Glossary of Political Parties and Terms

These labels and identities crop up constantly in discussions on Northern Ireland:

Alliance: a label used for a party composed of moderate Unionists, both Protestant and Catholic, but it loses out to the more extreme parties.

B Specials: a special, part-time reserve force within the RUC with special powers to search out IRA members, operating from the 1920s until the 1970s. Catholics maintain that they beat up alleged IRA members and intimidated ordinary Catholics.

Catholic: according to the 1991 Census 605,639 people belong to the Roman Catholic Church in Northern Ireland.

Civil Rights Movement: begun in the 1960s, inspired by the American Civil Rights campaigner Martin Luther King. The Civil Rights Association, founded in 1967, called for jobs, houses and one man, one vote. It was supported by both Catholics and Protestants, and the leadership of the Association has been described as 'middle-aged, middle-class and middle-of-the-road'. The Civil Rights Movement was hijacked by a more Republican and Socialist element and the mob violence that attended the Civil Rights marches. It eventually lost out to the IRA.

Direct Rule: The Government of the United Kingdom of Great Britain and Northern Ireland had always retained full powers of sovereignty on all matters over the Northern Ireland Government at Stormont. Thus, when the riots and bloodshed began to get out of control, and the Stormont Government seemed unable to implement reforms or control the police, Direct Rule was imposed in 1972. It was suspended in 1998 with the creation of a new Northern Ireland Assembly.

Fenian: a term for a Catholic that suggests s/he is a Republican.

Gerrymandering: refers to the policy of concentrating large numbers of Catholics with Republican views in unusually big electoral districts, whilst Protestant Unionists were in smaller districts. This meant that the Protestant Unionists were always certain to win a larger number of representatives, district by district. Gerrymandering gradually became the norm from the late 1920s until the electoral reforms at the beginning of the 1970s.

Internment: the arrest of alleged terrorist suspects for an indefinite period without trial.

IRA: the label used to describe the Irish Republican Army, which did not disband after the Civil War in Ireland ended (1920–21). The IRA is outlawed in the Republic of Ireland and the United Kingdom. The objective of its members is to fight by the gun and bomb until the whole of Ireland is free of the British, and the Six Counties reunited with the rest of Ireland. In 1969, with the start of civil disturbances, the IRA was reinvigorated. Firstly it reorganized itself and split into two. The Marxist Socialist-inspired members call themselves the Official IRA (OIRA), whereas the traditionalists call themselves the Provisional IRA (PIRA) after the 'Provisional' government of Ireland set up in the GPO after the Easter Rising of 1916. The ideals of the 'Provos' are straightforward: a United Republic of Ireland, whatever the cost in terms of violence. The Provisionals are generally referred to as the IRA, since the Officials have dropped out of the action, and declared a cease-fire in 1972.

Loyalist: refers to a Protestant who is prepared to use violence to prevent a United Ireland and maintain the Union with the UK.

Nationalist: refers to anyone who supports a united Ireland.

Protestant: refers to Church of Ireland members, Presbyterians and other non-Catholic denominations. In the same census, the Church of Ireland numbered 279,280 people, and Presbyterians numbered 336,891.

PSNI: Formerly the Royal Ulster Constabulary (RUC), which has now become the Police Service of Northern Ireland. This police force manages much of the security of Northern Ireland in co-operation with the British Army. The Catholic Nationalists in Northern Ireland traditionally regarded the RUC with dislike and suspicion, believing it to be biased by its largely Protestant Unionist membership. Catholics who joined it were singled out for death by the IRA, but it still managed to have eight per cent of (mainly English) Catholics in its ranks. The PSNI now has a different uniform and oath of allegiance.

Orange Order: a sectarian and largely working-class organization that originated as a secret Protestant working-class agrarian society known as the Peep-O'Day Boys. William of Orange (William III of England) became their hero, and the society changed its name to the Orange Order in 1795. Its members have a traditional fear of the Catholic majority in Ireland and are Unionist in politics. Orange Lodges are still active in Northern Ireland.

Republican: a supporter of United Ireland. Used as a synonym for an IRA supporter.

Republican Movement: this covers both Sinn Féin and the IRA.

Socialist, Democratic and Labour Party (SDLP): Formed in 1970 in Northern Ireland. Committed to achieving a United Ireland through peaceful and democratic means. It is not linked, except through its aims, to Sinn Féin, the political wing of the IRA, which is less choosy about its methods.

Summer Marching Season: the Orange and Hibernian marches during July and August. Each side commemorates opposing events in the history of Ireland. In the past, drums and equipment were lent between the two sides, but the present conflict has distilled into bitterness and hatred, and this has ceased. The Orange marchers in particular frequently take provocative routes through Catholic areas.

Taig: an offensive term used by Loyalists to describe Catholics.

Unionist: refers to supporters of the Union with Great Britain, who have no wish to share an Irish nationality with the Republic of Ireland. There are two main Unionist parties in Northern Ireland. The Official Unionists (UUP) were the original party and are, on the surface, more willing to discuss options to try and solve the crisis in the State. The Democratic Unionist Party (DUP), led by Ian Paisley, is more radical and Protestant. It is very anti any co-operation with the Irish Republic, and anti the pope.

UVF, UDA, UFF and **LVF**: The Ulster Volunteer Force and the Ulster Defence Association are illegal Protestant terrorist organizations that recruit from the working class. They're usually involved in revenge sectarian killings and assassinations of IRA members. The Ulster Freedom Fighters and Loyalist Volunteer Force are illegal Protestant paramilitary organizations that engage in bloody sectarian and Republican killings, and also they feud among themselves.

UDR: stands for the Ulster Defence Regiment. A regiment of the British Army, many of its soldiers are part-time, and drawn from the Protestant population in Ulster. Over 200 UDR soldiers have been killed by the IRA, often when off-duty.

Religion

04

Despite a small decline in the last few years, Ireland still has the largest number of regular churchgoers in Western Europe, and although many of the social factors which generally undermine religion are present, they do not seem to be having a huge effect as yet. The reminders and symbols of a religious faith and deep love of God are to be seen everywhere throughout the country.

The images that fill my mind are a child in white, showing off her dress after her first Holy Communion; rags caught in brambles around a holy well; cars parked up a country lane, everybody piling out for Mass, umbrellas held high and skirts fluttering. The Catholic people of Ireland invoke and refer to the Virgin Mary and to Jesus often in their everyday talk. Roadside shrines to the Virgin are decorated with shells and fresh flowers, and some people still stop what they are doing to say the Angelus at noon and at sunset. Grey neo-Gothic churches dominate the small country towns, whilst in the smaller villages the chapel or church is a simpler building, planted around with dark yews and beeches above which the ceaseless cawing of the rooks can be heard.

In Ireland most people will want to know what religion you are – whether Catholic, Presbyterian, Church of Ireland, Baptist, Methodist or Quaker. If your religion is still a mystery, they will very soon find out, not by a direct question, but in a very roundabout way of conversation and enquiry. There has long been a strong, although small, Jewish community in Ireland; and recently an increase in Islam and Buddhism. In the past, the Christian clergy would have encouraged their congregation to feel sorry for these 'poor heathens', and the greatest pity was reserved for those who did not believe in a God at all. This huge Catholic complacency is less obvious as Ireland develops into a more liberal and democratic society.

The history of Ireland has had much to do with this feeling of religious identity, and unfortunately, in the North this mix of politics and religion has produced individuals whose extreme Catholic or Presbyterian attitudes are reminiscent of 17th-century Europe. The bigotry that characterizes such attitudes has been a major factor in the political situation in the North today. Great efforts are made by some of the clergy to organize ecumenical meetings, but mostly their congregations ignore them. The challenges to the clergy in the North are enormous because, in this welcome period of peace, they must try to work together against sectarianism, and to promote reconciliation between the different Christian traditions.

Church leaders in Ireland realize that for the present position of religion in Ireland to continue, they will have to adapt to the many social trends that are changing Christian Ireland. Among the factors driving the trends are prosperity and an increase in materialism, a young, well-educated population, and a rise in the feeling that the individual should decide for him or herself on many of the moral issues on which the churches used to pronounce. This is especially true in matters of sex, marriage and family life. Under pressure from many groups, and a national referendum, the Republic has brought in divorce (albeit with many restrictions), and birth control measures are more widely available. The respect usually accorded to those in religious life has been shaken by a number of church scandals, and many people feel that the churches must become more open and accountable.

Pre-Christian Ireland

The Irish have been religious for five thousand years, and there are plenty of chambered cairns (mounds of stones over prehistoric graves) to prove it. The Celts who arrived in waves mostly between 500 BC and 300 BC seem to have been very religious, and had a religious hierarchy organized by Druids. These people worshipped a large number of gods, and central to their beliefs was the cult of the human head. They believed that the head was the centre of man's powers and thoughts. Their stonemasons carved two-headed gods, and the style of their work has a continuity which can be traced up to the 19th century. There are heads in the Lough Erne district which are difficult to date. They could be pagan, Early Christian or comparatively modern. The origins of the earlier Tuatha Dé Danaan are lost in legend: they may have been pre-Celtic gods or a race of invaders, themselves vanquished by the Celts. They are believed to have had magical powers and heroic qualities. Today they are remembered as the 'wee folk' who live in the *raths* and stone forts. Here they make fairy music which is so beautiful that it bewitches any human who hears it. The wee folk play all kinds of tricks on country people, from souring their milk to stealing their children, and so a multitude of charms have been devised to guard against these fairy pranks. I can remember being told about the fairies who used to dance in magic rings in the fields; the trouble was, if you tried to get near they would turn into yellow ragwort dancing in the wind.

Early Christian Ireland

Christianity is believed to have come to Ireland from Rome in the 4th century, although St Patrick is credited with the major conversion of the Irish in the 5th century. The Irish seem to have taken to Christianity like ducks to water, although much of our knowledge of early Christianity comes through the medieval accounts of scholarly (but possibly biased) clerics. One explanation for the ease with which Christianity took over is that the Christians didn't try to change things too fast, and incorporated elements of the Druidic religion into their practices. An example of this assimilation by the Christians is the continuing religious significance of the holy wells. Ash and rowan trees, both sacred to the Druids, are frequently found near the wells, and Christian pilgrims still leave offerings of rags on the trees as a sign to the Devil that he has no more power over them. *Patterns* (pilgrimages) and games used to be held at the wells, although they often shocked the priest, who would put the well out of bounds and declare that its healing powers had been destroyed. There are many everyday signs that the spiritual life of the Irish people harks back to pagan times. In cottages you might see a strange sign like a swastika, made out of rushes. This is a St Brigid's Cross, hung above the door or window to keep the evil spirits away. Fairy or sacred trees are still left standing in the field even though it is uneconomic to plough round them – bad luck invariably follows the person who cuts one down.

Monasteries in Early Christian Ireland

The first Christian churches were built of mud and wattle, and later of oak wood; the larger ones were painted inside with frescoes and decorated with linen hangings.

The need for chalices, altar vessals, bells and bible covers stimulated craftsmen to produce filigree and enamel work and carvings. By the end of the 5th century, a monasticism of the kind associated with the communities of the Desert Fathers in the Near East and Eastern Europe came to Ireland, and many place names with *disert* in them are indicative of each. Larger, more relaxed monasteries also flourished, and became the most important centres in the region. Each one followed the rule established by its founder. The episcopal organization set up by St Patrick was replaced by one in which the abbots were the more effective leaders in the Church.

By the end of the 6th century the Church was firmly monastic, with great monasteries such as Clonmacnoise in County Offaly and Clonfert in County Galway. These centres were responsible for big strides in agricultural development and were important for trade; they also became places where learning and artistry of all sorts were admired and emulated. The Ireland of 'Saints and Scholars' reached its peak in the 7th century. The monks sought an ascetic and holy way of life, although this was pursued in a warlike manner. The ultimate self-sacrifice was self-imposed exile, and so they founded monasteries in Scotland, England, France, Italy and Germany. The abbots, by the 8th century, had become all-powerful in Irish politics; many were tied by kinship to petty kings, and so were involved in their territorial disputes. Missionaries continued to leave Ireland and contribute to the revival of Christianity in Europe, and there was a blossoming of the arts with wonderful metalwork and painted manuscripts. By the 9th century, the monasteries were commissioning intricately carved stone high crosses, such as you can see at Ahenny in County Tipperary.

Religious Discrimination

Religious discrimination is long-established in Ireland. Over the centuries Catholics and Protestants have suffered by not conforming to the established church, although Catholics have undoubtedly received the greatest share of discrimination and persecution. The Huguenots (French Protestants), who were skilled workers and established the important linen industry, arrived when Louis XIV revoked the Edict of Nantes in 1686. The biggest group of dissenters were the Presbyterians: most of them were Scots who settled in Ulster during the 17th century. They had been persecuted in Scotland because of their religious beliefs and now they found that Ireland was no better; the Presbyterians were as poor as the native Irish, and many found life so hard that they emigrated to America. Quakers, Palatines (German Protestants), Moravians, Baptists and Methodists also settled in Ireland, but their numbers have declined through emigration and intermarriage.

Religion in Ireland Today

The 1991 population census reveals that, overall, 75.1 per cent of the Irish are Catholic, 14 per cent are Protestant, while the rest is made up of people who either were not inclined to state their religion, or who did not have any religion at all.

In the Republic, the Catholic majority of 91.6 per cent is obviously the controlling force in political and social life, and the Protestant minority has bowed out gracefully.

The Protestants used to represent almost 10 per cent of the population but this figure has declined to 3.1 per cent through mixed marriages and emigration.

In theory the modern state does not tolerate religious discrimination, and it is true that both Jews and Protestants have reached positions of importance and wealth in industry and banking. However, the Protestant classes had it so good during the hundreds of years of British rule that it is not surprising that for a short time there was a legacy of antipathy towards anyone connected with the mainly Protestant ascendency. Happily, the antipathy has nearly disappeared now. The Church is still very powerful; the bishops' exhortations on divorce, contraception, AIDS and so on are listened to with great earnestness by the politicians, and the sanctity of the family is held to be of the greatest importance. Of course, in Northern Ireland, the laws of the land are quite secular, being laid down by the British government, but divorce is still quite unusual there, too, and the principal UK legislation on abortion, the 1967 Abortion Act, has not been extended to the province.

The parish priest is of great importance in Irish society and is usually very approachable. You might meet him in the village bar having a drink and a chat. Nearly every family has a close relative who is a priest or a nun, and they leave in great numbers to serve overseas, taking their particular brand of conservative Catholicism with them. Schooling is mostly in the hands of the Church (incidentally, Ireland has a very high standard of literacy and general education), and thankfully the days of the cane and the cruel sarcasm of the priest-teachers described by so many Irish writers has disappeared. The people in the top positions in Ireland today mostly went to Christian Brothers Schools (look in the Irish *Who's Who*). So did many county councillors and petty officials who organize Ireland's huge bureaucracy. The old-boy network still gets favours done, grants approved, and planning permission granted.

In Northern Ireland, there is a divided system – although all schools are eligible for 100 per cent state funding, most Catholics attend Catholic 'maintained' schools and more Protestant children attend state 'controlled' schools. There's a small but growing number of mixed religion primary and secondary schools, attended by around two per cent of children. Irish people practise their religion faithfully in rural areas. The churches are full on Sundays, and visits to Knock, Croagh Patrick and Lough Derg are made many times in a person's lifetime. Holy wells are still visited, and Stations of the Cross go on even in ruined churches and friaries. But in the cities more and more young people and disillusioned individuals have moved away from the church, and some religious orders are forced to advertise for new priests. The numbing censoriousness of Catholicism and Protestantism in Ireland has become part of the island's image, just like the green hills and constant rain, but it is a theme which has been overplayed. Great community involvement and care comes directly from the churches, and the social events are great fun. The Irish are among the most generous when it comes to raising money for world disasters, and this charity work is usually channelled through the Church.

Death and weddings are always occasions for a bit of '*craic*', and there is also a party whenever the priest blesses a new house. Irish couples spend more on their engagement rings and weddings than their English counterparts; it is a really big occasion. The Irish wake for the dead has lost many of its pagan rituals – mourning with keening and games involving disguise, mock weddings, jokes and singing. Nowadays, the dead person is laid out in another room and people come to pay their last respects, and then spend the rest of the evening drinking, eating and reminiscing.

In 2001 a reliquary containing half the bones of Saint Thérèse of Lisieux came to Ireland on a 3-month tour, attracting huge crowds: according to the tour organizers, as many as 3 million people turned out to see the holy relics. Without a doubt, religious faith is alive and well in Ireland.

Irish Saints

Every locality in Ireland has its particular saint. The stories that surround him or her belong to myth and legend, not usually to historical fact. One theory is that all these obscure, miraculous figures are in fact Celtic gods and goddesses who survived under the mantle of sainthood. Included below is a short account of the lives of some of the most famous saints, about whom a few facts are known.

Brendan (c. 486–575), Abbot and Navigator

This holy man is remembered for his scholastic foundations, and for the extraordinary journey he made in search of Hy-Brasil, believed to be an island of paradise, which he had seen as a mirage whilst looking out on the Atlantic from the Kerry Mountains. His journey is recounted in the *Navigatio Brendan*, a treasure of every European library during the Middle Ages. The oldest copies are in Latin and date from the 11th century. The account describes a sea voyage that took Brendan and 12 monks to the Orkneys, Wales, Iceland, and to a land where tropical fruits and flowers grew. Descriptions of his voyage have convinced some scholars that he sailed down the east coast of America to Florida. Tim Severin, a modern-day explorer, and 12 others recreated this epic voyage between May 1976 and June 1977. In their leather and wood boat, they proved that the Irish monks could have been the first Europeans to land in America (the boat is at the Lough Gur Interpretative Centre, County Limerick; *see* p.166). Christopher Columbus probably read the *Navigatio*, and in Galway there is a strong tradition that he came to the west coast in 1492 to search out traditions about St Brendan. The saint's main foundation was at Clonfert, which became a great scholastic centre. Brendan is buried in Clonfert Cathedral, and he is honoured in St Brendan's Cathedral in Loughrea, County Galway, where the beautiful mosaic floor in the sanctuary depicts his ship and voyage.

St Brigid (died c. 525), Abbess of Kildare

Brigid, also known as Bridget, Bride and Brigit, is the most beloved saint in Ireland and is often called Mary of the Gael. Devotion to her spread to Scotland, England and the Continent. Traditions and stories surrounding her describe her generous and warm-hearted acts to the poor, her ability to counsel the rulers of the day, and her great holiness. Her father was a pagan from Leinster and she was fostered by a Druid.

She decided not to marry and founded a religious order with seven other girls. They were the first formal community of nuns and wore simple white dresses. St Brigid has her feast day on 1 February, which is also the date of the pagan festival Imbolg, marking the beginning of spring. She is the patron of poets, scholars, blacksmiths and healers, and is also inevitably linked with Brigid, the pagan goddess of fire and song. There is a tradition that St Brigid's Abbey in Kildare contained a sanctuary with a perpetual fire, tended only by virgins, whose high priestess was regarded as an incarnation and successor of the goddess. The two women are further linked by the fact that Kildare in Irish means 'church of oak', and St Brigid's church was built from a tree held sacred to the Druids. There's a theory that Brigid and her companions accepted the Christian faith, and then transformed the pagan sanctuary into a Christian shrine.

Kildare was a great monastic centre after Brigid's death, and produced the now lost masterpiece, the *Kildare Gospels*. Tradition says that the designs were so beautiful because an angel helped create them. The St Brigid's nuns kept alight the perpetual fire until the suppression of the religious houses during the Reformation. Brigid was buried in Kildare Church, but in AD 835 her remains were moved to Downpatrick in County Down, because of the raids by the Norsemen. She is supposed to share a grave with St Patrick and St Colmcille, but there is no proof of this. In 1283 it is recorded that three Irish knights set out to the Holy Land with her head; they died en route in Lamiar, Portugal, and in a church there her head is enshrined in a chapel to St Brigid. The word 'bride' derives from St Brigid. It is supposed to originate from the Knights of Chivalry, whose patroness she was; they called the girls they married their 'brides'.

St Columban (died 615), Missionary Abbot

Columban, also known as Columbanus, is famous as the great missionary saint. He was born in Leinster and educated at Bangor in County Down under St Comgall, who was famed for his scholarship and piety. Columban set off for Europe with 12 other religious men to preach the gospel and convert the pagans in Gaul (France) and Germany. He founded a monastery at Annegray, which is between Austria and Burgundy, in AD 575, and his rule of austerity attracted many. Lexeuil, a larger monastery, and Fontaines were both established within a few miles of Annegray. When Columban was exiled by the local king, he and his followers founded Bobbio in the Apennines, between Piacenza and Genoa. Bobbio became a great centre of culture and orthodoxy from which monasticism spread. Its great glory was its library, and its books are scattered all over Europe and regarded as treasures.

St Colmcille (c. 521–97), Missionary Abbot

Along with St Patrick and St Brigid, Colmcille, also known as Columba and Columcille, is probably the most famous of the Irish saints, a charismatic personality who was a scholar, poet and ruler, and spread the gospel to Iona and hence to Scotland. St Colmcille was a prince of Tyrconnell (County Donegal), and a great-great-grandson of Niall of the Nine Hostages, who had been High King of Ireland. On his mother's side he was descended from the Leinster Kings. He was educated by

St Finian of Movilla, in County Down, and also by Finnian of Clonard and Mobhi of Glasnevin. He studied music and poetry at the Bardic School of Leinster, and the poems he wrote which have survived are delightful. A few are preserved in the Bodleian Library, Oxford. He chose to be a monk, and never to receive episcopal rank. He wrote of his devotion: 'The fire of God's love stays in my heart as a jewel set in gold in a silver vessel.' In AD 545 he built his first church in Derry, the place he loved most. Then he founded Durrow and later Kells, which became very important in the 9th century when the Columban monks of Iona fled from the Vikings and made it their headquarters. In all, Colmcille founded 37 monastic churches in Ireland; he also produced the *Cathach*, a manuscript of the Psalms. At the age of 42 he set out with 12 companions to be an exile for Christ. They sailed to the island of Iona, off the west coast of Scotland, which was part of the Kingdom of Dalriada ruled over by the Irish King Aidan. He converted Brude, King of the Picts, founded two churches in Inverness, and helped to keep the peace between the Picts and the Irish colony. The legend that he left Ireland because of a dispute over the copy he made of a psalter of St Finian is very dubious. Apparently the dispute caused a great battle, although the high king of the time, King Diarmuid, tried to settle the dispute and had ruled against Colmcille, saying: 'to every cow its calf, to every book its copy'. The saint is supposed to have punished himself for the deaths he caused by going into exile. Colmcille was famous for his austerity, fasting and vigils; his bed and pillow were of stone. He died at Iona, and his relics were taken to Dunkeld (Scotland) in AD 849.

St Enda of Aran (died *c.* 535), Abbot

Famous as the patriarch of monasticism, he's described as a warrior who left the secular world in middle life. He had succeeded to the kingdom of Oriel, but decided to study for the priesthood. Granted the Aran Islands by his brother-in-law, Aengus, King of Cashel, he is said to have lived a life of great severity, and never had a fire in winter, as he believed that 'hearts so glowing with the love of God' could not feel the cold. He reputedly taught 127 other saints, who are buried close to him on the islands.

St Kevin of Glendalough (died *c.* 618), Abbot

Many stories surround St Kevin, but we know he was one of the many Irish abbots who chose to remain a priest. He lived a solitary, contemplative life in the Glendalough Valley. He played the harp, and the Rule for his monks was in verse. He is supposed to have prayed for so long that a blackbird had time to lay an egg and hatch it on his outstretched hand. His monastery flourished until the 11th century. In the 12th century St Lawrence O'Toole came to Glendalough and modelled his life on St Kevin's, bringing fresh fame to his memory. The foundation was finally destroyed in the 16th century.

St Kieran (*c.* 512–49), Abbot

St Kieran, also known as Ciaran, is remembered for his great foundation of Clonmacnoise, where the ancient chariot road through Ireland crosses the Shannon River. Unlike many Irish abbots he was not of aristocratic blood, for his father was a chariot-maker from County Antrim, and his mother from Kerry. St Kieran attracted craftsmen to his order, and Clonmacnoise grew to be a great monastic school, where, unusually for Ireland, the position of abbot did not become hereditary. Kieran died within a short time of founding the school. Many kings are buried alongside him, for it was believed that he would bring their souls safely to heaven.

St Malachy (1094–1148), Archbishop of Armagh

Malachy is famous as the great reformer of the Irish Church. He persuaded the Pope, Eugenius III, to establish the Archbishops of Ireland separately from those of England. He also ensured that it was no longer possible for important ecclesiastical positions to be held by certain families as a hereditary right. For example, he was appointed Bishop of Armagh, although the See of Armagh was held in lay succession by one family. It was an achievement to separate the family from this post without splitting the Irish Church.

The saint was educated in Armagh and Lismore, County Waterford, and desired only to be an itinerant preacher. His great talents took him instead to be Bishop of Down and Connor, and in 1125 he became Abbot-Bishop of Armagh. He travelled to France, where he made a lasting friendship with Bernard of Clairvaux, the reforming Cistercian. The Pope appointed him papal legate in Ireland, and whilst abroad he made some famous prophecies; one was that there will be the peace of Christ over all Ireland when the palm and the shamrock meet. This is supposed to mean when St Patrick's Day (17 March) occurs on Palm Sunday.

St Patrick (c. 390–461), Bishop and Patron Saint of Ireland

St Patrick was born somewhere between the Severn and the Clyde on the west coast of Britain. As a youth he was captured by Irish slave-traders, and taken to the Antrim coast to work as a farm labourer. Controversy surrounds the details of Patrick's life. Popular tradition credits him with converting the whole of Ireland, but nearly all that can be truly known of him comes from his *Confessio* or autobiography, and other writings. Through these, he is revealed as a simple, sincere and humble man who was full of care for his people; an unlearned man, once a fugitive, who came to trust God completely. Tradition states that after six years of slavery, voices told him he would soon return to his own land, and he escaped. Later, other voices called to him from Ireland, entreating him 'to come and walk once more amongst us'.

It is believed that he spent some time in Gaul (France) and became a priest; perhaps he had some mission conferred on him by the Pope to go and continue the work of Palladius, another missionary bishop who worked among the Christian Irish. It is believed that some confusion has arisen over the achievements of Palladius and Patrick. Patrick, when he returned to Ireland, seems to have been most active in the north, whilst Palladius worked in the south. He made Armagh his primary see, and it has remained the centre of Christianity in Ireland. He organized the church on the lines of territorial sees, and encouraged the laity to become monks or nuns. He was very concerned with abolishing paganism, idolatry and sun-worship, and he preached to the highest and the lowest in the land. Tradition credits him with expelling the snakes from Ireland, and explaining the Trinity by pointing to a shamrock. One of the most famous episodes handed down by popular belief is that of his confrontation with King Laoghaire at Tara, known as the seat of the high kings of Ireland, and the capital of Meath. It was supposedly on Easter Saturday in 432, which that year coincided with a great Druid festival at Tara. No new fire was allowed to be lit until the lighting of the sacred pagan fire by the Druids. St Patrick was camped on the Hill of Slane which looks onto Tara, and his campfire was burning brightly; the Druids warned King Laoghaire that if it was not put out, it would never be extinguished. When Patrick was brought before Laoghaire, his holiness melted the king's hostility and he was invited to stay. Although Laoghaire did not become a Christian, his brother Conal, a prince of the North, became his protector and ally.

Certain places in Ireland are traditionally closely associated with St Patrick, such as Croagh Patrick in County Mayo, where there is an annual pilgrimage to the top of the 2,510ft (765m) mountain on the last Sunday of July; and Downpatrick and Saul in County Down. The cult of St Patrick spread from Ireland to many Irish monasteries in Europe, and in more modern times to North America and Australia, where large communities of Irish emigrants live. The annual procession on 17 March, St Patrick's Day, in New York has become a massive event, where everybody sports a shamrock and drinks green beer. However, quite a few Irish believe St Colmcille should be the patron saint of Ireland, not this mild and humble British missionary.

Oliver Plunkett (1625–81), Archbishop of Armagh and Martyr

This gentle and holy man lived in frightening and turbulent times, when to be a practising Catholic in Ireland was to court trouble. He was born into a noble and wealthy family whose lands extended throughout the Pale. He was sent to study in Rome, and was a brilliant theology and law scholar. He became a priest in 1654 and in 1669 was appointed Archbishop of Armagh. Oliver was one of only two bishops in Ireland at that time, and the whole of the laity was in disorder and neglect. Apart from the hostility of the Protestants, the Catholics themselves were divided by internal squabbles. Oliver confirmed thousands of people, and held a provincial synod. He did much to maintain discipline amongst the clergy, to improve education by founding the Jesuit College in Drogheda, and to promulgate the decrees of the Council of Trent. Oliver managed to remain on good terms with many of the Protestant gentry and clergy, but was eventually outlawed by the British government. The panic caused by the false allegations made by Titus Oates in England about a popish plot was used by Plunkett's enemies, and he was arrested in 1678. He was absurdly charged with plotting to bring in twenty thousand French troops, and levying a charge on his clergy to support an army. No jury could be found to convict him in Ireland, so he was brought to England, where he was convicted of treason for setting up 'a false religion which was the most dishonourable and derogatory to God of all religions and that a greater crime could not be committed against God than for a man to endeavour to propagate that religion'. He was hanged, drawn and quartered at Tyburn in July 1681. His head is in the Oliver Plunkett Church in Drogheda, County Louth, and his body lies at Downside Abbey, Somerset.

The Old Gods and Heroes

The Celts

Nobody knows exactly when the first Celts arrived in Ireland; it was some time before 1000 BC, with the last wave of people coming around the 3rd century BC. The Greek chroniclers were the first to name these people, calling them *Keltori*. Celt means 'act of concealment', and it has been suggested that they were called 'hidden people' because of their reluctance to commit their great store of scholarship and knowledge to written records. Kilt, the short male skirt of traditional Celtic dress, may also come from this word.

The Celtic civilization was quite sophisticated, and much of the road-building attributed to the Romans has been found to have been started by the Celts. The Romans frequently built on their foundations. In Ireland, ancient roads are often discovered when bog is cleared.

Ireland's ancient and rich epic story tradition was strictly oral until the Christian era. Even then, it was well into the 7th century before the bulk of it was written down by scribes, who often added to or changed the story to give it some moral Christian interpretation. The reluctance of the Celts to commit their knowledge to writing is directly related to the Druids and their power, because the Druidic religion was the cornerstone of the Celtic world, which stretched from Ireland to the Continent and as far south as Turkey. Irish mythology is therefore concerned with the rest of that Celtic world, and there are relationships with the gods and heroes of Wales, Scotland, Spain and Central Europe.

The *Book of the Dun Cow* and the *Book of Leinster*, the main surviving manuscript sources, date from the late 11th century. Many earlier books were destroyed by the Viking raids, and entire libraries lost. The various sagas and romances that survived have been categorized by scholars into four cycles. First, the **mythological cycle**: the stories that tell of the various invasions of Ireland, from Cesair to the Sons of Milesius. These are largely concerned with the activities of the Túatha Dé Danaan, the pagan gods of Ireland. Next there is the **Ulster Cycle**, or deeds of the Red Branch Knights, which include the tales of Cú Chulainn and the *Táin Bó Cuailgne*. Then there is the **Cycle of Kings**, mainly stories about semi-mythical rulers; and finally the **Fenian Cycle**, which relates the adventures of Fionn MacCumhaill (Finn MacCool) and the warriors of the Fianna. Only qualified story-tellers could recite these sagas and tales under Brehon (Celtic) laws, and they were held in great respect. Several qualities emerge from these sagas and tell us a great deal about the society of Iron Age Ireland, and indeed Europe. The stories are always optimistic, and the Celts had evolved a doctrine of immortality of the soul.

The heroes and gods were interchangeable – there were no hard and fast divisions between gods and mortals. Both had the ability to change shape, and often reappear after the most gruesome deaths. The gods of the Dé Danaan were tall, beautiful and fair, although, later, in the popular imagination, they became fairies or the 'little people'. They were intellectual as well as beautiful, but as gullible as mortals, with all our virtues and vices. They loved pleasure, art, nature, games, feasting and heroic single combat. It is difficult to know whether they are heroes and heroines made into gods by their descendants. In the 11th century, Cú Chulainn was the most admired hero, particularly by the élite of society. Then Fionn MacCumhaill took over. He and his band of warriors became very popular with the ordinary people right up to the early 20th century. The English conquests in the 17th century and the resulting destruction and exile of the Irish intelligentsia meant that much knowledge was lost, though the peasantry kept it alive in folklore recited by the *seanachie* or village story-teller. Then, with the famines and vast emigration of the 19th century, the Irish language came under great threat and, with it, the folklore.

The stories were anglicized by antiquarians and scholars at the end of the 18th century and into the 19th century, who did much to record and translate the Irish epic stories into English and to preserve the Gaelic; many were Ulster Presbyterians. Names that should be remembered with honour are William Carleton, Lady Wilde, T. Crofton-Croker, Standish James O'Grady, Lady Gregory and Douglas Hyde. Their writings and records of Irish peasant culture have become standard works.

The question of where Irish myth ends and history begins is impossible to answer. Historical accounts are shot through with allegory, supernatural happenings and fantasy. Nothing at all has changed, as a similar mythical process is applied to modern Irish history.

Directory of the Gods

Amergin: a Son of Milesius. The first Druid of Ireland. There are three poems credited to him in *The Book of Invasions*.

Aonghus Óg: the God of Love, son of Dagda. His palace was by the River Boyne at Newgrange. Also known as Aengus.

Ard Rí: the title of High King.

Badhbha or *Badh*: goddess of battles.

Balor: a god of death, and one of the most formidable Fomorii. His one eye destroyed everything it gazed on. Destroyed by his own grandson, Lugh.

Banba, Fotla and Eire Dé Danaan: sister goddesses who represent the spirit of Ireland, particularly in Irish literature and poetry. It is from the goddess Eire that Ireland takes its modern name.

Bilé: god of life and death. He appears as Cymbeline in Shakespeare's play.

Bran: 'Voyage of Bran'. This is the earliest voyage poem, which describes through beautiful imagery the Island of Joy and the Island of Women. Also, the hound of Fionn MacCumhaill.

Brigid: goddess of healing, fertility and poetry. Her festival is one of the four great festivals of the Celtic world. Also a Christian saint who has become confused in popular folklore with the goddess.

Caílte: cousin of Fionn MacCumhaill. One of the chief Warriors of the Fianna, and a poet. A Christian addition to his story has returned him from the Otherworld to recount to St Patrick the adventures of the Fianna.

Conall Cearnach: son of Amergin, a warrior of the Red Branch, and foster brother and blood cousin of Cú Chulainn. He avenged Cú Chulainn's death by slaying his killers.

Conchobhar MacNessa: king of Ulster during the Red Branch Cycle. He fell in love with Deidre (*see* below) and died from a magic 'brain ball' which had been lodged in his head seven years before by the Connacht warrior, Cet.

Conn: one of the Sons of Lir, the ocean god, changed into a swan by his jealous stepmother Aoife. Also, Conn of the hundred battles, High King from AD 177 to 212.

Cormac MacArt: High King from AD 254 to 277 and patron of the Fianna, he reigned during the period of Fionn MacCumhaill and his adventures. His daughter was betrothed to Fionn MacCumhaill but eloped with one of Fionn's warriors, Diarmuid. His son succeeded him and destroyed the Fianna.

Cú Chulainn: the hound of Culann, also called the Hound of Ulster. He has similarities with the Greek hero, Achilles. He was actually called Sétanta until he killed the hound belonging to Culann, a smith god from the Otherworld. He promised to take its place and guarded his fortress at night. He became a great warrior whose battle frenzy was incredible. Women were always falling in love with him, but Emer, his wife, managed to keep him. He is chiefly famous for his single-handed defence of Ulster during the War of the Tain (Bull of Cuailgne) when Ailill and Medb of Connacht invaded (*see* Medb). He was acknowledged as champion of all Ireland, and forced to slay his best friend, Ferdia, during a combat at a crucial ford. Later Cú Chulainn rejected the love of the goddess of battles, Mórrigan, and his doom was sealed; his enemies finally slew him. During the fatal fight he strapped his body to a pillar stone because he was too weak to stand. But such was his reputation that no one dared to come near him until Mórrigan, in the form of a crow, perched on his shoulder, and finally an otter drank his blood.

Dagha: father of the Gods and patron god of the Druids.

Diarmuid: foster son of the love god, Aonghus Óg, and a member of the Fianna. The goddess of youth put her love spot on him, so that no woman could resist loving him. He eloped with Grainne, who was betrothed to Fionn MacCumhaill, and the Fianna pursued them for 16 years. Eventually the couple made an uneasy peace with Fionn, who went out hunting with Diarmuid on Ben Bulben, where Diarmuid was gored by an enchanted boar who was also his own stepbrother. Fionn had the power to heal him with some enchanted water, but he let it slip through his fingers. Aonghus Óg, the god of love, took Diarmuid's body to his palace and, although he did not restore him to life, sent a soul into his body so that he could talk to him each day.

Deidre: Deidre of the Sorrows was the daughter of an Ulster chieftain. When she was born it was forecast by a Druid that she would be the most beautiful woman in the land, but that, because of her, Ulster would suffer great ruin and death. Her father wanted to put her to death at once but Conchobhar, the Ulster King, took pity on her and said he would marry her when she grew up. When the time came she did not want to marry such an old man, particularly as she had fallen in love with Naoise, a hero of the Red Branch. They eloped to Scotland. Conchobhar lured them back with false promises, and Naoise and his brothers were killed by Eoghan MacDuracht. Deidre was forced to become Conchobhar's wife. She did not smile for a year, which infuriated her husband. When he asked her who she hated most in the world, she replied, 'you and Eoghan MacDuracht'. The furious Conchobhar then said she must be Eoghan's wife for a year. When she was put in Eoghan's chariot with her hands bound, she somehow managed to fling herself out and dash her head against a rock. A pine tree grew from her grave and touched another pine growing from Naoise's grave, and the two intertwined.

Donn: king of the Otherworld, where the dead go.

Emain Macha: the capital of the kings of Ulster for six centuries, which attained great glory during the time of King Conchobhar and the Red Branch Knights.

Emer: wife of Cú Chulainn. She had the six gifts of womanhood: beauty, chastity, eloquence, needlework, sweet voice and wisdom.

Female champions: in ancient Irish society women had equal rights with men. They could be elected to any office, inherit wealth and hold full ownership under law. Cú Chulainn was instructed in the martial arts by Scáthach, and there was another female warrior in the Fianna called Creidue. Battlefields were always presided over by goddesses of war. Nessa, Queen of Ulster, and Queen Medb of Connacht were great warriors and leaders. Boadicea of Britain was a Celtic warrior queen who died in AD 62, and this tradition survived with Grace O'Malley of County Mayo into the 16th century.

Ferdia: the best friend of Cú Chulainn, killed by him in a great and tragic combat in the battle over the Brown Bull of Cuailgne (or Cooley).

Fergus MacRoth: stepfather of Conchobhar, used by him to deceive Deidre and Naoise and his brothers. He went into voluntary exile to Connacht in a great fury with the King, and fought against Conchobhar and the Red Branch. But he refused to fight against Cú Chulainn, which meant the ultimate defeat of Queen Medb and her armies.

The Fianna: known as the Fenians. A band of warriors guarding the high king of Ireland. Said to have been founded in about 300 BC, they were perhaps a caste of the military élite. Fionn MacCumhaill was their greatest leader. In the time of Oscar, his grandson, they destroyed themselves through a conflict between the clans Bascna and Morna. In the 19th century the term was revived as a synonym for Irish Republican Brotherhood, and today it is used as the title for one of the main Irish political parties, Fianna Fail, which means 'Soldiers of Destiny'.

Fintan: the husband of Cesair, the first invader of Ireland. He abandoned her and survived the Great Deluge of the Bible story by turning into a salmon. Also, the Salmon of Knowledge who ate the Nuts of Knowledge before swimming to a pool in the River Boyne, where he was caught by the Druid Finegas. He was given to Fionn MacCumhaill to cook. Fionn burnt his finger on the flesh of the fish as he was turning the spit, sucked his thumb, and acquired the knowledge for himself.

Fionn MacCumhaill: anglicized as Finn MacCool. He was brought up by two wise women, then sent to study under Finegas the Druid. After acquiring the Knowledge of the Salmon, Fintan, he became known as Fionn, the Fair One. He was appointed head of the Fianna by Cormac MacArt, the High King at the time, in place of Goll MacMorna who had killed his father. His exploits are many and magical, and include creating the Giant's Causeway, in Co. Antrim. His two famous hunting hounds were Bran and Sceolan, who were actually his own nephews, the children of his bewitched sister. His son, Oísín, was the child of the goddess Sadb, but he suffered unrequited love for Grainne. In the story of the Battle of Ventry, Fionn overcomes Daire Donn, the King of the World. He is said not to be dead, but sleeping in a cave, waiting for the call to help Ireland in her hour of need.

Dé Fionnbharr and Oonagh: gods of the Dé Danaan who have degenerated into the King and Queen of the Fairies in folklore.

Fionnuala: the daughter of Lir. She and her brothers were transformed into swans by her jealous stepmother, Aoife. The spell was broken with the coming of Christianity, but they were old and senile by then.

Fir Bolg: 'Bagmen'. A race who came to Ireland before the Dé Danaan. They do not take much part in the myths.

Fomorii: a misshapen and violent people, who are the evil gods of Irish myth. Their headquarters seems to have been Tory Island, off the coast of County Donegal. Their leaders include Balor of the Evil Eye, and their power was broken for ever by the Dé Danaan at the second Battle of Moytura, in County Sligo.

Gaul: Celt. Gaulish territory extended over France, Belgium, parts of Switzerland, Bohemia, parts of modern Turkey and parts of Spain.

Geis: a taboo or bond which was usually used by Druids and placed on someone to compel them to obey. Grainne put one on Diarmuid.

Goibhnin: smith god, and god of handicraft and artistry.

Goll MacMorna: leader of the Fianna before Fionn MacCumhaill.

Grainne: anglicized as Grania. Daughter of Cormac MacArt, the high king. She was betrothed to Fionn MacCumhaill but thought him very old, so she put a *geis* on Diarmuid to compel him to elope with her. Eventually he fell in love with her (*see Diarmuid*). After Diarmuid's death, although she had sworn vengeance on Fionn, she allowed herself to be wooed by him and became his wife. The Fianna despised her for this.

Laeg: charioteer to Cú Chulainn.

Lir: ocean god.

Lugh: sun god who slew his grandfather, Balor, and the father of Cú Chulainn by a mortal woman. His godly status was diminished into that of a fairy craftsman, Lugh Chromain, a leprechaun.

Macha: a woman who put a curse called *cest nóiden* on all Ulstermen, so that they would suffer from the pangs of childbirth for five days and four nights in times of Ulster's greatest need. This curse would last nine times nine generations. She did this because her husband boasted to King Conchobhar that she could beat the king's horses in a race, even though she was pregnant. She died in agony as a result.

Medb: anglicized as Maeve. Queen of Connacht, and wife of Ailill. She was famous for her role in the epic tale of the cattle raid of Cuailgne (Cooley), which she started when she found that her possessions were not as great as her husband's. She wanted the Brown Bull of Cuailgne which was in Ulster, to outdo her husband's bull, the White-Horned Bull of Connacht. This had actually started off as a calf in her herd, but had declined to stay in the herd of a woman. She persuaded her husband to join her in the great battle that resulted. The men of the Red Branch were hit by the curse of the *nóiden* (*see* Macha), and none could fight except Cú Chulainn, who was free of the weakness the curse induced and single-handedly fought the Connacht champions. Mebh was killed by Forbai, son of Conchobhar, while bathing in a lake. The bulls over which the great battle had been fought eventually tore each other to pieces.

Milesians: the last group of invaders of Ireland before the historical period. Milesius, a Spanish soldier, was their leader but his sons actually carried out the Conquest of Ireland.

Nessa: mother of Conchobhar. A strong-minded and powerful woman who secured the throne of Ulster for her son.

Niall of the Nine Hostages: High King from AD 379 to 405, and progenitor of the Uí Neill dynasty. There is a confusion of myth and history surrounding him.

Niamh: of the golden hair. A daughter of the sea god Manannán Mac Lir. She asked Oísín to accompany her to the Land of Promise and live there as her lover. After three weeks, he discovered three hundred years had passed.

Nuada of the Silver Hand: the leader of the Dé Danaan gods, who had his hand cut off in the great battle with the Fomorii. It was replaced by the god of healing.

Ogma: god of eloquence and literature, from whom ogham stones were named. These are upright pillars carved with incised lines that read as an alphabet from the bottom upwards. They probably date from AD 300.

Oísín: son of Fionn and Sadh, the daughter of a god, and leading champion of the Fianna. He refused to help his father exact vengeance on Grainne (to whom Fionn was betrothed) and Diarmuid (with whom Grainne eloped), and went with Niamh of the Golden Hair to the Land of Promise. Oísín longed to go back to Ireland, so Niamh gave him a magic horse on which to return, but warned him not to set foot on land, as three hundred years had passed since he was there. He fell from his horse by accident and turned into an old, blind man. A Christian embellishment is that he met St Patrick and told him the stories of the Fianna, and they had long debates about the merits of Christianity. Oísín refused to agree that his Ireland was better off for it. His mood comes through in this anonymous verse from a 16th-century poem translated by Frank O'Connor.

Patrick you chatter too loud
And lift your crozier too high
Your stick would be kindling soon
If my son Osgar stood by.

Oscar or Osgar: son of Oísín. He also refused to help Fionn, his grandfather, against Diarmuid and Grainne. The high king of the time wished to weaken the Fianna and allowed the two clans in it, Morna and Bascna, to quarrel. They fought at the battle of Gabhra. Oscar was killed and the Fianna destroyed.

Partholón: the leader of the third mythical invasion of Ireland. He is supposed to have introduced agriculture to Ireland.

Red Branch: a body of warriors who were the guardians of Ulster during the reign of Conchobhar MacNessa. Their headquarters were at Emain (*Eamhain*) Macha. The Red Branch cycle of tales has been compared to the Iliad in theme. The main stories are made up of the *Táin Bó Cuailgne* (the Brown Bull of Cuailgne or Cooley). Scholars accept that the cycle of stories must have been transmitted orally for nearly a thousand years, providing wonderful descriptions of the remote past.

From Stone Circles to Castles

06

Ireland is fascinatingly rich in monuments, and you cannot fail to be struck by the number and variety of archaeological remains all over the country. They crown the tops of hills or stand out, grey and mysterious, in the green fields. Myths and stories surround them, handed down by word of mouth. Archaeologists too have their theories, and they are as varied and unprovable as the myths!

Man is known to have lived in this country since Middle Stone Age times (roughly from about 6000 BC). There are no structures left from these times but, following the coming of Neolithic or New Stone Age peoples, some of the most spectacular of the Irish monuments began to be built.

Here is a brief description of the types to be seen in order of age.

Stone Circles

The stone circles served as prehistoric temples and go back to Early Bronze Age times. Impressive examples may be seen at Lough Gur, County Limerick, and on Beltany Hill, near Lifford, County Donegal. Earthen circles probably served a similar purpose. One example is the Giant's Ring at Drumbo near Belfast, which surrounds a megalith. They have been variously interpreted as ritual sites and astronomical calendars. They are mainly found in the southwest and north. Associated with them are standing stones.

Megalithic Tombs

Neolithic colonisers with a knowledge of agriculture came to Ireland between 3000 and 2000 BC and erected the earliest megalithic chambered tombs. They are called the court cairns, because the tombs are made up of a covered gallery for burial with one or more unroofed courts or forecourts for rituals. Pottery has been found in these tombs. Court cairns are mainly found in the northern part of the country—north of a line between Clew Bay in the west and Dundalk Bay in the east. Good examples are the full-court cairns at Creevykeel, County Sligo, and Ballyglass, County Mayo (one of a group on the west shores of Killala Bay).

Linked to the court cairns is the simple and imposing type of megalith—the dolmen or portal dolmen. This consists of a large, sometimes enormous, capstone and three or more supporting uprights. The distribution of the dolmens is more widespread but tends to be eastern. There is one with a huge capstone at Browne's Hill, just outside Carlow Town. Another variety of megalith is the wedge-shaped gallery. There are numbers of such tombs in the Burren area in County Clare, where they are built from the limestone slabs so common in the region. Most excavated wedges belong to the Early Bronze Age—2000 to 1500 BC. They are now largely bare of the cairns or mounds which covered them. The people who built them advanced from being hunters to growing crops and keeping domestic animals.

The most spectacular of the great stone tombs are the passage graves. The best known is Newgrange, one of a group on the River Boyne, west of Drogheda, County Louth, which by its construction and the carvings on the stones is among the most important megalithic tombs in Europe. The graves belong to a great family of structures found from eastern Spain to southern Scandinavia. The decorative carving which covers many of the stones consists of spirals, lozenges and other motifs, and is thought to have some religious significance. Unchambered burial mounds also occur throughout the country. They date largely from the Bronze Age, but earlier and later examples are known.

Standing Stones

Also known as gallauns. Single pillar stones which also have a ritual significance, and occasionally mark grave sites. Others carry inscriptions in ogham characters.

Ring-forts

The most numerous type of monument to be seen in Ireland is the ring-fort, known also as *rath, lios, dun, caher,* and *cashel.* There are about 30,000 in the country. These originated as early as the Bronze Age and continued to be built until the Norman invasion. The circular ramparts, varying in number from one to four, enclosed a homestead with houses of wood, wattle-and-daub, or partly stone construction. Well-preserved examples of stone forts are those at Staigue, County Kerry, the royal site at Grianan of Aileach, near Derry, and the cashels of the Aran Islands. Collections of earthworks identify the royal seats at Tara, County Meath, and Emain Macha, County Armagh, where earthen banks are now the only reminders of the timber halls of kings. They, like Tara in County Meath, lie at the centre of a complex tangle of myth and tradition in the ancient Celtic sagas.

Hill-forts

Larger and more defensive in purpose are the hill-forts, whose ramparts follow contour lines to encircle hill-tops. To this class belongs the large green enclosure at Emain Macha known as Navan Fort, County Armagh.

Crannógs

Crannógs, or artificial islands, found in lakes and marshy places, are defensive dwelling sites used by farmers, with even earlier origins than the forts, but which continued in use sometimes until the 17th century. The Craggaunowen Centre in County Clare has a very good example, and many were found at Lough Gara, near Boyle, County Roscommon.

Early Irish Architecture

Before the Norman invasion most buildings in Ireland were of wood. None of these has survived. In the treeless west, however, tiny corbelled stone buildings shaped like beehives and called *clochans* were constructed. They were used as oratories by holy men. Some, possibly dating from the 7th century, still exist. *Clochans* are particularly common in County Kerry: there are many in the Dingle Peninsula and some very well preserved examples in the early monastic settlement on the Skellig Rock, off the Kerry coast. Also in Kerry is the best-preserved example of an early boat-shaped oratory, at Gallarus.

Most of the early mortared churches were modelled on wooden prototypes. They were very small, and from an early stage were built with stylistic features which have remained characteristic of Irish buildings: steeply pitched roofs, inclined jambs to door and window-openings. Many of these small churches would have been roofed with wood, or tiled or thatched, but some were roofed with stone. The problem of providing a pitched roof of stone over a rectangular structure was solved by inserting a semi-circular arch below the roof. The small space over the arch forms a croft. A fine example is St Kevin's Church at Glendalough, County Wicklow. These buildings lack features by which they can be accurately dated; a conservative dating would be from the beginning of the 9th century onwards.

Round Towers

Contemporary with these early Irish churches, and very characteristically Irish, are round towers, of which about 120 are known to have existed in Ireland. They are tall, gracefully tapering buildings of stone, with conical stone roofs, which were built as monastic belfries, with the door approximately 12ft (3.5m) from the ground. This is a clue to their use as places of refuge or watch-towers during the period of Viking raids between the 9th and 11th centuries. Food, precious objects and manuscripts were stored in them. The ladder could then be drawn up. There are about seventy surviving examples in varying degrees of preservation. A good example is the one on the Rock of Cashel, County Tipperary.

The monk who wrote these beautiful lines expresses the tensions of those days:

Bitter the wind tonight,
Combing the sea's hair white:
From the North, no need to fear
the proud sea coursing warrior.
                    version by John Montague

High Crosses

These carved stone crosses, usually in the typical 'Celtic' ringed form, contain a great variety of biblical scenes and ornament. They are found in most parts of the country in early monastic sites. The earliest type are simple crosses carved on standing stones. They are most common in the west and in the Dingle Peninsula, County Kerry. The development of low-relief carving began in the 7th century, and gradually became more complex, as seen in the cruciform slab at Carndonagh, County Donegal. It is carved with scenes of the Crucifixion, and interlaced ornament. The ringed high cross first appears at a later date; the earliest group of high crosses, dating from the 8th century, are in southern Kilkenny and Tipperary. Good examples are at Ahenny, County Tipperary, and Kilkieran, County Kilkenny. Also close are the Ahenny Crosses in County Tipperary. In this group the cross-shafts and heads are carved in sandstone with spirals and other decorative forms derived from metalwork, with figure-carvings on the bases. To the north, in the Barrow Valley, is another group, later in date and more roughly carved in granite. The Barrow group has an interesting innovation: the faces of the shafts and heads are divided into panels, in which a scene, usually biblical, is portrayed. The best of these crosses is at Moone, County Kildare.

Sandstone was used again for crosses in the 10th century; they still grace monastic ruins scattered across the Central Plain. The West Cross and Muiredach's Cross at Monasterboice in County Louth are the best examples. In each case the east and west faces are carved with scriptural scenes, while the north and south faces have spirals, vine-scrolls, and other decorations. Favourite subjects for the carver were the Crucifixion; the Last Judgment; Adam and Eve; Cain and Abel; and the arrest of Christ. Later elaborate crosses may be seen at Clones, County Monaghan, Drumcliff, County Sligo, Ardboe, County Tyrone, and Donaghmore, County Down.

By the end of the 11th century the cross had changed; the ring was often left off, and the whole length of the shaft was taken up with a single figure of the crucified Christ. Ecclesiastical figures often appear on the opposite face and on the base, and the decoration of the north and south faces usually consists of interlaced animals. Crosses of this style were being carved up until the mid-12th century. A good 11th-century cross exists at Roscrea, County Tipperary, and a good 12th-century cross at Tuam, County Galway.

Romanesque Architecture

Characteristics of this decorative style appear in Irish buildings of the 12th century. While remaining structurally simple, the Irish churches of the period have carved doorways, chancel-arches or windows, with ornament in an Irish variation of the style. The most impressive example of the style is the arcaded and richly carved Cormac's Chapel on the Rock of Cashel, County Tipperary, consecrated in 1134. The use of rib-vaulting over the chancel here is very early, not only for Ireland, but for the rest of Europe. Many of the characteristic features of the early churches, such as antae and sloping jambs, were kept throughout the Romanesque period. The use of the chevron, an ornamental moulding, is common in Irish-Romanesque work, and it is nearly always combined with rows of beading. The use of carved human heads as capitals to the shafts in the orders of the doorway may be seen in the portal at Clonfert, County Galway, which has some of the most richly carved Irish-Romanesque decoration. This style is also referred to as Hibernio-Romanesque.

Transitional Architecture

At the same time as the Romanesque style was so popular, another plainer type of church building was being introduced by the Cistercian order, whose first church in Ireland, Mellifont Abbey in County Louth, was influenced by churches of the Continental type, with simple, carved decoration. Examples of the 12th-century churches of this transitional style may be seen at Baltinglass, County Wicklow; Boyle, County Roscommon; and Jerpoint, County Kilkenny.

Gothic Architecture

With the coming of the Normans and the changes they wrought, the native tradition in building declined, and Gothic architecture was introduced in the 13th century.

The Irish Gothic cathedrals were on a smaller scale than their English and Continental counterparts; the grouping of lancets in the east window and south choir wall is typical of the Irish buildings of this time, such as the ruined cathedral of Cashel, County Tipperary. The restored Cathedrals of St Canice, Kilkenny, and St Patrick, Dublin, are also good examples. Gothic parish churches in the plain Early English style were built only in the anglicized parts of the country, for example at Gowran, County Kilkenny.

Because of the turbulent times during the 14th century there was very little building done in Ireland, but this changed in the 15th and 16th centuries when a native Gothic style began to emerge, particularly in the west. It is best seen in the Franciscan friaries and the rebuilt Cistercian abbeys of the period. A good example of the Franciscan style, with narrow church, a tall tapering tower, carved cloister and small window openings can be seen at the well-preserved ruin at Quin, County Clare. The Cistercian style, with a larger church, a huge square tower topped by stepped battlements, and a large carved cloister, can be seen at Kilcooly and Holycross, County Tipperary.

Castles

Although the Normans had built many castles before they came to Ireland, in the first years of the invasion they built fortifications of wood, usually taking over the sites of ancient Irish forts. The remains of these can be seen all over the eastern half of the country in the form of mottes and baileys. At the end of the 12th century the construction of stone fortifications on a large scale began. An early example of Norman building skill is at Trim, County Meath. It has a great square keep in a large bailey, defended by a high embattled wall, with turrets and barbicans. Other examples of this type are at Carlingford, County Louth, and Carrickfergus, County Antrim. A very attractive feature of the Irish countryside is the ruined 15th- or 16th-century tower house, which became common from about 1420. These fortified farms consisted of a tall, square tower which usually had a small walled *bawn* or courtyard. In most cases the *bawn* has disappeared, but well-preserved examples can be seen at Doe Castle near Creeslough, County Donegal; Pallas, County Galway; and Dunguire (Dungory), near Kinvara, County Galway.

Topics

07

The People

The people are thus inclined: religious, frank, amorous, sufferable of infinite paines, verie glorious, manie sorcerers, excellent horsemen, delighted with wars, great alms-givers, passing in hospitality.
Holinshed's *Chronicles*, 1577

This description so aptly fits the Irish today that there remain only a few superficial remarks on the subject. Conditions have changed radically. For a start, almost half of the population lives in the spreading cities. Still, compared to its near-neighbour, England, and to many other European countries, Ireland is a very rural place, and even city-dwellers have close links with their country background. Wherever they live, though, Irish people have a healthy disdain for time and the hustle and bustle of business. As you travel around, bear in mind the old Irish saying, 'When God made time he made plenty of it.' You will become aware of a great sense of shared identity and neighbourly feeling, particularly towards those in trouble, or the very old.

The traits peculiar to the Irish which always reassert themselves, wherever they are in the world, are numerous. Amongst them is a delight in words and wordplay (reading anything by Flann O'Brien or James Joyce will give you a taste of it); a love of parties and *craic* (a good time), music, dancing and witty talk; a ready kindness which never fails; great hospitality and an interest in your affairs which is never mere inquisitiveness, but a charming device to put you at your ease.

The Irish do however have a certain irascible spirit, quickly roused in the face of bland priggishness. They never forget an insult or a wrong, and this memory will go back for generations; it might have been a quarrel over land or the meanness of the local gentry. Oliver Cromwell is still remembered with hatred for his savage campaign in the 1650s. The Irish can also be untidy – in their houses and in the countryside, and ignorance or indifference towards aesthetic matters exists. Old buildings often go to rack and ruin, and vile ribbon development chokes the towns and the countryside around them. There is a phenomenon of rusty cars dumped in lonely glens, litter in any old place, and general messiness. Not for the Irish the freshly painted doors and gateways of the Anglo-Saxon.

Each province and county of Ireland produces more, individual traits. The north-erners have a reputation for direct speech and a certain fighting spirit. The Munster people are held in respect for their poetry. A Dubliner might be considered a bit of a know-all. The people of Connacht are famous for their hospitality and strength.

Finally, one last word in this briefest of outlines: the Irish still have a great sense of the spiritual. The Catholic Church is very strong (despite recent sex scandals, the secularization of the schools and the introduction of divorce) but so is the faith of Church of Ireland members and of the Presbyterians, to judge by the large numbers who attend their churches on Sundays. Religion is the great anchor that pervades all aspects of living. This, perhaps, partly explains why in Ireland there is sometimes little thought for the future, and life is lived for the moment.

The Fairy People

The Fairy People, or *Daoine Sidhe*, are a rich part of Irish folklore. According to peasant belief, they are fallen angels who are not good enough to be saved and not bad enough to languish in Hell. Some say they are the gods of the Earth, as is written in the *Book of Armagh*, or the pagan gods of Ireland, the Tuatha Dé Danaan (the Tuatha may also have been a race of invaders whose origins are lost in the mists of time). Antiquarians have different theories but, whatever they surmise, these fairy people persist in the popular imagination and are kept alive in tradition and myth.

The Fairy People are quickly offended, and must always be referred to as the 'Gentry' or the 'Good People'. They are also easily pleased, and will keep misfortune from your door if you leave them a bowl of milk on the window-sill overnight. Their evil seems to be without malice, and their chief occupations are feasting, fighting, making love and playing or listening to beautiful music. (The only hardworking person amongst them is the leprechaun, who is kept busy making the shoes they wear out through dancing.) It is said that many of the beautiful tunes of Ireland are theirs, remembered by mortal eavesdroppers. Apparently, Carolan, the last of the great Irish bards, slept on a *rath* which, like the many prehistoric standing stones in Ireland, had become a fairy place in folk tradition; for ever after, fairy music ran in his head and made him the great musician he was.

Some of the fairy types are not very pleasant. The following are brief descriptions of a few:

The **banshee**, from *bean sidhe*, is a woman fairy or attendant spirit who follows the old families, and wails before a death. The *keen*, the funeral cry of the peasantry, is said to be an imitation of her cry. An omen which sometimes accompanies the old woman is an immense black coach, carrying a coffin and drawn by headless riders.

The **leprechaun**, or fairy shoemaker, is solitary, old, and bad-tempered; he's the practical joker amongst 'the Good People'. He is very rich because of his trade, and buries his pots of gold at the end of rainbows. He also takes many treasure crocks, buried in times of war, for his own. Many believe he is the Dé Danaan god Lugh, the god of arts and crafts, who degenerated in popular lore into the leprechaun.

The ***leanhaun shee***, or fairy mistress, longs for the love of mortal men. If they refuse, she must be their slave; if they consent, they are hers, and can only escape by finding another to take their place. The fairy lives on their life while they waste away, and death is no escape. She has become identified in political song and verse with the Gaelic Muse, for she gives inspiration to those whom she persecutes.

The **pook** lives in solitary mountain places and old ruins, and is of a nightmarish aspect. It is a November spirit, and often assumes the form of a stallion. It comes from water and is only easy to tame if you can keep him away from the sight of it. If you cannot, he will plunge in with his rider and tear him or her to pieces at the bottom. Some authorities have linked the pook with a he-goat from *púca* or *poc*, the Gaelic for goat. Others maintain it is a forefather of Shakespeare's Puck in *A Midsummer Night's Dream*.

Tracing Your Ancestors

If you have any Irish blood in you at all, you will have a passion for genealogy. The Irish seem to like looking backwards. When they had nothing left – no land, no Brehon laws, no religious freedom – they managed to hold on to their pride and their genealogy. Waving these before the eyes of French and Spanish rulers ensured that they got posts at court or commissions in the army. There is thus no such thing as class envy in Ireland: everyone is as good as the next man, and everyone is descended from some prince or hero from the Irish past. It is the descendants of the Cromwellian parvenues who had to bolster up their images with portraits and fine furniture. Now the planter families have the Irish obsession with their ancestors too.

Information and sources for research are rather fragmented, and it would be best to write to the Genealogical Office in the National Library in Dublin before you come, to ask their advice, or contact the Irish Genealogical Project, which is also very helpful. For Ulster families, try the Ulster Historical Foundation. You must have first found out as much as possible from family papers, old relatives, and the records of the Church and State in your own country; your local historical or genealogical society might be

Sources of Information

Genealogical centres are also listed under 'Sports and Activities' sections, and in the main text of the book.

General Register Office (Births, Marriages and Deaths), Joyce House, 8–11 Lombard St East, Dublin 2, t (01) 671 1000, *www.groireland. ie*; Will supply birth, marriage or death certificates. Marriages of non-Catholics were recorded from 1845, and registration of all faiths from 1864. Search fees are reasonable. *Open Mon–Fri 9.30–12.30 and 2.15–4.30*; also at 49–55 Chichester Street, Belfast BT1 4HL, t (028) 9025 2000, *www.groni.gov.uk*.

National Library, Kildare Street, Dublin 2, t (01) 661 8811, *www.nli.ie*. Holds many sources: books, newspapers and manuscripts, including Griffith's *Primary Valuation of Tenements*, the Tithe Applotment Books, microfilm copies of Roman Catholic parish registers up to 1880 and a collection of landed estate records. *Open Mon–Wed 10–9, Thurs–Fri 10–5, Sat 10–1*.

Genealogical Office, at the National Library, 2 Kildare Street, Dublin 2, t (01) 661 8811, *www.nli.ie*. Handles enquiries into heraldry, genealogy and family history for the whole of Ireland, and will make searches for you for a small fee. They publish a useful leaflet, *Getting Started*, which introduces you to the records they hold. It is also the contact address for a list of research agencies in the Republic. *Consultations by appointment only; open Mon–Fri 10–4.45, Sat 10am–12.30pm.*

Registry of Deeds, Henrietta Street, Dublin 7, t (01) 670 7500, or lo-call t 1890 333001, *www.irlgov.ie/landreg/*. Holds records of land matters from 1708 onwards. You may carry out your research for a small fee. *Open Mon–Fri 10.30–4.30.*

National Archives, Bishop Street, Dublin 8, t (01) 407 2300, f (01) 407 2333, *www. nationalarchives.ie*. The Public Record Office in Dublin was burnt in 1922, and with it many of the Church of Ireland registers. This houses Griffith's *Primary Valuation of Ireland, 1848–63*, which records the names of those owning or occupying land and property, rebellion reports and records relating to 1798; it also holds records of transportees to Australia. *Reading Room open Mon–Fri 10–5; bring some ID in order to obtain a Reader's Ticket.*

Public Records Office of Northern Ireland, 66 Balmoral Avenue, Belfast BT9 6NY, t (028) 9025 1318, *http://proni.nics.gov.uk*. Tithe applotment records, valuation and church records, pre-1864.

Irish Genealogical Project, 7–9 Merrion Row, Dublin 2, *www.irishgenealogy.ie, info@ irishgenealogy.ie*. Gives information and able to help. Find out the full name of your emigrant ancestor, the background of his or her family, whether rich, poor, merchants or farmers, Catholic or Protestant. The family tradition of remembering the name of the parish or townland is a great help.

In America, immigrant records have been published by Baltimore Genealogical Publishing Company in seven volumes, and lists the arrival of people into New York between 1846 and 1851. In Canada, the Department of Irish Studies at St Mary's University, Halifax, is very helpful. In Australia, the Civil Records are very good: try the National Library, Canberra, the Mitchell Library, Sydney, and the Society of Australian Genealogists, Richmond Villa, 120 Kent Street, Sydney.

Music

Traditional Irish music is played everywhere in Ireland: in the cities and in the countryside. Government sponsorship helped to revive it, especially through Radio an Gaeltachta (Irish-language radio) in the west. Now there is great enthusiasm for it: a nine-year-old will sing a lover's lament about seduction and desertion without

advice to researchers and those who are commissioning research.

Ulster Historical Foundation, 12 College Square East, Belfast, t (028) 9033 2288, *www.uhf.org.uk, enquiry@uhf.org.uk.* Undertakes searches and has published a useful guide called *Ulster Libraries, Archives, Musuems and Ancestral Heritage Centres – A Visitor's Guide.*

Irish Genealogical Research Society, c/o The Irish Club, 82 Eaton Square, London SW1W 9AJ, England, *www.igrsoc.org.* A charity which promotes research and has a valuable library containing manuscripts of family histories, memoirs and pedigrees, useful for those whose research is pre-1864. They also publish an annual journal, *The Irish Genealogist.* They cannot undertake research for you. *Library open (at the above address) on Sat only, 2–6pm; adm £10.*

Irish Family History Foundation, Pat Stafford, Yola Farmhouse, Tagoat, County Wexford, t (053) 32610, *www.irish-roots.net.* A cross-border umbrella organization for local genealogical and historical societies. Their research centres are all over Ireland, with computerised information on Irish families; parish and appropriate civil records are currently being collected and filed. An initial search costs around €75. *Enclose an international reply coupon when contacting by post.*

Calgagh Heritage Centre, Butcher Street, Derry City, Co. Londonderry, t (028) 7137 1967, f (028) 7136 0921. Holds genealogical data from 1663 in its heritage library. There is an extensive computerised genealogical database, which currently holds over two million records. *Admission free.*

Clare Heritage Centre and Genealogical Society, Church Street, Corofin, Co. Clare, t (065) 683 7955, f (065) 683 7540, *http://clare.irish-roots.net, clareheritage@eircom.net.* Holds parish records for Co. Clare (post-1864); will research family history. *Open all year Mon–Fri 9–5.30.*

Cobh Heritage Centre, Cobh, Co. Cork, t (021) 481 3591, f (021) 481 3595, *www.cobhheritage.com, info@cobhheritage.com.* Offers a record-search service for around €25.

Eneclann, Unit 1, Trinity College Enterprise Centre, Pearse Street, Dublin 2, t (01) 671 0338, f (01) 671 0281, *www.eneclann.ie, genealogy@eneclann.ie.* Will undertake geneological and historical research on your behalf. An initial search assessment costs around €21.

Heraldic Artists Ltd, 3 Nassau Street, Dublin 2, t (01) 679 7020, f (01) 679 4717, *www.heraldicartists.com.* Bookshop in Dublin which stocks a lot of useful genealogical publications.

batting an eyelid to a grandfather whose generation scarcely remembered the Gaelic songs at all. Traditional music has strengthened its hold on the cultural life of the country, rather than sadly declining as it has done in England. Today Ireland has one of the most vigorous music traditions in Europe, and this is a big pull for many visitors. Irish ballads are sung the world over: many emigrants consider themselves exiles still, and the commercial record industry churns out the ballads. Most record covers tend to be decorated with grinning leprechauns and a few shamrocks for good measure.

Serious traditional music is not in this folksy style. Listening to it can induce a state of exultant melancholy or infectious merriment. Whatever way, it goes straight to your heart. The lyrics deal with the ups and downs of love, failed rebellions (especially that of 1798), soldiering, dead heroes, religion and homesick love for the beauty of the countryside. Not surprisingly, comparatively few deal with occupations or work.

The bard in pre-Christian society was held in honour and a great deal of awe for his learning and the mischievous satire in his poetry and music. After the Cromwellian and Williamite wars, he lost his status altogether; music and poetry were kept alive by the country people, who cheered themselves up during the dark winter evenings with stories and music. Sadly, nowadays the traditional Irish harp is scarcely used, except when it is dragged out for the benefit of tourists. The main traditional instruments used are the *uillean* pipes, which are rather more sophisticated than the Scottish bagpipes, the fiddle (violin) and the tin whistle. The beat and rhythm is provided by a hand-held drum made from stretched goat hide, called the *bodhrán*. The accordion, the flute, guitar and the piano are used by some groups as well, and are played singly or together. A popular feature of the traditional music scene are the *seisiúns* – informal sessions of music, ceilidhs and cabaret.

The airs, laments, slip jigs, reels and songs all vary enormously from region to region, and you might easily hear a Cork man or a Leitrim fiddler discussing the interpretation of a certain piece with heated emotion. Pieces are constantly impro- vised upon, and seldom written down; inevitably some of the content gets changed from generation to generation. Traditional fiddle music from Co. Donegal has long been among the best in the land. A form of singing that had almost died out by the 1940s is the *Sean-Nós*, fully ornamented and sung, unaccompanied, in Gaelic. Today the *Sean-Nós* section in music festivals is overflowing with entrants.

Today Ireland is producing some good musicians of a completely different type from the folk groups. The local bands that play in the bars play jazz, blues, and a rhythmical and melodious combination of pop and traditional instruments. Look in the local newspaper of any big town or ask in a record shop; they will know what gigs are on and probably be able to sell you a ticket as well. Some of the top names on the rock and pop scene come from Ireland, for instance, Van Morrison, U2, The Corrs, The Cranberries, Westlife and Sinéad O'Connor. The phenomenal success of *Riverdance*, which has toured the world and sold out in every venue, has given tradi- tional music and dance the glamour of Broadway.

You will have no difficulty in hearing traditional ballads or folk music in bars or hotels; players usually advertise in the local newspaper, or by sticking up a notice in the window. They are usually only too happy to let you join in, and as the atmosphere gets smokier the music really takes off. In 1951 **Comhaltas Ceoltoírí Eireann** was set up for the promotion of traditional music, song and dance. It now has two hundred branches all over the country, and their members have regular *seisiúns*, which are open to all. Ask at a tourist office or write to Comhaltas Ceoltoírí Eireann, 32 Belgrave Sq, Monkstown, Co. Dublin, **t** (01) 280 0295.

Boglands

Ireland is literally rich in boglands, formed over many hundreds of years. In the past boglands were despised, except as a source of fuel, but nowadays we know how rich they are in flora, fauna and also history: underneath the bog, well-preserved bodies, jewelled crosiers for bishops, golden cups, giant elks' antlers and brittle pots of butter have all been revealed as the turf is cut away. A vast quantity of folklore has grown up around them too, beautifully described in *Irish Folk Ways* by E. Fstyn Evans. In many fairy stories, humans are lured off their path and into the bog by strange lights at night. Indeed, walking on bogs can be very mucky and sometimes dangerous, so keep to the few paths and try to go with a local to guide you. Many writers describe the great peace and well-being to be had from a day out on the bogs, cutting turf. Fven now, a Dubliner clings to his cutting rights on a piece of Wicklow hill, for there is something eminently satisfying about cutting the sods of rich blackness, and then, later, during the bitter cold winter nights, heaping it onto the open fire.

About 14 per cent of Ireland's land surface is bog. The brooding immutability and the drizzling rain and winds which sweep it have surely contributed towards the Irish philosophy of fatality. There are two types – blanket and raised. The latter are mainly to be found in the midlands. In Ireland, wetness is a key factor in the formation of peat, which begins in lakes and ponds as plants invade the water. Sphagnum moss is the vital plant because it holds water like a sponge and has a great capacity for trapping nutrients. Peat builds up because the moss releases acid that inhibits the breakdown of dead plants.

The Irish economy has been bolstered by the boglands. The Government-owned turf company, Bord na Mona, was set up in 1946 and has drained vast areas of peat, cutting it by machines and using the fuel to generate electricity. The sphagnum in the upper layers is baled as horticultural peat and sold for use in gardens all over Britain. But the draining of the bogs has consequences for rivers, and for those living near them in valleys, for the bogs act like huge natural sponges that soak up rainfall and release it very slowly. Thus, if the bog is stripped away there is danger of flooding. Stripping is also ecologically costly, as gully erosion results. Some hand-cut bogs, when left, show signs of being colonized and healed by the bog-forming plants themselves, but this is unlikely to happen in machine-cut bogs. Sheep-grazing and burning also do damage. A balance must be found between economic needs and conservation needs, because at the rate the machines can cut the turf, there will be no more left within the next 20 years. All the insects, birds and animals that find a home in the bog will disappear if nothing is done, and we will lose the flight of the golden plover and the special mosses and flowers.

Historic Houses and Gardens

If you want to try to understand the Anglo-Irish, who have a very muddled status amongst most shades of opinion, the best thing to do is to look round one of their houses. The expression 'Anglo-Irish' has political, social and religious connotations. It is used to describe the waves of English settlers and their descendants who became so powerful in the land after the success of the campaigns of Elizabeth I of England. An optimistic view is held by some that 'Anglo-Irish' is a tag that should only be applied to literature, and indeed it does seem ridiculous that, after three hundred years of living in a place, these land-owning families are not counted as truly Irish. On the one hand, it is a fact that the sons of the Ascendancy were educated in England, served the British Empire as soldiers or civil servants, and saw themselves as different from the native Irish; whilst on the other, many of these people felt a great and patriotic love for Ireland, led revolts and uprisings against British rule and, starting with the Normans, became 'more Irish than the Irish', as the Latin saying goes.

Ireland's Big Houses were built by families who would be most offended if you called them English, although as far as the Gaelic Irish are concerned, that is what they are. 'The Big House' is another very Irish expression; it is applied to a landowner's house regardless of its size or grandeur. In fact, if you look through Burke's *Guide to Irish Country Houses* and the rather depressing, but fascinating, *Vanishing Houses of Ireland* (published by the Irish Architectural Archive and the Irish Georgian Society) you will get a very good idea of the variety and huge number of houses that belonged to the gentry. (Valerie and Thomas Pakenham's book *The Big House in Ireland* also gives fascinating and witty insights into life behind doors.)

The English monarchs always financed their Irish wars by paying their soldiers with grants of land in Ireland, and, as the country was so unruly, during the 17th century the settlers lived in fortified or semi-fortified houses. There are only a very few examples of Tudor domestic architecture. Portumna Castle, County Galway, is a ruined mansion of this type, but the most famous is Ormonde Castle in Carrick on Suir, County Tipperary, which has the remains of 16th-century stucco-work, including a plasterwork portrait of Elizabeth I. Look out also for the early 17th-century plasterwork if you visit Bunratty Castle, in County Clare. Another interesting house which it is possible to visit is Huntington Castle, County Carlow, a fortified Jacobean house built in 1620. The most impressive and the first Irish building in the grand Renaissance style is the late-17th century Royal Hospital at Kilmainham in Dublin, which has been rescued from dereliction and restored. It now houses the Irish Museum of Modern Art, and its state rooms are once more decorated with rich and costly furnishings.

The majority of Big Houses were built in the hundred years following the Penal Laws in the 1690s, when the Protestant landowners settled down to enjoy their gains. The civil and domestic architecture that survives from these times is both elegant and splendid, and is to be found in every county. The chief centre of this 18th-century architecture was, of course, Dublin. Even before the unfortunate Union of Ireland with England in 1801, it was a confident, learned and artistic capital. Today, in spite of the building developers, it has held on to its gracious heritage. When you are in Dublin, make a point of walking around the elegant residential squares of St Stephen's Green, Merrion Square and Fitzwilliam Square to the south of the city, and, on the north side, Parnell and Mountjoy Squares. The two great masterpieces of public building, the Custom House and the Four Courts, were built by James Gandon towards the close of the century, and they still dominate the skyline. A few distinguished buildings were added to the city in the 19th century, including Gandon's King's Inns, but after the Union, building in Dublin tended to stagnate.

A Big House usually consists of a square, grey stone block, sometimes with wings, set amongst gardens and parkland with stables at the back, and a walled garden. Sometimes it is called a castle, although the only attribute of a castle it may have is a deep fosse. A lingering insecurity must often have remained, for many are almost as tall as they are wide, with up to four storeys, rather like a Georgian version of the 16th-century tower house. The buildings are completely different in atmosphere here from their counterparts in England. They have not undergone Victorian 'improvements' or gradually assumed an air of comfortable mellowness over the centuries. It was an act of bravado on the part of the Anglo-Irish to build them at all, for they always had to be on the alert against the disaffected natives, who readily formed agrarian groups such as the White Boys. They never had enough money to add on layer after layer in the newest architectural fashion; their houses remained Palladian splendours or Gothick fantasies built during the Georgian age, when the old fortified house could at last be exchanged for something more comfortable.

The Big Houses that remain are full of beautiful furniture, pictures, *objets d'art* and the paraphernalia of generations who appreciated beauty, good horses, hard drinking and eating, and were generous and slapdash by nature. It is against this background of grey stately houses looking onto sylvan scenes and cosseted by sweeping trees that one should read Maria Edgeworth, supplying some details yourself on the Penal Laws, the famine, the foreignness of the landlords and their loyalties. The literature on the 'Big House' is huge, and if you read Thackeray, Trollope, Charles Lever, Somerville and Ross, and more Maria Edgeworth on the subject, you will not only be entertained but well informed. The Big House, the courthouse, the jail and the military barracks were all symbols of oppression and not surprisingly many of them got burnt out in the 1920s; but these houses echo with the voices of talented and liberal people: the wit of Sheridan, Wilde, the conversations of Mrs Delany, the gleeful humour of Somerville and Ross, whisper through the rooms as you wander around.

In England there is a whole network of organizations and legislation to protect the historic house. In the Republic of Ireland there are no exact equivalents of the National Trust or the Historic Building and Monuments Commission, and no National Heritage fund. This means there are no grants for repairs to buildings, and no effective legislation to protect them from dereliction or neglect. Even now the Big House is persistently regarded by the powers that be as tainted with the memories of colonialism and an oppressive age. They are labelled as 'not Irish', although the craftsmen who built and carved the wonderful details of cornicing, stucco-work and dovetailing, elegant staircases and splendid decoration were as Irish as could be. There are many desolate shells to glimpse on your travels, though it is still possible to go around quite a selection of well cared-for properties.

The Heritage Council is allocated a little money to help a few architecturally important buildings each year. It was set up by Charles Haughey and has helped to change official attitudes, but it is the Irish Georgian Society (*74 Merrion Sq, Dublin 2, t (01) 676 7053, www.archeire.com/igs/*) which so far has done most to secure the future of the Big House. Founded in 1958 to work for the preservation of Ireland's architectural heritage, the society has carried out numerous rescue and restoration works on historic houses. Other influential organisations include An Taisce, The National Trust for Ireland (*Tailors' Hall, Back Lane, Dublin, t (01) 454 1786, www.antaisce. org*); they have saved much of Georgian Dublin from the demolishers.

Later Architectural Forms

Palladian: used to describe a pseudo-classical architectural style taken from the 16th-century Italian architect, Palladio. Sir Edward Lovett Pearce introduced the style to Ireland, and it was continued by his pupil, Richard Cassels, also known as Castle. Carton and Castletown in Co. Kildare, and Russborough in Co. Wicklow are good examples of the Palladian style, in which the central block of each house is flanked by pavilions. One of the most perfect Palladian houses in the British Isles is Bellamont Forest in Co. Cavan, designed by Pearce, which is unfortunately closed.

Neoclassical: a style of building which is similar to that of Palladio, but was more directly inspired by the civilization of Ancient Rome. It became popular in the 1750s until the Gothic Revival.

Gothick: an amusing and romantic style which was popular in the late 18th century. It is spelt with a 'k' to distinguish it from the serious, and later, Gothic Revival. Gothick Castles were built by Francis Johnston and the English Pain brothers, who came over to Ireland with John Nash during the 1780s.

Gothic Revival: From the 1830s onwards many houses and churches were built in a style harking back to the Tudor and perpendicular forms; the popularity of these gradually gave way to the more severe style of the Early-English and Decorated Gothic. The English architect Augustus Pugin (1812–52) equated the Gothic with the Christian and Classicism with the pagan. He designed some Irish churches and cathedrals, including St Mary's Cathedral in Killarney. J. J. McCarthy (1817–82), an Irish architect, was very strongly influenced by Pugin; see his work at St Patrick's (RC) Cathedral, Armagh.

Hibernio-Romanesque: A style which was popular in Catholic church architecture from the 1850s onwards. It fitted in with growing national feelings to lay claim to an 'Irish style' which existed before the Anglo-Norman invasion. A good example of it can be seen at the RC Church in Spiddal, County Galway.

Irish Rococo Plasterwork: The great period of rococo plasterwork in Ireland began with the Swiss Italian brothers Paul and Philip Francini, who came to Ireland in 1739 to decorate the ceiling at Carton, Maynooth, for the Earl of Kildare. They were great *stuccodores* and modelled magnificent combinations of plaster figures, trophies, fruit and flowers. See their work at Castletown House, Celbridge, County Kildare and at Newman House, 85–6 St Stephen's Green, Dublin. Irish craftsmen quickly learned the technique, and between 1740–60 many beautiful ceilings were created. They tended to leave out figures, and concentrate instead on birds, flowers, and musical instruments. The ceilings are graceful yet lively, with a swirling gaiety that makes Adam ceilings, which later became the fashion, seem rather stilted. A fine example of a rococo ceiling and staircase is at 20 Lower Dominick Street, Dublin, where the composition of birds, flowers and fruits is perfect. Other splendid examples of this rococo exuberance can be seen at Russborough, County Wicklow, the Rotunda Hospital Chapel, Dublin, and Newman House, 85–86 St Stephen's Green, Dublin.

Selected Architects

Richard Cassels, also known as Castle (*c.* 1690–1751). Cassels is responsible for some of the most beautiful country houses in Ireland. He was of Huguenot origin (his family came from Germany to England), and part of the circle surrounding Lord Burlington, the wealthy and scholarly aristocrat who did so much to bring neoclassicism to Britain. Cassels came to Ireland in the 1720s and designed Powerscourt House, in County Wicklow, which so sadly was burnt down in the 1970s. He also designed Carton House in County Kildare, the Rotunda Hospital in Dublin, many houses in St Stephen's Green, and Leinster House. He is credited with the designs for Parliament House (now the Bank of Ireland building) in College Green. Cassels was also involved in designing the Newry Canal, begun in 1730, which linked the coalfield of Coalisland in County Tyrone to Newry, a distance of 18 miles (28.8 km). It was the first major canal in the British Isles. He designed the Doric Temple and the Dining Halls in Trinity College, Dublin.

James Gandon (1743–1823). Born in London of Huguenot origin, and apprenticed to William Chambers, the Scottish architect. He was invited to Ireland to build a new Custom House in Dublin. He arrived in 1781 and it was completed the same year. He was later commissioned to make extensions to Parliament House in College Green, and his Classical Four Courts were finished in 1802. He also designed the King's Inns, although he resigned from the project in 1808 because of irritation with the Lord Chancellor, and it was completed by his partner, Baker. His buildings – original and harmonious combinations of elegant neoclassical and Palladian Baroque styles – set the seal on Dublin's character at the time of Grattan's Parliament.

Francis Johnston (1760–1829). An architect in Armagh, and responsible for many of the fine buildings there, such as the Observatory. He moved to Dublin in 1793 where he designed the Chapel Royal in Dublin Castle, and the GPO in O'Connell Street. He also supervised the rebuilding of the House of Commons. He made a huge contribution to founding the Royal Hibernian Academy of Painting, Sculpture and Architecture in 1823, and he was its president for many years. He designed some Gothick castles such as Charleville Forest in County Cork.

Sir Charles Lanyon (1813–89). He was born in Belfast, and built the Custom House there in 1857. Lanyon was adept at creating country houses in the Italian style; imposing and florid buildings adapted from Italian palaces and villas of the High Renaissance Period.

Sir Richard Morrison (1767–1849). The Regency architect from West Cork who designed the neoclassical Fota House, in County Cork, where the estate buildings, including a huntsman's lodge, are scaled-down versions of the house. You can also see his fine courthouse in Galway City.

John Nash (1752–1835). English architect who designed grand country houses, amongst which are Killymoon Castle and Caledon in County Tyrone. His elegant neoclassical style can be seen in the planned terraces of Regent's Park, London, and in the Royal Pavilion, Brighton.

Sir Edward Lovett Pearce (1699–1733). Born in County Meath, and served as a soldier. He visited Venice in his early twenties, and made drawings of the buildings there and in other Italian cities. He was the leader of the Irish Palladians, and he designed the interior of the largest and most splendid of all Irish country houses, Castletown in County Kildare. Pearce became an MP and, in 1730, Surveyor-General. He worked on the Irish Houses of Parliament in College Green (the first purpose-built parliament house in the world, and now the Bank of Ireland), with his pupil Richard Cassels.

Robert West (c. 1730–90). Dublin architect and *stuccodore*. He was responsible for many of the fine houses in the Georgian squares of Dublin, including 20 Lower Dominick Street, which it is possible to visit, and No.85 St Stephen's Green, Dublin.

Gardens and Arboreta

If you love the colours, shapes, textures and scents of peaceful and mature gardens, you can have a marvellous time touring the many gardens of Ireland. The climate is a fortunate one for plants and trees because it is temperate and rainy; there is a variety of rocks and soils, and the winter is so mild it allows for the cultivation of tender plants. The grass grows well and makes generous areas of green, interacting with the formal hedges, herbaceous borders, impressive trees and romantic stretches of water which nearly always enhance the parkland of these gardens.

Gaelic Ireland does not have a long horticultural tradition. It began when the Anglo-Normans and later settlers introduced the idea of a pleasure garden, with its flowers and fruits. The unsettled state of Ireland, with its many hundreds of years of internal fighting and conquest, left little time for gardening until the 18th century. By then the country was calmer and the new 'Ascendancy' began to build themselves comfortable houses, formal gardens and parklands. They planted their estates with fine oak and beech woods, and it is usually fairly obvious today where the lands around you formed part of a demesne, because of the trees. Inevitably, these parks and gardens were regarded as symbols of conquest, and were often attacked by the landless peasants. An attitude still prevails in Ireland which does not value trees, except as firewood, and very few non-sacred ones are left to grow on the lands of the small farmer. That said, one of the most attractive features of the Irish landscape is the way your eye is drawn to the top of ancient *raths* or ring forts which are crowned by graceful trees. These grow undisturbed because of their association with the fairies. Many landlords planted exotic species of trees around these forts and on small hillocks in the 19th century, and they do much to beautify the landscape. The Huguenots who came to Ireland with William of Orange brought with them new fashions in evergreens, topiary, and flowers such as tulips, pinks and auriculas. Mazes were laid within clipped hedges, and there are still a few examples, as at Birr Castle in County Offaly and Kilruddery, near Bray, Co. Wicklow.

Most of the Irish gardens which survive were started in the 18th and 19th centuries. The Dublin Florists' Club, founded in 1746, was a great stimulus to the propagation of flowers and trees. It sounds a very convivial society whose members (mainly aristocrats, army men and clergy), met in taverns and drank endless toasts to the King, the Royal Family and 'the glorious memory' (of William III). After these loyal toasts exhibits of carnations and auriculas were passed around to be admired. Specimens were named and premiums offered to plantsmen by the society. More recently, Ireland has become famous for its roses, cultivated by very famous breeders such as Dickens and McCredy's, and for its daffodils, bred by Guy Wilson near Broughshane, County Antrim and Lionel Richardson of Waterford.

The mid 18th century saw the fashion for naturalized parkland take over from formal gardening. In the 19th century William Robertson, who started life as an Irish garden boy in County Laois, led the revolution against bedding plants and artifice and became the advocate of wild gardens – where the plant was suited to the situation and the garden to the nature of the ground. Mount Usher in County Wicklow and Anne's Grove Gardens in County Cork are fine examples of his style. For those who love rock gardens designed as miniature mountain landscapes, the garden at Rowallane in County Down is a delight. Mount Stewart, also in County Down, is full of the bizarre, including fanciful topiary. There is a charming Japanese garden at Tully (part of the National Hunt Stud), and Kilruddery and Powerscourt in County Wicklow are lovely examples of Italianate gardens with beautiful ironwork and classical statuary. The arboreta at Castlewellan, Fota, Birr and Powerscourt are very famous; and at Derreen in County Kerry the Australian tree fern has become naturalized. Howth Castle Gardens in County Dublin and Rowallane in County Down have superb rhododendron trees. Glenveagh Castle in County Donegal and Glin Castle Gardens in County Limerick are special favourites. Both are a happy mixture of formal and wild gardens, with huge walled gardens filled with flowers, vegetables and herbs. Both have wonderful natural settings. Another great favourite is Birr Castle Gardens, right in the heart of Ireland. If you are in Dublin, do not neglect to go to the Botanical Gardens in Glasnevin, which are really superb.

The list of treasures and rare species in Irish gardens open to the public is very impressive, and there are too many to mention here. Useful publications are *The Gardens of Ireland* by Tourism Ireland, *The Hidden Gardens of Ireland* by Marianne Heron (Gill & Macmillan) and *Irish Gardens* by Terence Reeves-Smyth (Appletree Press).The Royal Horticultural Society of Ireland (*Swanbrook House, Bloomfield Avenue,*

Morehampton Road, Dublin 4, t (01) 668 4358, www.rhsi.ie) holds flower shows, lectures, and garden visits. The Ulster Gardens Scheme (*contact the Northern Irish Tourist Board*) organizes open days in many gardens.

Potatoes and the Famine

Potatoes were the main food of peasants in the 19th century. The whole family would sit around a *rishawn* (basket) made of willows placed on the three-legged iron pot in which they had been boiled. The summer months were known as the hungry months, as the old crop of potatoes was finished. The last Sunday in July, or the first Sunday in August, was the ancient feast of *Lughnasa* (Lammas), a celebration of the start of the new harvest. Sometimes a delicious mixture of new potatoes, milk, onion, spices and melted butter would be eaten from the first digging of the new potatoes. This is known as *colcannon*. The potato crop enabled large families to live on tiny, subdivided holdings on the poorest land. The spuds were grown in lazy beds, the farmers using spades to build up ridges of soil on these stony hillside farms. You can still see the traces of lazy beds in hillside parts of Munster. Today they are no longer cultivated; many were abandoned in the famine times.

The potato blight, a fungal disease that struck between 1845–1849, had fatal consequences for the peasants living in this subsistence economy, especially in the west and southwest of the country. Huge suffering, death and disease followed, and the departure of millions of folk for Britain, Australia, Canada and America. The consequences of the famine and emigration were enormous, and still affect Ireland today. The population of Irish-speaking small farmers declined dramatically from 1847; nearly a quarter of a million emigrated every year. The landscape was emptied of people, villages were deserted, and the more prosperous farmers increased their land holdings. Very often all but the eldest son in a family emigrated; he was left to carry on with the farm, and he did not marry until very late in life, usually when his parents were dead. The wandering labourer who had an important place in society gradually died out as a class after the famine. These labourers had gone to hiring-fairs all over the provinces to be taken on by 'strong' or 'comfortable' farmers, as the better-off were called. Many were poets and storytellers and helped to keep oral traditions alive. The spade was the essential tool that each labourer carried with him, and every region in Ireland had its own variation of spade made by the blacksmith to suit local conditions. A Munster spade is typically a very long, narrow blade with fishtail ends.

'Clonakilty God help us' is an expression that originates from the time when that area westwards through Rosscarbery and Skibbereen, in County Cork, suffered terribly. At Knockfierna in west County Limerick there is a village that has been preserved as a memorial to the famine. Before it struck, about 1,000 people lived on the hill overlooking the Golden Vale. Afterwards, only 300 remained. These people lived in terrible conditions, doing back-breaking work to survive. Today there is no one left; only the huts remain. The Knockfierna Heritage and Folklore Group has developed the National Famine Commemoration Park here, which includes 15 dwellings on their original sites, around which you can still see the potato ridges.

Gaelic Games

Hurling (or hurley) and Gaelic football are uniquely Irish games, which are played widely in the counties of southwest Ireland. Both games are extremely fast and demand expert co-ordination, quick thinking, brawn, bravery and sure-footedness. It is probably fair to say that hurling requires the most skill and practice; Dr Johnson described it as 'hockey without the rules'. The game has been played all over the world wherever Irish migrants have settled. In Scotland it is called Shinty, and was introduced by Irish missionaries, along with Christianity. To watch a match in Dublin, Derry, Cork City, Galway or another of the 32 county grounds in Ireland would give you a huge buzz and some insight into Irish culture (matches are advertised in the local newspapers or you can get details from the local tourist office). Gaelic football, which uses the same pitch as hurling, is often described as a mixture of soccer and rugby, although it is much older than either of these games.

The first recognized version of hurling was recorded in County Meath in 1670, although it has existed in Ireland since pre-Christian times; the hero Cú Chulainn – hound of Cullen – was named thus after killing a guard dog by driving a hurling ball down his throat. Skill on the hurling field in these ancient times was equated with ability on the battlefield. By the 17th and 18th centuries the games were sometimes wild and violent, the rules were not set, and many regional variations existed.

Games are organized under the auspices of the GAA – Gaelic Athletic Association (*www.gaa.ie*) – which has been described as the 'greatest single bonding force in the Gaelic nation'. The GAA was founded in 1884 by Michael Cusack and Maurice Davin in a hotel meeting in Thurles. The Association standardized the rules in order to preserve the traditions of the games, in particular hurling, which was in danger of being gentrified and becoming a variant of hockey. Rugby was also becoming the accepted alternative to Gaelic football, especially amongst the middle classes. After the horrors of the Great Famine, many Irish customs and pastimes had fallen into decline, yet hurling was still very popular in much of southwest Ireland. The founding of the GAA was part of a general movement within the country, initiated by largely middle-class intellectuals, which sought to promote and esteem all things Irish. The literary revival and the language movement were part and parcel of this, but they did not achieve the mass following that grew up around the GAA, which was built on rural and Catholic support. Influential patrons of the GAA in its infancy were Dr Croke, the Archbishop of Cashel and Emly, Charles Stewart Parnell and Michael Davitt. The GAA organizes the two sports on a parish, county and provincial level. Among the most famous of the many different leagues and championships are the All Ireland Club Championship, the finals of which are played in Croke Park in Dublin on St Patrick's Day; the Railway Cup in early spring; and the Sam Macguire Cup.

Cork and Tipperary have a famous rivalry that has built up over the years and makes matches between them especially electric. Christy Ring of Cloyne, County Cork, and Nicholas English, who played brilliantly for Tipperary, spring to mind as hurling heroes; heroes indeed are the players in the minds of their parish, county and province. People line the roads and streets to welcome home their teams, and bonfires are lit to celebrate great victories. All the players are unpaid, and play just for the game and the glory.

Hurling is played with a *camán* or curved stick, and is variously known as *cambuc, camack, camac, crabsowl, shinney, hockie, hockey* or *hawkey* throughout the Celtic fringes of Britain. The Galway Statutes of 1527 include it as a prohibited game, describing it as 'the horlinge of the litill balle with hockie stickes or staves'. The Irish hurling stick is short with a wide blade and used to hit the ball in the air, to bounce it along on the stick or balance it there whilst running and being tackled aggressively. The stick is also used to hit the ball along the ground, although the breadth of the Irish stick means that the players cannot be as dextrous as their Scottish neighbours across the water, who play with a narrower stick. (The Ireland versus Scotland matches at Croke Park are legendary, the strengths and shortcomings of each method of hurling adding up to a match of equals.)

The ball in Gaelic football and hurling can be dribbled, punched, or kicked and carried in the hand for not more than four steps, after which it must be either bounced or 'solo-ed'. This means dropping the ball on to the foot or *camán* and kicking it back into the hand. In hurling you are not allowed to catch the ball more than twice. The goalposts for both games are the same shape as for rugby, although the crossbar is lower than on a rugby post. The ball used in Gaelic football is smaller than a soccer ball, while in hurling it is hard and leather-covered, like a hockey ball with raised ridges.

The growing popularity of soccer all over Ireland is seen as something of a threat to hurling and Gaelic football, as both these sports need commitment and training from an early age. The willing involvement of the religious orders, who used to run many of the educational establishments and helped train players after school, has not been replaced within the more secular organization. The dominance of Munster and the modern cult of counting success above everything is discouraging clubs that have never been very successful. The GAA once imposed Rule 21, which forbade any member of the RUC (now known as the PSNI) from participating in GAA events – unsettling for people who were worried about sectarianism and the politicization of sport. However, the GAA have now abolished this rule, and the Irish government recently gave them a grant of £20 million towards the refurbishment of Croke Park.

Food and Drink

Beyond the Potato

Eating out in Ireland can be a memorable experience, if chef gets it right. The basic ingredients are the best in the world: succulent beef, lamb, salmon, seafood, ham, butter, cream, eggs and wonderful **bread** – which is often homemade, and varies from crumbly nutty-tasting wheaten bread to moist white soda bread, crispy scones, potato bread and barm brack, a rich fruity loaf which is traditionally eaten at Hallowe'en. Irish **potatoes** are light and floury and best when just off the stalk, and crispy carrots and cabbages are sold in every grocery shop, often bought in from the local farms. If you stay in a country-house hotel, the walled garden will probably produce rare and exotic vegetables and fruit.

The history of Ireland has quite a lot to do with the down-side of cooking: over-cooked food, few vegetables, and too many synthetic cakes. The landless peasants had little to survive off except potatoes, milk and the occasional bit of bacon, so there is little traditional 'cuisine'. **Fish** was until recently regarded as 'penance food', to be eaten only on Fridays. Local people talk with amusement of those who eat oysters or mussels, and most of the fine seafood harvested from the seaweed-fringed loughs and the open sea goes straight to France, where it appears on the starched linen tablecloths of the best restaurants. But do not despair if you love fat oysters or fresh salmon, because they can always be got, either in the bars, the new-style restaurants which are really excellent, or straight from the fisherman. Remember, everything in Ireland works on a personal basis. Start your enquiries for any sort of local delicacy at the local post office, grocer or butcher, or in the pub.

Having got over the trauma of the famine, and since the relative prosperity of the 1960s, many people in Ireland like to eat **meat**: you cannot fail to notice the number of butchers or 'fleshers' in every town. Steak appears on every menu, and if you are staying in a simple Irish farmhouse, huge lamb chops with a minty sauce, Irish stew made from the best end of mutton neck, onions and potatoes, and bacon and cabbage casserole baked in the oven are delicious possibilities; fish, however, is becoming more and more readily available.

The standard of **restaurants** in Ireland is getting much better. This is especially true of those that are run by people from other European countries, many of whom set up here because of the beauty of the country and the raw ingredients. There are Irish cooks, too, who combine the local specialities and traditional recipes with ingredients and cooking methods from other cultures. Ballymaloe House in County Cork and Drimcong Restaurant in County Galway spring immediately to mind. Serious cooking is still a recent phenomenon, and many places will be trying to impress you (and the restaurant guides) with showy creativity – so expect to come across some bizarre sauces and combinations of ingredients. Eating out can be a massive disappointment. Too many restaurants still serve up musty and watery vegetables, overcooked meat, frozen fish, and salads of the limp lettuce and coleslaw variety. Also, eating out is not cheap, unless you have a pub lunch. To compete with the pubs, many restaurants do charge considerably less for lunch than dinner, so if it is convenient you can save a lot by having your main meal of the day in the afternoon.

To get around the serious problem of eating cheaply in Ireland, fill up on the huge breakfasts provided by the bed and breakfast places. If the lady of the house also cooks high tea or supper for her guests, take advantage of that as well. The food she produces is usually delicious and very good value. Irish people love their food, and are generous with it: huge portions are normal in the home and often in restaurants. It is a sign of inhospitality to give a poor meal. (They say, 'It was but a daisy in a bull's mouth'.) Bakeries usually sell tea, coffee and soft drinks along with fresh apple pie, doughnuts, cakes and sausage rolls. Roadside cafés serve the usual menu of hamburgers, chicken 'n' chips and so on. In the North they do a tearing trade in take-away foods. Most of the big towns have Chinese restaurants, pizza places and fish-and-chip shops. Vegetarians will find an increasing number of restaurants in Dublin and the larger towns that cater specifically for their needs. Also, vegetarians will find that even where no special menu exists, people are generally keen to provide suitable fare. If you are staying in a country house, you should telephone in advance to let them know you are vegetarian. You can sample the many delicious cheeses of Ireland by finding a good deli or wholefood shop, buying some bread and salad and taking yourself off to eat a picnic in some wonderfully scenic place. If it is drizzling, warm yourself up afterwards with a glass of Irish coffee in the local pub.

Restaurant Listings

You will normally find the service in Ireland friendly and helpful. A variety of good eating places are listed at the end of each county chapter; in the various culinary deserts which exist, those listed are the best of an indifferent lot. The establishments are categorized in the following cost brackets. Do bear in mind that proprietors and places change, so it is always best to phone before you arrive.

Luxury

Cost is no object – these restaurants serve creative and delicious food, cooked with fine ingredients. They are often in the dining-rooms of stately country houses or castles, where the silver and crystal sparkle and you are surrounded by fine pictures and furniture. Or they may be smart, fashionable places in the cities.

Expensive

Over €65 (UK£40) a head, excluding wine. Many country-house hotels come under this category, as do seafood restaurants around the coast and city establishments. Lunch in expensive places is often a very reasonably priced set meal, so ask about this if you do not want to fork out for dinner.

Moderate

€32–65 (UK£20–40) a head, excluding wine. The quality of the food may be as good as the more expensive places, but the atmosphere is informal and, perhaps, less stylish.

Inexpensive

Under €32 (UK£20) a head, excluding wine. This category includes bar food, lunchtime places and cafés. You can usually be sure of good homemade soup and one, simple course.

Eating Hours and Etiquette

Most restaurants do lunch and dinner but do check before you go. A few do only dinner and Sunday lunches. Some country places only open for the weekend during the winter months. Service is usually included in the bill at all restaurants. In the country towns and sometimes even in Dublin, you may find it difficult to pay by credit card. Check this out before you order your meal. If there is no liquor licence of any sort, the manager is usually quite happy to let you bring in your own wine or beer, if you ask. (The publicans – pub landlords – have a monopoly on licences, and many restaurants cannot get them without having to fulfil ludicrous requirements for space-planning).

Legal and Illicit Drinks

'The only cure for drinking is to drink more', so goes the Irish proverb. Organizations such as the Pioneers exist to wean the masses off 'the drink' – alcohol costs an arm and a leg, what with the taxes and the publican's cut; yet, nevertheless, an Irish bar can be one of the most convivial places in the world. The delicious liquor, the cosy snugs and the general hubbub of excited conversation, which in the evening might easily spark into a piece of impromptu singing, makes the business of taking a drink very pleasant. Pubs can also be as quiet as a grave, especially in the late afternoon when a few men nod over their pint, and an air of contemplation pervades.

You are bound to have been lured into trying **Guinness** by the persuasive advertisements you see all over the world (Guinness got to be what it is by the same sort of massive and diabolically clever advertising that made an institution of Coca-cola). Stout, or porter, is a beer made by drying the malt at a high temperature: browning it in effect, and providing the characteristic colour and taste, though there's considerably more to the art than just that. The export trade is thriving; but the place to get a real taste of the creamy dark liquor is in an Irish bar. It is at its most delicious when it is draught and drunk in a bar around Dublin, where it is made. Guinness does not travel well, especially on Irish roads. It is said to get its special flavour from the murky waters of the River Liffey, and you can go and find out for yourself if this is so by visiting the Brewery at St James Gate. The quality of taste once it has left the brewery depends on how well the publican looks after it and cleans the pipe from the barrel, so it varies greatly from bar to bar.

If it's obvious that you are a tourist, your Guinness may be decorated with a shamrock drawn on its frothy head. They've finally managed to get Guinness into a can, though it's only a pale reflection of the real thing. If you are feeling adventurous, try something called black velvet – a mixture of Guinness and champagne. And note that it isn't just Guinness. Down in Cork, Murphy's and Beamish make stout that's just as good, and available everywhere.

Whiskey has been drunk in Ireland for more than 500 years and the word itself is derived from *uisge beatha*, the Irish for water of life. It is made from malted barley with a small proportion of wheat, oats and occasionally a pinch of rye – so it's a blended whiskey, though without the distinctive taste of blended Scotch. On the whole Irish is better than American blended, and as good as Canadian. There are several brands: Jameson's, Paddy, Power, and Bushmill's (from the North) are all good.

Irish coffee is a wonderful combination of contrasts: hot and cold, black and white, and very intoxicating. It was first dreamed up in County Limerick in the 1940s. It's made with a double measure of Irish whiskey, one tablespoon of double cream, one cup of strong, hot black coffee, and a heaped tablespoon of sugar. To make it, first warm a stemmed whiskey glass. Put in the sugar and enough hot coffee to dissolve the sugar. Stir well. Add the Irish whiskey and then pour the cream slowly over the back of a spoon. Do not stir the cream into the coffee; it should float on top. The hot whiskey-laced coffee is drunk through the cold cream.

Poteen (pronounced 'pot-cheen') is illicit whiskey, traditionally made from potatoes, although nowadays it is often made from grain. Tucked away in the countryside are stills which no longer bubble away over a turf fire, but on a Calor gas stove. Poteen is pretty disgusting stuff unless you get a very good brew, and it probably kills off a lot of brain cells, so it's much better to stick to the legal liquid.

If you happen to stay in that wonderful country house, Longueville, near Mallow, you must order a bottle of dry fruity white **wine** from Ireland's only vineyard. It is delicious, and rare, because of Ireland's fierce frosts and the uncertainty of sunshine.

Bars

The old-fashioned serious drinking bar with high counter and engraved glass window, frosted so that the outside world couldn't intrude, is gradually changing. It used to be a male preserve. Farmers on a trip into town can be heard bewailing the weather or recounting the latest in cattle, land prices or gossip. What the inns have lost in character they compensate for, to a degree, with comfort. The bar of the local hotel is the place to find the priest when he is off-duty. My own favourite drinking establishment is the grocery shop which is also a bar, where you ask for a taxi/plumber/undertaker, only to find that the publican or his brother combine all these talents with great panache.

Licensing Hours

In the Republic, public houses are officially open Mon–Wed 10.30am–11.30pm, Thurs–Sat 10.30–12.30am, and on Sundays and St Patrick's Day from 12.30–11pm. In winter they close half an hour earlier. Plenty of places stay open later, although you'll have to get in before closing time, since they lock the doors and then carry on. The Garda don't seem to mind. There is no service on Christmas Day or Good Friday.

In Northern Ireland, public houses are open Mon–Sat 11am–11pm, and 12.30–10pm on Sundays. Also, you can always get a drink on Sundays at a hotel, though you are supposed to justify it by having a meal as well if you are not staying there. In the Republic, children are nearly always allowed to sit in the lounge bar with packets of crisps and fizzy orange to keep them happy, and they often appear in the evenings too when there's music.

If you do get into a conversation in a bar, a certain etiquette is followed: men always buy everybody in your group a drink, taking it in turn to buy a round; women will find they are seldom allowed to. Both sexes offer their cigarettes around when having one. If there are ten in your group, you will find yourself drunk from social necessity and probably out of pocket as well. The price in the Republic for wine, whiskey and beer is much higher than in the UK. A bottle of whiskey is about €18. If you are bringing a car from France or the UK, it might be as well to bring some booze in with you, or you could stock up in Northern Ireland. The customs allowance is 1½ litres of distilled beverages or spirits, 12 litres of beer and (if the alcohol is bought duty-paid) 4 litres of wine per person. Customs enforcement is not systematic.

Travel

Getting There

By Air

Most flights to the Irish Republic go to
Dublin, but there are also international
airports at **Cork**, **Shannon** (Limerick), **Galway**,
Sligo, **Kerry** (Killarney), **Knock** (in Co. Mayo) and
Waterford. The main airport in Northern
Ireland is **Belfast International** (aka Belfast
Aldergrove), but there is also another, smaller,
more central airport, **Belfast City**. There are
also flights to **Derry** (Eglinton Airport) and
Enniskillen. There are no direct flights from
Dublin to Belfast – the two towns are 3 hours
apart and well connected by road and rail.

From Britain

The Irish Republic's national airline, **Aer
Lingus**, handles an enormous number of
flights to the Republic from British and
European cities. If you are going to immerse
yourself in all things Irish, you might start
with this airline and its bright green planes.
Aer Lingus will take you to Dublin, Shannon or
Cork from at least one of the following:
Birmingham, Bristol, Edinburgh, Glasgow,
Leeds, London or Manchester (*see* below).
Other airlines also fly direct to Dublin, Cork
and Shannon from the four main London
airports (Heathrow, Gatwick, Luton and
Stansted), and there are numerous additional
flights to Irish cities from British regional
airports. A cheaper alternative is now offered

Airlines

From Mainland Britain

Aer Lingus, t (020) 8899 4747 or t 0845 973
7747, *www.aerlingus.ie*. Flights between
Dublin and Birmingham, Bristol, Edinburgh,
Gatwick, Glasgow, Heathrow, Leeds, London
City, Manchester, Newcastle and Plymouth;
also Shannon to London Heathrow, and Cork
to Birmingham, Heathrow and Plymouth.

bmi British Midland, t 0870 607 0555, or
t (01332) 854 854 *www.flybmi.com*. East
Midlands Airport, London Heathrow to
Dublin and Belfast, and Jersey to Dublin.

British Airways, t 0845 773 3377, *www.british-airways.com*. Heathrow and Gatwick to
Dublin and Cork, and Plymouth to Dublin.
Birmingham, Edinburgh, Glasgow,
Leeds/Bradford, Manchester, Sheffield and
Southampton to Belfast.

British European, t 0870 567 6676,
www.flybe.com. Exeter to Dublin, and
Birmingham to Shannon and Cork. Also
Birmingham, Bristol, Isle of Man, Leeds,
London and Newcastle to Belfast.

easyJet, t 0870 600 0000, f (01582) 443 355,
www.easyjet.com. Belfast to Edinburgh,
Glasgow, Luton and Liverpool.

Euroceltic Airways, UK t 0870 040 0100,
www.euroceltic.com. Waterford to London
Luton and Liverpool.

go, t 0845 605 4321, *www.go-fly.com*.
Edinburgh and Glasgow to Dublin; Stansted,
Edinburgh, Glasgow and Bristol to Belfast.

Keenair, t (0151) 448 0606, *www.keenair.co.uk*.
Flights from Liverpool to Cork, and from
Blackpool, via the Isle of Man, to Belfast.

Manx Airlines, t 0845 725 6256, *www.manx-airlines.com*. From the Isle of Man to Dublin
and Belfast; also Jersey–Cork and Dublin.

Ryanair, UK t 0870 156 9569,
www.ryanair.com. Dublin from Aberdeen,
Birmingham, Bournemouth, Bristol, Cardiff,
Edinburgh, Glasgow, Leeds, Liverpool,
London (Luton, Stansted and Gatwick),
Manchester, Teesside; also from Stansted to
Cork, Derry, Kerry, Knock and Shannon.

From the USA and Canada

Aer Lingus, USA t 1 800 IRISH AIR,
www.aerlingus.com. Boston, Chicago, Los
Angeles and New York to Dublin, and New
York and Boston to Shannon.

American Airlines, USA t 1 800 433 7300,
www.aa.com.

British Airways, USA t 1 800 247 9297, Canada
t 1 800 668 1059, *www.britishairways.com*.

Continental Airlines, USA t 1 800 525 0280,
www.continental.com. New York/Newark to
Dublin and Shannon.

Delta Airlines, USA and Canada t 1 800 221
1212, *www.delta.com*. Atlanta, New York and
Chicago to Dublin, and Atlanta to Shannon.

United Airlines, USA t 1 800 241 6522,
www.ual.com. Major US centres to London.

Virgin Atlantic Airways, USA t 1 800 862 8621,
www.virgin.com. Washington, New York, LA
and Florida to London and Manchester.

by budget carrier **Ryanair**, which has regular flights connecting Dublin with Birmingham, Cardiff, Glasgow, Leeds, Liverpool, London Luton and Manchester, as well as services from Glasgow and Stansted to the other Irish airports. Most British airlines run regular flights to Belfast from the UK.

Prices are always in a state of flux, but are reasonable by European standards; however, there is a bewildering array. As a guideline, an economy return from London to Dublin should cost around £40, London to Belfast around £22. The no-frills, low-cost carriers such as **Go** and **EasyJet** offer very low prices, and **Ryanair** offers extremely competitive fares, especially if you book online. London's *Time Out* and the Sunday newspapers are good places to start hunting for bargains. A travel agent or bucket shop can also help you to find the best deal.

From the USA and Canada

The main airports for transatlantic flights are **Dublin** and **Shannon**, which are served by direct scheduled flights from Atlanta, Boston, Chicago and New York. The main carriers flying direct to Ireland are Delta Airlines and Aer Lingus, but of course many others fly to European destinations, where you can pick up connecting flights. Often you can get a better price on these flights than you would pay if you flew direct.

Since **prices** are constantly changing and there are numerous kinds of deals on offer, the first thing to do is find yourself a travel agent who is capable of laying the current options before you. The time of year you choose can make a great difference to the price and availability of tickets. Expect to pay more and to have to book earlier if you want to travel at peak times, especially between June and August. Prices can range from around $500 for the best bargain deals to well over $1,000 for a plain ticket on a regular flight, so do some shopping around. A number of companies offer cheaper charter flights to Ireland – look in the Sunday travel sections of *The New York Times*, *Los Angeles Times*, *Chicago Tribune*, *Toronto Star* or other big-city papers. Remember to read all the small print as there are often catches, such as big cancellation penalties or restrictions about changing the dates of your flights; sometimes charter contracts include provisions that allow charter

Internet Travel

A good place to start looking for flights and bargain deals is on the Internet. There are countless websites; those listed below are a good starting point.

UK and Ireland
www.airtickets.co.uk
www.cheapflights.com
www.lastminute.com
www.skydeals.co.uk
www.sky-tours.co.uk
www.thomascook.co.uk
www.travelocity.com
www.travelselect.com

USA and Canada
www.air-fare.com
www.expedia.com
www.flights.com
www.orbitz.com
www.priceline.com
www.travellersweb.ws
www.travelocity.com
www.xfares.com (carry-on luggage only)
www.smarterliving.com

companies to cancel your flight, change the dates of travel and add fuel surcharges after you have paid your fare.

Shannon Airport, by the way, offers a variety of duty-free goods and Irish specialities: cut crystal glass, Connemara rugs, Donegal tweed and so on. If you don't want to get burdened with lots of presents and packages during your stay in Ireland, you can get everything here at the last minute.

Student and Youth Discounts

If you can produce an **International Student Identity Card** (ISIC), you can expect to get discounts of at least 25% on standard passenger rates for travel. There are student/under 26 rates for flights between Britain and Ireland, and similar concessions for transatlantic flights. You can get your card from the agencies below, who can also help you to find student deals.

Council Travel, USA, 205 E 42nd St, New York, NY 10017, t 212 822 2700 and branches across the States, or 1 800 226 8624, *www.counciltravel.com*. Student flights.

Airline Offices in Ireland
Aer Lingus, t 0818 365 000.
American Airlines, t 0845 601 0619.
British Airways, t 1 800 626 747.
British European, t 1 890 925 532.
Continental Airlines, t 1 890 925 252.
Delta Airlines, Dublin t (01) 407 3165,
    Shannon t 1 800 768 080.
easyJet, t 0870 600 0000.
Euroceltic Airways, t (051) 875 020.
go, t 1 890 925 922.
Keenair, t (021) 464 2217.
Manx Airlines, t (01) 260 1588.
Ryanair, t 0818 303 030.
United Airlines, t 0845 844 4777.
Virgin Atlantic Airways, t (01293) 450 150.

STA Travel, UK, 86 Old Brompton Road, London SW7, t (020) 7581 4132. and branches in all main university towns and campuses; USA, t 1 800 781 4040 and branches across the States, *www.sta-travel.com*. Flights etc.
Travel Cuts, Canada, 187 College St, Toronto, Ontario M5T, t (416) 979 2406 and branches across Canada, *www.travelcuts.com*. Canada's largest student travel specialists.

Getting To and From the Airports

Trains and/or buses run between the main airports and city centres. They're comfortable, frequent and economical; taxi drivers, by contrast, tend to ask a dramatically high price for a ride into the city.

Dublin Bus runs Airlink services (routes 747 and 748) between **Dublin Airport**, the Central Bus Station (Busáras), Connolly and Heuston railway stations and O'Connell Street every 10–15mins from 5.45am to 11.45pm. Aircoach also runs a service to city centre hotels and landmarks every 15mins from early morning to 10.20pm. You can also catch the cheaper but slower Citybuses (routes 41, 41A and 41C), which circulate between the airport and Eden Quay, outside Busáras.

There is a daily Airbus service from **Belfast International Airport** into Belfast's Europa Buscentre (Mon–Sat every 30mins, Sun every 30–60mins), and a regular train service from **Belfast City Airport** to Belfast Central Staion, as well as a regular Citybus (route 21). The quickest way to get from Belfast International Airport to Derry City is to take the Antrim

Airlink bus service (Mon–Sat 7.45am–7.45pm) to Antrim's railway station, from where you may catch one of the six daily trains to Derry.

Bus Eireann runs similar services from **Cork Airport** to Cork City, and from **Shannon Airport** to Limerick, 15 miles (25km) away.

By Sea

The **ferries** from the British west coast cross the Irish Sea at the shortest possible crossing points. Which port and crossing you choose will depend on where you are starting from, and where you wish to go in Ireland – which is not as obvious as it may seem. The Irish Sea is notoriously rough, and some crossings may be cancelled due to gales in winter.

The main crossings are as follows:
Rosslare Harbour (near Wexford) and south-east Ireland is served by Fishguard and Pembroke in South Wales, as well as regular services (every other day) from Cherbourg and Roscoff in Northern France.
Dublin Harbour and **Dun Laoghaire** are served by Holyhead, in North Wales, and Liverpool. Since early 1994 the Holyhead route is also served by a high-speed catamaran which crosses the Irish Sea in 1 hour 40mins. There is also a seasonal service to the Isle of Man.
Belfast and nearby **Larne**, in the North, are served by ferries and catamarans taking the short crossing from Cairnryan and Stranraer in southwest Scotland, and by ferries taking the longer journey from Liverpool. There is also a seasonal service to the Isle of Man.
Cork, the port for the southern Republic, is reached via Swansea, in South Wales, and from Roscoff, in France.

All the ferry ports are well connected to rail and coach transport (*see* opposite), and all the ferry services have drive-on/drive-off facilities for cars. **Prices** depend on time of year and length of crossing, how long you intend to stay in Ireland and, if you are taking your car, the number of passengers, car size and so on. Schedules can be complex too. Find a good travel agent and let them explore the options.

Note that at some peak times of the year – Easter, Christmas and especially around spring and autumn bank holidays – and on all sailings from Liverpool, the number of passengers on certain ferry crossings is controlled.

Ferry Companies

Irish Ferries, Dublin, t 0800 018 2211; Liverpool, t 0870 517 1717; London, t (020) 7499 5744, *www.irishferries.ie*. Holyhead–Dublin, 2 sailings daily all year, 3¼hrs; 3 catamaran sailings daily all year, 2hrs. Pembroke–Rosslare, 2 sailings daily all year, 3½hrs.

Isle of Man Steam Packet Company, Isle of Man, t 0870 552 3523; Dublin, t 1 800 551 743, *www.steam-packet.com*.Isle of Man–Dublin, 2–3 sailings per week Mar–Oct; 4½hrs; 2hrs 40mins by Sea Cat. Isle of Man–Belfast, 2–3 sailings per week, Mar–Sept; 2hrs 45mins by Sea Cat.Liverpool–Dublin, Mar–Oct daily; 4hrs by Sea Cat. Belfast–Troon, daily; 2½hrs by Sea Cat. Heysham–Belfast, April–Sept daily, 4hrs by Sea Cat. Stranraer–Belfast, several catamarans daily, all year, 1½hrs.

Norse Merchant Ferries, UK t (0151) 944 1010, *www.norsemerchant.com*. Liverpool–Belfast, 1 daily, all year, 8½hrs. Liverpool–Dublin, 1 daily, all year, 7½hrs.

P&O European Ferries, UK t 0870 2424 777, Ireland t 1800 409049, *www.poirishsea.com*. Cairnryan–Larne, 3 sailings daily, all year, 2hrs; 5 catamaran sailings daily April–mid Oct, less than 1½hrs.

Stena Line, reservations in the UK t 0870 570 7070; Dublin, t (01) 204 7777, *www.stenaline.ie*. Holyhead–Dun Laoghaire, 2 sailings daily all year, 3½ hrs; 3 catamaran sailings, 1½ hrs, plus an extra sailing on Sat. Fishguard–Rosslare, 3–6 sailings daily all year, 3½hrs; by catamaran 1½ hrs. Stranraer–Belfast, 2 ferry sailings daily, 1hr 45mins or 3½hrs; 5 catamaran sailings daily, 1¾hrs.

Swansea Cork Ferries, Swansea, UK t (01792) 456116; Cork Ferryport, Ringaskiddy, t (021) 276 000, *www.swansea-cork.ie*. Swansea–Cork, 10hrs (overnight crossing from Swansea, on alternate days). Takes you all the way to the west coast, and costs about the same as the shorter crossings.

All non-motorist passengers must have a '**sailing control ticket**' to board the ship at these times. These can be obtained when you book your crossing, or if you change your booking or have an open ticket, from the ferry offices. It is worth checking whether you need a control ticket before you start your journey.

Otherwise, crossings are easygoing. Unless they are packed, there is usually no problem if you miss a boat, even if you have a car. They'll just put you on the next one – but do ring ahead and let them know if you are delayed.

By Train

All the ferries crossing back and forth between Britain and Ireland are scheduled to link up with **trains** that go frequently and speedily from London to Fishguard, Liverpool, Holyhead and Stranraer. You can buy your **tickets** at any train station or booking office, or from National Rail, t 08457 484 950, *www.nationalrail.co.uk*. You can get couchettes on the night trains, or when it is quiet you can stretch out along the seats.

London (Euston) to Dublin via Liverpool/Dublin and Holyhead/Dun Laoghaire takes 6–11hrs; London (Paddington) to Wexford via Fishguard and Rosslare takes about 12½hrs; London (Euston) to Belfast via Liverpool about 16hrs; and London (Euston) to Belfast via Stranraer and Larne takes about 13hrs.

By Coach

Travelling by coach/ferry to Ireland is quite an endurance test. The journey seems endless, with lots of stops through Britain and Ireland to pick up other travellers, but it is cheap and takes you straight to destinations in the provinces, without changing on arrival in Ireland. The small coaches that go to and fro across the Irish Sea are flourishing private enterprises in the hands of local individuals. They leave all parts of Ireland for the chief cities of England, Scotland and Wales, full to the brim with Irish people returning to work or coming home on leave. Look for the smaller companies in Irish newspapers, which you can buy fairly easily in Britain.

London services leave from Victoria Coach Station. **Fares** from London can be as low as £20 return, or as high as £50. Ask about special student rates. The major coach companies for **Northern Ireland** are Eurolines/National Express and Ulsterbus in Belfast.

Coach Companies

Eurolines, t 0870 580 8080, Victoria Coach Station, Buckingham Palace Road, London SW1, *www.eurolines.com*. Connected with Bus Eireann and National Express, with regular services. London–Dublin: 3 daily, 11–12hrs. London–Waterford/Cork/Killarney (via Rosslare): 1 daily, overnight, 18hrs. London–Waterford/Limerick/Tralee (via Rosslare): overnight, 18hrs. Glasgow–Dublin: one daily, overnight, 10hrs. Leeds–Dublin: one daily, 11hrs. Bristol–Dublin: 3 daily, overnight, 12hrs. Birmingham or Bristol–Waterford/Cork/Killarney: 3 daily, 19–21hrs.

Ulsterbus, Belfast; from Ireland **t** (028) 9033 3000; from UK **t** (028) 9033 7002.

Entry Formalities

Passports and Visas

British citizens do not require a passport to enter the **Republic**. All the same, it can be useful to take a passport or some form of identification with you for completing formalities, such as hiring a car. Citizens of the USA and Canada must have a valid passport to enter the Republic, but no visa is required.

For **Northern Ireland**, entry formalities are exactly as they are for entry to the United Kingdom. US and Canadian citizens require a passport, but no visa. UK citizens do not need any form of identity documents, but it's as well to carry some since, if you are stopped in a security check, quick identification will speed the process.

Citizens (other than UK citizens) of the European Union, Australia and New Zealand need a full passport or identity card for entry into both the Republic and Northern Ireland. Passports are also required for visitors from other countries, and citizens of some may need visas too. Check with your nearest Tourism Ireland office, or with the visa departments of your local Irish or British embassies.

Customs

There is no customs inspection for travellers between the Republic and Northern Ireland or mainland Britain. Travellers do not have to pay tax or duty in the UK or Ireland on goods bought in other EU countries, as long as they are for personal use. This includes gifts, but the resale of goods may be illegal. Guidelines are issued for quantities of tobacco and alcohol regarded as reasonable for personal use; if you bring more than these amounts you must be able to satisfy customs officers that they are genuinely for your own use. The limits are: 800 cigarettes, 400 cigarillos, 200 cigars, 1kg of smoking tobacco, 10 litres of spirits, 20 litres of fortified wine, 90 litres of wine and 110 litres of beer. Under-17-year-olds cannot import tobacco or alcohol.

Duty free no longer exists within the EU borders. If arriving from outside the EU, however, duty-free remains, as do customs allowances, which are: 220 cigarettes or 100 cigarillos or 50 cigars or 250 grams of tobacco; 2 litres of still table wine; 1 litre of spirits or strong liqueurs over 22% alcohol, or 2 litres of fortified wine, sparkling wine or other liqueurs. The limit on all other goods including gifts and souvenirs is £145 for Northern Ireland, €92 for the Republic. Anything above these limits must be declared and tax paid.

Residents of the USA may each take home $400-worth of foreign goods without paying duty, including tobacco and alcohol allowances. Canadians can take home $500 worth of goods in a year, plus their tobacco and alcohol allowances.

Dog- and cat-owners can bring their pet to Ireland, as long as it comes directly from mainland Britain, the Channel Islands or the Isle of Man, and has been there for six months.

VAT Refunds

Any non-EU visitor can claim back the **VAT** (Value Added Tax) on goods bought in Ireland. To claim a tax refund, you must complete a form provided by the shop and present the form and goods to Customs when you leave. You must take your purchases home with you, within three months of purchase.

Customs Information

Irish Republic: t (01) 817 1920, *www.revenue.ie*.
UK: t 0845 010 900, *www.hmce.gov.uk*.
USA: t (202) 927 6724, *www.customs.ustreas.gov*.
Canada: t 800 461 9999, *www.ccra-adrc.gc.ca*.

Getting Around

By Air

It is possible to fly from one city to another in Ireland. However, this is a small island and the main destinations are well covered by rail and bus. **Aer Lingus** and **Ryanair** fly from Dublin to Cork, Shannon, Galway, Knock Airport in Co. Mayo, Sligo, Kerry (near Killarney) and Waterford (*see* pp.116–18 for details). **Aer Arann Express, t** 1 890 462726, or **t** (01) 814 5240, *www.aerarannexpress.com*. Dublin to Donegal, Sligo, Galway, Knock, Kerry and Cork, and to the Aran Islands from Galway.

By Train

In the Republic, trains are operated by **Iarnród Eireann** ('Iron Road Irish Rail'). Routes radiate out from Dublin and take you through sleepy little stations and green countryside. The system is rather like the British system of 50 or 60 years ago, with old signal boxes which still need people to operate them and keep an eye on things. People are always friendly on trains, and the ticket inspectors are far from officious. Services are reliable, and the fares are reasonable. Just the same, the network is not extensive, and especially lacking in the west and north; you will find trains useful mostly for getting to and from Dublin. Fares are nearly always more than those of buses, especially for one-way trips.

If you are planning an itinerary with lots of train trips in a short time, ask about the special rail cards, allowing unlimited travel over a given period of time. There are **Faircard** and **Weekender** deals for students, especially on return trips to or from Dublin (one of these even includes a free laundry service) as well as various discount tickets. The **Irish Explorer** ticket can be used for five days out of 15, is valid on the Republic's entire intercity and suburban rail network and costs €98. The **Irish Rover** has similar conditions and can also be used in Northern Ireland (€122/UK£75). The **Irish Explorer Rail and Bus** also includes travel on Bus Eireann; the Republic-only version costs €145, and a ticket covering both north and south is €158 (UK£98). At the top of the range is the **Emerald Card**, which can be used

Railway Companies
Iarnród Eireann, t 1850 366 222 or **t** (01) 836 6222, *www.irishrail.ie*. For information, timetables and tickets in the Republic.
NIR Travel Shop, Great Victoria Street Station, Belfast, **t** (028) 9023 0671; NIR enquiries **t** (028) 9089 9411; reservations **t** (028) 9089 9409. For rail travel in Northern Ireland.

for 15 days out of 30 and is valid for both trains and buses in both countries, cost €290.

Rail travel in Northern Ireland is run by **Northern Ireland Railways** (NIR), with services connecting Belfast to Coleraine and Derry and the ports. This system is fully integrated with Iarnród Eireann, and lines between Belfast and Dublin are operated jointly by Iarnród Eireann and NIR. It takes two hours to reach Dublin on the Belfast–Dublin non-stop express, and there are eight trains a day (five on Sundays).

Ireland is now part of the **Eurail Pass** and **Interail Pass** networks, which allow unlimited rail travel on European railways, including the Republic of Ireland but excluding the UK, and free ferry crossings from France to Ireland. To obtain the Eurail Pass you must be resident of a non-European country and buy it outside Europe; check *www.raileurope.com* for details. The Interail Pass is on sale to European residents, and is available in the UK from Rail Europe, **t** 0870 584 8848, *www.raileurope.co.uk*. There are also discount rates for under-26s.

For **steam train** enthusiasts there are plenty of places in Ireland where you can travel on one, as narrow gauge lines are reopened. The Northern Irish Tourist Board publishes a guide to steam railways which covers the whole of Ireland, and the Steam Traction Museum in Stradbally, Co. Laois, hosts 'steam rallies' in summer (*see* p.548).

By Bus

The bus service throughout Ireland is efficient and goes to the most remote places. The main companies are **Bus Eireann/Busáras** in the Republic, and **Ulsterbus** in Northern Ireland. Prices are reasonable, although on Bus Eireann they can be irrational, with a 20-mile journey sometimes costing as much as one of 100 miles. The best deals are with mid-week return tickets between the principal cities.

Bus Eireann offer discount **Irish Rambler** tickets for 3, 8 or 15 days costing €45, €100 and €145, respectively. There's a similar **Irish Rover** ticket, which is also good on Ulsterbus; again, the options are 3, 8 or 15 days and the respective prices are £37/€60, £84/€135 and £120/€195. They also operate chatty one-day and half-day tours throughout the Republic from many cities; ask for details at any of their Travel Centres, located in the bus company offices in Cork, Dublin and Galway. Addresses and phone numbers for individual bus stations are given in the 'Getting Around' sections of the relevant chapter. Local transport in Dublin and most places in Co. Dublin is handled by **Dublin Bus, t** (01) 873 4222.

The most convenient and reliable source for bus information is always the local tourist office. Bus Eireann have offices only in the largest towns, and there are many other smaller independent bus companies around. Two of the largest are **Nestor Bus**, which runs a Galway to Dublin service, or **Suirway**, which serves the southeast. Some private lines stop running in summer, as they depend on students for much of their income. You can pick up a Bus Eireann timetable at tourist offices and at some newspaper stands. Note that, in the Republic, bus destinations posted on the front of the bus are often given in Irish; Dublin, for example, may be seen as *Atha Cliath*, Galway *Gaillimh*, or Waterford *Port Lairge*. If in doubt, ask.

Ulsterbus runs frequent services to all parts of Northern Ireland. You can pick up time-tables at any Ulster bus station, or the tourist office in Belfast. The Ulsterbus head office is at the Europa Buscentre, on Great Victoria Street; the other main bus station is in Oxford Street. The Citybus tour service operates in Belfast only. Ulsterbus offers **Freedom of Northern Ireland** tickets for a day or a week, good on buses and trains in the North, and Irish Rover

> ### Bus Companies
> **Bus Eireann/Busáras**, Store Street, Dublin, **t** (01) 836 6111, *www.buseureann.ie*.
> **Citybus**, Belfast, **t** (028) 9045 8484.
> **Nestor Bus**, Galway, **t** (091) 797 144.
> **Suirway**, Waterford, **t** (051) 382 209.
> **Ulsterbus**, Europa Buscentre, Great Victoria Street, Belfast, **t** (028) 9032 0011, or **t** (028) 9031 5655, *www.ulsterbus.co.uk*.

tickets which are also good on Bus Eireann. For further details of special fares and bus excursions, see *On the Move*, published by the Northern Ireland Tourist Office.

Student and Youth Fares

You can expect to get discounts of at least 25% on standard passenger rates for travel with an ISIC card. You can also buy a **Travelsave Stamp** for around €8, which gets you some big savings: 50% off single adult tickets on B&I Line ferry crossings between Britain and Ireland, 33% discount off mainline rail fares in Ireland, 30% off single adult CIE provincial bus journeys and 50% off the return fare to the Aran Islands by boat. The stamp is available from USIT Now (Union of Students International Travel), from student travel offices in the UK, USA or Canada (*see* p.117), and at Irish or Northern Irish universities. **USIT Now**, 19 Aston Quay, Dublin 2, **t** (01) 679 8833; University of Limerick, Limerick Town, **t** (061) 332 079, *www.usitnow.ie*.

By Car

To explore Ireland with minimum effort and maximum freedom, bring a car. If you fill it up with people who share the ferry and petrol costs, it won't be too expensive. Buy a detailed road map and, if you have time, choose a minor road and just meander. It is along these little lanes that the secret life of Ireland continues undisturbed. The black and red-brown cows still chew by the wayside while the herdsman, usually an old man or a child, salutes you with an upward nod. You will come upon castles, and the ruins of the small, circular buildings called *clochans*, still breathing with memories, tumbled even further by the local farmer in search of stone; and there are views of hills which have never reached the pages of any guidebook.

Once upon a time, one of the best things about driving in Ireland was the lack of other cars, and the absence of ugly, if efficient, motorways with their obligatory motor inns and petrol stations. With the Republic's new prosperity, this has changed in many places. Traffic around the towns, especially Dublin, can be ferocious, while the government is committed to a big programme of new roads and road widenings that are guaranteed to make the problem worse, while eroding the country's natural beauty and its way of life. Car ownership in Ireland has risen in keeping with most European countries, but for now, some country roads are serene enough.

Watch out for the country driver who tends to drive right in the middle of the road, never looks in his mirror to see if anyone is behind, and probably won't indicate if he suddenly decides to turn left or right. The ones wearing old tweed caps are usually the worst offenders. There is also the other extreme: people who drive at crazy speeds on narrow roads. Cars frequently pull out of a side road in front of you and, just as you are getting up enough steam to pass, suddenly decide to turn off down another side road. Don't be alarmed by the sheepdogs which appear from cottage doorways to chase your car – they are well skilled at avoiding you.

If your car **breaks down** in any part of Ireland you will always be able to find a mechanic to give you a hand; whether it's late at night or on a Sunday, just ask someone. He or she will sweep you up in a wave of sympathy and send messengers off in all directions to find you someone with a reputation for mechanical genius. If it is some small and common part that has let you down, he will either have it or do something that will get you by until you come to a proper garage. One thing you will notice is that the Irish have a completely different attitude to machinery from most nationalities. In England, if you break down, it is an occasion for embarrassment; everybody rushes by hardly noticing you or pretending not to. In Ireland, if your car has broken down the next passing car will probably stop, and the problem will be readily taken on and discussed with great enjoyment. The Irish can still laugh at the occasional failure of material affairs.

Facts and Formalities for Car Drivers

In Ireland you **drive on the left** (when you are not driving in the middle of the road); the government has installed signs in seemingly random places around the country to remind us: *Conduire à gauche! Links fahren!* **Petrol stations** stay open until around 8pm, and the village ones are open after Mass on Sundays. If you are desperate for petrol and every station seems closed, you can usually knock on the door and ask somebody to start the pumps for you. Prices are roughly the same as in Britain, three or four times as much as in the US.

The **speed limit in the Republic** is 60mph (100kph) on ordinary roads, 70mph (113kph) on motorways, and 30–45mph (48–69kph) through the villages and towns, as posted. Note that speed limit signs in the Republic are always given in miles. Road signs showing distances to the next towns are charmingly given in either miles or kilometres, usually without telling you which one (the older, white signs with black borders are in miles; newer, enamelled aluminium signs in green or white are usually in kilometres). Otherwise, directional signs are mainly notable for their absence; out in the country you will get lost, and probably stay lost. Some signs, especially in Gaeltacht areas, will be written in Irish; of these, the most important to know is *Go Mall* – slow down. *An Lar* is the city centre, while *Gach treo eile* signifies 'all routes'.

The **speed limit in Northern Ireland** is 70mph (112 kph) on dual carriageways, 60 mph (96 kph) on country roads, 40 mph (64 kph) in built-up areas and 30 mph (48 kph) in towns.

Drivers and front-seat passengers must always wear a **seat belt** – it is illegal not to. Children under 12 should travel in the back. There are strict drink-driving laws in the Republic as in the North, and the police will use a breathalyser test if they suspect that you 'have drink taken'; the legal limit is roughly two pints of Guinness.

There are some excellent **motoring maps**: Bartholomew's quarter inch, obtainable from the AA and Bord Fáilte, gives good details of minor roads. The principal roads in Northern Ireland are marked A, lesser roads B; in the Republic they are N (national) and R (regional). Scenic routes are signposted and marked on the Bord Fáilte map. Place names on signposts in the Republic are usually given in English and in Irish; in the places where Irish only is used a good map will be useful.

Residents of the Republic of Ireland, Northern Ireland and Great Britain using private cars and motorcycles may cross the borders with very little formality. A **full, up-to-date licence** is all you need. Under EU regulations, private motor insurers will provide the minimum legal cover required in all EU countries, although they may need to be told before you travel. Always carry the **vehicle registration book**. If you have hired a car, be sure to tell the rental company that you plan to cross borders, and that you have all the necessary papers; the rental company should also deal with all the insurance headaches.

Due to the ceasefire, the rules governing border crossings and approved roads are changing. You should use an approved road to cross the border, or you may incur penalties. If in doubt, anyone in the border regions will know whether a back road is approved.

The army checkpoints have decreased considerably, but it is as well to carry your licence or some means of identification and slow down. Surprisingly, you are more likely to encounter a Garda checkpoint coming south than a British security checkpoint going north. **AA** (Automobile Association) or, in the North, **RAC** (Royal Automobile Club) offices will give you all the details of necessary formalities if you are not clear about anything. The **AAA** in the USA will be able to help with licence and insurance questions before you set off.

Parking meters are used to control car parking in the central zones of Dublin. The meters are in operation during specific hours from Mondays to Saturdays, when street parking is prohibited at non-metered sites. Yellow lines along the kerbside or edge of the roadway indicate waiting restrictions. In some large towns a **disc system** is used to control parking in the centre. Parking discs can be bought, usually in books of ten, at shops and garages near the car parks. Unexpired time on a parking disc can be used at another parking place. In **Belfast** it's best to head for a car park; in Northern Ireland, for security reasons, parking is not permitted in central city areas marked off as 'Control Zones', which are clearly indicated by yellow signs saying 'Control Zone. No Unattended Parking'.

Driving Associations

AA, Irish Republic t (01) 677 9481; UK t 0870 600 0371, *www.theaa.com*.
AAA, USA t (407) 444 4000.
Moto Europa, *www.ideamerge.com/ motoeuropa*. Everything you ever wanted to know about driving in Europe.
RAC, UK only t 0800 550 550, *www.rac.co.uk*.

Car Hire Companies

Argus Rent-a-Car, Dublin Airport, t (01) 814 4013. Budget car hire firm in the Republic.
Dan Dooley/Kenning, 42 Westland Row, Dublin 2, t (01) 677 2723.
Murrays Europcar, Baggot Street Bridge, Dublin 4, t (01) 614 2800; Dublin Airport, t (01) 812 0410, f (01) 812 0428, *www.europcar.ie*.
Payless Bunratty Car Rentals, Dublin Airport, t (01) 8445522, *www.iol.ie/paylessbcr*.
Avis, Ferry Terminal, Larne Harbour, Belfast, t (028) 2827 0381.
Hertz, Aldergrove Airport, Belfast, t (028) 9442 2533.

Car Hire

All of the big chains will meet you at the airports and the ferry ports of the Republic, but you can do better to wait and get a cheaper deal with a city centre branch, or even better, with one of the **local budget firms**. If you can book in advance you can get a car for as little as €150 (UK£110) a week subject to availability. Otherwise, rates for the smallest cars can go as high as €311 (UK£500) or more.

In Northern Ireland, the story is much the same. The chains all operate from both of Belfast's airports but it's much less expensive to hire a car from their city centre branches. Local firms (*see* phone book) can offer even better deals. Renting a car in Ireland is never cheap, but you might be able to bargain if business is slack. Look out also for fly-drive, or rail-sail-drive **packages** offered by some of the airlines and ferry companies: these usually represent major savings. Note that to hire a car you should normally be over 23 and in possession of a licence which you have held for at least two years without endorsement. The car hire company will organize **insurance**, but do check this. If you do not take extra collision-damage waiver insurance you can be liable to damage up to €1714 (UK£2790). Check that your contract covers both the North and the Republic if you plan to drive in both areas.

By Bicycle

Ireland is one of the most pleasant countries in which to cycle. Once you escape the highways the roads are quiet, there are still many birds and animals that live around the hedgerows, and in many places there is no pollution to spoil the air. This means, of course, that you'll encounter all the whiffs and pongs of the countryside, and in between the delicious gorse and honeysuckle perfumes will waft the strong, healthy smell of manure.

You can take your own bike onto the ferry for free, or you can rent one when you arrive. In the Republic the **Raleigh Rent-A-Bike** network connects some 70 centres throughout the country, with tandems, racing bikes, and ordinary touring bikes available for hire. For full details get the *Cycling Ireland* leaflet from the nearest Bord Fáilte office. This gives details of the main hire companies, lists Irish cycling holiday specialists, and also describes 23 suggested routes. Alternatively, contact the Raleigh Rent-A-Bike Division direct (*see* below). Raleigh network members and other bike hire shops are listed within the 'Getting Around' sections in each chapter.

The Northern Ireland Tourist Board produces a leaflet on cycling which lists tours, routes, and events for cyclists, plus a number of cycle hire companies. Rental rates are comparable to those in the Republic. You can also hire bikes at some youth hostels in the North; contact the YHANI. Note that bicycles hired in the Republic cannot be taken into Northern Ireland, and vice versa. Irish Cycling Safaris run well-organized and enjoyable holidays bicycling through scenic parts of the country.

Irish Cycling Safaris, 7 Dartry Park, Dublin 6, **t** (01) 260 0749.

Raleigh Ireland Limited, Raleigh House, Unit 1, Finches Park, Longmile Road, Dublin 12, **t** (01) 626 1333, **f** (01) 460 3096.

YHANI (Youth Hostels Association Northern Ireland), Belfast **t** (028) 9032 4733.

On Foot

If you enjoy **walking** in the countryside, Bord Fáilte and the Northern Ireland Tourist Board produce useful leaflets on public footpaths. The website *www.irishwaymarkedways.ie* is a mine of information for those wanting to walk in the Republic of Ireland.

From all accounts, **hitch-hiking** in the countryside seems to be a fairly safe but rather slow method of transport round the South. In the North you might find that people will not pick you up because years of the Troubles have made them cautious. It would be unwise to hitch around border areas anyway, and there are plenty of buses that will take you through. (**Women**, as always, should be especially cautious, and it is advisable, if they are determined to hitch-hike, for them to travel with a companion; *see* 'Women Travellers', p.150) On major roads write your destination on a bit of cardboard and hold it up. You will find you have to compete with local people who hitch regularly from town to town. Tony Hawkes made a wager in a pub that he could hitch-hike a circuit of Ireland carrying a refrigerator. He won the bet (and wrote a book about it – see **Further Reading**, p.653).

Getting to the Aran Islands

The Aran Islands to the west of Galway are probably the most famous of the islands lying off the west coast of Ireland, but there are many others, each with its own charms. You can reach most of these by boat services from the nearest mainland port – these range from regular car-ferry lines for some of the larger islands, to asking on a dock for a fisherman to take you over to the smallest ones. For more details, see pp.121 and 318.

Tour Operators

There are hundreds of tour companies offering all manner of enticing holidays in Ireland. Tourism Ireland has lists of the main operators in their brochures. Alternatively, contact your travel agent.

Special-interest Holidays

Travellers who want holidays with a special focus – ancestor-hunting, angling, bird-watching, farm and country, gastronomy, gardens, golf, horse-riding, sailing, a mixture of these or none of them – are well catered for in Ireland. The main specialist companies are listed in the tourist board brochures. Bord Fáilte also has brochures with details of organizations offering holidays 'designed to enable participants to acquire new leisure skills' – sports, gardening, cookery, arts and crafts – 'in a relaxed and green environment'.

Specialist Tour Operators

See also 'Summer Schools', in **Practical A–Z**, p.143.

In the UK

Angler's World Holidays, 46 Knifesmithgate, Chesterfield, Derbyshire, S40 1RQ, **t** (01246) 221 717, *www.anglers-world.co.uk*. Game fishing for salmon and sea-trout, dollaghan, gillaroo, sonaghen and ferox trout, and coarse fishing for bream, roach, rudd, tench and monster pike galore in the rivers, lakes and loughs of Ireland.

Back-Roads Touring Co., 14/a New Broadway, London W5 2XA, **t** (020) 8566 5312, *www.backroadstouring.co.uk*. Tours of Dublin, Killarney, Galway, Sligo and Donegal.

Enjoy Ireland, **t** (01254) 692 899, *www.enjoyireland.net*. Golfing, riding, angling and walking holidays.

HF Holidays, Imperial House, Edgware Road, London, NW9 5AL, **t** (020) 8905 9556, *www.hfholidays.co.uk*. Dingle Way and West of Ireland guided walking holidays, or stays in Killarney National Park, Co. Kerry.

On Course Travel, **t** (01372) 451 910, *www.ireland-oncourse.co.uk*. Horse racing holidays including Laytown Beach Races, Curragh Classics and Dublin winter races.

In Ireland

Ardress Craft Centre, Kesh, Co. Fermanagh, **t** (028) 686 31267. Holidays based around courses in arts and crafts (weaving, patchwork and painting).

Colclough Tours, 71 Waterloo Road, Dublin 4, **t** (01) 668 0109, *www.tourismresources.ie*. Informative tours anywhere in Ireland. Tailor-made itineraries, car with a driver-guide and accommodation ranging from traditional farmhouse to grandest castle. Tours can take in gardens, genealogy, ghosts, gourmet meals, and sites of historical importance.

Emerald Star Line Ltd, The Marina, Carrick-on-Shannon, Co. Leitrim, **t** (078) 20234, *www.emeraldstar.ie*. Cruising holidays on the River Shannon. Impressive on-shore facilities and variety of boats.

Go Ireland, Killorglin, Co. Kerry, **t** (066) 976 2094, *www.goireland.fexco.ie*. Guided and independent walking and cycling holidays in Co. Kerry.

Irish Country Holidays, The Discovery Centre, Rearcross, Co. Tipperary, **t** (062) 79330, *www.country-holidays.ie*. Opportunity to live as part of a small, rural community. You can spend your week in Ballyhoura, Co. Limerick, the Barrow/Nore area, Lough Corrib country, and west Cork. Each community has something special to offer in the way of landscape, customs and amenities.

Irish Cycling Safaris Ltd, Belfield Bike Shop, University College Dublin, Belfield House, Dublin 4, **t** (01) 260 0749, **f** (01) 706 1168, *www.cyclingsafaris.com*, *ics@kerna.ie*. Offers leisurely one-week cycling holidays, with bikes supplied, in many parts of Ireland, concentrating on the Cork/Kerry and Connemara regions.

Kerry Holidays, c/o Kerry Airport, Farranfore, Killarney, Co. Kerry, Ireland **t** (066) 976 322, UK **t** 0800 039 0088, *www.kerryholidays.com*. Fly-drive, B&B, self-catering and golf holidays.

Oideas Gael, Glencolmbkille, Co. Donegal, **t** (073) 30248, **f** (073) 30348 *www.oideas-gael.com*, *oideasgael@iol.ie*. Offers a workshop-type course in Irish culture and language, which includes folklore, singing, storytelling, set dancing and local history.

In the USA and Canada

Backroads, 801 Cedar St, Berkeley, CA 94710-1800, **t** 1 800 GO-ACTIVE, or **t** (510) 527 1555, *www.backroads.com*. Multi-sport: golf, walking and biking, with packages in Counties Kerry, Cork and Galway.

CIE Tours International Inc, 100 Hanover Ave, PO Box 501, Cedar Knolls, NJ 07927-0501, **t** 1 800 CIE-TOUR, or **t** (973) 292 3438, *www.cietours.com*. Escorted coach, self-drive or independent holidays, including 'Irish Pub and Folk' and 'Irish Legends' tours.

Classic Adventures, New York State, **t** 1 800 777 8090, *www.classicadventures.com*. Guided biking holidays in the southwest.

Golf International Inc., 14 E 38th St, New York, NY 10016, **t** 1 800 833 1389, *www. golfinternational.com*. A great variety of golf courses on customised or escorted tours.

Saga Holidays, **t** 1 800 343 0273, *www. sagaholidays.com*. Escorted coach tour, 'Around the Emerald Isle', for the over-50s.

Practical A–Z

Children

You will find that Irish bed and breakfast establishments welcome children. Many have family rooms with four or five beds, and charge a reduced price for them. Most supply cots and high chairs and offer a baby-sitting service, but always check beforehand. Some farm and country houses keep a donkey or pony and have swings and play areas set up.

Irish people love children, and easily tolerate seeing and hearing them in bars and eating places during the daytime. Children's menus are offered at a cheaper price and generally people will be helpful, but in some places they will not be so happy if you turn up with kids in the evening for dinner. If you are contemplating staying in some of the smart country house hotels, which are full of precious antiques, please check that it is a suitable place for children beforehand.

Climate

Ireland lies on the Gulf Stream, which makes the climate mild, equable and moist. No temperature of over 90°F or below 0°F has ever been recorded. Rainfall is heaviest in the high western coastal areas, where it averages over 80 inches (203cm) a year. On the east coast and over the central plain, rainfall averages between 30 and 40 inches (76 and 101cm). Rain is Ireland's blessing, yet, from the reputation it has in its own country and abroad, you might imagine it was a curse. It keeps the fields and trees that famous lush green, and the high level of water vapour in the air gives it a sleepy quality and softens the colours of the landscape. The winds from the east increase the haziness and mute the colours, but these are nearly always followed by winds from the northwest which bring clearer air and sunshine. So the clouds begin to drift and shafts of changing light touch the land. Nearly every drizzly day has this gleam of sunshine, which is why the Irish are always very optimistic about the weather. The driest parts of the country are counties Carlow,

Wexford and parts of Kilkenny and Waterford, the 'Sunny Southeast' as the tourist office imaginatively puts it, averaging fewer than 200 days with rain a year. Donegal, Tyrone, Londonderry, Sligo, Galway and the coastal parts of Cork, Clare and Kerry average over 250.

Snow is rare and seldom severe. Spring tends to be relatively dry, especially after the blustery winds of March, and the crisp colours and freshness of autumn only degenerate into the cold and damp of winter in late December. You can hope for at least 6 hours of sunshine a day over most of the country during May, June, July and August.

Disabled Travellers

Tourism Ireland produces useful booklets advising travellers with disabilities. Particularly commended is *Accessible Accommodation in Northern Ireland*. Useful advice for travelling in the North can also be obtained from Disability Action in Belfast.

The tourist board also publishes a comprehensive list of accommodation with access in its annual guides, available from its offices. In Dublin the National Rehabilitation Board can offer you information and assistance. The Irish Wheelchair Association can supply wheelchairs for the disabled.

In Britain, RADAR is an excellent source of information. The Holiday Care Information Unit offers advice for all travellers with special needs, and publishes a short information sheet on the Irish Republic.

Specialist Organizations in Ireland
Comhairle, 44 North Great George's Street, Dublin 1, t (01) 874 7503.
Disability Action, Belfast, t (028) 9029 7880, *www.disabilityaction.org*.
Irish Wheelchair Association, Blackheath Drive, Clontarf, Dublin 3, t (01) 818 6413, *www.iwa.ie/*. Services for disabled travellers; also guides for disabled holidaymakers.
National Disability Authority, Dublin, t (01) 608 0400, *www.nda.ie*.

Specialist Organizations in Britain
Holiday Care Service, 2nd Floor, Imperial Buildings, Victoria Road, Horley, Surrey RH6 9HW, t (01293) 774 535, f (01293) 771 500,

Average Daily Temperatures
Jan 4–7°C (39–45°F)
July–Aug 14–24°C (57–75°F)

www.holidaycare.org.uk. Up-to-date information on destinations, transport and helpful tour operators.

RADAR (Royal Association for Disability and Rehabilitation), 12 City Forum, 250 City Road, London EC1V 8AF, **t** (020) 7250 3222, **f** (020) 7250 0212, *www.radar.org.uk*. Publishes books with useful information for travellers with disabilities, including one on 'Access to Air Travel' and several holiday 'factpacks'.

RNIB (Royal National Institute for the Blind), 224 Great Portland Street, London W15 5TB, **t** (020) 7388 1266, *www.rnib.org.uk*. The RNIB's mobility unit offers a 'Plane Easy' audio-cassette which advises the blind or visually impaired on air travel. Will also advise on accommodation.

Specialist Organizations in North America

American Foundation for the Blind, 11 Penn Plaza, Suite 300, New York, NY 10001, **t** (212) 502 7600, or **t** 800 232 5463. The best source of information in the USA for visually impaired travellers.

Mobility International USA, PO Box 10767, Eugene, OR 97440, **t** (541) 343 1284, **f** (541) 343 6812, *www.miusa.org*. Information on international educational exchange programmes and voluntary services for the disabled.

SATH (Society for the Advancement of Travelers with Handicaps), 347 5th Av, Suite 610, New York, NY 10016, **t** (212) 557 0027, **f** (212) 725 8253, *www.sath.org*. Travel and access information, with a good website resource.

Eating Out

You will normally find service in Ireland friendly and helpful. A variety of good eating places are listed under 'Eating Out' in each chapter; in the various culinary deserts, those listed are the best of an indifferent lot. Restaurants are categorized in the price ranges below. For further details on eating habits, *see* **Food and Drink**, pp.109–14.

Restaurant Price Categories
luxury cost no object
expensive over UK£40/€65
moderate UK£20–40/€32–65
inexpensive under £20/€32

Electricity

The current is 220 volts AC, so you should bring a current converter if you have any American appliances or computers. Wall sockets take the standard British-style three-pin (flat) fused plugs, so Americans and other Europeans will need a plug adaptor too.

Embassies and Consulates

Australian Embassy, Fitzwilton House, Wilton Terrace, Dublin 2, **t** (01) 676 1517.
Australian High Commission, Australia House, Strand, London, WC2 B4L, **t** (020) 7379 4334.
British Embassy, 31 Merrion Road, Dublin 4, **t** (01) 205 3700.
Canadian Chancery and Consulate, 65 St Stephen's Green, Dublin 2, **t** (01) 417 4100.
Canadian High Commission, Grosvenor Square, London W1, **t** (020) 7258 6600.
New Zealand Consulate General, 46 Upper Mount St, Dublin 2, **t** (01) 660 4233.
South African Embassy, Earlsfort Court, Dublin 2, **t** (01) 661 5553.
US Embassy, 43 Elgin Road, Dublin 4, **t** (01) 668 8777.
US Consulate, 14 Queen's Street, Belfast BT1 6EG, **t** (028) 9032 8239.

Emergencies and Hazards

Emergencies

If you do find yourself in trouble in Ireland, you will find no shortage of sympathetic help. If you fall ill, have an accident or are the victim of some crime, people will rush to your aid. Whether they bring quite the help you need is another matter. If in doubt, get the advice of your hotel, the local tourist office or the police. In serious cases (medical or legal), contact your embassy or consulate (*see* above). Try to keep your head: in the case of medical treatment, take your insurance documents, inform the people treating you of your cover, and make sure you keep all receipts (or at least get someone reliable to do this for you).

The **emergency telephone number** (to call any of the emergency services) in both the Republic and the North is **t 999**. In the Republic you can also call **t 112**.

Beasts

If you decide to have a picnic in an inviting green field, just check that there is not a bull in it first. High-spirited bullocks can be just as alarming; they come rushing up to you, have a good look and knock you over in the process.

Midges

Toads and adders are said to have fled from Ireland at the sound of St Patrick's bell tolling from the top of Croagh Patrick mountain; unfortunately, the voracious midges of the west coast did not take their cue. They are very persistent on warm summer evenings, so remember to arm yourself with an insect repellent. There is plenty of choice in the chemist's if you forget. Wasps, hornets and horseflies also emerge in summer.

Motorists

Motorists in Dublin should always lock their cars, and leave them in authorized car parks. Many cars are stolen and taken for 'joy rides' by very young boys. Do not leave luggage or valuables in the car.

The Sea

A major hazard can be strong currents in the sea. One beach may be perfectly safe for bathing, but the one beside it positively dangerous. Always check with locals before you swim. There are lifeguards on most of the resort beaches; few elsewhere.

Also, don't eat the seaweed. No matter how clean the water looks, beware! It may make you sick to your stomach.

Walkers

Walkers who intend to go through bog and mountainous country should be warned that, even though it looks dry enough on the road, once into the heather and moss you will soon sink into waterlogged ground. Wear stout boots and bring at least an extra jersey. Sudden mists and rain can descend, and you can get very cold. You should not rely on mountain rescue teams to find you; if you do intend to go walking on a mountain range, leave word at your hotel or a put a note on your car as to where you plan to go. During the shooting season (grouse and snipe from August to 3 January, duck from September to

Calendar of Events

March

Dublin Film Festival. New Irish cinema, t (01) 679 2937, f (01) 679 2939.
Belfast Music Festival, t (028) 9032 5942.
St Patrick's Week. Events centre around St Patrick's Day (17 March), with parades, music, dance and theatre, especially in Dublin, Cork, Galway and Limerick, www.stpatricksday.ie.
World Irish Dancing Championships, contact Maire Nichobaid, t (01) 475 2220.
Irish Grand National, Fairyhouse, Co. Meath.

May

Fleadh Nua, Ennis, Co. Clare. Traditional music, song and dance. Comhaltas Ceoltoírí Eirean, 32 Belgrave Square, Monkstown, Co. Dublin, t (01) 278 1529; www.fleadhnua.com.
AIB Music Festival in Great Irish Houses. International soloists and orchestras perform in grand houses through the summer. Festival Administrator, 1st Floor, Blackrock Post Office, Blackrock, Co. Dublin, t (01) 278 1528, f (01) 278 1529.

Castlebar International 4-day Summer Walk (late June–July). Walking and traditional, pop and classical music, t (094) 24102.

June

Irish Derby, The Curragh, Co. Kildare.

July

Galway Arts Festival. One of the biggest, most popular festivals: theatre, arts and music, t (091) 583800, info@gafiof.ie.
RDS Kerrygold Irish Oaks, The Curragh, Co. Kildare.

August

Kilkenny Arts Festival. Music recitals, poetry, art, theatre and children's workshops. Maureen Kennelly, t (056) 63663.
Puck Fair, Killorglin. Lots of drinking and wild-ness revolving around a captured goat. Call Declan Falvey, t (066) 976 2366.
Fleadh Cheoil na Heireann. Up to 5,000 traditional musicians play impromptu sessions; usually held in summer (changes venues). Contact Comhaltas

31 January and pheasant from 1 November to 1 January), be careful of wandering into stray shot on the hilly slopes or in marshy places.

The Fairies

There is just one last possible hazard which you might only have dreamt about: the mischievous fairies might put a spell on you so that you never want to return to your own country. It's not a joke, for Ireland is an enchanting country and difficult to leave. As a rule, it's no use enquiring about charms against this enchantment, or any other; the answer is always the same: 'There used to be a lot of them in the old days, but the priests put them down.' You'll hear the same about *poteen*. Underneath, people have a sneaking belief in fairies – why, in a perfectly modern housing estate outside Sligo, is there a ragged mound which escaped the bulldozer and cement? Perhaps it is a fairy *rath*?

Have you ever heard where the fairies come from? Padraic Colum (1881–1972), the Irish-American author, found out from a blind man whom he met in the west, who believed in them as firmly as in the Gospels. Apparently, when the Angel Lucifer rebelled against God, Hell was made in a minute. God swept Lucifer and thousands of his followers down to it, until the Angel Gabriel said, 'O God Almighty, Heaven will be swept clean.' God agreed, saying, 'Them that are in Heaven let them remain so, them that are in Hell, let them remain in Hell; and them that are between Heaven and Hell, let them remain in the air.' And so the angels that remained between Heaven and Hell became the fairies.

Festivals

Tourism Ireland's annual *Calendar of Events*, available from tourist offices, presents you with a dazzling array of international festivals and small town extravaganzas, where everyone has a ball: jolly music pours into the street, farmers and tradesmen parade their goods and machinery, and there are endless bouncing baby competitions, discos and poteen, whiskey and stout drinking bouts.

See 'Calendar of Events', below, for details of some of the main annual festivals.

Ceoltóirí Eireann, 32 Belgrave Square, Monkstown, Co. Dublin, t (01) 278 1529, or t (068) 23036.

Rose of Tralee International Festival. Girls of Irish parentage and birth come from all over the world to compete for the title of 'Rose of Tralee'. Carnival parades, street dancing, fireworks, music, and the Tralee races. Rose of Tralee Office, Ashe Memorial Hall, Tralee, Co. Kerry, t (066) 712 1322, *www.roseoftralee.ie*.

Dublin Horse Show, RDS, Dublin.

Connemara Pony Show, Clifden, Co. Galway.

September

International Festival of Light Opera. A dozen light operas, one after the other, performed in Waterford's lovely old Theatre Royal. Waterford Light Opera Festival Office, Theatre Royal, The Mall, Waterford, t (051) 375 437/87440.

Matchmaking Festival. A festival in County Clare for local bachelors (and ladies in search of a husband), accompanied by drinking, noise and crowds. Takes place in Lisdoonvarna, Co. Clare, t (065) 707 4005,

f (065) 707 4406, *www.matchmakerireland. com*.

Eircom Dublin Theatre Festival (late Sept–Oct). See work by Irish writers and productions by well-known international theatre companies. Festival Director, 44 East Street, Temple Bar, Dublin 2, t (01) 677 8439, *www.eircomtheatrefestival.com*.

October

Wexford Opera Festival (Oct–Nov). Rare operatic masterpieces are performed in the town's Theatre Royal, with supporting events. Wexford Opera Festival, Theatre Royal, Wexford, t (053) 22144, f (053) 24289, *www.wexfordopera.com*.

Ballinasloe Horse Fair. One of Europe's oldest horse fairs. Can get wild. End July–Oct only. Contact Mary Phelan, t (0905) 44793, f (0905) 44132, *www.ballinasloe.com*.

November

Belfast International Festival. Concerts, films, opera and theatre in Northern Ireland's cultural capital.

Health and Insurance

Do remember that if you need **medical** or **dental** treatment in the Republic, you will be expected to pay for the treatment then claim back the costs from your insurance company. This, of course, may not be something you can discuss on the operating table. *In extremis* the international emergency services offered by companies such as Europ Assistance or Travel Assistance International, which are often incorporated into travel insurance packages, demonstrate their blessings. For all kinds of medical care, citizens of EU countries can benefit from the mutual agreements that exist between EU member countries. British citizens travelling to the Republic can make use of any GP who has an agreement with the Health Board, but to benefit from this you should take Form E111 with you, available from Post Offices and health centres in the UK in advance of your departure. The same scheme also applies to dentists and to hospitals.

The best advice is to always **insure** your holiday, and do so as soon as you book your ticket. Standard travel insurance packages issued by major insurance companies cover a broad range of risks, including cancellation due to unforeseen circumstances, transport delays caused by strikes or foul weather, loss or theft of baggage, medical insurance and compensation for injury or death. The cost of insurance may seem substantial, but it is negligible when compared to almost any claim, should misfortune befall you. That said, it is worth checking to see if any of your existing insurance schemes cover travel risks: certain British household insurance schemes, for example, include limited travel cover.

To make a **claim** for loss or theft of baggage, you will need evidence that you have reported the incident to the police. Check your insurance details for what is required of you in such circumstances. It is, by the way, useful to have more than one copy of your insurance policy – if your baggage is stolen, the document may go with it.

Heritage Centres

In the last ten years there has been a huge increase in these centres all over Ireland. The larger ones incorporate local history, flora and fauna, using audio visuals as an aid, or lifesize models and actors dressed in period costume, producing 'an experience to remember'. The Office of Public Works have purpose-built a few Interpretative Centres in places of great natural beauty and fragile ecology. Controversy has been provoked by the siting of one such centre in the middle of the Burren, Co. Clare. Inevitably such places destroy some of the beauty and peace with huge carparks, WCs, craft centres etc., however sympathetic the architecture and landscaping may be. Many of the small heritage centres double as genealogical centres and are situated in fine old buildings (mainly in towns), which have been restored by the efforts and enthusiasm of the local people.

Money

Currency

The **Republic of Ireland** has joined the European Monetary System, and on 1 January 1999, the **euro** (€) became its official currency, along with eleven other nations of the EU. That year, the value of the Irish punt (pronounced 'poont') was fixed, and it was subsequently phased out and then abolished in 2002. Euro coins and notes were introduced on 1 January 2002 and, as of 9 February 2002, became the only legal currency in the Republic and other European Monetary Union countries. In **Northern Ireland** the currency is still the **UK pound** (£), the value of which is generally around US$1.30–40.

The new **euro notes** are in denominations of 5, 10, 20, 50, 100, 200 and 500, with coins for €1 and €2. Each single euro consists of 100 cents; coins are used for 1, 2, 5, 10, 20 and 50 cents. At the time of writing, the euro is worth IR£0.79 (79 pence), or approximately UK£0.62 (62 pence) or US$0.90 (90 cents). Exchange rates are as follows, but do check current rates:

IR£1	€1.27
UK£1	€1.62
US$1	€1.11

As everywhere, the best exchange rates are available at banks, and the worst at hotels. Rates will also be less good at bureaux de change, though these are useful when banks are closed. They can be found in city centres, key tourist areas like Killarney, ferry terminals and the international sections of airports, including those at:

Cork: *open Mon–Fri 10–3;*
Dublin: *open summer 6.45am–10pm, winter 7.30am–8.30pm;*
Shannon: *open for service to all flights.*

Getting Cash and Using Credit Cards

You can obtain **cash** in local currencies from bank ATMs, usually sited in airports as well as towns and cities. Check with your bank or building society as to whether charges will be applied to your withdrawals, and which ATMs you may use. Leading **credit** and **debit cards** (Visa, Mastercard/Access, American Express and Diner's Club) are widely accepted in major hotels, restaurants and shops, but always check that your card will be accepted before you buy anything.

Traveller's Cheques

The main brands of traveller's cheques (American Express, Visa and Thomas Cook) are accepted by banks throughout the Republic of Ireland and Northern Ireland.
American Express Foreign Exchange Bureau, 41 Nassau Street, Dubin 2, **t** (01) 679 9000, **f** (01) 679 9445. *Open Mon–Fri 9–5;* also at International Hotel, East Avenue Road, Killarney, Co. Kerry, **t** (064) 35722, **f** (064) 36297. *Open Mon–Fri 9–5.*
Going Places, 57 Donegall Place, Belfast, **t** (028) 9033 4100. American Express traveller's cheques cashed here, commission-free.
Thomas Cook, 11 Donegall Place, Belfast, **t** (028) 9088 3900.

Banks

Small towns have at least one bank. They are open Mon–Fri 10am–12. 30pm and 1. 30–4pm in the Republic. Banks in the larger towns will usually have one day each week – normally market day or Thursday – when they will stay open until 5pm. Larger branches do not close for lunch. In the North banks also open at 10am and close at 4pm, but in Belfast and Londonderry they do not close for lunch.

The bank usually occupies the grandest building in town – the various banking groups seem to have some sort of conscience about historical buildings, which is very rare in Ireland. The moving of money is accompanied by massive security, which looks very out of keeping with the happy-go-lucky attitude in Ireland, but is necessary because bank raids have become so common.

Tipping

Tipping is not really a general habit in Ireland, except in taxis and in eating places where there is table service. Taxi-drivers will expect to be tipped at a rate of about 10% of the fare; porters and doormen 50 cents or so. There is no tipping in pubs, but in hotel bars where you are served by a waiter it is usual to leave a small tip. A service charge of 12%, sometimes 15%, is usually raised automatically on hotel and restaurant bills. Where this is not the case, a tip of this magnitude would be in order, if the service merits it.

Newspapers

The best newspaper to read while in Ireland is the *Irish Times*, a magnificent rag full of scholarly meanderings and insightful commentary, followed closely by the *Irish Independent* and the *Cork Examiner*. The *Irish Times* on Saturdays lists 'What is on' – exhibitions, festivals and concerts around the country. In Northern Ireland the most widely read morning newspaper is the *Belfast Newsletter*, which has a Unionist slant. The only evening paper, the *Belfast Telegraph*, is middle-of-the-road. Every small Irish town and county has its own newspaper. Wherever you're staying, have a read and watch the community life unfold.

Image is a glossy magazine along the lines of *Harpers & Queen*, and has information on fashion, interior decoration and restaurants. *Phoenix* is the Irish equivalent of *Private Eye*, and well-worth reading is *Magill*, a monthly news and current affairs magazine with excellent investigative journalism.

Packing

Whatever you do, come expecting rain – wellingtons, umbrellas and raincoats are essential unless you want to stay inside reading a book all day. Once you get out into the rain it is never as bad as it looks, and the clouds soon begin to clear. Bring warm jumpers, trousers, woollen socks and gloves for autumn, winter and early spring. The best thing to do is to expect the cold and wet and then get a pleasant surprise when it's sunny and hot – so sneak in a few T-shirts, just in case. Sometimes the sun shines furiously in March and April and you can end up with a very convincing tan. If you like walking, bring a pair of fairly stout shoes or boots – trainers end up bedraggled and let the water in. Fishing rods and swimsuits are worth packing, if you think you may have cause to regret leaving them behind. Bring a sleeping bag if you plan to stay at youth hostels.

Post Offices

Letterboxes are green in the Republic and red in the North. Some villages in the Republic list them among the historic monuments in their brochures – old ones with the monogram of Queen Victoria, now painted green. As you would expect, you have to put British stamps on letters posted in the North.

If you do not have a fixed address in Ireland, letters can be sent Poste Restante to any post office and picked up with some proof of identity. There is a post office in every village, often in the village shop. In general the Irish Post is admirably efficient; the gentlemen behind the counters will sometimes be amateur poets and historians. Remember that Ireland's most glorious battle was fought from a post office – the 1916 Rebellion.

Post offices are open 9am–5.30pm on weekdays, 9am–1pm on Saturdays, and closed on Sundays and public holidays. Sub-post offices often close on one day a week at 1pm. The GPO in O'Connell Street, Dublin, is open 8am–11pm, and in the mornings on Sundays and bank holidays.

Shopping

Shopping in Ireland is the most relaxing pastime. High-quality design and craftsmanship make for goods which will last you a lifetime. You can find them easily in the craft centres which have been set up all over the country. The **Crafts Council of Ireland**, based at Castle Yard, Kilkenny, t (056) 61804, f (056) 63754, *www.craftscouncil-of-ireland.ie*, *ccoi@craftscouncil-of-ireland.ie*, has given a great boost to many talented craft workers and helped them to market their wares and join forces in studios and workshops, sometimes in IDA (Industrial Development Authority) parks. Crafts are not cheap, because of the artistry and labour involved, but you can find bargains at china, crystal and linen factory shops if you are prepared to seek them out. Grinning leprechauns, colleen dolls, Guinness slogan T-shirts and shamrock mugs are stacked high in most gift shops if you want something cheerful and cheap, but do not ignore the real products from Ireland.

Opening Hours

Shops are usually open Mon–Sat from 9 or 9.30am to 5.30 or 6pm. Craft shops in scenic areas are usually open on Sundays as well, especially if they have a tearoom. In some towns there is an 'early-closing' day when businesses close at one; this is normally on a Wednesday, although it may be different in some areas. You shouldn't have much trouble finding food or petrol on Sundays; most supermarkets are at least open in the morning.

Irish Specialities

Connemara Marble: a natural green stone, found in the west, which ranges from bright field-green through to jade and oak-leaf

Public Holidays

January: New Year's Day (1st).
March: St Patrick's Day, Republic only (17th).
March/April: Good Friday, widely observed as a holiday, but not an official one;
  Easter Monday.
May: May Day (1st or early May);
  Spring Holiday, N. Ireland only (end May).
June: June Holiday, Republic only (first Monday in June).
July: Orange Parades, N. Ireland only (12th).
August: August Holiday Republic only (first Monday in Aug).
  Summer Holiday, N. Ireland only (end Aug).
October: October Holiday Republic only (last Mon in Oct).
December: Christmas Day (25th);
  Boxing Day/St Stephen's Day (26th)

colour, sometimes with stripes of brown. It is worked into jewellery and sold with other locally made objects, such as paperweights or chess sets.

Food and Drink: Soda, wheaten and potato breads are found everywhere in Ireland – McCambridge's brown bread is even available in airport shops. Smoked salmon and farmhouse cheese is sold in every shape, size and texture. Irish whiskey (note the 'e' in the Irish spelling) is slightly sweeter than Scotch; try Bushmills, Paddy's, Power's and Jameson's. Cork gin is considered to have a delicious tang of juniper. Popular liqueurs are Irish Mist, which contains whiskey and honey, Tullamore Dew and Bailey's Irish Cream.

Glass: Waterford Crystal is world-famous for its quality and design. Attractive crystal glass can also be bought at the factories in Cavan, Tyrone, Sligo and Cork. The hand-blown glass from the Jerpoint Glassworks in Co. Kilkenny is worth collecting.

Hand-knits and Aran Sweaters: Connacht, Donegal and the coastal stretches of Munster have the greatest variety. In the Clifden/Leenane region of Connemara, you can buy soft, striped wool rugs and cured sheepskins, which make good bedside rugs. Aran sweaters are made from tough wool, and are lightly coated in animal oils so that they are water-resistant and warm. They have differing patterns; in the past there were family patterns so that drowned fishermen could be recognized. Make sure you buy one which has the hand-knitted label – it makes all the difference.

Jewellery, Silver and Antiques: Claddagh rings (*see* p.304) are still the nicest of all love tokens, and are very evocative of the west. Antiques are now highly prized and expensive. Try to go to the July Antiques Fair at the RDS in Dublin.

Lace: Irish lace is one of the lightest and most precious of all the specialities to take home. It is fun if you can visit the convents and co-operatives where the lace is made. Try the Lace Cooperative, Carrickmacross, t (042) 966 2506/966 2088; the Good Shepherd Convent, 9 Good Shepherd Avenue, Limerick, t (061) 415183; and Kenmare Lace and Design Centre, Kenmare, t/f (064) 41491.

Linen: you can buy excellent Irish linen teacloths and fine linen sheets in Belfast.

Hand-embroidered handkerchiefs and table-cloths are for sale in Co. Donegal.

Pottery and China: talented potters work in rural communities all over Ireland, and the best places to find their work for sale is at IDA centres and craft shops. Look out for Roundstone in Connemara, Co. Galway, Belleek in Co. Fermanagh, Arklow in Co. Wicklow, and the work of Nicholas Mosse, sold at the Kilkenny Design Centre.

Traditional Musical Instruments: for *bodhráns* (a type of drum), try John McNeill, 140 Capel Street, Dublin, t (01) 872 2159, or try Malachy Kearns, Roundstone Musical Instruments, Michael Killeen Park, Roundstone, Co. Galway, t (095) 35875, *www.bodhran.com*. For *uillean* pipes and *bódhrans* visit The Bodhrán Maker, Spiddle Road, Spiddal, Co. Galway, but phone Michael Vignoles first, Mon–Fri 9–5, on t (091) 589 094, *www.irishpipesandbodhrans.com*.

Tweed: hand-woven from wool, tweed keeps you warm, but also lets your skin 'breathe'. Donegal tweed is particularly attractive, with its subtle shades. In Ardara and its environs you will still find thick, naturally dyed tweed. *Bainin* (pronounced 'bawneen') is an undyed tweed, and is often used for upholstery.

Woven Baskets: you can buy baskets made of willow or rush all over Ireland: bread baskets, turfholders, place mats and St Brigid Crosses – charms against evil.

Sports and Activities

Adventure Sports

The House of Sport, Longmile Rd, Dublin 12, t (01) 450 1633, can give you information for mountaineering, canoeing and many other sports. In the North, contact the Sports Council for Northern Ireland, Upper Malone Road, Belfast, BT9 5LA, t (028) 9038 1222.

Bird-watching

You can still hear the corncrake amongst the fields of Rathlin Island, or the choughs calling from the rocky headlands. Walking along the coastal mudflats in winter, whether you are in Co. Down or Co. Wexford, you will very likely see whooper swans. Ireland has more than 60 bird sanctuaries; contact the Wildlife Service, 51 St Stephen's Green, Dublin 2, t (01) 677 2815.

Field trips are organized by branches of Birdwatch Ireland; contact them at Ruttledge House, 8 Longford Place, Monkstown, Co. Dublin, t (01) 280 4322, the RSPB (Royal Society for the Protection of Birds), Belvoir Park Forest, Belfast, t (028) 9049 1547, or the National Trust (NI), Rowallane, Saintfield, Co. Down, BT24 7LH, t (028) 9751 030.

Canoeing

This is an exciting and compelling way to tour Ireland via the Liffey and the Barrow Rivers, with their smooth-flowing stretches, rapids and weirs. The other principal rivers are the Nore, Boyne, Slaney, Lee, Shannon, Suir and Blackwater. You can always camp by the waterside as long as you get permission from the owner. Contact the House of Sport (Attn: Michael Scanlon), Longmile Road, Dublin 12, t (01) 450 9838, for details of the many rivers and waterways, sea canoeing and tuition, or Canoe Association of Northern Ireland, 14 Ravelstone Avenue, Bangor, Co. Down, t (028) 9146 9907.

Caving

This activity has become more organized recently with the establishment of the Speleological Union of Ireland. The caving possibilities in the Cavan/Fermanagh area and in Co. Sligo are numerous. For more information contact the House of Sport, as above, or Rosarie Kernan of the Irish Orienteering Association, Dublin, t (01) 219 1951, or Duncan

Foster at the Speleological Union of Ireland, Radharc, Kilquade, Co. Wicklow.

Cruising the Inland Waterways

This is an unforgettable and exciting way to travel around Ireland. The main waterways are the **River Shannon**, which is navigable from Lough Key to Killaloe, and the **River Erne**, which has two huge island-studded lakes and is navigable for more than 50 miles (80km) from Belturbet to the little village of Belleek. The two are now linked due to the recent restoration and opening of the Shannon-Erne Waterway, along with the Grand Canal and the River Barrow (the canal links Dublin with the Shannon and the Barrow). Along the waterways you pass peaceful, lush scenery: tumbledown castles, abbeys and beautiful flowers and birds. In the evening you can moor up your boat for a meal and a jar and listen to some good traditional music.

The Erne waterway is beautifully wooded, with nature reserves and little islands to meander amongst. Lough Erne in all covers 300 square miles (777 sq km) of water. Cruiser hire companies operate around the lakes; contact the Erne Charter Boat Association. The Shannon-Erne waterway links the North and South and makes it possible to navigate along a 300km stretch. It is possible to get a one-way rental; contact Erincurrach Cruising.

On the **Shannon** there are several companies offering luxury cabin cruisers for self-drive hire, ranging from two to ten berths.

Boat Cruise Companies

Athlone Cruisers Ltd, Athlone, t (0902) 72892.
Celtic Canal Cruisers Ltd, Tullamore, Co. Offaly, t (0506) 21861.
Corrib Cruises, Cong, Co. Mayo, t (092) 46029/46292, or t 0876 796 470, *www.corribcruises.com*. For cruising and exploring Lough Corrib.
Emerald Star Line Ltd, The Marina, Carrick-on-Shannon, t (01) 679 8166, or t (078) 20234; Portumna t (0509) 41120.
Erne Charter Boat Association, Fermanagh Tourism, Enniskillen, t (028) 6632 3110.
Erincurrach Cruising, Blaney, Enniskillen t (028) 6864 1737, *www.boatingireland.com*.
Riversdale Barge Holidays, Riversdale, Ballinamore, Co. Leitrim, t (078) 44122.

Shannon Castle Line, Williamstown Harbour, Whtegate, Co. Clare, t (061) 927042, f (061) 927426, *www.shannoncruisers.com, sales@shannoncruisers.com*.
Shannon Sailing Ltd, Dromineer, Nenagh, Co. Tipperary, t (067) 24499, *www.shannonsailing.com*.

Day trips and **pleasure cruises** are also available on the Shannon. Contact:
Destination Killarney, t (064) 32638.
It is possible to take the *Killarney Waterbus* through the famous lakes on a trip lasting 1½ hours.

Jolly Mariner Marina, Athlone, Co. Westmeath, t (0902) 72892/72113, *www.iol.ie/wmeathtc/acl, acl@wmeathtc.iol.ie*.

All are fitted with fridges, gas cookers, hot water and showers; most have central heating. A dinghy, charts, binoculars and safety equipment are included on the river and lough routes. Groceries and stores can be ordered in advance and collected when you arrive. Skippers must be over 21, and the controls must be understood by at least two people in a group, but no licence is necessary. You receive an hour of tuition, or more if you need it. The average price for a six-berth cruiser ranges from €700 per week in April to about €1,800 in July–August. Ask for details from your travel agent or Irish tourist office.

You will find that there are excellent **pubs and restaurants** catering for the needs of the cruisers; ask at the local tourist office. Good pubs along the Shannon include Hughes Pub, Northgate Street, Athlone; Conlins, Church Street, Athlone; Garry Kennedy's, Portrow; Hough's Pub and Killeen's in Shannonbridge; the Sail Inn, Scarriff; the Jolly Mariner, Sean's Bar and the Green Olive, Athlone; the Crew's Inn in Roosky.

Some of the companies listed opposite also operate river cruises. Many others exist, wherever there are rivers and loughs; these are listed in the 'Sports and Activities' sections for each county.

Useful reading: *The Shell Guide to the Shannon*, *The Guide to the Grand Canal*, and the *Guide to the River Barrow*. Available from Eason and Son Ltd, 40 Lower O'Connell Street, Dublin 1, t (01) 873 3811.

Fishing

We are most grateful to Antony Luke for the following personal account. Antony has been returning on holiday to Ireland since 1963. He acts as a consultant on fishing matters to the corporate entertainment company Country & Highland, gives fly-fishing instruction, and organizes salmon-fishing parties. He has a cottage on one of the northern isles of Orkney where he keeps a lobster boat, and from where he runs a business exporting fish and shellfish.

Whatever the catch, one always returns from Ireland with a story and happy memories. The sport is excellent, and all visitors are treated with the usual great Irish hospitality and charm. Tackle shops are very helpful, and Tourism Ireland, the tourist board

for the whole of Ireland, issues a wealth of information, including dates of angling competitions and an excellent brochure on angling in Ireland. In general, fishing in Ireland is more available to the general public and less restricted than in Scotland. Notably, fishing on Sunday is permitted. Unlike the UK, there is no closed season for coarse fishing. Seasons for other types of fishing vary according to region and sometimes specific rivers. Costs are also comparatively low. Government licences are not hefty, but they are required for salmon and sea-trout fishing.

For the purposes of licensing, fishing in the **Republic** can be divided into four categories: game, for salmon and sea-trout (migratory); trout (non-migratory); coarse, for perch, roach, rudd, bream, tench, etc., and pike; and sea-fishing. Visitors require a licence for the first. It is possible to purchase individual or composite licences from Tourism Ireland offices in your country of residence. In the Republic, they can be bought from any Tourist or Fisheries Board office, from all government-run fisheries, and many tackle shops.

One of the finest aspects of the sport in Ireland is the variety of different fishing techniques that are to be found in quite small areas. It is possible to fish a lake system – either dapping or wet-fly – and a river on the same day. In the UK, this is only possible in a few places on the west coast of Scotland, and to some extent in the Hebrides. The great Irish limestone lakes such as Carra, Conn, Mask and Corrib offer some of the best trout-fishing in the world, especially at the time of the mayfly (mid-May to early June). On Corrib there is also salmon. A ghillied boat is necessary if you wish to fish these beautiful lakes scattered with many hundreds of small islands; Irish ghillies have a great knowledge of the shoals and bays where fish lie. They are often also highly entertaining.

Coarse fishing is immensely popular in the Republic, particularly with visitors from the UK, where there is a closed season from mid-March to mid-June. Vast expanses of water throughout the centre of the country are open to visitors, and pike-fishing here is amongst the best in Europe.

It would take a book longer than this one to list all the rivers and loughs for visiting game-fishers. On the whole, salmon-fishing is privately owned, but good association water is available for the general public. On the east coast, the Boyne, Liffey and Slaney rivers have early runs of salmon, and grilse run later – from mid-June. On the south coast, the Nore, Suir, Barrow and the Blackwater also have early runs of salmon, and grilse later. On the southwest coast, there are a number of rivers and lake systems, notably Lough Currane at Waterville and the Maine and Laune, including the Killarney Lakes. In the mid-west the list is endless, numbering such famous places as Ballynahinch, the Newport, which drains Lough Beltra, Delphi, the Moy and the mighty Shannon. Fishing on the Shannon was badly affected by the introduction of the hydro-electric scheme in 1929, but the Castleconnell beats are still worth a visit. The Corrib River drains the Corrib system and the famous Galway Weir. Thousands apply every year for a permit to fish here, but you may be lucky in the ballot for selection. If not, you can join the crowds at the Galway Salmon Weir Bridge and watch the ranks of salmon stream past.

Also in the mid-west, one of my favourite spots is the River Erriff, administered by the Central Fisheries Board. Running through a glacial valley in the heart of Connemara, it has a wild beauty, culminating in a cascade over the Aasleagh Falls and into the sea at Killary Harbour. Beats are on both banks and generous. Given good conditions, the Erriff can be as prolific as some of the most famous rivers. Visitors can either take a cottage or stay in the Aasleagh Lodge, which offers both dinner and B&B. Book early through the Manager, Erriff Fishery, Aasleagh Lodge, Leenane, County Galway.

Fishing Information

Central Fisheries Board, t (01) 837 9206, **f** (01) 836 0060. Contact this board to find out how to get the necessary fishing licence for the area in which you wish to fish.
Fermanagh Lakeland Visitors' Centre, Enniskillen, Co. Fermanagh, **t** (028) 23110.
Foyle Fisheries Commission, 8 Victoria Road, Derry City, Co. Londonderry, **t** (028) 7134 2100, **f** (028) 7134 2720. For game-rod licences.
Northern Regional Fisheries Board, Donegal Town, Co. Donegal, **t** (072) 51435, *koc@nrfb.ie*.

Sea-trout have been in sad decline over the past five years, especially on the west coast, and a number of well-known sea-trout fisheries have suffered badly due to 'sea lice' (which many claim is due to salmon farming). Considerable research is now being done by the Salmon Research Trust at Newport and things have shown a slight improvement. By contrast, runs of salmon and grilse have held up well in recent years.

Sea-angling is becoming increasingly popular with the hardy fisherman. The Central Fisheries Board issues a comprehensive booklet. More boats are available for hire than ever before, although they can be expensive for the individual; it is best to organize a group of four or more. Kinsale is one of the main centres for sea-angling. Here, when the sea warms a degree or so, odd species of tropical fish arrive. Out of Kinsale there is also good shark-fishing, and many other species such as conger, skate and, for the less choosy, huge bags of large pollack can be caught. On the west coast, Cleggan is another small port where boats can be hired. The area around Connemara is startlingly beautiful, and many self-catering cottages are available to rent.

Other main sea-fishing stations are Rosslare and Dungarvan in Co. Waterford; Youghal, Ballycotton, and Baltimore in Co. Cork; Cahirciveen and the Dingle Peninsula in Co. Kerry; Westport, Achill Island, Newport and Belmullet in Co. Mayo; and Moville in Co. Donegal. As a rule, all stations will be able to supply boats for hire, rods, tackle, etc.

Northern Ireland has a wealth of lakes, rivers and tributaries, and fine sport can be had in all areas. Seasons vary, as they do in the South, and costs are not high.

Lough Erne is well known for quality in all types of fishing. The upper water is mostly for coarse fish, while the lower holds salmon and trout. The River Foyle and its tributaries, some running into Lough Foyle, have good runs of salmon and sea-trout. The River Bann divides into two; the lower drains Lough Neagh and is famous for its salmon-fishing, but the lower beats are expensive. The Upper Bann rises in the Mountains of Mourne and fish run later. The popularity of **sea-fishing** has grown immensely in recent years; 24 species of sea-fish are caught regularly. The main centres

Golf Courses

Eastern Ireland

Carlow: an exceptional course.

Delgany: one of the nurseries of Irish golf; has produced several famous players, including Harry Bradshaw and Eamon D'Arcy.

Howth: clings precipitously to the hill's southern slopes; high quality golf and spectacular views.

Island Golf Course: on a peninsula across the water from Malahide; among rolling dunes.

Co. Louth Golf Course/Baltray, Drogheda: home to the East of Ireland Championships; reputed to have the finest greens in Ireland.

Luttrelstown: quality greens, beautiful landscaping; only 15 mins west of Phoenix Park.

Mount Juliet: host to the Murphy's Irish Open several years running; probably the best inland course in Ireland.

Mullingar: the scene of several international tournaments in recent years.

Open Golf Centre, at Newtown House, St Margaret's: 27 holes, plus a driving range with 4 pros available for lessons.

Portmarnock: the jewel of the Republic's crown, less than 30 mins' drive from Dublin.

Royal Dublin: along with the above, hosts the Irish Open Championship.

Woodenbridge and **Courtown**: two courses not far from the sea and well worth a visit.

Northern Ireland

Ballyliffin Golf Club: set amid daunting sand hills and surrounded by the Atlantic on three sides, the course is still inland in character.

Luttrelstown: south of Belfast, a beautifully landscaped course.

Portsalon and **Rosapenna**: 19th-century courses that still test the the giants, with stunning views of the Donegal coastline.

Royal County Down Golf Course, Newcastle: quite possibly the best links course in the world. Scenically stunning, the course lies right at the base of the Mourne Mountains.

Royal Portrush: near the Giant's Causeway; the only Irish course ever to have hosted the Open Championship. Only the most competent should tackle it on blustery days.

Valley Course: an entertaining few days can be spent in the Portrush and Portstewart area, for there are no less than five courses within a mile (1.6km) or so of one another.

Western Ireland

Ballyconneely Golf Club: another for a calm day, in the western reaches of Connemara.

---

that boats can be hired from are Portrush, Glenarm, Larne and Whitehead in Co. Antrim; and Bangor and Donaghadee in Co. Down.

Rod licences are issued by the Fisheries Conservancy Board (FCB) or the Foyle Fisheries Commission (FFC). Permission to fish from the owner of the water – often the Department of Agriculture, which is the ultimate authority for fisheries in the North – takes the form of a permit. Angling clubs which own waters not held by the Department issue daily tickets. All permits and licences for fishing in Northern Ireland, and a lot more information, are available from the Northern Regional Fisheries Board in Donegal. The Lakeland Visitors' Centre at Enniskillen is also very helpful. Tackle shops throughout the Province issue permits and tickets for, or information on, angling clubs (*see* opposite for useful contacts).

Golf

We are most grateful to Bruce Critchley for this expert guide to Ireland's golf courses. Bruce is one of television's golf commentators, following a successful amateur international career in the 1960s. Now a consultant to golf-course developers, he also, in association with his wife's company, Critchley Pursuits, arranges tours of British, Irish and Continental courses for both English and American enthusiasts.

With the possible exception of Scotland, Ireland can boast more courses per head of population than any other country in the world. As with Scotland, quality is in no way diminished by quantity and, in common with the rest of the British Isles, the greatest courses are situated at the seaside.

As host to the British Open Championship, names like St Andrews, Muirfield and Royal Birkdale are famous around the world. The likes of Portmarnock, Mount Juliet and Royal Portrush suffer nothing by comparison. But they are just the tip of Ireland's golfing iceberg, and no discerning golfer's experience is complete without a taste or two of what's littered around the shores.

Bundoran Golf Club: delightful clifftop course.
Donegal Golf Course, Murvagh: a splendid challenge; 7,000 yds (6,400m) off the back.
Galway Club: a more gentle test.
Lahinch: traditionally the home of the South of Ireland Championships.
Rosses Point: the prince of courses in this area, in the shadow of Benbullen; has hosted most of the country's major events.
Strandhill and **Inniscrone**: seaside courses.
Westport Golf Course: a test for the itinerant golfer, on the shores of Clew Bay.

Southwestern Ireland

Ballybunion: a real treasure; recently a second 18 has been added of equally high quality.
Bantry: no trip to this neck of the woods should miss this little nine-hole gem, over-looking the famous bay.
Dooks at Glenbeigh and the mighty links of **Waterville**: two widely differing courses on the Ring of Kerry. Glenbeigh, only 5,750 yards (5,260m) in length, is supposedly the third-oldest course in the country and follows the undulating dunes. Waterville is much more recent and, with the ocean on three sides, the wind is an ever-present factor.

Killarney: can there be any more beautiful setting for golf anywhere in the world? Perhaps the two courses don't quite match up to the view, but then very few would.
Shannon Golf Club: near the airport, a modern course, inland in character, with lovely views down to the River Shannon.
Tralee: Arnold Palmer has laid out an outstanding course here on Kerry's coastline.

Southern Ireland

Away from the pounding of the Atlantic Ocean, the courses in the south don't have the sand dunes out of which links courses are traditionally carved. Nonetheless, the natural beauty of the countryside lends a great back-drop wherever courses are constructed.
Bandon Golf Course: southwest of Cork city, set in the grounds of Castlebernard Castle.
Clonmel: spectacular views over the plains of Tipperary.
Doneraile: a little nine-holer that should not be passed up.
Little Island, Cork: the most spectacular here; holes alternate between the edge of the massive quarry and views over the estuary.
Midleton: to the east, well worth a visit.
Thurles: fine old oaks and elms command respect in its parkland setting.

Wherever you go in Ireland, golf courses abound, and whatever your standard you'll find something to enjoy. With facilities getting ever more crowded around the major cities of the world, Ireland offers golf as it used to be – the ability to get on a course in the hours of daylight, and green fees that are not going to break the bank.

If you are thinking of a golfing holiday, some of the courses do get busy in summer and it is always advisable to check with clubs in advance and, where necessary, get a confirmed tee time. Also, every travelling golfer should carry a handicap certificate as proof of competence. Trolleys will be for hire at most clubs and quite a few will be able to lay on caddies if ordered in advance.

Hang-gliding

Ireland is a hang-glider's paradise: shaped like a saucer with a mountainous rim. The wind blows from the sea or from the flat central plains. Most of the hills are bare of power-lines and trees, and the famous turf provides soft landings. Flying in the Republic is controlled by the Irish Hang-Gliding Association, The House of Sport, Longmile Rd, Dublin 12, t (01) 450 1633. In Northern Ireland, contact the Northern Ireland Hang-gliding Club, (Hon. Secretary Tom Purvis), 43 Ransevyn Park, Whitehead, Co. Antrim, t (028) 9337 2050, or the Sports Council for Northern Ireland.

Horse-racing

Irish people are wild about horses; they breed very good ones, and they race them brilliantly. You can go and watch them being exercised on the Curragh in Co. Kildare, a nursery of some of the finest racehorses in the world. Classic flat races which take place on the Curragh are the Airlie/Coolmore Irish 2000 Guineas, and Goffs Irish 1000 Guineas in May, the Budweiser Irish Derby in June, far and away the premier International flat race of the year; the Kildangan Stud Irish Oaks in July, and in September the Jefferson Smurfit Memorial Irish St Leger. Close to the Curragh is the Irish National Stud, with its magnificent and authentic Japanese Garden.

The flat racing season begins in March and ends in November, with occasional Sunday meetings; other important flat racing takes place at the modern Leopardstown course on the south side of Dublin. The main National Hunt (steeplechasing and jumping courses) are at Leopardstown, Punchestown, Navan, Gowran, Galway and, of course, Fairyhouse, where you can watch the exciting Irish Grand National on Easter Monday. The most fashionable event is the 3-day meeting held at Punchestown near Naas, Co. Kildare during the last week of April. The Dublin Horse Show, which is a principal sporting and social event in Ireland, includes showjumping competitions for the Aga Khan Trophy, the Nations Cup and the Grand Prix.

The weekly *Irish Field* and daily *Racing Post* and *Sporting Life* publish form, venues and times of all race meetings and point-to-points. Tourism Ireland's *Calendar of Events* also shows some racing fixtures.

Hurling

To read about this sport, *see* **Topics**, p.107.

Polo

The All Ireland Polo Club in Phoenix Park, Dublin, is one of the oldest clubs in the world. Matches take place Wednesday evenings, Saturday and Sunday afternoons, from May to the middle of September, plus sponsored 4-day tournaments from June to August.

Riding Holidays

There are many new residential schools and companies offering pony-trekking holidays. The Irish are putting their natural love of horses to good use, and the areas of beauty where you can ride include empty beaches that stretch for miles, heathery valleys, forests, empty country roads and loughside tracks. Accommodation and food are arranged for you. Full details from Tourism Ireland.

Sailing

The Irish coastline is uniquely beautiful, with diverse conditions and landscapes. The waters are never crowded, and the shoreline is completely unspoilt. On one of those sublimely beautiful evenings when the light touches each hill and field with an exquisite clarity, you will think yourself amongst the most privileged in the world. And if you want a bit of *craic*, there are many splendid bars and restaurants to be visited in the sheltered harbours. But the peace and calm of the sky, the land and the sea in the many inlets is deceptive, for the open seas in the northwest can be rough and treacherous, exposed as they are to the North Atlantic. A journey around the whole coastline should only be attempted by experienced sailors.

Ireland has a long sailing tradition, with more than 125 yacht and sailing clubs around the country. The Royal Cork Yacht Club at Crosshaven is the oldest in the world, and was founded in 1720 as the Water Club of the Harbour of Cork. Many of these clubs preserve their original clubhouses, and emanate a feeling of tradition and comfort. Visitors are made very welcome, and are encouraged to use the club facilities.

If you do not have your own yacht, it is possible to charter a variety of craft; whilst if it is your ambition to learn to sail, there are several small and friendly schools. In Ulster, information on yachting facilities, sailing schools and charter companies can be had from the Sports Council for Northern Ireland in Belfast (*see* p.135). In the Republic, contact the Irish Sailing Association, 3 Park Road, Dun Laoghaire, Co. Dublin, **t** (01) 280 0239.

Where to Sail

The Southwest: Ireland's southwest coastline, bordering the counties of Cork and Kerry, is a favourite with Irish sailors, and it has a good selection of charter companies, sailing schools and windsurfing facilities. The harbours are charming, and the peninsulas and islands around which you can sail are magnificent.

The West: Further west, in County Galway and County Mayo, there is exciting sailing around the Aran Islands, Clifden, Renville and Clew Bay and the many deserted islands with haunting, beautiful names.

The North: Here is the glorious coastline of Sligo and Donegal. You need to be an experienced sailor to sail in these waters, for charts are outdated and inaccurate, currents and shallows are sometimes treacherous, and there are few facilities for sailors.

The East: More wonderful sailing can be had on Strangford and Carlingford Loughs in County Down, and around the Antrim Coast. Just north of Dublin there are several excellent sailing centres which still retain the charm of fishing villages. Inland is the huge freshwater expanse of Lough Derg in the River Shannon system, where you can anchor in a sheltered bay or in one of the charming canal harbours.

Practicalities

There is no tax or duty if you bring in your **own yacht** for a holiday; a special sticker is issued by customs officials on arrival. Mariners should apply to the harbour master of all ports in which they wish to anchor. On arrival at the first port of entry, the flag 'Q' should be shown. Contact should then be made with the local customs official or with a *garda* (civil guard) who will be pleased to assist. Fees are very reasonable in marinas and harbours. It is illegal to land any animals without a special licence from the Department of Agriculture, but this does not apply to pets from Britain.

The main centres for **charter** are the south-west coastline, Clifden and Lough Derg. Private charter can be arranged at leading sailing centres elsewhere. Bare-boat and crewed charters are available on boats ranging from four- to seven-berth. The average cost of chartering a four-berth yacht ranges from €130 per person per week in the low season to €165 per person per week in the high season. For a complete list of yacht charter companies, contact Tourism Ireland.

Most of the **sailing schools** are residential and located in areas of scenic beauty. Many offer other outdoor sports such as board-sailing (wind-surfing), canoeing and sub-aqua. A full list of schools is available from Bord Fáilte in Dublin and from the Irish Association for Sail Training, Confederation House, 84–86 Lower Baggot Street, Dublin 2, **t** (01) 660 1011.

Useful Media

The Irish Cruising Club (address above) publishes *Sailing Directions* which covers the entire coast of Ireland, and includes details of the coast, sketch plans of harbours, tidal information and information about port facilities.

The *Directions* come in two volumes – one for the south and west, and one for the north and east. Available from most Irish booksellers. Also recommended is *Sailing Around Ireland* by Wallace Clark (Batsford), and *Islands of Ireland* by D. McCormick (Osprey, 1977). The BBC issues gale warnings and shipping forecasts on Radio 4 and the World Service.

Sub-aqua

Ireland's oceans are surprisingly warm and clear because they are right in the path of the Gulf Stream, so it would be very difficult to find a better place for underwater swimming or diving. *Subsea* is the official journal of the Irish Underwater Council, which publishes information about the affiliated clubs, articles on diving, etc. Write to the Hon. Secretary, Irish Underwater Council, 78A Patrick Street, Dun Laoghaire, **t** (01) 284 4601. Centres for experienced divers and equipment hire are in Co. Mayo, Co. Donegal, Co. Galway, Co. Kerry, Co. Clare, Co. Wexford, Co. Down. Ask for information in any tourist office. By the way, it is illegal to take shellfish from the sea.

Surfing

Due to the geographical position of Ireland great swells endlessly pound the west coast, producing waves comparable to those in California. The entire coastline of Ireland is thus ideal for surfing when the beach, tide and wind conditions are right. Many of the beaches in Counties Donegal, Sligo, Kerry, Waterford and Clare are considered first-rate for breakers. Hire centres are not numerous, although you can occasionally hire equipment from hotels and adventure sports centres, but it's best to bring your own board and wetsuit. Contact the Irish Surfing Association, 7 Marine Terrace, Tramore, Co. Waterford, **t** (051) 386582;1 Ardeelan Dale, Rossnowlagh, Co. Donegal, **t** (072) 52522, **f** (072) 52523. Contact for details of beaches and surfing centres.

Swimming and Beaches

There are lovely beaches (also called strands) wherever the sea meets the land – north, south, east or west. If you wish to go sea-bathing (it can be surprisingly warm because of the Gulf Stream), bear in mind that swimming is not a regulated sport, and that there are lifeguards only on the most popular beaches, if at all. Be aware of the possibility of a strong undertow or current, and always ask locally about the safest ones for swimming.

Walking and Mountaineering

The Irish mountains and hill areas are not high (few peaks are over 3,000ft/915m), but they are rugged, varied, beautiful and unspoilt. There are quartz peaks, ridges of sandstone, bog-covered domes, and cliff-edged limestone plateaux. Excellent walking trails have been or are in the process of being developed. General advice, information and a list of hill-walking and rock-climbing clubs can be obtained from the Mountaineering Council of Ireland at The House of Sport (see below), who can send you a full list of guides. Tourism Ireland offices also stock hill-walking info sheets for individual areas. The website *www.irishwaymarkedways.ie* is a mine of information on walking in the Republic.

The Ordnance Survey ½-inch-to-a-mile maps and a compass are essentials for serious walkers. Maps and guidebooks can be obtained at some bookshops or sports shops in popular walking areas, or from the National Map Centre, 34 Aungier Street, t (01) 476 0471.

Please remember there are very few tracks on Irish mountains; always let your hotel know where you are climbing or walking, or leave a note in your car. Mountain rescue in the Republic is co-ordinated by the Garda (Police) and in the North by the Police Service of Northern Ireland (PSNI). There are mountain rescue teams in the main mountain areas.

Walking and Mountaineering Centres

The House of Sport, Upper Malone Road, Belfast, t (028) 9038 1222. For details on climbing in the Mournes; handles grants and serves as an advice centre.

Irish Ways, Ballycanew, Gorey, Co. Wexford, t (055) 27479. Courses and holidays.

National Mountain and White Water Centre, Tiglin, Ashford, Co. Wicklow, t (0404) 40169, *www.tiglin.com*. Details of training courses in mountaineering.

Tullymore Mountain Centre, Bryansford, Nr Newcastle, Co. Down, t (028) 4372 2158. For climbing in the Mourne Mountains.

Youth Hostel Association, *An Oige*, 6 Mountjoy Street, Dublin 1. Courses and holidays.

Summer Schools

The phrase 'Ireland, land of saints and scholars' is delightfully apt when it comes to the tradition of learning. You can study and learn some fascinating subjects in a beautiful environment, and still feel as if you are on holiday. Tourism Ireland will send you an up-to-date list of programmes if you write and ask for the *Live and Learn* brochure. The courses range from the seriously intellectual to activity holidays. You can study for a month, two weeks or a few days, and the variety is tremendous. Some are run by Ireland's universities, and offer courses on literature, history, Gaelic, and archaeology. Private companies run arts and crafts courses, painting, English language courses and classes in traditional music and dancing.

One of the most enjoyable summer schools is the Yeats International Summer School in Sligo, well-run and set in wonderful countryside. Enjoyable lectures and tours are also offered by the Irish Georgian Society. Contact the Society at 74 Merrion Square, Dublin 2, t (01) 676 7053, f (01) 662 0290. For other courses, *see* overleaf.

Telephones and Internet

The **country code** for the Republic is t 353; for Northern Ireland t 44, if calling from outside the UK. However, if you are calling Northern Ireland from the Republic of Ireland, all 8-digit numbers can be prefixed with just t 048.

It is more expensive to telephone during working hours than outside them. Note that if you telephone from your hotel you are liable to be charged much more than the standard rate. Phonecards, sold by most newsagents, are a much cheaper, more convenient option.

Ireland shares the same **time zone** as Great Britain, and follows the same pattern of seasonal adjustment in the summer (i.e. Greenwich Mean Time plus one hour, from the end of March to the end of October).

The **Internet** has a wealth of information to help you prepare all the practical details for your holiday, such as accommodation, especially in the busy summer months, when festivals make rooms hard to come by in even the smallest of towns. It can also enhance

Summer Schools

Art/Painting

Achill Island School of Painting, Co Mayo; **t** (058) 56182. Early July–Aug.

Burren Landscape Painting, Co. Clare, **t** (065) 707 4208.

Irish Studies

University College Dublin, International Summer School for Irish Studies, in July; **t** (01) 475 2004, **f** (01) 716 7211 *www. ucd. ie/summerschool*, *summer.school@ucd.ie*.

Parnell Summer School, Avondale, Rathdrum, Co. Wicklow; **t** (01) 287 5124, **f** (01) 288 1060.

Humbert Summer School, Ballina, Co. Mayo; contact John Cooney, **t** (096) 22034, *cooneyjohn@eircom.net*. August.

Douglas Hyde Summer School, Ballaghaderreen, Co. Roscommon, **t** (0903) 37100, or **t** (0907) 60013. July.

Literature

James Joyce Summer School, UCD International Summer School Office, Newman House, 86 St Stephen's Green, D2; contact Dept of English, University College Dublin, D4, **t** (01) 706 8480/706 8323. July.

Bard Summer School, Clare Island, Clew Bay, Co. Mayo, **t** (01) 490 4879, *www.bard.ie*, *bard@bard.ie*. July.

Brian Merriman Summer School, Lisdoonvarna, Co. Clare; **t** (098) 27758, or **t** (01) 286 4107, *www.merriman.ie*, *eolas@merriman.ie*. Late Aug.

Yeats International Summer School, Yeats Memorial Building, Douglas Hyde Bridge, Sligo; **t** (071) 42693, **f** (071) 42780, *www.yeats-sligo.com*, *info@yeats-sligo.com*. Lectures, seminars, readings and tours.

John Hewitt International Summer School at St MacNissi's College, Carron Tower, Carnlough, Co. Antrim, **t** (028) 9038 0817, *sean.armstrong@johnhewitt.org*. July–August; named in honour of John Hewitt, an Ulster poet. Lectures, music, poetry, plays.

Goldsmith Summer School, Abbeyshrule and Ballymahon, Co Longford, **t** (0902) 32374, *linesend@iol.ie*. June.

Synge Summer School, Whaley Lodge, Rathdrum, Co. Wicklow; **t** (0404) 46131, **f** (0404) 46044, *syngesummerschool@oceanfree.net*, *ngrene@tcd.ie*. July.

Shakespeare Summer School, Ely House, Ely Place, Dublin 2; **t** (01) 832 1897; late August.

William Carleton Summer School, Clogher, **t** (028) 8776 7259. August.

Music

Scoil Eigse; contact *Comhaltas Ceoltoiri Eireann*, 32 Belgrave Square, Monkstown, Co. Dublin **t** (01) 280 0295, **f** (01) 280 3759. Traditional music and dancing; late August.

Willy Clancy Summer School, Miltown Malbay, Co. Clare, **t** (065) 708 4281. Mid-July.

South Sligo Summer School, Tubbercurry; **t** (071) 85010. Music and dance; mid-July.

O'Carolan Traditional Irish Music Summer School, Keadue, Co. Roscommon; **t** (078) 47204; **f** (078) 47511, *www.keadue.harp.net*, *ocarolan@eircom.net*. Late July–early Aug.

Joe Mooney Summer School, Drumshanbo, Co. Leitrim, **t** (078) 41213/41426. Late July. Traditional music, song and dance.

Other Courses

Oideas Gael **Irish Language and Summer School**, Glencolmcille, Co. Donegal, various times throughout the summer; **t** (073) 30248, *www.oideas-gael.com*. Culture, flute and *bodhrán*-playing, dancing, Irish language, pottery, hill-walking, archaeology.

Achill Archaeological Summer Field School, Dooagh, Achill Island, Co. Mayo, **t** (098) 43564, or **t** (098) 43343, or **t** (0506) 21627, *www.achill-fieldschool.com*.

Taipéis Gael, Malinbeg, Glencolmcille, Co. Donegal, **t** (073) 30325, *taipeisgael@eircom.net*. Tapestry and weaving; summer.

your knowledge of Ireland's history, politics and culture before you leave home. Internet cafés are blossoming in Ireland; airports and libraries also usually provide public access points and local tourist offices can direct you to the nearest ones.

Toilets

Public loos – *leithreas* – are often labelled in Irish: *Fir* (men) and *Mná* (women). They're usually pretty grim. Nobody minds if you slip into a lounge bar to use the loo, though it's a good excuse to stop for a drink as well.

Tourist Boards

Ireland was until recently served by two separate tourist boards: *Bord Fáilte* (or the Irish Tourist Board) in the Republic, and the Northern Ireland Tourist Board (NITB) in Northern Ireland. The new **Tourism Ireland** has now amalgamated these two for tourism services. Their offices will do literally anything to help and organize whatever is practical. They can supply you with a wealth of beautifully presented maps and leaflets, most of which are free, and they also publish fuller booklets on, for example, accommodation, for which there are modest charges. They can also find a hotel or B&B in your price range and book it for you.

The head office in Dublin is at Baggot Street Bridge, t (01) 676 5871, f (01) 602 4100, although it serves mainly for administration. A more useful office if you are in Dublin is the new Dublin Tourism Centre on Suffolk Street, just off Grafton Street, from Ireland t 1850 230 2330 for information, t (066) 979 2082 for reservations, *www.ireland.travel.ie*. You can contact Tourism Ireland in the North through the NITB, on t (028) 9023 1221, f (028) 9024 0960, *www.discovernorthernireland.com*.

There are some 80 tourist information offices scattered around the Republic, some of which open only during the summer season, although most are open throughout the year (some may close for a few days each week in winter). Addresses are given in boxes at the beginning of each county, and when counties are divided, at the beginning of that area.

Irish Tourist Offices Abroad

UK: All Ireland Desk, British Visitors Centre, Regent Street, London SW1Y 4XT, UK only t 0800 039 7000, or t (020) 7518 0800, f (020) 7149 39065, *www. tourismireland.com*;
98 West George Street, 7th Floor, Glasgow G2 1PJ, t (0141) 572 4030.
USA, 345 Park Avenue, New York, NY 10017, t (212) 418 0800, f (212) 371 9059, *www. shamrock.org, www.tourismireland.com*.
Canada (written and telephone enquiries), 160 Bloor Street East, Suite 1150, Toronto, Ontario, M4W 1BN, t (416) 929 2777, f (416) 929 6783.

Weights and Measures

1 kilogram = 2 lb
1 litre = 1.76 Imperial pints = 2.11 US pints
1 centimetre = 0.39 inches
1 metre = 39.37 inches = 3.28 feet
1 kilometre = 0.621 miles
1 hectare = 2.47 acres
1 lb = 0.45 kilograms
1 Imperial pint = 0.56 litres
1 US pint = 0.47 litres
1 Imperial gallon = 4.54 litres
1 US gallon = 3.78 litres
1 foot = 0.305 metres
1 mile = 1.609 kilometres
1 acre = 0.404 hectares

Where to Stay

Whether you are a traveller with plenty of loot to spend, or one who is intent on lodging as cheaply as possible, Ireland offers plenty of choice. Places to stay range from romantic castles, graceful country mansions, cosy farmhouses, smart city hotels and hostels which, although spartan, are clean and well-run. Many of these hostels have double or family rooms; are independently owned and require no membership cards.

At the beginning of each county chapter (and where counties are divided, at the beginning of each area), there is a list of recommended accommodation, split into price categories (explained below). With this list as a guide, it is possible to avoid the many modern and ugly hotels where bland comfort is doled out for huge prices, and to avoid the shabby motels and musty bed-and-breakfast establishments. Some counties are favoured with many desirable hotels and B&Bs, whilst a few are meagerly served. If that is the case where you are, your best bet for a pleasant stay is to stick to the farmhouse accommodation, which is usually adequate.

One thing you can be sure of is that the Irish are among the friendliest people in Europe, and when they open their doors to visitors they give a great welcome. The many unexpected kindnesses and the personal service that you will experience will contribute immeasurably to your visit. The countryside is beautiful, and there are many sights to see, but what adds enjoyment and richness, above all, to a tour of Ireland is the pleasant conversation and humour of the people.

Prices

Tourism Ireland registers and grades hotels and guest houses, and divides the many B&B businesses into Farm, Town and Country Houses. All of this is very useful, but apart from indicating the variety of services available and the cost, you really do not get much idea of the atmosphere and style of the place. The establishments listed in this book are described and categorized according to price, and include a variety of lodgings ranging from a luxurious castle to a simple farmhouse – all have something special to offer a visitor. This may be the architecture, the garden, the food, the atmosphere and the chat, the distance you are from a special tourist site, or simply the beauty of the surrounding countryside. The most expensive offer high standards of luxury, and the cheapest ones are clean and comfortable. Most are family-owned, with a few bedrooms, and none fits into a uniform classification, but they are all welcoming and unique places to stay. The price categories are of necessity quite loosely based, and some of the more expensive establishments do weekend deals which are very good value. Please, always check prices and terms when making a booking. Rates in the Republic are quoted in euros. Sterling (UK£) is the currency used in Northern Ireland.

Luxury

Cost no object; from €114 (UK£70) per person. Expect top-quality rooms with style and opulence. Furnishings will include priceless antiques, whilst the facilities and service provide every modern convenience you could wish for. Many of the four-star hotels in Dublin fall into this category, but there are also delightful castles and mansions, set in exquisite grounds, all over Ireland.

Expensive

From €76–114 (UK£47–70) per person. All bedrooms have their own bathroom, direct-dial telephone, central heating, TV and the other mod cons, but many have something else as well – charm, eccentricity, and a feeling of mellow comfort. There are places where you might sleep in a graceful four-poster hung with rich cloth, and wake up to the sort of hospitality where the smell of coffee is just a prelude to a delicious cooked breakfast, and the sharp, sweet taste of homemade jam on Irish wheaten bread.

Moderate

From €38–76 (UK£23–47) per person. Not as luxurious, but most of these places have private bathrooms and extremely good cooking and service. Again, some of them have a wonderful atmosphere combined with attractive décor, which is sometimes more atmospheric for its touch of age.

Inexpensive

Up to €38 (UK£23) per person. Whitewashed farmhouses, Georgian manses, rectories, old manor houses, modern bungalows and fine town houses come under this heading, along with the increasing numbers of holiday hostels. They are all very good value, good '*craic*', and you will often get marvellous, simple cooking. Not all of the bedrooms will have central heating or en suite facilities, but there will be perfectly good bathrooms close by and washbasins in the room.

Reservations

You can make a reservation direct with the premises, or use the Tourism Ireland offices in Ireland, Northern Ireland and Great Britain, who operate an enquiry and booking service. (Offices in other countries operate an enquiry service only.) Offices throughout Ireland will reserve a room for you for the price of a telephone call, but will only book you into registered and approved lodgings. A 10% deposit is payable, plus a charge of €4 for the service.

Make sure that you book early for the peak months of June, July and August. At other

Booking Websites

The Blue Book: *www.irelands-blue-book.ie*

Friendly Homes of Ireland: *www.tourismre-sources.ie*

The Hidden Ireland: *www.hidden-ireland.com*

Independent Holiday Hostels: *www.hostels-ireland.com*

Irish Hotels Federation: *www.irelandhotels.com*

Irish Tourist Board: *www.ireland.travel.ie*

Town and Country Homes: *www.commerce.ie/towns_and_country*

times of the year it is usually quite all right to book on the morning of the day you wish to stay (except in Dublin, which can be crowded in any season). Also, good places soon get known by word of mouth, so they are always more likely to be booked up in advance.

Literature

Tourism Ireland offices keep plenty of booklets on various types of accommodation. There is an illustrated hotels and guest houses guide called *Be Our Guest*; a *Farmhouse Bed and Breakfast Guide*; an *Illustrated Town and Country Homes* guide for B&Bs and a *Caravan and Camping Guide*. Other useful publications are the *Ireland Self-catering Guide*, *The Hidden Ireland Self-catering Guide* and *The Hidden Ireland Guide*, with accommodation in listed heritage houses, and *Friendly Homes of Ireland*. All these are available from any tourist office. The Northern Ireland Tourist Board stocks similar publications including a comprehensive list of accommodation called *Where to Stay*.

Hotels

The tourist boards register and grade hotels into five categories: **Four-star** stands for the most luxuriously equipped bedrooms and public rooms with night service, a very high standard of food and plenty of choice. Most bedrooms have their own bath and suites are available – the sort of place where delicious snacks are automatically served with your cocktails. This grading includes baronial mansions set in exquisite grounds or the rather plush anonymity of some Dublin hotels. **Three-star** grade stands for a luxury hotel which doesn't have quite so many items on the *table d'hôte*, nor does it have night service;

but the food is just as good and the atmosphere probably less restrained.

Two-star grade stands for well-furnished and comfortable; some rooms have a bath, cooking is good and plain. **Two-star** and **one-star** grades are clean, comfortable but limited, **two-star** offering more in the line of bathrooms and food. All Tourism Ireland graded hotels have heating and hot and cold water in the bedrooms. If you come across a hotel that is ungraded, it is because its grading is under review or because it has just opened, or does not comply with Tourism Ireland's requirements. The prices of hotels vary enormously, no matter what grade they are, and the grading takes no account of atmosphere and charm. Many of the most delightful and hospitable country houses come under one- or two-star grades, whilst some of the three-star hotels are very dull. All graded hotels are listed in the Tourism Ireland booklets. Northern Irish hotels are listed in their *Where to Stay* guide.

Guest Houses

These are usually houses which have become too large and expensive to maintain as private houses. The minimum number of bedrooms is five. The top grade **four-star** houses are just as good as their hotel equivalent, as are those graded lower down the scale, although the atmosphere is different. Some of the best places to stay are guest houses, particularly in Dublin.

If you decide to vary your accommodation from guest house to town and country house or farmhouse, you will discover one of the principles of Irish life: that everything in Ireland works on a personal basis. If you are on holiday to avoid people, a guest house is the last place you should book into. It is impossible not to be drawn into a friendly conversation, whether about fishing or politics. You will get a large, thoroughly uncontinental breakfast, and delicious evening meals with a choice within a set meal. Dinner is usually very punctual, at eight, after everyone has sat around by the fire over very large drinks. Lunch or a packed lunch can be arranged.

All grades of guest house have hot and cold water, and heating in the bedrooms. Four-star guest house rooms have private bathrooms, but their reputation is based on scrumptious food and comfortable surroundings. You can get full details of many of the finest guest houses in Tourism Ireland's booklets entitled *Be Our Guest* and *Where to Stay in Northern Ireland*. As a general guide, a comfortable, even luxurious night's sleep will cost between €25 (UK£15) and €80 (UK£50). A meal, where available, ranges from €12–30 (UK£7–18) on average. Sometimes the owners provide high tea; sometimes the only meal they do is breakfast.

Farmhouses, Town and Country Houses

Often these family homes complete your stay in Ireland, for you meet Irish people who are kind, generous and intelligent. This is also the most economical way to stay in Ireland if you don't want to stay in a tent or in a youth hostel. If you are not going to a place that is recommended, it is largely a matter of luck whether you hit an attractive or a mediocre set-up, but always watch out for the shamrock sign, Tourism Ireland's sign of approval.

Wherever you go, you should have a comfortable bed (if you are tall, make sure it is long enough; sometimes Irish beds can be on the small side), and an enormous breakfast: orange juice, cereal, eggs, bacon, sausages, toast, marmalade and a pot of tea or coffee.

Bed and breakfast per person ranges from around €25–40 (UK£18–30) throughout the Republic and the North if you are sharing a bedroom. You can get much cheaper weekly rates, with partial or full board. Very often you can eat your evening meal in the dining room of the B&B. Again, there will be masses to eat and it will be piping hot – so much better than many restaurants and cafés. There is often great flexibility about breakfast and other meals: they happen when it suits you, but you should give notice before 12 noon if you want to eat dinner.

Some houses serve **dinner** at around €12–30 (UK£7–18), and some offer 'high tea', which is less costly (between €8–12, UK£5–7). 'High tea' is a very sensible meal which has evolved for the working man who begins to feel hungry at about 6pm. You get a plate of something hot, perhaps chicken and chips, followed by fresh soda bread, jam and cakes and a pot of tea. Some houses provide tea and biscuits as a nightcap for nibblers at around 10pm.

More and more establishments have en suite bathrooms. You usually pay about €2.50 (UK£1.25) extra for this. If there is only a communal bathroom, you may be charged a trivial amount for hot water – although nowadays this is uncommon.

For people who are hitch-hiking or using public transport, the town houses are the easiest to get to and find; but the real favourites are farmhouses and country houses. The farms concentrate on dairy, sheep, crop farming or beef cattle and often a mixture of everything. Tucked away in lovely countryside, they may be traditional or modern. The farmer's wife, helped by her children, usually makes life very comfortable and is often ready to have a chat and advise you on the local beauty spots and good places to hear traditional music, or go for a *ceili*. Some of the town and country houses are on fairly main roads, but they are generally not too noisy as there is so little traffic about. The type of house you might stay in ranges from the Georgian to the Alpine-style bungalow, from a semi-detached to a 1950s dolls' house. There are a bewildering number of architectural styles in the new houses beginning to radiate out from small villages.

Renting a House or Cottage

This is very easy. Every regional office of Tourism Ireland has a list of houses and apartments to let, as well as the national *Self-Catering Guide*, with photos and descriptions of a wide choice of houses and flats. There is also a short list of self-catering houses at the back of the *Guest Accommodation* booklet. Places to rent range from converted stable blocks to modern bungalows.

In the North, ask the NITB for their self-catering bulletin or look in the back of the accommodation booklet and in newspapers. The Republic has a very popular 'Rent-an-Irish-Cottage' scheme with centres in Counties Limerick, Galway, Mayo, Tipperary and Clare. On the outside the cottages are thatched, whitewashed and traditional; inside they are well-designed with an electric cooker, fridge and kettle – all the mod-cons you could want. There are built-in cupboards and comfy beds and linen. Simple, comfortable, Irish-made furniture and fittings make it a happy blend of tradition and modern convenience. Cottages vary in size: some take eight, others five.

Easter and May, June, July and August are the most expensive times with prices hovering around €380–507 (UK£235–312) per week, but in October, sometimes the nicest month in Ireland weather-wise, a cottage can be very reasonable at around €250–330 (UK£153–200) per week. The local people take a great interest in you because they are all shareholders in the scheme and so do their best to make you content.

Renting Big Houses

There is a growing demand to stay in or rent an Irish castle and some of them are quite reasonable in price. There are some exclusive and attractive country houses where you can stay as the guest of friendly, interesting hosts, and where you can be sure of good food.

The National Trust has several gloriously restored properties in Northern Ireland. Castle Coole in County Fermanagh and Springhill in County Londonderry are favourites. It is also possible to rent holiday properties on some National Trust estates.

Youth Hostels

The Irish YHA is called *An Oige*, and has 44 hostels. These are distributed all over the Republic; there are a few in the Six Counties, often in wild and remote places, which are doubly attractive to the enterprising traveller. Members of the International Youth Hostel Federation can use all of these hostels in Ireland. You can join for €15 (UK£9); there is no

age limit, and your card can be used world-wide. Buy an International Guest Card, by purchasing six welcome stamps costing €2 (UK£1.20) each. The stamps may be bought one at a time at six different hostels.

Youth hostels are sometimes superb houses, and range from cottages to castles. They are great centres for climbers, walkers and fishers, and not too spartan; many have a comfortable laxity when it comes to the rules. You must provide your own sheet and sleeping bag. A flap or pocket to cover the pillows can be bought at the *An Oige* office, and the hostel provides blankets or sheet bags. All the hostels have fully equipped kitchens, and most also provide breakfast, packed lunches and an evening meal on request.

Charges vary according to age, month and location; during July and August it is slightly more expensive, and it is vital to book. This applies also to weekends. All *An Oige* and YHANI (Youth Hostel Association of Northern Ireland) hostels may be booked from one hostel to another, or centrally by contacting the head office listed below. Most of the hostels are open all year round.

There are several rail/cycling holidays on offer to hostel members. The average cost of staying overnight is around €10–12 (UK£6–7). All information, an essential handbook and an excellent map can be obtained from the *An Oige* Office, 61 Mountjoy Street, Dublin 7, t (01) 830 4555, f (01) 830 5808, *www.irelandyha.org*, *mailbox@anoige.ie*. For Northern Ireland, contact YHANI, 22 Donegall Road, Belfast, BT12 5JN, t (028) 9032 4733.

Besides the youth hostels, a large number of independent hostels have appeared in recent years. These are friendly, open to everyone (children are welcome in most hostels), and most have double and family rooms; some even have single rooms. They are also less likely than the youth hostels to have bothersome rules, such as curfews and no access to rooms during daytime. All hostels will rent you sheets and all hostels provide duvets and blankets. The average price for a dormitory bed in high season is €10 (UK£6). These hostels are listed in Tourism Ireland's *Accommodation Guide*, or you can get a list from the Independent Holiday Hostels of Ireland (IHH), 57 Lower Gardiner St, Dublin 1, t (01) 836 4700, f (01) 836 4710.

Big House Rentals

Country House Tours, 71 Waterloo Road, Dublin 4, t (01) 668 6463, f 668 6578, from the US t 1 800 688 0363, *www.tourismresources.ie*, *cht@tourismresources.ie*. Tours of public and private houses and castles.

Elegant Ireland, 15 Harcourt Street, Dublin 2, t (01) 475 1665/475 1632, f 475 1012, *www.elegant.ie*, *info@elegant.ie*.

The Hidden Ireland, t (01) 662 7166, f (01) 662 7144, US toll-free t 1800 688 0299, *www.hidden-ireland.com*.

National Trust, t 0870 4584411, f 0870 4584400, *www.nationaltrust.org.uk/cottages*, *cottages@ntrust.org.uk*.

Horse-drawn Caravans

You get a trustworthy and solid horse, a barrel-shaped caravan which sleeps four, and you can travel at a relaxing pace, usually about 9 miles (15kms) a day. Cost per week is from around €260 low-season to €700 in July and August. Contact Tourism Ireland, or:

Dieter Clissmann Horse-drawn Caravans, Carrigmore Farm, Wicklow, Co. Wicklow, t (0404) 48188, f (0404) 48288.

Kilvahan Horse Drawn Caravans, Cullenagh, Portlaoise, Co. Laois, t (0502) 27048, f (0502) 27225.

Slattery's Horse-drawn Caravans, 1 Russell Street, Tralee, Co. Kerry, t (066) 712 2364. Speak to Mr David Slattery.

Camping and Caravanning

The camping and caravan parks which meet the standards set by the tourist boards are listed in a booklet available from tourist offices (ask for *Caravan and Camping in Ireland*). Sites are graded according to amenities and many of them are in beautiful areas. Laundry rooms, excellent showers and loos, shops, restaurants, indoor games rooms and TV make camping easy and also more civilized, especially if you have children.

It is also possible to hire caravans and motor homes. For full details check the *Caravan and Camping* booklet. Overnight charges in the camping parks are around €8–10 (UK£5–6) per night, with a small charge per person at some parks and for electrical linkup. If you bring your own caravan or camping equipment to Ireland, and have Calor gas appliances, the only compatible ones on sale in Ireland are those supplied by Gaz. Some caravan parks accept dogs if they are on a leash.

Farmers will usually tolerate people turning up and asking if they can camp or park their caravan in a field. You must ask their permission first and tell them how long you want to stay. Be polite, do not get in the way and you will find that they will give you drinking water, lots of chat, and perhaps even some garden vegetables.

Women Travellers

Irish men have an attitude towards women which is as infuriating as it is attractive. They are a grand old muddle of male chauvinism, with a dash of admiration and fear for their mothers, sisters and wives. Irish women have a sharpness and wit which makes them more than a match for 'your man' in an argument, but at the same time they work their hearts and guts out.

If you are a lone female travelling through Ireland, you will find that Irishmen will often help with your luggage, your flat tyre and stand you for a meal or a drink without any questions. If a man tries to chat you up in a bar, or at a dance, it is usually just a bit of *craic*, and is not to be taken too seriously – the game is abandoned at once if you get tired of it. You might encounter a prevailing attitude that you ought to be travelling with somebody else – but it's only the women who will say so, saying, with a smile, that it must be a bit lonesome.

If you walk into an obviously male preserve, such as a serious drinking pub, don't expect to feel welcome, because you won't be, unless everybody is drunk, and by that time you would need to scarper. A bit of advice, which does not apply just to women, was pithily put by an Irish politician: 'The great difference between England and Ireland is that in England you can say what you like, so long as you do the right thing. In Ireland you can do what you like, so long as you say the right thing.' If you are hitch-hiking on your own, or with a female companion, you will get plenty of lifts and offers to take you out dancing that night. Your driver will never believe that you have to get on and be somewhere by a certain date, so the journey should pass with some pleasant banter. You would be better off hitch-hiking with someone else if possible; it isn't as common in Ireland today as it was in poorer times, although on the whole it remains fairly safe.

The Province of Munster

11

Munster

Highlights

1 Unique flora, limestone and ancient sites at the Burren, Co. Clare
2 The Beara Peninsula's stunning coast and brooding mountains, Co. Cork
3 Lovely walks at Derrynane House and Beach, Co. Kerry
4 Culture and shopping in Cork City
5 The imposing Rock of Cashel, ancient capital of Munster, in Co. Tipperary

Munster (*Cuige Mumhan*) is the largest province in Ireland, and is a mixture of everything that you consider Irish: the purples of the mountains melt into chessboards of cornfields, in which the stooks stand like golden pieces. Houses are whitewashed, glens are deep and the coastline is made ragged by the force of the Atlantic, with sandy bays and rocky cliffs. It is a land of extremes: a large, placid, fertile plain, brooding mountain scenery, luxurious vegetation, and harsh barren land. The stately River Shannon flows along the border of Tipperary and on out to the sea between County Clare and County Limerick. The extreme southwesterly coast is swept by westerly gales, and trees have been distorted into bent and twisted shapes. The moonscape of the Burren contrasts with the softness of Killarney; the dairy-land of Cashel of the Kings, where the lordly and the holy worshipped on a rock above the plains, contrasts with the thrashing sea around Dingle and the Iveragh Peninsula.

The Burren is the youngest landscape in Europe, and its carboniferous limestone hills have been shaped by intense glaciation. Spring gentian, mountain avens, hairy primrose, milkwort and orchids are amongst the wonderful variety of plants that flourish here. Wild goats still range it and keep at bay the ever-invasive hazel scrub. A great collection of southern and northern plants grow throughout the province. The best time to visit for them is May.

This is the land of the Mumonians; the 'ster' suffix is a Scandinavian addition to the ancient name of Muma, as it is with Ulster and Leinster. The people are warm, relaxed and musical; however, they are also backward-looking and quarrelsome. Dubliners say that Munster is a little England. The Anglo-Normans certainly had a part in moulding the towns, as did some of the adventurer types of the Elizabethan times, but Cork city has created many lively Irish minds, whether Celts or later arrivals.

Munster has always been cut off geographically from the rest of Ireland – by the mountains of Slieve Bloom, the bogs of Offaly and the River Shannon. This has helped to develop a great mythological tradition, with mother-goddesses figuring prominently in legend and place-names. There is Aire of Knockaney in County Limerick, and Aibell of Crag Liath. Anu is Mother of the Gods, whose breasts are represented in the Pap Mountains on the Kerry border. Most primitive of all is the ancient Hag of Beare, who spans many centuries and to whom many megalithic monuments are attributed. She is supposed to have written the marvellous 9th-century poem *The Hag of Beare*, which is a lament for lost beauty and the struggle between bodily pleasure and salvation through the Christian way of repentence:

Yet may this cup of whey
O! Lord, serve as my ale-feast –
Fathoming its bitterness
I'll learn that you know best.

Also strong in the mythological tradition is Donn Firinne, the ancestor-god to whom all the Irish will journey after death. His house is believed to be somewhere in this province. Munster has been commonly accepted as being divided into two parts

– between the ancient O'Brien Kingdom of Thomond and the MacCarthy Kingdom of Desmond. This was certainly a political reality between the 12th and 17th century.

County Limerick

A limerick is a nonsense verse, and Limerick is also a lovely county in Ireland. The county existed long before the five-line stanza, but since Edward Lear popularized them in his nonsense book, limericks have become world-famous. The origin of these poems is intriguing and open to debate, but it is claimed that in the 18th century a group of poets known as the Poets of Maigue, who lived near Croom, wrote these witty verses in good-natured sparring and as drinking songs. James Clarence Mangan, himself a great poet, translated them into English in the 1840s and they became popular in England. One of the poets, Sean O'Tuama, a tavern-keeper, wrote:

I sell the best brandy and sherry
To make my good customer merry
But at times their finances
Run short as it chances
And then I feel very sad, very.

One of his customers, Andy MacCraith, replied:

O Tuomy! you boast yourself handy,
At selling good ale and bright brandy,
The fact is your liquor makes everyone sicker,
I tell you that,
I your friend Andy.

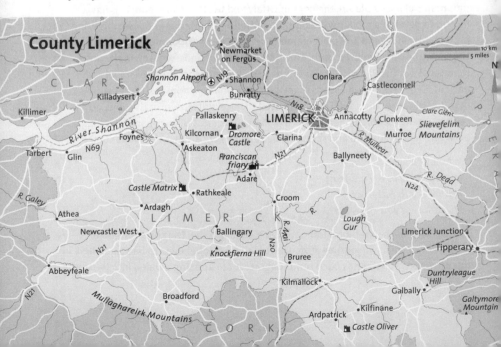

Getting There and Around

By Air
Bus Eireann (t (061) 474311) runs a regular service to Shannon Airport from the bus/train station on Parnell Street; the trip takes 45mins and is much cheaper than a taxi.

By Bus
Limerick City train and bus depots are on Parnell Street. Bus Eireann runs a reasonable service on lines to Cork, Ennis, Tipperary, Dublin and Waterford.
Bus Eireann, t (061) 313333, or **t** (061) 319911 (24hr talking bus timetable).

By Rail
From Limerick there are eight trains a day to Dublin, two to Cork, and two to Clonmel/Waterford/Rosslare; call **t** (061) 315 555.

By Bike
Emerald Cycles, 1 Patrick St, Limerick, **t** (061) 416983. Bike hire.

By Car
Traffic has become one of Limerick City's biggest problems, and getting in or out can be a nightmare; parking isn't easy either, and most of the city centre is a disc parking zone. If you must hire a car, try the following:
SIXT Rent-a-car, t 1850 206088;
  Shannon Airport, **t** (061) 472649;
  Ennis Road, Limerick, **t** (061) 206000.

Festivals

The dates of festivals vary a little each year, and there may be one-off festivals in some towns, so do check details with the tourist offices. For example, EV+A in Limerick City is a huge exhibition of visual art and dates vary every year.

March
Jazz Festival, Adare.
Irish Film Festival, Limerick.
International Church Music Festival, Limerick. Choral music in St Mary's Cathedral.
Band Music Festival, Limerick. Mixture of concert bands, marching bands and street entertainment, with a big parade (nearest Sun to St Patrick's Day).

May
Adare Country Fair. A gathering of hunters and fishermen.
Paddy Music Expo, Limerick. Showcase of traditional and contemporary Irish music (May Bank Holiday weekend).
Ballyhoura Walking Festival, Kilfinane.

June
Summerfest, Castletroy. RTE Classical Music Festival.

July
Ten Knights of Desmond Festival, Newcastle West.
Music Festival, Murroe (end July–early Aug).

August
Agricultural Show, Limerick.
Food Festival, Limerick .
Powers Irish Coffee Festival, Foynes.

September
Sionna, Limerick. Festival of traditional music.

October
Halloween Storyfest, Lough Gur. Storytelling, music and dancing.

County Limerick itself is a quiet farming community, dotted with the ruins of hundreds of castles and bounded on the north by the spreading River Shannon, and on its other sides by a fringe of hills and mountains. Limerick has the peaks of the Galtees in the southeast, the wild Mullaghareirk Mountains in the southwest and the rich Golden Vale in the east. There are lovely forest walks in all these places and sailing to be had on the Shannon. The visitor will be fascinated by Lough Gur and its wealth of archaeological remains, and the many ruined Norman castles and monasteries that still survive among the green fields and old farmhouses lying snugly in the valleys. The best dairy cattle in Ireland come from County Limerick, and it is also famous for its horse-breeding, largely due to the fertility of the pasture land.

The population of County Limerick is around 165,000, of whom well over half live in towns. Limerick likes to call itself the 'Birthplace of the Celtic Tiger'. When Taoiseach Sean Lemass liberalized Ireland's economic policies in the 1950s, the county was one of the first to take advantage. Shannon Development and the Free Trade Zone still provide a lot of jobs. Limerick City has a reputation for its vibrant cultural life, with a good university, excellent museums, art galleries and classical music concerts.

History

Not surprisingly in such fertile countryside, the monks founded important monasteries here. That they were rich is proved by the bejewelled Ardagh Chalice, discovered in a ring-fort in 1868 and now in the National Museum in Dublin. The Vikings, in search of new territory and loot along the Shannon Estuary, destroyed many centres of learning. They founded a colony which was to become the City of Limerick. Next came the Anglo-Normans, also attracted by the rich lands.

Among the principal families were the Fitzgeralds, the de Burgos, the de Lacys and the Fitzgibbons. But it was the Earls of Desmond, the heads of the Fitzgeralds, who owned the most and ruled like independent princes, eventually quarrelling with their Tudor overlords in England. They and their supporters are known as the Geraldines. In the 16th century the Tudors tried to centralize their authority; in consequence the Geraldines, who by now were completely Gaelicized, started a revolt in 1571 and maintained a constant guerrilla war against the crown and its agents. This ended in savage wars, repression and ruin for their house.

Throughout the following centuries up to the present day, Limerick has played a significant role in the numerous uprisings against English rule. In 1650 there was a 12-month siege of Limerick by Cromwell, which ended in capitulation. The Jacobite-Williamite war (1689–91) saw two more sieges in which the heroic General Patrick Sarsfield played his role (*see* 'Limerick City', below). William Smith O'Brien, a Limerick man, was one of the leaders of the abortive 1848 Rebellion, and three of the leaders of the 1916 Rising in Dublin were from the county. Edward Daly and Con Colbert were executed, but Eamon de Valera escaped that fate because of his American birth. Later he was one of the leaders of the War of Independence (1919–1921), and was President of Ireland from 1959 to 1973.

Limerick City

Limerick City at first sight has something rather drab about it which is hard to put your finger on, but it has the much-lauded Hunt Collection of art treasures, which is well worth making the journey for. It is largely Georgian in character – a grid pattern of streets has been superimposed onto the older town, which followed the curve of the River Shannon. The novelist Kate O'Brien came from the respectable middle class

Tourist Information

Limerick City: Arthur's Quay, **t** (061) 317522,
  f (061) 317939; *open all year.*
Shannon Airport: **t** (061) 471664; *open all year.*

Shopping

Crafts
The Convent of the Good Shepherd Sisters,
  Clare Street. Quality Limerick lace.
Irish Handcrafts, 26 Patrick Street. Woollens
  and tweeds.
Martin O'Driscoll, Limerick. Popular gold- and
  silversmith.
Niamh Hynes, Newgarden Road, Lisnagry,
  t (061) 377331. Pottery.
Potato Market, Merchant's Quay.
Shannon Airport Duty Free Shop. Only
  possible to visit when leaving the country.

Delicacies
Greenacres Deli, Carr Street, Milk Market.
  One of the permanent shops in the
  market (*see* p.161). Well worth visiting
  to stock up with picnic ingredients, as it
  sells a feast of Mediterranean and
  local foods.
Sona's Chocolates, 35 O'Connell Street, **t** (061)
  416963. Delicious chocolates made in
  Limerick by the unemployed, under the
  auspices of Sister Joan.

Sports and Activities

Art Galleries
Belltable Arts Centre, 69 O'Connell Street,
  t (061) 319866.
The Dolmen, Honan's Quay, **t** (061)
  417929.

Limerick Art Gallery, Pery Square, **t** (061)
  310633.
National Self-Portrait Collection, The
  University, Castleroy, Plassey, **t** (061) 333644.
  Open Mon–Sat 10–5.

Golf
Castletroy Golf Club, **t** (061) 335753.
Shannon Golf Club, Shannon Airport, **t** (061)
  471551.
Limerick Golf Club, Ballyclough, **t** (061) 414083.

Greyhound-racing
Market Fields, off Mulgrave Street **t** (061)
  415170. Racing on Mon, Thurs and Sat and
  occasionally Sun at 8pm.

Horse-racing
Limerick, four-day meeting in December.

Pony-trekking
Coonagh Equestrian Centre, **t** (061) 327348.

Where to Stay

Limerick City **t** (061–)
The Castletroy Park, Dublin Road, **t** 335566,
  f 331117, *www.castletroy-park.ie* (*expensive*).
  Modern four-star hotel with an uninspiring
  exterior, but suprisingly, it has the best
  accommodation in the city and good food.
Jurys Hotel, Ennis Road, **t** 327777, *www.jurys-*
  doyle.com/ireland (*expensive*). Modern
  and convenient.
Hanratty's Hotel, 5 Glentworth Street,
  t 410999 (*moderate–inexpensive*). Limerick's
  oldest hotel (1796), pleasant and up to date.
Railway Hotel, Parnell Street, **t** 413653,
  sales@railwayhotel.ie (*moderate–*
  inexpensive). Old-fashioned and very
  comfortable family-run hotel.

that moulded this city in the 19th century. She describes it as having 'the grave, grey
look of Commerce'.

Yet Limerick is doing its best to forget the hard times of the 1940s–60s, and has
recently been given a substantial facelift. It has a reputation for smart clothes shops,
and the Art School here has produced some talented clothes designers. For a city of
its size (52,000) it also has a buzzy nightlife. Previously high levels of unemployment
and emigration have significantly decreased recently as new industries have been set

Alexandra Guest House, 5–6 O'Connell Avenue, t 400433, *info@alexandra.iol.ie* (*inexpensive*). Attractive Victorian house with en suite rooms and only 5mins walk from the city centre.

Barrington's Lodge, George's Quay, t 416611 (*inexpensive*). Cheap but austere option.

Mount Gerard, O'Connell Avenue, t 31498 (*inexpensive*). Family B&B conveniently close to the city centre.

Self-catering

Shannon Development Tourist Office, t 362689. Handles bookings for most of the nicest properties in the county; everything from modern homes to thatched cottages, at varying prices. Call for a brochure.

Eating Out

Limerick City t (061–)

The Parlour Restaurant, Ennis Road, t 322777 (*moderate*). Finely decorated with a cosy atmosphere, and classic, creative dishes.

Green Onion Cafè, Ellen Street, t 400710 (*moderate–inexpensive*). Trendy and popular city centre café.

Belltable Arts Centre Café, 69 O'Connell Street, t 319866 (*inexpensive*). Tasty lunches and a great choice of cakes. Daytime only.

The Castle Lane Tavern, Nicholas Street, t 318044 (*inexpensive*). From the same stable that produced the Bunratty Banquets, this is reproduction traditional Irish that one would love to hate, but is in fact rather good.

Foley's Pub, Lower Shannon Street (*inexpensive*). Standard lunchtime meals such as ham and cabbage or Irish stew.

Greene's Cafe Bistro, 63 William Street, t 314022 (*inexpensive*). Central lunch spot with beautiful stained glass features and wholesome dishes.

Matt the Thresher, Birdhill, t 379227 (*inexpensive*). On the road into Limerick, Matt's serves excellent bar food and home-made bread; the bar stools are made out of tractor seats.

Vintage Pub, Ellen Street (*inexpensive*). Traditional pub with lunchtime snacks.

Entertainment and Nightlife

Pubs and Clubs

Brazen Head, O'Connell Street, t 417412. Popular pub and eatery, housing an after-hours club called 'Teds'.

Dolan's Pub and Restaurant, 3–4 Dock Road, t 314483, *www.dolans-pub.ie*, *accommodation@dolanspub.com*. Lively venue in the old docklands area, with decent pub grub and accommodation. Live gigs by national and international traditional musicians in the Dolan Warehouse.

The Works, Savoy Cinema Complex, t 411611. New, fashionable nightclub.

Traditional Music

The Belltable Arts Centre, 69 O'Connell Street, t 319866. Great live arts centre, with especially good theatre, film and exhibitions during Limerick's many festivals.

The Locke, George's Quay, t 413733. Old bar dates back to 1724; very relaxed atmosphere.

Nancy Blake's, Upper Denmark Street, t 416443. Great beer garden and live music venue attached.

Unversity Concert Hall, Limerick University, t 331549. Largest concert hall in Ireland, presenting a broad programme of excellent classical music.

up; and the cultural life is healthy, with an excellent arts centre. The city is very proud of its musical heritage, with a strong choral tradition, chamber music and marching bands. Suzanne Murphy, the opera singer, was born here. The people of Limerick are not so proud of the descriptions of their city in Frank McCourt's *Angela's Ashes* (a memoir of his childhood), but a walking and bus tour (*daily at 2.30 from St Mary's Action Centre, 44 Nicholas Street, Limerick, t (061) 318106*) points out some of the places mentioned in his grim, exuberant portrait of life in 1930s–40s Limerick.

Like Derry, Limerick is a symbolic city, full of memories, and there is lots to see that reveals Limerick's more ancient past. It was founded in AD 922 by the Norsemen, and has always been an important fording place on the River Shannon; in 1997 the city celebrated the 800th anniversary of its royal charter. More concrete evidence of the past is the massive round tower of King John's Castle, built in 1200, which is on the river guarding Thomond Bridge, and is one of the best examples of fortified Norman architecture in the country. The motto of the city is *Urbs antiqua fuit studiisque asperrima belli* ('an ancient city inured to the arts of war'). The history of the city is certainly stirring. In the wars of 1691 it was eventually surrendered to the Williamite Commander Ginkel after a fierce battering from his guns. The siege that preceded the surrender is stored away in the psyche of Irishmen. During the 1690s there were three struggles going on: the struggle of Britain and her Protestant allies to oppose the ascendancy in Europe of Catholic France, the struggle of Britain to subdue Ireland, and the struggle between the Protestant planter families and the Catholic Irish for the leadership of Ireland. The French supplied money and commanders to help Catholic James II wrest his crown back from the Protestant William of Orange (*see* **History**, p.42). The majority of the Catholic Irish supported the Jacobite cause and many joined up. It is part of Irish folk memory that the French commander St Ruth and King James were asses, and that the Irish commander Patrick Sarsfield was intelligent, daring and brave. The Irish army had been beaten at the Boyne under St Ruth and had retreated to Limerick, where the walls were said to be paper thin. William began a siege while he waited for the arrival of big guns, but Patrick Sarsfield led a daring raid on the siege train from Dublin and destroyed it. Sarsfield rode through the night with 600 horses into the Clare Hills, forded the Shannon and continued on through the Slievefelim Mountains. Finally, he swooped down on William III's huge consignment of guns and blew them skywards. His action saved Limerick from destruction for a time, when the siege was abandoned. When William did break through the Limerick walls, he sent in 10,000 men to wreak havoc, but the women and children of the city fought alongside their men, and they beat back the invaders. The second siege began the following year, and this time heavy losses were inflicted when the Williamite leader, Ginkel, gained control of Thomond Bridge. The promised help never came, and there was nothing to do but negotiate an honourable treaty. This Sarsfield did, and he agreed to take himself and 10,000 Irish troops off to France, in what became known as 'The Flight of the Wild Geese'. But the terms of the treaty were not carried out and the stone beside Thomond Bridge, where it was supposed to have been signed, is now known as 'The Stone of the Violated Treaty'. In the Roman Catholic Cathedral of St John is the Sarsfield Monument by the sculptor John Lawlor (1820–1901).

Old English Town and its Irish counterpart across the river are the most interesting parts of Limerick to wander in. **English Town**, the old Viking town of Limerick, is on an island formed by the Shannon and what is called the Abbey River (a branch of the Shannon). The Vikings and later the Normans tried to keep the native Irish from living and trading in the city area, so the Irish settled on the other side of the Abbey River – in **Irish Town**. A short circular walk takes you round the main places of interest. One great way to appreciate the beauty of the Shannon is to take a hovercraft trip up and down the river (*enquire at the tourist office, t (061) 317522*).

In the city centre is the tourist office and **Arthur's Quay Park**, between the Shannon and the city's sparkling new shopping district. From here, cross the river by Sarsfield Bridge, then turn right up Clancy's Strand, which gives you a good view of the city. This passes the **Treaty Stone**, a block of limestone, and leads to Thomond Bridge and the Old Town, passing by King John's Castle. You can visit **King John's Castle** (*open mid April–Oct, daily 9.30–4.30, Nov–Mar, Sun only 12–3 or by appointment; adm; t (061) 360788*), which has had two floors converted into an interpretative centre with displays of various instruments of early warfare and details of the castle's role in Irish history. The **Limerick Museum** (*open Tues–Sat 10–1 and 2.15–5; adm; t (061) 417826*), now installed in its new home next to the castle, houses an impressive collection of items from the Neolithic, Bronze and Iron Ages, as well as the city's civic treasures, including the famous 'Nail' or pedestal, formerly in the Exchange (now gone, except for a fragment of the façade in Nicholas Street), where the merchants of Limerick used to pay their debts (hence the expression 'paying on the nail').

Walk down Nicholas Street to **St Mary's Cathedral**, the only ancient church building left in the city, built in 1172 by Donal Mor O'Brien, King of Munster. Inside it has plenty of atmosphere, monuments and impressive furnishings including some superb 15th-century oak misericords (choir stalls) carved into the shapes of fantastic beasts such as the cockatrice and griffin. They are known as mercy seats because, although it looked as if the singers were standing, they could half sit or lean on a ledge. The oak for these and the barrel-vaulted roof came from the Cratloe Woods in County Clare. The cathedral was vandalized by Cromwell's soldiers, although it still has its pre-Reformation limestone high altar. Note the spectacular chandeliers. The Hiberno-Romanesque doorway on the west side is splendid, and the graveyard and garden surrounding the cathedral are charming. In summer a *son et lumière* show about Limerick is put on nightly at 9.15pm.

A few minutes' walk down Bridge Street and over the little Abbey River brings you to the best thing in Limerick – the **Old Custom House** in Rutland Street. This restored 18th-century building is now the home of the **Hunt Museum** (*open Mon–Sat 10–5, Sun 2–5; t (061) 312833*) and a rare example of the architecture of Davis Ducart. John Hunt was a noted art historian and Celtic archaeologist who died in the 1970s. He and his wife Gertrude had a remarkable European collection that they gathered over 40 years, containing a hoard of archaeological finds considered the second most important in Ireland. Beyond that, there is 18th-century silver: jewels, including early Christian brooches; paintings (one by Picasso); and Egyptian, Roman, Greek and medieval carved statues and artefacts, including the 9th-century bronze Cashel Bell, the largest in Ireland, found near Cashel town in 1849. As self-portraits go, the one by Robert Fagin with his half-naked wife is rather stunning; so, in a different way, is the bronze horse by Leonardo da Vinci. The fascinating and beautiful objects are too numerous to list, but you could easily spend most of a day there, taking a break in the café before going back for more. Around the corner in Michael Street, the **Granary** is a fine example of an 18th-century Georgian warehouse, which has been recently restored as the home of the City Library and Archive.

After the 1760s, when the city walls were dismantled, English and Irish Town merged and Georgian streets and squares were built. **John's Square** has the lofty spire of the Victorian Gothic St John's Cathedral, as well as a number of lovely old buildings of the mid-18th century, some of which are being restored after years of neglect. From here, a walk up Brennan's Row and a right on Sean Heuson Place brings you to the **Milk Market**; scene of a busy farmers' country market on Saturday mornings and an arts and crafts market on Fridays. There are also permanent shops open here.

More fine Georgian streets can be found on the southern edge of the city centre, around the **Crescent**, a development of the early 1800s at the southern end of O'Connell Street, and around **People's Park**. Close to the entrance of the park, off Pery Square, the **Limerick Art Gallery** (*t (061) 310633*) has a collection of modern Irish paintings and holds some very interesting exhibitions. Beautiful lace is made by the **Good Shepherd Sisters** in Clare Street, on the Dublin Road, (*t (061) 414918*). The **Belltable Arts Centre** (*see* 'Entertainment and Nightlife', p.158) is situated to the southwest and various Irish travelling theatre companies stop off here; it's well worth a phone call to find out what's on. There is also a small gallery that shows the work of many local artists and is part of the international EV+A Art Exhibition held at various venues around the city. Three art galleries are housed in the university at Castletroy, Plassey on the edge of the city, off the main Dublin road (N7); the **National Self-Portrait Collection** is the most worthwhile (*see* p.157). The university is also home to the Irish Chamber Orchestra and has a fine concert hall. For those interested in contemporary art, one of the best galleries is **The Dolmen** on Honan's Quay.

To the west of Limerick, only 16 miles (26km) away in County Clare, **Shannon Airport** got its start in the days when airliners couldn't cross the Atlantic without a stop for re-fuelling. Later, when the Irish invented duty-free and opened the first shop here (in 1947), it became the discount bazaar of Europe.

Around County Limerick

Along the Shannon and Round to the Mullaghareirks

From Limerick City, the N69 follows the Shannon Estuary to Askeaton, where the **Askeaton Friary** is a well-preserved 14th-century complex endowed by the Earls of Desmond. Between the N69 and the Shannon are two very prominent landmarks: the crumbling 15th-century **Carriggogunnell Castle** at Clarina, superbly set on a volcanic rock with a commanding view of the Shannon River, and, four miles further west, the romantic silhouette of **Dromore Castle** (*private*), designed by E.W. Godwin for the Earl of Limerick in 1870. In the vicinity of **Kilcornan**, Pallaskenry is the gutted ruin of Curragh Chase, which burnt down in 1942; the demesne is now a forest park. The minor Victorian poet Aubrey de Vere lived most of his long life here, and was often visited by Tennyson. One visit produced the poem *Lady Vere de Vere*. Aubrey de Vere

Tourist Information

Adare: Heritage Centre, Main Street, **t** (061) 396255, **f** (061) 396610; *open Feb–Dec.*

Shopping

Crafts

Lucy Errdige Crafts, Main Street, Adare, **t** (061) 396898. Knitwear and unusual crafts.
Orchard Pottery, Castleconnell, **t** (061) 377181. Stoneware with colourful Celtic designs.

Sports and Activities

Golf

Adare Manor Golf Club, Adare, **t** (061) 396204.
Newcastle West Golf Club, Ardagh, **t** (069) 76500.
Limerick County Golf and Country Club, Ballyneety, **t** (061) 351881, *www.limerick-county.com, icgolf@iol.ie.* Accommodation also available.
Abbeyfeale Golf Centre, Dromtrasna Collins, Abbeyfeale, **t** (068) 32033.

Pony-trekking

Clonshire Equestrian Centre, Adare, **t** (061) 396770.
Yerville Stables, Pallasgreen, **t** (061) 351547.

Where to Stay

Glin Castle, Glin **t** (068) 34173, *www.glincastle.com* (*expensive*). For those with a big budget and a taste for grandeur, this baronial pile is designed for sumptuous entertainment.
Adare Manor Hotel, Adare, **t** (061) 396566, *www.adaremanor.ie* (*luxury*). Original house of the Earls of Dunraven. Mixture of Victorian, Gothic and Tudor Revival fantasy, with beautiful grounds, horse riding, clay pigeon shooting and an 18-hole golf course designed by Robert Trent Jones.
Dunraven Arms Hotel, Adare, **t** (061) 396633, *www.dunravenhotel.com* (*expensive*). Old-world hotel, with appealing rooms, friendly staff and a huge pool and garden.
Ivy House, Craigue, Adare, **t** (061) 396270 (*inexpensive*). Pretty, ivy-covered, 18th-century country house.
Reens House, Ardagh, **t** (069) 64276 (*inexpensive*). 17th-century house on a farm.
Courtenay Lodge Hotel, Newcastle West, **t** (069) 62244, *res@courtenaylodge.iol.ie* (*inexpensive*). Ideal for golfers who want to be close to some of Ireland's best courses.
Echo Lodge, Ballingarry, **t** (069) 68508, *www.irelands-blue-book.ie/mustardseed.htm* (*expensive*). Outstanding service at this attractive 19th-century house on a hill.
Ash Hill Stud, Kilmallock, **t** (063) 98035, *www.ashhill.com* (*inexpensive*). Imposing 18th-century pile with large, comfortable

did many good works during the famine; he is buried in Askeaton. The house is in a very romantic setting, and walks are laid out in the arboretum and around the reed-filled lake (*open daily*). Also in Kilcornan you'll find the **Celtic Park and Gardens** (*open March–Nov 9–6; adm; t (061) 394243*), a collection of original and recreated Celtic buildings: a dolmen, holy well, ring-fort and a well-planned garden.

At **Foynes**, Limerick's little port, a very interesting hour can be spent at the **Flying Boat Museum** (*open April–Nov 10–6; t (069) 65416*). Between 1939 and 1945 Foynes was famous as a base for seaplanes crossing the Atlantic. The radio and weather room with its original transmitters, receivers and Morse code is fascinating. Many high-ranking British and American officers passed through Foynes during the Second World War, and the popular alcoholic 'Irish coffee' was concocted then. Nearby, **Boyce Garden**, Mount Trenchard (*open May–Sept 10–6; t (069) 65302*) is a one-acre garden overlooking the Shannon, with herbaceous borders, rock garden and pergola.

At **Glin**, a lovely village on the Shannon, you can visit **Glin Castle** (*open May–June, daily 10–1 and 2–4; other times by arrangement; guided tours every half-hour; t (068)* bedrooms, glorious plasterwork and shades of Anglo-Irish splendour – the front door leads straight into the stable yard. Set on a working horse farm; one self-catering apartment is also available.

Cooleen House, Bruree, t (063) 90584 (*inexpensive*). Very friendly service and fine, old-fashioned rooms in Mrs McDonoogh's whitewashed Georgian farmhouse.

Ballyteigne House, Rockhill, Bruree, t (063) 90575 (*inexpensive*). Mrs Johnson's warm hospitality and good food in a location convenient for Shannon Airport.

Castle Oaks House, Castleconnell, t (061) 377666, *info@castle-oaks.com* (*moderate*). Delightful Georgian house, convenient for golfers and anglers.

Millbank House, Murroe, t (061) 386115 (*inexpensive*), Mrs Keays welcomes guests at her attractive Georgian house in a farm setting. There's trout and salmon fishing on the river which flows through the farm.

Self-catering

Dunraven Arms Hotel, Adare, t (061) 396793. Attractive, modern town houses are run in association with this hotel.

FinnitersTown House, Adare, t (061) 396232. Attractive 18th-century home of the O'Grady Clan, set in farmland.

Springfield Castle, Drumcollogher, t (063) 83162. Fabulous historic home available for holiday lettings.

Eating Out

The Blue Door Restaurant, Adare, t (061) 396481 (*inexpensive*). Unpretentious modern bistro food.

The Wild Geese, Adare, t (061) 396451 (*expensive*). Heady combination of classic French and modern Irish cooking.

The Mustard Seed, Ballingarry, t (069) 68508 (*expensive*). Delicious and imaginative food in a new home at Echo Lodge; particularly memorable is their smoked salmon with walnut oil.

M. J. Finnegan's, Dublin Road, Annacotty, t (061) 337338 (*moderate*). A pub just east of Limerick, with a fine restaurant attached.

Acorn Restaurant, Castle Oaks House Hotel, Castleconnell, t (061) 377666 (*moderate*). Friendly ambience and local home cooking.

Worrall's Inn, Castleconnell, t (061) 377148 (*moderate*). Family-run restaurant with an extensive menu and wine list.

Entertainment and Nightlife

Bars and Pubs

Duggan's, Bridge Street, Newcastle West, t (069) 62283. Fine selection of pints.

Paddy the Farmers, Annacotty, t (061) 337171. Cosy pub, with plenty of *craic*, which has been voted Irish Pub of Distinction.

34173; *www.glincastle.com*), still the ancestral home of the Knights of Glin, part of the Fitzgerald tribe. (The present Knight of Glin is an art historian and stalwart campaigner on behalf of the historic buildings of this island, which are so often left to decay.) The castle is Georgian Gothic with castellations, and noted for its flying staircase, plasterwork and 18th-century furniture, portraits and landscape paintings. The gardens are beautifully planned and tended, and are a fitting extension of this romantic house. Exotic plants and the dark-leaved myrtle with its creamy, scented flowers love the mild climate; the walled garden is large and sloping and filled with fruit, herbs and vegetables for the house. The hens have gothic-style quarters and a headless Ariadne stands in a rustic temple. The Knight and his wife fill the house with paying guests (*see* 'Where to Stay', above), so they use up all their home produce. Many owners of large houses like Glin have opened them up not only for tours but for B&B and dinner. It is one way of keeping such places up, and a great way for tourists to enjoy the generous houses and grounds (*craft shop and restaurant at the Gate Lodge open April–Oct*). By the castle gates is the **Glin Heritage and Genealogical**

Research Centre (*t (068) 34001*). **Tarbert**, west of Glin in County Kerry, is the site of the car ferry across the Shannon that makes a very useful shortcut into Clare.

Following the border with Kerry southwards from Glin you come to **Athea**, a centre for traditional music, and a pretty place. All around are lovely hill walks and drives. **Abbeyfeale**, on the N21 south of Athea, surrounded by rolling hills, is another centre of traditional music, song and dance. It is also the gateway to Killarney and Tralee. To the east are the **Mullaghareirk Mountains** near the village of **Broadford**, which are mainly forested with the uniform evergreens so beloved of the Forestry Commission.

Central Limerick and the Maigue Valley

About 10 miles (16km) from Limerick, going southwest on the N20, **Adare** (*Ath Dara*: 'Ford of the Oak Tree') is set in richly timbered land through which the little River Maigue flows. This village has attracted visitors for many years. There is only one wide street, Main Street, set on both sides with pretty thatched cottages, many of which house antique shops, craft shops or restaurants. One of them is the local tourist office. The village is noted for its fine ecclesiastical ruins, but first notice the restored village washing-pool opposite the Trinitarian Abbey, just off Main Street. You can imagine the stories and scandal that might have been exchanged here as the village women washed their clothes. The finest ruin is the **Franciscan Friary**, founded in 1464 by Thomas, Earl of Kildare. (The village belonged to the Kildare branch of the Fitzgeralds or Geraldines.) The friary was attacked and burned by parliamentary forces, but its ruins are beautifully proportioned and can be viewed at a distance from the long narrow bridge of 14 arches (*c.*1400) on the outskirts of the village, on the N20 going north. If you want to go right up to it, check with the golf club office at the entrance, as it is in the heart of the Adare Manor Golf Club.

The modern village has grown up around the rest of the ecclesiastical buildings. The **Augustinian Priory**, now used as the Church of Ireland Church, was founded in 1315 by the Earl of Kildare. It was restored in 1807 by the first Earl of Dunraven. He and his family did much to protect the old buildings, and built the thatched cottages in Main Street in the 1820s. His family, the Dunravens, used to own the Gothic Tudor Revival-style manor house whose lush parklands surround the village. The Manor is now a luxury hotel with elegant formal gardens. The church has some interesting carvings of animals and human heads, and gives a good idea of what an Irish medieval church must have looked like. **Desmond Castle**, on the banks of the Maigue beside the bridge, was built in the 13th century on the site of an earlier ring fort. It is a fine example of feudal architecture with its square keep, curtain walls, two great halls, kitchen, gallery and stables.

The area around Adare is known as 'the Palatine' because of the number of Lutheran refugees from southern Germany who settled here in the 18th century, under the patronage of Lord Southwell. Their descendants, bearing such names as Ruttle, Shier, Teskey and Switzer, are still numerous in the area, and they are credited with introducing the rotation of crops. The British Government encouraged them to come and paid their rents for a number of years. **Rathkeale**, 17 miles (27km) west of Adare, is one of the largest towns in County Limerick and is in the centre of the dairy farming region. It is notable for its fine, early 19th-century courthouse and doorways in the main street. It has a small museum devoted to the history of the Palatines. **Castle Matrix** (*open June–Sept daily 11–5; adm; t (069) 64284*), about a mile to the southwest, is a fine Geraldine castle built in about 1410. The poet-Earl of Desmond, whose style epitomized the courtly love genre, lived here in the 1440s. The castle has been restored and is open for tours. It houses a unique collection of documents relating to the Wild Geese, Irish soldiers who served so nobly in the continental armies of the 17th and 18th centuries. It has the reputation for being the first place in Ireland where the potato was grown (of course Youghal makes that claim too). The story goes that the poet Edmund Spenser met Walter Raleigh here in 1580, and they became great friends. They were both young and as yet unknown, seeking to make their fortune in Ireland, where they had been granted land. When Raleigh returned from his successful voyage to America, he presented some potatoes to their host, Lord Southwell, who evidently cultivated them with some success. The Methodist movement in North America was initiated at Castle Matrix: Palatine refugees on the estate were converted by John Wesley, and in 1760 Philip Embury and Barbara Ruttle Heck sailed to New York and founded a church there. It is now the headquarters of the Irish International Arts Centre and Heraldry Society. A short distance southwest is **Ardagh**, famous for the chalice, brooches and bronze cup discovered in an ancient ring-fort. They are now in the National Museum in Dublin, and are superb. The chalice is wrought of gold, silver and bronze, ornamented with enamel, amber and crystal. Ardagh also has a newly constructed golf course on the road to **Newcastle West**, a busy market town. Parts of the Desmond Castle in Newcastle West have been restored and are open to the public (*adm*).

Croom, right in the middle of County Limerick and in a charming position on the River Maigue, is celebrated as the meeting place of the 18th-century Gaelic poets of the Maigue. Fortunately, their poetry is available in translation, and is unforgettable for its wit and feeling. It is here that the light verse of the 'limerick' was first popularized, to be taken up later by Edward Lear. An old castle of the Geraldines is hidden behind a wall on the southern approach to the village. Croom was frequently attacked by the O'Briens, whose territory it bordered. Their battle cry was '*Lamh laid ir abu*' ('the strong hand forever') and it was always met by the rallying cry of the Geraldines, '*Cromadh abu*' ('Croom forever'). The old mill with its huge water wheel has been converted into a **heritage centre** and has a good restaurant (*t (061) 397 130*).

Knockfierna Hill, 6 miles (10km) southwest of Croom, is a fine place for a walk. It is held sacred to the Dé Danaan, King of the Other World, or Death, Donn Forinne. From the summit, on a clear day, you can see a great expanse of Ireland, with blue mountains and the pale Shannon Estuary. It's also the site of the National Famine Commemoration Park, with 15 renovated dwellings dating from the time of the famine. You can walk up there at any time; ask for directions in Ballingarry.

Lough Gur and the Southeast

Lough Gur, 11 miles (17km) south of Limerick City and surrounded by low hills, is guarded by the remains of two castles built by the Earls of Desmond in an area rich in field-antiquities, which were revealed when the water level was lowered by drainage in the 19th century. According to legend, the last of the Desmonds is doomed to hold court under the waters of Lough Gur and to emerge, fully armed, at daybreak on every morning of the seventh year in a routine that must be repeated until the silver shoes of his horse are worn away. As if to echo the story, the lake itself is horseshoe-shaped. Man has been here since 3000 BC, and you can see stone circles, wedge-shaped graves, a *crannog*, a ring-fort and Neolithic house sites. The **Interpretative Centre** (*open May–end Sept, daily 10–5.30; adm; t (061) 385186; guided tours on offer*) has an excellent audio-visual show explaining the history of the Lough Gur area from the Stone Age. Ask about the guided walk that takes in all the archaeological remains.

Kilmallock, about 11 miles (17km) south of Lough Gur on the R512, is in the rich land of the Golden Vale. It was founded by Saint Mocheallog, and received a charter in the time of Edward III, during which period it was heavily fortified. Built by the Geraldines (Fitzgeralds), it was a centre of Desmond power between the 14th and 16th centuries, and was partially destroyed during the Desmond Rebellion. It was also involved in the Cromwellian and Williamite wars, when its fortifications were destroyed. The 15th-century **King John's Castle** still stands in the centre of town, while Blossom's Gateway is a remnant of the ancient walls. Unlike Adare, the buildings have either been pulled down or left to decay. There is a beautiful **Dominican Priory** dating from the 13th century. A pillar in the aisle arcade shows the ball-flower ornament – very rare in Ireland, though common during the 14th century in England. **Kilmallock Museum** (*open daily 1.30–5*) has a small collection of relics from the town's past, and models of medieval Kilmallock and its stone-age counterpart, recently excavated nearby. South of Kilmallock are the **Ballyhoura Mountains**, which straddle the border with County Cork, pleasant farming country with opportunities for pony trekking and walking.

The slight remains of a round tower can be seen beside a holy well at **Ardpatrick**. Two miles south, in the demesne of **Castle Oliver**, Marie Gilbert was born in 1818. She rose to fame as Lola Montez, the mistress of King Ludwig I of Bavaria. Approximately 12 miles (18km) to the east, outside the village of **Galbally**, a lovely walk may be made up **Duntryleague Hill**, where you can explore a megalithic passage tomb and the remains of a stone circle. **Bruree**, 4 miles (7km) to the west of Kilmallock on the R518, is the place where Eamon de Valera grew up. His mother came from here; his father was a Spaniard. De Valera was born in Manhattan, but when his father died his mother sent him back here at the age of two to be reared by his grandmother. The school he went to is now the **De Valera Museum** (*open Tues–Fri 10–5, Sat and Sun 2–5; adm*). Later he became a teacher of mathematics, and joined the Gaelic League, the beginning of his lifelong championship of the Irish language. He is referred to affectionately in Ireland as 'Dev'. An old corn mill with a huge millwheel makes a striking image as you enter the village from the west.

East of Limerick

Castleconnell, 6 miles (9km) from Limerick, is a pretty Georgian spa town on the Shannon. Tourists used to come here to walk to the Falls of Doonass, which are no longer exciting since the Shannon Scheme diverted most of the water away to drive the turbines at Ardnacrusha. Murroe and the Clare Glens are on the northeastern borders of Limerick, about 10 miles (16km) from Limerick City on the R506.

Murroe (also spelt Moroe) lies under the foothills of the **Slievefelim Mountains**, and is dominated by the 19th-century mansion of **Glenstal**, which was built by the Barrington family as a massive Norman Revival castle. They left it in 1921 after Winifred, a daughter of the house, was shot dead in an ambush while travelling with an army officer and a District Inspector of the RIC. The IRA maintained that it was an accident, and that they were only after the policeman, who was also shot. Now a Benedictine monastery, it is officially called **St. Columba's Abbey** but is always known as Glenstal. It is famous as one of Ireland's public schools, run by the monks, and a centre for the promotion of ecumenicalism. It has a remarkable collection of Russian icons. The wooded grounds are very beautiful in May and June when the rhododendrons are out. The monks will always make you welcome; they sell beautiful hand-turned wooden bowls and religious books.

The Barringtons donated the **Clare Glens**, 3 miles (5km) north of Murroe, to the County Councils of Limerick and North Tipperary for the pleasure of the public. The Glens are not so much glens as a scenic gorge with sparkling waterfalls; there is a nature trail which leads you through. A further 4 miles or so west, at **Clonkeen**, is a small rectangular church, about 12th-century, with a richly decorated Irish Romanesque doorway and north wall window.

County Kerry

Kerry is packed with some of the most beautiful scenery in Ireland, and the friendliest folk. It is a kingdom all of its own, whose people love to use words with skill, flamboyance and humour. An irregularly shaped county with long fingers of land reaching into the sea, it boasts the opulent lakes of Killarney at its centre, set amongst the wooded slopes of the Macgillycuddy's Reeks, the grandest mountain range in the land. To the west are the peninsulas of Iveragh and Dingle, dear to every traveller who lands amid their splendour, where mountains and sea are jumbled together in a glory of colour. The Beara Peninsula, which Kerry shares with County Cork, has an equal beauty but is relatively unexplored. Every year the small farmer recreates a pattern of golden hayricks and cornfields, and wild flowers grow in the hawthorn hedges and handkerchief fields where the black Kerry cow grazes, when she is not creating a traffic jam on the narrow country lanes. One exotic plant which has colonized the southwest to its advantage is the scarlet-blossomed fuchsia; other sub-tropical plants thrive too, due to of the warming effects of the Gulf Stream.

Off the coast are some fascinating islands that are possible to visit with some perseverance. On the Skellig Rocks, the word of God has been praised and celebrated for six hundred years. Valentia is a soft, easy island by comparison, connected to the mainland by a causeway; while the Blaskets, three miles out to sea, are beautiful but deserted: the community of subsistence farmers and fisherfolk that the islanders recorded in a couple of lyrical biographies is sadly gone.

County Kerry

The possibilities for enjoying yourself in County Kerry are many. If you are simply motoring around the narrow country lanes, you will see the most superb vistas of seascape, hill and valley. But do not try to do too much driving in one day, for the roads are very twisty and each bend holds more alluring beauty. The driver can end up doing too much and it is possible to explore it all too quickly. The hotels and restaurants of County Kerry are generally of a very high standard, and the seafood and salmon are all that could be desired. Sailing, deep-sea fishing, diving and water-skiing are all easy to arrange, as are golf, game fishing, horse-riding and walking in the heathery mountains. For those who most like to wander amongst gardens and into historic buildings, there are several properties open to the public.

One of the most famous is Derrynane House, the house of Daniel O'Connell, 'the Great Liberator'. Whatever you plan to do, expect some rainy weather and cloud, for Kerry is notoriously wet and warm. For those interested in the ancient past, Kerry is scattered with ogham stones, standing stones, forts and the beehive-shaped cells called *clochans*, the stone huts of holy men. Interpretative centres have opened up to educate those interested in local history and to cater for the coach tours.

History

A brief historical outline must start, as always, back in the time of the Bronze Age, some 4,500 years ago. Miners from Spain and Portugal were attracted by the precious metals to be found in the mountains, and it is still possible to find traces of their

Getting There and Around

By Rail

Kerry is linked to Dublin by a good rail line from Killarney and Tralee; t (064) 31067 in Killarney, t (066) 712 3522, or t 1850 388222 in Tralee.

By Bus

Bus Eireann provides a good bus service to many parts of the county. Regular buses from Tralee go to Dingle town, from where there are infrequent services to other points on the peninsula. From June to September Bus Eireann runs daily coach tours round the Ring of Kerry and the peninsula (from Killarney and Tralee).

Bus Eireann, Killarney t (064) 34777; Tralee t (066) 712 3566.

By Sea

If you are planning to go west you can avoid Limerick City by taking the **car ferry** at Tarbert, across the Shannon River to Killimer. The ferry sails from Tarbert every hour on the half-hour and from Killimer every hour on the hour; it takes 30mins. There is a ferry service around the Ring of Kerry from Dingle Tues–Thurs and weekends, which costs €12.70.

By Bike

Cycle Ireland, St Mary's Terrace, Killarney, t (064) 32536. Runs 8-day cycle tours.

Killarney Rent-a-Bike, Old Market Lane, Main Street, Killarney, t (064) 32578. Gives out a free map with rentals.

O'Neills, Plunkett Street, Killarney, t (064) 31970. Rents standard and tandem bikes, as well as fishing and camping gear.

Kerry Cycle Tours, Tralee, t (066) 712 3376.

Tralee Bike Hire, Ashe St, Tralee, t (066) 712 7527.

Foxy John Moriarty, Main Street, Dingle, t (066) 915 1316. A bar, hardware and bedding store and cycle hire centre.

Mountain Man, Main Street, Dingle, t (066) 915 2400.

O'Gorman's Cycle Hire, Ballydavid, Dingle, t (066) 915 5162.

Getting to the Islands

Tourism Ireland are loath to recommend anyone because of the insurance requirements. Bear in mind that the local boatmen may not be covered and the trip is at your own risk.

The Skelligs: Hire a boat from Waterville, Caherdaniel, Derrynane Pier, Portmagee or Valentia Island – a matter of trying your luck with the local fishermen. Michael O'Sullivan does the trip from Waterville, as well as fishing cruises; ask at the Oyster Bar, t (066) 947 4255. Sean Feehan arranges angling, diving and boat hire at Ballinskelligs Pier, as well as trips to the Skelligs, t (066) 947 9182. Due to the popularity of the Great Skellig, and the fragile nature of the ruins and paths, a limit has been set on how many people can visit at once – book ahead in July and August. A waterbus tour is available from the Skellig Experience Heritage Centre, Valentia Island, t (066) 947 6306.

Valentia Island: You can get here over the causeway, but there is also a ferry shuttle mines and their assembly places, which are marked with stone circles, rock carvings and wedge tombs. From the wealth of legend that remains of the later Bronze Age and early Iron Age (500 BC) it is possible to build up a picture of society as it was then. It was hierarchical, aristocratic and warlike. There were no towns, and cattle-raising and raiding dominated everything. Farmers lived in ring-forts and on *crannógs* for defensive reasons. Writing was confined to an archaic form of Irish, which you can see on the ogham stones scattered around the county. Kerry beaches were the landing places for many of the legendary invasions, voyages and battles of Ireland's past. The miners who sailed into the bays from Spain are recorded in legend, as are the other waves of settlers.

Christianity came in the 5th century and great changes began. The old tribal centres went into decline, and powerful new kingdoms emerged, often with an abbot-prince

service in season to the opposite end of the island from Reenard Point near Cahirciveen, t (066) 947 6141.
Blasket Islands: The Blasket Island Boatmen take day-trippers from Dunquin Harbour every half-hour in summer, t (066) 915 6422. Ask in Krugers Bar, Dunquin, t (066) 915 6127, about hiring a boat to the Great Blasket. Mountain Man, Main St, Dingle, t (066) 915 2400, offers bus and boat trips.

Festivals

March
Roaring 1920s Festival, Killarney (St Patrick's Week).

April
Pan-Celtic Festival, Tralee. Programme of varied music, dancing and street entertainment (mid-April).

May
Féile na Bealtaine, Celtic May Day festivals, Ballyferriter and Dingle.
Rally of the Lakes, Killarney.
Blessing of the Boats, Brandon.
Irish National Surfing Championships, Ballybunion.
Writers' Week, Listowel.
Walking Festival, Kenmare (late May–early June).
Siamsa Tíre, National Folk Theatre of Ireland, Godfrey Place, Tralee. Programme of evening entertainment based on Irish music, folklore and dance, t (066) 712 3055 (May–Sept).

June
International Bachelor Festival, Ballybunion (late June–early July).
Tralee Races, t (066) 713 6148.

July
Summer Festival, Castlegregory (mid-July).
Féile Lughnasa and Mt Brandon Pilgrimage, Cloghane/Brandon (last week).
Killarney Races.
Duchas House, Edward Street, Tralee. Evening performances of Irish music, song and dance, t (066) 712 4803 (July–Aug).

August
Music Festivals, Milltown and Cahirciveen (first week).
Rose of Tralee Competition, Tralee, *www.roseoftralee.ie*. Major festival and beauty contest (third week).
Puck Fair, Killorglin (10–12th).
Races and Regatta, Dingle.
Tralee Races, t (066) 713 6148.
Fleadh Cheoil na hEireann. Celebration of Irish culture, music, song and dance. Check website for annual change of location, *wwwfleadhcheoil.com* (last weekend).

September
Races and Harvest Festival, Listowel (third week).

October
Traditional Music Festival, Castleisland.

December
Wren Boys Festival, Dingle and Listowel (26th).

at their heads. A strong monastic structure grew up and some monasteries became great centres of learning. The monks learnt the art of writing and recorded the sagas and legends. Many of these centres were in inhospitable locations – the 'dysart' of some place names. In Kerry there is the wonderfully preserved 7th-century foundation on Skellig Michael.

In the upheavals and faction-fighting of the 11th and 12th centuries, three ruling families emerged in Kerry as definite clans: the MacCarthys south of Killarney; the O'Donoghues around Killarney; and the O'Sullivans around the Kenmare Rivers. These are names that crop up again and again in Kerry's history, right up to today. In the 13th century, with the arrival of the Anglo-Normans, the Fitzgeralds and other closely related fighting men established strongholds throughout the region. They became the Palatine Earls of Desmond (*Deas Munhan*: 'West Munster') and brought with them many tenants and fighting men who introduced the common Kerry names of Walsh, Browne, Chute, Landers, Ashe and Ferriter. The Earls of Desmond became so powerful that they were able to maintain an independence from the centralizing efforts of the English monarchs right up until the reign of Elizabeth I. They adopted many of the old Irish traditions, language, laws and dress; poetry and music flourished under their patronage. The last Earl took part in a rebellion against Elizabeth and lost his lands and his life, and even in this remote part of Ireland the Gaelic way of life began to disappear.

Another branch of the Fitzgeralds who crop up again and again in Irish history were the Earls of Kildare, eventually the Dukes of Leinster. The son of the first Duke, Lord Edward Fitzgerald, was a United Irishman and very involved in the plans for the Rising of 1798, although he died in prison, after the organization was infiltrated with informers.

The county was reorganized in 1606 into the shape we know today, and the new landowners were largely English Protestants. The political destruction of the 17th century is wonderfully recorded in the laments and satires of the poets of Munster. This short verse of David O'Bruadair (*c.* 1625–98) sums up what the poets felt:

Sad for those without sweet Anglo-Saxon
Now that Ormonde has come to Erin
For the rest of my life in the land of Conn
I'll do better with English than a poem.

version by John Montague

Kerry produced perhaps the greatest Irish leader there has ever been in the shape of Daniel O'Connell, who in 1829 won Catholic emancipation, not only for the Irish, but for all Catholics under British rule. He came from an old Gaelic family who had managed to hold on to their lands and to get along with their Protestant neighbours. The famine of 1847 and the emigration that followed reduced the population in Kerry as it did all over Ireland. Nowadays Kerry is a land of small farmers and relies on the tourist industry. Other industries include food processing, the manufacture of animal feed, pharmaceutical and small engine manufacturing, dairying and automotive manufacture. The population of County

Kerry is approximately 126,000, although this swells considerably during the tourist season.

Kenmare and the Beara Peninsula

The route in to County Kerry via County Cork is spectacular. However, instead of going straight to the large town of Killarney, you might like to start by exploring Kerry's portion of the quiet Beara Peninsula. Around **Lauragh** and the **Cloonee Loughs**, the waterfalls and lakes are lovely and relatively free of tourist crowds. An unmarked road off the R571 will take you up to a wonderful view over the Beara Peninsula, the Cloonee Loughs and Inchiquin Lough. Across the lough is **Uragh** (or Lauragh) **Wood**, a survivor of the primeval oak woods that once covered most of Ireland. The woods are a mixture of native oak and sessile oaks, which are distinguished by their curious hunched branches. There is a beautifully planted garden at **Derreen Woodland** (*open April–end Sept, daily 11–6; adm; t (064) 83103*) near Lauragh, on the road between Kenmare and Castletownbere (R571). The moist climate has given the plants a tropical vigour. As you walk through the winding paths and tunnels of deep shade cast by the delicate bamboo, blue eucalyptus and tousled rhododendrons, there are glorious glimpses of sea and wild mountain country. Stately North American conifers and New Zealand tree ferns also decorate the garden. The land, and thousands of acres around it, used to belong to Sir William Petty, who was responsible for the mapping of two-thirds of Ireland after the Cromwellian Conquest. He is blamed for denuding many of the oak woods over a large area, especially around Caragh, as fuel for his ironworks, although his descendants (who were further ennobled with the marquisate of Lansdowne) planted the gardens and woods you see today, and also laid out Kenmare.

This is marvellous walking country, and you can base yourself in **Kenmare**, a pretty, colourful 19th-century market town at the head of this long sea inlet. Savour the views of the rolling Kerry Hills, the Macgillycuddy's Reeks, the Caha Mountains on the Cork border and the broad estuary of the River Kenmare. Leave yourself at least a couple of hours to wander around Kenmare itself, which is full of excellent coffee houses, bars, restaurants, a heritage centre and craft shops. The colours of woven rugs, jerseys and tweeds perfectly echo the beautiful surrounding countryside. Fine silver jewellery and good-quality ceramics are to be found in the many craft shops stocking the work of local artists, and there is a wide range of books of Irish interest to enhance your knowledge of the host country.

It is worth seeking out the small Neolithic stone circle along the banks of the River Finnihy. To get there, walk up the road to the right of the Market House (which is home to the tourist office); the stone circle is signposted and you'll see it on the right overlooking the river. Back on the town square and above the tourist office is the **Heritage Centre** (*open April–Sept, Mon–Sat 10–6, also Sun 11–5 in July and Aug; adm*), where inside an exhibition explores the career of Sir William Petty.

During the last week of May, Kenmare is busy with keen walkers taking part in the Walking Festival. It is an ideal location because two of Ireland's long distance walking routes, the Kerry Way and the Beara Way, converge in the town. For further information on this festival, consult *www.kenmare.com/walking*, which also links to

Tourist Information

Kenmare: beside Heritage Centre, t (064) 41233; *open June–Sept.*

Shopping

Books
Noel and Holland Books, Bridge St, Kenmare.

Crafts
Black Abbey Crafts, 28 Main Street, Kenmare. A wide selection of locally made handcrafts.
Cleo's, 2 Shelbourne, Kenmare. For quality tweed suits, linen and woven rugs.
De Barra, Main Street, Kenmare. For traditional Celtic jewellery.
Kenmare Lace and Design Centre, The Square, Kenmare. Sells locally made lace.
Nostalgia, Henry St, Kenmare. Linen sheets.
Quill's Woollen Market, Kenmare. All manner of woollen goods.
Avoca Handweavers, Bunratty, and at Moll's Gap, Kenmare.

Delicacies
The Pantry, 30 Henry Street, Kenmare. For home-made bread, Capparoe goat's cheese and picnic ingredients.
The White House, Tuosist, Beara Peninsula. Peter and Lisette Kal make delicacies such as farmhouse cheeses and elaborate seafood dinners. Fishing and seal-watching trips in the surrounding bays also available.

Sports and Activities

Art Galleries
The Iverni Gallery, Kenmare, t (064) 41720.

Fishing
There is excellent deep-sea and brown trout fishing in the **Kenmare River Estuary**.

Kenmare Seafari, The Pier, Kenmare, t (064) 831 7120.

Golf
Kenmare Golf Club, Killowen, Kenmare, t (064) 41291. Parkland course.
Ring of Kerry Golf and Country Club, Templenoe, t (064) 420 0020.

Pony-trekking
Dromquinna Stables, Kenmare, t (064) 410 4320.

Tours by Car
Pro-Car, Kenmare, t (064) 42500.

Water Sports
Dromquinna Manor, Kenmare, t (064) 41657.
Kenmare Bay Diving Centre, Kenmare, t (064) 42238.
Kenmare Seafari, The Pier, Kenmare, t (064) 831 7120, *www.seafariireland.com*. Guided cruises introducing the local marine life; plus fishing, kayaking and water-skiing.

Where to Stay

The Park Hotel, High Street, Kenmare, t (064) 41200, *www.parkkenmare.com* (*luxury*). Château-style, award-winning hotel, with every modern comfort in rooms furnished with fine antiques.
Sheen Falls Lodge, Kenmare, t (064) 41600, *www.sheenfallslodge.ie* (*luxury*). Set in a beautiful location with sunny, low-key décor. The rooms are elegant, the food is lavish and imaginative and there is even a helipad for visiting dignitaries.
Dromquinna Manor, Kenmare, t (064) 41657, *www.dromquinna.com* (*moderate*). Very comfortable with lovely views over the water and waterskiing and horse-riding nearby.
Lansdowne Arms, William Street, Kenmare, t (064) 41368 (*moderate*). Family-run hotel.

the Caha Mountains Walking Festival that takes place in Glengarriff, Co. Cork, only 30 minutes away. Another attraction of note is the **Kenmare Lace and Design Centre** on the square (*open daily exc Sun 10–5.30; adm; t (064) 42636*), where you can look at a display of the locally made point lace and see demonstrations. During the tourist

Sallyport House, Kenmare, **t** (064) 42066, *www.sallyporthouse.com* (*moderate*). Smart, elegant and spacious old house that has been modernized and refurbished by the Arthur family. Set in peaceful surroundings overlooking Kenmare Harbour.

Shelburne, Kenmare, **t** (064) 41013 (*moderate–inexpensive*). Georgian farmhouse, five minutes' walk from Kenmare town centre. Run by two of the best restaurateurs in Kerry, Tom and Maura Foley. The rooms are individually furnished with antiques.

Atlantic Lodge, Kenmare, **t** (064) 42666 (*inexpensive*). Newly built, small, family-run hotel set in fields, five minutes' walk from the town. It has large rooms and a relaxed atmosphere.

Darcy's, Main Street, Kenmare, **t** (064) 41589 (*inexpensive*). One of Kenmare's several great restaurants with simple, en suite rooms above.

Hawthorne House, Shelbourne Street, Kenmare, **t** (064) 41035 (*inexpensive*). Extremely comfortable, modern house with all bedrooms en suite and lavish, delicious food.

The Lake House, Cloonee Tuosist, Kenmare, **t** (064) 84205 (*inexpensive*). Friendly pub and restaurant with accommodation above, run by Mary O'Shea. Highly recommended, especially for its beautiful lakeside setting.

Muxnaw Lodge, Kenmare, **t** (064) 41252 (*inexpensive*). Hannah Boland's attractive old house was built in 1801 and overlooks Kenmare Bay, within walking distance of town. There is an all-weather tennis court and good gardens and walks.

Eating Out

The Park Hotel, High Street, Kenmare, **t** (064) 41200 (*luxury*). Delicious French cuisine in grand surroundings. Ideal for a special occasion.

An Leath Phingin, 35 Main Street, Kenmare, **t** (064) 41559 (*moderate*). Italian chef, Maria, makes her own fresh pasta and scrumptious sauces. The stone-oven pizzas are also popular.

The Boathouse Restaurant, The Quay, Kenmare, **t** (064) 41788 (*moderate*). Fine seafood and sweeping views down by the harbour.

Darcy's Old Bank House, Main Street, Kenmare, **t** (064) 41589 (*moderate*). Well-established local favourite with constantly innovative specialities and colourful décor.

The Lime Tree, Shelbourne Street, Kenmare, **t** (064) 41225 (*moderate*). Recently reopened as an American-style café, with plenty of atmosphere.

Packies, 35 Henry Street, Kenmare, **t** (064) 41508 (*moderate*). Excellent fish restaurant; unpretentious, skilful cooking with the best ingredients.

Café Indigo and The Square Pint, The Square, Kenmare, **t** (064) 42356 (*inexpensive*). Very trendy daytime haunt for beautiful young locals and tourists, with an esoteric menu and minimalist decor. The pub below is good for traditional entertainment on the summer evenings.

The Horseshoe Bar and Restaurant, 3 Main Street, Kenmare, **t** (064) 41553 (*inexpensive*). Friendly, informal bistro.

The New Delight, Henry Street, Kenmare, **t** (064) 42350 (*inexpensive*). A treat for vegetarians in this wholesome café, serving imaginative food and organic wine.

The Purple Heather, Henry Street, Kenmare, **t** (064) 41016 (*inexpensive*). Good for lunch-time snacks, home-made soups and seafood. There is a very cosy fire in the bar.

The Wander Inn, 2 Henry Street, Kenmare, **t** (064) 42700 (*inexpensive*). Perfect for the classic combination of a plate of Irish stew, a pint of Guinness and traditional music.

season there are various operators in town to take you on two-hour-long boat cruises in Kenmare Bay and introduce you to the local marine wildlife.

On the main road to Cork is the village of **Kilgarvan**. The Michael J. Quill Centre there (**t** *(064) 85511*) is a craft shop and walking centre commemorating the founder of the Transport Workers Union of America, who was a native of the village. The **Kilgarvan Motor Museum** (**t** *(064) 85346; adm*) is a collection of classic and vintage cars including Rolls Royce, MGs and Alvis. On the outskirts of town on the Killarney road (N71) is **St Mary's Holy Well**, which is still much visited as the waters are reputed to have strong healing powers. The road from Kenmare to Killarney (N71) is twisty and very steep but the landscape is spectacular: you find yourself borne aloft green fields and rock-strewn hills. Once you have climbed to the top of the mountain and through Moll's Gap, you get wonderful views of Killarney's lakes and woods.

Killarney

Killarney is a resort town that only began to grow up in the 1750s, when tourism in Kerry first became popular. The town itself is not the attraction; it is the combination of lakes, woods, mountains and the stunning light and skies in the surrounding countryside which remain beautiful and unspoiled. If you are prepared to walk in the mountains and the National Park away from well-worn tracks, you will find that the luxuriant woods, the soft air, the vivid blue of the lakes and the craggy mountains above will have the same charm for you as they have had for countless travellers since the 18th century. Remember to bring a raincoat, since it nearly always rains, and expect at least one day when the mists will creep over everything.

Killarney does have one thing to offer sightseers: **St Mary's Cathedral**, built in silvery limestone in the 1840s. It is a very successful early English style building; austere and graceful, with good stained glass. It was not finished completely until the early 20th century, partly because it served as a refuge for the starving during the famine. You will find it in Cathedral Place, a continuation of New Street. Pugin's fine interior plasterwork was completely destroyed in a bit of post-Vatican II vandalism, except in one small chapel. Another fine church to visit is in College Street. It was built for the Franciscan order by Pugin in the 1860s. Look out for the vivid window by Harry Clarke. Facing the church is the **monument** to four Kerry poets who lived in the 17th and 18th centuries. It is worth searching out their poetry in the local bookshops; the translations into English are excellent.

It is quite fun to wander down some of the old lanes that survive from Victorian times, branching off the main street. There are plenty of banks, shops, craft shops, pubs and restaurants to choose from, but avoid staying in the centre as it gets so crowded. Those with a mechanical bent might enjoy what claims to be one of the longest **model railways** in the world, on Beech Road (*adm;* **t** *(064) 34000*) or the **Irish Transport Museum**, Scotts Gardens (*adm;* **t** *(064) 34677*).

Expect to be approached by the jarveys (coachmen), who gather with their ponies and traps on the street corner as you enter town on the N71; they will guide you around the valley and take you for as long or as short a trip as you want. Be sure to

Tourist Information

Killarney: Town Hall, Beech Road (beside town centre car park), **t** (064) 31633, **f** (064) 34506; *open all year.*

Shopping

Crafts

Blarney Woollen Mills, Main Street, Killarney.
Bricín Craft Shop, High Street, Killarney.
Kerry Glass, Fossa.
Kerry Woollen Mills, Beaufort, **t** (064) 44122. Although there is a shop, it is primarily the real thing – a woollen mill, producing proper scratchy blankets.

Sports and Activities

Art Galleries
Frank Lewis Gallery, Bridewell Lane, **t** (064) 34843.

Genealogy
Killarney Genealogical Centre, Cathedral Walk, **t** (064) 35946.

Golf
Killarney Golf Club, Mahony's Point, **t** (064) 31034.
Beaufort Golf Club, Beaufort, **t** (064) 44440.
Ross Golf Club, Ross, **t** (064) 31125.

Horse-racing
Look in the local newspapers, or in the back of Tourism Ireland's *Calendar of Events,* available from any tourist office.
Killarney, throughout May and July, **t** (064) 31125.

Open Farms
White Villa Farm Museum, Cork Road, **t** (064) 31414.
Muckross Traditional Farms, t (064) 31440.
Kennedy's Open Farm, Glenflesk, **t** (064) 54054.

Pleasure Cruises
Killarney Waterbus, t (064) 32638.
Lily of Killarney, t (064) 31068.

Pony-trekking
Killarney Stables, Ballydowney, **t** (064) 31686. For Killarney National Park.

Tours by Car
Castlelough Vintage Tours, t (064) 32496.
Dan Corcoran, t (064) 36666.
Jaunting Car Tours, Tangney Tours, **t** (064) 36852.

Where to Stay

Killarney t (064–)
Great Southern Hotel, t 31262, *www.greatsouthernhotels.com* (*expensive*). Stylish hotel with landscaped gardens and impressive facilities, including a choice of dining venues and leisure centre.
Killarney Park Hotel, Kenmare Place, **t** 35555, *www.killarneyparkhotel.ie* (*expensive*). Modern luxury in the heart of Killarney – marble floors, antique furniture, pool and huge suites.
Beaufort House, Beaufort, **t** 34440 (*moderate*). Pretty 18th-century house and gardens, with impressive antiques, 'World of Interiors'-type decoration, and massive bedrooms and bathrooms.

negotiate the price for the ride before you start and be prepared for a certain amount of chat. Most of them have a host of stories about the famous landmarks that have been polished and embroidered ever since Killarney first became a tourist destination. Some of it is tongue-in-cheek, as is this hoary old phrase about the constant rain: 'Twasn't rain at all, but just a little perspiration from the mountains'. The jarvey nowadays often carries a mobile phone to check on his next ride.

Some geography of the area: the underlying rock varies from old red sandstone to limestone, whilst the scooping action of glaciers in the ice-age created the precipitous mountain corries. Lower down, the indented lakes are softened by oak,

Castlerosse Hotel and Leisure Centre, t 31144, www.towerhotelgroup.ie (moderate). Great lake and mountain views from the self-catering suites or the main hotel, which caters well for disabled guests. Golf and accommodation packages and an inviting leisure centre offering Swedish massages.

Coolclogher House, Mill Road, t 35996, coolclogherhouse@eircom.net (moderate). Victorian house in a wonderfully secluded walled estate, with a great conservatory.

Earls Court House, Muckross Road, t 34009, f 34366, www.killarney-earlscourt.ie, info@killarney-earlscourt.ie (moderate). Comfortable Victorian furnishings, spacious rooms and delicious breakfasts, rounded off with efficient and friendly service.

Gleann Fia Country House, Deerpark, Dry Brusillarney, t 35035 (inexpensive). Recently built, Victorian-style guest house, set in a 30-acre wooded valley a mile from Killarney.

Killarney Royal Hotel, College Street, t 31853, www.killarneyroyal.ie (moderate). Boutique town house hotel.

Killeen House Hotel, Aghadoe, Lakes of Killarney, t 31711, www.killeenhousehotel.com (moderate). Friendly, cosy little hotel up in the hills of Aghadoe, 10 minutes from Killarney and away from the crowds. A golfer's paradise.

Randles Court Hotel, Muckross Road, t 35333, randles@iol.ie (moderate). Friendly, family-run manor house hotel.

White Gates Hotel, Muckcross Road, t 31164, whitegates@iol.ie (moderate). Lively, with an in-house pub, Kit Flaherty's, hosting traditional music and serves Irish fare.

Abbey Lodge, Muckross Road, t 34193 (inexpensive). Recently opened, a convenient B&B run by the welcoming King family.

Carriglea House, Muckross Road, t 31116 (inexpensive). Very close to Muckross House and the National Park, so you can avoid the busy centre of town. Comfortable rooms, with en suite bathrooms.

The Holiday Inn, Muckross Road, t 33000, call save t 1850 355 000, www.holidayinnkillarney.com (inexpensive). Excellent version of its type – family rooms, pool, gym, good food – but in an uninspiring setting on the outskirts of Killarney.

Eating Out

Killarney t (064–)

The Strawberry Tree, 24 Plunkett Street, t 32688 (expensive). Easily one of the best restaurants in Killarney.

The Celtic Cauldron, 27 Plunkett Street, t 36821 (moderate). Although at first it seems to cater for the tackiest type of tourism, it's completely redeemed by the food, inspired by traditional Celtic cookery.

Foley's Seafood and Steak Restaurant, 23 High Street, t 31217 (moderate). Serves delicious seafood, lamb and very good vegetarian dishes.

Gaby's Restaurant, 27 High Street, t 32519 (moderate). Mediterranean-style café with delicious seafood. Very popular locally and doesn't take bookings, so arrive early. Lunch served Tues–Sat, and dinner at 6pm.

The Laune, 103 New Street, t 32772 (moderate). Good for lunch, with extensive menu.

Cooper's Restaurant, Old Market Lane, t 37716 (inexpensive). Cosy, friendly atmosphere.

Sugan Bistro, Bunrower Lodge, t 33104 (inexpensive). Cheap, wholefood bistro near the railway station.

holly and arbutus, interspersed with the alien *rhododendron ponticum*, which splashes mauve among the dark leaves in late spring. The great Macgillycuddy's Reeks rise up to the west of the three famous lakes; to the southwest is the Mangerton Range. The Upper Lake is narrow, small and impressive, enclosed by the mountains, and scattered with wooded islands on which cedars of Lebanon stand high amongst the trees. A narrow passage leads into a connecting stretch of water called the Long Range, which flows under the Old Weir Bridge. Here the water rushes over some rapids, giving a frisson of excitement to those on a boat trip. The river then divides at 'the Meeting of the Waters'; the left branch flows into the Lower Lake, also called

Lough Leane; the right branch empties into Middle Lake, known as Muckross Lake. The limestone that underlies the Middle Lake has been worn away by the water into a series of fantastically shaped rocks and cliffs. Lower Lake contains the verdant island of Innisfallen, a wonderful place to stop for a picnic, and on the western side of the lake are O'Sullivan's Cascades which, with all the blessed rain, is always a pretty sight.

Excursions from Killarney: the Gap of Dunloe

A large part of the Killarney Valley is a national park, at the centre of which you will find Muckross House and Abbey (*see* opposite). The valley runs roughly north-south through a break in the Macgillycuddy's Reeks range of mountains, which runs east-west. Lough Leane lies north of the range, and the Middle and Upper Lakes mainly south of it.

The **Gap of Dunloe** is six miles west of Killarney and about eight miles in length, a wild gorge bordered by the dark Macgillycuddy's Reeks, the Purple Mountain and Tomies Mountain. The Macgillycuddy's Reeks include **Carrantuohill**, at 3,414ft (1,040m) the highest mountain in Ireland. Cars are not welcome on the dirt track during the tourist season, as the route is taken up with horse traffic, cyclists and walkers, and the horse traffic on the narrow, unpaved road will not allow you to pass. A standard **tour** can be booked in town or at the mouth of the Gap, consisting of a jaunting car ride through the Gap, and then a pleasant boat trip back to town through the lakes. This takes a full day and is idyllic in good weather (*costs about €19*). Seeing the sights by pony and trap, also known as a jaunting car, can be great fun, and during the trip you are regaled with stories by the jarveys. If the expense of a boat trip down the three lakes does not appeal, you can always hire a bike, walk or catch a bus. There are half-day bus trips, and ponies can be hired to explore the Gap of Dunloe, on the outskirts of Killarney. This is only advisable for experienced riders.

The mouth of the Gap starts at **Kate Kearney's Cottage** (Kate was a local woman, and reputedly a witch), a convivial refreshment house and coffee shop off the Killorglin road, six miles west of Killarney, and continues through to **Moll's Gap** on the Kenmare road (N71). Most people start from this end and hire a pony or sidecar. The journey through the Gap is spectacular, with steep gorges and deep glacial lakes. It's a good idea to approach it from the opposite way to the crowds, especially if you are walking or biking. Take the main Killarney–Kenmare road (N71); there is plenty to stop for en route. Notice the strawberry tree, or arbutus, growing among ferns and oaks, and the pink saxifrage on the wayside. All of the sights along the way are well signposted. You can stop and take an easy walk up the woodland path to the **Torc Waterfall**, found by following a rough road on the left just before a sign cautioning motorists about deer. The walk is very short, leading you through splendid fir trees to the 6oft (18m) falls. It is also possible to drive there and park. Go back on the main road for another little detour to some falls; continue past the Galway Bridge, where you can follow the stream up into the hills to the **Derrycunnihy Cascades**. Maybe you will come upon a few sitka (Japanese deer) or red native deer. The cascades are set in primeval oak woods, and this is a rich botanical site for ferns and mosses – the area even has its own Killarney fern, *trichomanus speciosum*.

Go back to the main road again (N71) and continue for six miles to **Ladies' View**, which gives you a marvellous view of the Upper Lake. Now turn off right before Moll's Gap and right again along the dirt track. You are now close to the Gap of Dunloe. A path leads you along the river to **Lord Brandon's Cottage** where tour groups coming from the Gap join the boats back to Killarney. To the west is a continuation of the Gap, the Black Valley, a sombre and remote corner of Kerry; nearly the entire population died off during the potato famine, and the place counts only a few lonely inhabitants today. Other walks include the Glen of Cummeenduff which leads to the heart of the Reeks, or the equally desolate and stunning Glen of Owenreagh.

This is some of the best, most arduous ridge-walking country in Ireland. Besides the places mentioned above, there is the **Kerry Way**, a hiking trail that begins in Killarney and passes Muckross Abbey and Lake before climbing to some dramatic scenery around Torc Mountain and Windy Gap. The trail goes on to Kenmare and from there clean around the Iveragh Peninsula – the hiker's version of the Ring of Kerry. If you do go walking, even for a short stroll, you should carry good waterproof gear, because the weather comes straight in off the Atlantic. Visibility is often very poor, with wreaths of mist on the hills.

Around Lough Leane

For those who prefer to be independent (and economical), hiking, walking or biking will take you to Ross Castle, Innisfallen Isle, the Gap of Dunloe, and Muckross Estate, Abbey and Castle. **Ross Castle** (*open May–Oct, daily 10–5; adm*) is 1½ miles (2½km) southwest of the town centre on a peninsula with pretty, wooded paths to the edge of Lough Leane. Evidence of copper deposits can be seen in the green waters here; these deposits were worked in the Bronze Age and the 18th century. Ross Castle is a fine ruin dating from the 15th century, consisting of a tower house surrounded by a *bawn* (fortified enclosure). The castle was built by the O'Donoghues, and taken by the Cromwellians, one of the last strongholds to fall. It has been restored and there are guided tours with much historical information. On its left is a 17th-century house built by the Brownes, who became Earls of Kenmare. From here you can hire a boat to **Innisfallen Isle** (*book in advance during the high season, €3.80–€5 per person*), an isle like a country in miniature, with hills, valleys and dark woods. Holly and other evergreens grow very thickly here. Near the landing stages are the extensive ruins of **Innisfallen Abbey**, founded about AD 600, as a refuge for Christians during the Dark Ages in Europe. *The Annals of Innisfallen*, a chronicle of world and Irish history written between AD 950–1380, are now in the Bodleian Library, Oxford. The monastery lasted until the middle of the 17th century, when the Cromwellian forces held Ross Castle.

About three miles south of Killarney is the Muckross Estate on the Kenmare road. Muckross House and Abbey are part of an 11,000-acre estate given to the nation by Mr Bowers Bourne of California and his son-in-law, Senator Arthur Vincent. They had owned the property for 31 years. The estate is now a national park and covers most of the lake district, with walks and drives to all the beauty spots, although cars are not allowed to some parts. **Muckross House** (*open mid Mar–Oct, daily 9–6, July–Aug, 9–7, Nov–mid Mar, Tues–Sun 11–5; adm, gardens free; for a small extra fee you can visit a* *traditional working farm within the estate;* **t** *(064) 31440*) was built in Tudor style in 1843 by Henry Arthur Herbert, whose family were landlords in this area. On the death of the last MacCarthy, Muckross passed to an Anglo-Norman family who eventually became known as Herbert. Queen Victoria stayed here when she visited in 1861. The main rooms are furnished in splendid Victorian style; the rest of the house has been transformed into a museum of Kerry folklore with a craft shop in its basement. You can see a potter, a weaver, a bookbinder and a blacksmith at their trades. There is a very informative film on the geology and natural beauties of the park, which is shown every half-hour. It is worth paying the extra to tour the traditional farm, especially if you have children with you; they will love the chickens, pigs, and the little black Kerry cows that give such sweet milk. The gardens around the house are delightful, and here you can see the native Killarney strawberry tree (*Arbutus unedo*), an evergreen with creamy white flowers followed by fruit that resembles strawberries.

Close by, overlooking the Lower Lake, is **Muckross Abbey**, a graceful early English ruin founded in 1448 for the Observatine Franciscans. After being dispossessed by Cromwell in 1652, the Franciscans had to go into hiding, but returned in more tolerant times and set up a boys' school and a new church in Killarney. In fact, this area is a stage set for everything the tourist wishes to see, and the natural beauty of the setting is enhanced by the superb gardens and arboretum. There is a gigantic yew tree in the centre of the cloister. The walks laid out in the park lead you through a mature oak and yew wood and to the very end of the peninsula, to the cliff known as Eagle Point, named after the golden eagles that used to be seen here. The path crosses the wooded **Dinis Island** (the Victorian cottage here serves good pizza). You are now 2½ (3.7km) miles from Muckross House, and if you do not want to retrace your steps, you can join the N71 Kenmare road (about a mile away).

If you are interested in seeing a fine example of **ogham stones**, take the main road for Killorglin (R562), past the Dunluce Castle Hotel. Turn right down a hill to a T-junction, and right again, over the bridge and up the hill. A signpost points left to a collection of ogham stones in a wired enclosure high on the bank. This is the best place in Kerry to see the weird ogham writing, the only form that existed in Ireland before the arrival of Christianity. The lateral strokes, incised into the stone and crossing a vertical line, give the name of a man long, long dead. **Dunloe Castle gardens** are well worth a visit (*adm by appointment or ask at reception;* **t** *(064) 44583*); it is claimed that your walk will take you around the world in a botanical sense, such is the variety of plants. The nearby village of **Beaufort** is very pretty, and there is a good golf course.

Another fine view of the Killarney lakes and mountains can be seen from **Aghadoe Hill** about 2½ miles from Killarney. It is not at all touristy. In pagan times, the hill was believed to be the birthplace of all beauty, and lovers still meet here. The legend goes that whoever falls in love on Aghadoe Hill will be blessed for a lifetime. From here one can be seen the voluptuous pair of hills known as the **Paps of Anu** (Danu), the mother of the gods. James Stephens is said to have remarked jokingly, 'I think those mountains ought to be taught a little modesty.'

Lower down the hill are the ruins of a round tower, a castle and the remains of a 12th-century church with a Romanesque doorway. To get there from the centre of Killarney, take the Tralee road until you see a sign for Aghadoe Heights Hotel. The view opens up around the hotel. One of the youth hostels is also in this direction. Halfway between Killarney and Killorglin are the **Kerry Woollen Mills**, established in the 17th century, which produces goods to be sold in the mill shop.

The Ring of Kerry

The narrow road that makes up the Ring of Kerry is 112 miles (180km) long, and takes about three hours to drive without any detours. Starting back at Kenmare, one can take the N70 and follow the coiling road south around the coast, stopping to enjoy the views, and perhaps setting off down the tiny R roads to get a better look at St Finan's Bay, Bolus Head and Doulus Head. The Ring ends at Killorglin.

You can, of course, travel the Ring anti-clockwise, starting from Killarney on the Killorglin road. The views are equally as good, but the route gets clogged with tourist traffic in July and August as the bus tours usually do the Ring this way round.

The Southern Ring: Parknasilla to Ballinskelligs

Parknasilla is a sheltered wee place, on the Kenmare River where it widens out into a sea inlet of islands and lovely bathing places fringed by woods and flowers. It has an excellent hotel with a well-established garden. The coves are favoured sunning places of the Atlantic seal. A lovely climb can be made up Knocknafreaghane (1,350ft/412m) and also the less demanding Knockanamadane Hill. **Sneem** is a quiet village, out of season, divided by the Sneem River. It has a good pub and was attractively laid out by an 18th-century landlord around a green, through which the river runs. On the green is a recently erected monument to De Gaulle, who once spent two weeks here; locals refer to it affectionately as 'De Gallstone'. Other modern sculptures are positioned around the place, the most memorable being the modern beehive huts with stained glass panels by James Scanlon, beside the church. There are several good restaurants to choose from.

About 10 miles west of Sneem, continuing on the N70, there is a signpost right to **Staigue Fort** (*open Easter–Oct daily; adm*), isolated at the head of a desolate valley, and between 1,500 and 2,000 years old. The circular stone fort rises out of a field, and a large bank and ditch surround it. Its thick dry stone walls are in good condition and the place has a tremendous atmosphere of ancient strength about it. It was probably built by late Bronze Age people, but has never been excavated or restored. Elaborate stairways lead to the defensive platform; it is fun to climb to the top, look out over the coast and wonder where it fits in amongst the myths and legends of these parts. (The farmer who owns the field requests a donation from those crossing his land.) Two miles away, at the Staigue Fort Hotel, is a small exhibition centre about the fort. Beyond Castlecove village on the N70 is **White Strand**, which is superb for bathing.

Tourist Information

Waterville: t (066) 947 4646; *open June–mid Sept.*
Caherciveen: t (066) 947 2589; *open all year.*

Shopping

Crafts

Waterville Craft Centre, Waterville.
Fuchsia Cottage Pottery, Dooneen, Caherciveen.
Sheeog Irish Handcrafts, Langford Street, Killorglin.

Sports and Activities

Art Galleries

Cill Rialaig Arts Centre, Ballinskelligs, t (066) 915 6100.

Beaches

White Strand, near Castlecove.
Derrynane Beach, near Caherdaniel.
Kells Bay, near Rossbeigh.

Fishing

There is excellent deep-sea fishing on Valentia Island and shore-angling all round the Ring of Kerry. Sea trout fishing is available on the Inny River; salmon fishing is also very popular, and brown trout fishing takes place on Lough Leane and Lough Avaul.
The Butler Arms Hotel, Waterville, t (066) 947 4144. For sea trout fishing.
Michael O'Sullivan, Waterville, t (066) 917 4255. For deep-sea and shore angling.
The Waterville Tourist Office, t (066) 947 4646. Excellent salmon fishing on Lough Currane near Waterville.
The Glencar Hotel, Glencar, t (066) 976 0102. For fishing the River Laune and River Caragh.

Golf

Waterville Golf Links, Waterville, t (066) 947 4102. Excellent links course.
Dooks, Glenbeigh, t (066) 976 8205. Once-great links course.
Killorglin Golf Club, Stealroe, Killorglin, t (066) 976 1979.

Tours

Countryside Tours, Glencar, t (066) 976 0211.
Into The Wilderness Tours, Glencar, t (066) 976 0101.

Walking

The Kerry Way. A long-distance, way-marked circular route around the Ring of Kerry. 133½ miles (215km) in nine stages.

Water Sports

Parknasilla Great Southern Hotel, Parknasilla, Sneem, t (064) 45122. Sailing and water-skiing available.
Activity Ireland and Skelligs Aquatics, Caherdaniel, t (066) 947 5277, *www.activity-ireland.com*. Offers scuba diving lessons and equipment. Also, sea angling and guided hill walking on the Kerry Way.
Derrynane Watersports Centre, Caherdaniel, t (066) 947 5266. Diving, sailing etc.
Des Lavelle, operating from Valentia, t (066) 915 6124. Diving school.

Where to Stay

Parknasilla Great Southern Hotel, Parknasilla, t (064) 45122, *www.parknasillahotel.com* (*expensive*). Comfortable hotel in a 19th-century mansion on the banks of the Kenmare River. Ask for a room in the older part.
Tahilla Cove, near Sneem, t (064) 45204, *www.tahillacove.com* (*moderate*). 1960s flat-roofed guest house with a Caribbean

---

West again on the N70, a mile from Catherdaniel, is **Derrynane House** (*open May–Sept, daily 9–6, Sun 11–7, Oct and April, Tues–Sun 1–5, Nov–Mar, Sat–Sun only, 1–5; adm; t (066) 947 5113*), the home of Daniel O'Connell, 'the Great Liberator', who won Catholic emancipation in 1829. It contains many of his possessions, including his desk, duelling pistols and rosary, amongst the plain furniture which he seems to have favoured, and is beautifully kept as a museum. The mellow simplicity of the house is very appealing, feel, in an idyllic location on the Ring of Kerry seashore.

Iskeroon, Caherdaniel, **t** (066) 947 5119, *www.iskeroon.com* (*moderate*). A large 1930s bungalow overlooking Derrynane Harbour in a very remote setting – you have to drive across a beach to get to it. Great seafood, turf fires, interesting books, and a semi-tropical garden leading to a private pier.

Butler Arms Hotel, Waterville, **t** (066) 947 4144, *www.butlerarms.com* (*expensive–moderate*). Intimate, family-run, pleasantly old-fashioned hotel. A lovely place to stay if you like salmon or trout fishing.

Club Méditerranée, Waterville, **t** (066) 74483 (*moderate*). Shedding its sun image, it has lots of activities for the fit.

Smugglers' Inn, Cliff Road, Waterville, **t** (066) 947 4330 (*moderate*). Friendy, family-run inn on the beach.

The Climbers' Inn, Glencar, **t** (066) 976 0101, *www.climbersinn.com* (*moderate*). Wild mountain location, 30mins and a million miles from Killarney. Cottagey, Laura Ashley-style bedrooms and a hostel behind it. Walking and climbing centre too, offering wilderness walking tours.

Glencar House Hotel, Glencar, **t** (066) 976 0102, *www.glencarhouse.com* (*moderate*). Remote, comfortable, clean and efficient country house hotel with stunning surroundings.

Caragh Lodge, Caragh Lake, **t** (066) 976 9115, *www.caraghlodge.com* (*expensive*). Comfy, well-furnished country house in a wonderful situation overlooking the lake, with a fine garden. Try to get rooms in the main house, not the yard.

Carrig House, Caragh Lake, **t** (066) 976 9100 (*moderate*). Good food and friendly accommodation in Frank and Mary Slattery's delightful, historic country house on the shore of Caragh Lake.

Glendalough House, Caragh Lake, Killorglin, **t** (066) 976 9156, *www.kerryweb.ie/ destination-kerry/glendalough* (*moderate*). Josephine Roder-Bradshaw is an excellent hostess and has furnished her house lovingly. Great views over the lake.

Mount Rivers, Carhan Road, Cahirciveen, **t** (066) 947 2509 (*inexpensive*). Comfortable rooms with en suite bath in Mrs McKenna's Victorian house.

Glanleam House, Valentia Island, **t** (066) 947 6176 (*moderate*). Splendid, sub-tropical gardens surrounding the Knight of Kerry's old home.

Ferntock, Killorglin, **t** (066) 976 1848 (*inexpensive*). This well-run, modern B&B is well situated for golf and the Puck Fair in August.

Self-catering

Patrick O'Leary, Sneem, **t** (064) 45132 (*inexpensive*). Two-bedroom house, pleasantly situated near the sea.

Eating Out

Stone House, Sneem, **t** (064) 45188 (*moderate*). Guesthouse producing reasonable Irish food. *Dinner only*.

The Blue Bull, South Square, Sneem, **t** (064) 45382 (*inexpensive*). Quality seafood in an old-style building; delicious seafood platters.

The Blind Piper, Caherdaniel, **t** (066) 9475126 (*inexpensive*). Good, lively atmosphere in this pretty hamlet.

Brennan's, 12 Main Street, Cahirciveen, **t** (066) 947 2021 (*moderate*). Good, modern cooking for lunch or dinner.

Nick's Restaurant and Pub, Lower Bridge Street, Killorglin, **t** (066) 976 1219 (*expensive*). Serves large portions of seafood and steaks. Often packed with local people singing 'My Irish Molly' round the piano; very friendly and great fun.

with its low ceilings and tiny Gothic-style chapel. Part of the house has been demolished, having got beyond repair. The video of his life is well worth watching and the historical background, very interesting. He believed that 'no political change whatsoever is worth the shedding of a single drop of human blood'.

The grounds have exceptionally fine coastal scenery, and form part of a national park of hundreds of acres. **Derrynane Bay** has one of the most glorious strands in the country, a wonderful place for a long walk. A shorter walk can be taken to Abbey Island and its ruined 10th-century abbey, along a cliff path with the rocky outline of the Skelligs framed by the sea and sky. Nearer to land are the isles of Deenish and Scarriff. Access to the abbey is only possible at low tide. Several O'Connell graves can be seen in the graveyard.

A few miles further round the coast, **Waterville** is the main resort of the Ring; palm trees and fuchsia imbue it with a continental air and hotels line the waterfront. The people speak Gaelic (the Munster variety) and **Ballinskelligs Bay** is a favourite place for Gaelic-speaking students, who stay in the B&Bs. The beach here and at St Finan's Bay is very beautiful, with splendid views. **Cill Rialaig Arts Centre**, Ballinskelligs, (**t** *(066) 915 6100*), is a small gallery and tea room associated with an international artists' retreat in the nearby recently restored famine village. Inland is **Lough Currane**, popular with fishing folk; the mountain streams that feed it are well known for brown trout. This area is a rich source of legend. The story goes that it was near Waterville that Cessair, the grand-daughter of Noah, landed with her father, two other men and 49 women. They were hoping to escape the Great Flood of the Bible story. The year, apparently, was 2958 BC. The women divided the three men amongst them but two of them died and the third, Fintan, was so reluctant to remain with the women that he fled and later turned himself into a salmon.

This peninsula was also the landing point of another invasion; the coming of the Celts. The 12th-century manuscript *The Book of Invasions*, or *Lebor Gabala*, describes it as follows: the Milesians arrived in Spain, where they built a watch-tower from which they saw Ireland, and it looked so green and beautiful that they set sail for it. Their poet, Amergin, sang a poem of mystical incantations when he first touched the Irish shore. The poem itself is rather beautiful, and this is part of what he sings:

I am the womb: of every holt,
I am the blaze: on every hill
I am the queen: of every hive,
I am the shield: for every head
I am the grave: of every hope.
version by Robert Graves

The Book of Invasions states that the Celts arrived on 1 May, 1700 BC. As you enter Waterville on the N70, on the skyline to your right is an alignment of four stones. This is supposed to be the burial place of Scene, wife of one of the eight leaders of the Milesians. Perhaps Staigue Fort has something to do with them.

The Skellig Islands

A trip to the Skellig Islands will take a whole day and is a high point of any visit to this part of the country. The jagged, rocky islands lie at the mouth of Ballinskelligs Bay and rise dramatically from the sea. Small Skellig is home to thousands of gannets and other sea birds, and its dark surface is splashed white – a mixture of birds and droppings. It is a nature reserve and boats do not land there. Great Skellig, or Skellig Michael, has on it an almost perfect example of an early monastic settlement, which was in use between the 6th and 12th centuries. The Gaelic word *sceilig* means 'splinter of stone', and you can only wonder at the skill of those who cut and shaped that stone. The remains still impress with their simplicity – seven beehive huts and oratories which convey something of the indefatigable striving of this community.

The **Skellig Heritage Centre** (*open May–Sept; **t** (066) 947 6306*), at Portmagee on Valentia Island, interprets the life of the monks on Skellig Michael through film, graphics and models. It also gives information about the birdlife, waterlife and the lighthouse service and has a shop. It is well worth visiting for the background knowledge it will give you before you go out to see for yourself.

There are environmental concerns about the number of visitors to the islands, so you may prefer simply to circle the island in one of the **tour boats** run by the Heritage Centre. If you wish to go yourself and stop off at the island for a couple of hours, boats can be hired at several places around the coast; from Waterville, the closest point, from Portmagee and also at Caherdaniel or Derrynane Pier. (*See 'Getting Around', p.169; landing times vary during the high season; check with the tourist office.*) The boats go out there only between mid-March and October, and whether you get there will be determined by the weather. Take a waterproof jacket, flat shoes, a picnic and, if you are keen on birdlife, a pair of binoculars. The trip out there can be very rough even on a fine day; the boat will soon be riding great waves of jade, iridescent water, illuminating something of the hunger for solitude that those holy men felt. Shearwaters glide past, known locally as 'mackerel cocks' for their knowledge of where the shoals are. Kittiwakes abound, and you may get a chance to see a huge gannet bomb into the water after a fish. You land to the noisy fury of the seabirds, and approach the monastery up a stairway of about six hundred steps, 540ft (164m) long, hacked out of stone over a thousand years ago. It is thought that St Finan founded the monastery on this barren rock, half a mile long and three quarters of a mile wide, in the 7th century. There was little these holy men could do there except pray and meditate, fish and grow vegetables. The way of life must have been hard; sometimes the waves crashing around the rock reach enormous heights. You can see beehive huts, stone crosses, the holy well, cisterns for storing rainwater, two oratories and cemeteries, and the ruins of **St Michael's Church** which, although it is of medieval origin, has not lasted as well as the cells. These are laid out close together on a small plateau and enclosed by a strong wall. The oratories and the medieval church are separated from the six cells or beehive huts by the holy well. Fresh water on this desolate island is provided by the rock fissures, which hold rainwater. The Vikings raided the monastery in AD 812 and 823, but in AD 995 Olaf Trygveson, the son of the King of Norway, is reputed to have been baptized here. When he became king he introduced Christianity to Scandinavia. The addition of Michael to the name of the island happened sometime in the 10th century. (St Michael being the leader of the Heavenly Host against the spirit of wickedness in high places, his name is invoked in many places throughout Europe, such as at Mont St-Michel in Normandy.) The monastery here grew independent of the authorities in Rome, as did the clerics in Ireland. The Celtic church refused to follow a 7th-century ruling about the time of Easter, and it was not until medieval times that the Skelligs fell into line. The monastic community appears to have withdrawn from the island in the 13th century, maybe because the weather got harsher or because it was attracting too many pilgrims. It remained a place of penitential pilgrimage, especially during the 18th century.

Inside the Ring: The Iveragh Peninsula's Interior

The Ring does not venture deeply into the interior of the Iveragh Peninsula, but you could do just that by travelling to the lake area of Caragh, Glencar and Lough Cloon, which will take at least half a day. This wild, mountainous landscape was the hunting ground of the legendary Fionn MacCumhaill (Finn MacCool) and it is absolutely delightful. Myriad little roads lead up to these parts.

Perhaps the simplest is the lonely road through the **Ballaghisheen Pass**, which is unnumbered and runs between Killorglin and Waterville. It actually branches off the N70 just north of Waterville by Inny Bridge. The Caragh River is famous for its early salmon, and the Macgillycuddy's Reeks cast their great height against the skyline all the way. There is an interesting walk to be had at the north end of **Lough Cloon**, where, up a small road to some farmhouses, and then right along a track, you will find an ancient settlement with ruined *clochans* (beehive huts) and terraced fields.

Further up in this wild country, turn right at Bealalaw Bridge and continue on until you come to a right fork over the Owenroe River, which takes you into the Ballaghbeama Gap and joins a larger road to Sneem. This takes you through a tortuous and breathtaking channel between two mountains, Knocklomena and Knockavulloge, named in Irish after the golden gorse that grows on their slopes. Traces of the early Bronze Age Beaker People have been found here in rock carvings. Alternatively, follow the Caragh River to Caragh Bridge and on to Killorglin. All these single track roads are lonely but so beautiful; huge boulders lie scattered like sheep on the slopes of the hills. Some were old turf tracks, or led to communities long gone since the famine times. The **Kerry Way**, a signed route for walkers, starts at Glenbeigh and follows a beautiful, desolate route through the Reeks. If you have come for the walking and climbing, note that the summits are challenging; do not attempt them without a good map and take all sensible climbing precautions (*see* also pp.178–9).

The Northern Ring: Caherciveen to Killorglin

A theatrical tower guards the bridge and the inlet at **Caherciveen**. It used to be the police barracks but is now a heritage and visitor centre. The design is grandiose Victorian, and was used for many other police barracks all over the British Empire; this one was built to take police reinforcements after the 1867 Fenian Uprising, and was later burnt down by anti-treaty forces in the Civil War. Now restored, the tower houses exhibitions which are full of interest and obviously have a lot of local input. From the barracks there is a three-mile floral walk along the coast to Cuas Crom. Daniel O'Connell was born here and the Catholic church has a dedication to him. The long main street has more pubs than you could believe possible, but not of the old-fashioned shop-cum-bar type: these are fast disappearing all over Ireland. It is often difficult to get a meal in any of them, especially off season.

This area is marked by turf-cutting and dominated by **Knocknadobar,** the holy mountain, also known as the hill of wells. From the summit at 2,267ft (690m), you get a wonderful view of the Dingle Peninsula and the Blasket Islands. St Finan's Well on its slopes was reputed to cure sick cattle, and people still take water from St Fursey's at the foot of the mountain.

Closer to the sea, **Valentia Island** and its quiet little harbour village of **Knightstown** is a pretty place to stay. The village was named after the Knight of Kerry, an improving landlord who owned most of the island. He opened a slate quarry in 1816, and the blue-grey slates were used to roof, among other famous buildings, the British Houses of Parliament. The quarry gave work to four hundred men and women, even during the famine. You can still see the old workings and spoil, although an enormous cavern has been converted into a grotto with Our Lady of Lourdes placed high up and St Bernadette gazing up at her. Another industry the knight set up was weaving; the small, excellent museum in the old school house details the natural dyes that were used, many from plants. The knight also planted a garden at **Glanleam House** *(open June–Sept, 11–7; adm; **t** (066) 947 6176)*. Tree ferns, bamboos and other sub-tropical species love it here, because the harbour is very well sheltered by Beginish and Church Island. Himalayan poppies and candelabra primulas give intense colour in the summer, and paths take you down to the sea. Other attractions on Valentia Island are detailed by the tourist office, which is close to the pier. You can obtain a map with marked walks; one of the best is a walk along the **Cliffs of Fogher** – massive, slaty shelves pounded by huge waves. You might decide to get out to the little islands in the bay. Shell middens and the remains of an ancient iron smelting industry have been found on the golden strand and dunes at the eastern end of Beginish. Deep sea fishing and diving can be organized on the island. In Victorian times this sleepy place was right at the hub of action, for Valentia was chosen as the site for the first transatlantic cable in 1858; locals could get in direct contact with New York but not with Dublin. The views across to the mainland are magnificent. The Skellig Heritage Centre is beside the road bridge that links the island to **Portmagee**; a very short ferry trip links Knightstown with Reenard Point, three miles west of Caherciveen (*see* opposite).

The N70 continues around the peninsula, passing close to Knocknadobar Mountain and along **Kells Bay**, which is a good place to bathe. This wildly romantic landscape is peopled with heroes from Ireland's legendary past; Fionn MacCumhaill and the warrior band, the Fianna, hunted these glens. Close by, in the locality of **Rossbeigh** and **Glenbeigh**, the landscape is rich in memories of Oísín, the son of Fionn, who came back here after his long sojourn in the land of youth. He had left with Niamh, a golden-haired beauty he had met on the Rossbeigh strand; he returned to the desolate glens of the Ballaghisheen Pass looking for his companions in the Fianna, and from this great height surveyed the glens and mountains. He did not understand that three hundred years had passed whilst he was enchanted, and that they were long dead. This area is also strongly associated with the story of Diarmuid and Grainne (*see* pp.82 and 84), who stayed in a cave at Glenbeigh.

It is fascinating to visit the **Bog Village Museum** *(open Mar–Nov, daily 9–6; adm; **t** (066) 976 9288)* just to the east of Glenbeigh, which depicts life in the rural 1800s.

The areas of bogland hereabouts support a wealth of specialized plants and insects with their acid-rich soil; the rich, coloured mosses include the sphagnum mosses which soak up the water and help create the bog, in which sundews and bog asphodel, dragonflies and butterflies flourish. A walk may be made to **Lough Coomasharn** and beyond. Branch off the N70, southwest of Glenbeigh, by turning left and crossing over the Beigh River, then turn right through the townland of **Ballynakilly Upper**. This leads you into a landscape of purple mountains and to the tarn itself, fishful of trout and char. A walk around the lough brings you to **Coomacarree Mountain** (2,541ft/772m). From its summit you can see a host of mountains, peak after peak, starred with lakes and ribboned by silver rivers, which drain into Dingle Bay. An easier walk on the Strand of Rossbeigh (Rossbehy in some maps) might be more appealing; the sand here often looks gold against sapphire in the glancing sun. There are other walks around **Caragh Lough**, a place popular with holidaymakers since Victorian times. It is strange to think that the bare bogland here was once covered in oak and holly trees; they were mostly destroyed by Sir William Petty, who used them as fuel for his ironworks in the 17th century. Only a fringe of trees survive around the lough now. Near the southeast of the lough is **Glencar**, a little village, and a wild glen. The Gaelic ruling family in these parts were the MacCarthys. It was from here that the head of the clan decided to take his title when he submitted to Elizabeth I, and became the Earl of Glencar.

Back on the N70, the Ring of Kerry ends with the attractive town of **Killorglin**, which grew up around an Anglo-Norman castle on the River Laune. The castle is now ruined, but you can explore a similar one nearby at **Ballymalis**. It has been partly restored, and you can climb to the top of the 16th-century tower, which is great fun (*always accessible*). Killorglin is famous for its cattle and horse fair, held in August, when vestiges of an ancient rite are enacted: a wild goat from the mountains is captured and enthroned in a cage in the centre of town. He is a symbol of the unrestricted merrymaking to follow. The event is known as the Puck Fair, and it may date from the worship of the Celtic God, Lug. Certainly, the *craic* is good; book in advance if you want to stay overnight in the town.

The Dingle Peninsula

This slender peninsula, the northernmost arm that Kerry stretches out into the sea, has become one of the most popular tourist destinations of the west. Dingle could be the Iveragh Peninsula in miniature, one with an equal helping of natural beauty. There is the same sort of spectacular coastal road; girdling impressive, grand, encircling mountains, and an even greater wealth of ancient remains and localities associated with Irish mythology. At the tip, instead of the Skellig Islands, there are the Blaskets.

Dingle comes from the Irish *daingean*, 'fortress', but nothing remains of one now. The local people speak Irish amongst themselves, though you will find that they will switch to English when you are around, for courtesy's sake. To the west of Dingle is wonderful, austere country battered by the Atlantic wind and sea.

Tourist Information

Dingle: t (066) 915 1188; *open April–end Oct.*
Castlegregory: Tailor's Row, Strand Street,
t (066) 713 9422; *open all year.*

Shopping

Crafts

Annascaul Pottery, Annascaul.
Brian de Staic, Green Street, Dingle. For
silver jewellery.
Irish Wild Flowers Ltd, 132 The Wood, Dingle.
Wild flower (seeds) gift gallery.
Lisbeth Mulcahy, Green Street, Dingle.
Knitwear, pottery, prints and weaving.
Penny's Pottery, Ventry. Lots of chunky
lavender-blue pottery.
Louis Mulcahy Pottery, Clogher, Ballyferriter.
For beautiful, large and very original pieces.

Delicacies

Norreen Curran, Green Street, Dingle.
Delicious smoked bacon and black pudding.
Ted Browne, Kilquane, Ballydavid. Smoked
salmon.

Sports and Activities

Archaeological Tours

Fios Feasa Holyground, Dingle, t (066)
915 2465.

Isabel Bennett, Ventry, t (066) 915 9012.

Fishing

There is excellent **deep-sea fishing** off
Ballydavid Head. Contact:
An Tiaracht, Dingle, t (066) 915 5429.
Mr N. O'Connor, Ventry, t (066) 915 9947.
Shore-angling is possible all round the
Dingle Peninsula. Contact:
The Dingle Tourist Office, t (066) 9151188.

Golf

Dingle Golf Club, Dingle, t (066) 915 6255.
Ceann Sibeal, Ballyferriter, t (066) 915 6255.
The westernmost course in Europe.
Castlegregory Golf and Fishing Club,
Stradbally, t (066) 713 9444. Nine-hole golf
course that also has a freshwater lake, filled
with brown trout, available to those with
their own boat and equipment.

Open Farms

Scanlon's Pet Farm, near Ballydavid, Dingle,
t (066) 915 5135.

Pony-trekking

Ballintaggart House, Dingle, t (066) 915 1454.
Dingle Horse Riding, Ballinaboula, Dingle,
t (066) 915 2199/2018.
Trekking Centre, Mountain View, Ventry,
t (066) 915 9723. 5–7-day trekking holidays.

Walking

Long-distance way-marked walks include:

Castlemaine to Slea Head

From the Ring of Kerry, Dingle is reached by continuing on the N70 to Castlemaine
and then to Annascaul on the R561, which passes the vast, beautiful sandy beach at
Inch. The most spectacular way to get to Dingle, however, is via Camp (west of Tralee)
on the R559, and the Glennagalt Valley – the Glen of the Madmen. Mad people were
taken here to recover, helped perhaps by the magnificent scenery between the
Beenoskee Massifs. (Incidentally, the Irish phrase for someone who has gone mad is
'he's away with his head'.) This is the way the old railway used to go, dropping down
to Annascaul on its way over to Dingle.

Entering the peninsula from Castlemaine, the coastal road (R561) passes beneath
the **Slieve Mish Mountains**, where there is not only wild beauty but a fund of
archaeological remains. The light glancing off the sea, traditional field patterns with
silvery stone walls and grey ribbed hills make this a scenic drive. Some new, big
houses have been built looking out to sea; this is happening all around the coastal

The Dingle Way. Circular route around the Dingle Peninsula. 110 miles (178km), 8 stages.
The Pilgrims Route from Dingle to Cloghane, 39 miles (64km).
Ryan's Daughter Route at Dunquin.

Walking Tours

Irish Walking Tours, Annascaul, **t** (066) 915 7382.
Hidden Ireland Tours, Dingle, **t** (087) 221 4002.

Water Sports

You can **dive** at Ventry and Dingle Bays; in the latter you'll find yourself accompanied by an amazing and much-loved friendly dolphin called Fungi who has been living there for a few years. You can walk 1km east of Dingle to the bay where he lives, or take a boat trip (about €10.20) out to see him, organized by a number of operators in Dingle harbour. **Surfing** is good at Inch Strand and Srudeen Strand, near Dingle; bring your own surfboard. If you want to **swim**, try Slea Head, Smerwick Strand, near Ballyferriter, or Stradbally.
Dingle Boatmen's Association, t (066) 915 1163.
Waterworld, Castlegregory, **t** (066) 713 9292, *www.waterworld.ie*. Ireland's largest scuba-diving centre, which organises visits to the Blasket and Magharee Islands. Dive holiday packages for all levels are available, as well as hill-walking and other energetic beach-based activities.

Where to Stay

Dingle Skellig Hotel, Dingle, **t** (066) 915 1144, *www.dingleskellig.com* (*expensive– moderate*). Family-friendly hotel with good leisure facilities.
The Captain's House, The Mall, Dingle, **t** (066) 915 1531, *homepage.tinet.ie/~captigh/guest-house.html* (*moderate*). B&B with a seafaring tradition, plenty of awards adorning the walls and wonderful turf fires. Self-catering option available in a seaside bungalow.
Doyle's Townhouse, John Street, Dingle, **t** (066) 915 1174, *www.doylesofdingle.com* (*moderate*). One of the most enjoyable, comfortable places to stay in the country. The rooms are full of individuality, and the sitting-room shelves and tables groan with interesting books over which you can linger by a warm fire. The bar and restaurant next door are famous for their conviviality and good food.
Greenmount Guesthouse, Dingle, **t** (066) 915 1414 (*moderate*). Mrs Curran's guesthouse has been recommended by readers. Enjoy freshly squeezed orange juice and lots of choice for breakfast.
The Old Stone House, Chiddaun, Dingle, **t** (066) 59882 (*inexpensive*). Comfortable little cottage.
Cleevaun, Milltown, **t** (066) 915 1108 (*inexpensive*). Modern guesthouse set in landscaped gardens overlooking Dingle Bay, a mile from Dingle town. Excellent food and

parts. Not only are the locals better off than they have ever been, and emigration has tailed off, but many newcomers are moving in, attracted by the beauty and way of life here in the southwest. The Phoenix wholefood café and B&B catch your eye as you drive along; such enterprises are indicative of the alternative way of life that many young Irish and foreigners try to put into practice. In the little towns, you will often spot a health food shop, advertisements for yoga classes are stuck up in the windows, and the Saturday morning country markets selling crafts, local vegetables and cheeses go from strength to strength.

From the great **Strand of Inch** you have views across the bay and over the mountains. This immense flat sheet of sand holds the water after the tide goes out and to walk on it while it reflects the sky is a remarkable experience. Unfortunately, people drive on to the beach, and litter the area around the entrance where there is a car park and touristy café-cum-craft shop. In the pubs, after 10pm, you can listen to traditional music or singing, which just happens when the locals get together.

very smart bedrooms, with tea and coffee facilities, hairdryers and TVs in rooms.

Crutchs' Hillville House Hotel, Kilcummin, near Castlegregory, t (066) 713 8118, *www.iol.ie/inf/hotels/o6638118.html* (*moderate*). Gorgeous scenery and peace and quiet at the bottom of the Connor Pass.

Aisling House, Castlegregory, t (066) 713 9134 (*inexpensive*). Wonderful guesthouse – clean and comfortable with a delicious breakfast.

Self-catering

Bog View Hostel, Annascaul, t (066) 915 8125. Converted school with turf fires which also does B&B and evening meals.

Ballintagart Hostel, Dingle, t (066) 915 1454. Converted 18th-century hunting lodge.

Penny Sheehy's traditional three-bedroom stone house in Ventry, t (066) 915 9962. She also has other comfortable properties.

Ms Naughton's modernized farmhouse, close to Ballyferriter. Sleeps six and prices start at €279 a week. Contact her at 20 Vineyard Hill Road, London SW19 7SH, t (020) 8946 4782.

Eating Out

Beginish Restaurant, Green Street, Dingle, t (066) 915 1588 (*expensive*). Enthusiastic staff and wonderful seafood; it has a conservatory at the back.

The Chart House, The Mall, Dingle, t (066) 915 2255 (*expensive*). Seriously good food.

Doyle's Seafood Bar and Restaurant, John Street, Dingle, t (066) 915 1174 (*expensive*). Set in a room reminiscent of an old Irish kitchen, with a stone floor and mellow wooden furniture. Treat yourself to deliciously prepared seafood chosen by the very friendly and welcoming proprietors, John and Stella Doyle.

Armada, Strand Street, Dingle, t (066) 915 1505 (*expensive–moderate*). Traditional west coast restaurant with a reputation for quality fare.

The Forge, Holy Ground, Dingle, t (066) 915 2590 (*moderate*). Steaks and seafood.

Graney's Fish and Chip Shop, Holy Ground, Dingle (*moderate*). Tasty, cheap take-aways.

The Half-door, John Street, Dingle, t (066) 915 1600 (*moderate*). Excellent, imaginative food. Very good value.

An Café Liteartha, Dingle, t (066) 915 2204 (*inexpensive*). A combined book-shop and café serving delicious open sandwiches while you browse through the bookshelves.

Lord Baker's, Main Street, Dingle, t (066) 915 1277 (*inexpensive*). Good quality bar food.

O'Riordan's, Castlegregory t (066) 713 9379 (*inexpensive*). Wonderful lunch spot – unusual dishes, memorable breads and good atmosphere.

Whelans, Main Street, Dingle, t (066) 915 1620 (*inexpensive*). Very good Irish stew and other traditional dishes.

At **Annascaul**, you can get a drink at the South Pole Inn, so called because a former proprietor, Tom Crean, was part of that brave team with Scott in the Antarctic. Dan Foley's Bar is another excellent drinking house, and Dan himself is a great source of local knowledge and folklore. To the northeast of Annascaul, on the right summit of Caherconree Mountain, is a rare example of an inland promontory fort. It dates from about 500 BC and is associated with Cú Chulainn, the great Ulster hero. (Notorious for his attraction to women, in this story he rescues a damsel in distress, and carries her off to the north of Ireland.) A drive or a walk of a few miles can be made to tranquil Annascaul Lake; the little tarred roads to it are empty of all but a few tractors, and you scarcely pass a house.

Dingle, a big fishing port and the westernmost town in Europe, has developed in a very attractive way; the population is about 15,000, but this can treble in the summer months. Gaily painted houses and busy streets lead you to the harbour, where the fishing boats move gently in the swell of the tide. The catches off this part of the coast are terrific, but the boats are small and high-tech methods have not yet arrived. This adds greatly to the charm of the scene. The Roman Catholic church in the centre of the town is a dim, calm place enlivened by narrow stained-glass windows and full of a feeling of welcome. In a different way the cafés and bars invite one to linger, and give the town a delightful holiday atmosphere. The choice of restaurants, pub food and traditional music is excellent. James Flahive's Bar by the harbour is full of clutter and old-fashioned furnishings, and in Dick Mack's in Green Lane you can buy not only a pint but also a selection of footwear. Ireland used to have many such places, but they are rapidly disappearing. A fast-food café with the most delicious ingredients is The River God (squid, home-made sausages); there are also good craft and book shops.

The local celebrity and major attraction, however, is undoubtedly Fungi, a playful bottle-nosed dolphin who wandered into the bay in 1983 and decided to stay. Boats in the harbour take tourists out to visit him daily: you can swim with him, wet suits are for hire and there is a life-size model of him on display at the **Dingle Aquarium** (*open daily 9.30–5, May, June and Sept until 6, July–Aug until 8.30; adm; t (066) 915211*). This is not just a tourist attraction but an informative and well laid out exhibition of the wonders of the deep. The highlight is a walk-through aquarium with all the stars of Kerry marine life in attendance, including small sharks.

Continuing west, **Ventry** has a lonely white strand on which, it is said, the King of the Other World, Donn, landed to subjugate Ireland. He had come to help the King of France avenge his honour, as Fionn had run off with his wife and daughter. The great Fionn MacCumhaill and his Fenian knights won the day, of course (*see* **Old Gods and Heroes**, pp.83–4). On the road to **Slea Head**, just off the R559 at Fahan and about 3 miles (6km) past Ventry, there is a group of early Christian *clochans*, 414 in all. Some were built by hermit monks, others are 19th-century. Up until recent times local farmers still built little *clochans* as storehouses for animals, and the continuity of style with the unmortared stone is such that it is difficult to tell the old from the new. Nineteen souterrains (underground passages and storage places), 18 standing stones, two sculptured crosses and seven ring-forts are strewn all over the slopes of Mount Eagle; the most prominent is the powerfully built **Doonbeg Fort**, which can be seen from the road, surrounded by the sea on three sides. The fort is dated to between 400–50 BC. It was well protected by several defensive earthen walls and an inner stone wall. Inside, local people and livestock would have gathered when under threat by rival tribal groups. There is a souterrain leading from the inside of the fort to the entrance.

The road from Fahan winds around the countryside from Eagle Mountain to **Slea Head**, from where you can see the Blasket Islands. The viewing places here allow you to stop and savour the views of traditional sheep fields, walls and dramatic headlands dark against the ever-changing light of the seas and skies. Aerial photographs reveal how the traditional land-holding patterns of these small farms are changing, and with them the landscape we all cherish. Signs invite you to visit the well known Louis Mulcahy Pottery, where you can watch a pot taking shape, and perhaps make a purchase from the good selection of ceramics on sale.

Dunquin and the Blasket Islands

The Blaskets are made up of several tiny islands plus the Great Blasket, all now uninhabited. Charles Haughey, the former Taoiseach and a fellow still surrounded by seemingly eternal investigations about alleged influence-peddling, owns one of them as a holiday retreat. Recently, plans to protect the islands by making them into a national park (including compulsory purchase) have been given the go-ahead, though strangely enough, Haughey's island will not be included.

Some beautiful writing has sprung from the **Great Blasket**, produced just before the islands' way of life collapsed in the 1940s. The young emigrated because of the harsh living conditions, and the Great Blasket has been uninhabited since 1953. Accounts of island life left to us record the warmth and the fun as well as the misery and heartbreak of their hard way of life. Their acceptance of death and life has great dignity, as does their sense of comradeship with the others on the island. There are three autobiographies written in the 1920s and 1930s: *The Islandman* by Tomas O'Crohan, *Twenty Years a-Growing* by Maurice O'Sullivan, and the autobiography of Peig Sayers. All are worth reading for the humour, pathos and command of the Gaelic language, which comes through even in translation.

The Blasket Centre in **Dunquin** (*open Easter–Sept, daily 10–6, July–Aug 10–7; adm; t (066) 915 6444*) focuses on the story of the Blasket Islands. Unlike Horace's inn, 'the interior is better than the exterior'. Even though it looks like an oversized public convenience from the outside (its primary function for many of the tour bus passengers that find their way there) the exhibition is excellent. An unusual attraction in Dunquin is '**The Enchanted Forest**' (*t (066) 915 6234*), a fairytale museum full of fantasy, fun and friendly bears taking a journey through a mythical forest of the seasons, in search of holidays. Incidentally, this little place became famous after the film *Ryan's Daughter* was filmed here, and there's a *Ryan's Daughter* walking route around Dunquin, as well as mementoes from the later film *Far and Away*.

You can visit the Blaskets from Dingle or Dunquin Harbour. Kruger's Pub in Dunquin is the place to enquire about boats and departure times. Regular ferries to the islands take about 25 minutes from Dunquin. You might be lucky and persuade a local to take you out there in a curragh, the boat used for centuries by the island men to catch the shining mackerel found in these waters. When you arrive, you will see that the Great Blasket is full of memories. If you have read the literature, you will recognize the White Strand where the islanders played hurling on Christmas morning. Sadly, the stone walls around the intensively farmed fields have now tumbled, and the village is a ruin. Tomas O'Crohan wrote at the end of his account: 'somewhere there should be a memorial of it all...for the like of us will never be again'. It is a pleasant walk up to the ruined hill-fort and there are wonderful views; you might also catch a glimpse of Blasket's new inhabitants – red deer, recently transplanted from Killarney.

Ballyferriter to Tralee

Back on the mainland again, heading north up round the peninsula, you arrive at **Ballyferriter**, a small village popular with holidaymakers because of the good beaches close by. It was named after the Anglo-Norman family of Ferriter who built the nearby ruined Castle Sybil. The most famous of that family was Pierce Ferriter, who wrote courtly love poetry; a soldier who was executed in Killarney when Cromwell and his forces rampaged through Ireland. There is a friendly co-operative here that grows parsley to export to France. They are also very keen on preserving their heritage, namely the Gaelic language, antiquities and beautiful scenery. Their displays on the archaeology, flora and fauna of the area can be seen at the **Chorca Dhuibhne Heritage Centre**, Ballyferriter (*open Easter and June–Sept; adm; t (066) 915 6333/6100*). At **Ballydavid** the ancient industry of curragh-making goes on. The beaches around here are magnificent, in particular **Smerwick Strand**. In any of these you might find Kerry diamonds – sparkly pieces of quartz that make a more attractive souvenir than anything you could buy.

Everywhere are signs of past wars and struggles. One such ruin is Dun an Oir, or Fort de Oro, built by Spanish forces in 1579 when they and some Irish dug themselves in during the rebellion against Elizabeth I. Lord Grey, her deputy, took the fort, and the garrison was massacred. The road that leads past Castle Sybil towards Ferriter's Cove is very pot-holed, not recommended if you are in a car; it is more comfortable to stroll amongst the superb views of the sea cliffs and Smerwick Harbour.

East of Ballyferriter, signs point the way to the **Oratory of Gallarus**, the most perfect relic of early Irish architecture, and a sight not to be missed (*always accessible, entry free*). You approach through a fuchsia-lined path amongst the green fields. This tiny, inverted, tent-shaped church may go back as far as the 8th century; no one knows. There is more art in it than meets the eye; despite their accidental appearance, all the stones in it were carefully shaped, and they fit together so well that not a drop of rain has got in for over a thousand years. The only missing parts of the original building are the crosses that stood at each end of the roof ridge. A visit here, along with a look at the reconstructed plans of the monastery at Ardfert (*see* p.198), provides a vision of the remarkable aesthetic of Irish building in the early medieval golden age – round, walled settlements, round huts and towers, and strange, striking shapes like that of Gallarus. It's fascinating to speculate how Irish architecture would have evolved, had the local traditions not been destroyed by the Vikings and supplanted by foreign forms under the English.

At the crossroads above Gallarus, take a sharp left for **Kilmalkedar Church**, built in Irish Romanesque style in the 12th century. There must have been an earlier pagan settlement here as there are some ancient carved stones around the site, including an ogham stone and an early sundial. Nearby, close to a ruined house for the clergy, is the Saint's Road up **Brandon Mountain** (Cnoc Breanainn – Brendan's Hill, 3,127ft/950m). This ancient track leads up to **St Brendan the Navigator's Shrine**. St Brendan climbed up to its summit to meditate and saw in a vision Hy-Brasil, the Island of the Blessed, and afterwards he voyaged far and wide looking for this ideal land, possibly even as far as America. People still climb up here on the last Saturday in June to pray. An easier climb can be made from the village of **Cloghane**, and the views from it are magical. It's not surprising that St Brendan saw Utopia from here.

The main (unnumbered) road from Dingle to Stradbally and that on to Tralee (R560) take you over the **Connor Pass**, the summit of which is at 1,500ft (497m), to reveal great views over Dingle Bay and Tralee Bay. There are dark loughs in the valley and giant boulders strewn everywhere. At the foot of the pass, a branch road leads off towards Cloghane and Brandon, both good bases for exploring and climbing the sea cliffs around Brandon Point and Brandon Head. It is worth buying a good specialist map in Dingle that marks all the ancient sites in this area. **Brandon Bay** looks temptingly calm at times, but it is a dangerous anchorage; mountains encircle it, and the road is high above the sloping fields that edge the long beach. The **Brandon Heritage Centre** (*adm; t (066) 713 8137*) has items of local interest and old photos of Brandon. Tomasin's Bar and Restaurant in **Stradbally** has framed newspaper cuttings that record the sinking of The Port of Yorrock, a barque from Glasgow returning from America which tragically went down with all hands. There is a memorial to the crew on Kilcummin Strand.

This area is well worth spending some time in if you base yourself in or near **Castlegregory**. You could explore the sandy spit of the peninsula that ends at Rough Point, whilst the **Magharee Islands**, made of limestone and sometimes called The Seven Hogs, are scattered even further northwards. To the south towers **Beenoskee Mountain** and beside it the slightly smaller Stradbally. Beenoskee summit gives you sublime views in every direction. Surfing and swimming are excellent here, and an interesting trip can be made to **Illauntannig**, one of the Magharee islands. On it are the remains of an old monastic ruin, surrounded by a *cashel*. The limestone gives the coast distinctive, rough-ridged and fluted shapes. On the spit is Lough Gill, a shallow, brackish lagoon where the Berwick swan and other water birds have made their home. A variety of flowers thrive on the water's edges, and in the lough itself are large yellow waterlilies. On the main road into Tralee you will pass Blennerville (*see* p.197).

Tralee

Tralee is the chief town and administrative capital of County Kerry, and is invariably jam-packed with cars and shoppers. It is famous outside Ireland for the sentimental Victorian song, *The Rose of Tralee*. The town was the chief seat of the Desmond family, but nothing remains of their strong castle. In 1579 the Earl of Desmond was asked to aid the Commissioners of Munster against the Spanish who had landed at Smerwick, but the Desmonds had no love for the English, and that night the representatives of Queen Elizabeth and their entourage were put to death by the Earl's brother. In the following year a ruthless campaign of retribution was waged against the Desmonds. Tralee was threatened and the Earl fired the town rather than leave anything that might be claimed as a prize by the Queen's men. In 1583 the Earl of Desmond, then an old man, was hunted from his hiding place in Glanageenty woods and beheaded. His head was sent to decorate a spike on London Bridge. The old Dominican priory that the Desmonds founded was completely destroyed by the Elizabethan courtier-soldier Sir Edward Denny, who was granted the town when the Desmond estates were seized.

The town has suffered continually from wars and burnings, and today is largely mid-19th-century in character, although there are some elegant Georgian houses in

Tourist Information

Tralee: Ashe Hall, **t** (066) 712 1288, **f** (066) 712 1700; *open all year.*

Shopping

Antiques
15 Princes St, **t** (066) 712 5635. Georgian house with seven rooms furnished with books, prints and antiques for sale.

Crafts
Carraig Donn Knitwear, Bridge Street, Tralee. **John J Murphy Weavers**, Currow Road, Farranfore, **t** (066) 976 4659.

Delicacies
Sean Cara, Abbey Court, Tralee. Excellent cheeses, home-made bread and lemon curd.

Sports and Activities

Art Galleries
The Wellspring, 16 Denny St, **t** (066) 712 1218.

Clay Pigeon Shooting
Castleisland Shooting Grounds, Limerick Road, Castleisland, **t** (066) 714 1709.

Donkey Rambles
Slattery's, Russell Street, **t** (066) 712 4088. Hires out a donkey, saddlebags and maps for €30 a day.

Golf
Tralee Golf Club, West Barrow, Ardfert, **t** (066) 713 6379. Links by Arnold Palmer.
Kerries Golf Course, The Kerries, **t** (066) 712 2112

Greyhound Racing
Oakview Park, Tralee, **t** (066) 712 5416, Tues and Fri at 8pm. Restaurant, **t** (066) 80008.

Horse-drawn Caravans
Slattery's, Russell Street, **t** (066) 712 9122.

Horse-racing
Look in the local newspapers, or in the back of the free calendar of events available from any tourist office.
Tralee: in June and Aug.

the centre. The courthouse has a fine Ionic façade, and in Denny Street there is an impressive 1798 memorial of a single man armed with a pike. In Ashe Street the Dominican **Church of the Holy Cross** is by Pugin, built after the monks had managed to re-establish themselves here, long after Sir Edward Denny destroyed their priory. The priory garden contains some ancient carved stones, amongst them the White Knight stone and the Roche slab which date from 1685, proof that the foundation was at least partly in existence in the rein of James II. The interior is very fine, especially the Chapel of the Blessed Virgin, with exquisite mosaics and altar charts by that great artist Michael Healy, who worked in the early 20th century. In Abbey Street there is a modern **church** with a lovely chapel dedicated to the Blessed Virgin Mary, which contains some of Healy's fine stained glass work.

The **Ashe Memorial Hall**, an imposing 19th-century building off Denny Street, is a very fine county museum (*open all year, Mon–Sat 10–6, Sun 2–6; adm;* **t** (066) 712 7777). The display, entitled 'Kerry, The Kingdom', traces the history of Kerry from 5000 BC, and the exhibits include archaeological treasures found in Kerry. There is some fascinating black and white film footage taken during the War of Independence and after, up until 1965. Thomas Ashe, after whom this building is named, was a native of Tralee, and active in the 1916 Uprising and the IRB. He was arrested and imprisoned in Mountjoy Prison, where he went on hunger strike as a protest at being treated as an ordinary convict, and not as a political prisoner. After he was roughly force-fed, fluid

Open Farms

Beech Grove Farm, Castleisland, t (066) 714 1217.

Farmworld, Camp, t (066) 915 8200.

Pony-trekking

El Rancho Riding Centre, t (066) 712 1840.

Kennedy's, Cahirwisheen, t (066) 712 6453.

Eagle Lodge Equestrian Centre, t (066) 713 7266.

Water Sports

The Aqua Dome, Ballyard, t (066) 712 8899.

Where to Stay

Tralee t (066-)

Castlemorris House, Ballymullen, t 718 0060 (*inexpensive*). Large, 18th-century house in extensive gardens, a short walk from the city centre. With a pleasant drawing room, spacious bedrooms, welcoming open fires and a friendly atmosphere.

Collis Sandes House, Oakpark, t 712 8658, *www.colsands.com* (*inexpensive*). Imposing

Victorian country house that also features wonderful, traditional musical entertainment in the evenings.

Finnegans, 17 Denny Street, t 712 7610 (*inexpensive*). 18th-century town house with a basement bistro/restaurant.

Tralee Townhouse, High Street, t/f 718 1111 (*inexpensive*). Conveniently located in the city centre.

Eating Out

Tralee t (066-)

Swedish Bistro, McCowan's Lane, off Castle Street, t 712 1711 (*moderate*). Impressive dishes served all day from an extensive menu.

Ashes Bar, Upper Camp, t 713 0133 (*inexpensive*). Very good seafood platter at lunchtime, with a more elaborate à la carte menu in the evening, and traditional music in the summer.

Roots Cafe, 76 Boherbue, t 712 2665 (*inexpensive*). Vegetarian café with a loyal, local following and imaginatively varied menu. Lunchtime only.

got into his windpipe and then his lungs, and he died a few hours later. He was a close friend and ally of Michael Collins, who described him as 'a man of no complexes. Doing whatever he did for Ireland and always in a quiet way'.

Another attraction is a life-size reconstruction of a street in medieval Tralee – you travel through it in a 'time-car', seeing and smelling what street life was like in the walled Desmond town, so different from the Tralee of today with its supermarket, multi-screen cinema complex and aqua-dome fun centre. The town park surrounding the museum and tourist office is well maintained with pretty trees and, of course, there is a rose garden, which is at its best during the Rose of Tralee Festival (*see* p.170).

Past the rose garden is the headquarters of **Siamsa Tire, the National Folk Theatre**, which presents performances of song, dance and mime in an idealized version of rural life. During the winter the venue is available to travelling theatres (*t (066) 712 3055*). Those with children can carry on around the corner to the **Science Works**, Godfrey Place (*t (066) 712 9855*), an interactive science museum.

The **Tralee steam train** (*runs May–Oct, on the hour 11–5*), a relic of the old Tralee and Dingle narrow-gauge railway, leaves from Ballyard station. The 3km jaunt takes you to **Blennerville Windmill**, the largest in the British Isles, complete with restaurant and craft shops (*open April–Oct, daily 10–6; adm*). **Blennerville** used to be the port for Tralee, although it is now silted up. The shipyard includes a visitor's centre (*open daily 9–6; adm*), with exhibits on traditional shipbuilding and the emigrant experience.

Blennerville was the initial site for the construction of the *Jeanie Johnston*, a replica of an 18th-century sailing ship built from the original plans (*www.iol.ie/kerry-insight/ jeanie-johnston/centre.html*). The original *Jeanie* was a passenger ship that carried emigrants to America in the years of the famine. The finishing touches to the replica are currently being carried out in Dingle and they hope to recreate the voyage to the USA and Canada soon. It is interesting to look at the intricate family tree of the Blennerhassetts, a family who ruled over these parts in the 18th century and renamed the place in their honour. One of them tried to abolish the Puck Fair in Killorglin, but luckily the locals refused to comply. One of the family's old homes is at Ballyseedy House, now a hotel. East of Tralee, near Castleisland is **Crag Cave**, signposted off the N21 Limerick–Tralee road (*open March–Nov, daily 10–5.30, July–Aug, 10–6; adm; t (066) 714 1244; www.cragcave.com*), an underground cave system discovered in 1983 that is at least 4km long, and is now now a big tourist attraction.

North Kerry

Spa to Kilflyn's Bog

North Kerry has none of the splendour of Dingle but rather a quiet charm, a taste of which you will get if you drive between Tralee and Tarbert on your way to County Clare. Places to visit in north Kerry include the village of **Spa**, once famous for its sulphurous waters, and **Fenit**, a small fishing port, from where the coastal views on a bright day are stunning. One attraction on a rainy day for those with children is **Fenit Seaworld** (*t (066) 713 8544*), the aquarium takes as its theme fishy life on and around a shipwreck. On a fine day, the trips and island barbecues on The Maherees in Tralee Bay offered by West Kerry Angling and Fenit Sea Cruise Centre, Fenit Pier (*t (066) 713 6049*) are bracing.

A very well-known ecclesiastical site, built on St Brendan's original foundation, is **Ardfert Cathedral** on the R551, a noble Norman building dating from the 13th century and partially restored (*open June–Sept daily 9.30–6.30; guided tours; adm*). Exhibits inside detail Ardfert's history as a monastic centre from the earliest times. The great nave remains without a roof, and the authorities have had to put up a sign to forbid locals from making any new burials inside. Besides the cathedral the grounds contain a picturesque graveyard with those vault-like graves that are common here, and the remains of the early Romanesque church that the cathedral replaced, which has a beautiful carved south window. Beside it is **Temple-na-griffin**, a late Gothic ruin. Ardfert was an important settlement in the early Middle Ages, and probably long before then. The surrounding countryside is full of ring-forts and other ancient relics, along with an austerely handsome 15th-century Franciscan **friary** and **church** just down the road from the cathedral.

Banna, about two miles to the west of Ardfert, is a place of dunes, caravans and a beach that is at least six miles long. It is known in Irish history as the place where Roger Casement was captured after landing from a German submarine. He had

Tourist Information

Listowel: St John's Church, t (068) 22590; *open June–Sept.*

Sports and Activities

Fishing
Celtic Sea Angling, Fenit, t (066) 713 6118.

Golf
Listowel Golf Club, Feale View, Listowel, t (068) 21592.
Old Course and Cashen Course, Ballybunion, t (068) 27146.

Horse Racing
Look in the local newspapers, or in the back of the free calendar of events available from any tourist office.There is racing at **Listowel** in September.

Pony-trekking
Curragh Cottage, The Spa, t (066) 713 6320.

Open Farms
Beal Lodge Dairy Farm, Asdee, Listowel, t (068) 41137. Sells farmhouse cheese.
Lixnaw Agricultural Museum, Lixnaw, t (066) 713 2202.

Seaweed Baths
Collins Family, North Beach, Ballybunion, t (068) 27469. *Open June– early Oct.*
Daly's Baths, Ladies' Strand, Ballybunion, t (068) 27559. *Open June–end Sept.*

Water Sports
There is good **swimming** to be had at Ballyheige and Banna Strand.
Atlantic Pleasure Craft, Fenit Pier, t (066) 712 3248. Hires speedboats, ski boats and jet skis.

Where to Stay

The White Sands Hotel, Ballyheige, t (066) 713 3102. Family-run hotel surrounded by wonderful west coast beaches. Jimmy Browne's Pub, in the hotel, frequently hosts traditional music sessions.
Listowel Arms, The Square, Listowel, t (068) 21500 *(moderate).* Old-fashioned country hotel and hospitality.
Harty Costello Townhouse, Main Street, Ballybunion, t (068) 27129 *(moderate).* Upmarket pub with accommodation, serving Ballybunion's golfers.
Iragh Ti Connor, Main Street, Ballybunion, t (068) 27122, *raghticonnor@eircom.net (moderate).* Warm and welcoming, with open fires, a cosy bar, period furniture and walled gardens.

Eating Out

The Oyster Tavern, The Spa, Fenit, t (066) 713 6102 *(expensive).* Excellent seafood in an unlikely setting.
Kate Browne's Pub, Ardfert, t (066) 34055. Extensive bar menu in a pub with lots of local character.
Allo's Bar and Bistro, 41 Church Street, Listowel, t (068) 22880 *(moderate).* Great food – far better than just pub grub.

travelled to Germany to enlist support and was returning with a cargo of arms, which were to be used in the Easter Rising. The plans went terribly wrong, and Casement was taken to London where he was tried, found guilty of high treason and hanged. His remains were returned to Ireland and he was given a state funeral in 1965. You can find the monument to him on the beach, past the caravan park.

Ballyheige is a small village on a continuation of Banna Strand; the white sand and views of Kerry Head make it popular with holidaymakers. The skeleton of a fin whale washed up on the beach a few years ago is preserved in the Maritime Centre (*t (066) 713 3666*). Going inland, signposted after the village of Ballyduff, is **Rattoo Round Tower** and ruined priory, rising from among the flat fields. The tower is one of the most perfect examples of its kind, and is in good condition. The graveyard has the usual mixture of old and new gravestones and is overgrown with delicate ivy and hart's-tongue fern. **Rattoo Heritage Centre** (*t (066) 712 9752; adm*) has a display on the local archaeology, history and folklore of north Kerry. On the main road between Tralee and Listowel at Kilflyn is 'A Day in The Bog' (*t (066) 713 2555*), which recreates an Irish bog farmer's life.

Writers and Seaweed Baths: Listowel to Tarbert

Listowel has ambitions as a cultural centre and puts on a Writers' Week every year in May, with a book fair, art and photography exhibitions and short-story-writing workshops (*dates change every year, check with tourist office for details*). This attractive town is situated on the River Feale, on the flat Kerry plain, with a ruined 15th-century castle in the square. It belonged to the Fitzmaurice family, Anglo-Normans who later showed consistent disloyalty to the Crown. Also in the square is a handsome Catholic church, and on the outskirts of the town is a racecourse. Many writers came from this area; of particular note are Bryan MacMahon, whose wonderful novel *Children of the Rainbow* will keep you entranced with its descriptions of the Kerry countryside; and prolific novelist and playwright John B. Keane, whose pub is on William Street. His novel *The Field* became an Oscar-winning film. Listowel has some remarkable plaster-work shopfronts by Pat McAuliffe (1846–1921), The Maid of Erin on Church Street being the most rococo. **St John's Arts Centre**, on The Square in the late Georgian Church of Ireland church, has a weekly programme of theatre, music, dance and exhibitions and occasional evening shows (*open daily 9.30–6; t (068) 22566*).

On the coast, some 10 miles (16km) northwest of Listowel on the R553, is the delightful and popular resort of **Ballybunion**. The golden sand is divided by a black rocky promontory on which perches the dramatic remains of a 14th-century castle. Besides good sea bathing, you can have a hot **seaweed bath**, which is very relaxing, leaves your skin feeling like silk and seems to take away any aches and pains; it is very popular with jockeys after the Listowel races. The seaweed baths are right down on the beach (*see* 'Sports and Activities', p.199). The views of Kerry Head and Loop Head in County Clare are magnificent and there are bracing long walks along the cliffs to Beal Point, which overlooks the Shannon Estuary. See if you can persuade a boatman to take you out to the intricate and connecting caves within the cliffs; the largest is known as the Pigeon Cave. Most people come here for the beach and the golf, and there are plenty of ugly hotels, enlivened by the bright oranges and ochres with which they are painted. B&Bs line the road towards the golf course, and bang next to the smart-looking club house is the parish burial ground, among the dunes and cropped grass. It's rather an incongruous sight, especially when the mourners meet the golfers. The **Heritage Centre and Museum** (*t (068) 27799*) at Greenfields on Church Road has some interesting relics from the Marconi Station and the Lartigue mono-railway that ran to Listowel.

Carrigafoyle Castle, north of Ballylongford, is a 16th-century O'Connor castle that stands by the shoreline. It was built of carboniferous sandstone, which has weathered well. It is always accessible and you can walk to the battlements by a winding stone staircase to get a stunning view. If you are taking the car ferry across to County Clare from Tarbert, you can stop to see the **Bridewell Courthouse and Jail** (*open April–Oct daily 10–6; adm; **t** (068) 36500*). The buildings have been restored with tableaux, exhibits and documents to show what justice and prison were like for local people in Victorian times when the British still ruled. Especially interesting are the accounts of life on transportation ships going to Australia, and the verse of the neglected poet Thomas MacGreevy (1894–1967) who came from around here. A short, signposted walk leads from the courthouse through mature mixed woods, part of the demesne of **Tarbert House** (*open May–Aug, Mon–Sat 10am–noon and 2–4pm, Sun am only; adm; **t** (068) 36198*), a fine, grey 18th-century mansion of the Leslie family that can be glimpsed from the avenue.

County Cork

Imagine quiet flowing rivers in green wooded valleys, a coastline which combines savage rock scenery with the softest bays, hillslopes which are purple in the late summer with heather, an ivy-clad castle standing amongst hayricks in a field, and you have captured something of County Cork. This is Ireland's largest county and includes some of the richest agricultural land in the northeast, the third largest city in Ireland, the important ocean port of Cobh, as well as the most beautiful coastal and mountain scenery in the country and a climate famously mild because of the warm Gulf Stream. It is also the most suitable spot to indulge in the relaxing pastimes of eating and drinking: you'll find some of Ireland's best hotels and rest-aurants located in attractive settings all over the county. There is wonderful sailing, deep-sea angling, and salmon- and trout-fishing amongst its 680 miles (1,094km) of indented coastline, with beautiful stately homes and gardens to visit, and, of course, the Blarney Stone to kiss. The growth of tourism has not yet spoilt the coast: it has just encouraged better-quality craft shops, pubs, restaurants and hotels. Many of the most discerning visitors are the Corkonians themselves, who work hard in the city and play in the pretty coastal resorts of Kinsale and Crosshaven.

The city is something else: the country people may be slow-spoken and laid-back, but the people have produced a cosmopolitan centre humming with energy and confidence, full of grand buildings and shops, industry and culture, aided by a wit and business sense that is hard to beat. Dubliners alternate between jealousy and heavy sarcasm in trying to describe the place – the best I heard was 'God's own place with the devil's own people'. Corkonians think nothing of nipping across to Paris for the weekend, and there is an air of cultural sophistication which seriously challenges Dublin's role as the cultural capital. The Triskel Arts Centre in the city centre is excellent and puts on a great variety of events all year round, whilst the Crawford Art Gallery has a memorable collection of Irish and English works.

Corkonians are a mixed bunch, consisting of the down-to-earth working class and the monied middle class, which includes a rather genteel Protestant element whose

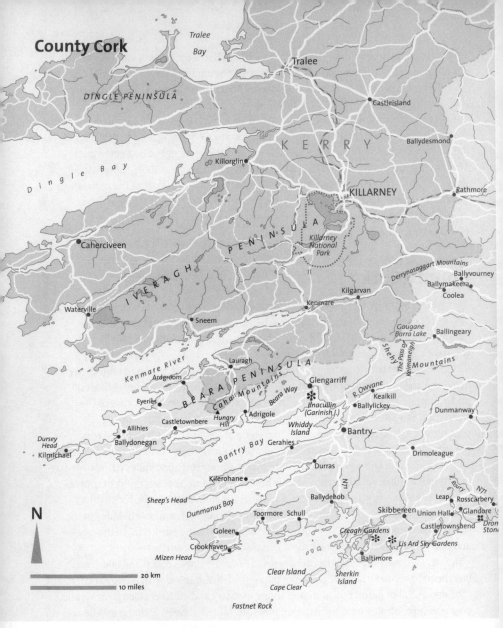

County Cork

Tralee Bay

Tralee

DINGLE PENINSULA

Castleisland

KERRY

Ballydesmond

Dingle Bay

Killorglin

KILLARNEY

Rathmore

Cahirciveen

IVERAGH PENINSULA

Killarney National Park

Derrynasaggart Mountains

Ballyvourney

Ballymakeera

Coolea

Waterville

Sneem

Kenmare

Kilgarvan

Gougane Barra Lake

Ballingeary

Kenmare River

Lauragh

Ardgroom

BEARA PENINSULA

Caha Mountains

Eyeries

Castletownbere

Hungry Hill

Adrigole

Beara Way

Glengarriff

Shehy Mountains

The Pass of Keimaneigh

R. Owvane

Kealkill

Ballylickey

Dunmanway

Ilnacullin (Garinish I.)

Whiddy Island

Bantry

Dursey Head

Allihies

Ballydonegan

Kilmichael

Bantry Bay

Gerahies

Durras

Drimoleague

Kilcrohane

Ballydehob

N71

Sheep's Head

Dunmanus Bay

Toormore Schull

Skibbereen

Leap

Rosscarbery

R. Ilen

N71

Union Hall

Glandore

Castletownshend

Drom Stone

Goleen

Creagh Gardens

Lis Ard Sky Gardens

Crookhaven

Mizen Head

Baltimore

N

Clear Island

Sherkin Island

Cape Clear

20 km

10 miles

Fastnet Rock

forebears manned the British Empire; as well as quite a few 'blow-ins' – English, Europeans and North Americans who have come for a variety of reasons and settled down to enjoy the way of life. You will notice these incomers especially in west Cork, where some have restored traditional cottages and farms; produce vegetables, arts and crafts, and practise an alternative lifestyle. The Cork accent is very strong, slow and sing-songy, and you may have to concentrate to understand it.

LIMERICK
Broadford
Mullaghareirk Mountains
Kilmallock
TIPPERARY
Galty Mountains
Ardpatrick
Castle Oliver
Liscarroll
Kilcolman Castle
Kildorrey
N73
Mitchelstown
Mitchelstown Caves
Knockmealdown Mountains
Buttevant
Doneraile
R. Awbeg
N8
Kanturk
N72
N20
Castletownroche
Glanworth
Kilworth
Mallow
Killavullen
Nagles Mountains
Castle Hyde
Fermoy
N72
Ballyduff
WATERFORD
Lismore
Millstreet
River Blackwater
Castlelyons
Conna
River Bride
Boggeragh Mountains
Glenville
N72
River Blackwater
CORK
N20
Blarney
Knockraha
Dungourney
Youghal
Macroom
Carrigadrohid
Dripsey
Coachford
Riverstown
Dunkathel House
Barryscourt Castle
N25
Inishcarra Reservoir
Farnanes
N22
Ballincollig
CORK
Carrigtohill
Midleton
Castlemartyr
Youghal Bay
Crookstown
Carrigrohane
Blackrock
N25
Ladybridge
Kilcredan
Ballymaloe House
Douglas
Passage West
Cobh
Monkstown
Ballinhassig
Ringaskiddy
Cloyne
Shanagarry
Garryvoe
Ballycotton
Carrigaline
N71
Crosshaven
Bandon
Inishannon
Myrtleville
Swansea & the continent
Bandon River
Ballynacarriga
Dunderrow
Rossmore
R. Argideen
Ballindee
Kinsale
Robert's Cove
Kilbrittain
Summercove
Castle Gardens
Charles Fort
Oysterhaven
Clonakilty
Timoleague
Ballinspittle
Courtmacsherry
Garrettstown
Inchydoney Island
Butlerstown
Old Head of Kinsale
Castle Freke
beg Circle
Galley Head

History

The well-watered and fertile lands of Cork attracted human settlement as far back as 6000 BC, when people lived by hunting, fishing and gathering roots and berries. Kitchen middens found around the shores of Cork Harbour date from this time. From the Megalithic period there are stone circles, standing stones and wedge tombs to explore; luckily these have survived because farmers did not touch them, believing them to be fairy places. Various waves of invaders brought different peoples, with the

Getting There and Around

By Air

There is a regular shuttle service from the bus station on Merchants' Quay to the airport, south of the city on the N27; the bus takes 20mins and is moderately cheaper than a taxi. Cork Airport has regular flights to Dublin and London, as well as Manchester, Paris and Amsterdam, and additional services in summer.

Cork Airport, t (021) 431 3131, *www.cork-airport.com*.

Cork Aviation Centre, t (021) 888 747. Air-taxi service offering aerial sightseeing tours.

By Rail

Cork is linked to Dublin and other areas by an excellent rail network. Trains run from Kent Station, including a suburban service to Cobh. For all passenger enquiries, bus or train, call **t** (021) 504888.

By Bus

Expressway buses service Dublin and other big towns, and there's a good local bus service in Co. Cork. Most local buses pass down St Patrick's Street. During summer, open-top bus tours of Cork and Blarney are available.

Cork City Depot, Merchant's Quay, Parnell Place, **t** (021) 506066/508188.

By Boat

There is a car and passenger ferry at Ringaskiddy, 3 miles (6km) from the city centre, on the road to Kinsale. Brittany Ferries has a Mar–Oct service to Roscoff in Brittany; in summer Irish Ferries go to Roscoff, as well as Le Havre and Cherbourg. There is also a crossing run by Swansea-Cork Ferries to Britain. *See* **Travel**, p.118, for more information.

By Bike

The Raleigh Rent-a-Bike network operates here. Local dealers are:

Kramer's Bicycles, Glengarriff Road, Newtown, Bantry, **t** (027) 50278.

Roycroft Bikes, Ilen Street, Skibbereen, **t** (028) 21235.

Shortcastle Cycles, Shortcastle Street, Mallow, **t** (022) 21843.

J. O'Donovan, McSweeney Quay, Bandon, **t** (023) 41227.

Bikes are also available for hire from the following:

Irish Cycle Hire, Cork Train Station, **t** (021) 455 1430.

Rothar Cycle Tours, 2 Bandon Road, Cork, **t** (021) 431 3133.

Mylie Murphy, 14 Pearse St, Kinsale, **t** (021) 477 2703.

Getting to the Islands

Cruises to offshore islands leaving from Kinsale are run by **Shearwater Cruises,** Seaview Farm, Kilbrittain, **t** (023) 49610, or, to reach specific islands, ferries are as follows:

Bear Island: Off Castletownbere, Bantry Bay. Two ferries run frequently during summer. Contact Colm Harrington, **t** (027) 75000; or Patrick Murphy, **t** (027) 75004.

Cape Clear Island: During the summer months, the island is serviced by two ferries:

Celts arriving between 800 and 500 BC. Written history dates from the coming of Christianity and later clerics recorded the sagas, annals and laws of this Celtic culture which had been left intact on the edge of the Roman Empire. St Ciaran of Cape Clear is titled 'first-born of the Saints of Ireland', and it is claimed that he arrived before St Patrick in the 5th century AD. Early church sites abound, and the metalwork and carved stone that survives from the 11th and 12th centuries testifies to the mastery and skill of the Celtic artist. The Norsemen or Vikings mounted many raids on the early Christian settlements from the late 8th century onwards. They soon founded their own ports, settling down to trade with the native Irish, accepted Christianity, and so gradually became amalgamated into Gaelic society, especially in the southeast. With the invasion of the Anglo-Normans in 1169 the continental religious orders were set up in rich and beautiful abbeys. Some of their ruins remain. The Anglo-Norman invasion also brought advanced building techniques to Ireland: the Norman warlords one departing Schull and one departing Baltimore. The Baltimore ferry runs at least twice daily, May–Sept, **t** (028) 39119. The Schull ferry operates daily, June–Sept; **t** (028) 28138.

Heir Island: Departs Cunamore Pier, off Bantry Road, Skibbereen, **t** (028) 38144.

Schull to Baltimore via Heir Island, Horse Island and Cape Clear Island: West Cork Coastal Cruises, **t** (028) 39153/39172, or (087) 268 0760. Departs Baltimore and Schull.

Sherkin Island: The ferry from Baltimore sails seven times daily during summer and takes about 10mins; **t** (028) 20125.

Whiddy Island: Off Bantry in Bantry Bay. Contact Danny O'Leary, **t** (027) 50310.

Festivals

April
International Choral and Folk Dance Festival, Cork (late April–early May).

May
Rugby Sevens Tournament, Kinsale (first Bank Holiday weekend).
Mussel Festival, Bantry (early May).
Denis Murphy's Weekend, Knocknagree, Mallow; music and dance (end of May).

June
Garden Festival, Cork (7–16th)
Cullen Pipe Band Contest, Cullen.
St John's Bonfire Festival, Glenville.

July
Classic Boat Regatta, Glandore.
Classical Music Festival, Castletownshend.
Arts Festival, Youghal (first week).
Cahirmee Horse Fair, Buttevant.

July–August
International Busking Festival, Youghal.
Regatta and Homecoming Festival, Kinsale.
Music Fair, Millstreet. Featuring major international stars.
Folk Festival, Mallow.

August
Regattas, Glandore, Glengarriff, Schull and Baltimore.
Ballydehob Gala (mid-Aug).
Feile Fhearmui, Fermoy and Rockchapel. Celebration of traditional music and dance.
Horse Races, Mallow.
Horse Show, Millstreet.

September
International Storytelling Festival, Cape Clear Island.

October
International Film Festival, Cork (mid-Oct).
Jazz Festival, Cork, *www.corkjazzfestival.com.*
Gourmet Festival, Kinsale.
Fringe Jazz Festival, Kinsale.

November
International Horse Show, Millstreet.

built sophisticated castles, usually on defensive sites which had been used before. Their followers lived in moated farmhouses. The Gaelic ruling families – MacCarthys, O'Sullivans, O'Mahonys, O'Driscolls and O'Donovans – generally lost out to the Norman Barrys and their followers. In the 15th century the ruling families built tower houses and many of these grand ruins remain to add drama and interest to the countryside and coastline (Blarney Castle is one of the best surviving examples). Comfortable domestic architecture did not develop until the 17th and 18th centuries, because until then the county was very unsettled, as the Celts and Anglo-Normans fought, made alliances with and against each other, and largely ignored the laws issued from London. It was only the area around Dublin, known as 'the Pale', that was really under the thumb of the English.

After the Elizabethan wars of the late 16th century, the land was colonized with families loyal to the crown, who supported the administrators sent to implement

English rule. Huge tracts of land were granted to adventurers; men like Richard Boyle, who became Earl of Cork, and Sir Edmund Spenser, who wrote *The Faerie Queene* at Kilcoman Castle. Beautiful Georgian houses survive from the 18th century, especially in the richer farmlands of Cork, a time when the new landowners began to feel secure in their properties and able to build, plant and garden. It is possible to stay in some of these fine houses, which are not huge, but perfect in proportion and decoration. Nowadays, many of these houses are being bought up by the increasingly prosperous Irish, and foreign buyers. There is a new regard for the craftsmanship of the mainly Irish workers who created them, and a reassessment of the landed gentry, who were not necessarily all as bad as they have been portrayed.

By contrast, the oppressive laws introduced to control the Catholic population in the 1690s, the Rising of 1798 and the ghastly famine of the 1840s all combined to create a peasantry that was poverty stricken. Large families relied almost totally on the potato, and the failure of the crop in successive years brought starvation, disease and death to thousands in County Cork. The fight for fair rents and fixity of tenure was pursued vigorously in the 1880s. The Irish War of Independence was fought with ferocity in County Cork, with burnings and cruelties on both sides. The Civil War split family loyalties in two, and it was especially bitter in County Cork where anti-treaty forces were in control. Michael Collins (1890–1922), the dynamic revolutionary leader and one of the men responsible for negotiating the Anglo-Irish Treaty of December 1921, was the son of a small farmer from Clonakilty. During the Civil War he was shot in the head by the anti-Treaty forces in an ambush between Macroom and Bandon.

Today, the memories of the Civil War are still alive, but the people are forward-looking and sophisticated. Industries such as whiskey-making, brewing, clothing, food-processing, computers and pharmaceuticals have boomed around Cork Harbour. The drug Viagra, among others, is made in Ringaskiddy for Pfizer, as well as artificial hips and knees produced for Johnson and Johnson; as you can imagine, there are a good many jokes that circulate in the local bars.

Cork City and Environs

The name Cork comes from the Gaelic *Corcaigh*, which means 'a marshy place'. Ireland's second city, with a population of 135,000, is built on marshy land on the banks of the River Lee, and has crept up the hills. Over the years nearly all the islands in this marsh have been reclaimed, their watercourses built over and the city walls removed. The river flows in two main channels, crossed by bridges, so that central Cork is actually on an island. It can be confusing if you are driving there for the first time, with its one-way roads and the crossing and recrossing of the river.

Until the Anglo-Norman invasion in 1179, Cork City was largely a Danish stronghold. It was famous from the 7th century for its excellent school under St Finbarr. The Cork citizens were an independent lot, and, although after 1180 English laws were nominally in force, it was really the wealthy merchants who were in charge. In 1492 they took up the cause of the Yorkists and Perkin Warbeck, and went with him to Kent where he was proclaimed Pretender to the English crown – Richard IV, King of England and Lord of Ireland. They lost their charter for that piece of impudence, but Cork continued to be a rebel city (although, rather curiously, it offered no resistance to Oliver Cromwell). William III laid siege to it in 1690 because it stood by James II, and it had to surrender without honour. In the 17th and 18th centuries it grew rapidly with the expansion of the butter trade, and many of the splendid Georgian buildings you can still see were built during this time. By the 19th century it had become a centre for the Fenian movement, which worked for an independent republic. During the War of Independence, 1919–21, the city was badly burned by the Auxiliaries, known as the Black and Tans after the colours of their uniform, and one of Cork's mayors died on hunger strike in an English prison. But Cork is also famous for a more moderate character, Father Theobald Matthew (1790–1856), who persuaded thousands of people to go off the drink, though the effect of his temperance drive was ruined by the potato famine and the general misery it brought. Cork still has a reputation for clannish behaviour amongst its businessmen and for independence in the arts and politics, but it would be hard to find a friendlier city to wander around, and you can easily explore it on foot.

City Centre

Cork's business and shopping centre is crowded on to an island between the twin channels of the River Lee, with elegant bridges linking the north and south sides of the city. The city's elegant skyline is still, like Derry's, 19th-century. Cork has spires and gracious wide streets; many of its fine buildings, bridges and quays are of a silvery limestone. **St Patrick's Street** curves close to the river; one side of the street is lined with old buildings, the other by uninspiring modern offices, shop fronts and an opera house built since the burning in 1920. Here you will find a statue of Father Matthew. The covered **English Market**, hidden behind the facades of St Patrick's Street, is rather like Smithfield Market in London and displays great pig carcasses and *drisheen* (a type of black pudding), as well as fresh fish, piles of vegetables, mouth-watering bread and olives of every description. It also has some superb eating places.

Paul Street, north of St Patrick's Street, once the Huguenot quarter, has become the trendy corner of Cork, with cafés, bookshops and buskers in an attractively redesigned pedestrian area. It joins **Cornmarket Street** and its open-air flea market, usually called **Coal Quay**, where you can bargain for trifles and observe the sharp-tongued store owners. Also off Paul Street is **St Peter and St Paul Church**, a Gothic-style building designed by the younger Pugin.

The **South Mall**, to the south of the island, and the adjoining **Grand Parade** have some pretty buildings. The tourist office, on the Grand Parade, offers free walking tours from June to September on Tuesdays and Thursdays at 7.30pm. In Washington Street, east of Grand Parade, is the magnificent Corinthian façade of the 19th-century **Court House**. Just off South Mall is **Holy Trinity Church**, on **Father Matthew Quay**, with a wonderful stained-glass window dedicated to Daniel O'Connell, 'the Great Liberator'. Between South Main Street and Grand Parade is the fine 18th-century **Christ Church**, used today to house the archives of the county. At the south end of the

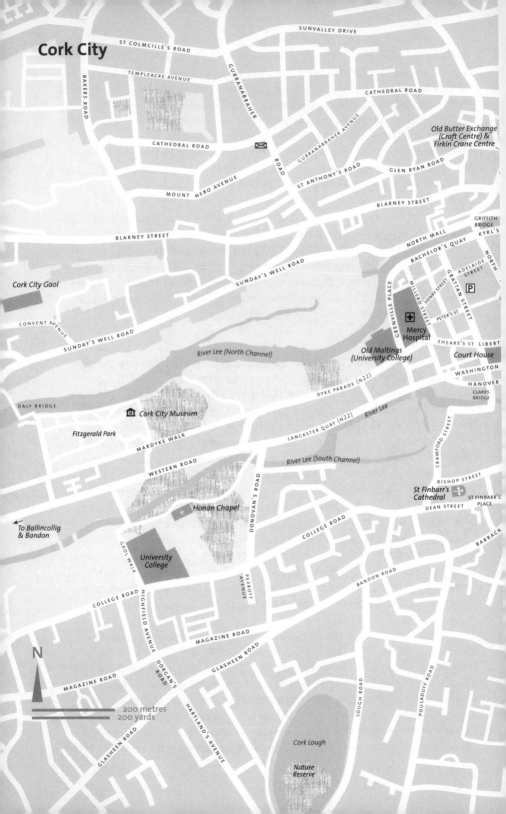

Tourist Information

Cork City: Tourist House, Grand Parade, **t** (021) 427 3251, lo-call **t** 1850 230330, **f** 427 3504; *open all year.*
Blarney: **t** (021) 438 1624; *open all year.*

Shopping

Antiques
The Flea Market, Cornmarket Street, Cork.
McCurtain Street, Cork. Antiques and bric-a-brac.
Dunkathel, Glanmire.

Books
The Mercier Bookshop, Academy Church Street, Cork. A wealth of books of Irish interest, and novels by Irish authors.

Crafts
Stephen Pearse Shop, Paul Street, Cork.
IDA Craft Centre, The Butter Exchange, Shandon. A wide selection of top quality crafts.
Blarney Castle Craftshop, Blarney.
Cork Crystal Glass Company, Blarney.

Delicacies
The English Market, located in Cork between St Patrick's Street, Grand Parade and Oliver Plunkett Street; good for food and flowers.
Natural Foods, 26 Paul Street, Cork. For bread.

Musical Instruments
Crowleys Music Centre, 29 McCurtain Street, Cork. Sells *bodhráns*.
A. Kennedy, St Johns, Clifton Road, Montenotte Park. Stocks *uilleann* pipes.
L. Egar, Ardmuire, Herbert Park, Gardiner's Hill. Selection of harps.

Tweeds and Knitwear
Blarney Castle Knitwear, Blarney.
Blarney Woollen Mills, Blarney.

Sports and Activities

Fishing
Angling Charters, Kaybille, Carrigaloe, Cobh, **t** (021) 481 2435. Organizes day or evening trips.

Golf
Douglas Golf Club, Douglas, **t** (021) 489 1086.
Ted McCarthy Municipal Golf Course, Mahon, **t** (021) 429 4280.
Blarney Golf Course, Stoneview, Blarney, **t** (021) 438 2455.
Muskerry Golf Club, Carrigrohane, **t** (021) 438 5297.
Cork Golf Club, Little Island, **t** (021) 435 3451.
Harbour Point Golf Complex, Clash Road, Little Island, **t** (021) 435 3094.
Fota Island Golf Club, Carrigtohill, **t** (021) 488 3700, *reservations@fotaisland.ie.*
Cobh Golf Club, Ballywilliam, Cobh, **t** (021) 481 2399.
Monkstown Golf Club, Monkstown, **t** (021) 484 1686.
Rafeen Creek Golf Club, Ringaskiddy, **t** (021) 437 8430.
Fernhill Golf Club, Carrigaline, **t** (021) 437 3103.

Greyhound Racing
Cork Greyhound Track, Curraheen Park, **t** (021) 454 3095, *www.igb.ie.* Wed, Thurs and Sat at 7.30pm.

Open Farms
Blarney Woodland Farm, Waterloo Rd, Blarney, **t** (021) 385733. A relaxing river nature trail through lush meadows and woodland.

Grand Parade is a monument to Ireland's patriot dead, and the tourist office. **Crawford Art Gallery** (*open Mon–Sat 10–5*; **t** *(021) 427 3377*; *www.synergy.ie/crawford*) in Emmet Place has a stunning collection of works by Irish artists such as Sean Keating, Orpen and Walter Osbourne. There are also some very good 18th- and 19th-century paintings – in particular, two magnificent paintings by James Barry, a native of the city, one of which is a self-portrait. The Gallery Café, well known throughout Ireland for its excellence, is just the place for a civilized lunch after the exhausting pastime of art appreciation. Nearby, are a couple of excellent craft shops

Pleasure Cruises

Cork Harbour Cruises, t (021) 427 7085. In summer, depart from Penrose Quay in Cork and the main pier in Cobh.

Water Sports

International Sailing Centre, 5 East Beach, Cobh, **t** (021) 481 1237, *www.sailcork.com*
Royal Cork Yacht Club, Crosshaven, **t** (021) 483 1210.
Cork Water Ski Club, Lower Dripsey, **t** (021) 433 4605.

Where to Stay

Cork City t (021–)

Hayfield Manor, Perrott Avenue, College Road, **t** 431 5600, **f** 431 6839, *www.hayfieldmanor.ie* (*luxury*). Modern building designed in a traditional style, graciously appointed, with a lovely pool, air-conditioning and various other pampering amenities.
Jury's Hotel, Western Road, **t** 427 6622, **f** 427 4477, *www.jurysdoyle.com* (*expensive*). Modern hotel offering sports facilities and a riverside garden.
The Metropole Ryan Hotel, McCurtain Street, **t** 450 8122, **f** 450 6450, *www.metropoleh.com /metro/welcome.htm* (*moderate*). Old-fashioned charm and excellent facilities, including three pools, two dining areas with great views over the River Lee, and the Met Tavern.
Isaac's, 48 McCurtain Street, **t** 450 8338 (*inexpensive*). Cheerful hostel with a self-service restaurant in a converted warehouse.
Sheila's, 4 Belgrave Place, Wellington Road, **t** 450 0940 (*inexpensive*). Conveniently central (north of the river) hostel.
Lotamore House, Tivoli, **t** 482 2344 (*moderate*). Comfortable bedrooms with en suite baths.

Maryborough House, Douglas **t** 436 5555, **f** 436 5662 (*luxury*). Beautiful 18th-century house with large, comfortable rooms and very good service.
Inchivarra House, Stoneview, Blarney, **t** 438 5549 (*inexpensive*). Run by the welcoming O'Dwyer family, this B&B offers all rooms en suite, a huge breakfast and is conveniently located for keen golfers.
The Commodore Hotel, Cobh, **t** 481 1277 (*moderate*). Old-fashioned seaside hotel.

Self-catering

Brookfield Holiday Village, College Rd, **t** 434 4032 (*moderate*).
Belfry Apartments, John O'Connell St, Cobh, **t** 481 5588, *www.selfcateringireland.com* (*moderate*).
Mrs Kowalski, Ashgrove Lodge, Cobh, **t** 812 483, 18th-century house, sleeps five. From €285 per week.

Eating Out

Cork City t (021–)

The Ivory Tower, Exchange Buildings, Princes Street, **t** 427 4665 (*expensive*). Upstairs restaurant in the heart of the city, perfectly run by its talented chef-patron.
Isaac's Restaurant (also known as **Greene's**), 48 McCurtain Street, **t** 455 2279 (*moderate*). Located in a fashionable 18th-century converted warehouse.
Jacques Restaurant, 9 Phoenix Street, **t** 427 7387 (*moderate*). Imaginative cooking, with particularly good vegetarian dishes.
Oyster Bar, Market Lane, off St Patrick's Street, **t** 427 2716 (*moderate*). Atmosphere of a gentlemen's dining room, with white-aproned waitresses. Excellent seafood.

to browse in. Opposite North Mall, on Cork Island still, the **Old Maltings** buildings have been adapted for the use of the University of Cork. This complex includes a small theatre called **The Granary**. Swans, the symbol of Cork City, are fed near here, so there are often large flocks of them. Close to the Maltings is the large Mercy Hospital, in Prospect Row, off Grenville Place, which incorporates the 1767 **Mayoralty House**, built as the official residence of the Mayor of Cork, with fine rococo interior plasterwork. It was designed by Davis Ducart, a Sardinian whose work can also be seen in the Limerick Customs House. Follow the river westwards along

Café Paradiso, 16 Lancaster Quay, Western Road, t 427 7939 (*moderate–inexpensive*). Great vegetarian food made solely from organic ingredients.

Clancy's Bar and Bistro, 15-16 Princes St, t 427 6097 (*inexpensive*). Relaxed, friendly atmosphere. Useful to remember if you are shopping or visiting the city centre.

Crawford's Art Gallery Café, Emmet Place, t 427 4415 (*inexpensive*). Run by one of the Allen Family of Ballymaloe Restaurant fame, it serves light, original food for lunch or early supper. Particularly good fresh orange juice and gooey cakes.

Eastern Palace, t 427 6967 (*inexpensive*). Chinese restaurant in the English Market; take advantage of their excellent €9–13 lunch menu. Zesty and imaginative food.

The Gingerbread House, Paul St Plaza, t 427 6411 (*inexpensive*). Takeaway or eat-in sandwiches, croissants, and cakes.

Gino's, Whinthrop St, t 427 4485 (*inexpensive*). Fabulous pizzas, famous amongst Corkonians. For big appetites.

Oz Cork, Grand Parade, t 427 2711 (*inexpensive*). A taste of Australia in the heart of the city. Very popular, so make a reservation.

Quay Co-op, 24 Sullivan's Quay, t 431 7026 (*inexpensive*). Good wholefood, vegetarian restaurant, open for lunch and dinner. Also a wholefood shop and bookshop.

The Triskel Arts Café, Triskel Arts Centre, 15 Tobin Street, t 427 2022 (*inexpensive*). Wide variety of filling lunchtime dishes, and very good soups.

The Vineyard, Market Lane, off St Patrick's Street, t 427 4793 (*inexpensive*). Traditional, old-fashioned bar ideal for a quiet drink.

Bawnleigh House, Ballinhassig, south of the city on the N71, t 477 1333 (*moderate*). Rather grim décor but don't be put off; the food is delicious and creative.

Entertainment and Nightlife

Pubs and Clubs

An Bodhrá, Oliver Plunkett Street. Specializes in traditional Irish music.

An Spailpin Fanach, South Main Street. Also a great venue for traditional music.

City Limits, Coburg Street. Offers different styles of music, occasionally comedy and disco nights.

The Forum, Grand Parade. Provides a big venue in a converted theatre for traditional and contemporary music.

The Lobby, Union Quay. The place to sample a decent pint of Murphy's Stout.

Theatre, Music and Film

Check the *Cork Examiner* and *Evening Echo* for current listings. In the evenings there is plenty to choose from.

Cork Opera House, Emmet Place, t (021) 270 022. Try to see a production by the **Theatre of the South**. They tend to produce only modern Irish writers' work, which can be very good. The theatre is open for about eight weeks every summer.

Everyman Palace Theatre, McCurtain Street, t (021) 501 673. This theatre does not restrict itself in any way – tragedy, farce and comedy, by any author as long as he or she is good. Go prepared for anything and you won't be disappointed.

Kino Cinema, Washington St, t (021) 427 1571. Shows first-run and classic films, catering for all tastes.

Triskel Arts Centre, Tobin Street, off South Main Street, t (021) 427 7300. Hosts a wide range of events – music, exhibitions, drama, film seasons, and poetry readings.

Dyke Parade and leafy Mardyke Walk, and then cut south across Western Road, and you will come to the Oxbridge-style **University College**, its buildings grouped around a 19th-century Gothic square. There is an important collection of ogham stones here. The only modern building in the complex is the **Boole Library**, opened in 1985. It is named in honour of George Boole (1815–1864), who was the first professor of mathematics here, and who is credited with working out the principles of modern computer logic.

The Roman Catholic **Honan Chapel** is a period piece of Celtic revivalism, copied from Cormac's Chapel on the Rock of Cashel and adorned with exquisite Irish revival stained glass. Close to the university is the **Cork City Museum** (*open Mon–Fri 11–1 and 2–5, Sun 3–5, closed Sat; t (021) 427 0679*), a pleasant Georgian house in the gardens of **Fitzgerald Park**, north of the Lee. It is worth visiting for local information and history, particularly on the War of Independence. There are displays of silver, glass and lace and, on the first floor, the Garryduff bird, a tiny wren of exquisite gold filigree from the early Christian period. Bus no.8 from the centre will drop you close by.

Cork is the home of two dark beers that rival Guinness – Murphy's and Beamish. **The Beamish and Crawford Brewery**, South Main Street, (*t (021) 491 1111; www.beamish. ie*) offers brewery tours throughout the year.

North of the River

St Patrick's Street leads to St Patrick's Bridge. Once over it, you enter a hilly part of the city. Some of the mostly 19th-century streets here are literally stairs up the steep slopes, and open only to pedestrians. Off Shandon Street, the bell-tower of **St Anne's Church**, the lovely **Tower of Shandon** with its two faces in white limestone and two in red sandstone, topped by a cupola and distinctive salmon weathervane, looks down into the valley. It has been nicknamed the 'four-faced liar' because the clock often tells a different time on each side. The church, which is open daily, was built between 1722 and 1726 to replace the church destroyed during the Williamite siege. The peal of the eight bells, which were made in Gloucestershire in 1750, are dear to every Corkonian heart. You may ring the bells of Shandon for a small fee, and conjure up Father Prout's lyrical poem about the spells that they wove for him 100 years ago:

'Tis the bells of Shandon
That sounds so grand on
The pleasant waters of the River Lee.

Skiddy's Almshouse, founded in 1584, stands in the churchyard. In about 1620, the Vintners Company of London settled a perpetual annuity of £24 on 12 widows of Cork. Down by the river is North Mall, which has some fine 18th-century doorways. The 18th-century **Butter Market** used to be in this area, as was the slaughterhouse for vast numbers of cattle, which were then salted and used as provisions for the British Navy and many European ships before they made the long voyage to America. The **Old Butter Exchange** is now a centre for craft studios. Beside it is the curiously named **Firkin Crane Centre** (the butter was packed in firkins, an old-fashioned measure) which is now used as a dance theatre. The Dominican **St Mary's Church** by the River Lee was completed in 1839 and has a magnificent classical façade. It is in a very prominent position, which immediately dates it as post-Catholic Emancipation: Catholic churches built before that time were built away from the main centre of towns and cities. Further north is **St Mary's Pro-Cathedral**, begun in 1808, which has a fine tower.

South of the River

South of the river, between Bishop and Dean Streets, is **St Finbarr's Cathedral**, which was built in the 19th century by wealthy Church of Ireland merchants on the site of the ancient church founded by St Finbarr. If you don't have time for much sight-seeing, this building and the Art Gallery are musts. The cathedral's great spires dominate the city, and it has a beautiful west front, with three recessed doors, elaborate carving and a beautiful rose window. The building itself is in the Gothic style of 13th-century France and was built between 1867 and 1879 by a committed medievalist, the English architect William Burgess. His eye for detail was meticulous as well as humorous, and the whole effect is vigorous – a defiant gesture to Catholic Ireland. Also on the south side, off Douglas Street, is the grey limestone tower of **Red Abbey**, a remnant of a 14th-century Augustinian friary. Close by, on Dunbar Street, is **South Chapel**, built in 1766 on an inconspicuous site. At this time, the penal laws may have relaxed, but a show of Catholicism was discouraged and disliked by the ruling classes. It contains most of its original fittings and furniture, and a sculpture of 'The Dead Christ' by John Hogan.

Back on Sullivan's Quay, the **Munster Literature Centre** (*t (021) 431 2955; www .sleeping-giant.ie/literature*) has gathered together an interesting pictorial exhibition of well known writers from Cork City and County: people such as Elizabeth Bowen, Frank O'Connor, William Trevor and Patricia Lynch (who wrote enchanting children's stories) are all represented. The centre also promotes young poets and writers and is a focus of literary activity in the south.

The Suburbs

The **Church of Christ the King** on Evergreen Road, to the south at Turner's Cross, was designed by an American architect, Barry Byrne, in the 1930s. The carved figure of Christ crucified with his arms spread above the twin entrance doors is very striking.

Riverstown House near **Glanmire**, 3 miles (6km) from the city centre, just off the Cork–Dublin road (*open May–Aug, Thurs–Sat 2–6; at other times by appointment; adm; t (021) 4382 1205*), was built in 1602, and has exquisite plasterwork by the Francini brothers. The brothers were Swiss-Italian stuccodores, who came to Ireland in 1734 and adorned the ceiling of the dining-room with allegorical figures representing Time rescuing Truth from the assaults of Discord and Envy. Dr Browne, the Archbishop of Cork, was responsible for remodelling the original house in the 1730s and it remained in his family until the early 20th century. It has been beautifully restored by its present owners, Mr and Mrs Dooley, with the help of the Irish Georgian Society.

This area is well endowed with large houses overlooking the Lee Estuary. One you can visit is **Dunkathel House**, also in Glanmire (*open May–mid Oct, Wed–Sun 2–6; adm; t (021) 482 1014*). It is a fine Georgian Palladian house, worth visiting to see, or even to buy, the antiques. Afternoon tea here is very pleasant too. The house was built by a wealthy Cork merchant in 1790, and has a wonderful bifurcated staircase of Bath stone. A permanent display of watercolours by Elizabeth Gubbins, a daughter of the house, is hung on the walls. She was a deaf mute who travelled widely, recording her experiences and the scenery as she went. There is a rare 1880s barrel-organ which is still played for visitors. Across the Glanmire Valley from Dunkathel is Brian Cross's attractive new garden, **Lakemount** (*open during the summer, daily 2.30-5; t (021) 482 1052*) on Barnavara Hill, Glanmire. Twenty minutes' walk from the city centre via Barrack Street and Bandon Road is the **Lough**, a freshwater lake with wild geese. **Douglas Estuary**, via Tivoli (15 minutes from the centre by car) has hundreds of black-tailed godwit, shelduck and golden plover. The **Cork Heritage Park** (*open May–Sept 10.30–5*) in Blackrock illustrates the maritime history of the city and its burning during the War of Independence, as well as the history of a Quaker merchant family, the Pikes, who lived there. Other interesting buildings on the estuary are **Blackrock Castle**, designed by the Pain brothers, and Father Matthew's Memorial Tower on the other side of the water, a Gothick folly.

Around Cork City

Approximately 5 miles (8km) southwest of Cork City on the N22 is **Ballincollig**, where you can visit the 19th-century **Royal Gunpowder Mills** on the banks of the River Lee (*open April–Sept, daily 10–6; adm; t (021) 874 430*). This factory produced huge quantities of gunpowder for the British army. The restored visitor centre details the history of the mills, and has an exhibition gallery, craft shop and a pleasant café.

Blarney is 5 miles (8km) northwest of the city on the R617. This small village has a fame out of all proportion to its size because it is the home of the Blarney Stone. According to legend, whoever kisses it will get the 'gift of the gab'. This magic stone is high up in the ruined keep that is all that is left of **Blarney Castle** (*open Mon–Sat 9–6 (till 6.30pm in May and Sept, 7pm June–Aug), Sun 9.30–5 (5.30 May–Sept); adm, t (021) 438 5252*). It is a magnet which attracts almost every visitor to Ireland, so expect to find the place (and the entire town of Blarney) crowded and full of knick-knacks. In the days of Queen Elizabeth I the castle was held by Dermot MacCarthy, the lord of Blarney, who had the gift of *plamas*, the Irish word for soft, flattering or insincere speech. Elizabeth had asked him to surrender his castle, but he continued to play her along with fair words and no action. In the end the frustrated Queen is supposed to have said, 'This is all Blarney – he says he will do it but never means it at all'. The MacCarthys forfeited their castle in the Williamite wars of 1690, and it was later acquired by the St John Jefferyes family. To kiss the Blarney stone, climb the stone steps up five flights to the parapet, where an attendant will hold your feet while you drop your head down to the stone. The stone is probably a 19th-century invention, and today you can even buy yourself a certificate which guarantees you have kissed it. The castle is well worth seeing for its own sake, as it is one of the largest and finest tower houses in Ireland, built in 1446 by the MacCarthy clan. The landscaped gardens surrounding it are also superb. You can also visit **Blarney Castle House and Gardens** (*open June–mid Sept, Mon–Sat, 12–6; adm; t (021) 438 5252*), a Scottish-style baronial mansion built by Charles Lanyon with a charming garden, ancient yew trees, scattered rocks and a lake.

Fota House and Estate (*open all year, Mon–Sat 10–5 Sun 11–5; adm; t (021) 481 2678; www.fotawildlife.ie*), over the Belvelly Bridge, is on magical little **Fota Island** in the

River Lee Estuary. The arboretum surrounding the house is luxurious and mature, with a collection of semi-tropical and rare shrubs. The gardens are now in the care of Duchas, the Heritage Service, and are being restored. The house, which is mainly Regency in style, was built as a hunting lodge, and has a splendid neoclassical hallway. The fine collection of Irish landscape paintings has been transferred to Limerick University Museum. There is also a bee garden and a **wildlife park** (*open Easter–Oct, 10–5, t (021) 481 2678*). The park is an ideal expedition for children as the animals (giraffes, zebras, ostrich, antelope, kangaroos, macaws and lemurs) roam freely – only the cheetahs are in a large pen. The splendid scimitar-horned oryx, extinct in its native North Africa, is being bred here.

Cobh

Cobh (pronounced 'Cove') is 15 miles (24km) southeast of Cork City on the R624 off the N25 and served by regular trains – though the shortest and most interesting way to reach it, if you can find your way through Cork's southern suburbs, is by the little car ferry at **Passage West**, a five-minute crossing to **Carrigaloe**, just beside Cobh. **Cobh** is the great harbour of Cork and handles huge ships. In the 18th century, it was a great naval base for the British. Later on, nearly all the transatlantic ships and liners stopped here – it was the last port of call for the *Titanic*, and the destination of the *Lusitania* when it was torpedoed nearby off Old Head. For many thousands of people, it was the embarkation port for the new world of North America and Australia. Despite the industry that surrounds it, Cobh is a rather nice place to stay, near to the city but without its bustle.

The colourful town centre is almost entirely 19th-century and is dominated by the Gothic **St Colman's Cathedral**, the work of Pugin and Ashlin. It dates from 1868, but it was not completed until 1919, and has a soaring spire and a glorious carillon of some forty bells which can be heard at 9am, 12 noon, 4pm, and 6pm (*open daily 10–6; adm; t (021) 481 1562*). Between 1848 and 1950 two and a half million people emigrated to America from here, with many a sad scene enacted by the quay. The history of the port and the story of the emigrants is recorded at the **Cobh Heritage Centre** (*open daily 10–6; t (021) 481 3591*), a converted Victorian railway station. A genealogical information centre has been set up here for those with Irish antecedents.

The view from the hill above Cobh facing south on to the harbour, peppered with islands (one of which is a prison) and edged with woods, is superb. If you want a stroll, make for the old **churchyard of Clonmel**, a peaceful place where many of the dead from the *Lusitania* are buried. Also buried here is the Rev Charles Wolfe, 1791–1823, who is remembered for one stirring poem, *The Burial of Sir John Moore*, which was extravagantly praised by Byron. Sir John Moore died a hero in the Peninsula Wars, but he was closely connected to Ireland through his role in quelling the 1798 Rebellion. Unlike many of his superiors, he was successful in disarming parts of the south with restraint, and he is remembered for his clemency and humanity; he found the behaviour of his own Irish troops disgraceful.

Not a drum was heard, not a funeral note
As his corse to the ramparts we hurried
Not a soldier discharged his farewell shot
O'er the grave where our hero we buried.

One of the finest public monuments in the country is the **Lusitania Memorial** in Casement Square, sculpted by Jerome Connor (1876–1943), who was born in County Kerry but raised in Massachusetts. It depicts two mourning sailors and, above them, the Angel of Peace. **Crosshaven**, 13 miles (21km) southeast of Cork city, on the Cork Harbour Estuary, a crescent-shaped bay filled with yachts and boats of every description, is the playground of the busy Cork businessmen and their families. There are delightful beaches at **Myrtleville** and **Robert's Cove** further along the coast.

West of Cork:
The Lee Valley and Gougane Barra to Bantry Bay

Heading west from Cork for Killarney, the N22 and the more scenic R618 meet at **Macroom**, a busy market town on the Sullane River. Macroom (*Maigh Chromtha*: 'Sloping Plain') once belonged to Admiral Sir William Penn, whose son founded Pennsylvania, and it has a small folk museum. This is a gorgeous part of Ireland, lush with green pasture and bright-flowered with fuchsia and heather. The Lee and Inishcarra Reservoirs swell the river. The R618 follows the lovely River Lee from Cork City through **Dripsey** (where the mills produce an excellent wool) and **Coachford**. Just beyond Macroom, to the south off the R584, is a marshy area of water known as the **Gearagh**, which is a haven for water-birds, and woodlands of oak, ash and birch. It forms part of the Lee hydroelectric works, and is an expansion of the river into a maze of rivulets. The overall effect is of dreary flooded land, but it is a bird-watcher's dream. If you are heading for Killarney, try to include the **Pass of Keamaneigh**, 5 miles (8km) west of Ballingeary on the R584 to Bantry, which takes you on a loop into the wild countryside. Follow the N22 up the Sullane Valley through **Ballymakeera** and Ballyvourney, passing the ruins of **Carrigaphuca**, a MacCarthy tower-house, on the way. Turn off the N22 where it is signposted Kilgarven and Kenmare on the left. In **Ballyvourney**, stop at the **Shrine and Holy Well of St Gobnat**, who has many devotees. She established a monastery here in the 6th century, after being led to this spot by a vision of nine white deer. St Gobnat is said to have kept the plague away from the village by consecrating the ground so that the plague could not pass. She is also known as the patroness of bees. In the church is a wooden 13th-century statue of Gobnat, which is displayed to pilgrims on her feast day, 11 February. *Tomhas Ghobnata* ('Gobnat's measure') is still observed: a length of wool is measured against her statue and then used for curing ailments. Nearby, in **Killeen**, is **St Gobnat's Stone**, an early cross pillar; carved on one face is a figure bearing a crozier. Having turned left off the N22, the road climbs up to **Coolea**, a tiny place which was the home of Sean O'Riada

Tourist Information

Macroom: Castle Gates Lodge, **t** (026) 43280. *Open May–Sept.*

Shopping

Crafts and Toys
Milmorane Basketry, Milmorane, Ballingeary, Macroom. Quality handmade baskets.
Prince August Toy Soldier Factory, Kilnamartyra, Macroom, *www.princeaugust. ie*. Ireland's only lead soldier factory, in a wild and remote setting.

Markets
A market is held at **Macroom**. Time your visit for a Tuesday morning when the market is in full swing and you can stock up with delicious farm-produced cheeses for your picnics.

Sports and Activities

Art Galleries
The Vanguard Gallery, New Street, Macroom, **t** (026) 41198.

Golf
Lee Valley Golf and Country Club, Clashenure, Ovens, **t** (021) 433 1721.
Macroom Golf Club, Lackduv, Macroom, **t** (026) 41072.

Open Farms
Muskerry Farm Museum, Ryecourt Meadows, Farnanes, **t** (021) 336 469, near Crookstown

on the Cork–Killarney Road. Horse-drawn machinery.
Lee Valley Open Farm, Droumcarra, Kilmichael, Macroom, **t** (026) 46232.

Water Sports
The Carrig Water Ski Club, Carrigadrohid, Macroom, **t** (021) 487 3027, *open May–Oct.* Has wheelchair facilities.

Where to Stay and Eat

The Auld Triangle, Killarney Road, Macroom, **t** (026) 41940 (*moderate*). Popular for its extensive à la carte dinner menu.
The Castle Hotel, Macroom, **t** (026) 41074, *www.castlehotel.ie* (*moderate*). Impressive service, choice and quality in this welcoming hotel, with its own leisure centre and award-winning restaurant.
Farran House, Farran, Macroom, **t** (021) 733 1215, *www.farranhouse.com* (*moderate*) Patricia Wiese's elegant country house is set in 12 acres of mature beech woods, and the rooms have huge bathrooms.
Bridelands Country House, Crookstown, Macroom, **t** (021) 733 6566 (*moderate*). Comfortable accommodation in this attractive old house.
Café Muesli, South Square, Macroom, **t** (026) 42455 (*inexpensive*). An interesting variety of vegetarian and Italian cuisine.
Gougane Barra Hotel, Ballingeary, **t** (026) 47069 (*moderate*). Quiet hotel in a perfect setting on the shores of beautiful Gougane Barra Lake.

(1931–1971), a composer and musician who did much to awaken a strong interest in Irish musical heritage by reviving traditional dances and tunes.

Continuing through the moorland, you come to a fork in the road: make a sharp left and you will ascend steeply to **Ballingeary** via Inchee Bridge. From here it is a short distance to **Gougane Barra**, 'The Rock-cleft of Finbarr'. This is a dramatic glacial valley with a shining lake in its hollow into which run silvery streams, and the source of the River Lee. In the lake is a small island, approached by a causeway, where St Finbarr set up his oratory in the 6th century. At the entrance to the causeway are **St Finbarr's Well** and an ancient cemetery. The island has a few 18th-century remains, some Stations of the Cross, and a tiny modern Irish Romanesque chapel which is often used for weddings. A popular *pattern* (pilgrimage) is made here every year on the Sunday nearest to the feast day of St Finbarr (25 September). After the **Pass of Keamaneigh,** strewn with massive boulders, you come into the colourful valley of the Owvane with a view of Bantry Bay. At **Kealkill,** 5 miles (8km) before Bantry, there is an ancient stone circle, reached by an exciting hilly road just off the R584; ask for directions, as it isn't easy to find.

Southwest Cork: Kinsale to Mizen Head

Kinsale and Around the Old Head

Kinsale (*Cionn Saile*: 'Tide Head') is 18 miles (29km) southwest of Cork City on the R600. A sheltered port on the Bandon Estuary, its fame was established years ago as a quaint seaside town with excellent restaurants and carefully preserved 18th-century buildings, clad often as not with grey slates to keep out the damp, or painted cheerful colours. In the last decade, it has become unquestionably the smartest, poshest and most expensive corner of rural Ireland, with music and cinema stars bidding up local real estate values, and wealthy Cork folk dining out in its restaurants.

A few far-sighted people restored the dilapidated buildings in the 1960s so that Kinsale avoided the usual fate of a town with a lot of ancient history and decaying houses – piecemeal demolition. It can become quite crowded in the summer, and some of the new holiday homes jar the eye a little, but for all that it's still a very agreeable place. There is a lot to see in the area, as well as good quality craft shops, delis, restaurants, antique shops and art galleries.

Kinsale was once an important naval port. In 1601 the Irish joined forces with Spain against the English after the Ulster chieftain Hugh O'Neill called for a national rising and support of the Catholic cause. He met with success at first, and appealed to Spain for help. In September 1601, a Spanish fleet anchored here with 3,500 infantry aboard. They planned to meet with the Gaelic lords O'Neill and Tyrconnell, who were marching south to meet them. In November, the forces of O'Neill met with the forces of Mountjoy, Elizabeth's deputy, who was beseiging the Spaniards. Within hours, the Gaelic army had been defeated at the disastrous Battle of Kinsale. This led to what is now called 'The Flight of the Earls', and put an end to the rebellion against Queen Elizabeth I and her reconquest of Ireland. It was the beginning of the end for Gaelic Ireland; anglicization was now inevitable. Although the peasantry still spoke Irish, the language of power was English. Afterwards, Kinsale developed as a shipbuilding port. It declared for Cromwell in 1641, but James II landed and departed from here after his brief and unsuccessful interlude fighting for his throne between 1689 and 1690.

St Multose Church is the oldest building in town, with parts of it dating from the 12th century. Inside, take a look at the Galway slab in the south aisle, and the old town stocks. The churchyard has several interesting 16th-century gravestones which in spring are covered in whitebells and bluebells, and in summer red valerian grows out of crevices in every wall. **Desmond Castle,** a tower house from the 1500s, was once used as a customs house and later as a prison for captured American sailors in the War of Independence, as well as for the French. The castle now accommodates an

Tourist Information

Kinsale, Pier Head, t (021) 477 2234, f (021) 774438; *open March–Oct.*
Skibbereen, North Street, t (028) 21766, f (028) 21353; *open all year.*
Bantry, t (027) 50229; *open June–Sept.*

Shopping

Art Galleries

Kent Gallery, Quayside, Kinsale, t (021) 477 4956.
The West Cork Arts Centre, Skibbereen, t (028) 22090. Established and emerging artists.
Harling Gallery, Cotter's Yard, Main Street, Schull, t (028) 28165.

Books

Fuchsia Books, Schull.

Crafts

Kinsale Crystal Glass, Market Street, Kinsale.
Bandon Pottery, St Finbarr's Place, Bandon.
Norbert Platz, Ballymurphy, Innishannon, near Bandon. For unique, handmade baskets.
Bantry House Craftshop, Bantry.
Rory Connoer, Ballylickey. Handmade knives.
Ardigole Arts, Droumlave, Ardigole.

Delicacies

Adele's, Schull. For cakes and breads.
Gubbeen Cheeses, Gubbeen House, Schull. Wonderful soft cheese, made on the farm.
Durras Farmhouse Cheese, Croomkeen, Durras. Semi-soft raw milk cheese.
Milleens Cheese, Eyeries, Beara Peninsula, t (027) 74079. Delicious garlic and plain semi-soft cheese. Call in advance.
Quay Food Co., Market Quay, Kinsale.
Ummera Smoked Products, Ummera House, Timoleague, Bandon, t (023) 46187. Call first to buy delicious smoked-salmon sausage.
Twomey's Butchers, 16 Pearse Street, Clonakilty. Famous Clonakilty black pudding.
Manning's Emporium, Ballylickey, Bantry. Local cheeses and whiskey cake.

Markets

Bandon, The market here on Fridays, 2–4, is a good place to stock up with delicious bread and cheeses, and the pottery in the main street sells wares of deep blue
Bantry. The town has a good country market on Friday mornings, and a fair in the market square on the first Friday of the month.
Carrigaline, the GAA Hall, Crosshaven Road, Carrigaline. Country market every Friday, 10–11. Good vegetables, home baking and gorgeous flowers.
Skibbereen. Market held every Friday 12 noon–2pm. A great place for cheeses, baked goods, conserves and fresh vegetables.

Pottery

Jagoes Mill Pottery, Farrangalway, Kinsale.
Keane on Ceramics, Pier Road, Kinsale.
Bandon Pottery, Lauragh, Bandon.
Courtmacsherry Ceramics, Courtmacsherry.
Rossmore Country Pottery, Clonakilty.
Ian Wright, Corsits Pottery, Kilnaclasha, Skibbereen.
Leda May Studios, Main Street, Ballydehob.
Great Barrington Pottery, Eyeries, Beara Peninsula.

Sports and Activities

Clay Pigeon Shooting

Claybird Ltd, Novohal, t (021) 887 149. In a stunning setting on the cliffs beside Kinsale.

Courses and Tours

West Cork Special Guided Tours, The White House, Lough Hyne, Baltimore, t/f (028) 20566.
Archaeological and Historical Tours of West Cork, *Teach Dearg*, Ballydehob, t (028) 37282.
The Ewe Art Centre, Goleen, near Mizen Head, t (028) 35492, *www.theewe.com*. Pottery courses in a relaxed environment. Craft shop, sculpture garden and self-catering cottages.

Fishing

The Kinsale Angling Co-op, 1 The Ramparts, Kinsale, t (021) 477 4946, *www. kinsaleangling.com*. For the Blackwater River.
Bandon Angling Association, Bandon t (023) 41674. For fishing in the Bandon River.
Fallon's Sport Shop, North Street, Skibbereen, t (028) 22246.

Baoite Mara Teo, Cape Clear, Skibbereen,
t (028) 39146.
Donal Healy Finaha, Castletownbere, t (027)
70217.

Golf

Fernhill Golf and Country Club, Carrigaline,
t (021) 437 2226.
Kinsale Golf Club, Kinsale, t (021) 477 2197.
Old Head Golf Links, Kinsale, t (021) 477 8444,
info@oldheadgolf.ie. Open April–Nov.
Bandon Golf Club, Castle Bernard, Bandon,
t (023) 41111.
Skibbereen and West Carbery Golf Club,
Skibbereen, t (028) 21227.
Bantry Golf Club, Bonenark, Bantry, t (027)
50579, *www.bantrygolf.com*
Glengarriff Golf Club, Glengarriff, t (027)
63150.

Outdoor Activity Centres

The Kinsale Outdoor Education Centre,
Kinsale, t (021) 477 2896, *www.oec.ie/kinsale.*
Instruction in all water sports.

Pleasure Cruises

Kinsale Harbour Cruises, t (021) 477 3188.
Sail Ireland Charters, Kinsale t (021) 477 2927.
Bare-boat or skippered yachts.

Pony-trekking

Kingston's Riding School, Kilgarriff, Clonakilty,
t (023) 33793.
Bantry Horse Riding, Coomanore South,
Bantry, t (027) 51412.

Walking

The Sheep's Head Way, 90km circular route
from Bantry.
The Beara Way, 196km circular route
around the Beara Peninsula from
Glengarriff.

Water Sports

Kinsale Dive Centre, Castlepark Marina,
Kinsale, t (021) 477 4959.
Oysterhaven Centre, Kinsale, t (021) 477 0738.
Aquaventures, Lifeboat Road, Baltimore,
t (028) 20511. An impressive new dive centre
with abundant marine life and wrecks,
including a German U-Boat and the infamous Kowloon Bridge.

Baltimore Diving and Water Sports Centre,
Baltimore, t (028) 20300.
The Baltimore Sailing School, The Pier,
Baltimore, t (028) 20141. Courses on ketches
and day boats.
Glenans Sailing Club, Baltimore, t (028) 20154.
Residential sailing courses.
Schull Watersports, Schull, t (028) 28554.
Dinghies and windsurfing.

Where to Stay

Sovereign House, Newmans Mall, Kinsale,
t (021) 477 2850, *www.sovereignhouse.com*
(*expensive*). Striking Queen Anne house
converted into a very comfortable guesthouse, with cobbled streets leading down to
the harbour.
The Blue Haven, Kinsale, t (021) 477 2209, *blue-
haven@iol.ie* (*moderate*). Best hotel in
Kinsale: small, cosy and comfortable with
excellent food.
Peryville House, Kinsale, t (021) 772 731
(*moderate*). Sophisticated accommodation,
with stunning views and super breakfasts.
Glebe Country House, Ballindee, Kinsale t (021)
477 8294 (*inexpensive*). Family-run Georgian
rectory, informal and relaxed.
Leighmoneymore, Dunderrow, Kinsale, t (021)
477 5312 (*inexpensive*). Friendly farmhouse
overlooking the River Bandon.
Kilbrittain Castle, Kilbrittain, t (023) 49601
(*inexpensive*). Small guesthouse in a restored
castle overlooking the sea. The decoration
may lack authenticity, but it is fun.
Lettercollum House Hostel, Timoleague,
t (023) 46251 (*inexpensive*). Budget option
with an excellent restaurant.
Travara Lodge, Courtmacsherry, t (023) 46493
(*inexpensive*). Comfortable rooms with views
of the bay and good home-cooking.
Butlerstown House, Butlerstown, south of
Courtmacsherry, t (023) 40137 (*moderate*).
Georgian country house with fine rooms
and excellent breakfasts.
Seacourt, Butlerstown, t (023) 40151
(*inexpensive*). Beautiful historic house (1760),
with views of the Seven Heads Peninsula.
The Lodge, Inchadowney Island, Clonakilty,
t (023) 33143 (*expensive–moderate*).
Luxurious hotel that comes complete with
thalassotherapy spa.

O'Donovan's Hotel, 44 Pearse Street, Clonakilty, t (023) 33250, *odhotel@iol.ie* (*inexpensive*). Wonderful old-fashioned hotel in the town centre, with a fine public bar.

Castle Salem, near Rosscarbery, t (023) 48381, *www.geocities.com/~castlesalem* (*inexpensive*). Atmospheric B&B, where William Penn once slept. Donations gratefully received to preserve this impressive 15th-century castle.

The Marine, Glandore, west of Rosscarbery, t (028) 33366 (*moderate*). Simple hotel with lovely views of the cove.

Maria's Schoolhouse, Glandore, t (028) 33002 (*inexpensive*). Great hostel hospitality and striking interior decoration.

The Old Mill, Leap, t (028) 33849 (*moderate*). Two delightful guest rooms in an enchanting mill.

Casey's, Baltimore, t (028) 20197, *caseys@eircom.net* (*moderate*). Best type of small hotel: welcoming and comfortable, with excellent food in the bar and restaurant.

Grove House, Skibbereen, t (028) 22957 (*inexpensive*). Pleasant Georgian house.

Schull Central B&B, Schull, t (028) 28227 (*inexpensive*). Efficiently run, comfortable B&B, central to the many amenities available in the town and all rooms en suite.

Heron's Cove, The Harbour, Goleen near Mizen Head, t (028) 35225 (*inexpensive*). Well-run B&B right on the water.

Fortview House, Gurtyowen, Goleen, t (028) 35324 (*inexpensive*). Friendly farmhouse in a remote setting.

Grove House, Ahakista, Durras, t (027) 67060 (*inexpensive*). Pretty old farmhouse on the Sheep's Head Peninsula. Sample the delicious honey from the garden and the free-range eggs.

Bantry House B&B, Bantry, t (027) 50047 (*moderate*). Converted wing of an interesting country pile (*see p.231*), where the plush library, snooker room/bar and extensive gardens are at guests' disposal throughout their stay.

Seaview Hotel, Ballylickey, near Bantry, t (027) 50073 (*moderate*). Cosy Victorian house with spacious bedrooms and two comfortable cottages in the grounds to rent.

Westlodge Hotel, Bantry, t (027) 50360, *www.westlodgehotel.ie* (*moderate*). Scenic location just outside town. Includes fully-refurbished leisure centre and gym.

Ardnagashel Lodge, Bantry, t (027) 51687 (*inexpensive*). Comfortable and modern, on the edge of a seaside demesne.

Hillcrest Farm, Ahakista, Bantry, t (027) 67045 (*inexpensive*). Traditional farmhouse with lovely views.

Shangri La, Glengarriff Road, Bantry, t (027) 50244 (*inexpensive*). Friendly, cosy house.

Magannagan Farm, Derryconnery, Glengarriff, t (027) 63361 (*inexpensive*). Good high teas.

Self-catering

Courtmacsherry Coastal Cottages, Courtmacsherry, t (023) 46198. Eight luxury coastal cottages, with use of hotel facilities, €190–670 per week.

Mrs Harte, Cahermore, Rosscarbery, t (023) 48227. Renovated farmhouse, oil-fired Aga cooker, sleeps six. €190–420 per week, depending on season.

Shiplake Hostel, Dunmanway, t (023) 45750. Vary Knivett's traditional farmhouse in the mountains, with a self-catering kitchen where you can cook up the organic vegetables sold by the owners. They also sell wholemeal bread and delicious pizzas.

The Castle, Castletownshend, t (028) 36100. Mrs Cochrane-Townshend has a selection of apartments in 18th-century buildings, €130–570 per week.

Hollybrook House, Skibbereen, t (028) 21245. Several 19th-century properties on wooded estate; €305 in season.

Blairs Cove House, Durras, t (027) 61041.

Eating Out

The Blue Haven, 3 Pearse Street, Kinsale, t (021) 477 2209 (*expensive*). Very good restaurant in this cosy hotel. Seafood is a speciality, and the steaks are good too.

Max's Wine Bar, Main Street, Kinsale, t (021) 477 2443 (*moderate*). Set in an attractive old house, offering a varied menu.

Casino House, Coolmain Bay, Kilbrittain, near Kinsale, t (023) 49944 (*moderate–inexpensive*). Specialises in French dishes.

Lettercollum House, Timoleague, t (023) 46251 (*moderate*). Eight tables and a delicious set menu. *Booking essential.*

Dillon's Pub, Mill Street, Timoleague, t (023) 46390 (*inexpensive*). Continental-style bar/café with good snacks.

Dunworley Cottage, Butlerstown, t (023) 40314 (*moderate*). Very popular locally. Its innovative and imaginative menus are also good for vegetarians. With Dunworley Cottage, the Rejas are moving the centre of good quality food westwards from Kinsale.

Kicki's Cabin, 53 Pearse Street, Clonakilty t (023) 33884 (*moderate–inexpensive*). Maritime-themed restaurant with unusual menus.

O'Donovan's Hotel, 44 Pearse Street, Clonakilty, t (023) 33250 (*inexpensive*). Plain cooking and pub grub. The bar has a huge Guinness mural, and a collection of old bottles and glasses.

The Rectory, Glandore, t (028) 33072 (*expensive–moderate*). Regency house with views over the harbour and excellent food in elegant surroundings.

The Baybery, Glandore Bay, Union Hall, t (028) 33605 (*inexpensive*). Serves wholesome food, and has handcrafted pine furniture and pottery for sale.

Mary-Anne's Bar, Castletownshend, t (028) 36146 (*inexpensive*). Serves excellent bar food in a friendly atmosphere. Beware of the rather boisterous Hooray Henrys at the height of the summer season.

The Mews, Baltimore, t (028) 20390 (*expensive–moderate*). Impressive, contemporary fare. *Dinner only*.

Casey's, Baltimore, t (028) 20197 (*moderate*). Bar and seafood restaurant with a wide choice of freshly caught fish and traditional music on Saturdays.

Custom House Restaurant, Baltimore, t (028) 20200 (*moderate–inexpensive*). Conjures up imaginative and excellent dishes, in a seaside setting.

Liss Ard Lake Lodge, Liss Ard, Skibbereen, t (028) 22635 (*luxury*). Refined cuisine, ranging from Mediterranean to oriental, in a lovely location.

Island Cottage, Heir Island, Skibbereen, t (028) 38012 (*moderate, plus the boat fee*). Great cooking in an unlikely, remote setting; the only restaurant in Cork you need a boat to reach. *Evenings only*.

Annie's, Ballydehob, t (028) 37292 (*moderate*). Good value set meals and special portions for children.

Levis's Bar, Ballydehob, t (028) 37118 (*inexpensive*). The old-fashioned type of bar which used to be common: a dim friendly room with two long counters; on one side the bottles and glasses, on the other side a mixture of groceries.

The Altar Restaurant, Toormore, Schull, t (028) 35254 (*moderate*). Very tasty pâté and seafood.

The Courtyard, Main Street, Schull, t (028) 28390 (*inexpensive*). Combined restaurant, bar, craftshop and deli, serving simple yet sophisticated lunches.

Heron's Cove Restaurant and B&B, Goleen, near Mizen Head, t (028) 35225 (*moderate*). Very good fish and shellfish dishes in a harbour setting.

Blairs Cove House, Durras, t (027) 61127 (*expensive*). Situated in the stable building of a Georgian mansion and run by a French-Belgian couple. Steaks and fish are grilled in front of you. *Dinner and Sun lunch only*.

Larchwood House, Pearson's Bridge, Bantry, t (027) 66181 (*moderate*). Good home-cooking in an informal atmosphere.

The Snug, The Quay, Bantry, t (027) 50057 (*inexpensive*). Eccentric bar opposite the harbour with simple home-cooked dishes.

Lawrence Cove House, Bear Island, Castletownbere, t (027) 75063 (*moderate*). Fabulous fish restaurant.

The Old Bakery, West End, Castletownbere, t (027) 70790 (*moderate*). Last espresso machine before New York.

Holly Bar, Ardgroom, Beara Peninsula, t (027) 74433 (*inexpensive*). Decent soup and sandwiches. A holly tree actually grows in the middle of the bar.

Entertainment and Nightlife

Traditional Music
The Lord Kingsale Bar, Main Street, Kinsale. Also hosts musical evenings.

The Shanakee Bar, Market Street, Kinsale. Popular venue for sessions.

'International Museum of Wine' which details the Irish links of some major vineyards in Europe. There is also the interesting **Kinsale Regional Museum** (*open daily 10–1 and 2–5.30; adm; town tours for groups over 8 if pre-booked; t (021) 477 7930*) in the Dutch-style old courthouse and market building, with a collection of material associated with the life of the town and port through the centuries, especially the Siege and Battle of Kinsale. By the harbour are the ruined remains of King James Fort, built some time after 1600. A much better example of a military fort can be seen on the opposite shore at Summercove: **Charles Fort** (*open mid April–Oct, daily 10–6; adm; t (021) 477 2263*) was built in the 1670s (in the time of Charles II) as a military strong point. It is shaped like a star and you can wander round its rather damp nooks and crannies. It was breached by Williamite forces under Marlborough after a 13-day siege. The severe 18th- and 19th-century houses inside were used as barracks for recruit training. The fort was burned by the IRA in 1921. Further to the east is the little port of **Oysterhaven**. It is possible to walk to Charles Fort: follow the Scilly Walk from the middle of Kinsale. It takes about 45 minutes.

To the south, on the R604, near **Ballinspittle**, is a ring-fort built around AD 600. This tiny village is now famous for its shrine to Our Lady: the statue of her is said to have moved in 1985, and since then, thousands of people have come to pray here. Already, there are miracles associated with the statue; unfortunately, later on in the same year of 1985, it was attacked by a Christian sect from California and badly damaged. It has been repaired but apparently has not moved since. There are some superb sandy beaches at the resort of **Garrettstown** on the wide expanse of Courtmacsherry Bay, a little further south on the R604, and splendid cliff scenery at the **Old Head of Kinsale** at the end of the road (to see it, and the old lighthouse on the point, you'll need to pay an admission fee to the golf course that occupies most of Old Head). The *Lusitania* was sunk off here, with the loss of 1,198 lives. Round the Old Head, just 7 miles (11km) outside the attractive village of **Summercove**, the remains of a 15th-century De Courcy castle known as **Ringnone Castle** overlooks the blue and white-flecked sea. A good drive or cycle ride can be made along the river from Kinsale to **Inishannon**, once an 18th-century Huguenot weaving village. You will pass several ruined castles on the way. Take the unnumbered route via **Ballindee** by crossing the Western Bridge. From Inishannon you can get to Bandon on the N71.

Bandon to Clonakilty

The market town of **Bandon**, 20 miles (32km) southwest of Cork City on the N71, was founded in 1608 by Richard Boyle, the Earl of Cork. Over the gate of the then-walled town it is said that there were once the words, 'Turk, Jew or atheist may enter here, but not a papist'. A Catholic wit responded, 'He who wrote this wrote it well, the same is written on the gates of hell'. The ownership of the town passed to the Dukes of Devonshire through marriage and they constructed most of its public buildings. The Maid of Erin Monument commemorates the Rebellions of 1798, 1848 and 1867. West of Bandon, the river skirts the demesne of **Castle Bernard**, originally called Castle Mahon. It was a large mansion with a Gothic façade, but it was burnt down in the summer of 1921, one of fifteen houses burnt around Bandon in the same week. The owner, Lord Bandon, was kidnapped by the IRA, but released a few days later after talks between De Valera, Arthur Griffith and the leaders of the Southern Unionists where safeguards for the Protestant and Unionist minority were agreed. The River Bandon and its tributaries make for good fishing and walking and, if you want to explore, **Kilbrittain**, **Timoleague** and **Courtmacsherry Bay** are unspoilt.

Courtmacsherry, a peaceful place with a lovely setting on the bay, is a sea-angling centre. Motorists can get a good view of the wooded valleys and rolling fields, which do not have the high hedges you find in Tipperary. Timoleague is dominated by the ruins of a **Franciscan Abbey** founded in 1312, overlooking the mud flats of the estuary. It has a fairly complete cloister and an outer yard, and is always accessible to the public. The mudflats are the temporary winter home of birds from the far north, Russia and beyond. On the banks of the Argideen River are the varied and lush **Timoleague Castle Gardens** (*open mid May–mid Sept, daily 11–5.30, by appointment; adm, t (023) 46116 or t (021) 483 1512*) with many rare and tender plants. The 13th-century Barry Castle is in ruins, but the more modern house sits comfortably amid the landscaped gardens. Both the Catholic and Protestant churches are worth seeing in the village, the latter for its Harry Clarke window and the former for its rich mosaic walls, decorated by an Indian Maharajah. Dillon's Pub is a good stopping place for a coffee or lunch. Back on the main road are **Lisselan Gardens** (*t (023) 33249*) on the Bandon side of Clonakilty, with a plethora of unusual and exotic trees and plants in an informal 25-acre landscape around the Big House.

Clonakilty, birthplace of Michael Collins (*see* below), received its first charter in 1292. It was a thriving linen town in the 18th century, but was given the label 'Clonakilty, God help us' during the Great Famine, such was the horror and suffering of the people there. Nowadays it is an attractive place, with traditional hand-painted signs swinging from the pubs and shops. You could linger in the **West Cork Regional Museum** on Main Street, or in the craft centre, or look at the statue of the pikeman, a monument to 1798. A **model railway village** (*open Feb–Oct, daily 11–5, July–Aug, 10–6; last entry 4pm; adm; t (023) 33224, www.clon.ie*) has been built on the Inchydoney Road, which recreates the world of the long-closed West Cork Railway. Clonakilty is also famous for its black puddings, which you can buy at Twomey's, the butcher's shop in Pearse Street. **Lisnagun Ring Fort**, (*open Mon–Fri 9–5, from 10 at weekends; adm*), a reconstructed 10th-century defensive farm, is signposted on the N71, just outside town on the Cork Road. At the other end of the spectrum is the model dairy farm with pedigree Holstein cows at **Lisselan Estate**, (*open April–Sept, Thurs 10–5 only; t (023) 34605*). Mature rhododendrons and other shrubs are planted around the simple French château-style house, built in 1851. Other attractions include a small stone circle at **Templebrian**, north of the village off the N71, and a fine, broad beach at **Inchydoney**. It is becoming a bit over-developed, but if you are looking for beach solitude there are plenty of other opportunities in the coves and inlets around Clonakilty. Inland from here, if you fancy a drive or bike ride away from the coast, you can follow small uncrowded roads going northwest amongst scenic farmland, past wooded demesnes, to **Ballynacarriga Castle**, a well-preserved ruin on the edge of a small lough, with a Sheila-na-gig on the outside wall, and fine stone carvings within.

The reputation of Michael Collins, the energetic and much loved strategist of the War of Independence, is growing with the years, rather as Dev (De Valera) himself prophesied. He was born a few miles outside Clonakilty, and bus tours now run from Clonakilty to **Woodfield**, the family homestead near Pike's Cross, where there is a small memorial to him. Only the older building remains, as the new farmhouse was burnt down in a revenge attack by a regular army officer, Major A.E. Percival, and his troops in 1921 after an IRA attack on Rosscarbery. Michael Collins went to see the ruins on the last day of his life and had a drink in his cousin's bar, where he met up with friends and relatives. He was confident that he would not be attacked in his own county, despite the warnings of friends who told him that something was planned. Later he was ambushed by anti-treaty forces and shot in the head on the road between Bandon and Clonakilty. A little further west is **Sam's Cross**, where there is a bronze roundel of him by Seamus Murphy.

Rosscarbery to Union Hall

The road then leads to **Rosscarbery**, which is a charming old-fashioned village with a pretty square, famous for its good eating houses, lively pubs, and a strange saying – 'Rosscarbery, where they buried the elephant' – that nobody seems to understand. It had a famous school of learning founded by St Fachtna in the 6th century, and a medieval Benedictine monastery. The very attractive 17th-century **Protestant church** is on the site of the old cathedral; it was mostly rebuilt in the 19th century, although the tower dates from 1612. It was raised to a bishopric in the 12th century. Inside the church is a marble statue of the sixth Baron Carbery in Elizabethan dress, and a fine carving on the west doorway. The nationalist Jeremiah O'Donovan Rossa (1831–1915) was born in the grounds of the Celtic Ross Hotel (which has delicious bar food). He was active in the Fenian movement, arrested in 1865, and sentenced to penal servitude, but was freed in 1871 on the condition that he left Ireland. He went to America where he published, among other things, recollections of his prison life. When O'Donovan Rossa died, he had an enormous funeral in Dublin, at which Patrick Pearse proclaimed, in his famous oration, 'The fools, the fools, they have left us our dead, and while Ireland holds these graves, Ireland unfree shall never be at peace'.

Castle Freke, the home of the Barons of Carbery, is a sad Gothic ruin to be found on the road out to **Galley Head**. It was in fine shape for the 10th baron's coming-of-age ball in 1913, for it had just been restored after a fire with reinforced steel window frames and reinforced concrete between the walls. The 10th Lord Carbery was rather a spoiled young man who is remembered for his daring loop-the-loop in his monoplane; his beautiful wife, Jose; and his devilment in shooting out the eyes of his neighbours in a group painting of the Carbery Hunt, which used to hang in the hall of Castle Freke. Like many Anglo-Irish, after the end of the First World War he left, sold the estate and settled abroad; for him it was Kenya, where he married twice more. Inland to the west, in the valley of the little River Roury, stands the ruin of **Coppinger's Court**, a ruined Elizabethan or Jacobean mansion, burned out in 1641, which gives shelter to cows in winter. It stands to the left, off an unclassified road between **Leap** (pronounced 'lep') and Rosscarbery. It was built by Sir William Coppinger who sprang to prominence after the defeat of the Irish chieftains and Spaniards at the Battle of Kinsale. At that stage he was valet to one of the O'Driscolls, but used the time and position to amass an empire from the confiscated lands of the defeated chieftains, only to lose it to Cromwell in his old age. Northwest of Rosscarbery, signposted off the N71 Skibbereen road, is **Castle Salem** (*open Feb–Nov, daily 10–5; tours at 10 and 2, call in advance; adm; t (023) 48381, www.castlesalem.com*), a 15th-century tower-house built for the MacCarthys and known as Benduff. It was confiscated from Florence MacCarthy in 1641 and given to a Cromwellian soldier, Major Apollo Morris, who became a Quaker and renamed it Castle Shalom (meaning 'peace'), which over the years has been corrupted to Salem. During the 17th century, a farmhouse was built into the thick castle walls, and now the entrance into the first floor of the castle is through a small door at the top of the farmhouse stairs. It is slowly crumbling away, but perhaps your entrance money will help to keep its roof on. It also offers B&B accommodation (*see* p.222). The graves of a community of Quakers are in the grounds.

From Roury Bridge, a country road (R507) winds to **Drombeg Stone Circle**, from where you can see across pastures and cornfields to the sea. Erected between the 2nd century BC and 2nd century AD, it may have been used for some kind of fertility rite and worship of the sun. A cremated body was discovered in the centre of the circle when it was excavated. Close beside the circle are the remains of an open-air roasting oven and cooking pit, so it must have been a place of feasting. The cooking pit would have been filled with water and hot stones added to bring the water to boiling point.

The beaches of **Owenahincha** and, to the east, the **Longstrand** have wonderful sand. **Union Hall** and **Glandore** are two pretty and colourful resort villages on a narrow inlet 5 miles (8km) west of Rosscarbery, whose harbours are filled with highly painted boats. Their grey-steepled Protestant churches add to their prettiness, although the congregations have dwindled to a handful. Glandore is fashionable with the rich; its south-facing seaside houses form a street known as 'Millionaire's Row'. Jonathan Swift was a visitor here while writing *Rupes Carberiae*. *Fuchsia magellanica* adorns the hedges here, as it does in so much of west Cork; the bright red-flowered plant was brought from Chile.

Castletownshend, Skibbereen and Islands Around Fastnet Rock

Round the next headland, **Castletownshend** is a neat Georgian village on a steep hill, in the middle of which grows a huge sycamore tree. The village's claim to fame is that it used to be the home of Edith Somerville (1858–1949), author of *The Real Charlotte* and the humorous *Reminiscences of an Irish RM* and other novels. She is buried in the pretty Church of Ireland graveyard here, with her cousin and co-author Violet Martin (1862–1915), who wrote under the pen name 'Martin Ross'. In their day, Castletownshend was made up of gentry who were all vaguely related to each other: the Coghills, the Chavasses and the Alymers all lived in good stone houses at various points throughout the village. At one end lived the Somervilles in Drishane House and, in the castle on the shore, lived the Townshend family. They still do to this day – you can even stay in The Castle (*see* p.222).

Park your car in the village and walk up to **St. Barrahane's Church** to visit the graves of Edith Somerville and Violet Martin and look down on the wooded Castlehaven shore. It is one of the prettiest graveyards in the country, planted with autumn-flowering cyclamen, gnarled cherry trees and the stately yew. The church itself has a very fine Harry Clarke window and a four-spired turret. The history of these Protestant families reveals itself in the gravestones and memorials in the church. They hoped for service to the British Empire and retirement to Ireland for their sons and, if they were lucky, intermarriage with local families for the daughters. Edith Somerville did not put her energies into marriage and children, and we are all the better off for it. She was the organist in the church and at one time master of the Carbery Hunt (which is still going strong).

On the outskirts of the village is a pleasant Catholic church on the road to Skibbereen, and further on is **Knockdrum Fort**, a stone-built cashel (*always accessible*). Opposite the fort is an alignment of standing stones known as 'the fingers' – a prehistoric calendar. A cul-de-sac follows the coast westwards to Castle Haven where, in the little glen leading up to the 18th-century rectory (of the first Somerville to come to Cork), there's a holy well dedicated to St Barrahane. it is still venerated: locals hang threads from the branches of the tree that overhangs it, and as the thread rots, their ailment disappears.

Skibbereen, linked to Castletownshend by the R596, is a market town famous for its weekly newspaper the *Southern Star*, previously called the *Skibbereen Eagle*. It's a good read and sheds light on local preoccupations. The old phrase, 'Skibbereen, where they ate the donkey', came about during the famine. From 1846 to 1848 over a million people died in Ireland, yet foodstuffs worth £17 million were being exported to England every year. The soup kitchens run by the gentry could not possibly feed the thousands of starving people who poured into Skibbereen from the countryside. Between Skibbereen and **Drimoleague**, off the R593, is an exciting and thoughtful enterprise called the **Liss Ard Foundation Gardens** (*open May–Sept, Sun–Fri 10–8, Oct–April, Wed–Sun 1–6; adm; t (028) 22368, www.lissard.com*): a combination of artistic spaces, water and wildlife gardens extending for forty acres. The 'sky garden' was designed by the American James Turrell. 3½ miles (5.6km) south of Skibbereen on the Baltimore Road are the **Creagh Gardens** (*open daily 10–6; adm; t (028) 22121*), a romantic and informal garden planted amongst woods which lead to the river estuary, best seen between April and June, although the grounds are lovely all year around. The walled garden is cultivated organically and contains a variety of hens and other fowl. All around Skibbereen, and particularly to the west, is some lovely country-side where knuckles and fingers of land reach out into the sea, breaking off into islands like Sherkin and Clear.

Baltimore is an attractive fishing village perched at the end of one of these fingers. It looks out on to the humpy shape of Sherkin Island and beyond to the wonderful expanse of **Roaring Water Bay** and '**Carbery's Hundred Isles**'. In the summer, the trawlers are outnumbered by sailing boats and the place is buzzing with visitors who come for the sea sports, hotels, bars, eating places and to visit the islands. Holiday cottages have been built here, as they have in many of these coastal villages, which sit uneasily with the local architecture, but there are not enough of them yet to spoil the area. It is also the place to get a boat for the islands – negotiate with the local fishermen or take the regular ferry boat.

The O'Driscolls ruled all this area, but by 1200 their power had dwindled and their chief kept up his revenues by plundering ships and exacting harbour dues. You will notice that many people you come across here have the surname O'Driscoll, and in the week before the annual regatta in August there is always an O'Driscoll get-together. The O'Driscolls built nine castles around Baltimore in order to secure themselves; these are now all dramatic ruins, especially those on Cape Clear and on Sherkin Island. This area has many tales of blood and treachery – one such story describes a retaliatory attack on Baltimore in 1537 by some soldiers from Waterford, after the O'Driscoll chief of the time had plundered a ship loaded with Spanish wine bound for Waterford City. Baltimore later became a rotten borough in the gift of Lord Carbery, sending two MPs to the British Parliament. After the famine, during which time people here suffered terribly, a boat-building industry was set up, and there are still two or three boat-builders locally. You can learn to sail at the sailing schools based here, or even better, if you have your own boat, arrive that way and explore the islands with their sandy beaches and tranquil green fields. Diving, sail-boarding and deep-sea fishing are all easy to organize. There are also regular ferries to the islands.

East of Baltimore on the mainland is the beautiful **Lough Ine**, just the place for a walk or picnic. Or you could walk from the village up to the navigational beacon at the tip of the peninsula – a beautiful spot, with dramatic cliffs of shiny slate, which breaks off in big sheets and piles up on the shore below. Lough Ine is a remarkable stretch of salt water connected to the sea by a very narrow channel, and the channel is partially blocked by a sill of rock, which prevents the lough from ever dropping below the halfway mark. Very little fresh water flows into it and it is extremely deep, especially on its western side. This unusual geography has produced a marine life more typical of the Mediterranean Sea: the red-mouthed goby fish, a variety of sponges, coral and the purple sea urchin thrive in its warm waters. Sea water rushes in and out of the channel with the pull of the tide and the water is very clear. In the shallows you can see the spiky sea urchins and the pearly saddle oyster in profusion. The lough is a nature reserve and divers have to obtain a government permit. The water is scattered with hump-backed islands and the road that leads down to the car park is edged in September with arches of brilliant red fuchsia. The hilly woods behind are often hung with dramatic wisps of cloud, great conifers mixed with beech give way to oaks and holly, and the walks are edged with ferns and bell heather.

Sherkin Island (*frequent ferry in summer, eight crossings daily, taking 10 mins each way; t (028) 20125*) encloses Baltimore harbour. It is very small with three sandy beaches. Murphy's Bar on the island rents bicycles, and you can head off to visit one of the excellent sandy beaches on the far side of the island, or the ruins of a 15th-century Franciscan Abbey which was destroyed by the expeditionary raid from Waterford in 1537. There are several B&Bs on the island and bars serving food.

Saint Ciaran was born on **Cape Clear Island** (*three daily ferries in summer, contact Cape Clear Holiday Centre, t (028) 39153, www.capeclearisland.com*) where the remains of a cross and holy well mark the site of his church. There are several other ancient stones at the eastern end of the island, in the townland of St Comillane; one is known as the trysting stone because of the hole bored through it. About one hundred and forty people live on the island, which is Irish-speaking. There is a B&B, a campsite, a couple of hostels, three bars, a small heritage centre and a pottery. Of special note is Ed Harper's goat's cheese and, even better, his ice cream (*t (028) 39126*). The cars that the islanders use are very ancient, and a lot of disused cars litter up the place. A visit to the island makes a wonderful day trip (it takes about 45 minutes on the ferry) but you might like to stay for a day or so to go walking or bird-watching. There is an important **bird observatory** here by the harbour and it is worth asking about organized bird-watching trips, as the island is on a major bird migration route and many birds are blown in by the autumn gales. You may well see manx shearwaters which live on the rocky islands off the Kerry coast; in the mornings and evenings during July and August huge numbers fly past skimming the water on their way back and forth from their feeding grounds.

The familiar **Fastnet Rock**, mentioned in the shipping forecasts, is just off Cape Clear, and you can get a fine view of it from the hill of Clear and its south-facing sea cliffs. This is especially dramatic in the winter, when the wind often reaches force 10 and the seas are huge with waves and spume. The list of ships lost in these waters makes chilly reading, but it is a diver's paradise. The diving centre in Baltimore organizes dives around the reefs of Fastnet.

Ballydehob to Mizen Head

Ballydehob is on the next finger of land, stretching into Roaring Water Bay and the Atlantic. It is a colourful little village, 10 miles (16km) away from Skibbereen on the N71 and distinguished by a fine 12-arch railway bridge, now defunct, which lies at the head of Roaring Water Bay. Quite a few 'blow-ins' have come to live around here: Germans, Dutch and English people who have bought up neglected cottages in spectacular situations. About 2 miles (3.2km) south at **Rossbrin Cove**, the ruin of an O'Mahony castle stands by the sea, home of the 14th-century scholar Finin. **Gurtnagrough Folk Museum**, 3 miles (5km) north of Ballydehob (*open most days during summer; adm; t (028) 37274*) contains a delightfully haphazard collection of bygone agricultural and domestic tools.

Schull (pronounced 'skull'), west of Ballydehob on the coast, is a small boating and tourist centre with a deep harbour; ferries run out to Clear Island and along the coast to Baltimore. Schull has a good selection of craft shops, food shops, restaurants and cafés. It also has a wonderful second-hand bookshop, Fuchsia Books, in which you could while away hours on the many books of Irish and local interest. It also has a small **planetarium**, as the night skies are so free of light pollution (*for details of opening times and star shows, t (028) 28552, or Schull Community College t (028) 28315*), and diving and sailing are also offered here. A spectacular road runs from Schull up to **Mount Gabriel** (1,339ft/407m). If you decide to climb it, be careful of the prehistoric copper mines dug into the slopes. The view is out of this world. The R591 curls round the head of lovely **Toormore Bay**, and past **Goleen** with its sandy beach (the Gulf

Stream means that swimming is quite possible here) and the Ewe Art Centre nearby (see 'Courses and Tours', p.220). The road winds on in its spectacular way to **Crookhaven** with its boat-filled harbour. O'Sullivans's Bar is a good place for a jar, its walls decorated with sketches of well-known locals. This was once a busy anchorage for fishing and sailing fleets. Marconi built the first transatlantic radio station here in 1902, before moving it to Valentia Island in Kerry.

Farther on, **Barleycove**, one of the best beaches in the southwest, stretches down to the splendid, sheer heights of **Mizen Head**, the southwesternmost point of Ireland. The soft red sandstone cliffs banded with white fall down to the sea while flurries of birds glide on the air currents beneath you. (The cliffs are high and nearly vertical, so be careful.) A lighthouse on the islet below is linked to the mainland by a suspension bridge. Many ships have been wrecked here in the past. The old fog signal station, now automatically controlled, has been opened to visitors by the former keeper as the **Mizen Head Signal Station Visitor Centre** (open April–Oct daily 10.30–5, weekends only in winter; adm; t (028) 35225). Further round is **Three Castle Head**, where on the edge of the sheer cliffs is a dramatic ruin, an O'Mahony castle. On its other side is a supposedly haunted lough. You can walk out to it, but do not bring any dogs, and ask permission at the farmhouse. (From the Barley Cove Hotel car park turn right, then left at the T-junction, right at the next junction, ignoring the sign for the Ocean View B&B on the left. Pass through the farm gate and on up the track.)

Durras and the Sheep's Head to Adrigole

From Mizen Head, the R591 goes to **Durras** at the head of **Dunmanus Bay**, which has another ruined medieval castle. The drive to Kilcrohane and **Sheep's Head**, over Seefin Pass then on to **Gerahies**, is magnificent and very untouristy. The views extend across Bantry Bay and the Beara Peninsula. The **Sheep's Head Peninsula** is relatively unvisited and, as you stand on the hilliest parts of the rocky promontory, little farmhouses lie below, built into the side of the slopes. The small village of **Kilcrohane** is famous for its early potatoes. A good walk or bike ride can be made along the Goat's Path and the north side of the peninsula. An unusual sight is **Matt O'Connor's Crane Farm** (open by appointment; t (027) 50011), 4 miles down the Goat's Path out of Bantry. From Durras, an amazing (but quite drivable) part-road part-track route leads past the Durras Cheese Farm and over the top of the peninsula down into Bantry.

Bantry has one of the finest views in the world, out over the bay. There is a deep water harbour between the Beara and Dunmanus Peninsulas, which in 1796 attracted a French fleet of 47 ships and 14,000 troops under General Hoche with Wolfe Tone on board. They were all set to support the planned United Irishmen's uprising, but what became known as the 'Protestant wind' foiled their attempt at landing and they had to return to France. Don't miss **Bantry House** (open March–Oct, daily 9–6, most summer evenings until 8; tea room and craftshop; adm; also B&B accommodation – see 'Where to Stay', p.222; t (027) 50047) which has a glorious view and is directly above the town so you do not see the ugly petrol stations below it. You can go around the house on your own, accompanied by the faint strains of classical music, with a detailed guide written by the owner, which you hand back when you have finished.

Rare French tapestries, family portraits and china still have a feeling of being used and loved. The house and garden have definitely seen better days, but nevertheless, this is one of the most interesting houses in Ireland open to the public, and certainly one of the least officious. The house was built in 1740, and added to in 1765. The owner, Mr Egerton Shelswell-White, is always at work on various restoration projects in and around the house. He is an enthusiastic patron of music, and many fine concerts are held in the library. The dining room is a stunning shade of bottle-blue, against which the gold-framed portraits and the china and silver look magnificent. Two of the portraits are of King George III and Queen Charlotte. They were painted at the sovereign's order and given to the first Earl of Bantry, from whom Mr Shelswell-White is descended, as a token of thanks for his efforts in helping repel the French invasion force of 1796. In the side courtyard of the house is an exhibition devoted to the 1796–78 Bantry Bay Armada. There is a 1:6 scale model of a frigate in cross-section and extracts from Wolfe Tone's journal. West of the town is the 9th-century Kilnaruane Pillar Stone, carved with figurative and interlaced panels, including one of a boat with oarsmen which some think is a depiction of St Brendan. (Take the N71 Cork road, turn left by the West Lodge Hotel.)

Glengarriff's humpy hills and wooded inlets look over limpid water and isles. The average annual temperature here is 11°C (52°F). **Ilnacullin**, alias Garinish Island (*open March–Oct, Mon–Sat 10–4.30 Sun 1–5, April–June and Sept, Mon–Sat 10–6.30 Sun 1–7, July and Aug, Mon–Sat 9.30–6.30 Sun 11–7; adm; t (027) 63040*), used to be covered only in rocks, birch, heather and gorse until it was made into 37 acres of garden by a Scotsman, John Allen Bryce, in 1910, and designed by Harold Peto. Now it is a dream island full of sub-tropical plants, with a formal Italian garden, rock gardens and a marble pool full of goldfish. It is an exceptional place, perfectly structured and full of outstanding plants; well worth the €6-plus return boat fares to the island. Bernard Shaw often stayed here. You will find that there are many boatmen willing to take you out to the island.

The village itself consists of a main street lined with craft shops selling woollens of every description, including soft sheepskins. Wonderful walks can be taken in the **Glengarriff Forest**, full of every shade of green – mossy trees and stones, ferns growing in every crevice and on the trees, mostly oak, beech and holly. Also growing in wild profusion is *Rhododendron ponticum*; here, as in Killarney, it has become a threat to native plants. There is a steep drive to **Barley Lake** (*Loch na Heornan*), which is up in mountainous bogland crossed by rushing streams. The tourist office stocks a local walking map.

You might walk in **Glengarriff Valley**, 'the bitter glen', and up to the hills hidden in the Caha Range, or continue westwards into the **Beara Peninsula** – one of the less touristy parts of the western coasts. The Beara presents rougher, rockier landscapes than its neighbours to the north and south, under the sombre peaks of the **Caha Mountains**, some of the highest in Ireland. From **Adrigole**, the first town west of Glengarriff, you can drive up the **Healy Pass Road**, with its lovely mountain scenery gazing down on the indented sea-line and the green woods. It is quite a testing zig-zag drive following the R574 road to Lauragh in County Kerry (*see* p.172).

The Tip of the Beara Peninsula

Castletownbere, the only town of any size, is a fishing village built around a deep water harbour where you can get a boat across to **Bear Island** (Bere on some maps). It is busy in the summertime with sailors, walkers and cyclists and festivals, especially during the regatta on the first weekend of August. **Hungry Hill** (2,251ft/686m) and **Sugarloaf Mountain** (1,887ft/575m) are very popular with climbers and hill walkers, offering beautiful views in every direction. To the west are the looming **Slieve Mickish Mountains** with equally lovely views. **Bear Island** is used by the Irish army for training; it has a pub, shop, splendid restaurant and B&B, and the opportunity for long, peaceful walks.

Just outside Castletownbere is the ruined castle of **Dunboy** on a small wooded peninsula. In fact there are two buildings here: the ancient ruin was the castle of the O'Sullivan Bere, the powerful chief of the O'Sullivans, who played a leading role in organizing the revolt against English rule. He fought in the disastrous Battle of Kinsale, and his castle was besieged by Sir George Carew. It held out bravely under the leadership of MacGeohegan, a subsidiary chief, but was eventually stormed and its inhabitants hanged. Donall waited in hiding for more help from the Spanish but, when he learnt that Philip III of Spain had abandoned all thoughts of another expedition, he decided Ulster was his safest refuge. He set off from Glengarriff in late December 1602 with 400 fighting men, 600 women and children and servants. They were continually attacked by the English and other hostile chiefs; only 35 survived to reach the protection of the O'Rourke chief in Leitrim Castle. Donall hoped for a pardon from James I in 1603, but got none, so he sailed to Spain with his family. Philip gave him honours and a pension, but he was murdered in Madrid by John Bathe, an Anglo-Irishman. J.A. Froude based his Irish historical romance *The Two Chiefs of Dunboy* (1889) on this story.

The other building on the peninsula is a 19th-century **mansion** in the Scottish Baronial style built by the Puxleys (*adm to the castle grounds*), a family who became very wealthy through copper-mining. They were burned out in 1921, although they had lived latterly mainly in England. Daphne du Maurier used them as an inspiration for her novel *Hungry Hill*. Exotic garden escapees grow wild in the hedgerows and roadsides here – gunnera, buddleia, orange monbretia – and every garden sports spiky New Zealand flax, and the pretty myrtle with its cinnamon-coloured bark.

A scenic drive can be made to the end of the Beara Peninsula, where another sparsely inhabited island, **Dursey**, at the tip of the peninsula, is connected to the mainland by a cable car. The cable car was set up in the 1970s and is designed to take either six passengers, or one person and a cow (*open Mon–Sat 9–11, 2.30–5 and 7–8; hours vary on Sun according to when and where mass is being celebrated*). The islanders graze cattle and try to earn a living through fishing. About twenty people live on the island full time, but Irish is no longer spoken here, although it was recorded in 1925 as being a Gaeltacht area. A road leads through the village of **Kilmichael** and across the middle of the island to a martello tower. Tracks lead around the cliffs to **Dursey Head** which has wonderful views: from here you can see the three rocks in the ocean known as the Bull, the Cow and the Calf.

As the road winds around the coast, there is barely a tree to be seen; only thorn and fuchsia hedges, and astonishingly beautiful coastal views all the way through Allihies, Eyeries and Ardgroom. Between Castletownbere and Allihies, at the junction where the road goes left for Dursey, is a wedge grave in a field, and from here you can see the beach at **Ballydonegan**. The village of **Allihies** is a tiny place along one street, with a fine hostel and friendly pubs. Fresh fish is fried up in the simple Atlantic restaurant, bikes can be hired from O'Sullivan's and the beach at Garinish is of white crystalline sand. There is a café and campsite by the beach and as yet the place is unspoiled. Allihies has always been a fishing village, but during the 19th century it was also a busy copper-mining centre which formed part of the Puxley empire. The mines closed in 1930 but used to employ 1,200 people, some of whom were skilled workers brought in from Cornwall to oversee the locals. This caused great resentment and the community boycotted the Cornish workers – their food supplies had to come from Wales on the boats which took the copper ore to Swansea. Their ruined stone cottages and the remains of a nonconformist chapel are still there. There is easy walking around the copper mines, which are above the village. Part of the **Beara Way** runs above Allihies; a track continues from the copper mine, and it is a glorious walk to Eyeries. (Have a look at *West Cork Walks* by Kevin Corcoran.)

The drive to Eyeries is as different as the weather; you might be impressed by churning seas, black rocks, rough bracken and wind-torn skies or, if the weather is fine, by the idyllic cerulean water, the brilliant green fields, the wild flowers and silvery rocks. The village of **Eyeries** is painted in strong Mediterranean colours, and behind it rises Maulin Mountain (2,044ft/620m). Above **Ballycrovane Harbour**, on a little hill, looms the tallest ogham stone in the country: it stands over 17ft (5m) high. Milleens, a distinctive and delicious farmhouse cheese, is made here. As you approach **Ardgroom** the seas are calmer, and in the bay you will notice the lines of seaweed-covered ropes and rafts that indicate mussel farming. The road continues to Lauragh and Derreen Gardens (*see* **County Kerry**, p.172).

East of Cork: Midleton and Youghal

Approximately 11 miles from Cork City, going east on the N25, is the attractive town of **Midleton**, which has benefited from the restoration of an 18th-century whiskey distillery, the **Jameson Heritage Centre**, off Distillery Road (*open May–Oct, daily 10–4, rest of the year weekdays only; tours at 12 noon and 3pm; adm;* **t** *(021) 461 3594*). It is a fine building, self-contained within 11 acres, and you can take a tour around all the major parts – mills, maltings, corn stores, stillhouses and kilns. The water wheel is still in perfect order, and you can see the largest pot-still in the world with a capacity of more than 30,000 gallons as well as sample some of the delicious stuff. It stopped being a working distillery in 1975, but there is a mass of information charting the history of Irish whiskey.

West of Midleton is the impressive 15th-century **Barryscourt Castle** (*open June–Sept, daily 10–5;* **t** *(021) 488 3864*) at **Carrigtohill**, which contains an exhibition on the history of the Barrys and the castle. It is a quadrangular keep with square towers surrounded by a lawn, overlooking the inner reaches of Cork harbour. The 18th-century farmhouse (**t** *(021) 488 3864/488 2218*) in its *bawn* sells crafts, antiquarian books and teas.

The fast main road (N25) to Midleton and Youghal means that many people do not explore the peninsula opposite Crosshaven. Turn off at Midleton and follow the R629 to **Cluain Uamha** ('Meadow of the Cave'), where an ancient bishopric was founded by St Colman in the 6th century. There are some large limestone caves close to the village, but it is chiefly interesting for its vast and ancient **cathedral**. This dates from the 13th century, and the **round tower** beside it is one of the only two similar examples in the county. You are allowed to climb to the top where the view is superb; its castellated top is more modern than the base. Among the monuments in the cathedral is an alabaster tomb to George Berkeley, the philosopher who was bishop here from 1734 to 1753, and a 17th-century Fitzgerald tomb. The carved decoration on the north door represents the pagan symbols of life.

The R629 from Cloyne leads down to **Ballycotton**, a little fishing village set in a peaceful, unspoiled bay. There is a pretty view out to the Ballycotton Islands, which protect the village from the worst of the sea winds, and a bird sanctuary on the

Tourist Information

Midleton: Jameson Heritage Centre, **t** (021) 461 3702; *open June–Sept.*
Youghal: Market House, on the harbour, **t** (024) 20170; *open June–mid Sept.*

Shopping

Crafts

Ballymaloe Craft Shop, Shanagarry.
Ballymaloe Kitchen shop, Shanagarry. For hand-made kitchen knives.

Delicacies

Ardsallagh goat's cheese and milk, Ardsallagh, Youghal. Also comes bottled with olive oil.

Pottery

Stephen Pearce Pottery, Shanagarry.

Sports and Activities

Courses

Ballymaloe Cookery School, Kinoith House, Shanagarry, **t** (021) 464 6785, *www.ballymaloe.com.* Cookery courses

from one day to three months, contact Darina and Tim Allen.
Long Weekend of Music in Ireland, Ballymaloe House, Shanagarry, **t** (021) 464 6785, *www.tradsessions.com*, *roryallen@ballymaloe.com.* A three-day musical event with workshops and performances by local musicians. Accommodation is in the superb Ballymaloe House Hotel (*see* below).

Golf

East Cork Golf Club, Gurtacrue, Midleton, **t** (021) 463 1687.
Water Rock Golf Course, Water Rock, Midleton, **t** (021) 461 3499.
Youghal Golf Club, Knockaverry, Youghal, **t** (024) 92787.

Greyhound Racing

Youghal Race Course, Youghal, **t** (024) 92305.

Open Farm

Leahy's Open Farm and Farm Museum, Condonstown, Dungourney, **t** (021) 466 8461. Feed the animals, play in the indoor games room or visit the agricultural museum. *Open Easter–Sept daily 11–6.*

extensive marsh by the estuary. Close by is the welcoming **Ballymaloe House** (signposted in **Castlemartyr** on the Cork–Waterford road), which is now a hotel, and is famous for its restaurant, cooking school and kitchen/craft shop . The cookery school is at Kinoith House and courses range from twelve weeks to one-day courses where you can concentrate on puddings or breadmaking (*see* 'Courses', p.235). The gardens (*open daily 9–6; adm*) are new, although laid out within the old grounds, and are designed to resemble a series of 'rooms', including a potager in geometric patterns, a formal fruit garden, a herb garden, a rose garden and herbaceous borders (*see* also 'Where to Stay', below). At **Ladysbridge**, near **Garryvoe**, is a grand, fortified house built of the local limestone, called **Ightermurragh Castle**. Over one of the fireplaces is a Latin inscription which tells that it was built by Edmund Supple and his wife, 'whom love binds in one', in 1641.

Two miles (3.2km) southeast in **Kilcredan**'s 17th-century Church of Ireland church are some fascinating limestone headstones with a variety of imaginative motifs. Sadly, the church has suffered the fate of many of that faith and is without a roof,and the carved tomb of Sir Robert Tynte has been ravaged by the weather. Just to the south is **Shanagarry**, famous for Stephen Pearce's pottery, and the old home of the father of William Penn, the founder of Pennsylvania. You can buy simple earthenware and

Outdoor Activity Centres

Trabolgan, Midleton, t (021) 466 1551, *www.trabolgan.com*. Indoor jungle safari, outdoor wooden wonderand, sub-tropical pool, adventure sports and pitch and putt. Day or residential visits welcomed.

Where to Stay

Glenview House, Ballinaclasha, Midleton, t (021) 463 1680, *www.dragnet-systems.ie/dira/glenview* (*moderate*). Pretty 18th-century house in lovely grounds, with tennis and croquet. Good food.

The Midleton Park Hotel, Midleton t (021) 463 1767 (*moderate*). Quite luxurious for the price. The décor is beautiful, the atmosphere relaxed and the restaurant food superb.

Spanish Point Seafood Restaurant, Ballycotton, t (021) 464 6177 (*inexpensive*). Seaside restaurant with accommodation.

The Old Parochial House, Castlemartyr, near Ladysbridge, t (021) 466 7454 (*moderate*). Elegantly restored Victorian house on the edge of the village.

Ballymaloe House, Shanagarry, t (021) 465 2531, *www.ballymaloe.com*, *res@ballymaloe.com* (*expensive*). Beautiful Georgian house

near the fishing village of Ballycotton; elegant rooms, friendly service, fabulous food and generous helpings. The whole Allen family are involved in the enterprise – you may be inspired to book into their cookery school. Sea- or river-fishing and horse-riding can be arranged.

Avonmore House, South Abbey, Youghal, t (024) 92617 (*inexpensive*). Elegant old house with beautiful rooms. A good bargain.

Eating Out

The Clean Slate, Midleton, t (021) 633 655 (*moderate*). Adventurous food in a striking building.

Finin's, Midleton, t (021) 631 878 (*moderate*). Attractive pub with an excellent restaurant.

The Farm Gate, Coolbawn, Midleton, t (021) 463 2771 (*moderate–inexpensive*). Fresh local ingredients and traditional dishes.

Ballymaloe House, Shanagarry, t (021) 465 2531, *www.ballymaloe.com* (*expensive*). Famed throughout Ireland for its superb food, this won't disappoint you.

Aherne's Seafood Restaurant, North Main Street, Youghal, t (024) 92424/92533 (*moderate*). Good atmosphere and delicious seafood dishes.

glazed pottery from Pearce's studio and tea rooms or at the Ballymaloe House craft shop, which is one of the best kitchen shops in the country.

Youghal (pronounced 'Yawl', from *Eochaill*: 'Yew Wood') is approximately 30 miles (48km) east of Cork City on the N25. It is an important medieval town which used to be a centre for the carpet industry, but has become one of the most attractive seaside towns in Ireland (ignore the less appealing buildings on the outskirts). It is set on the estuary of the River Blackwater, and has many fine bathing places and a long sandy beach. The river scenery between here and Cappoquin is memorable for its pretty woods, the silver twisting Blackwater and the attractive houses along its banks.

Youghal was founded by the Anglo-Normans in the 13th century and was destroyed in the Desmond Rebellion of 1579. The Fitzgeralds, Earls of Desmond, were a powerful Anglo-Norman family who joined forces with the Gaelic lords from Ulster to try and repulse the armies of Elizabeth I. Ruthless coercion and martial law put down the rebellion – 'man, woman and child were put to the Sword' wrote Raleigh's half-brother. The ruined town was handed over to Sir Walter Raleigh, as he had played an important part in the suppression, along with 42,000 acres of the Earl's forfeited estate in the Elizabethan plantation period. Raleigh became an 'undertaker', agreeing to repopulate his lands with English settlers and drive out the native Irish. He became mayor of the town and lived in a gabled house called **Myrtle Grove** (*open occasionally between June–Aug;* **t** *(024) 92274; adm*) at the end of William Street. He later sold Youghal to Richard Boyle who became the Earl of Cork. Thereafter, it was a prosperous place, supporting Oliver Cromwell and so avoiding another sacking. Raleigh reputedly planted the first potato in the garden, an act which was to have far-reaching consequences for Ireland's population.

In nearby Church Street is the 15th-century Church of Ireland collegiate **Church of St Mary**. The inside of this large cruciform church is crowded with interesting monuments, including one to the Earl of Cork, Richard Boyle. He looks very smug, surrounded by his mother, his two wives, and nine of his 16 children. A memorial stands to an extraordinary lady, the Countess of Desmond, who apparently died in 1604 at the age of 147 after falling out of a tree when gathering cherries. The church was built around 1250, rebuilt in 1461 by Thomas, the 8th Earl of Desmond, and restored in 1884, after lying partially derelict since the Desmond Rebellion. The most notable features are its early English west doorway, the massive pulpit with its canopy of carved bog oak, and the large stained glass east window (*c.* 1468) with the arms of the Desmonds, Sir Walter Raleigh, the Earl of Cork and the Duke of Devonshire. Nearby on Main Street is the ruined 15th century tower house, **Tynte's Castle**. Large sections of the old town walls still stand, up on the crest of the hill, but even in 1579 they were in a bad state, and were easily breached by the rebellious Earl of Desmond.

The old part of town lies at the foot of a steep hill, whilst the new part has grown along the margin of the bay. The main street is spanned by Youghal's landmark, a tower known as the **Clock Gate** and erected in 1771. Other buildings of note are the **Red House**, an early 18th-century Dutch style brick building, and, on the corner of Church Street, a group of medieval **almshouses** which have been restored. Youghal's harbour is close by. When you see it, try to imagine it fixed up with picket fences and clapboard siding to look like New Bedford, Massachusetts – that's what John Houston did to it when he filmed *Moby Dick* here in 1954, with Youghal's old salts, housewives and children pressed into service as extras. Paddy Linehan's Moby Dick bar, facing the harbour, is full of photos and mementos. The tourist office, in the old market house, includes a heritage centre with exhibits on Youghal's rich history. In summer they offer walking tours of the town. Across the road in Foxes Lane is a small folk museum.

Leaving Youghal for the east, you might wish to take a detour up the lovely **Blackwater Valley**, which has some of the best driving and walking country in Ireland – if you like wooded banks, green fields, old buildings and twisting, unfrequented roads. You may be tempted to follow the Blackwater River to Lismore in County Waterford, which is well worth a tour (*see* p.252). To the west, along the R666 back towards Fermoy, you will pass the turreted Gothic gateway and bridge of **Ballysaggartmore** (1834), all that is left of the Keily estate. These follies were built to the design of their gardener. (The old house itself was demolished in the 1930s.)

North of Cork: Fermoy to Mallow

Fermoy (*Mainistir Fhearmuighe*: 'Abbey of the Plantations'), 30 miles (48km) north of Cork City on the N8, used to be a garrison town for the British army. People hereabouts are familiar with every fascinating detail of salmon-catching. The town, built along both sides of the darkly flowing River Blackwater, has seen more prosperous days and retains an air of shabby gentility. Lord Fermoy, an ancestor of the late Princess of Wales, is said to have gambled away his Fermoy estates in an evening. The Protestant church, built in 1802, contains some grotesque masks; however, the Catholic church is rather elegant: it was designed by E.W. Pugin in 1867, with an interior by the Pain brothers.

Just outside Fermoy, overlooking the river to the west, is one of the most beautiful houses in Ireland, the late-Georgian mansion, **Castle Hyde** (*now owned by Michael Flatley of 'Riverdance' fame; not open to the public*). This was the ancestral home of Douglas Hyde, the first President of the Irish Republic and the founder of the Gaelic League, although he was actually born at French Park in County Roscommon. **Castlelyons**, a few miles outside the town (turn left off the N8 going towards Cork), is a quiet and pretty hamlet where intimations of past history compel you to stop. Here is the great ruined house of the Barrys, a Norman family, burned down in 1771, and the remains of a 14th-century Franciscan Friary. In the graveyard of Kill St Anne is a roofless 15th-century church, and within is the ruin of an 18th-century parish church. The classical **Barrymore Mausoleum** is quite impressive, especially the white marble bust of the Earl of Barrymore.

To the north, **Mitchelstown** is famous in Ireland for butter and cheese, an industry which employs a lot of people, although the cheese is rather boring – Cheddar and a sort of soft bland spread. It is also famous for its limestone **caves** (*open daily 10–6; adm; t (052) 67246*), which have good examples of stalactites and stalagmites, and are

Tourist Information

Fermoy: Avenue Tourism, Fermoy Resource Centre, t (025) 33699; *open all year.*
Mallow: Bridge Street, t (022) 42222; *open all year.*

Shopping

Delicacies
Ardrahan Cheese, Ardrahan House, Kanturk. Gouda-like cheese.

Markets
Mitchelstown; Thurs, 10.30–4.

Sports and Activities

Golf
Fermoy Golf Club, Corrin, Fermoy, t (025) 32694, *fermoygolfclub@eircom.net.*
Mitchelstown Golf Club, Limerick Road, Mitchelstown, t (025) 24072.
Doneraile Golf Club, Doneraile, t (022) 24137.
Mallow Golf Club, Ballyellis, Mallow, t (022) 21145.
Kanturk Golf Club, Kanturk, t (029) 50534.

Open Farms
Rambling House Farm Museum and Folk Park, Ruhill, Boherbue, Mallow, t (029) 76155.

Kanturk Rural Farm Museum, Mealehara, Kanturk, t (029) 51319/5092.
Millstreet Country Park, Millstreet, t (029) 70810. A 500-acre park with nature trails and reconstructions of archaeological sites.

Pony-trekking
Green Glens, Millstreet, t (029) 70707. Offers 1–6-day trail-rides.

Walking
Both the following are way-marked:
The Ballyhoura Way, 90km from Limerick Junction to John's Bridge near Kanturk; and **The Blackwater Way**, 168km from the lower slopes of the Knockmealdown Mountains near Clonmel to Muckross Park.

Where to Stay

Ballyvolane House, near Fermoy, t (025) 36349, *www.ballyvolanehouse.ie* (*expensive*). Run by Mrs Merrie Green and her friendly family. The lovely old Georgian house is set in beautiful grounds, and locally produced vegetables are used in the cooking.
Castlehyde Hotel, Fermoy, t (025) 31865 (*moderate*). Beautifully renovated 18th-century courtyard hotel full of character.
Conna House, Conna, Fermoy, t (058) 59419 (*inexpensive*). Comfortable 19th-century manor house, set in glorious gardens.

very extensive. (They are a further 10 miles (16km) to the northeast on the N8 to Cahir). The Lord of Kingston planned Michelstown in the grand manner with important buildings at the end of vistas. If you have some time to spare, walk through **Kingston Square** where there are 18th-century almshouses for decayed Protestant gentlefolk, and a central chapel designed by John Morrison of Cork. His son and grandson were also architects and responsible for some of the finest buildings in the county. A tree-lined street leads to the Church of Ireland church, which was designed by G.R. Pain.

The castle, which was the focus of all this grandeur, has unfortunately been demolished and first replaced with a huge dairy factory. The old castle was founded by the White Knights of Desmond, and passed to the Kingstons through marriage around 1660. It was replaced with a Gothic mansion by G.R. Pain in 1823, but the estates were heavily mortgaged owing to the extravagance of the Regency earl. Mary Wollstonecraft (1759–1797), author of *Vindication of the Rights of Women* and mother of Mary Shelley, spent time as a governess here; her libertarian and feminist ideas

Fuchsia House Hostel, The Square, Kilworth, Fermoy, t (025) 27565 (*inexpensive*). Minimalist hostel with almost monastic decoration in a quiet village square.

Ghillie Cottage, Fermoy, t (025) 32720 (*inexpensive*). Joy Arnold and Doug Lock are the friendly hosts at this charming cottage.

Glanworth Mill, Glanworth, Fermoy, t (025) 38555 (*moderate*). Lovely riverside inn with excellent food and literary bedrooms, including one cut into the cliff face.

Longueville House, Mallow, t (022) 47156 (*expensive*). With a maze and the only vineyard in Ireland to be found behind this house, this has long sloping views to the river, with the ruined Callaghan Castle in the front. The food is superlative, and the service attentive.

The Hibernian Hotel, Mallow, t (022) 21588, www.hibernianhotelmallow.ie (*moderate*). Delightful old family-run hotel in the town centre.

Assolas Country House, Kanturk, t (029) 50015, www.assolas.com (*expensive*). This 17th-century house is a superb place to get away from it all, set amongst mature trees that reach down to the river. Offers tennis, fishing and croquet and delicious food.

Glenlohane, Kanturk, t (029) 50014, www.glenlohane.com (*moderate*). Mrs Bolster has rooms in a comfortable Georgian house, set in beautiful parkland.

Self-catering

Cashman Family, Garrison, Kanturk, t (029) 50197. Charming thatched cottage that sleeps six comfortably. From €190 per week.

Eating Out

Castlehyde Hotel, Fermoy, t (025) 31865 (*moderate–inexpensive*). Imaginative bar food at lunch time and modern Irish cuisine in the evening.

Glanworth Mill, Glanworth, Fermoy, t (025) 38555 (*moderate–inexpensive*). Lovely riverside inn with a café, serving delightful soups, salads, and wickedly wonderful desserts at lunchtime; a smarter restaurant attached serves dinner. Accommodation is also available.

La Bigoudenne, 28 McCurtain Street, Fermoy, t (025) 32832 (*inexpensive*). Quintessentially French bistro.

Paki Fitz's, Cork Street, Mitchelstown, t (025) 84897 (*moderate*). Recently renovated, this venue offers everything: a café, a three storey bar serving bar food and a more sophisticated evening restaurant with an extensive menu.

Longueville House, Mallow, t (022) 47156 (*expensive*). Exciting cuisine in generous portions.

were deeply disapproved of by the family. By the 19th-century reign of Anna, Countess of Kingston, the land wars were brewing; her tenants wanted their rents reduced and refused to pay her. Her finances were already straitened; it was well known that you would get barely a raisin in her *barm brack* (a delicious moist currant bread) if you were invited to tea. In 1880, some 1,600 of her tenants demanded a rent reduction, and there was a huge demonstration in Michelstown in 1881. The dispute ended with evictions; most of the tenants paid up and were reinstated by the summer of 1882. But the whole thing started up again in 1887, and a meeting in Mitchelstown of Land Leaguers, tenants, nationalist MPs and Radicals from England turned into a riot which ended when two people were killed and twenty others were seriously wounded by shots from the police. There is a statue of John Manderville, a leader of the agitation for fair rents, and stone crosses to commemorate the dead in the Market Square. Elizabeth Bowen, the novelist, describes the last garden party at Mitchelstown in her recollections, *Bowen's Court*.

The countryside around becomes richer as you travel west and enter the Golden Vein, a fertile plain that extends north of the Galty Mountains. At Kildorrey, turn right off the N73 on to the R512 to go to **Doneraile**. Near here was the home of Elizabeth Bowen (1899–1973), whose works so beautifully describe the shades and subtleties of the Anglo-Irish. Her house, Bowen's Court, a beautiful 18th-century mansion, was demolished in the 1960s – a victim of the government's lack of interest in historic buildings at that time. Doneraile and Buttevant are in Edmund Spenser country, 40 miles (64km) north of Cork City, between the Blackwater and the Ballyhoura Mountains. Here the poet served the Crown in various positions, and wrote most of *The Faerie Queene*, trying desperately (and unsuccessfully) to flatter Elizabeth I enough to get the grant of a bigger manor that was closer to London. While spinning his learned Renaissance fantasies he also found time to write *A View of the Present State of Ireland* in which he advocated a policy that was uncomfortably close to genocide. Spenser had just been appointed Sheriff of Cork when a revolt broke out in 1598, and the Irish repaid him by sacking and burning his home and chasing him back to England, where he died the following year. His home, **Kilcolman Castle**, is now a sombre ruin and hard to find, in a field beside a reedy pool northeast of Doneraile. There is a sad essay by Yeats on Spenser and the irony of the poet as oppressor. 'Could he have gone there as a poet merely,' he wrote, 'he would have found among wandering storytellers...certainly all the kingdom of Faery, still unfaded, of which his own poetry was often but a troubled image.' From 1895 to 1913 Doneraile was the parish of Canon Sheehan, who wrote wise and funny books about Irish rural life. His statue stands outside the Catholic church.

Doneraile Court and Wildlife Park (*open mid April–Oct, Mon–Sat 10–8.30 Sun 11–7; t (022) 24244*) is a wonderful Georgian house which has been saved from ruin by the Irish Georgian Society. Here, Elizabeth Barry, wife of the first Viscount Doneraile, hid in a clock case to observe a masonic lodge meeting held in the house. Perhaps she laughed, but whatever happened she gave herself away, and all the masons could do to keep her quiet was to elect her as a mason – the only woman mason in history. A sadder story concerns a 19th-century viscount who kept a pet fox, which bit him and his coachman one day. The fox was found to have rabies, and both men travelled to Paris to be treated by Pasteur, but although the coachman continued with his treatment, Lord Doneraile gave it up. He soon developed the disease and died a terrible death in 1887. The beautiful surrounding parkland has been developed for tourists, and there are nature walks, cascades, and herds of deer in the park. Enter through the grand stone gates just outside the town. Nearby is the unique alkaline **Kilcolman Bog**, home to many birds, and you can visit it if you are involved in bird study. Contact the tourist office for details. At **Buttevant** during July is the Cahirmee Horse Fair, which has been held here for hundreds of years and is always good *craic*, with lots of other events happening at the same time.

Mallow, 10 miles (16km) south, used to be a famous spa where the gentry of Ireland came to take the waters and have a good time. In the 18th century the spa inspired the anonymous verse which begins:

Beauing, belling, dancing, drinking,
Breaking windows, damning, singing,
Ever raking, never thinking,
Live the rakes of Mallow...

The old spa house in Spa Walk is now a private home and the once-famous water gushes to waste. The town has some pretty 18th-century houses and a timbered, decorated Clock House. **Mallow Castle** is a still-impressive, though roofless, ruin of a fortified 16th-century tower house. The Catholic **St Mary's Church** has a pretty interior and Romanesque Revival façade. Davis Street is named after the poet and nationalist Thomas Davis (1814–1845) who was born in No.72. The Mallow Races, which happen intermittently throughout the spring, summer and autumn, are the only times the place really comes alive, although it is frequented by anglers, and the Folk Festival in July is very cheerful. Just outside the town is **Longueville House**, which produces delicious wine and is a place where you may eat and stay in great style (*see* p.240).

At **Castletownroche** on the N72, 10 miles (16km) east of Mallow, notice the pretty Church of Ireland church on a rise above the river. It is also worth stopping to wander around the ruins of Bridgetown Abbey, founded by FitzHugh Roche in the 13th century. To the north of the pretty church is **Anne's Grove** (*open Easter–end Sept, Mon–Sat 10–5 Sun 1–6; adm; t (022) 26145*) with its tranquil woodlands and walled garden. The sloping grounds surrounding the beautiful 18th-century house are planted in the style made popular by William Robertson in the late 19th century. Nothing appears contrived and the massed plants lead up winding paths to the river and gardens. Rhododendrons, magnolias, eucryphias, abutilons and primulas obviously love it here, so vigorously have they grown. Just south of the Blackwater River at Castletownroche is **Killavullen** where **Ballymacmoy House**, the original home of the Hennessys of cognac fame, has been restored. The extensive caves beneath the estate are already open during the summer. Northeast of Castletownroche is **Glanworth**, a sleepy village dominated by the imposing remains of Roche's castle above the River Funchion, on which stands an 18th-century watermill that has recently opened as an attractive inn.

From Mallow, the country lanes which take you through the **Boggeragh Mountains** are a maze, and rather fun if you have time to get lost for a while. They have a wild mystery, heightened by the green glow from the overgrown hedges which form an arbour overhead. The road from Mallow to Killarney meanders past the haunted shell of the O'Callaghan's castle at Dromaneen. **Kanturk**, to the north of the main road, is an attractive 18th-century planned town. **Kanturk Castle** is a huge building, begun around 1609, but never finished. It is said that the Privy Council ordered the work to stop and the owner, McCarthy, flew into a rage and ordered that the blue glass tiles with which the castle was to be roofed be thrown into the river.

A little diversion to the northwest will take you to **Liscarrol**. This small and remote village has the third-largest **Norman Castle** in Ireland, probably built by the Barrys. It also has the largest concentration of donkeys in the country, for it is the home of a **donkey sanctuary** (*open Mon–Sat 9–1 and 2–4.30; t (022) 48398*). Back on the main road (N72) to Killarney (which bypasses **Millstreet**, famous for its equestrian centre) the second road to the left after Rathmore, about a mile from the ton, goes to the base of the **Paps Mountains**, dedicated to the ancient fertility goddess Danu. At the end of that road, by the school, turn left and then first right where a small signpost points to 'The City'. This extraordinary site, enclosed by a dry stone *cashel* 10ft (3m) high, is the setting for what is perhaps the oldest uninterrupted religious ceremony in Europe. Certainly since the early Iron Age, people have gathered here in May. Time stands still; uninterpreted and without a gift shop in sight, this is the sort of place that makes a tour of Ireland memorable.

County Waterford

Waterford is a fertile county, with rugged mountain beauty and a pretty coastline dotted with fishing villages-cum-holiday resorts and interesting ruins. The southeast coast also has a reputation for being sunny. The county is traversed by two mountain ranges, the Comeragh and the Monavullagh, which are set with tiny lakes and planted conifer forests. The valley in which Waterford City lies is watered by the River Suir, which flows into the River Barrow, which in turn is fed by the River Nore. These sister rivers cross the county, which is furthermore bordered by the Blackwater and the great Atlantic sea. In *The Book of Invasions* (or *Lebor Gabala*), a mythological account of the pre-history of Ireland, the first Celts described the site where Waterford City grew up as 'a sweet confluence of waters, a trinity of rivers'. It was, however, Norsemen who founded the city of Waterford in about AD 850 and used it as a base from which to raid up the rivers to the rich valleys of Tipperary and beyond. The name 'Waterford' is of Danish origin.

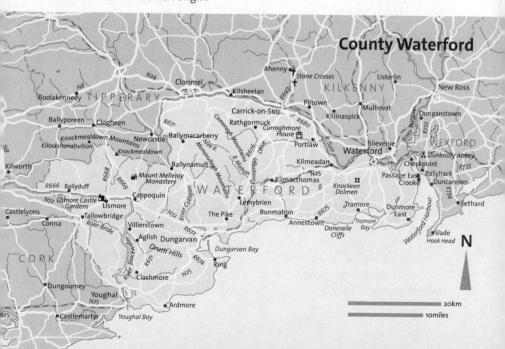

County Waterford

Getting There and Around

By Air
Euroceltic Airways, t 0818 300100, *www.euroceltic.com*. Daily service between London Luton and Waterford City.

By Rail
Mainline train services from Plunkett Station, just across the bridge from the city centre, connect Waterford City with Dublin, Limerick and Rosslare.
Iarnród Eireann, Waterford, t (051) 873401, *www.irishrail.ie*.

By Bus
Bus Eireann has at least twelve buses a day to Dublin and along the coast to Cork, less frequent services to the smaller towns, and a regular connection to the beaches at Tramore. Towns along the River Suir can be reached by Suirway. Buses leave from the Quay opposite the tourist office – take a taxi or walk across the bridge from the rail to the bus station.
Bus Eireann, Waterford, t (051) 879000, *www.buseireann.ie*.
Suirway, Waterford, t (051) 382422.

By Bike
The Raleigh Rent-a-Bike scheme is operated by the following:
Altitude Cycle and Outdoor, 22 Ballybricken, Waterford, t (051) 870356/850228, f (051) 858433, *altitude@indigo.ie*.

Murphy's Toys and Cycles, Main Street, Dungarvan, t (058) 41376.

Festivals

February
Merriman Winter School, Dungarvan, t (098) 27758, *www.merriman.ie*. Celebrates all aspects of Irish culture. Contact Úna Uí Chuinn, Secretary.

April
Sean Dunne Literary Festival, Waterford, t (051) 309983, *art@waterfordcorp.ie*. Readings, workshops and music to celebrate the Waterford writer.

May
Féile na nDéise, a traditional Irish music festival in Dungarvan, t (058) 45273.

August
Spraoi Street Festival, Waterford, t (051) 841808, *spraoi@eircom.net*. 'Ireland's biggest street festival', held on the bank holiday weekend in August; contact Miriam Dunne.

September–October
Waterford International Festival of Light Opera, at the Theatre Royal, Waterford, t (051) 357437, *www.operafestival.com*, *fglosec@eircom.net*. Contact Sean Dower.

History

A brief sketch of the county's history must start with the great race of builders from the Boyne Valley who built Newgrange in County Meath. They spread down to Waterford and left impressive monuments to their civilization. The manner of their decorative carvings is unmistakable and it has been tagged the 'Boyne Valley style'. Their tombs and portal dolmens are particularly concentrated around the seaside resort of Tramore; human remains that date from about 9000 BC have been discovered east of Cappoquin. When the Celts invaded in about 500 BC, the main tribe in Waterford seems to have been the Deisi, who launched successful raids on Roman Britain. They held territory between the Blackwater and the Suir, and such was their impact that Waterford county is still referred to as 'the Decies'.

The Norsemen kept to their patch round *Vadrafjord*, or Waterford city, occupying themselves with raiding and establishing trade links. The early Christian monks made a great impact on the Decies. St Declan of Ardmore is supposed to have pre-dated

St Patrick's mission in the first half of the 5th century. The Monastic foundation at Lismore dates from AD 635 and became famous throughout Europe as a centre of learning, with 20 centres of study within its complex. It was constantly raided and burned by the Norsemen from about AD 833.

In the 1120s, Lismore became the centre of a reformation movement under St Malachy, who wanted to bring the Gaelic church under the domination of the Pope. The Anglo-Normans entered into this scene in about 1167 because of an alliance Dermot MacMurragh, King of Leinster, made with them against the Norsemen of Waterford. This was part of a larger quarrel he was having with O'Rourke of Breffni. Waterford was besieged by the Norman commander Richard de Clare (also called Strongbow) and his men, and eventually fell. Strongbow married the King of Leinster's daughter, and many of his followers also married Irish girls. So the invaders stayed, intermarried with the Gaelic nobility and created a race who, as the years went by, abandoned their allegiance to the kings of England and became Gaelic in their customs. Religion and Reformation brought the English armies back to the shores of Waterford because the city merchants chose to support the Catholic faith. They got further involved in the overspill of the English Civil War, suffering several sieges which ended at last in 1690 with surrender to William III (William of Orange).

Waterford City

Waterford is snugly situated on a curve of the River Suir before it opens out into the sea. It has a reputation for good wine bars and the old parts of it are attractive, although the modern surrounds are very ugly, as is too often the case. A quick tour of the city should perhaps start with the **Waterford Crystal Glass Factory** (tours Jan–Feb, Mon–Fri 9–3.15, Mar–Oct, 8.30–4, Nov–Dec, Mon–Fri 9–3.15; t (051) 332500, f (051) 356624, visitorreception@waterford.ie), a mile or so (2km) west of the city on the Cork Road (N25). There are organized tours around the factory. Most visitors will have heard of Waterford Crystal, which has a worldwide market, and its beautifully patterned cut glass with many different styles. The industry was started in 1783 and pieces dating from that time are now extremely valuable. You can see a wonderful example in the cut-glass chandelier which hangs in the City Hall in the Mall.

The Mall is right in the heart of Waterford, and from here you can see most of the buildings of interest in the city. A tour could include the crystal factory, a quick look in at the City Hall, and then a browse in **Reginald's Tower** (open Easter–May and Oct, daily 10–5, June–Sept, daily 9.30–6.30; adm; t (051) 873501/304220), which guards the end of the Mall by the river. A massive circular fortress with a wall 10ft (3m) thick, it was built in 1003, and named after the Norse governor of the time. When the desperado Strongbow landed in 1170 and took the city, Reginald's Tower became a Norman stronghold and has since then served as a royal residence, a mint, a military barracks and a city prison. It now holds a very interesting display of old artefacts and memorabilia from Waterford's past.

Tourist Information

Waterford: 41 The Quay, t (051) 875823, f (051) 876720, *www.waterfordvisitorcentre.com*; *open all year*; also at Waterford Crystal Visitor Centre, Cork Road, t (051) 358397; *open all year*.

Shopping

Crafts
Aisling Crafts and Sweaters, 61 The Quay, Waterford, t (051) 873262.
City Square, Waterford, t (051) 853528, *www.city-square.ie*, *csquare@iol.ie*. In the city centre.
Dye Gallery, Dyehouse Lane, Waterford, t (051) 878166, f (051) 850399. Pottery.
Kelly's Ltd, The Quay, Waterford, t (051) 873557.
The Treasures Museum Shop, The Quay, Waterford.
The Waterford City Design Centre, 44 The Quay, Waterford. Offers some of the best Irish crafts and modern fashion.
Ardmore Pottery, The Cliff, Ardmore, t (024) 94152.

Crystal
Joseph Knox Ltd, 3–4 Barronstrand Street, Waterford, t (051) 875307/872723, *info@josephknox.com*.
Waterford Crystal Gallery and Factory, Kilbarry, Waterford, t (051) 332500, *visitor-reception@waterford.ie*. On the N25 west.

Sports and Activities

Golf
Faithlegg Golf Club, Faithlegg House, Waterford City, t (051) 382241, f (051) 382664.

Waterford Castle, The Island, Ballinaskill, t (051) 371633, f (051) 871634, *golf@waterford-castle.com*.

Internet Access
Voyager Internet Café, Parnell Court, Parnell Street, Waterford t (051) 843843, *www.voyager.ie*. Open Mon–Sat 10–7.

Pony-trekking
Collaghane Riding Centre, Dunmore Road, Waterford City, t (051) 878203, f (051) 878342, *info@waterfordcastle.com*.

Tours
Walking Tours of Historic Waterford, t (051) 873711, f (051) 850645. An organized tour of the city, starting from the Waterford Treasures Museum. *Mar–Sept 11.45–1.45*.

Where to Stay

Waterford City t (051–)
Waterford Castle, The Island, Ballinaskill, Waterford, t (051) 878203, f (051) 878342/ 879316, *info@waterfordcastle.com* (*luxury*). Two miles (3.2km) downstream from Waterford City, this Anglo-Norman castle is very luxurious, with an indoor pool and excellent sporting facilities.
Granville Hotel, Meagher Quay, Waterford, t (051) 855111/305555, *stay@granville-hotel.ie* (*expensive*). Smart, old-world and conveniently central.
Brown's Townhouse, 29 South Parade, t (051) 870594, f (051) 871923, *info@brownstown-house.com* (*moderate*). This late Victorian house is decorated in period style, with TV and tea-making facilities in ensuite rooms. Breakfast is served at a large dining room

Just down the Quay on Greyfriars Street is the **French Church**, originally a Franciscan foundation built in 1240. It got the label 'The French Church' because it was used by Huguenot refugees who came to Ireland after the Revocation of the Edict of Nantes in 1686. It has a lovely east window and some interesting carvings; the keys are kept in the adjacent **Waterford Museum of Treasures**, in the same building as the tourist office (*open April–Sept, 9.30–6 (June–Aug until 9), Oct–Mar, 10–5; adm; t (051) 304500, f (051) 304501*). This museum has a good collection of artefacts from Viking and Norman times and, in 'The Waterford Viking Show', tells of the city's heritage through table, with fresh fruit salad and home-made bread and jams accompanying a full fry-up. Conveniently located for city centre nightlife, its helpful proprietor is a generous, humourous, well-travelled web designer and native Waterford family man who was once in the Irish Guards.

Dooley's Hotel, 30, The Quay, Waterford, **t** (051) 873531, **f** (051) 870262, *www.dooley-hotel.ie*, *hotel@dooleys-hotel.ie* (*moderate*). Old-established, friendly.

Sion Hill House, Ferrybank, Waterford, **t** (051) 851558, **f** (051) 851678, *sionhill@eircom.net* (*moderate*). Early 19th-century house with lovely gardens covering four acres. Four ensuite bedrooms.

Eating Out

The Wine Vault, Lower High Street, Waterford City, **t** (051) 853444, *info@ waterfordwinevault. com* (*expensive*). Well-stocked wine bar, perhaps the finest in Ireland, in the cellars of an 18th-century wine merchant. Friendly service is given in the small, popular and excellent restaurant with a good nouveau-vegetarian and seafood selection, and substantial entrees. *Dinner only.*

Dwyers Restaurant, 8 Mary Street, Waterford, **t** (051) 877478 (*moderate*). In a converted barracks, cosy, comfortable ambience and good food. *Dinner from 6pm.*

Poppy's Restaurant, Park Road, Waterford City, **t** (051) 304844 (*moderate*). Fresh local seafood, Mediterranean salads and chargrilled specialities; popular with locals. *Lunch and dinner Tues–Sun.*

Rafferty's, Arundel Square, Waterford, **t** (051) 857774 (*moderate*). International

and American-style food, locally recommended.

Haricots Wholefood Restaurant, 11 O'Connell Street, Waterford, **t** (051) 841299 (*inexpensive*). Very good home-made soups, and, a rarity in Irish restaurants – freshly squeezed juice! Delicious home-made ice-cream and cakes. *Open Mon–Fri 9am–8pm, Sat 9–6, closed Sun.*

The Olde Stand, 45 Michael Street, Waterford, **t** (051) 879488 (*inexpensive*). Excellent pub food and a good upstairs restaurant.

Reginald Bar and Restaurant, 2 The Mall, Waterford, **t** (051) 855087 (*inexpensive*). Good pub grub behind Reginald's Tower.

Entertainment and Nightlife

Arts

Waterford Arts Centre, Garter Lane, 50 O'Connell St, Waterford, **t** (051) 55038/77153.

Waterford Show, City Hall, The Mall, Waterford City, **t** (051) 381020. A presentation of Irish music, story, song and dance. *Held May–end Sept on Tues, Thurs and Sat at 9pm.*

Traditional Music

The Ginger Man, Arundel Lane, Waterford, **t** (051) 875041. Traditional music every Mon, Tues and Wed; ballads on Thurs.

The Mansion House, Johnstown, Waterford, **t** (051) 857574. Stylish and traditional bar, comfortable for family and group occasions.

T&H Doolan's, George's Street, Waterford, **t** (051) 857646. Music most nights at this ancient pub.

music, dance and storytelling (*June–Aug at 8pm; for all ages, lasts 1½hrs*). Turn third left after the French Church and you come to **St Olaf's Church**, founded by the Norsemen in about AD 980 and rebuilt by Normans.

At the end of Greyfriars Street in Cathedral Square is the Church of Ireland **Christ Church Cathedral**, which was built in 1779 and is classical Georgian in style. Inside are several older monuments, one of them in remembrance of the 15th-century Lord Mayor Rice, who chose to depict himself in a state of decay with frogs, toads and other wriggling things emerging from his entrails. The cathedral was restored after fire in 1779 to plans created by a local architect, John Roberts. It was redecorated again in 1891. Another lovely building is the Chamber of Commerce in George Steet, built by the same architect as the cathedral. You can ask to see inside it. In September the Theatre Royal hosts the Waterford International Festival of Light Opera. Waterford City produced some great actors whose names are still revered in the acting world: Mrs Jordon in 1767, and Charles Kean in 1811. It is also where the Christian Brothers opened their first scholastic establishment in 1802. Edmund Ignatius Rice had his first foundation at Mount Sion in Barrack Street, since when the order has spread all over the world. **Mount Congreve Demesne and Wild Garden** (*guided tours by appointment only; adm exp; t (051) 384115/348103*) at Kilmeadan, 5 miles (8km) west of Waterford city, covers over 110 acres with one of the world's largest collections of rhododendrons.

Around County Waterford

Portlaw to Annestown

Portlaw, on the River Clodagh, northwest of Waterford on the R680, was founded as a model village by a Quaker family, the Malcolmsons, who had started up a cotton industry in the 19th century. Unfortunately many of the quaint houses have been modernized and become dull in the process. Beside the town is **Curraghmore House and Gardens**, the family home of the Marquis of Waterford (*open Jan Mon–Fri 9–1, May–mid July, Mon–Sat 9–1, and by appointment; t (051) 387101, f (051) 387101*). The family name is Beresford and they were once noted for their dominance in the Church and Government; one of them was called 'Sand Martin' because of his skill in picking sinecures and plum jobs for his many friends. (A characteristic of the sand martin is to share his nest with a numerous extended family.) Curraghmore is worth visiting just to see the splendid, grey 18th-century house in its parkland setting, with gentle hills rising behind. The specimen trees have reached a magnificent size; they were mainly planted in the 19th century. It is worth seeking out the 18th-century shell house made by the Countess of Tyrone.

Nearby on the Waterford Harbour is the village of Crooke. Roughly opposite and a little further down is Hook Head, interesting because the two – so it is claimed – are immortalized in the saying 'By Hook or by Crooke', a phrase first used by sailors. There is nothing much to see at Crooke, but **Passage East**, further up the estuary, is an atmospheric village which has been a ferry crossing for centuries and an important port. It was here that Strongbow landed in 1170, and here too that Henry II landed a year later with 4,000 men in 400 ships to make sure that Strongbow did not set up a rival kingdom and step into the shoes of his father-in-law Dermot MacMurrough, who had just died. He formally declared Waterford a Royal City, and tradition holds that it remained loyal to him and his heirs until the 16th century and the English Reformation. Today there is a car ferry across from Passage East to County Wexford.

Dunmore East, 10 miles (16km) southwest of the city, is a little seaside place, rather like a Devon fishing village, with beautiful little headlands made of old red sandstone carved into cliffs and safe bathing beaches. Sea pinks grow along the cliff edges,

Tourist Information

Tramore: Railway Square, t (051) 381572,
www.tramore.ie; open June–Sept.
Dungarvan: the Square, t (058) 41741; *open
all year.*
Ardmore: t (024) 94444; *open in summer only.*
Lismore: t (058) 54975; *open April–Oct.*

Shopping

Crafts
Waterford Woodcraft, Dunabrattin,
Annestown, t (051) 396110.
Ardmore Pottery and Craft Gallery, Ardmore,
t (024) 94152.

Crystal
Criostal na Rinne (Eamonn Terry), Ballinagoul,
Ring, t (058) 46174.

Sports and Activities

Fishing
For **sea-angling**, contact:
Dungarvan Sea Angling Club, Dungarvan,
t (058) 41298.
Dungarvan East Angling Charters,
Dunmore East, t (051) 383397, *workingboat@
indigo.ie.*

Golf
West Waterford Golf and Country Club,
Dungarvan, t (058) 43216/41475, f (058)
44343, *info@waterfordgolf.com.*
Faithlegg Golf Club, t (051) 382241.
Dungarvan Golf Club, Knocknagranagh,
Dungarvan, t (058) 43310,
f (058) 44113, *dungarvangolf@
cablesurf.com.*

Indoor Leisure Centres
Splashworld, Tramore, t (051) 390176. A water-
based adventure centre.

Pony-trekking
Melody's Riding Stables, Ballymacarberry,
t (052) 36147.

Walking
Walk through the Comeraghs on the
Munster Way, a marked trail, or St Declan's
Walk, a popular pilgrimage route that goes
from Lismore to Ardmore. Ask the tourist office
for details. Orienteering, bird-watching, hill-
walking and other activities are also organized
through the tourist offices in summer.
Shielbaggan Outdoor Education Centre,
Ramsgrange, t (051) 389550.

Water Sports
Excellent beaches for swimming are at
Tramore, Dunmore East, Ardmore and around
Dungarvan. Tramore is also a popular spot for
surfing.
Oceanic Manoeuvres, 3 Riverstown, Tramore,
t (051) 390944.
T–Bay Surf Centre, on the beach, Tramore,
t (051) 391297. Surf hire, beach facilities,
activity camps.
Dunmore East Adventure Centre, on the
harbour, Dunmore East, t (051) 383783.
Sailing, windsurfing, canoeing.

Where to Stay

O'Shea's Hotel, Strand Street, Tramore, t (051)
381246, f (051) 390144, *www.osheas-hotel.
com (moderate)*. Small family-run hotel,
close to the beach.
Castle Farm, Milstreet, Cappagh, near
Dungarvan, t (058) 68049, f (058) 68099

where there are some peaceful places to walk. Follow the coast path leading along
to Brownstown Head, where there are the remains of a fort. You will meet colourful
fishermen in the bars, although they can be quite clannish. Dunmore was the centre
of a thriving herring industry and the Irish terminal for a mail service from England in
the early 19th century.

Tramore, 10 miles (16km) around the coast to the west, is the place to go if you want
to meet Irish people on holiday rather than fellow foreigners. Its 3 miles (4.8km) of
sand are swept by the Gulf Stream, which makes the sea fun for bathers and surfers.

(*moderate*). This has a lovely restored 15th-century wing. It is not a smart castle, but Mrs Nugent has made it very homely. Tennis, trout fishing, and riding are available.

Kate's Cottage, Riverside, Tarr's Bridge, Dungarvan, **t** (058) 41040 (*inexpensive*). A modern yet cosy, thatched self-catering cottage in its own grounds, just over a mile from Dungarvan town centre. Contact Mrs Pauline Beresford. *Open all year.*

Round Tower Hotel, College Road, Ardmore, **t** (024) 94494 (*inexpensive*). Simple accommodation in an old convent, with a restaurant. *Open Sun lunch year round; lunch and dinner end May–end Sept.*

Richmond House, Cappoquin, **t** (058) 54278 (*moderate*). Comfortable Georgian country house, en suite rooms; also contains a very good restaurant (*expensive*).

Aglish House, Aglish, **t** (024) 96191 (*inexpensive*). Nice stone farmhouse, near the River Blackwater.

Ballyrafter House, Lismore, **t** (058) 54002 (*moderate*). Comfortable Georgian house; an ideal place to centre yourself for fishing or just exploring the lovely Blackwater Valley.

Blackwater Lodge, Upper Ballyduff, **t** (058) 60235, **f** (058) 60162 (*moderate*). A snug place for fishermen to swap stories in.

Bennett's Church, Old School House, Ballymacarberry, Nire Valley, **t** (052) 36217, or **t** 0882 571203, *richiem@tinet.ie* (*inexpensive*). Found on the Clonmel–Dungarvan road, an old converted school in a pretty setting, furnished by Martin and Una Moore with antiques. *Open all year.*

Clonanav Farm Guesthouse, Ballymacarberry, Nire Valley, **t** (052) 36141, **f** (052) 36294, *www.clonanav.com* (*inexpensive*). Larry and Eileen Ryan are experts on local walks and angling. They also offer self-catering

accomodation in nearby Orchard House, a 4-bedroom bungalow.

Self-catering

Cappagh House, Cappagh, Dungarvan, **t** (058) 68185. House with 1 double, 2 singles and a cot; contact Mrs Claire Chavasse.

Eating Out

McAlpin's Suir Inn, Cheekpoint, north of Passage East, **t** (051) 382220 (*inexpensive*). Good pub grub. *Evenings only.*

Hartley's Bistro, 21 Queen Street, Tramore, **t** (051) 857774 (*moderate*). Features seafood and game. *Evenings only.*

The Ship Restaurant and Bar, Dunmore East, **t** (051) 383141 (*moderate*). Casual, fun atmosphere. Good seafood.

Barron's Bakery and Coffee House, The Square, Cappoquin, **t** (058) 54045 (*inexpensive*). A good place for lunch.

Richmond House, Cappoquin, **t** (058) 54278 (*inexpensive*). This has won several awards for its globally-influenced modern Irish cuisine. *Open Tues–Sat 7–9pm.*

Entertainment and Nightlife

Traditional Music

Two very good spots can be found practically next to each other, just west of Dungarvan on the N25.

Bean a Leanna Pub, 86 O'Connell St, in the centre of Dungarvan, **t** (058) 44882. **Marine Bar**, Pulla Ring, west of Dungarvan, **t** (058) 46520.

Seanachie Restaurant, N25, west of Dungarvan, **t** (058) 46285 (*inexpensive*).

It has a well-developed amenity complex beside the promenade, a miniature railway and boating lake, attractions like 'Laserworld' and 'Splashworld', and a first-class racecourse. A quick and pleasant walk to the west of the town leads by a coastal path to some steep cliffs known as the Doneraile Cliffs.

The remarkable **Knockeen Dolmen** is nearby, but quite difficult to find. Follow the signs off the Tramore to Carrick on Suir road (R682). Drive until you meet a three-forked road. Take the right fork and drive uphill until you come to a white farmhouse. Opposite is a field gate and stile. The dolmen is in the shadow of the hedge on the far side of the field. It probably marks the grave of a local Deisi chieftain. This sort of tomb-building was going on when people moved from being hunter-gatherers to keeping domestic animals and growing their own food. Two large matching upright stones mark the entrance, with three smaller standing stones behind. The uprights support the heavy capstone, which is thought to have been raised up by a system of propping and levering. **Annestown**, on the R675 nearby, also has a lovely beach. So does **Bunmahon**, further west, a small fishing village which is perched above some magnificent cliffs.

Dungarvan and Ardmore

Dungarvan is a pleasant seaside town where the River Colligan broadens into Dungarvan Bay. There are the remains of an old Norman Castle and a pretty arched bridge. In the graveyard of the Church of Ireland church by the river is a curious 'holed' gable with circular openings. Two and a half miles (4km) northwest of the town, on the fork of the R672 and N72, is the **Master McGrath Memorial** erected in 1873: a plain stone structure with an elegant spire. The tablet is engraved not with the name of some famous Victorian, but with the image of a greyhound – the locals claim it is the first monument in the world to be dedicated to a dog. (Master McGrath won the Waterloo Cup for coursing on three occasions during the 19th century.) The animal is still remembered in ballads and by a brand of superior dog food. About 5 miles (8km) south on the R674 is the famous Irish-speaking village of **Ring**, the only *Gaeltacht* area in the southeast, where students take summer courses in Irish.

Ardmore, further west along the coast on the R673, combines a long and popular beach with an important ecclesiastical site. Just outside the village are the remains of a 7th-century monastic settlement founded by St Declan, possibly as early as the 5th century. Some say St Declan was busy converting the pagans to Christianity whilst St Patrick was still a slave herding cattle. The ancient remains are spread out over a small area and interspersed with more modern gravestones and memorials. They include the most graceful **round tower** in Ireland, built in the 11th century of cut stone. Its entrance door is 10ft (3m) above the ground, so that the monks could store precious things up there: in times of trouble they entered it by means of a retractable ladder. There is also the remains of a 12th-century Romanesque **cathedral**, with a wealth of figure-sculpture spread over almost the whole of the west gable. The figures are badly weathered but it is just possible to make out the Judgement of Solomon, Adam and Eve with the Tree and the Serpent, and the Adoration of the Magi. In the nave and chancel are some ogham stones from *c.* 400 AD which suggest this was a burial place even before St Declan arrived. The lower portion of the building is believed to incorporate part of an earlier 7th-century church. Besides the cathedral and the tower, there is St Declan's Oratory in the eastern part of the graveyard. It is reputed to be where he is buried, and on 24 July many locals still make a pilgrimage to it. St Declan's Oratory is typical of the small, dark dwellings in which the early fathers used to live. Apparently this preference for separate cells grouped together comes from the Coptic Egyptian influence in the Irish Church, along with a rejection of the bodily senses and a deep suspicion of women.

(St Declan's Oratory was not in fact built until the 9th century, but Irish architecture seems to advance very slowly.) This foundation was the recognized seat of a bishop as early as AD 1111.

About half a mile to the east is St Declan's **Holy Well**. It was renovated in 1789, and many people still visit it. There is a stone chair, three stone crosses and a stone basin for pilgrims to wash in. Most holy wells have pre-Christian associations of magical healing powers, which the early clerics modified to fit in with Christianity. Legend and fact become impossibly mixed up and this area is scattered with objects that have folk stories behind them. Down on the strand is a *crannog*, visible only when the tide is out. There too lies **St Declan's Stone**, at the end of the strand. It was supposed to have been used by the saint to carry his bell and vestments across the sea from Wales. It is reputed that if you crawl beneath it your aches and pains will be cured – although, of course, this manoeuvre is impossible for sinners. **St Declan's Way**, the old pilgrims' route between here and Cashel in Co. Tipperary is popular with walkers; this includes a 2½-mile (4km) route around Ardmore itself.

Inland: Cappoquin to Ballymacabry and the Nire Valley

An unmarked road runs from the southwest corner of the county, through Clashmore and Aglish to Cappoquin, following stretches of the Blackwater that are lined by stately grey houses. It also passes through **Dromana Wood**, a small bit of ancient forest that is embellished with a unique and delightful domed gatehouse at the northern end, a Victorian folly in a style of architecture that has been described as 'Hindu-Gothic'; and indeed, it resembles a miniature Taj Mahal. **Cappoquin**, famous for chickens, is at the head of the tidal estuary of the River Blackwater. Wooded hills surround it, whilst the northern slopes of the Knockmealdown Mountains rise to the north. This is an excellent place to fish for trout or roach.

Four miles (6.4km) to the north, off the R669, is the Trappist Cistercian Abbey of **Mount Melleray**. The monastery is modern, but in its precincts are five ogham stones. The order has built up an almost self-sufficient community which still keeps the old rule of monastic hospitality, so do not hesitate to accept if they offer you a meal – everyone is welcome. At the foot of the hill on the road to the abbey is **Melleray Grotto**, where a statue of the Virgin is said to move.

The N72 from Cappoquin to Lismore follows the River Blackwater, flowing smoothly between green fields and trees, overlooked by gracious houses. **Lismore** has one of the finest **castles** in Ireland, dating back in parts to the original built by King John in 1185. It belonged to Sir Walter Raleigh in 1589 and he sold it to the adventurer Richard Boyle, later the first Earl of Cork, who apparently said: 'I arrived out of England into Ireland, where God guided me hither, bringing with me a taffeta doublet and a pair of velvet breeches, a new shirt of laced fustin cutt upon taffeta, a bracelet of gold, a diamond ring, and twenty-seven pounds three shillings in monie in my purse.' His 14th child, Robert, is remembered as the Father of Chemistry, having established Boyle's Law in the late 17th century, which proves that air has weight – a milestone in the dissociation of chemistry from alchemy. In 1814 the Lismore Crozier and the 15th-century manuscript *The Book of Lismore* were discovered here in one of the walls (both are now on display in the National Museum in Dublin). Eventually the castle passed through the female line to the Devonshire family, who still own it. The present castle was rebuilt in the mid-19th century by the 6th Duke of Devonshire. *Lios mor* means 'great fort' in Irish, and this great pile of grey castellated stone hanging over the Blackwater River lives up to all one's expectations of what a castle should be. Unfortunately it is not open to the general public, although it can be rented, but the **gardens** are very lovely, especially the stately eight hundred-year-old Yew Walk (*entrance in the town of Lismore; open mid April–mid Oct, daily 1.45–4.45, from 11am in high season; adm; t (058) 54424*). It is said that Edmund Spenser wrote part of *The Faerie Queene* here. Try to visit in late spring, when the camellias and magnolias are in bloom.

Lismore is an ancient place of renown, both for learning and piety. Under St Colman in the 8th century it won the title of 'Luminary of the Western World', and men came from all over Europe to study here. The Norsemen, of course, were attracted to it like bees to honey, and looted the place frequently, but the monastery and abbey were finally destroyed by Raymond le Gros and his Norman mercenaries in 1173. The Gothic **Cathedral of St Carthach** is one of the loveliest in Ireland and is approached by a tree-lined walk. It dates from medieval times but was restored by the Earl of Cork in 1633. The graceful limestone spire was added in 1827. There is an interesting 1557 MacGrath tomb and a window by Burne-Jones, made by William Morris. The **Heritage Centre** in the Courthouse details the town's ancient history.

On the R668 a few hundred yards north of the castle, is a fine walk to **Ballysagartmore Towers**, a Gothic style gateway and tower which guards the entrance to a three arched bridge; a waterfall adds to the beauty of the scene. To the west of Lismore, the nearby village of Ballyduff on the Lismore–Fermoy road (R666) is another possible base for salmon or roach fishing. To the northeast, the **Nire Valley** is fantastic for views, pony-trekking and walking. On either side are mountain slopes, clear tumbling streams and woods. (It lies between the Comeragh and Knockmealdown ranges and can be approached from Clonmel to Ballymacarberry, or from the R671 off the N72 near Cappoquin.)

Ballymacarberry is a welcome spot for pony-trekkers and walkers exploring the Nire Valley and the heather-covered slopes of the Comeragh Mountains. The local bar is very friendly and hires out ponies, as does Melody's Riding Stables (*see* 'Sports and Activities', p.249). A superb car drive awaits you if you head for the village of Lemybrien at the junction of the Waterford/Carrick-on-Suir road and Dungarvan roads (R676 and N25). Just north of it is a highly scenic road through the mountains called the **Comeragh Drive**, which takes you up to the Mahon Waterfall. It is well signposted. Locals call the road to the falls the 'Magic Road'; at just the right spot, if you can find it, you can take your car out of gear and enjoy the bizarre impression that you are rolling uphill. **Rathgormuck**, on the R678 about 6 miles (10 km) from Clonmel, is a lovely little village on the northern side of the Comeragh mountains. It is a popular hiking centre, and boasts the remains of an early-medieval church and castle.

County Tipperary

To get a clear idea of the beauty of Tipperary – and it is very beautiful, even though it lacks a stretch of coastline – walk to the top of Slievenamon, which in early summer is scented with the almond fragrance of gorse blossom. Slievenamon is a county landmark; a conical mountain north of Clonmel that rises to 2,358ft (719m). Up there, you get the feeling of space and a wide, splendid view: to the south are the Comeraghs and silver ribbon of the Suir; to the west, the Galtees; and to the north, the Rock of Cashel rising out of the flat, rich farmland.

Slievenamon in Irish means 'mountain of the fairy women'. The story relates how Fionn and the Fianna warriors had dallied with fairy women, so when Fionn decided to wed, to prevent any of them becoming jealous, he said he would marry the one who reached the summit of the mountain first. However, the wily man had set his heart on Grainne, the daughter of King Cormac, and so he whisked her up to the top the evening before the race. When the panting winner reached the top, 'there sat the delicate, winsome Grainne, and not a feather of her ruffled'. So much for legend.

The refrain 'It's a long way to Tipperary' entered the battlefields of the Somme as a favourite British marching song during the First World War. So many people have heard of the county without knowing of its glorious countryside and its wealth of

Getting There and Around

By Rail
Mainline routes (Waterford–Limerick and Cork–Dublin) pass through the county and stop at Thurles, Cahir, Clonmel, Carrick-on-Suir and Roscrea. The two main lines cross at busy Limerick Junction station, just outside Tipperary town.
Iarnród Eireann, t (01) 836 6222, *www.irishrail.ie*.

By Bus
Bus Eireann services are limited to a few daily Tipperary–Waterford runs via Cahir, Clonmel and Carrick-on-Suir. Clonmel, Cahir and Cashel also have some direct connections to Dublin and Cork. A competing line, Kavanagh's, connects Dublin with Thurles, Cashel and Tipperary.
Bus Eireann, Waterford, t (051) 879000, *www.buseireann.ie*.
Kavanagh's, Cashel, t (062) 51563.

By Bike
The Raleigh Rent-a-Bike network operates throughout the county.
Classic Cycles, 8 Mary Street, Clonmel, t (052) 27827.

Mcinerneys, Main Street, Cashel, t (062) 61225.
OK Sports, New Street, Carrick-on-Suir, t (051) 640626.

Festivals

June
Clonmel Show, t (052) 22611, *news@sportingpress.iol.ie*. Horse show that includes jumping.

July
Cashel Cultural Festival, t (052) 22611, *news@sportingpress.iol.ie*.
Munster *Fleadh Cheoil*, t (01) 280 0295. Traditional Irish music, song and dance.
Kilcommon Festival, t (062) 78103. An eight-day affair in the rural highlands between Nenagh and Thurles. Traditional music and dance, Gaelic games, sheepdog trials and street entertainment.

August
Aonach Paddy O'Brien, Newtown, t (067) 42900, *eminogue@eircom.net*. Traditional music and arts festival, held in the name of a local composer and accordionist.

12th- and 13th-century church buildings and castles. For the angler there are rivers of brown trout; for the archaeologist, plenty of Stone Age and Iron Age sites. Horse lovers will be attracted by the hunting and the gourmet riding holidays around Lough Derg. This is also a fine place for the breeding of horses, gun-dogs and greyhounds. But, for passing travellers, it is the story of Cashel of the Kings and the strength of Cahir Castle which hold the imagination. Another treasure is the border town of Birr, up in the north of the county, where the gardens and arboretum of the castle are amongst the finest on the island, and there is soon to be a splendid scientific centre.

History

The history of this county is very closely linked to that of the great Ormonde family. The founder of the family in Ireland was Theobald Fitzwalter, who came over in 1185 with Prince John, and was later appointed to high office as Chief Butler to the Lord of Ireland. Thenceforth, the family surname was Butler, and its members generally remained faithful to the interests of the British crown. This was in direct contrast to their kinsfolk and arch enemies, the Geraldines. The Geraldines were close neighbours and split into two branches, Desmond and Kildare. Tipperary was divided into two Ridings; with Clonmel as the capital of the South Riding, and Nenagh as the capital of the North Riding. This division dates from some early administrative peculiarity.

Tipperary has always been a rich prize for the winners of battles and uprisings, because of its fertile farms and pastures. In the 18th century it was a county of landlords and relatively prosperous peasants. The region was settled during this time by Palatines who were fleeing religious persecution. The potato famine hit hard in the 1840s, and, later, during the uncertain times leading up to Independence, many landlords were burnt out.

Southern Tipperary

Clonmel and the Southeast

Clonmel ('The Honeyed Meadows'), in the south of the county on the N24, has a lovely setting by the River Suir and the Comeragh Mountains. An important town when the Norman family of Butler were all-powerful, today it is the largest in the county, with bustling shops and industries that produce everything from cider to computer parts. It has a prosperous, bright look about it, which is not surprising as most of Tipperary, particularly its central region around the Suir and the Golden Vale, is particularly fertile. The restored Franciscan Friary in the town centre has retained its old tower and a 15th-century Butler tomb with stone effigies of a knight and lady. **Tipperary County Museum**, in a grand 19th-century house in Parnell Street (*open all year, Tues–Sat 10–1 and 2–5; adm; t (052) 25399*), has town memorabilia and a gallery with some good 20th-century paintings. Parts of Clonmel's medieval walls still stand around William Street and Kickham Street; though picturesque, they weren't strong enough to keep Oliver Cromwell out in 1650, despite a spirited defence under

Tourist Information

Clonmel: Sarsfield Street, t (052) 22960; *open all year, Mon–Fri 9.30–5.*
Cashel: Main Street, t (062) 61333; *open April–Sept Mon–Sat 10–6.*
Cahir: Castle Street, t (052) 41453; *open May–Sept Mon–Sat 9–6, July–Aug daily 9–6.*

Shopping

Crafts
Rossa Pottery, Cashel, t (062) 61388.
Sarah Ryan Ceramics, Palmers Hill, Cashel, t (062) 61994.
Patsy Cahill, Mullinahone, t (051) 647056. Basketry.
South East Regional Craft Centre, Church Street, Granary, t (052) 26200.
Mandy Parslow Pottery, Clonbeg Lodge, Glen of Aherlow, t (062) 56011.

Glass
Tipperary Crystal, Ballynoran, on the N24, Carrick-on-Suir, t (051) 641188, *tippcrys@iol.ie, sales@tipperarycrystal.com.*

Health Foods
The Honey Pot, 14 Abbey Street, Clonmel, t (052) 21457. Shop and restaurant with organic vegetable market on Thursdays and Fridays.

Sports and Activities

Fishing
Brown trout and salmon fishing are good on the River Suir and its many tributaries.
Clonmel Salmon and Trout Anglers, Kavanagh's Sport Shop, Upper O'Connell Street, Clonmel, t (052) 21279.
Cashel Golden Tipperary Anglers Asscociation, Cahervillahow, Cashel, t (062) 72354.

Reiska Cahir, Cahir, t (052) 42729.

Golf
Clonmel Course, 3 miles (5km) outside Clonmel at Lyreanearle, t (052) 21138. A very pretty course.
Ballykisteen Golf and Country Club, Limerick Junction, near Tipperary, t (062) 33333.
Tipperary Golf Club, Rathanny, Tipperary, t (062) 51119.
Slievenamon Golf Club, t (052) 32213.

Horse-racing
In Tipperary, Thurles and Clonmel throughout the year.

Internet Access
The Olde Church, Bansha, t (062) 54980, *theoldechurchbansha@eircom.net. Open Mon–Fri.*

Pony-trekking
Davern Equestrian Centre, Tannersrath Lower, Clonmel, t (052) 22991.
Cahir Equestrian Centre, Ardfinnan Road, Cahir, t (052) 41426.
Lissava House Stables, Cahir, t (052) 41117.
Hillcrest Equestrian Centre, Glabally, t (062) 37915, *hillcrestcentre@eircom.net.* Trekking, lessons, etc.
Lisfuncheon Equestrian Centre, Lisfuncheon, Ballyporeen, t (052) 67121.

Walking
The **Cahir Way** is a signposted walking route from Cahir to Ballydavid through the Galtee Mountains. There are also trails between Carrick-on-Suir, Clonmel and Clogheen near 'The Vee', in the Knockmealdown Mountains.
Ms Jane Toomey, t (062) 33360, *tlg@iol.ie.* For information on the above routes.
Margaret O'Keefe, t (052) 33456. For details on trails around Slievenamon.

Hugh Duff O'Neill. Laurence Sterne, who wrote one of the first English experimental novels, *Tristram Shandy,* was born in Clonmel (in 1713); as was George Borrow, another English novelist (1803–81). The enterprising Italian pedlar Charles Bianconi, who gave Ireland its first public transport service when he ran his celebrated Bianconi Long Cars from Clonmel to Cahir in 1815, came to Clonmel as a poor vendor of holy pictures, and

Where to Stay

County Tipperary has really got its act together for well-run bed and breakfast in lovely country houses. The following establishments are in beautiful places, have comfortable rooms, and produce delicious food for breakfast and dinner.

Knocklofty House, Clonmel, t (052) 38222, f (052) 38300, *knocklofty@eircom.net* (*moderate*). Overlooks the river Suir, is central and very comfortable.

Mobarnane House, Fethard, t/f (052) 31962, *info@mobarnanehouse.com* (*moderate*). A newly renovated 18th-century family house with a late Georgian addition. The friendly owners offer a very high standard of service: excellent dinners and breakfasts are served with clockwork efficiency. Ask for local advice. *Not recommended for young children.*

Killaghy Castle, Mullinahone, t (052) 53112 (*inexpensive*). An 18th-century manor farmhouse with a Norman castle attached. Quiet location north of Slievenamon, with horse-riding close by. The village of Mullinahone is noted for its memorabilia and the grave of 19th-century novelist and revolutionary Charles J. Kickham. The castle is available for 18 people, self-catering, at approximately €3,800 per week; contact Mrs Sherwood.

Cashel Palace Hotel, Main Street, Cashel, t (062) 62707, f (062) 61521, *www.cashel-palace.ie, reception@cashel-palace.ie* (*luxury*). Elegant living in an historic and beautiful 18th-century house, just off the main street of the town.

Ros-Guill House, Kilkenny Road, Cashel, t (062) 61507 (*inexpensive*). Great views of the Rock of Cashel and tasty breakfasts.

Rock House, Dundrum Road, Cashel, t (062) 61003 (*inexpensive*). A restored 18th-century coach house; hostel and self-catering.

Indaville, Cashel, t (062) 62075 (*inexpensive*). Friendly and comfortable accommodation from Mrs Murphy.

Cashel Holiday Hostel, John Street, Cashel, t (062) 62330 (*inexpensive*). Cheerful hostel in an old town house; tours arranged.

Dundrum House, Dundrum, near Cashel, t (062) 71116 (*expensive*). Country hotel furnished with Victorian period furniture. Elevators make access easy for the disabled. Good food and excellent sporting facilities.

Cappamura House, Cappamura, Dundrum, t (062) 71127 (*inexpensive*). Nicely furnished rooms in a 300-year-old farmhouse; horses available.

Lismacue House, Bansha, t (062) 54106, f (062) 54126, *lismac@indigo.ie* (*moderate*). A beautiful lime tree avenue leads you to this gracious 17th-century house. The owners offer you a warm welcome, with excellent dinners and breakfasts and a real sense of Anglo-Irish tradition – not to mention tons of local advice.

Bansha House, Bansha, t (062) 54194, f (062) 54215, *banshahouse@eircom.net* (*moderate– inexpensive*). A comfortable Georgian home set in 100 acres of farmland, where brood mares and foals roam among the beech and lime trees. Its hospitable, welcoming owners, John and Mary Marnane, encourage visitors to relax or explore the 'walker's paradise' surrounding the house. They also rent a self-catering cottage nearby. *Dinner served upon advance request.*

Aherlow House Hotel, Glen of Aherlow, t (062) 56153/56147, f (062) 56212, *aherlow@iol.ie* (*moderate*). A popular local hotel which lies in the middle of a forest.

The Glen Hotel, Aherlow, t (062) 56146, f (062) 56152 (*moderate*). A family-run hotel, set among trees, near the Galty Mountains.

stayed. Near his original headquarters is Clonmel's **Museum of Transport**, at Richmond Mill in Emmet Street (*open all year, Mon–Sat 10–6, also June–Sept Sun 2.30–6; adm; t (052) 29727*). The Parish Church of St Mary has a fine east window. About 2 miles (3 km) east of town, off the N24 and near Marlfield, is **St Patrick's Well**. This is a noted local beauty spot, in a pretty glen and near the Scillogues twin lakes.

Self-catering

Anner Castle, Ballinamore, Kilsheelan, near Clonmel, t (052) 33365, *www. annercastle.com, annercastle@eircom. net*. Accommodation in a romantic 19th-century folly, set in landscaped parkland.

Ballyslateen, Golden, Cashel, t (062) 72287 (*inexpensive*). A lovely farmhouse offered by Betty Flood.

Cooper's Cottage, Raheen, Bansha, t (062) 54027, *cooperscottage@esat.clear.ie*. 19th-century cottage, in a convenient spot for seeing the Glen of Aherlow.

Lismacue, Bansha, t (062) 54106. A very comfortable 17th-century coach house. Sleeps 6, contact Mrs Nicholson.

Carrigeen Castle, Cork Road, Cahir, t (052) 41370 (*inexpensive*). Lovely cosy rooms.

Eco Booley, Clogheen, t (052) 65191, *www.ecobooley.com*. A pioneering eco-friendly cottage.

Eating Out

Mulcahy's Restaurant, 47 Gladstone Street, Clonmel, t (052) 22825 (*moderate*). Pub lunches.

Abbey Restaurant, Abbey Street, Clonmel, t (054) 36060 (*inexpensive*). Wholefood and vegetarian restaurant in an old warehouse. Good range of soups and stir-fry. *Daytime only*.

Honeypot, 14 Abbey Street, Clonmel, t (052) 21457 (*inexpensive*). Tasty wholefood restaurant, crunchy salads and bakes.

Chez Hans, Moore Lane, Cashel, t (062) 61177 (*expensive*). In an old church. Excellent food cooked by Hans, who is German. *Dinner only*.

Cashel Palace Hotel, Cashel, t (062) 61411 (*expensive– moderate*). Choose between the formal Four Seasons Restaurant and the attractive Cellar, where the traditional Irish

dishes are a speciality, and are more affordable in price.

Legends Guesthouse and The Kiln Restaurant, Cashel, t (062) 61292/63115 (*expensive–moderate*). French and Irish menu offered, and a pre-theatre option served for those attending Brú Ború, next door. *Lunch Sun only, dinner Tues–Sat 6.30–9.30*.

Granny's Kitchen, St Patrick's Rock, Cashel, t (062) 61861 (*inexpensive*). Children and vegetarians welcome in a traditional house. *Open 9.30–8 during summer, for breakfast, lunch and dinner*.

Baileys of Cashel, Main Street, Cashel, t (062) 61937 (*inexpensive*). Reasonable lunches and dinners in this guesthouse.

Dundrum House, Dundrum, t (062) 71116 (*expensive*). Excellently prepared, simple Irish cooking.

The Glen Hotel, Glen of Aherlow, t (062) 56152 (*moderate*). In the most spectacular position overlooking the wooded valley; reasonable meals.

Clifford's at The Bell, 2 Pearse Street, Cahir, t (052) 43232 (*expensive–moderate*). Nice and cosy, with vegetarian options and a pleasant view.

The Spearman, 97 Main Street, Cahir, t (062) 61143 (*moderate*). Good for a light lunch; dinner served 5.30–9.30.

Crock of Gold, 1 Castle Street, opposite Cahir castle, t (052) 41951 (*inexpensive*). Small restaurant above craft shop; handy for snacks and afternoon tea.

Entertainment and Nightlife

Brú Ború, beside Rock of Cashel, t (062) 61122, f (062) 62700. Traditional Irish music and dance show. *Open summer Tues–Sat 9pm*.

Further downriver, still following the N24, is the old town of **Carrick-on-Suir**, a thriving market town which in the past had a big wool industry, founded by the Duke of Ormonde in 1640. His family, the Butlers, had long made Carrick their stronghold, and Black Tom the 10th Earl of Ormonde built himself the fortified Elizabethan mansion home you can see, known as **Ormond Castle** (*open mid June–Sept, daily*

9.30–6.30; guided tours only; adm; t (051) 640787). He was loyal to Elizabeth I, and was evidently hoping for quieter times. There is nothing else quite like this Tudor mansion in Ireland, for when it was built the transition from the fortified castle to the undefended house had not yet begun, and when it did, the Tudor style gave way to other architectural fashions. It has been sympathetically restored, returning to the long gallery the great carved fireplace that adorned Kilkenny Castle for many years.

Ahenny ('Ford of Fire'), about 3½ miles (6km) from Carrick-on-Suir off the R697 and the border with County Kilkenny, boasts two elaborately carved stone crosses from the 8th century in a sleepy old churchyard. The bases are carved with wonderful figures; and the crosses themselves with spiral, interlaced and fret designs. The art of the high cross has developed here from abstract decoration to the telling of a story in stone. There is a message on the base of the larger North Cross depicting Christ giving the Apostles their mission; and on the base of the South Cross, the scene of Daniel in the lion's den. Around the neighbourhood are some very extensive slate quarries. Their vast spoil-heaps and water-filled holes are softened by many kinds of orchids and yellow irises, known locally in Gaelic as *felistroms.*

Near Fethard, about 6 miles (10km) north of Clonmel on the R689, is **Kiltinane Castle** and **Kiltinane Old Church**, where you can see some *Sheila-na-Gigs* smothered in ivy. **Fethard** itself, 3 miles (5km) further north, has a lovely old church with fine 15th-century windows and a square tower. There is also a 14th-century Augustinian abbey, which has a fine collection of gravestones and beautiful arches beside the sanctuary. It is always open to view. On the Cashel road (R692) just outside the village is a **Folk and Transport Museum** (*open all year, Sun 11.30–5, plus May–Sept, Mon–Sat 10–6; adm; t (052) 31516*) with some interesting items from the agricultural past, including a man-trap, for catching poachers. Three miles (4.8km) northeast of Fethard is the ruined **Knockelly Castle** with a fine 16th-century tower. Five miles (8km) south of the town is the ancient **Church of Donaghmore**, in a very ruined state. It still has a very beautiful carved Irish-Romanesque doorway.

Travelling north from Fethard towards the Slieveardagh Hills is **Killenaule**, on the R689. This village has an impressive example of a Gothic-style Catholic church. There is a good view of Slievenamon from here. Ten miles (16km) further north, again following the R689, you come to **Kilcooly Abbey** (*always accessible*), on an unnumbered road which follows the wall of Kilcooly estate. (Park your car outside the entrance gate, as requested, and walk a few hundred yards up the avenue. Take a path to the right, past the Church of Ireland church, and through a field which has a marvellous stone dovecote.) Kilcooly Abbey is one of the most outstanding examples of Cistercian building in County Tipperary. It was founded in 1183 and nearly ruined in 1445, with subsequent reconstruction. Despite being a muddle it is a very handsome ruin with a superb six-light east window. The exquisite tomb flags were carved by one Rory O'Tunney. The south doorway is set in the midst of a highly ornamented screen with a carved crucifixion and a scene of St Christopher bearing Jesus over a river, symbolized by a shoal of fish. Among the other carvings is one on the doorway of the south transept, of a coy mermaid holding a looking-glass – a motif also found in Connacht.

Cashel

South of Kilcooly, towards the middle of the county, is one of the landmarks of Ireland, the **Rock of Cashel** (*open mid June–mid Sept, daily 9–7.30, mid Sept–mid Mar, 9.30–4.30, mid Mar–mid June, 9.30–5.30; adm; t (062) 61437, f (062) 62988*): a steep outcrop of limestone rising out of the rich agricultural land of the Golden Vale, and crowned with the imposing ecclesiastical ruins of the ancient capital of the kings of Munster. The grouping of the bare, broken buildings against the sky is memorable and worth travelling many miles to see. There is an 11th-century round tower; a small chapel known as St Cormac's Chapel; a grand cathedral which was built in the 1230s; and a Vicars' Choral Hall, built around 1420. The Vicars' Choral Hall houses some exhibits including St Patrick's Cross. Outside on the rock is a replica of this cross, which was moved inside to protect it from erosion.

The Rock was the seat of ancient chieftains and later the early Munster kings, and upon this naturally well-defended high place there was very likely a stone fortress or *caiseal*. Legend records that in AD 450 St Patrick came to Cashel to baptize either Corc the Third or his brother and successor, Aengus. During the ceremony Patrick is supposed to have driven the sharp point of his pastoral staff into the king's foot by mistake, and the victim bore the wound without a sign, thinking that such pain was all part of becoming a Christian. From that time onwards, Cashel was also called St Patrick's Rock. Brian Boru, High King of Ireland, was crowned here in 977. In 1101 King Murtagh O'Brien granted the Rock to the Church, for its political importance had declined, and it became the See of the Archbishopric of Munster.

The Rock itself and the buildings are in the care of the Office of Public Works, and the guided tour of 40 minutes or so is very interesting. If you want to walk around on your own, you will find **Cormac's Chapel** on your right as you face the main bulk of the cathedral buildings, in the angle formed by the choir and south transept of the cathedral. It was built in the 1130s by the Bishop-King Cormac MacCarthy and is a fascinating building architecturally, in a style described as Hiberno-Romanesque. The most Irish thing about Cormac's Chapel is its steep stone roof. As for the rest – the twin towers, the storeys of blank wall arcading, the high gable over the north doorway and most of the stone-cut decoration – it could be German. Inside is a splendid but broken stone sarcophagus of 11th-century work. The ingenious pattern of ribbons and wild beasts with which it is decorated was probably reintroduced into Ireland by the Vikings. A gilt copper crozier head was found inside the sarcophagus. The head, which is now preserved in the National Museum in Dublin, is late 13th-century French, and richly ornamented with animal and fish forms in enamel, turquoise and sapphire.

The French and German influences at Cashel are not surprising: there are docu-mented links between Cashel and the Irish monasteries of Cologne and Ratisbon; before the chapel was built monks were always travelling to and from the Continent. The fascinating carved-stone heads are a feature of Romanesque architecture, also originating in France. One is reminded of the Celtic head cult, and perhaps both Irish and French carvings derive from ancient Celtic monuments, such as can be seen in Roqueperteuse and Entremont in southern France.

As you enter the complex of buildings through the restored **Vicar's Choral Hall** you will see the Cross of St Patrick, probably of the same date as the sarcophagus. Christ is carved on one side and an ecclesiastic, perhaps St Patrick, is carved on the other. The massive base on which it is set is reputed to be the coronation stone of the Munster Kings. The immense ruins of the cathedral built beside Cormac's chapel date from the second half of the 13th century, and were the scene of two deliberate burnings during the Anglo-Irish wars of the Tudors and Cromwell. In 1686 the cathedral was restored and used by the Church of Ireland, but then it was left to decay until Cashel became a National Monument and everything was tidied up. What remains now is a fine example of austere Irish Gothic architecture with a rather short nave, the end of which is taken up with what is known as **The Castle**, a massive tower built to house the bishops in the 15th century. Everything about the cathedral is superbly grand and delicate – in marked contrast to Cormac's Chapel.

The round tower is roughly 11th-century. You can see the top of it perfectly if you climb to the top of The Castle, plus a wonderful view of the Golden Vale, the hills to the east and west, and Slievenamon in the south. There is a gap in the hills to the north which is said to correspond exactly to the size of the Rock. Legend tells that the Devil bit off the Rock and spat it onto the plain below, hence the name of the mountain: Devil's Bit. Just below, on the plain, is **Hore Abbey**, built by the Cistercians from Mellifont. It is always accessible if you want to visit it. The Rock looks superb at night, particularly during the summer when it is floodlit. You should also visit **Cashel Folk Village**, nearby (*open daily during high season 10–7.30; t (062) 62525, f (062) 62322*), which recreates an Irish village of a century ago.

Cashel Town is a thriving place with a very good hotel, the Cashel Palace. It used to be the residence of the Church of Ireland archbishops and was built in gracious Queen Anne style in 1730. The architect was Edward Lovett Pearce (1699–1733), who also built the Irish Houses of Parliament in Dublin. It is worth having at least a coffee there so you can get a glimpse of the panelling and carving. The **GPA Bolton Library** (*adm; t (062) 61232*), in the precincts of the St John the Baptist Cathedral, has one of the finest collections of 16th- and 17th-century books in Ireland. There are several on exhibition, but you have to contact the Dean if you want to get inside the cathedral. The Roman Catholic **Church**, also called after St John the Baptist, is in direct contrast to the simplicity of the cathedral – exotic and full of statues. The shop fronts in Cashel's main street are very colourful and the plastic age has not made too much impact.

Cahir

Cahir ('Stone Fortress'), 8 miles (12.8km) south of Cashel at the meeting of the N8 and N24, is the nicest sort of Irish town, on the River Suir, with old-fashioned shops, colourfully painted houses and a wide main square, with plenty of space to walk and park. It has a magnificent, fully restored 15th-century castle on an island in the river, the largest of its period in Ireland. **Cahir Castle** (*open mid June–mid Sept, daily 9–7.30,* *mid Mar–mid June and mid Sept–mid Oct, 9.30–5.30, mid Oct–mid Mar, 9.30–4.30; guided tours; adm; t (052) 41011)* was granted to James Butler, the third Earl of Ormonde, in 1375 and through many vicissitudes it remained in that family until Victorian times. The Ormonde Butlers were a Norman family who became all-powerful in the county. They also became rather too independent of their monarch in England, and the massive fortifications of the castle came under fire from the cannon of the Earl of Essex in 1599. It was the only important success of his Irish Campaign. A visit to the castle is memorable as the guides are so enthusiastic and bring the defensive tactics of the Butlers to life. One's head is set spinning with the ingenuity of the portcullis and the holes for pouring burning oil. The Great Hall and other rooms within the castle are furnished and there is plenty of information about the lifestyle of the day. There is also an excellent audio-visual show outlining the archaeological and ecclesiastical sites of importance in the area. The town of Cahir has several old buildings including the town house of the last Butler, the Earl of Glengall, in the square. This is now a typical Irish country hotel, the Cahir House Hotel.

On the outskirts of Cahir is the restored **Swiss Cottage** (*open May–Sept, daily 10–6, mid Mar–April and Oct–Nov, Tues–Sun 10–1 and 2–4.30; guided tours only; adm; t (052) 41144)*, a delightful folly designed by John Nash for Lord and Lady Cahir in the early 19th century. It is the epitome of the rural idyll, with a higgledy-piggledy thatched roof and grotto chairs. The Church of Ireland church here was also by Nash.

The **Vee Road** (R668) from Cahir passes through some beautiful wrought iron gates and then plunges you deep in the countryside, eventually taking you through the Knockmealdown Gap and over the county border into Waterford. Ten miles (16km) south of Cahir you pass through Clogheen, before the road curves up the slopes thick with pine forest; then it suddenly turns back on itself in a wide hairpin, or 'V', and there's the most fabulous view over a patchwork of fields – from 1,114ft (340m) above sea-level. It is sometimes quite misty, and as you go down towards Lismore in County Waterford, you look through the rain and sparks of sunlight at shifting vales. Just before Lismore the trees, oak and beech, grow with tropical thickness, festooned with moss and ferns, then suddenly the spires of Lismore Cathedral appear against the skyline. Off the Vee Road, just west of Clogheen on the R665, **Ballyporeen** has become famous for its connection with the family of Ronald Reagan. His great-grandfather was baptized in the church here, and there is a pub named after him.

Four miles (6km) away at Coolagarran Roe, Burncourt, is the exciting **Mitchelstown Cave** (*open daily 10–6; adm; t (052) 67246)*, with fantastical dripstone formations, stalactites, stalagmites and columns. It is well signposted from Ballyporeen and 2 miles (3km) off the N8 Mitchelstown/Cahir road. The caves have been given a variety of names such as 'The Altar Cave', where the formations are remarkably ecclesiastical, and the two caves known as 'The Lords' and 'The Commons', after the Houses of Parliament in London. They were often used by rapparees, or rebels on the run. The prominant rebel, the Sugane Earl of Desmond, took refuge in them in 1601 but was betrayed to the English by his kinsman Edmond, the last White Knight, who received £1,000 for his treachery. A rare species of spider, *Porrhomma myops*, is found in the network of caves. You must explore with the guide, who is a fascinating source of stories and information. The **Glen of Aherlow** between the Galtee mountains and the Slievenamuck Hills is not really a glen, but a lush, colourful valley. The R663 runs parallel with the River Aherlow, and signs point to many tarns and lakes set in the beautifully shaped Galtees.

Tipperary and the Galtees

Tipperary, which lies in the Golden Vale, is a great farming centre. The town has a fine bronze figure of Charles Kickham (1828–82), a patriot and novelist. Read his novels *Knocknagow* and *The Homes of Tipperary* if you can. The Manchester Martyrs and John O'Leary (1830–1907), a Fenian leader and journalist, also have memorials worth looking at. The town's Catholic **church** is a Gothic limestone building.

The Galtees are a magnificent huddle of peaks, formed from a conglomerate mixture of old red sandstone and silurian rocks, and stretch from Tipperary into Limerick, where they merge with the Ballyhoura Hills bordering Cork. The ridge-walking is fantastic, especially around Lyracappul. The splendour between the Silvermine Mountains (still mined for silver and zinc) and Toomyvara, on your way to Nenagh, is worth exploring. Around here you will hear stories of Ned of the Hill, the local Robin Hood, who plundered the English planter families and composed the lovely song 'The Dark Woman of the Glen'.

Northern Tipperary

Thurles and Nenagh

Deep in the countryside between Thurles and Cashel, on the banks of the lazy Suir, and reached by a road (R660) hemmed in by hawthorn hedges, is **Holycross Abbey**. The abbey was built so that a portion of the True Cross presented by Pope Paschal II in 1110 to Murtagh O'Brien, King of Munster, might be properly enshrined. In 1182 the abbey was transferred to the Cistercians, who embellished it so magnificently that it became a popular place of pilgrimage. It was rebuilt and changed over many centuries, though most of the finest work belongs to the 15th century. Inside is a sedile of perfect workmanship, so delicate that it resembles the work of a woodcarver rather than a mason working in limestone. The abbey is in full use today, having been restored by skilled workmen, who had to give their best to equal the standard of past centuries. It is open for prayer all day, and there is a craft shop in the courtyard.

Three miles (5km) north of Holycross on the R660 is **Thurles**, a busy market town situated on a plain by the River Suir. It was important as a strategic base during the Anglo-Norman conflict. It is also famous for its sugar-beet factory, and for the founding of the Gaelic Athletic Association (GAA) in 1884 by Archbishop Croke: there is a statue of him in Liberty Square. He is buried in the fine cathedral in the town centre; this was modelled on the cathedral in Pisa, and has a pretty bell-tower. It is the centre of the Catholic archdiocese of Cashel, one of the four into which Ireland is divided. The town has a race-course and the remnants of two keeps, known as **Bridge Castle** (guarding the south side of the bridge) and **Black Castle** (in the town centre). There is also a new exhibition centre on Slievenamon Road, the **Tipperary Institute GAA Club** (*open all year Mon–Fri, also April–Sept Sat; t (0504) 23579, http://tipperary.gaa.ie*), devoted to Gaelic games such as hurling, football, camogie and handball.

Nenagh is the administrative capital of the north riding of Tipperary. It has an impressive 100ft (33m) circular keep called the **Nenagh Round**, which was built as part of a strong pentagonal castle in 1200 by the first of the Ormonde line, and is one of the best examples of its kind in the country. The Bishop of Killaloe did it an injustice in 1858 by adding a castellated crown, but it is still beautiful. Across the road in the 19th-century gaol and governor's house is the **Nenagh Heritage Centre** (*t (067) 33850*). Permanent displays and temporary exhibitions are held on view here; one, 'The Hurler', gives you an insight into that very national sport. The centre also provides a genealogical service. **Terryglass** and **Lorrha** are pretty villages beside Lough Derg. The former has a good craft shop. Lorrha is well worth a detour, for its architecture is still that of an unspoilt Irish village with a smithy, old school, and single-storey buildings. There are some remnants of 9th-century high crosses, a Norman motte, and a finely decorated doorway in the Norman church of the Canons Regular. At the other end of the village is an attractive Roman Catholic church. Nearby is a splendid tower house encompassed by a well cared-for lawn, and the remains of

Tourist Information

Nenagh: Connolly Street t (067) 31610; *open April–Sept, call t (067) 32100 at other times.*

Shopping

Crafts
Hanly Woollen Mill Shop, Ballyartella, Nenagh, t (067) 24278.
McQuaid's Traditional Music Shop, 38 Pearse Street, Nenagh, t/f (067) 34166.
Farney Castle Knitwear and Porcelain Visitor Centre, Holycross, t (0504) 43281, f (0504) 43357, *farneycastle@eircom.net*.

Delicacies
Cooleeney Cheese, Cooleeney House, Moyne, Thurles, t (0504) 45112. Delicious Camembert-style cheese. Check for availability.

Sports and Activities

Cycling
Premier Cycling Holidays, Nenagh, t (0509) 47134.

Fishing
Dromineer Bay Hotel, Nenagh, t (067) 24288.
Otway Lodge, Dromineer, t (067) 24273/24133.
Irish Sports, Killaloe, t (061) 376798.

Golf
Nenagh Golf Club, Beechwood, Nenagh, t (067) 31476.

Horse-racing
Ballintoher Equestrian Centre, Nenagh, t (067) 31400.

Walking
Ely O'Carroll Tourism, Brendan Street, Birr, Co. Offaly, t (0509) 20923.

Water Sports
Shannon Sailing Centre, New Harbour in Dromineer, t (067) 24499. Lough Derg cruises, boat hire and sailing, windsurfing and canoeing lessons.

Where to Stay

Kylenoe, Terryglass, t (067) 22015, f (067) 22275 (*moderate*). Attractive stone farmhouse; excellent breakfasts and dinners.

a 13th-century **Dominican priory** which has some lovely carved tombs of about 350 years old. Five miles (8km) from Nenagh is the holiday centre of **Dromineer** on the edge of Lough Derg. It has a fine ruined castle by the harbour, and the place has been sympathetically developed as a sailing, fishing, cruising and water-skiing resort. The wooded islands which cluster in the 25-mile (40km) long lough are fun to explore, and there are regular cruises if you do not want to navigate a boat yourself.

Roscrea and Surroundings

Two wonderful artefacts from the early Christian era have been found in these parts: the early-9th-century silver Roscrea Brooch, with its gold and amber decoration; and the mid-8th-century *Book of Dimma*, which contains the four Gospels and is enclosed in a shrine of bronze with silver plates ornamented with Celtic interlacing. Both treasures are now in Dublin. You can see the *Book of Dimma* in Trinity College, and the brooch in the National Museum. At the entrance to the little town of Roscrea, St Cronan's Church and Round Tower is all that remains of a monastery founded by St Cronan in the early 600s. The west façade of this 12th-century Romanesque church has survived and the rest was demolished to make way for an 1812 Church of Ireland church in the churchyard. There is a 12th-century high cross

Riverrun House, Terryglass, t (067) 22125, f (067) 22187, *riverrun@iol.ie* (*inexpensive*). Well-run B&B in the village.

Tir na Fiûise, Terryglass, t/f (067) 22041, *nheenan@eircom.net* (*inexpensive*). Quiet, pretty farmhouse on an organic farm just outside the village, where Inez and Niall Heenan go out of their way to help you enjoy your stay. They also have self-catering stone cottages to rent.

Ballycormac House, Aglish, Borrisokane, t (067) 21129, f (067) 21200, *ballyc@indigo.ie* (*moderate*). 300-year-old farmhouse lovingly restored by American ex-pats; exceptional breakfasts, and they do dinners too. The owners also organize activities for their guests.

Otway Lodge, Dromineer Harbour, Dromineer, t (067) 24133/24273, *flannery@eircom.net* (*inexpensive*). Comfortable, convenient location for those wanting to explore Lough Derg. Contact Mrs Shesgreen-Flannery.

Eating Out

Dwan's Brewery Pub and Restaurant, The Mall, Thurles, t (0504) 26007 (*moderate*). Home-brewed and special beers. Tours of the brewery and live music at weekends.

Matt the Thresher's, Birdhill, southwest of Nenagh, t (061) 379227 (*inexpensive*). All-day pub food. Organic bread, seafood and Limerick ham.

Paddy's Pub, Terryglass, t (067) 22147 (*inexpensive*). For a pub lunch and dinner. Traditional music at night and in the Derg Inn next door.

The Whiskey Still, Dromineer, t (067) 24129 (*inexpensive*). Traditional old pub, good grub and music.

Goosers Pub, Ballina, Killaloe, t (061) 376791 (*moderate–inexpensive*). Some of the best pub grub in the area, with a restaurant too.

Entertainment and Nightlife

Traditional Music

Hickey's Bar, Silvermines, t (067) 25003. Music year round.

Stapleton's Bar, Pallas Cross, Borrisoleigh, t (0504) 51281. Also with year-round music.

Lucky Bags, Kilruane, t (067) 41444. Music 3 times a week, on Tues, Sat and Sun.

Larkins, Garry Kennedy, Portroe, t (067) 23232. Music six nights a week.

there too. The Roman Catholic **Church of St Cronan** in Abbey Street is built on the site of a 15th-century Franciscan friary, of which the square tower and part of the church remain. The altar piece is very attractive. You must go to the **Roscrea Heritage Castle Complex** in Castle Street, which contains **Damer House** (*open June–Sept, daily 10–6; adm; for info on other opening hours and special exhibitions **t** (0505) 21850/21689, **f** (0505) 21904, www.heritageireland.ie*). This early 18th-century town house is in the curtilage of a 13th-century Norman castle built by the Ormondes. It was rescued by the Georgian Society and has a wonderful carved pine staircase which took years of loving care to restore. The panelling and proportions of the rooms are very attractive. The town Heritage Society now runs the centre with an annexe for cultural and historical exhibitions; it also has a craft and book shop and tourist information.

    Birr, on the north tip of County Tipperary, is one of the prettiest towns in Ireland, with wide Georgian streets and mature trees. It is a border town, actually just in County Offaly (*see p.547*). **Birr Castle** (*open all year, daily 9–6; adm; for info on exhibitions **t** (0509) 20056/20336/20023, **f** (0509) 21583, info@birrcastle.com*), built by the Parsons family, the Earls of Rosse, is magnificent. The landscaped park, with its lake and waterfalls, the formal garden, box hedges and huge magnolia tree, is entrancing. Coming through the gates is like entering a magic world where the trees are greener, the flowers more vivid and the fruit trees always laden. The castle itself is only open for rare events such as the Festival of Music in Great Irish Houses (*see p.130*). However, there is an exhibition hall which always has something of interest, usually to do with the Parsons family, after whom the town was once named. In 1845 a descendant built what was then the world's largest telescope, which you can see.

County Clare

    Until the 4th century Clare was part of Connacht, after which it became known as the Kingdom of Thomond. It is a wild and beautiful county, still marked with signs of a tempestuous past; there are 2,300 stone forts or *cahers* dating back to pre-Celtic times. Clare is bounded by water on three sides: the silvery Shannon Estuary and River widen into Lough Derg on its south and east side, its western side is edged by the pounding Atlantic Ocean, and on its northern border it meets County Galway. It is unspoilt by tourism, even though there is some unattractive ribbon development and the urban sprawl of Shannon Airport. The locals earn money from farming, tourism and fishing; the airport and the industries that have grown up around it also provide much employment to the surrounding area. It benefits further from the Shannon Scheme, the largest hydroelectric resource in the country. The population is approximately 94,000, with most people living in the flat central plain from which the county takes its name, *An Clar*. It is separated by the Shannon Estuary from County Kerry, its neighbour in the south, although there is a car ferry from Tarbert to Killimer.

    Most people go inland, almost to the centre of Ireland to find the Limerick bridge, and rush through Clare on their way to the delights of Connemara. But Clare's plunging cliffs and strange limestone karst landscapes attract the more adventurous.

County Clare

Galway Bay

Ballyvaughan Bay

Black Head

Inishmore

Inishmaan

Fanore

Ballyvaughan

Aran Islands

Burren Way

Corkscrew
Hill

The Burren

Aillwee
Caves

N67

Poulnabrone
Megalithic Tomb

Inisheer

Lisdoonvarna

Doolin

Ballykinvarga
Stone Fort

O'Brien's Tower

Kilfenora

Cliffs of Moher

R. Dealagh

Leamaneh Castle

Hags Head

Liscannor

St Brigid's Holy Well

Lahinch

Ennistymon

Liscannor Bay

R. Cullenagh

Atlantic

N67

Miltown
Malbay

N85

Spanish Point

Slievecallan

Ocean

Quilty

The Hand Cross Roads

Lake Boolynagreana

Doonbeg

R. Doonbeg

N68

Corbally

Cooraclare

Kilkee

N67

Kilrush

Killadysert

Carrigaholt

Killimer

Scattery Island

Loop
Head

Tarbert

River Shannon

10 km

5 miles

N

The west Clare coast ends in the dramatic Cliffs of Moher and, besides gazing at the sea, you can go sea-fishing, diving, walking, rock-climbing, golfing or dolphin-watching all along it. To the north, overlooking Galway Bay, the Barony of the Burren looks like a misplaced moonscape: white, crevassed and barren. But springy turf and calcium-loving plants grow in the earth-filled fissures, and cattle manage to graze quite happily around the cracks. The archaeological and botanical interest and the

mysterious evasive charm of this rocky place make many converts. There are numerous places to bathe and fish on this northern coast too, whilst the scenery and walking around the lakes and hills of Slieve Bernagh and the Slieve Aughty mountain range are some of the best in the county.

Walking and caving attract the more active, but many regard County Clare as the best place in Ireland to hear traditional music. Doolin, a little fishing village and port

Getting There and Around

By Air
Shannon Airport, t (061) 471 444, www.shannonairport.com.

By Bus and Rail
Buses leave from Ennis train station, with regular connections to Shannon Airport, Limerick, Galway and Dublin. The train service basically duplicates these lines. It is also possible to get to most of the smaller towns by bus – a few each day to Lahinch and Doolin on the coast, as well as Lisdoonvarna, the Cliffs of Moher, and most towns near Ennis.
Bus Information, Ennis, t (065) 682 4177, www.buseireann.ie.
Iarnród Eireann, t (01) 836 6222, www.irishrail.ie.
Burren Coaches, t (065) 707 8009.

By Sea
The Clare–Kerry ferry makes the crossing from Killimer to Tarbert. To reach the Aran Islands, contact Aran Island Ferries in Co. Galway.
Shannon Ferries, t (065) 905 3124. Departs from Killimer Mon–Sat on the hour, 7am–7pm (April–Sept until 9pm), Sun 9–7. Departures from Tarbert (Co. Kerry) are on the half-hour.
Aran Island Ferries, t (091) 568903, www.aranislandferries.com. Service runs from April to late Oct.

By Bike
Michael Tierney, 17 Abbey Street, Ennis, t (065) 682 9433. Ennis Raleigh Rent-a-Bike dealer.

Irish Cycle Hire, in the train station, Ennis, t (065) 682 1992.
Shannon Cycle Hire, Bunratty, t (061) 364 696.
Burren Cycling Holidays, t (065) 707 4300.
Shannon Cycle Centre, Newmarket on Fergus, t (061) 361280.

Festivals

April
Irish Dancing World Championship, Clare. (First week).

May
Fleadh Nua, Ennis. Festival of traditional music, dancing and singing, on the last weekend.

June
Festival of Traditional Singing, Ennistymon (early June).

August
Festival of Traditional Music, Feakle.
Carnival of Music, Lisdoonvarna (early Aug).
International Darlin' Girl From Clare Festival, Miltown Malbay.

September
Match-making Festival of Ireland, Lisdoonvarna (late Sept–early Oct), www.matchmakingireland.com. Spinster ladies come all the way from America for the fun.

November
Ennis Traditional Festival (first week).

for boats to the Aran isle of Inisheer was the place to hear it in the late 1970s, and still continues to attract many backpackers. However, spontaneous creativity and excellence are not tied to one place, and it has long moved on to other places in Clare.

History

The 12th-century *Book of Invasions*, or *Lebor Gabala*, connects Clare with the Fir Bolgs; but we know little about these shadowy people. Many centuries later, it was a Clare man, Brian Boru of the clan O'Brien, who conducted a vigorous campaign against the Vikings and defeated them at Clontarf in 1014. He became High King of Ireland in 1002 and built the Palace of Kincora as his royal residence in 1012. He was killed in his tent after the battle of Clontarf, and the fragile national unity he had created disappeared very fast.

In the tales of ancient Ireland the countryside was fraught with the battles of the land-owning Celtic clans: the O'Briens, the O'Deas, the MacNamaras and the MacMahons, who, when they were not waging fierce war on foreigners, passed the time by fighting among themselves. In 1172 the incumbent chief of the O'Briens, Donal Mor, enlisted the help of a new group of invaders in his war against the O'Conors of Connacht: a party of Norman mercenaries. Despite this initial foothold in the country, the Norman-English forces did not make much of a mark in County Clare until the accession of Henry VIII in 1534 and the acknowledgement of him as King of Ireland. The O'Briens were made Earls of Thomond and remained more or less loyal to the English crown until the Cromwellian conquest (see **History**, p.42). After that time, Clare and its neighbour, Connacht, became a seat of rebellion against English rule. Cromwell had heard that a substantial part of Clare had no trees to hang a man, nor enough water to drown him, nor enough earth to bury him; so he thought it would be just the place to banish the rebellious Irish, whom he had thrown off the land elsewhere. In the 19th century Daniel O'Connell was able to exploit this sense of injustice to win support for his campaign for Catholic emancipation. He was enthusiastically supported by the peasantry, who contributed the 'penny a month' that they could afford. The Great Famine and emigration hit Clare hard: the county's population fell from 286,000 in 1841 to less than half this number thirty years later.

East Clare and Ennis

Around Lough Derg

Broadford, **Tulla** and **Feakle** are all pleasant villages where you can stay and explore the Clare Lakelands. **Lough Graney** is especially beautiful, with its wooded shores. Most of the lakes are well stocked. Near Feakle the witty and outrageous 18th-century poet Brian Merriman earned his livelihood as a schoolmaster. Here too is the cottage of Biddy Early, the wise woman, stories of whom were collected by Lady Augusta Gregory for her book *Visions and Beliefs of the West of Ireland*.

From the neat and pretty village of **Mountshannon** on Lough Derg it is possible to get a boat to **Holy Island**, also known as Iniscealtra, about half a mile from the shore. Regular ferries run in summer or you could hire a boat at the harbour, which is a main stopping place on the lake for hire-cruisers and sailing boats. The view of **Tountinna Mountain** from the lough is magnificent. The giant cross on its summit was erected to the Irishmen who fell in the Troubles of 1916–22. This mountain is in County Tipperary; the Gaelic name is *Tul tuinne*: 'Hill Above the Wave'. The Christian settlement on the island is attibuted to St Cairmin, who lived here *c.* AD 640. Today there are five ancient churches, a round tower, a saint's graveyard, a hermit's cell and a holy well. St Cairmin's Church, beside the incomplete round tower, has a wonderful Hiberno-Romanesque chancel arch, impressive in its simplicity. St Mary's Church, much altered in the 16th century, contains a monument to Sir Turlough O'Brien and

Tourist Information

Bunratty: t (061) 360133; *open May–Oct.*
Ennis: Clare Road, t (065) 682 8366, f (065) 682 8350; *open all year.*
Shannon Airport: t (061) 471664, f (061) 471661; *open all year.*

Shopping

Crafts

Ballymorris Pottery, Cratloe.
Cratloe Woods House, northwest of Limerick.
Bunratty Folk Park, Bunratty Castle. Good selection of woven clothing, candles and prints.
Bunratty Village Mills, Bunratty. Shopping complex including a Tipperary Crystal shop, Meadowes and Byrne clothing store and a restaurant.
Shannon Airport Duty Free Shop. The first of its kind, only possible to take advantage of as you are leaving the country.
Ballycasey Craft Workshops, Ballycasey, close to Shannon Airport on the junction of the N18/N19. Great selection of tweeds, Arans, pottery, and woodwork.
Knappoque Castle, Quin.
Clare Business Centre, Ennis. Peadar O'Loughlin sells fiddles and violins.
Clare Craft and Design, Parnell Street, Ennis. Displays and sells the work of a number of local craftsmen.

Delicacies

The Bunratty Winery, Bunratty (behind Durty Nelly's Bar). Sells a particularly good mead.
Open Sesame Wholefood Shop, 35 Parnell Street, Ennis. Organic vegetables and local cheeses – wonderful smells.

Sports and Activities

Fishing

O'Callaghan Angling, Tulla Road, Ennis, t/f (065) 682 1374.

Golf

East Clare Golf Club, Scarriff, t (061) 921322.
Shannon Golf Club, Shannon Airport, t (061) 471551.
Dromoland Castle Hotel Golf Club, Newmarket on Fergus, t (061) 368144.
Ennis Golf Club, Drumbiggle, Ennis, t (065) 682 4072, *www.golfclub.ennis.ie.*
Woodstock Golf and Country Club, Woodstock House, Ennis, t (065) 682 9463.

Pleasure Cruises

Mountshannon Harbour, on Lough Derg. Great place from which to make boat trips up the lovely River Graney (also known as the Scarriff).
Ireland Line Cruisers, Ballina, Killaloe, t (061) 375011, *www.irelandlinecruisers.com.* Selection of well-equipped cruise boats for hire over flexible periods.
Shannon Castle Line, Williamstown Harbour, Whitegate, t (061) 927042, *www.shannon-cruisers.com.* Cruiser hire for 3 nights minimum. Instruction available.

Pony-trekking

Carrowbaun Farm Trekking Centre, Killaloe, t (061) 376754.
Lough Derg Equestrian Centre, Ballina, Killaloe, t (061) 376144.
Clonlara Equestrian Centre, Killaloe Road, Clonlara, t (061) 354172.
Cahergal House, Newmarket on Fergus, t (061) 368358.

his wife. This O'Brien was infamous for butchering the Spanish Armada survivors who were washed up on the coast of Clare. The festival at the holy well was famous for the Bacchanalian revelry that accompanied it. It was stopped by the priests some time in the 19th century, because the local squireens would steal the girls attending.

Around Killaloe and Bunratty

Killaloe sits on the Shannon River, surrounded by the hills of **Slieve Bernagh** and the **Arra Mountains**. It is connected to Ballina in Tipperary by an elegant bridge of 13 arches. Not far from the bridge, on the west bank of the river, is the gem of Killaloe,

Castlefergus Farm Riding Stables, Quin, t (065) 682 5914.

Ballyhannon Horse Riding, Ballyhannon House, Quin, t (065) 682 5645.

Clare Equestrian Centre, Ennis, t (065) 684 0136.

Sailing

University of Limerick Activities Centre, Killaloe, t (061) 376622. Watersports facilities and instructing available. Call well in advance to book sessions.

The Shannon Sailing Centre, Dromineer, Co. Tipperary, t (067) 24499. Windsurfing, canoeing, water-skiing, day cruises and sailing on Lough Derg.

Swimming

It's possible to swim at **Lough Graney**.

Walking

The Mid-Clare Way. A circular way-marked route from Quin, 100km.

Where to Stay

Smyths Village, Feakle, t (061) 924002 (*inexpensive*). Cosy fishing hotel.

Tinarana, Ballycuggeran, Killaloe, t (061) 376966, *info@tinarana.com* (*moderate*). B&B in a Victorian mansion, set in an extensive park; they can set you up with horses and boats and all manner of cures, since it is also a health farm.

Bunratty Castle Hotel, Bunratty, t (061) 707034 (*moderate*). Every instinct suggests that this should be a dreadful tourist trap, but in fact it offers excellent accommodation and traditional music every night. The bar can become very crowded.

Dromoland Castle, Newmarket on Fergus, t (061) 368144, *www.dromoland.ie* (*luxury*). Owned by the consortium that also operates Ashford Castle, this hotel has beautiful grounds, a golf course and delicious food. However, the atmosphere is a bit impersonal.

Thomond House, Dromoland, Newmarket on Fergus, t (061) 368304, *www.thomond-house.com* (*expensive*). Conor O'Brien, the 18th Baron Inchiquin, is the O'Brien of Thomond. His exquisite Georgian-style house overlooks Dromoland Castle and its lake, the original home of the O'Briens, which is also now a hotel (*see* above). There is salmon-fishing, deer-stalking, riding and golf; arrange in advance.

Carnelly House, Clarecastle, t (065) 682 8442, *www.carnelly-house.com* (*luxury*). Early Georgian house with a wonderful Francini ceiling. Elegant rooms and colourful, friendly hosts. Only 9 miles from Shannon Airport.

Ballykilty Manor, Quin, t (065) 682 5627 (*moderate*). Set in wooded grounds with fishing on the River Rine. It is often busy with 'functions' at the weekend that stretch late into the night. It was the home of the infamous Captain Blood, who attempted to steal the Crown jewels.

Ballymarkham House, Quin, t (065) 682 5726 (*inexpensive*). Fine country house.

Queen's Hotel, Abbey Street, Ennis, t (065) 682 8963, *stay@irishcourthotels.com* (*moderate*). Charming hotel overlooking a 13th-century Franciscan Abbey.

The Clare Hostel, the Cornmarket, Summerhill, Ennis, t (065) 682 9370 (*inexpensive*). Good hostel with a restaurant.

Lahardan House, Crusheen, Ennis, t (065) 682 7128 (*inexpensive*). Dilly Griffey's old family house; comfortable rooms with en suite baths and delicious home cooking.

St Flannan's Cathedral. This fine 12th-century building was built by Donal O'Brien on the site of an earlier church, founded in the 6th century by St Lua. There is a magnificent Hiberno-Romanesque door, better than anything of its kind in Ireland, that is said to be the entrance to the tomb of Murtagh O'Brien, King of Munster, who died in the same century that the cathedral was built. The bold, varied carvings of animals and foliage on the shafts and capitals and the chevrons on the arches are not merely decoration; they are modelled to make the entire conception whole.

Nearby is **Thorgrim's Stone**, the shaft of a cross bearing a runic and ogham inscription of about AD 1000. The view from the top of the cathedral tower is superb.

Self-catering

Feakle, east Clare Lakelands. 18th-century farmhouse with a pretty garden, €254–356 per week. Contact Christine Guilfoyle, Laccaroe, t (061) 924111.

Mountshannon Village, close to Mountshannon Harbour and Sailing Club. Traditional-style cottages, €254–571 per week, depending on the season. Contact Bridie Cook, Gortatleva Bushypark, Galway, t (091) 525295.

Ballyhannon Castle, near Quin. Beautifully restored 15th-century castle, with massive stone walls and crafted stout oak beams. Call Havens and Hideaways, t (01) 668 0109.

Mullagh, Ennis. Traditional farm cottage with sea-view, from €381 per week. Contact Marie Lernihan, Mullagh, Ennis, t (065) 708 7208.

Eating Out

Game Keeper's Restaurant, Smyth's Country Lodge Hotel, Feakle, t (061) 924000 (*moderate*). Impressive fare in an intimate setting.

Flappers, Tulla, t (065) 683 5711 (*moderate–inexpensive*). Interesting menus and flavoursome food in a simple setting.

Lantern House, Ogonnelloe, south of Scarriff, t (061) 923034 (*inexpensive*). Home cooking overlooking Lough Derg.

Galloping Hogan's, Ballina, near Killaloe, t (061) 376162 (*moderate*). Ideal for relaxed *al fresco* dining on tranquil Lough Derg.

Goosers Bar and Eating House, Ballina, near Killaloe, t (061) 376791 (*moderate*). Popular award-winning restaurant, with plenty of intimate character and inviting open fires.

MacCloskey's Restaurant, Bunratty House Mews, Bunratty, t (061) 364082 (*expensive*).

In the cellars of an attractive house built in 1846 by a hopeful son waiting to inherit the castle from his father. The décor and atmosphere reflect that feeling of a vanished, leisurely way of life. *Evenings only.*

Castle Banquets, t (061) 360788 (*moderate*). Medieval banquets at Bunratty and Knappoque Castles (*see* opposite and p.277).

Gallagher's of Bunratty, Bunratty, t (061) 363363 (*moderate*). Charming thatched cottage specializing in local seafood.

Mac's Pub, Bunratty Folk Park, Banratty t (061) 360788 (*moderate*). Good seafood and music in the evening.

Durty Nelly's, Bunratty, t (061) 364861 (*inexpensive*). Pub and eating house popular both with locals and visitors.

The Conservatory, Carrygerry Country House, Newmarket on Fergus, t (061) 363717 (*expensive*). Rustic charm that is worth seeking out.

The Cloister, Abbey Street, Ennis, t (065) 682 9521 (*moderate–inexpensive*). Old world bar. Good soups, local cheeses and nutty brown bread during the daytime; at night it becomes more formal as a restaurant.

Entertainment and Nightlife

Traditional Music

Clare is particularly famous for its music sessions, and Ennis boasts some good venues.

Brogan's, O'Connell Street, Ennis.

Cois na hAbhna, on the N18, Ennis, t (065) 682 0996. Music and dancing on Sat and Wed nights.

Kearney's Bar, Newbridge Road, Ennis.

You can see all the mountains that crowd round the gorge of Killaloe and the beautiful Lough Derg. In the grounds of the cathedral is **St Flannan's Oratory** with a lovely high stone roof; its Gothic doorway is a splendid contrast to the cruciform cathedral. The oratory, which dates from the 12th century, has a Romanesque west door, but the inside is dark and gloomy. The Roman Catholic church standing high above the town is believed by some to be on the site of Kincora, the great palace of Brian Boru where riotous banquets were the order of the day. (Others believe Kincora to have been at Beal Boru, an ancient earthen mound to the north of the town.) Inside the church are some fine stained-glass windows by Harry Clarke, who worked on many church windows in the early decades of the 20th century. His style is fantastical and fairylike, in the manner of the English illustrator Aubrey Beardsley, and the colours are exceptionally vivid. In the grounds is **St Molua's Oratory**, a very ancient ruin reconstructed here after being removed from an island in the Shannon before it was flooded by the Shannon Hydroelectric Scheme in 1929. Killaloe is a centre for fishing and boating; there are facilities for water-skiing and sailing, and a large marina. **Ballina**, over the bridge, has better bars and restaurants.

A mile or so out of Killaloe on the R463 is **Crag Liath**, known locally as the Grianan, overlooking the road northwards to Scarriff. It was written in 1014 in the annals of *Loch Ce* that this fort was the dwelling place of Aoibheal (also known as Aibell), the celebrated banshee (*bean-sidhe*, see **Topics**, p.95) of the Dalcassian Kings of Munster, the O'Briens. (In Irish, *Dal gCais* means 'Tribe of Cas'.) Aoibheal appeared to Brian Boru on the eve of Clontarf and told him that he would be killed the next day, though not in the fury of the battle. This is exactly what happened, for he was murdered in his tent when the battle was over and the victory his. It is a lovely, short climb to the fort (*always accessible*).

If you cross the Shannon at Limerick, you will find yourself heading for **Bunratty Castle** on the Newmarket road (N18). Allow yourself a day to tour the castle and the folk park here, for it is very interesting and well-conceived. Bunratty is a splendid tower-house standing beside a small stone bridge over the River Ratty; a perfect, restored example of a Norman-Irish castle keep. The present castle dates from 1460, though it is at least the fourth to have been built on the same spot. It was built by the McNamaras, who were a *sept* of the O'Briens, and it remained an O'Brien stronghold off and on until 1712, and played an important part in the struggle between the Anglo-Norman de Clares and the Thomonds. It was then occupied by the parliamentarian Admiral Penn, the father of William Penn who founded Pennsylvania. After years of neglect it was bought by Lord Gort in 1954, who restored it with the help of Tourism Ireland and the Office of Public Works. They have managed to recreate a 15th-century atmosphere and there is a wonderful collection of 14–17th-century furniture, tapestries and early portraits. The stairs to the upper apartments are very narrow and steep, which can make things difficult when the place is crowded, but you get a real feeling of what it was like to be one of the privileged in those times, and the mellow simplicity of the furnishings is very attractive. In the evenings the castle is a memorable setting for medieval-style banquets, which are great fun.

In the grounds surrounding the castle, the **folk park** (*open daily 9.30–5, July and Aug 9.30–7; teashop; adm; t (061) 360788*) displays examples of houses from every part of the Shannon region; many of them were re-erected here after being saved from demolition during the Shannon Airport extension. The various types of cottage range from the wealthier small farmer's house, with a small parlour, down to the cabin of a landless labourer. They are all furnished with authentic cottage pieces; one constant is the dresser-cum-henhouse, keeping the fowl snug in the house at night. Patchwork quilts, utensils, ornaments and pictures tell a million stories about life in the olden days, while outside the cottages you can wander around the vegetable patches and hay stooks, and watch the pigs, donkeys, doves and chickens. Inside some of the cottages there are people who can tell you about a lifestyle that has all but disappeared now; you may even get a taste of the scones baking on the open turf fire. You can see butter-making, basket-weaving and all the traditional skills that made people nearly self-sufficient. Village life is depicted too; the school, the musty-smelling doctor's house with its oil cloth on the floor, the post office selling stamps and sweets and various shops selling crafts and old linens, as well as a bar where you can have a good glass of creamy Guinness.

It is worth making an expedition to **Cratloe Woods House** (*open June–mid Sept, Mon–Sat 2–6; tea and craft shop; adm; t (061) 327028*), on the main Limerick/Shannon to Ennis Road (N18), about 5 miles (8km) from Limerick. Cratloe Woods is an ancient O'Brien house, and the only surviving example of an Irish long house that is still lived in as a home. The woods themselves are a remnant of the only primeval oak forest left in Ireland, and if you climb Woodcock Hill you will get a fine view. Timber from these woods was used for the roof of Westminster Abbey in London in 1399, and further back in the mists of time we know that the men of Ulster came down and cut the oaks and carried them back to make a roof for the Grianan of Aileach, near Derry.

Towards Ennis

Beyond Bunratty is the entirely modern sprawl of buildings that makes up Shannon Town and airport. The roads around here are large and busy, but they soon get smaller and more attractive as you get further into the county. On the road to Newmarket on Fergus, you will pass by **Kilnasoolagh Church**; try if you can to get in and see the exuberant baroque monument (*c.* 1717) by William Kidwell. It is a sculptured figure of an obese O'Brien – this time Sir Donat, the son of Maire Ruadh, who is rather a legend in Clare. She was a tough, hatchet-faced woman who kept her castle at Leamaneagh in the Burren against all the odds (*see* p.280). Their descendant was Lord Inchquin who built **Dromoland Castle**. This line of O'Briens became loyal servants of the Crown and they were rewarded well. But in the 19th century William Smith O'Brien (1803–1864) of Dromoland bucked the trend, became a leading member of the Young Irelanders and planned a revolt. He and others decided on an armed rising, despite the fact that many of them had been arrested and the preparations for the rising were not complete. In July 1848, O'Brien and a small party clashed with forty-six policemen in the widow McCormack's cabbage patch at Ballingarry, in County Tipperary. That was the end of the uprising; O'Brien was sentenced to death, but this was commuted to penal servitude, and later he was given an unconditional pardon.

Newmarket on Fergus takes its name from the aforementioned 19th-century O'Brien, Lord Inchiquin, who was very enthusiastic about horses. In the grounds of his neo-Gothic mansion, now a luxury hotel, is **Mooghaun Fort** (also spelled 'Maughaun'), one of the largest Iron Age hill-forts in Europe, enclosing 27 acres with three concentric walls. Maybe it was people from this fort who buried the enormous hoard of gold ornaments that was discovered nearby in 1854 by workmen digging the way for a railway line. Unfortunately much of it was melted down, probably by dealers, but a few pieces of 'the great Clare gold find' can be seen at the National Museum in Dublin. You can reach the fort through Dromoland Forest. Access is by foot via a forestry car park, signposted to the left off the N18 road between Newmarket on Fergus and Dromoland.

At **Craggaunowen** off the Quin–Sixmilebridge Road (R469) there is a reconstructed Bronze Age *crannog*, a ring-fort and farmers' houses, built on a pond next to a four-storey tower house. This house contains an important collection of medieval art donated by John and Gertrude Hunt, who were very involved in setting up the **Archaeological Park** (*open mid Mar–Oct, daily 10–6, mid Oct–Dec, daily 10–4; adm; t (061) 367178*). On display is the *Brendan*, a replica of the original boat used by St Brendan on his voyages. Tim Severin, a modern-day adventurer, sailed it to North America via Iceland and Greenland, with the purpose of demonstrating that St Brendan could have been the first to discover America in the 6th century. Rare and ancient breeds of poultry and livestock, including Kerry cattle, graze in the recon-structed pens and fields. The valley surrounding it is beautiful, and if you are there at teatime, the scones at the reception cottage are delicious. Nearby, at **Quin** (about 8 miles/13km northwest of Bunratty), is **Knappoque Castle**, run on the same lines as Bunratty Castle with medieval banquets in the evening (*open April–end Sept, daily 9.30–5; medieval banquets held twice-nightly at 5.30 and 8.45 from May–end Sept; adm; t (061) 360788*). The ribbon development between Sixmilebridge and Quin may disappoint you; this is a feature around all expanding towns in Ireland.

At the next crossroads, to the east of the town, a right turn leads to **Quin Abbey** (*always accessible*) which is very well preserved, and therefore thronged by countless coach parties. It was founded for the Franciscans in 1402 and incorporated with a great castle built by one of the de Clares. The monastic buildings are grouped around an attractive cloister and there is a graceful tower. Buried here is a famous duellist with the wonderful name of Fireballs MacNamara. Northeast of Quin, on the road between the R469 and the R352, you can walk up to the **Mound of Magh Adhair**. This was the crowning place of the kings of Thomond, and a battle was fought here in AD 877 between Lorcan, the Thomond king, and Flan, High King of Ireland.

Ennis

Ennis (*Inis*, 'River Meadow'), the busy and attractive county capital, is sited on a great bend of the River Fergus. The streets are narrow and winding, and in the centre is a hideous monument to the great Daniel O'Connell, who successfully contested the Clare seat in 1828 even though the repressive laws of the time disqualified Catholics from standing. Right in the middle of the town is **Ennis Friary**, a substantial ruin (*open late May–late Sept, daily 9.30–6.30; rest of the year key with caretaker, t (065) 682 9100*). The friary was founded for the Franciscans by Donchadh O'Brien, King of Thomond, just before his death in 1242. It is rich in sculptures and decorated tombs, although the building itself has been rather mucked about, with additions and renovations. On one of the tombs is the sculptured device of a crowing cockerel. Standing on the rim of a pot, he apparently cries in Irish, 'the son of the Virgin is safe', a reference to the story of the cock that rose from the pot in which it was cooking to proclaim that, 'Himself above on the Cross will rise again', to the astonishment of the two Roman soldiers who had questioned the prophecy. There is a small **museum** (*open Mon–Fri*) in a disused church in Harmony Row which specializes in objects associated with famous Clare people. De Valera has strong connections here, as he represented Clare from 1917–59. Fans of Percy French (1854–1920), the painter and entertainer, can look at the old steam engine immortalized in his song, 'Are you right there, Michael, are you right?' This song about the West Clare Railway and the engine's habit of stopping at places other than stations led to a libel action with the directors.

The Burren and the Clare Coast

North of Ennis

On the way from Ennis to Corofin (off the N85 to Ennistymon, and 2 miles off the R476) is the famous religious settlement of **Dysert O'Dea**. It was started in the 7th century by St Tola; but he probably lived in a cell of wattle and daub. The present ruin is a much-altered, 12th-century, Hiberno-Romanesque church with a badly reconstructed west doorway that now stands in the south wall. The door is sumptuously carved, and the arch has a row of stone heads with Mongolian features and proud but rather sad expressions. The idea for the heads came from northern France; monks and scholars moving between Ireland and the continent had much more influence on building and style than was once thought. Beside the church is the stump of a round tower, and about a hundred yards east is a **high cross** from the 12th century. Christ is shown in a pleated robe, and below him is a bishop with a crozier. A decisive battle fought here in 1318 drove the Anglo-Normans out of the area for several centuries, when the O'Brien chief of the time defeated Richard de Clare of Bunratty and expelled him. **Dysert O'Dea Castle** (*adm; t (065) 683 7401*) has a heritage centre and is the start of a short walk around the archaeological remains in its vicinity.

Corofin village lies between two pretty lakes, the Inchiquin and Atedaun. There is good game and coarse fishing here, and plenty of caves, for this is marginal shale and limestone countryside in which the River Fergus plays some tricks. The **Clare Heritage Centre** (*open all year, daily 10–6, closed Sun in winter; adm; t (065) 683 7955*) in the old Church of Ireland hall offers a 'trace your ancestors' service, and displays give a very interesting guide to rural Ireland 150 years ago. About 2 miles (3.2km) further up on the R476 is **Killinaboy** (also spelled Kilnaboy), a small village close to the northern tip of Lough Inchiquin. The remains of a round tower rest in the graveyard of a ruined **church** which dates from the 11th century. Over the south door is a *Sheila-na-Gig*, a grotesque and erotic figure of a woman. These *Sheila-na-Gigs* are often carved and fixed to ecclesiastical buildings, probably as a sort of crude warning to the monks and laity of the power of female sexuality. A mile northwest of Killinaboy at Roughan, just over a stile and in a field, is the **Tau Cross**, shaped like a T with a carved head in each of the arms. Several like this have been found in a Celtic sanctuary at Roquepertuse in France, and it is likely that it is pre-Christian.

If you wish to continue to avoid the main roads, several little roads from Killinaboy meander right into the heart of the Burren. Take the first road to the right after

Tourist Information

Cliffs of Moher: t (065) 708 1171; *open March–Oct.*
Lahinch: t (065) 708 2082; *open all year.*
Kilkee: t (065) 905 6112; *open June–Aug.*
Kilrush: t (065) 905 1577; *open May–Sept.*

Shopping

Crafts

The Burren Perfumery, Corron, **t** (065) 708 9102, *www.burrenperfumery.com*. An unlikely alchemist's laboratory in the middle of the Burren. They can also organize field trips to the Burren in the company of experts living in the area.
Aillwee Caves Complex, near Ballyvaughan. Crafts, books and Tim Robinson's map of the Burren.
The Manus Walsh Craft Shop, Ballyvaughan. Paintings, silver, jewellery and enamels.
Whitethorn Crafts, Ballyvaughan. Refurbished fish factory with a wide range of high quality ceramics, glass, jewellery and clothes.
Eugene Lambe, Fanore. Uillean pipes.
The Doolin Crafts Gallery, Doolin, **t** (065) 707 4309. Batik, books, fine art, ceramics, glass, clothing and an excellent café.
Liscannor Stone Story, Quarry and Rock Shop, St Brigid's Well, Liscannor, **t** (065) 708 1930. The history of Liscannor stone, and common, semi-precious and precious stones in the shop.
The Design Yard, Kenny Woollen Mills, Main Street, Lahinch. Designer woollens by Lyn Mar; tweeds, crystal and chinaware also available.

Delicacies

The Farmshop, Aillwee Caves Co. Ltd, Ballyvaughan. Food for picnics or to take home – all the delicacies are made by the Johnston family. They also bottle the natural spring water from the caves, produce honey and Ben makes his own cheese, Burren Gold.
Burren Smokehouse, Lisdoonvarna. Sells smoked salmon and offers guided tours.
Unglert's Bakery, Ennistymon. German rye breads and strudels.

Sports and Activities

Beaches and Bathing

Swimming is possible at **Fanore**, **Lahinch** (in the sea or in the 25m pool at the promenade leisure centre), **Spanish Point** and **Doonbeg**.

Courses

Willie Clancy Summer School, Miltown Malbay, **t** (065) 708 4281, *www.setdancingnews.net/wcss*. Held as a tribute to Clare's greatest piper, Willie Clancy (1921–73), a musician, folklorist and master carpenter. He was noted for his beautiful rendering of slow Irish airs on the *uilleann* pipes. The summer school comprises lectures, concerts, workshops in Irish dance and traditional music. *Commences on the first Saturday in July for 10 days.*

Fishing

Burke's Shop, Main Street, Corofin, **t** (065) 683 7677. Tom Burke will take you brown trout fishing on the lakes.
Atlantic Adventures, Cappa, Kilrush, **t** (065) 905 2133. For deep-sea fishing.

leaving Killinaboy, which will take you between Glasgeivnagh Hill and Mullaghmore. The **Cappaghkennedy** megalithic tomb is near the summit on Glasgeivnagh. At the next junction take a left and continue back in a wide circle to Carran and pass by the great stone fort of **Cahercommaun**. To get to it, turn left in Carran village and left again at the next junction. Look out for an avenue to the left which leads to a car park. From here you go a short way on foot. The fort is situated on a cliff edge across some ankle-breaking country, but while you pick your way across notice the flower life between the stones. A Harvard excavation team reached the conclusion that the fort was occupied during the 8–9th centuries by a community that raised cattle,

Golf

Irish National Golf Club, Doonbeg, **t** (065) 905 5051.
Kilkee Golf Club, Kilkee, **t** (065) 905 6048.
Kilrush Golf Club, Ballykett, Kilrush, **t** (065) 905 1138.
Lahinch Golf Club, Lahinch, **t** (065) 708 1003, *www.lahinchgolf.com*.

Pleasure Cruises

Dolphinwatch, Carrigaholt, **t** (065) 905 8156. Two-hour cruises in the Shannon Estuary to observe the large colony of dolphins there and eavesdrop on their conversations.
Gerald Griffin, Kilrush, **t** (065) 905 1327. Boat hire.

Pony-trekking

Burren Riding Centre, Fanore, **t** (065) 707 6140.
Willie Daly Riding Centre, Ennistymon, **t** (065) 707 1385.

Sailing

Traditional Galway Hookers, Ballyvaughan, **t** (091) 37539.

Spa and Seaweed Treatments

Sulphur baths, Lisdoonvarna, **t** (065) 707 4023. €8 for a bath in this little-changed Victorian spa well. Sulphur water is also available by the glass in the Edwardian pump room.
Thalassotherapy Centre, Gratton Street, Kilkee, **t** (065) 905 6742, *mulcahype@eircom.net*. Enjoy a seaweed bath, or a full range of other treatments.

Tours

Burren Outdoor Education Centre, **t** (065) 707 8066.

Burren Hill Walks, Ballyvaughan, **t** (065) 707 7168.
Christy Brown Tours, Lahinch, **t** (065) 708 1168.
Laly's Burren Tour, **t** (091) 562 905. Guided coach tours of the Burren, departing from Galway.

Walking

If you are planning to walk in **the Burren**, the best map of the area is a large-scale one by local cartographer Tim Robinson. It should be easy to buy locally. **The Burren Way** is a way-marked walk between Liscannor and Ballyvaughan, 42km.

Water Sports

Kilkee Diving Centre, The Pier, Kilkee, **t** (065) 56707, *www.diveireland.com*. Highly rated scuba diving, snorkelling and boat-handling courses available.

Where to Stay

Clifden House, Corofin, **t** (065) 683 7692, *www.clifdenhouse-countyclare.com* (*moderate*). Highly eccentric house full of character, and associated with Richard Burton, translator of the *Arabian Nights*. Has been described as 'being slowly coaxed into compromise with the 20th century'.
Caherbolane Farm, Corofin, **t** (065) 683 7638 (*inexpensive*). Simple but good cooking from the Cahill family.
Fergus View, Kilnaboy, Corofin, **t** (065) 683 7606 (*inexpensive*). Farmhouse with good home-cooking. Mary Kelleher makes all her own yoghurt and muesli.
Gregan's Castle, near Ballyvaughan, **t** (065) 707 7005, *www.gregans.ie* (*expensive*). Not

hunted red deer and cultivated some land for growing grain. This route brings you back to the main road (R480).

On the main road leading to Kilfenora (R476) is the ruined **Leamaneagh Castle** which belonged to the O'Briens. It is a lovely ruin with a tower dating from 1480 and an early 17th-century fortified house. Sir Conor O'Brien, who built the four-storey house, had a strong-minded wife called Maire Ruadh (Red Mary), many of whose exploits have passed into folklore. After Sir Conor died, she married an influential Cromwellian to ensure the inheritance of her son, Donat, and to prevent the expropriation of her lands. Legend has it that one day her new husband made an actually a castle, but an old manor house, with delicious food and comfortable rooms. Set at the top of Corkscrew Hills amidst green gardens, in fantastic contrast to the Burren's moonscape, with wonderful views over Galway Bay.

Lismacteigue, Ballyvaughan, t (065) 707 7040 (*inexpensive*). Thatched farmhouse in a ring-fort, on a green road in the Burren.

Ballinalacken Castle Hotel, Lisdoonvarna, t (065) 707 4025 (*moderate*). Beautifully situated overlooking the beach. Has recently upgraded from guesthouse to hotel.

Sheedy's Spa View Hotel, Lisdoonvarna, t (065) 707 4026 (*moderate*). Friendly, family-run hotel with a popular restaurant.

Ballinlacken Castle Country House, Coast Road, Doolin, t (065) 707 4025, *ballinlackencastle@eircom.net* (*inexpensive*). Mary and Denis O'Callaghan's beautiful guesthouse with spectacular views.

Paddy's Doolin Hostel, Doolin, t (065) 707 4006 (*inexpensive*). Modern, with a shop and kitchen facilities.

The Falls Hotel, Ennistymon, t (065) 707 1004, *www.fallshotel.net* (*moderate*). Has had a good reputation for 50 years, and it still has a spectacular view of the river. Full of atmosphere and faded charm.

Aberdeen Arms Hotel, Lahinch, t (065) 708 1100, *aberdeenarms@eircom.net* (*moderate*). Ireland's oldest golf links hotel.

Berry Lodge, Miltown Malbay, t (065) 708 7022 (*inexpensive*). Rita Meade's Victorian house has attractive rooms and excellent food.

Clohauincy House, Seafield, Quilty, t (065) 708 7081 (*inexpensive*). Good home-cooking by Mrs O'Connor.

Ocean Cove Leisure Hotel, Kilkee Bay, t (065) 682 3000, *www.lynchotels.com* (*moderate*). Well-situated to take advantage of all the water sports and golfing in the area.

Halpin's Hotel, 2 Erin Street, Kilkee, t (065) 905 6032 (*inexpensive*). Good service and comfort in this cosy hotel.

Crotty's Bar, Kilrush, t (065) 905 2470 (*inexpensive*). Traditional Irish music in a friendly, cosy traditional bar. Rooms are a little intimate and can be noisy, but it's a great place for atmosphere.

The Old Parochial House, Cooraclare, t (065) 905 9059 (*inexpensive*). Possibly as comfortable when the parish priest lived here, but he certainly never had the four-poster beds! They also have two attractive apartments.

Self-catering

Corofin. Charming if basic apartments in the carriage house of a Georgian manor, with wonderful surroundings; €381–540 per week. Contact Mrs Robson, Corofin, t (065) 683 7692.

Doolin. Thatched cottage near the sea; €152–355 per week. Contact Mrs Cullinan, t (065) 707 4349.

Kilkee. Fifteen 4-star holiday homes by the sea; €349–584 per week. Contact Atlantean Management Ltd, Kilkee, t (061) 401388).

Eating Out

The Gairdin, Market Street, Corofin, t (065) 683 7425 (*expensive*). Small restaurant with delightful modern cooking. *Dinner only.*

Linnane's Lobster Bar, New Quay, Burren, t (065) 707 8120 (*moderate*). Pub that specializes in lobster and oysters.

uncalled-for remark about Conor O'Brien, and Red Mary promptly pushed him out of the window.

The Burren

This district is generally called the Burren (*An Bhoieann*: 'The Stony District') after the ancient Barony of that name. It extends some 25 miles (40km) from east to west and 15 miles (24km) from north to south, between Galway Bay and the Atlantic Ocean, with the villages of Doolin, Kilfenora, Gort and Kinvarra forming its south-eastern border. An amazing thing about the Burren is that its 50 square miles are

Cassidy's of Carron, Burren, t (065) 708 9109 (*inexpensive*). Remote pub in the wildest part of the Burren, with excellent lunches using local produce like the farmhouse cheeses.

Gregan's Castle Hotel, near Ballyvaughan, t (065) 707 7005 (*moderate*). Delicious food all day in the Corkscrew Bar, where the cosy fire and low-beamed ceiling are especially welcoming after a long hike.

Tri na Cheile, Ballyvaughan, t (065) 707 7029 (*moderate*). Small and unpretentious; lots of seafood and a vegetarian dish as standard. Great atmosphere; very popular locally.

Aillwee Cave Restaurant, Ballyvaughan, t (065) 707 7036/77067 (*inexpensive*). Eating in a cave is rather a novel experience. Delicious soups, pies, cakes. *Lunch only*.

Monk's Bar, Ballyvaughan, t (065) 707 7059 (*inexpensive*). Delicious mussels and brown bread. Traditional music at night.

The Orchard Restaurant, in Sheedy's Spa View Hotel, Lisdoonvarna, t (065) 707 4026 (*expensive–inexpensive*). Surprisingly sophisticated food in this family-run hotel; they also do pub lunches.

Roadside Tavern, Kincora Road, Lisdoonvarna, t (065) 707 4494 (*inexpensive*). Wood-panelled pub-cum-smoking house. Delicious smoked trout, salmon and chowder.

The Cottage, St Brigid's Well, Liscannor, t (065) 708 1760 (*expensive–inexpensive*). Light lunches and more serious evening dining in a rustic setting.

Mr Eamon's, Lahinch, t (065) 708 1050 (*expensive*). Unpretentious, popular steak and seafood house.

Barrtrá Seafood Restaurant, Lahinch, t (065) 708 1280 (*expensive–moderate*). Simple but good seafood restaurant just outside Lahinch, with views of the bay.

O'Looney's, on the Promenade, Lahinch, t (065) 708 1414 (*moderate*). Good seafood, also bar food, sandwiches and music nightly.

The Black Oak Restaurant, Rineen, near Miltown Malbay, t (065) 708 4403 (*moderate*). Perched on the coast road, with beautiful views down on to Liscannor Bay and an extensive, international menu.

The Cape Restaurant, Armada Hotel, Spanish Point, t (065) 708 4110 (*expensive–moderate*). Hearty, traditional Sunday roast or informal bar food in a variety of settings with uninterrupted views over the Atlantic Ocean.

An Tintean Restaurant, Main Street, Doonbeg, t (065) 905 5036 (*moderate*). Seafood restaurant with Swiss chef. *Evenings only*.

Manuel's Seafood Restaurant, Corbally, Kilkee, t (065) 905 6211 (*moderate*). Fabulous views from here over the bay and, on the other side, the River Shannon and Kerry Mountains. *Dinner only*.

The Long Dock, Carrigaholt, t (065) 905 8106 (*moderate*). Good grub and great *craic* in a beautiful area.

Entertainment and Nightlife

Clare is particularly famous for its traditional music sessions. **Ennistymon** boasts some good venues, as does **Doolin**. Try the following:
McGann's, Roadford, Doolin.
O'Connors, Doolin.

dotted with signs of ancient habitation – stone forts, walls and megalithic tombs, which blend perfectly with a landscape strewn with strangely shaped rocks, left behind by glaciers. You really have to get out of your car and walk here, for the Burren's appeal is gradual rather than dramatic. The Burren is a plateau riven by valleys, some of which lead to the sea; others go nowhere. The Aran Islands rise from Galway Bay, sometimes appearing dark and close to shore, at other times in a shimmering misty haze, far away. They were once part of the Burren and share the same geology and flora. In late May the place becomes starred with sky-blue gentians, bloody cranesbill, geraniums and orchids. Arctic-alpine mountain avens sprawl lavishly over the rocks and Irish saxifrage tufts cover sea-sprayed boulders. Sheltered in the damp clefts of limestone are shade-loving plants such as the maidenhair fern. No one has yet been able to explain fully how such a profusion of northern and southern plants came to grow together, some of them unknown in continental Europe. The present temperate winters and limestone beneath the turf suit the plants; their colonies have grown up unhindered because the land has never been cultivated, only grazed by cattle.

The Burren is considerably rich in antiquities: portal and megalithic tombs, *cahers* and cooking places left by Stone Age farmers who cleared the hills of forest. It is probable that in those times the place was not such a desert. By medieval times, the hills were treeless, and the wide expanses of fissured rock exposed. The Burren certainly stimulates many questions. Botanists and geologists as well as tourists come here, but happily the plan to site an interpretative centre right in the middle of one of its most beautiful and untouched places was shelved after local people and environmentalists objected. How to maintain the traditional ways of farming which have preserved the unique character of the Burren is, as yet, an unresolved issue. The bulldozer is busy clearing the mythical landscape of ancient stone patterns, and mechanized spraying creates a sward of modern flowerless grasses. The farmers are encouraged in this by EU grants: after all, they have to make a living, and there is no support system in place to stop the destruction; only the opportunities for profit that farmers themselves can make in opening up their land and houses to tourists.

It would be easy to drive through the Burren, never stopping to see and feel its magic. You have to walk in its moss-softened hazel woods and see close up the profusion of colour and scented plants in early summer that somehow thrive on the thin soil of the limestone pavements. The black wiry fronds of the maidenhair ferns and the bright green hart's tongue hide in the shelter of the grikes, while wild goats and rabbits nibble at the succulent grass. Many of the stone ring-forts where the ancients kept their cattle for safety are covered in a mass of brambles or hazel, and you could easily pass them by.

Kilfenora is a place of ancient importance on the fringe of the Burren. It is worth staying a while, not only to look at the **Burren Display Centre** (*open Mar–Oct, daily 10–5, June 10–6, July–Aug 9–7; adm;* **t** *(065) 708 8077*), which explains the flora, fauna, butterflies and rock formations of the area, but also because in the graveyard of the ruined church are four 12th-century carved high crosses, all of the same excellent standard, which suggests they might have been produced by one workshop or even by one carver. The small, 12th-century church of St Fachnan is called 'the Cathedral', and its bishopric is still held by the Pope. A fifth cross with elaborate carvings, including that of the crucifixion, stands in a field to the west. Nearby is a holy well.

On the R480 to Ballyvaughan, 6 miles (9.7km) past Leamaneagh Castle, is the great dolmen of **Poulabrone** ('The Pool of Sorrows') with a massive capstone; it is one of the most photographed sites of the Burren. Excavations in 1986 produced the remains of 14 adults and six children and dated the tomb as middle-Neolithic. Not surprisingly, the farmer who owns the land on which it lies has decided to charge the crowds of people who trail up to it and occasionally leave their litter behind. A couple of men in a battered car will probably wave a plastic bucket at you for a donation to help keep the stone walls up and the gate up to the dolmen open. Also on the road to Ballyvaughan, a mile out of Kilfenora, is one of the finest stone forts in Ireland, known as **Ballykinvarga**. This has a very effective trap for those trying to launch an attack: *chevaux de frise*, which are sharp spars of stone set close together in the ground. (The great fort of Dun Aengus on the Aran Islands has a similar arrangement.)

At **Ballyvaughan**, an attractive fishing village on the north edge of the Burren, you can rent yourself an Irish cottage and explore **Black Head**, which looks over the shimmering Galway Bay with clear views of the Aran Islands and the Cliffs of Moher. The islands are made of the same grey limestone as the Burren and have the same bright flowers in the springtime. Ballyvaughan village is set in a green wooded vale, an oasis after the bleached plateaux of limestone, mighty terraces and escarpments to the south. The village has good craft shops, and the harbour is the starting point for boat trips to the islands. There are a couple of tower houses built in the 16th century to explore: Gleninagh, signposted between Ballyvaughan and Lisdoonvarna, was occupied by the O'Loughlins (often spelled O'Loghlen) until 1840; close by is a deserted and ruined village which in the 1930s still had a thriving community and 85 men fishing from their curraghs out in the bay. **Newtown Castle** (*open Easter–early Oct, daily 10–6; adm; t (065) 77216*), also an O'Loughlin stronghold, has been restored and is unusual in that it is round with a square base. You will find it down a lane, off the N67 and 2 miles (3.2km) south of Ballyvaughan. The castle tours take about forty minutes; a trail around the surrounding area includes bardic poetry recitals and extracts from ancient annals, as well as archaeology and geology.

While in Ballyvaughan, take some time to explore the Burren uplands and the inlets of **Ballyvaughan** and **Aughinish Bays**, quiet beaches where the oystercatcher whistles. A long hike can be made into the stony fastness of Turlough Hill or the higher Slievegarron, where all the Burren features make their appearance. The pass between Turlough and Corcomroe Abbey is called *Mám Chatha*, 'the Pass of Battle'. This is the path Donagh O'Brien took on his way to battle against his rival and kinsman Dermot O'Brien in 1317. He was forewarned of defeat by the Hag of the Burren as he passed Lough Rask, close to Bealaclugga. As she washed a grisly pile of heads and limbs in the waters she told him that his head was in the pile. She then rained foul curses upon him and disappeared in the air. Donagh tried to dismiss the prophecy but, sure enough, later that day he and his followers were killed. Dermot O'Brien went on to defeat Richard de Clare, which kept the Normans out of the Burren for nearly two hundred years. **Corcomroe Abbey** was founded by the Cistercians in 1195; in the north wall of the choir is an effigy of King Connor O'Brien. To the south on a hill are the remains of the three ancient churches of Oughtmama.

Aillwee Caves (*open Mar–early Nov, daily 10–6.30, July and Aug, 10–6.30; 3 guided tours daily; adm; t (065) 707 7036*) are 2 miles southeast of Ballyvaughan on the N67. All over the Burren there are hundreds of caves formed by the underground rivers, which give great sport for the speleologist. Aillwee Caves date back to two million years BC. When the river dried up or changed its course, they became the dens of wild bears and other animals. Today the entrance has been tamed to make it easier for the less intrepid, and the caverns are festooned with stalagmites and stalactites. The food shop and craft shop here are excellent, and the centre itself is built sympathetically to blend with its surroundings, though there is a charge to enter even the car park.

Clare's West Coast

By taking the corkscrew road to **Lisdoonvarna** (*Lios Duin Bhearna*: 'Enclosure of the Gapped Fort'), you get a series of lovely views of Galway Bay. Since the decline of Mallow, Lisdoonvarna is the most important spa in Ireland. The waters are said to owe much to their natural radioactivity; there are sulphur, magnesium and iron springs, a pump room and baths for those who come to take the waters. Hotels, guest houses and B&Bs have sprung up everywhere; the town could not be described as attractive, but it has a certain energy when the place is very crowded in the summer. Traditionally it was the place where moderately prosperous farmers came to arrange marriages for their children; and there is still much courting, inspired no doubt by the invigorating properties of the water. There are also plenty of dances and concerts during the spa season; the excitement peaks in September with the **Matchmaking Festival**, which is hyped up for all it's worth. There is a sandy cove at **Doolin**, 3 miles (4.8km) away, good for fishing but dangerous for bathing. This long straggling little fishing village (really two hamlets divided by a field) became famous for its traditional music in the late 1970s, and is still a mecca for music lovers and backpackers. Several hostels have sprung up to cater for all these visitors, and the pubs do a fine trade, with traditional music every night in the summer. On the outskirts of the village is the very fine **Doolin Craft Shop** (*t (065) 707 4309*). You can get a boat from here to Inisheer, the smallest of the Aran Islands, a crossing that takes about 40mins and goes three times a day in the summer months (*Doolin Ferries, t (065) 707 4455*).

In this area you find curious mineral nodules formed by limestone and shale that look just like tortoise shells. There are three of these built into the wall beside the Imperial Hotel in Lisdoonvarna. From here, the coast road (R478) leads to the **Cliffs of Moher**, which drop down vertically to the foaming sea. Seabirds somehow manage to rest on the steep slopes: there are guillemots, razorbills, puffins, kittiwakes, various gulls and choughs; and sometimes even peregrines can be seen. The cliffs stretch for nearly 5 miles (8km) and are made of the darkest yellow sandstone and millstone grit, which can be seen in bands near the top. On a clear day there is a magnificent view of the Twelve Bens, the mountains of Connemara and the three Aran Islands. **O'Brien's Tower**, on the cliff edge, was built in 1835 by Cornelius O'Brien, a local landlord around whom a lot of stories have been woven. In truth he was a bit of a do-gooder as well as being a builder of follies and bridges, not a ruthless tyrant and womaniser as he has been portrayed. He wanted the tower as an observation post from which to watch the turbulent seas, and he also got his peasants to build a three-mile-long wall of limestone flags to prevent visitors being sucked over the edge of the cliffs by the down-draughts. Behind it is an **Information Centre** (*open Mar–Oct*).

On the R478 southeast of the cliffs is **Liscannor**, a little fishing village where a few of the fishermen still use curraghs. It is on the north shore of Liscannor Bay, where the

River Dealagh flows into the sea. The famous limestone flags of Clare were exported from here, and it is easy to spot these lovely striated stones propping up a gateway, or used as lintels, roofing slates or paving. Under the waters of the bay, it is said, there lies a submerged city. Down on the shore of Liscannor Bay (just off the R478) is the tumbledown ruin of St Macreehy's Church (he was a destroyer of plagues, eels, and dragons), and there is also a holy well. John P. Holland (1841–1914), who invented the submarine, was born here, the son of a coastguard. Holland was a nationalist who went to America, where Irish friends and Clan na Gael helped him with funds to build and operate his invention. He hoped that it would be used in the War of Independence against England.

Liscannor is more famous for the **Holy Well of St Brigid**, about 2 miles (3.2km) west on the R478, near the Cliffs of Moher. The well is an important place of pilgrimage: on the last Saturday in July a vigil is held there; the *patron* (celebration) once continued on into Lahinch on the Sunday with racing and sports on the strand. It was the end of the 'hungry month' and the beginning of the festival of Lughnasa, when all the crops were harvested; so the *patron* was accompanied by a feast of new potatoes. Around the well an aura of faith and devotion lingers in the damp air and amongst the trivial offerings of holy pictures of bleeding hearts and saints are plastic statues of the Pope, rosaries and other bits and pieces left by the sick. You approach by a narrow stone passage after the amazing life-size painted plaster model of St Brigid next to the entrance of the well, which is sufficiently naturalistic to be macabre when first glimpsed. Sir Cornelius O'Brien is buried under the Victorian memorial and he also built the monument on the hill with the urn on top. The remains of his house and demesne are within sight of the well; apparently a curse was put on the place because he gave up going to mass.

Lahinch, a mile south of Liscannor, is a small seaside resort with a pretty arc of golden sand and waves big enough for surfing. The part of town devoted to entertainment is a bit tacky, but it has a fine promenade. During the War of Independence in 1920, Lahinch was partially burnt and two men shot by the Black and Tans and Auxiliaries, in reprisal for the ambushing and killing of four RIC by the republican army. The townspeople took refuge in the sand dunes. The **golf course** at Lahinch is championship-standard, but as a guest you are most welcome. There is an amusing story of one enthusiast who putted a winner and got the trophy. He remarked with the skill and colour only the Irish can summon, 'I declare to God I was that tense I could hear the bees belchin.' Club members use the goats as a barometer: if there are none on the links, they know that the weather is bad and it is not worth going out to play. On the promenade is a **Sealife Centre** (*t (065) 708 1900*), where you can see and experience the underwater life of the Atlantic Coast and the unusual Clare coastline.

Ennistymon, with its colourful shop fronts, is 2 miles inland on the N85, in a wooded valley beside the cascading River Cullenagh. The Falls Hotel, which was previously known as Ennistymon House, was the home of Francis MacNamara, a bohemian character and a friend of Augustus John, whose daughter Caitlin married the Welsh poet Dylan Thomas. MacNamara was a supporter of Sinn Féin and an advocate of free love. He generally shocked local sensibilities – the parish priest let fly at him from the pulpit for letting his children play naked on the beach at Doolin. In 1919 his father, who was an ardent unionist, was shot in the neck when one of his shooting parties was ambushed; later Francis' own house at Doolin was burnt by the Black and Tans.

Southwards, following the N67 down the coast from Lahinch, you come to **Spanish Point** (just off the R482), a good spot for surfing, where a great number of ships from the Spanish Armada were wrecked. Those sailors who struggled ashore were slaughtered by the locals on the orders of the Governor of Connacht, Sir Richard Bingham, and a local man, Sir Turlough O'Brien. **Miltown Malbay**, opposite Spanish Point on the N67, is noted for its Willie Clancy Summer School in July (*see* 'Courses', p.279). It is a splendid time to visit for all the fun, and the standard of traditional music in the bars is good all year round (*see* 'Festivals', p.270).

From Miltown Malbay, which was once a rather smart Victorian resort, you can have a swim at the silver strand of **Freach**, just to the north of the town, or climb **Slievecallan**, the highest point in west Clare, which has a megalithic tomb on its southeast slopes. On the way you could rest at the little lake at **Boolynagreana**, which means 'the summer milking place of the sun'. To get there, follow the R474 southwards for 6 miles (9.6km) to the Hand Cross Roads, and then walk over rough land for about a mile. All round these foothills the ancient agricultural practice of transhumance was pursued. This is known in Ireland as 'booleying' and involves moving livestock to mountain pasture during the summer months, although it has fallen into disuse with modern feeding methods.

Back on the coast road (N67) you will find **Quilty**, a strange name for an Irish village: it comes from the Gaelic *coillte*: 'woods', but there are no trees on this flat part of the coast. The great lines of stone walls are strewn with seaweed as it dries for kelp-making. The seaweed is either burned, and the ash used for the production of iodine, or exported for the production of alginates which make the rich, creamy head on Guinness. The church here is reminiscent of the early Christian churches, but in fact it was built in 1907 with money given by some French sailors who were rescued by the villagers when their ship was wrecked one stormy night.

Southwest Clare

Kilkee (*Cill Chaoidhe*: 'Church of St Caoidhe'), about 12 miles (19km) south on the N67, is a favourite resort for Irish holidaymakers, though a recent orgy of tasteless building has rather changed its Victorian ambience. It is built along a sandy crescent-shaped beach; the Duggerna Rocks, acting as a reef, make it safe for bathing at any stage of the tide. Within the rocks are natural swimming pools and further to the south is a large sea cave. A cliff walk starts from the seafront, from where you can get a good view of these sights. The coast southwest for about 15 miles (24km), from here to **Loop Head**, is an almost endless succession of caverns, chasms, sea-stacks and weirdly and wonderfully shaped rocks. The cliff scenery is on a par with the Cliffs of Moher. Walkers can explore the coast between Kilkee and Loop Head, a path of some 15 miles (24kms). There is a colourful legend about Ulster's hero Cú Chulainn, who was generally well loved by women, but this time was being pursued relentlessly by a termagant of a woman called Mal. Eventually he came to the edge of the cliffs on

Loop Head and leapt on to a great rock about 30ft out to sea. Mal was not to be outdone and made the same leap with equal agility and success. Cú Chulainn straightaway performed the difficult feat of leaping back to the mainland and this time Mal faltered, fell short, and disappeared into the raging ocean below. Out of this legend came the name Loop Head (Leap Head in Irish). As for poor Mal, she must have been a witch, for her blood turned the sea red and she was swept northwards to a point near the Cliffs of Moher called **Hag's Head**. The R487 takes you close to Loop Head, but you will really have to branch off down the minor roads to get a view of all its splendour. If dolphin-watching appeals, head for **Carrigaholt** where boat trips go out to a resident population of sixty bottle-nosed dolpins who hang around the Shannon Estuary. You can also go from Kilrush.

Kilrush (*Cill Rois*: 'Church of the Promontory') is a busy market town overlooking the Shannon Estuary. It has a large marina and a heritage centre that explores the role of the landlords, the Vandeleurs, in shaping the town. There is also the recently restored **Vandeleur Walled Garden Park** (*open daily 10–5.30; adm; t (065) 905 1760*), where you can walk through 420 tranquil acres of woodland. The Catholic church has some Henry Clarke stained glass windows. He was part of the movement to revive the art of stained glass in Ireland, nurtured by a workshop in Dublin founded by Sarah Purser. About a mile away is the harbour, centred around Cappagh Pier.

Two miles out into the estuary, **Scattery Island** (Cathach's Island), founded by St Senan in the 6th century, has some interesting monastic remains. An island in the broad Shannon was easy meat for the Vikings, who raided it several times. The round tower is very well preserved and has its door at ground level – the unsuspecting monks must have been surprised by the aggressive Norsemen. The five ruined churches date from medieval times. Boat trips from Cappagh to Scattery Island are available in the summer (*Scattery Island Ferries, t (065) 905 1237*), and the **Scattery Island Centre** in Kilrush, on the Marina on Merchant's Quay (*open mid June–mid Sept daily 9.30–6.30*), offers an introduction to the island before you go. The **Fergus Estuary**, where the mouth of the River Shannon gapes its widest, is a paradise of forgotten isles, untouched and deserted, with names like **Deer Isle, Canon Isle** and **Deenish**. You can base yourself near **Killadysert**, on the R473 going north to Ennis, and have great fun exploring them. If you make enquiries you may find someone to take you out there in a boat.

The Province of Connacht

12

Connacht

p.372
p.512
p.152

Highlights

1 Old ways of life on the Aran Islands, Co. Galway

2 The wild west of your dreams at the Connemara National Park, Co. Galway

3 Views from Croagh Patrick, the holy mountain, Co. Mayo

4 Strong intimations of W. B. Yeats at Lissadell House, Co. Sligo

5 The beauty of nature and the art of man at Ceide Fields, Co. Mayo

The province of Connacht (*Cuige Chonnacht*), also spelt Connaught, is made up of Counties Galway, Mayo, Roscommon, Sligo and Leitrim. Oliver Cromwell thought of Connacht as a Siberia to which he could banish the troublesome Catholic landowners. It was here on the crowded, stony farms that the famine struck the hardest in the 1840s. Today, it seems a wild paradise of mountains, heather and lakes into which the Atlantic makes spectacular entrances with black cliffs, golden beaches and island-studded bays. This is the wild west, which was for centuries remote from Dublin and fashionable values; where in some parts the local people still speak Gaelic, and where they have clung to their own traditions in spite of the past invaders and the more insidious advance of modern life.

On a bright day in this region, you might think that Cromwell did those 'transplanted Irish' a good turn: your aesthetic feelings are satisfied, and you can be sure that a good meal is waiting at the next hotel. The grey rocks, the scraggy sheep, the turf ricks and misty mountains are transformed into a tumble of brownish purple, with streaks of silver and blue where deep valley lakes reflect the sky. This is why the monks in early Christian times turned their backs on the court of Tara and the rich Celtic princes, and built their tiny churches on the windswept islands off the coast.

Farming and fishing in this part of the world is a risky business, and the history of Connacht reflects the barren countryside closely. The Norman invaders seem to have been less successful, or less persistent, here than in other provinces; or else they became Irish themselves, like the de Burgo family, who changed their name to Burke. It is rather ironic that the Connacht people, who so strongly ignored outside influences for hundreds of years, should be more Anglicized now because of TV and the tourist trade than they ever were under the British. But the areas known as the *Gaeltachta*, where Gaelic is still the first language, are protected by the government, and incentives by way of grants have encouraged people not to move off to America or England for jobs.

It would be a mistake, though, to think that all Connacht is wild mountain scenery. A large part of it belongs to the limestone plain which covers the centre of Ireland, making it saucer-shaped, with its mountains on the rim. The whole of Roscommon, part of Leitrim, South Sligo and much of Galway is made up of neat fields, trees and heather, dotted with lakes and watered by the lovely River Shannon. The Shannon rises in the Iron Mountains of Cavan and flows southwest into Leitrim, where it curves to form a moat round the eastern boundary of Connacht. This part of the province is wonderful, but it lacks the instant splendour of Connemara or the Joyce Country. The Shannon widens to engulf huge lakes, rather like a snake swallowing down its prey whole, and continues to coil down the countryside.

The climate of the west is mild, though a misty rain often falls and leaves you soaked through. The mountains seem to nudge the clouds above them into rain, but there is always a glimmer of sunshine about and in summer it can get superbly warm. Scarlet fuchsia grows along the coast roads in place of the overbearing hawthorn hedges. In parts where you would be hard put to find a blade of grass, a giant hogweed plant will grow in early summer; purple rhododendron grows here profusely. All of Connacht, but especially Connemara, is rather like a piece of tweed cloth with a thread of grey running through it – a speckled look, given by its many thousands of little stone walls.

History

Connacht has a lion's share of heroes, legends and battles. Back in the mists of pre-history, tradition holds that the Fir Bolgs, who had thought themselves alone on the island, bumped into the tall, fair Tuatha Dé Danaan and the resulting battle was fought on the plain of Moytura. The Fir Bolgs were defeated and had to retreat to the islands and mountains of the west. Here they built themselves the marvellous ring-forts of *Dun Aonghasa* and *Dubh-Chathair* on the Aran Islands, and clung on whilst the centre of power shifted from the Dé Danaans to the invading Celts. The legendary Dé Danaans are supposed to have brought with them the *Lia Fail*, or Stone of Destiny, which was used in Ireland as the coronation seat, and, some people claim, can still be seen at Tara in County Meath.

Connacht has produced two infamous queens. One told Queen Elizabeth I not to patronize her, and was a sea pirate who ruled from Clare Island. Her name was Grace O'Malley (*see* p.332). The other was Maeve (or Medb), a legendary Queen remembered in the epic tale of 'The Cattle Raid of Cooley' (*see* p.528). On the slopes of the hauntingly beautiful Ben Bulben, the legendary hero Diarmuid met an untimely death in a boar hunt arranged by his enemy Finn MacCool (*see* **Old Gods and Heroes**, pp.83–4).

County Galway

County Galway (*Gaillimh*) is the second-largest county in Ireland, and 50 per cent of its population still speak Gaelic as their first language. It stretches from the wild and beautiful region known as Connemara in the west, to the banks of the Shannon and Lough Derg in the east, and includes the island-studded Lough Corrib. It is truly a county of contrast. There is bog and rich farming land that a Meath man would not sniff at; whilst amongst the mountains and along the coast the tiny *clochans* of whitewashed stone cottages tell of a different way of life, where the Atlantic winds blow strongly and red hens scratch away amongst a seaweed-fertile soil.

For those of you in search of peace and solitude, miles of lonely valleys and hills and huge golden beaches await you. Anglers will be in paradise fishing on Lough Corrib, the other countless lakes and the salmon rivers of Owenglin and Dawros. Some very good restaurants have grown up and serve delicious fresh seafood in imaginative ways. As for drinking, the bars are the friendliest you could hope to find. Ancient Stone Age fortifications and early monastic churches add more fascination to the county. A trip to the Aran Islands is not only an adventure in itself, but gives you a chance to see Conor Fort on Inishmaan, built of massive great stones. Romantic ruins of 15th-century castles add their charm and stories to the landscape, and some have been restored for the public to look around. Galway City is an attractive and civilized place, with plenty of cultural life: music, theatre, good bookshops and cosy bars in which to discuss all you have seen and heard.

History

The names that crop up again and again in the history of County Galway are O'Flaherty, de Burgo, and Lynch. They each represent a different and conflicting group who battled it out for centuries. The O'Flahertys were a warlike Gaelic tribe from Connemara, also known as *Iar-Chonnacht*. The de Burgos were Norman adventurers who were granted the land around Galway City in 1226, at which time it was a small fort. Richard de Burgo fortified it stongly to keep out the O'Flahertys, but over the years the de Burgos became Irish in their ways and lost their allegiance to the Crown. During the reign of Edward I at the end of the 13th century, fourteen Anglo-Norman and Welsh families had settled in the town, and were passionate Royalists. They controlled all the civic powers and kept themselves to themselves, excluding any Irish from the town, including the de Burgos or Burkes as they were now called. (Quite when this name change happened is not recorded.) In 1518 the Corporation resolved that no inhabitant should receive into his house, 'at Christmas, Easter, no feast else, any of the Burkes, MacWilliams, Kellys, nor any *sept* else without licence of the Mayor and Council, on pain to forfeit £5, that O nor Mac shall strut nor swagger through the streets of Galway'. The chief of these fourteen families, or 'tribes' as they were known, were the Lynches, and through the enterprise and resourcefulness of such families Galway City became rich, trading in wine and other commodities with Spain. The tribes of Galway were able to hang on to civic power in their city until 1654, when Cromwellian forces took the city after a siege of months and shattered it. The Williamite wars in the 1690s brought about another siege and spelt the end of Galway's independence.

Galway City was the administrative centre for the west of Ireland during British rule in the 18th and 19th centuries. The famine years of 1845–49 bought desolation and horror to the countryside and massive emigration followed for several generations. However, the Congested Districts Board set up in 1890 to promote the development of traditional crafts and fishing industries started to improve matters. At the turn of the century, Nationalists used the west of Ireland as a powerful symbol of 'Real Ireland', because the people remained un-Anglicized and still spoke Gaelic despite widescale emigration and the national school system, which between 1831 and 1904 taught no Irish. After the establishment of the Irish State, the Congested Districts Board evolved into the *Roinn na Gaeltachta* (the Department of State responsible for Irish-speaking districts), and special grants were made available to encourage people to stay in the county. The IDA (Industrial Development Authority) has also had great success in attracting sophisticated industrial companies. Galway City has its own university, the second largest regional technical college in the country, and a flourishing arts community. The attempts to preserve the Irish language are bolstered by *Radio na Gaeltachta* and Irish summer colleges, where students from all over Ireland speak Gaelic, learn *ceili* dancing and stay in the houses of Irish-speaking families. The struggle to preserve the Gaelic speaking districts is always present: tourism and television undermine it, and the young continue to emigrate to other parts of Ireland and abroad. Many people have a sister or brother working in North America or England.

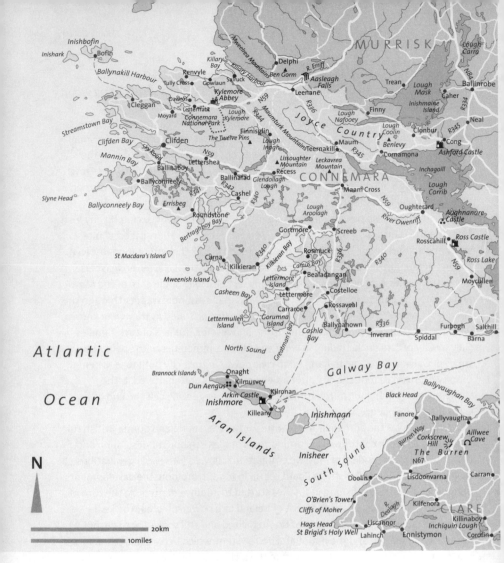

East Galway

Gort (*Gort inse Guaire*: 'Field on Guaire's Island'), the main town on the road from
Galway to Ennis, Shannon, Limerick and the south, stands in a natural gap between
the Slieve Aughty mountains and the Burren – the traditional road between Munster
and Connacht. Guaire was the name of the 7th-century king who built a castle here;
he was supposed to have been so generous that his right hand – his giving hand –
was longer than his left. One day as he sat down to a sumptuous meal, the plates of
food suddenly flew out of the windows; he naturally followed his meal on horseback,
intrigued by such magic. After a few miles he came upon St Colman, who had just
that minute finished a seven-year fast by gobbling up the feast. Instead of being
angry the king was impressed; he was even more so when he found Colman was a

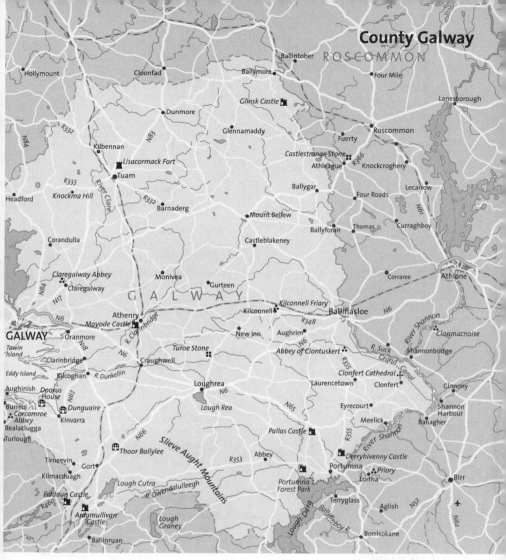

relation, and granted to him the lands of Kilmacduagh, where the saint founded a monastery. About 4 miles (7.4km) southwest of Gort on the R460, **Kilmacduagh** has one of the most interesting collections of church buildings in Ireland. There is a 12th-century monastic church which is called a 'cathedral'. It is roofless now but has good carvings; one on the jamb of the door is an incised comic face with earrings. The round tower near the small lake was built in the 11th or 12th century. It is one of the most perfect in Ireland; its angle has something in common with the Leaning Tower of Pisa. The monks used to build the door of such towers about 25ft (7.6m) from the ground, so that when marauders attacked they could whip up the ladders once they were safely installed with their treasures. In **Tirneevin**, just north of Kilmacduagh, is a small church with a very fine stained-glass window of Christ the Sower, by George Campbell.

Getting There and Around

By Air

Galway Airport has daily flights to Dublin on Aer Lingus and some to London. There is a bus connection from the rail/bus station in Galway City that is scheduled to meet flights.
Galway Airport, Carnmore, t (091) 755569, f (091) 752876, *www.galwayairport.com*.

By Rail

Galway Train Station, t (091) 564222, *www.irishrail.ie*. There are a few daily trains to Dublin.

By Bus

Buses depart from the train station, right in the centre off Eyre Square. Galway City is one of Bus Eireann's main hubs, and you can get to almost every town in Galway and the surrounding counties conveniently. For Dublin, you can do better with Nestor Bus; other private operators provide economical services to County Galway towns, especially in summer.
Galway Bus Information, t (091) 562000.
Nestor Bus, t (091) 797144. €14 return to Dublin.
Bus Eireann, t (091) 562000, *www.buseireann.ie*. Also offers day tours around Connemara and the Burren from Galway City in summer.

By Bike

Europa Bicycles, Earls Island, Galway City (also arranges tours), t (091) 563355.
Irish Cycle Hire, Victoria Place, Eyre Square, Galway City, t (091) 561498.

Kearney's Bicycle Hire, Headford Road, Galway City, t (091) 563356.
Renvyle Stores, Tullymore, t (095) 43485.
John Mannion, Bridge Street, Clifden, t (095) 21160.

Festivals

April
Cuirt Literary Festival, Galway City, t (091) 565886, *www.galwayartscentre.ie*.

May
Ballinasloe Coarse Angling Festival, t (0905) 42619, f (0905) 44474, *coconnor@tinet.ie*, *www.irelandholidays.co.uk*.
Fleadh na gCuach ('Cuckoo Festival'), Kinvara, *www.kinvara.com*. Traditional music and song festival incorporating art and drama.
Galway Early Music Festival, Galway City, t (091) 846356, or t (091) 753908, *www.galwayearlymusic.com, maura.ocroinin@nuigalway.ie, maireadk@eircom.net*.

June
Bloomsday, Nora Barnacle House, Bowling Green, Galway City, t (091) 564743. Open-air readings from the works of James Joyce, June 16th at 6.30pm.

July
Galway Arts Festival, t (091) 509700, *www.galwayartsfestival.ie, info@gaf.iol.ie*. Ireland's biggest arts festival.
Galway Film *Fleadh*, Town Hall Theatre, Galway City, t (091) 751655, *gafleadh@iol.ie*.

Around Gort there are many little streams which suddenly disappear into the limestone. The River Beagh emerges to flow through a ravine, called the Ladle, into the Punchbowl: a huge funnel-shaped hollow, surrounded by trees, with water swirling dangerously at the bottom. It is only a few yards from the road, and not difficult to see even if you are in a hurry. The Gort area is full of literary associations: in 1917, W. B. Yeats bought a ruined tower house for £35 and called it **Thoor Ballylee** (*open May–30 Sept, daily 10–6; adm; t (091) 563081*). Now Tourism Ireland have carefully restored it, and many rare first editions of Yeats' work are on exhibit there. He lived here until 1929, whereupon it fell into ruin once more. You will find it just off the N66 north of Gort. It is a romantic building with a wonderful view from the top. An audio guide to the tower and grounds is available in different languages. Lady Gregory's old

Galway Races, 2 miles (3.2km) from the city at Ballybrit Racecourse, *www.iol.ie/galway-races*. Held late July–early August. The most exciting meetings are held at the end of July and feature the Galway Plate and the Galway Hurdle – a mixture of high society and sweet-talking bookies.

Kiltartan Hedge School, Coole Park and Yeats Tower, Gort, t (048) 9064 9010, or from UK t (028) 9064 9010. Informal exploration of W.B. Yeats' Coole and Ballylee in the landscape that inspired his writing.

Traditional Echoes in Song and Dance, Inis Mor, Aran Islands, t (099) 61424, *info@irishculture.ch*, *www.irish-culture.ch*. A ten-day programme of set/ceili dancing, old Gaelic songs, session and party with islanders; boat trips, walks, etc.

August

Crinniu na mBad ('the Gathering of the Boats'), Kinvara, t (091) 637579. Traditional boat festival with curragh-racing, arts, sports, children's events and traditional music.

Connemara Pony Show, Clifden, t (095) 21863, *enquiries@cpbs.ie*. Annual show of Connemara ponies, by Connemara Pony Breeders Society.

September

Clarinbridge Oyster Festival, t (091) 796359. Lots of drinking, oyster-opening competitions, traditional music, dance and fun.

Clifden Community Arts Festival, t (095) 21644, *www.connemara.net/artsweek*. Top-quality arts events, poetry, lectures, recitals and exhibitions.

Galway Oyster Festival, Galway City, t (091) 527282. Centres around the oyster-opening championship which attracts international participants. The whole affair snowballs into dances, dinners, shows and speeches from local worthies, and maybe a celebrity or two.

Lady Gregory of Coole: An Autumn Gathering, t (091) 521836. Weekend of lectures, a play and discussions highlighting the folklorist, dramatist and joint founder of the Abbey Theatre.

The Quiet Man Festival, Clonbur, t (092) 46155, *paddyrock@esatclear.net*.

October

Baboro International Arts Festival for Children, t (091) 509705. Irish and international theatre, dance, music, workshops for 3–12-year-olds. Held in Galway City and around the county.

Ballinasloe International Horse Fair and Festival, t (0905) 44132. Traditional festival dating back to 1772.

Cooley-Collins Traditional Music Festival, Gort, t (091) 632370. Traditional music, *ceili* and storytelling for children in honour of two deceased local musicians, Joe Cooley and Kieran Collins. Adults welcome.

Maam Cross October Fair, Maam Cross, t (091) 552306. Sale of sheep, cattle and Connemara ponies via stalls, trailers and cars parked for miles on each of the four roads leading to Connemara.

December

Woodford Mummers' *Feile*, Woodford, held on 26th and 27th, t (0509) 49326.

home, **Coole Park**, is about 2 miles (3.2km) northeast of Gort (*mid June–Sept daily 9.30–6.30, Easter–mid June and Sept daily exc Mon 10–4.30; adm; t (091) 631804*). She was a writer and co-founder, with Yeats, of the Abbey Theatre in Dublin. Many remarkable people from the Irish literary scene stayed here, including Yeats, who found it a refuge when he was ill and little-known. Nothing is left of the house, which was demolished for the value of its stone, but the spreading copper chestnut that served as Lady Gregory's visitors' book still grows in the walled garden: you can make out the initials of A. E. (George Russell, the mystical painter), Jack Yeats, Sean O'Casey and a bold G. B. S. – George Bernard Shaw. Mementoes of Lady Gregory and the Celtic Revival can be seen at the **Kiltartan Gregory Museum**, at Kiltartan Cross north of Gort (*open June–Sept daily 11–6.30, Oct–May Sun only 1.30–5; adm; t (091) 631069/632346*).

Tourist Information

Thoor Ballylee: north of Gort, t (091) 631436; *open May–Sept.*
Ballinasloe: t (0905) 42131; *open July–Aug.*
Tuam: t (093) 25486/24463; *open July–Aug.*

Shopping

Crafts
Thoor Ballylee, t (091) 563081.
Dunguaire Castle, Kinvarra, t (061) 360788, or t 1800 269811.
Tuam Mill Museum Craft shop, Shop Street, Tuam, t (093) 25486.

Crystal
Clarinbridge Crystal, Clarinbridge, t (091) 796178.

Sports and Activities

Fishing
Coarse fishing for brown trout on the River Clare and Lough Rea, and on the River Suck for bream, rudd, perch and pike. For tackle and information, contact:
Sonny Martyn, Tuam, t (093) 24151.
Mr Salmon, Main Street, Ballinasloe, t (0905) 42120.

Golf
Galway Bay Golf and Country Club, Oranmore, t (091) 790500. Championship course.

Pony-trekking
Aille Equestrian Centre, Aille Cross, Loughrea, t (091) 841216. They also organize week-long trails in Connemara here.
Clonboo Riding School, Corandulla, t (091) 791362.
Rockmount Riding Centre, Claregalway, t (091) 798147. Located near Galway City.

Where to Stay

Doorus House Youth Hostel, Doorus, Kinvarra, t (091) 637512 (*inexpensive*). The site of Yeats' and Lady Gregory's famous conversation which led to the creation of the Abbey Theatre.
O'Deas Hotel, Bride Street, Loughrea, t (091) 841611, *www.commerce.ie/odeashotel*, *odeashotel@eircom.net* (*moderate*). Comfortable and unpretentious.
Hayden's, Dunlo Street, Ballinasloe, t (0905) 42347 (*moderate*). Lovely hotel with land-scaped gardens and fifty rooms.
Oranmore Lodge, Tuam Road, Oranmore, t (091) 794400, *www.oranmorelodge.com*, *orlodge@eircom.net* (*moderate*). Comfortable with good food. Typical hotel décor, with plush carpets.

Five miles (8km) south of Gort are the ruins of the 16th-century **Ardamullivan Castle**, an O'Shaughnessy stronghold. They were the ruling *sept* in these parts before they were dispossessed by Cromwell. Another of their strongholds is **Fiddaun Castle**, also ruined but with a fine *bawn*, 5 miles (8km) southwest of Gort.

Around Kinvarra

Kinvarra is a charming fishing village at the head of a bay where there is a restored 16th-century castle called **Dunguaire**, also known as Dungory (*open May–6 Oct, daily 9.30–5.30; adm; medieval banquets May–early Nov, twice nightly;* t (061) 360788, or t 1800 269811). It is sited on a little jutting promontory beside the bay; a tower house stands within the strong walls of its close-fitting *bawn*. On summer evenings you can savour the delights of a medieval banquet as you listen to readings from Irish literature. The Great Hall is rather bijou but the Irish dancing and singing are fun. To the north, through the windows of the castle, you look over the waters of Galway Bay to the hills of Connemara. To the south you can make out the grey and hazy hills of the Burren in County Clare. The road from Kinvarra goes past the head of the

Hazel House Farmhouse, Mausrevagh, Headford, t (091) 791204, *hazelhouse@ esatclear.ie* (*inexpensive*). A modern bungalow with a traditional Irish welcome from Mrs Cunningham, who provides tea and scones when you arrive. Matt, the man of the house, plays the accordion, banjo and fiddle, and he is happy to play to his guests.

Cregg Castle, Corrandulla, t (091) 791434, *creggcas@indigo.ie* (*moderate*). 17th-century castle, friendly and ideal for children. Traditional music in the evenings.

Ballindiff Bay Lodge, Linmnagh, Corrandulla, t (091) 791195 (*inexpensive*). On the edge of Lough Corrib. Good angling facilities.

Eating Out

The Blackthorn, Crowe Street, Gort, t (091) 632127 (*expensive–moderate*). Bar and upstairs restaurant open for dinner and *inexpensive* lunches. Live music Saturday nights.

Sullivans Royal Hotel, The Square, Gort, t (091) 631257, *www.irelandmidwest.com*, *jsullinsauc@eircom.net* (*inexpensive*). Home-cooked food.

Kinvara Coffee and Wholefood Shop, Kinvarra Harbour, Kinvarra.

Dunguaire Castle Medieval Banquet, Kinvarra, t (061) 360788, or t 1800 269811 (*expensive*).

Poetry readings as you wine and dine on typical Irish fare.

Paddy Burke's, Clarinbridge, t (091) 96107 (*inexpensive*). Oysters to be taken, in particular, with a glass of creamy stout. If you order a lavish amount of seafood, obviously, the price will creep up.

Moran's on the Weir, Kilcolgan, near Clarinbridge, t (091) 796113 (*inexpensive*). Seafood bar in an old cottage overlooking their own oyster beds in Galway Bay.

Meadow Court Restaurant/Bar, Loughrea, t (091) 841051, f (091) 842406, *www. meadowcourthotel.com* (*moderate*). International menu and seafood.

Haydens, Dunlo Street, Ballinasloe, t (0905) 42347 (*moderate*). Good pub snacks and an excellent dining room.

Aughrim School House Restaurant, Aughrim, Ballinasloe, t (0905) 73622 (*moderate*). Simple and good food.

Imperial Hotel, Tuam, t (093) 24188 (*inexpensive*). Hearty lunches.

The Oranmore Lodge, Tuam Road, Oranmore, t (091) 794400 (*moderate*). Rich Irish cooking.

The Moorings Restaurant, Main Street, Oranmore, t (091) 790462 (*moderate*). Good value.

Cre-na-Cille Public House, High Street, Tuam, t (093) 28232 (*moderate–inexpensive*). Game, meat and seafood.

peninsula, on which is **Doorus House**, where Yeats and Maupassant each stayed. (It is now a youth hostel.) Northwards from Kinvarra the N67 runs inland with little side-roads turning west to the island waters of Galway Bay. One of these roads leads to the ancient monastic site of Drumacoo, which is dedicated to a nun, Sister Sorrey. Here there is a very beautiful south doorway decorated in Early Gothic style, c. AD 1200. There is also a very weedy holy well outside the churchyard wall.

At **Clarinbridge**, on the main Galway–Limerick road (N18), the bars come alive in September with enthusiasts gathered there for the Oyster Festival. Whatever the time of year, though, you should take the tiny signposted side-road to Moran's on the Weir in Kilcoghan, for delicious Guinness and seafood of all sorts.

Around Portumna

Fifteen miles (24km) east of Gort on the R353 is **Portumna** (*Port Omna:* 'Landing Place of the Tree Trunk'). This market town stands at the head of the huge and intricate Lough Derg, the furthest downriver of the Shannon lakes and a major cruising centre, with plenty of shops and bars. To the west of Portumna is good walking country on the forested slopes of **Slieve Aughty**. The R353 from Gort bisects the mountain, and there are numerous unnumbered roads from which you can climb to a vantage point and see the extensive views of Lough Derg and the surrounding countryside. The climb up the Slieve Aughty mountains is not too strenuous an exercise, for the highest point is 1,207ft (368m). On the edge of the town is the forested demesne of the Earls of Clanrickarde, now a lovely **forest park** (*car park adm*) with nature trails and picnic spots bordering Lough Derg. The 17th-century **Portumna Castle** is being restored by the Office of Public Works (*open mid June–mid Sept, daily 9.30–6.30; adm; t (0509) 41658, or t (01) 647 2461*), and is probably the best example of Jacobean art in Ireland. A stone set in the crumbling walls of the double staircase bears an affectionate epitaph to a dog that died in April 1797: 'Alas poor Fury, she was a dog taken all in all, I shall not look upon her like again'. Near the castle is a Dominican friary, founded in 1410, with beautiful windows.

There are two castles in this area you should go out of your way to see (though neither is open to the public): Derryhivenny and Pallas. **Derryhivenny Castle** is 3 miles (4.8km) northwest of Portumna. Built in 1653 by Donal O'Madden, it is well preserved and one of the last tower houses built in Ireland. **Pallas Castle** is about 6 miles (9.7km) from Portumna on the Loughrea road (N65). Built in the 16th century by the Burkes, the lower storeys are defensive, as in most castles, and any openings are few and purely utilitarian – making them terrible places to have actually lived in. Amongst the lush and peaceful Shannon valley, about 15 miles (24km) northeast of Portumna and 10 miles (6km) northeast of Eyrecourt off the R355/6, is a monastery founded by St Brendan the Navigator in AD 563. There is a superb example of Irish Romanesque art in the doorway of the minuscule 12th-century church known as **Clonfert Cathedral** (*open daily*). Six receding planes are decorated with heads, foliage and abstract designs; within the pediment, sculptured heads peer down at you. The 15th-century chancel arch is decorated with angels, rosettes, and a mermaid admiring herself in a mirror. **Clonfert Catholic Church** houses a 13th-century wooden Madonna and child, found in a tree hole. It was probably hidden during Cromwell's time. **Meelick**, close by on the River Shannon, has mooring facilities for boats.

Around Lough Rea

Loughrea ('Town of the Grey Lake'), is a bright, colour-washed town, situated on a lovely lough. The pubs are venues for fine traditional music, which is very popular here. It started life as a stronghold of Richard de Burgo, whose family turned into Burkes and later Clanrickardes; you will often come across the name. The town is very affluent because at Tynagh there are lead and zinc mines. What you must not miss if you stop in Loughrea is **St Brendan's Catholic Cathedral**. It is not very inspiring from the outside, but inside the decoration epitomizes the development of ecclesiastical arts and crafts in Ireland from 1903 to 1957. The stained-glass windows are by Sarah Purser and other members of her Tower of Glass. This was a stained-glass workshop founded in 1903 in Dublin which attracted other talented artists such as Evie Hone. The statue of the Virgin and Child is by John Hughes, and the embroidered sodality banners are by Jack Yeats. The Carmelite monastery is a fine early 14th-century ruin, and next door to it is an active Carmelite abbey.

A most impressive curiosity is the **Turoe Stone**, which is found 4 miles (6.4km) north of Loughrea, signposted from the hamlet of Bullaun. It is a rounded pillar about 3ft (1m) high. A swirling mass of opposed spirals is carved upon the upper part. It must have had some ritual purpose; dating from the 1st century AD at the latest, it is the finest of its type in Ireland, and its decoration has been linked with the Celtic *La Tene* style of decoration that is found in Brittany, and also with the Omphalos Stone in Delphi which was seen as the navel or centre of the world by the ancient Greeks. The stone was moved to its present position from a ring-fort called Rath of the Big Man.

The family who live in the house close by have sought to benefit from the tourists, and opened the **Turoe Pet Farm and Leisure Park** (*open Easter–Sept daily 10–7, Oct–Easter weekends only 2–6, exc Dec 1–23, Thurs–Fri 6–8 and Sat–Sun 2–8; adm; t (091) 841580*) which has changed the ambience somewhat. There's a duck pond, small animals, a playground with swings and a collection of old farm machinery.

Around Ballinasloe

Ballinasloe (*Beal Atha na Sluaighe*: 'Town of the Ford of the Hostings'), 20 miles (16km) east on the N6, is famous for its **Horse Fair** in early October, when the quiet streets suddenly bustle with eight days of carnival events and show-jumping competitions (*see* 'Festivals', p.297). Horses are still put for sale on the fair green, but not in the number that the ballads reminisce about. (Horse fairs used to be common all over Ireland up until the 1950s, when the tractor and car took over.) A tower is all that remains of the castle, which used to command the bridge over the River Suck. The Suck is excellent for coarse fishing, and Ballinasloe Angling Week, one of the biggest coarse angling competitions in Ireland, takes place here annually. **St Michaels Church** contains some of the best stained-glass by Harry Clarke (1889–1931) and Albert Power (1883–1945), both highly regarded artists.

Kilconnell village, about 6 miles (9.7km) away on the R348 to Galway, has a Franciscan friary, founded in 1353 by William O'Kelly. In the 17th century it was unsuccessfully besieged by Cromwell. In the north wall of the nave are two 15th to 16th-century tomb chests, one with flamboyant tracery. The west tomb is divided into niches with the carved figures of Saints John, Louis, Mary, James and Denis. Under the tower the corbel shows a little carving of an owl in high relief. Tradition alleged that the incompetent French general, St Ruth, who led the Irish against King William in 1691, was buried here after the Battle of Aughrim. West of Ballinasloe on the N6 is the site of the battle, and the **Battle of Aughrim Interpretative Centre** (*open daily Easter–Oct, 10–6; tearoom; adm; t (0905) 73939*). The main causes and results of the battle are explored in displays, documents and an audio-visual show.

The well-preserved ruins of the **Abbey of Clontuskert** lie on the way to Laurencetown (R355). The abbey, which stands on the site of a monastery founded in the 9th century, was rebuilt by industrious Augustinian monks in the 14th century with money from the sale of 10-year indulgences. The monks ignored the Reformation and carried on until Cromwell finally wrecked the place. The abbey has an unusual and pretty west door of 1471, depicting saints, a mermaid and other creatures.

Around Athenry

Athenry (*Baile Atha an Ri*: 'Town of the King's Ford') is pronounced 'Athenrye', and was founded by Meiler de Bermingham, a Norman warlord, in the last half of the 13th century. The strong walls that were later built round it still remain in fragments. In the central square stands the remains of a 15th-century cross showing the Crucifixion on one side and the Virgin and Child on the other. **St Mary's Parish Church** was built in 1289, if not before. It became collegiate in 1484, and was suppressed in 1576 and burnt by Clanrickarde's sons (even though the mother of one of them was buried there). The graceful spire in the grounds dates from 1828. Now ruined but full of interest is the **Dominican priory** founded by de Bermingham in 1241. It has been a university and a barracks, and has been tidied up by the Office of Public Works. The tracery work of the east window, dated 1324, is very fine. The church was the burial place of the Earls of Ulster and many of the chief Irish families of the west, but their graves were destroyed by Cromwell's soldiers. In a recess a small carving of a monk grins forever, and there is an interesting grave slab dated 1682 to Thomas Tannain, on which are carved the bellows, anvil, auger, pinchers and horseshoes of his blacksmith's trade. In North Gate Street is a **heritage cottage**: a recreated traditional cottage furnished as it would have been early this century (*access through the tourist information point*).

Moyode Castle, 2 miles (3.2km) southwest of Athenry, is a ruined mansion with an ancient castle in its grounds. Here in 1770 the nucleus of what was to become the Galway Blazers Foxhounds was formed. The Big House, which is now a ruin, was taken over in the Nationalist cause by Liam Mellows and his Galway followers for several days during the Easter Rising in 1916. Mellows was a socialist leader who was executed during the Irish Civil War in 1922. **Claregalway** on the River Clare is now a suburb of Galway, where you'll find the remains of a 13th-century **Franciscan abbey**.

Around Tuam

Tuam ('grave mound'), pronounced 'Choom', is a very uninspiring place: the streets smell of beer and chips. But that was on a rainy dark day. Tuam has a long history and during the 12th century was the seat of the O'Connor kings of Connacht. The presence of a fine 12th-century cross in the town square and an imposing **Church of Ireland cathedral** are reminders of its past glory. Although the latter is a Gothic-revival structure, it still has a splendid, wide and lavishly carved chancel arch of rosy sandstone which dates from the 12th century. The imposing church door is surrounded by carved decoration; on one of the splays, the Devil is pulling Adam's ears. **Tuam Mill** in Shop Street (*open mid June–mid Sept, Mon–Sat 10–6; adm; t (093) 25486*), one of the last mills in the county, survives as a museum and heritage centre, and also provides tourist information in the summer. Four miles (6.4km) north of Tuam is **Tollenfal Castle**, ancestral home of the Lallys – one of whom was the famous French general Baron de Lally, who has his name inscribed on the Arc de Triomphe in Paris. It is not open to the public. **Lisacormack Fort**, 1 mile (1.6km) northeast on the Dunmore road

(N83), is the largest of the numerous earthworks scattered round this area. The fort is on private land. On the Ballinrobe road (R332), 2½ miles (4 km) from Tuam is **Kilbennan Church**, in Gothic style with 16th-century detail. Beside it is a 10th-century round tower. **Barnaderg Castle**, 4 miles (6.4 km) to the southeast of Tuam on the R332 to Barnaderg, is believed to be one of the last castles built in Ireland. On the keystone over the door is a *Sheila-na-Gig*.

Headford (*Ath Cinn*: 'Ford Head'), 10 miles (17km) west of Tuam, is set in countryside divided by stone walls. It is neat and tidy and a favourite angling centre, where you may stock up with fishing tackle and groceries. The surrounding countryside contains the ruins of many Norman castles. **Knockma Hill**, about 7½ miles (12km) east of Headford on the R333, is traditionally held to be the home of King Finbarr and his Connacht fairies, and the burial place of Queen Maeve (one of several, including Knocknarea Mountain in Sligo). It is the only hill for miles. **Ross Errilly Abbey**, just outside Headford, is an important and well-preserved 14th-century ruin; the cloister remains intact, although not ornate, and the domestic buildings are complete, exhibiting perfectly the arrangements of a Franciscan friary in the Middle Ages. There is a round hole in the floor of the kitchen: it is not a well but a fish tank, built so the monks would always have fresh fish on Fridays. Notice that often the Abbot knew how to choose the best architects, the finest land and best-stocked rivers for himself.

Galway City

Galway is a bustling city which has been the centre of trade for the whole of Connacht since the 13th century, despite a decline in the 18th and 19th centuries. The wine trade with Spain and the enterprise of its citizens has given it an independence and character which marks it out from the other provincial towns of Ireland. In recent times that character has become even more pronounced. With new high-tech industries and its growing prominence as a tourist centre, Galway has become the boom town of Ireland, and one of the fastest-growing cities in Europe. The mixture of Celtic tradition and cosmopolitan modernity make it a unique place indeed.

History

There has always been some sort of settlement here because of the ford on the Corrib River, but it never achieved any importance until the arrival of the Anglo-Normans. The de Burgos built a castle here in 1226. By the end of the 13th century many Welsh and English families had been encouraged to settle here, and they built themselves strong stone walls to keep out the now dispossessed and disgruntled de Burgos and the wild O'Flahertys. There were 14 main families and they became known as the tribes of Galway. Fiercely independent, they created an Anglo-Norman oasis in the middle of hostile Connacht. In 1549 they placed this inscription over the west gate: 'From the fury of the O'Flaherties, good Lord deliver us'. (It is no longer there.) They also put out edicts controlling the presence of the native Irish in the town. An Irish settlement thus grew up on the west side of the Corrib following

Tourist Information

Galway: *Aras Fáilte*, Forster Street, **t** (091) 537700, *info@irelandwest.ie; open all year.*

Shopping

Antiques
Antique shops in Galway city cluster around Cross Street.
Cobwebs, 7 Quay Lane, **t** (091) 564388, *www.cobwebs-galway.ie*, *cobwebs@eircom.net.*
Tempo Antiques, 9 Cross Street, **t** (091) 562282.
Twice as Nice, 5 Quay Street, **t** (091) 566332.

Books
Charlie Byrnes Bookshop, Middle Street, **t** (091) 561766.
Kenny's Bookshop, Tuam Road, **t** (091) 773311, *www.kennys.ie.*

Crafts
Fadu, Middle Street, **t** (091) 564429. Modern and traditional handmade pottery, wood, wrought iron and slate items.
Meadows and Byrne, Lower Abbeygate Street, **t** (091) 567776.

Crystal
Galway Irish Crystal, Merlin Park, **t** (091) 757311. With tours, a restaurant and showroom.

Delicacies
Food For Thought, 5 Abbeygate Street, **t** (091) 565854. Health foods.
Goya's Pastry Shop, 3 Kirwans Lane, **t** (091) 567010. For some of the best *pâtisserie* this side of Paris. Small coffee shop attached.

McCambridge's Grocery, 38 Shop Street, **t** (091) 562259. For cheese and preserves.
Sean Loughnane's Food Hall, Industrial Estate, Tuam Rd, **t** (091) 771236. Has a sandwich bar.

Jewellery
Claddagh Jewellers, Eyre Square, **t** (091) 563282, or **t** 1800 473 3259, *jewels@iol.ie.*

Markets
Saturday Morning Market, by St Nicholas' Cathedral. Sells cheese, herbs, vegetables, sausages and their own home-made jams.

Pottery
Royal Tara China, Mervue, Galway, **t** (091) 751301, **f** (091) 757574. Showrooms open to the public and a tea room, as well as guided tours.

Traditional Music
Zhivago's, 5–6 Shop Street, **t** (091) 568794.
Mulligan, 5 Middle Street Court, **t** (091) 564961.

Tweeds and Knitwear
Galway Woollen Market, 21 High Street, Galway, **t** (091) 562491.
O'Máille's, 16 High Street, Galway, **t** (091) 562696.

Sports and Activities

Fishing
Freeney's, 19 High Street, Galway City, **t** (091) 568794.
Duffy's, 5 Mainguard Street, Galway City, **t** (091) 562367.

completely different traditions. They spoke only Gaelic and earned a livelihood through fishing. The settlement is now renowned for the Claddagh Ring, which you will notice on the fingers of many Irish exiles: a circle joined by two hands clasping a heart, often used as a marriage ring. Nowadays the romantic but poverty-stricken Claddagh settlement which appealed to Victorian travellers is gone, and the thatched and whitewashed one-storey cottages have been replaced by a modern housing scheme. The chief tribe of Galway was the Lynch family and there is a colourful story about the Lynch who was mayor in 1493. The tribe had grown prosperous through trading in wine with Spain and Bordeaux; this Lynch had the son of a Spanish merchant staying in his house who aroused the jealousy of Walter, his son. Walter

Galway Fishery, Nun's Island, Galway, t (091) 562388.

Golf

Galway Golf Club, Blackrock, Renville, Oranmore, t (091) 790503.

Horse-racing

For details of the Curragh Races contact the tourist office in Galway, t (091) 537700.

Indoor Leisure Centres

Leisureland, Salthill, t (091) 521455. Water fun.

Pleasure Cruises

Corrib Tours, Old Steamers Quay, Furbo, t (091) 592447.

Pony-trekking

Feeney's Riding School, Tonabrucky, Bushypark, near Salthill, t (091) 527579.

Where to Stay

Galway t (091–)

There are B&Bs galore in Salthill, including a large selection on Fr. Griffin Road, within easy walking distance of the centre.

Great Southern Hotel, Eyre Square, t 564041 (*expensive*). Rambling, Victorian and central, with comfortable rooms and a rooftop swimming-pool.

Ardilaun House Hotel, Taylors Hill, Galway, t 521433 (*expensive–moderate*). Large mansion house converted into attractive hotel with wooded grounds. Good food.

Brennan's Yard Hotel, Merchant's Road, t 568166, *info@brennansyardhotel.com* (*expensive–moderate*). Comfortable, friendly

service and pleasant bedrooms with lots of stripped pine and locally made pottery.

Skeffington Arms Hotel, 28 Eyre Square, Galway, t 563173 (*moderate*). Small, central.

Barnacle's Quay Street Hostel, 10 Quay Street, t 568644 (*inexpensive*). Right in the centre of the action.

D'Arcy's B&B, 92 Fr. Griffin Road, t 589505 (*inexpensive*). New and good, with parking and all rooms en-suite.

Great Western House, Frenchville Lane, Eyre Square, t 561139 (*inexpensive*). Large, centrally located hostel.

Norman Villa, 86 Lower Salthill, t 521131 (*inexpensive*). Another good choice.

Killeen House, Bushypark, t 524179, f 528065, *killeenhouse@ireland.com* (*expensive–moderate*). Set in manicured gardens and within walking distance of Lough Corrib, this luxurious, modern guesthouse is run like a small hotel. Immaculate outside and in, each bedroom is decorated according to a theme, such as Edwardian or Regency. Staff are eager to please; good breakfasts.

Eating Out

Galway t (091–)

Claddagh Room, inside Great Southern Hotel, Eyre Square, t 564041 (*expensive*). Good seafood.

Park Room Restaurant, Forster Street, Eyre Square, t 564924 (*expensive*). One of Galway's finest restaurants for 25 years.

Nimmo's, Spanish Arch, t 563565 (*moderate*). Seafood. Atmospheric café downstairs and restaurant upstairs. Lovely location.

Royal Villa, 13 Shop Street, t 563450 (*moderate*). Good quality Chinese food.

stabbed the young guest to death, but because he was so popular nobody could be found to hang him. So his father, having pronounced the sentence, did the deed himself and, filled with sadness, became a recluse. Near the Church of St Nicholas, in a built-up Gothic doorway on Market Street, there is a tablet commemorating the event, which gave the verb 'to lynch' to the English language.

Galway City Centre

Galway was an important administrative centre during the days of the British, from the 17th century until Independence. It now has a strong cultural identity, with its own university where courses are followed in Irish and English, a large technical

Skeffington Arms Hotel, 28 Eyre Square, t 563173 (*moderate*). Sophisticated food.
Sev'nth Heav'n, Courthouse Lane, t 563838 (*moderate–inexpensive*). Irish-Cajun-TexMex; live music, and they stay open late.
Tigh Neachtain, 17 Cross Street, t 566172 (*moderate–inexpensive*). A great pub with above average bar food. Lunch weekdays only. Dinner is in the restaurant, upstairs.
Da Tang Noodle House, 2 Middle Street Mews, t 561443 (*inexpensive*). The real thing, and the only one in Ireland.
Food For Thought, 5 Abbeygate Street, t 565854 (*inexpensive*). Vegetarian restaurant beside a health food shop.
Fat Freddy's, The Halls, Quay Street, t 567279 (*inexpensive*). First-rate pizza and some innovative dishes; always packed.
Goya's Pastry Shop, 3 Kirwans Lane, t 567010. (*inexpensive*). Delicious cakes and coffee.
The Malt House, High Street, t 567866 (*inexpensive*). Excellent soups and snacks.
McDonagh's Seafood House, 22 Quay Street, t 565001 (*inexpensive*). Excellent eat-in or take-away fish and chips.
McSwiggan's, 3 Eyre Street, t 568917 (*inexpensive*). Seafood and veggie dishes.
Pierre Victoire, 8 Quay Street, t 566066 (*inexpensive*). Excellent value French food.
Taafe's Bar, 19a Shop Street, t 564066 (*inexpensive*). Pub with good food.

Entertainment and Nightlife

Jazz
Blue Note, 3 William Street, t (091) 589116.

King's Head, 5 High Street, t (091) 566630.
Quays Bar, Quay Street, t (091) 568347.

Theatre
Druid Theatre, Chapel Lane, t (091) 568617, *www.druidtheatre.com*. Produces very exciting performances; they have built up something of an international reputation for their mostly contemporary repertoire.
Taibhdhearc na Gaillimhe, Middle Street, t (091) 562024/530291. Interesting Irish-language theatre as well as traditional music and bilingual folk presentations. Home to the acclaimed Siamsa Festival of music, dance and drama in July and August.
Town Hall Theatre, Courthouse Square, t (091) 569777, *www.townhalltheatregalway.com*.

Traditional Music
Ballad-singing and traditional music in the local bars. During the summer months try the following:
The An Púcán Bar, Forster Street, t (091) 561528. Nightly.
The Crane Bar, 2 Sea Road, t (091) 587419. Nightly.
Lisheen Bar, Bridge Street, t (091) 563804.
The Quays, t (091) 568347. Mon and Tues nights.
The Roisin Dubh, 8 Dominick Street Upper, t (091) 586540. At weekends.
The Snug, William Street.
Taaffes, 19a Shop Street, t (091) 564066. Nightly.
Taylor's, 7 Dominick Street Upper, t (091) 587239. Nightly.

college and vigorous and high-quality theatre, traditional music and song. The city itself is small enough to walk around in a day. The planned 18th-century part centres around Eyre Square, which you come into immediately when approaching the city from the east. The Galway tourist office, *Aras Fáilte*, in Victoria Park, is just a block away, close to the railway and bus station. The **Gardens** in Eyre Square are dedicated to John F. Kennedy, who received the freedom of the city only a few months before his assassination. In the gardens are captured Russian cannons, brought home from the Crimean War by a famous regiment in the British Army, called the Connaught Rangers, as well as a fine steel sculpture by Eamon O'Doherty based on the sails of the Galway 'hookers' or fishing boats; and a statue to Padraic O'Conaire (1883–1928), who wrote short stories in Gaelic and pioneered the revival of Gaelic literature.

The liveliest part of Galway is the medieval centre, with narrow streets winding down from Eyre Square to the river. **Shop Street/High Street/Quay Street** is the spine of the district; lined with the city's most popular bars, restaurants and shops, it jumps day and night. Fragments of buildings and mutilated stone merchant houses still exist amongst the fast-food signs and modern shop fronts. You have to go and seek out the strange and memorable animal carvings and the fine doorways and windows that have survived. The best example is Lynch's Castle in Shop Street which now houses a branch of the Allied Irish Bank.

The **Church of St Nicholas** in Market Street is rather attractive, and worth a visit for its fine carvings. You may hear the eight bells peal, which make a lovely sound over the city. A proud tradition exists that Christopher Columbus stopped at the church for Mass on his way to discover America. No.8 Bowling Green, close by, is the **Nora Barnacle House Museum** (*open May–Sept, Mon–Sat 10–5; adm; t (091) 564743*), once the home of James Joyce's wife. The little museum contains memorabilia of the couple and their links with County Galway. A Saturday market of organic vegetables, German sourdough breads and local cheeses is held in its shadow, with an atmosphere that revives shades of medieval Galway. The modern **Catholic cathedral**, beside the salmon weir on the river, is an imposing hotchpotch of styles and dominates the skyline. It was completed in 1965. The weir is in fact one of the nicest places to go and idle away the hours. Shoals of salmon making their way up to the spawning grounds of Lough Corrib lie in the clear river – the only entrance from the sea to 1,200 miles (1,930km) of lakes.

Elizabeth Tudor confirmed the city's charter in 1579, and appointed the mayor as admiral with jurisdiction over Galway Bay and the Aran Islands. The town was fully walled with 14 towers, but now there is only a fragment left near the quay, called the **Spanish Arch**. The office of Mayor, which had been in decline and abolished in 1840, was restored and given statutory recognition in 1937. The mayor's silver sword and great mace dating from the early 17th century are on display in the Bank of Ireland, at No.19 Eyre Square. The mace, a fine piece of Galway silver, was returned to the city by the Hearst Foundation in the USA in 1961.

Near the Spanish Arch is the **Galway City Museum** (*open Mon–Sat, 10–1, 2–5; adm; t (091) 567641*). It has displays on the history of Galway and folk life. The **Kenny Art Gallery** in the high street holds exhibitions of ceramics, sculptures and paintings by contemporary artists. The **Grain Store** on Lower Abbeygate Street shows work in wood and metal. The **University of Galway Gallery** (*t (091) 24411*) also holds occasional exhibitions. The local newspapers, the *Galway Advertiser*, *Connaught Tribune* and the *Galway Sentinel* (which is free), as well as the tourist office, will have details of what's on. Good traditional music is played in the city's bars, and the atmosphere can verge on the raucous. Galway City is always a lively place, partly due to the youthfulness of its inhabitants, but the week of the famous **Galway Races**, in late July, the

Arts Festival (also July) and the Oyster Festival in September bring an extra sparkle and sense of enjoyment to the place.

Salthill is a seaside resort which merges with the city. Many local people holiday there or come on day trips. Hotels, fun-parks and bingo halls line the seafront; it's a bit run-down, like many old seaside resorts all over the British Isles. But at night the place lights up as the strip opens up its clubs and discos, catering primarily to the population of Galway City. Children can splash about all day at Leisureland (*open daily 8–10; adm; t (091) 521445*), with fun fair rides and amusements, or visit the new museum, Atlantaquaria (*t (091) 585100*), in the same complex.

Connemara

Connemara is not an area firmly drawn by boundary lines; it is the name given to the western portion of County Galway which lies between Lough Corrib and the Atlantic, bounded in the north by Killary Harbour.

Lough Corrib and Around

Here at Moycullen the real splendours of the west begin, although it is worth stopping only when you get to Oughterard. A pretty river, the Owenriff, runs through the charming town, which is right on the upper shores of Lough Corrib and a good place to base yourself if you are keen on salmon and trout angling. If you are coming from Costelloe on the coast road or going there from Oughterard, take the mountain road, which joins the two towns cross-country and gives you a vast panorama of watery landscape as you go up through a small hill pass.

Aughnanure Castle, 3 miles (4.8km) southeast of Oughterard (*open mid June–early Sept daily 10–6, early Sept–Oct weekends 10–6; key with caretaker rest of year; guided tours on request; adm; t (091) 552214*), is an O'Flaherty building and said to have been one of the strongest fortresses at the time Cromwell was blockading Galway. The six-storey tower stands on an island of rock. In the days of its prosperity a portion of the floor of the hall was made to collapse: one of the flagstones was hinged downwards and an unwelcome guest might well find himself tipped into the fast-flowing stream below. Nothing of the hall stands today: it too collapsed into the stream, as did the cavern over which it was built. But the castle has been restored, and you can climb right to the top.

Ross Castle (*not open to the public*), 5 miles (8km) southeast of Oughterard beside the shores of Ross Lake, was the home of the Martins, who bankrupted themselves trying to help out in the famine times of the 1840s. Follow the road from the village down to Lough Corrib for a lovely drive along its wooded shores. It leads you to the Hill of Doon and a good view of the largest island on the lake, Inchagoill (*Inis an Ghaill*: 'Island of the Devout Stranger'). This is the prettiest and most interesting of the hundreds of islands on Lough Corrib. There is a 5th-century church, Teampall Pharaic, and one of 10th-century origin further to the south which was reconstructed in 1860. There is also the Stone of Lugna, named after the navigator of St Patrick. This

Tourist Information

Oughterard: t (091) 552808, f (091) 552811; *open all year.*
Clifden: Galway Road, t (095) 21163, f (095) 21887; *open March–Oct Mon–Sat.*

Shopping

Crafts

Connemara Handicrafts, Ardbear, Clifden.
The Celtic Shop and Tara Jewellers, Clifden, t (095) 21064.
Connemara West Centre, Letterfrack, t (095) 41047. Woodwork, design, a workshop and a tea room.
Craft Centre, Spiddal, t (091) 83255. Has crafts, an art gallery and a coffee shop.
An Spideal, Spiddal, t (091) 553376, f (091) 553734. On the coast road, west of Galway.

Crystal

Connemara Celtic Crystal, t (091) 555172. On the outskirts of Moycullen.

Delicacies

Carabay Seaweed, Moycullen, t (091) 555112. Health foods.

Pottery

Connemara Pottery, Ballyconnelly Road, Clifden, t (095) 21254. China, pottery and a coffee shop.
Roundstone Ceramics, Roundstone, t (095) 35874. The handcrafted pottery here is imaginatively and colourfully decorated with mythical fishes, snakes and other weird and wonderful designs.

Traditional Music

Roundstone Musical Instruments, IDA Park, Roundstone, t (095) 35808. Specialists in locally hand-crafted goatskin *bodhráns*. They also have a shop in Main Street, Clifden, open in summer only.

Tweeds and Knitwear

Standûns Gift Shop, on the coast road at Spiddal, t (091) 553108. A large store with a wide selection of knitwear and Irish fashions, as well as pottery, glass and crafts.
Rosmuck Knitwear, Gort Mor, Rosmuck, t (091) 574172. Handwoven sweaters.
An Tinteán **Crafts Workshop**, Katie and Ann Hand Knits, Camus, Connemara, t (091) 574162/574076. Rugs, Aran sweaters, hats, crafts – all handmade by local weavers and knitters.
Leenane Cultural Centre, t (095) 42323. Knitwear, tweeds, crystal, pottery and jewellery; plus a restaurant and an exhibition from the local sheep and handicrafts industry. Overlooks Killary Harbour.

Sports and Activities

Beaches

It is possible to bathe all along the coast in the various inlets and coves. Fine, sandy beaches are found at Ballyconneely and Tullycross.

Fishing

For brown trout, sea trout, and salmon fishing on Lough Corrib, contact the tourist

2ft (72cm) high obelisk bears engraved Roman characters. It is fancifully claimed to be the earliest Christian inscription in Europe after the catacombs.

Clonbur is a centre for fishermen, situated on the limestone isthmus between Lough Mask and Lough Corrib. If you want to climb the Connemara, Maumturk or Partry Mountains, Clonbur is well-placed. One mile (1.6km) to the west rises the lovely mountain area known as Joyce Country, where it is said the Fir Bolgs assembled before they made their last stand against the Dé Danaan at the Battle of Moytura. In the foothills leading up to the highest peak, Benlevy (1,370ft/418m), is Lough Coolin, a peaceful, dreamy sort of place. You can drive there but the road is very narrow.

office in Galway City for details and
regulations.

Thomas Tuck, Western Garage, Oughterard,
t (091) 552335. Advice and help on boat hire
and fishing.

Delphi Lodge Fishery, Leenane,
t (095) 42211.

Erriff Fishery, Leenane, t (095) 42252.
For information on **sea-angling,** contact
the Western Region Fisheries Board, or
e-mail the NorthWestern Fisheries
Board at *info@nwfb.com.* There are
several boat owners who take out fishing
trips in Clifden.

Western Region Fisheries Board, Weir
Lodge, Earl's Island, Galway, t (091) 563118,
f (091) 566335.

John Brittain, t (095) 21073.

John Ryan, t (095) 21069.

Golf
Oughterard Golf Club, t (091) 552131.
Connemara Golf Club, Aillebrack, Clifden,
t (095) 23502.

Internet Access
Two Dog Café, 2 Church Hill, Clifden,
t (095) 22186. Sandwiches and coffee as
you surf.

Outdoor Activities
Killary Adventure Centre, Leenane,
t (095) 43411. Provides weekend or
week-long courses in canoeing, sailing
or rock-climbing.

Delphi Adventure Sports Centre, Delphi,
Leenane, contact Mr Noone, t (095)
42208. Canoeing, rock-climbing, surfing,
hill-walking and snorkelling.

Pleasure Cruises
Corrib Princess, Woodquay, Galway, t (091)
592447, *corribtours@eircom.net.* Offers tours
of Lough Corrib, twice daily in season.

Sea Cruise Connemara, t (091) 566736.
Catamaran.

Pony-trekking
Cashel House Hotel Riding Centre, Cashel,
Connemara, t (095) 31001.

Aillecross Equestrian Centre, Loughrea, t (091)
841216. Contact Mr Leahy.

Errislannan Manor, Connemara Pony Stud and
Riding Centre, Clifden, t (095) 21134.

Spa Treatments
The Mountain Lodge and Spa at Delphi,
Leenane, Galway, t (095) 42987.

Where to Stay

Moycullen House, Moycullen, t (091) 555621,
info@moycullen.com (*moderate*). An
Edwardian sporting lodge designed in Arts
and Crafts style, set in a lovely woodland
garden of azaleas and rhododendron which
overlooks Lough Corrib. Fishing and boating
also organized by your hosts, the Casburns.

Currarevagh House, Oughterard, t (091)
552312/552313 (*expensive–moderate*). This
country house is in the most beautiful
setting on the edge of Lough Corrib. A
charming and friendly atmosphere reigns
amongst the cosy Victorian rooms. The
passages are crammed with books, stuffed
fish and fishing tackle. The food is
comforting in an old-fashioned way, right
down to the dinky coffee percolators. Harry

The Joyce Country
Cornamona is on the northern corner of Lough Corrib on the Dooras Peninsula. It is
in one of the most popular Irish-speaking districts in North Connemara, on the edge
of the Joyce Country. This area is named after a race of Welshmen who settled in
Connacht after Richard de Burgo conquered it in the 13th century. The native
O'Flahertys and the Joyces eventually got on rather well and used to go and rough up
the 'plainsmen' on the isthmus, which became known as the Gap of Danger. Not one
of the roads around here is dull and the fishing on the little loughs, as well as Loughs
Mask and Corrib, is good. On the R345 to Maum is a spectacular ruin, **Hen's Castle,** on
an island in the Corrib. It is said to have fallen into ruin after an O'Flaherty ate the hen

and June Hodgson are extremely helpful and have some of the best wild brown trout fishing in Europe, which they will organize for guests.

Sweeney's Oughterard House Hotel, Oughterard, t (091) 552207 (*expensive– moderate*). An ivy-covered Georgian house by the river, with a good restaurant.

Connemara Gateway Hotel, Oughterard, t (091) 552328 (*expensive–moderate*). Pleasant, modern hotel with heated indoor pool and tennis.

Camillaun, Eighterard, Oughterard, t (091) 552678, f (091) 552439; *camillaun@ eircom.net* (*inexpensive*). This comfortable new wooden-floored home is perfect for the visitor who, after breakfast, wants to take one of the owners' boats from the River Owenriff (next to the garden) and float out on Lough Corrib to fish or explore Inchagoill Island. Dinner (*moderate*) by arrangement; contact friendly Deirdre and Greg Forde.

Ard Aoibhinn, Cnocan Glas, Spiddal, t (091) 553179 (*inexpensive*). Close to the sea, with comfortable rooms which have en suite bathrooms. Contact Mrs O'Malley Curren.

Col-Mar House, Salahoona, Spiddal, t (091) 553247 (*inexpensive*). A house in a lovely setting; especially good breakfasts. The Keadys are very friendly owners, who prefer old-fashioned ways.

Fermoyle Lodge, Casla (Costelloe), Connemara, t (091) 786111, f (091) 786154; *fermoylelodge@ eircom.net, www.fermoylelodge.com* (*moderate*). Travel through flat, rocky land beyond Oughterard or Spiddal and you'll find a stone with this country house's name carved into it. Hidden among trees, rhododenrons and a Victorian garden, with

even a stone staircase leading to a wooded area, is what was once a fishing lodge near a lake (or possibly a fairy's house). Mineral-rich water flows in the bath, and excellent meals are flavoured with delicacy under the influence of its delightfully embracing owners, Jean-Pierre Maire and his wife Nicola Stronach. A good stopping point before taking the ferry to the Aran Islands. Dinner (*expensive*) by arrangement.

Ballynahinch Castle Hotel, Ballinafad, Recess, t (095) 31006, *www.ballynahinch-castle.com, bhinch@iol.ie* (*expensive*). Magnificent setting at the base of one of the Twelve Bens, overlooking the Owenmore River. Relaxed and informal atmosphere; was once the residence of an Indian Maharajah.

Cashel House Hotel, Cashel, t (095) 31001 (*expensive*). A very luxurious but at the same time cosy house, full of fine furniture and *objets d'art* picked up at country house sales. Superb garden overlooking a beautiful sea inlet. Horse-riding can be arranged.

Zetland House Hotel, Cashel Bay, t (095) 31111, f (095) 31117 (*expensive*). A converted hunting lodge in an isolated setting overlooking the bay, run by John Prendergast, who trained at the Ritz in Paris. Superb food. Tennis, billiards and other activities.

Crocnaraw House, Moyard, t (095) 41068, f (095) 41068, *lucyfretwell@eircom.net* (*expensive*). Small and cosy country house, with tastefully decorated rooms and lots of pretty, striped Connemara woollen rugs. Delicious and well-prepared food.

The Ardagh Hotel, Ballyconneely Road, Clifden, t (095) 21384, f (095) 21314, *ardaghhotel@ eircom.net* (*moderate*). Dutch-run small hotel, wonderful food.

which had been given to his family generations before by a witch. Cold fact however states that the castle was built by the O'Connors.

At **Maumeen** (*Maimean*) in the Corcogemore Mountains (part of the Maumturk range) is **St Patrick's Bed and Holy Well**, reached by a footpath off the R336. Pilgrims have travelled here for centuries, as the well is reputed to have strong healing powers. The annual pilgrimage, on the last Sunday of July, has undergone a revival recently, with many people attending. **Lough Nafooey** ('Lake of the Spectre') is one of the most beautiful in Connemara. It is off a mountain road that leads up the Finny River, and can also be approached by another road halfway between Maum and Leenane off the R336. Lots of little streams run into the lake: the music of

The Quay House, Beach Road, Clifden, **t** (095) 21369, **f** (095) 21608, *www.thequayhouse. com, thequay@iol.ie* (*moderate*). Restaurant with rooms.

Ben View House, Bridge Street, Clifden, **t** (095) 21256, **f** (095) 21226, *www.connemara.net/ benviewhouse, benviewhouse@ireland.com* (*inexpensive*). Pleasant, old-fashioned Irish B&B in the centre of Clifden, with a variety of breakfasts on offer. The en suite rooms have TVs.

Fáilte, Ardbear, off Ballyconneely Road, Clifden, **t** (095) 21159 (*inexpensive*). Nice B&B run by the Kelly family, with good breakfasts.

Mallmore Country Guest House, Ballyconneely Road, Clifden, **t** (095) 21460 (*inexpensive*). Comfortable, friendly country house, close to Clifden. Contact Mrs K. Hardman.

Day's Hotel, Inishbofin Island, **t** (095) 45809 (*moderate*). Well-established, family-run, clean and friendly hotel right on the pier. The son runs the musical evenings. Children are welcome; facilities for divers.

Doonmore Hotel, Inishbofin, **t** (095) 45804 (*moderate*). Simple and clean with good local seafood.

Rosleague Manor Hotel, Letterfrack, **t** (095) 41101, **f** (095) 41168 (*expensive*). Pretty first-class hotel overlooking Ballinakill Bay. Delicious food and a friendly atmosphere.

Delphi Lodge, Leenane, **t** (095) 42296, *www.delphilodge.ie, delfish@iol.ie* (*expensive–moderate*). The ideal spot for fly-fishing (with courses for novices), this 1,000-acre estate includes mountain, water and bogland. The hospitable owner, Peter Mantle, makes every dinner an occasion to remember, with excellent food and old-fashioned service that has even pleased Prince

Charles. All of its rooms are doubles and elegantly comfortable. Dinner and lunch or packed lunches are available.

Killary House, Leenane, **t** (095) 42254 (*inexpensive*). Friendly farmhouse in superb situation; contact Mrs King.

Self-catering

Ireland West Tourism, Forster Street, Galway, **t** (091) 537700 (*inexpensive*). Located at Inveran on Galway Bay, a self-catering thatched cottage overlooking the sea.

Lucy O'Toole, Annaghvane, Bealadangan, **t** (091) 572120. Two 200-year-old traditional reed-thatched cottages by the sea. Three bedrooms; from €317 a week in low season.

Renvyle Thatched Cottages, Renvyle, Tullycross, **t** (095) 43464, **f** (095) 43994, *www.irishcottageholidays.com, anne@ conwest.iol.ie*. Nine modernized thatched cottages of various sizes, €190–570 per week.

Delphi Lodge Estate, Leenane, **t** (095) 42211. Cottages costing approx €200–500 per week.

Eating Out

Drimcong House Restaurant, Moycullen, **t** (091) 555115/555585, **f** (091) 555836 (*expensive*). The owners create the most delicious and original combinations of tastes here, yet never overdo the novelty. You can be sure that you will get the best of what the season offers. The restaurant itself is in a lovely 17th-century house, and there are always turf fires in the rooms. Vegetarian and children's meals are available.

gurgling water plays continually in early summer, accompanied by the smell of gorse and pine trees.

Connemara's Southern Coast

This section includes most of the Irish-speaking parts and stretches along the north of Galway Bay, and from there along the Atlantic to Carna. Its northern boundary runs from Gowlaun (*Gabhla*) through Maam Cross to Barna (*Bearna*). This part of the world is hilly and remote, for there are very few roads into it. From Galway to Spiddal (R336) it is disappointingly built-up, although you do get glimpses of the Aran Islands, looking far or near according to the clarity of the weather.

Boat Inn, The Square, Oughterard, t (091) 552196 (*inexpensive*). Does good pub food.

O'Grady's on the Pier, Barna Pier, Barna, t (091) 592223 (*moderate–inexpensive*). Breton and French-style seafood. *Open daily 4–10pm, Sat–Sun lunch from noon onwards.*

Boluisce Seafood Restaurant, Spiddal Village, t (091) 553286 (*inexpensive*). Delicious seafood snacks. Try the fish chowder with home-made brown bread.

Peacocke's Restaurant, Maam Cross, Recess, t (091) 552306, f (091) 552215 (*inexpensive*). Good lunches. *Open winter 9am–11pm, summer 9am–11.30pm.*

Cashel House Hotel, Cashel, t (095) 31001 (*expensive*). Super food in fancy country house surroundings. *Dinner only, booking essential. Not suitable for children.*

Zetland House Hotel, Cashel Bay, t (095) 31111 (*expensive*). Wonderful seafood.

Beola Restaurant, Roundstone, t (095) 35871 (*moderate*). Seafood a speciality.

Fire and Ice Restaurant, Station house Courtyard, Clifden, t (095) 22946, *fireandice @eircom.net* (*expensive–moderate*). Inventive cooking with local organic produce. House speciality is crispy duck with stir-fried egg noodles and plum sauce, plus excellent vegetarian dishes. Organic wines and delicious fresh breads, pastries and salad dressings – all made on the premises. Christmas hampers available. *Open mid Mar–Dec Tues–Sun 6.30–9.30pm, also May–Aug Sun 11.30–3.30.*

Erriseask House Hotel, Ballyconnelly, Clifden, t (095) 23553 (*expensive*). Unexpectedly imaginative cooking. *Open Easter and throughout high season.*

Quay House, Beach Road, Clifden, t (095) 21369 (*expensive*). Friendly, relaxed atmosphere in the old Harbour Master's house. Very high standard of cooking.

Ardagh Hotel, Clifden, t (095) 21384 (*expensive*). Delicious continental food and good value open sandwiches.

O'Grady's Seafood Restaurant, Market Street, Clifden, t (095) 21450 (*moderate*). Traditional seafood restaurant with a good menu and friendly service.

Destry's, Main Street, Clifden, t (095) 21722 (*moderate*). Lively bistro-style restaurant named after the Marlene Dietrich film. Laid-back with delicious modern cooking.

High Moors Restaurant, Doneen, Clifden, t (095) 21342 (*moderate*). Very good home cooking, with mostly home-grown ingredients. *Booking essential.*

Day's Hotel Bar, Inishbofin, t (095) 45809 (*inexpensive*). Good seafood and soups.

Portfinn Lodge, Leenane, t (095) 42265 (*moderate*). Great seafood.

Entertainment and Nightlife

Traditional Music

Mannion's Bar, Market Street, Clifden, t (095) 21780.

Teach Ceoil, Tullycross, t (095) 43446. Irish music house, summer only.

Day's Hotel, Inishbofin, t (095) 45809. Wed–Sun nights in summer.

Doonmore Hotel, Inishbofin, t (095) 45804. Wed–Sat nights in summer.

Rossaveal (*Ros An Mhil*) at the mouth of Galway Bay has a cabin-cruiser called *Aran Flyer* which runs regularly to Aran doing a brisk trade in turf, as Aran has no fuel resources of its own (*see* p.318). By now you may have noticed the black beetle-like boats which the fishermen in Connacht use. The type of *curragh* you see in Ireland varies considerably from the Donegal coast to the Kerry coast in the south. Here they are very light and it needs a skilful man to handle the long, heavy oars, which have no blade. It is astonishing how much they can carry: a load could include cement, or pigs and sheep with their legs tied and muffled.

From Rossaveal you follow the road north for just a few miles to **Costelloe**, which has a wonderful coral strand and a good salmon-fishing river. There is quite a meeting of the roads here and you can go either to Maam Cross or follow a little road to Carraroe (*An Cheathru Rua*). Back on the main road again you come to Screeb (*Scrib*). By turning left here you come to Lough Aroolagh and Gortmore (*An Gort More*). Here on a ledge of hillside above a small lake in the townland of Turlough you can go round the whitewashed **Pearse's Cottage** (*Teach an Phiarsaigh*), where the patriot used to write plays and poems (*open Easter and mid June–mid Sept daily 10–6; guided tours on request; t (091) 574292*). Patrick Pearse built this cottage as proof of his interest in Irish language and culture. He believed that if the Irish language died, Ireland would die as a nation.

Back on the R340, 4 miles (6.4km) further on, is the village of **Kilkieran**. Here is scenery typical of the west: scattered houses with no nucleus nor clear distinction from the next village. You can see the brooding island of Lettermore and, if the wind is in the right direction, smell the rich seaweed which is dried in a factory here. Kilkieran and **Carna** are lobster-fishing centres, and there is a research station for shellfish, but you will find it difficult to buy a lobster for yourself – most of the seafood caught goes abroad or to the hotels. A side-road from Carna over a bridge takes you to **Mweenish Island** with its beautiful sandy beaches.

You can get a boat from Carna to **St MacDara's Island** for a marvellous view across Bertraghboy Bay. MacDara was a 5th-century saint who was greatly honoured by the people of Iar Chonnachta, so much so that in the age of sailing boats, the fishermen used to dip their sails three times before passing the island.

Western Connemara

This is the district west of Maam Cross to the Atlantic, extending northwards to Killary Harbour and the Partry Mountains. It is a superb part of the world, much more exciting and untouched than the road that leads you round South Connemara.

Maam Cross to Roundstone

Maam Cross is a place that you see signposted constantly. In fact it is the most unprepossessing place, but it is the centre of magnificent scenery and everybody travelling round Galway ends up here. If you climb Leckavrea Mountain (1,307ft/402m) there are great views of the Twelve Bens, Maumturks and Lough Corrib. From Maam Cross you could take the N59 past Recess, and then the N59/R341 for Roundstone. **Recess** is a pretty village, where suddenly you come upon woods and Glendollagh Lough after driving through some spartan scenery. Lissoughter Mountain at 1,314ft (400m) is worth climbing and you can see over to Lough Inagh and the mountains either side. This is where the green Connemara marble is quarried. It was formed millions of years ago by the action of strong compressive forces and heat on limestone. The oldest rocks in the county are exposed in this central area: the Twelve Bens (or Pins) and the Maumturk Mountains.

Cashel village is on a minor road (R342) right on Cashel Bay, an inlet of Bertraghboy Bay. It became famous overnight when General de Gaulle spent his holidays there. All these inlets and the mountain roads leading into the interior are bathed in the most superb colours. The luxurious Cashel House Hotel is worth stopping at for a walk around the wonderful sub-tropical gardens or tea on the lawn.

Roundstone is a pleasant 19th-century village. The name is an awful English corruption of the Irish *Cloch na Ron*, which means 'Rock of the Seals'. There is a pretty harbour which looks across the water to the low-lying islands in Bertraghboy Bay and a friendly bar, O'Dowd's, where the fishermen contrast starkly with the Dubliners in their smart Aran sweaters. **Errisbeg Mountain** (987ft/300m) towers above the village. It is a short climb but the views are superb; look out for the flowers and plants, for this is a place beloved of botanists as well as artists. Two miles (3.2km) on towards Ballyconneely are two of the best beaches in Connacht. You will have seen their silver lines beside the blue sea if you climbed Errisbeg. They are called **Gorteen** and **Dog's Bay**. The latter is another terrible mistranslation from *Port na Feadoige*: 'Bay of the Plover'. **Ballyconneely** is on the isthmus about 9 miles (14.4km) from Roundstone. The coast road is called 'the brandy and soda road' because of the exhilarating air. Beside the wide Mannin Bay is Coral Strand, so called because of the white sand-like debris of a seaweed which looks like coral. Four miles (6.4km) south of Clifden is the site where Alcock and Brown came to ground after the first ever transatlantic flight.

Clifden (*An Clochan*: 'Stepping Stones') is generally called the 'capital' of Connemara. It has a population of only just over a thousand, but it is the biggest place around in a countryside of scattered hamlets and farms. The town sits in a sheltered bay, and if you walk half a mile (1.6km) to the Atlantic shore and gaze out, you are looking straight towards America. It is a well-planned early 19th-century town founded in 1812 by John D'Arcy, and the two spires of the Protestant church and the Catholic cathedral give it a distinctive outline. There are plenty of places to eat and much going on, including bands and craft and cookery exhibitions, and the wide streets overflow with people speaking Gaelic as well as an English which uses the idioms and expression of Gaelic.

Travelling around this part of Connemara, you pass through lakes, rivers, forests and mountains where there is little hint of pollution or industry. Even the machinery used on the farms is fairly traditional. At **Dan O'Hara's Homestead Farm**, part of **Connemara Heritage and History Centre**, just off the N59 in Lettershea (*open April–Oct daily 10–6; adm; t (095) 21246/21808, f (095) 22098, danohara@eircom.net*), you can see an eight-acre farm being run as it would have been in the 19th century. It's also an all-organic farm.

There is a lovely road signposted 'Sky Road' which takes you further north round the indented coast. Amidst sprays of fuchsia it climbs high above Clifden until it is above **D'Arcy's Castle**, the baronial-style ruin of the D'Arcy who founded the town. From here you can see the waves crashing onto the rock islets of Inishturk and Inishbofin, whilst beyond to the north is Clare Island. The road continues into the quiet, seaweed-fringed Streamstown Bay, where white Connemara marble is quarried.

Inishbofin Island

Inishbofin Island can be reached by boat, a 45-minute journey each way. The boats leave Cleggan pier two or three times daily April to October, once a week in winter.

Sailings depend on the weather, so always check ahead. There are two boats: the *Queen* (*tickets from King's Ferries, King's Shop in Cleggan, t (095) 44642/21520, f (095) 44327*), and the *Dun Aengus* (*tickets from the Spar supermarket, t (095) 44750*).

Inishbofin has a very varied history. In the 7th century St Colman founded a monastery here, remains of which can still be seen. In the 13th century the O'Malleys won the island from the O'Flahertys, adding to their seaboard empire. Grace O'Malley is said to have fortified it, although the locals say she could not dig through the rock to finish the deep ditch she was making. In 1652 Inishbofin was surrendered to the Cromwellians and was used as a sort of concentration camp for monks and priests. The fortress Cromwell built above the harbour has room for six cannons, but now there are only red-beaked choughs to sound the alarm. Inishbofin has two hotels, so it is easy to get something to eat while you are there (both hotels also rent bikes). A small **Heritage Centre** (*open summer noon–5pm*) is near Day's Hotel. The island's beaches are beautiful.

Letterfrack to Leenane

Letterfrack, a pretty village, was founded by the Quakers. There are wonderful bays for swimming and, along the coastal approach from Moyard onwards, there are excellent craftshops. Nearby is the sparkling Diamond Hill (1,460ft/445m). On the Renvyle peninsula north of Letterfrack, the **Connemara Sea Leisure: Oceans Alive Visitor Centre** includes an aquarium, marine museum and sightseeing cruises (*open Mar–Sept daily 9.30–7, Oct–April 10–4; adm; t (095) 43473*). **Connemara National Park** (*open all year*) extends over 3,800 acres (1,540ha), and is of outstanding ecological value, as well as being very beautiful. There is a **Visitors' Centre** (*open April–Sept 10–5.30, July–Aug 9.30–6.30; adm; t (095) 41054*) with exhibits and an audio-visual room which describes the geology, the flora and fauna of the area. Short- and long-distance walks have been laid out.

The Kylemore Valley lies between the Twelve Bens and the forested Doughruagh Mountains in the north. The Twelve Bens and Maumturks, with their beautiful varying shapes, are not much above 2,000ft (610m) at their highest. (If you are going climbing, note that even though it may be sunny and dry at sea level it will be very wet underfoot in the mountains.) On the floor of the valley, trees and rhododendrons grow beside the three lakes and the Dawros River, which are well stocked with salmon and sea trout. There is a splendid lakeside mock castle in the woods at **Kylemore Abbey**, which is now a girls' school and a convent for the Benedictine Nuns of Ypres. The nuns run a restaurant and an excellent craft shop and cultivate beautiful grounds around which you can wander, including a newly-restored Victorian walled garden (*gardens, craft shop and restaurant open mid Mar–Dec, 9–6; winter: gardens daily 10.30–4.30; tearoom and abbey open all year; adm; t (095) 41146, f (095) 41145, info@kylemoreabbey.ie*). The wealthy Liverpudlian merchant who built the castle also built a fine mock Gothic chapel, with pillars of Connemara marble. Nearby is a pre-Christian chamber tomb.

The road to the mouth of Killary Harbour (R334) is set between the dark blue fjord and stream-scored green hillsides, which give the effect of crushed velvet. This is one of the safest natural anchorages in the world, keeping an almost constant depth of 13 fathoms, and sheltered from the wind by the mountains around. The Erriff River comes tumbling over the Aasleagh Falls at the bridge just north of **Leenane**. This village, situated at the head of Killary Harbour, has plenty of accommodation if you want to base yourself here for walking or fishing. The **Leenane Cultural Centre** is just above the village on the N59. Besides acting as an outlet for local knitters, it also has information on local history, places of interest to visit and a **Sheep and Wool Museum** (*open Mar–Oct daily 10–7; t (095) 42323/42231, f (095) 42337*). Leenane featured as the location for the film *The Field*, and you will find constant references to it all over the village.

The Aran Islands

The people and the islands of Aran were described sensitively by the playwright John Millington Synge in his notebooks and in his play *Riders to the Sea*. If you read them, you will long to visit these windswept islands in Galway Bay. Liam O'Flaherty, another great Irish writer, was born here in 1897, two years before Synge first came to the islands. He describes the hard life of the island people in his short stories, *The Landing* and *Going into Exile*. Tim Robinson, a stranger who came and lived on the islands a few years ago, wrote a wonderful book called *Stones of Aran*, well worth searching out in Kenny's bookshop in Galway City. The Aran Islands today are much the same as they were in John Synge's time, although in the summer the irritations that tourism always brings diminishes some of their peace and unique culture, particularly on Inishmore.

The Islands

There are three Aran Islands: Inishmore ('Great Island'), Inisheer ('East Island') and Inishmaan ('Middle Island'). They can be reached by air from Galway City, by a regular ferry boat from Galway Harbour or Doolin in County Clare, or by motorboat from Rossaveal. Most tourists come for the rugged beauty, the sweeping views, and to visit the prehistoric and early monastic ruins. The landscape is similar to that in the Burren in County Clare and is made up of porous limestone. You will notice as you approach by boat that it is eroding into great steps. Gentian, maidenhair fern, wild roses and saxifrage blossom on the 11,000 acres (4,450ha) which make up the three islands, but only 6 per cent of the land is rated as productive. The soil has been built up over the years with layer upon layer of seaweed, animal manure and sand from the beaches, so that these limestone rocks can support a few cattle, donkeys and rows of potatoes.

The Aran Islands currently have a population of approximately 1,450 with 900 on Inishmore, 300 on Inishmaan and 250 on Inisheer. The young people tend to disappear to the mainland or further for jobs, and seldom come back. When John Millington Synge came to the islands between 1899 and 1902, he felt very aware that they were the hinterland of European culture, and he was strongly drawn to

Getting There and Around

By Air

Aer Arann flies to all three islands, and operates several daily flights all year from Connemara Regional Airport in Inverin (19 miles west of Galway, with connecting buses to the city centre for all flights). It takes about 10 minutes actual flying time; rates are approximately twice the cost of the ferry – though their special packages which include a night's B&B accommodation on the island make it a much better deal, especially if you want a look at the islands from the air. They will also arrange scenic flights for groups.

Aer Arann, Dominick Street, Galway, t (091) 593034, *www.aerarann.ie, aerarann@iol.ie*; also at Galway Airport, t (091) 755569; Inverin, t (091) 593034/593054; and Inishmore, t (099) 61109, f (091) 593238.

By Sea

Three companies operate ferries out to all three of the islands; the main port of call is Kilronan on Inishmore.

Doolin Ferries, t (065) 74455. From Doolin, in Clare, this and the above line runs services to the Inisheer and Inishmore, Easter–Sept. You can usually arrange a through ticket to make the islands a stepping-stone from Clare to Galway.

Aran Ferries, t (091) 568903, *www.aranisland-ferries.com, island@iol.ie*. They have two boats: the *Galway Bay*, which operates between Galway City and Inishmore, late May–Oct daily, and the *Aran Flyer*, which operates between Rossaveal and Inishmore, April–Sept daily. Timetables and bookings are available from the Galway Tourist Office, t (091) 537700.

Island Ferries, t (091) 561767/568903/572273. Offer services between Rossaveal and all three islands year round. In summer there may be six boats a day to Inishmore. Coaches depart from Galway 1½hrs before departure times of boats. The crossing takes 40mins–1 hour.

O'Brien Shipping, t (091) 567283/567676. Services to all three islands, June–Sept daily, departing from Galway docks at 10.30am, and departing from Aran at 5pm; in winter Tues, Thurs and Sat only at the same times. Return tickets on all lines are generally about €20.

By Minibus

There is now a regular public bus service on Inishmore, leaving from Kilronan, that can take you to most of the villages. Besides these, a number of islanders offer inexpensive minibus tours of the island from Kilronan.

By Bike

Bicycles can be hired at several places in Kilronan.

Aran Bicyle Hire, t (099) 61132.

By Jaunting Car

Details from Galway and Kilronan tourist offices.

the islanders' faith in God. This is what he wrote of a young girl on Inishmaan: 'At one moment, she is a simple peasant, at another she seems to be looking out at the world with a sense of prehistoric disillusion, and to sum up in the expression of her grey-blue eyes, the whole external despondency of the clouds and the sea.'

There are seven stone forts on the islands; four on Inishmore, two on Inishmaan and one on Inisheer, all believed to go back as far as the early Celtic period 2,500 years ago. Mythology states that they were built by the Fir Bolg after they were defeated by the Tuatha Dé Danaan at the Battle of Moytura (*see* **History**, p.37, and **Old Gods and Heroes**, p.84). The people who lived on the islands became Christians in the 5th century, converted by St Enda. Monastic schools were set up which became famous over the centuries, and people came from far and wide to study there. In the Middle Ages, the O'Flahertys of Galway and the O'Briens of Clare fought

Festivals

June–early July
Festival of Saints Peter and Paul, Inishmore. Music and curragh races.

Tourist Information

Comharchumann Forbartha Arann, t (099) 61354, **f** (099) 61454, *www.visitaranislands. com*, *info@visitaranislands.com*.
Inishmore: Kilronan, **t** (099) 61263; *open year round*.

Shopping

Crafts
Snámara Craftshop (Islanders' Co-operative), Main St, Kilronan, Inishmore, **t** (099) 61359.
Carraig Donn, Kilronan, **t** (099) 61033. Knitwear and gifts.
Inis Meain Knits, Inishmaan, **t** (099) 73009. Probably the nicest traditional jumpers in the country; they do an enormous export trade to Italy.
Aran Knitwear Co-op, Inishmore, **t** (099) 61140. For Aran sweaters.

Sports and Activities

Water Sports
Aran Watersports, Kilronan, **t** (087) 904 2777. For those interested in fishing or hiring a boat (or even a *curragh*). *Open May–Sept*.

Aran Deep Sea Angling, t (091) 68903. For a fishing charter.

Where to Stay

Aran Islands **t** (099–)
There are plenty of choices on Inishmore, mostly in and around Kilronan, but nevertheless in summer you'd do well to have a booking before you get on the boat. Some places outside Kilronan send people to meet visitors coming off the ferries.
Johnston–Heron Kilmurvey House, Kilronan, Inishmore, **t** 61218, **f** 61397 (*moderate–inexpensive*). A highly recommended place to unwind, an old stone house with friendly owners. Lies 20mins' walk from Dún Aonghasa. Good, simple meals are served.
Man of Aran Cottage, overlooking Kilmurvey Bay, Inishmore, **t** 61301, **f** 61324, *manofaran@eircom.net* (*moderate–inexpensive*). This cottage appeared in the famous film before it became a B&B. The owners are enthusiastic organic gardeners.
Mainistir House Hostel, Kilronan, Inishmore, **t** 61322 (*inexpensive*). There are a number of hostels similar to this, with great value accommodation. Multilingual, friendly atmosphere, good music and an excellent vegetarian restaurant.
Dun Aengus Hostel, on the beach at Kilmurvey, Kilronan, Inishmore, **t** 61318 (*inexpensive*).

endlessly over the ownership of the islands. The English ended the dispute by building and garrisoning a fort, **Arkin Castle**, in the late 16th century. It is along the shore of the bay as you arrive at Inishmore. It was occupied at various times by Royalists, Cromwellians, Jacobites and Williamites.

The Aran Islands are wild and rugged, with so many attractions you might wish to stay there for months. The views around the forts and churches are magnificent, and you can wander around the rough roads, amongst the limestone rocks, watching for the little flowers and plants that somehow manage to grow. There are beaches on Inishmore and Inisheer, and the water is comparatively warm. It is best to ask locally about the various beaches, and about sea-angling, which can be done from a curragh or the cliffs. Every summer evening there are ballad sessions in the public houses.

Ard Einne, Kilmurvey, Inishmore, t 61126, ardeinne@eircom.net (*inexpensive*). Serves fine dinners at reasonable prices and offers bike rentals and tours.

Ard Alainn, Inishmaan, t 73027, f 73027 (*inexpensive*). Typical Aran farmhouse where you get a fine welcome from Mrs A. Faherty. *No evening meals.*

Tigh Chonghaile, Moore Village, Inishmaan, t 73085, f (087) 989 7074 (*inexpensive*). Open year-round; contact Mrs Conneely.

Ard Mhuire, Inisheer, t 75005 (*inexpensive*). Tourist board-approved; contact Mrs Una McDonagh.

Ms. Maura Sharry, West Village, Inisheer, t 75024, maire.searraigh@oceanfree.net (*inexpensive*). B&B, attached to *Radharc Na Mara* Hostel. *Open all year.*

Radharc An Chlair, Castle Village, Inisheer, t 75019 (*inexpensive*). A cosy, friendly establishment with heart-warming cooking. Contact Mrs Poil.

Radharc na Mara Hostel, West Village, Inisheer, t 75087 (*inexpensive*).

Tigh Ui Chathain, Inisheer, t 75090 (*inexpensive*). Also approved by the tourist board; contact Ms. Catherine Hernon Keane.

Eating Out

Aran Islands t (099–)

Aran Fisherman Restaurant, Kilronan, Inishmore, t 61363/61104 (*expensive–* *inexpensive*). Set dinners. *Open winter daily around 1–9pm, summer daily 10–10.*

An tSean Cheibh ('The Old Pier'), Kilronan, Inishmore, t 61228, f 61437, oldpier@ ireland. com (*moderate*). Good home-baking and fresh fish. Also a good fish and chip shop in the same building. *Open daily May–Oct.*

Dun Aengus Restaurant, Kilronan, Inishmore, t 61104 (*moderate*). Traditional stone house serving seafood, steaks, international and vegetarian dishes. *Open daily 6–10pm.*

Man of Aran Cottage, Kilmurvey Bay, Inishmore, t 61286/61301 (*moderate– inexpensive*). A daytime café which serves soup, sandwiches and a lobster lunch. *Open Mar–mid Oct daily, weather permitting.*

Joe Watty's Pub, Kilronan, Inishmore, t 61155 (*inexpensive*). Good chowders. *Open summer time only.*

Mainister House Hostel, Kilronan, Inishmore, t 61322 (*inexpensive*). Wonderful vegetarian buffets, but be sure to book and turn up for 8pm, for it disappears fast.

Teach Osta, Inis Meáin, Inishmaan, t 73003 (*inexpensive*). This is the only pub on the island, and offers good bar food and conviviality.

Fisherman's Cottage, near the pier, Inisheer, t (087) 904 2777 (*inexpensive*). The island has this one good and reasonably-priced seafood restaurant. *Open May–Sept 11–4 and 7–9.30.*

Tigh Ned, near the pier, Inisheer. Traditional music, nightly during the summer.

Inishmore

Inishmore is the largest of the islands, being about 8 miles (12.9km) long. When you get off the steamer you can hire either a bicycle or a sidecar and jarvey to see the sights. The capital, **Kilronan**, has become rather touristy, but the people remain cheerful and courteous. **Ionad Arainn** is a museum of folklife in Kilronan (*open June–Aug 10–7.30, mid Mar–May and Sept–Oct 11–4; adm; t (099) 61355, f (099) 61454*), with material about the Gaelic League. Kilronan is linked by road to a chain of villages, and if you want to get to a friendly drinking-house after the gruelling voyage, Daly's pub in **Killeany** (*Cill Einne*) is the place. Amongst the fields separated by loose stone walls (the effect is rather maze-like), you will come upon ancient ecclesiastical sites and the forts. The people of Aran, who could be descended from the Fir Bolgs, never bother with gates – they are too expensive to import. Instead, if they are herding livestock through different fields, they take down the stone walls and then calmly build them up again when the animals have got through.

Dún Aonghasa or Dun Aengus (*open Mar–Oct daily 10–6, Nov–Feb daily 10–4; t (099) 61008*) is on the south coast, on the summit of a hill which rises straight up from the sea. It covers some 11 acres (4.5ha) and consists of several concentric ramparts, 18ft high and 13ft deep (5.5m by 4m), which form a semi-circle with the two edges ending on the brink of the cliffs that fall nearly 350ft (107m) to the Atlantic. The approach is designed to cripple you if you do not advance with caution, for outside the middle wall, sharp spars of stone set closely in the ground form a *chevaux de frise*. Be warned that the site is not enclosed and you could quite easily fall from the cliffs.

Dun Eoghanacha, another stone ring-fort, is to the south of the village of Onaght on the northeast coast, and is circular in shape. The fields to the west and south are full of ancient remains. One and a half miles (2.5km) west of Killeany is **Dubh Chathair** – some of which must have disappeared over the steep cliffs, for it was once even larger than Dun Aonghasa. At Kilchorna, Monasterkieran and Teampall an Cheathrair are more evocative ruins. **Monasterkieran**, just northwest of Kilronan, has the ruins of a transitional period church, early cross slabs, an ancient sundial and a holy well. Kilchorna, about a mile southwest of Kilronan, has two *clochans*. **Teampall an Cheathrair** ('The Church of the Four Comely Saints'), is near the village of Cowrugh. It is a small 15th-century building outside of which four great flagstones mark the supposed graves of the saints. **Teampall Bheanain**, just south of Killeany, is 6th-century, only 10ft by 7ft (3m by 2m), and a unique example of an Early Christian church. With the coming of Christianity and St Enda in AD 483, the island became known as Aran of the Saints: at Killeany, 2 miles (3.2km) southeast of Kilronan, there are the graves of 120 of them. All Enda's followers seem to have reached the glorious state of sainthood after living their lives in the narrow confines of *clochans*. The site also contains the remains of a small, early church and the shaft of a finely carved high cross. A few yards to the northwest of the doorway is a flagstone which is said to cover the grave of St Enda.

Inishmaan

Inishmaan is not usually visited by tourists, who tend to go to Inishmore if they're only on a day-trip. If you do go to Inishmaan or Inisheer, see if you can go by *curragh*. It is an exciting experience to drop into the frail-looking craft and leave the security of the mail boat. (*Curraghs* are made of laths and canvas, which is then tarred over.) You can see the huge **Fort of Dun Conor** (*Dun Chonchuir*) from the sound as you approach the shore of Inishmaan. It is in the middle of the coastline and faces out to Inisheer. Its three outer walls have disappeared, with the exception of the remnants of the inner curtain, but the massive fortress wall, built of stones which only a race of giants could lift easily, is almost intact. Nearby is a freshwater spring which never dries up, called **St Chinndheirg's Well**. It is supposed to have curative properties. In the same area is one of the most interesting churches on the island, known as **Cill Cean Fhionnaigh** ('Church of the Fairheaded One'). It is one of the most perfect primitive Irish churches in existence, and there is another holy well here.

Inisheer

As you come through Foul Sound towards **Inisheer**, you see **O'Brien's Castle** on the rocky hill south of the landing place – a 15th-century tower set in a stone ring-fort. Inisheer is the smallest island, only about 2 miles (3.2km) across, but it greets you with a broad, sandy beach. It also boasts a tiny **10th-century church** dedicated to St Gobhnait, the only woman allowed on the three islands when the saintly men ruled these shores. Situated to the southeast of the landing place is the **Church of St Kevin** (*Teampall Chaomham*). This ancient building is threatened by shifting sand, but the locals clear it every year on the saint's feast day, 14 June. It has a Gothic chancel, and an earlier nave. Islanders are still buried in the ground around the church.

Synge wrote this of the men of Inisheer: 'These strange men with receding foreheads, high cheek bones, and ungovernable eyes seem to represent some old type found on these few acres at the extreme border of Europe, where it is only in the wild jests and laughter that they can express their loneliness and desolation'.

County Mayo

Mayo is a large county which towards the east is made up of limestone plains. These are interrupted by the sandstone hills of the Curlews and, further north, by the Ox Mountains or Slieve Gamph. From Ballinrobe in the southeastern corner to Ballintobber and Claremorris, heading for the central plains around Lough Mask, you might turn a corner and see the most unexpected things: perhaps a hedgehog or an otter, a beautiful shining lake, or a vast grey dolmen. If you stray to the southwest of the county, to the stunningly beautiful coastline, and explore right up to the Mullet Peninsula and Portacloy, you will find yourself amongst some of the most spectacular and lonely scenery in the west. Quartzite, schist and gneiss rocks form dramatic mountains and cliffs, and the Atlantic is a wonderful backdrop for the fuchsia-covered inlets, the beaches, the soft green *drumlins* and the stretches of wild boggy country.

Mayo is one of the loveliest counties, especially the loughs of Furnace and Feeagh, the hillside country looking to the Holy Mountain, Croagh Patrick, and the wild Nephin range. Between the lonely mountain bogs are some charming villages, excellent eating places and comfortable houses in which to stay.

History

Historically, County Mayo ('Plain of Yew Trees') has its share of fascinating archaeological remains – mainly court cairns in the northwest of the county. The legendary battle of Moytura, between the Tuatha Dé Danaan and the Fomorians, was fought on the Mayo plains in the 303rd year of the world. The written history of Mayo starts, as it does for the whole of Ireland, with the coming of Christianity and St Patrick, who fasted for 40 days on the mountain which is now called Croagh Patrick in his honour. Important monastic remains are scattered about the county. Their names, such as Cong and Ballintubber, reverberate with past associations of learning and devotion to God. Ballintubber Abbey has celebrated Mass daily since it was founded in

1216, and was a stopping place for pilgrimages on their way to climb the holy mountain of Croagh Patrick. The Celtic people arrived in about 300 BC, and gradually evolved into *septs* with identifiable surnames such as O'Connor and O'Malley. The Anglo-Norman invasion in the 12th century bought a new influx of peoples with names such as Joyce, Burke (originally de Burgo), Walsh and Prendergast. In time they became more Irish than the Irish, often marrying the Celtic Irish and allying themselves with various factions. The English monarchs eventually determined to subjugate Ireland since most of the Anglo-Normans had lost their loyalty to the Crown. From 1600 English rule was firmly established. The county was 'shired' in about 1570 and called Mayo after a small hamlet within its eastern borders.

After the Cromwellian victories of the 1640s many Irish from all over the country were dispossessed of their fertile lands and sent 'to hell or Connacht'. Many hundreds of small landowners arrived in Mayo and had to make a living out of the bleak moorland and bogs. In the following century the Rebellion of 1798 brought great hope and ultimately great loss of life to Mayo. The whole country rose up against English rule, and the French Directory in Paris, who were eager to export their revolution, sent

Getting There and Around

By Air

Knock International Airport, which is actually south of Charlestown: five flights a week to Manchester and one to Stansted, Birmingham and Jersey; for information, call t (094) 67222.

By Rail

Each of these has three trains daily to Dublin.
Westport Station, t (098) 25253.
Castlebar Station, t (094) 21222.
Ballina Station, t (096) 71818.

By Bus

You can get around by bus to almost anywhere within Mayo, or points beyond, but they are never as frequent or convenient as they might be. There are a number of obscure local lines; as always, the tourist offices are the best source for bus information.
Bus Eireann, Ballina, **t** (096) 71800, *www.buseireann.ie.*

By Bike

O'Connor's, Main Street, Cong, **t** (092) 46008.
Bike World, Castlebar, **t** (094) 25220.
Sean Sammons, The Fuel Yard, James Street, Westport, **t** (098) 25471.
Achill Sound Hotel, Achill Island, **t** (098) 45245.
O'Malleys, Dooagh, Achill Island, **t** (098) 43125.

Getting to the Islands

To Clare Island: O'Malley Ferries make five runs a day from Roonagh; **t** (098) 25045; you can also buy tickets from Westport Tourist Office, **t** (098) 28288. Mr Chris O'Grady also operates a service out to the island, and can organize sea-fishing and boating; call the Bay View Hotel, Clare Island, **t** (098) 28228.
To Inishturk and Caher: Also from Roonagh point. Service is somewhat informal; negotiate with local fishermen, or Chris O'Grady (*see* above). The *Caher Star* and *Lady Marilyn* make trips in summer from Roonagh via Inishturk, **t** (098) 45541.

To Inishglora and Inishkea: There is no regular service to these islands, and you'll have to find someone with a boat to take you over, such as Matthew Geraghty in Belmullet, **t** (097) 85741.

Festivals

May

Heineken Green Energy Festival, Castlebar, **t** 1890 925100.
Castlebar International Blues Festival. Held over May–June, **t** (098) 26206.

June

Westport Horse and Pony Show, t (098) 26206.
Westport International Sea Angling Festival and Horse Show. Late June, **t** (098) 27297/27344.
Castlebar International Blues Festival. Bank holiday weekend.

July

Ballina Festival and Arts Week, t (096) 79814/79862.
International Four-day Walking Festival. Held in Castlebar, **t** (094) 24102.
Croagh Patrick Pilgrimage, Westport, **t** (098) 25711. At the end of the month.
Mu Iranny **Mediterranean Heather Festival**, **t** (098) 36287. Sheepdog trials, community sports, angling, entertainment.

August

Geesala Festival, Ballina, **t** (097) 86742. Traditional festival with equestrian sports.
Westport Horse Fair, t (098) 25616/26206.

September

Westport Arts Festival, t (098) 66502.

October

Westport Harbour Seafood Festival, t (098) 29000/26534.

more than a thousand French troops to join the United Irishmen. The French General Humbert landed in Killala, and inflicted a humiliating defeat on the English General Lake at Castlebar. The Irish peasants were armed only with pitchforks and other rudimentary weapons, but in the euphoria of victory a 'Republic of Connacht' was set up with John Moore (ancestor of George Moore, the novelist) as its president. But massive English reinforcements soon put an end to the new Republic, and the uprising all over Ireland was vigorously put down. Many people were hanged.

During the Napoleonic Wars, all horses were commandeered for the British Army, and that was when the donkey, which is so associated with this part of the country, was introduced. The potato blight between 1845 and 1847 bought huge suffering and loss of life. The peasants barely survived in a good year, but several years of partial crop failure and then the complete loss of their staple crop meant that families died in their thousands. In the years that followed, many emigrated. Great bitterness and loss of hope followed until the land-leaguers started to organize tenant resistance to evictions and land clearance in the 1860s. (Speculators had moved in to buy land off impoverished landowners, and they had few scruples about evicting peasants.) Michael Davitt, a Mayo man from Straide, and Charles Stewart Parnell were the leaders of the land agitation, and eventually the government bought huge tracts of land and redistributed it to the people who worked it. An incident during this time of agitation gave a new word – 'boycott' – to the English language. What happened was this. In 1880, the local people refused to co-operate with Lord Erne's land agent at Lough Mask House. The harvest was ripe for cutting, but nobody would lift a hand to help him. The agent's name was Captain Boycott, and the affair drew a lot of attention to the issue of land rights.

Today much of the population of County Mayo earns money from tourism, in some form or another, and from keeping hill-sheep and fishing. Foreign companies have been encouraged by the state to set up here, and at Killala, in north Mayo, there is a huge Japanese chemical textile plant. The land is sparsely populated, and people are very friendly and helpful. The Mayo Gaeltacht covers parts of northwest Mayo including Curraun, parts of Achill and the Mullet Peninsula, plus a small area around Tourmakeady – the centre of the Gaeltarra Eireann knitwear industry.

Eastern Mayo

Cong to Ballinrobe

Mayo has many holy sites and one of them, **Cong** ('Isthmus'), is beside the island-studded Lough Corrib, just over the border from County Galway. The Corrib and Mask lakes are connected by a river which flows underground for part of its course. At some stage a canal was built so that you could take a boat between the lakes, but the water never stayed in the porous limestone.

Cong is a very friendly place, and has a reconstructed medieval **market cross**, one of the nicest ancient **abbeys**, and a most attractive modern Catholic **church**. They are beside each other down by the tree-lined river. The graceful stone of the old abbey merges somehow with the flat, grey asbestos of the new parish church. It was founded in the 7th century by St Feichin and became the favourite place of the

Tourist Information

Cong: t (092) 46542; *open May–Sept daily.*
Knock: t (094) 88193; *open May–Sept.*
Knock Airport: t (094) 67247; *open June–Sept.*
Castlebar: t (094) 21207; *open May–Sept.*

Shopping

Crafts

Westport: shops on the High Street, the Mall, Shop Street, James Street, Bridge Street.
The Sun House, Swinford Road, Foxford, t (094) 56506, *sunhouse@tinet.ie.* For porcelain, stoneware and jewellery gifts.
Hats of Ireland, Breaffy Road, Castlebar.

Delicacies

Stauntons Health Shop, Cavendish Lane, Castlebar, t (094) 23959, *www.stauntons.ie.* Health foods.

Knitwear

Foxford Woollen Mills, Foxford; t (094) 56104. Also in Westport.

Sports and Activities

Fishing

The salmon and brown trout fishing is superb on Loughs Mask, Carra and Corrib.

North Western Regional Fisheries Board, Ballina, t (096) 22788, f (096) 70543, *nwrfb@iol.ie.* For more information.

Golf

Ashford Castle Hotel, Cong, t (092) 46003. Has a golf course in its grounds.
Ballinrobe Golf Course, Clooncastle, Ballinarobe, t (092) 41118.

Pony-trekking

Claremorris School of Equitation, Galway Road, Claremorris, t (094) 62292.
Turlough Equitation Centre, Castlebar, t (094) 26646.
Cong Horse-riding, t (092) 46024.

Sailing

Glenans Sailing Centres, Collanmore Island, Westport, t (098) 26046.

Tours

Clew Bay Heritage Centre, The Quay, Westport, t (098) 26852. Historical walking tours in summer.

Walking

The **Western Way**, the 45-mile (73km) signposted trail over the mountains to Westport, starts at Oughterard. It is linked to the **Foxford Trail**, leading through the mountains to Loughs Conn and Cullin.

O'Connors, Kings of Connacht, who for a time were also high kings of Ireland. There are four fine doorways left and the cloisters, which were restored in the late 19th century by Benjamin Lee Guinness. The monks became very rich here because they possessed a fragment of the True Cross (it is now in the National Museum in Dublin).

Also in Cong, on Abbey Street, is the **Quiet Man Cottage** (*open Mar–Nov daily 10–5; rest of the year by appointment; adm; t (092) 46089, www.quietman-cong.com, quiet.man.cong@iol.ie*), used as a set in the 1951 John Ford film with John Wayne. It was a major event in these parts – partly because they had to bring electricity to the town to make filming possible. Cong was a busy place in Neolithic times; you can see a tomb called **The Giant's Grave** off the R345 west of town and a **stone circle**, also off the R345, on the way to Neal. The demesne of **Ashford Castle** (*t (092) 46003*), built by Benjamin Lee Guinness, borders the river here. Ashford is a mid-19th-century fantasy castle, with castellated towers, overlooking Lough Corrib. It is now a hotel, but anyone may walk in the beautiful grounds for a small fee. The underground tunnel through which the river flows can be reached by various openings with intriguing names.

Where to Stay

Ashford Castle, Cong t (092) 46003,
f (092) 46260, *www.ashford.ie*,
ashford@ashford.ie (*luxury*).
Opulent Victorian furnishings. Very
}comfortable, with stunning grounds,
but rather impersonal because of its large
rooms. There is Irish entertainment in
the Dungeon Bar; and the health club,
sauna, and sailing on Lough Corrib are all
available to guests.
Belmont Hotel, Knock, t (094) 88122,
f (094) 88532, *www.belmonthotel.ie*,
belmonthotel@eircom.net (*moderate*).
Offers natural health therapy packages.
Award-winning restaurant.
Knock House Hotel, Ballyhaunis Road, Knock,
t (094) 88088, f (094) 88044, *hotel@
knock-shrine.ie* (*moderate*). New hotel in
parkland.

Self-catering

The Old Rectory, Cong, t (092) 46227. Stone
coach house built in 1817 with two
bedrooms, around €300 per week. Contact
Mrs Marshall.
The Old Granary, Culduff, Foxford,
t (094) 51183, *www.culduffcottages.com*,
culduffcottages@eircom.net. Three
well restored self-catering farmhouses,
from €300 in low season. Contact
Mr Keane.

Eating Out

Ashford Castle, Cong, t (092) 46003
(*expensive*). Irish food in a sumptuous and
impressive setting.
Echoes, Main Street, Cong, t (092) 46059
(*moderate*). Cheerful home-cooking with
well-reputed meat and fish dishes and
desserts. *Open summer, daily 6.30–10pm,
winter, Thurs–Sun 7–10pm, closed
Jan–mid Feb.*
Garden Restaurant, Breaffy House Hotel,
Breaffy Road, Castlebar, t (094) 22033
(*moderate*). Good hotel-restaurant. *Open
daily 7.30–10am, 1–2.15pm and 7–10.45pm.*
Lantern Restaurant, Thomas Street, Castlebar,
t (094) 23502 (*moderate–inexpensive*).
Cantonese, Thai and northern Chinese
cooking. *Open Sun–Thurs 6pm–12.30am,
Fri–Sat 6pm–1am.*
Mulligans Pub, James Street, Claremorris,
t (094) 71792 (*inexpensive*). Traditional Irish
pub with good steaks. *Open noon–8.45pm.*

Entertainment and Nightlife

Traditional Music

Padraic Horkan's, Main Street, Swinford, east
of Castlebar, t (094) 51189. A wonderful old-
fashioned place.

Pigeon Hole is the most impressive. You climb down steep steps to the underground
stream, which is said to contain two white trout, supposed to be an enchanted
maiden and her lover. **Captain Webb's Hole** was named after an individual who
pushed his unfortunate mistresses down it. Apparently the thirteenth mistress had
the sense to push him into the hole instead.

Between Cong and Ballinrobe on the R345/R334 is a bizarre site, the **Neale**
(pronounced 'nail'). It is approached through the gates of an old estate set in an area
that is rich in ring-forts. The Neal demesne contains a medieval tomb-carving with a
19th-century inscription claiming that 'the gods go back to the year of the world
2994'. To get a glimpse of the private ruin of **Lough Mask House**, 4 miles (6.4km)
southwest of Ballinrobe, turn right off the R334 just as you leave town, and go
through the little hamlet of Ballinchalla. This was the home of the Charles Boycott
who was ostracized by his tenants during the land agitation of the 1880s. About
2 miles (3km) from town is the great stone fort of **Cahernagollum**, and a mile (1.6km)
further on is **Killower Cairn**, dating from the Bronze Age.

Castlebar to Knock

On the N84 travelling north to Castlebar, you pass by the fretted shores of Lough Carra. On the eastern shore is the ruin of **Moore Hall**, burned in 1923; it was the home of George Moore (1852–1933), the novelist. He was something of a terror in Irish literary circles, and fell out with W. B. Yeats and Lady Gregory, moving to England for the last 20 years of his life. He is buried on an island in the lake. The demesne is now a forest park with a picnic site, walks and lakeside scenic views.

A mile (1.6km) south of Castlebar is **Ballintubber Abbey**, off the N84 to the east (*open daily 9am–8pm; donation; t (094) 30934, btuabby@eircom.net*). Known as 'the Abbey that Refused to Die', it the only one founded by an Irish king that has survived intact. The fame of Ballintubber goes even further back to the time of St Patrick, who baptized his converts in a holy well there and founded a church. In the early 13th century the king of Connacht, Cathal of the Wine-red Hand, built the abbey for the Augustinian order. When the guest house to the abbey was excavated many burnt stones were found near the stream over which it was built, revealing how the monks had heated their water: by throwing in red-hot stones. There is a pilgrim path from here to Croagh Patrick, 20 miles (32km) away to the west. The foot-weary pilgrims must have been in need of a good wash when they returned. Nearby, at Mary Moran's Cottage, a crafts and information centre on the N84, you can visit **The Celtic Furrow**, a guided tour/exhibition on the Celtic calendar, festivals and folklore (*open May–Oct, daily 10–6; adm; t (094) 30709*).

Another noted place of pilgrimage is **Knock**, situated in the Plain of Mayo, 7 miles (11.3km) from the freshwater fishing centre of Claremorris. In 1879 the Virgin Mary, St Joseph and St John appeared here to 14 people. Although it rained heavily on the witnesses, the area around the apparition remained dry. The quiet little village of Knock has today become very commercialized, with chapels, monuments and a huge basilica; holy water comes from chrome taps and there are endless car parks. Over 750,000 visitors and pilgrims visit the shrine annually – it even has its own airport. At **Knock Folk Museum** you can hear the story of the Knock Apparition. The exhibition reflects local customs from the 1870s.

Castlebar is the administrative centre of Mayo and is busy enough to have a small airport. The town started as a settlement of the de Barrys. It became more important in 1611 when James I granted it a charter, and is remembered for the ignominious scattering of the British garrison in 1798 when the French General Humbert advanced with a motley crowd of French and Irish troops. The event is known today as the 'Races of Castlebar'. John Moore, the first and only president of the Connacht Republic, is buried in the Mall and there is a memorial to 1798 beside his grave.

Western Mayo

Delphi Valley to Louisburgh

At the head of the Killary inlet separating Galway and Mayo are the handsome **Aasleagh Falls**. Here you can take a beautiful and lonely route up to Louisburgh

Tourist Information

Westport: James Street, t (098) 25711,
f (098) 26709, *www.visitmayo.com*,
westport@irelandwest.ie,
westportheritagecentre@irelandwest.ie;
open all year.
Achill: t (098) 45384; *open June–Aug.*

Shopping

Crafts
From many shops in Westport, on the
High Street, the Mall, Shop Street and
Bridge Street.
Westport Crystal, the Quay, Westport, t (098)
27780. Handmade crystal.
The Gift Shop, Bridge Street, Westport. Crystal
and pottery.
Foxford Woollen Mills, Bridge Street, Westport,
t (098) 27844. Pottery and knitwear.

Delicacies
On Thursday mornings there is a
farmers' market, held in the Town Hall
in Westport.

Woollen Goods
Carraig Donn, Bridge Street, Westport,
t (098) 26287. Knitwear and gifts; Aran
sweaters a speciality;
also at Lodge Road, Westport, t (098) 25566;
and Belmullet, t (097) 20947.
Waterfront Gallery, The Harbour, Westport,
t (098) 28406.

Sports and Activities

Fishing
For **sea-fishing**, contact the following:
V. Keogh, The Helm Bar, The Quay, Westport,
t (091) 26194.
Mary Hughes, Newport, t (098) 41562.
Peter McGee, Newport, t (098) 41313.
Tony Burke, on Achill Island t (098) 47257.
  Coarse fishing is available for salmon and
trout near Newport. Tackle and advice from:
Newport House Hotel, t (098) 41222.
Delphi Fishery, Leenane, t (095) 42213.

Golf
Westport Golf Club, t (098) 28262. A lovely
course between the sea and Lough Patrick.
Achill Island Golf Club, Keel, Achill Island,
t (098) 43456.

Horse-drawn Caravans
Mayo Horse-drawn Caravan Holidays,
Belcarra, Castlebar, t (094) 32054. Caravans
hired, with full self-catering facilities.

Internet Access
Dunnings Cyber Café, The Octagon, Westport,
t (098) 25161, *dunning@aun.ie*.

Otter Watching
Island Otterwatch, Claggan, Kilmeena,
Westport, t (098) 41048. Spend a day on
the lookout for otters, dolphins and
seals around Clew Bay with
Shay Fennelly.

---

through the pass of Bundorragha (R335), with the Mweelrea Mountain on your left
and Ben Gorm on your right. You soon come to **Delphi**; an apt name, for the
mountains and the wilderness have a sort of wisdom that you can sense in the peace
around you. Lord Sligo was so impressed by its resemblance to Delphi in Greece that
he renamed it from Fionnloch. Three lochs lie beside the road: Fin Lough ('Bright
Lake'), Doo Lough ('Dark Lake') and Glencullin Lough ('the Lake of the Holly Tree Glen').
  Louisburgh (pronounced 'Lewisburg') is a pretty village near to Clew Bay. The purple-
blue mountain ranges give the village a marvellous backdrop; and it has numerous
pubs offering traditional music on different nights. The story of Granuaile, or Grace
O'Malley (*see* box, p.332), is documented in the **Granuaile Centre** here (*open May–Oct
Mon–Sat 10–7; adm;* t *(098) 66341*), with an excellent interpretative exhibition on
permanent display. There are fine sandy **beaches** at Old Head and further to the
southwest at Carrowniskey. If you take a minor road from Louisburgh and travel west

Outdoor Activities

Achill Adventure and Leisure Island Holidays,
t (0902) 94801. Canoeing, wind-surfing, snorkelling, rock-climbing, hill-walking and orienteering.

Pony-trekking

Drummindoo Stud and Equitation Centre,
Castlebar Road, Knockranny, Westport,
t (098) 25616.
Carrowholly Stables, Carrowholly, Westport,
t (098) 27057.

Spa Treatments

Rosmoney Spa and Seaweed Baths,
Rosmoney, Westport, t (098) 28899.

Walking

Croagh Patrick Walking Holidays, Westport,
t (098) 26090. Guided hill-walking tours.

Water Sports

Glenans Irish Sailing School, based on Collanmore Island, Kilmeena, Westport,
t (098) 26046. Sailing and other water sports facilities available.

Where to Stay

Delphi Lodge, Delphi, t (095) 42211 (*moderate*). Very comfortably converted sporting lodge in a wonderfully wild position, with its own salmon fishery.
Cuaneen House, Carrowmore, Louisburgh,
t (098) 66460 (*inexpensive*). Modern

farmhouse in a beautiful location overlooking Clew Bay. Good home-cooking and very friendly family, the Sammons.
Bay View Hotel, Clare Island, t (098) 26307 (*moderate*). The only place on the island to stay: friendly and comfortable.
Carrabaun, Westport, t (098) 25569 (*inexpensive*). Bed and breakfast. Also, a pretty, quiet, one-bedroom self-catering cottage available, €241–342 per week; contact Mrs Loughry.
Rosturk Woods, Mulrany, Westport, t (098) 36264 (*inexpensive*). Comfortable, elegant family house on Clew Bay. Children welcome; contact Mrs Stoney.
Newport House, Newport, t (098) 41222 (*expensive*). Superb country house hotel in a creeper-covered Georgian house overlooking the river. Irish 18th-century furniture adds to the elegance and beauty of the house: notice the Rococo Chippendale mirror hanging over the fireplace in the dining room. Old-fashioned formal service and delicious food, including their own home-smoked salmon.
McDowell's Hotel, Slievemore, Dugort, Achill Island, t (098) 43148 (*moderate*). Family-run and full of atmosphere.
Achill Island House, Newtown, Keel, Achill Island, t (098) 43355 (*inexpensive*). Simple, near the beach. Contact Sheila Mangan.
Teach Mweewillin, Corraun, Achill Island,
t (098) 45134 (*inexpensive*). Modern hillside bungalow overlooking Achill, owned by Margo Cannon.

for a couple of miles over some low hills you will come to Roonah Quay. There are some nice places to stay here and quite a lot to see. **Kilgeever Abbey** is 2 miles (3.2km) east and has an ancient well and church. Pilgrims to Croagh Patrick still include it in their itinerary. **Murrisk Abbey,** founded by Tadhg O'Malley in 1457, is 7 miles (11.3 km) further to the east on the R335 to Westport, and has a beautiful east window.

Croagh Patrick is a sacred and beautiful mountain where St Patrick is believed to have spent 40 days and nights in fasting and prayer. For this feat of endurance he is said to have extracted a promise from God that the Irish would never lose the Christian faith he had brought them. The mountain is made up of quartzite which breaks up into sharp-edged stones, so it is not very comfortable walking – some pilgrims do it in bare feet. Even if you are not interested in the religious aspects of the mountain, climb it just to see the magnificent views of Clew Bay below. The **Croagh Patrick Information Centre** is at Teach naMiasa, Murrisk (*open from 17 March*

Island House, Dookinella, Keel, Achill Island, **t** (098) 43180 (*inexpensive*). Very adequate lodgings; contact Josephine Patten.

Self-catering

Westport House Estate, Westport, **t** (098) 25430. Renovated self-catering apartments within the Old Coach House, and farm cottages on the Westport Estate. Sleeps 6–10; from €325 a week.

Eating Out

Durkans Weir House and Restaurant, Chapel Street, Louisburgh, **t** (098) 66140 (*expensive–moderate*). Bar food and a popular seafood restaurant. *Open daily 12–9pm for bar food; restaurant open June–Sept and Dec daily.*

The Lemon Peel, The Octagon, Westport, **t** (098) 26929 (*expensive*). Modern bistro-style restaurant which is good value. *Open Tues–Sat 5.30–10pm, Sun 6–9pm.*

La Bella Vita, High Street, Westport, **t** (098) 29771 (*expensive–moderate*). Bistro restaurant serving authentic Italian food. *Open Tues–Sun 6–10pm.*

The Urchin, Bridge Street, Westport, **t** (098) 27532 (*moderate*). Good Irish food served all day, with evening a la carte (*after 6pm*).

Quay Cottage, The Harbour, Westport, **t** (098) 26412 (*moderate*). Folksy seafood restaurant. Very cosy, with good bread and a vegetarian menu as well. *Open Tues–Sat from 6pm for dinner only.*

Newport House, Newport, **t** (098) 41222 (*expensive*). It is a treat just to see inside this house, with its elegant furniture. The food is good too, especially the home-cured fish.

McDowells Hotel, Slievemore Road, Dugort, Achill Island, **t** (098) 43148 (*moderate*). Home-cooking.

The Boley House, Keel, Achill Island, **t** (098) 43147 (*moderate–inexpensive*). Good, well prepared and thought-out menus in a stone cottage. Salmon, seafood, steaks. *Dinner only; open summer daily 6–10pm.*

Calvey's Restaurant, Keel, Achill Island, **t** (098) 43158 (*moderate–inexpensive*). Good vegetarian dishes, seafood, beef and lamb from their own farm.

The Chalet, Keel, Achill Island, **t** (098) 43157 (*inexpensive*). Fish and chips.

Entertainment and Nightlife

Traditional Music

Matt Molloy's Bar, Westport, **t** (098) 26655. This is owned by a member of the Irish folk group, The Chieftains; if you can't get in, there will be plenty of other choices in summer.

The West Bar, Bridge Street, Westport, **t** (098) 25886.

McDowell's Hotel, Slievemore Road, Doogort, Achill Island, **t** (098) 43148.

daily through the peak season; **t** *(098) 64114,* **f** *(098) 64115, croaghpatrick@ ireland.com*); tired walkers will find the café, craft shop and shower facilities particularly welcome.

The Islands of Clare, Inishturk and Caher

Clare Island (pop. 140) has more land given over to farming than the other islands, though its higher slopes are covered in heather. It has superb cliffs up to 300ft (91m) high, but even these are overshadowed by the Knockmore Mountain, which drops from 1,550ft (472m) in a few hundred yards to join the cliffs. You could easily spend a couple of days on Clare although there's not a huge amount to occupy you – you may just come and have a picnic. As you come into the small stone pier you will see **Grace O'Malley's Castle**, converted into a coastguard station during the 19th century but now a ruin. The large, square stone tower still dominates the bay. There is a holy well

Grace O'Malley, Warrior and Pirate Queen

This part of the coast and the islands off it are associated with the warrior woman who outshone all her male contemporaries in qualities of leadership: Granuaile, otherwise known as Grace O'Malley. A pirate captain, whose symbol was the seahorse, her territory included Clare, Caher, Inishturk and Inishbofin. Her family had been Lords of the Isles for two hundred years, and in the 40 years that it took the Tudors to extend their power to Ireland Granuaile was the mainstay of the rebellion in the west. At the age of 45 she gave birth at sea to her first child, Toby. An hour later, her ship was boarded by Turkish pirates. The battle on the deck was almost lost when she suddenly appeared wrapped in a blanket and shot the enemy captain with a blunderbuss. Her men rallied, captured the Turkish ship and hanged the crew. She was also in the habit of mooring her ships by tying them together, passing the main rope through a hole in her castle walls and retiring to bed with the rope wound round her arm, in order to be ready at the first alarm. In her last years she was forced, aged 63, to sail up the Thames to parley with Elizabeth I. Elizabeth offered her a title, but Grace replied that she was a queen in her own right. Finally, they made a deal: Grace would retain some of her old lands, including Clare, and in return she would keep down piracy. People still talk of Grace today, even though she died in 1603.

at **Toberfelabride**, but the gem of Clare is its abbey, which is about 1½ miles (2.4km) west of the harbour. **Clare Abbey** is a 15th-century church with a tower, and is believed to be a cell of the Cistercian monastery of Abbeyknockmoy in County Galway. The most notable thing about the **friary** (*always accessible*) is the trace of fresco painting on the plastered ceiling of the vaulted roof; they seldom survive in medieval Irish churches. Grace O'Malley is buried here: on a plain arch leading from the roofless nave to the chancel there is a coat of arms topped by a horse rampant with the words '*Terra Marique potens O'Maille*' ('O'Malley powerful on land and sea'). You can walk to the **lighthouse** at the north end where there are spectacular views from the cliffs.

Inishturk has a wonderful beach on its south side, and its little farms are full of wild flowers. About 90 people live here and make a living from fishing. **Caher Island** evokes the mood of early monastic settlements better than any other, especially since it is now uninhabited. It is a lovely grey-green place of walls, donkeys, sheep and green pastures. The **church** here is small and roofless. Around it are 12 stone crosses, the most recent of which is not less than a thousand years old. One on the hilltop shows a human face, another a pair of dolphins. In the graveyard is **St Patrick's Bed** with impressions said to be the mark of his hands, feet and hips. Few pilgrims come nowadays to lie in his bed and hope for a miraculous cure.

Clew Bay: Westport and the Corraun Peninsula

From Louisburgh, the R335 winds its way to Westport with lovely views of Clew Bay. The sea-angling grounds here are among the best in Europe. **Westport** is an attractive 18th-century planned town, unusual in the west. James Wyatt, the well-known Georgian architect, designed it for the Marquess of Sligo, and included a pretty walk called the Mall which runs beside the River Carrowbeg and is overhung with trees. In summer the place is overflowing with people attracted by the town's many festivals. Here too, you can walk around one of the few stately homes of the west of Ireland – **Westport House** (*open Easter–May, Sat–Sun 2–5, June, daily 1.30–5.30, July–Aug, Mon–Fri 11.30–5.30 Sat–Sun 1.30–5.30, 3–23 Sept, daily 2–5; adm; t (098) 27766/25430*). The house is west of the town and is full of old Irish silver, family portraits and lovely furniture, and there is a miniature zoo in the grounds. It was built by Colonel John Browne and his wife, ancestors of the present Marquess of Sligo. He was a Jacobite, and she was the great, great grand-daughter of Grace O'Malley. **Newport**, on the N59, has a superb country house hotel overlooking the river. Newport House used to be the home of the O'Donnells, once the Earls of Tir Connell, who were often in the forefront of opposition to English rule. The modern Irish Romanesque style **church** of St Patrick has some Harry Clarke stained glass windows depicting the Last Judgement.

The coastline around here is full of little islands and inlets. However, about ½ mile (0.8km) outside Newport on the N59, take a little road signposted to Furnace; this leads you into the wild mountain country of the **Nephin Beg** range. When it's sunny the lakes go a deep, sparkling blue; and the air is bracing, rather like Switzerland. If you decide to explore the wild territory of the interior between Glen Nephin and Bangor Erris, follow the old mountain road on past the lakes and past Glennamong Mountain (2,063ft/629m) until it joins the R312. Then turn northwards until it joins the N59 at Bellacorick. The route is very beautiful; fuchsia and rhododendron mingle with the stone walls and rock. Continuing along the N59, turn off to **Burrishoole Abbey**, a 15th-century ruin (*always accessible*), and a very charming and peaceful place where the sea laps all about. The next stop-off is further along the coast at **Rockfleet Castle** (also known as Carrickahooley), a complete tower house that stands on seaweedy rock overlooking Newport Bay. This four-sided 15th-century castle was built by the Burkes and passed to Grace O'Malley by means of a trick. She married Richard Burke on the understanding that either of them could end the marriage after a year. She used the year to garrison the castle with her own men and kept it when she declared the marriage ended.

When you get to **Mulrany** on the neck of the **Corraun Peninsula** you will find a long strand looking out to Croagh Patrick across Clew Bay. This area is very popular in the summer, for the climate is mild. Rhododendrons bloom luxuriously and myriads of yellow flags grow in the fields, which are another common and lovely sight in Connacht – although the local farmers wouldn't agree. The Corraun Peninsula is a wild knob of land through which you can pass on the way to Achill Island. The single-track road around it is a fine introduction to Achill Island, which has all the most attractive characteristics of Connacht. Amongst them are the sleepy whitewashed cottages you can see across the water and the smell of burning turf floating on the breeze. Placid-looking donkeys are everywhere.

Achill Island

Achill is connected to the mainland by a bridge, and because it is one of the easiest islands to reach, it is the most touristy. The island covers 53 square miles (137.25 sq km) and is the largest of the Irish islands. The best introduction to it is to take the **Atlantic Drive**. This is signposted clearly as you leave the little hamlet of Achill Sound beside the causeway. You pass a small, ruined 12th-century church and then a charming tower house, **Kildownet**, which is supposed to have belonged at some time to Grace O'Malley. The road follows the line of the shore round the south tip and passes **Achillbeg Island**, which contains the remains of an old hermitage.

Keel is a big village with restaurants and craft shops and a large, sandy beach. The west-facing **Cliffs of Menawn** to the south of Keel have been wrought by the sea and wind into fantastic shapes, which are best viewed from a boat. Particularly noteworthy are the **Cathedral Rocks**, which are covered in fantastic fretwork. If you walk 3 miles (4.8km) to the end of Menawn Strand, you come to a holy well; and if it is low tide you can see the arches and pillars of the rocks clearly. Above, Mweelin Mountain rises up. It is an easy climb, if approached from Dookinelly. **Keem Bay** is a lovely sandy cove obvious from the cliff road, and is a favourite haunt of the basking shark.

Doogort is a little fishing hamlet in the shadow of Slievemore Mountain (2,204ft/672m). The hamlet has a contentious history. In the early 19th century, a Protestant missionary outpost was established here in order to convert the local Catholics. The Mission acquired title to the rights of three-fifths of Achill in a short time, and resentment amongst the Achill people ran high. This was intensified when, apparently, soup and bread was given out to islanders during the famine only if they became Protestants. The Mission closed down in the late 19th century, but it did help start the first hotel on the island. Along the coast here are the **Seal Caves**. You can hire a boat to get to them and enjoy the superb bathing beaches.

Northern Mayo

From Mulrany the N59 runs over a vast bog; the edges are enlivened by splashes of purple rhododendrons and a few fir trees. Turf, which for hundreds of years has been cut from the bog, is used much less nowadays in heating and cooking since bottled gas has made life much easier for the housewife. But many farmers and country people have rights to turf turbaries, which they cut every year. The tool used to cut the neat sods from the bog is called a slane; as they are cut the sods are arranged in little piles to dry. The pattern of the piles varies from area to area, but they often resemble little *clochans*.

Bangor Erris is a small place on the long, lonely road to Belmullet. This region is still known as Erris, one of the ancient Norman baronies of Ireland. **Belmullet** is one of the loneliest towns in Connacht. It stands on a slender piece of land just wide enough to prevent the Mullet from becoming an island. All the commerce of the peninsula is channelled through this town, so on market day it is surprisingly full. If you want to base yourself here before exploring the wild and lonely peninsula, there is plenty of accommodation. Belmullet is famous for sea-angling, and there is an international fishing festival here in August. The Mullet is almost divided into little islands by the deep bays which cut into it on either side. The beaches and fishing are excellent and

Tourist Information

Belmullet: Erris Tourist Information Centre,
t (097) 81500; *open all year.*
Ballina: t (096) 70848; *open late March–Sept.*

Shopping

Crafts

Terrybaun Pottery, Bofeenaun, near Pontoon,
Ballina, t (094) 56472. Earthenware.

Tweeds and Knitwear

Gaeltarra Knitwear, Tourmakeady, t (092)
44015.
Flannery Knitwear, Graughill, Pullathomas,
Belmullet, t (097) 84607.

Sports and Activities

Fishing

Coarse fishing on the River Moy, one of the
best salmon rivers anywhere, and on Loughs
Conn and Cullin. **Sea-angling** is also available.
Moy Fishery, c/o Mount Falcon Hotel, Ballina,
t (096) 21332.
Lough Conn, Healy's Hotel, Pontoon, t (094)
56443.
Vincent Sweeney, Blacksod, Ballina, t (097)
85774. For sea-fishing advice and equipment.

Golf

Ballina Golf Club, Mossgrove, t (096) 21050.

Where to Stay

Highdrift, Haven View, Ballina Road, Belmullet,
t (097) 81260 (*inexpensive*). Modern
bungalow; contact Mrs A. Reilly.
Rathoma House, Killala, t (096) 32035
(*inexpensive*). Pleasant farmhouse in the
depths of the country. Lots of activities, and
Mrs Carey will arrange horse-riding for you.
Enniscoe House, Castlehill, near Crossmolina,
Ballina, t (096) 31112, f (096) 31773
(*expensive*). Georgian house set in parklands
on the shores of Lough Conn. Grand,
spacious rooms are filled with family furniture, with four-poster and half-tester beds in
the pretty bedrooms. There are huge log

fires and superlative cooking using seasonal
ingredients. The grounds include an
ornamental garden and an organic garden
(*adm*). Mayo North Heritage Centre adjoins
the gardens (*see* p.338). Woodcock shooting
is available in the winter for small groups.
Boats and ghillies for the lough can easily be
arranged. Self-catering cottages in the
grounds are available for short lets. Contact
Ms Annette Maughan.
Kilmurray House, Castlehill, Crossmolina,
Ballina, t (096) 31227 (*inexpensive*). Friendly,
cosy old farmhouse. Mrs Moffat organizes
and cooks the meals very well, and her
husband is a keen fisherman.
Breege Padden, Quignalegan House, Sligo
Road, Ballina, t (096) 71644 (*inexpensive*).
Family B&B, recommended by readers.
Pontoon Bridge Hotel, Pontoon, t (094) 56120/
56699, f (094) 56688, *fishing@ pontoon-
bridge.com* (*expensive–moderate*). Simple
three-star hotel, popular with fishermen.
Healy's Hotel, Pontoon, t (094) 56443, f (094)
56572, *healspontoon@eircom.net* (*moderate*).
Quiet place with a lovely setting on the
shore of the lough; great for anglers.

Eating Out

Unfortunately restaurants are pretty dismal
in this area, so you might be advised to head
over to Westport, Cong or Castlebar.
Western Strand Hotel, Main St, Belmullet,
t (097) 81096 (*moderate*). Evening meals only.
Anchor Bar, The Georges Street, Killala, t (096)
32050 (*inexpensive*). Pub lunches.
Dillon's Bar and Restaurant, Dillon Terrace,
Ballina, t (096) 72230 (*moderate*). Locally
famous for salmon. *Bar food 12–8.30,
restaurant open 6–10pm.*
Pontoon Bridge Hotel, Pontoon t (094) 56688
(*expensive*). One of the better places for
food; its restaurant overlooks the lakes.

Entertainment and Nightlife

Traditional Music

The Broken Jug, O'Rahilly Street, Ballina,
t (096) 72379.

there are superb views of Achill, the Nephin Beg range, and the mystical islands of Inishglora and Inishkea. The grey and red-necked phalarope nests in the crevices and rocks along the coast, and the peninsula is scattered with prehistoric remains. Out in Blacksod Bay lies the wreck of *La Rata*, a large Spanish galleon which went down in the wild seas of September 1588 – part of the Armada which threatened England. The islands of Inishglora and Inishkea are uninhabited, and hardly ever visited by tourists. Getting out to them is a matter of negotiation with local fishermen, and they can only be reached in calm weather. A walk around each one takes at least one hour. Always bring your own picnic and drinks.

Along the spectacular coastline from Blacksod Bay to Ballina you can follow the **North Mayo Sculpture Trail**. Fifteen contemporary works, based on aspects of Irish folklore and the landscape, are scattered on various sites. The tourist office can provide a list of them.

Inishglora and the Islands of Inishkea

On **Inishglora** ('Island of the Voice'), the Children of Lir regained their true form after being turned into swans by their jealous stepmother. The spell was to be broken when St Patrick's bell was heard ringing out over Ireland, but, unhappily for the Children of Lir, their immortality only lasted whilst they were swans. They came ashore, blind, senile and decrepit, to die almost at once.

Inishglora has been a sacred island for thousands of years. It is only one mile from the Mullet Peninsula, and its ecclesiastical remains are associated with St Brendan the Navigator. Some of the buildings definitely date from the 6th century. The most complete is the 12th-century **St Brendan's Chapel**, which is built of dry-stone masonry. Close by are the ruins of a church for men and a church for women. The holy well here is supposed to turn red if the water is touched by a woman's hand. Once it was believed that the more serious a dead man's crimes, the more important it was to have him buried on an holy island. This not only improved his chances of salvation, but ensured that he could not come back to haunt you, since the spirits of the dead cannot pass over water. It is said locally that on Inishglora lots of bones are uncovered where the soil is washed away by rain and sea-spray.

Southwest lie the islands of **Inishkea** ('Isle of the Lonely Heron'). Legend tells of Mulhenna, who was unfaithful to her husband and was banished here for a thousand years, condemned to take the form of a heron. South Island has a little deserted hilltop village, though fishermen camp here when they are working offshore. The islanders moved to the mainland after ten men were drowned in 1927 during a freak gale. Moondaisies, grass, sheep and sandy beaches will be your reward if you come out here. Both islands have the remains of ancient churches, incised stone crosses and some prehistoric signs of occupation. **Duvillaun More**, the most distant of this chain of islands, lies off the southern tip of the Belmullet peninsula, and is only accessible when the sea is calm. There are remains of monastic settlements here too, including a holy well.

The Northern Coast

On the mainland again, make your way up to the fishing hamlet of Pollatomish on Sruwaddacon Bay. Take the unnumbered road west of Barnatra on the R314. Close to the cliff edge is **Dooncarton Stone Circle** and megalithic tomb. Further north is the little harbour village of **Portacloy**, which is surrounded by high cliffs. **Ceide Hill** and the surrounding area is probably one of the world's most extensive stone age monuments. The **Céide Fields Visitor Centre** (*open mid Mar–May, daily 10–5, June–Aug, 9.30–6.30, Sept, 9.30–5.30, Oct, 10–5, Nov, 10–4.30; site open for advance bookings Dec–Mar; adm; t (096) 43325*) has opened just off the R314 to explain the archaeology and geology of the area. Hidden in the bogs is evidence of a well-organized farming community dating from more than 5,000 years ago, and extensive patterns of stone-walled fields and corrals have been revealed.

On the R314 in the northeastern corner of the county, **Ballycastle** is typical of the villages in the west. The streets are wide, the air smells faintly of turf, and everybody seems to be asleep. The cliffs of **Downpatrick Head** are full of wheeling birds, terns, gulls, skuas, razorbills and guillemots, plus less active ones such as puffins; all seem to have nests somewhere on the edges of the cliffs. There are picnic tables set out overlooking the Atlantic, but it does not look as if anyone has ever eaten off them, and now the birds and seapinks have taken over, visited by the occasional hare. There is wire fencing on the head to prevent you from falling into the crevasses and holes around the cliff edge. One of the most spectacular holes is a puffin hole called Poulnachantinny. Once upon a time St Patrick was having a fight with the Devil, and dealt him such a blow with his crozier that the Devil was hammered clean through the rock and down into the sea-cave below. In their fight they also knocked a bit of the headland off into the sea – the stack of **Doonbristy** is proof. An old promontory fort was built on Doonbristy, before it became separated from the headland. It is a ruin now, of course. There is a *pattern* to the holy well and ruined church of St Patrick on Garland Sunday in May.

About 2 miles (3.2 km) northwest of Ballycastle on the R314 is **Doonfeeney Graveyard**, where there is a ruined church and a standing stone, about 18ft (5.5m) high, with a cross carved on it. A large ring-fort stands close by where, according to old beliefs, fairies hold their revels. The graveyard is scattered with ancient stone slabs and it is a quiet, secret place. In spring, on the way east to **Killala Bay** (still following the R314) the banks of the roadside are covered in daisies and primroses. Killala was the scene of the landings in 1798, when Humbert brought 1,100 French soldiers, plus supplies and artillery, from France to support the rebels. The bay is rather like a lagoon, having calm sheltered waters. Before you get to the town, a road to the left leads you past **Rathfran Abbey**, a ruined but fine Dominican friary dating from 1274. **Killala** town is very pretty and rather higgledy-piggledy, with a round tower rising from the middle. The tower is of a later date than the abbey, and the doorway is almost 13ft (4m) from the ground. It is now thought that such towers were the work of skilled builders who moved around the country from site to site. This tower is of a blue limestone with a greenish cap.

Two miles (3.2km) west is a 15th-century ruin called **Moyne Abbey** – although it was in fact a friary – on the estuary of the lovely salmon river, the Moy, reputedly one of the best in Europe. Just a mile or two upstream is another abbey, **Rosserk**, which is rather more complete and is regarded as one of the finest Franciscan friaries in the country. It has some good carvings on the double piscina, one of which is of a round tower. The buildings include a square tower, nave, chancel, south transept, cloister and conventional buildings. There is a lovely arched doorway and east window.

Ballina and the Loughs

Ballina (pronounced 'bally-nah') is a port town on the estuary of the River Moy and is a good place to stay if you are in Ireland for the fishing. It is an excellent shopping centre as well, especially after the remoteness and lack of choice in Erris – though these days Ballina is perhaps best known as the home town of former president Mary Robinson. West of Ballina at Enniscoe, Castlehill, is the **Mayo North Heritage Centre** (*open all year; t (096) 31809*), off the R315 and 2 miles (3km) south of Crossmolina. It is in the outbuildings of Enniscoe House, which is also an attractive and comfortable place to stay (*see p.335*).

Foxford, 10 miles (16km) due south of Ballina, is a convenient place to stay if you are fishing on the Loughs Conn and Cullin. Its thriving wool and tweed mill in St Joseph's Place operates the **Foxford Woollen Mills Visitor Centre** where you can see rugs, blankets and tweeds being made (*open all year, Mon–Sat 10–6 Sun 12–6, Suns in winter, 2–6; t (094) 56756, shop t (094) 56104, foxfordwoollenmills@eircom.net*). This area is very attractive; the summit of Nephin Mountain is of whitish quartzite so it looks perpetually snowcapped, and when the sun is shining it is a lovely background for the deep-blue waters of Lough Conn. **Pontoon** is on the isthmus between the two loughs, and there are two hotels there.

It is worth stopping at **Straide**, if you are going to Castlebar. Straide is the birthplace of Michael Davitt (1846–1906), who started the Land League. His family were evicted from their small farm when he was five, and they emigrated to Lancashire, where he worked as a child in the cotton mills and lost his right arm in the machines. The **Michael Davitt National Memorial Museum** (*open Mar–Oct, daily 10–6; adm; t (094) 31022 for more details*) here has a large collection of historical documents and photographs relating to the League. Opposite is a ruined **Franciscan abbey**, founded in the mid-13th century, which has a wonderful series of sculptures. The *Pieta* is especially good; the Virgin sits with the limp body of Christ in her lap, guarded by two angels. There is an elaborate 15th-century tomb chest in the same style with figures of saints.

County Roscommon

Roscommon is a wonderfully green and fertile county, with shining sheets of water encircling it and scattered throughout. It is the only county in Connacht without a seashore, but the many lakes and rivers give it a different charm from that of its windswept Atlantic neighbours. The placid River Shannon forms its eastern boundary,

County Roscommon

N

20km
10miles

SLIGO

LEITRIM

MAYO

ROSCOMMON

LONGFORD

GALWAY

WESTMEATH

OFFALY

Lavagh
Achonry
Banada
Tubbercurry
Charlestown
Ballymote
Castlebaldwin
Derry
Carrowkeel
Ballyfarnon
Keadue
Drumshanbo
Lough Allen
Kesh
Lough Arrow
Lough Meelagh
Ballinafad
Curlew Hills
Drumcong
R294
Gorteen
Mullaghroe
Boyle
Lough Key
Leitrim
R284
Lough Gara
Lough Key Forest Park
Carrick-on-Shannon
Knock Airport
Ballaghaderreen
Ballinameen
Killukin
Jamestown
Drumsna
N4
Frenchpark
Hill Street
Clougher
N5
Elphin
Drumod
R202
Loughglinn
Rathcroghan
Kilglass Lough
Roosky
Lough O'Flynn
Clonalis House
Ballyhaunis
Tulsk
Strokestown
Lough Forbes
N60
Castlerea
Carnfree
R367
Termonbarry
N5
N60
Cloonfad
Ballintober
Four Mile House
Cloondara
N4
Ballymore
Lanesborough
Glinsk Castle
Dunmore
Roscommon Castle
Roscommon
LONGFORD
Glennamaddy
Fuerty
Ballymurray
N83
Castlestrange Stone
Athleague
Knockcroghery
Inishcloraun
Newtown Cashel
R366
Galey Castle
Saint's Island
Barnaderg
Ballygar
Four Roads
Lecarrow
Lough Ree
R332
Mount Bellew
N61
Curraghboy
Inchmore
Monivea
Ballyforan
Thomas
WESTMEATH
Gurteen
Castleblakeney
Glassan
Killinure Lough
Corraree
Athlone
Bealin
Kilconnell
Ballinasloe
N6
Killogeenaghan
New Inn
Aughrim
R348
Old Town
River Shannon
Clonmacnoise
N6
Abbey of Clontuskert
R. Suck
Shannonbridge
Blackwater Bog
Ferbane
R355
Grand Canal
Loughrea
Laurencetown
Clonfert
Clonony
OFFALY

Getting There and Around

By Rail

The rail link between Dublin and Sligo passes through Boyle. The Dublin–Westport–Ballina line passes through Roscommon Town and Castlerea; both lines have about three trains a day.
Roscommon Train Information, t (0903) 26201.

By Bus

Express bus services from Dublin to Roscommon Town, Strokestown, Elphin, Ballaghaderreen, Ballanagare and Boyle. There is also a good local bus network.
Bus Eireann Information, Athlone, t (0902) 73322.

By Bike

Bicycle hire, sales and repair are available from:
Brendan Sheerin, Main Street, Boyle, t (079) 62010.
Buckley's Cycles, Astor Buildings, Roscommon, t (0903) 27318.
Gerry Kelly, Ballybride, Roscommon, t (0903) 25181.
Riverside Cycles, Bridge Street, Boyle, t (079) 63777.

Festivals

May

Strokestown International Poetry Festival, t (078) 33759. Poetry competitions and international poets performing readings and workshops.

July–August

Country and Western Carnival, Boyle, t (086) 254 5176. Always a favourite.
Boyle Arts Festival, t (079) 640690/63085, *info@boylearts.com.*
O'Carolan Harp and Traditional Irish Music Festival and School, Keadue, Boyle, t (078) 47204/47247, *www.keadue.harp.net,* *ocarolan@eircom.net.*
Rosfest, Roscommon Summer Festival, Roscommon Town, t (086) 232 6419. Music, arts, culture and street entertainment.
Castlerea International Rose Festival, t (0907) 20067. Top bands perform in the street.
Tulsk Summer Fair, t (078) 39195.

October

Eileen Og Harvest Festival, Castlerea, t (0907) 55175.

Tourist Information

Boyle: t (079) 62145; *open May–Sept.*
Roscommon: t (0903) 26342/26532, *www.roscommon.ie, tourism@roscommon.ie, www.visitroscommon.com, info@ irelandwest.ie; open mid May–mid Sept.*
Athleague: t (0903) 63602.

Shopping

Crafts

Una Bhan Craft Shop, Main Street, Boyle, t (079) 63033.
Raftery's Gift and Antique Centre, Main Street, Castlerea.
Eight 'Til Late, Market Square, Roscommon.
Newsround, The Square, Roscommon.

engulfed as it is by the beautiful Lough Ree for several miles. The River Suck, beloved of coarse fishermen, forms the boundary with County Mayo in the west, and Lough Key, Lough Gara and Lough Arrow encircle the county in the north. In the east and west there is bogland, but in the centre rich pastureland divides into fine cattle and sheep farms. The flood meadows on either side of the Suck provide the perfect environment for bird-watching. Great flocks of widgeon come here to graze, as do whooper swans, golden plovers, black-tailed godwits and white-fronted geese. Snipe, curlew and lapwing are also common. The familiar, beautiful cry of the curlew, as it turns and wheels above the green fields, is a sound that is peculiarly reminiscent of the Irish countryside.

Time Pieces, Main Street, Roscommon, t (0902) 25408. Clocks, jewellery and crafts.
The Bastion Gallery, 6 Bastion Street, Athlone, t (0902) 94948.

Sports and Activities

Cycling

For details on cycle routes in County Roscommon, contact Athleague Visitor Centre, t (0903) 63602, or check out the Suck Valley Tourism Group's website: *http://suckvalley .firebird.net*.

Fishing

Coarse fishing on the River Suck and its tributaries at Glinsk, Castlecook, Ballygar and Ballyforan. Also on Errit Lake, Hollygrove Lake, and in the Ballyhaunis area, Eaton's Lake, and Lakehill Lake. Fishing for **brown trout** on the upper stretches of the River Suck, River Derryhipps, and on Lake O'Flynn, a 600-acre (242ha) limestone lake. For more information contact the Roscommon tourist office, or the following:
Angling and Visitor Centre, Athleague, t (0903) 63602, *tench@indigo.ie*.
Cavetown Angling Club, t (079) 68037.
Ballaghaderreen and District Angling Club, t (0907) 60077.
Ireland West Tourism, t (091) 563081.
Christopher Wynne, Main Street, Boyle, t (091) 790499. For fishing information, ghillies or supplies of tackle and bait.
Mr Fitzpatrick, t (079) 62444. For supplies.

Golf

Boyle Golf Course, t (079) 62594.
Roscommon Golf Club, t (0903) 26382.

Open Farms

Glendeer Open Farm, between Rosscommon and Athlone, t (0902) 37147, *www.iol.ie/ wmeathtc/glendeer*. Open April–Sept, Mon–Sat 10–6 and Sun 12–6.

Pleasure Cruises

On Lough Key, during the summer only. Check the website *www.visitroscommon.com* or contact local tourist offices for more information.
Tara Cruisers, The Moorings, Knockvicar, Boyle, t (078) 67777.
Shannon-Erne Waterway Holidays, Cootehall, near Carrick-on-Shannon, Co. Leitrim, t (079) 67028, *www.sew-holiday.com*.
Viking Tours, Athlone, Co. Westmeath, t (0902) 73383, *vikingtours@ireland.com*.

Pony-trekking

Una Bhan Rural Tourism Cooperative, King House, Military Road, Boyle, t (079) 63033. They also organize fishing, bike tours and other activities like old-fashioned farmhouse skills.
Munsboro Riding Holidays, Munsboro Lodge, Sligo Road, Roscommon, t (0903) 26449.
Kiltoom Stables, Kiltoom, near Athlone, t (0902) 89511.

Where to Stay

Royal Hotel, Bridge Street, Boyle, t (079) 62016, f (079) 62505 (*moderate*). Town centre inn on the river, in business for over 200 years.
Riversdale House, Knockvicar, near Boyle, t (079) 67012 (*inexpensive*). Period farmhouse in the middle of the country,

There are many prehistoric monuments to see – burial mounds, megalithic tombs and ring-forts, and the most powerful Norman and Gaelic leaders of the medieval period built strong castles and abbeys here which have survived, although in a ruined state. The Cistercian abbey in Boyle is perhaps the most impressive, but the countryside is scattered with charming Church of Ireland churches dating from the 17th and 18th centuries, which nowadays have hardly a congregation at all.

The Protestant English and Scottish invaders who built these churches also planned and constructed impressive estates. The wealth of design and craftsmanship which went into making these large houses and their parks is only just beginning to be appreciated today; for years they were branded as the symbols of oppression by a race with its own lake and river fishing, run by the Burke family.

Glencarne House, Ardcarne, near Carrick-on-Shannon, t/f (079) 67013 (*moderate–inexpensive*). Fine Georgian farmhouse with comfortable rooms, lovely old furniture and well-cooked meals. Very close to Lough Key Forest Park; contact Mrs A. Harrington. *Book in advance for dinner.*

Clonalis House, Castlerea, t/f (0907) 20014, *clonalis@iol.ie* (*moderate*). An opportunity to stay with descendants of Ireland's last High Kings, Pyers and Marguerite O'Connor Nash, at this Victorian-Italianate house in a lovely wooded estate. Shooting and fishing can be arranged, as can dinner (*luxury*), with 24hrs notice. They also have converted four bedroom mews houses available to rent on Clonalis Estate, €406 per week in high season.

The Abbey Hotel, Galway Road, Roscommon, t (0903) 26240, f (0903) 26021, *cmv@indigo.ie* (*expensive*). Attractive Georgian building with 20 en suite bedrooms.

Gleeson's Townhouse, Market Square, Roscommon, t (0903) 26954, f (0903) 27425, *gleerest@iol.ie* (*moderate*). Centrally located, with well-appointed rooms and a restaurant.

Self-catering

Abbey House, t (079) 62385. Lovely old houses available to rent on the grounds of Boyle Abbey; €280 per week in high season. Contact Christina and Martin Mitchell.

Rookwood, Athleague, just south of Roscommon, t (0903) 63810. 18th-century gate lodge by the river; €200 per week in high season. Contact Mary Glennon.

Eating Out

Cromleach Lodge, Lough Arrow, Castlebaldwin, t (071) 65155 (*expensive*). Set in the hills above Lough Arrow and in County Sligo, although close to Boyle. Traditional, hearty Irish cooking. *Dinner only.*

Donnellan's, Clarendon House, Knockvicar, Boyle, t (079) 67016 (*moderate*). Good children's menu. *Open summer Tues–Sun, winter Thurs–Sun.*

The Royal Hotel, Bridge Street, Boyle, t (079) 62016 (*moderate*). Coffee shop which serves salads and snacks; the restaurant is more exotic. *Open Sun–Thurs 12.30–3 and 6–9, Fri–Sat 6–9.30.*

James Clarke, Patrick Street, Boyle, t (079) 62064 (*inexpensive*). Traditional pub selling delicious Irish coffee.

Abbey Hotel, Abbeytown, Galway Road, Roscommon, t (0903) 26240/26505 (*expensive*). 18th-century house with excellent French-style cooking. *Open daily 8–10am, 12.45–2.30pm and 6–9.15pm.*

Knights Restaurant, Stone Court, Roscommon, t (0903) 25620 (*expensive*). Has a good reputation for French, Italian and Asian fusion cooking.

Gleeson's Restaurant, Market Square, Roscommon, t (0903) 26954 (*moderate*). Try breakfast in the 'Manse' restaurant, or eat in the café for lunch, afternoon tea or dinner.

The Royal Hotel, Castle Street, Roscommon, t (0903) 26317 (*moderate*).

The West Deli, Castle Street, Roscommon, t (0903) 25382 (*inexpensive*). Soups, salads, hot main dishes. *Open until 7.*

that has a long memory for wrongs and past injustices. One such great house, near Boyle, belonged to the King family of Rockingham.

You could spend a melancholy few days touring the ruined Big Houses of County Roscommon, as you can everywhere in Ireland. The list of sad remains in this county is long: Kilronan Castle near Ballyfarnon, Mantua near Castlerea, Mount Plunkett near Athlone, Mount Talbot, Athleague, the Bishop's Palace in Elphin, and Ballanagare House in Ballanagare. Ballanagare House was built by the O'Connors, who were high kings of Ireland in pre-Norman times. Their main seat at Clonalis near Castlerea – an attractive late 19th-century house – is open to the public, and houses a collection of early-Irish papers and books (*see also* 'Where to Stay'). However, Stokestown Park

House, the ancestral home of the Mahons, will lift your spirits. In 1979 the local garage-owner bought it in partnership with the present curator and began a programme of restoration. It is one Big House with a bright future, full of hope and with plenty of community involvement to sustain it. The other great Gaelic family of Roscommon were the MacDermotts; the head of the family was known as the MacDermott Prince of Coolavin. They survived as property-owners right up to the early 20th century.

Northern Roscommon

Keadue to Boyle

Keadue is near the Sligo and Leitrim borders. It is in one of the most attractive parts of the county, with the **Slieve Anierin Range**, also known as the Arigna Mountains, rising to the east. The R284 mountain road from Sligo to Ballyfarnon, further north, gives one a magnificent view over **Lough Meelagh** and Lough Skean. Between Keadue and Ballyfarnon the same road passes close to the edge of Lough Meelagh, where on the shore there is an ancient church site and a holy well called **Kilronan**. Both are associated with St Lasair and St Ronan. St Lasair was the daughter of St Ronan, who founded the original church in the 6th century. It has been burned down twice, and was last rebuilt in the 17th century. You are far away from the bustle of life here in the enchanted and weed-high graveyard. In the ruined church is a modern monument to Turlough O'Carolan, who died in 1733, and was the last in a line of harpists and poets who used to have such status in the Gaelic kingdoms. He is supposed to have composed the melody that is used for 'The Star Spangled Banner'. He was born blind, and somehow came to the home of Mrs MacDermott Roe of Alderford, Ballyfarnan, who befriended and educated him. She provided him with a horse so that he could wander the country playing his harp at the Big Houses. He is buried in the graveyard and to commemorate his memory the O'Carolan Festival is held annually in August. Nearby, surrounded by the ash trees so sacred to the Druids in ancient times, is a clear **well** which flows into the lough. Rosaries and rags ornament the ground, and a large rectangular stone slab is supposed to heal those suffering from backache. The cure entails crawling under the slab, which is balanced on two other stones. A *pattern* is made to the well on the first Sunday of September every year.

Boyle is an attractive town, situated between Lough Key and Lough Gara. The Curlew Hills rise to the northwest and the River Boyle flows through it. The main street was once the avenue to the castle of the King family who later moved to Rockingham House (*see* below). By the river bank is **Boyle Abbey** (*open early April–Oct, daily 9.30–6.30; during rest of year key with caretaker in Abbey House B&B; adm; t (079) 62604*), a ruined Cistercian abbey, founded in 1161 and closely associated with its brother house, the great Mellifont Abbey in County Louth. It was not completed until 1218 and reflects the change of fashion from the round arches of the Romanesque period to the pointed lancet of the early English Gothic style. There is a mix of different styles of arches and lavishly decorated capitals. The monastery was suppressed in 1569 and occupied by Cromwellian soldiers later on; you can see their names carved on the door of the porter's room. Looking onto the River Boyle is **Frybrook House** (*open June–Sept daily 2–6;adm;* **t** *(079) 63513*) which has beautiful 18th-century plasterwork. It is right next to the Main Street in which another 18th-century house, **King House**, has recently been restored and opened as an Interpretative Centre (*open May–mid Oct, daily 10–6, April and late Oct, weekends only 10–6; adm;* **t** *(079) 63242,* **f** *(079) 63243, kinghouseboyle@hotmail.com*). It was once the seat of the King family. An exhibition explores the history of Celtic chiefs, such as the MacDermotts, and the 17th-century English families who amassed huge estates.

East of the town is the great demesne of **Rockingham House**, which belonged in the 18th century to the King family of Rockingham. The Kings later became the Earls of Rockingham and abandoned the house, which subsequently served as a military barracks for the Connaught Rangers, a British army regiment, and then later the Irish army. The house burnt to a shell in 1957 but has now become a tourist attraction. Unfortunately, the character and splendour of the place has been rather lost. The park is now planted with conifer trees which form part of the beautiful **Lough Key Forest Park**, 4¾ miles (3km) east of Boyle on the N4 (*open all year; car park adm;* **t** *(079) 62212*). Here there are walks, a bog garden, picnic sites, a caravan and camping park, boating, fishing and cruising.

About 2 miles (3.2km) away at **Drumanone** is one of the largest dolmens in Ireland, known locally as **Druid's Altar**, which may have been a monument to someone living in the Bronze Age. It is beside the R294, just beyond the railway line, and is found by following a grassy lane to a railway crossing. Close by, on the waters of Lough Gara, three hundred *crannogs* (artificial islands) have been found. These were used by Iron Age farmers as defensive sites for themselves and their cattle. Some were in use up until the 17th century. Thirty-one dug-out wooden boats were also excavated here.

Frenchpark and Around

Southeast of Lough Gara is **Frenchpark**, the birthplace of Douglas Hyde (1860–1949), founder of the Gaelic League and the first president of Ireland. His great cultural and social achievement was to collect stories and folklore from the peasantry. Some of the stories were at least a thousand years old, and had been transferred orally from generation to generation. They were in grave danger of being lost altogether as the use of Gaelic was declining. He was born in the rectory here and retired to **Ratra House** (*not open to the public*) in his old age. You pass the house as you enter Frenchpark from the direction of Ballaghaderreen on the N5. The Church of Ireland church and graveyard in which he is buried is typical of many: a grey, simple Planter's Gothic with a garden of gravestones, flowers and grasses. It is now the **Douglas Hyde Interpretative Centre** (*open May–Sept Tues–Fri 2–5, weekends 2–6; donation requested;* **t** *(0907) 70016*). **Frenchpark House** was built to the designs of Richard Castle (or Cassels), Ireland's greatest Palladian architect. Its interior was dismantled in the 1950s, and the ruin demolished in the 1970s. In the grounds is a five-chambered souterrain. Like all souterrains it is difficult to date, but was used between the Bronze Age and the 5th century AD.

Six miles (9.7 km) southeast of Frenchpark is the **Hill of Rathcroghan**, a beautiful place just off the N5 going southeast to Tulsk. Rathcroghan is a flat-topped, almost circular mound of about 68 yards (62m) in diameter. In the 1st century the legendary AD Queen Maeve, or Medb, also known as a warrior and earth goddess (*see* p.84), had a palace here. A little to the south of the mound is an enclosure known as the **Graveyard of the Kings**. This contains the remains of stone sepulchral chambers and, along with Kells in County Meath and Brugh (Newgrange) in County Louth, is well known as one of the three royal burial places of prehistoric Ireland. In the graveyard is an old redstone pillar known as the **Pillar Stone of Daithi**. Daithi was a pagan king of Ireland who, according to the *Book of Leinster*, conquered Scotland, invaded the Continent and died in the Alps from a stroke of lightning in about AD 428. Forts are scattered all around this area, to a radius of 3 miles (4.8km).

Three miles to the southeast of Rathcroghan, just outside Tulsk, is **Carnfree**, the inauguration mound of the O'Connors, kings of Connacht. It is not much to look at – a grassy mound of earth and stones about 8ft (2.4m) high and 40ft (12m) in circumference; but the views from it are wonderful. It is reputed to be the burial ground of Conn of the Hundred Battles and the three Tuatha Dé Danaan queens: Eire, Fotla and Banba. Here at Croghan, Queen Maeve launched her expedition to capture the Brown Bull of Ulster (*see* p.528). It is difficult to imagine these legendary figures and this place as the seat of power, for the plain is crisscrossed by stone walls and modern farms. In the village of **Tulsk** itself is the *Curachan Aí* Visitor Centre (*open April–Sept, Mon–Sun 10–6; Oct–Mar, Mon–Sat 10–5; t (078) 39268, f (078) 39060, www.cruachanai.com*), an educational museum that arranges tours of the *Cruachan* ('Royal Palace') of Queen Maeve. The tours evoke a sense of the importance of this burial place for the kings of Connacht, said to be one of the most significant of Europe's Celtic royal sites.

Castlerea to Roosky

Just northwest of **Castlerea**, a market town which lies on the attractive wooded land near the River Suck, stands **Clonalis House** (*open June–mid Sept, Tues–Sun 11–5; adm; t (0907) 20014*), the ancestral home of the O'Conor clan. The family can trace itself back to Feredach the Just, a petty king who reigned in AD 75. The O'Conors produced 24 kings for Connacht, and 11 high kings for Ireland. At Clonalis an inauguration stone, not unlike the Stone of Scone, symbolizes the O'Conors' royalty and prestige. The existing Victorian house was built in 1880; the old 18th-century house is now derelict after storm damage in 1961. The land itself has belonged to the O'Conor family for at least 1,500 years, in spite of war and the Penal Laws. Besides furniture and family portraits, the house contains a unique collection of Early Irish documents. Amongst them is a copy of the last Brehon (Gaelic) Law judgement, handed down in about 1580. Also on show is the harp of Turlough O'Carolan, who composed beautiful and haunting airs and three *planxtys* (lively pieces of dance music) for his O'Conor patrons. Within Castlerea itself, **Hell's Kitchen Railway Museum**

and Bar makes for an amusing diversion (*open all year, Mon–Sat 10–6; t (0907) 20181*). Sean Browne's private collection of railway memorabilia has spilled over into the bar, with a restored A55 locomotive built into the wall.

Four miles (6.4km) southeast of Clonalis on the R367 is **Ballintober of Bridget** (named after St Bridget's Well), where there is a ruined **O'Conor castle** (*always accessible*) that withstood many sieges, including one by the Cromwellians. The 13th-century castle was the O'Conor's principal seat after the Anglo-Norman invasion in the 12th century until the beginning of the 18th century, when they moved to Clonalis. It is now an extensive ruin, quadrangular in shape, with towers at each corner and two other towers defending the main entrance on the east.

Glinsk Castle (*always accessible*), south of Ballintober and just over the border into County Galway, is well worth a visit. Glinsk is the shell of one of the best fortified houses in Connacht, with four storeys of mullioned and transomed windows and stacks of chimneys, now used by the starlings and crows. Sir Ulric Burke, who died in 1708, is supposed to have built it, but its machicolated appearance suggests an earlier design. It is approached on an unnumbered road, between the R360 just south of Ballymore or the R362. Turn left at the Kilcroan crossroads.

Returning northeast via the R367, through Tulsk and onto the N5, is **Strokestown**. It sits at the foot of Slieve Bawn, which at 864ft (263m) is quite something in this low-lying countryside. The town is very handsome, with a wide main street laid out by Maurice Mahon, who was created Baron Hartland in 1800, and was impressed by the Ringstrasse in Vienna. Inside the former Church of Ireland church is **St John's County Heritage Centre** (*open Mon–Fri 2.30–4.30; adm free; t (078) 33380*). The church was built in 1819, reputedly to the design of Sir John Nash, and has a fine octagonal nave. If you want to trace your Roscommon ancestry, the centre offers a research service.

One of the most fascinating Big Houses that has survived intact is **Strokestown Park House** (*open April–Oct, daily 11–5.30; adm; t (078) 33013, f (078) 33712, www. strokestownpark.com*), on the eastern outskirts of the town. Strokestown was the ancestral home of the Mahon family from 1660 to 1979. Most of the house was designed by Richard Cassels in the 1730s, but it contains both 17th- and 19th-century interiors. The house and lands were bought by the present owners intact, with all its centuries-old paraphernalia; there is a still-room where the mistress of the house dried herbs and concocted remedies for minor illnesses; and the nursery is full of lovely old toys. The kitchen gallery is a very unusual thing to find in Ireland. From here, the mistress of the house could observe and communicate with her cooks and underservants without having to trail down to the kitchen herself. Weekly menus were dropped from the balcony every Monday. The ballroom-cum-library still has its original furniture. The stables, with magnificent groin-vaulted ceilings and Tuscan pillars, now house a Famine Museum, a startling contrast after the splendours of the mansion. In the parkland surrounding the house pheasants and sheep graze, unconcerned by the occasional car and village boys who have made it their own adventure land. A new pleasure garden has been made within the walls of the old, with a richly coloured herbaceous border, yew arbours, walks and a maze.

Roscommon and Around

Roscommon is the county town and the main shopping centre of the county, as well as a popular angling resort. It is dominated by the castle, the friary and the **old jail** in the Main Street. The last hangman of the jail was not a man, but a woman known as Lady Betty, who was supposed to have agreed to do this grisly job to save her own head from the noose. The Georgian **courthouse**, opposite, has lovely rounded windows rescued by the Bank of Ireland. In the 8th century St Coman founded a monastery here from which the town gets its name, but there is sadly nothing left of it today. South of the town centre, off Abbey Street, is the ruined **Dominican friary** founded by Felim O'Conor, king of Connacht in 1253. His tomb is sculptured with figures representing gallowglasses – fierce warriors from the west of Scotland, hired by the Irish kings to fight the Norman and English invaders.

Roscommon Castle, north of the town off Castle Street (*always accessible*), was built in 1269 by Roger d'Ufford, Lord Justice for Ireland. Four years later it was razed to the ground by the Irish, built anew, and taken again by the O'Connors in 1340, who held it for more than two hundred years. It is a typical Anglo-Norman fortress, quadrangular, with a tower at each angle and one on each side of the gateway. It began to fall into decay in the last years of the 17th century. The Roman Catholic **Church of the Sacred Heart** off Abbey Street is built of local cut limestone and was completed in 1925. Over the main door are lovely glass mosaics constructed by the famous Italian firm of Salviati & Co. It also has a replica of the famous processional Cross of Cong, made in Fuerty in 1123 of oak decorated with animal designs in bronze gilt.

Five miles (8km) to the west of Roscommon on the R366 is the village of **Fuerty** itself, with the remains of a Franciscan church in which at least a hundred priests were massacred in Cromwellian times by a Colonel Ormsby. The colonel, who was buried here, was known as *Riobard na nGligearnach* ('Robert of the Jingling Harness'), whose cruelties are still remembered in local stories. Between Fuerty and Athleague on an unnumbered road by the River Suck is the **Castlestrange** demesne. The house is a ruin, but under some trees is an egg-shaped Iron Age boulder known as the Castlestrange Stone. It is covered in whorls and spirals which seem to have been potent ornamental symbols, and were often used in the pre-Christian Celtic La Téne style. The land is privately owned, but it is unlikely that anyone will object to you visiting the stone.

The N61 from Roscommon to Athlone stays close to Lough Ree, but not close enough to get a proper look at it. If you cut down a small country lane to **Galey Castle**, just beyond Knockcroghery village, you will see the island of Inishcloraun in Lough Ree, where the legendary Queen Maeve retired to ponder on her eventful life and to find some peace (*see* **Old Gods and Heroes**, p.84). She used to bathe in a clear, fresh pool here, but an enemy pursued and killed her with a stone. From **Lecarrow** another minor road leads you down to the **Castle of Rindown** (*always accessible*), a great fortress in the 13th century with a rectangular keep within curtain walls. In the shelter of its stone walls a medieval Norman village grew up. A defensive ditch was built across the peninsula on which it was built, and it became one of the bases for the conquest of Connacht. Now it is an ivy-covered ruin and place of peace: hardly a soul wanders down the mile-long stretch.

County Sligo

Writing in the 19th century about her tour of Ireland, Mrs S. C. Hall dismisses Sligo in a few words with these lines: 'in scenery and character it so nearly resembles the adjoining county of Mayo that we pass over Sligo'. Nothing could be further from the truth. Sligo is somehow civilized, unlike the other counties in Connacht: there is order among the lakes and the glens, the great table mountains and open beaches.

From an artistic standpoint Sligo is Yeats just as Wessex is Hardy, for there is hardly a knoll or stream in the county that did not stir his imagination. His brother Jack (1871–1957) used paint instead of words to capture the faces of old men at the Sligo

Getting There and Around

By Air

There is a daily service between Sligo and Dublin during the week.
Sligo Airport, Strandhill, t (071) 68280/68318, *info@sligoairport.com*.

By Rail

Daily service from Sligo to Dublin via Boyle, t (071) 69888.

By Bus

Bus Eireann operates daily from Sligo to Dublin, Ballina, Derry and Galway. Local bus services also link the villages of Inniscrone and Tobercurry.
Sligo Bus Station, Lord Edward Street, t (071) 60066.

By Bike

Call North West Tourism, t (071) 43149, for details of their 'Hiking and Biking Guide'. For bike hire and equipment, try the following:
Gary's Cycles, 5 Quay Street, Sligo Town, t (071) 45418, f (071) 43149, *gary@iol.ie*.
Flanagan Cycles, Market Yard, Sligo Town, t (071) 44477.

Festivals

February
Yeats Weekend Winter School, t (071) 60291, *info@yeats-sligo.com*.

June–July
Sligo Arts Festival, Sligo Town, t (071) 69802.
Sligo County *Fleadh*, Ballintogher, t (071) 64250.
Seisiún, Sligo Town. Traditional festival of music, story-telling and dance, t (071) 64250.
South Sligo Summer School of Traditional Music and Dancing, Tubbercurry, t (071) 85010.

August
Ballymote Heritage Weekend, t (071) 83380.
Gurteen Agricultural and Horse Show, Gurteen. Held at the end of the month, t (071) 65082.
Joe Fallon Traditional Festival, Collooney, t (071) 30962.
Michael Coleman Traditional Festival, Gurteen, t (071) 82250/82599.
Warriors Festival, Strandhill, t (071) 68633. This incorporates the **Culleenamore Horse and Pony Races** and the **Warriors' Run** to Queen Maeve's legendary grave, on Knocknarea Mountain.

October
Ballintogher Feis, Ballintogher, t (071) 64250.
Sligo International Choral Festival, Sligo Town, t (071) 60780.

November
Sean Nós **Singing**, Coleman Heritage Centre, Gurteen, t (071) 82599, f (071) 82602, *ceolaracoleman@eircom.net*.

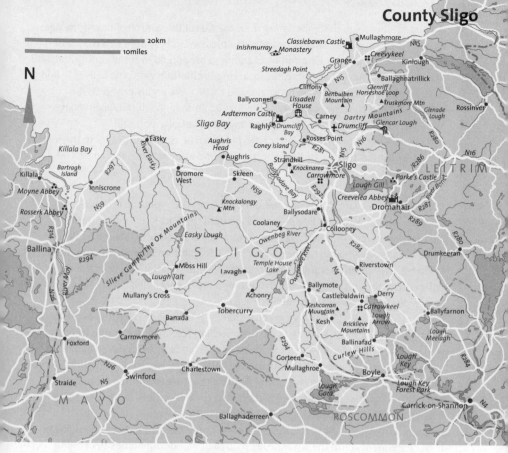

races; or the special quality of the light that bathes figures on the beaches – a light that is very like that which plays around the coast of Brittany. Jack is always quoted as saying, 'Sligo was my school and the sky above it', and it was William Butler Yeats' wish that he should be buried under 'bare Ben Bulben's head'. All the places which inspired Yeats are still largely untouched; they are brought to your notice occasionally by discreet Tourism Ireland notices which quote the name and the line from the poem in which they are mentioned.

The two brothers became intimately bound up in Sligo through their maternal grandparents, the Pollexfens, who were millers and small shipowners. They used to spend their school holidays with them, travelling from London where their father, John, tried to earn a living as a portrait painter. They occupy such an important part in the artistic and literary history of Ireland in the early 20th century that one can hardly do justice to them in a guide book. Suffice it to say that if you obtain a copy of William Butler's collected poems and make sure you visit the county museum to see the paintings by Jack, you will know why.

Besides being so beautiful Sligo is famous for its traditional fiddle music, for fishing and for its fabulous hoard of prehistoric remains. In the vicinity of Carrowmore there is a huge cemetery with tombs dating from the Mesolithic and Neolithic Stone Ages. Close by is the romantic Knocknarea Mountain, crowned by Maeve's Cairn, one of the highlights of a Sligo tour. Ring-forts and *crannogs* are spread over the county and date from the Bronze Age. At this time, the local king or chieftain would have lived in and ruled from the fort. There were no towns, and cattle were highly prized. So it is understandable that the epic story of the *Táin Bó Cuilnge*, in which Queen Maeve plays such a central part, should describe a war over a bull (*see* p.528).

The people are mainly sheep- and cattle-farmers. The climate is similar to the rest of Ireland; and it has the wonderful light that is found all along the west coast.

History

The chief Gaelic families of Sligo were the O'Haras, O'Conors and O'Dowds; and since the Anglo-Normans did not reach Sligo until the mid-13th century, these families continued with their own private quarrels and territorial struggles. When the Normans did arrive, in the persons of the Fitzgeralds and the Burkes and their followers, they failed to maintain their grants of land. Therefore, up until the early 17th century, the Celtic culture and native Brehon laws continued to function alongside the English administrative structure.

From 1585 onwards there was a gradual change in land ownership and in the Celtic order of society. Elizabethans and later Cromwellian soldiers were granted lands, which in numerous cases were unoccupied church lands, or lands which had never been permanently settled. The population of Ireland was very small at that time, and many of the farmers moved their cattle from one pasture to another. Of course, some tribal lands were confiscated and granted to new settlers, but on the whole English families settled into Sligo fairly peacefully. The names Phibbs, Crofton, Perceval, Ormsby, Parke, Irwin, Gore, Jones and Cooper date from these times. Today their descendants farm the land and keep up their wonderful homes by opening them up to guests. You can stay with the O'Haras at Coopershill House or the Percevals at Temple House (*see* 'Where to Stay', p.357). Each family represents a strand of Sligo's history.

Sligo Town was badly sacked and burned in the 1641 Rebellion, and later was held for the Jacobites in the wars of the 1690s. The whole county suffered terribly during the famine of the 1840s. Thousands died or emigrated to the New World; this struck the death knell for the Gaelic peasant culture, which had so far survived the vicissitudes of the centuries since the English invaded. Gaelic ceased to be the everyday language of the peasants, and many of the folk stories and traditions would have been lost forever if it had not been for enthusiasts and antiquarians such as Lady Gregory (1852–1932) and Yeats. They and others collected much folk material and later, in 1904, they and J. M. Synge (1871–1909) set up the Abbey Theatre in Dublin, which produced many Irish sagas.

In the 18th and 19th centuries Sligo Town was a large port. Its industries were distilling, brewing, linen manufacture, milling, rope and leather-making. The famine hit the economy very hard, and it took years to recover. Today, the county is prosperous, with most people working in agriculture.

Sligo Town and Environs

Sligo, with only 17,000 souls, is the largest town in the northwest of Ireland. It has a great deal of colourful charm, and a feeling of centuries-old importance and prosperity. People come from their farms in the countryside to shop, socialize, go to the cinema or theatre and to attend the large hospital. The town centres around two bridges over the River Garavogue. There are attractive 18th-century buildings and some rather ugly 20th-century office blocks, hotels and supermarkets. The streets are always busy and quite congested with traffic, so if you have a car it would be wise to park it in the car park off Wine Street.

In the **Anglican cathedral** in St John Street, designed by Richard Cassels, is a brass memorial to Susan Mary Yeats, the mother of William and Jack. The cathedral itself dates from the 14th century, and has been restored several times. It is a cruciform shape, in the perpendicular style, with a huge tower. The **Catholic cathedral**, made out of local limestone, is next door. This Romanesque building has a beautiful high altar, and a fine peal of bells. It was completed in 1874. **Sligo Abbey**, a graceful ruined Dominican priory off Abbey Street, was founded in 1252 but was rebuilt in the 15th century after being burnt. It then suffered the usual fate of Irish monasteries, and was destroyed by the Cromwellians. The abbey ruins have been tidied up and some conservation work has been carried out by the Office of Public Works. Inside are monuments to the local Gaelic nobility, and some fine cloisters. The tower and the cloister, the east window and the high altar were added in the 15th century. The key to the abbey is available at any time from the caretaker; directions to his house are on the entrance gate. **Sligo Town Hall** and **Courthouse** were erected in the late 19th century, and you can visit them in the course of an interesting walking route devised by and available from the tourist office. As you wander, you may notice the shabby back yards of the houses sloping down to the River Garavogue, although the owners of the shops and pubs in the streets have made an effort to look after their handsome Edwardian fronts.

You can easily spend a delightful couple of hours in the **County Museum and Art Gallery** housed in the County Library building in Stephen Street (*open Tues–Sun 10.30–12.30 and 2–4.30; adm*). The custodians are charming, and the collection of pictures by Jack Yeats, Paul Henry, Nora McGuinness, Sean Keating and others is inspiring. The **Sligo County Museum** (*open July–Sept, Tues–Sun 10.30–noon and 2–4.30, Oct–June, 2–4.30pm only; adm; t (071) 42212*) in the building attached to the library has exhibits of prehistoric interest, items on folk life and on the Anglo-Irish war of 1919–1921. It also has a special section on the Yeats family – William, Jack and sisters Lily and Holly. At one time they set up a publishing press and started different cottage industries. W. B. Yeats won the Nobel Prize in 1923 and this is proudly displayed. The **Sligo Art Gallery** (*t (071) 45847/42693*), in the Yeats Memorial Building at Hyde Bridge, holds impressive travelling art shows by national and international artists. It also contains papers and books of special interest to Yeats scholars. There is also a new gallery, the **Model Arts and Nilard Gallery** on The Mall (*t (071) 41405*), which is a venue for travelling exhibitions and is developing an art collection of its own.

Tourist Information

Sligo: Temple Street, t (071) 61201; *open
all year*;
also at the Yeats Building, Hyde Bridge,
t (071) 38772; *open all year*.

Shopping

Books
Book Nest, Rockwood Parade (beside river),
t (071) 46949.
Keohane's, Castle Street, Sligo, t (071)
42597/47740. Irish interest books.
The Winding Stair, Hyde Bridge, t (071) 41244.

Crafts
Attic Crafts, Wine and Quay Streets, Sligo,
t (071) 44660. Local work.
Carraig Donn, O'Connell Street, Sligo, t (071)
44158. Aran sweaters and other knitwear.
The Cat & the Moon, 4 Castle Street,
Sligo, t (071) 43377. Pretty handicrafts
and jewellery.
Michael Quirke, Wine Street, Sligo, t (071)
42624. Sculptures in wood from
mythological themes.

Delicacies
Cosgrove's, 32 Market Street, Sligo,
t (071) 42809. Old-fashioned deli, crammed
with goodies.
Gourmet Parlour, Bridge Street, Sligo, t (071)
44617. Delectable chocolate cakes and
breads. They also offer a catering service.
Tír Na Nóg, Gratton Street, Sligo, t (071) 62752.
Fresh vegetables, Irish cheeses, seaweed,
herbs, shampoos and soaps.

Pottery and Crystal
Michael Kennedy Ceramics, Church Street,
Sligo, t (071) 62586.
Sligo Craft Network, 19 Castle Street, Sligo.

Sligo Crystal, 2 Hyde Bridge, Sligo, t (071)
43440.

Tweeds and Knitwear
Mullaney Bros, 9 O'Connell Street, Sligo, t (071)
40718. Tweeds and cashmeres.

Sports and Activities

Boat Hire
Blue Lagoon Bar, Sligo, t (071) 42530. Boat hire
on Lough Gill.

Fishing
For advice on **coarse fishing** in the
Owenbeg River and Glencar Lough, on **sea-
angling** and for tackle and equipment,
contact the following:
Barton Smith, 4 Hyde Bridge, Sligo Town,
t (071) 42356/46111.
Irish Angling Services, Ballyconnell, Co. Cavan,
t (049) 952 6258.
Shannon Regional Fisheries, t (062) 455171.
For Northern Fisheries waters information
and share certificates.
For **sea-angling** advice and boat hire,
contact:
Tommy McCallion, Rosses Point, t (071) 42391.
Lomax Boats and Angling, Mullaghmore,
t (071) 66124.

Golf
County Sligo Golf Club, Rosses Point, t (071)
77134. Championship links course.
Strandhill Golf Club, Strandhill,
t (071) 68188.

Internet Access
Cyco Internet Café, 19 O'Connell Street, Sligo,
t (071) 40082. *Open Mon–Sat 10–7.*
Galaxy Cyber Café, Millbrook, Riverside,
Sligo, t (071) 40441. *Open daily
10am–midnight.*

The town is lucky in having the large municipal **Doorly Park**, bordering the River
Garavogue. It has some lovely walks with wonderful views of Lough Gill and the
mountains. Inside the park is **Sligo Racecourse**, where races take place in April, June
and August. One of the highlights of a tour of Sligo is a boat ride to watch the pretty
wooded lake scenery of Lough Gill pass by (*see* 'Sports and Activities', above). It is of
course possible to drive right around Lough Gill, taking the R286 to Dromahair in

Pleasure Cruises

Wild Rose Waterbus, t (071) 64266, or t 0872 598869. Cruises on Lough Gill accompanied by recitations of Yeats' poetry, visiting *The Lake Isle of Innisfree* and Parke's Castle. The 60mins' tour departs from Doorly Park or Parke's Castle in Sligo Town, Mar–Oct.

Pony-trekking

Sligo Riding Centre, Carrowmore, t (071) 61353.

Seaweed Baths

Celtic Sea Baths, Strandhill, Sligo, t (071) 68686. A treat not to be missed.

Surfing

Catch some waves at **Strandhill**. For advice, information and equipment contact:
Call of the Wild, Stephen Street, Sligo, t (071) 46905.
Malibu Surf Shop, Strandhill, t (071) 68302.

Tours

There are signposted **walking tours** around Sligo Town and **guided tours** every weekday in summer; contact the tourist office for details.

Where to Stay and Eat

Sligo Town t (071–)

Hillside, Kilsellagh, Enniskillen Road, Sligo, t 42808, f 44461 (*inexpensive*). Comfortable old farmhouse, home cooking and log fires in the company of the Stuart family. *Open Easter–Oct.*

Primrose Grange House, Knocknarea, outside Sligo, t 62005 (*inexpensive*). This farmhouse was built as a charter school in the 18th century and has a splendid position overlooking the glen and the sea. Mrs Carter has won an award for the breakfasts.

Coriander Restaurant, Stephen Street, Sligo, t 44135 (*expensive–moderate*). Stylishly decorated restaurant near Hyde Bridge in the town centre. Locally-grown produce is used in imaginative seafood and meat dishes. Snacks are served in the **Dooney Bar**, next door.

Fiddlers Creek, Rockwood Parade, Sligo, t 41866 (*expensive–moderate*). Serves a variety of traditional or Louisiana-style steaks, and dishes such as crispy honey roast duckling, wild mushroom tagliatelle, salmon, swordfish and sea bass. In-house DJs and live bands four evenings a week.

Bistro Bianconi, 44 O'Connell Street, Sligo, t 41744 (*moderate*). Pasta and pizza to take away or eat in. Pleasant modern interior.

Hargadon's, O'Connell Street, Sligo, t 70933 (*inexpensive*). Atmospheric pub with cosy snugs, old advertisements and mirrors decorated with gold painted slogans of whiskey and Guinness. Lunchtime pub fare.

Kate's Kitchen, 3 Castle Street, Sligo, t 43022 (*inexpensive*). Deli salads and sandwiches to take away.

Entertainment and Nightlife

Theatre

The Factory, Sligo, t (071) 70431. Productions from the Blue Raincoat Theatre Company.
The Hawk's Well Theatre, Temple Street, Sligo, t (071) 61526/61518, *www.hawkswell.com*, *hawkswell@eircom.net*. Revivals and contemporary Irish theatre.

Traditional Music

Fureys, Bridge Street, Sligo, t (071) 43525. Mon, Tues, Thurs and Sun evenings.
Leitrim Bar, the Mall, Sligo, t (071) 43721.
McGarrigle's Bar, O'Connell Street, t (071) 71193. Thurs and Sun evenings. Lunch also.
McLaughlin's, t (071) 44209. Nightly sessions.

County Leitrim and then the R287 to the N4, going back into Sligo Town. Don't forget to go around **Parkes Castle**, just over the border in County Leitrim (*see* p.369).

Strandhill and Carrowmore

If you take the R292 going west of Sligo Town, after 3 miles (4.8km) you come to **Strandhill**, a popular village resort on the rocky coast (also reached by city bus from

Sligo). It has rather too much concrete and is not greatly attractive, but the strand is superb. The hard sand stretches for miles and the waves are good for bodysurfing. Huge dunes dominate the shore to the southwest of the sea-front car park, and you might find beach pebbles with interesting fossil remains. Just as you enter Strandhill on the R292 is **Dolly's Cottage** (*open July–Aug daily 2–6;* **t** *(071) 68034/67564*), a typical example of an early 19th-century rural dwelling. It consists of a few simply furnished rooms, a mud floor, and a thatched roof.

From every direction in this area you can see **Knocknarea Mountain**, which is topped by Maeve's Cairn. To climb it, continue along the R292 for a few miles and take the little road marked 'Glen', which ascends the lower slopes. (You will know if you have gone too far because just beyond the turning for the Glen road is a restaurant called Glen Lodge.) From the Glen road, you get a lovely view of the hummocky green fields down to the shore. You will come to a farm where it is possible to leave your car, as long as you are tactful and polite. The walk to the summit (1,978ft/603m) is along a track of curiously moulded limestone, with orchids and primroses growing either side. The cairn itself is 33ft (10m) high by 197ft (6m) wide, a huge mound of weather-beaten stone. It is reported to be the burial place of Maeve, Queen of Connacht, who challenged the forces of Ulster to a battle over a bull. The story is contained in the *Táin Bó Cuilgne*, the longest and most important of the Ulster cycle of heroic tales (*see* p.528). The origins of the *Táin* are ancient and pre-Christian, although it was actually written down by monks in the 12th century. Maeve is thought to have lived around the time of Christ, but the cairn may well be Bronze Age. Archaeologists believe that within it there may be a passage tomb similar to that at Newgrange in County Meath, which was built by Stone Age farmers in about 3000 BC. As yet no one has excavated it, probably because it would be very expensive to undo its massive structure – and it would be very sad if they did.

Continue on through the crossroads at Knocknarea Church, and instead of rejoining the R292 take the turn southeast. You are now on the right road for **Carrowmore**, about 3 miles (4.8km) further on. This amazing Megalithic Stone Age cemetery spreads over many small fields. The excavated burial chambers contain cremated remains dating from 3000 BC. There are circles, passage graves and dolmens – each one has a little notice warning that it is a national monument, but unfortunately since the 19th century over a hundred have been destroyed, and only 40 remain.

Heading back towards Sligo town you see **Cummeen Strand**, which stretches up to Rosses Point. This expanse of sand and water is mentioned in Yeats' poem *Red Hanrahan's Song*; here the River Garavogue flows into the sea. You can walk or drive out to **Coney Island** from the Strandhill side when the tide is out. (Coney is supposed to have given its name to the New York pleasure island.) Only a few people live on it, and the beaches surrounding it are tranquil. You will be able to watch wild duck and waders; during the winter months brent geese feed on the mud flats.

Rosses Point to Glencar

Rosses Point, a seaside village and resort, is 5 miles (8km) north of Sligo and reached by city bus from Sligo or by following the R281 along the curve of Sligo Bay.

The village is long and straggling with plenty of pubs and places to eat. It has a first-class golf course, used for the West of Ireland Amateur Open Golf Championship every year during the Easter weekend. At Dead Man's Point the yacht club and an open-air swimming pool are a hive of activity and colour and, during the summer, pleasure boat trips around Sligo Bay leave daily from Rosses Point pier. There are many Dead Man's Points all over this part of the coast, probably because the tides are treacherous. This one is supposed to owe its name to a long-dead foreign seaman who was buried rapidly at sea because the boat had to be away before the tide changed. He slid into the water accompanied by a loaf of bread, just in case he was not quite dead.

A trip to **Glencar** is a very pleasant excursion if you are staying in Sligo Town. Leave Sligo on the N16 for Manorhamilton, and after about 10 miles (16km), a left turn will signpost you to **Glencar Waterfall**. The road takes you along the edge of Glencar Lough, and steep-sided mountains rear up against the sky. The Differeen River feeds the lough whilst the Drumcliff River runs out the opposite end. This spot is popular with salmon and sea trout anglers. A small car park marks the path to the waterfall, which drops 49ft (15m); it is particularly impressive after heavy rains. In Yeats' poem 'The Stolen Child', he talks of the Glencar pools 'that scarce could bathe a star'. The pools are now bordered by a concrete path but are still very beautiful, with the noisy stream and a mass of rhododendrons around them.

Around County Sligo

North Sligo

Drumcliff and Lissadell House

If you follow the N15 northwards towards Donegal, after 5 miles (8km) you will find yourself in **Drumcliff**. This ancient Christian monastic site still has the remains of the old monastic enclosure and a fine 10th-century high cross carved with biblical scenes. St Columba (*see* pp.75–6 and 370) founded a monastery at Drumcliff in the 6th century before sailing away to Iona. The road divides the site in two with the cross on your right and the stump of a round tower on the left. The graveyard of the Church of Ireland church, also to your right, contains the **grave of W. B. Yeats**. Yeats' great-grandfather was the rector of this simple Georgian Protestant church, and the poet is buried here, under his beloved Ben Bulben. He has a very plain headstone with his own epitaph 'Cast a cold eye on life, on Death/Horseman, pass by'.

Just past Drumcliff, to the west an unnumbered road via Carney leads you to **Lissadell House** (*open June–mid Sept, Mon–Sat 10.30–12.30, 2–4.15; guided tour; adm; t (071) 63150, lissadellhouse@aol.com*), with its grounds swallowed up by Forestry Commission conifers. The house is the home of the Gore-Booths, a family who came to Sligo during the early 17th century. Like many of the Irish gentry, the Gore-Booths were great travellers and worked all over the British Empire. They brought home all

Shopping

Crafts
Lake Isle Crafts and Teas, Innisfree, Ballintoher.
The Mews Art Gallery and Coffee Shop,
Rathcormac, t (071) 43689.

Pottery
Benbulben Pottery, Rathcormac, t (071) 46929.

Sports and Activities

Fishing
Coarse and game fishing can be found on
the Owenmore River and the lakes in its
system, which produce marvellous pike, bream
and rudd. The sister river of the Owenmore,
the Owenbeg, is known for its sea trout, as is
Glencar Lough. Sea-angling can be done from
the shore at Inniscrone Strand, Inniscrone Pier,
Easky Quay, Kilrusheighter Strand,
Mullaghmore Pier, Mermaids Cove and Milk
Haven.
Lough Arrow Boats, t (071) 65491. Boat rental.
Brendan Merriman, Mullaghmore, t (072)
41874.
Mayfly Holidays, t (071) 65065. Also for boat
rental on Lough Arrow.

Golf
Inniscrone Golf Club, Inniscrone, t (096) 36297,
f (096) 36657. A high quality course amidst
magnificent scenery.
Tubbercurry Golf Club, t (071) 85849.

Pleasure Cruises
There are waterbus tours available on Lough
Gill, or excursions can be made to Inishmurray
Island. The boat goes out to the island
April–Oct. Contact:
Rodney Lomax, Mullaghmore, Cliffony, t (071)
66124.
Peter Power, Mullaghmore, t (0872) 576268.
Tommy McAllion, Rosses Point, t (071) 42391.
Wild Rose Waterbus, t (071) 64266. Tours of
Lough Gill; see also p.353.

Pony-trekking
Ard Chuain Equestrian Centre, Corballa, near
Ballina, t/f (096) 45084.
Horse Holiday Farm Ltd, Temple Mount,
Grange, t (071) 66152, f (071) 66400,
hhf@eircom.net. Daily pony hire or 7- to 14-
day trail rides through the mountains and
along the magnificent coastline. You stay in
B&Bs en route or, with a more expensive
package, in country house hotels.
Woodlands Equestrian Centre, Tubbercurry,
t (071) 84207, f (071) 84220.

Seaweed Baths
Kilcullen's Seaweed Baths, Cliff Road,
Inniscrone, t (096) 36238, f (096) 36895. A
luxurious and very relaxing experience;
there is a nice tea room attached. Open
May–Oct and winter weekends.

Surfing
Easkey and Inniscrone are good spots. For
advice, information and equipment contact:

sorts of weird and wonderful things, and Lissadell is a rich repository of furniture,
pictures and books. Sir Robert Gore-Booth built the house during the troubled years
which culminated in the famine of the 1840s, and mortgaged the estate to help the
poor during the famine. His son Sir Henry is famous for sailing to the rescue of the
Arctic explorer Leigh Smith. The following generation included Eva and Constance,
both of whom were great friends of W. B. Yeats, who stayed in the house frequently
during the second decade of the 20th century. Constance married a Polish artist and
became Countess Markievicz, and became deeply involved with the struggle for Irish
independence. Having won a seat for the Sinn Fein party, she, like the rest of them,
refused to take up her seat in Westminster and sat instead for the Revolutionary
Parliament called the Dail Eireann as the minister for Labour. The building is in plain
Georgian style with a cavernous porch. It is in a lovely situation looking onto the sea,
Knocknarea and Ben Bulben, but it is also very large and a little run-down. In the

Easkey Surf and Information Centre, Easkey, t (096) 49020.

Where to Stay

Ardtarmon House, Ardtarmon, 11 miles northwest of Sligo on the Drumcliff–Raghly road, t (071) 63156, *www.ardtarmon.com* (*moderate*). A peaceful country house setting with mountain views where a 19th-century ambience permeates your stay. Simple breakfasts are prepared by friendly proprietors Charles and Christa Henry, who operate the estate and whose family home this is. There is an easy walk to the sea nearby. *Dinner available with advance notice.*

Beach Hotel, The Harbour, Mullaghmore, t (071) 66103 (*moderate*). Comfortable old hotel in a lovely setting on the seafront; pool, gym and sauna included.

Markree Castle, Collooney, t (071) 67800, f (071) 67840, *www.markreecastle.ie, markree@iol.ie* (*luxury*). County Sligo goes in for rather grand country houses. This castle, with its impressive castellated façade, has three interconnecting reception rooms with tall mirrors and Louis Philippe-style plasterwork dating from 1845. The castle has been sympathetically restored by the owners, Charles and Mary Cooper, who have built up a reputation for imaginative food and a pleasant ambience in the **Knockmuldowney Restaurant**, with its extensive wine list. Rooms are very comfortable with private bathrooms, and the views over the surrounding countryside are superb. Formal gardens lead down to the River Unsin.

Temple House, Ballymote, t (071) 83329, f (071) 83808, *www.templehouse.ie, accom@templehouse.ie* (*moderate*). A rambling mansion which was made even grander in the 1860s by a nabob ancestor of the present occupants. It has a lovely, slightly faded Victorian feel, with original half-tester beds in huge bedrooms, ancient curtains and oriental *objets d'art*. The Perceval family are committed to organic farming, and their breakfasts are particularly delicious. Fresh produce is served in the dining room (*luxury*), with lamb and beef from the estate farm and dishes such as Cashel blue cheese tart followed by pear croustade. Boats are available to fish for pike and perch on Temple House Lake. Shooting for woodcock, snipe and duck on the estate can be arranged. Please be aware that Sandy Perceval is chemically sensitive, so scented cosmetics and perfumes should not be worn. *Dinner available with advance notice; vegetarian dishes available with notice.*

Coopershill House, Riverstown, t (071) 65108, f (071) 65466, *www.coopershill.com, ohara@coopershill.com* (*luxury–expensive*). This Georgian mansion set in its own wooded parkland contains the most delightful aspects of a gentleman's residence. Spacious rooms are filled with furniture and books, and are warmed by crackling log fires. The bedrooms

centre is a two-storey hallway lined with Doric columns leading to a double staircase of Kilkenny marble. Downstairs in the vast kitchen you can have tea and coffee made under conditions reminiscent of the 1920s; there is no drinking-water or electricity in this part of the house, and buckets of water have to be lugged down the stairs. The forestry lands around Lissadell House have picnic sites and in the winter months you may be lucky and see skeins of barnacle geese wheeling in the sky, since there is a huge colony of them here. The two south-facing beaches that border the forest are reputedly the warmest in the county.

Raghly and the Gleniff Horseshoe Loop

The road past Lissadell continues west towards the tiny fishing harbour of **Raghly**, which is surrounded by stunning views of Drumcliff Bay and the mountains all around. On the way there you will pass **Ardtarmon Castle**, built in the 17th-century as contain four-poster beds and a connecting bathroom. A clean and crisp air is maintained by owners Brian and Wendy O'Hara. Dinner is also available.

Ross House, Riverstown, **t** (071) 65140 (*inexpensive*). Comfortable and friendly farmhouse accommodation from Mrs Hill-Wilkinson. Good for children, with lots of activity on the farm.

Cromleach Lodge, Castlebaldwin, **t** (071) 65155, **f** (071) 65455, *www.cromleach.com*, *info@cromleach.com* (*luxury–expensive*). Looks a bit souless from the outside, but is in fact very comfortable. Delicious breakfasts are served before charming views over Lough Arrow.

Arrow Lodge, Kilmactranny, southeast of Castlebaldwin, **t** (079) 66298, **f** (079) 66299, *www.arrowlodge.com*, *rob@arrowlodge.com* (*moderate–inexpensive*). Fishing lodge with simple but pleasant rooms.

Self-catering

North West Tourism, Sligo, **t** (071) 61201. Cottages on Lissadell House estate. North West Tourism books a number of other properties in the area, including a restored gamekeeper's cottage on Lough Gill.

Ardtarmon House, Ardtarmon, **t** (071) 63156, *www.ardtarmon.com* (*moderate*). Five self-catering cottages that are attached to the estate (*see above*).

William Coleman, Lavagh, Tobercurry, **t** (071) 84053 (*expensive–moderate*). Two-bedroom thatched cottage near Tubbercurry and the mountains.

Eating Out

Knockmuldowney Restaurant, Markree Castle, Collooney, **t** (071) 67800 (*luxury*). Tasty food, an excellent wine list and friendly service in an atmospheric early-19th-century castle. *Dinner 7–9pm, except when booked for large wedding parties (usually Sat eves); Sun lunch 1–3pm.*

Glebe House, Coolaney Road, Collooney, **t** (071) 67787 (*moderate*). Homely French cooking with lots of herbs and vegetables from the garden. *Dinner only from 6.30pm; book in advance.*

Yeats Tavern, Drumcliffe, **t** (071) 63117 (*moderate–inexpensive*). Offers good salads and facilities for children, with a bar-café and restaurant area.

Cromleach Lodge, Castlebaldwin, **t** (071) 65155, **f** (071) 65455, *www.cromleach.com*, *info@cromleach.com* (*luxury*). Michelin-rated; *see* above. *Dinner only.*

Entertainment and Nightlife

Traditional Music

Ellen's Pub, Maugherow, near Grange, **t** (071) 63761. A tourist attraction in its own right, with a thatched roof and frequent *seisúns*.

Beach Bar, Aughris, **t** (071) 66703.

The Thatch, Ballisodare, **t** (071) 67288. Well known for its *seisúns*; lies by the bridge on the Dublin road.

Traditional Restaurant, Gorteen.

a semi-fortified manor house by an ancestor of the Gore-Booths. It is privately owned and has been restored.

Continuing along the coast on this tiny unnumbered road, on your left you will see **Knocklane Hill**. This was the site of a Celtic promontory fort and a martello tower, built as a lookout post in the uncertain times of the Napoleonic era. It is a short and exhilarating climb to the top of the hill, and on a fine day you will be rewarded with unsurpassable views. The beaches along this stretch of coastline are very isolated and there is much bird-life. Sand used to cover much of the headland until bent grass was sown in the 19th century by Lord Palmerston, the British prime minister. The beach at **Streedagh**, signposted to the left, has magnificent sand dunes, and the limestone rocks contain fossil coral formed about four million years ago. All around the coast are wrecks of the warships of the Spanish Armada. 'The Rock of the Spaniards', just north of Streedagh, was the place where in 1588 three Armada ships foundered.

Contemporary accounts tell us that 1,100 bodies were laid out on the beach at a time, and that most of the men who reached the shore were stripped and killed.

It is not surprising that the people of **Inishmurray**, 4 miles (6.4km) off the coast, abandoned their lands and houses in the 1950s, for life here was very hard. This island used to be famous for its brand of *poteen*. Now it is famous for the Early Christian relics that have survived: beehive huts, small rectangular stone oratories, open-air altars, pillars and tombstones are dotted all over the island. The **monastery** in the middle of the island was probably built on a Druidic site, for one of the oratories is known as the Temple of Fire, and round about are quite a few stones, known as 'cursing stones', that are thought to have been used in Druidic rituals. Trips out to the island can be organized easily throughout the summer months from Mullaghmore (*see* 'Sports and Activities', p.356).

North of Cliffony a rock peninsula projects into Donegal Bay. Its sandy beach has encouraged the growth of the small resort of **Mullaghmore**. On the headland here you will see a Victorian Gothic castle – **Classiebawn**, once the home of Earl Mountbatten of Burma. This place became the focus of attention in 1979 when the Earl and members of his family were killed by an IRA bomb on their boat in the bay below. The house is not open to the public. Return to the N15, and at the hamlet of **Creevykeel** by the crossroads, stop to look at a court tomb that is regarded as one of the finest in Ireland. It consists of a circular ritual court bounded by upright stones. Opposite the entrance are two burial chambers under a lintel which date from between 3500 and 3000 BC.

Cross over the N15 and continue for 5¾ miles (9km) along the unnumbered road leading to Ballaghnatrillick Bridge. Cross the bridge and take the right-hand turn onto the **Gleniff Horseshoe Loop**. This road runs into the heart of the Dartry Mountains, with their tumbling streams and desolate limestone cliffs. A left turn takes you to Truskmore Mountain, which rises to 2,115ft (645m). From the car park for the RTE transmitter station, a short walk takes you to the top for a wonderful view. Close to the summit are the entrances to Ireland's highest caves. These form part of an ancient underground system truncated by the glacier that formed the Gleniff valley. One of these caves is supposed to be where Diarmuid and Grainne slept when they were fleeing from the wrath of King Fionn MacCumhaill. Diarmuid and Grainne are the Irish equivalent of Tristan and Iseult: every cave, dolmen and *cromlech* seems to be named after them (*see* **Old Gods and Heroes**, pp.82 and 84). From here, you can follow the loop road around to Cliffoney and back on to the N15, or turn left along the old route and rejoin the N15 at the Mullaghnaneane crossroads.

West Sligo

Killala Bay, Sligo Bay and into the Ox Mountains

The western parts of County Sligo make up a variety of handsome seascapes, mountainous bogland and pretty lakes. The coastal stretch has been developed for holiday-makers, whilst the mountains behind are wild and relatively unexplored. The

R297 branches off the N59 between Sligo and Ballina in County Mayo and meanders through the villages along the coast. **Inniscrone** (or Inishcrone) is a holiday resort on Killala Bay with a long, sandy strand that is ideal for bathing. It also has a marina with berths for yachts and deep-sea fishing boats for hire. There is an excellent bath-house offering salt-water seaweed baths and steam baths in your own little wooden box (*see* 'Sports and Activities', p.356). The pier and breakwater provide excellent fishing and bird-watching, and there is lovely walking country up the Moy estuary to Ballina. At the north end of town and in ruins is **Nolan's Castle**, an early 17th-century semi-fortified manor house.

This area is dotted with the ruins of castles, some of which have romantic associations. **O'Dowd's Castle**, 3 miles (4.8 km) to the south of Inniscrone, is one such ruin. A local story tells of how one of the O'Dowds captured a mermaid and stole her magic cloak, and so was able to change her into a mortal woman. She bore him seven children but always longed to return to the sea. When she at last regained her cloak she changed back into a mermaid, took her children to a place called Cruckacorma, in Scurmore, and transformed them into pillar stones. She then returned to the sea. (The pillar stones are actually on a tumulus, and are known locally as 'the Children of the Mermaid'). Two miles (3.2km) north of Inniscrone is **Castle Firbis**, the ruined stronghold of a family well known for their poetry and annals. The MacFirbis Clan were the hereditary poets and historiographers to the O'Dowds between the 14th and 17th centuries. They had a school of learning here where many important manuscripts were compiled. The most important to survive are *The Yellow Book of Leacan* (*c.* 1391), now in Trinity College, Dublin; *The Great Book of Leacan*, compiled between 1416 and 1480, now in the Royal Irish Academy, Dublin; and *The Book of Genealogies of Ireland*, compiled between 1585– and 1671, and now in University College, Dublin. One of the last MacFirbis scribes was employed by Sir James Ware (1594–1666) to prepare transcripts and translations from the Gaelic. Ware, an antiquary and historian, was responsible for preserving and collecting valuable historical material on Gaelic Ireland. As a member of parliament and the auditor-general for Ireland, he was in a good position to help native Celts like the MacFirbis clan.

Easky is a fishing village 8 miles (12.9km) from Inniscrone on the coast road. The village is guarded by two martello towers, built to raise the alarm if Napoleon tried to invade. It is famous for its waves in winter and it has become something of a surfer's hangout, although there are also other water sports facilities. Two miles (3.2 km) east on the R297, by the roadside, is the split rock also known as **Fionn MacCumhaill's Fingerstone**. This is said to have been split by MacCumhaill's sword – Irish heroes always have superhuman strength – and is very impressive. It may in fact have been created in the Ice Age. Legend tells that the rock will close on anybody who dares to pass through the split three times.

From Dromore West the R297 road joins the N59. Take the mountain road, signposted on the left, along a scenic route to Easky Lough. If you continue on into the Ox Mountains, then just after the hamlet of Moss Hill you can turn right for Gleneask and **Lough Talt**. The views in this wild and isolated country are fabulous and it is possible to walk from Lough Easky to Mullany's Cross. Ask in the local tourist office for

Irish Walks Guide 3, Northwest, by Simms and Foley, which details this route. The R294 traverses the region and leads to the market town of Tubbercurry (*see* p.362). Just before you reach it, at **Banada** is the ruin of **Corpus Christi Priory**, beautifully situated on the River Moy. The priory was the first Irish house of the Augustinian Friars of the Regular Observance and was founded by the O'Haras in 1423.

Skreen to Coolaney

Another lovely route can be taken into the Ox Mountains from **Skreen**, which is a tiny little place just off the N59 between Ballysodare and Dromore West. It is worth stopping off at the **Church of Ireland graveyard** to see the carved box tombs which date from between 1774 and 1866. The Black family tomb is a masterpiece of carving. On the north side it shows a ploughman in a top hat, tail coat, buckled shoes guiding a plough. The west end has a cherub's head and a skull and crossbones carved in high relief. The minor road leads you past tumbling streams and grand mountain scenery, past Lough Achtree and on to the scenic route signposted 'Ladies Brae'. Reforestation has changed the face of the mountains: the subtle browns, greens and purples have given way to the standardized green of the sitka spruce and lodgepole pine. But the skies and the shapes of the mountains are still magnificent and the forests will one day yield a good cash-crop. As you journey closer to **Coolaney** the road runs close to the Owenbeg River, which makes a very pleasant picnic spot. And as you enter Coolaney you might notice the Pack Horse Bridge, which has many arches but is in a very bad state of repair, with several trees growing up in it.

Just outside Coolaney, about 1½ miles (2.4km) east on an unnumbered road leading to Collooney, is the **Holy Well of Tobar Tullaghan**, also known as Hawk's Well. This tranquil place used to be a place of pilgrimage for many; during the medieval period it was regarded as one of the Wonders of Ireland, apparently gushing forth fresh water at one moment and salt water at another. It is still thought that the water in the well ebbs and flows with the tide. Close to Collooney and just off the N4 is **Markree Castle**, which was until very recently an example of a huge and derelict Gothic-style pile. Now it has opened as a hotel (*see* 'Where to Stay', p.357), and has been beautifully restored. This is an especially satisfactory state of affairs because Charles Cooper is a descendant of the Coopers who acquired the estate in the 17th century. The castle was built in 1802, when the 18th-century house was transformed by the designs of Francis Johnston (1760–1829).

Aughris to Ballysodare

The coastal stretch between Ballysodare and Skreen is very pretty. Visit the little fishing harbour of **Aughris** and walk around Aughris Head; and then have a jar in the Beach Bar, which is famous for its Saturday-night traditional music sessions. The bar has been badly modernized, but you can admire the views from a cosy bench outside. The cliff ledges of Aughris Head hold the nesting places of many different bird species, and Dunmoran Strand to the east is a lovely sandy beach. **Ballisodare** is a bit of a thoroughfare for traffic leaving Sligo Town for Ballina, but it has the remains of a pre-Romanesque church and a 7th-century monastery founded by St Feichin of Fore in County Westmeath. The church overlooks the wooded edge of Ballisodare Bay. Close by is the ruin of a 15th-century church, almost buried in rubble from the quarry.

South Sligo

Tubbercurry and Ballymote

Tubbercurry (also known as Tobercurry) is a busy market town which holds the Western Drama Festival. The festival is very well thought of for the quality of the productions and the range of different styles and interpretations. The town is also a good centre for anglers, being close to Loughs Gara, Key, Arrow, Easky and Talt. Brown trout, pike and perch are the usual catches. Another excellent fishing centre to the north is **Ballymote**, which also has a ruined square Norman **castle** (*always accessible*) which was used as a major defensive post up until the 1690s. You get to it through the car park of the St John of God's Nursing Home near the railway station. Whilst you are in the area, you could take the opportunity to stay in the intriguing 18th-century **Temple House**, situated off the N17 about 5 miles (8km) to the northeast (see 'Where to Stay', p.357). Close by is **Achonry**, an early Christian monastic site in a very ruined state which boasts a cathedral, the **Church of St Nathy** (CI). It dates from 1823, and on its east side are the ruins of a 15th-century church with a lofty square tower.

Gorteen and Lough Gara

To the southeast of Tubbercurry is the village of **Gorteen** (or Gurteen), which is recognized by traditional music-lovers as the centre of the distinctive Sligo flute-and-fiddle style. Sometimes you can hear the evocative airs and dancing tunes at the **Traditional Restaurant** and the **May Queen** in the centre of the town. Impromptu dancing may start up, which is the greatest fun. Courses are offered in traditional musical styles, songwriting, instrument playing and Sean Nós singing at the **Coleman Heritage Centre** in Gorteen (*t (071) 82599, f (071) 82602, www.colemanirishmusic.com*). On the R294, 2 miles (3.2km) southeast of Gorteen at the Mullaghroe crossroads, is a 16th-century square stone **castle** consisting of a walled enclosure with six square towers and the remains of a curtain wall. It was the stronghold of the O'Garas, a ruling Gaelic family of that time. Fergal O'Gara was a patron of the monks who compiled the *Annals of the Four Masters* between 1623 and 1626. **Lough Gara** itself is set with many tiny islands, some of them man-made *crannogs* which were inhabited by Iron-Age farmers.

Keshcorran and Carrowkeel

Over wooded and boggy lands to the northeast of Gorteen is the summit of **Keshcorran**, from where there are fantastic views of the surrounding countryside. (Get there by travelling cross-country on the minor road from Mullaghroe to Kesh. Just before you get to Kesh, cross the R295 running between Ballymore and Boyle.) Keshcorran has many caves on its west face, all associated with legendary characters such as Cormac MacArt, the wise and generous high king who ruled over the heroes of the Fianna (*see* p.82). On Garland Sunday (the last Sunday in July) locals still gather by the caves for prayers and chat in a tradition that stretches back thousands of years to celebrations in honour of the Celtic God Lugh. Close by on a hill-top of the Bricklieve Range are the Bronze Age passage graves of **Carrowkeel**. You reach these via an untarred mountain road, just off the N4 between Castlebaldwin and Ballinafad, which takes you round the base of the hilltop on an approach from the northwest for a couple of miles (3.2km). Clearly the burial chambers were elaborately planned and set in round cairns, with commanding views of the land. The cruciform passage graves are narrow and roofed with large lintel stones, whilst the larger chambers are roofed with corbelled stone.

County Sligo has many interesting archaeological remains that possibly link up with the mythological stories of Ireland's past. The great and legendary battle between the Fomorians and the Tuatha Dé Danaan, which is related in the *Book of Invasions*, or *Lebor Gabala*, is reputed to have taken place near here, and it is said the slain were buried here. Fourteen cairns are located on the spurs of promontories, but there is also a 'village' of 14 *clochans*. It is possible to enter a few of the tombs, one of which is lit up by the setting sun on the longest day of the year. This contrasts with the great passage tomb at Newgrange in County Meath, which is lit by the sun at sunrise on the shortest day of the year. Also in this area is the **Sligo Folk Park**, at Riverstown (*open May–Oct daily, Nov–April by appointment; coffee shop; t (071) 65001, f (071) 65983, www.sligofolkpark.com*), a community of traditional houses and cottages portraying a bygone Irish lifestyle.

County Leitrim

Leitrim is a very individual county, with a secret, forgotten feel to it; it is a good place for a quiet holiday. The region is long and narrow, with a foothold in the sea and stretching back to mountains, hills and streams. It is divided in two by Lough Allen, one of the many lakes of the Shannon river. It shares the beauty of Lough Gill and Lough Melvin with County Sligo, and has countless lakes of its own. The lakes are, by all accounts, teeming with bream, pike, perch, salmon and trout. The renovation of the 19th-century Ballinamore and Ballyconnell canal provides the link between the Shannon and the Erne, and cruisers can able to travel for 470m (750km) along tranquil inland waterways.

If you are a walker and anxious to be alone, the mountains around Manorhamilton are full of beauty; you will pass the remains of many deserted cottages on the slopes where only sheep and cattle graze. The people of Leitrim are mainly small farmers and the land has attracted quite a few outsiders or 'blow-ins', who are keen to own a smallholding and try organic methods. Trees thrive here and the district immediately north of Lough Allen is planted with conifers. South of Slieve Anierin the county is covered by a belt of *drumlins*. These teardrop-shaped hills were left behind by retreating glaciers and are composed of gravel debris. Most of the Leitrim boundary with County Roscommon to the west is formed by the winding River Shannon.

History

Before the county was 'shired' in around 1585 by Elizabethan administrators, it was known as West Breffni. The principal *sept* of this area was O'Rourke, whose members lived around the tiny settlement of Leitrim. In the centuries leading up to the Anglo-Norman conquest the O'Rourkes were continually involved in dynastic struggles for the high kingship of Ireland. In the 12th century, Tighernan O'Rourke was allied to Rory O'Connor, the high king. Dermot MacMurragh, the King of Leinster, coveted his position, and a struggle began. MacMurragh raided Breffni in 1152, and stole Devorgilla, O'Rourke's wife. This led to the banishment of MacMurragh in 1166, and the arrival of the Normans in 1169 to help him win his kingdom back. For Ireland, it was the beginning of a long and traumatic relationship with England. However, Breffni was hardly affected by the Normans, who kept to the south, and the Gaelic system under the lordship of the O'Rourkes lasted until Elizabeth I mounted her conquest of Ireland. Brian O'Rourke, the chieftain of the time, was one of the few Irish recorded who tried to rescue some of the Spanish sailors wrecked off the Sligo-Leitrim coast after storms drove the 1588 Armada onto the rocks. As a reprisal he was taken prisoner and hung at Tyburn in 1590. His son, known as Brian of the Battleaxes, fought endlessly against the English and joined in the Nine Years' War against the Elizabethan Conquest with the Ulster Lords O'Neill and Red Hugh O'Donnell. Their defeat at the Battle of Kinsale in 1601 spelled the end of their power; and the O'Rourke estate and castles were handed over to English and Scottish planters. The names Hamilton, St George, Harrison, Gore and Clements date from that time.

The Gaelic system took a long time to break down. Turlough O'Carolan, the famous blind harper, composer and poet (1670–1733) lived in Mohill for a while, succoured by the Gaelic system of patronage and welcomed into the houses of peasants and gentry with his music. The Irish people everywhere still spoke Gaelic and remained fervent Catholics, which set them far apart from the new colonialists. The 1798 Rebellion bought bloodshed to Leitrim as the peasants joined in the French General Humbert's march to Ballinamuck, County Longford, from Mayo. Many of them were slaughtered. The potato famine and emigration took its toll in the 1840s and by 1851, the population had dropped from 155,000 to 43,000. Today the population is about 28,000. One of the heroes of the Irish struggle for independence came from Leitrim: Sean MacDiarmada (1884–1916), who was born in Kiltyclogher, was one of the seven signatories of the proclamation of the republic in Easter Week 1916. He was court-martialled and executed in May 1916.

North Leitrim

Around Manorhamilton

Manorhamilton is situated at the meeting of four valleys in a setting of steep limestone hills and narrow ravines. It was built by Sir Frederick Hamilton, whose fine 17th-century mansion, now a ruin and cloaked in ivy, overlooks the town. At **Manorhamilton Castle Heritage Centre** (*open May–Sept, Tues–Sat 11–6 Sun 2–7; craft*

County Leitrim

shop, café, herb garden, picnic area; adm; **t** (072) 55249) you can find out about the
O'Rourke, O'Conor and Maguire clan revolt against Sir Frederick in 1641. It's also a good
place from which to explore the various roads that spiral out from Manorhamilton.
You can take a boggy little road signposted right, a few miles down the main road to
Belcoo (N16). It leads to some *cashels* known as **Tallyskcherny**, built in about 500 BC.

Getting There and Around

By Rail
Carrick-on-Shannon is connected with Boyle, Sligo, and Dublin. There are three daily trains during the week, and two on Sunday.
Carrick Station, t (078) 20036.

By Bus
Expressway buses link Carrick-on-Shannon with Dublin and Sligo, and there is a good local network.
Sligo Bus Depot, t (071) 60066.

By Bike
Gerharty's, Main Street, Carrick-on-Shannon, **t** (078) 21316. Bike hire.

Festivals

May–June
Community Arts Festival, Carrick-on-Shannon, **t** (078) 20673.
Homecoming Festival, Cloone, **t** (078) 36045.

July
Joe Mooney School of Traditional Music, Song and Dance, Drumshanbo, **t** (078) 44091.
Mohill Arts Festival, t (078) 31174.
Newtown Gore Festival, t (049) 433 3582.

August
Ballinamore Annual Festival, t (078) 44091.
Michael Shanley Traditional Weekend, Kiltyclogher, **t** (078) 20489.

September
Carrick-on-Shannon Fishing Festival, **t** (078) 20489.

October
North Leitrim Walking Festival, **t** (078) 44091.

Tourist Information

Carrick-on-Shannon: The Marina, **t** (078) 20170, or **t** (071) 61201, *www.leitrimtourism.com*, *www.northwest.travel.ie*; *open mid Mar–Oct*.

Shopping

Crafts
Leitrim Design House, Market House Centre, Carrick-on-Shannon.
The Sculpture Centre, Manorhamilton, **t** (072) 55098.

Health Foods
Oasis Health Foods, Bridge Street, Carrick-on-Shannon, **t** (078) 21560.

Sports and Activities

Boat Hire
Crown Blue Line, Carrick-on-Shannon, **t** (078) 50176.
Emerald Star Line, The Marina, Carrick-on-Shannon, **t** (078) 20234.
Riversdale Barge Holidays, Ballinamore, **t** (078) 45112.

Cycling
For information on the **Kingfisher Cycle Trail**, log on to *www.cycleireland.com*, or contact North West Tourism, **t** (071) 61201.

Fishing
Information on **coarse fishing** in the county: **North West Regional Fisheries Board, t** (096) 22623/22788.
Northern Regional Fisheries Board, **t** (072) 51435.
The Creel, Main Street, Carrick-on-Shannon, **t** (078) 20166. Tackle and information.
The Drowse/Laureen Fisheries, Kinlough, **t** (072) 41055.
Rossinver Fishery, Eden Point, **t** (072) 540229.

The land around here belonged to the O'Rourke chieftains who took part with O'Neill and O'Donnell in the last great rebellion of the Irish nobility against Elizabeth I, in the last decades of the 16th century.

North of Manorhamilton the Bonet Valley narrows towards the source of this pretty river into an equally pretty lake, the **Glenade**. This is a superb example of a glacial

Golf

Ballinamore Golf Club, t (078) 44346.
Carrick-on-Shannon Golf Club, t (079) 67015.

Internet Access

Gartlans Cybercafé, Bridge Street, Carrick-on-Shannon, t (078) 21103, *gartlan@iol.ie*.

Outdoor Activity Centres

Lough Allen Adventure Centre, Ballinagleragh, t/f (078) 43292.

Pony-trekking

Hayden Equestrian Centre, Carrick-on-Shannon, t (078) 38049.
Moorlands Equestrian Centre, Drumshanbo, t (078) 41500.

Steam Train Rides

Cavan and Leitrim Railway, Dromod, t (078) 20089.

Walking

In the **Cairns Hill Forest Park**, near Dromahair.

Where to Stay

Stanfords Village Inn, Main Street, Dromahair, t (071) 64140 (*inexpensive*). Traditional Irish bar with bottles stacked high to the ceiling, hard stools and a cosy fire. Away from the *craic* in the bar are comfortable, clean rooms.
Cromleach Lodge Country House, Castlebaldwin, Co. Sligo, t (071) 65155 (*expensive*). Just over the border in neighbouring Sligo. Beautiful views over Lough Arrow, excellent traditional cooking.
The Bush Hotel, Carrick-on-Shannon, t (078) 20014, f (078) 21180, *bushhotel@tinet.ie* (*moderate*). Small, friendly and central, with solid Irish cooking.
Glencarne House, Ardcarne, Carrick-on-Shannon, t (079) 67013, f (079) 67013 (*inexpensive*). Although just over the border in County Roscommon, this solid stone

farmhouse is only 3 miles (4.8km) from Carrick-on-Shannon. Your hostess, Agnes Harrington, is an excellent cook and has a good eye for attractive objects and furniture.
Glebe House, Ballinamore Road, Mohill, t (078) 31086, *glebe@iol.ie* (*moderate*). 19th-century rectory. Fishing and riding can be arranged by the Maloney family, and there's a pony for the children. Minimum stay 2 nights.
Riversdale Farm Guesthouse, Ballinamore, t (078) 44122, f (078) 44813 (*moderate–inexpensive*). Edwardian farmhouse with light and spacious rooms, swimming pool and sauna, good home-cooked food, and delightful hosts, the Thomases. They also run **Riversdale Barge Holidays**, so you can take a trip up the Shannon–Erne Waterway. The farmhouse base has an indoor swimming-pool and squash court.

Eating Out

Stanfords Village Inn, Main Street, Dromahair, t (071) 64140 (*inexpensive*). Cosy Irish pub with a simple restaurant overlooking a garden. Set dinner.
Maguire's Cottage, Drumshanbo, t (078) 41033 (*moderate*). Friendly restaurant with open fire and traditional furnishings. Big helpings of steaks, prawn cocktail, salads. *Open Easter–Nov evenings only from 6pm*.
Cryan's Pub, Bridge Street, Carrick-on-Shannon, t (078) 20409 (*inexpensive*). Basic pub lunches. The coffee shop next door sells quiche and pizza.
Lough Rynn Estate Restaurant, Mohill, t (078) 31427 (*inexpensive*). Restaurant with traditional food and fast-food outlet offering snacks. There is also a craft shop, nature trails, guided tours and angling on the estate. *Open end April–mid Sept*.
Glenview, Ballinamore, t (078) 44157 (*moderate*). Restaurant as part of a B&B. Lovely setting beside the Woodford river. Call in advance.

valley. The R280 runs beside its waters which are thickly edged with trees. The hills are high in the east, and to the west a line of crags rise from the grassy slopes. The road slopes down to **Kinlough**, a neat little village on Lough Melvin only 3 miles (5km) from the sea. If you want to taste the delights of **Bundoran**, a highly developed seaside resort in Donegal, it is only a few miles further on. The many-islanded Lough Melvin extends for 8 miles (13km) and a scenic road follows its southern side from Kinlough to Rossinver. A sign by the road points to **Rossclogher Abbey and Castle**. The small ruined abbey was founded by St Mella, and the deserted castle was a stronghold of MacClancy, a sub-chieftain of the O'Rourkes. In 1588 nine survivors of the Spanish Armada took refuge here. You have to leave your car or bicycle and walk over long grass to reach both buildings, but it is worth it, for the view of the lough is superb. Notice the line of rushes, probably a causeway, going out to the castle, which is on a little island or *crannog*. The abbey is easy to wander around, but you have to cross shallow water to reach the castle and it is easiest viewed from the shore. At **Rossinver** at the head of the southern end of the lake, the remains of a 13th-century church and a monastery of St Mogue are to be found, which date from the 6th century, with a holy well nearby. The modern gravestones look somewhat out of place.

The road south to Kiltyclogher passes over the ancient earthwork called the Worm Ditch or the **Black Pig's Dyke**, which extends intermittently from Bundoran in the west to Newry in County Down. It was probably built by the Scotti, people who lived in the north between 300 and 200 BC, to prevent encroachment from the south. Legend as usual tells a much more colourful story: the ditch was formed by the slithering of a huge serpent over the land; or if it was not a serpent, then it was a monstrous pig that snuffled and rooted around, throwing up the earth as it went.

In the centre of **Kiltyclogher** village stands Albert Power's statue of Sean MacDiarmada, who was executed for his part in the 1916 uprising. The cottage where he was brought up is a short distance away in the townland of Corranmore (*open to the public by arrangement; t (072) 53249*). Follow the R283 to a rock at **Laughty Barr** where people used to go to hear Mass during the times of the Penal Laws. Signposted from the road is **Kiltyclogher Megalithic tomb**, a court cairn built between 2000 and 1500 BC and known locally as Prince Connell's Grave.

Around Dromahair

Dromahair is a very pretty village about 8 miles (12.9 km) from Manorhamilton, through which the River Bonet flows until it gets to Lough Gill. The N16/R286 road from Manorhamilton has the most beautiful views of Lough Gill, and in the wooded country around (approached from the R286/R287) are the ruins of **Creevelea Abbey**, founded in 1508 by Margaret, wife of Owen O'Rourke. The abbey has a pretty pillar with a carving representing St Francis talking to birds in a tree. The branches and roots of the tree grow in Celtic patterns.

In the middle of the town are the sparse remains of **Breffni Castle**, stones from which were used to build another mansion known as the Old Hall beside it in 1630. The old castle was the chief stronghold of the O'Rourkes and it was from here that in 1152 Devorgilla, wife of Tighernan or Tiernan O'Rourke, eloped with Dermot MacMurragh at the age of 44. But she regretted her action, for Dermot turned out to be even crueller than Tiernan, and one day she slipped back to be reconciled with him. Her elopement was the turning point in Irish history, for it led to the flight of Dermot MacMurragh and his alliance with Henry II, which resulted in the Anglo-Norman invasion of Ireland.

On the scenic R286 around Lough Gill, on the way to Sligo, there are plenty of lay-bys where you can park and look out over the water to the many islands. Following this route you pass the 17th-century **Parke's Castle** at Fivemilebourne (*open Mar 29–May, Tues–Sun 10–5, June–Sept, daily 9.30–6.30, Oct, 10–5; guided tours; adm; t (071) 64149*), a fine example of a planter's insecurity. The manor house was well fortified against the Irish and is surrounded by high *bawn* walls with picturesque turrets and steep sloping roofs. It has been restored and contains a permanent exhibition which provides information on many of the monuments in the area. You might also want to take a cruise on the *Wild Rose* waterbus that operates on Lough Gill (*see* p.353).

From Dromahair take the R289, which joins the R280, for Drumkeeran and Drumshanbo. This road twists through hills, past Lough Belhavel and Lough Allen. Along the roads you will notice signposts naming the various lakes and the sort of fish you are likely to catch. Lough Allen is noted for its large pike; fish over 30lb (13.6kg) are not uncommon. There is good bream fishing from the banks of the 20 lakes within the 5 mile (8km) radius of Drumshanbo. **Drumshanbo** itself is a tidy and well-kept town, one that keeps close to its culture and traditions; you can learn about these at the Visitors' Centre, *Sliabh an Iarainn* (*open Easter–Oct, Mon–Sat 10–6, Sun 2–6; adm; t (078) 41522*). The Slieve Anierin range, or Iron Mountains, dominate the landscape. Iron was mined here two hundred years ago, but the industry ceased when the timber in the neighbourhood, which was the source of fuel for the smelting furnace, was used up.

South Leitrim

Carrick-on-Shannon was always an important crossing place. During the plantation of Leitrim in the reign of James I it was fortified and garrisoned to protect the new settlers. It is the county town, a pretty place and the centre of river cruising on the Shannon. Within 6 miles (9.6km) there are 41 lakes; and fishing is free and unrestricted. Many coarse fishermen make it their base.

Worth a look is the **Costelloe Memorial Chapel**, the second smallest chapel in the world, erected by Edward Costelloe in 1877 in remembrance of his wife. Both are now buried there in crumbling coffins, which are visible behind glass in sunken pits at either side of the entrance. Drop into Armstrongs next door, which sells drink amongst all the shoes and jumpers. It looks like nothing has changed here since Edward Costelloe passed away. Following the N4 over the border into County Roscommon, you will come to the **Lough Key Forest Park** (*open all year; restaurant and mooring facilities for boats; car park adm; t (079) 67037*). The park is very beautifully laid out with bog gardens and nature trails, and there are boat trips on the lake. Still following the N4 towards Dublin, you keep close to the Shannon and pass through **Jamestown**, founded in the reign of James I. The next village of interest is **Drumsna**, which is on a hill overlooking the Shannon. The river scenery is lovely. When the Shannon was used for transporting produce, Drumsna was quite an important

St Columba the *Enfant Terrible*?

Colourful stories have grown up around the lives of all Irish saints which have no historical foundation. The following is one such story about St Columba.

Among saints, St Columba seems to have been a bit of a rebel. Once, whilst he was a guest of St Finian, he borrowed a psalter and secretly copied it out. Finian found out and said that the copy should be his, but Columba refused to hand it over. The high king was asked to settle the dispute and he ruled in favour of Finian, saying that just as every calf belongs to its cow, so every copy belongs to the book from which it is made. St Columba did not accept the king's judgement and gathered an army. He fought the king and won, but with the loss of three thousand lives. Columba's friend, St Molaise of Inishmurray, advised him to leave Ireland for ever as a penance, and convert as many people as he had caused to die. (For more about St Columba, or Colmcille, *see* pp.75–6.)

trading centre. Anthony Trollope lived here for some time and wrote his novel *The MacDermotts of Ballycloran*.

Dromod and **Roosky** are pretty little villages on the edge of the Shannon. If you retrace your steps to Dromod and take the R202 to **Mohill**, you come into *drumlin* country, a place of little hills whose hollows are filled with lakes. Mohill is a favourite angling centre. Between here and Dromod, 6 miles (9.6km) off the N4 Sligo–Dublin road on the shores of Lough Rinn is a lovely estate which was once owned by the earls of Leitrim. The Victorian walled, terraced gardens of **Lough Rynn House** are very attractive (*currently undergoing renovation, check opening hours in advance; usually open mid June–mid Sept, daily 10–7; adm includes tours; t (078) 31427, f (078) 31518*), with many beautiful redwoods and rhododendrons as well as 600 fishable acres (243ha) of Lough Rinn. The estate was rescued by an American, Mike O'Flaherty, who saw it advertised in a real estate office in the USA, flew over, and bought it. **Fenagh**, up in the hills, has the ruins of two medieval Gothic churches. They are all that remain of the monastery St Columba (*see* box above) founded and which, under the rule of his close friend St Caillin, became internationally famous as a school of divinity. This is a lovely lake-starred area where you can fish to your heart's delight. Close to the little village of **Drumcong** on the R210, on an island in Lough Scur, is a ruined Elizabethan castle which in the past was often attacked by the O'Rourkes of Breffni. Above the lough is **Sheebeg**, a small hill with a prehistoric mound on its summit. It is one of the many resting places accorded to the legendary Fionn MacCumhaill. On the road (R209) back to Carrick-on-Shannon is the sister hill of **Sheemore**, which also has a pre-historic cairn and a huge cross to mark Holy Year 1950. Both are easy to climb.

The Province of Ulster

13

Ulster

40km
20miles

N

INISHOWEN

Rathlin Island

❶ Giant's Causeway

Portrush   Ballycastle

Coleraine

Rathmullan
Inch Island

Letterkenny

DERRY
LONDONDERRY

Ballymena   Larne

ANTRIM

DONEGAL

Strabane

Glencolmcille

Donegal

Antrim   Carrickfergus

Lough Derg

Cookstown

Newtownabbey

TYRONE

Rossnowlagh

Omagh

Lough Neagh

❺

BELFAST

Bangor
Newtown-ards

Lower Lough Erne

❷

Devenish Island   Monastic Ruins

❸

Sligo

Enniskillen

FERMANAGH

ARMAGH

DOWN

Downpatrick

Upper Lough Erne

Monaghan

SLIGO

MONAGHAN

Newry

LEITRIM

Castleblaney

Cavan

CAVAN

Dundalk

ROSCOMMON

LOUTH

LONGFORD

p.290

p.512

NORTHERN IRELAND
ULSTER

CONNACHT

REPUBLIC OF IRELAND

LEINSTER

MUNSTER

Highlights

1 Spectacular basalt columns rising out of the sea at The Giant's Causeway
2 Peaceful Devenish Island, Co. Fermanagh
3 Characterful gardens at Mount Stewart House, Co. Down
4 Glorious boat trips to Tory Island
5 A satisfying foray into history at the Ulster Museum, Belfast

The Ulster border has meant much through the ages: Cú Chulainn, the Hound of Ulster, was perhaps its most famous guard when he defended it against the host of Ireland during the epic battles of the Brown Bull of Cooley. Myth has always been used throughout Ulster's history by those keen to validate their points of view, and the boundaries of Ulster (or *Ulaid*) have shifted continuously up until the 16th century.

However, it is interesting to contemplate how myth and history support each other over this enmity between North and South. Irish archaeologists have just concluded that a great earthen wall was built two thousand years ago to separate Ulster (*Ulaidhstr*: Land of the Ulstermen) from much of the South of Ireland. It consisted of two pairs of double ramparts – the largest of which was 90ft (27m) wide, 18ft (5.5m) high and 1½ miles (2.8km) long, and formed part of a defensive border along the line of the upper reaches of the Shannon River. It is thought that the wall was built by tribal rulers in central Ireland to prevent the warlike tribes of Ulster from crossing two of the major fords across the Shannon, at Drumsna and Carrick in County Leitrim. The Drumsna wall cuts off a loop of the Shannon and is broken only by an entrance complex which formed a huge gateway into tribal territory – probably the Kingdom of Connacht.

Another earthwork, built in the third or second century BC and known as the Black Pig's Dyke, stretches intermittently from Donegal Bay to the Dorsey and Newry Marshes in the east. This time the defence was built by the Ulstermen against the Southerners. It is likely that the two earthworks reflect different stages in the armed conflict between these two major prehistoric tribal groupings. It may even be that the legendary Connacht Queen Maeve, or Medb, built the defences during the great battles over the Brown Bull of Cooley (*see* p.528).

The Northern Ireland you will see today has suffered most in the towns from the last 30 years of the Troubles. This has paradoxically brought about planned and attractive public housing and buildings for the most part, although, as with the rest of Ireland, there are few exceptionally pretty towns. But the countryside is as beautiful and has been made accessible through the development of forest parks and the guardianship of bodies such as the British National Trust. The North is also different because it was industrialized during the 19th century, and so endured the uglier stages of capitalist development, while Southern Ireland is only now building factories and pulling itself out of its agriculturally based economy.

Having said all that, the visitor should not ignore Northern Ireland, thinking it is a foreign and probably dangerous country within Ireland – because it certainly is not. One great plus point for the North is its teeming lakes and rivers; coarse fishermen find nothing like it anywhere else in the British Isles.

The vast majority of Northern Irish people are friendly, hard-working, witty and kind. The North and the South, as the two states of Ireland are colloquially referred to, co-operate in many areas, especially the arts and tourism. A major example of this has been the reopening of the 19th-century Ballinamore and Ballyconnell canal, which links the Shannon and Fermanagh lake systems. It fell into disuse over a hundred years ago, and its restoration has been funded by both governments, the EU and the International Fund for Ireland.

The six counties which make up the North are Antrim, Armagh, Down, Fermanagh, Londonderry and Tyrone. They are included in the ancient province of Ulster together with Cavan, Monaghan and Donegal, which are part of the Irish Republic.

History

Some experts on the Irish race maintain that in ancient times the North was full of Picts and the South full of Milesians – another Celtic tribe from Spain whose invasion is recorded in the ancient manuscript, the *Lebor Gabala*, or *Book of Invasions*. They probably arrived in about 200 BC. What is more sure is that later, in the 17th century, Ulster was the most systematically planted province because of its continued fierce resistance to the English, and the hardy Scots were introduced into the province to provide a loyal garrison.

The sign of Ulster is the Red Hand. This symbol is the result of the race for the overlordship of Ulster between the Gaelic MacDonnells and the Norman de Burghs in the 12th century. The first to reach land would take the prize, and, as the contestants struggled through the shallows off the Antrim coast, MacDonnell, fearing that de Burgh who was leading the race would win, cut off his own hand and threw it far onto the strand where it lay covered in blood. The symbol of this fair land is thus oddly prophetic of the many bloody struggles for its conquest.

The two great clans of the west are descended from the sons of the great High King of Ireland, Niall of the Nine Hostages (AD 379–405). Their names were Conal and Eoghan and they gave their name to districts in this part of the province: Tyrconnell and Tyrone. When Brian Boru, the high king in the 11th century, instituted surnames in Ireland, the followers and descendants of Conal and Eoghan took the names O'Donnell and O'Neill respectively, and it was they who rebelled against English rule.

County Fermanagh

This is the lakeland of Ireland, bounded with limestone mountains in the southwest and scattered with *drumlins* which speckle the lakes with islands. A third of the county is under water, covered by the lake system of the Erne with its mass of lakelets in the upper lough, and the great boomerang of Lower Lough Erne. Then there are the two Lough MacNeans in their mountain fastness, which together with the county's share of Lough Melvin have until recently discouraged incoming populations, so it is a place of long-lasting traditions and folklore. Even today, few strangers settle in this area, although the lakes attract summer visitors.

The countryside in which these beautiful lakes are scattered is mostly composed of little rushy farms where sheep and cattle graze. The higher ground is covered in hazel scrub, whilst in the limestone upland to the western edge of the country the soil is so poor that natural species have survived undisturbed by the tractor or fertilizers of the farmer. There are some lovely ash woods at Hanging Rock and Marble Arch. Here too are the famous Marble Arch Caves on Cuilcagh Mountain, which you can explore with a guide. The county also has two exquisite Georgian mansions under the care of the National Trust – Castle Coole and Florence Court. The coarse fishing is legendary, and every year in May fishermen have great fun at the Guinness Classic Fishing Festival, which spreads events all over the myriad lakes. You can explore the lakes by chartering a cabin cruiser, and there are plenty of opportunities for water-skiing.

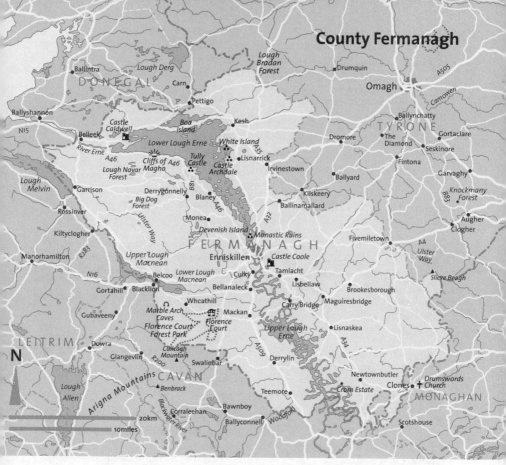

The waterways of the Upper and Lower Erne are now connected to the great waterway of the Shannon by the Ballyconnell and Ballinamore canal, which passes through some very unspoilt scenery.

History

The history of this county is similar to that of the rest of Ulster. The Maguires were the chief Gaelic family here before the plantation. In the 17th century, Scottish 'undertakers' arrived (this name is derived from their 'undertaking' a pledge to provide a population loyal to the English crown). Many grand houses were built by landowners in the 18th century. Fermanagh has a vast and largely unrecorded ancient history, which you will get glimpses of through the beautiful carvings and stone statues still to be seen in graveyards and the Enniskillen Museum.

Those of a reflective turn of mind will be fascinated by the pagan idols; their impassive stone heads are to be found on the islands and peninsulas of Lough Erne. Usually they are mixed up with the gravestones of the newer religion, Christianity. The two seem to mingle quite happily. There are many remains of Christian hermitages; on Devenish Island, on Lough Erne, there is a superb collection of ecclesiastical ruins dating from the 6th century. The headlands of the loughs are

Getting There and Around

By Air

From Belfast International Airport and Enniskillen Airport.

Enniskillen Airport, St Angelo, Trory, Enniskillen, t (028) 6632 3110. Located four miles from Enniskillen, with flights to Jersey and Zürich; plans are under way to develop further routes to the UK and Europe.

By Rail

There is no train service within Fermanagh.

By Bus

Six Ulsterbus express buses run daily from Belfast to Enniskillen; two from Dublin. There are good local bus links from Enniskillen to country areas.

Enniskillen Bus Station, Wellington Road, t (028) 6632 2633.

By Car

Lochside Garages Ltd, Tempo Road, Enniskillen, t (028) 6632 4366. For car hire.
M & N Motors, Irvinestown Road, Enniskillen, t (028) 6632 4712. Car sales and rental.

By Bike

Bicycle hire from:
Lakeland Canoe Centre, Castle Island, t (028) 6632 4250.
Marble Arch Cycle Hire, in Tarmon, Blacklion and Florencecourt, t (028) 6634 8320.

Festivals

There are lots of tiny festivals and sporting events in villages thoughout the summer. Ask at the tourist office. The following are among the most interesting.

May

Fermanagh Classic Fishing Festival, t (028) 6632 3110.
Scottish Pipe Band Competition, t (028) 6638 8202/6632 4078.

June

Border Trek Cycle Event. A 50-mile cycle for peace, t (028) 9032 1462/6632 3110.
Fiddlestone Festival. Traditional festival in Belleek, t (028) 6865 8201.
Lisnaskea Feis, t (028) 6772 1610.

July

Lady of the Lake Festival, in Irvinestown, t (028) 6862 1656, *www.ladyofthelake festival.com*. Named after a mystical woman who is said to once have made her way among the islands of Lower Lough Erne clad in a flowing gown, filled with light and carrying wild flowers.
Summer Drama Season, Ardhowen Theatre, Enniskillen, t (028) 6632 5440.

August

Lough Melvin Open Trout Angling Championships, t (028) 6865 8095/ 6865 8248.
Enniskillen Agricultural Show, t (028) 6632 2509.
Kesh Carnival/Maid of Glendurragh Festival, t (028) 6863 2158.

October

Antique and Fine Art Fair, Enniskillen, t (028) 6632 7360.
Eddie Duffy Traditional Music Festival, t (028) 6864 1679.

December

International Mumming Festival, Enniskillen, t (028) 6632 5050.

wooded and often enough their interest is enhanced by the ruins of Plantation castles from the 17th century.

This county and the town of Enniskillen suffered greatly after the Troubles began in 1969. The most notable tragedy was an IRA bomb in 1987 which killed 11 people in Enniskillen. Today there is much hope here for a new era, ushered in by the Good Friday Agreement and the Northern Ireland Executive. Fermanagh has never been a rich county. Its population has always lived by farming, fishing and now tourism.

Enniskillen and Around

Enniskillen is built on a bridge of land between Upper and Lower Lough Erne. At first sight the medieval conglomeration of town and castle makes you think this is a very ancient town, but modern shops, supermarkets and offices soon spoil the illusion. Before the plantation the Maguires held sway over this lakeland area and used it as the centre for their watery dominions. Enniskillen's name comes from Cathleen, one of the women warriors of the Fomorian invaders. Her husband Balor was head of a pirate gang quartered on the rock island of Tory, off the Donegal coast. He later resurfaced as the Celtic god of darkness, whose one eye could strike you dead (*see* **Old Gods and Heroes**, p.81). Enniskillen is famous for its home regiments – the *Air of the Inniskillings* became the tune of 'The Star Spangled Banner'. Visit the **County Museum** (*open all year, Mon 2–5, Tues–Fri 10–5, plus May–Sept, Sat 2–5, July–Aug, Sun 2–5; adm; t (028) 6632 5000*), which is housed in Maguire's Keep, a 15th-century building. Attached to it is the **Water Gate**, a fairytale building with towers and fluttering standards. The museum is one of the best and friendliest of local museums. It displays some of the strange head sculptures found in the locality, and explains the history of Fermanagh from the Middle Stone Age to the end of the Early Christian period. There is also an audio-visual display on the Maguires of Fermanagh. British

Tourist Information

Enniskillen: Fermanagh Tourist Information Centre, Wellington Road, t (028) 6632 3110.

Shopping

Crafts
Belleek china, fishing-fly brooches and Irish lace in giftshops in Enniskillen main street.
Fermanagh Craft Consortium and Design Centre, The Buttermarket, Down Street, Enniskillen, t (028) 6632 4499.

Pottery
Ann McNulty Pottery, Unit 1, The Buttermarket, Enniskillen, t (028) 6632 4721.
Belleek Pottery, Belleek, t (028) 6865 8501, *www.belleek.ie*. Ireland's most famous pottery, producing fine glazed porcelain.

Sports and Activities

Cycling
The **Kingfisher Cycle Trail** is a fully way-marked trail which runs over 230 miles through counties Fermanagh, Leitrim, Cavan,

Donegal and Monaghan. Contact the Tourist Office in Enniskillen for more details.

Fishing
Fermanagh Tourist Information Centre, Enniskillen, t (028) 6632 3110. Stocks permits, licences and a booklet on local waters.

Golf
Castle Hume Golf Club, Enniskillen, t (028) 6632 7077.
Enniskillen Golf Course, Castle Coole Estate, t (028) 6632 5250. Good club house, excellent course.

Water Sports
Lakeland Canoe Centre, Enniskillen, t (028) 6863 24250. For canoeing.

Where to Stay

Killyhevlin Hotel, Dublin Road, Enniskillen, t (028) 6632 3481, f (028) 6632 4726 (*expensive*). Comfortable, modern hotel overlooking Lough Erne. The bar is a great chatting place for fishermen. Very good lunchtime carvery and excellent dinners at *moderate* prices.

regiment enthusiasts will be interested in the soldiering relics of the Royal Inniskilling Fusiliers which can be seen in the same building.

You should take a walk through the centre of Enniskillen, which is rather a jumble: the winding main street takes on about six names during its course. You might be impressed enough to buy the local souvenir brooches, made from fishing flies. In the old **Buttermarket** you can buy a variety of handcrafted goods (*see* 'Shopping' p.377). The **Church of Ireland cathedral** dates from the mid-17th century, but was extensively remodelled in the 19th. In the chancel and choir hang the colours of the Royal Inniskilling Fusiliers together with the pennons of the Inniskilling Dragoons, which were recruited in the town. Close by is St Michael's Catholic Church, which was built in 1875 to plans by John O'Neill, although the spire (designed by the original architect) dates from 1992. Inside are some fine paintings depicting scenes from the life of Christ. Four are by the Scottish artist Charles Russell (1852–1910), whilst the Holy Family scene is by Michael Joseph Healy (1873–1941). For a good view of the town and surrounding area, you could climb the 108 steps to the top of the **Coles Monument** (*open May–Sept, daily 2–6; adm; t (028) 6632 5050*). It was built between 1845 and 1857 in Forthill Park at the eastern end of town.

Just outside Enniskillen to the northwest is the **Portora Royal School**, founded in 1608. As a public school it had Oscar Wilde and Samuel Beckett among its more

Killyreagh House, Tamlaght, Enniskillen, t (028) 6638 7122 (*moderate*). Comfortable 19th-century country house, owned by Lord and Lady Anthony Hamilton. Fishing, riding and tennis arranged.

Dromard House, Dromard, Tamlaght, Enniskillen, t (028) 6638 7250 (*moderate–inexpensive*). Comfortable rooms in a converted stable loft.

Corrigan Shore, Clonatrig, Bellanaleck, Enniskillen, t (028) 6634 8572 (*inexpensive*).

Riverside Farm, Gortadrehid, Culkey, Enniskillen, t (028) 6632 5822 (*inexpensive*). The River Sillies at the bottom of the farm holds the record for coarse fishing. Friendly and comfortable; contact Mrs Fawcett.

Eating Out

Scoff's, Belmore Street, Enniskillen, t (028) 6634 2622 (*expensive*). Ostrich steaks and nouvelle cuisine served in this popular restaurant. *Booking essential at weekends.*

Franco's Pizzeria, Queen Elizabeth Road, Enniskillen, t (028) 6632 4424 (*moderate*). Pasta, pizza, fish and vegetarian dishes.

Oscar's, Belmore Street, Enniskillen, t (028) 6632 7037 (*moderate*). Salmon and local trout are served in this small popular restaurant with its good atmosphere and good food. *Children welcome.*

Saddler's, 66 Belmore St, Enniskillen, t (028) 6632 6223 (*moderate*). Lovely pub food.

Blakes of the Hollow, 6 Church Street, Enniskillen, t (028) 6632 2143/6632 5388 (*inexpensive*). Pub offering snacks.

Crow's Nest, 12 High Street, Enniskillen, t (028) 6632 5252 (*inexpensive*). Oysters, cottage pie and ham. Live music every evening, but can get noisy.

Pat's Bar, 1 Townhall Street, Enniskillen, t (028) 6632 7462 (*inexpensive*). Good lunches.

Entertainment and Nightlife

Theatre
Ardhowen Theatre, Enniskillen, t (028) 6632 5440.

Traditional Music
Blakes of the Hollow, Church Street, Enniskillen, t (028) 6632 2143/6632 5388. Weekend sessions in this fine pub, with its original Victorian decor.

famous pupils. About 1¼ miles (2.4km) southeast of the town, on the main Belfast road (A4), is **Castle Coole** (*house open 16 Mar–May, weekends and bank hols, June daily exc Tues, July–Aug daily, Sept weekends only, 12–6pm; parkland open May–Sept, daily 10–8, Oct–April, daily 10–4; adm; t (028) 6632 2690, www.nationaltrust.org.uk*), an assured neoclassical house which has recently been restored by the National Trust, who replaced the Portland stone blocks of the façade. It was built between 1790 and 1797 with an agreeably simple symmetry; the main block with its colonnaded wings was designed by James Wyatt. Inside, 18th-century furniture is still in the rooms for which it was made. English plasterer Joseph Ross, who had worked for Adam at Syon and Harewood, made the long journey to supervise the creation of the ceilings. The building accounts of the house survive, and, since the cost of the construction exceeded the estimates restraint may have been exercised in the decoration, keeping it elegant but simple. In the surrounding parkland there is a lake which has a very long-established colony of greylag geese. It is said that if they leave Castle Coole, so will the Lowry-Corrys, Earls of Belmore, whose seat it is.

Northern Fermanagh

The Islands in Lower Lough Erne

Lower Lough Erne stretches in a broad arc with a pattern of 97 islands, with Belleek at one end and Enniskillen at the other. Ripe for exploration, Lough Erne's scattered islets hold many treasures. You should not miss **Devenish**; here St Molaise founded a monastic community in the 6th century, which was probably a more perilous venture than usual in that remote water kingdom, where paganism persisted long after Christian practices had taken hold in more accessible parts.

However, there is a legend which credits these parts with a visitation by a character from the Old Testament, for the prophet Jeremiah is said to have his grave in the waters of Lough Erne. His daughter was married to the son of a high king of Ireland, and she brought as her dowry the Stone of Destiny, the coronation stone of Scone, the same stone that Fergus, who also cropped up in County Antrim (*see* p.409) took to Scotland.

Devenish island has a complete round tower, with an elaborately decorated cornice. Another ruin on the island incorporating some outstanding decoration is the 12th-century Augustinian **Abbey of St Mary**. Here St Molaise rested from his labours, listening spellbound to bird song which, it was said, was the Holy Spirit communicating. The reverie lasted a hundred years, and when he looked around the abbey had been built. You will find it a few miles outside Enniskillen off the main road to Omagh (A32). (For transport to the island *see* 'Sports and Activities', p.381.)

Another island with more tangible supernatural associations is **White Island**, in Castle Archdale Bay, north of Enniskillen, famous for its eerie statues. All eight of them are lined up in a row against the wall of a 12th-century church. Like many of the sculptures found in Fermanagh and nearby districts, there is a pagan quality about these objects. There are conflicting theories about just what they represent.

Shopping

Crafts

Ardess Craft Centre, Kesh, t (028) 6863 1267.
Sells a range of local pottery, woven rugs
and other crafts; also they run spinning and
weaving workshops.

Crystal

Belleek Crystal, Main Street, Belleek, t/f (028)
6865 8631. Watch glasses, vases and lamps
of lead crystal being hand-cut at
Fermanagh's only crystal factory. Mail order
service available.

Pottery

Belleek Pottery Visitor Centre, t (028) 6665
8501, f (028) 6665 8625, www.belleek.ie.
A 20-minute guided tour of the pottery; its
parian china and early designs are collectors'
items. You can even eat off the stuff in the
Pottery Restaurant.

Sports and Activities

Bird-watching

The waterways are the home of kingfishers
and great crested grebes. The Erne basin is an
important breeding ground for redshank,
snipe, lapwing and curlew.
Eddie McGovern, Fermanagh Tourist
Information Centre, Wellington Road,
Enniskillen, t (028) 6632 3110.

Boat Hire

The area comprises over 300 square miles
(800 sq km) of island-studded lakes and rivers,
with over 70 free jetty-moorings and only one
lock. Many companies rent out cruisers by
the day or week. Prices range from around
£385 a week for a four-berth cruiser in the
low season and £1,000 for an eight-berth
in the high season. They welcome complete
novices and give free lessons on how to
handle boats. You can get a complete list from
the tourist office in Wellington Road,
Enniskillen, t (028) 6632 3110.
Manor House Marine, Killadeas, t (028)
6862 8100.
Erincurrach Cruising, Blaney, Enniskillen,
t (028) 6864 1737. Operates a one-way boat
rental between the Erne and the Shannon.

Cycling

Kingfisher Cycle Trail Tour, t (028) 6632 0121/
6632 3110, f (028) 6632 5511, www.cycleire-
land.com, pat@cycleireland.com. A 30–40
mile ride along the trail from Belleek, over
Boa Island to Kesh, down through
Irvinestown to Enniskillen and over to
Florence Court.

Fishing

The Fermanagh lakelands are renowned for
their coarse fishing. Brown trout and salmon
fishing are also excellent in the rivers and
loughs. Lough Melvin is notable for three
unusual species of trout: the gillaroo, the
sonaghan and the ferox.
Lough Melvin Holiday Centre, Garrison,
t (028) 6865 8142. Angling holidays.

Pleasure Cruises

The *Kestrel* leaves from the Round 'O' Quay in
Enniskillen for cruises round the islands every
day from July to September, and includes a
stop at Devenish Island. It is possible to hire
the *Kestrel* for private groups.

Possibly they are of Christian origin employing archaic pre-Christian styles, dating
from between the 7th and 10th centuries.

Boa Island, joined to the mainland by a bridge at each end, is the largest of the
islands. Its name comes from *Badhbha*, war goddess of the Ulster Celts, and
traditionally it remained the centre of the Druidic cult long after Christianity had
arrived in Ireland. In the old cemetery, **Caldragh**, at the west end of the island, there is
a strange 'Janus' figure with a face on each side. Such figures (several have been found
in the Fermanagh area and in Cavan) are thought to have had ritual significance; a
hollow in the figure's head may have held sacrificial blood.

Boats over 10hp must be registered with the Portora Locks Warden. You could also try: *Inishcruiser*, Share Centre, Lisnaskea, **t** (028) 6772 2122. Equipped with a bar and facilities for up to 60 people.

Ferry to White Island from Castle Archdale. *April–June Sun 2–6, July–Aug daily 11–6.*

Ferry to Devenish Island from Troy point, 3 miles north of Enniskillen (A32/B82). *Easter–Sept daily at 10am, 1, 3 and 5pm.*

Pony-trekking

Due to the foot-and-mouth epidemic in 2001, equestrian sports have practically stopped as a sport in much of County Fermanagh. The nearest horse-riding centre is in Fivemiletown, County Tyrone (*see* p.392).

Water Sports

Water-skiing and canoeing is available through the cruiser-hire companies listed above, or:

Drumrush Watersports Centre, Drumrush Lodge, Lough Erne, Kesh, **t** (028) 6863 1578.

Tudor Farm, Goal Island Road, Kesh, **t** (028) 6863 1943.

Where to Stay

Tempo Manor, Tempo, **t** (028) 8954 1450, **f** (028) 8954 1202, *www.tempomanor.com* (*expensive*). Victorian Manor house overlooking gardens and lakes.

The Cedars, Castle Archdale, Irvinestown, **t/f** (028) 6772 1493 (*moderate*). Guest house.

Lakeview House, Drum Crow, Blaney, **t** (028) 6864 1263 (*moderate*). Farmhouse with lough view.

Castle Archdale Youth Hostel, Irvinestown, **t/f** (028) 6862 8118 (*inexpensive*). Family rooms and group accommodation in an historic listed building.

Ardess House, Kesh, **t** (028) 6863 1267, *www.ardesshouse.co.uk* (*inexpensive*). Wholefood cooking from Mrs Pendry. Courses are run at the craft centre in the grounds.

Lusty Beg Island Chalets, Boa Island, **t** (028) 6863 2032 (*luxury–moderate*). Bed and breakfast as well as self-catering chalets, which sleep 6.

Self-catering

Innish Beg Cottages, Innish Beg, Blaney, Derrygonnelly, **t/f** (028) 6864 1525. Five cottages with views over Lower Lough Erne. Rowing boat for hire and private shoreline. Around £180 per week.

Shannon-Erne Luxury Cottages, Teemore; book through Rural Cottage Holidays, Central Booking Office, **t** (028) 9024 1100, **f** 9024 1198 (*expensive*). Six traditional-style cottages on the banks of the canal. Each sleeps 4.

Eating Out

Mahon's Hotel, Irvinestown, **t** (028) 6862 1656 (*moderate*). Meals served all day, but a limited choice.

The Waterfront, Irvinestown, **t** (028) 6862 1938 (*moderate–inexpensive*). Very good food but again, a limited choice.

The Cedars, Castle Archdale, Drumall, Lisnarrick, **t** (028) 6862 1493 (*moderate*). Excellent steaks.

Fiddlestone Bar, Belleek. Sandwiches.

The Northern Shore of Lough Erne

Killadeas is a fishing village looking on to Lough Erne. In the graveyard of the chapel there are some ancient, sculptured stones. One called the Bishop's Stone depicts a man with a crozier and bell. It is certainly pre-Norman. There is also a carved stone figure in the churchyard which dates from the 9th century. The country around the lough is full of the dips and hollows of the glacial-drift *drumlins*. Just beyond the lough is **Castlearchdale Country Park** (*open from early morning till dusk*) on the B82. It is an old demesne now opened up for walking in the beautiful forest along nature trails, and for camping, boating and fishing (*open July–Sept, Tues–Sun 11–7,*

Easter–June, Sun 12–6). The old castle is a pretty ruin. From the jetty you overlook White Island and **Davy's Island**; it is a good place for setting off by boat to some of the nature reserve islands. Perhaps the loveliest aspect of this part of the shore is the flowers that decorate the water's edge.

Kesh is a busy little fishing village on the A35 where you can hire cruise boats. There is a boat-building industry here specializing in traditional broad-beamed eel boats, as this is a centre for eels (though subsidiary to Lough Neagh). From Kesh you can make your way to the pretty little island of **Lustybeg**, which has holiday chalets for hire and B&B accommodation. Another 'Janus' figure was discovered here, which is now in the Enniskillen Museum. Following the curve of the shoreline west you reach **Pettigo**, which is just in County Donegal, with newer houses straggling on and over the border into Fermanagh. Pettigo is an angling village which has grown up by the River Termon about a mile from where it flows into Lough Erne. It was on the pilgrims' route to Lough Derg, which lies in Donegal about 4 miles (6km) away, so it is busy in summer. The ruins of the 17th-century **Castle Magrath**, with its keep and circular towers at the corners, are on the outskirts of the village, next to the rectory. The B136 joins up with the A47 here and leads you to the ruined **Castle Caldwell**, which is situated on a wooded peninsula jutting out into the lough – a romantic situation for a romantic and enterprising family. One of the Caldwells had a barge on which music used to be played for his pleasure. Unfortunately, a fiddler overbalanced on one of these occasions and was drowned. You can see his fiddle-shaped monument with its warning:

On firm land only exercise your skill
There you may play and safely drink your fill.

In the 19th century the Caldwells promoted the original porcelain industry at nearby Belleek, using clay found on their estate. Visitors can wander in their gardens above the shore, admiring the view that in 1776 made Arthur Young, the agriculturalist, exclaim that there was 'shelter, prospect, wood and water here in perfection'. You can use the wildfowl hides to watch the plentiful ducks, geese and other birds; these grounds also have the largest breeding colony of black scooters in the British Isles.

At **Belleek** (*Beal Leice:* 'Flagstone Ford') you reach another border village. For anglers there's a joky saying that you can hook a salmon in the Republic and land it in Northern Ireland. But it's more famous for its lustreware, which is produced for ornament rather than anything utilitarian. The 19th-century **pottery** (*see* p.380) is very attractive; it has a small museum and guided tours. Also in Belleek is **Explorerne**, an exhibition centre detailing the history of Lough Erne through exhibits and video (*open May–Sept, daily 11–5; adm;* **t** *(028) 6865 8866, tic@fermanagh.gov.uk*).

The Southern Shore of Lough Erne

On your way along the southern shore the road (A46) hugs the waterline, for limestone cliffs loom overhead, rising to the height of 2,984ft (909m) at Magho. From the **Lough Navar Forest** (inland via Derrygonnelly on the B81) viewpoint you can see the splendid sight of the lough spread out in front of you, with the hills of Donegal in the distance, and the ranges of Tyrone, Sligo and Leitrim in a grand panorama. The forest entrance, opposite Correl Glen, is about 5 miles (8km) west of Derrygonnelly. It takes you on a 7-mile (11km) scenic road which is full of nature trails and little lakes, and has a camp site. The Ulster Way footpath runs through the forest up to a height of 1,000ft, and runs down to Belcoo, between Upper and Lower Lough MacNean. This mountainous area is full of caves.

The plateau on the southern shore is covered with forest lands, and behind them are the Cuilcagh Mountains rising to the south. If you stick to the loughside you will pass the plantation-era **Tully Castle** (*open April–Sept, Tues–Sat 10–7 Sun 2–7, rest of year, 2–7; adm*) and, further inland towards the south, a better-preserved castle at **Monea** (*free access always*). Both show the Scottish style brought to this country by settlers. Monea's front shows two circular towers which are square on the top storey, and the crow-stepped gables add to its Scottish air.

Southern Fermanagh

Up into the Western Mountains

For spectacular sights nature has more on her side than architecture, so head towards the mountains in the west. You can take winding roads cross-country from Monea, but for a simpler route take Enniskillen as a starting point and follow the A4. At **Belcoo** you reach a village lost in the mountains, situated on a narrow strip of land separating the two Lough MacNeans. In this place *patterns* to St Patrick's Well are held on Bilberry Sunday, the last Sunday in July and also the date of the Celtic *Lughnasa*, or festival of fertility; a lingering tradition which gave Brian Friel the name for his play *Dancing at Lughnasa*.

If you go back by **Lower Lough MacNean** you will see the **Hanging Rock** from the minor road which goes to Blacklion across the border. Limestone has endowed this place with caverns. They stretch in a sort of underground labyrinth through the Cuilcagh Mountains, and some remain to be explored. **Marble Arch Show Caves** at Marlbank, Florencecourt (*open Mar–Sept, daily from 10am, weather permitting; last tour 4.30pm; adm exp; call ahead before setting out, t (028) 6634 8855*) have been designated a European Geo-Park in recognition of their geological importance. A 1¼-hour tour includes an underground boat trip. Take a jumper and flat shoes.

The wooded demesne of Florence Court is situated under the steep mountain of **Benaughlin**, which means 'peak of the horse'; the white limestone showing through the scree at the foot of the eastern cliff did indeed once portray the outline of a horse, though it has now become difficult to distinguish. **Florence Court** (*open April–May and Sept, Sat–Sun 1–6, June–Aug, Wed–Mon 1–6; grounds open all year 10–7; adm; t (028) 6634 8249*), home of the Coles, Earls of Enniskillen, is about 8 miles (13km) southwest of the town they helped to fortify in Plantation times, on the A4 and A32 Swanlibar road. Built in the mid-18th century for Lord Mountflorence, the

Shopping

Antiques
Forge Antiques, Circular Road, Lisbellaw.
Sheelin Irish Lace Museum and
Sheelin Antiques, Bellanaleck, t (028)
6634 8052. Award-winning antique
lace museum.

Sports and Activities

Bird-watching
There is a wealth of bird life for the
enthusiast: the waterways are home to
kingfishers and great crested grebes, and the
Erne basin is an important breeding ground
for redshank, snipe, lapwing and curlew.
Eddie McGovern, Fermanagh District
Council TIC, Wellington Road, Enniskillen,
t (028) 6632 3110.

Fishing
The Fermanagh lakelands are renowned
for their coarse fishing. Brown trout and
salmon fishing are also excellent in the
rivers and loughs. See 'Sports and Activities'
in Northern Fermanagh for more
information, p.380.

Golf
Enniskillen Golf Club, Castle Coole Estate,
t (028) 6632 5250.

Pleasure Cruises
The Share Centre, Lisnaskea, t (028) 6772 2122.
Organizes tours of Upper Lough Erne on
the Inishcruiser; they also have a Viking
Longship, but only use it on request.
Open Easter–Sept.
Carrybridge Boat Company, Lisbellaw,
t (028) 6638 7034.

Potholing
Marble Arch Caves, Florence Court,
t (028) 6634 8855.

Where to Stay

Lanesborough Arms, High Street,
Newtownbutler, t (028) 6773 8488
(moderate). Refurbished 18th-century
town house.
Tullyhona House, Marble Arch Road, Florence
Court, t (028) 6634 8452 (moderate–
inexpensive). Old house set in its own
grounds beside Upper Lough Erne, with
children's play areas. Fine home-cooking.

Self-catering
Rose Cottage, Florence Court; call National
Trust Central Reservations, UK t (01225)
791199, www.nationaltrust.org.uk (expensive). Cottage on Florence Court demesne.
Crom Cottages, Crom Estate (National Trust)
near Lisnaskea, t (028) 6773 8118; or NT
Central Reservations, t (01225) 791199,
www.nationaltrust.org.uk (expensive).
Seven converted cottages available.
Belle Isle Estate Cottages, Lisbellaw;
contact Rural Cottage Holidays (see below)
or Mr C Plunket, t (028) 6638 7231,
f (028) 6638 7261, www.belleisle-estate.com
(luxury). Traditional cottages – a garden
cottage, coach house and bridge house – on
a lovely estate at the northern end of Upper
Lough Erne, sleeping 4–6, with spacious,
modern interiors.

Eating Out

Florence Court House, t (028) 6634 8249
(inexpensive). Quiche, stews, wheaten bread.
Lunch only.
The Sheelin, Bellanaleck, t (028) 6634 8232
(moderate). Excellent for lunch or dinner.
Traditional cottage with climbing roses
round the door, with a delicious and
original menu.
Le Bistro, Ernside Centre, t (028) 6632 6954
(moderate).
Wild Duck Inn, Lisbellaw, t (028) 6638 5032
(inexpensive). Pub grub.

house has sadly suffered fire damage, but there is still some fine rococo plasterwork.
It is beautifully situated in woodland with views across to the Cuilcagh Mountains. In
the gardens is the original Florence Court yew, from whose seedlings grew Taxus
baccata fastigiata, now found all over the world.

Upper Lough Erne

Upper Lough Erne and the maze of waters from the Erne river system provide quite a challenge for the explorer, so arm yourself with a good map. This area bridges the less water-strewn area of east Fermanagh whose pretty towns you may pass through. Some bear names of founder planter families. **Brookeborough** is on the A4, near the home of the Brooke family, who were prominent in Northern Irish affairs. Basil, the first Viscount Brookeborough (1888–1973), was Prime Minister of Northern Ireland, and is remembered, perhaps unfairly, for his *laager* mentality towards Roman Catholics, whom he said he 'wouldn't have about the place'. The town of **Maguiresbridge** is named after the reigning chieftains, who were deposed by the planters.

This area is rich in folk tradition; you might meet someone with the secret of a cure, either for animal or human ailments. If you are interested in the distinctive sculptures you may have seen at the Enniskillen Museum or elsewhere, go and search out **Tamlaght Bay** near Lisbellaw on the A4, where at **Derrybrusk Old Church** you can see some more strange carved heads on a wall. At nearby **Aghalurcher Churchyard**, near Lisnaskea on the A34, you can see gravestones carved with what seems to be a rather macabre funerary motif, typically found in Fermanagh: the skull and crossbones.

The Crom Estate (*open April–end Sept, Mon–Sat 10–6 Sun 12–6; car park fee*) on the shores of Upper Lough Erne is a huge acreage of woodland, parkland and wetland. It is under the protection of the National Trust and is an important nature conservation area. You approach it on a minor road off the A34 in Newtownbutler. **Lisnaskea**, also on the A34, is rather an interesting market town with a restored market cross whose ancient shaft has fine carving. In the middle of the town is a ruined 17th-century castle built by Sir James Balfour, which was burnt down in the 19th century. On the main street is a folklife display at the **library** (*open Mon, Tues and Fri 9.15–5, Wed 9.15–7.30, Sat 9.15–12.30; adm free; t (028) 6772 1222*). A cruise boat leaves from the jetty here for 1½-hour tours of Upper Lough Erne (*see* opposite).

The upper reaches of Lough Erne are scattered with 58 little 'islands'. These prettily named islands are really tiny districts or townlands, and not islands at all. Some of them are inhabited, though on an increasingly part-time basis. A sad story illustrates the difficulties associated with island living: a postman living on Inishturk Island froze to death when his boat was trapped in ice during the hard winter of 1961. **Cleenish Island** can be reached from Bellanaleck on the A509 by a bridge. There are some remarkable carved headstones in the graveyard. Even more interesting is the collection of carved slabs on **Inishkeen**, accessible by causeway from Killyhevlin.

Belle Isle is a townland which claims to be the spot where the *Annals of Ulster* were compiled in the 15th century by Cathal MacManus, Dean of Lough Erne. **Galloon Island** is large, with another ancient graveyard where you may, if you persevere, discern the curious carvings on the 9th- or 10th-century cross shafts which depict a man hanging upside down. Some think that this might be Judas Iscariot, or perhaps St Peter.

County Tyrone

This is the heart of Ulster, the land named after Eoghan (Owen), one of the sons of High King Niall of the Nine Hostages, who lived in the 4th century AD and was the progenitor of the O'Neill dynasty. The least populated of the six counties, Tyrone is celebrated in many a poignant song by emigrant sons. The Sperrin Mountains cover a large part of the north, the highest at 2,240ft (678m) being Sawel, which is on the border with County Londonderry. In these lonely hills locals have panned for gold for hundreds of years – excitement has recently been generated by the discovery of large deposits. Lough Neagh forms Tyrone's eastern border for a few miles in the east, but the county's attractions are its chattering burns, its flora and fauna and peaceful glens. There is much to attract the walker and naturalist in the Sperrin Mountains.

In the southeastern area it is well-wooded, and there is a much quoted tag about 'Tyrone among the bushes, where the Finn and Mourne run'. The land in this region is

Getting There and Around

By Air
Belfast International Airport and Dublin Airport are about 70 and 86 miles (112 and 137km) from Omagh respectively. Enniskillen Airport is not very far away (*see* p.376), as is the City of Derry Airport, t (028) 7181 0784. Belfast City Airport, t (028) 9045 7745, also has services. (An airbus service operates to and from Belfast city centre, t (028) 9033 3000.)

By Rail
There is no railway line in Tyrone. The nearest stations to the county are in Portadown, t (028) 3835 1422, and Derry City.

By Bus
Translink/Ulsterbus maintains a good service to all parts of the county. Express Coach and Bus Eireann also link County Tyrone to other parts of Ireland.
Omagh bus station, t (028) 8224 2711.
Strabane bus station, t (028) 7138 2393.
Bus Eireann, t (074) 21309.
Derry City bus station, t (028) 7126 2261.

By Car
Gallen Vehicle Hire, 96 Drumlegagh Road South, Omagh Town, t (028) 8224 6966.
P.G. McGillion, 132 Melmount Road, Sion Mills, t (028) 8165 8275.
Tattyreagh Car Hire, 110 Tattyreagh Road, Fintona, t (028) 8284 1731.

By Bike
Conway Cycles, 1 Market Place, Omagh, t (028) 8224 6195; also at 157 Loughmacrory Road, Carrickmore, t (028) 8076 1258.

Festivals

May
Magherafelt and District Mad May Festival.
West Tyrone *Feis*. Irish dancing and music.

June
Fair Day Carnival, Strabane, t (028) 7138 2204. Street entertainment in vintage Strabane.
The Strawberry Fair, Sion Mills, Strabane, t (028) 8165 8350. Traditional village fête.

July
Clogher Valley Agricultural Show, Augher.
Midsummer Festival, Ulster History Park.
Omagh Agricultural Show.
Ulster American Folk Park Festival, t (028) 8225 6330.

August–September
Glenelly Sheep and Dog Trials, Plumbridge, Strabane, t (028) 8164 8744.
Johnny Crampsie Weekend, Strabane, t (074) 41106, www.johnnycrampsie.com. Traditional Irish music and workshops.
Magherafelt Folk and Hillwalking Festival.
Storytelling Festival, Rural College, Draperstown, t (028) 7962 9100.

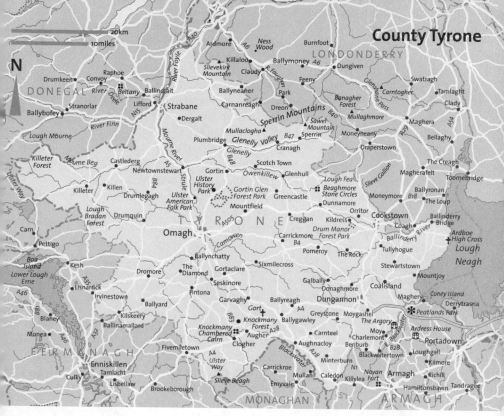

more fertile and well-planted with trees; the farmers here keep cattle and sheep. Many of the farmhouses are still of whitewashed stone with gaily painted doorways. The linen industry is important at Moygashel and there are many small businesses in the main towns, such as milling and crafts. The plantation families have their traditions and Big Houses in the southeast too. Some of the loveliest, such as Caledon, are still occupied by their original families, whilst the most unusual, Killymoon Castle, was saved from ruin by a farmer who bought it for £100 in the 1920s. (Neither of these houses is open to the public.)

Tyrone is an undiscovered county for many tourists, but it inspires pride in its native dwellers. Tyrone people are known for their music and their talent with language, both the spoken and written word. Notice how many writers and poets come from this part of the world: William Carleton, John Montague, Brian Friel and Flann O'Brien.

History

County Tyrone's past can be illustrated by concentrating on the lands and estate of Caledon, a small village close to the border with County Monaghan. This was O'Neill territory, and the natives fought the English vigorously from the mid-17th century on; but by the 18th century the region had been planted with Scottish undertakers. The story of Captain William Hamilton is typical of many of the new landlords. A Cromwellian soldier and one of the Hamiltons from Haddington in East Lothian,

William was granted the Caledon estate of Sir Phelim O'Neill after the Battle of Benburb in 1646. By 1775 the Hamilton line, which had intermarried with the Osserys – Earls of Ossery and Cork – had become very extravagant. As a result of their debts, the property was sold to a Derry merchant's son, James Alexander, who had acquired a vast fortune in the service of the East India Company. The most distinguished member of this family (which still owns the estate) was Viscount Alexander of Tunis.

Tyrone's history lives on in its language: some expressions recall Gaelic, although it is no longer spoken here, and a few turns of phrase will take you back to the days of Elizabeth I. For example, a 'boon' is a company of people in the house, to 'join' is to begin, to 'convoy' is to accompany, and 'diet' is the word for food. The small farmers in this area are for the most part descended from Scottish Presbyterians, although in the Sperrins there are many Catholic descendants of the O'Neills and their *septs*.

Northern Tyrone

Strabane and Environs

Strabane (*An Srath Ban*: 'The White Holm') is a border town and almost the twin of Lifford, across the Foyle in Donegal. The Finn and the Mourne join to form the Foyle here as well. Strabane is a bustling town with friendly people. It is also the birthplace of John Dunlap, printer of the American Declaration of Independence. You should try to visit **Grays Printers' Museum** (*open April–end Sept, Tues–Sat 2–5; adm; t (028) 7188 4094*), the 18th-century printing shop in Main Street where Dunlap worked. There is a collection of 19th-century hand-printing machines in full working order. Another Strabane-born notable is that curious wit Brian O'Nolan, alias Flann O'Brien. He wrote *The Poor Mouth, At-Swim-Two-Birds* and other stories, and his column in *The Irish Times* between 1937 and 1966 became a byword for a debunking type of humour.

Just to the northeast of Strabane, at **Dunnamanagh** (also spelled 'Donemana'), on the town's outskirts, you'll find **Silverbrook Mill** (*on Brook Road, t (028) 7139 7097*), which comprises an 18th-century corn mill and a 19th-century flax mill. You might also visit the **Tom Agnew Pottery**, nearby (*see* 'Shopping').

The Tyrone Hills

East of Strabane you pass into the **Tyrone Hills**, which consist mainly of the Sperrin mountain range and extend into County Londonderry. This is perfect walking country, full of glens and mountain passes to beyond Plumbridge (which is at the western end of the beautiful Glenelly Valley) and Cranagh. The **Sperrin Heritage Centre** (*open daily April–Oct; adm; t (028) 8164 8142*) is situated on Glenelly Road, between the villages of Cranagh and Sperrin. Here there is a comprehensive and interesting display of Sperrin wildlife, showing all the animals, birds and plant species that you might see whilst walking in the glens around here, like the hen harrier or the cloudberry, which grows on a single patch west of Dart Mountain.

One of the great saints of Ireland, St Brigid, is strongly associated with this area; there are not many houses which do not have a St Brigid cross hanging above the

Tourist Information

Strabane: Abercorn Square, **t** (028) 7188 3735; *open April–Sept.*

Castlederg: 26 Lower Strabane Road, **t** (028) 8167 0795; *open Easter–Oct.*

Cranagh: Sperrin Heritage Centre, 274 Glenelly Road, Plumbridge, **t** (028) 8164 8142; *open April–Oct.*

Omagh: 1 Market Street, **t** (028) 8224 7831; *open all year.*

Shopping

Antiques
Melmount Auctions, Unit C, Ballycolman Industrial Estate, Strabane, **t** (028) 8224 6271.
Kelly's Antiques, Old Mountfield Road, Omagh.
Viewback Antique Auctions, 8 Castle Place, Omagh, **t** (028) 8224 6271.

Pottery
Tom Agnew Mill Pottery, Brook Road, Donemana/Dunnamanagh, **t** (028) 7139 8377. Produces useful objects for everyday living in wonderful muted shades of stoneware.

Sports and Activities

Fishing
On the River Blackwater, near Omagh, for brown trout, sea trout and salmon, and on the Mourne River System which includes the Strule, Owenkillew and Glenelly. Licences from Foyle Fisheries Commission or local fishing tackle shops.

Baronscourt Estate, Newtownstewart, **t** (028) 8166 1683. Also offers pike fishing in the estate's lakes. *Book well in advance.*

Foyle Fisheries Commission, Derry, **t** (028) 7134 2100.

Department of Culture, Arts and Leisure, Inland Fisheries Division, Strabane District Council, **t** (028) 9025 8861. Fishing permits.

C.A. Anderson and Company, Hardware Merchant, 64 Market Street, Omagh, **t** (028) 8224 2311, **f** (028) 8224 9539. For fishing permits.

Golf
Newtownstewart Golf Club, **t** (028) 8166 1466.
Omagh Golf Club, **t** (028) 8224 3160. An 18-hole parkland course.
Fintona Golf Club, Fintona, **t** (028) 8284 1480. Best parkland 9-hole in Ireland.

Internet Access
Omagh Library, 1 Spillar's Place (off Dublin Road), **t** (028) 8224 4821.

Pony-trekking
Clanabogan Riding Stables, 85 Clanabogan Road, Omagh, **t** (028) 8225 2050.
Ardmourne House Stables, **t** (028) 8167 0291.
Ashlee Riding Centre, **t** (028) 7188 2708.
Carricklee Riding Centre, **t** (028) 7188 3221.
Tullywhisker Riding School, **t** (028) 8165 8267.

door to ward off evil. These crosses look rather like the ancient symbol, the swastika, and are made of rushes. The B48 from Gortin to Omagh passes through the wild and beautiful **Gortin Glen Forest Park**, where there are nature trails amongst the conifer trees. The Ulster Way also passes through. The country lanes around about are bright with gorse and primroses in spring, and the lambs make a very pretty sight. Another visitor centre, the **Ulster History Park** at Cullion (*open April–Sept, Mon–Sat 10.30–6.30 Sun 11.30–7, Oct–Mar, Mon–Fri 10.30–5; adm; **t** (028) 8164 8188*), traces human settlement and society from 8000 BC to the 17th century.

A couple of miles southeast of Strabane on the pretty, unnumbered Plumbridge road, at Dergalt, is the **Wilson Ancestral Homestead** (*open July–Aug, Tues–Sun 2–5, at other times call for opening hours; adm; **t** (028) 7138 2204*). This comparatively humble dwelling is where President Woodrow Wilson's grandfather (among many other children) was reared before he set off for the States to become a newspaper editor.

Shooting

Rough and clay pigeon shooting is available over the Sperrin Mountains. Book well in advance.

Baronscourt Estate, Newtownstewart, t (028) 8166 1683.

Collow Quarry Shooting Grounds, 44 Bradan Road, Drumquin, t (028) 8283 1625. Clay pigeon shooting.

Walking

In the valleys of the Glenelly, Owenreagh, Owenkillew and Camowen Rivers; in the 12 Sperrin forests, and Gortin Glen Forest Park with its nature trails and wild deer. The **Ulster Way**, a signposted walking trail, goes through the Sperrins. Strabane Tourist Information, Castlederg Visitor Centre and the Sperrin Heritage Centres sell maps and guides to the area for walkers and cyclists between April and October. The Department of Culture, Arts and Leisure of Strabane District Council offers them at other times of the year, t (028) 7138 2204.

Where to Stay and Eat

Badoney Tavern, 16 Main Street, Gortin, t (028) 8164 8157 (*inexpensive*). Good pub lunches and snacks.

Hawthorn House, 72 Old Mountfield Road, Omagh, t (028) 8225 2005 (*moderate*). Open daily for breakfast, lunch and dinner. Recommended for its excellent gourmet food. Accommodation is also available.

Golden Hill, 32 Tattykeel Road, Omagh, t (028) 8225 1257, *goldenhill@sperrins.com* (*inexpensive*). Lovely scenic location where visitors are especially welcome.

An Creagán, Creggan, Omagh, t (028) 8076 1112, f (028) 8076 1116. Eight traditional-style self-catering cottages; each sleeps 6. From £330 per week in high season.

Aughalane *Clachan*, Aughalane, Omagh, t (028) 9024 1100. Self-catering cottages which sleep 2–5 people; from £290 per week in high season.

Mote Cottage, Omagh, t (028) 8224 4589. Traditional whitewashed cottages with flowers around the door. Sleeps 2, self-catering; from £225 per week in high season.

Mellon Country Inn, 134 Beltany Road, Omagh, t (028) 8166 1224, f (028) 8166 2245 (*moderate*). Good steaks.

Entertainment and Nightlife

Traditional Music

Teach Ceoil in Rouskey, and the **Fernagh** *Ceili* **House**. Evenings of *craic*, traditional music, dance, stories and poetry. Enquire at the Omagh tourist office or *Commhaltas Ceoltoiri Eireann* in Omagh, t (028) 8224 2777, f (028) 8225 2162.

An Creagan Visitor Centre, t (028) 8076 1112. *Dún Uladh* Heritage Centre of Ulster, Ballinamullan, Omagh, t (028) 8224 2777.

Newtownstewart, on the A5 10 miles (16km) south of Strabane, is a 17th-century plantation town. It is attractively laid out on a large main street. Nearby on the B84 lies the **Baronscourt Estate**, which has a fine mansion house and gardens which you can tour (*by appointment only, t (028) 8166 1683*). There is coarse and game fishing available on the estate, and pony-trekking and golf nearby.

The **Ulster American Folk Park** (*open Easter–Sept, Mon–Sat 11–6.30 Sun 11.30–7, rest of year, Mon–Fri 10.30–5; last entry 3.30; adm; Mellon Road, Castletown, t (028) 8224 3292*) is between Newtownstewart and Omagh, sandwiched between the A5 and the Plumbridge road. Named Visitor Attraction of the Year 2000–2001, it was developed in order to illustrate the life that emigrants left in Ireland and that which they encountered in their new land, by reconstructing the buildings they inhabited. The ancestral home of the Mellons and the boyhood home of Archbishop John Hughes of New York are very spartan and simple, and established showpieces. There is a fair bit of outdoor walking, so take along some good strong shoes and a raincoat. East of Omagh, at Creggan, you will find the **An Creagán Visitor Centre** (*open daily April–Sept, 11–6.30, Oct–Mar, 11–4.30; adm; t (028) 8076 1112, f 8076 1116*) with bog trails, archaeological exhibits and a restaurant. Several archaeological walks and events are held throughout the year here.

Omagh

Omagh, the capital of Tyrone, is separated from the other large town of the county, **Cookstown**, by the Black Bog. This accounts for the turfcraft souvenirs you may find – which make an alternative to the more usual Irish linen hankies or crochet. Some people tell you that there is something French about this town, with its twin-spired church and its reputation for liveliness. Brian Friel, the playwright, is a native. (Any of his plays are worth making a special effort to see; he gives a profound and lyrical insight into Irish culture.). Other writers from this area are Benedict Kiely, Alice Milligan and William Forbes Marshall. The town is a good spot for fishing on the Camowen and Owenreagh Rivers. Those wanting to hear musical talent should time their visit to coincide with the West Tyrone *Feis* in May, also known as the Omagh *Feis*, which has plenty of Irish music and dancing.

Since 15 August 1998, Omagh has been known as the site of the most devastating single act of violence in the history of the Troubles: 29 people were killed by a bomb that day in the city centre. There is now a small memorial garden at the site, on Drumragh Avenue beside Strule Bridge, where one may spend some time in quiet reflection.

Southern Tyrone

From Omagh to Cookstown

Omagh is near other forest areas: **Seskinore Forest**, near Fintona, and **Dromore Forest**, further west. Should you wish to strike across the moor country you can go by Mountfield on the A505 from Omagh, which will take you by the Black Bog, a nature reserve; any other little roads you encounter may take you past some of the many antiquities which testify to Bronze or earlier Stone Age inhabitants of this area.

At **Pomeroy**, 15 miles (24km) east of Omagh on the B4, high in the mountains and equidistant from Cookstown and Dungannon, there are the remains of seven stone circles. More famous are the **Beaghmore Stone Circles**, outside Cookstown and near Dunnamore; these intricate alignments on a northeast axis represent the remarkable architecture of the late Stone Age or early Bronze Age. Their formation has been likened to a clock pointing for the last six thousand years towards the midsummer sunrise. They certainly look very impressive in the wild landscape that surrounds them. To get there, take a minor road off the A505 through Dunnamore and travel on a few miles, going north. Near to Cookstown at Corkhill is **Wellbrook Beetling Mill**

Tourist Information

Cookstown: 48 Molesworth Street, t (028) 8676 6727; *open April–Oct.*
Dungannon: Killymaddy Tourist Information Centre, 190 Ballygawley Road, t (028) 8776 7259; *open all year.*

Shopping

Glass

Tyrone Crystal, Killybrackey, t (028) 8772 5335. The glassworks give you a guided tour, and you can buy seconds very cheaply.

Sports and Activities

Fishing

On the River Blackwater for brown trout, sea trout and salmon. Licences from Foyle Fisheries Commission, Derry, or local fishing tackle shops. For the Ballinderry River, you need a Fisheries Conservancy Board game rod licence and a permit (from tackle shops or tourist offices in Caledon, Cookstown, Omagh, Moy and Aughnacloy).
Loughs Agency, Derry City, t (028) 7134 2100. Information on fishing in Creeve Lough, near Benburb, White Lough, near Aughnacloy, and brown trout fishing in Brantry Lough.

Kilmaddy Tourist Information Centre, t (028) 8776 7259. Offers details.
Anderson's, 64 Market Street, Omagh, t (028) 8224 2311.
Treanor's, Main Street, Gortin, t (028) 8166 8543.

Golf

Killymoon Golf Club, Cookstown, t (028) 8676 3762. An 18-hole parkland course.
Aughnacloy Golf Club, Aughnacloy, t (028) 8555 7050.

Open Farms

Altmore Fisheries, 32 Altmore Road, 3 miles south of Pomeroy, t (028) 8775 8977. *Open daily.*

Pony-trekking

Moy Riding School, 131 Derrycaw Road, Moy, t (028) 8778 4440.
Hilltop Stables, Eglish, t (028) 8775 3925.
Crocknagrally Forest Stables, 100 Croneen Road, Fivemiletown, t (028) 8952 1991.

Shooting

Seskinore Game Farm, Seskinore, t (028) 8284 1243.
Logue's Hill Clay Pigeon Club, near Cappagh. Book through Killymaddy Tourist Information Centre, t (028) 8776 7259.

(open April–June and Sept, daily 2–6, July–Aug, daily exc Tues 2–6, Oct–Mar, weekends and bank hols 2–6; adm; 20 Wellbrook Road, t/f (028) 8675 1735), a water-powered hammer mill for beetling, which is the final stage of linen manufacture. The mill is situated in a lovely glen with walks along the Ballinderry River and the mill race.

Cookstown is situated in the middle of Northern Ireland, near the fertile heartland which traces its course beside the Bann in Londonderry and continues down by Lough Neagh. There are two Nash buildings in its environs. On the outskirts southeast of the town is **Killymoon Castle**, a battlemented towered construction which contrasts with the simple Church of Ireland parish church known as St Laurane's at the southeast end of the main street. The conspicuous Puginesque Catholic church, sited on a hill in the middle of town, provides a good landmark. Arriving at Cookstown, you will be impressed by the long, wide main street; those of a cynical turn of mind may think it a good street for leading a charge against insurgents. Cookstown has a strong Nationalist tradition, exemplified by the energetic Bernadette Devlin, now McAliskey, who was active in the Civil Rights Movement and elected to the British Parliament

Walking

Forest parks with nature trails include **Favour Royal**, just southwest of Caledon on the Monaghan border, **Gollagh Woods**, and **Fardross Forest**, near Clogher, where you can see red squirrels. Riverside walks can be taken by **Wellbrook Beetling Mill**, near Cookstown.

Where to Stay

Braeside House, 23 Drumcovis Road, Coagh, Cookstown, t (028) 8673 7301 (*inexpensive*). Two rooms available in an old house.

Grange Lodge, 7 Grange Road, near Dungannon, t (028) 8778 4212, f (028) 8778 4313 (*moderate*). Comfortable Georgian house by the Blackwater River, with outstanding breakfasts. Contact Mrs Brown.

Charlemont House, 4 The Square, Moy, Dungannon, t (028) 8778 4755 (*inexpensive*). Georgian townhouse with period furnishings and lots of atmosphere. The lovely garden has a view of the Blackwater River at the back. Contact Mr and Mrs McNeice.

Corick House, 20 Corick Road, Clogher, t (028) 8554 8216, f (028) 8554 9531 (*expensive–moderate*). 17th-century house, full of history, in lovely grounds.

The Valley Hotel, 60 Main Street, Fivemiletown, t (028) 8952 1505 (*moderate*). Comfortable and cheery.

Self-catering

Blessingbourne Luxury Flats, near Fivemiletown, t (028) 8952 1221 (*expensive*). You can imagine you are staying in the time of leisurely house parties when you stay near this attractive Victorian mansion set in wooded grounds. Captain R. M. Lowry has three self-catering apartments, with very comfortable rooms.

Eating Out

Tullylagan Country House, 40 Tullylagan Road, near Cookstown, t (028) 8676 5100 (*moderate*).

Cookstown Courtyard, 56 William Street, Cookstown, t (028) 8676 5070 (*inexpensive*). Set lunch, home-made pies and puddings.

Tyrone Crystal Café, Killybracken Road, Dungannon, t (028) 8772 9953 (*inexpensive*).

Tommy's Bar, 9 The Square, Moy, t (028) 8778 4755 (*inexpensive*). A very authentic pub.

Suitor Gallery, 17 Grange Road, Ballygawley, t (028) 8556 8653. Good home-baking..

The Caledon Arms Hotel, 44 Main Street, Caledon, t (028) 3756 8161 (*inexpensive*).

Rosamund's Coffee Shop, Station House, Augher, t (028) 8554 8601 (*inexpensive*). Serves home-made stew during the day.

aged only 21 in 1969. There is also a strong Scottish Protestant tradition with the descendants of those who settled here in the 17th century.

Places to visit nearby include the loughside **Ardboe High Cross**, about 10 miles (16km) east on the shore of Lough Neagh. The cross is a 10th-century monument with 22 remarkable sculptured scriptural panels covered with scenes from the Old and New Testaments. These scenes are easily recognizable, unlike those on many of the other high crosses you may see, which are usually so weathered that you need to concentrate to read the theme. South of Cookstown, **Tullaghogue Rath** (pronounced 'Tullyhog') is where the great O'Neill chieftains were inaugurated. In 1595 Hugh O'Neill gave in to the British, and seven years later the Lord Deputy Mountjoy had the throne smashed to prevent any future ceremonies.

At the foot of Tullaghogue hill, in what is now Loughry Agricultural College, is the mansion where Jonathan Swift stayed while writing *Gulliver's Travels*; the portraits of his two loves, Stella and Vanessa, still hang in the house. It is sometimes possible to visit it; ask at the door. **Drum Manor Forest Park** close by, to the east of Cookstown on the A505, has a butterfly garden and a forest trail for the disabled (*open all year daily 10am–dusk; adm; parking fee; t (028) 8676 2774*).

Dungannon and Along the Blackwater River

Dungannon, a city on a hill, looks like your average planter town; with a planned main street and a Royal School founded in the time of James I of England. It was, in fact, the centre for the O'Neills until the Flight of the Earls deprived the Gaels of their native leaders (*see* **History**, p.40). It is now a quietly prosperous town with a long-established textile industry specializing in Moygashel fabrics, and a glass factory producing Tyrone crystal. At the beginning of the 17th century, in order to promote good Protestant education, James I of England and Ireland (James VI of Scotland) provided Royal Schools as well as charters for land. You may notice the **Royal School, Dungannon** which is on Northland Row in the centre of the town. The present building dates from 1786, and outside it is a statue of one of its most famous 'old boys', Major General John Nicholson, whose exploits in India inspired such respect that there was even a sect called 'Nikkul Seyn'. Another Indian connection is the **police station** in the town centre, which looks like a castle with projecting apertures for missile-throwing. Apparently it was built according to plans for a fort in the Khyber Pass because some clerk in Dublin got into a muddle. This is the usual explanation for many of the exotic-looking stations that are scattered about Ireland.

Tyrone has its River Blackwater, though it is not in the same league as the other Blackwater, which flows through Cork and Waterford. It creates a watery border with County Armagh and flows through **Moy** – with its Italian-styled square created by one of the Charlemont family – to **Benburb**, an ancient stronghold with a splendid ruined castle. The parish **church** (Church of Ireland) is 17th century and there are some fine tombstones in the graveyard. In 1646 the Irish forces led by Owen Roe O'Neill gained a significant victory here over English Puritan and Scottish troops.

The Blackwater flows in a series of fine pools and little falls to **Caledon** on the A28, with its unspoiled Georgian look. Intriguing to the traveller is the **Clogher Valley**, which is border country with the Republic and so enjoys that anomalous status of being either frontier outpost or lost territory. This place evidently has a long history of habitation, for many ancient earthworks have survived. In the townland of **Gort**, between Ballygawley and Augher, is the ancient graveyard of Errigal Keerogue, with a fine high cross and a superb view over the countryside.

Just north of Augher, off the B83, is the **Knockmany Forest**, a government-run forestry plantation on Knockmany Hill. At the top, look for the **Knockmany Chambered Cairn**, said to be the burial place of Queen Aine, Queen of Oriel, a 6th-century kingdom whose centre was Clogher. The cairn is a passage grave dating from Neolithic times. This type of monument consists of a stone-built passage leading to a terminal chamber, often cruciform in shape, and covered by a mound or cairn of stones. The remarkable thing about this grave is its incised decoration, in patterns of concentric circles, zig-zags and other designs, which are similar in style to the great earthworks in the Boyne Valley, County Meath. This country, besides being a fisherman's haunt, is well forested. The 19th-century landlords who once owned vast tracts of land have disappeared, but their old estates, such as Favour Royal and Fardross, gave their names to public parkland and forests where it is possible to camp and have picnics. At **Favour Royal**, you can walk from the river to St Patrick's Well and Chair at Altadaven – a secret, mossy place.

Augher and Clogher are within striking distance. **Augher** lies between the Blackwater River and Augher Lake. You can see the 19th-century **Castle of Spur Royal** just to the west of the village as you pass by on the A4. **Clogher** village is on a site of prehistoric importance, as well as being of great ecclesiastical significance. It was the original seat in the 5th century of the diocese of Clogher, one of the oldest bishoprics in Ireland. In the porch of **St MacCartan's Cathedral** there is a curious stone called the *Clogh-oir*, or 'Gold Stone'. There are two 9th-century high crosses in the graveyard, and you can climb the tower and get a stunning view of the Clogher Valley (ask at the rectory for access). Behind this centre of ancient Christianity is the even older hill-fort of **Ramore** (*always accessible*). Archaeologists have investigated it for evidence about the Iron Age, and perhaps the mysterious *Clogh-oir* comes from an idol of those times. It was certainly the site of the palace of the kings of Oriel; the tradition of the dynasty survives but not the dates, other than that they were pre-5th century. The hill-fort itself is now just a grassy mound.

Benburb has a picturesque castle ruin on a cliff overhanging the Blackwater River; this early 17th-century castle replaced an earlier O'Neill stronghold. The demesne surrounding the castle is freely accessible and the Servite Priory in the grounds has a popular open day on the third Sunday in June. **Benburb Valley Heritage Centre**, on Milltown Road (*open East–Sept, Tues–Sat 10–5 Sun 2–5; t (028) 3754 9885*), operates from the 19th-century linen mill on the banks of the Ulster Canal. You may like to take a tour around the mill and learn about the linen industry in Ireland; it also has a hostel and a café.

County Londonderry

This is a rich and varied region. The traditions of political argument and protest vie with the gifts of learning and song in the people who inhabit this friendly land. The countryside ranges from stormy sea coast and wild mountain ranges to sheltered valleys, well-wooded from years of far-sighted planting. The coastline from Magilligan to Downhill is scattered with golden strands. Historic Derry is a spire-dreaming city which arouses fierce passions in the hearts of its inhabitants.

The city and the whole county are fostering a renaissance of peace and heightened business activity after suffering several decades of the Troubles, which started in the 1960s. New housing, sports centres and a £15 million theatre have been built, and regeneration schemes have been implemented to replace destroyed shops with new city centre hotels, businesses and riverside apartments. Further rejuvenation has come through its Craft Village, Heritage Centre, and award-winning Tower Museum. People in the province are determined to live and work together harmoniously, and the traditional tribal areas are becoming less so with each passing year. The economy of County Londonderry is heavily subsidized by the British government, but there is still high unemployment in places like the Bogside. Several international companies have set up factories and there are the traditional shirt-makers, although these are now struggling in the face of competition from Third World countries.

Getting There and Around

Derry is a terminus for railway and bus services, and is a useful halfway house for those moving east or west.

By Air
City of Derry Airport, t (028) 7181 0784, *www.derry.net/airport/*. For flights to Manchester, Glasgow, Dublin and London Stansted.
Belfast International Airport, t (028) 9442 2888, *www.bial.co.uk*.
Belfast City Airport, t (028) 9045 7745, *www.belfastcityairport.com*.

By Sea
P&O ferries offer the shortest, fastest crossing (60mins) between Scotland and Larne. Seacat, Stena HSS and Norse Irish Ferries operate crossings to Belfast. For further information, *see* **Travel**, pp.118–9.

By Rail
Translink, t (028) 7134 2228. Mainline services from Belfast to Derry link several coastal towns along the way.

By Bus
Ulsterbus, t (028) 7126 2261. Connects Derry with Belfast.
Londonderry and Lough Swilly Bus Company, t (028) 7126 2017. Goes into County Donegal too.
Belfast Europa Bus, t (028) 9033 0000. Has a daily, hourly service from Belfast to Derry.
Dublin *Busáras*, t (01) 836 6111. Offers a Dublin–Derry Express bus service.
Airporter, t (028) 7126 9996. Express bus service to Belfast City and International airports.

By Car
Desmond Motors, Derry City, t (028) 7136 7137.
Hertz, Derry City, t (028) 7181 1194.

By Bicycle
Happy Days Cycle Hire, 245 Lone Moor Road, t (028) 7128 7128.

Festivals

March
St Patrick's Day, t (028) 7136 5151. March 17th.
City of Drama Festival, t (028) 7136 5151.
Buth an Earraigh, t (028) 7176 4132. Irish language festival.

June
Walled City Festival, t (028) 7136 5151. Outdoor carnival.

July–August
Maiden City Festival, Derry, t (028) 7134 6677, or look in local newspapers – *The Derry Journal* or *The Sentinel*.
Orange Order Parades, Derry (12th July).
Foyle Cup, t (028) 7126 7432. Youth soccer tournament.
Gasyard Wall *Feile*, t (028) 7126 2812. Events in the city, including music, workshops and exhibitions.

October
Banks of the Foyle Halloween Carnival, t (028) 7126 7284. Held 17–31 October.

November
Foyle Film Festival, t (028) 7126 7432.
Craft Fair, Derry, t (028) 7136 5151, ext. 6911.
Sperrins Autumn Storytelling Festival, The Rural College and Derrynoid Conference Centre, Draperstown, t (028) 7962 9100, *ruralcol@iol.ie*; Magherafelt District Council, t (028) 7939 7979, *info@sperrinstourism.com*.

December
Ferryquay Gate. Anniversary of the shutting of Derry's gates during the siege of 1689, on the Saturday nearest the 18th.

County Londonderry

N

20km
10miles

Dunree Head · INISHOWEN · Inishowen Head · Giant's Causeway · Whitepark Bay · B146
Cooley · Greencastle · Port · Ballintrae · Dunseverick · Ballintoy
Lough Swilly · R238 · Moville · Magilligan Point · Ramore Head · Portrush · A2 · Castle · Bushmills · Ballinlea · A2
Crana River · Buncrana · Redcastle · Mussenden Temple · Portstewart · Dunluce Castle
Rathmullan · R241 · White Castle · Magilligan · Downhill · Castlerock · Coleraine
Scalp Mountain · Bellarena · Moss-Side
Inch Island · Muff · Lough Foyle · Benvarden · Dervock
Burt · Culmore · Binevenagh Mountain · Ballybogy
Newtown-cunningham · Grianan of Aileach · A2 · Derry City Airport · Springwell Forest · A29 · Balleymoney · The Drones
R13 · DONEGAL · DERRY · Eglinton · Ballykelly · Limavady · Ulster Way · Ringsend · A54 · A26
Ardmore · A6 · Loughermore · Burnfoot · Cam Forest · Aghadowey · Finvoy
Raphoe · Ness Wood · River Roe · Garvagh · A54
Killaloo · LONDONDERRY · ANTRIM
Slievekirk Mountain · Claudy · Ballymoney · A6 · Dungiven · Augustinian Priory · Kilrea · Rasharkin
Lifford · Strabane · Ballyneaner · Feeny · B74 · Swatragh · Carntogher · Tamlaght
N15 · Dergalt · Carnanreagh · Park · Dreon · Banagher Forest · Glenshane Pass · River Bann · Ballymena
Mullaclogha · Sawel Mountain · B40 · Mullaghmore · Maghera · A54 · Galgorm
Plumbridge · Glenelly Valley · B47 · Sperrin · Moneyneany · Bellaghy · Gracehill
Mourne River · Cranagh · Draperstown · Ballyinderry Lough Beg · Newferry
Scotch Town · The Creagh · A26
Newtownstewart · Gortin · Owenkillew · Glenhull · Magherafelt · Toomebridge · Randalstown · M22
A5 · Strule · Ulster History Park · Lough Fea · Slieve Gallion · A6
Drumlegagh · B84 · Gortin Glen Forest Park · Greencastle · Beaghmore Stone Circles · Ballyronan · Shanes Castle
Ulster American Folk Park · Mountfield · Moneymore · B18 · The Loup · Antrim
Drumquin · Dunnamore · Orritor · Springhill
Omagh · T Y R O N E · Creggan · Kildress · Cookstown · Ballinderry Bridge · Lough Neagh
A505 · Drum Manor Forest Park · Coagh · Belfast Airport
Carrickmore · Ballinderry River

Derry City

Derry (*Doire*: 'Oak Grove') is a symbolic city situated on the River Foyle. Before the 1960s it was probably best known for its association with the pretty 'Londonderry Air' (better known as 'Danny Boy'), but has until recently been one of Northern Ireland's trouble-spots. The strife is not unprecedented, for it has survived three sieges.

The city is a place well worth visiting. On most of the approaches to its centre you will see its image across the water: a fine walled city, built around the curve of the Foyle. Some ugly buildings have been allowed to mar its elegant profile, but not as yet too many, and the docks are no longer crowded with thousands of folk sailing to a brand new world, as they were in the 19th century. A walk around the historic walls gives you a good view of the docks and the wide River Foyle. Big ships still harbour in the port, located three miles downstream of Derry, although in the days of the British Empire they carried exotic cargo such as silk from Bombay. To the northwest of the

Tourist Information

Derry: 44 Foyle Street, t (028) 7126 7284,
f (028) 7137 7992, t/f (028) 7136 9501,
www.derryvisitor.com, *www.discover
northernireland.com*; *open all year*.

Shopping

Antiques
The Whatnot, 22 Bishop Street, t (028)
7128 8333.

Art Galleries
The McGilloway Gallery, 6 Shipquay Street,
t (028) 7136 6011. Irish paintings, mainly
landscape.
The Orchard Gallery, Orchard Street,
t (028) 7126 9675. Examples of contemporary
Irish art.

Books
Bookworm, 18–20 Bishop Street, t (028)
7128 2727. Terrific section on books of
Irish interest.
Foyle Books, Craft Village, 12a Magazine
Street, t (028) 7137 2530. Second-hand
bookseller.

Crafts
The Donegal Shop, 8 Shipquay Street, t (028)
7126 6928.
Faller the Jeweller, 12 Strand Road, t (028) 7136
2710.
Tower Museum Gift Shop, Union Hall Place,
t (028) 7137 4404.

Sports and Activities

Golf
City of Derry Golf Club, 49 Victoria Road,
t (028) 7134 6369.
Foyle International Golf Centre, 12 Alder Road,
t (028) 7135 2222,
mail@foylegolf.club24.co.uk.

Indoor Leisure Centres
Brooke Park Leisure Centre, Rosemount
Avenue, t (028) 7126 2637.

Lisnagelvin Leisure Centre, Ritchill park,
Waterside, t (028) 7134 7695.
St Columb's Park Leisure Centre, Limavady
Road, t (028) 7134 3941.
Templemore Sports Complex, Buncrana Road,
t (028) 7126 5521.

Outdoor Activity Centres
Ness Woods, off A6 to Belfast, Derry. Nature
trails, waterfall.

Pony-trekking
Ardmore Stables, 8 Rushall Road, Ardmore,
t (028) 7134 5187.

Walking Tours
City Tours, 11 Carlisle Road, t (028) 7127 1996.
McNamara's Famous Guided Walking Tours,
t/f (028) 7134 5335. Tours of the city.
Northern Ireland Tours and Guides Ltd, 70
Marlborough Street, t (028) 7128 9051, f (028)
7130 9051. Contact Stephen McPhilemy.
Top Dog Tours, Tirmacool, Buncrana, Co.
Donegal, t 0868 046134. Tours of Derry City.

Where to Stay

Derry City t (028–)
Hastings Everglades Hotel, Prehen Road,
t 7134 6722, f 7134 9200, *res@egh.
hastingshotels.com* (*expensive*).
Overlooking the River Foyle. Bland
but comfortable.
Beech Hill Country House Hotel,
32 Ardmore Road, t 7134 9279, f 7134 5366,
www.beech-hill.com, info@beech-hill.com
(*expensive*). Lovely grounds and
well-known for good cuisine.
The Trinity Hotel, 22–24 Strand Road,
t 7127 1271, f 7127 1277, *www.thetrinityhotel.
com, info@thetrinityhotel.com* (*moderate*).
Modern city centre hotel.
Quality Hotel Da Vinci's, 15 Culmore Rd,
t 7127 9111, f 7127 9222, *www.derryhotels.
com, info@davincishotel.com* (*moderate*).
70 room hotel complex, 10mins walk
from the city.
Elagh Hall, Buncrana Road, t 7126 3116
(*inexpensive*). 18th-century farmhouse,
2 miles (3.2km) from the city centre,

overlooking the hills of Donegal. Contact Mrs Elizabeth Buchanan.

Manor House, 15 Main Street, Eglinton, (near Derry City Airport), t 7181 0222 (*inexpensive*). Attractive manor house; contact Mrs Davidson.

Derry City Hostel, 4 Magazine Street, Derry, t 7128 4100 (*inexpensive*). This YHANI hostel is currently the only accommodation inside the city walls.

Eating Out

Derry City t (028–)

Ardmore Restaurant, Beech Hill Country House, 32 Ardmore Road, t 7134 9279 (*expensive*). Delicious, imaginative food, such as home-made tagliatelle and sumptuous puddings.

Linenhall Bar, 3 Market Street, t 7137 1665 (*expensive–moderate*). Lunches.

Fitzroy's, 2–4 Bridge Street and 3 Carlisle Road, t 7126 6211. Popular city centre brasserie.

India House, 51 Carlisle Road, t 7126 0532 (*moderate*). Spicy, well-cooked and reasonably priced menu.

Oysters, 162 Spencer Road, Waterside, t 7134 4875 (*moderate*). Lunch and dinner available in this restaurant, recommended for its warmth, good service and excellent cosmopolitan menu.

Browns Restaurant, 1 Bonds Hill, t 7134 5180 (*moderate*). Diverse menu based on good quality lamb, fish and veg.

Badger's, 16 Orchard Street, t 7136 0736/7136 3306 (*moderate*). Grills, salads; lively bar and restaurant. *Open Mon–Thurs 12–7, Fri–Sat 12–9.30pm, Sun 12–5.*

La Sosta Ristorante, 45a Carlisle Road, Derry, t 7137 4817 (*moderate*).

Beckett's Bar, 44 Foyle Street, t 7136 0066 (*moderate*). Recommended for its good pub lunches and evening meals.

Dungloe Bar, 41 Waterloo Street, t 7126 7716 (*inexpensive*). Pub grub and traditional music.

Indigo, 27 Shipquay Street, t 7127 1011 (*inexpensive*). Relaxed café-bar with tasty Asian influences on the menu, and vegetarian options.

Metro Bar, 3 Bank Place, t 7126 7401 (*inexpensive*). Soup, stews.

Entertainment and Nightlife

You'll find live traditional music in the pubs around Waterloo Street.

Pubs and Clubs

Linenhall Bar, 3 Market Street, t (028) 7137 1665.

Grand Central, 27 Strand Road, t (028) 7126 7826.

The Metro, 3 Bank Place, t (028) 7126 7401.

Henry Joy McCrackens, 10 Magazine Street, t (028) 7136 0177. Describes itself as 'a chapel of cocktails and monastery of music'.

River Inn Bar, 36 Shipquay Street, t (028) 7137 1965.

Badgers, 16 Orchard Street, t (028) 7136 0736. Award-winning pub.

Monico Lounge, 4–6 Custom House Street, t (028) 7126 3121. One of Derry's oldest pubs, just beside the Derry Walls.

Theatre and Cinema

The Playhouse, 5–7 Artillery Street, Derry, t (028) 7126 8027, *thederryplayhouse@ hotmail.com*. Non-sectarian community arts centre with performances and workshops.

Orchard Street Cinema, Derry, t (028) 7126 2845. Shows mainly art-house films.

Strand Multiplex Cinema, Strand Road, Derry, t (028) 7137 3900. Seven-screen cinema for new release movies.

Arts Centres

Comhaltas Ceoltoiri Eireann, 15 Crawford Square, t (028) 7128 6359, *derryaoh@ hotmail.com*. Traditional Irish culture, with music, singing, *ceilidh* and set-dancing.

The Verbal Arts Centre, Mall Wall and Stable Lane, Bishop Street Within, t (028) 7126 6946, *info@verbalartscentre.co.uk*. Northern Ireland's only centre devoted to literature and the storytelling tradition.

The Nerve Centre, 7–8 Magazine Street, t (028) 7126 0562. Multimedia centre with in-house cinema.

old city walls is the historical, Republican Bogside, with its much-repainted and photographed 'Free Derry' monument and murals. Irish nationalists and Catholics usually call the city 'Derry'; for Northern Irish Protestants it's 'Londonderry' (although in general both county and city are known as 'Derry'). One solution among the PC has been to write 'London/Derry', leading local jokers to label it 'Stroke City'.

History

The land on which the settlement of Derry grew up was granted to St Columba (St Colmcille), by Aimire, Prince of the O'Neills, in AD 546. The saint built a monastery on the oak-crowned hill. He eventually left and founded many other religious settlements, the most important of which was on Iona, the isle off the west coast of Scotland. From here Christianity spread over Scotland and the north of England. St Columba wrote, homesick for this place:

> Derry, mine own small oak grove,
> Little cell, my home, my love.
> Oh. Thou Lord of lasting life,
> Woe to him who brings it strife.

He never outgrew his love for the city, and would have sympathized with emigrant families who left Derry for America during the 18th and 19th centuries, among them the forebears of such famous figures as Davy Crockett and President James K. Polk.

Derry suffered at the hands of the Norsemen, and then an expedition burned the abbey in 1195. By the end of the 16th century, the English built a fort in Derry, in order to attack the O'Neill of the time, and later a small town was built from the ecclesiastical ruins. This was completely destroyed in 1608 by Cahir O'Doherty and his supporters. It was after this that James I granted the city and the county to the London Livery companies, who rebuilt the walls and planned the streets, which still remain. Derry thus acquired its 'London' prefix.

Derry is the most complete walled city in Ireland, with early 17th-century walls about a mile (1.6km) in circumference, pierced by seven gates, six bastions and many cannon. It was first besieged during the rebellion of 1641, then during the Cromwellian wars of 1649, and finally there was an historic siege in 1689. This siege still plays a very important part in the mind of the Ulster Unionist, for it sums up the courage and righteousness of the Protestant settlers who resisted with the cry, 'No surrender.' The city was being assailed by James II, who had lost his throne in England and was trying to repair his fortunes in Ireland with the help of Louis XIV of France. Thirteen apprentice boys rushed to the gates of the city and shut them in the faces of his approaching army. This secured Londonderry for William III, who had been invited to take over from James II by the English parliament. The siege that followed resulted in many deaths, for the city had no stores of food. Citizens ate rats, dogs and even the starch for laundering linen. A boom was placed across the River Foyle to prevent food supplies reaching the city, but after 105 days it was eventually broken, and the city was relieved by the forces of the Lord Deputy Mountjoy, commanded by Captain

Browning, at Shipquay on 28 July. Every year now the anniversary of the shutting of the gates is celebrated on the Saturday nearest 18 December, and the Raising of the Siege on 12 August. There are marches around the city, with bands and drummers.

City Centre and City Walls

Derry has many attractions to offer the visitor: interesting museums and charming old streets. Great efforts have been made to improve the cultural life of the city, and its own spontaneous creativity in theatre, poetry and the arts has brought a welcome energy. One of the greatest changes has been the development of three huge retail complexes – Quayside, Foyleside and the Richmond Centre – which are a fair indicator of a new-found commercial confidence in a stable future for the city. Another major development is the relocation of the **Verbal Arts Centre** (*see* 'Arts Centres', p.399) to a building beside the city walls. The centre is a valuable resource, for it encourages and supports all forms of written and spoken creative expression.

The **walls** of Derry have been restored, making for a very interesting walk around the old part. They are entered by seven gates, and all along the circuit are views towards the Foyle, or into the Bogside and beyond to the hills. Information plaques mark every structure of note along the walls – accompanied by unofficial graffiti. If you start at **Shipquay Gate** opposite the Guildhall, you will see some of the cannon used in the seige of 1689. Walking on in a westward direction you come to **Ferryquay Gate**, where the gates were slammed and locked by the determined apprentice boys in the face of James II's troops. Moving on, you soon come to the long low plantation Church of Ireland **Cathedral of St Columb** (*chapter house museum open all year Mon–Sat, summer 9–5, winter 9–1 and 2–4; adm;* **t** *(028) 7134 2303*), which lies between Fountain Street and Bishop Street on Clooney Terrace, and is an example of planters' Gothic. The building was founded by the Corporation of London in 1633, and restored in 1886. It was the first specifically Protestant Cathedral to be built in the British Isles after the Reformation. The roof rests on stone corbels carved into heads which represent past bishops of Derry. The philosopher George Berkeley (1685–1753) was Dean here between 1724 and 1732, and the well-known cleric, the Earl of Bristol, was Bishop between 1768 and 1803. He was extremely rich and cultured, favoured Catholic Emancipation and opposed the tithe system. The bishop's throne incorporates the chair used at the consecration of the cathedral in 1633. There are a number of exhibits illustrating the spirit of the 17th-century siege; and the stained glass windows depict incidents from it. The small museum inside is well worth visiting for its relics of the seige and mementos of Cecil Frances Alexander, composer of such famous hymns as 'Once in Royal David's City' and 'There is a Green Hill Far Away'.

Bishop's Gate, nearby, has fine stone carvings. It actually dates from 1789 when the original was replaced with this triumphal arch. The terraced housing area behind the walls here is the Fountain, a dwindling Protestant preserve, the only one this side of the city. Now, as you turn the corner, you can see the Double Bastion with its cannons which still point out over the Bogside, where the Jacobite army was camped. There is a wonderful view from here, and you can clearly see the Bogside's large wall murals.

(The area immediately below the walls is a football pitch, well-used by the youngsters from the area.) If you continue, you will come to **St Augustines Church**, set amongst mature trees; somewhere here is the site of St Columba's (St Colmcille's) monastery, which, as the plaque proudly says, means 1,400 years of continuous Christian settlement. On the corner opposite is the Apprentice Boys' Hall; along the walls here are plane trees, planted to commemorate the apprentice boys. Overlooking the Bogside is the base of a monument to the Reverend George Walker, who rallied the dispirited Derry people to continue their defiance. The original statue was destroyed by an IRA bomb in 1973, and when a replacement was commissioned the IRA vowed they would blow that one up as well (it now resides safely behind a high fence, a few metres along the street past the Apprentice Boys Hall). The rest of the wall brings you back down Magazine Street, with its attractive 18th-century houses, to Shipquay Gate again; notice the fine **Presbyterian Church** in Upper Magazine Street with its classical lines. This area has been much rebuilt, since hardly a single building was left undamaged in the ceaseless IRA bombing campaign of the 1970s. The **Craft Village**, off Shipquay Street (*contact Inner City Trust for information, t (028) 7126 0329*), a representation of Derry between the 16th and 19th centuries, is worth a look, not least for a coffee break in one of the cafés – or a browse amongst the craft shops. **The Courthouse** (1813), in Bishop Street, is a good example of Greek Revival architecture; as the city's main symbol of British justice, it received a great deal of IRA attention, and the scars of numerous car-bombs are still evident.

To visit the **Bloody Sunday Memorial** pass through the Butcher's Gate. It is down to the right, close by the road. This commemorates 30 January 1972, when a civil rights march ended in 13 deaths after the Parachute Regiment opened fire on the marchers – government inquiries into the incident are continuing even now in the Guildhall (*see* **History**, p.59). Close by, just outside the city walls, is the 18th-century **Church of St Columba**, also called Long Tower Church. It is built on the site of a 12th-century monastery called Templemore. Saint Columba is further commemorated in a boys' school of that name further down the street. **St Eugene's Roman Catholic Cathedral**, off Infirmary Road and Great James Street, has a fine east window and high altar. It was built in Gothic style in 1873. **The Calgach Heritage Centre** in Butcher Street (*open Mon–Fri 9.30–4; adm; t (028) 7137 3177*) preserves genealogical data from 1663 in its heritage library, but its main attraction is a multimedia exhibition, 'The Fifth Province'. This tells the history of the Celts in the area, and is based on the mythical idea of a fifth Irish province: the shared heritage and state of mind that connects those of Irish descent, no matter where they live.

Southeast across the Craigavon Bridge is the Waterside, which remains largely Protestant. The **Tower Museum** (*open July–Aug, Mon–Sat 10–5, Sept–June, Tues–Sat and bank hols 10–5; adm; t (028) 7137 2411, towermuseum@derrycity.gov.uk*) in O'Doherty Tower, Union Hall Place, preserves the treasures of the Corporation of London, including a two-handed sword said to belong to Sir Caher O'Doherty, who raided Derry in 1608. This is an outstanding museum, the winner of several awards, and it does help you to grasp both the complex history of ancient Derry and the effects of the Troubles. Artefacts from the Spanish Armada ships wrecked off the coast in 1588 are also on display. Leave time to go to the less fashionable but enthralling **Harbour Museum** in Harbour Square (*open Mon–Fri, 10–1 and 2–4.30; t (028) 7137 7331*), where ship models in glass cases, a replica of a 30ft curragh in which St Colmcille (Columba) would have sailed to Iona and Derry's maritime history are set out on view.

Within the walls you will notice some attractive Georgian houses, some with medieval foundations. At the top of the hill on the Diamond, the central square of the old town, excavations were undertaken to try to uncover an early settlement, possibly the Columban foundation. However, they only revealed domestic material from the early 17th-century settler population. The old workhouse is now the **Workhouse Library Museum** in Glendermott Road (*open July–Aug, Mon–Sat 10–4.30, Sept–June, Mon–Thurs and Sat 10–4.30; adm; t (028) 7131 8328*), with exhibits on the famine; upstairs is the original workhouse dormitory in the same condition as it was for the poor souls who were sent there. In another room is the 'Atlantic Memorial Exhibition', which draws on the importance of the Foyle and Derry during the Second World War; Britain, Canada and the US all had navy bases here. Other museums of interest are the **Foyle Valley Railway Centre** on Foyle Road, close to Craigavon Bridge (*open Tues–Sat, 10–4.30; adm free, charge for train ride; t (028) 7126 5234/7137 7331*), where you can take a trip in a 1934 diesel railcar on the 3-mile track beside the Foyle. At the **Amelia Earhart Centre**, at Ballyarnet Country Park (*open Mon–Fri 10–4; adm free; t (028) 7135 4040, ameliaearhart@compuserve.com*) is a museum commemorating the first woman pilot to fly solo across the Atlantic, who accidentally landed nearby in 1932 after mistaking the city for Paris. You may wish to trace your family history via the **Heritage Library** (*open Mon–Fri 9–5; 14 Bishop Street, t (028) 7126 9792*), which holds all of County Londonderry's genealogical records.

Around the County

Eglinton to Magilligan

The A2 takes you along the Foyle Plain and by-passes Eglinton (the site of Derry City Airport) to travel through **Ballykelly**. This town was settled by people brought in by the Fishmonger's Company of London in 1618. There are two handsome churches here, the **Tamlaghtfinlagan Parish Church**, which is 18th-century Gothic with a graceful spire and fine tombstones; and the neoclassical **Presbyterian Church**. The next town along the coast, still following the A2, is **Limavady**, beautifully situated in the Roe Valley with fine mountain scenery to the north and southeast. Before the Fishermongers Company arrived, Limavady was an important centre of the territory of the O'Cahans, a *sept* under the lordship of the O'Neills, although no trace remains of their castle now. The town is associated with the famous 'Londonderry Air', noted down by Miss Jane Ross in 1851 from the playing of an itinerant piper. William Connolly, speaker of the Irish House of Commons before the Act of Union in 1800, and builder of Castletown House near Dublin, was the son of a Limavady blacksmith.

Precious gold representations of a masted boat, collars and a necklace fashioned in the Celtic La Tène style were found at **Broighter** near the coastal marshes surrounding

Tourist Information

Limavady: 7 Connell Street, t (028) 7776 0307,
www.discovernorthernireland.com; open all
year.
Coleraine: Railway Road, t (028) 7034 4723,
f (028) 7035 1756; open all year.

Shopping

Antiques
Forge Antiques, 24 Long Commons, Castlerock,
t (028) 7035 1339.

Crafts
McCluskey Pottery, 11 Gortgarn Road,
Limavady, t (028) 7776 4579.
Patricia Gavin, Endymion, t (028) 7131 1060.
Creates elegant clothes in tweed and other
textiles. Call for an appointment.

Sports and Activities

Fishing
You'll find coarse fishing on the River Bann.
Deep-sea fishing is available between Lough
Foyle and Portrush. Game fishing for brown
trout and salmon is available on the Agivey,
Clady, Roe, Bann and Faughan Rivers.
Foyle Fisheries Commission, 8 Victoria Road,
Derry City, t (028) 7134 2100, f (028) 7134
2720. Provides game-rod licences.
Glenowen Co-operative, t (028) 7137 1544.
Guides, licences, package fishing trips.

Golf
Benone Golf Course, Downhill, t (028)
7775 0555.
Castlerock Golf Club, 65 Circular Road,
Castlerock, t (028) 7084 8314.
Radisson Roe Park and Golf Resort, Limavady,
t (028) 7772 2222.

Outdoor Activities
Roe Valley Country Park, t (028) 7772 2074.
Centre for walking, fishing, canoeing,
rock-climbing and orienteering.
The Ulster Gliding Club, Sea Coast Road,
Bellarena, t (028) 7775 0301. For gliding
enthusiasts.

Pony-trekking
Hill Farm, Castlerock, t (028) 7084 8629.

Walking
The Sperrins Sky Way, a twenty-mile route,
starts at Barony Bridge, Moydamlaght Forest,
near Draperstown, and runds along the
Sperrin Ridge, finishing at Eden, east of
Plumbridge, in County Tyrone.

Where to Stay

Streeve Hill, 25 Dowland Road, Drenagh,
Limavady, t (028) 7776 6563, f (028) 7776
8285, hidden.ireland@indigo.ie (moderate).
Lovely early-18th-century house run by Mrs
Welch, with delicious food and walks in
parkland and the 'moon garden'.
Ballycarton House, 239 Seacoast Road,
Limavady, t (028) 7775 0216 (inexpensive).
Modern farmhouse in very scenic area
close to Magilligan Nature Reserve. Contact
Mrs Craig.
Ballyhenry House, 172 Seacoast Road, Myroe,
Limavady, t (028) 7772 2657 (inexpensive).
Farmhouse with Mrs Kane's good home-
cooking and comfortable rooms.
The Old Rectory, 4 Duncrun Road, Bellarena,
t (028) 7775 0477 (inexpensive). Pretty house
beneath Binevenagh Mountain.
Downhill Hostel, 12 Mussenden Road,
Castlerock, t (028) 7084 9077 (inexpensive).
A most comfortable and sociable hostel,
located right on a glorious stretch of
beach, west of Castlerock. Facilities
include an old communal kitchen and
laundry room. Dormitory and family
rooms available.
Camus House, 27 Curragh Road, Coleraine,
t (028) 7034 2982 (moderate). Listed
17th-century house overlooking the River
Bann; contact Mrs Josephine King.
Brown Trout Golf and Country Inn, 209
Agivey Road, Aghadowey, south of
Coleraine, t (028) 7086 8209 (expensive).
In pretty grounds near the river, with
good food.
Greenhill House, Aghadowey, Coleraine,
t (028) 7086 8241, f 7786 8365
(inexpensive). Pretty Georgian farmhouse;
good home-cooking from Mrs Hegarty.

Ardtara Country House, 8 Gorteade Road, Upperlands, near Maghera, t (028) 7964 4490, f (028) 7964 5080 (*expensive*). Fine 19th-century house, comfortable and welcoming.

Laurel Villa, 60 Church Street, Magherafelt, t (028) 7963 2238 (*moderate*). Run by friendly Blue Badge guide Eugene Kielty and his herb-growing wife Geraldine, this house was once the home of a Victorian doctor, and is furnished with antiques. It is well-situated for day trips to the Antrim coast, Belfast, Derry and the Sperrin Mountains. Guided tours of South Derry, based on the works of Seamus Heaney, are your host's speciality.

Dungiven Castle, Main Street, Dungiven, t (028) 777 42428, f (028) 777 41968, www.dungivencastle.com, enquiries@dungivencastle.com (*inexpensive*). Carefully restored Gothic Tudor style castle with hostel accommodation. Offers en suite family and dormitory rooms, a fully-equipped kitchen, reading room, lounge area and 22 acres of parkland – brilliant for those on a budget.

The Flax Mill Hostel, Mill Lane, Gortnaghey Road, Dungiven, t (028) 7774 2655 (*inexpensive*). Converted stone mill, 16 beds, traditional music in pub close by.

Drumcovitt House, 704 Feeny Road, Feeny, t/f (028) 7778 1224, drumcovitt.feeny@btinternet.com (*moderate*). Lovely 18th-century house in scenic countryside. They also have a self-catering cottage, **Drumcovitt Barn**.

Self-catering

Lough Beg Coach Houses, Ballyscullion Park, Bellaghy, t (028) 7938 6235, f (028) 7938 6416 (*expensive–moderate*). Six well-appointed cottages on a large estate bordering Lough Beg. Sleep 6, with games room, horse-riding and lovely walks. Full Irish breakfast and dinner can be ordered.

Eating Out

Radisson Hotel, Roe Park, Limavady, t (028) 7772 2222 (*expensive*). Sophisticated menu in golf-resort hotel.

Lucille's Kitchen, 17 Catherine Street, Limavady, t (028) 7776 8180 (*inexpensive*). Sandwiches and hot snacks on offer.

Salmon Leap, 53 Castleroe Road, Coleraine, t (028) 7035 2992/7034 2992 (*moderate*). Good buffet lunch.

Strawberry Fayre, 1 Blagh Road, Coleraine, t (028) 7032 0437 (*moderate–inexpensive*). Excellent food on offer here, with quality lunches and teas made from fresh produce and natural ingredients. Salads, fruit, local meats and home-baked breads and desserts. *No smoking*.

Morelli's, 54–57 The Promenade, Portstewart, t (028) 7083 2150 (*inexpensive*). With the Italian name, what else but good ice-cream and pasta dishes.

Brown Trout Golf and Country Inn, 209 Agivey Road, Mullaghmore, Aghadowey, t (028) 7086 8209 (*inexpensive*). Well-established, with good pub food.

Ardtara House, 8 Gorteade Road, Upperlands, Near Maghera, t (028) 7964 4490 (*expensive*). Creative menu using the freshest ingredients.

Gardiners, Garden Street, Magherafelt, t (028) 7930 0333 (*moderate*). Popular with locals, the ambitious chef-owner of this restaurant loves to cook – and his creations show it. Good for lunch and dinner.

Café Slice, Rainey Street, Magherafelt, t (028) 7963 3980 (*inexpensive*).

Mary's Bar, 10 Market Street, Magherafelt, t (028) 7963 1997 (*inexpensive*). Good pub food.

Ditty's Home Bakery, 44 Main Street, Castledawson, t (028) 7963 3944 (*inexpensive*). Pies, excellent bread, lasagne; also in Magherafelt.

Entertainment and Nightlife

Arts and Theatre

Flowerfield Arts Centre, 185 Coleraine Road, Portstewart, t (028) 7083 3959.

Riverside Theatre, Cromore Road, Coleraine, t (028) 7032 3232.

the estuary of the River Roe. They are now in the care of the National Museum, Dublin. Further up the coast, underneath the forest-covered Binevenagh Mountain, is the triangle of **Magilligan Point**. A Martello Tower, built during the Napoleonic wars, guards the entrance to Lough Foyle. The strand is well known for its shells, the herbs that grow among the dunes, the birds, and for the plagues of rabbits commemorated in a special Magilligan grace. The names of local villages such as Bellarena and the Umbra recall the foundering of the Armada; folklore would have you believe that some of the darker-hued Magilliganites are of Spanish descent. This part of the world also has connections with the Irish music tradition. At the end of the 18th century, interest in the Gaelic cultural achievement began amongst a group of scholarly men. Foremost among them was Edward Bunting, who did so much to preserve Irish airs and ancient music, and organized a great assembly of Irish harpists in Belfast in 1792. One of the oldest, a blind man called Denis Hempsey, or O'Hempsey (c. 1695–1807), lived near Magilligan, and provided Bunting with many old tunes and airs. **Benone Strand** is an extension of Magilligan, a glorious seven-mile sandy arc.

Downhill to Coleraine

From Limavady you can cut inland through the Roe Valley to Dungiven on the B68 and pass through the Country Park, which has many fine picnic spots and walks by the River Roe. However, if you want to take advantage of the superb coastline you should go on from Magilligan, following the A2 to Downhill and on up to the pretty Victorian seaside resort of **Castlerock**, which has a superb sandy beach stretching for miles, a bowling green, a golf course and tennis courts. A really worthwhile expedition can be made to the **Palace of Downhill** and **Mussenden Temple** (*open mid Mar–May and Sept, Sat–Sun 11–6, June–Aug and Easter, daily 11–6; glen and grounds always open; adm free; t (028) 7084 8728, www.nationaltrust.co.uk*). This ruined castle, just off the A2 at Downhill village, was built in the late 18th century by the famous Earl-Bishop, Frederick Augustus Hervey (1730–1803), one of the most interesting and enlightened Church of Ireland bishops. The palace itself is sited on a windswept hill with wonderful views of the Inishowen hills and the Antrim headlands. Hervey was extravagant and well-travelled. He built up a great art collection with the episcopal revenues from his Derry bishopric (which in the 18th century was the second-richest in Ireland), and had a second princely residence at Ballyscullion near Bellaghy, which is totally ruined. The landscaped estate which still remains includes the Mussenden Temple perched on a cliff overlooking the sea, the ruins of the castle, family memorials, gardens, a fish pond and woodland and cliff walks. The bishop was a great advocate of toleration, contributing generously both to Catholic and Presbyterian churches. One of his amusements was party-giving. If you go down to the Mussenden Temple, the story of the great race he organized between the Church of Ireland and the Presbyterian ministers is told. There was suspicion that he was more of a Classicist than a Christian: his temple, on a cliff edge, is modelled on the Roman temple of Vesta, and suggests a somewhat independent interpretation of religion.

Eastwards along the coast is **Portstewart**, a seasoned little resort town which is overlooked by the castle-style convent (*not open to the public*). Inland from

Portstewart is **Coleraine** (*Cuil Raithin*: 'Fern Recess'), which is supposed to have been founded by St Patrick. Most of what you see was developed by the Irish Society of London. Whiskey from Coleraine is now made by Bushmills Distillery (*for information about tours of Old Bushmills Distillery, call **t** (028) 2073 1521*); it is still held with high regard and is supplied to the House of Commons.

The Coleraine campus of the University of Ulster is a centre for talks and tours during the summer, and there is a good **theatre** here called the Riverside. The campus has a rare collection of Irish-bred daffodils and narcissi which are in full bloom in mid- to late-April (*always accessible*). The River Bann runs through the town and was the scene of early habitation. At **Mountsandel Fort**, on Coleraine's outskirts, Mesolithic flints have been found which indicate the presence of the earliest settlements in Ireland. There is much archaeological evidence to suggest that they date from 7000 BC. Later, the mound of Mountsandel became a royal seat of local Celtic kings, and finally, a Norman fort. If you visit the British Museum in London you will see some of those Bannside antiquities, the most spectacular of which is a huge hoard of Roman coins that were evidently seized by Irish pirates. On the A2, northwest of Coleraine, is **Hezlett House** (*open April–May and Sept, weekends and bank hols 12–5, June–Aug, Wed–Sun 12–5; adm; **t** (028) 7084 8567, www.nationaltrust. co.uk*), a thatched 17th-century cottage that was once a rectory, and has a cruck (or truss) roof.

The Bann Valley: Bellaghy to Moneymore

You can follow the River Bann through its valley by taking the A54. The valley is farmed by industrious farmers, many of them descendants of the Scots and English who were tenants of the London Companies and arrived in the region in the early 17th century. The countryside is very pretty in a cultivated way. At the **Garvagh Museum and Heritage Centre** on Main Street, you can see farming implements and Stone Age artefacts (*open June–Aug, Thurs and Sat 2–5, **t** (028) 2955 7924*).

The Lower Bann River broadens out into Lough Beg after leaving Lough Neagh. In the marshy area around the lake you will find **Church Island**, so called because of its ruined church and holy well. A spire has been constructed among the ruins – one result of Earl-Bishop Hervey's building ventures. He wanted to be able to see the spire from his palace at Ballyscullion. The local people still leave offerings at the holy well on the island. The birdlife around the lake is superb; many water-fowl, snipe and swans can be seen.

Seamus Heaney, the poet, comes from this area, and the strength of his feelings for this land is apparent in his poetry. You can find out more about him at the **Bellaghy Bawn** in Castle Street, Bellaghy (*open April–Sept, Mon–Sat 10–6, Sun 2–6, rest of year closes at 5; adm; **t** (028) 7938 6812*), a fortified farmhouse built for the London Vintner's Company in around 1618. Inside this fine *bawn* are a series of rooms through which you are taken on a tour of local history since prehistoric times. There is a video presentation by Seamus Heaney, in which he explains how local places and experiences have influenced him. There is a café and library with some of Heaney's manuscripts and original works, as well as works by other Northern poets and artists.

Moneymore, further south, is a sister town to Draperstown, having been developed by the same London Company of Drapers. You can visit the **Plantation of Ulster Visitor Centre** at 50 High Street (*open summer, daily 10–5, winter, daily 10–4; call in advance to arrange a guide; adm; t (028) 7962 7800, www.flightoftheearlsexperience.com*), an educational centre where you can learn about the plantation period and see their 'Flight of the Earls' audio-visual show.

One mile (1.6km) outside Moneymore on the B18 is the most attractive of residences, **Springhill** (*open July–Aug, Fri–Wed 2–4, April–June and Sept, weekends 2–6; adm; t (028) 8674 8210*). This house was built in the late 17th century as a fortified manor house by the Lennox-Conynghams, a settler family, with its outbuildings in Dutch style. It is a proper country gentleman's house with soft, shadowed interiors, a lovely library and portraits, including one with a following gaze. There is a small costume museum and implements on show in the outbuildings. The grounds are beautiful; the yew thicket is said to be a vestige of the ancient forest of Glenconkeyne, and there is a herb garden – essential for any household in the 17th and 18th centuries.

Through the Sperrins: Maghera to Dungiven

Here you are on the edges of the Sperrin mountains, which this county shares with Tyrone. **Maghera**, in the mountain heartland of the county, is a small and busy town at the foot of the Glenshane Pass. It is said to be the meeting place of the mountain and plains people, rather like Dungiven on the other side of the mountain. It is also famous as the birthplace of Charles Thompson, who helped to draw up the American Declaration of Independence while he was Secretary to Congress. At the southeast end of the town there is an ancient **church of St Lurach** (*always accessible*) with a square-headed doorway, dating from the 12th century. The massive lintels are decorated with a carved, interlaced pattern, and a sculpture of the crucifixion.

The steep, straight road through the **Glenshane Pass** will take you on to Dungiven, or you can explore the charming countryside around Draperstown and go on to **Feeny**, travelling on the B40. You will pass by **Banagher Forest Glen**, which is a nature reserve. Close by, to the west, is **Sawel**, at 2,240ft (683m) the highest mountain in the Sperrin range. North of the forest, off the B74 from Feeny, is **Banagher Church**, founded by a St Muriedach O'Heney. The church itself is probably 12th century, with a square-headed doorway and massive lintels. In the graveyard is a stone-roofed tomb or oratory with the figure of O'Heney in relief – the saint bequeathed to his descendants the power to be lucky with the sand from his tomb. The church is always accessible to the public.

On the southeastern side of **Dungiven**, on the A6, is a fine ruin of an **Augustinian priory**; only the chancel with a Norman arch remains. The elaborate altar tomb erected in the late 14th century is very striking. It is carved with a figure in Irish dress grasping a sword, and commemorates an O'Cahan, whose family were the lords of this territory before the plantation.

County Antrim

The Antrim coast has a well-deserved reputation for being one of the loveliest and most spectacular in Europe. The coast road (A2) passes through exquisite little fishing villages and areas of protected beauty. The famous Giant's Causeway – one of the wonders of the natural world – the wild beauty of Fair and Torr Heads, and the ruined

Getting There and Around

By Air
Belfast International Airport, t (028) 9442 2888, *www.bial.co.uk*. The airport is about 25 miles (40km) from Larne.

By Sea
See also **Travel**, pp.118–9.
P&O Ferries, t 1800 409049. Stranraer or Cairnryan in Scotland are about 2½ hours by ferry from Larne.
Isle of Man Steam Packet Company, Isle of Man, **t** 08705 523 523, *www.seacat. co.uk*. Take the Seacat between Troon and Belfast.

By Rail
There are frequent train services from Belfast to Larne, which connect with ferries, and with buses travelling to the villages in the glens.
Northern Ireland Rail, t (028) 9089 9411.

By Bus
Ulsterbus operates the **Antrim Coaster**, which runs in summer between Belfast and Portstewart, stopping at most towns around the Antrim coast. Ulsterbus and the Old Bushmills Distillery operate an **open-topped bus** between 27 June and 28 August from Coleraine along the Giant's Causeway, via Portstewart, Portrush, Portballintrae, Bushmills, and back.
Ulsterbus, t (028) 7032 5400.

By Car
Avis, Ferry Terminal, Larne Harbour, **t** (028) 2827 0381.
Hertz, Aldergrove Airport, **t** (028) 9442 2533.

By Bike
The Raleigh Rent-a-Bike network operates in Ballymena:
RF Linton and Sons, 31 Springwell Street, Ballymena, **t** (028) 2565 2516.
The Skerries Pantry, 6 Bath Street, Portrush, **t** (028) 7082 4334.
Portrush tourist office, t (028) 7082 3333.
Check with for cycle shops offering rental in summer season.
Cushendall Activity Centre, t (028) 2117 1340.

Ardclinis Outdoor Adventure Centre, 11 High St, Cushendall, **t** (028) 2177 1340.

Getting to Rathlin Island
There are daily boat crossings to the island, running from June to September. For the rest of the year, a limited service is arranged by the Harbour Tourist Office in Ballycastle.
Rathlin Island Ferry, t (028) 2076 9299.
June–Sept, four crossings daily, at other times twice daily. The boat leaves Ballycastle at about 10.30am every day and returns in the afternoon.
Ballycastle Harbour Tourist Office, 7 Mary Street, **t** (028) 2076 2024. For general information.

Festivals

March
Ballymoney Drama Festival. Contact Town Hall, High Street, Ballymoney, **t** (028) 2766 2280, ext. 227.

May
Northern Lights, Ballycastle. Music festival and street entertainment, held late in the month.
Ballyclare May Fair. Horse trading, community fair and other events, **t** (028) 9034 0000.
Larne Irish Dancing Festival. One week of Irish dance competitions, for all ages, **t** (028) 2826 0088.
Feis nGleann. Gaelic music, crafts and sports in the Glens of Antrim during May and June, **t** (028) 2076 2024.

July
Lughnasa Medieval Fair and Craft Market, Carrickfergus Castle, held mid-month, **t** (028) 9336 6455.

August
Ould Lammas Fair, Ballycastle. On the last weekend of the month, this is Northern Ireland's oldest traditional market fair, **t** (028) 2076 2024.
Heart of Glens Festival, Cushendall, **t** (028) 2076 2024. Mid-August, traditional Irish music.

Dunluce Castle, all contrive to make a trip here more than worthwhile. A little way inland are the Nine Glens of Antrim, which have been celebrated in poetry and song the world over because of their scenic beauty. Especially beautiful is Glenariff, with its waterfalls, the 'Mare's Tail' being the most spectacular. The glen is an excellent example of a post glaciation U-Valley; it is virtually geometric. The valley of the River Bann extends along the Londonderry border to Lough Neagh, the largest inland sheet of water in Britain: 150sq miles (388sq km) in all.

The weather on the east coast is variable, as it is in all parts of Ireland, although it is more inclined to be sunny and dry with a brisk breeze off the sea. The traveller who can brave the cold Atlantic water will enjoy the breakers which roll into Whitepark Bay and the fine sandy beaches around Portrush. The cyclist will find the roads quite strenuous, with hills and hairpin bends, but will be well rewarded with the views; whilst the walker can follow the Ulster Way, a marked trail which explores the Antrim Coast and Glens. A splendid adventure is to take the boat out to Rathlin Island and spend the day watching the huge sea bird population on the cliffs there, and revel in the island's unspoilt beauty.

History

Antrim lies very close to Scotland, with only a narrow strip of water in between, so it is not surprising that there are strong links between the two. Even the accents of the peoples are similar. Before the Celts invaded, the Scotti people moved easily between Scotland and Ireland, crossing the Moyle or North Sea Channel here. (This is the shortest ferry link to the mainland, and the same shifting of populations goes on today.) The word 'Scots' is derived from the 4th-century Irish verb 'to raid', and the Romans called Ireland 'Scotia' because it was from here that all the raiders came. It was not until the 12th century that its meaning was transferred to the country now called Scotland.

Up until the 6th century the ancient Kingdom of Dalriada extended from the Antrim coast, including the islands of Rathlin and Iona, to the west of Scotland. By the late 14th century the clan MacDonnell held the balance of power, and their territory straddled both sides of the Atlantic up until the Elizabethan era. The time of the Dalriadic kings and the Scotti people is shrouded in half-myth and legend, but it has given rise to some interesting theories on who the true natives of this land are – some of which have been used as cultural propaganda. The Scottish Presbyterians, whose forebears were settled here in the Jacobite plantations, have claimed that they were coming back to their original home, and that the Catholic Celts who were driven into the mountains were in fact the interlopers who had come up from the south.

Whatever the theories of the past may be, today the Jacobite plantations continue to have an effect, in that there are pockets of staunch Presbyterians loyal to Britain who would man a Unionist army given half a chance. These Unionists live mainly in the rich plains, whilst there is a Catholic Nationalist fringe along the coast and in the glens; the two do not mix easily.

Stepping back into the mists and fantasy of legend, there are stories of Fionn MacCumhaill (Finn MacCool) and of Oisín, his son; stories of the sons of Uísneach who died for Deidre's beauty; and of the Children of Lir, condemned to spend their lives as swans on the waters of the Moyle. The place-names of prehistoric remains, glens, mountains and caves abound with allusions to these myths.

Antrim's Eastern Coast

From Belfast to Larne

The Antrim Coast Road runs from Belfast to Larne. If you begin in Belfast, take the A2 loughside road passing the industrial districts and comfortable suburbs of Whiteabbey and Greenisland to the oldest town in Northern Ireland, **Carrickfergus**. The town takes its name from one of the Dalriadic kings, Fergus, who foundered off this point on one of his journeys between Antrim and Scotland. The kings of Scotland were descended from his line and, therefore, the kings and queens of England. He is said to have brought his coronation stone from Ireland to Scone. Certainly the rock of red sandstone, embedded with pebbles, is like rock found along the Antrim coast. The town is lovely, very well kept and pedestrianized in parts with some good craft shops.

Carrickfergus Castle (*open April–Sept, Mon–Sat 10–6 Sun 2–6 (exc June–Aug, Sun 12–6), Oct–Mar, Mon–Sat 10–4 Sun 2–4; adm; t (028) 9335 1273*) is the most prominent sight in the town: a massive, rectangular, unbuttressed four-storey tower built by John de Courcy in the years after 1180. (John de Courcy and his kinsmen were very successful Normans who conquered much of Counties Down and Antrim.) In 1210, King John of England slept here during his tour of Ireland. The de Courcys renewed their oaths of allegiance to him at this time, but in reality were very much a law unto themselves. The castle has been a museum since 1928, and houses an impressive array of weapons and armour on display, plus the history of such Irish regiments as the Inniskilling Dragoons. The video presentation and costumed guides give a lively insight into the 800 years' history of one of the best examples of a Norman castle in Ireland. Beside this splendid fortification lies the grand marina, where there are pleasure boats for hire.

Carrickfergus has an old **parish church** founded by St Nicholas in 1185, and rebuilt in 1614. The famous Ulster poet Louis MacNiece (1907–63), who was associated with the group which included Cecil Day Lewis, W. H. Auden and Stephen Spender, wrote of the skewed alignment of the aisle:

The church in the form of a cross but denoting
The list of Christ on the cross in the angle of the nave.

MacNiece's father was once the rector here. There's also a monument to Sir Arthur Chichester here, one of the loveliest pieces of 17th-century craftmanship in Ulster; the Chichester family were given extensive lands in Ulster at the time of the Ulster Plantation in the 17th century. The **Knight Ride** (*open April–Sept Mon–Sat 10–6, Sun 12–6; t (028) 9336 6455*), in Antrim Street, is a heritage exhibition and ride through history in the best Disney tradition. You can buy a joint ticket for this and the castle.

Tourist Information

Belfast: Belfast Welcome Centre, 35 Donegall Place, t (028) 9024 6609, *www.visitnorthernireland.com*; *open all year.*

Carrickfergus: Knight Ride, Antrim Street, t (028) 9336 6455, *www.carrickfergus.org*, *ntrainer.tourism@carrickfergus.org*; *open all year.*

Larne: Narrow Gauge Road, t (028) 2826 0088; *open all year.*

Cushendall: 25 Mill Street, t (028) 2177 1180; *open daily 10–1.*

Ballycastle: 7 Mary Street t (028) 2076 2024; *open all year.*

Giant's Causeway: Visitor Centre, 44 Causeway Road, Bushmills, t (028) 2073 1855; *open all year.*

Portrush: Dunluce Centre, Sandhill Drive, t (028) 7082 3333; *open April–Sept.*

Shopping

Crafts

Try looking around at the **Giant's Causeway** (*open Mar–Dec*) and in the **Cushendun National Trust Shop** (*open April–Sept, at other times by arrangement*).

Delicacies

Good bakeries are to be found all over County Antrim; you'll find especially good soda and potato breads. The local specialities, **Dulse** (seaweed) and **yellowman** (confectionery), can be found in Ballycastle grocery shops.

Wysner Meats, 18 Ann Street, Ballycastle, t (028) 2076 2372. Wonderful sausages and black pudding.

The Old Bushmills Distillery, Bushmills, t (028) 2073 1521. Whiskey tours and free sampling.

Sports and Activities

Fishing

Very good all along the Antrim Coast. For a full list of information contact Tourism Ireland, or contact the Ulster Cruising School. For local sea-fishing contact:

Ulster Cruising School, Carrickfergus Marina, Carrickfergus, t (028) 9336 8818, *ulstercruisingschool@hotmail.com*.

Red Bay Boats, Cushendall, t (028) 2177 1331. Contact Frank O'Neill.

Tackle Shop, 74 Main Street, Portrush, t (028) 7082 2209. Contact Joe Mullan.

Golf

Cairndhu Golf Course, Ballygally, Larne, t (028) 2858 3324. 18-hole parkland course.

Ballycastle, t (028) 2076 2536. A lovely seaside 18-hole course.

Bushfoot Golf Course, Bushmills, t (028) 2073 1317.

Royal Portrush Golf Course, t (028) 7082 2311. Three links courses, rated as having one of the finest dunes courses in the world.

Open Farms and Pony Trekking

Watertop Open Farm, 188 Cushendall Road, Ballyvoy, Ballycastle, t (028) 2076 2576. Ride on horseback through the hill farm. *Open end June–Sept.*

Steam Train Rides

Railway Preservation Society of Ireland, *www.rpsi-online.org*. Excursions on vintage trains up the coast as far as Portrush, on the *Portrush Flyer* from York Street in Whitehead. Book via Carrickfergus Tourist Information Office, t (028) 9336 6455. every Sunday June–Aug

Tennis

Ballycastle Tennis Club, t (028) 2076 3022.

On your way north out of Carrickfergus you pass **Kilroot**. Here in the ruined Church of Ireland church, Dean Jonathan Swift (1667–1745), best remembered for his satirical book *Gulliver's Travels*, began his clerical life. The road to Larne takes you along by the lough, which is almost landlocked by Island Magee, a small peninsula with popular beaches such as Brown's Bay and Mill Bay. There is a ferry from Larne to Ballylumford on Island Magee and it is fun to walk along the Gobbins, basalt cliffs on the east side

Where to Stay

Manor Guest House, 23 Olderfleet Road, Larne, t (028) 2827 3305, f (028) 2826 0505, *welcome@themanorguesthouse.com* (*inexpensive*). Guest house on the seafront.

Drumnagreagh Hotel, 408 Coast Road, Glenarm, t/f (028) 2884 1651 (*moderate*). Small hotel with stunning views.

Margaret's House, 10 Altmore Street, Glenarm, t (028) 2884 1307 (*inexpensive*). Welcoming old house, close to the hills and beach.

The Londonderry Arms Hotel, 20 Harbour Road, Carnlough, t (028) 2888 5255, f (028) 2888 5263, *ida@glensofantrim.com* (*moderate*). This was originally built as a coaching inn by the Marchioness of Londonderry, whose mother was the Countess of Antrim. It later came into possession of her grandson, Sir Winston Churchill, who sold it in 1926. It has a delightful old-world atmosphere.

Cushendall Youth Hostel, 24 Layde Road, Cushendall, t (028) 2177 1344, f (028) 2177 2042 (*inexpensive*). North of the village in the glens; some family rooms.

The Villa, 185 Torr Road, Cushendun, t (028) 2176 1252 (*inexpensive*). Victorian villa, set off the road in own gardens, comfortable and close to the beach.

Colliers Hall, 50 Cushendall Road, Ballycastle, t (028) 2076 2531 (*inexpensive*). Guest house one mile outside Ballycastle.

Ballycastle Backpackers Hostel, 4 North Street, Ballycastle, t (028) 2076 3612 (*inexpensive*). Seafront houses.

Sheep Island View Hostel, 42a Main Street, Ballintoy, t (028) 2076 9391 (*inexpensive*). Handy position for seeing the Causeway coast; comfortable new hostel with ocean views, bikes for rent. Dormitory accommodation in a camping barn is also available.

Whitepark Bay International Youth Hostel, 157 Whitepark Road, Whitepark Bay, Ballintoy, t (028) 2073 1745 (*inexpensive*). Excellent facilities, with views onto the beach; some family rooms.

Rathlin Guesthouse, The Quay, Rathlin Island, t (028) 2076 3917 (*inexpensive*). Very friendly base, run by Mr and Mrs McCurdy, from where you can explore the beautiful island.

Ahimas, 243 Whitepark Road, near Ballintoy, Bushmills, t (028) 2073 1383 (*inexpensive*). A traditional cottage, tastefully modernized. Organic garden produce is used for the vegetarian meals, and yoga and reflexology are available upon request.

Whitepark House, Whitepark Bay, Ballintoy, t (028) 2073 1482, *bob@whiteparkhouse.com*, *www.whiteparkhouse.com* (*moderate*). 17th-century house on a hill overlooking the Atlantic, luxuriously furnished by the owners with mementoes from their Asian travels. Possibly the best full-Irish vegetarian breakfasts are offered, along with those for meat-eaters. Good conversation beside the evening fire, with tea and biscuits is also likely. Three rooms share bathrooms.

Bushmills Inn, Main Street, Bushmills, t (028) 2073 2339, f (028) 2073 2048 (*expensive–moderate*). Comfortable, good service, excellent food.

Causeway Hotel, 40 Causeway Road, Giant's Causeway, Bushmills, t (028) 2073 1226/2073 1210, f (028) 2073 2552 (*expensive–moderate*). Delightful family-run hotel.

Craig Park, 24 Carnbore Road, Bushmills, t (028) 2073 2496, f (028) 2073 2479 (*inexpensive*). Comfortable country house near the Giant's Causeway.

Maddybenny Farmhouse, 18 Maddybenny Park, Loguestown Road, Portrush, t/f (028) 7082 3394 (*inexpensive*). Easy-going atmosphere, with a great breakfast. Holiday cottages (£250–450) and horse-riding.

of the peninsula. Before you get to Larne you will pass one of the glens that break through the Antrim plateau – **Glenoe**, with four waterfalls. It is now under National Trust care. The little village of **Glynn** is actually on the shore of Larne Lough, and was the setting for a film called *The Luck of the Irish*.

Although there are some hideous buildings and unecological views created by the industrial sites round **Larne**, it is an important port and the gateway to the Antrim

Glenkeen Guesthouse, 59 Coleraine Road, Portrush, t (028) 7082 2279 (*inexpensive*). Good value B&B just out of the centre of town, all rooms en-suite.

Self-catering

Briarfield, 65 Dickeystown Road, Glenarm, t (028) 2884 1296. Cottage sleeping 4; from £150 per week, low season.

Rural Cottages Holidays Ltd, Tourism Ireland, t (028) 9024 1100, f (028) 9024 1198. All of the following cottages can be booked through this company. They are all attractive traditional dwellings, restored and furnished to a high standard. Cost varies with the season, but a cottage sleeping 6 is around £410 per week:

Bellair Cottage, Glenarm. In the glens above Glenarm, a whitewashed farmhouse, sleeps 6;

Strand House, Cushendun. In pretty National Trust village, sleeps 7;

John O'Rocks, Cushendun. Just a few steps from a sandy beach, sleeps 6.

Eating Out

Ginger Tree, 29 Ballyrobert Road, Glengormley, Newtownabbey, t (028) 9084 8176 (*expensive*). Delicious Japanese food.

Dobbins Inn, 6 High Street, Carrickfergus, t (028) 9335 1905 (*moderate*). Rich à la carte food and bar meals.

The Londonderry Arms, Carnlough, t (028) 2888 5255 (*moderate*). Very good fish; and wonderful views of the sea and glens.

National Trust Tearooms, Cushendun (*inexpensive*). Light meals during the day, 12–6. Also at the Giant's Causeway, t (028) 2073 1582, and Carrick-a-Rede. *Open Mar–Sept/Oct, daytime only*.

Marine Hotel, Ballycastle, t (028) 2076 2222 (*moderate*). Simple but good cooking.

Rathlin Guesthouse, The Quay, Rathlin Island, t (028) 2076 3917 (*inexpensive*). Serving good snacks such as sandwiches, or high tea.

McCuaig's Bar, The Quay, Rathlin Island, t (028) 2076 3974 (*inexpensive*). Pub grub.

Smuggler's Inn Hotel Restaurant, 306 Whitepark Road, Giant's Causeway, t (028) 2073 1577 (*moderate*). A la carte and high tea. Also does B&B.

Sweeney's Wine Bar, Seaport Avenue, Port Ballintrae, t (028) 2073 2404 (*inexpensive*). Grilled meats and vegetarian meals on offer here.

Bushmills Inn, Dunluce Road, Bushmills, t (028) 2073 2339 (*expensive–moderate*). Delicious cold salmon and salads in an excellent bistro-style restaurant.

The Ramore Restaurant, The Harbour, Portrush, t (028) 7082 4313 (*expensive*). You can promise yourself a superb meal here, for the skilled chef has won many awards. Good value food is also served during the day in the wine bar upstairs. *Children welcome until 8.30pm.*

Magheraboy House Hotel, 41 Magheraboy Road, Portrush, t (028) 7082 3507 (*moderate*). Hearty meals for hungry people.

Harbour Bar, Harbour Road, Portrush, t (028) 7082 2430 (*moderate*). Great atmosphere, excellent food.

Entertainment and Nightlife

Traditional Music

The Central Bar, 12 Ann Street, Ballycastle, t (028) 2076 3877.

McCarrolls Bar, Ballycastle, t (028) 2076 2123.

The Harbour Bar, Portrush, t (028) 7082 2430.

coast proper, so you cannot very well avoid it. There are railway services at regular intervals to and from York Street Station in Belfast. These connect with the sailing times of the boats between Larne, and Stranraer and Cairnryan. It's the shortest sea crossing from Ireland to Scotland, taking only 70 minutes once you are in open sea.

On **Curran Point**, a promontory south of the harbour, you can see **Olderfleet Castle**, a corruption of the Viking name *Ulfrechsfiord*. The castle is 13th-century and ruined, with free access. If you have time to kill waiting for a ferry, a brisk 15-minute walk will take you past the Cairnyan ferry dock to Chaine Memorial Road, where a replica of a medieval round tower, 95ft (29m) tall, looks out to sea. Around here, so many Middle Stone Age artefacts have been found that the term 'Larnian' is often used to describe the Mesolithic culture of Ireland. You may not be surprised to learn that the discovery of so many early sites in the Black North (i.e. in 'Protestant' areas like Larne or Mountsandel, near Coleraine), has given rise to an interesting, if unproven, historical theory that there were anthropological differences between the two warring factions of the northeast – the aboriginal Protestants (heirs of the Dalriadic kingdom who came back from Scotland to claim their land), and the Celtic Catholic invaders.

From Ballygally to Ballycastle: Through the Glens of Antrim

Beyond Larne, still on the A2 coast road, some 60 miles (96km) of wonderful maritime scenery stretches ahead of you. This area is like a pictorial textbook, with examples of nearly every rock formation and epoch. For the average visitor this means views of lovely mountains, looming white cliffs, glens, trout streams and beaches. For the geologist it is fascinating: there are Archean schists over 300 million years old which formed the first crust over the once-molten earth, lava fields, glacial deposits, raised beaches and flint beds. The red sandstone which colours the beaches was formed from the sands of a desert which existed 110 to 150 million years ago in the Triassic epoch. This was succeeded by a sea which formed Lias clays, which in turn changed into chalk by a later invasion of the sea. This happened between 120 and 170 million years ago, and now Fair Head's white headlands remind us of it.

After the Ice Age, the **Glens of Antrim** were formed by the movement of the inexorable glaciers which gorged out the valleys. It is best to imagine the glens as being part of a giant hand with ten fingers, with the spaces in between forming a series of short steep valleys running out towards the sea. The glens drain in a north-easterly direction and look straight across to Scotland. They were isolated from the rest of County Antrim by the difficult terrain of the Antrim plateau with its bogs and high ground near Glenarm. Today on the Garron plateau it is still possible to lose oneself and to see wild ponies and goats grazing.

The A2 coast road links each of the nine glens. From south to north, they are Glenarm, Glencloy, Glenariff, Glenballyeamon, Glenaan, Glencorp, Glendun, Glenshesk and Glentaisie. The glens are rich in legend and history; most of the favourite characters of Irish legends make an appearance somewhere. The Children of Lir, who were changed into white swans by their wicked stepmother, were sentenced to spend three hundred years swimming on the bleak Sea of Moyle – an ancient name for this stretch of the North Channel, which lies along the northeastern shores of the glens. Thomas Moore (1779–1852) tells their sad story in the 'Song of Fionnuala':

> Silent, oh Moyle be the roar of thy waters,
> Break not ye breezes your chain of repose,
> While mournfully weeping Lir's lonely daughter
> Tells to the nightstar her sad tale of woes!

Deidre and the sons of Uisneach landed near Ballycastle after they had been in exile, and were lured from there to their death at Emain Macha, near Armagh. Fionn MacCumhaill (Finn MacCool) mistakenly killed his faithful hound Bran in Glenshesk, and his son Oísín (Ossian) is buried in the glens. His grave is marked by a stone circle in **Glenaan**. Other relics of the past are the megalithic monuments built by agricultural people about 5,000 years back, and the *raths* dotted all over the area. These were lonely farmsteads 1,500 years ago.

The remoteness of the glens has caused the people of these parts to have a great sense of regional unity and an affinity with their neighbours on the Scottish coast. They also retained the Irish language until the last quarter of the 19th century. When the Gaelic League set out to revive the Irish language early last century, they held a great *feis* (festival) in 1904 at which people competed in Irish dancing, singing and instrumental music, story-telling, crafts and hunting. A summer *feis* has been held every year since, in one of the nine glens.

From Larne you follow the A2 beneath cliffs and through the Black Cave Tunnel to **Ballygally**. Here there is a very Scottish-style castle, now a hotel. It is well worth a look inside to see the interior of a Scottish *Bawn* House. You can also have a drink in the bar, which is in the dungeon.

A couple of miles inland you can get a panorama of the Scottish coast, with the beehive outline of Ailsa Craig from the Sallagh Braes. **Glenarm**, 'Glen of the Army', is one of the oldest of the glen villages, dating from the 13th century. The castle here belongs to the MacDonnells, who are descended from Sorley Boy MacDonnell, Queen Elizabeth's great enemy. It is not open to the public, but if you go into Glenarm Forest you can look back at this turreted castle, which reminds many of the Tower of London. Those who are looking for folk music may well find it in the village itself.

The MacDonnells, the McQuillans and the Rush Bush

The glens have had a turbulent history. Originally Richard de Burgh, Earl of Ulster, conquered them, and they were sold to the Bissetts in the early 13th century. Five generations later the last of the Bissetts, Margery, the daughter of Eoin Bissett and Sabia O'Neill, became the sole heir to the glens. At this time John More MacDonnell of Kintyre, Lord of the Isles, was looking for a wife and he came to woo her. They were married in 1399, and from then on the glens have been in possession of the MacDonnells, who became known as the MacDonnells of Antrim.

The MacDonnells did not keep the glens easily however; they spent a lot of time fighting other claimants to their territory, particularly the McQuillans, the O'Neills and Sir Arthur Chichester. In 1559 Sorley Boy MacDonnell tricked the McQuillans by spreading rushes over the bog holes which lay between the hostile camps above Glendun. When the McQuillans and their allies, the O'Neills, led a cavalry charge, their horses sank into the swamps and their riders became easy prey to the arrows and axes of the MacDonnells. The MacDonnells still live at Glenarm Castle today (they were made Earls of Antrim in the 17th century), and a traditional saying goes, 'A rush bush never deceived anyone but a McQuillan'.

This part of the coast is full of chalk and limestone. Glenarm exports it from the little harbour, and there used to be quarries at **Carnlough**, which is the town at the foot of **Glencloy** ('Glen of the Hedges') although it is not particularly interesting. This area has long been inhabited and farmed, with dry-stone walls enclosing the land. Although Carnlough attracts local holiday-makers because of its sandy beach, solitude can be found on **Garron Moor** and in the other little glens.

On your way around the Garron Point to Red Bay you will notice a change in the geology – from limestone to the Triassic sandstone, exposed on the shore. All along the A2 coast road you will find breathtaking sea views. The road was built from 1834 to ease the hardships of the glens' people as a work of famine relief – but it also gave them a route out, resulting in a much diminished population.

Glenariff ('Ploughman's Glen'), is the largest and most popular of the glens, with its waterfalls: *Ess na Larach* ('Tears of the Mountain') and *Ess na Crub* ('Fall of the Hoof'). With names like these, you can understand how easy it was for poets to praise these valleys. **Waterfoot** is at the foot of the Glenariff River, by the lovely Red Bay, so called because of the reddish sand washed by the streams from the sandstone. There are caves that were once inhabited in the cliffs above. The village is often the venue for the Glens of Antrim *Feis*. In the glen you will see steep climbing mountains and a narrowing valley floor which gives some aptness to Thackeray's description, 'Switzerland in miniature'.

This is perfect ground for nature rambles, with lovely wild flowers and the moorland of **Glenariff Forest Park**. This magnificent national nature reserve has a camp site and visitor centre in the glen. There is a beautiful walk beside the waterfalls and cascades of the glen. You can spend an hour or a whole day hiking here, and it is best to bring walking boots.

Along the east flank of the valley you can see the remains of a narrow-gauge railway which a century ago transported iron. On the west side, at the Alpinesque cliffs of Lurigethan, you can look for the mound of **Dunclana Mourna**, home of Fionn MacCumhaill and his son, the poet Oísín. According to legend, the warrior Fionn was the leader of a mighty tribe called the Fianna; he was renowned for his wisdom gained through eating the Salmon of Knowledge; for his shining beauty (Fionn means 'fair'); and for his bravery. His deeds are recounted in the legends and epics of Scotland, as well as Ireland.

Continuing on the coast road, we get to **Cushendall**, called the capital of the glens. It lies at the foot of the **Glenballyeamon** ('Edwardstown Glen'), a somewhat lonesome glen, and the two glens **Glenaan** ('Glen of the Colt's Foot', or 'Rush Lights') and **Glencorp** ('Glen of the Slaughter'). Cushendall is delightfully situated on the River Dall, and there is an excellent golf course and camping facilities and a good bar called Pat's. An interesting building is **Turnley's Tower** at 1 Millstreet, right at the crossroads of the town. Built in 1820 as a 'Place of confinement for idlers and rioters', it had a garrison of one man, who lived in the tower until quite recently.

On **Tieveragh Hill** you can get marvellous views over the coast, and muse on the fact that you might be standing on the capital of the fairies – apparently they live inside it. (It is actually a rounded volcanic plug.) **Oísín's Grave** is at the end of a path on the lower slopes of Tieve Bulliagh about 2 miles (3km) west of Cushendall, in Glenaan. It is in fact a megalithic tomb and stone circle but, as usual in Ireland, it has a lovely story associated with it. The Celtic Orpheus, Oísín, was entranced by a vision of the golden-haired Niamh, and followed her to her father's kingdom of Tír na Óg. He returned to find his companions dead and St Patrick preaching. He died unconverted, for the priests' music was not sweet to him after that of his father, Fionn MacCumhaill.

Further up the road is **Beagh's Forest**, which stands in splendid open country. From here you can look back at the mountains Trostan and Slievenanee, where St Patrick is said to have spent many lonely hours in his youth watching sheep. A mile out of the village, on the way to Cushendun and by the sea, are the ruins of **Layde Church**, which contains many MacDonnells monuments and was in use up to 1790.

Cushendun village and its beach are in the care of the National Trust. Clough Williams-Ellis, who designed the pretty cottages here, also designed the seaside village of Portmeirion in Wales. There are marvellous walks around the village and surrounding area. The River Dun is famous for salmon and sea trout, but you have to ask the local Cushendun fishing club for permission to fish.

Within the hidden glen of **Glendun** ('Brown Glen') and its wood, Draigagh, there is a massive rock carved with a crucifixion scene, supposedly brought over from Iona. The poet John Masefield, whose wife came from here, was perhaps thinking of this glen when he wrote 'In the Curlew Calling Time of Irish Dusk', for it is full of wildlife and flowers. Continue along the A2 northwards to **Ballypatrick Forest**, where there is a scenic drive, a camp site, picnic area and walks. Opposite the entrance to Ballypatrick Forest is **Watertop Open Farm**, where you can see the animals at close quarters and hire a pony for trekking.

You have not finished with the glens yet, but you have some wonderful views from the headlands coming up. Go by **Torr Head**, traversing a twisty road from Cushendun through Culraney Townland, which remained an enclave of Scots Gaelic speakers until about 70 years ago. Here you can look to the Mull of Kintyre, only about 15 miles (24km) away on the Scottish coast. You can understand why this part of Ireland felt nearer to Scotland than any other kingdom. Between here and Fair Head is **Murlough Bay** where the kings of Dalriada had their summer residence. There are no remains, but the tree-fringed beach is charming. The best way to reach it is from Drumadoon. At **Fair Head**, reached from Ballyvoy, you can look down from the highest cliffs in the northeast, but still more impressive is the heather-covered top with its three lakes.

Ballycastle is a particularly attractive resort town. Although it's fairly lively, with lawn tennis courts in the old harbour, golf and other amusements nearby, this is the landscape for two of the saddest Irish stories. According to legend, the Children of Lir, condemned to imprisonment as swans by their wicked stepmother, haunted these waters. At the east end of the Ballycastle sands is a rock called *Carrig-Usnach*, where the ill-fated Deidre landed with her lover and his two brothers, the sons of Uisneach, at the treacherous invitation of King Conor, who had lured them back from Scotland.

The Northern Coast:
Ballycastle to the Giant's Causeway

Ballycastle is divided into the market end and the harbour end. The diamond-shaped market place is the site of the Ould Lammas Fair held at the end of August. Visitors from the nearby Scottish islands travel over for this ancient, famous fair. It was given a charter in 1606 and is, therefore, the oldest of Ireland's big traditional fairs. There are large cattle and sheep sales and about five hundred stalls selling hardware, food and crafts; and there's fun at night, with dancing in the street. There is a rhyme that goes:

Did you treat your Mary-Ann
To dulse and yellowman
At the Ould Lammas Fair in Ballycastle?

Ballycastle Museum (*open July–Aug, daily 12–6, at other times by appointment;* **t** *(028) 2076 2024, www.moyle-council.org, ballycastle@nitic.net*) in Castle Street is worth a visit. Ballycastle was a stronghold of the MacDonnells, and at the ruined **Bonamargy Friary**, east of the town, the great coffins of some of these redoubtable chiefs lie in the vault. Also associated with the town was the Boyd family who developed the coal mines; the entrances to these may be seen if you go across the golf course to the foot of Fair Head.

The harbour has a memorial to Count Marconi and his assistant, George Kemp, who in 1898 established radio contact between Ballycastle and Rathlin Island. The town is also famous for its tennis tournament on the grass courts which overlook the sea. There is a fine beach, friendly pubs, and plenty of old-fashioned shops where you can find seaside essentials like film, shrimping nets, buckets and spades. There is a forest drive around the beehive-shaped **Knocklayd Hill** and good fishing in the River Margy.

County Antrim is very well endowed with home bakeries, and the potato bread known as 'fadge' is quite a speciality around Ballycastle. Also sold here are the 'dulse and yellowman' of the Fair rhyme; 'dulse' being dried seaweed, salty and chewy, and 'yellowman' being one of the most delicious confections you can imagine – a bit like the honeycomb inside of a Crunchie bar. Ballycastle is a splendid touring centre, and the other glens which make the quorum of Nine Antrim Glens can be visited from here. **Glenshesk** ('the Sedgy Glen') is well wooded, lying east of Knocklayd Hill. **Breen Wood**, at the head of the Glen, is a nature reserve with very old oaks which probably witnessed the fights between the O'Neills and MacDonnells for mastery of the area. On the other side of the Hill of Knocklayd lies the last glen, **Glentaisie**, called after Taisia, a princess of Rathlin. She seems to have been something of a warrior, having won a great battle on this broad glen which now carries the main road (A44) from Ballycastle to Armoy.

Another short expedition that can be made from the town is to **Kinbane Head**, a couple of miles to the northwest and a stronghold of Colla MacDonnell, Sorley Boy's brother. Now it stands as a picturesque ruin on its narrow white promontory, reached from the B15 going to the Giant's Causeway. A better known tourist attraction is the swinging **Carrick-a-rede Rope Bridge** (*open April–Sept, daily 10–6, July–Aug, daily 10–8; tearoom; adm; t (028) 2076 2178/2073 1159*), north of Ballycastle and about a mile on from Kinbane Head. The bridge is narrow, bouncy and made of planks with wire handrails, and it is thrilling to cross. The views are tremendous, and a small salmon fishery still operates on the ocean side.

One of the prettiest towns on the coast is **Ballintoy**: if you catch it on a good day it looks like a Mediterranean fishing village with its white church and buildings. You can walk west from here to **Whitepark Bay**, a great curve of beach with sand dunes which is a National Trust property. On the edge of the cliffs is **Dunseverick Castle**, of which only one massive wall remains. In under the cliffs is the little hamlet of **Portbraddan** with a tiny church dedicated to St Gobhan (patron saint of builders), said to be the smallest church in Ireland. You will get a good close-up view of traditional salmon netting at this hamlet of four houses. The nets are set out to catch the salmon as they swim along the coast to find the river where they were spawned. You should take your time here; beachcombers can find fossils, flower enthusiasts can examine the dunes, and there is even evidence of a Stone Age settlement at the east end.

Rathlin Island

Fair Head gives you a good view of **Rathlin Island**, which is also called Raghery by the local people. It is said that Fionn MacCumhaill's mother was on her way to get some whiskey for him in Scotland, and she took a stepping stone to throw in on her way across the Moyle. This became Rathlin. The L-shaped island lies about 8 miles (13km) from Ballycastle, and 14 miles (22km) from the Mull of Kintyre, and rises with white cliffs from the sea. It is populated by families who retained their Scots Gaelic longer than any other community; and it has a fascinating history, mostly of battles over the island's strategic position. Pirates and smugglers throughout the centuries have used it as a refuge and a hiding place for contraband. According to local legend, it was a good hideout for Robert the Bruce: he had to take refuge in one of the caves underneath the east lighthouse, and here he saw the determined spider that inspired the saying, 'If at first you don't succeed, try and try again.' This was in 1306 when, with renewed resolve, he fought for and gained the Scottish throne at Bannockburn. In Early Christian times the island's remote position provided a tranquil home for monks, until the Vikings came to plunder it in the 9th century. There are traces of a monastic settlement and a stone sweat house at Knockans, between Brockley and the harbour; and a prehistoric mound-fort known as Doonmore, near the Stone Age settlement at Brockley. East of the harbour is a Celtic standing stone.

As you approach Rathlin in the boat, you will see the beautiful white cliffs of the island and the endless wheeling of the sea birds which rest all over it. The most dramatic place to watch them is from the west lighthouse where the volcanic rock stacks are covered with puffins, fulmars, kittiwakes, razorbills, shearwaters and guillemots. Buzzards, waders, wild geese, ravens and peregrine falcons can be seen at different times of the year.

The island is otherwise inhabited by about seventy people who farm and fish, and there is a guesthouse and restaurant. If you decide to pitch a tent, do ask at the appropriate farmhouse first. There are no cars for hire on Rathlin, which is a blessing, and the roads are silent except for the odd tractor and car belonging to one of the families who live there. The island is small enough to walk around in a (long) day or, even better, you can hire a bicycle. The verges of the roads are starred with wild orchids and there are hardly any bushes, let alone trees, to block the magnificent views of mountainy bog and little lakes. You might hear a corncrake calling, which is rare enough nowadays. You should be able to arrange to go lobster-fishing with one of the locals; the best place to ask is in the pub on the quay. There is good sport to be had catching eels around the wreck of the cruiser *Drake*, which was torpedoed in the First World War. There is good shore fishing, and deep-sea angling boats may be hired at Ballycastle, Ballintoy, and Portballintrae. The journey to Rathlin takes just 45 minutes, but if the weather turns bad you may not be able to return to the mainland the same day (*see* 'Getting Around', p.410).

The Giant's Causeway and Environs

The **Giant's Causeway** is a UNESCO world heritage site (the only one in Ireland), and this accolade only confirms what tourists have known for centuries: that the mix of black basalt columns, white chalk, sea, moorland and sandy beaches makes for a spectacular coastline. About 60 million years ago there was great volcanic activity, and basalt lavas poured out to cover the existing chalk limestone landscape. It actually baked the chalk into a hard rock – very unlike the soft chalk of southern England. These lava flows and eruptions were separated by several million years, allowing tropical vegetation and soils to accumulate. The cooling of the basalt lavas was very variable. When exposed to the air or water, they cooled rapidly and formed skins like that on the top of custard. If they cooled slowly at depth, they shrank to form even polygonal columns like the Giant's Causeway. Here the Ice Ages eroded the cliffs, and graceful arches have been formed by the action of the sea and weather.

There is a 2-mile (3½km) circular walk past the strange formations. The National Trust, which manages the Causeway, has made great efforts to make the site accessible to the thousands who visit each year, retaining the beauty and natural habitat of the area. No souvenir shops and ice-cream vans mar the scenery as they do in other parts of this beautiful coastline. The Trust now owns 104 acres (42ha) of the North Antrim cliff path between the causeway itself and the ruins of Dunseverick Castle beside Whitepark Bay. You will find the Giant's Causeway on the B146, a looproad off the A2 between Ballycastle and Bushmills. Car parking is provided, and a shuttle bus covers the one kilometre from there to the Causeway itself; otherwise access is on foot only. The **Visitors' Centre** (*open July–Aug, daily 10–7; earlier closing time during the rest of the year; guided tours June–Sept, by appointment only at other times; adm for car park; t (028) 2073 1855*) at the entrance includes a tea room, shop and information on the geology and history of the area. Next to the Centre is the **Causeway School Museum** (*open July–Aug, 11–4.30; t (028) 2073 1777*), which takes you back to a small country school circa 1920.

You can walk a couple of miles north along another coastal path to **Port Ballintrae**, a picturesque fishing village, and past a huge strand with strong Atlantic rollers, called

The Legend of The Giant's Causeway

Irish myths are very clear about how the Giant's Causeway was created. It was built by the great hero, Fionn MacCumhaill (Finn McCool): a warrior, magician and poet who was over 52 ft tall. Fionn had a feud with a Scottish giant called Benandonner, who lived on the Scottish island of Staffa. They challenged each other to a fight, and Fionn began to build the Causeway to get to his rival. He was so exhausted by this great labour, however, that he fell asleep as soon as he was finished. The next day Fionn's wife, the giantess Oonagh, saw the massive Benandonner pounding towards them down the Causeway, demanding to know where Fionn was. Quick-thinking Oonagh covered Fionn over and, pointing to his still sleeping form, told the Scot to stop being so noisy before he woke up the baby. Benandonner, unable to imagine how big Fionn had to be if this was the size of his child, turned tail and ran back to Staffa, tearing up most of the Causeway behind him.

Runkerry. Here, a Spanish galleon, the *Girona*, was sunk off the Giant's Causeway. It contained the most valuable cargo yet found (now in the Ulster Museum, Belfast).

Bushmills, which lies on the A2 inland from Port Ballintrae, is famous for its whiskey distillery which claims to be the oldest in the world. Whiskey (coming from the word *usquebaugh*, or *uisce beatha*: 'sweet water') is one word that the English have taken from the Irish. Before whiskey became a genteel drink, the 'best Coleraine' was admitted to be a connoisseur's drink. Peter the Great was amongst many to appreciate the Northern Irish liquor on his study tour of Europe in 1697. **Bushmills Distillery** can be visited (*open April–Oct, Mon–Sat 9.30–5.30 Sun 12–5.30, rest of year, Mon–Fri only; a tour of the distillery takes about one hour; adm; t (028) 2073 1521*).

Move on via the A2 to Northern Ireland's biggest seaside resort, **Portrush**. Before you reach this uninspiring mecca of amusement arcades and fish and chips, visit **Dunluce Castle**, sometimes translated as Mermaid's Fort (*open April–Sept, Mon–Sat 10–6 Sun 2–6 (exc June–Aug, Sun 12–6), Oct–Mar, Tues–Sat 10–4 Sun 2–4; adm; t (028) 2073 1938*), whose bold ruins keep watch over the magnificent coastline. You can see it from the A2, 3 miles (5km) before you reach Portrush. Its long, romantic history is set out in a leaflet available at the entrance. Its kitchen actually fell into the seas while it was inhabited. Anyone approaching it along the shore (you can scramble from the White Rocks, a range of chalk cliffs accessible from the main road) may see the rare meadow cranesbill flower called the Flower of Dunluce.

Portrush is on a promontory jutting out into the Atlantic. It has a small harbour which is popular with yachtsmen sailing in the west, and from here you can take boat cruises to see the Causeway Coast and the Skerries, a group of rocky islands where the great auk (now extinct) used to nest. Crowded in summer, it's not the most appealing place along the coast to stay – except for golfers, trying out the renowned Royal Portrush course. But the town's Victorian/Edwardian main buildings have their own contribution to make to the unique flavour of a Northern coastal resort.

Just west is the more personable resort of **Portstewart**, which also boasts excellent golf courses, as well as a huge stretch of sandy beach. An adventurous option in good weather is to hire a bike and cover a loop from Portrush to the Causeway, down to Bushmills for a well-earned whiskey, and back; it is possible to cover all of this in a single energetic but rewarding day.

Mid-Antrim

As you set off through mid-Antrim via **Ballymena** you will be passing through the richest farmland in the North. The farmers here are among the most modern and hardworking in Ireland. If you are here during the summer you will see the Loyalist flag, with a white background and red hand on a red cross, fluttering from many a household. This area has also benefited from the linen industry, which was boosted in

Tourist Information

Ballymena: 76 Church Street, t (028) 2563 8494; *open all year.*
Ballymoney: Ballymoney Borough Council, t (028) 2766 2280; *open all year.*
Antrim: 16 High Street, t (028) 9442 8331; *open all year.*
Belfast: Belfast Welcome Centre, 35 Donegall Place, t (028) 9024 6609, *www.visitnorthernireland.com*; *open all year.*

Shopping

Crafts
Orchard Crafts, Castlecroft, Main Street, Ballymoney.
Forge Pottery, 18 Milltown Road, Antrim, t (028) 9446 5349.
Irish Linen Centre, Lisburn, t (028) 9266 3377.

Delicacies
Good bakeries are to be found all over the county, with especially good soda and potato breads.
Lough Neagh Fishermans' Co-operative Society, Toomebridge, t (028) 7965 0618. Fresh eels.

Markets
Ballymena, at the market car park beside the leisure centre, on the Larne Road link. Held on Saturdays, the market has stalls selling vegetables and clothes.

Sports and Activities

Animal Sanctuary
TACT Talnotry Cottage, 2 Crumlin Road, Crumlin, t (028) 9442 2900. The owners look after injured birds and small mammals. For tea in their ornamental garden, call in advance. *Open Mon–Fri 12–3, Sun 2–5, other times by appointment.*

Fishing
The Bann, Main, Braid, Clough and Glenwhirry rivers have an abundance of brown trout and salmon. Lough Neagh has its own variety of trout, called 'dollaghan'. The Inver, Glynn, Bush, Carey, Margy, Dun and Roe are all excellent for sea trout, salmon and brown trout. Call local tourist offices for details.

Open Farms
Leslie Hill Open Farm, Macfin Road, Ballymoney, t (028) 2766 6803/2766 3109.

Pleasure Cruises
On Lough Neagh and the River Bann.
Ulster Cruising School, Carrickfergus, t (028) 9336 8818, *ulstercruisingschool@hotmail.com.*

Steam Train Rides
Railway Preservation Society of Ireland, t (028) 2826 0803. Runs the *Portrush Flyer* between Belfast and Portrush each summer. The 2hr journey costs about £15 one way; call for details and dates, as they change every year.

the late 17th century by the Huguenot weavers, who sought refuge here from the religious intolerance of Louis XIV of France. Louis Crommelin is credited with having started the industry; northeast of Ballymena is the village of **Newtown-Crommelin** which is named after him. It is now a lonely sheep-rearing settlement, though in the past bauxite was mined on the moors around it. **Ballymena** itself is a very prosperous town; the rumour is that all the farmers roundabout have bank accounts in the tax haven of the Isle of Man. (A riddle once asked – 'Why are pound notes green?' – and answered – 'because Ballymena men pick them before they are ripe'.)

Another spot worth stopping at is the little Moravian settlement of **Gracehill**, just outside Ballymena, where you can see some of the communal buildings dating from the 18th century around the green. These Moravians came from Eastern Europe. Their Protestant sect, also known as the United Brethren, was founded in Saxony before

Where to Stay

Galgorm Manor, Ballymena, t (028) 2588 1001, f (028) 2588 0080 (*luxury*). A spectacular 17th-century castle with lovely lawns transformed into a plush hotel.

Adair Arms Hotel, Ballymoney Road, Ballymena, t (028) 2565 3674, f (028) 2564 0436 (*moderate*). Attractive old 23-room hotel.

Moore Lodge, Kilrea, Ballymoney, t (028) 2954 1043 (*expensive*). Very upmarket, with excellent fishing on the River Bann. Contact Sir William and Lady Moore.

Dunaird House, 15 Buckna Road, Broughshane, t (028) 2586 2117 (*inexpensive*). Welcoming, modernized farmhouse, all en suite bedrooms.

Dunadry Hotel and Country Club, 2 Islandreagh Drive, Dunadry, Antrim, t (028) 9443 4343, f (028) 9443 3389 (*expensive*). Comfortable, modern hotel near Belfast International airport.

Keef Halla Guest House, 20 Tully Road, Nutts Corner, Crumlin, t/f (028) 9082 5491 (*inexpensive*). Comfortable and modern, 5 minutes from Belfast International airport.

Self-catering

Rural Cottages Holidays Ltd, Tourism Ireland, t (028) 9024 1100, f (028) 9024 1198. All the following self-catering cottages can be booked through this company. They are all attractive traditional dwellings, restored and furnished to a high standard. Cost varies with the season, but a cottage sleeping 6 is around £410 per week at the top rate:

Slemish Cottage, Broughshane. 100-year-old farmhouse with lovely views, sleeping 6;

Manns Cottage, Broughshane. Equally attractive, sleeps 10;

O'Harabrook, Old Dairy, Ballymoney. Three apartments in stone-built outhouses on large farm; each apartment sleeps 6.

Eating Out

Galgorm Manor, Ballymena, t (028) 2588 1001 (*expensive*). Opulent dining.

Manley Restaurant, State Shopping Centre, 70a Ballymoney Road, Ballymena, t (028) 2564 8967/2564 9360 (*moderate*). Cantonese and Peking cooking.

Water Margin Restaurant, 8 Cullybackey Road, Ballymena, t (028) 2564 8368 (*moderate*). Cantonese cooking.

Leslie Hill Open Farm, Ballymoney, t (028) 2766 6803 (*inexpensive*). Scones, cakes and teas.

Brown Jug, 27 Main Street, Ballymoney, t (028) 2766 4212 (*inexpensive*). Salads, quiche. *Daytime only.*

Dunadry Inn, 2 Islandreagh Drive, Dunadry, t (028) 9443 4343 (*expensive*). The wine bar here is open during the day. It is conveniently close to the airport, and unexpectedly good.

Piper's Quay, 88 Bridge Street, Lisburn, t (028) 9262 8816 (*moderate–inexpensive*). Locally recommended.

Café Rio, Market Square, Lisburn (*inexpensive*). Snacks, coffee.

they came to Ireland in 1746. The village is linked to **Galgorm** by a bridge over the River Main. You can glimpse the 17th-century Galgorm Castle, which is surrounded by a lawn and stately trees. The little village itself is delightful, with thatched cottages along one main street which runs by the river to the castle.

Off the A26 to Coleraine, just on the outskirts of **Ballymoney**, is **Leslie Hill Open Farm** (*open April–May and Sept, Sun and public holidays, 2–6; June, Sat and Sun, 2–6; July and Aug, Mon–Sat, 11–6, Sun, 2–6; adm; t (028) 2766 3109*). The 18th-century farm buildings include the Bellbarn (a threshing barn), a dovecote, a typical cattle byre and the payhouse. You can also see the old stables which now house newborn piglets. The famous traveller and agriculturist Arthur Young visited Leslie Hill in 1776, and much admired the lovely grounds, pretty lake and island. The estate has been lived in by the Leslie family for 350 years, and the Big House is a classic Georgian stone-cut building dating from 1760 (*only open to groups; advanced booking advised*). A few miles to the north in the tiny village of Benvarden Dervock, **Benvarden House and Garden** (*open June–Aug, Tues–Sun 2–6; adm; t (028) 2074 1331*) is worth a visit with its attractive 18th-century garden and pleasure grounds.

When you make your way down to Antrim Town and Lough Neagh you will see the distinctive shape of **Slemish Mountain**, east of Ballymena, where St Patrick spent his youth after being captured by Irish pirates. To get to it, take the B94 from Broughshane; turn left after a mile, right after 3 miles (5km) (signposted), right after half a mile, and follow the road between dry-stone walls to Slemish car park. From the top, which is a steep climb of about 700ft (213m), you get a wonderful view. This lonely, extinct volcano has been a place of pilgrimage on St Patrick's Day, 17 March, for centuries. At **Broughshane**, a mile beyond the village on the A42, is **Carncairn Daffodils Centre** (*adm free*) where you can buy bulbs which have frequently won prizes in the Chelsea Flower Show. At **Dreen**, near Cullybackey, is the ancestral home of US President Chester Arthur (1881–5). It is a thatched cottage which has been restored and furnished (*open April–Sept, in the afternoons; adm*).

Two miles south of Templepatrick on the A6, southeast of Antrim Town, is **Patterson's Spade Mill** (*open April–May and Sept, Sat–Sun 2–6, June–Aug, Wed–Mon 2–6; adm; t (028) 9443 3619*). It is the only water-driven spade mill left in Ireland, and you can see a traditional forge where nine regional types of spades are produced, although in its heyday the Mill used to produce around 300 different types. It has been restored by the National Trust and there is a fascinating guided tour; the busy, glowing workshop is full of exciting bangs and clangs showing the way things used to be done – you can even go away with your own sturdy spade.

Antrim Town stands a little way back from Lough Neagh. The town has an old nucleus with a 9th/10th-century round tower in almost perfect condition on Steeple Road (north of the centre), but it is now being encircled by new housing and shopping centres. The ruined **Antrim Castle and Gardens** (*open Mon–Fri 9.30–9.30, Sat 10–5, Sun 2–5; t (028) 9442 8000*), c. 1662, are worth a visit. The former stable block is now an arts centre, but of the castle itself only a tower remains, the rest having been destroyed by fire in 1922. The gardens have been carefully restored and include geometrical borders in the 17th-century Anglo-Dutch style and a wooded walk.

Shane's Castle, outside Randalstown, is a ruin on a private estate, which is now open to the public. It is on the site of the ancient stronghold of Edenduffcarrick. The castle was for many centuries associated with the O'Neills of Clandeboye; the sculptured head in the south wall of the tower, about 30ft from the ground, is known as the Black Head of the O'Neills. There is a traditional saying that if anything should happen to the head, the O'Neill family will come to an end.

Lough Neagh, the largest stretch of inland water in the British Isles, is surrounded by flat marshy land, so you do not get a good view of it from the road. Legend tells how Fionn MacCumhaill took up a sod of land to throw at another giant, which left behind a hole. This became Lough Neagh, and the sod formed the Isle of Man. The lough is famous for its eels, which spawn in the Sargasso Sea, swim across the Atlantic, and struggle up the Bann in springtime, all 20 million of them (although now they are captured at Coleraine and brought to Lough Neagh in tankers). The eels take about 12 years to mature, and the main fishery is at **Toomebridge**, a very large co-operative managed by local fishermen and farmers. **Newferry**, at the top of Lough Beg, is a haven for coarse fishermen as well as water skiers.

Lisburn, in the Lagan Valley, in the southern tip of County Antrim, has a Planters Gothic **cathedral**. Louis Crommelin lived here and there is also the excellent **Lisburn Museum and Irish Linen Centre** (*open all year Mon–Sat 9.30–5; t (028) 9266 3377*) which includes a re-creation of a linen-weaving workshop; specialist linen is manufactured here, and is available to buy. (For more information on the Irish Linen Centre, *see* p.452) You might also visit the **Hilden Brewing Company** (*t (028) 9266 3863*), where you can tour Ireland's oldest independent brewery and taste its best ales.

Belfast

Belfast is probably known to most people through the exposure brought by the Troubles. Press and television news reports have recorded the bombings, the military involvement and the sectarian murders, giving the impression of a war-torn city, constantly in a state of unrest and dangerous to visit. This is simply not the case. For visitors it is surprising how normal the streets are, full of people shopping at Marks & Spencer and other proliferous British chain stores. Military patrols and armoured police vehicles are now a rare sight, where once they were an everyday part of the city's life. Belfast people share a cautious optimism about the peace process, and while old sectarian divisions die hard, there is almost unanimous support for a permanent political resolution to the violence. They are very friendly, and will answer any queries with the characteristic good humour of the Irish.

There are many opportunities to see good theatre, art shows, classical and pop concerts, whilst the strong intellectual and historical atmosphere makes for good conversation and well-stocked bookshops. The well-educated young are still leaving for opportunities abroad, but many are coming back with a wealth of experience. Belfast is losing its parochial image and becoming more European-minded, and the

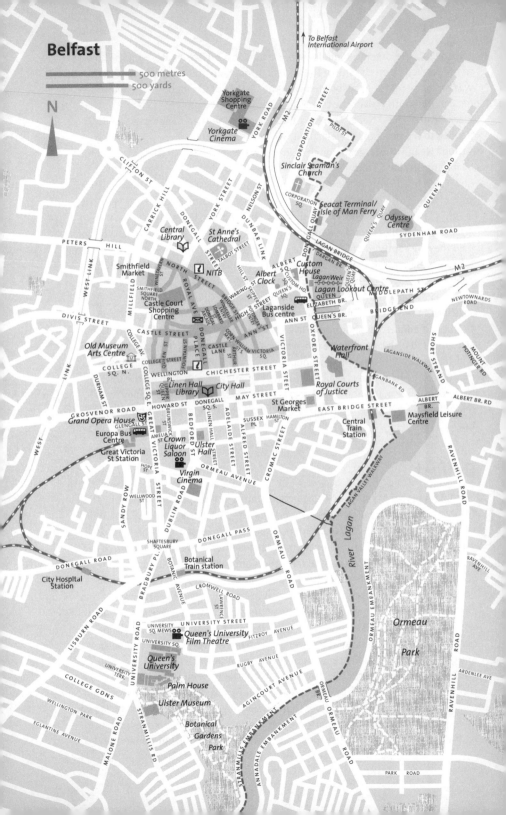

Getting There and Around

By Air

Belfast International Airport, t (028) 9442 2888. 19 miles (30km) from the city centre, at Aldergrove. The airport coach leaves every half-hour from the Europa Bus Centre. Belfast City Airport, t (028) 9045 7745. 4 miles (7km) from the city, served by local UK airlines only. Take a train to Sydenham Halt from either of the railway stations, Citybus no.21, or a taxi from Donegall Square.

By Sea

Larne–Cairnryan: P&O European Ferries, t 0870 242 4777. The Larne ferry service always links in with a train to Belfast. The station is just beside the terminal building. Belfast–Liverpool: Norse Irish Car Ferries, t (028) 9077 9090. Belfast–Stranraer: Hoverspeed Sea Cat, t 08705 523 523. Four crossings per day; journey takes 1½ hours. Belfast–Douglas: Isle of Man Steam Packet, t 08705 523 523. May–Sept only.

By Rail

From **Belfast Central Station**, East Bridge Street, or **Great Victoria Street Station**; trains go to all destinations. Note there are **no left luggage facilities** in any Northern Ireland railway station. **Translink, t** (028) 9089 9411, *www.translink.co.uk*. For all enquiries.

By Bus

The **Europa Centre** on Great Victoria Street serves destinations in Counties Armagh, Tyrone, Londonderry, Fermanagh and West Down, the Republic and ferry services to the UK. Go to the **Laganside Bus Centre** on Donegall Quay (east of the Albert Clock) for all destinations in eastern County Antrim and North Down. Ulsterbus operates within the city suburb and throughout the province; coaches also go to the Republic and mainland UK. **City buses** are red and cover most routes. **City Stopper** buses nos.523–538 also serve the Falls Road and Lisburn Road. **Ulsterbus**, Europa Centre, Great Victoria Street, t (028) 9033 3000. Enquiries and timetables.

There are no left luggage facilities. *Open daily 7.30am–8.30pm.*
Citybus Enquiries, t (028) 9024 6485.

By Car

Parking is forbidden in the centre of Belfast; large notices are displayed on the pavements and there are double yellow lines at the edge of the road. Excellent car parks and pay-and-display areas ring the centre of the city; the tourist office has a list and map.
Avis, 69–71 Gt Victoria St, t (028) 9024 0404.
Budget, 96–102 Great Victoria Street, t (028) 9023 0700.
Dan Dooley, 175B Airport Road, Aldergrove, t (028) 9445 2522.
Europcar, City Airport, t (028) 9045 0904; International Airport, t (028) 9442 3444.
Hertz, International Airport, t (028) 9442 2533.
McCausland Car Hire, 21–31 Grosvenor Road, t (028) 9033 3777.

By Taxi

Taxi **ranks** can be found at City Hall in Donegall Square, Upper Queen Street, Wellington Place and Castle Street.
Belfast Taxi, t 0786 090 1899.
Black Taxi, t (028) 906 2264.

By Bike

McConvey Cycles, 183 Ormeau Road, t (028) 9033 0322, *www.mcconvey.com*; also at 467 Ormeau Road, t (028) 9049 1163.
Life Cycles, 25 Smithfield Market, t (028) 9043 9959.
Recycle, 1–5 Albert Square, t (028) 9031 3115.

Festivals

March

Draoicht Children's Festival, West Belfast.

April

Easter Celebrations, at Ulster Folk and Transport Museum, Cultra, Holywood, t (028) 9042 8428.

May

Belfast City Summer Festival, including the Lord Mayor's Show, May–June, t (028) 9032 0202.

Cathedral Quarter Arts Festival, t (028) 9023 2403, www.cqaf.com, cqaf@hotmail.com.
The Best of Ireland, Ulster Folk and Transport Museum, t (028) 9042 8428, www.index.com/uftm. Traditional music and crafts.
Ulster Drama Festival, The Lyric Theatre, t (028) 9038 1081, www.lyrictheatre.co.uk.

June
Shankill Festival. Social, cultural and recreational events, t (028) 9031 1333.

July
Story-telling Weekend, at Ulster Folk and Transport Museum, t (028) 9042 8428. Story-telling and traditional music.
Orange Order Parades (12th).

August
Ardoyne Fleadh, t (028) 9075 1056. Local and international performers, ceili.
Feile an Phobail, t (028) 9031 3440. Annual festival with music, drama, Irish language events, carnival, parade.
Rare Breeds Show and Sale, Ulster Folk and Transport Museum, t (028) 9042 8428, www.index.com/uftm. Ireland's largest; rare, minority and re-established farm breeds.

September
Belfast Film Festival, t (028) 9032 5913, www.belfastfilmfestival.org.

November
Belfast Arts Festival, at Queens University. Festival Box Office, t (028) 9066 7687 for information, t (028) 9066 5577 for bookings, www.belfastfestival.com, festival@qub.ac.uk. Three weeks of music events, films, plays, poetry and art exhibitions, successful fringe shows from Edinburgh and internationally known stars. Events take place mainly around the university area.

Tourist Information
Belfast Welcome Centre, Donegall Place, t (028) 9024 6609.
Tourism Ireland Information Centre, 59 North Street, t (028) 9023 1221, f (028) 9024 0960, www.discovernorthernireland.com,

www.ireland-travel.ie, visitorservices@nitb.com; open Mon–Sat, 9–5.15. Extended opening hours in summer.
Belfast Visitor and Convention Bureau, 73–5 Great Victoria Street, t (028) 9023 9026, www.gotobelfast.com.

Useful Contacts
Emergency Services, t 999.
Belfast City Hospital, Lisburn Road, t (028) 9032 9241.
General Post Office, at Castle Place and Shaftesbury Square. Open Mon–Fri 9–5.30, Sat 9–9.
AA, 108–110 Great Victoria Street, t 08705 989 989; 24-hour rescue service t 0800 887766.
RAC, 14 Wellington Place, t 08705 722722; 24-hour rescue service t 0800 828282.
Youth Hostel Association, 22 Donegall Road, t (028) 9032 4733/9031 5435, f (028) 9043 9699, info@hini.org.uk.
USIT/Belfast Student Travel, t (028) 9032 4073/9032 7111.

Shopping
The centre of Belfast is full of shopping arcades and pedestrian malls, and all the British high street stores are well-represented. Shuttle buses can take you to and from the car parks, and a large number of city buses stop at the City Hall, which is very central. The more unusual shops are situated in Bedford Street, Dublin Road, and Donegall Pass, where you will find design outlets, antiques and bric-a-brac. Expensive women's clothes shops are to be found amongst the cafés and food stores on the Lisburn Road.

Antiques
Alexander the Grate, Donegall Pass, t (028) 9023 2041.
Blue Cat, Bedford Street, t (028) 9023 5204.
Oakland Antiques, Donegall Pass, t (028) 9032 0176.
Past and Present, Donegall Pass.

Books
Bookfinders, 47 University Road, t (028) 9032 8269.

University Bookshop, 91 University Terrace, opposite Queens College, t (028) 9066 6302.

Waterstone's, 8 Royal Avenue, t (028) 9024 7355; also 44 Fountain St, t (028) 9024 0159.

Clothes

House of de Courcy, 487 Lisburn Road, t (028) 9020 0205. International designer clothes for women.

Paul Costelloe, 45 Bradbury Place, t (028) 9023 9496. Stocks Irish designers.

Smyth and Gibson, Bedford Street, t (028) 9023 0388, www.smythandgibson.co.uk, shirts@smythandgibson.co.uk. Top quality Irish shirts made in Derry.

Crafts

Craftworks, Bedford Street, t (028) 9024 4465.

The Wicker Man, 12 Donegall Arcade, Castle Place, t (028) 9024 3550, www.thewickerman.co.uk.

The Workshops Collective, 1a Lawrence Street, t (028) 9020 0707.

Delicacies

Feasts, 39 Dublin Road, t (028) 9033 2787. Irish farmhouse cheeses, charcuterie and four different kinds of fresh home-made pasta.

French Village Bakery, 70 Stranmillis Road, t (028) 9038 1671. Traditional wheaten bannock, wheaten loaf and 'Belfast Baps', as well as enormous croissants and baguettes.

Irish Linen

Irish Linen Stores, Fountain Centre, College Street, t (028) 9032 2727.

Smyth's Irish Linens, 65 Royal Avenue, t (028) 9024 2232.

Markets

St George's Market, at the end of May Street, t (028) 9027 0386. Fresh fruit, vegetables, fish, crafts, new and vintage clothes and other wares. Held in the 19th-century 'Variety Market' building. Tuesdays and Fridays from 7am–1pm.

Musical Instruments

Matchetts Ltd, Wellington Place, t (028) 9032 6695, f (028) 9057 2133, www.matchettsmusic.com. Chain of shops selling traditional instruments, sheet music and accessories made in Ireland.

Sports Equipment

Graham Tiso, 12–14 Corn Market, t (028) 9023 1230.

S.S. Moore, 6 Chichester Street, t (028) 9032 2966/9032 9196.

Surf Mountain, 12 Brunswick Street, t (028) 9024 8877.

Sports and Activities

Art Galleries

The Troubles seem to have generated a creative urge amongst Ulster artists which is both exploratory and introspective. Artists such as Tom Carr, T. P. Flanagan, Brian Ferran, Basil Blackshaw and Brian Ballard have produced excellent works. They paint various subjects, often Ulster scenery, also nudes, and interpretations of Irish myths. Entry to all the private, commercial galleries is free.

Bell Gallery, 13 Adelaide Park, t (028) 9066 2998.

Crescent Arts Centre, 2–4 University Road, t (028) 9024 2338. Also includes the Fenderesky Gallery, open Tues–Sat.

Emer Gallery, 463 Lisburn Road, t (028) 9066 6912/9066 8386.

Old Museum Arts Centre, 7 College Square North, t (028) 9023 5053.

Ormeau Baths Gallery, 18 Ormeau Avenue, t (028) 9032 1402. Worth visiting for the shows, which are usually by Irish and Ulster artists. Open Tues–Sat 9–5.

Tom Caldwell Gallery, 40 Bradbury Place, t (028) 9032 3226.

Townhouse Gallery, 125 Great Victoria Street, t (028) 9031 1798. Prints and etchings.

Ulster Museum, Botanic Gardens (off Stranmillis Road), t (028) 9038 3000.

Golf

Balmoral Golf Club, Lisburn Road, t (028) 9038 1514. 18 holes.

Blackwood Golf Centre, Crawfordsburn Road, Clandeboye, t (028) 9185 2706.

Carrickfergus Golf Club, 7 miles (12km) north-east of Belfast on the A2, t (028) 9336 2203. 18-hole course.

Rockmount Golf Club, Carryduff, t (028) 9081 2279.

Royal Belfast Golf Club, Station Rd, Craigavad, t (028) 9042 8165. The oldest of the only four 'Royal' clubs in Ireland.

Indoor Leisure Centres

Maysfield Leisure Centre, East Bridge Street, t (028) 9024 1633. Central; and has a pool, gym, squash and sauna.

Internet Access

Revelations Café, Bradbury Place, t (028) 9032 0337, www.revelations.co.uk, info@revelations.co.uk.

Tours

Guided **walking tours** include those of pubs, historic Belfast, the University area and the Laganside walk; **bus tours** are also available. The Belfast Welcome Centre Distributes a free leaflet, called 'Walk this Way', about the tours. **Citybus**, t (028) 9030 1732/9024 6485. Tours taking in all the main sights of Belfast, including Stormont and Belfast Castle, and a 'Living History Tour', around the areas of Belfast associated with the Troubles.

Where to Stay

Belfast t (028–)

Luxury

The Culloden Hotel, 142 Bangor Road, Craigavad, t/f 9042 5223, or f 9042 6777. One of the nicest hotels, on the northeast of Belfast Lough. Very plush with lovely grounds and luxurious old-style furnishings.

Europa Hotel, Great Victoria Street, t/f 9032 7000. Very central, modern hotel which in the past was bombed so many times that everybody lost count. Recently redecorated.

Expensive

Belfast Hilton, 4 Lanyon Place, t 9027 7000. New, modern hotel; right up close to the Waterfront Hall, but has wonderful views.

Clandeboye Lodge Hotel, 10 Estate Road, Clandeboye, t/f 9185 2500. Luxurious hotel adjoining Blackwood Golf Course.

Dukes Hotel, 65–67 University Street, t/f 9023 6666. Quiet, central, close to restaurants.

McCausland, 34–38 Victoria Street, t 9022 0200. Rooms are rather small.

Ramada Hotel, 117 Milltown Road, Shaw's Bridge, t 9092 3500, f 9092 3600, www.ramadabelfast.com, mail@ramadabelfast.com. A bit souless, but this full service hotel has all mod cons and is conveniently located for travellers, on the ring road, 5 miles from the city centre.

The Wellington Park Hotel, 21 Malone Road, t 9038 1111, f 9066 5410. Modern and comfortable, close to the Botanic Gardens, with secure car parking.

Moderate

Ash-Rowan Town House, 12 Windsor Avenue, t 9066 1758/1983/3227. 10 minutes from the city centre; cosy and attractive.

Camera Guest House, 44 Wellington Park, t 9066 0026, f 9066 7856. Comfortably elegant Victorian terraced house. Contact the friendly proprietress, Caroline Drumm.

Greenwood Guest House, 25 Park Road, t 9020 2525, f 9020 2530, www.greenwoodhouse.co.uk. Jason and Mary Harris offer excellent full Irish breakfasts at their Victorian town house. The house overlooks Ormeau Park. Children welcome, babysitting available.

Lisdara Town House, 23 Derryvolgie Avenue, Malone Road, t 9068 1549. Comfortable 1870s town house in quiet residential avenue, within easy reach of the city centre.

Inexpensive

All of these offer good value B&B in the quiet, leafy streets of the university district. They are often busy in summer, so book ahead.

Eglantine Guest House, 21 Eglantine Avenue, t 9066 7585.

The George, 9 Eglantine Ave, t 9068 3212.

Liserin Guest House, 17 Eglantine Avenue, t 9066 0769.

Queen's University Common Room, College Gardens, University Road, t 9066 5938, f 9066 4501.

Windermere Guest House, 60 Wellington Park, t 9066 2693.

YWCA Hostel, Kent Street, t 9024 0439. Good and central.

Self-catering

The Ark, 18 University Street, **t** 9032 9626. Terraced house, close to city centre.

Queen's Elms, Queen's University, 78 Malone Road, **t** 9038 1608, **f** 9066 6680. Rooms are mainly singles; access to cooking facilities.

Eating Out

Belfast **t** (028–)

Expensive

Belle Epoque, 61 Dublin Road, **t** 9032 3244. French food in traditional style.

Cayenne, Lesley House, 7 Shaftesbury Square, **t** 9033 1532. Imaginative menu and reasonable set lunches. *Book ahead, closed Sun.*

Deane's, 36–40 Howard Street, **t** 9056 0000. Successful, well-run restaurant with a more affordable **brasserie** (*moderate*) in the basement, which also serves excellent food.

Nick's Warehouse, 35 Hill Street, Cathedral Quarter, **t** 9043 9690. Popular, modern restaurant, highly recommended for its freshly prepared gourmet dishes. *Open Mon 10–5, Tues–Fri 10–10, Sat 6–10, closed Sun.*

Moderate

Antica Roma, 67 Botanic Avenue, **t** 9031 1121. Lively décor; imaginative pasta and sauces.

Belfast Castle, Antrim Road, **t** 9077 6925/9037 0133. Lovely city views.

Ginger's, 271 Ormeau Road, **t** 9049 3143. Superb Southeast Asian-inspired cooking, including freshly baked breads, vegetarian dishes and inventive recipes incorporating ginger. Internationally reputed. *Book in advance; open Tues–Sat 5–9.30, Sat 12–3.*

Gipsy Queen Vegetarian Restaurant, 13–17 Amelia Street, **t** 9024 5489. Freshly made vegetarian and vegan dishes are GMO-free and organic. Informal, unique restaurant.

Sun Kee, 28 Donegall Pass, **t** 9031 2016. The best Chinese restaurant in Belfast.

Inexpensive

Fitzy's, 25–27 University Road, **t** 9024 7725. Studenty bistro-cum-gourmet pizzeria. *Open Mon–Sat 12–2.30, 5pm–late, Sun 5–9.30pm.*

La Salsa, 23 University Rd, **t** 9024 4588. Lively, informal; frozen margaritas and surprisingly good Mexican food. *Evenings only.*

Maggie May's, 50 Botanic Avenue, **t** 9032 2662. Big servings, good value veggie meals.

The Other Place, 79 Botanic Avenue, **t** 9020 7200. Good hamburgers, chips and Ulster fry.

Scarletts, 423 Lisburn Road, **t** 9068 3102. Snack menu and bistro.

Speranza, 16 Shaftesbury Square, **t** 9023 0213. Pizzas, pasta.

Villa Italia, 37–41 University Road, **t** 9032 8356. Lively and popular. *Evenings only.*

Cafés

Belfast has some good cafés serving exotic, well-prepared food or simple, affordable meals; yet few have effective non-smoking areas, and some have yet to master the art of a good cappuccino.

Bewleys Oriental Café, Donegall Arcade, **t** 9023 4955.

Bonnie's Museum Café, 11a Stranmillis Road. Pies, filled baguettes, soups.

Bookfinders Café, 47 University Road, **t** 9032 8269. In a bookshop; vegetarian meals.

Cargoes, 613 Lisburn Road, **t** 9066 5451. Mediterranean salads, café in delicatessen.

Equinox, 32 Howard Street, **t** 9023 0089. Café in a sophisticated interior design and gift shop. Excellent salads, coffee, milkshakes.

Roscoff Café, 27 Fountain Street, **t** 9031 5090. Great for breakfasts and snacks; also at 12–14 Arthur Street, **t** 9031 0108, with an express takeaway and a more relaxed area.

Smyth & Gibson, Bedford Street, **t** 9023 0388. Famous Derry shirtmakers with a coffee outlet downstairs that does try for decent latte and cappuccino, and it's non-smoking.

Entertainment and Nightlife

Pubs and Bars

The atmosphere in the bars mentioned below is friendly and warm. Traditional, folk and popular music is played in some places whilst specialities such as champ and stew are served in others. The best sources of information for music events are the *Belfast Telegraph*

or *That's Entertainment* and *Artslink*, available
from tourist offices and hotels.

Apartment, 2 Donegall Square, t (028) 9050
9777. Coffee and cocktails, meals and snacks
in this hip and stylish bar in the city centre.

Crown Liquor Saloon, 46 Great Victoria Street,
t (028) 9027 9901. A fine Victorian
extravagance (*see* opposite), faithfully
restored and maintained by the National
Trust. Irish stew and oysters at lunchtime.

The Duke of York, 11 Commercial Court, 103
Victoria Street, t 9031 1088/9024 1062. Live
music in the evenings.

Lavery's Bar and Gin Palace, 12 Bradbury Place,
t (028) 9087 1106. An old favourite for a wide
range of age groups. Pub grub.

McHugh's, 29–31 Queen's Square, t (028) 9050
9990. A charming bar and restaurant in
Belfast's oldest building, popular with
tourists and young professionals.

The Morning Star, 17 Pottinger's Entry, t (028)
9032 3976. Attractive old pub which serves
excellent meals.

Morrison's Spirit Grocers, 21 Bedford St, t (028)
9024 8458. Cleverly decorated theme bar.

White's Tavern, 2–4 Winecellar Entry, t (028)
9024 3080. Live music on Thursdays.

Live Music

Front Page, 108 Donegall Street, t (028) 9032
4924. Food and live music.

Kitchen Bar, 16–18 Victoria Square, t (028)
9032 4901. Traditional Irish bar with real ale
and Ulster food, and Irish and Scottish
traditional music on Friday nights.

The Rotterdam, 54 Pilot Street, t (028) 9074
6021. Folk and traditional music.

Nightclubs

The Limelight, 17 Ormeau Avenue, t (028) 9032
5968. Promotes new bands, attracts a young
crowd. U2 and Oasis have played here.

M Club, 23–31 Bradbury Place, t (028) 9023 3131.

Robinson's Bar, 38–42 Great Victoria Street,
t (028) 9024 7447. Has some truly awful duos
and bands but also the occasional gem.

Arts Centres

Cultúrlann Macadam O'Fiach, 216 Falls Road,
t (028) 9096 4180, *diane@culturlann.org*.
Irish-language arts centre, with performance and different forms of media.

Cinema

The Curzon, Ormeau Road, t (028) 9064 1373.

The Movie House, Yorkgate Centre, York Road,
t (028) 9075 5000.

Queen's University Film Theatre,
7 University Square Mews, t (028) 9024
4857. Avant-garde, art house films are
shown here in a narrow lane off
Botanic Avenue.

Strand Cinema, 152–4 Holywood Road,
Strandtown, t (028) 9067 3500.

Virgin, at the north end of Dublin Road, t (028)
9024 3200. Big multiplex.

Poetry

Ulster has also produced poets of
international renown; Seamus Heaney
started writing here when he was at Queen's
University in the 1960s, as did Paul Muldoon
at a later date. During the **Belfast Arts Festival**
in November you could be lucky and hear
them and other talented poets reading their
work (*see* under 'Festivals').

Theatres and Concert Halls

Belfast Waterfront Hall, 2 Lanyon Place, t (028)
9033 4455/9033 4400, *www.waterfront.co.
uk*. Concert hall which accommodates
about 2,200 people. Major stars from
the classical and pop music world
perform here.

The Grand Opera House, Great Victoria Street,
t (028) 9024 1919/9024 0411.

Lyric Theatre, 55 Ridgeway Street, off
Stranmillis Road, t (028) 9038 1081. Serious
Irish, European and American drama.

The Old Museum Arts Centre, 7 College Square
North, t (028) 9023 5053. Avant-garde dance,
theatre, comedy.

St Anne's Cathedral, Donegall Street, t (028)
9032 8332. Venue for occasional lunchtime
recitals; wonderful sung services on Sunday.

The Ulster Hall, Bedford Street, t (028)
9032 3900. Another venue for concerts
and comedy shows. The hall has a
wonderful organ; there are a series of
subscription concerts and lunchtime recitals
in the summer.

Whitla Hall, Queen's University, t (028)
9027 3075. Classical music concerts
throughout the year, particularly during
the Arts Festival.

bars and cafés more sophisticated. The new Waterfront Hall and Hilton seem to be new symbols for Belfast, just as the Europa Hotel and the Opera House became symbols of surviving the bomb and bullet during the worst of the troubles in the 1970s.

Belfast (*Beal Feirst*: 'Mouth of the Sandy Ford') is the administrative centre of the six counties that make up Northern Ireland. It has one of the most beautiful natural settings of any city, ringed by hills which are visible from most parts of the town, and hugging the shores of the lough. It has been a city officially only since 1888. In the 19th century it grew from an insignificant town by a river ford into a prosperous commercial centre and port, with great linen mills and the famous shipyards of Harland & Wolff. The Titanic, built here and so tragically sunk by an iceberg, was considered an outstanding engineering feat.

Architecturally, Belfast is made up of some grand Victorian public buildings and the red-brick streets which characterize many British towns. The prosperous-looking houses which make up the smart Malone Road area and line the lough on either side were built by the wealthy middle class who had benefited from the linen industry. The workers in the factories and shipyards divided themselves between the Catholic Falls Road area and the Protestant Shankill Road. Unemployment became worse as the linen and ship-building industries declined, nurturing the conditions in which the terrorist armies could thrive. The division of these working class areas from the city centre was made explicit by the Westlink motorway, which runs north-south and creates a boundary line through the west side of the city.

Central Belfast

The city centre is pedestrianized, for security reasons, but you will see nothing else out of the ordinary unless you are extraordinarily unlucky. It has been spoiled by awful shopping arcades and the usual range of British high street shops, which, on the up-side, does mean that shopping is convenient and there are a few decent cafés. There are also a few specialist interior décor, furniture and Irish design shops worth looking out for (*see* 'Shopping', pp.430–1). The city centre is quite compact and is easy to walk around, and the area is often lively long after nightfall.

Belfast is a 19th-century town and lacks Dublin's grace; some say this is owing to the plutocratic city fathers. Two of the most attractive buildings are on Great Victoria Street: the **Grand Opera House** and the **Crown Liquor Saloon**, the latter a gas-lit High-Victorian pub decorated with richly coloured tiles. It has been preserved by the National Trust, but has not been gentrified, and its old clientele still drink there (at night it can be noisy and a bit rough). The Opera House was also designed in High-Victorian style (by Robert Matcham, the famous theatre architect) with rich, intricate decorative detail, including carved elephants. It was restored in the 1970s by the architect Robert McKinstry, and painted on the ceiling is a fine fresco by Cherith McKinstry. Even if you don't have an evening to spare, both buildings are worth a quick look around, and the Crown is generally good for a quiet pint with lunch.

Although many of the splendours of Belfast date from its period of mercantile importance, there was a great quickening of spirit here in the 18th century. United Irishman Henry Joy McCracken, whose family first published *The Belfast Newsletter* in 1737 (the longest-running newspaper in the world), was a son of the city. Other 18th-century personalities include William Drennan, who coined the phrase 'the Emerald Isle' and founded the **Royal Academical Institution**. This distinguished building lies between College Square East and Durham Street, and was designed by Sir John Soane, the eminent London architect, classical scholar and collector. It was built between 1808 and 1810 in a style that is classical in proportion. The institution is now a school, but it is possible to look around it. The prospect is a little spoiled by the great College of Technology, built on the corner of the lawn.

The **City Hall** (*guided tours available; adm free; t (028) 9027 0456*) in Donegall Square, built between 1896 and 1906 in Portland stone, is a grand composition with a central dome and corner towers borrowed from Wren's St Paul's Cathedral. Unfortunately the 18th-century Donegall Square has been replaced with a medley of different styles since the 19th century. The **Linen Hall Library** (*open Mon–Wed and Fri 9.30–5.30, Thurs 9.30–8.30, Sat 9.30–4; t (028) 9032 1707; www.linenhall.com, info@linenhall.com*) is one of the last survivors in the British Isles of the subscription library movement, so important to civilized Europe in the late 18th/early 19th century. Still a rich storehouse of books of Irish interest, it also has a comfortable room where you can sample periodicals, magazines and the day's flurry of newspapers. The librarians are polite and helpful, and the prints which line the walls echo the feeling of an earlier age.

Just along the way is the Robinson Cleaver Building, overlooking Donegall Place. This flamboyantly Victorian department store now houses a mixture of boutiques. The **Customs House** and **Courts of Justice** in Custom House Square and the **Ulster Hall** in Bedford Street with its impressive organ are all rather grey self-important buildings in heavy Victorian style. In Corporation Square is the **Sinclair Seamen's Church**, designed by Charles Lanyon and built in 1853. The pulpit incorporates the bows, bowsprit and figurehead of a ship, the organ displays starboard and port lights, and the font is a binnacle. **St Anne's Cathedral** in Donegall Street was built in 1899 in Romanesque style, of the Basilican type. It is very imposing inside with some fine stained-glass windows and mosaics. In the nave is the tomb of Lord Carson, the Northern Unionist leader, who died in 1935.

On the eastern bank of the Lagan River at Queen's Quay you'll find the **Odyssey Centre**. Inside there is a new interactive children's museum, **whowhatwherewhenwhy – W5** (*open all year Mon–Sat 10–6, Sun 12–6; adm; t (028) 9046 7700, www.w5online. co.uk*). Kids can have great fun making giant cloud rings, playing the Laser Harp and watching the Fire Tornado. Farther upstream, at the **Lagan Weir and Lookout Centre** on Donegall Quay (*open April–Sept, Mon–Fri 10–5 Sat 12–5 Sun 2–5, Oct–Mar, Tues–Fri 11–3.30 Sat 1–4.30 Sun 2–4.30, closed Mon; adm; t (028) 9031 5444*), you can take a plat-form view of the busy Lagan waterway, and find out about local industrial and folk history. South of here, following the Lagan, is the newly built and prestigious **Belfast Waterfront Hall**, a large concert hall and conference centre.

About 10 minutes' walk away from Donegall Square, going south down Great Victoria Street, is the leafy university area. This neighbourhood best reflects the character of the city, and is by far the most pleasant part of town in which to stay. Lisburn Road, in particular, has seen dozens of new cafés and art galleries spring up in the wake of the cease-fire, and the student population ensures the area's vitality.

You pass the imposing Tudor-style red-brick Queen's University building to go into the **Botanic Gardens** (*gardens open from 8 to sunset; Palm House Mon–Fri 10–5, weekends 2–4*). The gardens are small but beautifully laid out with formal flower beds. The restored Victorian Palm House is a splendid combination of graceful design and clever construction. Richard Turner, the Dubliner whose ironworks produced it, was also responsible for its design. It is made of sections which comprise the earliest surviving cast-iron and curvilinear glass architecture in the world. Inside the Palm House are tender and exotic plants. Another building within the grounds worth visiting is the Tropical Ravine, which houses a large collection of tropical plants.

Set inside the Botanical Gardens is the **Ulster Museum** (*open Mon–Fri 10–5, Sat 1–5, Sun 2–5; adm free exc for special exhibitions; **t** (028) 9038 3000, www.ulstermuseum. org.uk*). It has a variety of well-displayed and informative collections ranging from giant elk antlers to patchwork, jewellery and Irish antiquities. Of special interest is the outstanding modern art collection with a good representation of Irish artists including Sir James Lavery, whose wife was the Irish *cailín* (colleen) on the old Irish pound notes. The museum also has a unique collection of treasure from the wreck of the Spanish Armada vessel, the *Girona*. In 1588 Philip II of Spain ordered the greatest invasion fleet ever assembled to put an end to the growing power of England. Of the 130 ships that set sail, 26 were lost on, or just off, the coast of Ireland. In 1968 a fabulous hoard of gold and silver coins, heavy gold chains, rings, ornamented crosses, a beautiful gold salamander pendant set with rubies and a filigree brooch were all recovered off the coast of Antrim. As recently as 1999 a set of delicate gold and jewelled cameos was made complete by the addition of the twefﬆh cameo. The temporary exhibitions are invariably excellent, and there is a programme of lectures, art films, talks and children's weekend activities. It also has a café overlooking the gardens. The streets leading off the University are attractive and tree-lined with some good restaurants and cafés, small art galleries and design shops – all a far cry from the wastelands of the 'other' Belfast, beyond the Westlink motorway.

If you want to see the **Republican enclaves** in west Belfast, which are brightened by gaudy wall paintings and political slogans, take a black taxi. These run like miniature buses and serve areas such as the Falls, where public buses do not venture. Unemployment and poverty are obvious in the streets here, and although tourists are generally welcome they do stand out, despite efforts to provide visitor facilities. These neighbourhoods are economically and socially depressed, and visitors should exercise caution, as they might in parts of London or New York. The communities are closed to strangers and it would not be wise to go drinking in the pubs or illegal clubs, nor to walk about these parts at night. The **Unionist** working-class area in west Belfast lies beside the Falls, in the notorious Shankhill Road, which has political murals of its own. The so-called 'peace line', a high barrier, divides the two communities. **Sandy Row**, a short distance from Great Victoria Street and Shaftesbury Square, is another working-class Unionist area. It seems less threatening to walk around, and there are plenty of little bakeries and small shops which gives it a bustling air. The bulk of the enclaves where the kerbstones are painted red, white and blue are over the river to the east, along Newtownards Road.

The Suburbs of Belfast

Parliament House, Stormont, can be seen from the Newtownards Road (A20) about 2 miles (4km) east from the city centre. It is a very imposing Portland stone building in English Palladian style, with a floor space covering 5 acres (2ha) and it stands in a park of 300 acres (121ha). Next door is **Stormont Castle**, built in Scottish baronial style, which houses government departments.

There are many fine parks around Belfast. In south Belfast, in the Upper Malone Road (B103) area, is **Barnett's Park**. Within the attractive parkland is an early 19th-century house with an art gallery, a permanent exhibition on Belfast parks and a restaurant (*open all year, Mon–Sat 10–4.30; adm free*). Nearby is **Dixon Park** (*open daily till dusk; adm free; for information call the City Council, t (028) 9032 0202*), where rose-fanciers will get a chance to view the Belfast International Rose Trials, the finals of which take place in the third week of July. The park borders the River Lagan, and in summer about 100,000 roses are in bloom.

Continuing up the Malone Road, those interested in Neolithic sites should visit the **Giant's Ring**, near Ballylesson, about a mile south of Shaw's Bridge (*always accessible*). The Giant's Ring is a circular grassy embanked enclosure over 600ft (187m) in diameter, with a chambered grave in the centre. The dolmen in the centre is called Druid's Dolmen. The original purpose of the site is disputed but it was probably ritualistic; its date is unknown. The giant it is named after is possibly Fionn MacCumhaill, a favourite to tag onto such places (*see* **Old Gods and Heroes**, pp.83–4). In old times, farmers used to stage horse-races in this huge circle. **Shaw's Bridge** is very picturesque and spans the River Lagan. It was originally built *c.* 1650, and is to be found off the B23. You can walk for 10 miles (16km) along the towpath of the River Lagan, past the public parks. Start at the Belfast Boat Club, Loughview Road, Stranmillis, and end at Moore's Bridge, Hillsborough Road, Lisburn.

On the northern side of the city, on the Antrim road (A6), the baronial-style **Belfast Castle** appears unexpectedly from the wooded slopes of Cave Hill. It was built by the third Marquess of Donegall in 1870. His family, the Chichesters, were granted the forfeited lands of Belfast and the surrounding area in 1603; the Gaelic lords of the area, the O'Neills, lost everything and fled to the Continent. The planted grounds of the castle are open to the public, and always accessible. There is a pleasant restaurant open for full meals or snacks in the Castle itself and a Heritage Centre with exhibits on the flora and fauna of **Cave Hill** (*call the castle for more details, t (028) 9077 6925*). An easy climb to the summit of Cave Hill (1,182ft/368m) gives stunning views over the city and Belfast Lough. There are five caves and the earthwork of MacArts Fort, named after a local Gaelic chieftain of the Iron Age. It was here that the United Irishmen, Wolfe Tone and his followers, took their oaths of fidelity in 1798 (*see* **History**, pp.45–6). **Belfast Zoo** (*open April–Sept, daily 10–6, Oct–Mar, 10–3.30; on city bus routes nos.8, 10, 45–51; adm; t (028) 9077 6277, www.belfastzoo.co.uk, strongej@belfastcity.gov.uk*), located on the slopes below Cave Hill, is beautifully planted with flowers, shrubs and trees. The zoo has won awards for its emphasis on large enclosures, its breeding programme, and mainly small-animal collection. It is great fun to view the penguins and sealions from underwater, and there is a rare opportunity to see a bespectacled bear and a red panda.

There are several interesting places within easy reach of Belfast which are worth a visit. Northeast of the city, follow the A2 past some of the world's largest cranes in the shipyards, and the aircraft works at Sydenham, until you arrive at the wooded suburb of **Cultra**, about 6 miles (9km) from the city centre near Holywood . Here, in a parkland of nearly 200 acres (80ha), is the **Ulster Folk and Transport Museum** (*open July–Sept, Mon–Sat 10–6 Sun 11–6, Mar–June, Mon–Fri 10–5 Sat 10–6 Sun 11–6, Oct–Feb, Mon–Fri 10–4 Sat 10–5 Sun 11–5; adm; t (028) 9042 8428; train from central Belfast stops at Cultra Station, in the grounds of the museum*). The museum, technically in County Down, provides a unique opportunity for visitors to explore Ulster's past. It is the best museum of its type in Ireland, and gives a wonderful insight into what life in the countryside was like all over Ireland until 60 years ago. It is open-air, with representative buildings of rural Ulster: a linen scutch mill, a blacksmith's forge, a spade mill and farmhouses built in different regional styles. These are all furnished appropriately, with real fires burning in the grates. An old-fashioned cinema should be completed in 2002.

At **Helen's Bay**, a couple of miles (3.2km) north of Cultra, two lovely beaches joined by a path flank **Crawfordsburn Country Park**, with a stream flowing through the woods to the sea. The wooded demesne of Clandeboye Estate has protected this area from the work of housing developers. In the distance the delightful **Helen's Tower** can be seen, erected in Victorian times by the first Marquess of Dufferin and Ava to the memory of his mother. The 19th-century English poet Alfred Lord Tennyson's lines are inscribed in the tower:

Helen's Tower, here I stand
Dominant over sea and land.
Son's love built me and I hold
Mother's love in letter'd gold...

It was erected at a time of destitution caused by the famine of 1845, and gave employment to many. It has become a symbol of Ulster; another Helen's Tower was raised in northern France near Albert to commemorate the appalling losses suffered by the men of Ulster in the First World War. The **Somme Heritage Centre** (*t (028) 9182 3202*) on the A21 Newtownards– Bangor road carries on the theme. Clandeboye Estate is opened from time to time for charitable purposes and specific events, but it is not possible to see inside the tower.

County Down

Sea-bordered and close to mainland Britain, this county has excited the envy and lust of waves of invaders. Its farmlands are amongst the richest in Ireland; it has an attractive coastline, the famous Mourne Mountains, and a wealth of historical buildings. For sailing enthusiasts there is the beautiful and sheltered water of Strangford Lough; for anglers, exciting sea-fishing off Ardglass and Portavogie. And there are plenty of opportunities for hill-walking, golfing, bird-watching and swimming. The climate has a reputation for being sunnier than other parts of Ulster. There are many farmers and fishing folk, although, this close to the city of Belfast, there are quite a few dormitory towns, light industries and also big roads. The county

Getting There and Around

By Air and Sea
See Belfast, p.429.

By Rail
Northern Irish Railways run a suburban service to Holywood and Bangor, and to Belfast via the Dublin Enterprise Rail Link, which stops in Newry. **Translink, t** (028) 9089 9411, *www.translink.co.uk*.

By Bus
Ulsterbus, t (028) 9033 3000. Excellent services to all parts of County Down.

By Bike
The Raleigh Rent-a-Bike network operates throughout County Down. Your local dealer is: **Ross Cycles**, 44 Clarkill Road, Castlewellan, **t** (028) 4377 8029; also at Unit 9, Slieve Donard Shopping Complex, Railway Street, Newcastle, **t** (028) 4372 5525.

Festivals

March
St Patrick's Day, t (028) 4461 2233, *events@downdc.gov.uk*. Celebrations at Downpatrick, Newry and Cultra on the 17th.

June
Castleward Opera. Contact Castleward, Strangford, **t** (028) 4461 2233, **f** (028) 4461 2350, *events@downdc.gov.uk*.

Green Living Fair, Castle Espie, **t** (028) 9187 4146. Ireland's biggest environmental event, on sustainable living.
Ulster Harp Derby, Down Royal Race Course, **t** (028) 4176 2166. A day at Ireland's oldest racecourse.

July
Booley Fair, Hilltown. Demonstrations of vanishing skills such as weaving, stone-carving, shoeing horses and other smithy work. Traditional music and dancing, street stalls and sheep fair. Held early–mid July.
Orange Marches. Held all over County Down.
Kingdom of Mourne Festival, Kilkeel, Cranfield and Annalong, **t** (028) 4176 2166.
Northern Ireland Game Fair, Ballywalter Park, Ballywalter, **t** (028) 9048 3873. Illustrates how farming, sporting and conservation can work together to preserve the countryside.

August
Fiddlers Green Festival, Rostrevor. Five-day festival.
Heart of Down Pipe Band Championship, **t** (028) 4461 2233, **f** (028) 4461 2350, *events@downdc.gov.uk*.

September
Aspects, North Down Heritage Centre, Bangor, **t** (028) 9127 8032. Literary festival.

October
Brent Wildlife Festival, Castle Espie, **t** (028) 9187 4146. Festival of arts and the environment.

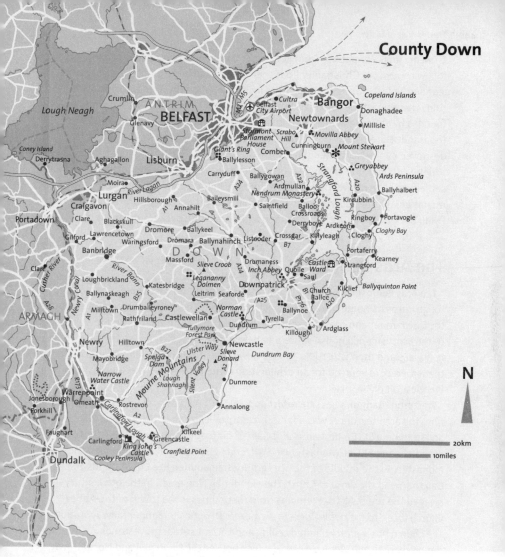

County Down

is rich, however, in monuments from pre-history; there are cairns, standing stones, and dolmens dating from 3000 BC scattered around the Strangford Lough and Lecale district, and evidence of man in the form of middens and flint tools dating from 6000 BC.

History

St Patrick is strongly associated with this county. After spending his boyhood as a slave in County Antrim, he spent 21 years in France preparing himself for his mission to bring Christianity to Ireland. In AD 432 he began his journey back to County Antrim, but was forced by bad weather conditions to land at the Slaney River between Strangford and the River Quoile. He founded an abbey nearby at Saul, near Downpatrick, where he died on 17 March AD 461. He is buried in the vicinity of Down

Cathedral in Downpatrick. From St Patrick's work, and that of his missionaries in the following century, Christianity flourished and Ireland became a centre of great learning. In fact, during the Dark Ages in Europe, when the Roman Empire was in ruins, the monasteries of Ireland kept the light of Christianity alive. The monastery founded by St Comgall in Bangor in the middle of the 6th century boasted three thousand students, but this famous place, like so many others in Ireland, was destroyed by the Norsemen (Vikings) in AD 824.

In the 17th and 18th centuries, County Down was planted with Scottish and English settlers, and the native Irish retreated into the hilly country around the Mourne mountains. North County Down remains, like Antrim, a cornerstone of Loyalist Ulster, flying the Ulster flag with its red hand against a white background (*see* p.374).

The Ards Peninsula

The **Ards Peninsula**, which runs along the length of the east shore of Strangford Lough, takes its name from rocky coast (*Ard*: 'Rock'). This finger of land curving round the Down mainland contains some of the most charming villages and towns created by the Scottish and English settlers. In between these towns are earlier sites: *raths*, holy wells and monastic ruins. You are never more than 3 or 4 miles (5 or 6km) from the sea. Prepare yourself for an exhilarating climate, for this is the sunniest, driest and breeziest bit of Ulster.

Start from **Bangor**, a seaside resort popular with the Edwardians, as you will see from the architecture. It was a famous centre of learning in the 6th and 7th centuries, and from here Sts Columbanus and Gall set off to found Luxeuil Monastery in Burgundy, and St Gall Monastery in Switzerland. St Comgall, who founded this monastery in the middle of the 6th century, trained men like Columbanus and Gall to spread the word of Christ. The plundering Norsemen in the 9th century ravaged the town. All that remains from these times is the tower of the **Abbey Church** (*open to the public Tues–Thurs mornings*) opposite Bangor railway station. The church has a pretty painted ceiling and ancient settler gravestones. An interlude can be spent in the Victorian castle, which houses the town hall and **North Down Heritage Centre** (*open all year during normal working hours; t (028) 9127 1200*), with a permanent display on Bangor as an ancient place of learning. Apart from the Edwardian seafront, which has a great many B&Bs and small hotels, and a fine marina for yachtsmen, there is not much to attract one to Bangor. The tacky shops and beach have an over-used look, although there is a lively market in the square on Wednesdays.

Donaghadee, a pretty seaside town with an attractive 19th-century harbour and a good number of pubs, used to be linked with Portpatrick in Scotland by a regular sailing boat. It has the feeling of an old port where generations of men and women have waited for the wind and the tide to change. The poet John Keats stayed at Grace Neill's Bar on the High Street, as did Peter the Great of Russia. ('Gracie's' is the oldest pub in Ireland, established in 1611, and is still one of the most attractive pubs in the

Tourist Information

Bangor: t (028) 9127 0069; *open all year.*
Groomsport: t (028) 9145 8882;
 open April–Sept.
Ards: t (028) 9182 6846; *open all year.*
Portaferry: Castle Street, t (028) 4272 9882,
 f (028) 4272 9822, *tourism@*
 ards-council.gov.uk; *open April–Sept.*
Newtownards: Kingdoms of Down,
 40 West Street, t (028) 9182 2881,
 f (028) 9182 2202, *www.kingdomsofdown.*
 com, *info@kingdomsofdown.com*;
 open all year.

Shopping

Antiques
 Shops can be found in the Main Streets of
Greyabbey, Portaferry and Holywood.

Crafts
The Bay Tree Pottery and Gallery, 118 High
 Street, Holywood, t (028) 9042 6414.
Iona, 27 Church Road, Holywood, t (028) 9042
 8597. Lovely craft shop which also sells
 organic vegetables.
Ards Crafts, 31 Regent Street, Newtownards,
 t (028) 9182 6846.

Delicacies
 There are excellent bread and cake shops
throughout the county.
Briggs Restaurant, Groomsport, t (028) 9146
 4288.
Panini, at 25 Church Road, Holywood, t (028)
 9042 7774. Italian delicatessen, for the
 makings of a picnic.

Sports and Activities

Beaches
 The beach at **Millisle** has a blue flag award
for cleanliness.

Fishing
 Sea-angling in **Strangford Lough** for tope,
skate, haddock, conger eel. Fishing trips can be
arranged at Portaferry tourist centre.
Norsemaid Sea Enterprises, 152 Portaferry
 Road, Newtownards, t (028) 9181 2081,
 f (028) 9182 0194, *www.salutay.com*,
 salutay@btinternet.com. Offers shore-
 angling as well as other water sports (*see*
 below); contact Peter Wright.
Nelson's Boats, 146 Killaughey Road,
 Donaghadee, t (028) 9188 3403. Contact
 Quinton Nelson.

Golf
Carnalea Golf Club, Bangor, t (028) 9127 0368,
 f (028) 9127 3989.
Donaghadee Golf Course, Warren Road,
 Donaghadee, t (028) 9188 3624, f (028)
 9188 8891.
Scrabo Golf Club, 233 Scrabo Road,
 Newtownards, t (028) 9181 2355, f (028) 9182
 2919, *scrabogc@compuserve.com*.

Internet Access
Emerald Tiger, 32–34 Main Street, Greyabbey,
 t (028) 4278 8453.

Open Farms
Ark Open Farm, 296 Bangor Road,
 Newtownards, t (028) 9181 0445. Rare breeds
 including Irish Moiled Cattle.

Pleasure Cruises
 Weather permitting, cruise boats leave from
Bangor and **Donaghadee** in summer at 10.30,
2.30 and 7.30pm for short cruises. Information
is posted on the piers, or call Bangor Tourist
Centre on t (028) 9127 0069. For trips to the
Copeland Islands, call t (028) 9188 3403.

Water Sports
Bangor and Strangford Sailing School, 13
 Gray's Hill, Bangor, t (028) 9145 5967/9754
 1592. For sailing in Strangford Lough.

town.) You can go stream-fishing at night in the summer with a white feather as a
lure. Or go out to the **Copeland Islands** – long, low islands covered with spring turf
and rabbit's trails, enchanting in spring and summer. It is possible to reach them and
also to go out stream-fishing on a regular boat. Following the coast road through

Norsemaid Sea Enterprises, 152 Portaferry
Road, Newtownards, **t** (028) 9181 2081,
f (028) 9182 0194, *www.salutay.com,
salutay@btinternet.com*. Sailing, sub-aqua
and scuba-diving, sea- and shore-angling;
contact Peter Wright.

Where to Stay

See also **Belfast**, 'Where to Stay', pp.432–3.
Clandeboye Lodge, 10 Estate Road,
Clandeboye, near Bangor, **t** (028) 9185 2500,
f (028) 9185 2772, *info@clandeboyelodge.com*
(*expensive*). Luxury hotel on the Clandeboye
Estate, with an 18-hole golf course.
Rayanne House, 60 Demesne Road,
Holywood, **t** (028) 9042 5859, **f** (028)
9042 3364 (*expensive*). Guest house with
comfortable bedrooms, delicious breakfasts
and an award-winning restaurant.
Beech Hill Country House, 23 Ballymoney
Road, Craigantlet, Holywood, **t** (028)
9042 5892, *beech.hill@btinternet.com*
(*moderate*). Georgian-style bungalow in a
peaceful extension.
Portaferry Hotel, 10 The Strand, Portaferry,
t (028) 4272 8231, **f** (028) 4272 8999,
www.portaferryhotel.com (*expensive–
moderate*). Old-fashioned, yet
well-appointed, in a lovely situation.
The Narrows, 8 Shore Road, Portaferry,
t (028) 4272 8148, **f** (028) 4272 8105,
www.narrows.co.uk (*moderate*). Recent
development with sea views, restaurant and
a walled garden.
Adair's, 22 The Square, Portaferry, **t** (028) 4272
8412 (*moderate–inexpensive*). A very simple
and clean place to stay.
Barholm, 11 The Strand, Portaferry, **t** (028) 4272
9598, *barholm@dial.pipex.com* (*inexpensive*).
Youth hostel.
Edenvale Country House, 130 Portaferry Road,
Newtownards, **t** (028) 9181 4881, **f** (028) 9182
6192, *edenvalehouse@hotmail.com*
(*moderate*). Pretty Georgian house in the
country with comfortable period bedrooms.

Eating Out

See also **Belfast**, 'Eating Out', p.433.
Fontana, 61a High Street, Holywood, **t** (028)
9080 9908 (*expensive–moderate*). Excellent
mediterranean and oriental dishes.
*Open Tues–Fri 12–2.30 and 5–9.30, Sat
6.30–10, Sun 11–3.*
Shanks Restaurant, Blackwood Golf Club, 150
Crawfordsburn Road, Bangor, **t** (028) 9185
3313 (*expensive*). Rich, varied menu; reputedly
one of the best restaurants in the area.
Villa Toscana, Toscana Park, West Circular
Road, Bangor, **t** (028) 9147 3737 (*moderate*).
Superb Italian food.
Heatherlea Tea Rooms, 94 Main Street, Bangor,
t (028) 9145 3157 (*inexpensive*). Good quiche,
pies and salads.
Briggs Restaurant, Groomsport, Bangor, **t** (028)
9146 4288 (*inexpensive*). Bar snacks and
main meals. Good plain cooking.
Baytree Coffee House, Audley Court, 118 High
St, Holywood, **t** (028) 9042 1419 (*moderate*).
Friendly place; serves breakfast, salads,
steaks, vegetarian dishes and cakes.
Grace Neill's Bar and Restaurant, 33 High
Street, Donaghadee. **t** (028) 9188 2553
(*moderate*). Adventurous food with
generous portions. *Lunch 12.30–2.30,
dinner from 6pm, lunch only on Sun.*
Bow Bells, 5 Bow Street, Donaghadee, **t** (028)
9188 8612 (*inexpensive*). Coffee shop with
good baking.
Portaferry Hotel, 10 The Strand, Portaferry,
t (028) 4272 8231 (*moderate*). Seafood,
delivered straight from the fishing boats
of Portavogie.
The Narrows, 8 Shore Road, Portaferry, **t** (028)
4272 8148 (*moderate*). Locally recommended.
Mount Stewart House, National Trust
Tearooms, Portaferry Road, Newtownards,
t (028) 4278 8387 (*inexpensive*). On the
Strangford Shore, a place for light lunch and
high tea. *May–Sept.*
Roma's, 4 Regent Street, Newtownards, **t** (028)
9181 2841 (*inexpensive*). Italian food.

Millisle down to **Ballyhalbert** you will pass golden strands. There are pebbly beaches further on at **Cloghy Bay**. Notice the Scottish influence: snug, unpretentious houses and carefully worked fields. Many of the road names – taken from the townlands, early units of land-holding – are intriguing: Ballydrain, Ringboy, Balloo, Bright, and

Scollogs Town. The National Trust maintains much of the little village of **Kearney**, which has pretty whitewashed cottages and coastal walks.

The most picturesque town on the Ards is **Portaferry**, situated where the tip of the Ards forms a narrow strait with the mainland of Down. On the waterfront you look across to **Strangford** village. The street here is wide, with brightly painted old houses. In Castle Street is the **Exploris Aquarium** (open Mon–Fri 10–6 Sat 11–6 Sun 1–6, Sept–Mar closes 5pm; adm; **t** (028) 4272 8062), where in spacious tanks you can see many of the sea animals that inhabit Strangford Lough; there is also plenty of interesting background information on the geology and plant life of the lough. On summer evenings you might be lucky and hear some open-air music. A ferry runs between Portaferry and Strangford every half-hour, and the journey of five minutes is well worth it for the view up Strangford Lough. If you are an artist, you may be so won over by the charms of this part of the peninsula that you will want to enrol in one of the painting courses held here in the summer.

The Strangford Shore

On the A20, which hugs the Strangford Shore, you can enjoy the beauty of this nearly landlocked water. Scattered with small islands, this area is of special interest to naturalists. The National Trust has a wildlife scheme operating which covers the entire foreshore of the lough, totalling about 5,400 acres (2,000ha). Vast flocks of wildfowl gather here, as do seals and other marine animals. There are bird-watching facilities at Castle Espie, Mount Stewart Gashouse, and Island Reagh (see p.447). Strangford was named by the Viking invaders after the strong tides at the mouth of the lough (strang means 'strong'). In Norman times, the wealthy knights encouraged the monks to settle amongst the lovely scenery.

At **Grey Abbey** (An Mhainistir Liath: 'the Grey Monastery'), you can visit one of the most complete Cistercian abbeys in Ireland (open April–Sept, Tues–Sat 10–6 Sun 2–6, Oct–Mar, Tues–Sat 10–4 Sun 2–4; adm; **t** (028) 9054 3037). Built in the 12th century by Affreca, the wife of John de Courcy, it represented the new monastic orders that were introduced to repress Irish traditions. The Pope was determined to stop the independence shown by the Irish abbot-prince, who combined temporal and spiritual power and often ignored pronouncements from Rome. A Physick Garden has been developed, planted as it may have been in medieval times; it was a vital guard for the monks against illnesses (adm). The pretty 18th-century house, Rosemount, is not open to the public. **Kircubbin**, a fishing village much used by yachts and leisure boats, has the interesting ruined church of Innishargie and associations with the 1798 rising.

Approximately 15 miles (24km) east of Belfast, on the A20 to Newtownards, following the lough, the demesne wall of **Mount Stewart**, the boyhood home of Robert Stewart, Lord Castlereagh, appears (house open for guided tours only, April–Oct, Wed–Mon 1–5; temple open April–Oct, weekends and bank hols 2–5; gardens open April–Sept, daily 11–6, Oct–Nov, weekends 11–6; **t** (028) 4278 8387/4278 8487). The 18th-century house and grounds are now in the care of the National Trust. Edith, Lady Londonderry, 7th Marchioness (1879–1959) and one of the foremost political hostesses of her generation, created the wonderful gardens some 70 years ago for her children. There are some lovely topiary animals, colourful parterres and wonderful trees. If you ever come across her children's story *The Magic Inkpot*, you will recognize some of the place names from around here. Also in the grounds is the **Temple of the Winds**, inspired by the building in Athens and built in 1780 for picnicking in style. In the Mount Stewart schoolhouse you can buy patchwork and handmade cottage furniture. The tea-room in the house itself is painted beautifully with the animals from Noah's Ark. Lady Londonderry nicknamed all the famous men and women who were her friends after animals in the Ark – it is fun to guess who was whom.

To complete the tour of the Ards, a quick visit to **Newtownards** will be rewarding, particularly for medievalists. The town square is also impressive and worth a visit. On the outskirts of the town, on the road to Millisle, is **Movilla Abbey** (*always accessible*), built between the 13th and 15th centuries. There was an earlier establishment here founded in the 6th century by St Finian, a contemporary of the great Irish saint, Columba (Colmcille). Unfortunately the two men did not get on; apparently St Columba stealthily copied St Finian's psalter, and they had a battle over it which caused many deaths (*see* **Connacht**, p.370). Columba was an O'Donnell prince as well as a cleric, and he was so dismayed at the bloodshed he had caused that he exiled himself and founded the famous church at Iona, an island off the coast of Scotland. From here Christianity spread to most of Scotland. The psalter he had copied became the warrior *Book of the O'Donnells* and was borne before them into battle; it is now in the National Museum, Dublin.

Newtownards has a 17th-century market cross and a fine town hall. You won't fail to notice the prominent tower on **Scrabo Hill**, a memorial to one of the Londonderry Stewarts and a good lookout point. The tower (*open Easter and June–Sept, Sat–Thurs 10.30–6; free access to park; t (028) 9181 1491*) stands on a granite outcrop and has 122 steps to the top. All around are woodland walks and the remains of old quarries where wildlife thrives. You might see a peregrine falcon. There is also a small visitor centre with an audio visual show. Close to the pretty little village of Saintfield is another wonderful garden in National Trust care. This is **Rowallane** (*open Mar 17–Oct, Mon–Fri 10.30–6 Sat–Sun 2–6, Nov–Mar 16, Mon–Fri 10.30–5; adm; t (028) 9751 0131, www.nationaltrust.org.uk*), famous throughout the horticultural and botanical world for its shrubs and trees. The best time to see it is early spring when the azaleas and rhododendrons are a riot of colour. There are also some interesting pillars and other structures in the garden made from Mourne stone, large round boulders of deep grey.

Mid-Down

Mid-Down is *drumlin* country until you reach Slieve Croob, around Ballynahinch. Harris, a local historian who described Down in the 18th century, had a rather droll phrase for the countryside contours, likening them to 'eggs set in salt'. Cap this with C. S. Lewis' recipe for his native county: 'earth-covered potatoes'. (The Belfast-born writer and critic became famous for his children's stories, *The Chronicles of Narnia*.)

Tourist Information

Downpatrick: t (028) 4461 2233; *open all year.*
Hillsborough: t (028) 9268 9717; *open all year.*
Lisburn: t (028) 9266 0038; *open all year.*
Banbridge: Newry Road, t (028) 4062 3322,
f (028) 4062 3114, *banbridge@nitic.net*;
open all year.

Shopping

Antiques
Shops at Balloo House, Killinchy; in
Killinchy Street, Comber; also in Moira,
Saintfield and Hillsborough.
The Gallery, Gilford Castle, Gilford;
also in Main Street, Hillsborough.

Crafts
The National Trust, Castle Ward;also at
Strangford, t (028) 4488 1204.
Discovery Glass Workshop, High Street,
Comber, t (028) 9187 0181.
Cowdy Crafts, Main Street, Hillsborough,
t (028) 9268 2455.
Ferguson Linen Centre, Banbridge, t (028)
4062 3491. The world's only manufacturer of
double damask linen; exhibition and tours.

Delicacies
There are excellent bread and cake shops
throughout the county.
James Nicholson, 27a Killyleagh Street,
Crossgar, t (028) 4483 0091. Excellent wines
in an elegant shop.
McCartney's, 56 Main Street, Moira, t (028)
9261 1422. Champion sausage-maker.

Sports and Activities

Beaches
Bathe at **Tyrella Strand** or **Dundrum Bay**.

Bird-watching
At the Castle Espie hide, and at Salt and
Green Islands, Mount Stewart Gas House and
Island Reagh – all on Strangford Lough. For
more details, call:
The Wildfowl and Wetlands Trust, 78
Ballydrain Road, Comber, t (028) 9187 4146.

Castle Espie, 78 Ballydrain Road, Comber,
t (028) 9187 4146, *castleespie@wwt.org.uk.*
Strangford Wildlife Centre, t (028) 4488 1411.
Delamont Country Park, t (028) 4482 8333.

Fishing
Coarse fishing in the River Quoile basin.
Contact the local tourist office for details.
Sea-angling is available in Strangford Lough
for tope, skate, haddock and conger eel.
Shore-angling is available off Ardglass.
Norsemaid Sea Enterprises, 152 Portaferry
Road, Newtownards, t (028) 9181 2081,
f (028) 9182 0194, *www.salutay.com*. Sea and
shore-angling in Strangford Lough; contact
Peter Wright.
Nelson's Boats, 146 Killaughey Road,
Donaghadee, t (028) 9188 3403. Fishing in
Strangford Lough; contact Quinton Nelson.
Captain R. Fitzsimons, Harbour Master, t (028)
4484 1291. Covers the Ardglass area.

Golf
Ardglass Golf Club, t (028) 4484 1219, *golf-
club@ardglass.force9.co.uk.*
Downpatrick Golf Club, t (028) 4461 5947.

Pony-trekking
Drumgooland House Equestrian Centre, 29
Dunnanew Road, Seaforde, t (028) 4481 1956,
frank.mcleigh@btinternet.com.
Lime Park Equestrian Centre, 5 Lime Kiln
Road, Maghaberry, west of Lisburn, t/f (028)
9262 1139, *limeparkequestrian@5limekiln.
fsnet.co.uk.*

Sailing
In Strangford Lough. There is a sailing school
on Sketrick Island in Strangford Lough where
there are residential or day-long courses on all
aspects of sailing.
Down Yachts, 37 Bayview Road, Killinchy,
t (028) 9754 2210. Sailing boat charter;
contact Terry Anderson.
East Down Yacht Club, Comber Road,
Killyleagh, t (028) 4482 8375,
crockard@dnet.co.uk.

Tours
Leprechaun Tour Guiding, 6–8 Main Street,
Gilford, near Banbridge t (028) 3883 1236.

Walking

The **Ulster Way** goes through Comber and along the shores of Strangford Lough, around the coast through Ardglass and Newcastle into the Mournes. There are lovely walks too on National Trust property in the Murlough Nature Reserve, near Newcastle, in the arboretum of Castlewellan, and at Tullymore Park, Newcastle.

Where to Stay

Old Schoolhouse Inn, 100 Ballydrain Road, Comber, t (028) 9754 1182, f (028) 9754 2583, *www.theoldschoolhouse.com*, *info@ theoldschoolhouse.com* (*moderate*). All rooms en-suite, dinner available.

Dufferin Arms, 35 High Street, Killyleagh, t (028) 4482 8229, f (028) 4482 8755, *dufferin@dial.pipex.com* (*moderate*). Comfortable B&B.

Tyrella House, Clanmaghery Road, Tyrella, Downpatrick, t/f (028) 4485 1422, *www.hidden-ireland.com/tyrella* (*moderate*). Georgian country house with a private sandy beach. Riding and grass-court tennis. Contact Mr and Mrs Corbett.

Pheasants Hill, 37 Killyleagh Road, Downpatrick, t/f (028) 4461 7246, *www.travel-ireland.com/irl/pheasant.htm* (*moderate–inexpensive*). Modern farmhouse on a smallholding; nature reserve nearby.

Havine Farm House, 51 Ballydonnell Road, Downpatrick, t (028) 4485 1242, *www.visitcoastofdown.com/havinefarm* (*inexpensive*). Comfortable farmhouse with pretty beamed ceilings in the bedrooms, and Mrs Macauley's great home-made cakes.

Drumgooland House, 29 Dunnanew Road, Seaforde, t (028) 4481 1956, f (028) 4481 1265 (*inexpensive*). Comfortable and friendly.

Self-catering

Killyleagh Castle Towers, Killyleagh, t/f (028) 4482 8261 (*expensive*). Self-catering in a 17th–18th century castle.

Potter's Cottage, in Castle Ward estate, Strangford, *www.nationaltrustcottages.co.uk* (*moderate*). Self-catering cottage which sleeps 4. Bookings through the National Trust, t (01225) 791199, or t 0870 458 4400.

Eating Out

Daft Eddys, Sketrick Island, Whiterock, Killinchy, t (028) 9754 1615 (*inexpensive*). Pub on an island reached by a causeway. Good soups and steaks.

Seaforde Inn, 24 Main Street, Seaforde, t (028) 4481 1232 (*moderate*). Venison sausages and mussels.

The Lobster Pot, 9–11 The Square, Strangford, t (028) 4488 1288 (*moderate*). Very good set meals and pub grub. Oysters and other shellfish a speciality.

Cuan Bar and Restaurant, 6 The Square, Strangford, t (028) 4488 1222 (*moderate*). Venison, quail, plus hot & cold buffet.

Primrose Bar, 30 Main Street, Ballynahinch, t (028) 9756 3177 (*inexpensive*). Good sandwiches.

Hillside Restaurant and Bar, 21 Main Street, Hillsborough, t (028) 9268 2765 (*moderate–inexpensive*). Salad bar, soups, plus oysters in season. Has a good reputation locally. *Open 12–2.30 and 5–9*.

The Plough Inn, The Square, Hillsborough, t (028) 9268 2985 (*inexpensive*). Recommended by locals, pub grub and upstairs seafood bistro. *Pub open daily 12–2.15 and 6–9.30; bistro open daily 12–2.15 and 5–8*.

Yellow Door Restaurant, 2 Bridge Street, Gilford, t (028) 3883 1543 (*expensive*). Roasted wild boar. Cheaper set lunches.

The Oriel Restaurant, Gilford, t (028) 3883 1543, *orielrestaurant@aol.com* (*expensive–moderate*). Fun restaurant with good food. *Open Tues–Fri 12.30–2.30 and 6.30–9.30, Sat 6.30–9.30, Sun 12.30–2.30*.

Gilberry Fayre, 92 Banbridge Road, Gilford, t (028) 3883 2098 (*inexpensive*). For breakfast, lunch and afternoon tea; a friendly welcome, freshly baked cakes and renowned shortbread.

Entertainment and Nightlife

Down Civic Arts Centre, 2–6 Irish Street, Downpatrick, t (028) 4461 5283. Arts venue.

To explore mid-Down you might start from **Comber**, a pleasant town with a prominent statue of Robert Gillespie, one of Ulster's military heroes in the Indian campaigns. Near here, off the A22 to Killyleagh, you can visit **Nendrum** (*open April–Sept, 10–7; always accessible; t (028) 9054 3037, sc@doeni.gov.uk*). This is one of the most romantic of the monastic sites, founded by a pupil of St Patrick on Mahee Island, and reached by a causeway through Island Reagh. It consists of a hilltop crowned with three circular stone walls, a church, a round tower stump, a sundial and cross slabs. It also has a small museum. If you have time it is worth taking a little detour at Balloo to **Ardmullan**. Whiterock yacht club is always a hive of activity and it looks out onto the islands of Strangford Lough – including Braddock Island where there is a bungalow designed by T. W. Henry, brother of the better-known painter Paul Henry. The little village of **Killyleagh** has a lovely-looking castle, still lived in by its original family, who came from Ayrshire in the mid-17th century. It is the oldest inhabited castle in Ireland, and is not open to the public. Pop concerts are sometimes held in the castle grounds. On the A22, a couple of miles out of Killyleagh, is **Delamont** (*open daily 9–dusk; t (028) 4482 8333*). It is a country park with fine views of Strangford Lough and the Mournes. Among its attractions is a heronry which you can view from a hide, lovely walks and a restored walled garden. You can also go pony-trekking. Going west on the B7 you come to the **Ulster Wildlife Trust** at Crossgar (*open Mon–Fri 10–4; t (028) 4483 0282*). Here you can learn about wetland raised bog and meadowland flora and fauna. The Victorian conservatory is planted to attract butterflies and guided walks are also available.

If you continue down the west side of Strangford, you cross the River Quoile and arrive at **Downpatrick**, an attractive Georgian town built on an old hill-fort which reputedly belonged to one of the Red Branch Knights (*see* **Old Gods and Heroes**, p.86). It is sited at the natural meeting-point of several river valleys, and so has been occupied for a long time, both suffering and benefiting from the waves of settlers and invaders – missionaries, monks, Norsemen, Normans and Scots (the army of Edward Bruce). **St Patrick's gravestone**, a large bit of granite, may be seen in the Church of Ireland Cathedral graveyard, although this is not the reason why the town carries his name. The association was made by the Norman John de Courcy, a Cheshire knight who was granted the counties of Antrim and Down by Henry II in 1176, and who established himself here at this centre of St Patrick's veneration by promoting the Irish saint. De Courcy donated some relics of Sts Patrick, Columba and Brigid to his Foundation and gave the town its name, adding Patrick to *Dundalethglas*, as it was previously called. During the Middle Ages Downpatrick suffered at the hands of the Scots: in 1316 it was burnt by Edward Bruce, and later it was destroyed by the English during the Tudor wars. In the early 18th century, stability returned to the town under the influence of an English family called Southwell, who acquired the Manor of Downpatrick through marriage. They built a quay on the River Quoile and encouraged markets and building. The **cathedral**, which had lain in ruins between 1538 and 1790, reopened in 1818. It is very fine inside, with impressive stained-glass windows. The **Saint Patrick Centre**, on Market Street (*open Oct–Mar, daily 10–5, Mar 17 and June–Aug, Mon–Sat 9.30–7 Sun 10–6, April–May and Sept,*

*Mon–Sat 9.30–5.30 Sun 10–5.30; adm; t (028) 4461 9000, f (028) 4461 9111, info@
saintpatrickcentre.com, www.saintpatrickcentre.com*), uses the saint's own words to
tell the story of his life and work in the context of the period in which he lived. The
Southwell Charity School and Almshouse in English Street near Down Cathedral is a
handsome early-Georgian building in the Irish Palladian style, and is now a home for
the elderly. Nearby, in the old county jail in the Mall, is the **Down County Museum**
(*open all year Mon–Fri 10–5 Sat–Sun 1–5; t (028) 4461 5218*), which contains very interesting exhibits of Stone Age artefacts and local history. There are also useful starting
points for leads on relics associated with St Patrick, which you might find elsewhere in
the county.

Other Places Associated with St Patrick

Just a mile and a half northeast of Downpatrick, at the mouth of the Slaney, is
St Patrick's Church in Saul, on the spot where St Patrick founded his first church after
deciding to return to Ireland to convert the people. A memorial church of Mourne
granite was built here in the 1930s to commemorate this. On Slieve Patrick nearby is a
giant statue of the saint also made of granite. Another place of association with
St Patrick is the 6th-century Raholp Church, between Downpatrick and Strangford
village on the A25. It was founded by Tassach, a disciple of St Patrick, who gave him
the last rites and carried his body to its burial place.

To the east of Downpatrick, off the B1 some 2 miles (3km) outside, are the **Struell
Wells** (*always accessible; adm free*). There must have been worshippers at this pagan
shrine, a group of holy wells, long before the arrival of St Patrick, who is thought to be
closely associated with them; in all events, the waters are still well-known for their
curative properties. To the west of Downpatrick, on the A24, is the little village of
Seaforde. In the grounds of the Big House here is an attractive **butterfly house** (*open
April–Sept, Mon–Sat 10–5, Sun 1–6; adm; t (028) 4481 1225*). It also has a hornbeam
maze and specialist nursery. It is fun to climb the newly built Moghul Tower and look
down on the richly coloured and patterned walled garden, shop and tea-room. The
area is rich in bird and plant life.

Cloghy Rocks Nature Reserve on the coast, south of Strangford village, is particularly
rich in inter-tidal plants, and has an ever-changing variety of seabirds and wildfowl.
Common seals can often be seen basking on the rocks at low tide. Near Downpatrick,
just off the A25 and guarded by Castle Ward at its southeastern end, is the **Quoile
Pondage Nature Reserve** (*Wildlife Centre open April–Aug, daily 11–5, Sept–Mar, Sat–Sun
1–5; t (028) 4461 5520*). This was formed as the result of a barrage at Castle Island to
prevent flooding caused by the tidal inrush of the sea from Strangford Lough into the
river. The freshwater vegetation which has established itself here as a result is of
great interest to the botanist. And for the ornithologist, a great variety of indigenous
and migrant birds feed and nest here. In springtime you can see great crested grebes
preening and displaying their crests. **Inch Abbey**, off the A7 (*open April–Sept, Tues–Sat
10–7, Oct–Mar, Sat 10–4 Sun 2–4; adm; t (028) 9054 3037*), is a very beautiful ruined
Cistercian abbey on an island in the Quoile Marshes. It was founded in the 1180s by
John de Courcy.

Going on the A25 in an easterly direction, 1 mile west of Strangford village, you will pass by **Castle Ward** (*open 16 Mar–Aug, daily 12–6, Sept–Oct, weekends 12–6; grounds open all year daily until dusk; adm, car park fee; t (028) 4488 1204*). The character and aspect of this house are worth a detour: it is a compromise between husband and wife, expressed in architecture. Built in the 1760s by Bernard Ward, afterwards Lord Bangor, and his wife Lady Anne, it has a neoclassical façade and a Gothic castellated garden front. The interior echoes this curious divergence of tastes: the reception rooms are gracefully classical, following his Lordship, and the library and her Ladyship's rooms are elaborately neo-Gothic in the Strawberry Hill manner conceived by Horace Walpole. The ceiling in the boudoir caused the poet John Betjeman to exclaim that it was like 'standing beneath a cow'. The property is in the hands of the National Trust and there are a number of other attractions: a Palladian-style temple which overlooks an early 18th-century lake, an early tower house and lovely grounds. A goldsmith's studio provides souvenirs for those who are looking for more valuable mementoes than snapshots. In June the rooms of this gracious house are full of music during the **Castle Ward Opera Festival**. Close by and just off the A25 is **Loughmoney Dolmen**, which is probably over four thousand years old. It is typical of dolmens scattered round this district.

Strangford village, which can be reached by a coastal footpath, is a few miles on. This is where you can catch the ferry across to the Ards village of Portaferry. No less than five small castles are within reach of Strangford, testifying to its strategic importance: Strangford Castle, Old Castle Ward, Audley's Castle, Walshestown and Kilclief. The nicest way to see them is from the lough, when the ferry is in mid-stream. **Kilclief Castle** (*open July–Aug, Tues–Sat 10–7 Sun 2–7; adm*), which is easy to find on the A2 between Strangford and Ardglass, is very well preserved and in state care. It was built before 1440 and is a grey-stone tower house. More castles can be seen around the fishing village of **Ardglass**, an important port in medieval times and now a centre for herring fleets. The best-preserved among them is **Jordan's Castle** (*open July–Aug, Tues–Sat 10–7, Sun 2–7; adm; t (028) 9054 3037, sc@doeni.gov.uk*), a 15th-century tower house with four storeys.

Also in the Strangford area is an 18-hole golf course, and there is good sea-angling off the coast here. The tree-lined village of **Killough**, about 1 mile (1.6km) from Ardglass, was developed as a grain port by the Ward family in the 18th century. There is a good beach and, further down at St Johns Point, an old ruined church. There are also some very good **strands**, notably Tyrella on the Dundrum Bay. Interesting prehistoric monuments in this area are **Ballynoe Stone Circle** and **Rathmullen Mote**. They are both within easy reach of Downpatrick, situated amongst the maze of little roads in the triangle between the A25, A2 and B176.

Hillsborough and the Linen Homelands

Heading towards Belfast on the A25/A1, you'll find the town of **Hillsborough**. The Anglo-Irish Agreement was reached here. It is one of the most English-looking villages in Ulster, with fine Georgian architecture, several excellent antiques shops in the Main Street, tasteful craft shops and numerous restaurants. To the south of the town in parkland is a massive **fort** built by Sir Arthur Hill, an English settler, in the 17th century (*open all year, Mon–Sat 10–7, Sun 2–7; in winter closes at 4 and also closed Mon*). **Hillsborough Castle**, which was the official residence of the Governor of Northern Ireland until 1973 and mostly houses various officials, stands in the parkland too. The wrought-iron gates which bar one's approach from the town are exquisite. **St Malachy's**, the Church of Ireland parish church, is in handsome planter's-style Gothic and was built by the Hill family in 1774. If you are lucky enough to get inside, you'll see that it is typical of the cool, unadorned churches of that style with box pews and 18th- and 19th-century wall tablets. It has a well-cared-for atmosphere; very different from the fate of so many Church of Ireland buildings in the Republic, which have become redundant because of dwindling congregations.

The **Linen Homelands** – Banbridge, Craigavon and Lisburn – is a convenient tag which describes an area of immense economic importance in the history of Northern Ireland. Nearly everybody in Ulster was involved in some way in the 19th and early 20th century in the growing and manufacture of linen, and especially so around the Upper Bann and Lagan River. The **Irish Linen Centre and Museum** (*open all year, Mon–Sat 9.30–5, plus April–Sept Sun 2–5; t (028) 9266 3377*) in Lisburn, with its exhibition 'Flax to Fabric', is well worth a visit. If you have time, take the Linen Homelands Tour, which visits a water-powered scutching mill, a working linen factory, and the Centre itself (*contact Banbridge Tourist Office, t (028) 4062 3322*).

South Down

South Down is a mainly mountainous area, and extends across to the south Armagh border, girded to the south and east by a beautiful coastline. The rather splendid fjord-like inlet, Carlingford Lough (a name of Scandinavian origin), cuts through the middle of the upland area. It follows a fault line forming the Gap of the North, the main north–south throughfare since ancient times.

In this trough, astride the ancient road from Armagh to Tara, lies the town of Newry. Within a 25-mile (40km) circle, some 48 peaks rise in a purple mass of rounded summits. The scenery around these, the **Mourne Mountains**, is not wild or rugged (Bignian and Bearnagh are the only two craggy peaks); their gentle undulations inspire peace and solitude. Few roads cross the Mournes, so this is a walker's paradise: endless paths up and down through bracken and heather, unspoilt lakes and tumbling streams, the wild flowers of moor and heath, birds and birdsong, all under an ever-changing sky.

Of the many walks possible, perhaps the loveliest are up to **Silent Valley**; or to **Lough Shannagh** from above Kilkeel; to the glittering crystals of **Diamond Rocks**; to the summits above Spelga Dam; and of course to **Slieve Donard** itself, where on a fine clear day you can see across the water to England. For the benefit of the more hearty, it is worth mentioning the 20-mile (32km) **boundary wall** that links the main peaks. Quite a constructional feat in itself, it used to be followed on the Annual Mourne Wall Walk, until erosion by thousands of pairs of feet caused the event to be cancelled.

Tourist Information

Newcastle: Newcastle Centre, 10–14 Central Promenade, t (028) 4372 2222, f (028) 4372 2400, *newcastle@nitic.net*; *open all year.*
Kilkeel: 6 Newcastle Street, t (028) 4176 2525, f (028) 4176 9947, *kda@kilkeel-tic.freeserve. co.uk*; *open all year.*
Warrenpoint: t (028) 4175 2256; *open all year.*
Newry: t (028) 3026 8877; *open all year.*

Shopping

Crafts

Parrot Lodge Pottery, 131 Ballyward Road, Castlewellan. Fish, birds of paradise, objects functional and surreal.
Loch Ruray House, 8 Main Street, Dundrum. Showcase for local crafts.

Delicacies

There are excellent bread and cake shops throughout the county. Try:
Victoria Bakery, Castle Street, Newry. Delicious wholemeal loaf and barmbrack.

Sports and Activities

Fishing

Game fishing for brown trout and salmon on the River Bann near Hilltown, Spelga Dam, and Shimna River in Tullymore Forest Park. Contact the local tourist office. For local knowledge of Carlingford Lough, contact:
Norsemaid Sea Enterprises, 152 Portaferry Road, Newtownards, t (028) 9181 2081, f (028) 9182 0194, *www.salutay.com.*

Golf

Royal County Down (Links) Course, 36 Golf Links Road, Newcastle, t (028) 4372 3314, f (028) 4372 6281, *golf@royalcountydown.org.*

Open Farms

Slievenlargy Open Farm, 5 Largy Road, Kilco, near Castlewellan, t (028) 4377 0083. Rare breeds of cattle, sheep, pigs and ponies.

Pony-trekking

Mount Pleasant Horse Riding, 15 Banannstown Road, Castlewellan, t (028) 4377 8651, f (028) 4377 0030.
Mourne Trail Riding School, 96 Castlewellan Road, Newcastle, t (028) 4372 4351, *www.mournetrailridingcentre.com*, *mgtnewsam@aol.com.*
Ring of Gullion Centre, Lough Road, Mullach Ban, t (028) 3088 9311. Activities for the young on traditions and the environment.

Walking

In the Mourne Mountains. The **Ulster Way** goes through Comber and along the shores of Strangford Lough, around the coast through Ardglass and Newcastle into the Mourne Mountains. The tourist office in Newcastle gives out details of Mournes walks. There are also lovely walks on National Trust property in the Murlough Nature Reserve, near Newcastle, in the arboretum of Castlewellan, at Castleward, Rowallane and Tullymore Park, Newcastle.
Sports Council for Northern Ireland, House of Sport, Upper Malone Road, Belfast, t (028) 9038 1222. Contact the Field Officer for more details on walking in the Mournes.

Perhaps the best place to start from when visiting this area is **Newcastle**, one of Ulster's more lively seaside resorts, although popularity has destroyed some of its charm. It has a lovely long sandy beach, and behind it there is the **Royal County Down Golf Course**, a fine championship course (*see* 'Sports and Activities', above). Near Newcastle lies the magnificent forest park of **Tollymore** (*open daily 10–sunset; t (028) 4372 2428*). It has many lovely – though well-trodden – forest trails and nature walks on the lower wooded slopes and along the River Shimna.

Before following the coast round, it is well worth heading northwards to visit one or two places. **Castlewellan** has two market places: one oval, one square. This neatly laid out town is surrounded by well-wooded demesnes, one of which is **Castlewellan Park**

Where to Stay

Hastings Slieve Donard Hotel, Downs Road, Newcastle, t (028) 4372 3681, f (028) 4372 4830, *www.hastingshotels.com* (*expensive*). Close to golf links.

Burrendale Hotel, 49 Castlewellan Road, Newcastle, t (028) 4372 2599, f (028) 4372 2328 (*moderate*). Modern, popular with bus tours.

Newcastle Youth Hostel, 30 Downs Road, Newcastle, t/f (028) 4372 2133, *www.hini.org.uk* (*inexpensive*). Centrally heated apartment and family rooms beside the sea, at the foot of the mountains.

Glassdrumman Lodge, 85 Mill Road, Annalong, t (028) 4376 8451, f (028) 4376 7041 (*expensive–moderate*). A superb place to spend the night, though on the pricey side. Next door in the restaurant you can have a delicious meal (*see* below).

Ryan B&B, 19 Milltown Street, Burren, Warrenpoint, t/f (028) 4177 2506 (*inexpensive*). 3 en suite rooms.

Rathglen Villa, 7 Hilltown Road, Rathfriland, t (028) 4063 8090 (*inexpensive*). Contact Mrs Maginn.

The Maggi Minn, 11 Bishops Well Road, Dromore, t (028) 9269 3520, *maggiminn@bigfoot.com* (*moderate*). Modern country house with views of the Mournes. Mrs W. Mark's delicious Ulster fry is served for breakfast; dinner is also available.

Sylvan Hill House, Dromore, t/f (028) 9269 2321 (*inexpensive*). 18th-century house and good food from Mrs Coburn.

Self-catering

Seeconnell Cottages, 104 Clanvaraghan Road, Castlewellan, t/f (028) 4377 0050, *www.seeconnell.com* (*moderate*). Cluster of traditional cottages in a quiet mountain valley, sleeping 5–7.

Hannas Close Cottages, Kilkeel, t/f (028) 4176 5999, *www.travel-ireland.com/hannas*. Six traditional cottages in a country lane, with wonderful views of the Mournes. £355 per week high season.

Eating Out

Bucks Head Inn, 79 Main Street, Dundrum, t (028) 4375 1868 (*moderate*). Seafood and steaks.

Glassdrumman Lodge Restaurant, 85 Mill Road, Annalong, t (028) 4376 8451 (*expensive*). Memorable food, especially the steak and fish dishes. The family who run it grow their own vegetables and keep their animals in free-range conditions.

Aylesforte House, 44 Newry Road, Warrenpoint, t (028) 4177 2255 (*moderate*). Exotic eastern-style menu.

Brass Monkey Bar and Restaurant, 16 Trevor Hills, Newry, t (028) 3026 3176 (*moderate*). Opens at 10.30am for coffee, then good steak, chicken and fish dishes for lunch and dinner.

Deli Lites, 12 Monaghan Street, Newry, t (028) 3026 1770 (*inexpensive*). Lots of breakfast options, soups, salads and even fair coffee.

O'Reilly's Bar, 7 Rathfriland Rd, Dromara, t (028) 9753 2209 (*moderate*). Excellent seafood served here.

(*with café and visitor centre; open daily 10–dusk; t (028) 4377 8664*), home to the world's largest maze, and now a forest park renowned for its arboretum and lovely gardens. The arboretum was begun in 1740, and there are some magnificent trees. A sculpture trail created from natural materials from the park and lake makes a lovely walk. North of Newcastle, about 2 miles (3km) away, is **Murlough National Nature Reserve** (*always open; car park free; t (028) 4375 1467*) where you can explore the sand dunes. Exposed to the wind, the dunes are a peaceful haven for waders, waterbirds and shore-birds. Sweet-smelling wild flowers grow unhindered, and in the summer wild strawberries weave across the sand. **Dundrum** is not far beyond. On the outskirts of this once flourishing fishing port, now more of a coal quay, a half-mile

(1km) northwest of Dundrum on a wooded hill, are the extensive ruins of a Norman motte and bailey **castle**, enclosing a magnificent partly ruined stone castle with a circular keep (*grounds accessible at all times; keep open April–Sept, Tues–Sat 10–7, Sun 2–7; adm; t (028) 9054 3034*). Staircases, parapets, towers and a massive gatehouse make this an ideal picnic spot and adventure playground for children. It was built in about 1177 as one of John de Courcy's coastal castles.

Newcastle to Rostrevor

Now travel along the coast from Newcastle to Rostrevor on the A2. From here there's a fine view of the Mournes, with Slieve Donard rising majestically up as the centrepiece. Heading south out of Newcastle, past the now quiet harbour, you come to the **National Trust Mourne Coastal Path**, which runs for 4 miles (6km) from the very popular Bloody Bridge picnic site, along the rocky shoreline to Dunmore Head. The mountain path beside the Blood Bridge River is a starting point for hillwalkers into the Mournes. Here are the splendid mountains of Slieve Donard (2,796ft/850m) and Slieve Commedagh, which face each other, and the rockier peaks of Slieve Bignian and Slieve Bearnagh, between which lie Silent Valley and its reservoir of water for Belfast. A network of by-roads runs deep into the foothills behind Annalong and Kilkeel. Here you'll find the unspoilt, undisturbed Mourne way of life – stone cottages, people at work in their pocket-handkerchief fields, the elderly passing the time of day, children playing. It is not hard to imagine it all in the days before roads were made.

Back again on the coast road: round the corner lies the little village of **Annalong**, set against a backcloth of mountains. The little old harbour still flourishes: boats are being repainted, nets repaired; everyone is doing something, but no one hurries. You can visit **Annalong Corn Mill**, (*open Feb–Nov, Tues–Sat 11–5; adm; t (028) 4376 8736*), a working mill, which overlooks the harbour and has a herb garden and café. **Kilkeel** is a surprisingly busy, prosperous town, home of the coast's main fishing fleet. It is on the site of an ancient *rath*, and the ruins of a 14th-century church still stand in the square. Just to the northeast of the town is a fine **dolmen** whose capstone measures over 10ft by 8ft (3m by 2.5m). The B27 road climbs up and across the Spelga Pass towards Hilltown. It has many vantage points for viewing both the mountains and the coastal scenery. The A2 branches right about 4 miles out of Kilkeel; this unnumbered road, known as The Head Road, will take you to the Silent Valley and Ben Crom reservoirs. There is a visitor centre, craft shop and café here, and it is busy in the summer.

Continuing on round the coast, the land levels out quite a bit. Leave the A2 and explore the peninsula of Cranfield Point and Greencastle, reached by narrow roads. Down to the left lies the long strand of **Cranfield**. Greencastle, the ancient capital of the 9th-century Kingdom of Mourne, is visible on the horizon and strategically sited at the entrance to Carlingford Lough. Its position was recognized by the Anglo-Normans who built a strong castle here, **Greencastle Fort** (*keep is open April–Sept, Tues–Sat 10–7, Sun 2–7; grounds accessible at all times; t (028) 9054 3037*). The tall, rectangular, turreted keep and some of the out-works are all that remain of this impressive 13th-century stronghold. From the topmost turret of the castle there are splendid views across the lough to the Republic.

The road swings round still more, ever twisting and turning as it makes its way along the indented coast. The houses are larger, their gardens bigger and better kept. Clearly this was, and still is, a prosperous area. Sheltered by high hills and set against a purple and green backcloth of pine forests, the town of **Rostrevor** enjoys a mild and sunny climate, hence the profusion of brightly coloured flowers in the gardens, many of them of Mediterranean origin. It has a lovely long seafront and superb views across the lough, but sadly no sandy beach. It is a quiet place to use as a base for walking in the Mourne Mountains or in the pine-scented Rostrevor Forest. A mountain road climbs northwards, passing the little old church of Kilbroney with its ancient cross, and levelling out to follow the valley of the Bann and emerge at Hilltown. The many tumbling little streams, stony paths and patches of woodland make for excellent picnic sites en route.

Not far from Rostrevor is **Warrenpoint**, a lively and popular resort. It is spacious and well planned, with a very big square and a promenade over half a mile (800m) long, the town being bounded by the sea on two sides. There is a well-equipped marina, golf and tennis facilities, and lots of live music in the pubs. Prior to the mid-18th century there was little here save a rabbit warren – hence its name. The **Heritage Centre** in Bridge Road (*open April–Oct, Tues–Sun*) has items of local historical interest. A little to the north, on a spur of rock jutting out into the estuary, lies the square, battlemented tower house of **Narrow Water Castle**, which is privately owned (*guided tours normally available July–Aug, Tues–Fri 11–4.30; call Warrenpoint tourist office in advance, t (028) 4175 2256*). It was built in the 17th century on the site of a much earlier fortification.

From here the road improves dramatically and before long you reach **Newry**, an old and prosperous town sited where St Patrick planted a yew at the head of the strand – hence its name, which in Gaelic is *An Hir*: 'Yew'. It enjoys a strategic site astride the Clanrye River. Newry has been a busy mercantile town for centuries, and trade was boosted in 1741 when the Newry Canal – believed to be the oldest canal constructed in the British Isles – connected Newry to Lough Neagh and Carlingford Lough. Today the canal is stocked with fish, and plans are afoot to open it up to boats, but a huge amount of work has to be done first. The long prosperity of this old town is clearly reflected in its large and imposing town houses and public buildings, though many are now rather dilapidated.

St Patrick's Parish Church Is possibly the earliest Protestant church in Ireland. The 19th-century **Cathedral of St Colman** boasts some beautiful stained glass windows. The town hall is impressively sited astride the Clanrye River, which forms the county boundary. There is much Georgian architecture, and many shops with small-paned windows and slate-hung gables. Some of Newry's oldest houses are to be found in Market Street. Remnants of far earlier centuries are the monastery, the castle and the Cistercian abbey. In the Arts Centre on Bank Parade is the small **Newry Museum** (*open all year, Mon–Fri 10.30–4.30; adm free; t (028) 3026 6232*), which contains many varied and interesting exhibits.

Two miles (3km) north of the town, near Crown Bridge, there is a very fine motte and bailey, giving rise to a crown-shaped mound. And at **Donaghmore** 3 miles (5km) on, in the parish graveyard, there is a fine 10th-century carved cross on the site of an earlier monastery, under which lies a souterrain. **Slieve Gullion Forest Park**, 4 miles (6.4km) southwest of Newry in County Armagh, has a wonderful 7-mile (11km) drive with views of lakes, which takes you nearly to the top of Slieve Gullion itself. A path continues upwards to 1,900ft (580m), where you can explore two Stone Age cairns.

Around Hilltown

Heading from Newry back across to Newcastle you pass just north of the Mournes. The view across to the mountains is superb and ever-changing. The road is very twisty so it is nice to stop and appreciate the many panoramic vantage points. There are two towns worth visiting. The first, **Hilltown**, the more southerly where the mountain roads from Kilkeel and Rostrevor converge, is a small angling village located at a cross-roads on top of a hill. The views here are breathtaking. Just over 2 miles (3.2km) northeast of Hilltown, in Cloughmore on Goward Hill, is a huge dolmen known as **Cloughmore Cromlech**. Underneath its three massive upright supports and 50-ton granite capstone, there is a double burial chamber in which traces of bones were once found. The road to Kilkeel (B27) passes close to the Silent Valley reservoir – a deep valley between the peaks of the Mournes. The road, known as the Spelga Pass, demands careful driving as it rises and twists amongst the spectacular scenery. However, if instead you decide to go north on the B25, you will come to a less dramatic landscape.

Easily spotted in the distance by its distinctive mushroom-shaped water tower lies **Rathfriland** – a flourishing market town set high on a hill, commanding a wide view of the Mournes and the surrounding countryside. This area from Loughbrickland to Rathfriland is called Brontë Country, because here lived the aunts, uncles and, when he was young, the father of novelists Charlotte, Emily and Anne Brontë. Emily is supposed to have modelled Heathcliff in *Wuthering Heights* on her wild great-uncle Welsh, who travelled to London with a big stick to silence the critics of his nieces' books. Nearby, at Drumballyroney school and church is the small **Brontë Homeland Interpretative Centre** (*open March–Sept, Tues–Fri 11–5, Sat–Sun 2–6; adm; t (028) 4063 1152*). Patrick Brontë, the father of the girls, was the parish schoolmaster here. The family homestead is at Emdale.

County Armagh

The smallest county in Ulster, Armagh's scenery is nevertheless varied: from the gentle southern *drumlins* to wild open moorland, and the grander mountains and rocky glens further east. The Gaelic tradition of splitting land between all the family gives a familar pattern to the landscape. Here, an intricate network of dry-stone walls gathers what fertility may be had into fields with barely enough room for a cow to turn in. As you travel north towards the reclaimed wetlands on the shore of Lough Neagh, the orchards and dairy pastures become more extensive and are dotted with small lakes and the rivers that once turned the wheels of the flax mills.

In general, the people are fairly prosperous farmers, although the Troubles of the last twenty years have taken their toll of misery and death. People here feel very strongly about politics, and there is very little middle ground, so you may find it easier to avoid the subject.

Highlights of the county include Ardress House and The Argory, both National Trust properties which give great insight into the more settled times of the 18th and 19th centuries. For the fisherman there are tremendous catches of bream in the Blackwater River, and walkers can enjoy the quiet tranquillity of Clare Glen.

You might be lucky and see a game of road bowls, an old Irish sport that is played here and in County Cork. The area has the reputation for being very rainy, but if you time your visit during May you will see the country at its prettiest, especially around Loughall with its apple orchards in full blossom. Public transport is excellent throughout the county, and the main Belfast to Dublin railway line passes along its eastern border, stopping along the way.

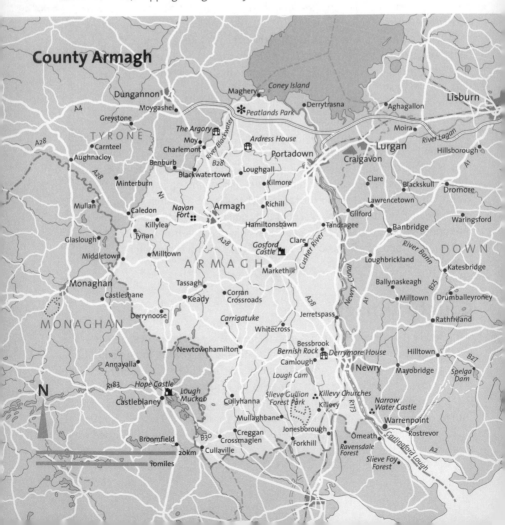

Getting There and Around

By Train

There is a frequent service between Dublin and Belfast stopping at Portadown and Newry. (The express service does not stop at all).

Translink, t (028) 9089 9411, *www.translink.co.uk*.

By Bus

Ulsterbus Express buses run from Belfast to Armagh, Mon–Fri every hour 6.30am–6.30pm; on Sundays there are only two.

Armagh City Bus Station, t (028) 3752 2266.

By Bike

The Raleigh Rent-a-Bike network operates in Armagh:

Raymonds, 65 Bridge Street, Portadown, t (028) 3835 2828. Your local contact.

The Cyclery, Grant House, 56 Edward Street, Lurgan, t (028) 3834 8627.

Festivals

March

St Patrick's Day. Huge parade in Armagh City, with a concert in St Patrick's Hall.

May

Apple Blossom Festival, Armagh City, t (028) 3752 2282.

June

Fleadh Ceol, Comhaltas Ceoltori Traditional Music Festival. County-wide.

July

Scarva Sham Fight, t (028) 3883 2163. Symbolic reenactment of the Battle of the Boyne between two horsemen in period costume – William of Orange and James II.

August

All Ireland Intermediate Road Bowls Festival, held on roads around Armagh City.

History

One of the most fascinating aspects of County Armagh is its history. On the outskirts of Armagh City is the legendary *Emain Macha*, also known as Navan Fort. This was the crowning place of the Sovereigns of Ulster (350 BC to AD 332), and it was from here that the legendary Red Branch Knights sallied out to display their prowess and do great deeds of chivalry. The greatest of these knights was Cú Chulainn, who is supposed to have received his training at the fort (*see* **Old Gods and Heroes**, p.82). Of course, this ancient history is clouded with mystery and legend; it is part of Ulster's mythology and identity, just as Fionn MacCumhaill and the Fianna are part of that of the rest of Ireland. Legends aside, we do know that when Fergus was King of Ulster in the 4th century, *Emain Macha* was burned and pillaged by forces from Tara, County Meath, and was never restored. Afterwards, the then small city of Armagh established itself as the ecclesiastical capital of Ireland. In the 5th century, St Patrick built his first stone church here, and around it other churches, colleges and schools grew up. The city developed into a great centre of religion and learning until the 9th and 10th centuries, with the incursion of the Vikings. Today it is a fine city of attractive 18th-century buildings, built in settled, prosperous days, with an excellent museum.

Armagh City

Armagh (*Ard Macha*), now sprawled over seven hills, was a centre of Christian learning and tranquillity when Rome was in ruins and London glowed with endless fires started by the barbarians. Today there is little to show of the ancient city; its

Tourist Information

Armagh: St Patrick's Trian Centre, 40 English Street, t (028) 3752 1800, f (028) 3752 8329, *www.armagh-visit.com, armagh@niticnet*; *open all year.*

Shopping

Crafts

Appleby Connections, Armagh, t (028) 3751 0825.

Cloud Cuckoo, Ogle Street, Armagh, t (028) 3751 0771.

Quinn's Antiquities, 27 Dobbin Street, Armagh, t (028) 3751 0947. Antiques and bric-a-brac.

St Patrick's Trian, 40 English Street, Armagh, t (028) 3752 1801.

Markets

There are a couple of markets in Armagh City:

Shambles Market, Cathedral Road. Tuesday and Friday, 9–5.

Variety Market, Market Street. Tuesday and Friday 9–5.

Sports and Activities

Golf

County Armagh Golf Club, 7 Newry Road, t (028) 3752 5864. 18-hole golf course.

Where to Stay

Armagh City t (028–)

The Charlemont Arms Hotel, 63 English Street, t 3752 2028, f 3752 6979 (*moderate*).

De Averell Guest House, 3 Seven Houses, English Street, t 3751 1213, f 3751 1221 (*moderate*). Georgian town house with a good basement restaurant.

Drumsill House Hotel, 35 Moy Road, t 3752 2009, f 3752 5624 (*moderate*). Modern and bland but comfortable.

Armagh City Youth Hostel, 36 Abbey Street, t 3751 1800, f 3751 1801 (*inexpensive*). New purpose-built and well-sited hostel. High security and a good range of facilities, but utterly sterile.

Deans Hill, t 3752 4923, f 3752 2186 (*inexpensive*). Pretty 18th-century house with lovely gardens, close to the Observatory. Two en suite rooms, one with a four-poster; contact Mrs Armstrong.

appearance is distinctly Georgian; yet it is still the ecclesiastical centre of Ireland. Armagh is a lovely city to walk around with its fine buildings, especially in the Mall and in Beresford Row. The **Courthouse** dates from 1809 and is the work of Francis Johnston, as are many buildings here; he was a local architect who later achieved fame in Dublin. It was bombed in 1993, but has since been completely restored. Many of the most interesting places to visit are just a brisk walk away.

A visit to the **Armagh County Museum** in the Mall East (*open Mon–Fri 10–5, Sat 10–1 and 2–5; adm free; t (028) 3752 3070, acm@nics.gov.uk*) helps to fill in the city's background. Here, a 17th-century painting shows the old wide streets, space for markets and the prominence of the early hill-top Cathedral of St Patrick. There is also a wide range of regional archaeological exhibits, a local natural history section, and an art gallery which has works by the Irish mystic poet and artist George Russell (1867–1935), better known as A. E. Russell. The **Royal Irish Fusiliers Museum** (*open Mon–Fri 10–12.30 and 1–4; adm; t (028) 3752 2911, amanda@rirfus-museum.freeserve. co.uk*), with displays of old uniforms, weapons and medals, is also in the Mall.

The two cathedral churches are unmistakable features of the city's skyline, for they each crown neighbouring hills. Founded by St Patrick, the ancient **Church of Ireland Cathedral** (*open April–Oct, 9.30–5, Nov–Mar, 9.30–4; adm free; t (028) 3752 3142*) is in

Hillview Lodge, 33 Newtownhamilton Road, t 3752 2000, f 3752 8276 (*inexpensive*). Reliable B&B with six en suite rooms.

Self-catering

The Chalet, Dean's Hill, 34 College Hill, t 3752 2099. Sleeps 4; contact Mrs Armstrong.

Eating Out

Armagh City t (028–)

D'Arby Byrne Restaurant, Palace Demesne, t 3752 9634 (*moderate*). Set in beautiful grounds, serves coffee, lunch, afternoon tea. *Open Mon–Sat 10–4.30, Sun 12.30–2.30.*

Rainbow, 13 English Street, t 3752 5391 (*moderate–inexpensive*). Morning coffee, lunch and afternoon tea; bistro menu in the evenings. *Open Mon–Sat 9–5.30, Fri–Sat 7.30pm–9.30pm.*

Calvert Tavern, 3 Scotch Street, t 3752 4186 (*inexpensive*). Good pub grub: open sandwiches and grills. *Food served until 10pm.*

Hester's Place, 12 Upper English Street, t 3752 2374 (*inexpensive*). Irish stew, great Ulster fry. *Open Mon–Sat 9–5.30.*

Jodie's, 37a Scotch St, t 3752 7577 (*inexpensive*). Cheerful surrounds, usually has some vegetarian options. *Open weekdays (exc Wed) for lunch; weekends for dinner.*

Navan Centre, 81 Killylea Road, t 3752 5550 (*inexpensive*). Hot meals, snacks and coffee.

The Pilgrim's Table, 38 English Street (inside St Patrick's Trian complex), t 3752 1801 (*inexpensive*). Reputedly the best lunch in town, with pleasant surroundings.

Entertainment and Nightlife

Theatre and Cinema

Armagh City Filmhouse, Market Street, t (028) 3751 1033. New 4-screen cinema complex.

Market Place Theatre and Arts Centre, t (028) 3752 1821. Brand new arts centre, with drama, music and dance, two theatres, a gallery and restaurants and bars.

Traditional Music

Charlemont Arms, Armagh, t (028) 3752 2928. One Thurs per month.

Palace Stables Heritage Centre, t (028) 3751 1248. Armagh Pipers Club once a month.

the perpendicular style with a massive central tower. Its present appearance dates mainly from the 18th century, but its core is medieval. Before medieval times the city suffered terribly from the Viking raids, and the cathedral and town were sacked at least twenty times in five hundred years. Inside the cathedral is a memorial to Brian Boru, the most famous high king of all Ireland, who visited Armagh in 1004 and was received with great state. The precious *Book of Armagh* (*c.* AD 807), which is now in Trinity College, Dublin, was placed in his hands and his visit noted in the book. He presented 20 ounces of pure gold to the church. Ten years later he hammered the Vikings at the battle of Clontarf in 1014, which put a stop to their encroachment into inland areas (*see* **History**, pp.38–9), but Brian Boru was killed in his tent after the battle was won. His body and that of his son were brought back to be buried here and the memorial to them is in the west wall.

The other heirloom of those ancient days is St Patrick's Bell, which is enclosed in a cover dating from the 12th century; it can also be seen at the National Museum in Dublin. The moulding on the west door is very fine, and there is a good stained-glass window in the choir. Notice the carved medieval stone heads high up on the cathedral's exterior and the mysterious statues in the crypt. The surrounding streets run true to the rings of the Celtic *rath* or fort in which St Patrick built his church – directed, it is said, by a flight of angels. On the corner of Abbey Street is **Armagh Public Library** (*t (028) 3752 3142*), also known as Robinson's Library, which contains some rare books, maps and a first edition of *Gulliver's Travels*, annotated by Jonathan Swift himself. Richard Robinson, Archbishop of Armagh, was a very influential figure in the building of the 18th-century city. There is an exhibition and historical centre in English Street, **St Patrick's Trian**; it derives this name from an ancient division of the city (*open all year; adm for exhibitions; t (028) 3752 1801, info@stpatrickstrian.com*). Inside, 'The Armagh Story' is illustrated through the ages by an audio visual show and an exhibition on the life and work of St Patrick, and his connections with Armagh. The 'Land of Lilliput' is a child-orientated exhibition, which has a giant model of Gulliver as the centrepiece. The centre also has art exhibitions, tourist information, and is home to **Armagh Ancestry** (*open Mon–Sat 9–5*), a central source for chasing up ancestors in Armagh county.

Across the valley are the twin spires of the Catholic **Cathedral of St Patrick**. This is a complete contrast to its more sombre Protestant neighbour, with its profusion of magnificent internal gilding, marbles, mosaics and stained glass. The building was started in 1849 and finished in 1873; the passing of the years is marked by a collection of cardinals' red hats suspended in the Lady Chapel.

Armagh has the most advanced facilities for astronomical studies in the British Isles. The institution owes its pre-eminence to Archbishop Richard Robinson, who founded and endowed the **Armagh Observatory** in 1790. It is complemented by the **Armagh Planetarium and Hall of Astronomy** on College Hill (*open all year, Mon–Fri 10–4, Sat–Sun 1.15–4; adm for shows and exhibition; observatory dome and grounds free; t (028) 3752 3689, www.armagh-planetarium.co.uk*), which has Ireland's largest public telescope and hosts presentations in its star theatre. (Star shows are put on more frequently in the summer; it is advisable to ring and book for these.) In the grounds you'll find the Astropark, which is a scale model of the universe. The Observatory was designed by Francis Johnston, who is also responsible for the Georgian terrace on the east side of the Mall.

On the south side of the city is the Palace demesne. The **Palace Stables Heritage Centre** (*open all year, daily; adm; t (028) 3752 9629, stables@armagh.gov.uk*) is a restored 18th-century building in the demesne of the Bishop's Palace. The 'Day in the Life' exhibition features typical scenes of life here in 1776 in the time of Archbishop Robinson. Craft exhibitions, fairs, lectures, art shows, music, dance and story-telling events are all held here.

The ancient fort of *Emain Macha*, now called **Navan Fort**, dates from 600 BC and is about 2 miles (3km) west of Armagh City on the A28. The fort was a centre of pagan power and culture, and is famous for its association with the Red Branch Knights. When Fergus was King of Ulster in the 4th century, *Emain Macha* was burned, its timber structures completely destroyed. By the time St Patrick came to *Ard Macha* (Armagh), this Bronze Age centre of power had lain in ruins for over a hundred years. Today, the grassy *rath* extends over about 12 acres (5ha). It is easy to walk or take a bus there from town, and you are rewarded with a pleasant view over the city when you arrive. Once in danger of being destroyed to make way for a quarry, the site has become a chief tourist attraction. An excellent interpretative centre, the **Navan Centre** (*open all year, Mon–Sat 10–5, Sun 12–5; adm; t (028) 3752 5550, www.navan.com, navan@enterprise.net*) has opened close by with a restaurant and shop. The centre is in the shape of a Bronze Age fort, and very unobtrusive; it is definitely worth a detour. The no.73 bus from Mall West in Armagh will drop you outside.

Around Armagh

The Shores of Lough Neagh to Tandragee

To the northeast of Armagh is the industrial part of the county, with the old linen town of **Portadown** and the new town of **Craigavon**. Though lacking in beauty they do benefit from their proximity to Lough Neagh and the River Bann with man-made lakes, boating ponds and a dry ski-slope. Craigavon's two large artificial lakes are used for water sports and trout fishing. There are two golf courses. An interesting trip can be made to **Moneypenny's Lockhouse** (*open April–Sept, Sat–Sun 2–5; t (028) 3832 2205*), Newry Canal, Portadown. It contains an exhibition on the history of this 18th-century canal, and the lifestyle of the lockhouse keeper. It is a peaceful walk from Portadown, along the banks of the canal from Shillington's Quay car park, Castle Street.

Near Portadown a network of little roads runs through a charming district, covered with fruit trees and bushes. In May and June the gentle little hills are a mass of pink and white apple and damson flowers. There is an **Apple Blossom Festival** in May with fairs, concerts, and exhibitions in Keady, Richhill, Tandragee and Loughgall. The orchards were a part of the old Irish agricultural economy long before the English settlers came here; though many of the fruit farmers are descended from Kent and Somerset families, well-used to growing fruit. Their main crop is Bramley apples.

The retreating glaciers many millions of years ago left behind deposits of clay and gravel which form little hills known as *drumlins*, of which there are many in this part. The teardrop *drumlin* country is intersected by trout-filled lakes and streams, high hedges and twisting lanes. In **Richhill** you will find some furniture workshops and a fine **Jacobean manor** with curling Dutch gables. It is not open to the public but the sight it makes within the pretty well-kept village is worth stopping for. The village of **Kilmore** has what is probably the oldest church in Ireland. In the heart of the present little parish church stands the lower half of a round tower dating from the first half of the 3rd century.

Right in the centre of this fertile district is the quaint village of **Loughgall**, with strung out along the main road, many of its little houses painted in the soft shades of blossom and their gardens bursting with colour. The small **Orange Museum**, at Sloan's House in Main Street (*open by appointment only; call Armagh Tourist Centre t (028) 3752 1800*), displays mementoes commemorating the founding of the Orange Order here in 1795. Ireland in the late 18th century was a place of localised secret societies, mostly made up of poor agrarian Catholics, mobilised by land hunger, tithes and local issues. The ferment caused by the concessions of Grattan's Parliament

Tourist Information

Craigavon: Civic Centre, Lakeview Road,
t (028) 3831 2400, *info@craigavon.gov.uk*;
open all year.
Lurgan: Waves Leisure Complex, Robert Street,
t (028) 3832 2906; *open all year.*
Crossmaglen: Community Centre, The Square,
t (028) 3086 8900; *open Mon–Fri 9–5.*

Shopping

Antiques
Heritage Antiques, Main Street, Loughgall,
t (028) 2889 1314.
Huey's Antique Shop, The Tavern, 45 Main
Street, Loughgall, t (028) 3889 1248.
Meredith Antiques, main Street, Loughgall,
t (028) 3852 8739.
Charles Gardiner, 48 High Street, Lurgan,
t (028) 3832 3934.

Crafts
The National Trust Shop, The Argory, Moy,
t (028) 8778 4753.
Mullaghbawn Folk Museum, Tullymacrieve,
Forkhill, t (028) 3088 8108.
Peatlands Park, t (028) 3885 1102. Hand carved
figures made from compressed peat.

Markets
Livestock Market, Newtownhamilton. Held
on alternate Saturdays.

Sports and Activities

Bird-watching
On Oxford Island and Coney Island for
birdlife and fishing. There is no ferry
service to Coney Island: hire a boat
from Kinnego Bay or Maghery
Country Park.
Lough Neagh Discovery Centre, Oxford Island,
Craigavon, t (028) 3832 2205. Bird-watching
and walks.

Cycling
Craigavon Borough Council is
developing cycle routes on paths and
minor roads.
Lough Neagh Discovery Centre, Oxford Island,
t (028) 3832 2205.
McCurniskey Cycles, Drominee, t (028) 3088
8593. For bike hire.

Fishing
Between Benburb and Blackwater town
an extensive river park makes fishing and
water sports of all kinds possible. Fishing is
also available on the Cusher and Callan Rivers,
which are tributaries of the Blackwater
River. Contact the Armagh Tourist Office,
t (028) 3752 1800.

Golf
Craigavon Golf and Ski Centre, Turmoyra Lane,
Lurgan, t (028) 3832 6606.
Tandragee Golf Club, Markethill Road,
Tandragee, t (028) 3884 1272. 18-hole course.

Open Farms
Tannaghmore Gardens and Farm, Silverwood,
Craigavon, t (028) 3834 3244. Victorian rose
garden and rare animal breeds.

Pleasure Cruises
From Kinnego Bay, Lough Neagh.
Paddy Prunty, Harbour Master, Kinnego
Marina, Oxford Island, t (028) 3832 7573.
Also offers sailing courses.

Pony-trekking
Ring of Gullion Centre, Lough Road,
Mullaghban, west of Slieve Gullion, t (028)
3088 9311, f (028) 4308 9022, *enquiries@
rogequestrian.com.*
Crossmaglen Equestrian Centre, t (028)
3086 1661.

Walking
The **Ulster Way**, a sign-posted trail which
traverses the mountains and coastline of
Ulster, goes through Armagh. A large stretch

towards Catholics in 1793, giving them the vote and more civil liberties, made
sectarian tension in this part of Ulster particularly acute. A confrontation between
the Protestant 'Peep o' Day Boys' and the Catholic 'Defenders' at Diamond Hill outside

along the Newry Canal between Newry and Portadown is very scenic. **Carnagh** and **Slieve Gullion Forest Park** (*open 10–dusk*) have way-marked walks. Details from the Tourist Office in Armagh.
Sports Council for Northern Ireland, t (028) 9038 1222. For more details on the Ulster Way.

Water Sports

Craigavon Water Sports Centre, Lakeview Road, Craigavon, t (028) 3834 2669. Watersports of all types.

Where to Stay

Drumcree House, 38 Ashgrove Road, Portadown. t/f (028) 3885 2189 (*inexpensive*). Four rooms; two en suite. High tea and dinner available.
Waterside House, Oxford Island, Lurgan, Craigavon, t (028) 3832 7573 (*inexpensive*). Hostel located in the conservation area overlooking Lough Neagh; wide range of watersports and activities.
Planter's Tavern, 4 Banbridge Road, Waringstown, east of Craigavon on the A26, t (028) 3888 1510 (*expensive*). Modern motel-style hotel.
Ballinahinch House, 47 Ballygroobany Road, Richhill, t/f (028) 3887 0081 (*inexpensive*). Victorian famhouse with spacious rooms and old world ambience. Contact Mrs Kee.
McDees, Blackwatertown Road, Drumcullen, Benburb, t (028) 3752 6088 (*moderate*). B&B a few minutes' drive out of town, with a notably modern interior; attention to detail in everything, from bed-linen to breakfast.

Self-catering

Benbree, Forkhill, t (028) 3088 8394. Sleeps 6; from £200 per week.
Mountain View, Mullaghbane, t (028) 3088 8410. Sleeps 4–6; from £200 per week.

Eating Out

Seagoe Hotel, Upper Church Lane, Portadown, t (028) 3833 3076, f (028) 3835 0210, www.seagoe.com (*moderate*). Beef and Irish stews.
Ardress House, 64 Ardress Road, Portadown, t (028) 3885 1236 (*inexpensive*). Picnic teas are available on Sundays in summer.
Lough Neagh Lodge, Maghery Road, Dungannon, t (028) 3885 1901 (*moderate*). Wild trout, steaks, eels.
Cafolla, 2 Carnegie Street, Lurgan, t (028) 3832 3331 (*inexpensive*). Fish and chips.
The Famous Grouse, 6 Ballyhagan Road, Loughgall, t (028) 3889 1778 (*moderate*). Reasonably priced and cosy restaurant. Try the pub grub at lunchtime or the à la carte menu in the evening.
Moneypenny's Restaurant, 9–19 Church Street, Tandragee, t (028) 3884 0219 (*moderate–inexpensive*). International dishes served in a gracious atmosphere, where you can dine either in the bar or restaurant. *Open daily exc Tues 12.30–2.30, Wed–Sun 5.30–9.30.*
The Old Barn, 5 Mowhan Road, Markethill, t (028) 3755 2742 (*expensive–moderate*). Traditional and world recipes served in a well restored building. *Open Mon–Sun 11–3, Fri–Sun 7pm onwards.*
The Court Rooms Restaurant, 7 Main Street, Markethill, t (028) 3755 1855 (*inexpensive*). Serves home-made desserts that are scrumptiously sweet. *Open Mon–Tues 10–5, Wed–Thurs 10–9, Fri–Sat 10–10, Sun 12.30–3 and 5–9.*
Old Thatch, 3 Keady Street, Markethill, t (028) 3755 1261 (*inexpensive*). Good cakes and coffee.
Hearty's Folk Cottage, Glassdrummond, near Crossmaglen (*inexpensive*). Afternoon teas, arts and crafts and traditional music. *Open Sun afternoons only.*
The Argory, Moy, t (028) 8778 4753 (*inexpensive*). A good tearoom. *Open June–Aug.*

Loughgall led to the founding of the Orange Order, which has played such a large part in modern Ulster politics. **Dan Winter's Cottage and Ancestral Home** (*open spring and summer weekends and bank hols;* t (028) 3885 2777) is at the centre of the site where the Battle of the Diamond took place in 1795; it bears the scorch marks where the building was set alight. Inside there are maps of and relics from the battle, and it is furnished in the vernacular style. (It may also be the longest thatched cottage in Ireland, at 94 feet.)

Not far away is **Ardress House** (*open Easter, April–May and Sept, weekends and bank holidays 2–6, June–Aug, Wed–Mon 2–6; t (028) 3885 1236, www.nationaltrust.org.uk*). This is a 17th-century manor much altered by George Ensor (who married the owner of this once simple farmhouse), so that it is now Georgian in character. It is in Annaghmore on the Portadown–Moy road (B28), 3 miles (5km) from Loughgall. Its elegant drawing room has one of the most beautiful decorative plasterwork ceilings in Ireland. The work is in Adam style and both the ceiling and the mural medallions have been carefully restored and sympathetically painted. Set in lovely parkland, it is now in the care of the National Trust. There is a farmyard display, picnic area, woodland walks and a small formal garden.

Coney Island, one of the few islands in Lough Neagh, is also a National Trust property. It lies to the north, not far from the mouth of the Blackwater, and can be reached by boat from Maghery. Apart from the excellent fishing, this thickly wooded, reedy island of 8½ acres (3.5ha) is also worth visiting for its huge and varied birdlife. St Patrick used the island as a retreat and there is also a rather overgrown holy well. Be prepared for the Lough Neagh flies, which are food for the pollan, a fish unique to these waters and absolutely delicious fried in butter. **Peatlands Park** (*park open 9–dusk, visitor centre open April–Sept, Sat–Sun 2–6, June–Aug, Mon–Fri 2–6; t (028) 3885 1102*), with its narrow-gauge railway, is close by on the Lough Neagh basin, and shows educational videos and outdoor exhibits on peat ecology. Further east again is the **Lough Neagh Discovery Centre** (*open April–Sept, daily 10–7, Oct–March, Wed–Sun 10–5; take exit 10 off the M1 at Oxford Island; t (028) 3832 2205*), which explains the geology and natural history of the area; it is possible to go bird-watching in the hides and go on guided nature walks. There are picnic areas, a café and a shop.

Returning southwards along the River Blackwater, which forms the county boundary, is **The Argory** (*open mid Mar–May and Sept, weekends 12–6 bank hols 1–6, June, daily 1–6, July–Aug, daily 12–6 bank hols 1–6; adm; t (028) 8778 4753, uagest@ ntrust.org.uk*), which lies 2½ miles (4km) from Charlemont on a tiny little road off the B28. Standing in woodland and parkland, this rather lovely early-19th-century neoclassical house overlooks the river. It is of particular interest in that its contents have remained almost completely undisturbed since the turn of the century. Much more of a home than a museum, it is full of treasures gathered over the years from all corners of the earth. The large cabinet organ at the top of the grand cantilevered staircase is unique. So too is the acetylene gas plant which still lights the house: every room has its own ingenious old light-fittings. Outside you can wander through the stable buildings, semi-formal gardens and along woodland and river walks. The village of **Charlemont**, once an important parliamentary borough, is 2.5 miles (4km) upstream. It has an 18th-century cut-stone bridge and a 17th-century ruined fort with star-shaped walls typical of that period, built by Lord Mountjoy, Lord Deputy of Ireland in 1602.

Flax-milling has ceased, but flour-milling still thrives in **Tandragee**, a pretty, well-kept town with brightly painted houses. It is of considerable age and was founded by the O'Hanlons, chieftains of these parts before the plantations of James I. The old castle and the town were destroyed in the Civil War of 1641. The present castle is barely more than a century old and now houses the **factory** which produces Ulster's foremost crisp, 'Tayto'. It is possible to go on an intriguing tour of what the locals call 'Tayto Castle' (*open daily for tours, Mon–Thurs 10.30–1.30, Fri at 10.30am; adm free;* **t** *(028) 3884 0249, www.tayto.com, rbro@tayto.com*).

Clare Glen and South to Slieve Gullion

Clare Glen, one of the prettiest glens in the country, is 4 miles (6km) away to the east of Armagh City. A fine trout stream winds under old bridges and past a now-silent mill. There are lovely walks around here and it is on such country lanes as these that you might come across a game of 'bullets' or **road bowls**. This game is played with 28oz (795g) balls made of iron, which are thrown along a quiet winding road. The aim is to cover several miles in the fewest shots. Children are stationed along the course to warn motorists, and the betting and excitement among the onlookers is infectious.

On the Newry road (A28) you pass the village of **Markethill** on the right, and **Gosford Castle**, a huge early 19th-century mock-Norman castle, on the left (*castle open daily 10–dusk; grounds daily 8–dusk; adm;* **t** *(028) 3755 1277*). The magnificent grounds are also open to the public and owned by the Forestry Commission. The walled cherry garden, the arboretum, unusual breeds of poultry, nature trails and forest parks make it an enjoyable place to while away some time. Further south and keeping to the more attractive minor roads, you come across the village of **Bessbrook**. This is a model linen manufacturing town, neatly laid out in the 19th century by a Quaker; it still has neither pub nor pawn shop. The design of the model town of Bournville, near Birmingham in England, which is famous for its chocolate industry, is based entirely on Bessbrook. The remains of the huge mill, dams, weirs and sluices stand deserted, but nearby the impressive cut-stone Craigmore Viaduct still carries the main railway line to Dublin. Just outside Bessbrook is **Derrymore House** (*house open for guided tours only, Easter and May–Aug, Thurs–Sat 2–5.30; grounds open May–Sept, daily 10–8, Oct–April, 10–4; adm;* **t** *(028) 3083 0353, www.nationaltrust.org.uk*), a small, thatched manor house set in parkland. Built in 1776, it was witness to the signing of the Act of Union in 1801, and is now in the care of the National Trust.

Travelling south from Bessbrook, the land becomes poorer, the fields smaller, the hedges higher and the roads have more of a twist to them. Soon the hills of south Armagh appear in the distance dominated by the peak of **Slieve Gullion**. This rugged group of hills is steeped in history and legend. Described as 'the mountains of mystery', the average tourist never hears of them, which is a pity as the whole region has magnificent scenery, beautiful lakes, streams and unspoilt little villages. There have been many bloody incidents in this area, labelled 'bandit country'; the population is predominantly Catholic and Nationalist, and the situation here before the ceasefire was extremely tense. **Crossmaglen** has a dicey reputation, but with the ceasefire holding the situation has improved. In general, you can enjoy exploring the delightfully unkept countryside, so different from the tamer lands in the north. Caught between Camlough Mountain and Slieve Gullion lies the beautiful ribbon-like **Lough Cam**. The surrounding hedges and shorelines are the homes of many flowers and birds, and there is good fishing on the Fane River, Lough Cam and Lough Ross.

From the other side of Lough Cam, the road climbs up through the trees to the extensive, recently developed **Slieve Gullion Forest Park**. From the top of Slieve Gullion, panoramic views of the encircling mountains that make up the Ring of Gullion and the distant hills of Belfast and Dublin spread out before you. Slieve Gullion (*Sliabh gCuillin*: 'Mountain of the Steep Slope'), is often shrouded in mist, and according to local folklore it is magical. Legend tells us that Chulainn was a chief who owned a fierce watchdog which was slain by a boy of 15. The young hero was afterwards called Cú Chulainn ('Hound of Chulainn'). On the southern slopes there is an ancient church known as **Killevy Church**. There are actually the remains of two churches here, each from different periods; this holy place was founded as a nunnery as far back as AD 450. Nearby is a holy well and prehistoric passage grave.

Close to the County Louth border, just off the N1, about 1.5 miles (2.4km) south of Jonesborough and east of the bridge, is one of the earliest datable Christian monuments in Ireland. The inscribed **Kilnasaggart Pillar Stone** is early 8th century, and carved with crosses. It commemorates a local dignatory, and the inscription is in Gaelic. **Moyry Castle**, a three-storey ruin nearby, dates from 1601. It was built by Lord Mountjoy, and was ruined in the struggle between the English forces under him and the Irish forces under Hugh O'Neill during the Elizabethan wars. Both the villages of **Forkhill**, with its trout stream, and **Mullaghbane**, with its tiny folk museum, furnished as a south Armagh farmhouse, are picturesquely situated in their own valleys between the hills. This region is famous for its traditional music, and one place you can be sure to find some is at the **Ti Chulainn Cultural Centre** at Mullaghbane (*open July–Aug, Mon–Sat 10–5.30, Sun 1–6; t (028) 3088 8828, tculainn@dial.pipex.com*), which has occasional live performances of traditional music, song and dance.

Crossmaglen and Through The Fews to Tynan

Southwest from here is **Crossmaglen**, with its staggeringly large market square. The town is the centre of the recently revived cottage industry of lacemaking. Again, there are earthworks to explore: a superb example of a treble-ringed fort, remains of stone cairns, and a *crannog* (artificial island) on Lough Ross. You are now actually following the old coach road from Dublin to Armagh, itself the ancient link between Emain Macha and Tara (another ancient centre of power), in County Meath. At Dorsey, to the east of the town, there is the largest entrenched enclosure of its kind in Ireland. Constructed as a defensive outpost for *Emain Macha*, this huge earthwork encloses over 300 acres (121ha) and lies astride the route. Some of the earth ramparts still remain. It is part of the ancient earth dyke known as the **Black Pig's Dyke**, which extends over most of the borders of Ulster.

On the B30, a short distance from Crossmaglen, an interesting stop can be made at the old church of **Creggan**. It dates from 1731 and the tower was added in 1799. The

O'Neill vault contains over seventy skulls of this ancient family, whose present clan leader is Don Carlos O'Neill of Seville. In the church grounds is a visitor centre with an exhibition on the poets and people of Creggan. Three 18th-century Gaelic poets are buried in the graveyard, one of whom, Art McCumhaigh (1738–1773), wrote a very poignant *aisling*, or vision poem, entitled *The Churchyard of Creagán*, in which the poet encounters the vision of a woman. They bemoan the decline of the Gaels of Tír Eoghain, and the ascendency of John Bull, whilst the poet's last wish is to be buried with Creagan's sweet Gaels. North of Creggan is **Cullyhanna** and the **Cardinal Tomas O'Fiaich Heritage Centre** (*open Sun–Fri; t (028) 3086 8757*). This powerful and strong-minded prelate played his part in the recent history of Ulster, and there is an exhibition of his life, a collection of south Armagh songs and poems to listen to and a research library.

Leaving behind the mountains of south Armagh, you enter the attractive upland country known as **The Fews**. The isolated village of **Newtownhamilton** was founded in 1770, but the neighbourhood is associated with the legendary story of Lir, for it was here that the ocean-god King Lir had his palace. Do not go straight back to Armagh, but branch off the B31 to the west and climb **Carrigatuke Hill**. From the top an outstanding view of the area as far as Meath to the south and even Roscommon to the southwest lies before you. This small area across and down to the border is a miniature Lake District with lots of little irregular lakes caught between tiny hills, vestiges of glacial movement and deposition. Many of the lakes are studded with islands. **Lake Tullnawood** is very picturesque. Just north of boot-shaped Clay Lake is the small market town of **Keady**. It was once a very important linen centre, hence the number of derelict water mills in the district. Nearby at **Tassagh Glen** there is a mill and a huge viaduct that spans the wide valley. Under the viaduct's arches you can picnic among wild flowers, rose briars and red-berried rowan. From here it is only about 6 miles (10km) back to the city of Armagh. To the west of Armagh, beyond the little hill-top village of Killylea, lies the pretty village of **Tynan**. In the middle of the main street stands a fine sculptured stone cross, over 13ft (4m) high and dating from the 10th century. There are other ancient crosses in the nearby extensive demesne of **Tynan Abbey**; enquire at the estate if you wish to see them.

County Donegal

Donegal (*Dun na nGall*: 'Fort of the Foreigner') is a microcosm of all Ireland, and is the fourth largest county. In the west is the Gaeltacht, with its mountains, heathery moors and boglands, home of the dispossessed Celt. In the east, there are rich pasturelands, plantation towns, and long-settled families which were originally Scottish or English. Set northwest against the Atlantic, much of its beauty comes from its proximity to the sea: from the sweep of Donegal Bay, the maritime cliffs around Slieve League, the intricate indentations of the coast up to Bloody Foreland, and the northern peninsulas formed by long sea loughs, around 200 miles (320km) of coast in all. Donegal is a county of beautiful countryside; the ancient mountain

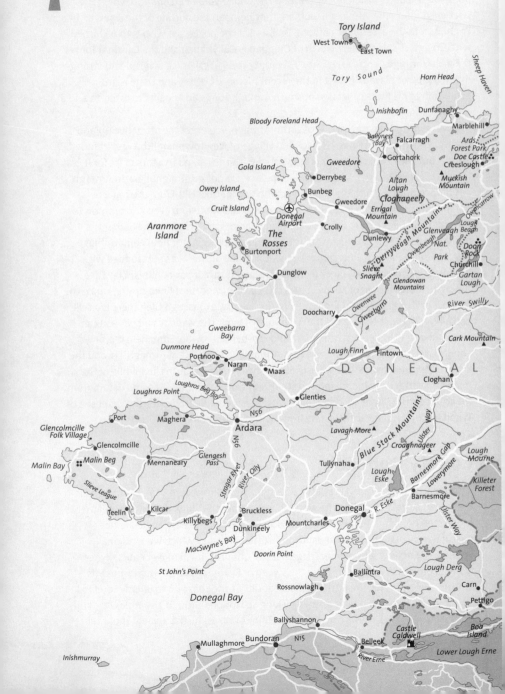

County Donegal

Getting There and Around

By Air

Daily services fly from Glasgow and Manchester to the City of Derry Airport, and there are also daily flights from Dublin to Sligo Airport, about 40 minutes' drive from Bundoran. There are numerous flights to Donegal Airport from Glasgow, and daily flights from Dublin.

City of Derry Airport, near Eglinton, t (028) 7181 0784, *www.derry.net/airport*. Lies about 40 minutes' drive from Letterkenny. Connections to Paris and Brussels.

Donegal Airport, Carrickfinn (between Dungloe and Crolly), The Rosses, t (075) 48284, *www.donegalairport.ie*.

Sligo Airport, Strandhill, Co. Sligo, t (071) 68280, f (071) 68396. *www.sligoairport.com*.

By Rail

Daily services from Belfast to Derry, and Dublin to Sligo.

Translink, Belfast, t (028) 9089 9411, *www.translink.co.uk*.

By Bus

Express bus services from Dublin to Letterkenny by Bus Eireann. If you want to travel to less populous areas of Donegal, you will have to take local buses.

Bus Eireann, t (074) 21101/21309.

Lough Swilly Bus Company, Derry, Co. Londonderry, t (028) 7126 2017. Links the various towns such as Ballyshannon, Burdoran, Donegal, Killybegs and Letterkenny.

Fedah O'Donnell Coaches, t (075) 48114. Daily to Galway and Belfast airport.

O'Donnell Buses, t (075) 48356.

North West Busways, t (077) 82619. Links Buncrana and Letterkenny.

John McGinley, t (074) 35201. Between Irishowen, Letterkenny and Dublin, Glasgow and Donegal.

McGeehan's, t (075) 46150. Runs from Donegal town to Dublin, with regular services to Glencolmcille and Dungloe; also serves Ardara, Killybegs, Kilcar and Carrick.

By Bike

The Raleigh Rent-a-Bike network operates here. Your local dealers are:

The Bike Shop, Waterloo Place, Donegal Town, t (073) 22515.

Church Street Cycles, Letterkenny, t (074) 26204.

Getting to Tory Island

A passenger ferry operates daily between Tory and Bunbeg (75mins), Magheraroarty (40mins) and Portnablagh (Wednesday only). Contact Donegal Coastal Cruises for times of sailings, t (075) 31991, or t (074) 35061. Sailing is subject to the weather and tide.

ranges are older than any others in Ireland, and the light of Donegal brings alive the subtle greens and browns of the landscape, and the strength of blue in the sky and sea. There are some exciting walks and climbs for the experienced. Because of the mountains in central Donegal, the weather is often quite different in the south west quarter.

Each part of Donegal has its own charm and beauty: the rocky flats of the Rosses studded with tiny lakes, the varied scenery of Inishowen, the curved beaches and mountains of Tirconnell and the rich cattle lands which border the River Foyle. Compared to many of the urban parts of Ireland, Donegal is still a land of wilderness and rock, where a lone farmhouse hugs the hill and its resident sheepdog hurtles out onto the road to chase the car that dares to intrude upon his kingdom.

Yet increasingly, as in other coastal parts of Ireland, there has been a growth in the numbers of homes and holiday chalets, which are often built right along the coast. County Donegal has traditionally been the holiday destination of urban Northerners from Belfast and its surrounds; many leave their caravans in Donegal

Getting to Arranmore Island

There is a regular ferry that takes approximately 25 minutes; there are approximately 6 sailings per day, year-round, t (075) 20532.

Festivals

All festival dates vary from year to year. For details of all these contact the Letterkenny tourist office, t (074) 21160. For details of festivals in the Inishowen district, call t (077) 74933.

March
Hillwalking Festival, Ardara, t (075) 41518/41830. Mid-month.

April
Hillwalking, Glencolmcille, t (073) 30248.

May
Killybegs Sea Angling Festival, t (073) 31137. Held May–June.

June
Weavers' Fair, Ardara, t (073) 41103.
Buncrana Folk Festival, Inishowen. Late June.

July
Orange Order Parade, Rossnowlagh (12th).
Ramelton Festival.

Earagaul Arts Festival, Letterkenny.
Buncrana Music Festival, Buncrana, t (077) 62737, or t (086) 686 8976.

July
Ballyshannon Folk and Traditional Music Festival, t (072) 51088, *www.donegalbay.ie*. July–Aug.
Orange Procession, Rossnowlagh (12th).
Donegal Town Summer Festival. July–August.
Dungloe Festival. A family festival of music and song, July–Aug.
Rathmullan Regatta.

August
Kilcar Street and Sea-angling Festivals, t (073) 38185.
Fiddle Festival and Fiddle Music Summer School, in Glencolmcille, t (073) 30248.
Busking Festival, Milford, t (074) 33137.

September
Harvest Fair, Glenties.
Muff Festival. One of the oldest and largest country fairs in Ireland for music and singing, north of Derry.
Music, Poetry and Singing, Traditional Cottage, Muff, t (077) 84024.
Traditional Music Festival, Carrick, t (073) 39333.
Oyster Festival, Moville and Greencastle.

and, as prosperity grows, they are buying into the new developments. The uglier by-products of Ireland's more general prosperity and industrial development is apparent around **Letterkenny**, which grows rapidly every year. The baby boom in Ireland has been experienced in this county more than anywhere else, which (almost) makes up for the rural depopulation that scourged the countryside after the famine of 1845–49. Of course, the new generation is not being brought up on the old homesteads in lonely picturesque valleys, but in the numerous bungalows and housing estates which line the roads near the factories that the Irish Government has enticed in with substantial financial assistance.

Tourist attractions are being developed with the restoration of buildings of architectural or historical interest, such as Lifford Old Courthouse and the Corn and Flax Mill at Newmills, near Letterkenny. The archeological and early Christian remains in County Donegal are numerous; St Colmcille, Ireland's most famous native saint, was born here at Gartan, and Glencolmcille is closely associated with him.

Some people say that Donegal is the 26th county in a 25-county state, meaning that there is an individuality and independence up here which Dublin likes to ignore. This Ulster county has the largest number of Irish native speakers of any county in Ireland, though, curiously enough, 'Official Irish' is based on the Leinster dialect. The Ulster dialect has more in common with Highland Gaelic than with the southern strain. There are strong links with Scotland; many districts of Glasgow are reputed to be like parishes of west Donegal, and you will see buses going from places like Annagry all the way to Glasgow. Part of Donegal is officially Irish-speaking (the Gaeltacht).

History

The county has a large proportion of Neolithic and Early Bronze Age remains. The main monument which survives from prehistoric times is the Grianan of Aileach, near Burt, a superb structure dating in parts back to the Iron Age, 1700 BC and perhaps earlier. The northern Ui Neill kings occupied it as their royal seat *c.* AD 700. In Donegal the two important branches of this clan were the O'Neills and the O'Donnells, who became great rivals. The chief of the O'Donnells was known as the Prince of Tirconnell. In about 850, the Vikings settled in Inishowen and along the northwest coast (hence the Gaelic name of the county). The main County Donegal clans clashed endlessly, and the Norman warlords laid waste to Inishowen, and built Greencastle on Lough Swilly. The wars between the O'Donnells, the O'Dohertys and other Irish *septs* continued for centuries, but towards the end of the 16th century two chiefs, Red Hugh O'Donnell and Hugh O'Neill, combined their powers in an effort to prevent the English from taking over. They were defeated at the battle of Kinsale in 1601 and made their way to the Continent in 'The Flight of the Earls'. This took place from the shores of Lough Swilly, near Rathmullan, in 1607 (*see* **History**, p.40). The Plantation began with Scots and English undertakers being given land and founding towns.

Between 1632 and 1636, the *Annals of the Four Masters* were compiled by Franciscan monks at Bundrowes, near Bundoran. These annals are a valuable source of Irish history. In 1841, the population of Donegal was at its height of 196,448. Then disaster struck with the Great Famine, which affected the west and north of Donegal very badly. In 1921 Ulster was partitioned, and Donegal was cut off from its natural hub of Derry.

South Donegal

Bundoran to Donegal Town

If you come up from Sligo along the superb sweep of Donegal Bay you will encounter one of Ireland's older seaside resorts, **Bundoran**. On the long main street there is a typically uninspiring hotchpotch of hotels, amusements and souvenir shops. Nearby are wonderful beaches and the Bundoran Golf Course, one of the best-known courses in Ireland.

For those who are avoiding populous resorts, **Ballyshannon**, 5–6 miles (8–9½km) up the coast from Bundoran, is ideal. It is said to have been founded in 1500 BC when the

Tourist Information

Bundoran: t (072) 41350; *open June–Sept Mon–Sat.*
Donegal Town: t (073) 21148; *open April–Oct.*

Shopping

Books

Four Masters Bookshop, The Diamond, Donegal Town, **t** (073) 21526.

China and Crystal

Celtic Weave China, Cloghore, Ballyshannon, **t** (072) 51844.
Barry Britton, Rossnowlagh, **t** (072) 52220. Crystal wares.

Crafts

Donegal Town Craft Village (just outside the town on the road to Sligo), **t** (073) 22225. Donegal tweed, woodwork, batik, pottery, uillean pipes, stonework, ironwork and jewellery.
Laurence Herron, The Heritage Centre, Donegal Town **t** (075) 41704. Sculptures made of local bog wood.
Niall Bruton, Donegal Craft Village, Donegal Town, **t** (073) 22225. Handcrafted jewellery.
The Present Company and Crooked House Gallery, Quay Street, Donegal Town, **t** (073) 21999.
Studio Donegal, Donegal Town, **t** (073) 38194. Hand-weaving.
Glencolmcille Folk Village Shop, **t** (073) 30017. Soaps, flower wines, St Brigid's crosses and honey.
Taipeis Gael, Glencolmcille, **t/f** (073) 30325. Naturally dyed, spun and woven tapestry. Week-long tapestry courses also available.
Triona Design, Ardara, **t** (075) 41422. Tapestry.

Health Foods

Simple Simon, The Diamond, Donegal Town, **t** (073) 22087/22687.

Tweeds and Knitwear

John Molloy Ltd, The Diamond, Donegal Town, **t** (073) 22882, *www.johnmolloy.com*, *jmolloy@iol.ie*;

also at Ardara (factory), **t** (075) 41133; Glencolmcille, **t** (073) 30282.
Magee of Donegal, The Diamond, Donegal Town, **t** (073) 22660, *www.mageeshop.com*.
Cindy Graham, Handweaver, St John's Point, Dunkineely, **t** (073) 37072. Subtle blends of colours inspired by the Donegal landscape.
The Tannery, Mountcharles, **t** (073) 35675.
Studio Donegal Handwoven Tweed, Kilcar, **t** (073) 38194.
Bonners, Ardara.
Kennedy of Ardara, Ardara, **t** (075) 41106.

Sports and Activities

Beaches

Blue flag beaches: **Bundoran, Rossnowlagh** and **Naran/Portnoo**. Those best for bathing are **Silver Strand**, at Malin Bay, and **Glencolmcille**.

Courses

Taipéis Gael, Glencolmcille, **t** (073) 30325, *taipeisgael@eircom.net*. Hosts week-long arts courses in summer.
Oideas Gael, Glencolmcille, **t** (073) 30248, **f** (073) 30348, *oidsgael@iol.ie*. Offers courses in dancing, flute and *bodhrán* playing, archaeology, hillwalking, pottery, tapestry, weaving and marine painting.

Fishing

Sea-angling is available in most parts of County Donegal, especially in the Killybegs region. Boats are also available for hire in Ardara and Portnoo. For charters, contact:
Bundoran Sea Angling, **t** (072) 41874. Contact Brendan Merrifield.
Ballyshannon Marine Ltd, **t** (086) 833 1665/ 872 4370.
Donegal Bay Charters, Donegal Town, **t** (073) 23191, *donegalbay@ireland.com*
Killybegs Angling Charter, **t** (073) 32444.
Killybegs Boat Hire, **t** (073) 31288.

There are also many salmon and trout rivers and loughs in Donegal. For information on **game fishing** in the south and southwest area, contact:
The Northern Regional Fisheries Board, Ballyshannon, **t** (072) 51435.

Golf
Bundoran Golf Club, t (072) 41302. This course is over 100 years old, and is one of the best in the country. It runs along the high cliffs above Bundoran beach.

Indoor Leisure Centres
Waterworld, Bundoran, **t** (072) 41172. *Open Easter–Sept.*

Internet Access
The Blueberry Tearoom, Castle Street, Donegal Town, **t** (073) 22933.

Outdoor Activity Centres
Malinmore Adventure Centre, Malin Bay, Glencolmcille, **t** (073) 30123. Scuba-diving, canoeing, boat trips.

Pilgrimages and Retreats
A Franciscan Friary is located in Rossnowlagh, and offers guest house accommodation. Opened as the **Centre of Peace and Reconciliation**, it is a quiet, reflective place where you can join in a retreat if you wish, **t** (072) 51342/52035.

St Patrick's Penance, Lough Derg, has been a place of pilrimage since early Christian times. It is open only to pilgrims during the summer season; call **t** (072) 61518/61546.

Pleasure Cruises
One-hour waterbus cruises on **Donegal Bay;** sailing times posted on Donegal Pier, **t** (073) 23666. Waterbus trips on **Lough Assaroe,** with storytelling, **t** (075) 31699.

Pony-trekking
Homefield Equestrian Centre, Bundoran, **t** (072) 41288/41977, **f** (072) 41049, *homefield@indigo.ie.* Trail-riding holidays arranged.

Walking
Hill-walking on Slieve League. Details about walking the **Ulster Way,** a signposted route, can be obtained from the Planning Department, DCC, Lifford, or the Long-distance Walking Route Committee, Cospair, 11th floor, Hawkings House, Dublin 2. Walking on the Ulster Way has to be well-organized as the landowners must be asked for permission first; they are very anxious about insurance claims against them.

Oideas Gael, Glencolmcille, **t** (073) 30248, **f** (073) 30348, *oidgael@iol.ie.* Walking holidays are organized by this company.

The Blue Stack Way, Ardara, **t** (075) 41518, *www.thebluestackway.com, bstack@indigo.ie.*

SOS Walking, Gortahork, **t/f** (074) 35206, *info@sosdonegal.com.* Donegal walking tours and ceili nights.

Where to Stay

St Ernans House Hotel, St Ernans Island, Donegal Town, **t** (073) 21065, **f** (073) 22819 (*expensive*). Charming situation on a wooded tidal island. The décor is rather too colour co-ordinated, but it is still a lovely place to stay.

Rhu Gorse, Lough Eske, near Donegal Town, **t** (073) 21685, *rhugorse@iol.ie* (*moderate*). Modern, family-run country house, overlooking Lough Eske and the Blue Stack Mountains.

Ardnamona House, Lough Eske, near Donegal Town, **t** (073) 22650 (*inexpensive*). Magical views over landscaped gardens, with wonderful food and hospitality from the Clarks. Famous for its rhododendrons, and for originally being the family home of the 20th century poet Rupert Brooke. Small functions and parties catered for.

Portnason House, Ballyshannon, **t** (072) 52016 (*moderate*). Georgian house, close to the sea.

Sand House Hotel, Rossnowlagh, **t** (072) 51777, **f** (072) 52100, *www.sandhouse-hotel.ie* (*luxury*). Excellent manor house hotel: friendly, comfortable, with delicious food and lots of sports, especially surfing.

Castlemurray House Hotel, St John's Point, Dunkineely, **t** (073) 37022, **f** (073) 37330, *www.castlemurray.com, castlemurray@eircom.net* (*moderate*). Comfortable, small hotel with fine French food prepared by its dedicated chef-owner, and lovely views.

Bruckless House, Bruckless, **t** (073) 37071, **f** (073) 37070, *bruc@iol.ie* (*moderate*). Charming 18th-century house with oriental influences in its decor, overlooking Donegal Bay. Mr and Mrs Evans will point you in the right direction, whether your interest is walking, prehistoric monuments or just exploring. Simple, comfortable rooms and a mature garden. *French and Chinese spoken.*

Gallagher's Farm Hostel, Bruckless, t (073) 37057 (*inexpensive*). Hostel in converted farm buildings.

Dooey Hostel, Glencolmcille, t (073) 30130 (*inexpensive*). Large, friendly hostel.

Campbell's Holiday Hostel, Ardara, t (075) 51491, *campbellshostel@eircom.net* (*inexpensive*). Youth hostel.

The Green Gate, Ardvally, Ardara, t (075) 41546 (*inexpensive*). Traditional cottage B&B. Paul Chatenoud charms visitors into a sense of what life must have been like in Donegal a century ago (apart from the bathrooms and central heating). Best seen in the warm months, when you can enjoy the glorious surroundings. *Smokers welcome.*

Self-catering

Ardnamona Cottage, Lough Eske, t (073) 22650 (*inexpensive*). Pretty self-catering cottage in a traditional yard, surrounded by lovely arboretum and scenery. Contact Mrs Clarke.

Eating Out

Le Chateaubrianne, Sligo Road, Bundoran, t (072) 42160 (*expensive*). Seafood, steak, poultry. Sunday lunch menu is cheaper.

Maggie's Bar, Ballyshannon, t (072) 52449 (*inexpensive*).

The Smuggler's Creek, Rossnowlagh, t (072) 52366 (*expensive*). Dinner menu includes fish and duck; Sunday lunch is cheaper. Traditional music on Saturday nights and Sunday afternoons. *Open at noon daily.*

Harvey's Point Restaurant and Country Hotel, Lough Eske, Donegal Town, t (073) 22208, *reservations@harveyspoint.com* (*moderate*). Continental food in beautiful surroundings.

Harbour Restaurant Quay, Quay Street, Donegal Town, t (073) 21702 (*moderate*). Seafood, lasagne.

The Blueberry Tearoom, Castle Street, Donegal Town, t (073) 22933 (*inexpensive*). Some good vegetarian choices including

quiche and lasagne; makes a fair attempt at real coffee. Also has internet access. *Open for breakfast, lunch and dinner.*

McGroarty's Pub, The Diamond, Donegal Town, t (073) 22519 (*inexpensive*). Good pub food.

Castle Murray House Hotel, St John's Point, Dunkineely, t (073) 37022 (*expensive*). Superb French cooking in lovely hotel with beautiful views. Very popular.

Bay View Hotel, Killybegs, t (073) 31950, *bvhotel@iol.ie* (*moderate*). Mainly a seafood restaurant.

Kitty Kelly's, Killybegs Road, Kilcar, t (073) 31925. Friendly welcome in this cottage restaurant that does tasty variations on Irish standards like lamb stew.

An Chistin, Ulster Cultural Foundation, Glencolmcille, t (073) 30213/30248 (*inexpensive*). Specializes in seafood, salads, soups. *Open for lunch and dinner March–Oct.*

Glencolmcille Folk Village Tearoom, t (073) 30017 (*inexpensive*). Home-made scones, bread and soups. *Open Easter–Oct.*

Nancy's Bar, Ardara, t (075) 41187 (*inexpensive*). Delicious oysters and burgers. *Summer only.*

Entertainment and Nightlife

Traditional Music

Look in the local newspapers for traditional and popular music sessions, which change venue all the time.

Thatch Pub, Dorrian's Imperial Hotel, Main Street, Ballyshannon, t (072) 51147/51010.

The Smuggler's Creek, Rossnowlagh, t (072) 52366. Traditional music Saturday night and Sunday afternoons.

The Scotchman, Donegal Town, t (073) 22022.

Piper's Rest, Main Street, Kilcar, t (073) 38205.

Corner House, Ardara, t (078) 31078. Frequent sessions here under the wing of this pub's musician owners, Ann and Peter Oliver. Their talented offspring are professional Irish dancers.

Nancy's Bar, Ardara, t (075) 41187. Traditional music weekends after St Patrick's Day and almost nightly June–mid Sept.

Glen Tavern, The Greenans, Glenties, t (075) 51170.

Scythians settled a colony on a little island in the Erne estuary. The Scythians were an offshoot of the Phoenician peoples who were supposed, in one version of the early history of Ireland (there are many), to have colonized areas of the north. It has its own poet, the bard of Ballyshannon, William Allingham, whose lines,

> *Up the airy mountain,*
> *Down the rushy glen,*
> *We daren't go a hunting*
> *For fear of little men.*

must have been chanted by many generations of children. **The Lakeside Centre**, Belleek Road, on the shore of Assaroe Lough, provides wool weaving demonstrations and lots of water sports. During the summer months a waterbus plies its way up and down the lough on story-telling trips for children (*see* 'Sports and Activities', p.476); the trip lasts about one hour. **Abbey Assaroe Mill** (**t** *(072) 51580*), just outside Ballyshannon and off the R231 Rossnowlagh road, was built by the Cistercians in the late 12th century, and has now been restored by local enthusiasts. It houses a local craft gallery, a coffee shop and interpretative centre.

Nearby are the sands of **Rossnowlagh**. If you are here around 12 July you may witness the last-remaining Orange procession on this side of the Northern Ireland border. Otherwise, Rossnowlagh is known for its surfing. At the **Franciscan Friary** (Centre of Peace and Reconciliation, *see* 'Sports and Activities', p.476), before you reach the pretty little town of Ballintra, you will find the diminutive **Donegal Museum** (*open daily 10–6*; **t** *(072) 51342*), run by the Donegal Historical Society. It has a few interesting items, including a piece of Muckish glass made from mica mined in the Muckish Mountains, which you will see as you go further north.

Donegal Town is the meeting point of roads which travel into the heart of Donegal, to the north and to the west. Situated on the River Eske, with a long history of habitation for its strategic site, it is a crowded, busy place even without the tourist buses which congregate near the hotels on the Diamond. (A diamond – or 'square' to most visitors – is an area where fairs and gatherings were held, and in the Plantation period it was placed in the shadow of the castle so as to guard against the fighting that was the accompanying feature of these occasions.) The town is nowadays one of the best places to buy Donegal **tweed**. Try Magee's shop in the Diamond, and the craft village on the Ballyshannon Road.

Donegal Castle (*open May–Oct, daily 9.30–5.45; adm*; **t** *(073) 22405*), once a stronghold of the O'Donnells, the Princes of Tirconnell, and then taken over by the planter Brooke family, is a handsome stone ruin that dates from the 15th century. It incorporates a square tower and turrets built by the O'Donnells in 1505, and the Jacobean house built by Sir Basil Brooke in 1610. Also of interest is the monument in the Diamond to the Four Masters. *The Annals of the Four Masters* is a history of old Ireland written by three brothers called O'Clery and O'Mulconry, who were scholars and monks. The brothers were tutors to the O'Donnells and stayed for a while at the nearby abbey, situated where the River Eske and the sea meet. They wrote this great work between 1632 and 1636. It records an Irish society that was fast disappearing as the English and Scottish were settled in Ireland. You might be interested in the **Donegal Railway Heritage Centre**, at The Old Station House (*t (073) 22655*), which takes a nostalgic look back at Donegal's narrow-gauge railways.

Further inland from Donegal Town lies the pilgrim's shrine of **Lough Derg**. Although most holy tradition in Donegal is associated with St Columba (Colmcille), the island is known as **St Patrick's Purgatory**, and between June and August it is the scene of one of the most rigorous Christian pilgrimages. People come here from all over the world to do penance, just as they did hundreds of years ago. The pilgrims stay on a small island on Lough Derg for 36 hours. They eat and drink only bread and water, stay up all night praying, and wear no shoes whilst making the Stations of the Cross. Information can be obtained from the Priory, St Patrick's Purgatory, Lough Derg, Pettigo (*t (072) 61518*). You can't actually visit St. Patrick's Purgatory unless you are a pilgrim, but it's quite a sight from the lough shore and certainly worth stopping for. Closer at hand is the lovely **Lough Eske**, where there is good fishing for trout. It is close to beautiful walks in the low range of hills called the **Blue Stack Mountains**. Overlooking Lough Eske is a superb rhododendron garden at **Ardnamona House**, best seen from April to mid-June. Ardnamona is also a very good guest house, amongst the most memorable of places to stay in Ireland (*see* 'Where to Stay, p.476). There is an admission charge for the gardens.

Donegal Town is a few miles away from the **Gaeltacht**, which begins after Killybegs. The Gaeltacht forms the officially recognized Irish-speaking area where government grants encourage the local people to stay put. Here you can walk into a shop or bar and catch fragments of true Irish, one of the oldest recorded Aryan languages. It is a strange language: rich, almost soft, but shot through with harsher, guttural tones. It is poignant, moving, but not melodious. The spoken English of Gaelic-speakers is, on the other hand, soft and poetic, as though through translation they have made a second language of it.

Around the Coast: Mountcharles to Glenties

Follow the N56 through **Mountcharles**, with its splendid view of Donegal Bay, **Bruckless** and **Dunkineely**. These were all centres of the now-defunct lace industry, and are still good places to buy hand-embroidered linen and the subtle patterned Donegal jumpers and rugs. There is a fine collection of early Irish portraits at **Ballyloughan House**, Bruckless (*contact Mrs Tindal; t (073) 31507*). The narrow, winding and climbing road leads you to **Killybegs**; in the summer, bordering hedgerows bloom with honeysuckle and fuchsia, and as you get further west the sweet, acrid smell of peat hangs on the damp air. Here you reach the most important fishing port in Ireland, which is set to expand even further to the tune of sixty-two million euros so that it can accommodate even bigger fishing vessels. There are plenty of sea-angling boats for hire here, and in July the place is full for the Sea Angling Festival. In the Catholic **church** there is a fine sculptured medieval grave slab of Noall Mór MacSwyne, which was found near St John's Point (this, by the way, is a lovely peninsula with a beautiful beach and views, signposted left from Dunkineely). The highly paid fishing and processing industry has brought great prosperity. It is quite a sight to watch the catches of haddock, plaice and sole being unloaded. The famous **Donegal Carpet Factory** started up here in the 1890s, headed by a Scots weaver, Alexander Morton. The hand-knotted carpets were often designed for palaces and embassies all over the world. The factory (*on the Kilcar road out of Killybegs, **t** (073) 31688*) has re-opened, and is producing original designs in pure wool; the showroom is worth visiting.

Beyond Killybegs you encounter some of the grandest scenery in Donegal; the great cliffs of Bunglass, Scregeigther and **Slieve League** are amongst the highest in Europe, rising to 1,972ft (601m). If you walk along the cliffs from Bunglass along One Man's Pass, a jaggedy ridge, on a clear day you will see fantastic views right down to County Mayo. The determined bird-watcher should be able to see puffins and cormorants, and the botantist should be able to find Arctic alpine species on the back slopes of Slieve League. The village of **Teelin**, under Slieve League, is popular with students on Irish language courses, whilst **Kilcar** is the site of the *Gaelterra Eireann* factory of fabrics and yarns. The wools are hard-wearing and flecked with soft colours, and you can buy them here in the craft shop and all over County Donegal. This is also a centre for handwoven tweed, and you might also like to visit **Studio Donegal** (*t (073) 38194*), handweavers in the village.

Glencolmcille should be visited next. A local priest called Father McDyer established a rural co-operative here to try to combat the flight of youth from the village through emigration. He helped the local economy greatly and there is a craft shop where you can buy handmade products such as jams, soaps and wines made from gorse or bluebells. The village has also become one of the most important centres for Irish culture and music, with its wealth of visitors who come in search of the best traditional pub 'session' in Ulster. **Glencolmcille Folk Village and Museum** constitutes three cottages, each representing different periods of Irish life (*open Easter–Sept, Mon–Fri 10–6 Sun 12–6; tearooms open during season; adm; t (073) 30017, f (073) 30334, folkmus@indigo.ie*). There is also a 3½mile (5km) **pilgrimage walk** along the valley here, around 15 cross slabs and pillars, which is known as the Stations of the Cross. It includes many of the ancient sites of the area, and begins with a Stone Age court-grave, which is among other attractively carved gravestones in the yard of the 14th-century St Columbcille's Church. The Stations of the Cross are still performed on 9 June, St Columba's Day. Notice the beautifully built stone and turf sheds with their thatched roofs which abound in this area. The countryside is full of prehistoric antiquuities, dolmens, cairns (including a famous horned cairn called Clochanmore), and ruins of churches connected with St Columba.

From Glencolmcille an expedition can be made along a winding, narrow road to the tiny bay and long-deserted village of **Port**. The sea cliffs have been fashioned into wonderful shapes, including a huge sea-stack of 148 metres. For Ireland's most beautiful beach, however, it's 5miles (8km) along the road southwest following the clifftops to the Silver Strand at **Malin Bay**. This gorgeous bay is sheltered by high cliffs all around, and the water is as clear as Waterford crystal. At the village of Malinmore you will find **Glencolmcille Woollen Mill** (*t (073) 30070, f (073) 30183*), which is known for its handwoven traditional and contemporary knitwear, designer products and crafts; it also has a demonstration area and a shop.

On the other side of the mountain, through the spectacular Glengesh Pass, you arrive at **Ardara**, another centre for Donegal tweed and Aran sweaters. Some lovely sweaters at very reasonable prices can be bought here (or at Glencolmcille). The new **Heritage Centre**, on the Main Street (*open Easter–Oct, daily 10–6; t (075) 41704, f (075) 41262*), tells the history of tweed in the area. Nancy's Bar, also on Main Street, is famous for its fresh oysters and atmosphere.

If you follow the road to **Maghera Caves**, signposted just outside Ardara on the road to Donegal Town (N56), you will come to another of the most beautiful beaches in Ireland. The single-track road from here unfolds a series of wonderful views of mountains, the sea inlet of **Loughros Beg Bay**, traditional farms, and near the end, a waterfall. The walk to the caves and beach takes you through someone's farm and over sand-dunes, so don't overload your picnic baskets.

If you travel a few miles on to the next little peninsula of Dunmore Head you will come to **Portnoo** and **Naran**, two popular beaches for holidaymakers from Northern Ireland. At Naran, you can park or hire caravans. There is a fascinating fort near here, built on an island in Doon Lough (beside Naran). It is over two thousand years old and is a very impressive sight – a circular stone fort which spreads over most of the island. It can easily be seen from the lough shore. At the neck of this peninsula you go from **Maas**, a small fishing resort, to **Glenties** (*Na Gleannta*: 'The Valley' – so called because of its position at the junction of glens), which is a good place for knitwear. There is a striking **church** designed by the innovative contemporary Irish architect, Liam McCormick, who is responsible for many fine churches in County Donegal. This one was built in the 1970s. Patrick McGill (1891–1963) the novelist and poet was born here; his semi-autobiographical novel *Children of the Dead End* sold very well in England, but was considered anti-clerical in Ireland.

Northern Donegal

Gweebarra Glen to Gortahork

All along the northwest coast you will see mountain ranges broken by long river valleys which reach into the hinterland. Any route along these valleys brings you across the harsh mountainous areas where beauty is bleak and the cost of wresting a living from the poor soil is no longer acceptable.

There is a rather zig-zag road from Fintown to Doocharry which brings you into the **Gweebarra Glen**. Northeast of this, between the Derryveagh and Glendowan Mountains, the valley extends into **Glenveagh**, which is now part of a National Park. However, you should keep heading out towards the sea on the road to Dunglow (also spelled 'Dungloe' – the 'g' is silent) if you want to see '**The Rosses**', as this area is called. The Irish name is *naRosa*, meaning 'Headlands', and is a good clue to the landscape. Although this area is going through a housing boom, it is still one of the most charming routes you can take to the north coast; loughs large and small are scattered

Tourist Information

Letterkenny: Blaney Road, t (074) 21160, f (074) 25180; *open all year.*

Shopping

Crafts
Lakeside Centre, Dunlewy, t (075) 31699.
The Pottery and Tea Room, Moyra, Falcarragh, t (074) 35330.
The Gallery, Dunfanaghy, t (074) 36224. Paintings, antiques and knitwear.
Avalon Craft Shop, 19 Academy Court, Letterkenny, t (074) 27939.
Design Studio, Port Road, Letterkenny, t (074) 25312.
Cavanacor Craft Centre and Gallery, Ballindrait, Lifford, t/f (074) 41143. Crafts, pottery and contemporary watercolours by local, national and international artists.

Jewellery
Geraldine Hannigan, 4 Port Road, Letterkenny, t (074) 25312. Jewellery, crafts.

Pottery
Robert More, Cashel, Creeslough, Letterkenny, t (074) 38130. Celtic-style pottery.
Cavanacor Studios, Cavanacor House, Ballindrait, Lifford, t/f (074) 41143. Joanna O'Kane creates delicate off-white bowls, plates and sculptures.

Tweeds and Knitwear
McNutts of Downings, t (074) 55643.
Falcara Ireland, Falcarragh, t (074) 35861.

Sports and Activities

Beaches
There are blue flag beaches at **Marblehill** and **Portsalon**.

Fishing
Sea-fishing is good in most parts of County Donegal, especially in Rathmullan. Boats are available for hire in Dunglow, Dunfanaghy and Falcarragh. For charters, contact:
Port-na-Blagh, Dunfanaghy, t (074) 66197.

Fisherman's Village Lodge, Downings, t (074) 55080, *info@rosguill.com.*
Rathmullan Enterprise Group, Rathmullan, t (074) 58131/58129.
There are many rivers and loughs in Donegal for **game-fishing**; the Clady River, which runs through Bunbeg and Gweedore, is renowned. Out of season, call t (072) 51435, or for info on areas in northern Donegal, contact:
Loughs Agency, Northern Regional Fisheries Board, t (048) 8166 2267.
Foyle Fisheries, Derry, t (028) 7134 2100.

Genealogy Centre
Donegal Ancestry, The Quay, Ramelton, t (074) 51266, *donances@indigo.ie.*

Golf
Rosapenna, t (074) 55301. The best part of this championship links course runs in a low valley along the ocean.
Portsalon, t (074) 59459. This course runs above the beautiful Ballymastocker Bay.
Otway, near Rathmullan, t (074) 58319. A fun 9-hole course on the edge of the Swilly.

Outdoor Activity Centres
Gartan Outdoor Education Centre, Churchill, near Letterkenny, t (074) 37032, f (074) 37254. Canoeing, rock climbing, windsurfing.

Pony-trekking
Dunfanaghy Riding Stables, Arnold's Hotel, Dunfanaghy, t (074) 36208.
Tirconaill Stables, Kilmacrennan, t (074) 39252.
Golden Sands Equestrian Centre, Rathmullan, t (074) 58124.
Inishfree Equestrian Centre, Atlantic View, Braade, Kincasslagh, near Letterkenny, t (075) 48226.
Black Horse Stables, Cashelshannaghan, Letterkenny, t (074) 51327.
Finn Farm Hostel and Trekking Centre, Cappry, Ballybofey, t (074) 32261.

Walking
Hill-walking is good on **Muckish** and **Errigal**. Details about walking the **Ulster Way** can be obtained from the Planning Department, DCC, Lifford, or the Long-distance Walking Route Committee, Cospair, 11th floor, Hawkings House, Dublin 2. Walking on the Ulster Way

has to be well-organized as the landowners must be asked for permission first. Walk with a ranger or by yourself on **Glenveagh Estate**; or take walking holidays organized by *Oideas Gael*, Glencolmcille, **t** (073) 30248, **f** (073) 30348, *oidsgael@iol.ie*. County Donegal now has **mountain rescue teams** based at Gortahork, Gweedore and Falcarragh; in emergencies **t** 999.

Water Sports

Laurence Strain, Forguar, Millford, **t** 9074) 53686. For deep-sea diving.

Where to Stay

Greene's Hostel, Cornmare Road, Dunglow, **t** (075) 21943 *(inexpensive)*. Youth hostel.

Viking House Hotel, Belcruit, Kincasslagh, **t/f** (075) 43295 *(moderate)*. Modern hotel owned by singer Daniel O'Donnell. A la carte and children's meals available.

Glen Hotel, Aranmore Island, **t** (075) 20505 *(moderate)*. Family-run, by the sea and friendly. A la carte and children's meals available. Irish spoken.

Screagan Iolair **Hostel**, Crolly, Near Gweedore, **t** (075) 48593 *(inexpensive)*. Remote hostel, but with free pick-up service from the N56.

Errigal Youth Hostel, Dunlewy, Gweedore, **t** (075) 31180, *mailbox@anoige.ie* *(inexpensive)*. Rated by the tourist board.

Bunbeg House, The Harbour, Bunbeg, **t** (075) 31305 *(inexpensive)*. Guesthouse with restaurant and tea rooms, overlooking Bunbeg harbour.

Teach Campbell, Magheraclogher, Derrybeg, **t** (075) 31545 *(inexpensive)*. In the middle of the *Gaeltacht*, a modern house set by the pounding Atlantic. Excellent home cooking.

Ostan Thoraigh **Hotel**, Tory Island, **t/f** (074) 35920 *(moderate)*. Cosy hotel on this wonderful island. A la carte meals available.

Grace Duffy, East Town, Tory Island, **t** (074) 35136 *(inexpensive)*.

Radharc na Mara **Hostel**, Tory Island, **t** (074) 65145 *(inexpensive)*. Youth hostel.

Shandon Hotel, Marble Hill Strand, Port-na-Blagh, near Dunfanaghy, **t** (074) 36137 *(moderate)*. Large family hotel with leisure centre and fine food.

Arnold's Hotel, Dunfanaghy, **t** (074) 36208, *arnoldshotel@eircom.net* *(moderate)*. This is a fine, old-fashioned hotel, set in a pretty village overlooking Sheep Haven.

Corcreggan Mill Hostel, Dunfanaghy, **t** (074) 36507/36409, **f** (074) 36902 *(inexpensive)*. Basic hostel in a renovated mill and simulated railway station, 1¼ miles (2km) out of town. There is also an organic garden.

Baileant Sleibhe, Downings, **t** (074) 55661 *(inexpensive)*. One of the rooms here boasts a four-poster bed; contact Grania O'Neill.

Tra na Rosann, Downings, **t** (074) 55374 *(inexpensive)*. An Oige youth hostel.

Croaghross Cottage, Portsalon, **t/f** (074) 59548, *www.croaghross.com*, *jkdeane@croaghross.com* *(moderate–inexpensive)*. Elegant, modern country house overlooking Ballymastocka Strand. Six rooms; 1 en suite suitable for the disabled. Good cooking. Also a self-catering holiday cottage. Contact John and Kay Deane.

Fort Royal Hotel, Rathmullan, **t** (074) 58100, **f** (074) 58103, *www.fortroyalhotel.com* *(luxury)*. Another fine period house, with more of a family atmosphere to it.

Rathmullan House Hotel, Rathmullan, **t** (074) 58188, **f** (074) 58200, *www.rathmullanhouse. com* *(luxury)*. 18th-century country house set on the edge of Lough Swilly. Beautiful gardens and excellent food in the dining room. Very cosy bar with a turf fire, a heated swimming-pool and a sandy beach.

Pier Hotel, Rathmullan, **t** (074) 58115 *(inexpensive)*. A favourite with the locals and foreign fishermen, there is plenty of atmosphere in this small family hotel. A la carte and children's meals available.

Frewin, Letterkenny Road, Ramelton, **t** (074) 51246, *www.accommodationdonegal.net*, *flaxmill@indigo.ie* *(moderate)*. This luxurious Victorian stone manor house was once a rectory. The elegant bedrooms have large bathrooms and woodland views. Dinner available by arrangement.

Ardeen, Ramelton, **t/f** (074) 51243 *(inexpensive)*. Comfortable, friendly house; contact Mrs Campbell.

House on the Mall, The Mall, Ramelton, **t** (074) 51255, *m_bgallagher@yahoo.com* *(inexpensive)*. Period home overlooking the River Lennon. Vegan breakfasts available.

Castle Grove Country House, Castlegrove, Letterkenny, t (074) 51118, f (074) 51384 (*expensive*). Marvellous Georgian house in wooded grounds overlooking Lough Swilly. Well-appointed rooms and good food.

Gortfad, Castlefinn, Lifford, t (074) 46135 (*inexpensive*). Lovely old farmhouse which is full of antiques, with lovely food. Contact Mrs Taylor.

Finn Farm Hostel, near Ballybofey, t (074) 32261 (*inexpensive*). Well-run and clean.

Eating Out

Danny Minnies, Teach Killindarra, Annagry, t (075) 48201 (*moderate*). Near Dunglow. Fish platters and à la carte.

Lobster Pot, Burtonport, t (075) 42012 (*inexpensive*). Seafood.

Bunbeg House, The Harbour, Bunbeg, t (075) 31305 (*moderate*). Cosy and family-run; healthy snacks and simple vegetarian meals, plus heartier food. Also has accommodation.

Collins Bar and Restaurant, Main Street, Dunfanaghy, t (074) 36205 (*moderate*).

Danann's Restaurant, Main Street, Dunfanaghy, t (074) 36150 (*moderate*). Seafood a speciality.

Dunfanaghy Workhouse, Dunfanaghy, t (074) 36540 (*inexpensive*). Coffee shop that's a wine bar in the evening, with traditional music. *Seasonal*.

Rathmullan House Hotel, Rathmullan, t (074) 58115 (*expensive*). Fresh, original cooking with vegetables from the walled garden. Sunday lunch is good value.

An Bonnán Buí, Pier Road, Rathmullan, t (074) 58453 (*moderate*). Small bistro; excellent food with a South American flavour.

Pier Hotel, Rathmullan, t (074) 58188 (*moderate*).

Mirabeau Steak House, Ramelton, t (075) 51138 (*moderate*). Georgian town house with unpretentious cooking.

Bakersville, Church Lane, Letterkenny, t (074) 21887 (*inexpensive*). Yummy croissants, cakes, bread and sandwiches.

Galfees Restaurant, The Courtyard, Letterkenny, t (074) 27173 (*inexpensive*). Good, with a cheaper menu during the day and early evening.

The Silver Tassie Hotel, Ramelton Road, Letterkenny, t (074) 25619, *silvertassie@ eircom.net* (*moderate*). Good value, with large helpings; cheap lunches.

Pat's Pizza, Market Square, Letterkenny, t (074) 24901 (*inexpensive*). Cheap and good.

Castlegrove Country House Hotel, Ramelton Road, near Letterkenny, t (074) 51118 (*expensive*). First-rate cooking.

Cavanacor Tea Room, Rossgier, Lifford, t (074) 41143 (*inexpensive*). Home-made scones.

Jackson's Hotel, Ballybofey, t (074) 31021 (*moderate*). Excellent salmon and ham. Also does good bar lunches.

Kee's Hotel, Stanorlar, Ballybofey, t (074) 31018 (*moderate*). Wholesome food, good service and cheaper bar food.

China Tower, Main Street, Ballybofey, t (074) 31468 (*inexpensive*). Chinese and European.

Entertainment and Nightlife

Live Music

Look in the local newspapers for traditional and popular music sessions, which change venue all the time. *Ceili* (traditional) music can be heard in the pubs of Falcarragh.

An Teach Ceoil, Fintown.

Leo's Tavern, Crolly (signposted *Croichsli*). Famous for its traditional music; various members of Clannad learnt their skills here.

Lakeside Centre, Dunlewy, t (075) 31699.

Tábhairne Hudi Beag, Bunbeg, t (075) 31016.

Dunfanaghy Workhouse, Dunfanaghy, t (074) 36540. Summer only.

The Bridge Bar, Ramelton, t (074) 51119.

Central Bar, Main Street, Letterkenny, t (074) 24088.

Mount Errigal Hotel, Ballyraine, Letterkenny, t (074) 22700. Venue for dances and music.

Ionad Cois Locha, Dunlewey, t (075) 31699. Traditional music sessions, June–Aug.

Theatre and Cinema

An Grianan Theatre, Port Road, Letterkenny, t (074) 20777.

Century Cinemas, Leckview Lane, Pearse Road, Letterkenny, t (074) 25050.

Balor Theatre, Ballybofey, t (074) 31840.

through the hilly country, and the beaches are lovely. If you make your way to Burtonport, an attractive fishing port, there is a regular ferry to **Aranmore Island**. You can have a good day's exploration of the island: there is good cliff scenery in the northwest, and it has a rainbow trout lake, Lough Shure. **Cruit Island** can be reached from the mainland by a connecting bridge. From here you can look out at Owey Island, and across at Gola Island with their deserted cottages. Despite the difficulties the islanders had to face, such as hard weather, no services and bureaucratic indifference to their needs, most of them did not want to leave their homes, and many return for the summer or for fishing. Several cottages are being restored as holiday homes. Boat hire must be negotiated with the local fishermen; none of them likes to be tied down to taking people out on a regular basis. Try the pubs and ask around. **Bunbeg** has an attractive 19th-century harbour and, close by at **Carrickfinn**, is Donegal airport, with daily flights to Glasgow and Dublin. The locals speak Irish and it is a favourite area for Irish summer schools. Further north, past Bloody Foreland, in the heart of the *Gaeltacht* is **Gortahork** ('Garden of Oats'), a small town on one arm of Ballyness Bay. It has a great strand which curves out into the sea, nearly locking the shallow bay in from the ocean. If you are here in the evening you can see cattle fording the waters back to the home farms. You might visit **Teach Mhici Mac Gabhann** (*t (074) 35555*), a 17th-century thatched cottage that was the birthplace of author Mickey McGowan.

Errigal and Muckish Mountains

Looking inland from Gortahork you cannot help but notice the glorious outlines of the mountains. Errigal is cone-shaped, and Aghla More and Aghla Beg form a spaced double peak. Muckish means 'pig's back' in Irish, and you will see it is aptly named. You can approach these mountains from this angle, or you could take the road from Bunbeg, past the secret **Dunlewy Lough**, overlooked by a roofless white church. The **Ionad Cois Locha**, or Lakeside Centre, at Dunlewey (*open Easter–Oct, Mon–Fri 10–6, Sun 11–7; t (075) 31699*) has a fine craft shop and tea room, a farm museum, animals and demonstrations in carding, spinning and weaving wool. You can also go on a story-telling trip on the lough, surrounded by its beautiful glens. Hidden behind this is the **Poisoned Glen**, so called either because the water in the lough is unfit to drink because of certain poisonous plants at the water's edge, or, so another story goes, because of the name some French travellers gave it, having caught some fish there. The hill and mountain climbs in this part are quite strenuous, but if you are fit you can tackle them.

Climb **Errigal** from the roadside, and after about an hour you will reach a narrow ridge of 2,400ft (731m), from which you will see Dunlewy Lough on one side and Altan Lough on the other side. Climb **Muckish** from the Gap or the western end. If you go straight for it from the Falcarragh side you may find yourself going up by the old mine-works, for the mountain was worked for its mica, to be used in glass-making; this is rather a dangerous but interesting ascent. The people who lived in the cottages in these lonely sheep glens used to weave Donegal tweed in the evenings, and pass the time singing and composing poetry. The old weaver poets had a good phrase for Muckish, calling it 'an oul turf stack', and so it is: flat-topped with its outline broken only by the remains of a cross. Looking across to Tory, you will see a huge hole, which is supposed to have been made when St Columba threw his staff from the top of Muckish.

Tory Island

It's possible to catch a regular ferry to **Tory Island** either from the pier at Magheraroarty or from Downings. Bad weather often makes the 7-mile (11km) journey impossible in winter, but if you have time to go, this windswept and barren island is endlessly fascinating. On a sunny day Tory feels rather like a Greek island with its whitewashed cottages and bright blue and red doors.

The island has two villages, called East Town and West Town. **East Town** is laid out in the traditional *clochan* or family grouping pattern of settlement. Close to the shore in **West Town** is the remanants of St Colmcille's Early Christian monastery. Here you can see a decapitated round tower and a T-shaped cross, known as a Tau Cross. There is only one other in Ireland, which is displayed in the Burren Centre, County Clare. At the eastern end is **Balor's Fort**, a great rock sticking out into the sea. Balor was the god of darkness, with one eye in the middle of his forehead. Mythology says he was one of the Formorii leaders (*see* pp.81 and 84).

In the summer you can buy snacks at a tearoom and the café close to the island's only public bar. There is a small hotel, a hostel and several B&Bs. The population is about 130 and thriving with a school and simple Catholic church. The island has become well-known for its fishermen artists who mostly use house paints to create their naïve-style paintings of seascapes and birds. They have been promoted by the landscape artist and portrait painter Derek Hill, whose house and collection of pictures is open to the public at the Glebe Gallery, Churchill (see p.490). You can buy their work at a small exhibition gallery on the island, although some of the more famous island painters exhibit and sell in Belfast and London.

Falcarragh to Doe Castle

Back to the coast between Falcarragh and Dunfanaghy is the great granite promontory of **Horn Head**. From a Falcarragh viewpoint it does indeed look like a horn or rock. You can do a complete circuit by taking the little road signposted 'Horn Head Coastal Drive' by the bridge at the top of the main street in **Dunfanaghy**, an attractive village overlooking Sheep Haven, which is experiencing a rash of building as moneyed folk from Northern Ireland build new holiday homes. The road leads you past old **Hornhead House** (*not open to the public*), which was drowned by sand when the bent grass was cut, and then climbs around the rocky farms, giving you dazzling views across Sheep Haven to Melmore Head in the east and back, towards Bloody Foreland Head. The road passes a 1940s military lookout post, and from here it is possible to walk to the **Little Horn**, a magnificent cliff which plunges down into the sea. From here there is a good walk ahead of you to an old tower, which takes about 40 minutes – you will need waterproof boots. You can peer over the 300ft (91m) cliff to see if the puffin population is in residence. There are also some caves and blow holes.

Dunfanaghy itself has a couple of good family hotels and, on the outskirts, the **Workhouse Heritage Centre and Art Gallery** (*open Mar–Oct, Mon–Fri 10–5 weekends 12–5; adm; t (074) 36540*) tells the famine story and exhibits local artists' work.

Sheep Haven is a complicated indentation with beautiful golden sands and a wooded shore. **Marblehill**, with its special provision for caravans, is a favourite place for holidaymakers. The mystic poet-politician George (A. E.) Russell used to stay here in **Marblehill House**. It is possible to rent apartments in the house and stableyard which overlooks the marvellous long curving beach.

Further on, the **Forest of Ards** provides some scenic walks and splendid views. At **Creeslough** you can admire another modern church designed by Liam McCormick. Its shape echoes the view of Muckish that you have from there. Otherwise it's a busy village with good shopping and pubs. On the road to **Carrigart** is one of the most romantic castles in Ireland: **Doe Castle**, set on the water's edge (*currently undergoing restoration*). It belonged to the MacSwineys (or MacSwynes), who came over from Scotland in the 15th century. They came to help the O'Donnells fight the encroaching Normans, and the constant small battles which took place with the O'Neill clan. They were part of the influx of mercenary soldiers known as 'gallowglasses' (*see* p.40). The castle was occupied right up until 1890. It had been taken by the English in 1650, and changed hands several times. In 1798 General George Vaughan Harte purchased it; he had been a hero in the Indian Wars, and his initials are carved over the main door. Scramble up the defensive walls for a superb view: overlooking Sheep Haven on one side, and on the other, the pretty bridge and waterfall of Duntally.

Downings to Portsalon

To get to the **Rosguill Peninsula** you cross a neck of sand similar to the causeway at Horn Head, and arrive at **Downings**. This fishing village is in the holidaymakers' zone of **Rosapenna**, a long-established resort with a good golf course and harbour. You can sail out to the islands of Tory and Inishbofin from Downings; ask about boats in the local post office down by the harbour. Very good tweed is made in this area; try McNutt's shop above the harbour. The beach beside the golf course is huge and unspoilt, and is ideal for a long walk and a swim, if you are hardy. The coastal ciruit (R245) leads to the spectacular **Atlantic Drive**. A branch road off this takes you past the **Tra Na Rossan Youth Hostel**, the only house designed by Lutyens in Ulster, and up to the wilder beaches of **Melmore Head**. There are several beaches along this road.

Leaving **Carrigart**, another centre for local crafts, the loughside road takes you down to Mulroy Bay, a narrow-necked lough bordered by the Fanad Peninsula on the opposite side and strewn with wooded islands. Behind Carrigart rises the Salt Mountain. A little moor-bound road crosses this range and comes out near Cranford. High in these mountains is the deepest lough in Ireland, **Lough Salt**. To take advantage of the panorama you should go up to the lough from the Letterkenny–Creeslough road (N56) and look out to the bays stretching from Horn Head to Fanad.

Down the road is **Millford**, a pretty town on a hill near some good fishing at Lough Fern. From Millford you can explore the **Fanad Peninsula** on the old road, which takes you past the Knockalla range by Carrowkeel and into the hidden reaches of **Mulroy**

Bay, by Tawny. In this secluded land there survives a very idiosyncratic Gaelic – although it was not untouched by the settlements of the 17th century. Even in their isolation, the Irish and the Scottish settlers remained distinct. At the far eastern point you can see Fanad Lighthouse, which guards the entrance of Lough Swilly and looks across to the Inishowen hills.

The tiny village of **Portsalon** is beautifully situated over **Ballymastocker Bay**, an immense curve of strand. Like all the settlements on the Swilly, it is curiously linked to the opposite view on Inishowen by the water in its landscape, in a way reminiscent of the Greek idea of the sea being a bridge. Rita's Bar, with its blazing fire, is a famous place to retire to after a walk along the beach. The golf course here is well worth playing, and the views are wonderful, although Portsalon is being spoilt by a profusion of holiday houses and caravans. Just a little way north, along the pretty road to Fanad Head, is the garden of **Ballydaheen** (*open May–Sept, Thurs and Sat 10–3; adm; t (074) 59091*). Protected by sheltering belts of trees, the garden's various 'rooms' and styles have flourished, and the views out to the Swilly are lovely. A planted walk leads down to The Seven Arches, a series of interconnecting caves on a tiny rocky beach. The house at the centre of the garden is Japanese in inspiration, and some of the planting and design reflects this.

Rathmullan to Newmills

A terrific coastal drive, which joins the R247, has been built with fabulous views over Lough Swilly and the Urris Hills. This brings you to Rathmullan, nestling in a sheltered plain which borders the Swilly as far as Letterkenny. The whole of **Lough Swilly** has played an important role in many of history's famous episodes. It is deep enough to accommodate modern war-fleets, as it did in the First World War. It has also been the departure route for the Gaelic aristocracy: in 1607 the Earls of Tirconnell and Tyrone took their leave for France from here. Lough Swilly has been called 'the Lake of the Shadows', an apt enough description, although from the Irish it means 'Lake of Eyes' or 'Eddies' (*Loch Suilagh*).

Rathmullan ('Maolán's Ring-fort') is a charming town with sandy beaches and lovely views across Lough Swilly. There are often fishing boats moored here as well as leisure craft, and, in the summer, little boys dive off the barnacled sides of the pier. It is, however, also being rapidly spoilt with tightly packed holiday houses, built close to the beach. Kinnagoe Bay, which carries on from Rathmullan Beach, is losing its charm, and the Blue Flag status of the beach has been lost because of water pollution.

The ruined **Carmelite friary** in the town has a romantic air that is borne out by the story behind it. In 1587 Red Hugh O'Donnell was staying in a castle here owned by the MacSwiney clan from Fanad. A wine merchant's ship happened to be lying in the bay, and the reputation of its cargo enticed the young reveller onto the ship. Treachery became apparent as the ship slipped its mooring and carried young O'Donnell off to Dublin Castle, a prisoner of Queen Elizabeth I. He was a great hostage to have captured, for his father was the Lord of Tirconnell, the powerful Sir Hugh O'Donnell, and the son could be used to keep him loyal to the English. More information is available from the excellent **Flight of the Earls Heritage Centre** (*open Easter–mid Sept, daily; adm; t (074) 58178*), in the Martello tower by the pier.

One of the most lovely routes in Ireland is the road between Rathmullan and its neighbour, **Ramelton**. It is often spelt on maps as Rathmelton, which translates as 'Mealtan's Fort', but the town you will see is a relatively unspoilt Plantation town built by the Stewart family, one of the so-called undertakers of the Plantation (meaning that they undertook to supply fighting men and build fortified dwellings to subdue and keep the 'wild' Irish at bay). It developed as a prosperous market town, with goods coming up the Lennon estuary from as far away as Tory Island. Ramelton was nearly self-sufficient in the 18th-century, with locally made whiskey, linen and leather goods and other small industries, and the Ramelton merchants built themselves fine houses in the Mall. (Letterkenny stole a march on the town fathers when the railway came, and now, it is the boom town.) The town is famous for its annual **festival** in July, with its cheerful floats and Queen of the Lennon competition, and for its **pantomime** in February. It is also famous for its thriving bottling industry and a soft drink of cloying sweetness, called McDaid's Football Special. The bottling plant, which is in a fine 19th-century warehouse overlooking the River Lennon, was used for a recent film, *The Hanging Gale*, set in famine times. The foundations of the building date back to the original O'Donnell Castle. **The House on the Brae**, on the Tank road, has been restored by the local Georgian Society. It is sometimes used for temporary art exhibitions. American Presbyterians will be interested in the old **Meeting House** in the Back Lane which is early-18th-century. It was here that the Reverend Francis Makemie (1658–1708) used to worship. He was ordained in 1682 and emigrated to America where he founded the first Presbytery in 1706. It has been restored and houses temporary exhibitions, Donegal's **Genealogy Centre** and a library.

Letterkenny is a thriving town, with factories on the outskirts and new housing enclaves, yet it still manages to maintain a country town appearance, with one long main street that loops round into the Swilly Valley. You can use this town as a centre for expeditions east and west. The **Donegal County Museum** on the High Road (*open Mon–Fri 10–4.30, Sat 1–4.30; t (074) 24613*) has a permanent collection of artefacts from early history and folk life, as well as being a venue for travelling exhibitions. In **Newmills**, 6km west of Letterkenny, an old **Corn and Flax Mill** has been restored (*open mid June–Sept, daily 10–6.30; adm; t (074) 25115*), with a visitor centre and a riverside walk to a scutcher's cottage and forge.

Glenveagh, Churchill and Kilmacrennan

If you go through Letterkenny up the Swilly Valley you reach the countryside where St Columba spent his first years. St Columba was the great Irish missionary who founded a church at Iona. He was born in about AD 521 on a height overlooking the two Gartan Loughs. A large cross just on Glenveagh Estate marks the spot. Gartan Clay, which can only be lifted by a family who claim descent from the followers of Columba, has powerful protective properties; soldiers fighting in the First World War carried it. You should follow the road around the lough; and if you take one of the forest trails on the Churchill side, a glorious prospect awaits you. The long glen which begins at Doochary on the west coast penetrates this far along the Derryveagh Mountains and into the scenic Glenveagh, parallel to the Valley of Gartan.

Glenveagh National Park (*Glenveagh*: 'Valley of the Birch'), west of Churchill, is beautiful and isolated with a 19th-century fairy-tale castle outlined against the mountains on the loughside (*open Easter–Oct, daily 10–6, closed Fri Oct–Nov; last adm 5.15pm; restaurant, tearooms and visitor centre; adm*; **t** *(074) 37088*). The gardens here have been developed by Henry McIlhenny, a millionaire whose grandparents came from these parts, and a visit is recommended. It would be difficult to find another such garden which combines the exotic and natural with such ease. Henry McIlhenny gave the wild, heathery acres of Glenveagh to be used as a National Park. Deer roam the glen and peregrine falcons nest in the rocky ledges.

Close by in **Churchill** itself, the artist Derek Hill has given his house and art possessions to the nation. It is signposted from the village and is known as **Glebe House** (*open May–Sept, daily except Fri 11–6.30; adm*; **t** *(074) 37071*). This plain Georgian house is packed with exquisite and curious *objets d'art*. The gallery's fine international collection includes paintings by Jack B. Yeats, Bonnard, Kokoschka, Basil Blackshaw, Annigoni and Victor Passmore. The gardens are beautifully laid out with shrubs and trees down to the lough's edge. It would be a great pity to miss Glenveagh, St Columb's and the Glebe Gallery, so make it a full day's outing. (If you feel that this may effect a surfeit of castles, galleries and gardens, nevertheless, make sure you tour Glenveagh.) Close to Churchill is the **Colmcille Heritage Centre**, beside the Gartan Outdoor Education Centre, which has a very informative display on days gone by.

On the way back from Glenveagh to Letterkenny you pass through **Kilmacrennan** ('Church of the Son of Enan'), named after one of St Columba's nephews. There are some ruins of a 15th-century friary, but the fame of the place rests on the claim that it was here that Columba received his education. You can have tea at the traditional thatched cottage of **Lurgyvale** with its displays of old rural implements. Near here, the Princes of Tirconnell were inaugurated, at **Doon Rock**, about 2 miles (3.2km) on the road to Creeslough. At the curious **Doon Well**, those hopeful of being cured have left tokens; most of them are now rags, although there is a story that a visiting film star left her lipstick.

Raphoe, Lifford and Environs

If you are travelling east from Letterkenny bound for the North, you will pass through the more prosperous midlands of Donegal, whose centre is south of here in **Raphoe**, an ancient town with a venerable cathedral, ruined Bishop's Palace and a pretty village green. Your fellow passengers on the road will probably be bound for the mart, the key of most Irish farmers' lives, and another indication of the importance of Raphoe. St Adomnan who lived in the 7th century founded an early monastery here. He was an O'Donnell like his ancestor St Columba. He wrote a life of Columba which reveals a lot about early Christian society – at one synod they passed a law exempting women from regular military service. At **Beltany**, between Raphoe and Lifford, just beyond the River Deele, is a stone circle which has some kind of mystical alignment. Archaeologists who examined the site in 1921 suggested the building had an astronomical purpose because the standing stone in the southwest is an almost perfect equilateral triangle. Its circumference measures 450ft (140m). There are 64 out of a possible 80 stones still standing, and a pleasant view from the top.

Lifford is the administrative centre of the county. The 18th-century courthouse with its **Seat of Power Visitor Centre** (*open Mon– Sat 10–6, Sun 2–6; t (074) 41733*) is attractive. It is open to the public and houses a genealogical centre, a café and a clan centre, which traces the importance of Lifford and the Plantation periods and the role of the dominant clans, including the O'Donnell princes, in the history of Donegal. If you find it open, go inside the **Clonleigh Parish Church** in the middle of the town. Here in an attitude of prayer are the Jacobean stone figures of Sir Richard Hansard and his wife, who gave money for the church to be built.

Outside Lifford, just off the Letterkenny Road at **Ballindrait**, is **Cavanacor Historic House and Craft Centre** (*open Easter–Sept, Tues–Sun 12–6; other times by appointment; pottery studio open all year; adm; t (074) 411 43*). This 17th-century house, with its fortified yard, was the ancestral home of James Knox Polk, the 11th President of the USA. The house contains late-17th- and 18th-century furniture, and it is possible to tour some rooms and the small museum. Its exhibits are associated with the American Connection and with the historic visit of James II, who dined under the sycamore at the front of the house during the seige of Derry in 1689. The home-made teas are splendid and you may browse among the attractive crafts, pottery and watercolour paintings. Near Ballybofey you will find the **Isaac Butt Heritage Centre** in Cloghan (*opening hours erratic, so call in advance; t (074) 33108*), which has a small exhibition of local life and an old school, restored to reflect the period in which Isaac Butt, the founder of the Home Rule movement, lived.

The Inishowen Peninsula

Inishowen (*Inis Eoghain*: 'Eoghain's Island') reaches out to the Atlantic between Loughs Swilly and Foyle, a kingdom of its own. As its name conveys, it forms a different territory to the rest of Donegal, which is part of Tirconnell. This is O'Doherty country. After leaving Letterkenny you pass through the rolling plains round Manorcunningham and Newtowncunningham to the neck of the peninsula at **Burt**. An unforgettable sight of this unexplored, almost islanded land can be obtained from the **Grianán of Aileach** (or Aíligh), an ancient stone hill-fort. Turn right by an unusually roofed modern Catholic church, another of Liam McCormick's, and climb the unclassified mountain road which gives you views onto the Swilly. Why the Grianan of Aileach is not as well known as Tara in County Meath, considering its spectacular position and its associations, must be one of the curious twists in the recording of history. Besides the circular stone fort and its terraces, there are three stone and earth ramparts, and underneath the Hill of Aileach there are said to be underground passages connecting the hill-top with Scalp Mountain, which overlooks the village of

Tourist Information

Buncrana: t (077) 62600; *open June–Aug, Mon–Sat.*
Inishowen: Carndonagh, **t** (077) 74933, *info@visitinishowen.com; open all year Mon–Fri, mid June–Aug daily.*

Shopping

Crafts
Curious Glass, Burt, **t** (077) 68633. Glassware.
Mary Barr, Main Street, Buncrana.
Crana Artists Network, Tullyarvan Mill, Buncrana, **t** (077) 61613.

Tweeds and Knitwear
Irish Knitting Centre, Lisfannon, Buncrana, **t** (077) 62365. Traces the history of traditional patterns.

Sports and Activities

Beaches
There is a blue flag beach at **Culdaff.**

Fishing
There are many salmon and trout rivers and loughs in Donegal – the Crana River is renowned for its salmon. **Sea-fishing** is also available on Inishowen.
Northern Regional Fisheries Board, t (072) 51435.
Loughs Agency, t (048) 8166 2267.

Inishowen Boating Co, Malin, **t** (077) 70605, **f** (077) 70764. For sea angling charters.

Golf
North West Golf Club, Fahan, **t** (074) 61027, **f** (077) 63284. A gentle, rolling, sandy course overlooking the Swilly.
Ballyliffin, Inishowen, **t** (077) 76119, **f** (077) 76672, *ballyliffin@eircom.net.* The most northerly golf club in Ireland, with lovely views over the Atlantic; 18 holes.

Indoor Leisure Centres
Leisureland, Redcastle, **t** (077) 82306.

Pony-trekking
Inch Island Stables, t (077) 60335.
Lenamore Stables, Muff, **t** (077) 84022.

Walking
Hill-walking is available on **Scalp Mountain.** Contact the tourist office for details.
Oideas Gael, Glencolmcille, **t** (073) 30248, **f** (073) 30348, *oidsgael@iol.ie.* Walking holidays.

Where to Stay

Malin Hotel, Malin, Inishowen **t** (077) 70645, **f** (077) 70770 *(moderate).* Small but comfortable, family-run hotel.
Barracin, Malin Head, **t** (077) 70184 *(inexpensive).* On the untouched and beautiful Inishowen Peninsula, 4 miles (6.4km) from Malin village, this modern bungalow

Fahan, about 6 miles (7.6km) further down the peninsula. There is an old story that the sleeping heroes of the past lie within the hill, to be wakened at Ireland's hour of need. The fort dates from about 1700 BC and, according to the *Annals of the Four Masters*, it was the seat of power for the Northern O'Neill kings from the 5th to the 12th centuries. It was destroyed by their enemies in AD 675 and 1101. The fort guards all approaches, which is why it affords such good views over the Foyle and the Swilly. At the foot of the hill, in the disused church of Ireland, is the **Grianán of Aileach Visitor's Centre** (*open June–Aug, daily 10–6, Sept–May, 12–6; adm; t* (077) 68000, *f* (077) 68012), with a good lunch stop in its restaurant and some interesting exhibits.

Inch Island, signposted off the main Buncrana–Londonderry Road, is a beautiful place. At the crossroads by the local shop, take the right turn to **Inch Fort** and **Brown's Bay** and look across the limpid water to Fahan, or you might go for a swim.

overlooks the sea. There are lots of country pursuits and your hostess, Mrs Doyle, produces excellent home-cooked food.

Malin Head Hostel, Malin, t (077) 70309 (*inexpensive*). Clean and comfortable, with an organic garden and orchard available for visitor use.

Sandrock Holiday Hostel, Malin Head, t (077) 70289 (*inexpensive*). Overlooking strand; bunk beds in an en suite dormitory.

Greencastle Fort Guesthouse, Greencastle, Inishowen, t/f (077) 81279 (*moderate*). Napoleonic sea fort with a martello tower, and its original cannon positions. It has a bar and a seafood restaurant which overlooks the sea. Contact Mr and Mrs McGonagle.

Redcastle Hotel, Redcastle, Inishowen, t (077) 82073, f (077) 82214 (*expensive*). Heavy décor has rather ruined the charm of this old Plantation house. Lovely setting, however, and popular with the Northern Irish.

Self-catering

Mamore Cottages, Clonmany, t (077) 76710, f (071) 60360. Traditional Irish cottages with open fires. Sleep 7; €255–325 per week.

Rock Cottage, Goorey Rocks, Malin, t/f (077) 70612. Cottage which sleeps 2–4, from €153–250 per week.

Eating Out

Kealy's Seafood Restaurant, Greencastle, Inishowen, t (077) 81010 (*expensive*). Award-winning seafood from James Kealy. Lunches are more moderately-priced.

St John's Restaurant, Fahan, Inishowen, t (077) 60289 (*moderate*). Beautifully cooked seafood and vegetables, including their famous seafood pancakes; the owner, Reggie Ryan, is urbane and welcoming. You can be sure of a feeling of well-being in his comfortable Georgian house; a welcome spot in the mountain wildness.

The Corncrake, Malin Street, Carndonagh, Inishowen, t (077) 74534 (*moderate*). *Dinner only.*

McGrory's of Culdaff, Inishowen, t (077) 79104 (*inexpensive*). Bar food and traditional music Tues and Thurs. Accommodation available.

Old Church Restaurant, Grianan of Aileach Visitor's Centre, Burt, Inishowen, t (077) 68000 (*inexpensive*). Good value lunches and snacks in a converted church.

Entertainment and Nightlife

Live Music

Look in the local newspapers for traditional and popular music sessions, which change venue frequently.

Teach Ceoil, Ballyliffin, t (077) 76124. A house of music and traditional entertainment during July and August on Tues and Thurs evenings; contact Clement Sweeney.

McGrory's, Culdaff, t (077) 79104. Well-known music venue (and guest house); Tues and Thurs.

The Flough, Muff, t (077) 84024. Songs, dances, poems, home-baking. *Mainly in summer.*

There is an O'Doherty Clan Centre here, the **Doherty Research Centre** (*t (077) 63998*). **Fahan** is famous for its St Mura's Cross in the Church of Ireland graveyard. This 7th-century two-faced cross with mythological birds and ecclesiastical figures is all that remains of the rich Abbey of St Mura. Here in the rectory in 1848, looking across to Inch Top Hill, Cecil F. Alexander wrote 'There is a Green Hill Far Away'.

There is a beautiful beach with lovely views all around which stretches up to **Buncrana**, a standard seaside resort with the usual run of amusement arcades. The Crana River is noted for salmon fishing and there are some pretty walks which lead close to the dilapidated early 17th-century Buncrana Castle and the O'Doherty keep. Just outside Buncrana, at Lisfannon, on the Derry road, is the **Irish Knitting Centre** (*t (077) 62365*), which traces the history of traditional patterns. Also of interest is the restored **Tullyarvan Mill** in Buncrana (*t (077) 61613*), on the Crana River; it is the base for Artlink, a community art group, and provides a space for temporary art exhibitions and traditional music functions. It is to be found off the scenic coast route signposted 'Inis Eoghain 100'; the mill is signposted on the right after the bridge. Close by at Dunree is the **Fort Dunree Military Museum** (*open June–Sept, Mon–Sat 10–6, Sun 1–6; adm; t (074) 24613*), a restored coastal defence battery depicting 200 years of coastal and military history. It has a wonderful view and a fascinating account of Wolfe Tone's plans to land with French help and take Derry in 1798.

Buncrana to Muff

Take the R238 through the mountains to the spectacular **Mamore Gap**, and gaze back at the view of the Fanad Peninsula. There are plenty of good beaches on the way if you go the longer coastal road, such as **Linsfort** and **Dunree**. On the other side of the Gap, past **Clonmany**, are the beaches around the Isle of Doagh. This is unspoiled country, full of fuchsia hedges and little whitewashed cottages. At Clonmany you'll find the **Doagh Visitor Centre** (*open Easter–Oct; adm; t (077) 76493*), an outdoor museum of life as it was here in the 1870s. In the Church of Ireland graveyard at **Carndonagh** are some interesting monuments, including the Marigold Stone which has the same ornamentations as St Mura's Cross, and by the roadside opposite the church is one of the most far-famed crosses in Ireland, said to be the oldest low-relief cross in the country (AD 650). This richly decorated and well-preserved cross must have been erected by a prosperous and settled community in those far-off times. The most northerly village in Ireland, **Malin**, has a pretty green and has twice been named 'Ireland's tidiest town'. It is a good example of a well-preserved 17th-century Plantation village, with a fine church. Nearby is lovely **Five Fingers Strand**.

If you want to see the most northerly tip of Ireland, **Malin Head**, which will be familiar to those who listen to radio shipping forecasts, take a road passing extensive sand dunes and you will come to a pebbly cove where you can pick up semi-precious stones. The old signal tower at Banba's Crown, at the very tip of Malin Head, was the last sight of Ireland for many of the emigrants as they left by ship. From Malin Head you can see lighthouse islands. From here to Glengad Head are cliffs rising to over 800ft (246m). To the east of **Culdaff** are some fine sandy beaches.

All this area is fine walking country; the cliff scenery is interspersed with great stretches of sandhills. You can choose whether to walk around Malin Head itself, or southwards towards **Inishowen Head**. Or visit yet another cross, 2 miles (3.2km) to the south of Culdaff in **Clonca**. This impressive shaft, called **St Boden's Cross**, is almost 12ft (4m) in height and is carved with a scene depicting the miracle of the loaves and the fishes. On the road from Culdaff to Moville, in **Carrowblagh**, is an example of an ancient **sweat-house** – the Irish form of a sauna. The almost enclosed room was heated like an oven, and, having sweated thoroughly, you were next immersed in cold water. This was said to be the cure for aching bones and temporary madness.

Greencastle is a beach resort with the remains of a 14th-century castle built in 1305 by Richard de Burgh, the Red Earl of Ulster, who needed it as a strategic base from which to try and dominate the O'Donnells of Tirconnell (most of Donegal) and the

O'Dohertys of Inishowen. The **Maritime Museum** (*open June–Sept daily 10–6; adm; t (077) 81036*) in the old coastguard's house is full of interest, with a room on the Armada and Emigration. Further down the coast you come to **Moville**, formerly a point of departure for many emigrants to the New World. It is now a leisure resort with a well-planted green, lined with seats from which you can comfortably gaze at the sea or have a picnic.

At **Cooley**, 1½ miles (3km) to the northwest, is a 9ft-high (3m) cross and the remains of a chapel with a corbelled stone roof. The area between Moville and Muff has many planter castles. They are known as castles, but are actually Big Houses, and you get glimpses of them through the trees as you pass by. One of them, Redcastle, is now a luxury hotel; some would consider it ruined with all its modern embellishment. Behind them rise rather forbidding mountains, though if you venture on the mountain roads you come across lost *clochans* and megalithic monuments, where yellow raspberries cluster beneath the hedges in July.

County Cavan

Cavan is a dreamy, unspoilt county. It is completely landlocked, yet there are attractive stretches of water everywhere, scattered as it is with lakes and rivers abounding with fish. It is a favourite county for coarse fishermen, many of whom come over from England for the huge catches. For the city-dweller in search of quiet it is a perfect holiday place.

The countryside is pretty and interspersed with woods. The hills or *drumlins* left behind by a glacier in earlier times offer plenty in the way of wild glens. The highest mountain in the county is Cuilcagh, at 2,100ft (640m). On its southern slopes is the source of the great Shannon River, which flows out to the sea as far away as County Clare. Along the winding roads you will hardly meet a soul, for the population is only 53,000. Most people are farmers, and many offer bed and breakfast accommodation.

Cavan is an undiscovered county to those who are not in the angling league, and this is undeserved. The ancient history of the county lingers on in the form of charming, ruined castles and abbeys and mysterious stone monuments from the Bronze and Iron Ages. Being in the lakelands, there are a number of *crannog* sites and figures left over from pagan times. One of the most curious finds from west Cavan is the three-faced Corleck Head, a rare example of a pagan Trinity figure, which now resides in the National Museum in Dublin. Christianity percolated slowly through this lakeland maze, and even up to the 17th century some recorded devotions to saints had a pagan flavour. A principal shrine of the Celtic gods in Ireland was at Magh Sleacht near Ballyconnell, but there is nothing left of it now.

History

Cavan, as it is defined today, is a fairly young county, created in 1584 by the British Lord Deputy. Previously, it was part of the ancient Kingdom of Breffni, and its Gaelic

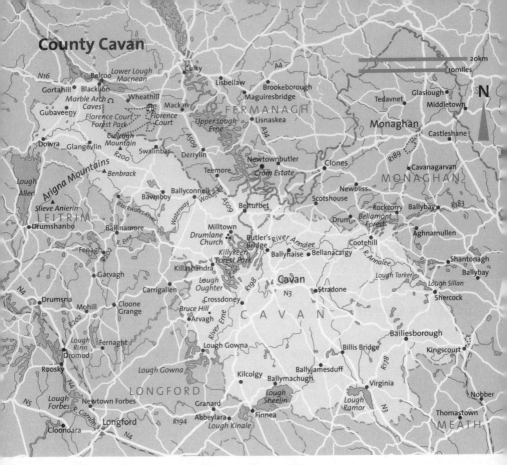

rulers were the O'Reillys. The O'Reillys managed to hold on to power until the division of the county amongst Scottish and English settlers in the 1600s.

In the 19th century the county suffered greatly from the famine and the consequent mass emigration. It did have a small linen industry, now defunct, as elsewhere in the North. Along with County Donegal and County Monaghan it is separated politically from the rest of Ulster. This happened in 1921 with the division of Ireland into the 26-county state and the continuing allegiance of the other six Ulster counties to Britain.

Cavan Town and Around

Cavan (*An Cabhan*: 'The Hollow'), the county town, is an inconspicuous place. It was once important as an O'Reilly stronghold in the ancient kingdom of East Breffni. Their castle, **Clough Oughter** (pronounced 'ooter') is a well-preserved example of an Irish circular tower castle and is situated about 3 miles (5km) outside Cavan on an island in Lough Oughter. You approach it from the Crossdoney–Killashandra road and the wooded splendour of Killykeen Forest Park. It is possible to get out to the island if you hire a boat. This 13th-century tower is built over a *crannog* and looks very

Getting There and Around

By Rail

There is no train service in County Cavan.

By Bus

Expressway buses stop in Cavan en route between Belfast, Enniskillen, Galway and Dublin. Small towns are served by local buses. Cavan Bus Depot, t (049) 433 1353.

By Bike

Fitz Hire, Bridge Street, Belturbet, t (049) 952 2866.

Festivals

March

Cavan Drama Festival.

May

County Cavan *Fleadh Cheoil*.

June

Festival of the Lakes, Killashandra, t (049) 433 4429. Music, dance, children's entertainment, powerboat racing and angling competitions.

Killinkere Whit Jamboree, Killinkere, t (049) 48102, or t 0863 112289. Car races, concerts and a busking competition.

Virginia Street Fair, t (049) 854 8299. Vintage cars, machinery, music.

July

Belturbet Festival of the Erne, t (049) 952 2781. Large family festival with water sports, music and heritage events. Held late July–early Aug.

August

Knockbride Vintage and Heritage Festival, Bailiesborough, t (042) 966 5282. Displays of vintage cars and machinery.

October

Cootehill Arts Festival, t (049) 555 2150. Music, arts and crafts, drama, literature.

Tourist Information

Cavan: Farnham Street, t (049) 433 1942, *www.cavantourism.com, cceb@tinet.ie*; open Mar–Oct.

Shopping

Crafts

Carraig Crafts, Mountnugent, t (049) 854 0179.

Celtic Crafts, Ballyconnell. *Open April–Oct Mon–Fri 10–6 Sun 2–6, Nov–Mar by request only.*

St Kilian's Heritage Centre Craft Shop, Mullagh, t (046) 42433.

Crystal

Cavan Crystal Factory, Dublin Rd, Cavan Town, t (049) 433 1800, *www.cavancrystaldesign. com, sales@cavancrystaldesign.com.* Factory tours Mon–Fri.

Delicacies

Back to Nature, Main Street, Cavan Town, t (049) 436 1019. Good picnic supplies are available from this health food shop.

Corleggy Farmhouse, Belturbet, t (049) 952 2219, *www.corleggy.com, corleggy@eircom.net.* Besides buying their delicious goats' cheese flavoured with herbs and peppers, you will also enjoy seeing this old-style farm where pigs wander about the yard, unlike the majority of porkers in Ireland.

Main Street, Kingscourt. Another farmhouse cheese is *Dun a Ró*, a Gouda-like cheese, which you'll find sold in the shops here.

romantic, viewed from the lakeside. Its history is more sinister. It was used as a prison by the Confederates in the 1641 rebellion, and Eoghan Roe O'Neill, the great leader of the Confederates, died here in 1649, poisoned, it is thought, by his Cromwellian opponents. North of Cavan Town, **Lough Oughter** is the name given to

Sports and Activities

Fishing

There is **coarse fishing** in most of Cavan's loughs. Particularly good are Loughs Oughter, Inchin, Gowna and Bunn. The Woodford and Annalee Rivers are also excellent. Look out for Hugh Cough's excellent book on coarse fishing in County Cavan.

Shannon Region Fisheries, t (049) 36144.
Northern Regional Fisheries Board, Corlesmore, Ballinagh, **t** (049) 433 7174.
International Fishing Centre, Loughdooley, Belturbet, **t** (049) 952 2616. Tackle and bait.
Butlersbridge Trout Anglers, Annagh Lake, Butlersbridge, **t** (049) 436 2110.

Golf

County Cavan Golf Club, Drumelis, **t** (049) 433 1283, **f** (049) 433 1541, *www.cavangolf.ie.*
Belturbet Golf Club, Redhills, **t** (049) 22287.
Slieve Russell Hotel, Ballyconnell, **t** (049) 952 6444, **f** (049) 952 6474, *www.quinnhotels. com.* Championship golf course.
Blacklion Golf Club, t (072) 53024.
Deer Park Lodge Hotel, Virginia, **t** (049) 47371. Golf available in the hotel grounds.

Pleasure Cruises

The opening of the **Shannon–Erne waterway** has been a boon for tourism, and no doubt more new restaurants and bars will appear.
Shannon–Erne Waterways, t (078) 44855.

Pony-trekking

Cavan Equestrian Centre, Shalom Stables, Lath, Cavan, **t** (049) 433 2017.
Redhills Equestrian, Killynure, Redhills, **t** (049) 435 5042.
Alan Kells, Castlehamilton Court, Killeshandra, **t** (049) 433 4432.

Steam Train Rides

Cavan and Leitrim Railway, t (078) 38599, *www.cavanandleitrimrailway.com,* *dromod@eircom.net.* Old-fashioned vintage train ride. *Runs Sept–June 10–2.30, July–Aug 10–5.30, Sun all year 1–5.30.*

Walking

The **Cavan Way** is a 15-mile (24km) marked trail which runs from Blacklion to Dowra and passes prehistoric monuments, a sweathouse near Legeelan and wonderful views. It also goes close to the Shannon Pot, the source of the Shannon (350yds/300m south of the trail). Information and leaflets from West Cavan Community Council, Blacklion, **t** (049) 433 1799, Tourism Ireland and on the useful website *www.irishwaymarkedways.ie.*

There are easier walks in **Killykeen Forest Park,** 2 miles (3km) north of Killashandra on the R201; at **Mulrick,** 1½ miles (2.5km) south-west of Lough Gowna village, on the edge of the lough; in **Dún a Ró Forest Park;** and at **Castle Lake,** a mile (1.6km) north of Bailiesborough on the R178.

Where to Stay

Lisnamandra Farmhouse, Crossdoney, just west of Cavan Town, **t** (049) 433 7196, **f** (049) 433 7111 *(inexpensive).* Ten minutes' drive from Lough Oughter, this award-winning traditional-style farmhouse has a very restful atmosphere, with comfortable rooms and home cooking from Mrs B. Neill.
Rockwood House, Cloverhill, Belturbet, **t** (047) 55351, **f** (047) 55373, *jbmac@eircom.net* *(moderate–inexpensive).* This house is a reconstruction of a rectory that stood here in the 1860s, and is surrounded by woodland and gardens.
Slieve Russell Hotel, Ballyconnell, **t** (049) 952 6444, **f** (049) 952 6474 *(luxury).* Built by a local millionaire, this hotel has marble columns, fountains and jacuzzis as well as a championship golf course.
Riverside House, Cootehill, **t** (049) 555 2150 *(inexpensive).* Old farmhouse overlooking

an entire region of small- to medium-sized lakes, an offshoot of the River Erne complex. This is a well known coarse fishing area. **Lough Inchin** is noted for pike fishing, though recently roach have been introduced. The **Killykeen Forest Park** (**t** *(049) 433 2541*) is a good access point to the loughs.

the tree-lined River Annalee. It has elegant, high ceilings and plasterwork and open fires in the main rooms. Your hostess, Una Smith, is an expert on all fishing matters, and there is a boat with engine available; she also cooks delicious five-course evening meals.

Cabra Castle Hotel, Kingscourt, t (042) 966 7030, f (042) 976 7039 (*luxury*). 15th-century pile with landscaped gardens and a golf course. Self-catering units available.

Virginia Park Hotel, Virginia, t (049) 854 6100, f (049) 854 7203, *www.bichotels.com/ parkhotel*, *virginiapark@eircom.net* (*luxury*). Attractive old hunting lodge beside Lough Ramor, built in 1750; with a modern 9-hole golf course.

St Kyran's, Dublin Road, Virginia, t (049) 854 7087 (*inexpensive*). Simple B&B in a lovely setting on the shore of Lough Ramor. Contact Mrs Bernie O'Reilly.

Sunnyside House, Lough Gowna, t (043) 83285 (*moderate*). A friendly, well-run B&B in what was, at the end of the 19th century, a doctor's residence. It has a rose, herb, fruit and vegetable garden, and is popular with fishing folk. Dinner available.

Self-catering

Cornacrea, Cavan, t (049) 433 2023. Nice stone house in the country, 3 miles outside Cavan Town. 4 bedrooms in two apartments; €210–230 per week, contact Doreen Clarke.

Killykeen Forest Chalets, Killykeen Forest Park, t (049) 433 2541, f (049) 436 1044, *www.coillte.ie*. Wooden chalets and log cabins in Killykeen Forest Park, €245–600 per week.

Eating Out

The Imperial, Main Street, Cavan Town, t (049) 73027/73029 (*moderate*). Roomy and comfortable, serves generous portions of good food on a daily menu, with steak a speciality. *Lunch 12–3, dinner 4–9.*

Kloisters Restaurant, Main Street, Cavan Town, t (049) 437 1485, f (049) 437 1486 (*moderate–inexpensive*). Good atmosphere and plentiful, flavoursome helpings; a wide menu choice, from seafood to pizza.

White Star, White Star, Main Street, Cavan Town, t (049) 433 1477 (*inexpensive*). Rustic, old-fashioned decor; tasty pub lunches only.

Casey's Steak Bar, Main Street, Ballinagh, t (049) 433 7105 (*moderate*). The best steaks in Ireland, according to some.

Derragarra Inn, Butler's Bridge, t (049) 433 1003 (*inexpensive*). Attractive pub by the river. Lots of seafood and traditional music on Fridays during the summer.

The Olde Post Inn, Cloverhill, t (047) 55555 (*moderate*). Renovated old post house with atmospheric gas lamps. The pork is always good, since the pigs are fed on the whey of Corleggy cheese.

MacNean Bistro, Blacklion, t (072) 53022 (*expensive–moderate*). Imaginative cooking such as fillet of ostrich with *rösti*; they mostly use locally grown organic produce. The desserts are highly lauded.

The Park Hotel, Virginia, t (049) 854 6100 (*moderate*). Imaginative and ambitious cooking.

Entertainment and Nightlife

Live Music

Louis Blessing's Pub, 92 Main Street, Cavan Town, t (049) 433 1138. Sometimes has jazz.

McGinnity's, Bridge Street, Cavan Town, t (049) 433 1236. Traditional music; a winner of the Regional Pub of the Year Award.

White Star, Main Street, Cavan Town, t (049) 433 1477. Traditional Irish music nights.

Ramor Theatre, Virginia, t (049) 854 7074.

White's Bar, Lochgowna, t (043) 83105. Occasionally they have traditional music.

There are some worthwhile diversions around Cavan, including a private folk museum called **The Pighouse Collection** (*call in advance for guided tour; adm;* t *(049) 433 7248*), a vast accumulation of clothing, tools, kitchenware, and the other necessities of Irish rural life, some of it going back 300 years; the name comes from the pigsty where they used to keep it all. It is located in Corr House, Cornafean, near Crossdoney (take the R198 west out of Cavan Town). On the road to Arvagh, continuing along the R198, is **Bruce Hill** (755ft/260m), which is worth climbing for the view. During the times of the Penal Laws, when Catholics were forbidden to build churches, Mass was celebrated here in the open air. If you like ornate cut glass you might take the opportunity to buy a bit of Cavan crystal from the factory shop on the Dublin Road (N3), on the outskirts of town. For those interested in prehistoric sites, a few miles out of Cavan on the R188 northwest to Blacklion on Shantemon Hill, off the Cootehill Road, are **Finn MacCool's Fingers**, standing stones within which the princes of Breffni, the O'Reillys, were crowned. (Many prehistoric standing stones are named after the heroes of Irish legend.) **Ballyhaise** is a pretty, neat village on the River Annalee, reached by an unclassified road off the R198 going north out of Cavan Town. It has a rather grand arcaded market hall. Nearby is **Ballyhaise House**, built in 1733 and designed by Richard Cassels, who also designed Leinster House in Dublin. It is worth asking to go around it (it is now an agricultural college) to see the lovely oval saloon and plasterwork. It is also worth stopping in **Butler's Bridge**, another pleasant village on the Annalee, to lunch at Derragarra Inn (*see* p.499). The fishing is reputed to be good here too.

North Cavan

Another lakeland town is **Belturbet** on the N3 north of Cavan. It is now a thriving angling and boating centre, and was once a depot for the traffic on the Ulster Canal, which might be somewhat revived now that the canal has been reopened. A boat trip along here is like driving on Irish roads fifty years ago, it is so unspoilt; you will barely even see a house. At **Milltown**, on the north end of the loughs, is a site associated with the 6th-century St Maodhóg; the site later became an Augustinian monastery, though today little remains but the ruined **Drumlane Church** and a truncated round tower. Look out for the faint carving, on the north side, of a cock and a hen. The church has a lovely Romanesque doorway. Going northwest along the N87 you reach **Ballyconnell**, which is now a stopping place on the Shannon–Erne waterway, set on Woodford River. The 17th-century Protestant church here has a carved stone with a human head which came from a medieval monastery. In the grounds of the church are the outlines of two diamond-shaped fortifications dating from the Williamite Wars. The village is a pleasant base for fishing or hill-walking. Three miles (5km) southwest at **Killycluggin** is a stone circle which once contained an ornamental phallic stone. You can see it on display at Cavan County Museum (*t (049) 854 4070, www.cavanmuseum.ie, ccmuseum@eircom.net*).

For walkers, 5 miles (8km) to the west on the N87 is the tiny hamlet of **Bawnboy**, which is on the way to some pretty glens and mountains. You can climb 1,148ft (350m) to **Glen Gap** between the peaks of Cuilcagh and Benbrack. For a panoramic view of the neighbouring counties, take the N87/R200 to Glangevlin (also known as Glengevlin), and go through Glen Gap to the summit of the Cuilcagh Mountains.

Blacklion, a small village on the Fermanagh border, is delightfully situated between Upper and Lower Lough MacNean in the limestone foothills of the Cuilcagh Mountains. It has a frontier post into Northern Ireland but, more importantly for walkers, from here you can walk up to **Lough Garvagh, Giant's Cave**, and **Giant's Leap**. These names refer to legendary figures whose origins are lost in the mists of time. For instance, nobody knows who built the fine *cashel* 3 miles (5km) away at Moneygashel Post Office near **Burren**, south of Blacklion. It consists of three beautifully built stone walls. The central *cashel* is 82ft (25m) in circumference and has a rampart 10ft (3m) thick, with internal and external stairways. Inside the south *cashel* is a beehive-shaped **sweat-house** – a kind of Irish sauna that was still popular a century ago. Burren was an important Neolithic centre, and if you have the time to seek them out there are numerous dolmens in the neighbourhood, including the aforementioned 'Giant's Cave', and a 'rocking stone'.

The **Cavan Way**, a signposted trail, passes prehistoric monuments, a sweat-house near Legeelan, and wonderful views (*see* 'Sports and Activities', p.498). It also goes close to the **Shannon Pot** (350yds/300m south of the trail), the 'eye', where an underground river surfaces to become the source of the mighty River Shannon. Just over the border from Blacklion in County Fermanagh are the famous **Marble Arch Caves** (*see* 'County Fermanagh', p.383). **Swanlinbar**, further to the southeast of this hilly country, is another frontier village. It was once known as the Harrogate of Ireland because of its sulphur baths. **Dowra**, at the western tip of Cavan, sits beside the Shannon at a point where the great river is still barely a stream; to the east of it you can inspect another long surviving section of the great ancient earthwork called the **Black Pig's Dyke** that stretches across much of northern Ireland.

Eastern Cavan: Cootehill to Ballyjamesduff

Cootehill, on the county border about 15 miles (24km) northeast of Cavan Town, is a market town named after the Coote family, who 'planted' the area with their followers in the 17th century. The Church of Ireland church at the end of its long main street is in the attractive planters' Gothic style. Nearby, to the north of the town in Bellamont Forest, is **Bellamont House**, built by Thomas Coote and designed by the famous Irish architect Sir Edward Lovett Pearce in 1730. It is a beautiful Palladian mansion which fell into decay and was lovingly restored by an Englishman. It has been claimed by an Australian descendant, but at the moment its future is uncertain and it is not open to the public. This is a great pity, since the interiors are spectacular.

The village next-door, **Shercock**, is rather pretty, with a fine plain Presbyterian meeting house set on the shores of **Lough Sillan** – a good lake for coarse fishing. This is a wooded and lake-studded country. Seven and a half miles (12km) away to the southeast is **Kingscourt**. Look in the Catholic church for the delightful stained-glass windows designed by the Dublin artist Evie Hone (1894–1955). Just over a mile (2km) away is **Dún a Ró Forest Park**, where you can picnic by the pretty Cabra River. There are planned walks and nature trails here. You might see a wild deer amongst the trees. It was the former demesne of the Pratts of Cabra – their castle home is now a hotel.

Beautifully situated on the edge of Lough Ramor is **Virginia**, a village founded in the reign of King James I but named after his aunt, Queen Elizabeth I. It is the most southerly of the Ulster Plantation villages. Dramatist Richard Brinsley Sheridan lived here, and so did the parents of the other famous Sheridan, General Philip Sheridan of the American Civil War. Although the Protestant population has dwindled since pre-Independence, the centrepiece of the village is still the Protestant **church**, which is approached down a straight avenue of clipped yews. There are some pretty, rusticated cottages in the main street. It is a very attractive and well-planned town, with graceful trees; and the shops have traditional painted signs. The lough is beautiful, and is full of little islands.

To the northwest is **Ballyjamesduff**, home of the **County Cavan Museum** (*open June–Oct, Tues–Sat 10–5 Sun 2–6; adm; t (049) 854 4070, f (049) 853 1384, www.cavan-museum.ie, ccmuseum@eircom.net*), in a magnificent 19th century building, with historical displays, medieval carvings, and some of the clutter from the Pighouse Collection. Ballyjamesduff was made famous by the song written by the humorous writer and singer Percy French in the early years of the 19th century. At one time French worked as Inspector of Drains with the Cavan County Council. His songs are beloved of Irish emigrant communities all over the world:

> *There are tones that are tender, and tones that are gruff,*
> *And whispering over the sea*
> *Come back, Paddy Reilly, to Ballyjamesduff,*
> *Come back, Paddy Reilly, to me.*

County Monaghan

This pleasant, sheltered county is caught at the top betweeen the counties of Armagh and Fermanagh. There are no really high hills, just lots of little ones that form a gentle, rolling countryside. To the north lies a small fringe of mountains. The central area is hillocky with fairly rich farming land, and is in many ways reminiscent of County Down. Set among the hills to the south, at almost every bend of the road, lie small well-wooded lakes and sedgy bogholes. The little cultivated fields, trimmed hedges, tiny lakes, the profusion of wild flowers and the hordes of green and red dragonflies make it a land of satisfying detail.

In contrast to the smallness of scale, there still remain a few large estates, with their landscaped parks, lakes, formal gardens and age-old trees. You get glimpses of these Big Houses and the forgotten ones, which are crumbling into ruins. Copper beech trees seem to have gone wild everywhere in Monaghan; they are quite a rarity in Ireland. A native of the place swore to me that this was the last retreat of the Fir Bolgs, who were squeezed out of the rest of Ireland by the Dé Danaan and the Celts.

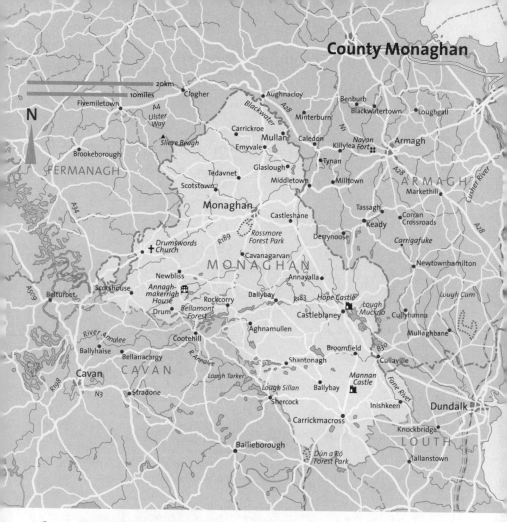

County Monaghan is well known to coarse fishermen because of the wealth of lakes; otherwise it has been little visited by tourists. The locals are hoping to change this, and quite a few attractions have been developed. Lough Muckno, near Castleblaney, offers many sporting activities and accommodation. In the southwest the Rural and Literary Resource Centre in Innishkeen is a magnet for admirers of the poet Patrick Kavanagh. To the northeast of the county, the pretty village of Glaslough has an excellent equestrian centre. Close by is Castle Leslie, a Victorian pile overlooking the lough and surrounded by beautiful trees. The northeastern corner of county Monaghan, bounded by the Blackwater River and the N2 and known as the Parish of Truagh, is one of the most untouched areas in the county – the roads are so unused that the grass grows up the middle. Many of them would have led into County Tyrone or County Armagh before the Troubles began. You will find pretty mountain scenery and views which stretch over Ulster and beyond.

Getting There and Around

By Rail
There is no rail service in County Monaghan.

By Bus
Frequent Bus Eireann express buses run from Dublin, Donegal, Armagh, Belfast and Derry. There are excellent local bus services to the smaller villages. Try also the private operators, such as McConnons.
Monaghan Bus Station, t (047) 82377.
McConnons, t (047) 82020. Daily service to Dublin.

By Bike
Snipe Cycle Hire, Monaghan, t (047) 52125.
Emyvale Cycles, Knockafubble, Emyvale, t (047) 88108. Contact Paddy McQuaid.
The Bicycle Shop, Shopping Arcade, Main Street, Carrickmacross, t (042) 31967.
The Cycle Shop, Ivy Lane, Carrickmacross, t (042) 63653.

Festivals

February–March
Castleblayney Drama Festival, t (042) 974 0454.

July
Muckno Mania, Castleblayney, t (042) 974 6087. Arts and music festival.

August
Ballybay Celtic Festival, t (042) 974 1050.

September
Rhythm and Blues Festival, Monaghan, t (047) 71114, www.harvestblues.net.

November
Patrick Kavanagh Weekend, Iniskeen, t (042) 937 8560.
Castleblayney Heritage Week, t (042) 974 6087.

Tourist Information

Monaghan Town: Market House, t (047) 81122, www.monaghantourism.com, www.ireland-northwest.travel.ie; open March–Oct.

Shopping

Crafts
Killycracken Wrought Iron, Castleblayney, t (042) 974 9810. Iron furnishings by Ashley Hill.
Grainne O'Reilly, The Old Schoolhouse, Annalitten, Castleblayney, t (042) 974 3322. Fashion, textiles, lampshades.
Iron Weave Ltd, Annyalla, Castleblayney, t (042) 974 6614. Ironware by Liz Christy.
Reimur Forged Crafts, Faragy, Shantonagh Post Office, Castleblayney, t (042) 966 9359. Blacksmith Thomas O'Reilly.
Irish Celtic Art, Rockville, Creeve, Latton, Castleblayney, t (086) 880 0781. Yoram Drori's woodcarving and repro art.

Delicacies
Emyvale is famous for its quail; contact Monaghan Tourism, t (047) 71818.

Health Foods
Nature's World, Church Square, Monaghan Town, t (047) 966 3421.

History
County Monaghan as it is now is a 16th-century creation. As the English conquered territory, they 'shired' it, hoping to make it easier to manage and more anglicized. Here, they joined the territories of the two ruling families, the MacMahons and the McKennas. Other powerful families were the Duffys, O'Carrolls and the Connollys, whose power was finally broken after the 1642 rebellion, when the lands of the Irish chieftains were divided between the English and Scottish 'undertakers', so called because in return for a grant of land they undertook certain duties to keep

Lace

Clones Lace Guild, Fermanagh Street, Clones, t (047) 51729. Crocheted lace, as well as a display of antique lace and a coffee shop.

Canal Stores, Clones Development, Clones, t (047) 51718.

Carrickmacross Lace Gallery, on Market Square, Carrickmacross, t (042) 966 2506/ 966 2088.

Sports and Activities

Courses

Cassandra Hand Summer School of Clones Lace, t (047) 51729, maireslace@ eircom.net. Maire Treanor teaches traditional Clones lace-making on a course held in June.

Fishing

Good coarse fishing in the numerous lakes especially Lough Ooney, Muckno, and the lakes beside Ballybay. Game fishing on the Finn, Fane and Monaghan Blackwater Rivers.

Talbot Duffy, t (042) 41692. In the Ballybay area.

Jimmy McMahon, Carrick Sports Centre, Carrickmacross, t (042) 61714. Advice and bait.

Golf

Nuremore Hotel Golf Club, Carrickmacross, t (042) 966 1438, f (042) 966 1853, www.nuremore-hotel.ie, muremore@eircom.net. 18-hole course.

Rossmore Golf Club, Monaghan, t (047) 81316. Also has 18 holes.

Outdoor Activity Centres

Lough Muckno Adventure Centre, Castleblaney, t (042) 974 0752, or t (086) 313 1612, mucknoadventurecentre@yahoo. co.uk. Open to day visitors. Sailing, canoeing, tennis, swimming, fishing and windsurfing.

Wildlife Educational Centre, Clontibret, between Monaghan and Castleblayney, t (047) 80632/80987, peademorgan@ esatclear.ie.

Pony-trekking

Greystones Equestrian Centre, Castle Leslie, Glaslough, t (047) 88100.

Castleblayney Equestrian Centre, t (042) 40418/69137.

Carrickmacross School of Equitation, t (042) 966 1017.

Walking

The Ulster Way, a signposted track for walkers, joins up here. Certainly County Monaghan is a peaceful place for a fishing or walking holiday. Hilton Park near Scotshouse is the perfect place to stay in style and comfort, and for those on tighter budgets there are plenty of hospitable bed-and-breakfast establishments. For details contact:

Sliabh Beagh Rural Tourism Centre, t (047) 89014, www.knockatallon.com, knockatallon@eircom.net.

Blaney Ramblers Hillwalking Club, t (042) 974 6554.

Where to Stay

The Hillgrove, Old Armagh Road, Monaghan, t (047) 81288 (moderate). Of the same stable as the Slieve Russell in Cavan; comfortable and very welcoming.

Monaghan loyal to the English crown. The descendants of those Gaelic families still live in the region today, whilst the undertaker families have disappeared or married into the local population. For over two hundred years, a smouldering resentment over land ownership made the relationship of peasants and landlord very uneasy, but this largely disappeared with the Land Acts of 1881, when the British government put up money for tenants to buy their own holdings.

In the 19th century County Monaghan benefited from the linen industry, and it was famous for its trade in horses, many of which were exported to Russia for the use of

Ashleigh House, 37 Dublin Street, Monaghan, **t** (047) 81227 (*inexpensive*). Centrally located B&B.

Castle Leslie, Glaslough, **t** (047) 88109, *www.castleleslie.com*, *ultan@castle-leslie.ie* (*expensive*). Elegant rooms furnished with antiques in Monaghan's most notable historic home (*see* opposite); dinner available upon request.

Pillar House, Glaslough, **t** (047) 88125, **f** (047) 88269 (*moderate*). Simple, family-run, hotel-like B&B.

Nuremore Hotel, Carrickmacross, **t** (042) 966 1438, **f** (047) 966 1853, *www.nuremore-hotel.ie* (*luxury*). Modern hotel in spacious grounds. The award-winning restaurant serves food with French-Irish influences. Popular with golfers, with a fine 18-hole course; also a gym and a big indoor pool.

Shirley Arms, Main Street, Carrickmacross, **t** (042) 966 1209, **f** (042) 966 3299 (*moderate*). Hotel in the town centre.

Hilton Park Country House, Scotshouse, Clones, **t** (047) 56007, **f** (047) 56033, *www.hiltonpark.ie* (*expensive*). This historic stately house set in the middle of luxuriant parkland is a superb place to stay if you are feeling extravagant. The rooms are furnished in keeping with the period of the house, and the food has a reputation for quality, with home-grown produce on the menu. Fishing and shooting in season, golf and lake-swimming are all available to guests.

Creighton Hotel, Fermanagh Street, Clones, **t** (047) 51055, **f** (047) 51284 (*moderate*). Family-run, traditional 19th-century hotel on Clones' main thoroughfare. A la carte and children's meals available.

Glynch House, Newbliss, Clones, **t** (047) 54045, **f** (047) 54321 (*moderate*). Comfortable rooms in an 18th-century Georgian house designed by Richard Harrison. Highly recommended. Dinner available; contact Mrs O'Grady.

Eating Out

The Four Seasons Hotel, Coolshannagh, near Monaghan Town, **t** (047) 81888 (*moderate*). Comfortable and friendly.

The Hillgrove Hotel, Old Armagh Road, Monaghan Town, **t** (047) 81288 (*moderate*). Traditional dinner and carvery.

Andy's Restaurant, 12 Market Street, Monaghan Town, **t** (047) 82250 (*moderate–inexpensive*). All manner of very well-cooked foods, including ostrich.

The Squealing Pig Bar and Restaurant, Monaghan Town, **t** (047) 84562 (*moderate–inexpensive*). Has a good reputation. *Open daily 10.30am–10pm.*

Castle Leslie, Glaslough (*see* above) **t** (047) 88109 (*expensive*). An old-world dining experience in truly opulent surrounds; one to consider as a special treat during your visit to Ireland. *Advance booking only.*

The Nuremore Hotel, Carrickmacross, **t** (042) 966 1438 (*expensive*). Showy food.

Hilton Park Country House, Scotshouse, Clones, **t** (047) 56007, **f** (047) 56033 (*expensive*) (*See* above).

Entertainment and Nightlife

Theatre

Garage Theatre, Monaghan Town, **t** (047) 81597, *garagetheatre@eircom.net*.

the Imperial army. Now both the linen and the horse trade have gone, along with the old rail and canal links. However, the county is well served by express buses going to and from Dublin and County Donegal, there is a good local bus network, and Monaghan is now noted for its furniture-making, poultry, and mushroom production. The locals are mostly involved in farming activities. Many of the country's chickens, ducks and even the rather exotic quail are produced for the table in County Monaghan. The people are fairly prosperous, and agriculture has been boosted tremendously by membership of the EU. The moist and mild climate produces good grass for cattle rearing, and there are many small mixed farms. The population is about 51,000.

Monaghan Town

Monaghan Town is a good place from which to start one's tour of the county. Built on an old monastic site, this market town has some very fine urban architecture, especially round the market square, called the **Diamond**. The large **Market House** dates from 1792. There is also a surprising amount of red brick in the smaller streets off the square. It is a very busy, prosperous town with lots of shops and a good restaurant in the square. The small **Monaghan County Museum**, founded in 1974 (*open Tues–Sat 11–1 and 2–5; t (047) 82928, comuseum@monaghancoco.ie*), on Hill Street on the west side of Market Street, won the EEC museum award in 1980. The museum has amongst its treasures the Clogher Cross, a fine example of Early Christian metalwork, with its highly decorative detail. There are objects collected from the nearby lake dwellings, including sandals and glass beads. There are also displays dealing with everything from lace-making to railways. The pedimented Market House holds the tourist office and a gallery with varying exhibitions. The 1860s Roman Catholic **St Macartan's Cathedral**, on the N2 to Dundalk, was designed by J. J. McCarthy, whose work is in the Gothic Revival style of Pugin – although sadly a modern 'improvement' has been to remove the original altarpiece. The **St Louis Convent Heritage Centre** (*open Thurs–Tues 10–12 and 2.30–4.30, Sat–Sun 2.30–4.30; t (047) 83529, f (047) 84907, stlouisheritage@eircom.net*) traces the fascinating history of this order throughout the world. The building itself is beautiful, and there is a *crannog* in the grounds.

Three miles (5km) to the southwest, on the R189 to Newbliss, is **Rossmore Forest Park** (*car park fee; t (047) 89915*), a former estate with beautiful grounds that are open to the public; there are picnic sites, forest and lakeside walks to be enjoyed.

North Monaghan

Only a small part of the county lies to the north of Monaghan town. It gently rises up from the flood plain of the Blackwater, to the high moorland of Slieve Beagh. Near the village of Glaslough, on the shores of a small grey lake, is the **Castle Leslie** demesne (*open May–Sept, daily 12–7; adm; t (047) 88109, ultan@castle-leslie.ie*). Sir Shane Leslie wrote superb ghost stories here in the early decades of the 20th century. The house, which is still lived in by the Leslie family, is in the Italianate style and full of art treasures; and it is possible to take a tour, or have an elaborate dinner and stay the night there (*see 'Where to Stay', opposite*). After dinner, the cloaked mistress of the house will guide you by candlelight around its haunted rooms, a performance of fun and drama. There is also a pleasant tearoom in the conservatory.

To explore the tangle of little roads in this area known as Truagh Parish you will need a detailed local map. To the west of Emyvale is the pretty **Lough More** with good stocks of brown trout; and the mountain scenery of Bragan where the local people go to cut their turf. Northeast of here is the townland of **Mullanacross**, and in the graveyard of the ruined and ancient Errigal church are some superbly carved 18th-century gravestones. They depict the stag, the emblem of the McKennas, and biblical animals. Just across the road is a holy well, sacred to St Mellan, the patron saint of these parts. Further to the southeast you come across the deserted village of **Mullan**, which has some fine stone houses.

South Monaghan

To the southeast of Monaghan town lies **Castleblaney**, on a narrow strip of land at the head of **Lough Muckno**. This is the county's largest stretch of water with perhaps the best coarse fishing there is, though all the lakes around here vie for that award. Founded in the reign of James I, Castleblaney is now a prosperous town. The plain Georgian **Court House** is rather fine, and in the wooded demesne of **Hope Castle** there are nature trails and picnic sites (*car park fee*). The castle once belonged to the 17th-century Blayneys, who developed the town, but was bought in the 1870s by Henry Hope, who is remembered as the owner of the Hope diamond – the largest blue diamond in the world, but reputed to bring ill-luck to its owner. The Hopes sold up in 1916.

Heading west from Castleblaney on the R183, meandering between the hills and fish-filled lakes, you come down to the town of **Ballybay**, on the shore of Lough Major. The Catholic and Church of Ireland churches rise up attractively, each on its own hill overlooking the grassy lakes and farmland. Ballybay was noted for its horse fair, which sadly has become defunct with the age of the tractor. Flax-growing and tanning used to be very important industries here, but now they too have virtually disappeared.

Fifteen miles (24km) southeast of Ballybay is **Carrickmacross**, a market town famous for its handmade lace, a cottage industry which was established at the beginning of the century. The very fine lace, appliqué work on tulle, is much sought after. Examples can be seen in **The Lace Co-operative**, Carrickmacross (*open April–Oct; book in advance for workshops and demonstrations; t (042) 966 2506*). The Roman Catholic **church** here has ten splendid windows by the stained-glass artist Harry Clarke, whose work was inspired by the Pre-Raphaelite style.

About 3 miles (5km) north on the Castleblaney Road at Donaghmoyne is **Mannan Castle**, a great hilltop motte and bailey (*free access*). It was constructed in the 12th century, and in 1224 it was encased in stone, some of which can still be seen. Southwest of here, in County Cavan, is Dun a Ró Forest Park (*see* pp.501–502), a great place for walks. The hilltop car park gives good views towards the Mourne Mountains.

About 5 miles (8km) to the southeast of Carrickmacross, near the border with County Louth, is the small village of **Inishkeen**. St Dega founded a monastery here in the 6th century, and you can see the remains of the old **abbey** and its 40ft (12m) high round tower with a raised doorway. Patrick Kavanagh was born here in 1904 and is buried in the graveyard of St Mary's church, which features **The Patrick Kavanagh**

Rural and Literary Resource Centre (*open Mon–Fri 11–5, Sat–Sun 2–7; adm; **t/f** (042) 937 8560, www.patrickkavanaghcountry.com, infoatpkc@eircom.net*). His masterly poem, *The Great Hunger*, is a very sad and ironic evocation of rural life in Ireland. The **Folk Museum** is now part of the Patrick Kavanagh centre, and deals with local history, folk life, and the old Great Northern Railway, which ran through the village.

Rockcorry to Clones

To the west of the county there are hundreds of small roads and lanes to explore with lakes caught in between, like a spider's web in the morning dew. Quite near the County Cavan border on the R188 lies the small village of **Rockcorry**, which has some fine 19th-century stone dwellings built for destitute widows. Here too, on the southwestern edge of the village, is the **Dartry Estate** with its open parkland, little lakes and much woodland, now all in the care of the Forestry Commission. It was once a beautiful estate but is less attractive now, with massive scars from tree-felling and an air of neglect. There are picnic sites and forest walks, but the Big House is a ruin. Nearby, lakes with names like Coragh, Mullanary and Drumlona are full of fish.

Further west is the pretty riverside village of **Newbliss**, and 5 miles (8km) to the northeast again is the town of Clones. Between the two towns, near Kileevan, lies the country church of **Drumswords**. Dating from AD 750, it has now sadly fallen into disrepair, but one window still has the remains of fine basket tracery. South of Newbliss, just off the R189, is **Annaghmakerrigh House**, which was once the home of Sir Tyrone Guthrie (1900–71). Sir Tyrone, a famous theatre, television and radio producer, left his estate to the nation on condition it be used as a house for those who lived by the arts. Many artists and writers come to spend some time in such a congenial place. You may walk through the forest near the house, and down to the lake. It is very peaceful with pretty parkland and trees.

Clones was once linked to Monaghan by the old Ulster railway and Ulster canal. In the days before the First World War it was a thriving town, but it is now rather run-down, although it is still an important agricultural centre. The town is, however, the main centre of traditional **hand-crocheted lace**. The tradition was brought here in the 1850s by Cassandra Hand, a local rector's wife, as a means to of providing relief from the famine, and was based on Italian lace styles. Sadly, today the industry is in decline, but you can still buy Clones lace, thicker than its counterpart from Carrickmacross, through the **Ulster Canal Stores** on Cara Street (*t (047) 52125, clonesdevelopment@eircom.net*).

Built on an ancient site, Clones has some fine remains, some of which have been whisked away to the National Museum. It retains an overgrown *rath* with three concentric earthworks, an abbey, a well-preserved 75ft (23m) round tower, and a finely carved Early Christian sarcophagus, which is probably a MacMahon family tomb. In the church graveyard are some fine 18th-century **gravestones** carved with skulls and crossbones. The key is available from Pattons pub nearby. Presiding over the triangular marketplace, perversely called the Diamond, stands an ancient, much-inscribed **cross**. It is carved with scenes from the Bible, and is probably 12th century. There are many fine old houses, particularly the imposing **market house**, which now houses the library. Charles Gavan Duffy (1816–1903), one of the leaders of the Young Ireland movement of the 1840s and later Prime Minister of Victoria in Australia, was born here. It's also the birthplace of Barry McGuigan, the former world champion featherweight boxer.

The Province of Leinster

14

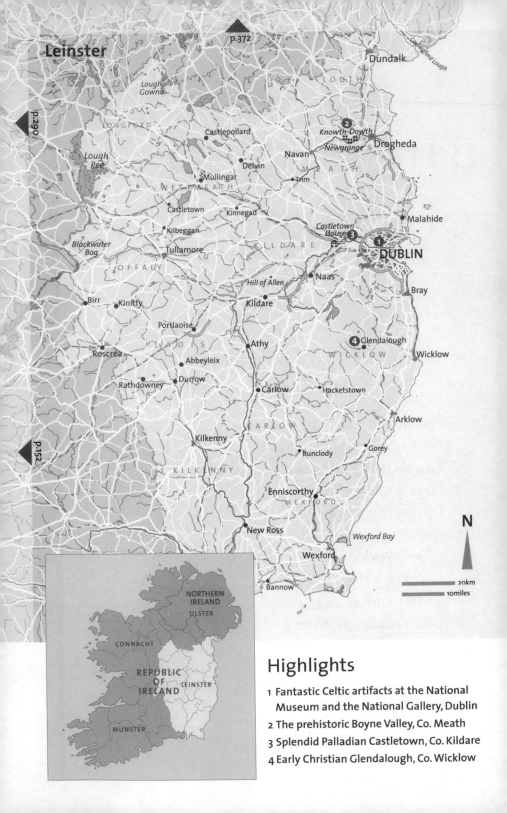

Leinster

p.372
p.290
p.152

Lough Gowna

LONGFORD

Lough Ree

Dundalk

Castlepollard

Knowth Dowth
Newgrange
Drogheda

Navan

MEATH

Delvin

Trim

WESTMEATH

Mullingar

Castletown

Kinnegad

Malahide

Kilbeggan

Castletown House

DUBLIN

Blackwater Bog

Tullamore

KILDARE

OFFALY

Hill of Allen

Naas

Bray

Birr

Kinitty

Kildare

Portlaoise

Athy

Glendalough

LAOIS

Wicklow

Roscrea

WICKLOW

Abbeyleix

Rathdowney

Durrow

Carlow

Hacketstown

Arklow

Kilkenny

CARLOW

Bunclody

Gorey

KILKENNY

Enniscorthy

WEXFORD

New Ross

Wexford Bay

Wexford

Bannow

N

20km
10miles

NORTHERN IRELAND
ULSTER

CONNACHT

REPUBLIC OF IRELAND
LEINSTER

MUNSTER

Highlights

1 Fantastic Celtic artifacts at the National Museum and the National Gallery, Dublin
2 The prehistoric Boyne Valley, Co. Meath
3 Splendid Palladian Castletown, Co. Kildare
4 Early Christian Glendalough, Co. Wicklow

Leinster (*Cuíge Laighean*) has always had a reputation for wealth, because of its fertile land. Many aristocrats lived on estates here, within a day's ride from Dublin; the city, which is the symbolic centre of the province, grew larger as industry and people were attracted to it. The province includes the ancient Kingdom of Meath, and its pre-Christian kings were the most powerful in the land. Each successive wave of invaders since the Vikings have founded towns and built themselves strong castles in this beautiful and varied region. It has a long sea coast, stretching from Dundalk Bay in County Louth to Hook Head in County Wexford. Essential ports and trading places grew up along it, but Dublin, which became the centre of British rule, has always maintained its position as the most important. Today, the population of Dublin and its swelling suburbs is one million and a half, so the farms of the province are engaged in supplying the huge city market with milk, vegetables, cattle and poultry. Brewing and other industrial ventures have grown up in the Greater Dublin area, but the rest of Leinster is comparatively rural, and the locals are either farmers or white-collar workers who commute to town.

The southeast coast has a reputation for being sunny, although the climate is fairly similar all over Ireland. Dublin is considered very cold and damp in winter. Tourist facilities are generally very good because restaurants and lodgings have responded to the sophisticated tastes of Dubliners. In fact, most travellers who come to Leinster head straight for Dublin City – a magnet which promises the most fun, history, culture and comfort. They might make a few sallies out into the countryside, perhaps to beautiful Glendalough in County Wicklow, the fascinating Boyne Valley burial grounds, or Tara, the seat of the high kings in County Meath. But Dublin City draws them all back, and the rest of Leinster pales into insignificance.

If you arrive in Ireland at Rosslare, in County Wexford, the province gets a fairer chance of being explored. There are many beautiful places in Counties Wexford, Wicklow, Kilkenny and Carlow. Centuries of history are marked by castles, monasteries, mansions and the more mysterious landmarks left behind by the Celts and those who went before. Leinster has more than its fair share of them, and many are open to the public. Castletown in County Kildare and Russborough in County Wicklow are the most impressive. The Bog of Allen, which takes up most of County Kildare and County Offaly, is counterbalanced by the gentle, rolling hills of the Blackstairs. The spiky mountains and rounded summits of the Wicklow range, the bogland and mountain pools make a happy contrast to the noisy crowds of Dublin. On a clear, blustery day it is not difficult to imagine yourself a million miles from civilization, even though the city is only an hour's drive away.

County Meath and County Louth

These two counties share many characteristics. Both are made up of rich farming land; both have some very exciting Neolithic, Celtic and Early Christian remains. Both were extensively settled by the Anglo-Normans, who built some fascinating castles and monasteries.

R183 • Lough Muckno • Aghnamullen • Castleblaney • Cullyhanna • ARMAGH • Narrow Water Castle • DOWN • Mullaghbane • Warrenpoint • Killevy • River Annalee • Butler's Bridge • Cootehill • MONAGHAN • Creggan • Jonesborough • Omeath • Rostrevor • Ballyhaise • Bellanacargy • Broomfield • B30 • Crossmaglen • Forkhill • Ravensdale Forest • Slieve Foy Forest • A2 • R. Annalee • Shantonagh • Cullaville • Carlingford Lough • Cavan • Lough Tarker • Mannan Castle • Faughart • Carlingford Mountain • Carlingford • Stradone • N3 • Lough Sillan • Ballybay • CAVAN • Shercock • Carrickmacross • Inishkeen • Dundalk • Cooley Peninsula • Knockbridge • Cooley Point • Bailiesborough • Dún a Ró Forest Park • Tallanstown • Billis Bridge • Kingscourt • Castlebellingham • Ballyjamesduff • R178 • LOUTH • Mallymachugh • Drumcondra • Ardee • Dunany • Lough Sheelin • Virginia • Nobber • Dunleer • Finnea • Lough Ramor • N3 • Thomastown • N2 • Collon • Monasterboice • Clogherhead • Sliab na Cailleach • Church of St Kieran • Carnaross • River Blackwater • Old Mellifont Abbey • Tullyallen • Termonfeckin • Loughcrew • Crossakeel • R163 • Wilkinstown • Rathkenny • Hill of Slane • Baltray • Castlepollard • Kells • N3 • Stackallen • Knowth • Dowth • Drogheda • Fore • Benedictine Priory • Clonmellon • Slane • Newgrange • Bettystown • Lough Lene • Collinstown • Navan • Duleek • River Nanny • Laytown • Crookedwood • St Munna's Church • Delvin • N51 • Kentstown • Balrath • Gormanston • Crazy Corner • Athboy • Dunderry • MEATH • Balbriggan • Mullingar • Trim • Tara • Ardgillan Demesne • WESTMEATH • King John's Castle • River Boyne • Kilmessan • Skerries • The Downs • Laracor • Dunsany • Royal Canal • Ratoath • Oldtown • Ballyboghil • Lusk • Rush • Kinnegad • Rathmolyon • Mullagh • Black Bull • Swords • Donabate • Lambay Island • Ballinabrackey • River Boyne • Dunboyne • Dublin Airport • Malahide • 20km • 10miles • KILDARE • Kilcock • Maynooth • DUBLIN • Portmarnock

N

County Meath is drained by the River Boyne and its tributary, the Blackwater, and is planted with fine deciduous trees. Cattle and horses move about the fields of well-kept estates, and there are many Big Houses, built during the 18th century. The River Boyne is wide and slow and very beautiful. It is famous for the great Battle of the Boyne in 1690, when James II, relying on French and Irish forces to help him regain his English throne, was outnumbered and outflanked by the Protestant William of Orange. The low hills of Slane and Tara give lovely views over the countryside, and are vibrant with the memories of an ancient Ireland. Both figure in the mythology of the country and have been important since the Neolithic era. County Louth shares part of the Boyne Valley, and enters the sea at Drogheda. It too has its well-planted estates, especially on the grassy plain around Ardee. But it has a wilder side, too. Going north are the heathery slopes of the Cooley or Carlingford peninsula; and the rocky coastline of Clogherhead lies to the east.

Getting There and Around

By Rail

The main Dublin to Belfast railway line runs through Drogheda and Dundalk.

Drogheda Station, t (041) 983 8749.

By Bus

From Dublin, Bus Eireann Expressway buses run hourly to Navan, Drogheda and Slane. Some Belfast–Dublin buses stop in Drogheda and Dundalk.

Bus Eireann, Drogheda, **t** (041) 983 8749.

By Bike

The Raleigh Rent-a-Bike network operates here at the following shops:

Quay Cycles, 11 North Quay, Drogheda rail station, **t** (041) 983 4256.

Irish Cycle Hire, Mayoralty Street, Drogheda, **t** (041) 873 3622.

Festivals

Late May–June

Dundalk International Maytime Festival, Dundalk, **t** (042) 933 5253, *dundalkfestival@eircom.net*. Cultural and sporting events, such as art, theatre, dancing, concerts; also includes children's events.

June

Moneley Oyster Pearl Regatta, Carlingford. Contact Dundalk and Carlingford Sailing Club, **t** (042) 937 3238. Races are held late in the month.

Blackrock Annual Raft Race, on the Promenade/beach, Blackrock, **t** (042) 932 1098. Local fundraising event, with carnival and fancy dress.

July

Kells Heritage Festival, t (046) 41097.

August

Carlingford Oyster Fest, Carlingford, **t** (042) 937 3033. Oyster festival with arts, crafts and fun for families.

Mid-August

Moynalty Steam Threshing Festival, Kells, **t** (046) 44390, *crocawella@eircom.net*.

Strand Races, between Laytown and Bettystown, mid-month.

October

O'Carolan Harp, Cultural and Heritage Festival, Nobber, Meath, **t** (046) 52115.

Both counties have experienced a huge rise in population in the last few decades, as they are within commuting distance of Dublin. Luckily, you can often as not avoid the traffic on the major roads as there are lots of tiny country routes with few cars on them.

History

The ancient history of this area is rich and colourful; it has Tara and the passage graves of Newgrange. Since the Anglo-Norman invasion in the 13th century, events have followed a pattern similar to that of the rest of Leinster. The Normans built themselves well-fortified castles, and later English settlers made themselves pleasant estates and farms amongst the rich agricultural land. The most famous confrontation between the Jacobite and Williamite armies took place along the Boyne river in 1690.

Louth and Meath suffered marginally less than others during the famine years of the 1840s, although, as was the case all over Ireland, the fate of the peasants depended to a great extent on whether or not they had a good landlord. Today this area is prosperous with industry in the towns, whilst many of the locals in the countryside work in the horse-breeding industry.

The Boyne Valley

The **Boyne Valley** is gloriously green, with a crumbling estate at every corner of the road, and ancient tumuli at every curve of the river. The valley was the centre of power in Ireland for thousands of years. The wealthy and organized farmers of Neolithic times built their burial chambers at Newgrange, Dowth, and Tara long before the Egyptians built their Great Pyramid. When the Celts arrived in waves, approximately between 500 and 100 BC, they recognized these burial mounds as very powerful and assimilated them into their culture. The Hill of Tara became a royal enclosure, whilst the burial chambers along the Boyne became the dwelling places of the Celtic god of love, Aonghus.

A bicycle tour would be the ideal way to see the Boyne Valley. You can easily cover all the ancient places and monasteries in a few days at a leisurely pace; and in summer it is the most enjoyable way to travel along the country lanes, laced with cow parsley.

Kells

Kells (*Ceanannus Mor* on the road signs) is not actually in the Boyne Valley, but in the wooded valley of the Blackwater. The village has a vast wealth of history behind it. Most people who come to Ireland go to see *The Book of Kells*, now in Trinity College, Dublin. The beauty and richness of this illuminated 8th-century manuscript never cease to amaze. **Kells Monastery**, in which it was so beautifully made, is no more, but there are many fine ruins to contemplate.

The High King of Ireland, Dermot (or Diarmuid) granted this defensive fort to St Columba in AD 550. (It is said to have been the residence of Cormac MacArt, a high king during the 3rd century AD.) St Columba (or Colmcille in Gaelic) was the princely monk who founded the first monastery on Iona in AD 563, and whose missionary zeal subsequently converted most of Scotland to Christianity. The religious centre he established became very important, and in AD 807 the Columba monks moved back here from Iona after being repeatedly pillaged by the Vikings.

Today, in the graveyard of the Church of Ireland **church of St Columba**, you can see a 9th-century round tower that is in a good state of preservation; and the wonderful scriptural stone cross of St Patrick and St Columba, opposite. The circular ditch around the now-ruined monastery is reflected in the modern-day street patterns. The round tower at Kells has some dark associations, as a claimant to the high kingship of Ireland was murdered in it in 1076. The **high cross of St Patrick and Columba**, one of four in the graveyard, has a wealth of decoration and another Crucifixion scene. **St Columba's house**, nearby, is a high-roofed oratory with very early barrel-vaulting and is similar to St Kevin's house at Glendalough in County Wicklow (*key from No.1 Lower Church View when closed*). It was probably built in the 9th century and is roofed with stone, the walls being at least 3ft (90cm) thick. Beside it is a well. There is a replica of *The Book of Kells* in the modern Church of Ireland church, the tower of which dates from 1578.

In the town, the landmark used to be a 10th-century **market cross** which had been moved there from the graveyard – until a car ran over it in 1996. They plan to erect a

Tourist Information

Kells: Kells Heritage Centre, Navan Road, Kells, t (046) 49336.
Trim: t (046) 37111; *open Sept–May*; also at Meath Heritage Centre, Mill Street, t (046) 36633.
Drogheda: t (041) 984 5684; *open April–Dec.*
Bru na Boinne: Bru na Boinne Visitor Centre, Donore, t (041) 988 0305.
Newgrange: t (041) 988 0300; *open all year.*

Shopping

Antiques
Sarah Gilsenan Antiques, Newmarket Street, Kells, t (046) 40183. Antique furniture and jewellery.

Crafts
Courtyard Craft Centre and Café, Cookstown House, Kells, t (046) 40346. Locally handcrafted ceramics, linen, textiles, woodwork, glass, jewellery, basketware and metalwork.
Trim Visitor Centre, Mill Street, Trim, t (046) 37227, f (046) 38053, *trimvisitorcentre@ eircom.net, www.meathtourism.ie.* Handmade silver jewellery, ceramics, textiles, leather goods, crystal glass and soaps.
Callan and Harte, 31 Railway Street, Navan, t (046) 21459. Prints, ceramics and other gift items.
Mary McDonnell Craft Studio, 4 Newgrange Mall, Slane, t (041) 982 4722. Quilts, wall hangings, ceramics and jewellery. During the winter it houses the local **organic food market**, every Friday 3–6pm.

Claidhobh O'Gibne, Drogheda, t (041) 41960. Celtic wood carvings.
Elaine Hanrahan, Millmount Craft Centre, Drogheda. Jewellery.
Lizzy Anne, 7 Millmount Craft Centre, Drogheda, t (041) 38244.

Furniture
John McGrane, Delvin Farm Antique Galleries, Gormanstown.

Sports and Activities

Fishing
Beach fishing for bass and flounder is best at Laytown.
Sportsden, Trimgate Street, Navan, t (046) 21130.

Golf
Headfort Golf Club, Navan Road, Kells, t (046) 40146/40857.
Royal Tara Golf Club, Bellinter, Navan, t (046) 25244/25508.
Laytown, t (041) 982 7170.

Pony-trekking
Kells Equestrian Centre, Normanstown, Carlanstown, Kells, t (046) 46998/46638, f (046) 46024. Riding and instruction for all ages, six days a week.
Bachelor's Lodge Riding Centre, Kells Road, Navan, t (046) 21736, *lowryfam@eircom.net.*

Open Farms
Newgrange Farm, off the N51 from Navan or Drogheda, near Slane, t (041) 982 4119. Working farm, with tours around its 17th-century buildings and herb garden.

replica on the spot, and have placed the repaired original in the **Kells Heritage Centre**, at Headfort Place (*open May–Sept, Mon–Fri 10–5.30, Sun and bank hols 1.30–6, Oct–April, Tues–Sat 10–5; audio-visual presentation every 30mins; adm; t (046) 47840*). In the 1798 Rising, this cross was used as a gallows. Its top has been broken off, but the fine carving of the scriptural scenes makes it well worth studying. On the head and shaft are scenes representing the Crucifixion, the Resurrection, Daniel in the Lion's Den, and the Fall of Man.

West of Kells, off the Crossakeel Road, is the **Hill of Lloyd Tower**, which looks rather like a lighthouse. It was built by the Marquis of Headford as a project to give

Lily Angela Murtagh, Fordstown, Navan, t (046) 34135, *info@causeyexperience.com*, *www.causeyexperience.com*. Recreation of traditional life on a farm, with hands-on experiences.

Walking Tours

Noel French, Meath Heritage Centre, Mill Street, Trim, t (046) 36633. Guided tours of the area.

Where to Stay

Lennoxbrook House, Carnaross, Kells, t (046) 45902 (*inexpensive*). Nice old farmhouse owned by the welcoming Mullins family. Rooms are full of pretty antique furniture, and the food is good. Trout fishing is available locally.

Loughcrew House, near Oldcastle, t (049) 854 1356/854 1922, f (049) 854 1722, *chaper@tinet.ie* (*expensive–moderate*). Set amid parkland and historic gardens, this luxurious country house offers accommodation in four elegant en suite rooms, with advance notice. Lies 5km south of Oldcastle on the Mullingar Road, near Loughcrew Cairns.

The Gate Lodge, Clonleason House, Fordstown, t (046) 34111, f (046) 34134 (*luxury*). Georgian cottage combining country house elegance with coziness in a secluded lane.

The Station House Hotel, Killmessan, t (046) 25239 (*moderate*). A converted 1850s railway station. Very pleasant.

Seamrog, Tara, t (046) 25296 (*moderate–inexpensive*). Mrs Joan Maguire offers B&B right beside the Hill of Tara

together with her insight into the area's more recent history, since her family have owned the nearby café, bookshop and tourist shop for several generations.

Ardboyne Hotel, Dublin Road, Navan, t (046) 23119 (*expensive–moderate*). Modern and friendly.

Mountainstown, Castletown, Kilpatrick, Navan, t (046) 54154/54195 (*expensive–moderate*). Beautiful 17th-century house on a wooded estate, with delicious food. It even has peacocks on the lawn. *Minimum stay 2 nights.*

Conyngham Arms, Slane, t (041) 982 4155 (*moderate*). Snug hotel, right in the middle of the village.

Minnamurra House, Dublin Road, Drogheda, t (041) 984 1437(*inexpensive*). Very convival, with Ursula McEntee's children bouncing in every direction.

Red House, Ardee, County Louth, t (041) 685 3523 (*moderate*). This attractive Georgian house lies in lovely parkland, and is well run by Jim and Linda Connolly, with comfortable rooms. Indoor heated swimming pool and sauna.

The Gables, Dundalk Road, Ardee, Co. Louth, t (041) 685 3789 (*inexpensive*). Offers simple accommodation, with a fine restaurant serving hearty food.

Annesbrook House, Duleek, t (041) 982 3293 (*moderate*). 18th-century mansion with a Greek Revival portico. George IV once slept here.

Old Mill House, Julianstown, t (041) 982 9133, *www.theoldmill-julianstown.com* (*moderate*). Converted flour mill on the River Nanny. Pleasing atmosphere and private fishing for residents.

relief to the needy in famine times. About 3½ miles (5.3km) northwest of Kells on an unmarked road near Castlekeeran, on the banks of a tributary of the Blackwater, is the ruined 14th-century **Church of St Kieran**. There is an ogham stone and two 9th-century crosses in the area around the church, and also a very attractive holy well. You may only drink from it, for if you wash in it the well would lose its holy properties – a rather sane law of hygiene. These remains are all that is left of an early hermitage called the 'Dysart of St Ciaran' – Ireland's first monks called their isolated monasteries 'deserts' in imitation of the lonely desert homes of the first Christian anchorites in the Middle East.

Self-catering

Seabank, Laytown, t (041) 98 28104/48761, f (041) 982 7955, *reservations@cottages-ireland.com*. Thatched cottages on the seashore. Liz Lyons has other seafront houses as well, from stately Victorian accomodation to modern bungalows.

Eating Out

There are a few excellent eating places in this region, but also a mass of vile hotel menus and takeaways. The following should stand you in good stead:

Vanilla Pod, Headfort Place, Headfort Arms Hotel, Kells, t (046) 40063, *www.headfortarms.com* (*expensive–moderate*). International menu. *Open Tues–Sun, dinner and Sunday lunch only.*

Bounty Bar, Bridge Street, Trim, t (046) 31640 (*inexpensive*). The oldest pub in the county, serving snacks.

The Station House Hotel, Kilmessan, t (046) 25239 (*moderate*). Tasty food: fish, lamb, and beef with herbs and sauces in this former train station. *Dinner and Sunday lunch.*

Hudson's Bistro, 30 Railway Street, Navan, t (046) 29231 (*moderate*). Casual place with international menu. *Dinner only.*

The Loft, Trimgate Street, Navan, t (046) 71755 (*moderate*). Light meals, music and a good atmosphere.

Dunderry Lodge Restaurant, Dunderry, Navan, t (046) 31671 (*luxury*). This little restaurant has acquired a tremendous reputation, and Dubliners think nothing of driving out to it for a meal. The restaurant is in converted farm buildings, with good décor, Mediterranean-influenced food and wine.

Newgrange Farm and Coffee Shop, Slane, t (041) 982 4119 (*inexpensive*). Home-made soups and sandwiches.

The Buttergate Restaurant and Wine Bar, Millmount, Drogheda, t (041) 983 4759 (*moderate*). Good, plain food made more sophisticated by imaginative sauces.

Kieran Brothers Deli and Restaurant, 15 West Street, Drogheda, t (041) 983 8728 (*inexpensive*). Delicious ham and smoked salmon. Self-service lunch.

The Gables, Dundalk Road, Ardee, t (041) 53789 (*expensive*). Small restaurant; an imaginative menu and large, country portions.

Forge Gallery Restaurant, Church Street, Collon, t (041) 982 6272 (*expensive*). Delightful little restaurant combined with an antique shop. Particularly good for vegetarians. *Dinner only.*

Old Mill Hotel, Julianstown, t (041) 982 9133, *www.theoldmill-julianstown.com* (*expensive*). Irish and continental cooking from local produce.

Entertainment and Nightlife

Arts Centres

Damsha na Boin, t (046) 32381. Dance and storytelling twice each week.

Traditional Music

Monaghan's, Carrick House, Kells, t (046) 40100.

Blackwater Pub, Kells. Monday night hears traditional Irish and modern country music.

Black Bull Inn, Dublin Road, Drogheda, t (041) 983 7139. Music on the weekends.

Sliab na Cailleach and Athboy

If you continue on the R163 out to the furthest reaches of County Meath, in the Loughcrew Mountains, you can visit a Neolithic site that must have been as important as the Brú na Bóinne in its day, though one that gets little attention from either tourists or archaeologists.

Sliab na Cailleach (pronounced 'shleev nah cahloe', meaning: 'Mountain of the Hag'), is known as the Hag's Chair, and is the highest part of the Loughcrew chain, offering views over several counties, the Irish Sea and the Atlantic. Neolithic people chose this conspicuous spot for three major groupings of passage-grave mounds, smaller mounds and standing stones. Locally the passage-graves are called cairns, for the rubble of stones that surround them; originally they must have gleamed like the one at Newgrange. Most of the sites are in open fields, and you may explore them at your leisure; in fact you could spend several days here. Some of the passages are locked; the key and a plan of the sites can be obtained from **Brù na Bòinne Visitors Centre** in Newgrange (*t (041) 988 0300*). There are two major sets of monuments, called Carnbane East and Carnbane West. Of special interest at Carnbane East is 'Cairn T', oriented towards the equinoctial sunrises (on September 21/22 and March 21/22); this is said to be the **Tomb of Ollamh Fódla** (pronounced 'Ola Fola'), a legendary king and high-poet who was the first law-giver of Ireland, and who built some of the works at Tara and instituted the autumn festival there.

Athboy, to the south of Kells, was founded by the Plunketts, a Norman family who produced St Oliver Plunkett (1625–81), a wise and brave Archbishop of Armagh who was hanged, drawn and quartered at Tyburn after being falsely accused of complicity in the popish plot of Titus Oates in England in 1678 (*see* p.78). About 2½ miles (4km) outside Athboy is **Rathmore Church**, which was built in the 15th century by a Plunkett. It has fine stone carvings and monuments, and a fragmentary 16th-century cross.

Trim

Trim is the usual starting point for a tour of the Boyne Valley. It was the capital of the Kingdom of Meath, which was granted to Hugh de Lacy by Henry II at the time of the Norman Conquest. You should approach it from the Dublin road (R154) if you can, for suddenly all the ruins, towers and moats through which the River Boyne winds burst upon you.

Trim Castle, also called King John's Castle (*open mid June–mid Sept, daily 10–6; adm; t (046) 38618, f (046) 38619*), was built in 1172 by Hugh de Lacy and is the largest Anglo-Norman castle in Ireland. This imposing, well-preserved ruin dominates the town, covers 2 acres (0.8ha) and consists of a massive square keep, with side turrets in the middle of each face, and a huge curtain wall with circular towers at regular intervals. There are two gateways, one of which still has a drawbridge, portcullis and barbican. The castle was at the centre of every battle during the Middle Ages and at one time the future King of England, Henry V, and the Duke of Gloucester were imprisoned here by Richard II.

The first Duke of Wellington went to school in Talbot Castle, off High Street. His father, the 1st Earl of Mornington, built **Dangan Castle** south of Trim, which is now completely ruined, and there is a handsome 15th-century tower attached to the 19th-century Church of Ireland **cathedral**. Also on the outskirts of Trim, on the Kildalkey road, are **Butterstream Gardens** (*open April–Sept, Tues–Sat 11–6; adm; t (046) 36017*) which have been described as 'the Sissinghurst of Ireland'. Structured, imaginative and modern, it is planned as a series of rooms with a wonderful display of colour through spring and summer. About two miles (3.2km) away is the village of **Laracor**, where Dean Jonathan Swift and Stella lived for a while. He must have been a curious rector; at least, not the sort the locals felt at ease with.

Tara

The **Hill of Tara** is to be found on a small road off the R154, just south of Trim *(Visitors' Centre open 1 May–31 Oct, daily 10–6, mid June–mid Sept, 9.30–6.30; audio-visual presentation; adm; book guided tours in advance July–Aug, or through t (041) 988 4026 at other times of the year; t (046) 25903)*. The turn for it is known as Pike's Corner and you pass through the hamlet of Kilmessan. All that is left of Tara, the ancient palace of the high kings of Ireland, is a series of earthworks on a green hill in green fields, so do not be disappointed; the wooden buildings have long disappeared. Though the earthworks date to the second millennium BC, the site was taken over by the Celts, and only seems to have been abandoned some time after Christianity came to Ireland in about the 6th century AD – it is said that the 6th-century Saint Ruadhan put a curse on it.

According to tradition, from the beginning of history Tara was the seat of kings who controlled at least the northern half of the country. It is central to many legends and mentioned in early annals, sagas and genealogies such as the 12th-century *Book of Leinster*. One of the characters frequently mentioned in them is Cormac MacArt, a semi-mythical high king who is associated with the legendary time of Tara's great fame in the 3rd century AD. Shut your eyes and imagine the pagan rites which were enacted, and later the great triennial *feis*, where tribal disputes were settled and laws were made. The *Book of Leinster* describes Tara in its heyday as being full of warriors who combined fierceness with elegance. The great wooden buildings resounded with the clamour of people going about their business, with music, feasting and the whinnying of the Fianna's sleek horses. The pastures around would have been thick with herds of cattle representing the wealth and importance of the high king. The Great Assembly Hall was built by Cormac, 'the Irish King Solomon', who presided over the massive banquets and laid down lists of protocol – even meat was portioned out according to rank: the king, queen and nobles of the first rank ate ribs of beef, buffoons got shoulder fat, and chess-players shins; harpers and drummers got pigs' shoulders as their portion, whilst historians were entitled to the haunches.

The most important of the earthworks that remain are the **Mound of the Hostages** and the '**Banquet Hall**', a pair of long parallel banks that may have been a Neolithic processional avenue. There are a number of tumuli, including the **Rath of the Synods**, where Patrick and the early saints are supposed to have held the first church synods; another is called '**Cormac's House**', upon which stands the **Lia Fáil** (apparently the real 'Stone of Destiny', the coronation stone of the ancient kings). Sixty-odd years ago, one of the mounds was dug up by enthusiastic but misled British Israelites, who believed that the Ark of the Covenant was buried in one of the large mounds. They got the information from a secondhand bookshop in Charing Cross Road, and no one did anything to stop them.

Dunsany and Navan

Dunsany, near the Hill of Tara, is the family house of the Catholic branch of the Plunketts. They are an example of a Catholic Norman family, Barons of the Pale, who survived the vicissitudes of Irish political life because one branch of the family was

Protestant and protected their interests. The **Church of St Nicholas**, in the demesne of **Dunsany Castle**, is a 15th-century ruin (*open June–July, Mon–Sat 9–1; advance bookings only out of season; adm; t (046) 25198, office@dunsany.com*). It has a beautifully sculptured fort with the figures of angels, apostles and saints on the basin and shafts. The castle, a 19th-century neo-Gothic mansion, is still lived in by the Dunsany Lords. One celebrated Lord Dunsany (1878–1957), known for his mystical short plays such as *The Glittering Gate* and *The Gods of the Mountain*, also wrote some very fine novels exploring his love for Ireland, its vanishing ways, and the beauty of its countryside.

North of Tara, on the N3, is the busy town of **Navan**, which is Norman in origin. In **St Mary's Catholic Church** there is a good wooden carving of Christ crucified dating from the 18th century. The sculptor, Edward Smyth, would have been at some risk carving such a subject during those penal times. The **Motte of Navan** dominates the town and the crossing on the River Blackwater. It is probably a natural mound of gravel deposited in the Ice Age, though legend says it was the burial tomb of a queen. The Norman baron of Navan built a bailey on top of it. There is a very pretty walk to Slane on the towpath of the old Navan to Drogheda Canal, which continues to Stackallen. The entrance to the walk is through a gateway on the left side of the Boyne road which leads from the market square. In this area are the pretty country roads leading to Balrath, Black Lion and the attractive Church of Ireland church at Kentstown, just off the R153. **Grove Gardens and Tropical Bird Sanctuary**, at Fordstown (*open Feb–Sept, daily 1–6; tearoom; adm; t (046) 34276, grove@iolfree.ie*), contains one of Europe's largest collections of clematis roses within its 14 acres, along with the bird sanctuary and exotic animal mini-zoo.

Slane

Slane, just northeast of Navan on the N2 and the River Boyne, once belonged to other Barons of the Pale, the Flemings. The Flemings lost out when they supported James II in the Williamite wars of the 1690s; their lands were forfeited, and a County Donegal family, the Conynghams, were awarded them in their stead. Burton Conyngham built the picture-book Gothic **Slane Castle** (*open 10 Sept–20 Oct, daily 12–5; adm; t (041) 982 4163/4207, slanecastle@oceanfree.net*), with its fine gates, in the 1780s. It looks dreamlike when seen from the Navan–Slane road as you cross the River Boyne. It was designed by James Watt and Francis Johnston and has some magnificent rooms and a splendid circular library; the grounds are occasionally used as a venue for pop concerts. Look out for the the the **four Georgian houses** in the village arranged in a square. Local legend says they were built for the four spinster sisters of one of the Conynghams, who could no longer stand their inquisitive chattering and quarrelling. They detested each other but could not bear to be parted, so he thought of this perfect solution; you can imagine them watching each other through lace curtains.

A few hundred yards outside Slane on the Ardee road (N2), is a very ancient site known as the **Hill of Slane**, famous in legend and as a site of early Christianity. St Patrick is said to have kindled a fire here in the 5th century AD. The Druids forbade any but themselves to light a fire there, and by doing so St Patrick brought himself to the notice of the High King of Tara and converted him. The present monastic remains date from the 15th and 16th centuries. Some of the Flemings, Barons of Slane, are buried there. On the Drogheda road (N51) just outside Slane is the **Francis Ledwidge Cottage and Museum** (*open daily 10–1 and 2–5.30, closes at 3.30 Nov–Jan; adm; t (041) 982 4244*). Ledwidge was a labourer who wrote fine poetry, and although he was a Nationalist he joined up to fight in the First World War, 'neither for principle nor a people nor a law, but for the fields along the Boyne, for the birds and the blue skies over them'. He was killed in Belgium in 1917. If you take the Slane–Drogheda Road (N51), and about 2½ miles (4km) from Dowth turn left off the main road, you will pass **Townley Hall**, a fine Georgian house, now attached to Trinity College, Dublin. There is a lovely forest trail and walk in the grounds. Further on at the bridge at **Oldbridge**, you can follow the signposted route of the Battle of the Boyne, 1690; a pleasant riverside drive.

Brú na Bóinne

On the other side of the river, along a twisting road, you will come to the most spectacular ancient site in Ireland, the burial sites known as **Brú na Bóinne**, 'the Palace of the Boyne'. This piece of land is enclosed by the river on three sides. There are at least 15 passage graves from Neolithic times, some of them unexcavated. The three main sites are called Newgrange, Knowth and Dowth. The **Visitors' Centre** is an attraction in itself (*open Nov–Feb, daily 9.30–5, Mar–April and Oct, 9.30–5.30, May and the second half of Sept, 9.30–6.30, June–mid Sept, 9.30–7; adm; last tours begin 1½ hours before closing; signposted from the N51, t (041) 988 0300, www.heritageireland.ie*), a striking piece of architecture with excellent exhibits on the creation of the monuments and the lives of their builders. Try to see it after your tour of the 'palace' because it has most of the answers to the questions you will want to ask about the sophistication of the building. And try to avoid going on weekends in summer when the place is crowded: it is impossible to appreciate the age or the impressive atmosphere when you are squashed sideways against a sacred stone. Unfortunately, the visit to the actual sites is the most over-bureaucratized tourist experience to be had in Ireland; they'll stick a badge on you with a tour time, load you on a bus to the sites for a weak guided tour, and haul you back to the Visitor's Centre before you've had any time to look around. Newgrange and Knowth have separate tours and schedules.

Newgrange

Newgrange, on its hilltop, is visible for miles around: a 340-ft diameter mound sparkling with white quartz like a beacon in the landscape. Somebody went to a lot of trouble to bring these white stones here; the closest place where they are found is in the Wicklow Mountains. Their use as a wall around the sides of a mound is unique to Ireland. Naturally, most of them fell down over the millennia, and restorers in the 1960s and 70s had a long and careful task putting them back into place. The round stones that make such a lovely pattern among the quartz may not be in their original positions; here the restorers had to guess. Another change they made is the semicircular bay faced with dark stone at the entrance, designed to accommodate large crowds of visitors. Originally, to enter, one would have to climb over the famous decorated slab that lies across the doorway, carved with an undulating pattern of spirals and lozenges. Like everything else at Newgrange, this stone has occasioned all manner of speculations: some see it as a kind of map of the Brú na Bóinne sites, others as an object for religious meditation, an obscure hint of what Newgrange might have meant to the people who built it.

Outside, a few standing stones remain from what was probably an unbroken ring around the mound, its purpose unknown. The tour will take you inside, down the narrow, 19m passage that does not quite reach the centre of the mound. At the end is a three-lobed chamber, typical of Neolithic constructions all over Western Europe. It is covered by a cupola of corbelled stone that has kept the place dry for 45 centuries; the builders cut grooves in the upper side of the stones to carry away the water. Many of the stones in the chamber are carved with designs similar to those at the entrance – beautiful, exasperating designs that show serious intent and meaning, without allowing us to decipher it. Neither can we guess much about what went on here on Newgrange's big day, the winter solstice, when the first rays of the rising sun penetrated the artfully positioned 'roof box' over the entrance and illuminated the entire passage for a few minutes (on the tour they'll recreate the effect with artificial lighting). Right now, they say, there's a ten-year waiting list to visit here on that occasion and they have stopped taking names.

Built around 3500–3000 BC, Newgrange is not only one of the most impressive works of the Neolithic age, but one of the oldest, antedating the great circle at Stonehenge by at least a millennium. In its layout, it resembles other passage-graves around Europe, notably Gavr'inis, near Carnac in Brittany, and its carved motifs echo those found in the temples of Malta, some of which were built at around the same time. When you visit Newgrange, think of it not as an isolated peculiarity from long ago, but one of the finest monuments of a culture that stretched around the Atlantic and Mediterranean shores from Malta to Scandinavia – Europe's first great civilization, a world of remarkable artistic and scientific achievements that endured for over 3,000 years.

Knowth, Dowth and the Battle of the Boyne

Knowth (*open May–Oct*), which can be visited on a separate tour from the Brú na Bóinne Visitors' Centre, is approximately the same size as Newgrange and contains a second, smaller passage in addition to the main one. Only part of the site is open to the public whilst archaeological excavations are completed, but you can see the wonderfully lavish kerbstones placed round the mound, decorated with spirals and lozenges. These may be common in Neolithic sites throughout Europe, but the Neolithic Irish carved many more of them than anyone else, and nearly half of the works so far discovered are at Knowth. Unlike Newgrange, Knowth is surrounded by nearly a score of smaller tumuli, and their placement is being studied closely for hints of astronomical or religious significance. Knowth seems to have been used for one purpose or another as late as the Middle Ages, and there are souterrains underneath that were probably dug by early Christians. **Dowth**, the third of the great mounds, has a passage made diametrically opposite to the one at Newgrange so that it is illuminated by the midwinter sunset. The archaeologists haven't done much work here yet, and the site is not currently open to the public. If they ever do reopen it, be prepared for a certain amount of scrambling if you want to see the two tombs inside and the early Christian souterrain at the entrance.

Nearly in the shadow of these ancient relics lie fields known from a very different episode in Irish history. On the N51 back towards Drogheda, near Tullyallen, a marker commemorates the **Battle of the Boyne**, where the troops of William of Orange succeeded in crossing the river and routing a smaller army loyal to James II in July 1690. It wasn't the end of the struggle, but as a psychological turning point, it is the event still celebrated each year by the Orange marchers in the north.

Drogheda

Drogheda, the largest town in County Meath, conjures up images of the cruelty of Cromwell, for which he is notorious in Ireland, but it has also been a famous place in Ireland since the Normans settled there in around 1180, and today it is bustling with energy (and eternal traffic jams). The old Drogheda Society has adapted some of the buildings of **The Millmount**, an 18th-century military barracks on a motte, as a museum (*open all year, Mon–Sat 10–6, Sun 2.30–6; adm; t (041) 983 3097*). It has many interesting exhibits including 18th-century guild banners, a 1912–22 room, information on the old industries of spinning, weaving, brewing, shoe- and rope-making, a folk kitchen and an extensive geological collection. **St Lawrence's Gate**, a twin-towered, four-storey gate stands on the road going to Baltray. It is the best preserved of all the remaining gates in this once-walled town. Off West Street, in the **Church of St Peter**, is the preserved head of St Oliver Plunkett, Archbishop of Armagh, who sadly became caught up in the panic of 'the Popish Plot' fabricated by Titus Oates in 1678. The 'Plot' was a smoke-screen manufactured by powerful men in England to discomfit Charles II and his Catholic heir, James II. Plunkett was drawn into it because of his fearless pursuit of duty in a country full of treachery and unease, where Catholicism was essentially outlawed. He was canonized in 1975, the first new Irish saint since St Lawrence O'Toole, more than seven hundred years ago.

Legal history in relation to Irish historic buildings was made here in 1989. Two of the finest 18th-century buildings in Drogheda were tumbled in spite of a court injunction to prevent the demolition. The judge then issued a High Court order, preventing any further demolition and requiring the owners to rebuild and restore the buildings. You can see them on Lawrence Street – one the town house of Lord Justice Singleton, the other Dr Clarke's Free School. Both were probably designed by Sir Edward Lovett Pearce in the 1730s.

Around Drogheda

Old Mellifont Abbey (*open May–Oct, 10–6; adm; t (041) 982 6459*) is a graceful ruin six miles (9.6km) west of Drogheda. It was built in 1142 by the first Cistercians to come to Ireland from Clairvaux in France. Their arrival and the new ideas in architecture and church organization introduced here were the result of the efforts of

St Malachy, who as Archbishop of Armagh did much to bring the Irish Church more in line with Rome. There is an interesting lavabo, a few arches of a Romanesque cloister, and a 14th-century chapter house. The Cistercians are still in the area at New Mellifont. **Monasterboice**, a 5th-century monastic settlement, contains the most perfect high cross, the **Cross of Muireadach**, made in the early 10th century. Nearly every inch of the cross is covered in scenes from the Bible – the only way the poor and illiterate could 'read' the scriptures. The West Cross is almost as handsome and less squat. You can climb the damaged **round tower** – the tallest ever built, at 358ft (110m).

Collon (pronounced 'cooh-lun'), a small place on the N2 south of Ardee, has a Church of Ireland **church** which is a miniature pastiche of King's College Chapel, Cambridge. It was at **Ardee**, now a very attractive market town, that Cú Chulainn slew his friend Ferdia in a four-day combat to stop the raiding party stealing the Bull of Cooley for Queen Maeve. Ardee was an outpost of the Pale, often used by the English as a base for attacking Ulster; that is why you will find two old **castles** along the main street. One of them, Ardee Castle, is under restoration to house a new museum.

South of Drogheda, **Duleek** has a ruined 12th-century abbey, on the site of a church founded by St Patrick himself, as well as a medieval high cross. Between Drogheda and Dublin are numerous beach resorts. Laytown is the home of the **Sonairte National Ecology Centre**, located at The Ninch (*open Mon–Fri 11–5 and Sun 11–6; adm; t (041) 982 7572*), with an organic farm, environmental exhibits, winery, nature trail, adventure playground and a wholefood coffee shop. The quiet, undiscovered village of **Termonfeckin**, along the coast, has its own 10th-century high cross.

The Cooley Peninsula

The Cooley Peninsula in the extreme north of County Louth is one of the most beautiful, untouched places in Ireland. First go to **Carlingford**, which looks across its lough to the Mourne Mountains. This town is full of castellated buildings; it is said to have possessed 32 'castles' in the days of the Pale, when almost every house on the border was fortified in some way. The ruins of the Anglo-Norman **King John's Castle**, with arrow slits in the outer walls, is impressive. It was built in 1210 by John de Courcy and is similar to Carrickfergus Castle in County Antrim. The Norsemen founded this town, and it was a place of great strategic importance in medieval times. Nowadays, it is nothing more than a little village with a 16th-century arched **Tholsel**, a **mint**, and **Taaffe's Castle**, which is multi-storied and attached to a modern house. The **Holy Trinity Centre**, in a restored medieval church, provides more local history.

You can have a marvellous walk across the **Cooley Mountains** (*for information call Dundalk Tourism, t (042) 35457*) along the slopes of Slieve Foye and Ravensdale Forest. You will find Slieve Foye 2 miles (3.2km) northeast of Carlingford, on the R173 to Omeath. Omeath has a ferry to Warrenpoint in County Down and fishermen sell shellfish in stalls by the boat. This is an area associated with the great story of the Bull of Cooley known as 'The Tain Saga' (Tain is pronounced 'tawn'), which is the oldest vernacular epic in western literature, and was written down by monks in various

Tourist Information

Carlingford: behind O'Hare's pub, t (042) 937 3888; *open Mon–Fri 10–7.*
Dundalk: t (042) 933 5484; *open all year.*

Shopping

Crafts
Ceramic Art, Tholsel Lane, Carlingford.
Riverstown Old Corn Mill, Cooley, Dundalk.

Delicacies
The Continental Meat Centre, Mullaharlin Road, Dundalk, t (042) 932 6643.

Sports and Activities

Fishing
Bellingham Castle, Castlebellingham, t (042) 937 2176. For salmon fishing on the River Glyde.
Peadar Elmore, North Commons, Carlingford, t (042) 937 3239. Contact to hire boats for Carlingford Loch.

Walking
The Tain trail, an 18-mile (30km) circular signposted route through the Cooley Mountains. Tourism Ireland publishes an information leaflet, available at any tourist office.

Water Sports
Carlingford Adventure Centre, Thosel Street, Carlingford, t (042) 937 3100. Organizes windsurfing, sailing and canoeing as well as tours and hiking, year round. By car, take the R173 from Dundalk, on the Cooley Peninsula.

Where to Stay

Ballymascanlon Hotel, Dundalk, t (042) 937 1124, f (042) 937 1598, *www.ballymascanlon.com (expensive–moderate).* Victorian country house set in an 18-hole parkland golf course, and much favoured by the clergy for ecumenical conferences. In the grounds is a fine example of a portal dolmen, as well as a pool, gym and tennis courts. Families welcome.
Jordan's Town House & Restaurant, Newry Street, Carlingford, t (042) 937 3223, f (042) 937 3827 *(expensive).* All rooms have views over the harbour.
Ghan House, Carlingford, t (042) 937 3682, f (042) 937 3772, *www.ghanhouse.com, ghanhouse@eircom.net (moderate).* High luxury at this 18th-century B&B manor, with views over the Lough and the Mornes. The renowned restaurant *(expensive)* offers dishes from local ingredients.
Carlingford Centre and Holiday Hostel, Tholsel Street, Carlingford, t (042) 937 3100, f (042) 937 3651 *(inexpensive).* Cheap and basic. *Book well in advance.*

Eating Out

Ballymascanlon Hotel, Dundalk, t (042) 71124 *(expensive–moderate).* Irish and French cooking.
Jordan's Town House & Restaurant, Newry Street, Carlingford, t (042) 937 3223 *(expensive–moderate).* Good, simple cooking using the best of local ingredients, including pig's trotters. An 'early bird' menu is also available.
Oystercatcher Bistro, Market Square, Carlingford, t (042) 937 3922 *(moderate).* Tasty seafood.

versions from Early Christian times to the medieval period (*see box*, overleaf, and **Old Gods and Heroes**, pp.84–5). The stories contained in the *Tain Saga* are full of fantastic heroism and impossible deeds; Cú Chulainn defends Ulster, and through his 'warp spasm' is able to change from a beardless youth to a furious, blood-lusting warrior.

Seek out **Faughart Hill**, which is just north of Dundalk, signposted a few miles off the Dundalk to Newry Road on the left. From here, the whole of Leinster spreads out below you. This is where Edward Bruce was killed in battle in 1318. He had been sent by his brother, Robert Bruce, King of Scotland, to make trouble for the Anglo-Normans

The *Taín Bó Cuilnge*, or The Cattle Raid of Cooley

Queen Maeve and her husband were measuring up their worldly possessions, and found that they were equal in all things except one: he owned the most magnificent white bull, which outclassed anything she could produce. Maeve knew, however, that there was a fine brown bull in the Kingdom of Ulster that was its equal, and she was determined to have it. At certain times of the year the guardians of Ulster, the Red Branch Knights, became as feeble as kittens because of a spell put on them. Choosing this time, she and her raiding party thought the whole expedition would be easy. However, at a crucial fording point the young and untried hero, Cú Chulainn, who was free of the spell, challenged each Connacht man to fight, and slew them all. Maeve, undaunted, decided to get the bull for herself and succeeded. When she got the bull home, though, it went into a mad frenzy and fought with the white bull until the earth shook. Finally, the brown bull of Cooley caught the white bull by the horns and shook it to pieces, causing a loin to fall by the Shannon (and thus giving the town of Athlone its name). Maeve is said to be buried at the top of Knocknarea Mountain in County Sligo (*see* p.354).

in Ireland, thereby lessening the pressure on himself. You can see the Wicklow Hills rippling across the plain to join the Slieve Bloom and the Cooley Hills behind. This part too is touched by myth – Cú Chulainn was born in these heather-coloured hills. In Faughart graveyard, there is a **shrine to St Brigid**, patroness of Ireland. St Brigid is a semi-mythical figure who has pagan associations; she was a powerful Celtic goddess who was responsible for sacred wells, livestock, the home, poetry and learning. When the Christian missionaries arrived, they christianized Brigid, made her a saint, and her feast day was put on 1 February, which was the pagan Celtic festival of *Imbolc* ('Lactation of Ewes'), the beginning of spring. It was in such a way that the Christian monks were able to make themselves and their religion acceptable in Ireland.

Her shrine is very garish and consists of a well, St Brigid's Pillar and a stone surrounding a bank. People still come here to do stations – prayers centring around devotion to the saint.

County Longford

For the coarse fisherman, this flat, watery county has a particular attraction. It is right in the middle of Ireland, and lies in the basin of the Shannon River. Many small streams make their way westwards through the county to join the Shannon, and the place is resplendent with lakes: Lough Gowna in the north and Lough Kinale near Granard. Both have some pretty islands, and the county is well planted with trees. The county also has strong associations for the literary. Oliver Goldsmith (1728–24) was born in Pallas. He wrote 'The Deserted Village', the classic poem so beloved of anthologies, and the play *She Stoops to Conquer*, which took the London stage by storm in 1773 and is constantly revived. Maria Edgeworth (1767–1849) was a well-educated and thoughtful woman whose work was read with respect by Sir Walter

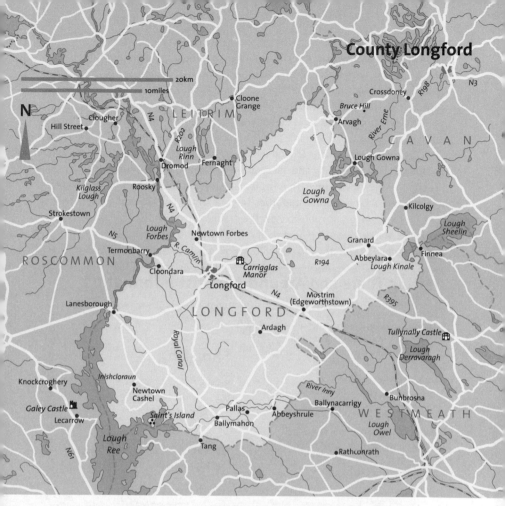

County Longford

Scott and Jane Austen. Her novels on Irish life in the 19th century are superb. She administered a large estate and did much to help during the famine years of the 1840s in her area of Longford. Padraic Colum (1881–1972), a poet and dramatist who worked for the revival of Gaelic literature, was born in Longford Town.

In the past Longford was known as Annaly, after a 9th-century prince who ruled over it. His tribe were the O'Farrells (one member of this famous family later became one of the founding fathers of Argentina). In 1547, the greater part of Annaly was formed into the new county of Longford. Today, the people of County Longford are mainly farmers or work in agriculture-related industries.

Northern Longford

Longford town is set on the River Camlin. It is a pleasant (if somewhat run down) town, which grew up around a fortress belonging to the O'Farrells – this has long since disappeared. You cannot fail to notice the dominating 19th-century limestone

Cathedral of St Mel, with its lofty towers. There is a modern **public library** in the Annaly car park, with a good local studies section and a comprehensive collection of titles by Oliver Goldsmith, Maria Edgeworth and Padraic Colum. The town is the administrative centre of the county and has quite good shops, particularly for picnics.

Five miles (8km) to the west is **Cloondara**, a pretty village on the Royal Canal. It was formerly the Royal Canal terminal and the link with the River Shannon, and there is a fine cut-stone canal harbour. Cloondara has a *Teach Cheoil* (Irish music house), where traditional Irish music, song and dance are performed in kitchen surroundings during the summer. **Newtownforbes**, three miles (4.8km) northwest of Longford, boasts a fine 17th-century mansion, **Castleforbes**, the seat of the Earls of Granard. It overlooks Lough Forbes and it is possible to view the grounds if you write to the Estate Office. **Carrigglas Manor** (*open May–Sept, daily 11–3; stable yard museum, tea rooms and gardens; adm; t (043) 45165, f (043) 42882, www.carrigglas.com*), 3 miles (4.8km)

Getting There and Around

By Rail
The main Dublin–Sligo line passes through Edgeworthstown (Mostim) and Longford Town, with three or four trains a day.
Iarnród Eireann, t (01) 836 6222, *www.irishrail.ie.*

By Bus
Expressway services from Dublin to Longford Town, Athlone, Granard and Ballymahom.
Longford Garage, t (043) 45208.

Festivals

April
International Coarse Angling Festival, in Abbeyshrule.

July
Longford Festival.
Abbeyshrule International Fly-In Air Show. Annual air show, with competitions held.

August
Granard Harp Festival. A renowned festival dating right back to 1781. Competitions are held on the second Saturday of the month.

Tourist Information

Longford: Main Street, t (043) 46566; *open May–Sept.*

Shopping

Books
The Longford Bookshop, Ballymahon Street, Longford, t (043) 47698.

Crafts
Tom McGuiness, Main Street, Longford, t (043) 46305. Crafts and sweaters.

Health Foods
Healthy Options, 3 Main Street, Longford, t (043) 47776.

Sports and Activities

Archery
Old Bond Estate, Killoe, Longford, t (0353) 432 3327. Archery facilities within an attractive walled garden and woodland.

Fishing
The Cut in **Lough Ree** near Lanesborough is famous for its big bream, rudd, perch and pike. **Lough Gowra** is a coarse fishing centre. An expedition may easily be made from here to Strokestown House, in County Roscommon (*see* p.346).

from Longford Town on the R194 (Longford to Granard road), is a romantic Tudor-Gothic mansion with castellated turrets. It was built for the Lefroys, a French Huguenot family, in 1837 by Daniel Robertson. The ceilings in the main rooms are beautifully corniced and moulded. The stable yard was built in 1790 by James Gandon, the architect of the Dublin Four Courts. The Lefroys still live in the house and it contains most of its original furniture. Antique costumes are on display in a museum in the stable yard.

Granard, on the R194 near Lough Gowra, is a bustling market town and angling centre for the River Inny, and for Loughs Gowra and Sheelin. Its name, *Grian-ard*, suggests that it was once a place of sun worship. There is a motte to the southwest of the town, crowned by a statue of St Patrick. Nearby at Abbeylara is part of the intriguing prehistoric earthworks known as the **Black Pig's Dyke**, which once stretched from Donegal Bay to County Louth.

Denniston Edward & Co, Centenary Square, Longford, t (043) 46345. For equipment and supplies.

Golf
Longford Golf Club, t (043) 46310.

Pleasure Cruises
On the Shannon and Lough Ree.
Athlone Cruisers, at the Jolly Mariner, Athlone, t (0902) 72892.

Pony-trekking
Chez Nous **Riding Centre and Guest House**, Arva Road, Drumlish, t (043) 24368.

Where to Stay

The Longford Arms, Main Street, Longford, t (043) 46296, f (043) 46244 (*expensive–moderate*). Reasonable, central.
Viewmount House, Dublin Road, Longford, t (043) 41919, f (043) 42906, info@viewmounthouse.com (*moderate*). This period Georgian house is a delight, with its elegant bedrooms, woven rugs, antique beds and beautiful views over gardens and fields.
Shannon Side House, Termonbarry, near Cloondara, t (043) 26052 (*inexpensive*). Comfortable house on the edge of the Shannon. Mr Keenan is an expert on fishing matters and has a boat available.
Toberphelim House, Granard, t (043) 86568, f (043) 86568, tober2@eircom.net

(*moderate*). Pleasant old farmhouse and a friendly family, the Smyths, who are also family-friendly.

Eating Out

There are also some worthwhile eateries over the border, in County Westmeath.
The Longford Arms, Main Street, Longford, t (043) 46296 (*moderate*). Pub lunches and à la carte menu.
Café au Lait, Main Street, Longford, t (043) 47483 (*inexpensive*). Excellent salads, quiches and soups. *Open until 6pm*.
Aubergine, 1 Ballymahon Street (upstairs above Market Bar), Longford, t (043) 48633 (*moderate–inexpensive*). Recommended highly by locals for lunch, vegetarian dishes.
Torc Café and Shop, Ballymahon Street, Longford, t (043) 48777 (*inexpensive*). Good for light lunches, snacks, cakes and chocolates. Busy at lunchtimes.
The Rustic Inn, Abbeyshrule, t (044) 57424 (*inexpensive*). Good value, family-run restaurant. Plain food and steaks.

Entertainment and Nightlife

Traditional Music
Camlin Lounge, Cloondara, t (043) 26039. Music twice a week during the summer, once a week during the rest of the year.

Southern Longford

Ballymahon, south of Longford Town, is Oliver Goldsmith country, and his connection with these parts is proudly remembered. Ballymahon itself is a good place from which to explore the River Inny and the Shannon. **Pallas**, 5 miles (8km) to the east of Longford Town, is Oliver Goldsmith's birthplace. All this countryside is charming, with soft green fields and hedges of hawthorn, sloe and holly. This area is said to have had a seminal influence on Goldsmith's work. This is an extract from 'The Deserted Village':

> *Sweet was the sound, when oft at evening's close*
> *Up yonder hill the village murmur rose;*
> *There, as I passed with careless steps and slow,*
> *The mingling notes came soften'd from below:*
> *The swain responsive as the milkmaid sung,*
> *The sober herd that low'd to meet their young;*
> *The noisy geese that gabbled o'er the pool,*
> *The playful children just let loose from school;*
> *The watchdog's voice that bay'd the whisp'ring wind,*
> *And the loud laugh that spoke the vacant mind;*
> *These all in sweet confusion sought the shade,*
> *And fill'd each pause the nightingale had made.*
> *But now the sounds of population fail,*
> *No cheerful murmurs fluctuate in the gale,*
> *No busy steps the grass-grown footway tread,*
> *For all the bloomy flush of life is fled.*

Few are aware of Goldsmith's work in a field of even more lasting significance; as the editor of one of the first collections of nursery rhymes, John Newbury's *Mother Goose's Melody* of 1760, the poet may have invented some of the old standards himself. Certainly he recast many of them into the forms we know today, and in the Newbury edition he added learned commentary and moral maxims to aid children with their studies. Of the Old Woman who lived under a Hill, he wrote: '...the very Essence of Truth. She lived under a hill, and if she is not gone she lives there still. Nobody will presume to contradict this'. And for the Three Wise Men of Gotham, in which had the bowl been stronger the song would have been longer, he adds, 'It is long enough'.

Abbeyshrule, near Pallas on the banks of the Inny, has the sad remains of a Cistercian abbey, and to the northeast lies **Ardagh**, a lovely village surrounded by woods, where it is said that St Patrick founded a church, which is open to visitors. Not far from here at Kenagh is the **Corlea Trackway Visitor Centre** (*open June–Sept, access by guided tour only; adm;* **t** *(043) 22386 or in winter* **t** *(01) 661311 ext 2386*), interpreting a timber trackway dating from 148 BC that was found in this area, beneath the bog.

Edgeworthstown (Mostrim), just outside Longford on the N4 running south, is not a very noteworthy place, except that Maria Edgeworth and her innovative father lived here. Richard Edgeworth reclaimed bogs and improved roads on his large estate, had four wives and 22 children, advocated Catholic emancipation and educated his daughters. The quality of life for the peasant living in Ireland 150 years ago was miserable, and Maria cleverly showed the causes of this through the thoughts of the faithful servant Thady Quirk in *Castle Rackrent*. Uncaring greed, absenteeism and the exploitative methods of the middlemen are exposed in this great tale of moral fiction. She and her father are buried in the churchyard of St John's, as is Isolda Wilde, Oscar Wilde's sister. The Edgeworths' family home is now a nursing home and has been terribly altered.

Lanesborough is famous for its coarse fishing, and is on the northern tip of Lough Ree. You may tour the power station which is fuelled by turf – one fossil fuel Ireland has a lot of. **Newtown Cashel**, a few miles south, is a pleasant town with a village green and stone walls. There is a lovely view of Lough Ree from the outskirts of the village, with the sympathetically restored **Abbey of Saints Island** to the south. This Augustinian monastery flourished in the 14th century, and today you can get to it by boat from Elfleet Bay, Lanesborough, in the summer. There are a variety of marsh birds around the lough, and good fishing. Another attractive island on the loch is **Inchcleraun** (also known as Inisclothran), which has the remains of a monastery founded at the beginning of the 6th century by St Diarmuid. On the highest point of the island is the Belfry Church, a Romanesque church with a square tower at the west end. There are the remains of several other churches grouped together and some Early Christian graves. The island is associated with the mythological Queen Maeve, who was killed by a stone fired from the sling of Fergus whilst she was bathing off the shore (*see* **Old Gods and Heroes**, p.85). It is easy to hire a boat out here during the summer from Coosan Point, Athlone or from Elfleet, Lanesborough.

County Westmeath

Westmeath (*Iarmhidh*) is one of the most fascinating counties for those who enjoy Irish history, fishing, and exploring. The wooded lake country is scattered with magnificent old-fashioned pubs and ruins. It has a quiet beauty. The land is fairly level with four large, spreading lakes: Loughs Owel, Ennell, Derravaragh and Lene. It shares the beautiful Lough Sheelin in the north with County Cavan. The many other tiny lakes are humming with insect, bird and fish life, and are set amongst gorse and hazel-covered countryside. Untouched, unspoilt bogland makes up quite a section of the county, and it has its own unique bog flora and fauna. Coarse fishermen catch bream, rudd, pike, eels and tench, and, where the Shannon River expands into the islet-scattered Lough Ree, cruise boats can be hired. Many of the locals are cattle-farmers, although there is some light industry around Athlone and Mullingar.

History

In pre-Norman times the county was part of the Gaelic territory of Teffia and of the Province of Meath, and the Irish names which were recorded then are still common in

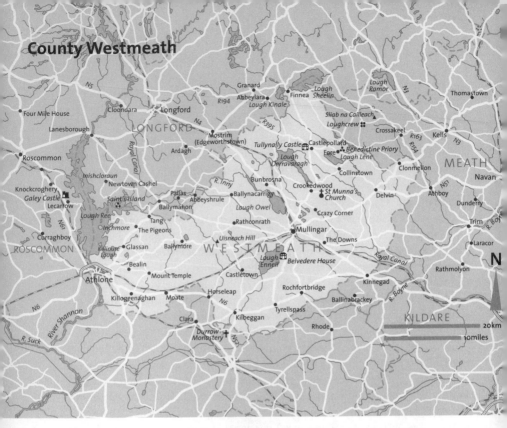

the locality. These are the O'Flanagans, MacAuleys, MacGeoghegans, O'Dalys, O'Melaghlins and O'Fenelons. These *septs* were often at odds with each other, raiding cattle and encroaching on each others' territory. In approximately AD 300, the palace of the *ard rí* (high king) was at Uisneach, a small hill in the centre of the county from which you can see a long distance over the surrounding countryside. Nothing remains of the palace. The *ard rí* moved back to Tara in County Meath in about AD 350. Yet this area was the chosen home of the high king again in the early 11th century, when Malachy II lived on the eastern shore of Lough Ennell. A large earthen mound marks the site of his fort, which is known as Dun-na-Sgiath.

Christianity came in the 5th century, and monasteries were founded by disciples of St Patrick in the following two centuries at Killare and Fore, and on Hare Island in Lough Ree. The Vikings raided up the Shannon and fought with the local Gaelic rulers. There is a story of how King Malachy slew the Viking chieftain, Turgesius, by throwing him into Lough Owel. When the Normans arrived after their successes in Waterford and Dublin in about AD 1170, they built themselves strongholds, and some of these can be seen today in the shape of mottes and baileys. Later they built stone castles and, from the 15th century onwards, tower houses. The Gaelic tribes of the region did not allow the Normans to settle in peacefully: there were constant skirmishes and the usual muddle of complicated alliances between Norman and Gaelic lords. Under the rule of the Plantagenet kings it had been administered as part of Meath,

Getting There and Around

By Rail
The county is served by two rail routes: the Dublin–Sligo line which stops at Mullingar, and the Dublin–Galway line which stops at Athlone; both have three or four trains a day in either direction.
Mullingar Station, t (044) 48274, *www.irishrail.ie*.

By Bus
Frequent express bus services stop at Kinnegad, Mullingar, Moate and Athlone. The local bus service stops at Killucan, Multyfarnham, Glassan and Kilbeggan.
Mullingar Bus Depot, t (044) 48274.

By Bike
Buckley Cycles, Main Street, Athlone, **t** (0902) 78989.

Festivals

May
All Ireland Amateur Drama Festival, Deane Crowe Theatre, Athlone, **t** (0902) 72333/92129. Busy festival, with many side-shows.

July
Mullingar Bachelor's Festival, held in the second week of the month.
Brideswell International Celtic Festival, Brideswell, Athlone. Popular folk music festival with musicians, singers and dancers from all over the Celtic world.

November
John McCormack, Golden Voice of Athlone. International classical singing competiton in Athlone named after a local son, who was the greatest lyric tenor of his day.

Tourist Information

Mullingar: Dublin Road, **t** (044) 48650; *open all year*.
Athlone: t (0902) 94630; *open Easter–mid Oct*.

Shopping

Antiques
Locke's Distillery Museum, Kilbeggan, **t** (0506) 32134, **f** (0506) 32201, *lockesmuseum@iol.ie*.

Crafts
Mullingar Pewter Limited, Great Down, The Downs, **t** (044) 48791, *mullingarpewter@eircom.com*. Guided tours of the factory on weekdays; children welcome.

Health Foods
Nuts 'n' Grains, Oliver Plunkett Street, Mullingar, **t** (044) 45988.

Tweeds and Knitwear
Tom Birminghams Man's Shop, 37 Oliver Plunkett Street, Mullingar, **t** (044) 40760.

Sports and Activities

Boat Hire and Pleasure Cruises
Cruiser and rowing-boat hire from:
Athlone Cruisers, the Jolly Mariner, Athlone, **t** (0902) 72892.
Adventure Viking Cruise, 7 St Mary's Place, Athlone, **t** (0902) 73383, **f** (0902) 73392, *www.vikingtoursireland.com*. Cruises to Lough Ree and Clonmacnoise on a replica Viking ship, departing from the Strand Fishing Tackle Shop (*see* below).
Greville Arms Hotel, Mullingar, **t** (044) 48563.

Fishing
Brown trout fishing is good on **Lough Sheelin,** and for coarse fishing try **Loughs Owel, Ennell** and **Derravaragh.** There is also very good pike fishing all over **Lough Ree.**
Strand Fishing Tackle Shop, St Endas Place, The Strand, Athlone, **t/f** (0902) 79277, or **t** (086) 8254141, *powell@iol.ie*. Information, tackle, bait and boats for fishing Lough Ree.
O'Malley's, 33 Dominick Street, Mullingar, **t** (044) 48300, *dpomalley@eircom.net*. For tackle and advice.

Golf
Athlone Golf Club, Hodson's Bay, **t** (0902) 92073.
Mullingar Golf Club, Belvedere, **t** (044) 48366.

Pony-trekking

Ladestown House, Mullingar, t (044) 48218. Trail rides along the lake.

Mullingar Equestrian Centre, Athlone Road, Mullingar, t (044) 48331/40569, f (044) 49004, *info@ mullingarequestrian.com*.

Where to Stay

Greville Arms Hotel, Pearse Street, Mullingar, t (044) 48563, f (044) 48052 (*moderate*). Traditional-style hotel.

Mearescourt House, Rathconrath, Mullingar, t (044) 55112 (*moderate*). Mansion house set in pretty parkland. The Pendred family provide good home cooking and comfortable rooms.

Woodlands Farm, Streamstown, Mullingar, t (044) 26414 (*inexpensive*). Very typical of Irish farmhouses, Mrs Maxwell's is crammed with holy pictures, is welcoming and has delicious food.

Mornington House, Multyfarnham, near Mullingar, t (044) 72191, f (044) 72338, *www.mornington.ie* (*moderate*). Lovely country house within peaceful grounds, where two dogs act as the welcoming party. The house is near Lake Derravaragh, to which you can walk; Anne and Warwick O'Hara are very knowledgeable about local history if you enjoy conversation. Home-grown vegetables and herbs are served at dinner, which might be enjoyed before a log fire.

Lough Derravaragh Camping and Leisure Park, Multyfarnham, near Mullingar, t (044) 71500 (*inexpensive*). For camping enthusiasts.

The Village Inn, Tyrellspass, t (044) 23171 (*moderate*). A cosy, period town house hotel, part of an elegant crescent around the village green. The service and food are excellent.

Temple Country House, Horseleap, Moate, t (0506) 35118 (*moderate*). Charming Georgian farmhouse with lovely bright rooms and an elegant dining room. Much of the wholesome food comes from the farm or vegetable garden. Relaxation therapies are also available.

Eating Out

Oscar's Restaurant, Oliver Plunkett Street, Mullingar, t (044) 44909 (*expensive– moderate*). Highly recommended by locals. *Open 6–9.30 for dinner every evening, plus Sunday lunch 12.30–2.*

Crookedwood House, Mullingar, t (044) 72165 (*moderate*). Cellar restaurant which has won awards for its excellent, plain cooking. *Dinner only and Sunday lunch; closed Mon.*

The Glassan Village Restaurant, Glassan, t (0902) 85001 (*moderate*). Lovely plain cooking, with lots of seafood options. *Dinner and Sunday lunch only.*

Tyrellspass Castle, Tyrellspass, t (044) 23105 (*moderate*). Medieval banquets and excellent Sunday lunches.

Le Château, St Peters Port, Athlone, t (0902) 94517 (*moderate*). Friendly and good value.

Conlon's Restaurant, 5–9 Dublingate Street, Athlone, t (0902) 79929 (*moderate*).

The Glassan Village Restaurant, Glassan, Athlone, t (0902) 85001 (*moderate*). Straightforward but tasty Irish cooking, with seafood a speciality.

The Wineport Lakeshore Restaurant, Glassan, t (0902) 85466 (*moderate*). Very popular spot.

The Jolly Mariner, Coosan Road, Athlone, t (0902) 72113 (*inexpensive*).

Danny Byrne's, 27 Pearse Street, t (044) 43792 (*inexpensive*). Victorian style pub and restaurant that is good for lunch.

The Cottage, Kinnegad, t (044) 75284 (*inexpensive*). Snack lunches and fresh scones.

Entertainment and Nightlife

Live Music

The following offer both traditional and jazz music:

Anthony Hughes', Pearse Street, Mullingar, t (044) 48237.

Danny Byrne's, Pearse Street, Mullingar, t (044) 43792.

Three Jolly Pigeons, Tang, Lissoy, Athlone, t (0902) 85162.

but in 1542 the part known as 'Westmeath' was split off from Meath because it was so difficult to control.

The 17th century bought great difficulties and much bitterness to the Gaels in the region. The Cromwellian wars of the 1640s resulted in huge amounts of land being confiscated, and as is the same all over Ireland, today the local people still remember who the land once belonged to. The new landowners soon settled in and built themselves fine houses. But the last decade of the 17th century was fraught with the Jacobean/Williamite war. The war was a disaster for the Jacobites and the Catholic peasantry who fought with them; more land was confiscated and given to those who had supported William III, and the Penal Laws to control the Catholic population were passed (*see* **History**, pp.44–5). There is a poem called *The Battle of the Aughrim*, written in 1927 by Richard Murphy, an excellent narrative poet from County Galway, which you should certainly try to read. It succinctly sums up the situation on the eve of the Battle of Aughrim in July 1691 by entering into the imagined thoughts and emotions of a Cromwellian landowner. Aughrim was one of the most decisive battles fought in the history of Ireland. William III's army of 18,000 men, under the command of Ginkel, met the Jacobite army of 24,000 men, under the command of a French general, St Ruth, and whipped them soundly.

Athlone

Athlone, half of which is in County Roscommon but is dealt with here, is a good touring centre that straddles the River Shannon and immediately spreads into the lovely Lough Ree. Athlone (*Ath Luain*: 'Ford of Luain'), has always been important as the crossing place on the Shannon between the kingdoms of Leinster and Connacht; many raids were launched from here by the fierce Connacht men who wanted the fat cattle of Meath. Later, when the Anglo-Normans had established themselves in Leinster, Athlone became the last strong outpost of that civilization, for behind it and around it stretched the world of the Gaels. Its castle was built by King John, and from it the English attempted to govern Connacht. Over the centuries, the castle and walls had to be rebuilt many times, but the most memorable stories concern the Siege of Athlone, when the town was held for James II against the Williamite forces. Sergeant Custume (after whom the present barracks is named) and 10 volunteers gave their lives in hacking down the temporary wooden bridge over which the enemy was about to swarm into the breach in the walls. Unluckily for the Irish, their leader, a French general called St Ruth, was a prize idiot, and, having secured what he thought was victory, decided to throw a grand party, even though Patrick Sarsfield, our Limerick hero, begged him to take the rumours of further attack seriously. Thus the Williamite forces were able to take the city whilst the Irish troops were drunkenly sleeping over their cups.

Today Athlone is a thriving market town, a major rail and road terminus, and has a harbour on the inland navigation system. It is full of good food shops and places where you can have a good jar and listen to traditional or jazz music. One of the most striking buildings in the town is the enormous Roman Catholic **Church of St Peter and St Paul**, off Grace Road, built in the Roman Renaissance style. It was erected in the grounds of the old military barracks and opened for worship in 1937. On the west bank overlooking the bridge, almost opposite the church, is **Athlone Castle** (*open May–Sept, daily 10–6; adm; t (0902) 72107, castle visitors' centre t (0902) 94630*). This was built in the 13th century and has always been a strong military post. Although it has been strengthened over the centuries, it retains its classic Norman design. It was used as a military post until 1969 when it was declared a national monument, and a museum was established in the central keep. The museum has interesting exhibits on the folk life and the archaeology of the area, as well as exhibits on the siege of Athlone and on the town's favourite son, the great tenor John McCormack. For one week in late April/early May, Athlone is brimming with people who come for the All-Ireland Amateur Drama Festival and its side-shows.

If you want to immerse yourself further in times past, wander into **St Mary's Church** in Church Street where, frozen into stone statues, Tudor squires kneel with their ladies in perpetual prayer. The atmosphere is like that of a village church in England. The tower bell is one of those removed at the despoiling of Clonmacnoise.

The town's transport and heritage museum at Ballinahown, **An Dún** (*open Easter–Oct, daily; t (0902) 30106*), contains a unique private collection of farm and transportation devices.

Lough Ree

If you are staying in Athlone, you may find time to explore the many islands in Lough Ree (*see* 'Sports and Activities', p.535). Ask down at the marina about hiring a boat to Hare Island, Inchmore, Inchbofin, Iniscleraun and Saint's Island, all of which were homes to saints in ancient times. **Hare Island** is very attractive, and contains the ruins of a church founded by St Ciaran in the 6th century before he moved to Clonmacnoise in County Offaly. **Saints Island**, in the eastern part of the lake, has the ruins of a well-preserved monastery and church (*see* 'County Longford', p.533) If you follow the N55 to **Glassan** a few miles outside Athlone, you get a lovely view of inner Lough Ree and its wooded islands and shoreline. Glassan is a pretty little place where artisans' cottages are smothered with roses and clematis in summer. All the little country roads from here down to the left lead to Lough Ree and little coves such as Killinure and Killeenmore. Scholars and the tourist board have claimed the area between Glassan and Tang as 'Oliver Goldsmith Country'. Goldsmith (1729–74) was the son of a clergyman, and was actually born over the border at Pallas in County Longford (*see* p.532).

Bealin to Mullingar

If you follow the N6 east, you enter rich cattle-raising and dairy country. The little country roads around here are really rural and very enticing, with many fine demesnes and ruins set in wooded fields, and the roads are nearly empty of cars, so you can really enjoy motoring or, even better, cycling.

At **Bealin**, on a little road between Athlone and Mount Temple, is a sculptured cross from the 8th century called the **Twyford Cross**. It is almost 7ft (2m) high and was found in a nearby bog. **Moate** is an important market town, and is traditionally supposed to be named after the mound of **Mota Grainne Oige**, which rises beside it. (Mota was the wife of O'Melaghlin, an early Celtic chief of the district.) The mound was definitely used as a defensive site by the Normans when they arrived in the 12th century. There are many small commercial sand pits in the esker – a long, winding ridge formed during the Ice Age – near Moate. Along the ridge runs one of the ancient roads of Ireland, going to Tara in County Meath; the surface of it is covered in hazel, hornbeam, bracken and gorse. In Moate itself you'll find the **Dún na Sí Cultural Centre and Heritage Park** (*open April–Oct, Mon–Thurs 9–5; adm; t (0902) 81183, f (0902) 81661*), a folk centre with old farm machinery and a recreation of traditional past life, including music, dancing and storytelling, alongside a genealogical centre where visitors may trace their roots.

If you are on your way to Dublin, you might stop in **Horseleap** on the N6. This place gets its name from an event that occurred when the Norman Baron de Lacy was being chased by a party of native Gaels (the MacGeoghegans) – he made his horse jump over the castle drawbridge. In the village is a partly damaged Norman motte and bailey which dates from 1192. Also there is a well-preserved 16th-century tower house which was built by the MacGeoghegans, a ruling Gaelic family whose lands remained fairly intact up to the time of Cromwell in the 1640s.

The next village along the N6 is **Kilbeggan**. It has an old distillery, founded in 1757, which has been restored as the **Locke's Distillery Museum** by an enthusiastic local committee (*open April–Oct, daily 9–6, Nov–Mar, 10–4; t (0506) 32134, f (0506) 32201, lockesmuseum@iol.ie*). The huge water wheel is back in operation. On the Tullamore road a few miles out is the ruined **Durrow Abbey**, a famous monastery founded in the 6th century by St Columba. Amongst its attractions are a holy well and, in the disused graveyard, the **Durrow High Cross** (*see* 'County Offaly', p.548).

Back on the N6 to Dublin is **Tyrellspass**, a very pretty village, laid out as a crescent around the central green in the 18th century by the Countess of Belvedere. The area was ruled by an Anglo-Norman family, the Tyrells, until Cromwellian times. The castle, a private residence, was built by them in the 15th century. Richard Tyrell was a late-16th-century hero who annihilated a large Elizabethan force near here with the help of a small band of men. **Belvedere House, Gardens and Park** (*open April–Nov, daily; adm; t (044) 49060, info@belvedere-house.ie;*) lies between Tyrellspass and Mullingar on the shores of Lough Ennell. It was built for Robert Rochfort, Lord Belfield, afterwards 1st Earl of Belvedere, in about 1740. It was probably built by Richard Cassels, Ireland's foremost Palladian architect. The house is small and comprises a three-bay recessed centre between projecting bay ends. The plasterwork on the ground floor is superb, with cherubs and classical figures amidst fruit, flowers, clouds and stars. The 1st Earl was a vindictive man who kept his young wife a prisoner in a nearby house for 31 years after her alleged adultery with his younger brother. The gardens are superb with many old-fashioned shrubs, 18th-century follies and ruins.

Twelve miles (19km) west of Mullingar on the Ballymore Road, beyond Loughanavally, is **Uisneach Hill**, the 'Navel of Ireland', with an ancient boulder called the Catstone, or the 'Stone of Divisions', traditionally the spot where the four provinces of Ireland meet. *Uisneach* (pronounced 'Ush nock') in mythology was a seat of the high kings before Tara, but archaeologists have found nothing on the site but thick layers of ashes, suggesting that this was a place for important national ceremonies, perhaps Beltane (May Eve) with its fire festival. Uisnech would be the perfect spot for a bonfire; from the top of the hill you can enjoy a view said to take in no less than twenty counties.

Mullingar was a garrison town and has now become a noted angling centre with a busy, brightly painted main street, several excellent pubs and grocery shops that sell items such as Brie and salami. It is one of the nicest market towns in Ireland, and has a feeling of energy which is often lacking in some of the more dreary towns scattered through the middle of the country. The area around Mullingar is great shooting, fishing and hunting country, and the new squires who lead the way are German and French (which might explain the Brie). A lovely anonymous rhyme relates an episode in Mullingar:

> There was an elopement down in Mullingar
> But sad to relate the pair didn't get far.
> 'Oh fly,' said he, 'darling, and see how it feels.'
> But the Mullingar heifer was beef to the heels.

The Seven Wonders of Fore and Castlepollard

Five and a half miles (8.9km) from Mullingar on the R394, east of Crookedwood village, is **St Munna's Church** (*key kept at the house opposite the graveyard*). This fairytale church was built in the 15th century and has a castle-like tower and battlements. In **Crookedwood**, at the southern tip of Lough Derravaragh, the scenery is really charming, for it looks over the glittering lake. Take the little road through Collinstown to **Fore**, once an important ecclesiastical centre, situated between Loughs Lene and Bane and freely accessible. Fore has the same magical atmosphere as Glendalough in County Wicklow, but has not really been looked after. For a welcome bit of blarney, stop in at the Seven Wonders Pub and ask them about the 'Seven Wonders of Fore'; they'll send you on a tour of seven sites associated with miracles of St Feichin, including wood that will not burn, water that won't boil, and **St Feichin's Church** in the western graveyard, which dates from the 10th century and is remarkable for its huge doorway; a cross in a circle marks the massive lintel, raised by the saint's prayers. The well-preserved Benedictine priory is one of the Wonders – the original church was built on a bog by St Feichin in AD 630. The one standing today was built by Walter de Lacy, a powerful Anglo-Norman, in the beginning of the 13th century on the remains of an earlier abbey. Another wonder, St Feichin's anchorite cell on the hillside, was occupied by a hermit as late as 1764, and later became a family vault for the Grenville-Nugents of Delvin. From the hills around Fore there are some lovely views of Meath, Cavan and Longford.

Castlepollard is an attractive 19th-century town with a triangular green. Close by, on the Granard Road (R395), are the beautiful grounds of **Tullynally Castle** (which used to be Pakenham Hall), the seat of the Earls of Longford (*open mid June–July, 10–6; gardens open May–Aug, 2–6; adm; t (044) 61159, f (044) 61856, tpakenham@eircom.*

net). Seen from a distance in its romantic setting, Tullynally makes you think of a castle in an illustrated medieval manuscript. The hall became a Gothick Castle in the 1790s; the new castellated additions were designed by Francis Johnston for the 2nd Lord Longford, whose family, the Pakenhams, had bought the property in 1655. Inside the castle is a fine collection of family portraits, furniture, and memorabilia. Maria Edgeworth, the novelist, was an enthusiastic visitor here and described it as, 'the seat of hospitality and the resort of fine society'. The present family are extremely literary: Lady Antonia Fraser is of this family and her brother, the present Viscount, is also a respected historian. The grounds are beautiful and the castle looks down to Lough Derravaragh, which is one of the loughs associated with the story of the Children of Lir: it was here that the children's jealous stepmother transformed them into swans.

County Offaly and County Laois

To many travellers the only significance of these two counties is that you travel through them on your way to Tipperary or Cork. They lie in the centre of Ireland's saucer-shape, in the flat plains and boglands, separated from Galway and Roscommon on the west by the Shannon. Both counties are delightfully untouched by organized tourism, there are no bus tours to speak of; even travellers to the famous monastic site of Clonmacnoise will find it as quiet and still as did the 6th-century monks who sought out this island of tranquillity along the river.

Most of County Offaly is bogland, which is alive with its own special flora and fauna. It is bordered in the west by the River Shannon, and there is plenty of scope for cruising along its beautiful waters, and through the Grand Canal which divides the county in two. In the southwest, Offaly shares with County Laois the glens of the Slieve Bloom Mountains. They are not a great height – 2,000ft (610m) at their highest point – but they have a grandeur of their own, amongst the flat watery boglands around them.

Both counties have a great wealth of Early Christian sites, and some superb examples of 18th-century big houses. The villages grew up around such landlord properties and are still, on the whole, very attractive. Birr is a gem of a planned 18th-century town, and the Parsons family who laid it out still own the magnificent gardens and arboretum their ancestors planted. You can spend hours in it, marvelling at the exotic species and grand design.

County Laois is bordered on its east by the Grand Canal which runs alongside the River Barrow at Monasterevin, finally merging into the Barrow at Athy in County Carlow. The River Nore flows through Laois on its western side, so there is plenty of scope for the coarse fisherman.

History

Perhaps because of the bogland, our knowledge of Stone Age man in these parts is scarce. However, at Lough Boora near Kilcormac excavations in 1977 discovered traces

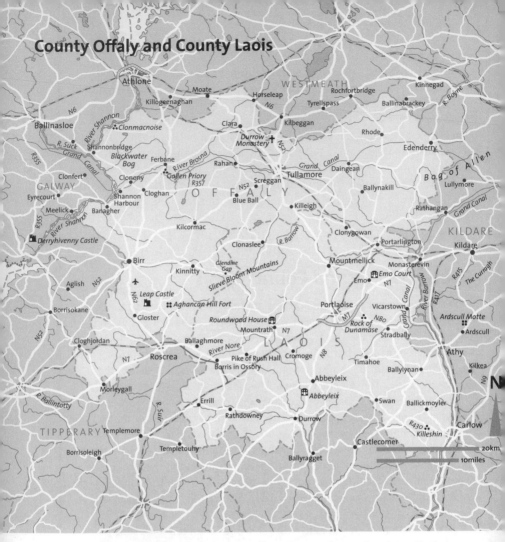

of nomadic activity from some 7000 years BC. There is plenty of evidence that man was around in these parts during the Bronze Age (2000 BC), as weapons and ornaments have been found, those at Banagher being particularly famous. The Iron Age and the arrival of the Celts is marked by numerous hill-forts such as Aghancon, near Leap Castle. The *septs* which eventually emerged were the O'Connors, O'Molloys, O'Dempseys, MacCoghlans, Foxes and O'Carrolls in County Offaly; and the O'Moores, Fitzpatricks, and O'Dunnes in County Laois.

When the Anglo-Normans arrived in 1169 they could never establish themselves securely here, and gradually retreated back to the Pale, a small area of land around Dublin, Meath and Louth. In the 16th century, the English started their experiment of planting disloyal parts of Ireland with loyal English. The boundaries of County Offaly and County Laois began to take shape with bits taken from the older Kingdoms of Ossory (now Kilkenny), Meath, Thormond and Munster. When plantation did not work

Getting Around

By Rail

Portlaoise is on the main line from Dublin to Cork and Limerick, and there are at least eight trains a day in each direction. Trains on the Dublin–Galway line pass through Portarlington and Tullamore.

Tullamore, t (0506) 21431.
Portlaoise, t (0502) 21303.
Portarlington, t (0502) 23128.
Ballybrophy, t (0505) 46331.

By Bus

Central Bus Information, t (061) 313333.

By Bike

Raleigh's Rent-a-Bike scheme operates here. Contact:
M. Kavanagh, Railway Street, Portlaoise, **t** (0502) 21357.

Festivals

June

Durrow Carnival Weekend. Traditional music, ceilidhs, concerts and street entertainment.

July

French Festival, Portarlington, Laois. Celebrates the French Huguenot influence on the town.
Laois Fleadh, Clonaslee.

August

Stradbally Steam Rally, Laois. Working steam engines, carousels and stalls; held early in the month, for more information **t** (0502) 25444 or www.rishsteam.ie, ette@gofree.indigo.ie.
Birr Vintage Week, Offaly. 'Old Time Fayre', with art exhibitions, antiques, parades, street entertainment, fireworks and singing competitions; contact O. Enright, **t** (0509) 20293.

October

Laois Arts Festival. Festival with music, all kinds of arts, literature and theatre performances.
John Keegan Weekend, Shanahoe, near Abbeyleix, Laois. Annual celebration of the life and works of the nineteenth century poet, writer and storyteller; call **t** (0502) 63355 for more information.

well enough, the Crown ordered the transplantation of the chief tribes and their followers to County Kerry, around Tarbert. By the 1620s families such as the Parsons, now the Earls of Rosse, had taken over the strongholds of the native Gaelic chiefs; in this case, the O'Carrolls of Ely in County Offaly.

Today, the people living in these counties work mainly in small industries such as the manufacture of vitrified clay pipes, or for Bord na Móna, the Irish turf development authority, which employs over five thousand people. Most of them have small farms which they work on a part-time basis.

Clonmacnoise

Clonmacnoise, at Shannonbridge, on the banks of the River Shannon, is one of Ireland's most celebrated holy places (open Nov–mid Mar, daily 10–5.30, mid March–mid May, 10–6, mid May–mid Sept, 9–7, late Sept and Oct, 10–6; guided tours; adm; **t** (0905) 74195, **f** (0905) 74273). In AD 545 St Ciaran founded a monastery here which became one of the most famous of all the monastic settlements in Ireland. T. W. Rolleston (1857–1920) adapted a beautiful early Gaelic poem, simply entitled 'Clonmacnoise', which suggests what a great centre of worship and learning it was, and the place it holds in the Celtic twilight view of history:

In a quiet water'd land, a land of roses,
Stands Saint Kieran's city fair;
And the warriors of Erin in their famous generations
Slumber there.

There beneath the dewy hillside sleep the noblest
Of the clan of Conn,
Each below his stone with name in branching Ogham
And the sacred knot thereon.

There they laid to rest the seven Kings of Tara,
There the sons of Cairbre sleep –
Battle-banners of the Gael that in Kieran's plain of crosses
Now their final hosting keep.

And in Clonmacnoise they laid the men of Teffia,
And right many a lord of Breagh;
Deep the sod above Clan Creide and Clan Conaill,
Kind in hall and fierce in fray.

Many and many a son of Conn the Hundred-fighte
In the red earth lies at rest;
Many a blue eye of Clan Colman the turf covers,
Many a swan-white breast.

The monastery was well sited on a major ford on the Shannon, on a huge esker ridge which stands well above the boggy plain. It became a centre of great learning in medieval times and was patronized by the O'Connor Kings. Turlough and Rory were buried there. The monastery suffered terribly from Viking raids and inter-dynastic wars between different *septs*. The coming of the Normans spelt the decline of Clonmacnoise, for they built a fort by the river, and an English garrison was built at Athlone. It further fell into a decline after the Reformation, and was sacked in 1552 by the English garrison at Athlone.

Today the remains are extensive and include nine churches, a cathedral, three fine high crosses, two round towers, and some decorated early grave slabs – they date from the 8th, 9th and 10th centuries. Many of the names on them are found in the annals, the ancient manuscripts of Ireland. A few of them are displayed in the reception area as you enter the monastery. The ruins are dispersed in a large grassy enclosure, and each building is well described. It takes at least an hour to walk around them.

Of particular note is the 10th-century **West Cross** with its decorative panels of figure-carving. The lowest panel on the east face of the shaft shows two figures clasping a post on which a bird perches. These have been interpreted as St Ciaran, the founder, and the local king, Diarmuid, who granted the land for the monastery. It is said that Diarmuid helped to build the first wooden church with his own hands, and

Tourist Information

Clonmacnoise: **t** (0905) 74134, *open April–Oct.*
Birr: **t** (0509) 20110, also **t** (0509) 20923,
www.elyocarroll.com; *open May–Sept.*
Tullamore: **t** (0506) 25015; *open all year round.*

Shopping

Brassware
Banagher Brass and Copper, Cuba, Banagher,
t (0509) 51381.

Charcuterie
Rudds, Busherstown House, Moneygall,
t (0505) 45077. Home-made sausages and
traditional smoked bacon.

Health Foods
Natural Stuff, O'Connor Square, Tullamore,
t (0506) 41308.

Sheepskin
Eric Stanley, Woodville Farm, Shinrone, Birr.
Sheepskin slippers and jackets.

Sports and Activities

Bird-watching
In the flood meadows on either side of the
Little Brosna River look out for golden plover,
wigeon, whooper swans, curlews, lapwings
and black-tailed godwits.

Bog Tours
It is possible to take a tour of the **Blackwater
Bog**, an 8km circular tour aboard the
Clonmacnoise and West Offaly Railway,
t (0905) 74114/74172, **f** (0905) 74210,

www.bnm.ie, bograil@bnm.ie. The starting
point is at the Bord na Mona Blackwater
Works, Shannonbridge; departures are every
hour, on the hour, between 10 and 5. *Open
April–Oct; trips on the hour from 10 to 5pm.*

Fishing
J. Hiney's Pub & Tackle, Main Street, Ferbane,
t (0902) 54344. For coarse fishing.

Golf
Birr Golf Club, The Glens, Banagher Road, Birr,
t (0509) 20082.
Castle Barna Golf Club, Daingean, **t/f** (0506)
53384, *www.castlebarna.ie, info@
castlebarna.ie.*
Esker Hills Golf and Country Club,
Ballykilmurray, Tullamore, **t** (0506) 55999,
f (0506) 55021, *www.eskerhillsgolf.com,
info@eskerhills.com.*

Outdoor Activity Centres
For orienteering in the Slieve Blooms.
Outdoor Education Centre, Birr, **t** (0509)
20029, **f** (0509) 21090, *birroec@indigo.ie.*
**Brendina O'Meara, Shannon Adventure
Canoeing**, The Marina, Banagher, **t** (0509)
51411, *advcaneo@iol.ie.* Canoeing trips.

Pleasure Cruises
Celtic Canal Cruisers, Tullamore, **t** (0506)
21861. Cruiser hire.
Historic Cruising Tours, 17 Woodlands, Birr,
t (0509) 51411, *advcanoe@iol.ie.* Cruises on
Lough Derg.

Pony-trekking
Annaharvey Farm and Equestrian Centre,
Tullamore, **t** (0506) 43544, **f** (0506) 43766,
annafarm@oil.ie.

was rewarded for his piety by the high kingship of Ireland. The largest church, the
cathedral, has a fine north doorway (*c.* 1460) of limestone with foliate carvings and
figure-sculpture. All the churches have Romanesque features; **Teampul Finghin** on the
northern border of the site has a beautiful chancel arch in three orders, decorated
with chevrons and animal heads. It dates from the second half of the 12th century.
A small **round tower** rises from the chancel. There is a small tourist office in the car
park, a coffee shop and some picnic benches are arranged around the entrance to the
reception area. A pilgrimage is held here on 12 September, the feast of St Ciaran.

Noel Cosgrave, Birr Equestrian Centre, Kingsborough House, Fortal, Birr, t (0509) 21961, f (0509) 20479.
Kinnitty Castle Equestrian Centre, Kinnitty, Birr, t (0509) 37318, f (0509) 37284.

Swimming Pools

Banagher Swimming Pool, Banagher. Outdoor pool.
Birr Swimming Pool, Roscrea Road, Birr, t (0509) 20343. Indoor pool.

Walking

The Slieve Bloom Way, a signposted circular route of 31 miles (50km), starts at Glenmonicknew Forest car park. Ask for information at any tourist office, or contact the following:
Slieve Bloom Walking Centre, Kinnitty Village, t (0509) 37299, f (0509) 37351, ardmore-house@eircom.net. With a guided walking tours programme, maps and information.
B.Doheny, Wild Earth Trails Ltd, The Elms, Spollenstown, Tullamore, t (0506) 22410, wildearthtrails@oceanfree.net. Eco tours, environmental safaris, wildlife trailing, cycling and walking.

Where to Stay

The Old Rectory, Deerpark, Shannon Harbour, t (0902) 57293 (inexpensive). Cosy country house near the lively cruising port; contact Mrs N. O'Hara.
Spinners Town House and Bistro, Castle Street, Birr, t (0509) 21673, f (0509) 21673, www.spinners-townhouse.com (moderate). Set in a renovated warehouse around a garden courtyard, this modern, stylish B&B has 13 rooms decorated in muted tones. The bistro

offers tasty dishes made from locally-produced ingredients at an affordable price.
Kinnitty Castle, Kinnitty, t (0509) 37318, f (0509) 37284, www.kinnittycastle.com, kinnitty@tinet.ie (luxury). Atmospheric rooms in a 17th-century neo-Gothic castellated mansion in the country. Dinner is served in the Georgian restaurant (moderate).
Moorhill House, Clara Road, Tullamore, t (0506) 21395 (moderate). Charming Victorian house; excellent restaurant.
Shepherd's Wood, Screggan, Tullamore, t (0506) 21499, jgott@esatelear.ie (moderate). A 1930s house surrounded by woodland.

Eating Out

County Arms Hotel, Railway Road, Birr, t (0509) 20791 (moderate). Georgian country house hotel. Reasonable food.
Dooly's Hotel, Emmet Square, Birr, t (0509) 20032, www.doolyshotel.com (moderate). Adequate, rather pretentious food in the restaurant but with a good coffee shop.
Riverbank Restaurant, Riverstown, Birr, t (0509) 21528 (moderate). On the banks of the Little Brosna River, a mile from Birr.
The Stables Restaurant, Oxmantown Street, Birr, t (0509) 20263 (moderate). Basic menu offering steaks.
Brosna Lodge Hotel, Banagher, t (0509) 51350 (moderate). Bland but good value cooking.
The Vine House, Banagher, t (0509) 51463 (moderate). Good value, simple cooking.
Moorhill House Restaurant, Clara Road, Tullamore, t (0506) 21395 (moderate). Restaurant in the converted stables of a Victorian country house.

Southern Offaly and Tullamore

If you travel south towards Birr from Clonmacnoise and Shannonbridge on the R357, you will pass a lovely little castle at **Clonony**, built in Henry VIII's time. It is a four-storey tower house with a 19th-century reconstructed *bawn*. Gravestones uncovered here belonged to the Ormonde Butlers. **Shannonbridge** has a power station, artillery fortifications dating from the Napoleonic period and a superb reputation for coarse fishing. It also has an excellent pub and supermarkets to supply the cruiser trade. Just outside Shannonbridge, Bord na Móna, the National Peat Board, has set up a unique attraction, converting one of its old working rail lines into the **Clonmacnoise and**

West Offaly Railway, upon which you can travel on a 5½-mile guided tour of the Blackwater Bog, and learn everything about the complex natural history of bogs and their importance to Ireland (*see* 'Sports and Activities', p.545).

Nearby is **Shannon Harbour**, where the Grand Canal and the Shannon River meet. You moor your boat underneath the ruins of an old hotel. Many an emigrant said their goodbyes here before sailing to America. The boglands around **Ferbane** and **Boher**, just south of the river, are fascinating in their way, and the medieval church remains in these tiny places are very interesting. At **Banagher**, you will see a Martello tower guarding the western side of the river, built as a lookout to warn against a possible Napoleonic invasion. The attractive town is linked with the novelist Anthony Trollope, who was stationed here as Post Office Surveyor in 1841. Just outside Banagher, the picturesque **Cloghan Castle** (*open by appointment only, call to confirm opening hours; adm; t (0509) 51650, www.cloghancastleoffaly.com*) was built in the 14th century on the site of a monastery that flourished seven centuries before. Now brought back to life by restorationist Brian Thompson, who lives there, it is furnished with a fascinating collection of antiques, weapons and armour going back to the time of Cromwell.

Birr is a must on any tour of Ireland: the castle gardens are superb, and the town itself is beautifully laid out with wide, Georgian streets and squares. The hand of the Parsons family is obvious in this; it is the planned, landlord towns which have grown old gracefully. Birr stands on land granted to Laurence Parsons in 1620 and used to be called Parsonstown. In Emmet Square is Dooley's Hotel, a very old coaching inn. The Galway Hunt were tagged 'The Galway Blazers' after setting fire to the hotel during a night of celebration in 1809. West of Emmet Square is **John's Mall** with its Georgian houses. Notice the fine fanlights above the doors. There is a pleasant walk downstream following the river, and to the right of Oxmanton Bridge is St Brendan's Church and the Convent of Mercy, designed by Pugin. The entrance to **Birr Castle** (*grounds open daily, 9–6; adm; t (0509) 20336, f (0509) 21583, www.birrcastle.com, info@birrcastle.com*) is in William Street, and there are over 100 acres (40ha) of pleasure grounds laid out by Laurence Parsons, the 2nd Earl of Rosse (1757–1841). The castle itself is not open to the public. Various exhibitions are held in the gallery, in the grounds during the summer, and you can see a gigantic reflecting **telescope** built in 1845, in its day the largest in the world; this is the centrepiece of the newly-opened **Historic Science Centre** (*opening hours as per Birr Castle; adm*), with exhibitions on the contributions of the Irish to the various sciences. The 3rd Earl of Rosse planned and constructed it himself. The gardens are famous for their elegant shrubs, magnolias and box hedges which are as tall as trees, and the park for its variety of Chinese and Himalayan trees. There is a proper kitchen garden, which is a rarity nowadays. Birr Castle hosts a number of events each summer, ranging from concerts and astronomy weekends to a 'Georgian cricket match' in period costume.

In the southern corner of Offaly, near Gloster, is **Leap Castle**, which guards the valley from Leinster into Munster (*open by appointment; adm; t (0509) 31115, or t 0872 344064*). This large tower house, restored in about 1750 by the Darby family, is rather a spooky place – parts of it have lain in ruins ever since a fire in 1922. It is said to be the most haunted castle in Ireland, and one of its ghosts is renowned for being very smelly. The present owner hopes to restore it – the house that is, not the smell.

Tullamore is the county town of Offaly; a prosperous place which has grown up on the banks of a small river. The Grand Canal also passes through it, and it is a major cruiser base. Irish Mist and Tullamore Dew whiskey are manufactured here, and there are good shops and restaurants. Six and three-quarter miles (11km) west, at **Rahan**, is a lovely old canalside pub called The Thatch. Take the N52 out of Tullamore for 5 miles (8km) and take the second turning on the right. You can combine a drink here with a visit to the ancient **churches** of Rahan (*always accessible*). Two of them are 12th-century and in the Romanesque style. One of them is very well-preserved, and joined to a later church built in 1732. The chancel arch has elaborate piers, carved into human heads with flowing hair.

About 5 miles (8km) north of Tullamore, off the N52, is the site of **Durrow Monastery** (*open daily 9am–1pm*), which was founded by St Columba (Colmcille) in the 6th century. It is most famous for the *Book of Durrow*, a 7th-century illuminated maunuscript, now housed at Trinity College, Dublin, and for the Crozier of Durrow, which is now in the National Museum, Dublin. Nothing remains of the monastery today except a 10th-century high cross and some fine early tombstones.

County Laois

County Offaly used to be known as 'King's County' after Phillip II, Spanish Consort of Mary Tudor. County Laois (pronounced 'Leash') was 'Queen's County', after Mary herself. She 'planted' this area with loyal supporters in 1556, but this policy did not bring peace, and early in the 17th century many of the rebellious Irish *septs* were banished to County Kerry. The new colonists built lovely houses and attractive villages. Houses of note include Abbeyleix, Roundwood House and Emo Court.

Portlaoise to Portarlington

The county town is **Portlaoise**, which has nothing much to recommend it, except that it is an important rail junction. It has a certain notoriety, as there is a well known prison in the neighbourhood. Of great interest is the **Rock of Dunamase**, just outside the town on the Stradbally road (N80). This is an ancient defensive fort, and the annals record that it was plundered by the Vikings in AD 845. It came into Anglo-Norman hands through the marriage of Aoife, daughter of the King of Leinster, to the warlord Strongbow. It was blown sky-high by Cromwellian artillery in 1650. The climb to the top is easy and the views are wonderful. At **Stradbally** there is a **Steam Traction Museum** (*adm; for opening hours call t (0502) 25114*). There is a steam rally every August bank holiday weekend. **Vicarstown** and **Monasterevin**, both on the River Barrow section of the Grand Canal, are peaceful cruiser harbours.

North of Portlaoise is the canal town of **Portarlington**. The town was founded at the end of the 17th century and became an important centre for Dutch and French Protestant refugees. In 1696 Henri de Massue, Marquis de Ruvigny, also the Earl of

Tourist Information

Portlaoise: **t** (0502) 21178; *open all year round.*

Sports and Activities

Fishing

Ballaghmore Lake, Ballaghmore House, Borris-in-Ossory, County Laois, **t** (0505) 21366.

Walking

The **Slieve Bloom Way**, a signposted circular route of 31 miles (50km), starts at Glenmonicknew Forest car park. Ask for Tourism Ireland information at any tourist office, or contact:

Slieve Bloom Walking Centre, Kinnitty Village, County Offaly, **t** (0509) 37299, **f** (0509) 37351, *ardmorehouse@eircom.net*. Guided walking tours programme, maps and information.

Where to Stay and Eat

Ivyleigh House, Bank Place, Portlaoise, **t** (0502) 22081, **f** (0502) 63343, *www.ivyleigh.com*, *info@ivyleigh.com* (*expensive*). Situated in the centre of town, a luxurious Georgian guest house where the emphasis is on quality, which is reflected in its four tastefully decorated en suite rooms.

Roundwood House, Mountrath, **t** (0502) 32120, *www.hidden-ireland.com/roundwood/* (*moderate*). A 1740s Palladian mansion run by a delightful family, the Kennans, who will instantly make you welcome. The atmosphere is relaxed and comfortable. Children are welcome, and have part of the top floor to amuse themselves in. The food is delicious.

Preston House, Abbeyleix, **t** (0502) 31432 (*moderate*). Ivy-covered stone B&B, run by Allison Dowling, which was originally a school. Now furnished with antiques, the restaurant is locally recommended. *Closed Christmas and Feb.*

Morrissey's Bar, Abbeyleix, **t** (0502) 31233 (*inexpensive*). Charming pub and grocery shop with old cake tins and a stove. Good for stout and sandwiches.

Galway, was granted title to the lands round here; he was one of William III's foreign favourites, who excited much jealousy among English courtiers. The connection is commemorated by the so-called French style of the old town houses; their gardens stretch down to the river rather than into the street.

It's worth stopping at the magnificent neoclassical **Emo Court** (*grounds open all year during daylight hours; house open mid June–mid Sept, daily 10.30–5; adm fee for house; **t** (0502) 26573, **f** (0502) 21450*), on the Dublin to Cork Road (N8) between Monasterevin and Portlaoise. Designed in 1795 by James Gandon, it contains a very impressive domed rotunda room. Siena marble and gilded capitals add to the richness. It was rescued and restored by Mr Cholmeley Harrison in the 1960s, and the house has recently been restored further by the National Heritage Service. The 18th-century gardens, with some new planting incorporated, are laid out between the house and a large lough, with grassy paths that lead you to a series of vistas.

Mountmellick, Mountrath and the Slieve Bloom Mountains

To the western side of the county are the Slieve Bloom Mountains, an island of mountain wilderness, with wooded glens, waterfalls, boglands and magnificent views, all of which are very well signposted. **Mountmellick** was founded in the 17th century by Quakers and grew prosperous on cotton, linen and wool industries. The town is curled into a bend of the River Owenass and today still retains an 18th-century feeling. **Mountrath**, further to the south, is another attractive town which was founded in the 1600s by Charles Coote, an active entrepreneur, whose family built houses all over Ireland. He established charcoal-burning ironworks which ate up the natural forests. Today the Irish State has planted thousands of acres of sitka spruce and pine in Laois which, although rather monotonous, will one day yield a good cash crop.

Close to Mountrath is **Roundwood House**, a fine Palladian mansion which has won many awards as a first-class guest house. The owners would be delighted to show you around. The house is to be found by following the N7 from Dublin to Mountrath, and then following signs for the Slieve Bloom Mountains. It is about 3 miles (4.8km) out of town. The Irish Georgian Society rescued Roundwood House from ruin in the 1970s, and the Kennan family continue the good work. Notice the unusual staircase carved in Chinese Chippendale style. Beyond Borris in Ossory, following the N7 to Roscrea, is **Ballaghmore Castle**, which was a Fitzgerald outpost on the borders of old Ossory, and has a *Sheila-na-Gig* high up on its walls. In the Slieve Bloom Mountains, the **Ridge of Capard** has outstanding views. It is reached from Rosenallis Village. **Glendine Gap** is also spectacular; from here you look over the four provinces of Ireland. One of the ancient highways of Ireland, the Munster Road, crosses the area from north to south through Glenlitter, Glynsk and the Tulla Gap. The pine marten, Ireland's rarest mammal, is found in these glens.

Southern Laois

In the southern tip of County Laois is the attractive town of **Durrow** (on the N8), which was owned at one time by the Duke of Ormonde. **Castle Durrow**, now a convent, was built in 1716. You can ask to look around it. To the south is the pretty village of **Cullahill**. In the village is a fine old gabled **castle** (*not open to the public*) built by the Fitzpatricks, lords of the area before the Normans arrived. Going back north again, following the N8, is the town of **Abbeyleix**. Nothing remains of the Cistercian monastery, founded here by Conor O'Moore in the 12th century, which became part of the Earl of Ormonde's vast possessions in Elizabeth I's reign. The town is well laid-out, and in the south is the beautiful Adam house built by Viscount de Vesci after a design by William Chambers (*not open to the public*). There is a lovely pub called Morisseys on Main Street, a good stop for a sandwich and a glass of stout. It has a lovely old-fashioned stove, used in winter.

At **Timahoe**, on the R426 between Portlaoise and Swan, there is a 12th-century **round tower** (*always accessible*) which is over 100ft (30m) high, with a double door decorated with stone heads in a Romanesque style.

County Kildare

Kildare is a county of bog and plain, divided by the Liffey in the northeast, and the basin of the Barrow in the south. The Bog of Allen, a huge raised bog formed over five thousand years ago, spreads to the northwest. The county is crossed by the Grand Canal, which links Dublin and the Shannon River at Banagher; its towpath provides lovely walks away from the traffic and fumes of the roads, and excellent coarse fishing. Being so near to Dublin, Kildare is one of the most populated counties, yet it is possible to explore the canal villages and its many castles, stately houses and gardens, and still feel you are in the heart of the country. Do not linger too long in the towns, many of which tend to get jammed with traffic during the rush-hours as they are situated on major through-routes to Dublin.

Most people have heard of The Curragh, a plain of over 5,000 acres (2,000ha) just east of Kildare Town, where some of the fastest horses in the world are bred and exercised. It was formed in the Ice Age, when the ice ground the surface of the

Getting There and Around

By Rail
Sallins, Kildare Town and Athy are on the main line from Dublin to Waterford, while the main line to Sligo and Galway passes through Maynooth, along with frequent trains.
Iarnród Eireann, t (01) 836 6222, www.irishrail.ie.

By Bus
Maynooth, Newbridge and Kildare are stops on many routes into Dublin.
Bus Eireann, t (01) 836 6111, www.buseireann.ie.

By Bike
The Raleigh Rent-a-Bike network operates in Kildare.
John Cahill and Son, Sallins Road, Naas, t (045) 879655, f (045) 874055.

Festivals

January–February
Féile Bhríde. Festival of St Brigid, at St Brigid's Cathedral, Kildare, t (045) 522890.

March
Kildare Drama Festival, t (045) 521907.

April
Irish National Hunt Festival, Punchestown Racecourse, t (045) 897704.

May
Robertstown Canal Festival. Held in the first week, and also the first week in August.
Prosperous Coarse Fishing Festival.
Leixlip Salmon Festival. Including a mock battle with Vikings, held in late May/June, t (01) 624 3085.

June
Derby Festival, Kildare. A week of music and celebrations around the horse race.
All-Ireland Turf Cutting Competition, Ticknevin.
Music in Great Irish Houses. Festival held in various locations, t (01) 278 1528 (see also Practical A–Z, p.130).

July
Bluegrass Music Festival, Athy.
Maynooth Summer Festival. Music, drama, dance, football and a treasure hunt.

August
Monasterevin Canal Festival. Held over the bank holiday weekend.

limestone plain to a powder. This mixed with vegetable remains to produce a rich pasture, famed for making the bones of horses grazed on it very strong. You may wish to visit the National Stud and Irish Horse Museum at Tully near Kildare Town. Or there is great fun to be had attending the races, both at the Curragh and Punchestown where, besides having a flutter, you can admire a Bronze Age standing stone, 23ft (7m) in height, which is in the grounds of the racecourse. This county also contains two of the grandest houses in the country: Carton House, ancient seat of the Earls of Kildare; and the next-door estate of Castletown House, a very fine Palladian mansion.

History
The history of the county is fascinating, for its fertile river plains have attracted many invaders. The first recorded inhabitants are a Celtic people, the Ui Dunlainge, who may have originated from Cornwall. They built great hill-forts, the remains of which can be seen at Mullaghmast in the south, Knockaulin in the centre, and the Hill of Allen in the west. Knockaulin, near Kilcullen, dates from the late Bronze Age, and shares, along with Tara in Meath and Emain Macha in Armagh, a legendary importance in the folk memories of the Irish people. Christianity came in the 5th century, and the monks built their churches near the centres of Celtic pagan

power. Moone, near the fort of Mullaghmast, has an 8th-century stone cross which is wonderfully carved with scenes from the Bible. The Ui Dunlainge split off into branches, becoming rivals and fighting for territory. The Norsemen arrived in early AD 900 and established their power in Dublin and the northeast of Kildare.

The Anglo-Normans under the leadership of Richard de Clare, called Strongbow, came in the 12th century. They had been invited over by Diarmuid MacMurragh, King of Leinster, to help him regain his kingdom. Strongbow did indeed help him to capture Dublin and defeat his enemies but, as the *Book of Leinster* records, 'he died after the victory of unction and penance; thence forward is the miserable reign of the Saxons, amen, amen' (*see* **History**, p.39). The Normans soon squeezed out the Celtic tribes, who took to the Wicklow Mountains, where they became the O'Tooles and mounted attacks on the Norman colony.

By 1300 Kildare was dominated by the Norman Fitzgerald Earls of Kildare, known as the Geraldines. For a time in the late 15th century, they were so powerful and wealthy that they were the uncrowned kings of Ireland. Gerald, the 8th Earl, who was known as the Great Earl, was made Deputy of Ireland in 1481 by Edward IV, who reasoned that if all Ireland could not rule this man, he would let him rule all Ireland. Inevitably, however, the Tudor kings viewed the power of the Fitzgeralds with increasing resentment. By 1534 they had completely fallen out with the English government, and the 9th Earl died in the Tower of London. His son, Thomas, renounced his allegiance to Henry VII and attacked Dublin Castle. (He is known as 'Silken Thomas' because his followers had silken fringes on their helmets.) His army was routed and he retreated to his stronghold at Maynooth. But in March 1535 Sir William Skeffington took it and the garrison was given the 'Maynooth pardon': in other words, they were executed. Thomas had escaped the bloodshed, but he eventually submitted and was given a guarantee of personal safety. This was not fulfilled and he too was sent to the Tower, and was hanged, drawn and quartered with his five uncles in 1537.

The Kildares lost much of their power again with the Cromwellian wars and plantation, although their estates were restored by Charles II. They survived the Williamite wars of 1689–91 and built Carton House. Many of the old Norman families did not fare so well, and were replaced by new loyal colonists known as 'planters'. They were Protestant, and built themselves fine houses with beautiful craftsmanship. The Great Famine of 1845–49 and the various uprisings put an end to all of this. Dublin has grown hugely in this century, especially in the last 20 years, so that most of the villages of northern Kildare have become dormitory suburbs of Dublin. People say 'we used to go to Dublin, but now Dublin has come to us.'

Northern Kildare

Naas and Around to the Grand Canal

Naas (pronounced 'Nace'), only 21 miles (34km) from Dublin, is a busy industrial town, on the edge of the Wicklow Mountains, with good shopping and a hunting and horse-racing centre. In Irish it is known as *Nas na Riogh*, meaning 'Meeting Place of the Kings'. It used to be one of the seats of the kings of Leinster, and was the centre of the Irish kingdom of Ui Dunlainge. All that remains of their fort is a motte: a large hill in the middle of the town. At **Kill**, 1½ miles (3km) away off the N7 to Dublin, is Goffs,

Tourist Information

Naas: 38 South Main Street, t (045) 898888; *open all year.*

Shopping

Crafts
Brenda O'Brien, Dun Buain Lodge, Kill, Naas. Pottery.

Health Foods
Naturally, 29 North Main Street, Naas, t (045) 871372.

Markets
Friday Country Market, Town Hall, Naas. Held between 10.45 and noon, with fresh vegetables and herb cheeses on sale.

Sports and Activities

Fishing
In Prosperous and all along the Grand Canal. Contact:
Mrs Travers, Curryhills House, Prosperous, Naas, t (045) 868728,

Horse-racing
Look for details in the national newspapers, or in the racing calendar in the back of the Tourism Ireland *Calendar of Events,* published every year.
Punchestown, t (045) 897704, **f** (045) 987319, *www.punchestown.com.*
Naas, t (045) 897391, **f** (045) 897486, *www.naasracecourse.com.*

Pleasure Cruises
Grand Canal Hotel, Robertstown, **t** (045) 860260. The *Eustace* operates from here, offering trips along the Grand Canal.
Lowtown Marine, Robertstown, **t** (045) 860427. Rent a boat on the canal.

Pony-trekking
Osbertstown Riding Centre, beside Sallins Railway Bridge, Naas, **t** (045) 879074.
Kill International Equestrian Centre, Kill, **t** (045) 877208.

Where to Stay

Moyglare Manor, Maynooth, **t** (01) 628 6351 *(expensive).* An elegant Georgian house built in 1775, and supposed to be the dower house to the Carton Estate. Expect immaculately kept bedrooms, antiques, a friendly, clubby bar, delicious food and fresh flowers everywhere. Garden suite available.
Curryhills House Hotel, Prosperous, Naas, **t** (045) 867728 *(moderate).* Georgian farmhouse with a lovely atmosphere and good food.
Kildare Hotel and Country Club, Straffan, **t** (01) 601 7200 *(luxury).* One of Ireland's finest country mansions, with a fitness centre, a highly-rated restaurant and its own golf course, designed by Arnold Palmer.
Barberstown Castle and Country House, Straffan, **t** (01) 628 8157, **f** (01) 627 7027, *castleir@iol.ie (expensive).* An attractive jumble of Norman, Elizabethan and Edwardian architecture.

Eating Out

Curryhills House, Prosperous, Naas, **t** (045) 868728 *(moderate).* Predictable but good-value menu.
Michaelangelo Restaurant, Main Street, Celbridge, **t** (01) 627 1809 *(moderate).* Irish/Italian food. *Evenings only.*
Kildare Hotel and Country Club, Straffan, **t** (01) 601 7200 *(expensive).* Sophisticated, with superb food; Michelin-starred restaurant.
Moyglare Manor Hotel, Maynooth, **t** (01) 6286351 *(expensive).* Has a romantic ambience and lots of seafood. *Open for dinner and Sunday lunch.*

the old established horse auctioneers which sell 50 per cent of all Irish-bred horses. John Devoy (1842–1928), the Irish-American newspaper man and Fenian, was born here. He was influential in organizing publicity in America, and worked in the early 20th century to help the Irish Freedom Movement with money and propaganda, through such organizations as Clan na Gael.

Jigginstown House, just a mile (1.6km) southwest on the Kildare Road (N7), is now a massive ruin. It was built by Thomas Wentworth, Earl of Strafford, when Charles I proposed to visit him. The visit never came off and 'Black Tom', one of the most unpopular men in Ireland, was executed in 1641 by the Roundheads before it was finished. It would have been the largest unfortified house ever built in Ireland, but only the cellars were completed. If you are in need of a little refreshment, an old-fashioned pub called Fletcher's, with cosy snugs and wooden floors, should fill that gap nicely.

Punchestown is famous for its standing stone and its races. The stone is 3 miles (4.8km) southeast of Naas, off the Woolpack Road, and is 23ft high (7m) with a Bronze Age burial chamber at its base. To the northwest are the quiet canal villages of Prosperous and Robertstown. The Grand Canal was built in the 1760s and carried agricultural produce between Dublin and the River Barrow at Athy. The railways destroyed the villages' passenger and commercial trade, but today the Grand Canal and the Naas Canal, a branch of the Grand, have been restored. The canalside has some very attractive walks and drives, and cruisers are for hire at Tullamore in County Offaly (*see* p.545).

Robertstown is ideal for a quiet and leisurely visit. The locals are very proud of the town's 18th-century associations, and the waterfront has been restored to look as it did in the days when travellers used to alight from their boats for an overnight stop. Some of the barges have been restored, and you can go for short trips on the canal. Eighteenth-century banquets are recreated in the Grand Canal Hotel, which no longer functions as a hotel, but is used for all sorts of entertainments. The evening begins with a horse-drawn barge cruise, and culminates with the feast. During weekends in July and August, there are concerts, lectures on the Georgian and canal eras, and lots of festivities. Between Clane and Prosperous is a Victorian garden at **Coolcarrigan** (*open for groups by appointment only; adm for house and gardens; t (045) 863512/863524*). It is best seen in spring and autumn, as there are some magnificent trees.

Stucco Splendour: Castletown and Environs

Celbridge, 8 miles (5km) north of Naas, is a must for all lovers of Georgian country houses, for within a few miles are both Castletown House and **Carton House**. Sadly, the future of the latter is rather precarious at the moment and it is difficult to view. It was once the seat of the Earls of Kildare, a powerful Norman family who became very Irish, and the grounds were laid out by Capability Brown as a park where 'art and nature in just union reign'. The house was designed in the 1730s by Richard Cassels, a French Huguenot who did a lot of work in Ireland. There is a Shell House in the grounds. Mrs Delaney, who is still remembered for her diaries which recorded the privileged life of the Protestant ascendency, helped to decorate the house when she stayed at one of the many house parties held at Carton during the mid-18th century.

Castletown House, at the eastern end of Celbridge village (*open mid April–Sept, Mon–Fri 10–6 weekends and bank hols 1–6, in Oct, Mon–Fri 10–5 weekends and bank hols 1–5, in Nov, Sun 1–5 only; adm; t (01) 628 8252, f (01) 627 1811*), is approached through a fine avenue of lime trees. This splendid Palladian mansion was built for William Connelly, speaker of the Irish House of Commons from 1715 to 1719, and contains some elaborate plasterwork by the Francini Brothers, who taught Irish craftsmen the art of stucco. It has the only 18th-century print room in Ireland, and some superb 18th-century furnishings. One of the hunt balls held during the week of the Dublin Horse Show takes place in its gracious rooms. From the windows of the Long Gallery you can see the extraordinary Connelly Folly, an obelisk supported on arches, built by the widow of Speaker Connelly to provide relief work after a particularly hard winter. In 1994 Castletown became the property of the state and is now run by the Office of Public Works. It is one of the venues for the Music in Great Irish Houses Festival, held in June (*see* **Practical A–Z**, p.130). A few miles southwest of Celbridge between the N7 and the R403 is the pretty village of **Straffan**, which has a wonderful **Steam Museum** (*open Easter Sunday–Sept, Tues–Sat 2.30–5.30; adm; t (01) 627 3155 or t (01) 628 8412*), with rare examples of industrial steam engines and locomotives and a good tea-room.

Maynooth, a couple of miles north of Celbridge, has ancient associations with the great Geraldine family, the Fitzgeralds, later Earls of Kildare and Dukes of Leinster. The fine ruins of the 12th-century **Castle Fitzgerald** may be explored if you get the key from Castleview House, across the road from the castle. A gate house, a massive keep and a great hall survive. This is where Sir William Skeffington, acting for Henry VIII, presided over the killing of the Geraldine followers when he took the castle in 1535. Today Maynooth is more closely associated with **St Patrick's College**, next to the castle, which has been turning out Catholic priests since 1795, although it is now a lay university as well. Funnily enough, it was established by the British, who did not like the idea of the Irish priests studying abroad where they might pick up revolutionary ideas. The buildings are late-Georgian in style, with a Gothic Revival addition by J. J. McCarthy, a pupil of Pugin, one of the architects who rebuilt the British Houses of Parliament. Visitors can see the **Ecclesiastical Museum** (*open weekdays 11–5, Sun 2–6; adm*) which includes vestments made by Marie Antoinette for an Irish chaplain, gardens and an audio-visual presentation.

Just west of Maynooth, at Kilcock's **Larchill Arcadian Gardens** (*open May–end Sept, daily 12–6; adm; t (01) 628 4580*), there is a rare example of an 18th-century style of garden called a *ferme ornée*, an 'embellished farm', perhaps inspired by the famous one at Versailles where Marie Antoinette played milkmaid and enjoyed the Arcadian fantasies of that delicately jaded era. The owner of Larchill, Michael de las Casas, completed a loving restoration and won the annual Irish Conservation Award for his trouble. The work included rebuilding a lake, with ten classical follies on islands, and a walled garden. Rare breeds of farm animals have been installed in quarters that are follies in themselves.

Leixlip (pronounced 'Leeks-lip') is on the banks of the Liffey; its name comes from the Danish *Lax-laup*, which means 'salmon leap'. Before the falls were utilized for hydroelectric power, it was a wonderful sight to see the salmon do just that. The 12th-century Norman **castle** is owned by Desmond Guinness, the force behind the Irish Georgian Society, which has done so much to preserve the rich treasury of 18th-century buildings in Ireland. (It is not open to view.) Leixlip has grown hugely as Dublin spreads ever outwards. The swift waters of the Liffey in this area are a great challenge to sportsmen, and canoeists come here from all over the world.

Southern Kildare

The Curragh to the Bog

Kildare Town is on the edge of the Curragh, and is now an important centre for horse-breeding. It is said that St Brigid spread her handkerchief over enough land on which to build a convent, and the ruling king had to grant it to her. Her nunnery thrived during the 6th century, but by the 7th century it had become a monastery.

The Church of Ireland **cathedral** on the hill in the middle of the town dates in parts from the 13th century, and stands on the site of a 6th-century church. This venerable pile of stones has been pillaged and burned many times, and lay in ruins between 1641 and 1875. (A roof-restoration appeal is now being run.) The cathedral has some fine monuments, and a three-light west window with scenes from the lives of Brigid, Patrick and Colmcille, the three Patron Saints of Ireland. Beside it there is a 10th-century **round tower** with an 18th-century top, which you can climb.

The thousand-acre **National Stud** at **Tully** (*open 12 Feb–12 Nov, weekdays 9.30–6, Sat and public holidays 10.30–6, Sun 2–6; adm for stud and gardens; t (045) 521617*), just outside Kildare Town on the R415, was started by Colonel Hall-Walker (later Lord Wavertree). He bred the famous Derby winner Minoru, and many others. In 1915 he presented the estate and horses to the Crown, and it was handed over to the Irish state in 1943. Its importance in the blood-stock and racing world is without parallel. The National Stud is open for guided tours in the summer, and there is a **Horse Museum**. Lord Wavertree, a Scotsman whose family made their money from beer, was brilliant with horses but a notable eccentric in his methods. On the tour they'll point out the skylights he had installed in all the stables; a firm believer in astrology, he wanted the stars to exert their influence on his horses to the full. One thing that motivated him was a lifelong fascination for all things Japanese; he brought over two of that nation's most renowned landscape architects in 1906 to lay out a spectacular **Japanese Garden**, still perfectly maintained and one of the most popular attractions in Ireland. The gardens symbolize the life of man from cradle to the grave, and include a Zen meditation garden.

The green spring grass of the **Curragh** stretches for miles, with the blue hills of Dublin on the horizon. The pasture that grows on its limestone plain is said to be the best in the world for building horses' bones. But it is the skill of the breeders in choosing the sires which has made Curragh bloodstock so successful, and the

Tourist Information

Kildare Town: Market House, Market Square, t (045) 522696/521240; *open June–Sept.*

Shopping

Crafts

Kildare Woolen Mills, Kildare.
Curragh Pottery, Lumville, Curragh.
Irish Pewter Mill and Craft Centre, Timolin.

Sports and Activities

Horse-racing

Look for details in the national newspapers, or in the racing calendar in the back of the Tourism Ireland *Calendar of Events*, published every year.
The Curragh Racecourse, t (045) 441205, *www.curragh.ie.*

Pleasure Cruises

Canalways Ireland, Spencer Bridge, Rathangan, t (045) 524646.

Pony-trekking

Red Hills Equestrian Centre, Kildare, t (045) 55042.

Where to Stay

Tonlegee House and Restaurant, Athy, t/f (0507) 31473, *www.tonlegeehouse.com* (*moderate*). Just off the Kilkenny road, outside Athy. An elegant 18th-century country house with en-suite rooms and a restaurant, which offers dishes made with organic vegetables from their own garden as well as local fish and game.

Ballindrum Farm, Athy, t (0507) 26294 (*inexpensive*). Comfortable accommodation on Mr and Mrs Gorman's working farm; good breakfasts and dinner available.

Woodcourte House, Moone, Timolin, near Athy, t (0507) 24167 (*inexpensive*). Modern bungalow in quiet countryside. Situated near a nice bar called the Moone High Cross Inn. There is a tennis court available

and arts and crafts weekends are organized. Evening meal available; contact Mrs Donoghue.

Griesemount, Ballitore, t (0507) 481205 (*moderate–inexpensive*). Small and genteel B&B in a Georgian house, run by Robert and Carolyn Ashe.

Kilkea Castle, Castledermot, t (0503) 45156, f (0503) 45187, *www.kilkeacastle.ie, kilkea@iol.ie* (*luxury*). Built by Hugh de Lacy in 1180, this is the oldest inhabited castle in Ireland and has views over the tranquil gardens. Good health and sporting facilities.

Kilkea Lodge Farm, Castledermot, t (0503) 45112 (*moderate*). Charming 18th-century farmhouse. Riding holidays arranged; contact Mr and Mrs Greene.

Doyles Schoolhouse Restaurant and B&B, Castledermot, t (0503) 44282 (*moderate*). Delightful eating place with excellent cuisine and comfortable rooms; run as a country inn.

Eating Out

The Red House Country Hotel and Restaurant, Nua, t (045) 431516 (*moderate*). French food, home-grown vegetables. *Evenings only.*

Tonlegee House, Athy, t (0507) 31473 (*expensive*). Imaginative and delicious cooking. *Dinner only.*

Moone High Cross Inn, Bolton Hill, Moone, t (0507) 24112 (*moderate*). Friendly, old-fashioned pub. Better than average pub food including home-cooked roasts, sandwiches and scrumptious apple pie.

D'Lacy's, in Kilkea Castle, Castledermot, t (0503) 45156, *www.kilkeacastle.ie* (*expensive*). Local produce and fresh vegetables are served in a dining room where the atmosphere must be due to long use.

Doyles School House Restaurant, Castledermot, t (0503) 44282 (*moderate*). A small friendly restaurant with a simple and delicious table d'hôte.

The Hideout, Kilcullen, t (045) 481232 (*moderate*). Cavernous bar with a good restaurant.

excitement at the races when their skill is put to test is phenomenal: the chat is fast and furious, porter is downed in the tents, and the horses are splendid, thundering along in the green distance. Numerous meetings are held between March and November. The most famous are the Irish Sweep Derby in midsummer, the Irish 2,000 Guineas, the Irish Oaks and the Irish St Leger. The Curragh is also famous for the country's largest army camp.

The **Hill of Allen** (676ft/206m), south east of Rathangan, is famous in Irish legend as the other world seat of Fionn MacCumhaill (*see* pp.83–4). The summit is 15 minutes' walk from the road, and at the top is a 19th-century **folly** built by a Sir George Aylmer, 'in thankful remembrance of God'. The hill, together with Naas, and *Dun Aillinne* (Knockaulin), which is just northwest of Kilcullen on the N9, was a residence of the kings of Leinster. Straight lines joining them form an equilateral triangle, with sides 9 miles (14.5km) long. **Rathangan**, a quiet canal town, stands on the edge of the Bog of Allen, one of the largest raised bogs in this part of Ireland. At nearby Lullymore you can learn all you ever wanted to know about bogs – and more – at an interpretative centre called **Peatland World** (*open weekdays 9.30–5, weekends 2–6; adm; t (045) 860133, f (045) 860481*). **Newbridge** (*Droichead Nua*) to the east is an industrial centre on the Liffey. Outside it and near the Dominican College is an ancient motte.

From Athy to Kilcullen

Athy ('Ford of Ae'), south of Kildare Town on the R417, has developed from a 13th-century Anglo-Norman settlement at a fording point on the River Barrow. The Ae of the Gaelic name for the town was a king of Munster, who was killed trying to take control of the ford in the 11th century. A privately owned 16th-century castle looks over Crom-a-boo bridge. (The name refers to the war-cry of the Desmond branch of the Fitzgerald family.) There is a lovely old **market house** in the town which can be viewed from the outside only, as it is now a fire station. The pentagon-shaped modern Dominican church is built of massed concrete, and has attractive stained-glass windows. **Athy Heritage Centre** (*open year round, Mon–Sat 10–6, Sun and bank hols 2–6, Nov–Feb closed Sun; t (0507) 33075, f (0507) 33076, athyheritage@tinet.ie*) is found in the early 18th-century town hall, and has multimedia displays on the town's history.

Half a mile (0.8km) out of town on the R417, the 13th-century **Woodstock Castle** still survives in the form of a rectangular tower. A short expedition can be made to another historical spot, the **Ardscull Motte**, some 4 miles (6.4km) north of Athy off the N78. It was used by Edward Bruce in 1315 to defeat an English army. **Moone High Cross** (*always accessible*), one of the most famous and beautiful of all the high crosses, is 8 miles (12.9km) from Athy, in the demesne of Moone Abbey House, beside the little village of Timolin on the N9. The cross, also known as St Colmcille's Cross, is 17½ft (5.3m) high and has 51 sculptured panels depicting scenes from the Bible.

Castledermot, south of Moone on the N9, is famous for the remains of its **Franciscan abbey**, high crosses and round tower. The **tower** is tall and slender, and facing it is a lovely 12th-century Romanesque doorway. A modern copy of it in the church is in use. The two attractive sculptured granite **high crosses** are in the graveyard. Castledermot was a place of great importance, once upon a time: a walled town in which Hugh de Lacy built an Anglo-Norman fortress. Edward Bruce fought for it in the 14th century, but was defeated; and Cromwell sacked it in 1649. There are some remains of the stone walls, and Carlow Gate still stands. A few miles outside the town is **Kilkea Castle**, once the home of the Earls of Kildare, now a luxury hotel and health farm.

At **Timolin**, the art of pewter has been restored at the **Irish Pewter Mill and Craft Centre** (*open Mon–Fri 10–4, workshop open for visits 11–5;* **t** *(0507) 24164*). The neighbouring village of **Ballitore** was once a flourishing Quaker settlement; the old **Meeting House** survives, now a library and museum, with exhibits on Quaker life. The nearby Ballitore School was famous for its high standard of education; Edmund Burke, the 18th-century political writer and orator; Napper Tandy (1740–1803), the United Irishman; and Cardinal Cullen (1803–1878), who was instrumental in setting up a Catholic university in Dublin, were all pupils. **Crookstown Mill** (*museum open Mon–Sat 11–6; mill open daily 10–6; adm*), by the river, has been restored, and there is a collection of industrial archaeology and exhibitions on milling and the life of the community in the 19th century.

Nearby, west of the village, is the **Rath of Mullaghmast**, an earthern Stone Age fort, rich with folklore. It is said that Garret Og Fitzgerald, the 11th Earl of Kildare, sleeps here and emerges once every seven years. A grisly massacre took place on this spot in 1597. It was also the setting for one of Daniel O'Connell's mass meetings in 1843 when he was campaigning for the repeal of the Act of Union, which had taken place between England and Ireland in 1801.

Close to the River Liffey and just southeast of the Curragh Camp are two tiny villages. **Old Kilcullen**, just off the N9, is the site of an Early Christian monastery, with fragmentary 8th-century crosses like those at Moone. There is also a ruined round tower. West of the tower, across the N78, is the Iron Age **Hill Fort of Knockaulin** (also called *Dun Ailinne*). From both of these sites you can get a wonderful view of the Barrow Valley. The petty chieftains of this area, who had ambitions to become kings of Leinster, associated themselves with the power and royal connections of the fort long after it had been abandoned as a royal centre in the first centuries AD. They referred to themselves as Kings of Dun Ailinne. The monks were doing the same thing by building Kilcullen monastery so close to the mill.

County Dublin

Ireland's capital city sprawls over a large part of this county and threatens to dominate it completely, but if you wish to be guided by the example of fun-loving Dubliners you will follow them to the jaunty sea resorts along the coast, to the lavish gardens of Howth Castle, or to the unique collection of Irish furniture and portraits at Malahide Castle. When you are in the National Gallery, search out Nathaniel Hone's picture, *Cattle at Malahide*, for he has caught the glancing light of the east coast perfectly. James Joyce disciples who are travelling by themselves around the *Ulysses* landmarks in Dublin should not neglect the museum of Joyceana in the Martello tower, and Sandymount, where Gertie McDowell showed Mr Bloom her garters. Further to the south sweeps the lovely Killiney Bay, whilst to the north of Dublin, the flat, tidy fields of the Skerries and Rush slope down to the sea, and the wide arm of Dublin Bay ends at the beautiful peninsula of Howth Head. Most of the population of the county commute to Dublin City to work, although there is a certain amount of vegetable-growing and dairy farming. Many of the little villages described have become dormitory towns of Dublin. Some of the new developments are not particularly attractive: the poorer housing is traditionally badly built, but this has improved enormously. Dublin City has its beggars, housing ghettos and problems with theft and drugs just like any other capital city; but it also has a wealth of

County Dublin

10km
5 miles

N

Kentstown
Balrath
Gormanston
Balbriggan
Ardgillan Demesne
Tara
Skerries
Dunsany
Oldtown
Ballyboghil
Lusk
Rush
Ratoath
M E A T H
Lambay Island
Newbridge House
Donabate
Mullagh
Black Bull
Swords
Malahide Castle
I R I S H
Dublin Airport
Malahide
Dunboyne
Talbot Botanic Gardens
Portmarnock
S E A
Maynooth
N2
Leixlip
Nose of Howth
Castletown House
Lucan
Howth Castle
Howth
Celbridge
Dublin Bay
Douglas (Isle of Man)
Holyhead
Straffan
Liverpool
DUBLIN
Grand Canal
Blackrock
Holyhead
KILDARE
Rathfarnham
Monkstown
Dun Laoghaire
Marlay Park
Dalkey
Kill
Dalkey Island
Fernhill Garden
Killiney
River Dodder
Glencullen
R116
Killiney Bay
Kilbride
Glencree
R117
Blessington
Enniskerry
Bray
Powerscourt Estate
Bray Head
WICKLOW
R107

Getting There and Around

By Air

A variety of airlines fly into Dublin Airport, which is 8 miles (10km) from the city. A **bus service** runs between the Central Bus Station (Busáras) and Dublin Airport. The **Aircoach** runs every 15mins from early morning to 10.20pm (around €5). It's considerably cheaper than a taxi. You can also get the cheaper, but slower, **city buses** (routes 41, 41A and 41C), which circulate between the airport and Eden Quay, outside Busáras. A further bus service runs between the airport and Heuston Station, for train connections. *See also* **Travel**, p.118.

Dublin Airport, t (01) 814 1111, *www.dublin-airport.com*.

Aer Lingus, 40–41 Upper O'Connell Street, flight enquiries **t** (01) 886 8888, reservations **t** (01) 705 3333, *www.aerlingus.ie, bookings@ aerlingus.ie*. They have several city offices.

British Airways, t 1800 626747.

British Midland, Merrion Centre, Merrion Road, **t** (01) 283 8833.

Ryanair, 3 Dawson Street, D2, enquiries **t** 1550 200200, reservations **t** 609 7800, *www. ryanair.com*. Budget airline; probably offers the cheapest flights.

By Boat

Ferries from Holyhead arrive at either **Dun Laoghaire** (Stena) or **Dublin ferry port** (Irish Ferries). Bus numbers 7, 7A and 8 run from Dun Laoghaire to O'Connell Bridge, which is in the centre of Dublin; the No.7 continues over the bridge to Eden Quay outside the bus station. There is also a DART train from Dun Laoghaire to Pearse (rail) Station, on Westland Row, until around midnight. If you arrive at the Dublin ferry port, you'll find buses to the bus station and city centre on the Alexandra Road – all buses with *An Lar* ('city centre') signs are going there.

Stena Line, at Dun Laoghaire ferry port, **t** (01) 204 7777.

Irish Ferries, 2–4 Merrion Row, D2, **t** 1890 313131.

By Rail

There are two main railway stations in Dublin city: **Heuston**, west of the centre on St John's Road, serves the south, southwest and west of the country, as well as commuter trains to County Kildare. **Connolly** station, north of the Liffey on Amiens Street, near the bus station, serves Wexford, Sligo and Belfast (where for Derry you must change trains), and has a connection with the main DART (Dublin Area Rapid Transit) line and commuter lines to Maynooth, Mullingar and Longford.

Iarnród Eireann Travel Centre ('iron road Irish rail'), 35 Lower Abbey Street , Dublin, **t** (01) 836 6222. For all rail information. *Office open Mon–Fri 9–5, phone lines open Mon–Fri 8.30–6, Sat 9–6, Sun 10–6.*

By Bus

All intercity Expressway buses run by Bus Eireann end up in *Busáras* (the central bus station), at Store Street, on the north side of the Liffey, three streets east of O'Connell Street.

The Travel Centre, Busáras, Store Street, Dublin 1, **t** (01) 836 6111. Information on all services is given here; you can also contact the tourist offices. *Offices for Irish services open Mon–Fri 9–4, phone lines open Mon–Fri 8.30am–7pm; Eurolines offices and phone lines (for services to the UK and rest of Europe) both open Mon–Fri 9–5.30.*

By Bike

CGL, 9 Townyard Lane, Malahide, **t** (01) 845 4275. Bike hire.

Festivals

April

Howth Jazz Festival. Usually takes place over the Easter bank holiday weekend; lots of gigs in local halls and bars.

June

AIB Music in Great Irish Houses. A festival of chamber music, with around 10 evening concerts held in great houses in the Dublin area (*see* also **Practical A–Z**, p.130).

July

Irish Open Golf Championship, Portmarnock.

Georgian architecture, a lively atmosphere and a charm that is peculiar to the city itself. Its beautiful setting beside the sea, within such easy reach of beaches and mountains, gives its people a great escape route when they need it, even if it is only for a few hours. Many Dublin writers – Flann O'Brien, James Joyce and Samuel Beckett to name just three – drew great inspiration from the countryside around them.

Around the County

North County Dublin

On the coast at the northern tip of the county, **Skerries** and **Balbriggan** are noted for their dry, sunny climate and their safe, sandy beaches. Many locals are involved in the fishing industry. **Ardgillan Castle**, between Balbriggan and Skerries (*park open daily, 10–dusk; castle open July–Aug, daily 11–6, April–June and Sept, Tues–Sun 11–6, Oct–Dec and Feb–Mar, Tues–Sun 11–4.30, Jan, Sun only 2–4; adm to castle; t (01) 849 2212*), is a lush public park of 194 acres of pasture, woods and gardens, amidst which is a well-maintained estate built in 1738. The main rooms are open to the public and are furnished in Victorian style; upstairs is an exhibition of historical maps of Ireland. At **The Naul** (*An Aill*: 'The Cliff' or 'The Rock', after the cliff on which the Norman-built Black Castle stands), to the west, you'll find the **Seamus Ennis Centre** (*t (087) 657 8849*). Named after one of Ireland's most acclaimed traditional musicians, collectors of folklore and broadcasters, it is a focal point for traditional culture in the Fingal area of County Dublin.

Rush, another attractive fishing village, overlooks **Lambay Island** with its 500ft (152m) cliffs rising out of the sea. You have to get permission to land there from the owner, for it is the sanctuary of many rare birds, but the beauty of the island can still be seen by sailing around it. About 3 miles (5km) west of Rush is **Lusk Heritage Centre** (*open mid June–mid Sept, Fri only 10–5; adm; t (01) 833 1618*), including a round tower, a medieval tower with an exhibition on County Dublin churches, and an 1839 Church of Ireland church which contains some fine medieval tombs.

At **Donabate** off the N1 is the splendid **Newbridge House** (*open April–Sept, Tues–Sat 10–1 and 2–5 Sun 2–6, Oct–Mar, weekends 2–5; adm; t (01) 843 6534*), one of the finest and most authentically maintained Georgian manors in Ireland. It was built in 1737 for Charles Cobbe, later Archbishop of Dublin. The authenticity extends to the restored dairy, forge, servants' houses and other buildings, all furnished as they might have been 200 years ago. There is also a working farm, managed according to traditional methods. In the house, the drawing room and its early-Georgian furniture and curios are unique, as is the collection of antique dolls and a doll's house with 14 rooms. There is also a small museum, made up of curiosities brought from all over the world and displayed in specially designed cabinets.

Malahide, a few miles further south, is another seaside resort, with a wonderful old castle which was the seat of the Talbots from 1185 to 1973. Today, **Malahide Castle** (*open April–Oct, Mon–Sat 10–5 Sun 11–6, Nov–Mar, Mon–Fri 10–5 Sat–Sun 2–5; adm; t (01) 846 2184/846 2516, f (01) 846 2537*) is publicly owned, and a part of the National

Tourist Information

Balbriggan: George's Square, **t** (01) 841 4884
Malahide: Malahide Castle, **t** (01) 845 0490.
Tallaght: 3rd Level, The Square, infoline **t** 1850 230330. *Open all year.*
Dun Laoghaire: New Ferry Terminal, infoline **t** 1850 230330. *Open all year.*

Shopping

Auctioneers
Buckley Galleries, 27 Sandycove Road, Dun Laoghaire, **t** (01) 280 5408, **f** (01) 284 4717. Auctions every Thursday at 2.30pm.

Crafts
Malahide Castle Craft Shop, Seaview, Yellow Walls Road, Malahide, **t** (01) 846 2516. Pottery, musical instruments and woven cloth.

Delicacies
Cavistons Delicatessen, 59 Glasthule Road, Sandycove, **t** (01) 280 9120, *www.cavistons.com*. An old-fashioned-style deli with fresh fish, Irish cheeses and smoked salmon.
Country Cellar, 8 Patrick Street, Dun Laoghaire, **t** (01) 280 3338. Health foods.

Sports and Activities

Beaches
Balscadden Beach, Howth: sandy but shallow.
Portmarnock: long and sandy, with donkey rides in the summer.
Malahide: long and sandy.
Donabate: famous for its dunes.
Portrane: has a bird sanctuary at the north end, and, like Donabate, has lovely dunes.
Killiney: this beach is good for long walks; part of it is stony.

Fishing
Trout fishing on the River Dodder and Bohernabrenna Reservoir.

Golf
Portmarnock, **t** (01) 846 0611, *www.portmarnockgolfclub.ie*. A premier tournament course.
The Open Golf Centre, Newton House, St Margaret's, **t** (01) 864 0324, *opengolf@iol.ie*. Off the main Ashbourne–Slane road, adjacent to the airport. 27 holes, open to visitors 7 days a week on a pay-and-play basis. Also has driving range and tuition.
The Royal Dublin Golf Course, North Bull Island, Dollymount, **t** (01) 833 6346/833 7153, *royaldublin@clubi.ie*.
Luttrelstown Golf Course, Castleknock **t** (01) 808 9988, *golf@luttrellstown.ie*.
Malahide Golf Club, south of Malahide Village, **t** (01) 846 1611, *malgc@clubi.ie*.

Horse-racing
Ireland's major tracks are close by in County Kildare (*see* p.554). Check *In Dublin* and evening newspapers for details.
Leopardstown Racecourse, 6 miles south of Dublin city centre, **t** (01) 289 3607, *www.leopardstown.com*.
Fairyhouse Racecourse, Ratoath, Co. Meath, **t** (01) 825 6167.

Portrait Collection is housed there. *The Boswell Papers*, which give us such an insight into 18th-century travel, were found here in a croquet box. The castle is made up of three different periods, the earliest being a three-storey tower house dating from the 12th century. The façade of the house is flanked by two slender towers built in about 1765. Inside is the only surviving original medieval great hall in Ireland, hung with Talbot family portraits. The display of Irish 18th-century furniture is fascinating and shows the sophistication of the craftsmanship and artistry existing in Ireland at the time. The grounds are superb, especially the part now known as the **Talbot Botanic Gardens** (*open May–Sept, daily 2–5; guided tours Wed at 2; adm; **t** (01) 816 9910*), laid out with thousands of species, many of them exotic plants from the southern

Internet Cafés
Cyberspace, Café Bleu, 88B Lower George Street, Dun Laoghaire, *cyberspace@internet-eireann.ie.*
Net House, 28 Upper Georges Street, Dun Laoghaire, **t** (01) 230 3085, **f** (01) 230 3076, *www.nethousecafes.com.*

Pony-trekking
Calliaghstown Riding Centre, Calliaghstown, Rathcoole, **t** (01) 458 9236.

Water Sports
Fingall Sailing School, Upper Strand Road, Broadmeadow Estuary, Malahide, **t** (01) 845 1979, *fingall.maritime@indigo.ie.* Junior, youth and adult courses in sail training and windsailing.
Wind and Wave Watersports, 16a The Crescent, Monkstown **t** (01) 284 4177. Windsurfing.

Royal Marine Hotel, Marine Road, Dun Laoghaire, **t** (01) 280 1911, low call **t** 1850 298298, *www.gresham-hotels.com, royalmarine@eircom.net* (*luxury*). Old-fashioned, comfortable and friendly. The best rooms are situated in the old building.
Chestnut Lodge, 2 Vesey Place, Dun Laoghaire, **t** (01) 280 7860 (*moderate*). Gracious Georgian house with lovely comfortable rooms, good breakfasts and a very friendly atmosphere in which nothing is too much trouble. It is situated close to Dun Laoghaire ferry port.
Sandycove Guesthouse, Sandycove Seafront, Dun Laoghaire, **t** (01) 284 1600 (*inexpensive*). B&B close to the DART station, beaches and Dun Laoghaire port.
Annesgrove, 28 Rosmeen Gardens, Dun Laoghaire, **t** (01) 280 9801 (*inexpensive*). A clean and cosy guesthouse; contact Mrs A. Dalton.

Where to Stay
Belcamp-Hutchinson Country House, Carrs Lane, Malahide Road, Balgriffin, D17, **t** (01) 846 0843, **f** (01) 848 5703 (*moderate*). This charming country house offers a sense of comfortable elegance. All are made welcome by proprietress Doreen Gleeson, who offers breakfasts at any hour if you are catching a flight. Relaxing surroundings, with gardens, a tree-swing and colour co-ordinated ensuite rooms with mod cons.
Seaglade House, 4 Convent Road, Port-marnock, **t** (01) 846 0179 (*moderate–inexpensive*). Very friendly and comfortable.

Eating Out
The Red Bank Restaurant, 7 Church Street, Skerries, **t** (01) 849 1005 (*expensive*). Superb fish.
Silks, The Mall, Malahide, **t** (01) 845 3331 (*moderate*). Good Chinese restaurant.
Malahide Castle, Malahide, **t** (01) 846 3027 (*inexpensive*). Good daytime soups and snacks.
Old Street Wine Bar, 3 Old Street, Malahide, **t** (01) 845 1882 (*inexpensive*). Wine by the glass and simple meals, like a traditional Dublin coddle.
King Sitric, East Pier, Howth, **t** (01) 832 5235 (*luxury*). Famous for its seafood.

hemisphere brought here by Lord Talbot de Malahide between 1948 and 1973. Also on the grounds is the **Fry Model Railway Museum** (*open April–Oct, Mon–Sat 10–5 Sun 2–6, Oct–Mar, Sat and Sun 2–5; adm;* **t** (01) 846 3779). The handmade models were built by Cyril Fry, a railway engineer and draughtsman in the 1930s.
They are laid out on a track which passes many miniaturized Dublin landmarks, including Heuston Station and the River Liffey with all its bridges, trams, barges and boats. A final attraction in the Malahide Castle Demesne is **Tara's Palace**, a magnificent doll's house constructed by some of Ireland's best craftsmen, with Castletown House, Leinster House and Carton rebuilt to one-twelfth of their true size.

The Old Schoolhouse, Coolbanagher, Swords, t (01) 840 2846/4160, *sincater@indigo.ie* (*moderate*). Informal bistro with pretty Victorian conservatory.

Ayumi-Ya Japanese Restaurant, Newtownpark Avenue, Blackrock, t (01) 283 1767 (*expensive*). Excellent seafood, vegetarian stir-fry, noodles and tempura.

Bijou, 47 Highfield Road, Rathgar, t (01) 496 1518 (*moderate*). Supper club meets bistro, with Asian and European influences. Beautifully cooked food, well presented. *Dinner 5–11pm; early bird menu with two courses for €15 between 5–6.30pm.*

Taylor's Tree Rock, Grange Road, Rathfarnham, D16, t (01) 494 6908/ 494 2999 (*inexpensive*). Traditional Irish food and entertainment.

Outlaws, 62 Upper George Street, Dun Laoghaire, t (01) 284 2817 (*inexpensive*). Cheerful spot serving good steaks, chicken and burgers.

Purty Kitchen, Old Dun Laoghaire Road, t (01) 284 3576 (*inexpensive*). Good food with a strong emphasis on seafood and tempting salads; music nightly.

Caviston's Seafood Restaurant, 59 Glasthule Road, Sandycove, t (01) 280 9245 (*moderate*). This delicatessen has a small restaurant with extremely good seafood. *Lunch only.*

P.D.'s Woodhouse, 1 Coliemore Road, Dalkey, t (01) 284 9399 (*moderate*). Nice friendly atmosphere and oak wood barbecued food.

The Queens, 12 Castle Street, Dalkey, t (01) 285 4569 (*inexpensive*). Pub serving good sandwiches and seafood chowder. Pleasant on a sunny day.

China Szechuan Restaurant, 4 Lower Kilmacud Road, Stillorgan, t (01) 288 4817 (*moderate*). Authentic Szechuan food.

Fox's Pub, Glencullen, t (01) 295 5647 (*inexpensive*). Good seafood pub on the Wicklow border.

Entertainment and Nightlife

Cabaret
Abbey Tavern, Howth, t (01) 839 0307.

Cinema
UCI Cinema, The Square, Town Centre, Tallaght, D24, t (01) 459 8400/459 8170. Multi screen complex.

UCI Cinema, 84 Greencastle Road, Coolock, D17, Malahide, t (01) 848 5130, f (01) 848 5127. Ten-screen cinema, with special midnight shows on Friday and Saturday nights.

Live Music
Polly Hops, Lucan Road, Newcastle, t (01) 628 0295. Traditional music here.

The Purty Kitchen and Bar, Old Dunleary Road, Dun Laoghaire, t (01) 284 3576. Music every night: rock, country or traditional.

Theatre
Lambert Puppet Theatre, Clifton Lane, Monkstown, t (01) 280 0974, *www.lambertpuppettheatre.com*. In the suburbs, also with a puppet museum.

Swords, just inland from Malahide, has a very interesting monastic settlement founded by St Columba in AD 563. The monastery flourished, even though it was raided by the Norsemen, and became so rich that it was known as 'The Golden Prebend'. To protect their precious manuscripts and jewelled croziers, the monks built a round **tower**, 74ft (22.5m) high, the remains of which you can see in the Church of Ireland grounds. The church is 14th-century with a square tower. They can be viewed from the outside only. The archbishops of the 12th and 13th centuries were often as well-armed as any baron, and the Archbishop of Dublin built a strong fortification at Swords for himself; the 12th-century **Archbishop's Castle** is five-sided and has been shored up against further ruin. Its courtyard is enclosed by strong walls, flanked by

square towers. **Portmarnock,** 5 miles (8km) further south along the coast, has a beach
3 miles (4.8km) long nicknamed 'velvet strand'. Two miles (3.2km) inland at Balgriffin,
just off the R107, is **St Doulagh's Church,** which incorporates a 12th-century
anchorite cell and a small subterranean chamber covering a sunken bath, known as
St Catherine's Well. The stone-roofed chancel dates from the 12th century. A square
tower was added in the 15th century. The Velvet Strand stretches up the neck of the
Howth Peninsula, whilst a mile (1.6km) out to sea is **Ireland's Eye,** a great place for a
picnic; you can take a boat out there from the pier in Howth Harbour during the
summer months. Its name comes from the corruption of *Inis Eireann,* which
means 'Island of Eire'. The old stone church on the island is all that is left of a
6th-century monastery.

Howth (with the 'o' pronounced as in 'both') comes from the Danish word *hoved,*
meaning 'head'. Before the Anglo-Norman family of St Lawrence muscled their way
into the area, Howth was a Danish settlement. An important ferry port until
superseded by Dun Laoghaire, its harbour today is full of pleasure craft. **Howth Castle**
still remains in the hands of the St Lawrence family. The public are allowed to walk
around the bright **tropical gardens** *(open 8am–sunset, adm free);* in late spring the
rhododendrons are a glorious colour. It is said that Grace O'Malley, the famous
16th-century pirate-queen from County Mayo (see p.332), stopped at Howth to
replenish her supplies of food and water and decided to visit the St Lawrences. The
family were eating however, and she was refused admittance. Enraged by this rude-
ness, she snatched Lord Howth's infant son and heir and sailed away with him to
Mayo. She returned the child only on condition that the gates of the castle were
always left open at mealtimes, and a place set at the table for the head of the
O'Malley clan – a custom that is still kept today. The **National Transport Museum** in
Howth Castle Demesne *(open June–Aug, Mon–Fri 10–5, Sept–May, Sat–Sun only 2–5;
adm; t (01) 832 0427)* has specimens of everything that ever rolled on an Irish road,
from Victorian-era carriages to early trams and fire engines.

South County Dublin and the Coast

Blackrock is a pleasant middle-class suburb south of Dublin, with a pretty public
park overlooking the sea. In the 19th century, Martello towers were built all along this
wharf to warn of a possible invasion by Napoleon. At **Monkstown,** about a half-mile
(0.3km) south, is the headquarters of *Comhaltas Ceoltoírí Eireann,* the cultural
movement set up in 1951 to preserve and nurture traditional Irish entertainment. In
the summer a variety of shows of traditional music, singing and dancing is held here
every week. The building also includes a music library.

Dun Laoghaire (pronounced 'Dun Lay-reh' or 'Dun Lyoora', or 'Dun Leary', depending
on who's doing the pronouncing), is a terminus for car ferry services from Britain. This
Victorian town with its bright terraced houses was traditionally a holiday resort, and
is pleasant to stroll around before exploring the wilder delights of the Wicklow
Mountains. Dun Laoghaire is named after Laoghaire, who was High King of Ireland
when St Patrick converted him in the 5th century. For a time this busy port was called

Kingstown, after George IV visited Ireland in 1821, but the name was dropped at the establishment of the Free State. The houses along **Marine Parade** are very handsome, painted different colours, and with intricate ironwork and Regency detail. The two great granite **piers** were built between 1817 and 1859. Both make for an invigorating walk; Sundays are especially good for people-watching. It is an important yachting centre, and the Royal Saint George and Royal Irish Clubs are situated here.

The **National Maritime Museum** is in the Mariner's Church, Haigh Terrace (*open May–Sept, Tues–Sun 1–5; adm; t (01) 280 0969*). The **Sacred Heart Oratory Dominican Convent**, George's Street, (*access by appointment only*) is a little gem of the Celtic Revival style, decorated by Sister Concepta Lynch in a combination of Celtic and Art Nouveau style. Marine Parade, laid out with trees and flowers, takes you to the **James Joyce Museum** at The Joyce Tower in Sandycove (*open April–Oct, Mon–Sat 10–1 and 2–5, Sun 2–6; adm; t (01) 280 9265/827 2077*). In fact this Martello tower, from the Napoleonic Wars, was rented by Oliver St John Gogarty, whose witty book *As I Walked Down Sackville Street* is a must for all true Hibernian enthusiasts. Joyce stayed with him for the weekend and used the visit in the opening scene of *Ulysses*. Gogarty ('stately plump Buck Mulligan'), and James Joyce later quarrelled – now their names are perpetually linked. Few people have actually read the whole of *Ulysses*, and for a long time it was banned by the Irish censor for revealing too much of the earthy Dublin character. But the tower is a shrine where visitors can worship and ponder over the collection of Joyceana. Just beside the tower is the Forty Foot Pool, where in *Ulysses*, Buck Mulligan had a morning dip. Made for the Fortieth Foot infantry regiment, it was traditionally a nude, men-only bathing spot, but now you have to wear a bathing suit after 9am. Aficionados swim here all year round, even on Christmas Day.

Dalkey, adjoining Dun Laoghaire, is a small fishing village where Bernard Shaw used to stay and admire the skies from Dalkey Hill. In the 15th and 16th centuries it was the main landing place for passengers from England. In the main thoroughfare, Castle Street, are the remains of fortified mansions from that time, plus **Dalkey Castle and Heritage Centre** (*open April–Oct, Mon–Fri 9.30–5 weekends and bank hols 11–5, Nov–Mar, weekends and bank hols only 11–5; adm; t (01) 285 8366, f (01) 284 3141*), where the history of the castle back to the Middle Ages is described by the area's famous resident author, Hugh Leonard. A boat may be hired from Coliemore Harbour to **Dalkey Island**, where there is a Martello tower and the remains of an ancient church. The Vico road runs along the coast, unfolding beautiful views of Killiney Bay. From the village centre you can walk to **Sorrento Point**, where you get a panoramic view of the distant coastline, the Sugar Loaf Mountains and the sweep of Killiney Bay itself. If you climb **Killiney Hill** you will have an even clearer view of the bay, the mountains and the Liffey Valley.

You pass through the little village of Glencullen on the R117 if you wish to go higher into the Dublin Hills, which merge into the Wicklow Mountains at Enniskerry. You can take the old 'Military Road' up into the Wicklow glens, or go back towards Dublin on the R116 through forest and hill. On the way to Rathfarnham, a pleasant suburb about 25 minutes from the city centre, is **Marlay Park** (*gardens open Nov–Jan, daily 10–5, Feb–Mar, 10–6, April and Oct, 10–7, May, 10–8, June–Aug, 10–9; adm free; t (01) 493*

4059). Formerly the estate of David La Touche, an 18th-century banker, it was left to the county for public use. Dublin County Council has developed it, with a **crafts centre** in the converted stables, where you can buy some lovely things. The craft workers include a bookbinder, a harpmaker, a woodcarver, an antique restorer and a potter. The parkland is laid out with lakes, woods, a golf course and miniature railway. The house itself is still being restored. **The Wicklow Way**, a long-distance, signposted walking trail over the mountains, starts in Marlay Park. **Sandyford**, a neighbouring suburb, contains the green shades of **Fernhill Gardens**, at Lamb's Cross (*open Mar– Sept, Tues–Sat 11–5, Sun 2–6; adm; t (01) 295 6000*). Giant Wellingtonia redwood trees form a sheltered walk, the front field is a wild meadow where cowslips grow, and in the walled garden is a Victorian vegetable and flower garden. There is also a rare example of a Victorian level garden and a fine rhododendron collection. **Lucan**, a suburb to the west of the city, used to be a minor Bath, and is placed on a beautiful stretch of the Liffey. James Gandon (1743–1823), Ireland's most famous architect, lived here and is buried in Drumcondra graveyard. The village is now very built up.

Dublin City

... The Dublin girl that's born an' bred,
Above all Ireland holds her head,
Still upper lip's her beauty.
No holy poke, she likes a joke,
She shies at nayther drink nor smoke,
An' at cards she knows her duty.

The Dublin boy that's born and bred,
Above 'em all high holds his head
For swagger, sport, an' cunning.
He's neither North, South, East, nor West,
But a blend of all that each holds best,
An' the tips he gets are stunning...

Here's Granua Aile, boys. Drink her down.
Quick end to all her troublin'.
May beauty, wit, and wisdom crown
Her Parliament in Dublin.
                    Dublin doggerel

Dublin, if not her parliament, has a worldwide reputation for culture, wit, friendliness and beauty, and this image perpetuates itself as the casual Dublin charm works its way into the heart of every visitor. Irish people themselves call it 'dear dirty Dublin', and at first glance you may think that they are right and discount the affection in their voices when they talk about it. For there is no doubt that Dublin can be a bit of a disappointment, and you may ask yourself what on earth all the fuss is about:

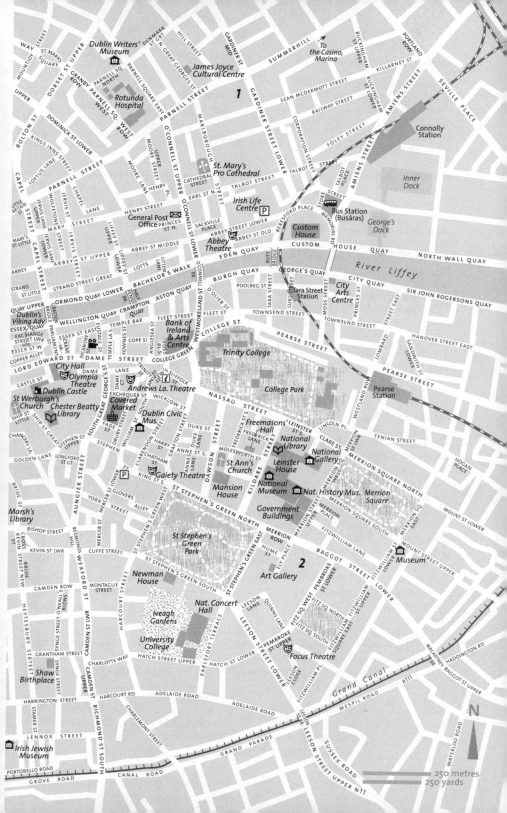

Getting Around

The best and cheapest way of getting around Dublin is by **walking**, because most of the museums, shops and galleries are fairly near to each other. Dublin is a compact city; the central area clusters around the River Liffey and occupies about two square miles. Most of the museums, galleries, theatres, architectural sights and restaurants are within this small area.

The **Liffey** separates the north side from the south. It is spanned by several bridges, the most central being **O'Connell Bridge**. The streets along the River Liffey are called quays, and they change names between bridges. St Stephen's Green, Trinity College, Grafton Street and the Castle area are south of the river. O'Connell Street, Henry Street and Parnell Square are north. Grafton Street and Henry Street are pedestrianized. **Phoenix Park** (1,760acres/712ha) is under 2 miles (3km) from the city centre, to the northwest. The **Grand Canal** crosses the city and joins the River Liffey, enclosing the southern part of the city centre in a gentle curve.

By Bus and Train

Dublin Bus controls all public bus services in the Greater Dublin Area (which includes parts of Wicklow, Kildare and Meath). The DART feeder system is run by **Iarnród Eireann**, and commuter services are controlled by **Bus Eireann**. Their buses run until about 11.30 or midnight, and are a very convenient way to get around, though you'll find the going slow enough through the centre. A route map is available from the Dublin Bus Travel Centre, and any of the tourist offices will help you find your way. Bus fares are based on distance; you should try and have the correct change, although it's not a disaster if you don't. A one-day rail and bus pass is available for €4.50, or €7.20 for a pass that includes the DART.

DART (Dublin Area Rapid Transit) electric trains serve 25 suburban stations near the coast from Howth to Bray. A DART day ticket is available from Iarnród Eireann for about €6, but you probably won't need it unless you are doing a lot of exploring in the suburbs. Right now work is under way on extensions to the system: two street-level tram lines, which are due to be completed in 2007. The first will run from Tallaght to Abbey Street and the second from Sandyford to St Stephen's Green.
Dublin Bus Travel Centre, 59 Upper O'Connell Street, t (01) 873 4222, *www.dublinbus.ie.*
Iarnród Eireann, t (01) 836 6222, *www.irishrail.ie.*

By Taxi

Found outside hotels and railway stations, and in special taxi parking areas in Central Dublin. There are 24-hour ranks at St Stephen's Green and O'Connell Street; it's often difficult to flag down a cab on the streets. Taxis should always have meters. They charge extra per piece of luggage, per person and at night.
Blue Cabs, t (01) 676 1111.
Metro Cabs, t (01) 668 3333/478 1111/677 2222.
Pony Cabs, t (01) 661 0101.
VIP Taxi and Courier Service, t (01) 478 3333.

By Car

Parking is difficult (and occasionally impossible) in the centre of town, but there is a new computerised system with strategically placed screens telling you which car parks have spaces. The main **car parks** are in Frederick Street and the St Stephen's Green Shopping Centre, and there is metered parking around St Stephen's Green and Merrion Square. On the north side you might find a parking place in the Irish Life Shopping Centre, entrance off Lower Abbey Street. **Driving** in Dublin is delightfully disordered, so be on your guard. It is mostly a matter of nerve and panache. Using your horn is the worst insult, so keep it as a last resort. Car theft and burglaries are an increasing problem, perhaps exaggerated by Dubliners who aren't used to the phenomenon, but it's a good idea when you book a hotel to check whether there is secure parking.

Most of the major **car hire** chains are represented at the airport, along with a wide choice of local firms.
AVIS, Dublin Airport, t (01) 605 7500, f (01) 605 7565, *flserck@iol.ie.*
Budget Rent A Car, Dublin Airport t (01) 844 5150, *reservations@budgetcarrental.ie.*
Dan Dooley/Kenning, 42 Westland Row, Dublin 2, t (01) 677 2723.

Hertz Rent-A-Car, Dublin Airport, t (01) 844 5466.

Murrays Europcar, Baggot Street Bridge, Dublin 4, t (01) 614 2800; Dublin Airport, t (01) 812 0410, f (01) 812 0428, *www.europcar.ie*.

Payless Bunratty Car Rentals, Dublin Airport, t (01) 844 5522, *www.iol.ie/paylessbcr*.

By Bike

The Bike Store Ltd, 58 Gardiner Street, D1, t (01) 872 5399.

Dublin Bike Hire, 27 North Great George's Street, t (01) 878 8473.

Harding for Bicycles, 30 Bachelors Walk, D1, t (01) 873 2455.

Joe Daly Cycles, Lower Main Street, Dundrum, D8, t (01) 298 1485.

Little Sport Ltd, 3 Merville Avenue, Fairview, D3, t (01) 833 2405, f (01) 833 0044.

Festivals and Events

February–March

Six Nations Rugby. Held over two Saturdays at Landsdowne Road; always a good party in the years when the Scots visit.

March

National St Patrick's Day Festival (17th). Celebrations and parades starting on O'Connell Street. There are lots of events and music around this date; log onto the official website for the festival at *www.stpatricksday.ie*.

April

Dublin International Film Festival. Held early in the month; highly recommended.

May

Green Energy International Music Festival. A huge event, with past headliners including the Cranberries, Tracy Chapman and Joe Strummer. Call t (01) 456 9569 for more information.

June

Bloomsday. June 16th is Dublin's own peculiar holiday, the anniversary of the day (in 1904) on which all the action of Joyce's *Ulysses* took place. Various events are held in the places visited by Leopold Bloom – some are scheduled, some aren't. People wear Edwardian costume, make recitations, and some just come along for the pub crawl. The day begins at 8am by the Tower in Sandycove; contact the James Joyce Centre for more information, t (01) 878 8547, *www.jamesjoyce.ie, joycecen@iol.ie*.

AIB Music in Great Irish Houses. A festival of chamber music, with around 10 evening concerts held in great houses in the Dublin area. *See also* **Practical A–Z**, p.130.

August

Kerrygold Horse Show. International equestrian event in Ballsbridge, t (01) 668 0866.

September

All-Ireland Hurling and Football Finals, t (01) 836 3222.

Dublin Jazz Festival. Week-long, held at a number of venues in the city.

Dublin Fringe Theatre Festival, t (01) 872 9433, *www.fringefest.com*.

International Puppetry Festival, t (01) 280 0974.

October

Dublin Theatre Festival, t (01) 877 8439.

Dublin City Marathon, t (01) 670 7918.

December

Dublin Grand Opera Winter Season, Gaiety Theatre, South King Street, t (01) 677 1717, *www.gaietytheatre.com, www.opera-ireland.ie*.

Tourist Information

The main **Dublin Tourism** office occupies an entire restored church in Suffolk Street; it's all very modern and efficient, but they don't have a lot of printed information to hand out and you could be waiting forever. Just take a number and have a seat. They also change money, and book hotels and theatre tickets. For information through the wires, the best you can do is telephone their toll-free recorded information line; or try their website, *www.visitdublin.com*.

Dublin Tourism Centre, St Andrew's Church,
Suffolk Street (off Grafton Street, near Trinity
College), t (01) 605 7700, information line
t 1850 230 330; *open Mon 9–5, Wed–Sat
9.30–5.30.*
*Bord Failté Eireann/*Tourism Ireland,
Baggot Street Bridge (south of the centre,
on the Grand Canal), D2, information line
t 1850 230 330, *www.ireland.travel.ie;
open Mon–Fri 9.30–5.15;*
also at 14 Upper O'Connell Street (north of
the Liffey); *open all year.*
Dublin Airport; *open daily 8am–10pm.*
Dun Laoghaire: New Ferry Terminal; *open daily
8–1.*
Tallaght: The Square, D24; *open daily 8–1.*

Practical A–Z

Banks
Banks are open Monday–Friday 10–4, and on
Thursday until 5pm.

Bureaux de Change
At the airport, tourist offices and banks.
Thomas Cook, 51 Grafton Street, D2, t (01) 677
7399.
American Express, 61–63A South William
Street, D2, t (01) 617 5588.

Chemists
Both the following are open until 10pm:
O'Connell's, 55 Lower O'Connell Street, t (01)
873 0427.
Leonard's, 106 South Circular Road, D8, t (01)
453 4282.

Emergencies
In an emergency, dial t **999** or t **112.**
Garda Confidential Line, t 1800 666111.
Women's Aid, t 1800 341900.

Hospitals
St Vincent's University Hospital, Elm Park,
D4, t (01) 209 4533.
St James's Hospital, James' Street, D8, t (01)
453 7941.

Internet Cafés
Central Cyber Café, 6 Grafton Street, D2, t (01)
677 8298, f (01) 677 8299, *www.globalcafe.ie,*

*info@centralcafe.ie. Open Mon–Fri
8am–11pm, weekends 10am–8pm.*
Cyberia Café, Temple Lane South,
Temple Bar, D2, t (01) 679 7607,
www.cyberia.net.
Does Not Compute, Unit 2 Pudding Row,
Essex Street West, Temple Bar, D8,
t (01) 670 4464, f (01) 670 4474, *www.
doesnotcompute.ie, info@
doesnotcompute.ie. Open 24hrs.*
Global Internet Café, 8 Lower O'Connell Street,
D1, t (01) 878 0295, f (01) 872 9100,
*www.globalcafe.ie, info@globalcafe.ie.
Open Mon–Fri 8am–11pm, Sat 9am–11pm,
Sun 10am–11pm.*
Internet Exchange Café, 3 Cecilia Street, D2,
t (01) 670 3000; 10 Fownes Street, D2, t (01)
635 1680.
Planet Café, 23 South Great George's
Street, D2.

Police (*Garda Siochana*)
Dublin Metropolitan Area HQ, t (01) 269 3766
and t 1800 666 111.

Post Offices
The **GPO** (General Post Office) is in the
centre of O'Connell Street (*open until 8pm*);
there are branches in Parnell Street and
Summerhill, north of the Liffey, south of it at
Upper Baggot Street, Lower Baggot Street,
Clare Street, Earlsfort Terrace, Pearse Street,
Merrion Row, Montague Street and South
Anne Street.

Student Travel Agency
USIT, 19–21 Aston Quay, t (01) 602 1600/
602 1700. They also book accommodation
and run a hostel. *Open Mon–Fri 9–5.30,
Sat 10–1.*

Telephones
Payphone centres are located in the
General Post Office, O'Connell Street, and
beside the Gaiety Theatre on South King
Street. More and more of these are
cardphones, the cards for which may be
bought in the post office and selected
newsagents. The big hotels are other reliable
sources for public telephones.
The local dialling code for the whole of
County Dublin is t (01–).

YHA

Irish Youth Hostel Association (An Oíge), 61 Mountjoy Street, D1, t (01) 830 4555.

Media

Newspapers and Listings

In Dublin magazine was started by a group of students, and became so successful that you can now buy it at every news stand. *Hot Press* is another essential source, with good arts and music reviews. The *Evening Herald* also contains cinema listings, while the *Irish Mirror* has a Friday supplement that is good for music and nightclubs. Read the *Irish Times* for reviews of plays, concerts and films. Every Saturday it also lists special happenings in Dublin and the provinces.

Websites

Good websites for information on city life include *The Dubliner* magazine's stylish website, *www.thedubliner.ie*, and *The Irish Times* website, *www.ireland.com/dublin*, which lists events daily. The official Dublin Tourism website, *www.visitdublin.com*, offers excellent coverage as well.

Guided Tours

On Foot

Signposts have been erected around the city to guide you through the historical sights on foot; there's the Georgian Trail, the Cultural Trail, the Old City Trail and the Rock 'n' Stroll Trail. Contact Dublin Tourism on Suffolk Street, D2, for more details, t 1850 230 330. If you need more assistance there are guided walking tours on offer, listed below.

Historical Walking Tour of Dublin, t (01) 845 0241. Assemble at the front gate of Trinity College. *Sat and Sun at noon.*

Old Dublin, t (01) 679 4291. Assemble at Bewley's, Grafton Street or Dublin Writer's Museum, 18 Parnell Square; *call for times.*

The 1916 Rebellion Walking Tour, t (01) 676 2493. Departs from the International Bar, 23 Wicklow Street, and takes you around all the sites asociated with this traumatic event. *Saturdays at 11.30am.*

Revolutionary Dublin 1916–23, t (01) 662 9976. Conducted by Trinity College graduate students; covers the same ground and more. *Daily tours, call for times.*

Besides these normal tours, Dublin can also offer several **pub tours**, where the walking becomes increasingly less steady; there is a charge, and you'll need extra cash for the Guinness.

The Dublin Literary Pub Crawl, 37 Exchequer Street, D2, t (01) 670 5602, f (01) 670 5603/454 5680, *www.dublinpubcrawl.com*, *info@dublinpubcrawl.com*. Meets at The Duke pub on Duke Street. Tickets are sold on a first-come-first-served basis. *Easter–Oct, nightly at 7.30pm; Nov–March, Thurs–Sat 7.30pm; Sun all year at noon and 7.30pm.*

The Musical Pub Crawl, t (01) 478 0193. Two knowledgeable musicians lead you through several traditional music bars. *Call for tour times.*

By Bus

For a less strenuous way of seeing the sights, Dublin Bus offers open-top bus 'hop on-hop off' tours. With these you can get on and off anywhere, and the ticket is good for the entire day. The start is Dublin Bus headquarters (*see* below). Buses run the circuit every 15mins. They also offer full- and half-day tours of North County Dublin, with a stop at Malahide Castle (*daily, 10am from O'Connell Street*), and the southern coast into County Wicklow (*daily, 11 and 2, from O'Connell Street*).

Dublin Bus; headquarters: 59 O'Connell Street (between Henry and Parnell), t (01) 873 4222, *www.dublinbus.ie*.

Sports and Activites

Greyhound Racing

Shelbourne Park, D4, t 1850 646566, *www.shelbournepark.com.*
Harold's Cross, D6, t (01) 497 1081.

Hurling and Gaelic Football

The Gaelic Athletic Association's website, *www.gaa.ie*, gives detailed descriptions of the two games and their rules. See them both played in Dublin at Croke Park, Parnell

Park and Phoenix Park. *See also* **Topics,**
pp.107–108.

Rugby and Football
See a game at **Landsdowne Road**, one mile
south of the city centre, where in February or
March you can catch the mighty Six Nations
Rugby tournament.

Shopping

The smartest and best shopping is
to be found in a small area around
Grafton Street and the little streets leading
off it, just northeast of the river. North of
the Liffey, **Henry Street** is the busiest
shopping street in Dublin – and generally
cheaper than the upmarket Grafton Street
area. The flagship of this area is Clery's, on
O'Connell Street.

Antiques
The antique shops in Molesworth,
South Anne Street and Kildare Street are well
thought of and sell top-quality furniture, silver
and ornaments. For more junky stuff and
bargains try Francis Street, in the Liberties,
where there are individual antique shops and
an antiques arcade.

A Star is Born, Clarendon Street. Try here for
antique and second-hand items. *Open
Saturdays only.*

Iveagh Market, just across the road from
the Tivoli Theatre. A fine 19th-century
covered market, now very shabby
and occupied by second-hand
clothes dealers.

Jenny Vander, in the George's Street
Arcade. Also for good second-hand clothes,
lovely antique pieces of clothing and
costume jewellery.

Auctioneers
De Vere's Art Auctions, 35 Kildare Street, D2,
t (01) 676 8300, f (01) 676 8305. For mostly
Irish paintings.

Herman and Wilkinson, 161 Lower Rathmines
Road, D6, t (01) 497 2245. Fortnightly
auctions of silver, paintings and furniture.

James Adams and Sons, 26 St Stephen's Green,
t (01) 676 0261.

Whyte's, 30 Marlborough Street, t (01) 874
6161. For stamps and coins, old prints, maps
photos etc.

Books
An open-air **book market** is held in Temple
Bar Square (*weekends 10am–6pm*), and at the
time of writing, there are plans afoot to open
a **daily market** on Capel Street Bridge in
September 2002.

Cathach Books, 10 Duke Street, t (01) 671 8676.
A large, independent bookseller.

Dublin Writers' Museum, 18 Parnell Square, D1,
t (01) 872 2077. The bookshop in here
provides an out-of-print and antiquarian
book search service.

Eason & Son, Lower O'Connell Street, t (01) 873
3811. With several other branches in the city.

Fred Hanna's Bookshop, 28–29 Nassau Street,
D2, t (01) 677 1255. Independent bookseller.

Greene's Bookshop Ltd, 16 Clare Street, D2,
t (01) 676 2554, *info@greenesbookshop.com*.
For rare and out-of-print books.

Hodges Figgis, 57 Dawson Street, D2,
t (01) 677 4754.

Waterstone's, Dawson Street, D2,
t (01) 679 1415.

Winding Stair Books, 40 Lower Ormond Quay,
D1, t (01) 873 3292. Has an excellent café and
three floors of second-hand books, plus a
lovely view.

Clothes
Many of the UK's high street clothing
chains – Next, Principles, Marks & Spencer –
have set up in Grafton Street. (*See also*
'Department Stores', below.) For
something in **Irish tweed**, and for
high-quality craft design, head for Nassau
Street, at the College Green end of
Dawson Street.

Alias Tom, Duke Street, t (01) 671 5443.
Designer men's clothes.

A-Wear, 26 Grafton Street, t (01) 671 7200 and
also at Henry Street, *www.a-wear.ie*.
Inexpensive; stocks a diffusion range by
Quin and Donnelly. The prices here are very
keen and will appeal to all ages.

The Blarney Woollen Mills, 21–3 Nassau Street.
Tailored skirts and jackets, soft jersey dresses
and jumpers, scarves and luxurious woollen
coats, in a good range of colours – from the

clear primaries to tweeds full of subtle shades like the Irish countryside, although some of the designs are a little staid.

Cleo, 18 Kildare Street, a little way off Nassau Street D2, t (01) 676 1421. A good designer tweed shop.

FX Kelly, Grafton Street. For men's designer clothes.

Kennedy McSharry, Nassau Street. Beautifully tailored suits from Donegal tweed.

Kevin and Howlin, 31 Nassau Street, t (01) 677 0257. Tweed heaven – they sell lovely caps, scarves and suits for men.

Se Si Progressive, Temple Bar. Worth a visit for its inexpensive clubby gear, with new, young designer talent.

Sybil Connolly, Merrion Square. The doyenne of Irish designers.

Commercial Art Galleries

The following galleries put on shows by Irish artists. You might even decide to invest and take a painting home.

City Arts Centre, 23 Moss Street, D2, t (01) 677 0643. Young emerging artists. The centre also has a pleasant café.

Green on Red, 26 Lombard Street, D2, t (01) 671 3414. Contemporary paintings and sculpture.

Kerlin Gallery, Anne's Lane, off South Anne Street, D2, t (01) 670 9093. Shows established and new talent – a lovely gallery space.

Oriel Gallery, 17 Clare Street, D2, t (01) 676 3410. Mostly traditional and figurative early-20th-century.

Rubicon, 10 St Stephen's Green, t (01) 670 8055. Mostly contemporary.

Solomon Gallery, Powerscourt Townhouse Centre, D2, t (01) 679 4237, solomon@indigo.ie. Pretty pictures – occasionally verges on the twee.

Taylor Galleries, 16 Kildare Street, t (01) 676 6055. Established artists.

Crafts

Anthony O'Brien, 14a Ailsbury Road, D4, t (01) 260 4064. Pottery.

Designyard, 12 East Essex Street, Temple Bar. In a converted warehouse, this is the new hotspot for designer jewellery, ceramics, furniture and glass.

Irish Georgian Society, 74 Merrion Square, D2, t (01) 676 7053. Visit here for historical placemats and books, and so on.

The Kilkenny Shop, Nassau Street, t (01) 677 7066. Sells excellent glass, pottery, rugs and sweaters.

Tower Craft Design Centre, Pearse Street, D2, t (01) 677 5655. Craft-workers produce glass, jewellery, woodcarving, pottery, weaving and other lovely things.

Delicacies

Asia Market, 18 Drury Street, t (01) 677 9764. Very good for exotic ingredients.

Bretzel Kosher Bakery, 1A Lennox Street, D8, t (01) 475 2724. Just up from Fitzpatrick's, near the Grand Canal, is this famous baker's which doles out treats such as gingerbread men, walnut loaves and challah, shiny twisted plaits of bread.

Butler's, Grafton Street. Irish chocolates; not quite as good as the Belgian ones, above.

Caviston's, In the Epicurean Food Hall, Liffey Street Lower, t (01) 878 2289. An old-fashioned deli selling fresh fish, Irish cheeses and smoked salmon. (They also have a restaurant in Sandycove, see p.566.)

Cooke's Bakery, Francis Street, and 32 Dawson Street. Indulge yourself with fabulous cakes, breads and cheese.

Down to Earth, 73 South Great Georges Street, D2, t (01) 671 9702. Health foods.

Fitzpatricks, 40 Camden Street, D8, t (01) 475 3996. A cheerful wholefood grocer.

Foodies, Poolbeg Street, D2, t 677 9140. Fresh soup, pies and quiches.

Leonidas, Royal Hibernian Way. For yummy Belgian chocolates.

Magill's, 14 Clarendon Street, t (01) 671 3830. A wonderful old-fashioned place smelling of charcuterie and sourdough breads.

Patrick Guildbaud, 42 The Liffey Trust, Sheriff Street, D1, t 855 5299. French bakery.

Temple Bar Food Market, held every Saturday morning in Meeting House Square. For edible Irish goodies, this is your first stop. Local farmers' organic produce, home-baked breads and pastries, and exotic treats you would have trouble finding elsewhere.

Department Stores

Brown Thomas, 88–95 Grafton Street,
t (01) 605 6666. A first-class
department store. Always carries Irish
designer labels such as Paul Costelloe,
Louise Kennedy, John Rocha and Michaelina
Stacpoole. The designer room is excellent,
as is the Wardrobe department for less
expensive options.

Clery's, O'Connell Street, t (01) 878 6000.
Famous, old-fashioned, independent
department store.

Powerscourt Town House Centre, Design
Centre, 59 South William Street, t (01)
679 5718. A must for any serious shopper,
this is an innovative shopping mecca
that is generally regarded as a
showpiece marriage between
conservation and commerce. The building
is elegantly Georgian, and was constructed
over two hundred years ago as a town
residence for Lord Powerscourt, an 18th-
century nobleman. A glass dome over the
old courtyard makes a wonderful space
for cafés and restaurants. Small craft
shops, fashion shops, antique shops and
jewellers have spaces in the old house.
Names to look out for include **Emma
Stewart Liberty** and **Patrick Flood** (silver-
smiths) and the **Design Centre**, which
sells clothes by up-and-coming and
established designers including Mariad
Whisker, Louise Kennedy, Lainey Keogh
and Deirdre Fitzgerald, who design
gorgeous and luxurious knitwear.
If you need refuelling, the perfect solution
is to order a dessert cake from **Chompy's** or
go veggie at **Fresh**.

St Stephen's Green Shopping Centre, on
the corner of St Stephen's Green and
Grafton Street. This huge glass mall has a
wide variety of small shops and a huge
Dunnes store (something like
Marks & Spencer). It also houses the
Crafts Centre of Ireland, t (01) 475 4526,
craftscentreireland@eircom.net.

The Westbury Centre, round the corner
from the Powerscourt Centre. Has an
Aladdin's cave of a lingerie shop, a
leather studio, a good Costa Coffee shop,
and **Angles**, a shop with the best of
contemporary Irish jewellery.

Music

Claddagh Records, 2 Cecilia Street, D2,
t (01) 677 0262, f (01) 679 3664,
www.claddaghrecords.com,
claddagh@crl.ie. Specialists in traditional
Irish music.

Waltons, 69–70 South Great Georges Street,
D2, t (01) 475 0661. Irish and world
musical instruments.

Street Markets

Cow's Lane Natural Food Market, at Temple
Bar. A range of food stalls selling certified
organic fruit, fish from the Atlantic ocean,
cheeses, breads and preserves. *Open
Saturdays 10–6*.

Dublin Food Co-op, in St Andrew's Centre,
114–116 Pearse Street, D2, t (01) 873 0451.
Whole and organic foods, held every Sat.

Moore Street Market. This is the place for
fruit and vegetables, although some of the
produce is rather suspect, so watch out for
the rotten ones. It is also a good place to
observe Dublin life. Here the warmly
wrapped pram people wait with their wares:
in place of a gurgling infant, veteran market-
traders, usually women, use prams to carry
jewellery, fish, turf, concrete blocks, flowers
and evening newspapers. You can buy their
vegetables, fruit and the most gaudy of
Taiwanese toys. The 'perambulators' are not
strictly allowed, as they do not pay rent,
unlike the properly established stands; and
if the boys in blue appear, they melt away
into the crowds. Some of the prams are as
old as 70 years, and are still going strong.

Mother Redcap's Market, on Back Lane near
Christchurch. Pottery, books and bric-a-brac.
Check out The Gallic Kitchen, for delicious
pies and cakes and Ryefield Foods, for
farmhouse cheeses.

Where to Stay

Dublin t (01–)

City Centre: South of the Liffey

Clarence Hotel, 6 Wellington Quay,
t 670 9000, f 670 7800 (*luxury*). Traditional
thirties hotel, owned by rock group U2,
with lovely wood-panelling, a fashionable

bar and friendly staff. Recently refurbished and well situated at the edge of the Temple Bar area.

Conrad International Dublin, Earlsfort Terrace, D2, **t** 602 8900, **f** 676 5424 (*luxury*). Top-of-the-range modern Hilton hotel with excellent facilities and a pleasant atmosphere.

Georgian House Hotel, 18 Baggot Street Lower, D2, **t** 661 8832, or **t** 1850 320260 (*luxury*). Own phone, TV, telephone, in a Georgian house which has been altered internally to create snug, pastel-coloured rooms. Very central, so you can walk everywhere. Private car park in back garden.

The Morgan Hotel, 10 Fleet Street, Temple Bar, D2, **t** 679 3939, **f** 679 3946, *www.themorgan. com* (*luxury*). Quiet, private accommodation with modern designer elegance, in the heart of Temple Bar. Staff are helpful, friendly and discreet, and continental breakfasts are served in your room. Rooms are also provided with TV, CD/hi-fi, minibar, and tea- and coffee-making accoutrements.

Shelbourne Hotel, St Stephens's Green, D2, **t** 676 6471, **f** 661 6006, *shelbourneinfo@ fort-home.com* (*luxury*). Lovely old-fashioned hotel in which the Irish Constitution was drafted. Also has a very elegant drawing room and a gem of a bar.

Westbury, Clarendon Street, off Grafton Street, D2, **t** 679 1122, **f** 679 7078 (*luxury*). Modern hotel, top of the range and conveniently central.

Buswell's Hotel, Molesworth Street, D2, **t** 676 4013 (*luxury–expensive*). An old-fashioned, cheerful family hotel. Very Central.

Longfields Hotel, Fitzwilliam Street Lower, D2, **t** 676 1367 (*expensive*). Georgian town house, quiet and intimate, with period furnishings and an excellent restaurant.

Number 31, Leeson Close, D2 **t** 676 5011, **f** 676 2929, *number31@iol.ie* (*expensive–moderate*). Stylish modern décor, comfortable and with a secure car park.

Earl of Kildare Hotel, 47 Kildare Street, **t** 679 4388 (*moderate*). A good hotel with a perfect location, near Grafton Street and Trinity College.

Barnacle's Temple Bar House, 19 Temple Lane, Temple Bar, **t** 671 6277, **f** 671 6591, *templeba@barnacles.iol.ie* (*inexpensive*). Centrally located hostel with self-catering and laundry facilities.

Brewery Hostel, 21 Thomas Street, D8, **t** 473 1512 (*inexpensive*). Well-equipped new hostel near the Guinness Brewery.

Kinlay House Hostel, 2–12 Lord Edward Street, D2, **t** 679 6644, **f** 679 7437, *kinlay.dublin@ usitworld.com* (*inexpensive*). Near Christ Church. Big and well-equipped.

City Centre: North of the Liffey

Gresham, Upper O'Connell Street, D1, **t** 874 6881 (*expensive*). Built in the days when a first-class hotel had big bedrooms and huge baths, this still has the atmosphere of the twenties and thirties. Best bedrooms are at the front. Car parking for residents.

Leeson Inn, 24 Lower Leeson Street, D2, **t** 662 2002, **f** 662 1567 (*expensive–moderate*). Stylish and convenient.

The Schoolhouse Hotel, 2–8 Northumberland Road, D4, **t** 667 5014, or **t** 1850 344000, **f** 667 5015, *www.schoolhousehotel.com, school@ schoolhousehotel.iol.ie* (*expensive–moderate*). Excellent, with a good bar called **The Inkwell**.

Castle Hotel, 2 Gardiner Row, **t** 874 6949 (*moderate*). Attractively furnished rooms with TV.

Merrion Square Manor, 31 Merrion Square, D2, **t** 622 8551, *merrionmanor@eircom. net* (*moderate*). Hotel with Georgian-style décor.

Anchor Guest House, 49 Lower Gardiner Street, **t** 878 6913 (*moderate–inexpensive*). Georgian house B&B, conveniently located near the bus station.

Dublin International Youth Hostel, 61 Mountjoy Street, D7, **t** 830 1766 (*inexpensive*). Central, clean and friendly.

Isaacs Hostel, The Dublin Tourist Hostel, 2–5 Frenchman's Lane, D1 (beside the bus station), **t** 855 6215, **f** 855 6574 (*inexpensive*). Built as a wine warehouse on the Liffey in the 1700s, this is a very clean, central, friendly place, with excellent restaurant facilities and a patio garden. Basic dormitory and single rooms. The restaurant is good value.

Jacob's Inn, 21 Talbot Place, **t** 855 5660 (*inexpensive*). Modern hostel, near the bus station.

Outside the Centre: Dublin City South

Jury's, Ballsbridge, D4, **t** 660 5000, **f** 660 5540, *ballsbridge_hotel@jurysdoyle.com* (*luxury*). Large, modern chain hotel with executive wing.

Sachs Hotel, 19 Morehampton Road, Donnybrook, D4, **t** 668 0995, **f** 668 6147 (*luxury–expensive*). Small, traditional hotel in a Georgian terrace. Ample parking.

Ariel House, 52 Lansdowne Road, Ballsbridge, D4, **t** 668 5512, **f** 668 5845 (*expensive–moderate*). A charming Victorian house with lots of antiques. The bedrooms in the older part of the house are more individual. Breakfast is served in the conservatory.

Waterloo House, 8–10 Waterloo Road, D4, **t** 660 1888, **f** 667 1955, *waterloohouse@ eircom.net* (*expensive–moderate*). A small, friendly hotel in a residential Georgian street, nearly unchanged by the tacky elements of the Celtic Tiger and within walking distance of the city centre. Breakfasts are carefully prepared and served in a plush garden dining room by meticulous staff. Perfect for those who require privacy, cleanliness and efficiency.

McMenamins Townhouse, 74 Marlborough Road, Donnybrook, D4, **t** 497 4405, **f** 496 8585 (*moderate*). A warm welcome awaits you here, as well as a night's peace, in a residential street not far from University College Dublin. Your helpful, hospitable host Padraig McMenamin knows all about Donnybrook's history, and his wife Kay serves up excellent home baking at breakfast. Special breakfasts are available for vegetarians, and tea-making facilities are in each room.

Merrion Hall, 56 Merrion Road, Ballsbridge, D4, **t** 668 1426, **f** 668 4280, *merrionhall@iol.ie* (*moderate*). Family-run guesthouse with pretty bedrooms, a friendly atmosphere and a delicious breakfast which includes home-made yoghurt.

Avalon House, 55 Aungier Street, D2, **t** 475 0001, *www.avalon-house.ie* (*inexpensive*). Old building converted into a modern hostel with twin, family and dormitory rooms. Central, clean and efficiently run.

Haddington Lodge, 49 Haddington Road, Ballsbridge, D4, **t** 660 0974 (*inexpensive*). Elegant Georgian house; contact Mrs Egan.

Hilton House, 23 Highfield Road, Rathgar, D6, **t** 497 6837 (*inexpensive*). Large Victorian house in a quiet secluded area; contact Mr or Mrs Doyle.

Outside the Centre: Dublin City North

Dorchester Guest House, 69 North Circular Road, D7, **t** 838 5204 (*inexpensive*). Very friendly and comfortable B&B in a quiet area near Phoenix Park, with safe parking.

Eating Out

Dublin t (01–)

Dining in Dublin is an extremely popular occupation, so always make sure you book a table in advance.

City Centre: South of the Liffey

Luxury

Patrick Guilbaud, 21 Merrion Street Upper, **t** 676 4192. Excellent classic French cuisine, awarded two stars by Michelin, in a modern formal interior.

Expensive

Clarence Hotel Tea Rooms, 6–8 Wellington Quay, **t** 670 7766. A fashionable and fun place to eat a set dinner (but not tea). Lots of salads.

Cooke's Café, 14 South William Street, D2, **t** 679 0536. One of the nicest, most intimate restaurants in Dublin. Lovely Italianate interior and superb modern Italian/ Californian cooking. Home-baked focaccia breads with olive oil dips and patisserie to die for – try the Calvados tart. There's also a very good value early evening set menu.

La Stampa, 35 Dawson Street, D2, **t** 677 8611, *www.lastampa.ie*. Fashionable and graceful brasserie, set in the splendid rooms of the former Guildhall.

L'Ecrivain, 109 Lower Baggot Street, D2, t 661 1919. Friendly little basement restaurant serving imaginative French food. Popular with local business people and particularly buzzy at lunchtime.

Les Frères Jacques, 74 Dame Street, D2, t 679 4555. Atmospheric and romantic restaurant. French food and friendly staff. Try the lobster ravioli.

Thornton's, 1 Portobello Road, D8, t 454 9067. Canal-side setting with modern Irish food.

Moderate

Avoca Café, inside Avoca Handweavers, Suffolk Street, D2, t 677 4215, *info@avoca.ie*. Excellent café with organic produce used where possible, and tempting baked desserts. *Open Mon–Sat 9.30–5.30*.

Bad Ass Café, 9–11 Crown Alley, Temple Bar, t 671 2596. Diner-style spot for pizza, chops and burgers, famous because Sinead O'Connor used to waitress here.

The Chameleon, 1 Lower Fownes Street, D2, t 671 0362. Popular Indonesian restaurant.

The Chilli Club, 1 Anne's Lane, South Anne Street, D2, t 677 3721. Proper Thai cooking by a Thai chef – the lemongrass soups have a real kick, whilst the curries vary in terms of spiciness.

Citron, Fitzwilliam Hotel, St Stephen's Green, D2, t 418 5525. Affordable Mediterranean food and fast service within a bright yellow colour scheme.

Chompy's, Powerscourt Town House Centre, South William Street, t 679 4552. American-style deli-restaurant with good desserts.

Elephant and Castle, 18 Temple Bar, D2, t 679 3121. Burgers, omelettes and really good bumper sandwiches. Always busy, and good for brunch on Sundays.

Good World Chinese Restaurant, 18 South Great Georges Street, t 677 5373. Nice any time, and great for *dim sum* on a Sunday.

Imperial, 13 Wicklow Street, t 677 2580. Smart Chinese restaurant with good value set lunches and *dim sum*.

Nico's Restaurant, 53 Dame Street, D2, t 677 3062. Busy and friendly Italian restaurant with a theatrical atmosphere.

Saagar, 16 Harcourt Street, D2, t 475 5012. One of the best Indian restaurants in Ireland, with some innovative dishes as well as the old favourites. *Inexpensive* for lunch.

Yamamori, 71–75 South Great George's Street, t 475 5001. Good Japanese noodle house with a *cheap* lunch special.

Inexpensive

Bewley's Café, 78–79 Grafton Street, D2 (also on Westmoreland Street), t 677 6761. Where Dubliners have met, talked and enjoyed delicious coffee and cakes (especially the *barm brack* or almond buns) for generations, although recent remodelling seems to have affected the food and mars what was once a real slice of Dublin life.

Blazing Salads, 42 Drury Street, D2, t 671 9552. Imaginative and streets ahead of average vegetarian cooking. Excellent soups, salads and home-made desserts. Caters for yeast-/gluten-/sugar-free diets. Organic wine and fresh-pressed vegetable juices.

The Boulevard Café, 27 Exchequer Street, D2, t 679 2131. Handy for shopping day lunches.

Captain America's Cookhouse and Bar, 1st floor, Grafton Court, Grafton Street, D2, t 671 5266. For those who miss burgers and milkshakes. Loud music.

Chez Jules, D'Olier Street, D2, t 677 0499. Another Parisian-style bistro, very informal with chequered tablecloths and a scrubbed wooden floor.

Cornucopia, Wicklow Street, D2, t 677 7583. Vegetarian restaurant serving wholesome bakes and soups; caters for restricted diets.

Fitzers, in the National Gallery of Art, Merrion Square, t 661 4496. Tempting salads and pasta dishes. Just the place to relax after exploring the gallery.

Gotham Café, 8 South Anne Street, t 679 5266. Pizza, pasta and more. Open quite late.

Govinda's, 4 Aungier Street, D2, t 475 0309. A good vegetarian restaurant serving Indian and wholefood bakes, soups and mild curries.

Irish Film Centre, 6 Eustace Street, t 679 5744. Continental-style café filled unsurprising salads and fresh breads in their self-service lunch bar.

National Museum Café, Kildare Street, D2, t 602 1269. Simple and tasty. Coddle, salads and cakes.

Newcomers Sup, South William Street, D2. Soup kitchen.

The Old Stand, 37 Exchequer Street, D2, t 677 7220/677 5849. Bar food, famous for its steaks.

Pasta Fresca, 22 Chatham Street, D2, t 679 2402. Crowded fresh pasta shop which serves its own produce at a limited number of tables. Simple dishes with a good variety of sauces.

Pizzeria Italia, 23 Temple Bar, t 677 8528. Tiny, cheerful restaurant with counters. Really good classic pastas and pizzas, cooked by real Italians; don't miss the garlic mussels.

The Queen of Tarts, Dame Street, t 670 7499, and also in the City Hall. Excellent patisserie and coffee shop.

Soup Dragon, 168 Capel Street, D1, t 872 3277. Soup kitchen with an ever-changing menu – let the Thai chicken soup or haddock chowder tickle your tastebuds.

The Stag's Head, Dame Court, D2, t 679 3701. Boiled bacon and cabbage, Irish stew.

The Stone Wall Café, 187 Exchequer Street, D2, t 672 7323. Pasta and salads during the day, Mediterranean and Asian food at night.

City Centre: North of the Liffey

101 Talbot, 101 Talbot Street, D1, t 874 5011 (*moderate–inexpensive*). Cheerful atmosphere, mediterranean and eastern-inspired cooking. Good for vegetarians and popular with theatre-going folk.

Chapter One, in the Basement of the Writers' Museum, 18–19 Parnell Square, D1, t 873 2266 (*expensive–moderate*). Smart, atmospheric restaurant with a French and modern Irish menu efficiently delivered to your table.

The Winding Stair, 40 Lower Ormond Quay, D1, t 873 3292 (*inexpensive*). Soup and sandwiches in a charming café-cum-bookshop with a lovely view over the Liffey.

Dublin City South

Locks Restaurant, 1 Windsor Terrace, Portobello, D8, t 454 3391 (*expensive*). This cosy place overlooks the Grand Canal and has an assured and friendly feel to it. Some of the dishes are adventurous and wholesome, with extensive use of organic produce from County Wicklow.

The Old Dublin Restaurant, 90–91 Francis Street, D8, t 454 2028 (*expensive*). A very appealing and well-presented menu which inclines towards the Oriental and east-European – mainly Scandinavian and Russian. They serve lovely *kasha* barley or savoury rice; and vegetarian *satsiv*, which is a crispy version of curried fresh vegetables.

The Orchid Szechuan Restaurant, 120 Pembroke Road, Ballsbridge, D4, t 660 0629 (*expensive*). Excellent Chinese food in this restaurant, recommended by locals.

Satchels Restaurant, in The Schoolhouse Hotel, 2–8 Northumberland Road, D4, t 667 5014, www.schoolhousehotel.com (*expensive*). Good bistro food, served in an impressive beamed hall.

Fitzer's Restaurant, 24 Upper Baggot Street, D4, t 677 1155 (*moderate*). Sassy food from the Pacific rim and the Med. Also at 5 Dawson Street.

The Grey Door, 22/23 Upper Pembroke Street, D4, t 676 3286 (*moderate*). Russian and Scandinavian food.

Kitty O'Shea's Restaurant, 23–25 Grand Canal Street, D4, t 660 8050 (*moderate*). Also good for Sunday brunch.

Marrakesh, 11 Ballsbridge Terrace, D4, t 660 5539 (*moderate*). Small, authentic Moroccan restaurant. Traditional dishes include delicious soups, generous helpings of couscous and a choice of *tagines*.

Roly's Bistro, 7 Ballsbridge Terrace, Ballsbridge, D4, t 668 2611 (*moderate*). Lovely interior; a fun and fashionable café atmosphere with food to match. *Advance booking essential*.

Ryan's, 28 Parkgate Street, D8, t 677 6097 (*moderate*). Cosy Victorian pub serving fine bar fare, especially the salad plates.

Burdocks, 2 Werburgh Street, D6, t 454 0306 (*inexpensive*). Excellent take-away fish and chips to eat in the park around the corner.

Entertainment and Nightlife

Bars and Pubs

Dublin's pubs and bars are famous for their warm, convivial atmosphere, their snugs, whiskey, mirrors and food – and, of course, their Guinness. If you haven't experienced them, then you certainly haven't experienced the true Dublin. The following are recommended.

The Bailey, Duke Street, t 670 4939. Another literary stop-off.

The Barley Mow Pub, Francis Street, D8. This has no connection with The Old Dublin Restaurant, next door, but you can have a drink here whilst a waiter takes your order.

Clarence Hotel Bar, Essex Street, D2, t 670 9000. Friendly staff, and fashionable with theatre and film people; owned by the group U2.

Davy Byrnes, 21 Duke Street, D2, t 677 5217. Busy with tourists on the literary trail. But they do make good sandwiches.

Dawson Lounge, 25 Dawson Street, D2, t 677 5909. Quirky basement bar.

Doheny and Nesbitt's, 5 Lower Baggot Street, D2, t 676 2945. Victorian décor. Frequented by lawyers and politicians.

The Globe, 11 South Great Georges Street, D2, t 671 1220/670 5765. Café popular with the young and beautiful – good sandwiches and cappuccinos at lunchtime.

Grogan's, 15 South William Street, D2, t 807 8980. Aspiring writers, artists, etc.

The International Bar, 23 Wicklow Street, D2, t 677 9250. Nice in the afternoon; music at night.

Kehoe's Pub, 9 South Anne Street, D2, t 677 8312. Authentic and quirky with a good snug.

Long Hall, 51 South Great George's Street, D2, t 475 1590. Crammed with knick-knacks and lovely mirrors. Nice barmen.

McDaids, 3 Harry Street, t 679 4395. Traditionally a literary haunt; hosts jazz on some nights.

Mulligans, Poolbeg Street, D2, t 677 5582. This bar has earned a reputation for high-quality Guinness, and is popular with journalists.

Neary's, 1 Chatham Street, off Grafton Street, D2, t 677 8596. Good sandwiches and a theatrical atmosphere.

Palace Bar, 21 Fleet Street, D2, t 677 9290. This one was a writers' haunt once upon a time in the 1950s.

Ryan's Bar, 28 Parkgate Street, D7, t 677 6097. Well-preserved Victoriana, cosy snugs and very good pub food, especially at lunchtime.

Stag's Head, 1 Dame Court, D2, t 679 3701. Cosy interior snug with friendly staff; good for sausages, chips and Guinness at tea-time.

The Shelbourne Hotel, Horseshoe Bar, 27 St Stephen's Green, D2, t 663 4500. An elegant spot, and popular with lawyers, politicans and journalists.

Toner's, 139 Lower Baggot Street, D2, t 676 2606. Victorian fittings and a mixed crowd. Nice toasted cheese sandwiches.

Bars with Music

Folk, Jazz and Rock

Bad Bob's, 35–37 East Essex Street, D2, t 677 5482. Country.

Baggot Inn, 143 Baggot Street, D2, t 676 1430. Music seven nights a week.

International Bar, 23 Wicklow Street, D2, t 677 9250. Two floors, with something different on each.

J. J. Smyth's, 12 Aungier Street, D2, t 475 2565. Mostly jazz.

McDaid's. 3 Harry Street, D2, t 679 4395. Blues upstairs.

O'Dwyers, 7 Lower Mount Street, D2, t 676 1617.

Whelans, 25 Wexford Street, D2, t 478 0766. Music almost every night: indie, rock, bluegrass, country and some styles that you never dreamed existed. Legends like Leo O'Kelly play there.

Traditional Music

Traditional music can be heard on different nights at each venue. Sessions are free, unless a big name is playing. Check in the local newspaper or with the bar. If you wish to learn more about traditional Irish music, pay a visit to *Ceol*, the Irish Traditional Music Centre, at Smithfield Village, Smithfield, D7, t 817 3820, f 817 3821, *www.ceol.ie*, *info@ceol.ie*.

Brazen Head, 20 Lower Bridge Street, D8, t 679 5186. The oldest bar in Dublin.

Harcourt Hotel, 60 Harcourt Street, D2, t 478 3677, or t 1850 664455. Sessions every night with musicians from all over Ireland.

Hughes, 19 Chancery Street, D7, t 872 6540. One of the best.

Kitty O'Shea's, 23 Upper Grand Canal Street, D4, t 660 8050.

O'Donoghues, 15 Merrion Row, D2, t 676 2807.

O'Shea's Merchants Bar, 12 Lower Bridge Street, D8, t 679 3797. Traditional Irish and ballad music and song; you'll also find set-dancing here.

Mother Redcaps, Back Lane, beside Tailors' Guildhall, Christchurch, D4, t 453 8306. Folk music also.

The Oliver St John Gogarty, Temple Bar, D2, t 671 1822.

Rumm's, Shelbourne Road, D4, t 667 6422. Pub food and nightly traditional music.

Slattery's, 179 Capel Street, D1, t 872 7971. A very popular place.

The Temple Bar, 47 Temple Bar, D2, t 672 5287.

Cabaret and Comedy

The cabaret scene is often a straggling descendent of music hall, with old-time Irish songs and jokes.

Ha'penny Bridge Inn, 42 Wellington Quay, t 677 0616. Comedy some weeknights; they also have live music.

International Bar, 23 Wicklow Street, t 677 9250. Mad Cow Comedy Club on Wed nights.

Jury's Hotel, Ballsbridge, D4, t 660 5000. A bit touristy during the summer months.

Murphy's Laughter Lounge, 4 Eden Quay, D2, t 874 4611. Comedy club.

Cinema

Film is extremely popular in Dublin, indeed, the Irish attend the cinema more frequently than any other Europeans. All cinemas are listed in the papers.

Ambassador Cinema, Parnell Square, D1, t (01) 872 7000.

Irish Film Centre, 6 Eustace Street, Temple Bar, D2, t 679 5744. Foreign and art-house releases. The film festival in March is organized from here. There is also a nice café with good snacks.

Imax, Parnell Centre, Parnell Street, D1, t 817 4222, f 817 4230.

Light House Cinema, 13 Anglesea Street, D2, t 679 9585. Art-house and foreign films.

Savoy Cinema, Upper O'Connell Street, t 874 8487. First-runs.

Screen Cinema, D'Olier Street, t 672 5500. Independent, less commercial films.

UGC Cinemas, Parnell Street, D1, t 872 8400. 10-screen, first-run house.

Classical Music and Shows

When big stars of whatever sort come to town they may appear at the RDS Concert Hall in suburban Ballsbridge; some big rock concerts use the Point Theatre at East Link Bridge, or even the Lansdowne Road Stadium. In any case, details of all will be in *In Dublin* or the newspapers.

Bank of Ireland Arts Centre, College Green, *www.boi.ie/html/gws/about_us/ community/arts/*. Classical music.

Gaiety Theatre, South King Street, t 677 1717, *www.gaietytheatre.com*. For opera. Log on to the Opera Ireland website, *www.opera-ireland.ie*, for information on the opera season.

Hugh Lane Gallery, Charlemont House, Parnell Square North, D1, t 874 1903, f 872 2182, *www.hughlane.ie*. Another place for classical music; hosts lunchtime concerts.

The National Concert Hall, Earlsfort Terrace, D2, t 417 0000, *www.nch.ie, info@nch.ie*. The National Symphony Orchestra is based here, and there is a full schedule of other concerts most of the year, not only classical but jazz, pop and touring shows from abroad.

Nightclubs

Dublin has been voted 'hippest city in Europe' by several fashion magazines, in particular for its nightclub scene. This seems extreme, but there is no doubt that Dublin at night can be fun. Most of the clubs stay open until 2–3.30am. They are also by their very nature fairly transient, so do check in advance.

Annabel's, Burlington Hotel, Upper Leeson Street, D4, t 660 5222. Mainstream, with professional, grown-up clientele.

The Dublin Pod (Place of Dance), Harcourt Street, D2, t 478 0225. Hard jungle and house for posers, tucked inside a train station.

Gaiety Theatre, South King Street, t 677 1717, www.gaietytheatre.com. Several levels including jazz, blues and salsa, dance and 60s/70s retro in a relaxed atmosphere. They also have reggae nights.

The Kitchen, East Essex Street, t 677 6635, www.the-kitchen.com. U2-owned club, hot, hip and friendly with an open-house music policy – which means anything from hardcore house and techno to drum 'n' bass.

Klub Zazu, Eustace Street, D2, t 670 7655. Playing classic dance music on two levels – accessible and popular.

Lillie's Bordello, Adam Court, off Grafton Street, t 679 9204. The longest established of Dublin's currently fashionable clubs, frequented by models, visiting rock stars and other beautiful people. Wide-ranging in age; be prepared to queue.

The Mean Fiddler, 26 Wexford Street, D2, t 475 8555. A wide choice of live gigs and club nights. Indie, dance, rock and punk.

Olympia, 72 Dame Street, D2 t 677 7744. This club is housed in a delightful old former music hall, and hosts a wide range of music.

The Red Box, Harcourt Street, D2, t 478 0166. Huge dancefloor with house, techno and disco nights.

Ri Ra, Dame Court, D2, t 677 4835. Funky, unpretentious and good for late-night drinking; two floors of music plus a quieter bar upstairs.

Theatre

It is worth spending money on the theatre in Dublin. Things really takes off during the festival in October, with new plays by Irish authors, some of which have become Broadway hits. The most convenient place to book tickets is at the stall in Brown Thomas's in Grafton Street. You can also get them at the tourist offices on Suffolk Street and O'Connell Street, or from the theatres themselves. Performances in the evening usually begin around 8pm, and most theatres are not open on Sundays. Student and pensioners can get a discount on tickets in some theatres.

Abbey Theatre, Lower Abbey Street, D1, t 878 7222. The famous theatre founded by the indomitable Lady Gregory and W. B. Yeats. The old building burned down; the new one also houses the **Peacock Theatre**, which concentrates on contemporary playwrights, whereas the Abbey sticks predominantly to the old Irish classics. The new theatre house is functional and modern in design with a great array of portraits of Dublin literati. The Abbey has made the Irish turn of phrase famous throughout the world with plays such as *Playboy of the Western World* by J. M. Synge and *Juno and the Paycock* by Sean O'Casey. It can be hard getting tickets, so book ahead.

Andrew's Lane Theatre, 12 St Andrews Lane, t 679 5720. A variety of dramatic fare; adventurous, modern pieces in the **Andrews Lane Studio**.

City Arts Centre, 23 Moss Street, t 677 0643. Exciting productions here too.

Focus Theatre, 6 Pembroke Place, off Pembroke Street, D2, t 676 3071. Fringe theatre.

Gaiety Theatre, South King Street, D2, t 677 1717, www.gaietytheatre.com. A splendid, tiered Victorian theatre, showing more traditional plays, and it provides a venue for opera, musicals and pantomime.

Gate Theatre, 8 Parnell Square, D1, t 874 4045. Stages productions of international and classic dramas; famous names such as Orson Welles and James Mason began their acting careers here, and current productions often go on to New York.

International Bar, Wicklow Street, t 677 9250. Has a cellar area devoted to comedy.

Olympia Theatre, 72 Dame Street, t 677 7744. Drama, ballet, musical as well as late night concerts.

Project Arts Theatre, 39 East Essex Street, Temple Bar, D2, t 679 6622, booking t 1800 260 027, f 679 2310, www.project.ie, info@project.ie. Perhaps some of the most experimental and stimulating theatre in Dublin, with art exhibitions alongside.

Samuel Beckett Centre, Trinity College, t 702 1239. Often has exciting lunchtime theatre.

SFX City Theatre, 23 Upper Sherrard Street, D1, t 855 4090. Fringe productions.

Tivoli Theatre, Francis Street, D8, t 454 4472. Stages musicals and plays, usually excellent.

the rosy-coloured Georgian squares and delicate, perfectly proportioned doorways are jumbled up together with some grotesque adventures into modern architecture. Fast-food signs and partially demolished buildings mingle with expensive and tacky shops, and the housing estates can be depressing. The tall houses north of the Liffey were divided into run-down flats, although many are now being done up and through the doors and windows you catch glimpses of their former glory – elegant staircases and marvellous plasterwork.

Modern Dublin was bent on knocking down the past or ignoring it so that it crumbled away on its own, especially during the 1970s. Should you ask about Wood Quay, official indifference reveals itself. Wood Quay was the complete 9th- to 11th-century Danish settlement of houses, walls and quays which was recently excavated, giving great insight into the lives of those first Dubliners. The Dublin City Corporation actually built their ugly modern office block on top of it, despite sustained protests from those who felt the old city should be preserved. On the positive side, the Custom House Quay development, which also houses a financial centre, is a fine attempt at regeneration of the docklands area. And the last few years have seen a quickening of interest in preserving the lovely old buildings of the past. The Dublin Millennium Celebrations in 1988 caused a great sprucing up, and Dubliners took great pride in their city's history and heritage. In 1991 Dublin was the European City of Culture, which encouraged more refurbishment. There is still an amount of unco-ordinated planning. Dublin is threatened with road-widening plans, and what amounts to a motorway has been built, cutting through the city centre.

You will find that gradually the charm and atmosphere of Dublin – and atmosphere is what it is all about – begins to filter through that first, negative impression. Get up early, explore the ancient medieval streets around Dublin Castle in the morning sunshine, and breakfast at Bewley's Café. Walk down Grafton Street, where noisy, laughing shoppers mingle with some genuine eccentrics. Relax, go with the flow and notice the pleasant things about Dublin which have been staring you in the face all along.

History

The Greek philosopher Ptolemy mentioned Dublin in AD 140, when it was called Eblana, but it really came to prominence under the Danes during the 9th century, because of its importance as a fording place and as a base for maritime expeditions. They established themselves on a section of ground between the River Liffey and Christ Church. The name Dublin comes from the Irish *Dubhlinn*: 'Dark Pool'; although the Irish form in official use at the moment is *Baile Atha Cliath*: 'Town of the Hurdle Ford' – this refers to an ancient river crossing near the present Heuston Station.

The marauding Vikings arrived in AD 840 and established a fortress and a settlement along the banks of the Liffey estuary. From a simple base for raiding expeditions, Dublin grew to a prosperous trading port with Europe. The local Gaelic rulers were very keen to grab it for themselves, but it was not until the Battle of Clontarf in 1014 that the dominance of the Danes was severely curtailed. They were finally driven out in 1169 by the Anglo-Normans under Strongbow (Richard de Clare), who took Dublin by storm and executed the Viking leader. The arrival of the Anglo-Norman foreigners began the occupation of Ireland by the English, which lasted for seven hundred years. Dermot MacMurragh, King of Leinster, invited the invasion by asking Henry II of England for the help of Anglo-Norman mercenaries in his battle for the high kingship of Ireland. They came, and their military campaigns were so successful that they soon controlled not only Wexford and Waterford but most of Leinster and, of course, Dublin. Once here, the Normans had no intention of leaving. In 1172 Henry II came to Dublin to look over his kingdom, and to curb the powers of his warlike vassal lords.

From then on, Dublin played a dominant role as the centre of English power. The Anglo-Normans fortified themselves with strong castles, and the area surrounding Dublin where they settled was known as The Pale. Anything outside was dangerous and barbaric – hence the expression, 'beyond the Pale'. For a short and glorious period in the late 18th century Ireland had its own parliament here, 'Grattan's Parliament' (1782–1800); the élite who sat within it had many liberal ideas, such as the introduction of Catholic emancipation. One could speculate that the course of Ireland's history might have been happier if this independent parliament had been allowed to develop. A great surge of urban building took place during this time. Grattan was typical of the liberal landowners who wanted legislative reform, and is remembered for his powers of oratory. Unfortunately, the influence of the French Revolution, and the growth of the United Irishmen frightened the British Government. The 1798 Rising was a realization of their worst fears, and the British Parliament resumed direct control of Irish affairs in 1800. This meant that the resident and educated ruling class left Dublin, and took with them much of its dynamism and culture. The struggle for independence from English rule manifested itself in violent episodes and street clashes in the 19th century, with violence becoming more common in the early 20th century. During the 1916 Rising, buildings and lives were shattered by Nationalists fighting with British troops, which erupted again during the Civil War that followed the peace with England. Many of those buildings, such as the Customs House, the masterpiece of James Gandon (1743–1823), have been restored to their former grandeur.

It was under the rule of the so-called Anglo-Irish Ascendancy that Dublin acquired her gracious streets and squares, which amaze one with their variety. Many of the houses were built in small groups by speculators when Dublin was the fashionable place to be – hence the variety. Each door is slightly different and the patterns of the wrought-iron balconies and railings change from house to house. You will not see ironwork like this in London, as most railings were ripped up and melted down during the Second World War.

The size of Dublin increased very slowly during the 19th and early 20th centuries, due in part to the lack of countrywide industrialization, the famine and emigration. The population started to grow in the 1950s with a shift from rural to urban areas; today Dubliners suffer from a lack of housing, inadequate sewage treatment, increasing crime, and a huge traffic problem caused by urban sprawl and the neglect of public transport, which is now being addressed. The population of young people in Ireland, and in Dublin particularly, is high. Greater Dublin has a population of over one million, and plenty of families are living on the dole; some of the suburban housing estates are among the poorest and most troubled in Europe.

Still, since the 1990s booming Dublin has become the power behind the 'Celtic Tiger' economy. It is a city full of new money and high-tech industries, one growing outwards in all directions. Tourists pour in, drawn by the city's traditional charms and even more by the continuing world-wide popularity of all things Irish. Changes to the city itself are noticeable. New museums and attractions have appeared, and there is some redevelopment in the city's docklands and around O'Connell Street. Dubliners are showing signs of finally reforming their notorious neglect of the inner city and its historic architecture; a symbol of this is Temple Bar, the riverfront area transformed by private initiative into a thriving and attractive entertainment district after the government tried – unsuccessfully – to demolish it. Dublin isn't a city given to grand gestures and showy mega-projects. Its people are cautious and mindful of traditions; they like things to stay as they are.

Throughout the centuries Dublin has produced great writers: Jonathan Swift (who suggested in his satirical yet frighteningly plausible essay *A Modest Proposal* that the ruling class in Ireland should eat all newborn babies to cure the problems of poverty and overpopulation), Bishop Berkeley, Edmund Burke, Thomas Moore, Sheridan, Le Fanu, Wilde and Goldsmith, to name but a few. Towards the end of the 19th century Dublin became the centre of the Cultural Movement, which resulted in the formation of the Gaelic League, which became entangled with the Nationalists' aspirations of the time. How much influence this movement had on the next flurry of great writers it is hard to say, but George Bernard Shaw, George Moore, James Stephens, Yeats, James Joyce and later Samuel Beckett drew much of their inspiration from the streets of Dublin. This is an extract from *No Mean City* by Oliver St John Gogarty (1878–1957), a writer, wit and surgeon who details Dublin's famous men:

Dublin, Dublin of the vistas. What names come to mind, names filling more than two centuries from the days of the gloomy Dean Swift, who left his money to found a lunatic asylum 'to show by one sarcastic touch no nation needed it so much', to Mrs Bernard Shaw, who left her money to teach manners to Irishmen; and some say (they would in Dublin) that, in spite of all his acumen, the man for whom it was principally intended failed to see the sarcastic touch; Oliver Goldsmith; Bishop Berkeley, who wrote 'Westward the course of Empire takes it way' and went his way to Rhode Island and gave his name to Berkeley, California; Hamilton, who discovered proleptically the Quaternion Theory by the banks of the Royal Canal; Burke, who thundered in defence of American liberation; Molyneaux, whose nationalism caused his books to be burned by the common hangman; Fitzgerald, who anticipated Marconi in the discovery of aetherial waves; Mahaffy, who was the greatest Humanist of his time as well as the expeller from Trinity College of Oscar Wilde to Oxford; down to Yeats, A. E., and lastly James Joyce, in whose Anna Livia Plurabelle the whole history of Dublin may be discerned by thought, this time cataleptic. All these men lived in Dublin, but most of them died elsewhere. Dublin, that stick of a rocket which remains on the ground while its stars shoot off to light the darkness and die enskied.

Trinity College

The **O'Connell Bridge**, the most important of the bridges that cross the Liffey, is a good spot to get your bearings and begin a tour of Dublin. On the riverbank the monuments of the city line up, the Four Courts on one side, the Custom House on the other. Across the river is the famous O'Connell Street, while on the southern side, narrow, busy Westmoreland Street invites you into the heart of the city.

The former Parliament House stands where Westmoreland meets College Green, and is nowadays the **Bank of Ireland** (*open during banking hours Mon–Fri 10–4, Thurs until 5; free guided tours of the House of Lords Tues at 10.30, 11.30 and 1.45 except on bank hols; adm; t (01) 677 6801*). The brainchild of Lovat Pearce, who designed it in 1729, it was finished in 1785 by James Gandon, Dublin's most notable architect. It was between these walls that Grattan stunned everybody with his oratory when he demanded constitutional independence from the English Parliament. Later, in 1800, a well-bribed House voted for the Union, and Parliament House became redundant. It is an imposing classical building with Ionic porticos. Inside you may see the coffered ceiling of the old House of Lords; a Waterford chandelier dating from 1765; and two fine 18th-century tapestries depicting famous Protestant victories, the Battle of the Boyne and the Siege of Derry, as well as the parliament's Golden Mace. The bankers celebrate their trade in the adjacent Bank of Ireland Arts Centre, Foster Place, with the **Story of Banking Museum** (*open Tues–Fri 10–4*).

Just opposite Parliament House is the entrance to **Trinity College**, through Regent House, and during term-time the students are clustered around it, joking, chatting, or handing out political leaflets. As you enter through the imposing 1759 façade, you leave bustling Dublin far behind and come upon a giant square, laid out with green lawn and cobbled stone, and surrounded by gracious buildings. Stop to look at the **Museum Building** (which has only a small geological collection) for the stone carving by the O'Shea brothers; they also created the amusing monkeys which play round what used to be the Kildare Street Club, the brick palazzo on the northeast corner of Kildare Street.

The other buildings in the quadrangle are 18th-century and are described below, but first pass through the peaceful grounds into the second quadrangle, as your main objective will probably be to visit **Trinity College Library** to take a look at the priceless *Book of Kells* (*open all year, Mon–Sat 9.30–5, plus Oct–May, Sun noon–4.30, June–Sept, 9.30–4.30; adm; t (01) 608 2320*). The library is on the right of the second quadrangle and dates from 1712. It has been a copyright library since 1801 and contains an enormous number of manuscripts, including the diaries of Wolfe Tone and the manuscripts of John Millington Synge. The library is a fine building and contains the Long Room, which has a barrel-vaulted ceiling and gallery bookcases. The area underneath the Long Room, known as the Colonnades, has been remodelled, and the *Book of Kells* is permanently displayed there. Every day one of the thick vellum pages of the book is turned to present more fantastic and intricate designs. Someone once said that the book was made up of imaginative doodles. The man who copied out the gospels and enlivened them with such 'doodles' was able to draw so perfectly that sections as small as a postage stamp reveal no flaws when magnified. The book is probably 8th-century and comes from an abbey in Kells, County Meath. Have a look too at the *Book of Durrow*, the *Book of Armagh* and the *Book of Dimma*, which are also beautifully illuminated. Next door is the **Berkeley Library** which contains over two million books. It was built in 1967 to designs by Paul Koralek, who also did the skilfully designed **Arts Building**, erected in 1978. An audio-visual show, '**The Dublin Experience**' (*open late May–early Oct, daily 10–5; adm; t (01) 608 2320*), is held in the Arts building. It tells the story of the city from its Viking beginnings to the present day.

Trinity College was founded in 1592, in the reign of Elizabeth I. The land on which it was erected had once been occupied by the Augustinian monastery of All Hallows, founded by Dermot MacMurragh in the 12th century. The squares are made up of a mixture of buildings, ranging from early 18th-century to the present-day. The red-brick **Rubrics**, beyond the campanile in the middle of the quad, is the oldest bit still standing and dates from *c.* 1700. Oliver Goldsmith had his chambers here, as do present-day students and professors. Trinity College has a long and venerable history; so many famous scholars, wits and well-known men of Ireland were educated here. It was freed from its Protestant-only restrictions in 1873, and Catholics were allowed to study here, but Paul Cullen, the Catholic archbishop of the day, threatened any that did with excommunication. The university remained the preserve of the Protestant gentry for some time (although that is far from the case now), but distinguished itself by admitting women students as early as 1903, as well as non-Christians. The **Provost's House** (on the left of the main entrance) is a fine 18th-century mansion. One of its most famous occupants was John Mahaffy (1839–1919) a great scholar and clergyman, as was essential for the fellowship of the college. He was also, in the last year of his life, a knight. His witty dinner talk was legendary, but he could also be very wounding. Apparently he impressed on Oscar Wilde the importance of good social contacts and brilliant conversation, and declared that James Joyce's *Ulysses* was 'the inevitable result of extending university to the wrong sort of people'.

On the right as you enter the first cobbled quadrangle is the **Theatre**, or Examination Hall, which was built between 1779 and 1791 with an Adam-style ceiling, and a gilt oak chandelier. On the left is the **Chapel**, built in 1798. Both buildings were designed by William Chambers, the Scottish architect who never actually set foot in Dublin. (*The Theatre and Chapel can be seen on request; ask at the Porter's Lodge.*) Beyond the Chapel is the **Dining Hall**, designed by Richard Cassels in 1743. It was nearly destroyed by fire in 1984 and has now been restored. The quick responses of the staff and students ensured the survival of the portraits and other works of art which now grace its walls again: they formed a human chain to get them safely out. Quite often there is music of some sort in the Junior Common Room, and the **Douglas Hyde Gallery**, in the Arts Building, often mounts retrospective exhibitions of major Irish artists.

As it passes Trinity College, Westmoreland Street becomes **Grafton Street**, an attractive pedestrian way that is the choice shopping street of Dublin. On its way it passes the ornate **Bewley's Coffee Shop**, a Dublin institution since 1840 – so much so that it has its own museum upstairs (there is another branch on Westmoreland Street). On the side streets west of Grafton, you can find the **Dublin Tourism Centre**, a formidably busy tourist office with the air of an airport terminal, which is housed in an imaginative restoration of the long-abandoned Protestant St Andrew's Church (1860). **Powerscourt Town House** in South William Street, built in 1771, was typical of Georgian town houses of the Ascendency. It has fine Rococo and Adamesque plaster-work which has survived in the conversion of the house and surroundings into the **Powerscourt Shopping Centre**. This triumph of enlightened development is a pleasure to visit; it houses a large crafts co-operative and has a variety of restaurants including a very good vegetarian one, called 'Fresh', which is right at the top. Here you can see Ireland's finest boutiques (including the Irish Design Centre) and speciality shops, enclosed under a great glass-roofed courtyard (*see* 'Shopping', p.576–8). Next to the Centre at 58 South William Street is the **Dublin Civic Museum** (*open Tues–Sat 10–6, Sun 11–2; free; t (01) 679 4260*), a collection of old newspapers, cuttings, prints, pictures and coins which build up a very clear picture of old Dublin. You can also see some Viking artefacts found in the recent excavations, and Admiral Nelson's head – from the column the IRA blew up in O'Connell Street (*see* p.598).

St Stephen's Green

St Stephen's Green (*open 8am–dusk*), at the top of Grafton Street, is one of the loveliest and certainly one of the best-loved city parks you will ever see. In the middle is a romantic landscaped park with a lake and waterfall, ducks and weeping willows. Every age and type of Dubliner uses it to wander in, and enjoy the trees and flowers. Its cool, green gardens make a perfect setting for a picnic. At the western edge of the green is Henry Moore's graceful monument to W. B. Yeats. Another monument is to Lord Ardilaun – Sir Arthur Guinness, the fellow whose signature is on the bottle. He not only paid for the improvements, but put through a bill in Parliament to purchase the park and open it to the public in the 1880s. Originally the area had been common land; in the 1660s the English fenced it in and converted it into a private residential square. The surviving Anglo-Norman aristocracy, Cromwellian adventurers and the new gentry (mainly composed of those who had profited from the seizure of forfeited lands), then built their grand houses around the square and adjoining streets.

Today, one of Dublin's biggest regrets is her many decades of utter carelessness in looking after her architectural heritage. It is certainly true in the streets around Stephen's Green. Two of the original houses that survive belong to University College Dublin, an institution founded by the Catholics in the 1860s as a counter to the Protestant Trinity College. **Newman House**, at 85 St Stephen's Green, D12 (*open June–Aug, Tues–Fri 12–5, Sat 2–5, Sun 11–2; adm; t (01) 706 7422*) is named after Cardinal John Henry Newman, the great theologian of the 19th-century Catholic revival who founded the University. These two buildings contain some of the finest late Baroque and Rococo plasterwork in Ireland; poet Gerard Manley Hopkins, who was a professor of Classics at the university, died here after many years residence. No.85 was built in 1738, designed by Richard Cassels, and it contains the ravishing Apollo room, a masterpiece of stucco decoration by the Francini brothers. No.86 was built in 1765 for the MP Richard Chapell Whaley, father of the notorious Buck Whaley, whose memoirs of 18th-century Dublin are still a good read. The house has very good plasterwork by Robert West; the hall is decorated with motifs of musical instruments.

If you are passing the famous Shelbourne Hotel on St Stephen's Green, you may notice a shuttered garden, just to the left of it. The **Huguenot Graveyard** is a secret place. Even Dubliners hardly know it is there. You can peer through the gates and see the mellow gravestones which mark the names of French Huguenots who successfully merged into the Irish way of life after a couple of generations. Ten thousand Huguenots arrived in Ireland to escape persecution for their religous beliefs, between the 1650s and 1700s. They had a great civilizing influence on early 18th-century Dublin, which was then very small and only just beginning to develop its own cultural activities after the turbulence of the 17th century. The Huguenots expanded the wine trade, started silk and poplin industries, and introduced a Horticultural Society, where they used to toast their favourite flowers.

Around Merrion Square

The beautiful Georgian **Merrion Square**, just east of St Stephen's Green, is one of the best-preserved in Dublin, and was the home of many famous literary people and politicians. Sir William and Lady 'Speranza' Wilde (Oscar's parents) lived at no.1; Daniel O'Connell at no.58; W. B. Yeats at nos.52 and 82; George Russell, known as A. E., at no.84; and Sheridan Le Fanu at no.70. With the Irish Parliament just next door, most of the square's homes have been converted into offices of the government, or interests that like to be close to it. **Leinster House**, on the western edge of the square, was finished in 1745, built to the design of Richard Cassels, who was responsible for so many lovely houses in Ireland – Russborough House in Wicklow, for instance. Leinster House has two different faces, one looking out over Kildare Street, and the other on to the pleasant garden of Merrion Square. It was the town house of the Dukes of Leinster and was originally known as Kildare House. Leinster House is now the seat of the Irish Parliament, which consists of the *Dáil* ('Lower House', pronounced 'doyle') and the *Seanad* ('Upper House', or 'Senate').

The National Gallery stands just opposite the fountain (*open Mon–Sat 10–5.30, Thurs until 8.30, Sun 2–5; tours on Saturday at 3pm and Sunday at 2.30, 3 and 4pm; adm free; t (01) 661 5133*). A statue of George Bernard Shaw greets you in the forecourt. He bequeathed one third of his estate to the gallery because he learnt so much from the pictures. Certainly this is one of the most enjoyable, first-class small galleries in the world. It has just been very sympathetically redecorated and many pictures rehung. There are over two thousand works on view, including a small collection of superb work by Renaissance painters; Spanish, French and Italian 16th- and 17th-century painters; and Dutch Masters. The Irish Room includes some elegant portraits by Lavery, Orpen and many others, work by J. B. Yeats (father of W. B. Yeats) and well-regarded wild and colourful oils by Jack Yeats (brother of W. B. Yeats). Gainsborough is well represented with 10 major works. Upstairs in the Arts Reference Library there is a good collection of Irish watercolours. The gallery restaurant is a good place for lunch or early supper, and the shop selling postcards and art books is also excellent.

The Irish Architectural Archive at 73 Merrion Square (south side), a wonderful example of a Georgian town house, opens its reading room to the public (*Mon–Fri 10–5. adm free; t (01) 676 3430*).

The **National Museum of Ireland**, in a grand Victorian edifice, occupies two sites: most of the block south of Leinster House (*entrance on Kildare Street; open Tues–Sat 10–5, Sun 2–5; adm free; t (01) 677 7444, f (01) 677 7828*) and Collins Barracks in Benburb Street, D7 (*see p.601*). It is the treasure house of Ireland, and absolutely vital for anyone who has not yet realized that Ireland between AD 600 and 900 was the most civilized part of northern Europe. It has the finest collection of Celtic ornaments and artefacts in the world, and items recently excavated from the Danish settlement in Wood Quay. The Historical Collection traces the history of Ireland from the 18th to the mid-20th century. In the Antiquities Department you can see the beautiful filigree gold whorl enamelling and design which reached perfection in the Tara brooch and the Ardagh Chalice. The many beautiful torcs, croziers and decorated shrines on display will leave you amazed at the sophistication and skill of the craftsmen in those days. Also very interesting are the findings of the Stone and Early Bronze Ages.

Linked to the museum is the **National Library**, which is also in Kildare Street. It has over half a million books and a fascinating collection of Irish-interest source material. There is usually an exhibition on in the entrance hall and the staff are very helpful. The **Genealogical Office** is across the street, in a stately building that was once an Anglo-Irish men's club (*open Mon–Fri, 10.30–12.30 and 2–4.30; adm free; t (01) 603 0200*). The **Natural History Museum** on Merrion Street (*open Tues–Sat 10–5 and Sun 2–5; adm free; t (01) 677 7444*) has barely changed in decades; it has a charming, musty atmosphere, with thousands of stuffed birds, fish and animals, and some fascinating elk skeletons. The **Royal Irish Academy**, at 19 Dawson Street, has one of the largest collections of ancient Irish manuscripts, one of which is on view (*open Tues–Fri 9.30–5; adm free; t (01) 676 2570*). **Ely Place** is more melancholy and just a stone's throw away, between Merrion Row and Baggot Street. It was once very grand, but is now wrapped in a gloom which strip-lighting, glimpsed through the elegant windows, does nothing to dispel. **Ely House** is now owned by the Knights of Colombanus, a charity organization.

Fitzwilliam Square (1791), two streets south of Merrion Square, is the last of Dublin's residential squares, and contains more well-preserved examples of 18th-century architecture with pretty doors and fanlights above. **29 Fitzwilliam Street Lower**, just off the square, is furnished in the style of a middle-class family of the period 1790–1820 (*open Tues–Sat 10–5, Sun 2–5; guided tours; adm; t (01) 702 6165*). The house is owned by the ESB, the state electricity company, which restored it as a sort of penance after knocking down much of the rest of the neighbourhood for their unsightly office block in the 1960s.

Walk a street or two northeastwards from Merrion Square, and the atmosphere changes rather dramatically. This is Dublin's docklands, a drab patch of abandoned wharves and gas works. Like its London counterpart, this docklands is facing an inevitable recycling into a business centre; a few modest towers have already appeared, but so far there's little evidence that the transformation will bring any aesthetic improvement. The **Waterways Visitor Centre**, on the basin where the Grand Canal empties into the Liffey (*open June–Sept daily 9.30–5.30, Oct–May Wed–Sun 12.30–5.30; adm; t (01) 667 7510, waterwaysireland@ealga.ie*) tells the story of the construction and architecture of the waterways, their role in the history of Ireland, and describes their flora and fauna. The **Grand Canal** marks the extent of the Georgian city south of the Liffey, and the towpath which runs alongside it across the southern edge of the city centre takes you past wildfowl and over humpbacked bridges.

Around Dublin Castle

West of Trinity College and Stephen's Green, back towards the quays, you will come to an area lacking in governmental glitter and fancy shops – but this is the true heart of the city, where Dublin began under the Vikings a thousand years ago. **Dublin Castle**, on Dame Street (*open Mon–Fri 10–5, weekends and bank hols 2–5; adm; t (01) 677 7129, www.historic-centres.com/dublin, dublincastle@eircom.net*), long the seat of British rule in Ireland, is well worth a visit, not only because of the place it has in Irish history, but for the beautifully decorated State Apartments and for the Church of the Holy Trinity, designed by Francis Johnston, in the Lower Castle Yard. The various buildings which make up the castle complex are still reminiscent of a fortified city within its own walls. The original medieval walls and towers, begun under King John in 1204, may be gone but the squares of faded red-brick houses with their elegant Georgian façades are a unity still. Many of the present buildings date from 1688, after the earlier castle was destroyed by fire, with most of the upper yard being built in the mid-18th century. From the 18th century onwards a vice-regal court grew up around the Lord Deputy and his administrators, and there were receptions, balls and levees for the gentry and Dublin merchants. It was far removed from the lives of the ordinary people of Ireland. At that time Dublin Castle was the seat of an alien power, and to the young Republican activists of the 19th and early 20th century it was understandably a symbol of tyranny. It was handed over to the provisional government of Ireland in 1922, and is used today for rituals such as the inauguration of the President. The guided tour begins in the upper yard with the **State Apartments**. The lavish decoration, grand chimney pieces and beautiful antique furniture are a feast for the eyes. There is a Throne Room for visiting British monarchs, and a long Portrait Gallery with their pictures. Particularly attractive are the blue and white Wedgwood Room and the Bermingham Tower with its Gothic windows. St Patrick's Hall, site of the inaugurations, has paintings of historical scenes; this leads to the newest – and oldest – attraction in Dublin Castle, the **Undercroft**. Foundations of the original Viking fort and parts of Dublin's first city wall were discovered here during recent excavations.

The **Record Tower** is one of the oldest parts of the castle, though it was substantially rebuilt in 1813. It was from here that, in 1592, Red Hugh O'Donnell, one of the last great Gaelic leaders, managed to escape to the Wicklow Hills (*see* his story under **Ulster**, 'County Donegal', p.488). The other blocks in the quadrangle have been refurbished inside and out, but sadly the proportions and original woodwork have been mucked about. **The Church of the Holy Trinity**, also called the Chapel Royal, was designed by Francis Johnston in 1807. The outside is decorated with scores of sculpted heads of Irish saints and historical figures, while the interior has elaborate vaulting, exuberant plasterwork and oak wood carving.

Within the gardens of the castle sits the **Chester Beatty Library** (*open May–Sept Mon–Fri 10–5, Oct–April Tues–Fri 10–5, Sat 11–5, Sun 1–5; t (01) 407 0750, www.cbl.ie*). Sir Alfred Chester Beatty (1875–1968) was an American mining millionaire and collector who decided to make Dublin his home. The library and its art museum together have one of the finest private collections of oriental manuscripts and miniatures in the world, as well as albums, picture scrolls, and jades from the Far East. The highlights are the Korans, the Persian and Turkish paintings, the Chinese jade books and the Japanese and European woodblock prints.

Just outside the Castle, facing Dame Street, **City Hall** (*open Mon–Sat 10–5.15, Sun 2–5; adm; t (01) 672 2204*) occupies a building on Cork Hill, constructed in 1769 as the Royal Exchange. It currently houses a new exhibition on the history of Dublin. On the opposite side of the castle, facing Werburgh Street, **St Werburgh's Church** is worth visiting for the massive Geraldine monument and the pulpit, a fine piece of carving, possibly by Grinling Gibbons (*open to the public by arrangement Mon–Fri 10–4; visitors are invited to contribute to the upkeep; entrance by the north door, 8 Castle Street, t (01) 478 3710*). Lord Edward Fitzgerald of the United Irishmen and the leader of the 1798 rebellion is interred in the vault here. This church was for a long time the parish church of Dublin, and, before the Chapel Royal in the Dublin Castle complex was built, British viceroys were sworn in here.

Just across Lord Edward Street is **Christchurch Cathedral** (*open daily 10–5; adm; t (01) 677 8099*). The church was founded by King Sitric and Bishop Donatus in 1038, rebuilt by Strongbow in the 12th century, and heavily restored in the 19th century after part of the walls collapsed – there isn't much solid ground for building in central Dublin. The magnificent stonework and graceful arches are well worth a look, as is the effigy representing Strongbow, who was buried in the church – or at least, part of him was. The crypt is the oldest surviving portion of the building; it contains the old punishment stocks, called the 'cat and mouse'. The arch which joins the cathedral to the Synod Hall frames a view of Winetavern Street and the River Liffey. The Synod Hall in Christchurch is now home to **Dublinia** (*open April–Sept, daily 10–5, Oct–March, Mon–Sat 11–4 Sun 10.30–4; adm; t (01) 679 4611*), a multimedia exhibition of medieval Dublin life. with a model of the city as it changed over the centuries and life-size tableaux. **St Audoen's Church** (*t (01) 677 0088, visits@ealga.ie; adm*), in Cornmarket, off High Street (the continuation of Lord Edward Street), is Dublin's only surviving medieval church. The bell tower, restored in the 19th century, has three 15th-century bells. Notice the beautiful Norman font, and make a wish at the lucky stone.

St Patrick's Cathedral (*open daily 9–6, except Nov–Feb, Sat 9–5 and Sun 9–3; adm;* **t** *(01) 453 9472/745 4817*), a short distance south in Patrick's Close, marks the site of a holy well that was associated with the saint. The largest church in Ireland, it was founded in 1190 and is Early English in style. It was built outside the city walls, on what was marshy ground, by a powerful Norman bishop who was also a baron in order to outshine Christchurch (like Christchurch, it is Church of Ireland). In the 14th century it was almost completely rebuilt after a fire, and during the 17th century it suffered terribly from the fighting during the Cromwellian campaign, and was not restored until the 1860s. Benjamin Guinness, the drinks magnate, provided the initiative and funds for this great undertaking. It is an inspiring experience to attend a choir recital here, for its huge dimensions make a perfect auditorium for the song of red-frocked choir boys. It is here that Dean Swift preached his forceful sermons in an effort to rouse some unselfish thoughts in the minds of his wealthy parishioners; over the door of the robing room is his oft-quoted epitaph, 'He lies where furious indignation can no longer rend his heart.' Swift's death mask, chair and pulpit are displayed in Swift Corner and nearby is the grave of Stella, Swift's pupil and great love. Notice the monument to Richard Boyle, first Earl of Cork, and the monument to the last of the Irish bards, O'Carolan.

Marsh's Library, near the cathedral in St Patrick's Close (*open Mon and Wed–Fri 10–12.45 and 2–5, Sat 10.30–12.45; adm;* **t** *(01) 454 3511, marshlib@iol.ie*), is the oldest public library in the country. Founded in 1707, it has changed little since, and provides a rare example of an 18th century library. Dean Swift once owned the copy of Clarendon's *History of the Great Rebellion*, and you can look at his pencilled notes. The entrance is very welcoming, with herbaceous plants softening the stone steps, and a feeling of hallowed learning inside. The library is classical in proportion and has a superb collection of Latin and Greek literature.

Temple Bar

Temple Bar is sold as Dublin's 'left bank' in the brochures; it is, but only if you're rowing upstream. The area is named after Sir William Temple, a provost of Trinity College in the 17th century. It was neglected for a long time and was nearly razed by town planners to build a bus depot. While they were deliberating, artists moved in and rented out studio spaces very cheaply, although now there is a continual battle with property developers, who want to oust the low-rent artistic element, even though the desirability of the area is mainly due to its bohemian atmosphere.

The area is home to various alternative bookshops, bars, clubs and restaurants, and the **Project Arts Centre** on Essex Street, Dublin's new, cutting-edge theatre, which also houses exhibitions and musical performances. The **Irish Film Centre** (**t** *(01) 677 8788,* **f** *(01) 677 8755*), on Eustace Street, shows the classics and has a film bookshop as well as the National Film Archive. The **Temple Bar Information Centre** (**t** *(01) 671 5717,* **f** *(01) 677 2525, info@temple-bar.ie*), also on Eustace Street, can tell you what's going on. For a live, interactive recreation of Dublin (or 'Dyflin') in the 9th century, visit **Dublin's Viking Adventure** in Essex Street West (*open Mar–Oct, Tues–Sat 10.30–4.30,*

Nov–Feb, Tues–Sat 10–1 and 2–4.30; adm; t (01) 679 6040, f (01) 679 6033), with Viking history, archeaological finds and a life-sized longship.

The Guinness Storehouse and the Liberties

Where else but in Dublin would one of the main landmarks of the town be a brewery? In this case, they claim it is the largest one in the world, one that makes fully half of all the beer (stout, really) consumed in Ireland. **The Guinness Storehouse** brewery, at St James's Gate, is just west of the city centre (*open Oct–Mar, daily 9.30–5, April–Sept daily 9.30–7; adm; t (01) 453 6700, f (01) 408 4927*). An informative tour of the birthplace of Guinness is offered; you can visit a rooftop bar with panoramic views of the city of Dublin and try some of the stuff for free, watch a video of the processes that go into making it, and visit a museum in the old hop-store. The shop sells all sorts of 'black gold' souvenirs to take home with you.

The **Liberties** is the old residential area around the brewery, and many of the workers come from this self-sufficient part of town. It was called 'The Liberties' because it stood outside the jurisdiction of the medieval town, and had its own shops and markets. In the late 17th century, French Huguenots set up a poplin and silk-weaving industry along the river valley (known as the Coombe) of the Poddle, a now-defunct river which used to flow through the Liberties and joined the Liffey at Wood Quay. The area still has great character; despite the new apartments and trendy shops springing up in places, it's very much a working class district, and the people who live in it are the Dubliners of ballad and songs. Some families have lived here for many generations. In the late 18th century, faction-fighting was common-place between the Liberty Boys, or tailors and weavers of the Coombe, and the Ormond Boys, butchers who lived in Ormond Market. Sometimes the fighting would involve up to a thousand men. One landmark of the neighbourhood is **St Catherine's Church** (*no access*) in Thomas Street. This fine 18th-century church has a lovely Roman Doric façade. It is occasionally used for concerts and is owned by the Dublin Corporation.

A few streets west of Guinness and the Liberties is the Kilmainham neighborhood and the **Royal Hospital and Irish Museum of Modern Art**, on Military Road across from Heuston Station (*open Tues–Sat 10–5.30, Sun 12–5.30; adm free; t (01) 612 9900, info@modernart.ie*). The restoration of this wonderful classical building is one of the most exciting things to happen to Dublin in recent years. The Government footed the enormous bill, and has earned much prestige through its role in saving it. The hospital was founded by James Butler, Duke of Ormonde, a very able statesman who survived the turbulent times of the Great Rebellion of 1640 and Cromwell's campaigns. He remained loyal to the Stuart kings, and was well rewarded by Charles II on his succession in 1660. The duke was a pragmatist, and was responsible for securing the passing of the Act of Explanation in 1665, which largely approved the Cromwellian land confiscations. But he also did some very charitable works, amongst them the building of this hospital for pensioner soldiers, similar in style to that of Les Invalides in Paris. The Royal Hospital is the largest surviving 17th-century building in Ireland and the most fully classical. Arranged around a quadrangle, it includes a Great

Hall hung with rich and splendid royal portraits. The chapel has a magnificent Baroque ceiling of plasterwork designs of fruit, flowers and vegetables. The museum has a small permanent collection, mostly of contemporary artists. Temporary exhibitions of new artists and 20th-century greats are held in the long galleries.

Kilmainham Gaol on Inchicore Road, D8, where Parnell, de Valera and the leaders of every Irish revolt from 1798 to 1922 spent time, is now a historical museum (*open April–Sept, daily 9.30–4.45, Oct–Mar, Mon–Fri 9.30–4, Sun 10–4.45; adm;* **t** *(01) 453 5984,* **f** *(01) 453 2037, visits@ealga.ie*). The leaders of the 1916 rising were executed (without trial) in the courtyard. Although rather a grim building, it is nevertheless interesting and quite moving; there is a guided tour, exhibits and an audio-visual presentation on the prison's history. Kilmainham was used as the prison in the film *In The Name of The Father,* starring Daniel Day Lewis.

North of the Liffey

The broad thoroughfare of **O'Connell Street**, Dublin's Champs-Elysées, has, like its Parisian counterpart, come down in the world a little. After suffering considerable destruction in the Easter Rising, and more in the Civil War, it gradually ceased to be the swanky showcase of the city that it was intended to be. But despite the tatty shop fronts and fast-food signs, it is still one of the most urbane and elegant streets you will find. And, like Paris, Dublin is beginning to pay some attention to its famous boulevard once again; plans for its renewal are now being discussed, although so far there is nothing concrete.

When O'Connell Street was created in the 18th century, it was purely residential, with a stately mall running up its centre to the Rotunda Hospital. The construction of the Carlisle (now O'Connell) Bridge over the Liffey changed it into a main thoroughfare, and fine department stores, theatres and office blocks replaced the houses. The monuments lining the centre of the street still add glory to it, as do the variety of architectural styles, which you notice if you lift your eyes above shop level. The (mainly Victorian) statues you see are: Daniel O'Connell (1745–1833), the lawyer who won Catholic emancipation (the street was named after him in 1927; before that it was called Sackville Street); William Smith O'Brien (1803–64), the Nationalist leader; Sir John Gray (1816–75), owner of *The Freeman's Journal* and a Nationalist, who was knighted for organizing Dublin's water supply; James Larkin (1867–1943), the trade union leader; Father Theobald Mathew (1790–1856), who advocated and set up temperance clubs; and Charles Parnell (1846–91), a great parliamentary leader whose career was destroyed by the scandal of his affair with a married woman, Kitty O'Shea.

Lord Nelson, who defeated the French at Trafalgar, used to grace a column outside the GPO, but this was damaged by an IRA explosion in 1966 and subsequently demolished. Currently there is a competition under way for replacing the monument, and proposals so far range from creating something modernistic and radically different to simply rebuilding the column as it was – with somebody else on top. Near the site there used to be a very different kind of monument, a modern sculpture of Anna Livia Plurabella, Joyce's eternal feminine personification of both the river Liffey and the women of Dublin, reclining in her fountain – artistic controversy surrounded her as soon as she was put here in 1988, and she was removed in 2001.

The **General Post Office** (*open Mon–Sat 8–8, Sun and bank hols 10–6.30; t (01) 705 7000*), at the centre of the street, is memorable not for its beauty but for the events of 1916, when Pádraig Pearse and his men seized the building on Easter Monday and proclaimed the Irish Republic from its steps. The rebels held out for five days, while the British surrounded the building and shelled it from a gunboat in the Liffey, wrecking it and much of O'Connell Street in the process. In the days that followed, the leaders of the rising, including Pearse and James Connolly, were summarily shot (*see* **History**, p.54). Inside is a memorial to the 1916 heroes in the form of a bronze statue of the dying Cú Chulainn. The GPO's historical role in the struggle for an independent Ireland has made it a venue for all manner of protest meetings.

Two streets behind, there is a colourful street market on **Moore Street**, while on the other side of O'Connell, on Marlborough Street, the (Catholic) **Pro Cathedral of St Mary** is a Greek Revival Doric temple built between 1815 and 1825; the Catholics would have preferred to build it right on O'Connell Street, but times were still too bigoted for that. There is a lovely sung mass at 11am on Sundays that is a long-standing Dublin tradition; the great tenor John McCormack used to sing in it. Down near the Liffey end of Marlborough Street is the famous **Abbey Theatre**, where the plays of Synge and O'Casey had their premieres – often to the accompaniment of riots, by moral-minded Catholics who packed the house to break up the show. The current grim building replaced the original, which burned down in 1951.

The Custom House is just around the corner on the quay, near Butt Bridge. Many consider this the most impressive building in Dublin. A quadrangular building with four decorated faces, it now houses the Customs and Excise and Department of Local Government. It was designed by James Gandon and completed in 1791. Unfortunately, its impact on the waterfront is lessened by a railway bridge which passes in front of it and the new development behind. Gutted by fire in 1921 during the civil war by the Republican side, it has been perfectly restored so that the graceful dome, crowned by the figure of commerce, still rises from the central Doric portico. Inside is a Visitors' Centre, with a small museum on Gandon and the history of the building (*open mid Mar–Nov, Mon–Fri 10–12.30 Sat and Sun 2–5, rest of the year, Wed–Fri 10–5, Sun 2–5; adm; t (01) 878 7660, f (01) 878 8013*).

Parnell Square

Found at the northern end of O'Connell Street, this square began its life as another of Dublin's residential squares; and in the 18th century it was the most fashionable address in town. Today it is known for its cultural institutions and for the conspicuous landmark of the **Rotunda Hospital**, the first specialized maternity hospital in the world (1752). The Rococo Chapel in the hospital is very sumptuous, with large-scale allegorical figures and curving plasterwork decorated with cherubs and putti. (Arrangements to view it must be made in writing to the Hospital Secretary, Rotunda Hospital, Parnell Square, D1.) The hospital has always had an unusual connection with the performing arts; its founder staged concerts to finance his project, including the first performance of Handel's 'Messiah'. The hospital's auditorium holds the Ambassador Cinema, and another part of the building is home to the Gate Theatre, an important venue for new Irish plays since the 1920s. **The Garden of Remembrance** (*always accessible*), behind the theatre, commemorates Irish freedom. The central feature of the garden is a sculpture of the legendary Children of Lir, by Oísín Kelly.

The **Hugh Lane Gallery of Modern Art** occupies a fine Georgian house at No.1 Parnell Square (*open Tues–Thurs 9.30–6, Fri and Sat 9 30–5, Sun 11–5; adm free; t (01) 874 1903, f (01) 872 2182, www.hughlane.ie*). The bulk of the collection was formed by Sir Hugh Lane in the early 20th century (W. B. Yeats wrote a poem about his bequests), and the gallery has a small but wonderful collection of works by well-known artists: portraits of Yeats, Synge and other famous Irish figures and a bust of Lady Gregory by Epstein. The magical stained-glass window by Harry Clarke, 'The Eve of Saint Agnes', is after a poem by John Keats. Within the gallery, the Francis Bacon Studio is a complete reconstruction of Bacon's studio at 7 Reece Mews, Kensington, London. The entire contents of the room were donated to the gallery after his death.

The **Dublin Writers' Museum**, No.18 Parnell Square North (*open all year, Mon–Sat 10–5, Sun 11–5, during June–Aug until 6; adm, combined tickets with the Joyce Museum and Shaw Birthplace are available; t (01) 872 2077*) is housed in another beautifully restored 18th-century building. The permanent displays introduce you to centuries of Irish literature, illustrated by letters, photographs, first editions and memorabilia. The **Irish Writers Centre**, within the museum, has a varied programme of lectures, readings and workshops. The museum also has a very good bookshop and restaurant. Yet another Georgian house in the area has become the **James Joyce Cultural Centre** (*open Mon–Sat 9.30–5, Sun 12.30–5; adm; t (01) 878 8547, f (01) 878 8488, joycecen@ iol.ie*), at 35 North Great George's Street, housing exhibitions, a library, a bookshop and a café.

The Four Courts, St Michan's and the Collins Barracks

At the **Four Courts**, down by Ormond Quay (*open Mon–Fri 10.30–4.30 exc Aug and Sept; t (01) 872 5555*), you get one of the most characteristic views of Dublin. The Four Courts was designed by Gandon, the architect of the Custom House, and completed by Thomas Cooley (1776–84). It was almost completely destroyed in the Civil War of 1921 but it has since been restored. The Law Courts were reinstalled here in 1931. The central block has a Corinthian portico and a copper green dome, and is flanked by two wings enclosing quadrangles. You may look inside the circular waiting hall under the dome. The **Public Record Office** next door was burnt down completely in 1921, with an irredeemable loss of legal and historical documents.

St Michan's on Church Street, west of the Four Courts, is a 17th-century structure on the site of an 11th-century Danish church. Most people are interested in getting to the **vaults** (*open Mar–Oct, Mon–Fri 10–12.30 and 2–4.30, Nov–Mar, Mon–Fri 12.30–3.30, Sat 10–12.45; guided tours; adm; t (01) 872 4154, f (01) 878 2615*), where bodies have lain for centuries without decomposing. Here the air is very dry due to the absorbent nature of the limestone foundations. The skin of the corpses remains as soft as in life and even their joints still work. Layers of coffins have collapsed into each other, exposing arms and legs; you can even see a crusader from the Holy Land. The body of Robert Emmet, one of the leaders of the 1798 rebellion, is said to be buried here. The only things that do live down in this curiously warm and fresh atmosphere are spiders, who feed on each other. There are so many types that people come from afar to study them. It is said that a Dublin lad has honourable intentions if he takes his girl there. The interior of the church itself is very fine and plain. A superb wooden carving of a violin intermingled with flowers and fruits decorates the choir gallery, and is supposed to be by Grinling Gibbons. Whoever carved it was a genius, and it is sad that so many people ghoulishly go only to the vaults.

Just around the corner on Bow Street, you can recover from your experience if necessary in the **Old Jameson Distillery** at Smithfield, (*open daily 9.30–6; adm; t (01) 807 2355*). Though the big copper tanks are no longer in use, everything is kept as it was for the guided tours. There's also an exhibition on the history of Irish whiskey, a 15-minute film and, most important, a generous tasting of all the different Irish.

A few streets to the west, just north of the Liffey on Benburb Street, stands **The National Museum at Collins Barracks** (*open Tues–Sat 10–5, Sun 2–5; adm free; t (01) 677 7444*), an 18-acre site that was known as the Royal Barracks when it was the head-quarters of the British military in Ireland. The main building, built in 1701, was restored by the National Museum to hold its collections of decorative arts, including furniture and relics of Irish history. In a sense this is Ireland's Smithsonian and it holds a little bit of everything, from Etruscan vases to an oar belonging to one of the lifeboats from the *Lusitania*.

Phoenix Park

Phoenix Park is huge, the largest city park in Europe. It is nearly within walking distance of central Dublin. (Cross the river northwards and walk west along the quays to Conyngham Road; or catch a bus from O'Connell Street) The Dubliners are very proud of the park – with good reason. There are sports fields, woodland, small lakes, duck ponds and the Dublin Zoo, and it finds room in its 1,760 acres (712ha) to house *Aras an Uachtarain* (the residence of the President), the residence of the American Ambassador, police headquarters and a hospital.

The name of the park comes from a corruption of the Gaelic *Fionn Uisce*, which means 'Bright Water', from a spring which rises near the Phoenix Column at the Knockmaroon Gate. To English ears the pronunciation of the Gaelic sounded rather like 'phoenix'. The Phoenix Column was put up in 1747 by Lord Chesterfield, who was the viceroy of the time, and who had the impetus and foresight to plant this part of the park with trees. The land was offered by Charles II to one of his mistresses, which illustrates to what degree Dublin, and indeed the whole of Ireland, was up for grabs in the 17th century. Luckily, the Duke of Ormonde (who built Kilmainham Hospital) suggested that it should be granted to the City of Dublin itself. Two hundred years later, in 1882, the Chief Secretary, Lord Frederick Cavendish, and the Under Secretary were stabbed to death by Nationalists in the park.

The park is memorable as a place where cattle still graze and deer can be glimpsed through the trees. It is open to the public at all times, and the **Visitor Centre** (*open*

April–May, daily 9.30–5.30, June–Sept, daily 10–6, Oct, daily 9.30–5, Nov–Feb, weekends only 9.30–4.30, and mid–end Mar, 9.30–5; adm; t (01) 677 0095), next to a 17th-century tower house, houses a multimedia exhibition on the history of the park over the last 6,000 years. Near the main entrance to the park on Parkgate Street stands the **Wellington Monument**, a 65m (211ft) obelisk completed in 1861. The Duke of Wellington was born in Dublin, though with his lifelong disdain for Ireland and the Irish he did not appreciate being reminded of it. Beyond this lie the **People's Flower Gardens**, and at the northern end is the old **Phoenix Park Race Course**, which is no longer in use. Between lies **Dublin Zoo** *(open Mar–Oct, Mon–Sat 9.30–6, Sun 10.30–6, Nov–Feb, Mon–Sat 9.30–5, Sun 10.30–5; adm; t (01) 677 1425, or toll free t 1800 924848)*, one of the oldest zoos in Europe, set in attractive grounds with artificial lakes. All the usual favourites are in attendance, along with a special Arctic section and a discovery centre for children.

Other Attractions in Dublin City

Shaw Birthplace, 33 Synge Street, D8, south of the centre near the Grand Canal *(open May–Oct, Mon–Sat 10–1 and 2–5, Sun 11–1 and 2–5; adm; t (01) 475 0854)*. It isn't much, this tidy middle-class home where the future genius spent a mildly unhappy childhood, but restored to what it might have looked like in the 1860s, it is a worthy introduction to the life of Victorian Dublin.

Irish Jewish Museum, 3 Walworth Road, D8, off the South Circular Road *(open Oct–April, Sun 10.30–2.30, May–Sept, Tues, Thurs and Sun 11–3.30; adm; t (01) 453 1797)*. Ireland today may have a Jewish population of less than 2,000, but their long and interesting history is recounted in this restored former synagogue.

The **War Memorial Gardens**, Island Bridge, off the South Circular Road (just before Islandbridge; the gardens are signposted to the left). Designed by Edwin Lutyens in 1931, this is a very architectural garden. You approach it by formal avenues which centre on the warstone at the heart of the garden. Circles and ovals commemorate the 49,400 Irish soldiers who died in the First World War. There are two sunken gardens, surrounded by terraces, roses, flowers and shrubs.

National Wax Museum, Granby Row, D1 *(open Mon–Sat 10–5.30, Sun 12–5.30; adm; t (01) 872 6340)*. No big tourist city would be complete without one, and Dublin's is neither more nor less grotesque than the average, except perhaps for the tableau of Jesus and the apostles reproducing Leonardo da Vinci's *Last Supper*.

Pearse Museum, St Enda's Park, Grange Road, Rathfarnham, D16 *(open daily 10–1, also in afternoons Feb–April and Sept–Oct 2–5, May–Aug 2–5.30, Nov–Jan 2–4; adm; t (01) 493 4208)*. The poet-patriot ran a Gaelic school here before the 1916 rising.

The Museum of Childhood, 20 Palmerston Park, Rathmines *(open Sun only, 2–5.30; t (01) 497 8696)* has a charming private collection of antique dolls and toys.

Dillon Garden, 45 Sandford Road, Ranelagh, Dublin 6 *(open Mar and July–Aug, daily 2–6, April–June and Sept, Sun only 2–6; adm; t (01) 497 1308, www.dillongarden.com)* is a lovely city garden with secret areas of light and shade, clematis-draped arches, borders filled with flowers, tubs of sweet-smelling lilies, and wild flowers and roses.

The Casino at **Marino**, north of the city centre off the Malahide Road (*open June–Sept, daily 10–6, May and Oct, daily 10–5, Feb–April and Nov, Sun and Thurs 12–4; adm; t (01) 833 1618*). This 18th-century miniature classical temple of three storeys was designed by Sir William Chambers, between 1762 and 1771, for Lord Charlemont (there isn't any gambling – casino means simply 'cottage' in Italian, and fancy ones were a fad among 18th-century aristocrats). It is one of Ireland's architectural gems. The public park nearby was part of Lord Charlemont's estate, the main house being demolished in 1921. It was exceedingly fortunate that this beautiful building did not go the same way. It has recently been restored and opened to the public. So ingenious was the architect that from the outside it only appears to be one storey high. The basement is actually below street level, whilst the ground and first floor are not distinguished in the façade. Inside are splendid inlaid floors, delicate plasterwork ceilings and silk-covered walls. Close by is **Croke Park**, the national temple of sport where the all-Ireland hurling and Gaelic football finals are played.

National Botanic Gardens, Botanic Road, Glasnevin, D9 (*open summer, Mon–Sat 9–6 Sun 11–6, winter, Mon–Sat 10–4.30 Sun 11–4.30; adm free; t (01) 837 7596/837 4388*). Founded in 1795 by the Royal Dublin Society, the range of beautiful plants and mature trees here make it a wonderful place to walk. There is a magnificent curvilinear glasshouse over 400ft (122m) in length, built and designed by the Dublin ironmaster Richard Turner between 1843 and 1869 (*currently under restoration*). Adjacent to the gardens is Prospect Cemetery, resting place of many famous Dubliners, including Michael Collins, Daniel O'Connell and Charles Stewart Parnell.

Drimnagh Castle, Long Mile Road, Drimnagh, D12, southwest of the centre (*open April–Oct, Wed, Sat and Sun 12–5, Oct–Mar, Sun only 2–5; adm; t (01) 451 8316, f (01) 450 5401*). In a quiet suburban neighbourhood, this modest medieval castle, the only one in Ireland with a moat, has an exquisite formal 16th-century garden.

County Wicklow

County Wicklow has everything that is thought of as Irish in its landscape: wild heather-covered glens and forests, high mountain peaks, deep loughs, ancient churches, stately houses and silvery beaches. Yet it is within only half an hour's drive of Dublin City. Dubliners call it 'the garden of Ireland'. Certainly it is their playground, and many come out to walk in the hills and picnic in the many beautiful places. Nothing could be more in contrast to the hustle and bustle of Dublin life.

In the winter the Wicklow hills are severe and savage, their bare conical shapes softened by snow. In the summer these same hills are clothed in verdant oak, beech and fir; the loughs are blue, and the little streams which tumble from the hills make delightful music. Pubs and restaurants are of a high standard, and if you want to be organized into rock-climbing, canoeing or orienteering there are two adventure centres hidden away in the glens. The coastline has great charm. The Victorian resort towns of Bray and Greystones have many amenities, and it is possible to

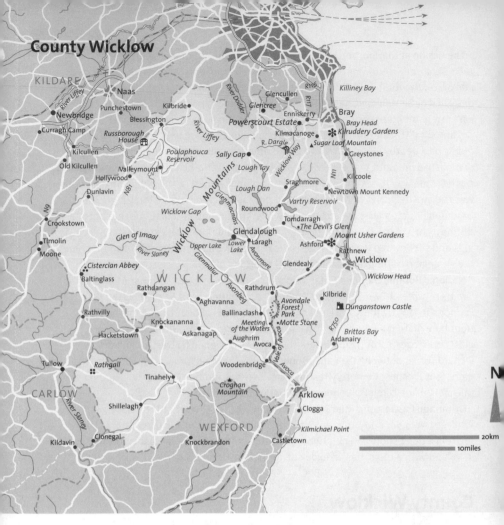

County Wicklow

20km

10miles

walk for miles from Dalkey to Wicklow Town between the railway and the sea, with nothing to interrupt the peace except the occasional train. The rugs made in the Avoca Woollen Mills are wonderful, a perfect combination of the colours you will almost certainly see around you in the countryside, and are something to cherish when you go home.

The monastic remains of Glendalough are amongst the best in Ireland, as are the gardens at Powerscourt and the magnificent furniture and pictures at Russborough House. So, if you do not have much time in Ireland, County Wicklow might give you just a taste to bring you back again.

The county has a growing population of well over 100,000, many of whom work in Dublin. Greystones and Blessington are the main commuter towns. The towns of Bray and Arklow have a wide range of industries, including the Arklow pottery. In the mountains, hill-farming with sheep is practised, whilst the eastern coastal strip and the land in the southwest supports richer farms.

Getting There and Around

By Rail
The main lines from Dublin to Wexford and Waterford runs through Wicklow via Bray, Wicklow, Rathdrum and Arklow. DART trains run to Dublin from Bray.
Iarnród Eireann, **t** (01) 836 6222, *www.irishrail.ie*.

By Bus
Bus Eireann provides services to County Wicklow from Dublin, Rosslare Harbour and Waterford. Most towns in northern Wicklow are also served by Dublin Bus.
Bus Eireann, **t** (01) 836 6111, *www.buseireann.ie*.
Dublin Bus, 59 Upper O'Connell Street, D1, **t** (01) 873 4222/872 0000, *www.dublinbus.ie*.
St Kevin's Bus, **t** (01) 281 8119. Runs twice daily between Dublin and Glendalough, via Bray

By Bike
Bray Sports Centre, 8 Main Street, Bray, **t** (01) 286 3046, or **t** (01) 282 8394.
Tommy McGrath, Rathdrum, **t** (0404) 46172.

Festivals

March
Arklow Music Festival. Competitions.

April
Parnell Spring Day, Rathdrum.

May
Avoca Melody Fair. Music and song festival.
Wicklow Gardens Festival. Celebrated in 50 private gardens and heritage properties.
Bray Jazz Festival.

June
Dunlavin Arts Festival. A parade, flower and agricultural shows, crafts and plenty of *craic*.
The International Cartoon Festival, Rathdrum.
Glen of Imaal Deer Fair.

July
The Bray Seaside Festival. Family-run festival with races, a 'barney' show, festival queen ball, hurling, live bands and fireworks.
Horticultural Rose Show, Delgany.

Wicklow Town Regatta Festival.
Arklow Seabreeze Festival. Includes a renowned pig race.
Arklow Garden of Ireland Festival.

August
Bray Festival of Dance and Music.
Arklow Maritime Festival.
Tinahely Agricultural Show, at Fairwood Park. Livestock, show-jumping, crafts and music.

September
Music Under the Mountains, Holywood. Folk music; past acts have included The Chieftains and Altan and Dervish.

October
Bray Seafood Festival.
Oscar Wilde Autumn School, Bray. Readings and talks by leading writers, **t** (01) 286 4943.

Tourist Information

Bray: **t** (01) 286 7128/286 6796, **f** (01) 286 0930; *open all year*.
Glendalough: **t** (0404) 45688; *open June–Sept*.
Wicklow Town: **t** (0404) 69117, *www.wicklow.ie*, *wicklow@eircom.net*; *open all year*.
Arklow: **t** (0402) 32484, *www.arklow.ie*; *open June–mid Sept*.

Shopping

Crafts
Powerscourt House Shops, Enniskerry, **t** (01) 204 6066. High quality goods.
Rustic Works, the Square, Enniskerry.
Handcrafted Irish Jewellery, Blessington Business Centre, Main Street, Blessington, **t** (045) 865041.
Harvest Loom Celtic Crafts, Laragh, Glendalough, **t** (0404) 45721, *info@ harvestloom.ie*.
Glendalough Woollen Mills, Glendalough, **t** (0404) 45156.

Markets
The movement to re-establish village markets has really caught on in Wicklow:
North Wicklow County Market, St Patrick's Hall, Kilcoole. *10.30–11.30am every Saturday*.

Roundwood Sunday Market, Parish Hall, Roundwood. Home-baking, country butter and flowers. *Mar–Dec 3–5pm*.
Blessington. *Saturday afternoons 2.30–4.30pm*.
Avoca, at the Parish Hall. *July–Aug, Sun 2.30–5pm only*.
Arklow, at the Masonic Hall. *Saturday 10.30–noon*.
Macreddin Village, Brook Lodge Hotel, Aughrim. *First Sunday of every month*.

Pottery

Ballinastoe Studio Pottery, Ballinastoe, Roundwood, t (01) 281815. Quality work.
Brian Kehogh Pottery, Mount Usher Gardens, Ashford, t (0404) 40313.
Arklow Pottery Factory, South Quay, Arklow, t (0402) 39442. *Open for tours and shopping Mon–Fri 9.30–4.30*.
Wicklow Vale Pottery, Arklow, t (0402) 39442.
Belinda Brayshaw, Rathdrum, t (0404) 46839.

Tweeds and Knitwear

Avoca Handweavers Mill Shop, Kilmacanogue, t (01) 286 7466. Tweeds, rugs and sweaters.

Sports and Activities

Fishing

Dargle Anglers Club, Bray Sports Centre, Main Street, Bray, t (01) 286 3046. For fishing salmon and sea trout on the Dargle.
Ray Dineen, Tara House, Redcross, t (0404) 41645. Brown trout at Blessington.
J. Byrne, t (0404) 67716. Further advice.

Golf

Woodbrook Golf Club, Bray, t (01) 282 4799.
Powerscourt Golf Club, Enniskerry, t (01) 276 0503. Championship 18-hole course.
Charlesland Golf and Country Club, Greystones, t (01) 287 8200.
Greystones Golf Club, Greystones, t (01) 287 4136.

Holistic Treatments

The Chrysalis Holistic Centre, Donard, north of Baltinglass, t (045) 40413, *www.holistic.ie/chrysalis*. Various therapies such as Reiki and Indian head massage.

Horse-drawn Caravans

Clissmann Horse-drawn Caravans, Carrigmore Farm, Wicklow, t (0404) 48188, *mary@clissmann.com*. Contact Dieter Clissman.

Pony-trekking

Brennanstown Riding School, Hollybrook, Kilmacanogue, Bray, t (01) 286 3778.
Bel-Air Hotel Riding School, Ashford, t (0404) 40109.

Outdoor Activity Centres

Clara-Lara Funpark, Rathdrum, t (0404) 46161. Waterslides and boats for children.
The Tiglin National Mountain and White Water Centre, Ashford, t (0404) 40169. Field courses in mountaineering, orienteering, canoeing, surfing and skiing.

Walking

The Wicklow Way starts in County Dublin at Marley Park and climbs rapidly into the Wicklow Mountains, switching from glen to glen. The long-running Wicklow Mountains **Spring and Autumn Walking Festivals** are run by the Wicklow Tourist Office, call t (0404) 69117. For local walking trips contact:
Damien Cashin, Outdoor Activities, Tomdarragh, Roundwood, t (01) 281 8212.
Barry Dalby, 155 Beachdale, Kilcoole, t (01) 287 5990.

Where to Stay

Powerscourt Arms Hotel, Enniskerry, t (01) 282 8903, f (01) 286 4909 *(moderate)*. Attractive town hotel where they serve good Guinness.
Avonbrae Guesthouse, Rathdrum, t (0404) 46198, f (0404) 46198 *(inexpensive)*. Family-run village guesthouse; they'll help to arrange hill-walking and other activities.
Rathsallagh House, Dunlavin, t (045) 403112, f (045) 403343, *info@rathsallagh.com (luxury)*. Comfortable farmhouse with good food and chat. Facilities include hunting, billiards, golf, croquet, swimming and sauna.
Downshire House, Blessington, t (045) 865199, f (045) 865335 *(moderate)*. Small and central.
Poulaphouca House, Poulaphouca, Holywood, t (045) 864412 *(moderate)*. Attractive guesthouse with a traditional bar from the 1890s.

Old Rectory, Wicklow Town, t (0404) 67048, *rectory2000@eircom.net* (*expensive*). Cosy rooms, delicious breakfasts and dinners.

Lissadell House, Ashdown Lane, Wicklow, t (0404) 67458, *lissadellhse@eircom.net* (*inexpensive*). Friendly Irish-German couple, the Klaues, with a comfortable house.

Tinakilly House, Rathnew, t (0404) 69274, f (0404) 67806, *reservations@tinakilly.ie* (*expensive*). Very stylish Victorian house, with delicious food. *No children under seven.*

Hunter's Hotel, Rathnew, t (0404) 40106, f (0404) 40338, *hunters@indigo.ie* (*moderate*). Attractive old coaching inn, run by the same family for five generations.

Ballyknocken House, Glenealy, near Ashford, t (0404) 44627, *cfulvio@ballyknocken.com* (*moderate–inexpensive*). Pretty farmhouse. Advice given on walks, and there's a pony on the farm. *Children welcome.*

The Brook Lodge Inn, Macreddin Billage, near Aughrim, t (0402) 36444, f (0402) 36580, *www.brooklodge.com* (*expensive–moderate*). Country hotel with fresh organic produce served for breakfast and afternoon tea.

Moneylands Farm, Arklow, t (0402) 32259, *mland@eircom.net* (*inexpensive*). Lillie Byrne offers B&B in a Georgian farmhouse, plus three restored self-catering farm buildings.

Plattenstown House, Coolgreany Road, Arklow t (0402) 37822, *mcdpr@indigo.ie* (*inexpensive*). Peaceful and comfortable country house run by Mrs McDowell.

Self-catering

Mrs McLoughlin, t (01) 459 1403, *tsj@oceanfree.net* (*moderate*). Attractive 2-bedroom house at Glendalough.

Fortgranite Estate, Baltinglass, t (0508) 81396, f (0508) 73510 (*moderate*). Old stone 2-bedroom house in a pretty setting.

Eating Out

The Tree of Idleness, Seafront, Bray, t (01) 282 8183, or t (01) 286 3498 (*expensive*). Run by a Greek-Cypriot, so lots of feta cheese, olive oil and herbs. Has long had a good reputation. *Open Tues–Sun evenings.*

Avoca Handweavers, Kilmacanogue, near Bray, t (01) 286 7466 (*inexpensive*). Home-made soups, vegetable bakes and cakes.

The Hungry Monk, Greystones, t (01) 287 5759, or t (01) 287 7892 (*expensive*). A family-run fish restaurant, with an impressive wine list. Good spot for Sunday lunch. *Open all year Wed–Sat 7–11pm, Sun 12.30–8pm.*

Poppies Restaurant, The Square, Enniskerry, t (01) 282 8869 (*inexpensive*). Salad lunches and home-baking. Lively at the weekends.

Harvey's Bistro, Newtownmount Kennedy, t (01) 281 9203 (*moderate*). Homely cooking.

Roundwood Inn, Roundwood, t (01) 281 8107, or t (01) 281 8125 (*expensive*). 17th-century inn. Bar food – filling Irish stew to oysters – and à la carte in the restaurant. Very large helpings. *Open Tues–Sat 1–2.30 and 7.30–9.30, Sun 1–2.30; booking essential.*

Mitchell's, Laragh, Glendalough, t (0404) 45302 (*moderate*). In an old, restored schoolhouse. Wicklow lamb and lovely home-baked cakes. Open for afternoon tea.

The Old Rectory, Wicklow Town, t (0404) 67048 (*expensive*). Original food decorated with herbs and flowers. During the Wicklow Gardens Festival they do a ten course 'Floral Dinner'. *Dinner only.*

Tinakilly House, Rathnew, t (0404) 69274 (*expensive*). Ambitious *cuisine française* in an elegant dining room. *Open 12.30–2 and 7.30–9, reservations essential.*

Hunter's Hotel, Rathnew, t (0404) 40106 (*moderate*). Famous for cream teas and marvellous Irish cooking. Lovely garden. *Open daily 8.30–10, 1–3 and 7.30–9.*

The Strawberry Tree, The Brook Lodge Inn, Macreddin Village, near Aughrim, t (0402) 36444, *brooklodge@macreddin.ie* (*expensive*). Only free-range, organic and wild foods are served in this award-winning restaurant. *Dinner Mon–Sun 7pm.*

The Stone Oven, 65 Lower Main Street, Arklow, t (0402) 39418 (*inexpensive*). Bakery and coffee shop specializing in German breads.

Entertainment and Nightlife

Esplanade (Doona Lawn) Hotel, Bray, t (01) 286 2056. Country-rock and folk singing during the summer months, Thurs–Sun evenings.

History

Historically, County Wicklow was part of the kingdom of the Leinster kings, the MacMurraghs, whilst the Vikings established towns at Arklow and Wicklow. The modern boundary lines were drawn up by the English during the reign of Elizabeth Tudor. The mountain *septs* of Wicklow earned themselves a reputation for guerilla warfare when the Anglo-Normans arrived in 1167: they wore the Normans down with constant skirmishes, and contained them within the Pale – a small fortified area around Dublin where the English king had control. O'Byrne and O'Toole were the two clans who made life so awkward for the Normans, and they continued to do so for centuries. During the reign of Elizabeth Tudor in the 1570s, Fiach MacHugh O'Byrne constantly harried the English forces and won some small victories that rallied the Gaelic cause in these parts for 20 years. The next great revolt was in 1798, and in Wicklow the Irish folk, led by Michael Dwyer (1771–1826), armed themselves with pikes to fight the English forces. The uprising was suppressed, and Michael Dwyer surrendered in 1803. He was spared execution because of the humanity he had shown in various engagements, and was sentenced instead to transportation to New South Wales, where he later became High Constable of Sydney. (You can go round his cottage home in the Glen of Imaal, *see* pp.611–2.) The English government then built the Military Road which runs through the mountains from north to south, and is still in use today. It helped them to flush out the rebels. The Great Famine of the 1840s reduced the population from 126,000 to 100,000, and it further declined with emigration to America and Australia. Charles Stewart Parnell (1846–91) was the vigorous and effective voice of the Irish in the British parliament. His estate and house at Avondale is now a museum. The political campaigns he fought bore fruit in the Wyndham Land Acts, which made government loans available to tenant farmers to buy the land they had leased. Sadly, his career was bought down by his affair with Kitty O'Shea, a married woman; the scandal rocked Catholic Ireland, and he lost support.

Around Bray

Bray is one of Ireland's principal coastal resorts and has golf, horse-riding, swimming and cinema – all sorts of amenities, although it seems a bit run-down and seedy at the moment. **Bray Heritage Centre**, in the old court house (*open every day, 10–4; t (01) 286 6796*) contains a fine array of photographs, records, maps and artefacts relating to the area. The town has a safe beach of shingle and sand. There are good walks to Bray Head, and a cliff walk of about 3 miles (5km) to Greystones.

Greystones is a smaller resort, an old fishing village rather more attractive than Bray, but still just as full of Dubliners and slowly being swallowed up by the capital's sprawl. South of it, on the N11, home gardeners will enjoy the **National Garden Exhibition Centre**, with 16 individual gardens by noted designers to inspire the rest of us (*open daily 10–6, Sun 1–6; adm; t (01) 281 9890*). **Kilruddery Gardens**, between the N11 and R761 south of Bray (*gardens open April–Sept, daily 1–5, house open May–June and Sept, 1–5; adm; t (01) 286 2777/286 3405, f (01) 286 2777*), were laid out in the 17th century. Here a pair of long canals reflect the sky, and a high beech hedge encircles a pool and fountains. There is also a fine parterre edged with box and filled with pink moss roses. The house, which opens to the public at the same time as the gardens, is an 1820 Elizabethan Revival mansion built for the 10th Earl of Meath. It has fine plasterwork.

The **Glen of Dargle** to the west of Bray off the N11 is another lovely place to walk. A narrow pathway runs beside the Dargle River, and a road follows the glen to the south. A huge rock, known as the 'lover's leap' juts out over the wooded gorge through which the river runs. Here, at Enniskerry, is **Powerscourt Estate**, with one of the finest formal gardens in Ireland, with Italianate and Japanese-style gardens, and a Monkey Puzzle Avenue (*open Mar–Oct, daily 9.30–5.30, Nov–Feb, 10.30–dusk; adm; t (01) 204 6000, www.powerscourt.ie*). Tragically, the house – one of the most beautiful in Ireland – was gutted by fire in 1976 after being carefully restored by the Slazenger family (of tennis-racket fame). However, the gardens remain and the setting of the house, facing the Sugar Loaf Mountain, makes it an unforgettable sight: you walk towards it thinking it is still intact, but it is in fact a mere shell. The Slazenger family have not given up on it, though, and are planning further restoration. On the Powerscourt Estate is the breathtakingly beautiful **Powerscourt waterfall**, the highest in Ireland. The water falls from 400ft (122m) into a fine stream, which winds its way through numerous walks. **Enniskerry** itself is a fine estate village with good food, shops and clothes boutiques. It is an excellent base for excursions into the surrounding hills. Nearby, **Coolakay House and Agricultural Display** (*open in summer daily; t (01) 286 2423*) is a museum of Irish farm life over the centuries.

Wandering Along the Wicklow Way

From Enniskerry, follow the road through the Scalp, a glacier-formed gap. The forests surrounding the Scalp have some lovely trails. If you want to glut yourself on forest scenery take the Military Road, which runs through the mountains from Rathfarnham to Aghavannagh. This road bisects the county and takes you through mysterious glens and remote valleys; you see turf-cutting country and some stupendous mountain scenery. One of the most spectacular glens is **Glencree**, which curves from near the base of the Sugarloaf Mountain to the foot of the Glendoo Mountain. Through it flows the Glencree River, which later joins the Dargle. The wild and beautiful **Sally Gap**, near the source of the River Liffey, is a cross-roads, from which you can follow the old Military Road to Laragh, the road to Roundwood or the valley road to Manor Kilbridge and Blessington. Dubliners come at weekends to cut their turf at Sally Gap.

Laragh is a pleasant little village where roads from the north, south, east and west meet. Near here, northeast on the R755, is the village of **Roundwood**, which is reputedly the highest village in Ireland, being 780ft (238m) above sea level. It is close to the Vartry Reservoir, which supplies water to Dublin City, and to the wild scenery around Lough Dan. The high ground in these mountainous areas was the realm of the 'mountainy men' – the Irish who had been deprived of their lands on the plain by the English settlers. Up here in the hills the rule of Dublin Castle had little influence.

Glendalough

The important Early Christian site of **Glendalough**, the 'Glen of Two Lakes', has overwhelmed people with its peace and isolation for many centuries, and is an enclave of holiness amongst the wilderness. Its setting is unforgettable and uniquely Irish, sitting high in the hills, with two small lakes cupped in a hollow, a tall round tower and a grey stone church. There are the remains of a famous monastic school, founded by St Kevin in the 6th century; and remains of churches spread between the upper and lower lakes; and the little river. A **Visitor Centre** (*open daily, summer 9.30–6, winter 9.30–5; adm; t (0404) 45325*) has been built beside the car park as you enter. There are very interesting exhibits and an audio-visual show to inform you before you explore the remains yourself. The churches, with a monastic gateway (the only one in Ireland) and a round tower, are clustered together by the little Glenealo River. On the southeast corner to the upper lake, by Poulanass Waterfall, is **Reefert Church** where the O'Toole rulers were buried. On the southern shore is the **Church of the Rock**. Between Reefert Church and the lower lake are five crosses, which some say marked the boundaries of the monastic land and later became station crosses in the Pilgrims' Way. The story goes that St Kevin came here to recover from the effort involved in rejecting the advances of a beautiful girl named Kathleen. However, she chased him to the monastery, and he had to hit her with stinging nettles to lessen her ardour. Another version of the tale, recounted by Thomas (Tom) Moore, is that he cooled her off by pushing her into the lake. Despite Kevin's wish to be a hermit, his refuge became a centre of learning and later a place of pilgrimage. You can see **St Kevin's Kitchen**; the **church** with its corbelled roof; and the ruins of the **cathedral** with its 12th-century chancel. **St Kevin's Bed** is on the southern cliff-face of the upper lake, and is a very dangerous climb that is not recommended, since intrepid visitors who have attempted it have often had to be rescued. This is the cell where St Kevin stayed before the seven churches of the settlement were built. The views of the lakes are remarkable. **St Saviour's Monastery**, about 430yds (400m) northeast of the cathedral, is also very handsome. It is said to have been founded in the 12th century by St Lawrence O'Toole. The chancel arch is a lovely bit of Romanesque architecture: three orders resting on large clustered piers, decorated with dog-tooth, chevron and floral ornament. Human heads and animals decorate the capitals and bases.

Rathdrum and Through the Vale of Avoca

Continuing south for 5 miles (8km) on the Military Road you go through **Rathdrum**, which has some good untouched pubs such as P. Cullen's Bar in the Main Street, and enchanting woodland in the Avondale valley. The 'big' **Avondale House** (*open Mar–Oct 11–6; adm; t (0404) 46111*), south of town, was the birthplace and lifelong home of that great Irishman, Charles Stewart Parnell, who fought for Home Rule and the land rights of the peasants in the 19th century. Recently restored to its appearance in Parnell's time, it is now open as a museum and the estate is a forest park, through which two nature trails have been signposted. Three rooms in the late 18th century house are devoted to displays of Parnell memorabilia.

The scenery continues to be delightful as you travel south through the **Vale of Avoca**, where the Avonmore and Avonbeg Rivers meet, and immortalized in the Romantic poetry of Thomas Moore's 'The Meeting of the Waters'. Copper is mined in the valley still. The meeting is marked by a very ugly pub with a glassy ballroom tacked on to its back wall; but the atmosphere inside is difficult to beat since everybody is there to have some fun. Traditional bands play here at the weekends, and some of them are excellent.

You can understand the appeal of such scenery to the Romantic poets of the late 19th century, amongst them William Wordsworth, who did an Irish tour. About 2½ miles (4km) northeast of Avoca village and the rivers, and high above them, is the **Motte Stone**, a glacial boulder of granite perched on the summit of the 800ft (244m) Croneblane Ridge. It commands a spectacular view and it used to be used by travellers as a milestone because it is halfway between Dublin and Wexford. Along the valley road are shops selling the well-known Avoca-weave rugs, which make lovely presents. You can visit **Avoca Handweavers** in Avoca village, the oldest working mill in Ireland and one of Wicklow's most popular attractions (*open all year; t (0402) 35105*). **Woodenbridge**, at the end of this 'sweet vale', was the site of a gold rush in 1796, and supplied much gold for Ireland's earliest goldsmiths. Nearby, the Croghan Mountain was the scene of another 18th-century gold rush.

Blessington to Baltinglass

West Wicklow is relatively unexplored, and ruggedly attractive. Travelling southwest out of Dublin on the N81 you come to **Blessington**, a small town on the northern arm of the **Poulaphouca Reservoir**. This huge reservoir, formed by the damming of the River Liffey, is picturesque enough to warrant a visit. Other attractions are **Russborough House** and its art collection (*open Easter and Oct, Sun and bank hols 10.30–5.30, May–Sept, daily 10.30–5.30; picnic area, tea room, shop and children's playground; gardens with maze and rhododendron garden, visits by appointment only; adm; t (045) 865239, f (045) 865054*). The house was designed by Richard Cassels in the 1740s for the Earl of Milltown, and its silvery Wicklow granite has aged magnificently. It is Palladian in style, with a central block and two semi-circular loggias which link the wings. The main rooms are decorated with elaborate plasterwork. The house was purchased by Sir Alfred and Lady Beit in 1952, and their art collection is one of the chief attractions of Ireland. It includes paintings by Rubens, Gainsborough, Murillo, Reynolds, Vernet, Velasquez and Guardi. Unfortunately the house has been burgled on a couple of occasions (once by the IRA) and some treasures have been lost; others were given to the National Gallery in Dublin. More unfortunately, visits are limited to a 45-minute guided tour, so you won't have much time to look at the ones that are left.

South from Blessington, you will come to **Poulaphouca Lake**, which forms the Wicklow Gap, and the lovely **Hollywood Glen**, before you arrive at Laragh. The nearby **Glen of Imaal** is also beautiful, though part of it is used as a military firing range – look out for the signs. In the Glen, on the Knockanarrigan to Rathdangan road, the **Michael Dwyer Cottage Museum** at Derrynamuck (*open mid June–mid Sept, daily 2–6;*

adm; t (0404) 45325/45352) commemorates the leader of the 1798 Rising. British troops had him surrounded in this old farmhouse, but he still managed to escape.

Baltinglass, which lies 19 miles (30km) south of Blessington on the N81, is in the Slaney Valley. The remains of a 12th-century **Cistercian abbey** lie to the north of the town. Six Gothic arches on either side of the nave remain to delight the eye. Above the town to the east rises Baltinglass Hill, at the top of which are the remains of a large cairn containing a group of **Bronze Age burial chambers**. It is an easy climb and there is a splendid view over the countryside.

Wicklow Town to Arklow

The pleasant and resolutely sleepy county town, **Wicklow**, overlooks a crescent-shaped shingle bay. The English name is a corruption of the Danish *Wyking alo*, 'Viking Meadow'. Maurice Fitzgerald, a Norman warlord, built the ruined **Black Castle** on the promontory overlooking the sea at the eastern end of the town. He was granted the lands here by Henry II in the 12th century, but he did not have a very comfortable existence, for the castle was constantly raided by the O'Tooles and O'Byrnes. Soon to open is a new museum in the former **Wicklow Gaol**, fittingly dedicated to 1798, the famine, transportation of rebels and criminals, and all the other depressing events of Irish history this grim old building witnessed. The 18th-century Church of Ireland **church**, off the main street, has a fine carved Romanesque doorway in the south porch. The ruined **Dunganstown Castle**, about six miles (9.6km) south on an unclassified road, is far more spectacular than anything in the town. At **Ashford**, a couple of miles north of Wicklow Town on the main Dublin to Wexford road, is **Mount Usher Gardens** (*open 17 Mar–Oct, daily 10.30–6; adm; t (0404) 40116/ 40205, f (0404) 40205, mount_usher.gardens@indigo.ie*), a wonderful example of a naturalised garden. On the banks of the river Vartry, it is famous for its eucalyptus and encryphia, and the woodland walks here provide beautiful vistas of azalea, rhododendrons and spring bulbs.

By taking the R750, it is possible to stay close to the coast all the way from Wicklow to Arklow, passing lovely sandy beaches sheltered by dunes. Both Wicklow town and Arklow have beaches of their own, popular enough in summer, but you would be better off looking for the nicer ones in between, especially the fine long strand at **Brittas Bay**. Another Danish settlement in the 9th and 10th centuries, **Arklow**, grew up at the mouth of the River Avoca. It is now a popular resort town, as the beaches surrounding it are safe for bathing. There is a golf course and a sports centre, and boat rides on the river start from behind the car park, off the main street, during the summer.

The remains of a 12th-century **castle** stand on the Bluff overlooking the river. It was built by Theobald Butler, and became one of the four strongest fortresses of the Ormonde family. Later it was sacked by the Irish, then ruined by Cromwell in 1649. Father Murphy, the leader of the insurgents in the 1798 rising, was repulsed in Arklow with heavy losses, and there is a monument to his memory marking the site where he died. **Arklow Maritime Museum**, in the Old Technical School, St Mary's Road (*open in summer, daily exc Sun 10–1 and 2–5; adm; t (0402) 32868*), details this town's surprisingly rich career, which has involved boat-building, fishing and plenty of smuggling. There's everything a small-town maritime museum should have, down to the model ship made of matchsticks by an old sailor.

County Wexford

If you are invading Ireland from the south, as the Normans did, you will land at Rosslare Harbour – the warmest, driest part of the whole country. The countryside of Wexford is said to be similar to that of Normandy, with low hills, rich valleys and extremely tidy farms. Some of the thatched cottages have upper floors, which is something you do not find elsewhere in Ireland. Perhaps it is a sign of the relative prosperity of the peasants, and the influence of the English settlers in the 16th century. Vegetables and fruit are grown in the light, sandy soil, farm implements are manufactured, and bacon is cured. The population is approximately 100,000.

Along the coast there are gloriously sandy beaches and some old resort towns. Many Irish families still take their holidays here rather than in southern Europe. Tower houses dating from the 14th century are a common feature; some are ivy-clad, but others blend into the farmhouses and yards which have grown up around them. Happily, these centuries-old buildings have been treated with a bit more care than is usual in Ireland. There are some magnificent monastic remains and old castles to explore, as well as Kennedy Park, planted with shrubs and trees from all over the world to honour John F. Kennedy.

For the garden lover there are several small and beautiful gardens, open by arrangement with their owners. Bird lovers will find herring gulls, kittiwakes, razorbills, puffin colonies, petrels, gannets, Greenland white-faced geese and terns in the numerous bird sanctuaries which have been established around the coast. Wexford is internationally famous for its Opera Festival, which was established in 1951 and specializes in rarely produced works. This week of first-class music and performers takes place in the autumn, and Wexford town buzzes with life.

History

County Wexford has a full history, due to its closeness to mainland Britain and Europe. It has been the landing place of many; and in past centuries trade across the sea was constant. This brief sketch starts in about 350 BC, when the Celts arrived from Europe in waves. They absorbed many of the existing customs, but they also imposed their own legal, religious and cultural beliefs. Their ruling élite divided into hereditary royal families who ruled over small politically defined areas, and were often at odds with their neighbours. What is now Wexford had a hereditary enmity with the kingdom of Ossory, which roughly corresponds to County Kilkenny. The monks arrived in about the 5th century and, with ease it seems, took over the mantle of respect and power from their pagan predecessors.

The arrival of the Norsemen or Vikings in AD 819 was a blow to the rich monasteries, which were plundered and sacked. The Norsemen liked it here and stayed,

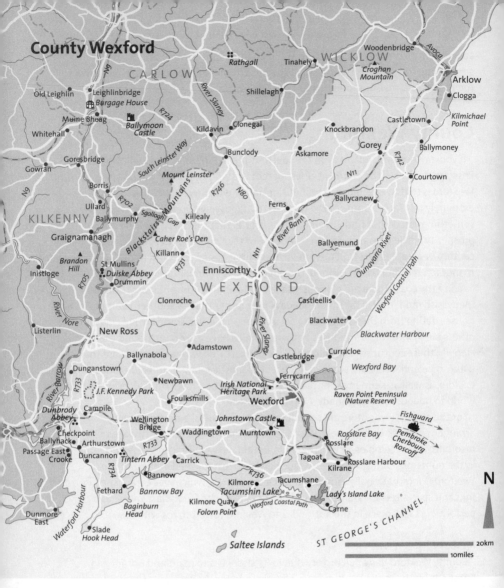

County Wexford

establishing a settlement called *Waesfjord* ('Muddy Fjord'), now known as Wexford Town. All over Ireland, the story is the same: it is the Norsemen and the Anglo-Normans who founded the towns, never the Celts.

The *sept* which seemed to produce the most dynamic leaders was that of the MacMurraghs. They played a great part in Ireland's history, and made alliances with Norsemen, Welsh and Anglo-Norman mercenaries when it suited them. Surnames did not exist in Ireland until the 11th century, but it was a MacMurragh king who in 1068 laid siege to Bristol – the only Irish monarch to threaten an English city. His descendant, Diarmuid (or Dermot) MacMurragh (1110–71), is reviled in Irish history for having invited the Anglo-Normans over to help him in his territorial struggles. In fact,

Diarmuid was following a well-used practice in hiring Flemish, Norman and Welsh mercenaries; but these ones stayed on, and laid claim to the whole of Ireland. The names Fleming, Prendergast, Fitzhenry and Roche are still a reminder of these people, and can be seen around the county on shop and pub signs. The MacMurraghs produced another great leader in the late 14th century: Art MacMurragh Kavanagh became king of what is now Carlow, Wexford and the old kingdom of Leinster. He was so powerful that Richard II was forced into leaving his precarious throne in England to lead two campaigns against him in 1394 and 1399. Both were failures, and he lost his own throne into the bargain. The Normans were gradually absorbed into the

Getting There and Around

By Sea
Rosslare Harbour handles passenger and car ferry boats from Fishguard, Pembroke and the French ports of Le Havre and Cherbourg. There's not much of anything in Rosslare Harbour, though you'll find taxis for nearby Wexford (there are only a few, so disembark quickly if you need one), and often Bus Eireann coaches bound for Waterford or Dublin are timed to meet the boats. See also **Travel**, pp.118–9.

By Rail
Mainline services from Dublin to Wexford and Rosslare, stopping at smaller places en route.
Iarnród Eireann, t (01) 836 6222, *www.irishrail.ie*.

By Bus
Bus Eireann Expressway buses from Dublin go to Wexford Town and Rosslare hourly, and from there westwards to Waterford and Cork. For details of local services, call Waterford **t** (053) 22522.
Bus Eireann, t (01) 836 6111, *www.buseireann.ie*.

By Bike
Hayes Cycles, 108 South Main Street, Wexford, **t** (053) 22462, *hayescycles@ eircom.net*.
The Bike Shop, 9 Selskar Street, Wexford, **t** (053) 22514.
Kenny's, Slaney Street, Enniscorthy, **t** (054) 33255, or **t** (087) 232 1137, *kennysfb@unison.ie*.

Festivals

March–April
Spring Music Festival, Wexford. Classical music, **t** (053) 23923.

April–May
Viking Festival, Wexford, **t** (053) 23401.

June–July
Strawberry Fair, Enniscorthy, **t** (054) 33256. Ten days celebrating the strawberry harvest.

July
Eileen Aroon Festival, Bunclody, **t** (054) 77600.
Kilmore Quay Seafood Festival. Celebrations include fresh seafood, races and live music, **t** (053) 29922.
Wexford Hooves and Grooves Festival. With horse-racing and live entertainment.
Sandworld, Duncannon. Sand-sculpting competition, with international teams taking part, **t** (051) 389434.

August
Blessing of the Fleet, Kilmore. An annual event, **t** (053) 29922.
Gorey Summer Fair, t (055) 20640.
Courtown Failte Festival, t (055) 22148.
Kilmuckridge Mardi Gras Festival, **t** (053) 30163.

September
Blackstairs Blues Festival, t (054) 35364.

October–November
Wexford Opera Festival. Contact the Wexford Festival Office, Theatre Royal, Wexford Town, **t** (053) 22400, *info@wexfordopera.com*.

Gaelic way of life. Up until the beginning of the 20th century, in the ancient Norman Baronies of Forth and Bargy in the southeast corner, the locals spoke in the Flemish-sounding Yola dialect. Some words are still in everyday use; for example, *stour*, meaning a truculent woman. Later, settlers were brought in over the centuries by the British government and given land in payment for military services. Wexford is perhaps the most 'planted' of all the Irish counties; but the 'foreigners' moved in gradually, and not with the systematic force with which the Scots moved into the north. The Rebellion of 1798 is remembered in the many memorials placed around the countryside and towns; its 200th anniversary was a major event throughout Ireland, but especially in Wexford, where a new museum dedicated to it was opened in Enniscorthy. There is great emotive value placed on it still, for it was such a brave and pathetic struggle: thousands of peasants armed with pitchforks held off the well-trained forces of the English for six weeks, until they were defeated at Vinegar Hill with huge losses (*see* **History**, pp.46–7).

Northern Wexford

Along the east coast is the pretty village of **Castletown** and the family resort of **Ballymoney**. There are numerous sandy coves here, perfect for bathing. **Courtown**, on the R742, is a harbour resort on the Ounavarra River with two miles of sandy beach. **Blackwater** is a very pleasant coastal village that has won numerous 'tidy town' competitions. This national award, run by the Tourist Board, inspires proud villagers to spruce up their paintwork and tidy their gardens each year. Courtown is said to be the *Ardladhru* ('Fort of Ladhru'), frequently mentioned in the Gaelic sagas. (Ladhru was one of the principal Celtic leaders at the time of their first landings.) There is a fine hill-top earthworks just outside the village. **Curracloe Strand**, on the way back to Wexford, is super for walking or bathing. It has 6 miles (9.7km) of golden beach and pretty white-washed houses. The **Raven Point Peninsula**, stretching from Curracloe to Wexford Harbour mouth, is a protected nature reserve, with 3 miles (5km) of sand dunes, forest, bird and plant life.

Enniscorthy

Along the side of the Blackstairs Mountains you sometimes meet a lone deer making its way between here and the Wicklow Mountains. The tiny farms on these slopes are more reminiscent of the West than the neat prosperity of the rest of Wexford. Stop in **Killann** (on the R731 from New Ross) at **Rackards Pub**, one of the friendliest traditional pubs in Ireland; a local haunt, it has no hint of 'the singing pubs for tourists' theme. The Rackard family are famous for their skill at hurling – four of them were in the team that won the Leinster Trophy in 1951. Killann was an important ecclesiastical centre in medieval times, though nothing much remains.

Enniscorthy is the most attractive town in County Wexford. It is a thriving market town on the River Slaney, presided over by Vinegar Hill, from where there is a great view of the river and the rich farming land around. You might time your arrival for the

Tourist Information

Enniscorthy: The Castle, t (054) 34699; *open mid June–Aug.*
Gorey: Lower Main Street, t (055) 21248; *open all year.*

Shopping

Pottery

Kiltrea Bridge Pottery Ltd, Kiltrea Bridge, Cairn, Enniscorthy, t (054) 35107.
Badger Hill Pottery, Enniscorthy, t (054) 35060.

Sports and Activities

Golf

Courtown Golf Course, Kiltennel, near Gorey, t (055) 25166, f (055) 25553, *courtown@iol.ie.*
Enniscorthy Golf Club, Knockmarshall, t (054) 33191.

Walking

Wexford **coastal path**, from Kilmichael Point to Ballyhack, stretches over 138 miles (221kms) – ask for details from the tourist office.

Where to Stay and Eat

Salville House, Enniscorthy, t (054) 35252, *salvillehouse@eircom.net* (*inexpensive*). Large, simple bedrooms overlooking a pretty wood, run by the Parker family.

Clohamon House, Bunclody, t (054) 77253 (*moderate*). This charming 18th-century house is set in an estate of 180 acres (40ha) in the lovely Slaney Valley, on a hill with a view of Mount Leinster. There is private fishing for salmon or trout on the Slaney River, and a Connemara Pony stud. Delicious food and comfortable period rooms with four-poster beds. Lady Maria Levinge is a charming hostess with good knowledge of local goings-on.

Woodville, Bunclody, t (054) 77982. Pauline Walker's restored farmhouse lies near Mount Leinster; 3 bedrooms, self catering.

Clonehouse, Ferns, t (054) 66113 (*moderate*). Pretty farmhouse belonging to Betty and Tom Breen, with well-prepared, simple food and clean, attractive rooms.

Marlfield House, Gorey, t (055) 21124 (*expensive*). Modern restaurant serving *haute cuisine* in a fine Regency country house. Lobster from a tank, oysters and scallops, veal, delicious seafood, and local fresh ingredients. *Booking essential.*

Entertainment and Nightlife

Ar mBreacha ('Our Roots'), Raheen, Ballyduff, t (054) 44148, *www.iol.ie/~story/*, *story@iol.ie.* For something a little bit different, evenings of Irish stories, music and dancing at the House of Storytelling on the first Tuesday of each month, and each Tuesday night in July and August. *Please call in advance.*

Strawberry Fair in early July. Enniscorthy was one of the hot spots of the 1798 rising, and the town has commemorated it with the newly opened **National 1798 Visitors' Centre** where you can learn the entire story through exhibits and audio-visual presentations (*open Mon–Sat 9.30–6.30, Sun 11–6.30; adm; t (054) 35540/37596, 98com@iol.ie*). **Wexford County Museum** (*open all year, summer Mon–Sat 10–6 Sun 2–6, winter 2–5, Dec–Jan Sun 2–6 only; adm; t (054) 35926*) is in the **castle**, built by Raymond le Gros and later owned by the Roche family. It has an interesting folk section. All around County Wexford it is traditional for mummers (or rhymers) to act out the characters of Irish heroes by dancing to the rhythm of Irish reels. They dress themselves in straw suits and tinsel and act out the perpetual struggle of good over evil. This tradition actually originated in England; in other parts of Ireland, custom differs. Like all country customs, it is in decline, but the mummers still 'visit' the houses of local people at Christmas time, and you might be lucky and see them perform at the Wexford Opera Festival.

Bunclody (N80), on the borders with County Carlow in the northwest of the county, is a very pretty mountainside town. Many people stay here to go walking on the Blackstairs Mountains. It has a very attractive Church of Ireland church. Nearer to Enniscorthy, on the N11, is **Ferns**. This town is rather like Swords in County Dublin – full of memories and former glory. In the 12th century the King of Leinster, Dermot MacMurragh (the one who invited the Normans to invade), made it his capital and founded a rich abbey there, but after the Norman conquest the town declined. It has been pillaged and burnt so often that there is little left of it. Yet it is a fascinating place with a vast, ruined **cathedral**, a segment of which is now the Church of Ireland cathedral. A 13th-century Anglo-Norman **castle** built by William de Valence, which has a fine chapel in its southeast tower, was built on the site of the ancient fortress of the kings of Leinster. It was destroyed by the O'Connor and O'Rourke forces in their conflict with Dermot MacMurragh, and it was here that he waited for his allies, the Normans, sending guides to Baginburn to show them the way. Dermot is buried here in the ruins of the **Augustinian priory** that he founded. The High Cross covered in a fretwork pattern marks his grave. An interesting quirk of fate links Ferns with another man who may have changed the course of history: in the graveyard of the modern Catholic church is the grave of Father Ned Redmond, who as a young priest in France saved Napoleon Bonaparte from drowning during his student days.

Southern Wexford

Wexford Town
Wexford Town is one of the most atmospheric of all Irish places. It was originally settled by a Celtic Belgic tribe called the Manapii, about 350 BC, and later by the Vikings who gave it the name *Waesfjord*. They ruled from the 9th to the 12th century and built up a flourishing port around the River Slaney and its outlet to the sea. Then the Normans, allies of Dermot McMurragh, captured it and built walls, castles and abbeys in their usual disciplined pattern. Many of the winding streets are so narrow that you could shake hands across them. Cromwell left as bloody a reputation behind him here as in Drogheda. He occupied the town in 1649 during his campaign to subdue the 'rebellious Irish', and destroyed many of the churches.

Most people come to Wexford for the Opera Festival, held every year in October. Programmes of lesser-known operas are produced with world-famous soloists, an excellent local chorus and the RTE Symphony Orchestra. Its reputation for originality and quality is held worldwide. Many fringe events, exhibitions, revues, and plays take place at the same time (*see* 'Festivals', p.615).

The centre of town is a small square called the **Bull Ring** – a reminder of the Norman pastime of bull-baiting, which was held on this spot – and contains a figure of an Irish pikeman, commemorating the Wexford insurgents of 1798. Some bits of the Norman

Tourist Information

Wexford: Crescent Quay, **t** (053) 23111;
open all year.
New Ross: t (051) 21857; *open mid June–Aug
Mon–Sat 10–6.*

Shopping

Crafts
You'll find good craft shops in Wexford Town
and at the John F. Kennedy Park.
Butlersland Craft Centre, Butlerstown,
New Ross.
Basketry Studio, Saltmills, **t** (051) 397618.
Bevel Country Furniture, Fethard, **t** (051)
397463.
Ceadógán Rug Shop, Barrystown, Wellington
Bridge, **t** (051) 561349.
Kilmore Quay Country Crafts, t (053) 29704/
29885.
Westgate Design, North Main Street,
Wexford Town.
Nicola Marray Knitwear, Waddington,
t (053) 39599.

Delicacies
Atlantis, Redmond Square, Wexford,
t (053) 22337. Freshly caught fish, sold from
a caravan.
Greenacres, 56 North Main Street,
Wexford, **t** (053) 22975. Good vegetables,
wholefoods and a small but very good
meat counter.
Rainbow Wholefoods, Walkers Mall, North
Main Street, Wexford, **t** (053) 24624.
Carrigbyrne Cheese, Adamstown,
t (054) 40560. Delicious hexagonal
Brie-type cheese.

Pottery
Lavery Pottery, at the John F. Kennedy Park,
south of New Ross, **t** (051) 388544.

Sports and Activities

Fishing
For **deep-sea fishing** charters, contact one of
the following:
Wexford Boat Charters, Kilmore Quay, **t** (053)
45888, *wexboats@iol.ie.*
Southeast Charters, Duncannon, **t** (051)
389242.

Golf
Rosslare Golf Club, Rosslare Strand, **t** (053)
32203.
St Helen's Bay Golf and Country Club, Kilrane,
t (053) 33669/33234.

Internet Access
FDYS Training Centre, Frances Street, Wexford
Town, **t** (053) 23262.
Wexford Library, Redmond Square, Wexford
Town, **t** (053) 21637.

Open Farms
Ballylane Visitor Farm, New Ross (off N25),
t (051) 425666. Orienteering courses.

Pleasure Cruises
Celtic Canal Cruisers, Tullamore, County
Offaly, **t** (0502) 21861. For cruises up the
River Barrow;
Also found at New Ross, **t** (051) 421723,
April–Oct.

Pony-trekking
Seaview Farmhouse Pony Trekking, Seaview,
St Kearns, **t** (051) 562239.
Horetown Equestrian Centre,
Foulksmills, **t** (051) 565786. Combine a
hunting course, picnic rides, hacking
and beginners' courses with a stay in
a lovely 17th-century
manor house.
Shelmalier Riding Stables, Forth Mountain,
Trinity, Taghmon, **t** (053) 39251.

town walls walls remain, along with one gate, now the **Westgate Heritage Centre**.
Here you can see an audio-visual presentation on the history of Wexford (*open
May–Oct, weekdays 10–2 and 2.30–5, Sat 10–2; adm; **t** (053) 46506*). Near West Gate, off
Abbey Street, is **Selskar Abbey**. It was built in the late 12th century, and the remains
consist of a square, battlemented tower and a church with a double nave and part of
its west gable. The 19th-century **church** (*always accessible*) stands on the spot where

Walking

Wexford coastal path, from Kilmichael Point to Ballyhack, stretches over 138 miles (221kms) – ask for details from the tourist office. During the summer evenings a **walking tour** of Wexford Town, led by a local historical society member, departs from Whites and Talbot Hotel – confirm with the tourist office.

Water Sports

Rosslare Sailboard and Watersports Centre, t (053) 32566. Sailboards, canoeing and more. *Open June–Aug.*

Ramsgrange Shielbaggan Outdoor Education Centre, New Ross, t (051) 389550. Offers sailing and snorkeling, canoeing, archery and rock-climbing.

Wexford Harbour Boat Club, t (053) 22039. For water-skiing and sailing.

Where to Stay

Rosslare Harbour and the road leading north to Wexford have a huge number of hotels and B&Bs, so you shouldn't have too much trouble finding a place if you get off the ferry in the evening. Even so, in summer it's best to book ahead.

Whites Hotel, George Street, Wexford Town, t (053) 22311 (*moderate*). Central and comfortable; it was the smartest hotel in town for years. It is now largely modern but incorporates part of an old coaching inn.

Ferrycarrig Hotel, Ferrycarrig Bridge, Wexford, t (053) 20999/20982 (*expensive*). This is a brand new hotel built on the Slaney Estuary. Nice views and good leisure facilities.

Newbay House, near Wexford Town, t (053) 42779 (*moderate*). Log fires, excellent meals and pine/period furnishings in Joan Coyle's 1820s house, only 2 miles (3.2km) from Wexford Town and 20 minutes from Rosslare. There are lovely gardens to stroll in.

Clonard House, Clonard Great, near Wexford, t (053) 47337 (*inexpensive*). Late-Georgian house with a staircase that curves into the ceiling because the money ran out for the top floor. Kathleen Hayes offers simple, delicious food, with perfect views and farmland to the sea.

Kilrane House, Kilrane, Rosslare Harbour, t (053) 33135 (*inexpensive*). A comfortable house run by Mrs Whitehead, only 2 minutes from Rosslare Harbour.

Dunbrody Country House, Arthurstown, t (051) 389600, f (051) 389601, *dunbrody@indigo.ie* (*luxury*). Georgian house set in a spacious park near the sea, which retains its period decoration and courteous service. The superior cuisine comes from the ex-chef of the Shelbourne Hotel in Dublin. *Breakfast available 7.30–noon, dinner from 6.30pm.*

Kilmokea Country Manor, Campile, t (051) 388109, f (051) 388776, *kilmokea@indigo.ie* (*luxury*). This near-perfect place is set beside a walled garden in 7 acres on Great Island, in the Barrow Estuary. Private trout fishing and horse-riding grounds, cream teas and aromatherapy massages are offered.

Creacon Lodge, New Ross, t (051) 421897 (*expensive–moderate*). Situated close to the John F. Kennedy Park, Josephine Flood's cosy house has tiny mullioned windows and creeper climbing up the walls.

Horetown House, Foulksmills, t (051) 565771 (*moderate*). Old fashioned 17th-century manor house in beautiful parkland setting. Mrs Young offers good plain food in the Cellar Restaurant, and facilities include an equestrian centre in the courtyard.

Self-catering

Clougheast Castle, Broadway, Carne, south of Rosslare, t (053) 31441 (*expensive–moderate*). Sue Davis offers an 18th-century coach house in a castle courtyard.

the first treaty between the Anglo-Normans and the Irish was ratified in 1169. Wexford's waterfront is a dowdy, long-neglected part of town that is currently being redeveloped. Notice the **Commodore John Barry Memorial** on Crescent Quay: he was born 10 miles (16km) away at Ballysampson, and is remembered as the father of the US Navy, and the first to capture a British ship in the Revolutionary War. A double of this statue stands in front of Independence Hall in Philadelphia. Lady Wilde (1826–

Ballyhealy Castle, Kilmore, t (053) 35566 (*expensive–moderate*). A fine 13th century Norman tower; a listed monument which has been furnished by Herbert Kellerer with antiques. Near the beach, 3 bedrooms.

Killowen House, Dunganstown, New Ross, t (027) 51184, *ricoff@eircom.net* (*moderate*). Cottage and an apartment, both very attractive, with tennis and gardens. Contact Bernie Coffey.

Eating Out

Mange 2, 100 South Main Street, Wexford t (053) 44033 (*expensive–moderate*). Simply but stylishly furnished with red walls and wooden tables, this restaurant offers excellent French-inspired cuisine with efficient service.

La Dolce Vita, Westgate, Wexford, t (053) 23935, (*expensive–moderate*). Superb Italian food.

Heavens Above, The Sky and the Ground, 112 South Main Street, t (053) 21273 (*moderate*). A delightful restaurant above a well-loved pub. Excellent food and an enormous wine list makes this place a must.

La Riva, Crescent Quay, Wexford, t (053) 24330 (*moderate*). Bistro-style restaurant serving super seafood, steaks and home-made pasta dishes as you overlook the harbour.

Tim's Tavern, 51 South Main Street, Wexford, t (053) 23861 (*moderate–inexpensive*). Lovely old-style, intimate restaurant, noted for its traditional Irish cooking as well as French and vegetarian specials. *Children welcome.*

Cappuccinos, 23 North Main Street, Wexford (*inexpensive*). Very popular lunchtime snack spot, with hot ciabatta sandwiches among the wide-ranging options.

Oyster Restaurant, Strand Road, Rosslare Strand, t (053) 32439 (*moderate*). Scallops and black sole are a speciality.

Kingsbay Inn, Arthurstown, t (051)3 89173 (*inexpensive*). Good bar food.

Lobster Pot, Carne, south of Rosslare, t (053) 31110 (*moderate*). A cosy and popular bar and restaurant. Great seafood and pub grub served all day.

Galley River Cruising Restaurant, The Quay, New Ross, t (051) 421723 (*expensive*). Six-course meals whilst you cruise on the River Barrow.

Neptune, Ballyhack Harbour, New Ross, t (051) 389284 (*moderate*). Overlooking the harbour. Good value dinner menus. Seafood is their speciality, and you can bring your own wine.

Cedar Lodge Restaurant and Hotel, Carrighbyrne, Newbawn, New Ross, t (051) 428386, f (051) 428222, *www.prideofeirehotels.com* (*inexpensive*). On the main Wexford–New Ross road. Good-quality food.

Horse and Hounds Inn, on the N25, Ballynabola, t (051) 428482 (*inexpensive*). Gargantuan portions of simple food; good stew. They also offer accommodation.

Entertainment and Nightlife

Traditional Music

In Wexford Town it is nearly impossible to stay bored or sober for long.

The Sky and the Ground, South Main Street, Wexford, t (053) 21273. This was once an old shop and pub in the 1960s, and they've left everything the way it was, including the groceries. Convivial, with a snug and good traditional music played every night Sun–Thurs.

Wavecrest Lounge, Commercial Quay, Wexford, t (053) 22849.

Wren's Nest, Custom House Quay, Wexford, t (053) 22359.

The Centenary Stores, Charlotte Street, t (053) 24424. Mon and Wed evenings and Sun mornings, with folk/blues on Tues evening.

96), mother of Oscar and known as 'Speranza', was born in the Old Rectory, Main Street. Sir Robert McClure (1807–73), who discovered the Northwest Passage in the Arctic, is another famous Wexford son.

There are mud flats close to the town at **Ferrybank**, which were reclaimed from the sea in the 1840s. The **Wexford Wildfowl Reserve** (*open mid April–Sept, daily 9–6, Oct–April, daily 10–5; guided tours on request; adm free; t (053) 23129*) provides over

2,500 acres (1,000ha) of mud flats, or 'slobs', for a huge variety of bird life in winter.
Vast numbers of Greenland white-fronted geese rest and feed here. There is a lecture
hall, library and observation tower in the public area of the reserve. About 2½ miles
(4km) north of Wexford Town, at Ferrycarrig, is the **Irish National Heritage Park**
(*open April–Nov, daily 9.30–6.30; adm; t (053) 20733, inhp@iol.ie*). Here you will find
reconstructions of life as it was in the past, from 7000 BC to the medieval period. It is
a scholarly and exciting exhibition, with full-scale replicas of the dwellings, places of
worship, forts and burial grounds over the ages, and contains everything from a
prehistoric *crannog* to an incredible Viking ship.

Three miles (4.8km) south of Wexford, near Murntown, is **Johnstown Castle** (*open
daily 9.30–5.30; adm in summer; t (053) 42888*). Built in 19th-century Gothic style, it is
now a State Agricultural College and visitors can tour round the landscaped gardens
and lakes. There are three lakes and a walled garden, as well as the old estate farmyard, now home to the college's **Irish Agricultural Museum** (*open all year, Mon–Fri 9–5,
also April–Oct, weekends 2–5; adm; t (053) 42888*).

The Southern Coast: Rosslare to Hook Head

Five miles (8km) north of Rosslare Harbour, the ferry port, is the resort of **Rosslare**,
with 6 miles (9.7km) of curving strand. The coastline beyond, approached from the
R736, is well worth travelling around. On **Lady's Island** there are ruins of an
Augustinian priory and a Norman castle built in 1237. The rare roseate tern can be
heard here, if seldom seen, and woolly cottonweed still grows on the sea bar, a plant
which died out on the south coast of England a couple of centuries ago. The island is
sacred to the Blessed Virgin and is still a favourite place of pilgrimage. In **Tacumshane**,
a tiny village of a few houses and a petrol station-cum-shop, is an example of a
working **windmill** with an attractive thatched top. This is part of the ancient Barony
of Forth, and the technology for the windmill was brought here by the families of
Flemish and Norman mercenaries. (Mr Michael Meyler of the petrol station has the
key to the mill, and will let you see round it.) At Tagoat is **Yola Farmstead Folk Park**
(*open May–Oct, daily 10–6, Mar–April and Nov, weekdays only 10–4.30; adm; t (053)
32610/32611, yolafst@iol.ie*) with a craft centre and a great tea room.

Kilmore Quay is an attractive thatched fishing village where you can get a boat,
weather permitting, to the **Saltee Islands**. Nobody lives on the islands, which are
verdant with waist-high bracken. Though they are private property and visits are
prohibited, boatmen on the Quay will take you out for a trip around them. The
puffins and other waterfowl are magnificent, and there is a curious coronation
place on the island, erected by the self-styled King of the Saltees in 1943. The view
from Kilmore Harbour along the headlands looks rather like the 19th-century
Dutch-influenced landscapes of the Norwich School of painters. The **Guillemot
Maritime Museum** is housed in what was Ireland's last working lightship (*open
Easter–end May and Sept, weekends noon–6, June–Aug, daily noon–6; adm; t (053)
21572, wexmaar@hotmail.com*).

Keeping close to the sea on the R736, turn left after Carrick to visit historic **Bannow**,
the first corporate town established by the Normans. The town is now buried deep

under the shifting sands, a process which began in the 17th century, though the benighted steeple and a couple of chimneys still returned MPs to the Irish Parliament until 1798. All that is left today of this proud Norman town is the ruin of St Mary's Church and an old graveyard. On the way to Hook Head, at the crossroads of the R733 and R734, you pass **Tintern Abbey** near Saltmills (*open mid June–late Sept, daily 9.30–6.30; t (051) 562650, visits@ealga.ie*), which is said to have been founded in AD 1200 by William the Marshall, Earl of Pembroke, in gratitude for surviving a terrible storm in St George's Channel. 'Mastless, a wreck unhelmed', he and his wife vowed that if they were saved they would found an abbey wherever they landed. The vessel beached itself in this lovely creek. The Office of Public Works has nearly finished restoring the magnificent Cistercian ruin, but it is still accessible to the public.

Nearby **Fethard** is a quiet resort, and there is a lovely walk over the sea pinks and grass to the ruined ramparts at **Baginburn**, which the Normans hastily built to repel the Norsemen and the Gaels. The Normans won the day by driving a herd of cattle into the advancing army. It is claimed that at the Creek of Baginburn, Ireland was lost and won. Certainly, the Norsemen of Waterford and MacMurragh's Ossory enemies were slaughtered, and those captured were thrown over the cliffs. Raymond le Gros held the earthworks until he joined Strongbow before the siege of Waterford in 1170. The road continues down to the tip of **Hook Head**, where the 700-year-old **Hook Lighthouse** (*open for guided tours Mar–Oct, daily 9.30–5; t (051) 397055, thehook@ eircom.net*) still keeps the light burning (*see* also p.248). The colourful and lively village of **Ballyhack** has a five-minute car ferry across the river to Passage East in County Waterford and a large **tower house** (*open in summer*). At **Duncannon** there is a star-shaped **fort** (*open June–mid Sept daily 10–5.30; guided tours on request; adm; t (051) 389 454, duncannonfort@ireland.com*) built in 1588 as a defence against the Spanish.

Around New Ross

Near to **Campile**, on the R733 and beside the winding River Barrow, is **Dunbrody Abbey**. This is is one of the most underestimated ruins in Ireland. It was built by the monks of St Mary's, Dublin, in 1182. A vast pile of weathered grey stone, it was suppressed in 1539. The west door is magnificent, and so are the lancet windows over the high altar. A small visitor centre can be found opposite the abbey (*open May–Sept, daily 10–6, July–Aug, until 7; adm; t (051) 388603*). It has a tea-room, a small museum, picnic site and a fully grown maze. Close by is **Dunmain House** (*open May–Sept, Tues–Sun, 2–5.30; adm; t (051) 562122*), a 17th-century building that has retained many of its original features; it is covered with slates, quite a common sight as you move further south in Ireland. **Kilmokea Country Manor and Gardens** (*open daily 9–5; guided tours, please ring ahead; adm; t (051) 388109, f (051) 388 776, kilmokea@indigo.ie*), near Campile, is a Georgian rectory with superb grounds. There is a rock garden, an Italian garden, a traditional herbaceous border, a lupin border, wide lawns with topiary hedges and a water garden set in beautiful woodland.

The Kennedy ancestral home is in **Dunganstown**. In 1848 Jack Kennedy left his family homestead for a new life in America after the dreadful years of the famine.

From there the success story needs no further telling: suffice it to say that his great-grandson is remembered all over the world, and especially in Ireland. The homestead is now a ruin. **New Ross** on the River Barrow has some ancient gabled houses and a medieval feel to it. It was built by Isobel, Strongbow's daughter, and has seen fighting against Cromwell and during the 1798 rebellion. Although there was much brutality on both sides, the massacre of Scullabogue during the 1798 rebellion is still not forgotten. Hundreds of British prisoners were burnt alive by the frightened rebels after they had fled from the fight in New Ross. It is possible to cruise for two or three hours on the rivers Nore and Barrow over a meal (*see* 'Eating Out', p.621). **The Kennedy Centre**, at the Quay in New Ross (**t** *(051) 425239*), provides genealogical records for those compiling family histories in the area, and the JFK Trust financed the building of the *Dunbrody* (*open April–Sept, daily 9–6, Oct–Mar, 12–5*; **t** *(051) 425239, **f** (051) 425 2401, jfktrust@iol.ie*), a 176ft replica of one of the ships that took immigrants to America during the famine. Early in 1999 the ship left the New Ross docks for its maiden voyage to Boston, and it is now docked here in the town. Also here is the **Berkeley Forest House Costume and Toy Museum** (*open May–Sept, Sat only; adm*; **t** *(051) 421361*), which has a collection of rare and delicate dolls and costumes – the lady who runs it makes tiny and exquisite dolls' hats. Just south of New Ross, off the R374, is the **John F. Kennedy Park and Arboretum** (*open Oct–Mar daily 10–5, April and Sept, until 6.30, May–Aug, until 8; adm*; **t** *(051) 388171*), with marvellous young trees and over 4,500 species of shrubs grouped according to where they are found in the world.

County Carlow

County Carlow is the second-smallest county in Ireland, and lies between Counties Wicklow, Wexford and Kilkenny. It is flat with undulating plains of rich farmland, although its borders to the south, east and west touch the hilly uplands of mountainous areas. To the southeast are the Blackstairs Mountains on the Wexford Border; in the west, the River Barrow threads through a limestone region which forms the boundary with Kilkenny; in the northeast the River Slaney flows through granite fringe shared with the Wicklow Mountains.

The rich river valleys contain many remains from the Anglo-Norman past in the form of castles and tower houses. There are Early Christian monastic ruins as well. The wide, twisting rivers provide opportunities for salmon and trout fishing, and you can cruise on the River Barrow. There is unstrenuous walking in the Slievemargey Hills above Carlow Town, and the South Leinster Way, a signposted long-distance walk, starts in Kildavin and passes through some fine mountain countryside in the Blackstairs range, before dropping down to follow the towpath of the River Barrow, with all the different bird life and tranquillity that the river world offers.

Travelling through the sleepy villages and the verdant countryside, one is struck by how unspoilt it is. The farms look old-fashioned; the hedges and trees have been left to decorate the fields and side roads. If you come from a highly industrialized country

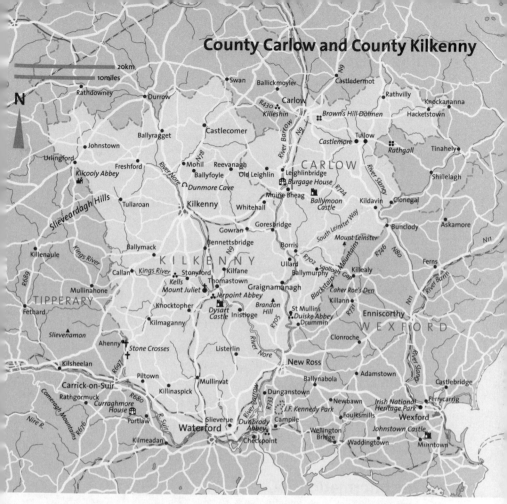

County Carlow and County Kilkenny

such as England, where farming is big business and almost every inch of land has been ploughed up, Carlow is very appealing. It also seems to have escaped the indiscriminate building of modern bungalows, which so often mar the wild beauty of Connacht and the counties along the western seaboard. It is still far enough away from Dublin to be ignored by commuters. Most people who live in the county work in agriculture or at the big sugar beet factory in Carlow Town.

History

In the 7th century Saint Moling founded a great monastic centre at St Mullins on the River Barrow. Later, many of the towns were Anglo-Norman strongholds, and were held for the king of England. In the 14th century, their position of power was challenged by a great chieftain, Art MacMurragh Kavanagh, who became King of Leinster and waged many successful battles against Richard II of England. MacMurragh was initially put down by a huge expeditionary force led by Richard, but as soon as he had submitted and a treaty been agreed, he mounted another attack.

Getting There and Around

By Rail
Mainline trains to Waterford from Dublin pass through Carlow.
Carlow Station, t (0503) 31633.

By Bus
There are a few buses each day from Carlow Town for Dublin, Kilkenny and Waterford on Bus Eireann or Rapid Travel Express Coaches. Private firms serve the other county towns.
Bus Eireann, t (051) 879000, www.buseireann.ie.
Rapid Travel Express Coaches, t (0503) 43081.

By Bike
Coleman Cycles, 19 Dublin Street, Carlow, t (0503) 31273.
Celtic Cycling, c/o Lorum Old Rectory, Bagenalstown, t (0503) 75282, info@celticcycling.com.

Festivals

May–June
Carlow Eigse Arts Festival, Bridewell Lane, t (0503) 30065, eigsecarlow@eircom.net. Music, exhibitions, recitals and dances.

Tourist Information

Carlow: t (0503) 31554; open all year, Mon–Sat.

Shopping

Crafts
Pembroke Gallery, Pembroke Street, Carlow, t (0503) 41562.

Cloydagh Woodcraft, Milford, t (0503) 32294. Visits by appointment.
Wild Irish Crafts, Kilquiggan, Tullow, t (0503) 56228.

Shamrock Seed
Honeysuckle Products, The Watermill, Hacketstown, t (0508) 71375, f (0508) 71499. Herbal suppliers.

Sports and Activities

Fishing
Try the River Barrow for brown trout and coarse fishing. Angling centres can be found in Muine Bheag (Bagenalstown) and Tullow.

Golf
Carlow Golf Club, Carlow Town, t (0503) 31695, f (0503) 40065, carlowgolf@tinet.ie.

Outdoor Activity Centres
Adventure Canoeing, t (0509) 31307. For canoeing on the Barrow River.

Pleasure Cruises
Celtic Canal Cruisers, Tullamore, County Offaly, t (0502) 21861. Also for boat hire.

Pony-trekking
Carrigbeg Stables, Bagenalstown, t (0503) 21962.

Walking
A good route is along the South Leinster Way; the tourist office can supply you with detailed maps. There is a forest walk by a canal at Bahana, 3 miles (4.8km) south of Barrow Bridge, Graignamanagh (on an unclassified road to St Mullins).

He joined with the O'Neills of Ulster and the Earl of Desmond and, at the Battle of Kellistown in 1399, King Richard's heir, Roger Mortimer, was routed and killed. Richard's preoccupation with Ireland and his extensive losses gave his enemies in England a chance to organize against him, and Bolingbroke usurped his throne. Richard returned to imprisonment and death, and MacMurragh got his kingdom back.

For the next 135 years the authority of the English crown was reduced to the narrow 'Pale' around Dublin. Carlow Town was for a time its most southern outpost, and

Where to Stay

Royal Hotel, Dublin Street, Carlow, t (0503) 31621, f (0503) 31125, *royal@iol.ie* (*moderate*). Old established hotel in the middle of Carlow Town. Quiet and comfortable with an attractive garden.

The Lord Bagenal Inn, Main Street, Leighlinbridge, t (0503) 21668, *www. lordbagenal.com, info@lordbagenal.com*. Small hotel with the owner's collection of paintings on the walls, and helpful staff who prepare generous breakfasts. Amenable to smokers and families, with a children's playroom that is open until 8pm.

Lorum Old Rectory, Kilgreaney, Muine Bheag (Bagenalstown), t (0503) 75282, f (0503) 75455, *www.lorum.com, lorum@indigo.ie* (*moderate*). The ideal place for those with children, with plenty to do on Mrs Smith's farm; plus outdoor toys, dogs, pet sheep and croquet in the garden. Tasty meals and pretty, old-fashioned rooms.

Sherwood Park House, Kilbride, Tullow, t (0503) 59117, f (0503) 59355 (*moderate–inexpensive*). Near Altamont Gardens, a peaceful Georgian house with extensive parkland. Rooms are furnished with brass-end canopy beds. Cosy open fires and home cooking; contact Mrs Owens.

The Watermill, Rathvilly, t (0503) 61392 (*inexpensive*). Delightful restored 16th century mill on the River Slaney, with home cooking and vegetables from Mr and Mrs Tononi's garden, plus free fishing.

Self-catering

Ballydarton House, Cloneen, Nurney, t (0503) 27140. 17th-century farmhouse.

Eating Out

The Beams Restaurant, 59 Dublin Street, Carlow Town, t (0503) 31824 (*expensive*). Three hundred-year-old coaching inn with a bistro serving modern Irish cuisine: fresh seafood, game and home-grown vegetables. Attached to the restaurant is an excellent wine and cheese shop.

Royal Hotel, Dublin Street, Carlow, t (0503) 31621 (*moderate*). Good food in the centre of town.

Brookes, Tullow Street, Carlow (*moderate–inexpensive*). Wine bar-restaurant, favoured by locals.

Teach Dolmain, Tullow Street, Carlow, t (0503) 30911 (*inexpensive*). Bar food and traditional music.

Ballykealey House, Ballon, near Carlow, t (0503) 59288 (*moderate*). Country house style restaurant.

The Lord Bagenal Inn, Main Street, Leighlinbridge, t (0503) 21668, f (0503) 22629, *www.lordbagenal.com, info@ lordbagenal.com* (*moderate*). Very popular pub-restaurant serving a good, varied menu, accompanied by an excellent wine list.

The Green Drake Inn, Main Street, Borris, t (0503) 73116 (*moderate–inexpensive*). Simple meals from local produce.

Entertainment and Nightlife

Traditional Music

Teach Dolmain, Tullow Street, Carlow, t (0503) 30911. Thursday nights.

Tully's Bar, Tullow Street, Carlow, t (0503) 31862.

Joyce's Bar, Borris, t (0503) 73114.

heavily fortified. The Cromwellian confiscations of the 1650s, the Williamite wars of the 1690s and the penal laws had their dire effect on the Gaelic culture and society of Carlow, as they did elsewhere in Ireland. The 1798 rebellion against English rule claimed many lives, for the rebel army consisted of peasant mobs who were no match for the trained and well-armed British forces. Most of the leaders of this uprising are still remembered locally, among them Father John Murphy, who was executed in the Market Square of Tullow, a small place east of Carlow Town. There is a monument to him there, and he is still remembered by local folk. The Great

Famine in the 1840s hit hard, and local life thereafter followed the usual pattern of death and emigration.

Carlow Town

Carlow Town is at the crossing of the River Barrow in the northwest of the county, and is steeped in history. It was an Anglo-Norman stronghold, and much later it was the scene of a bloody scrimmage in the 1798 rebellion (*see* **History**, pp.46–7). Nowadays it is involved in the processing of sugar beet, which was introduced in 1926 as part of the Irish self-sufficiency programme. Sights include the **Norman castle**, probably early 13th-century, with its two drum towers. Its ruins were further reduced by a Dr Middleton, who built a lunatic asylum here in 1814. It is in private hands, but permission to look around it is readily given. (Ask at the house near the castle, which is right in the centre of the town near the east bank of the River Barrow.) There is the prominent Catholic, Gothic Revival **Cathedral of the Assumption**, completed in 1833, off College Street, and a handsome **courthouse** with a Doric portico, after the Parthenon, at the junction of Dublin Street and Dublin Road (*open during working hours*). You may like to visit **Carlow County Museum** in the Town Hall on Centaur Street (*open weekdays 11–5, Sat and Sun 2–5; adm; t (0503) 40730*), which has displays on folk life, archaeology and local history.

Around the County

Outside Carlow, 2 miles (3.2km) to the east, is the largest capstoned dolmen in Ireland, the **Browne's Hill Dolmen** (*always accessible*). This is very impressive and is estimated to weigh over a hundred tonnes. **Killeshin**, 3 miles (4.8km) west of Carlow town off the R430, is a ruined 12th-century church with an exceptionally fine Romanesque doorway. In the graveyard you will find the oldest decorated font in Ireland.

Moving southwards, following the river Barrow, you come to Leighlinbridge and Old Leighlin on the N9. They are both pleasant spots. **Leighlinbridge** has a superb stone bridge with a Norman castle on its eastern side, which was built in 1181. On the unclassified road leading to Old Leighlin is **St Laserain's Church**, which has a very attractive bell-tower. **Old Leighlin** has the remains of a 7th-century monastery and fine cathedral. It was the centre of a bishopric from the 12th century until the diocese was joined with Ferns in County Wexford in 1600. The 12th-century **Cathedral of St Laserain** has some fine 13th- and 15th-century architectural details, and in the graveyard are St Laserain's stone cross and a holy well. In the grounds of **Burgage House** near Leighlinbridge is a large *rath* known as **Dinn Righ**, an ancient residence of the kings of Leinster. You can ask to visit it.

If you want to do some inland water-cruising, all Ireland's rivers are beautiful and unspoilt. In Carlow, it is possible to cruise through Carlow Town, St Mullin's and Muine Bheag. The River Barrow connects with the Grand Canal to Dublin, and links up with the Shannon. **Muine Bheag**, formally Bagenalstown, was destined by Walter Bagenal to become an Irish Versailles – a plan which never came off (perhaps he ran out of money). About 2 miles (3km) away on the R724 is the impressive ruin of **Ballymoon**

Castle (*always accessible*), built in the 14th century and one of the earliest Anglo-Norman strongholds built in Ireland. Legend says that it has never been conquered. It has two very strong square towers of great strength – the cut-granite walls are over 8ft (2.5m) thick.

Borris is another pretty river town surrounded by the woods of Borris Castle. This is where the descendants of Art MacMurragh Kavanagh, 14th-century ruler of Leinster and scourge of Richard II, once lived. One of the famous members of his family, Arthur, who lived in the 19th century, was born without limbs; and yet he was a great sportsman and could ride, fish, shoot and sail, and he was also MP for Carlow. His daughter died in 1930 in the **Step House**, which is opposite the gates of the castle. The MacMurragh Kavanaghs are still well-remembered here.

The kings of Leinster are supposed to have been buried at **St Mullins**, a very pretty village off the R729 on the way to New Ross. It is beautifully situated on the River Barrow, and was once a site of great ecclesiastical importance. St Moling, Bishop of Ferns, founded a monastery here in the 7th century, and there are the remains of several ancient churches and an abbey. His little stone cell, the stump of a round tower, a holy well, the remains of a small nave and chancel church and an old weathered stone cross are grouped together around the abbey.

The Blackstairs Mountains to the southeast of the county are gentle and rolling; there is a pretty pass through the **Sgollogh Gap** (R702). The R746 leads to Bunclody in County Wexford at the northeast end of the mountain range. On an unclassified road to the north of Bunclody is **Clonegal**, a small village situated on the River Derry. In the centre is a fine Elizabethan building, **Huntingdon Castle** (*open June–Aug, daily 2–6, Sept, Sun only 2–6; guided tours; adm; t (054) 77552*), which has belonged to the Robertson family for centuries. The courtyard is rather fine, and it has a modern sculpture museum. In the basement is a temple to the Goddess Isis, a rich medley of eastern statues and colour, and there's a magnificent yew walk in the grounds.

Following the N80/81 and the River Slaney northwards you come to **Tullow**, the biggest town in the county and an angling centre for those fishing the Slaney for salmon and trout. If you are interested in archaeology, the *raths* ringing the town are worth a visit. **Castlemore**, the most important, lies a mile (1.6km) to the west. Three miles (4.8km) east of the town, just off the R725, there is the ancient stone fort of **Rathgall**. This has four ramparts; the outer ring is 1,000ft (300m) in diameter. Both sites are always accessible. **Altamont Gardens**, 5½ miles (9km) off the Tullow–Bunclody Road (*open April–Oct, Sun only 2–6; or by appointment; adm; t (0503) 59444*), is a superb place to spend a few hours, with a formal garden, herbaceous borders, a water garden, and good teas. In autumn there are masses of naturalized cyclamen.

A short drive northeast of Tullow lies **Hacketstown**, situated in the Wicklow foothills. This was the scene of a desperate engagement between the insurgents and the yeomanry in 1798 (*see* **History**, pp.46–7). The tiny village of **Rathvilly** on the N81 to the west has a spreading view of the distant mountain ranges – the Blackstairs and the Slieve Blooms. It has a reputation to keep up, having won the All-Ireland title for the tidiest town three times over.

County Kilkenny

The countryside round Kilkenny is lush and well-cultivated, and is reminiscent of England. So too are the villages, with their neatness and mellowed cottages. History colours the landscape wherever you are in Ireland, but in this county there is more visible evidence than in most of the interaction between Norman and Gael, and the later English landlords and Welsh miners. The Anglo-Normans invaded Ireland in 1169, and quickly established themselves as the ruling power. These lords of conquest built themselves motte and bailey castles to hold their new territory, and as the centuries advanced and they grew more confident and wealthy, large and fine castles proclaimed their success. In Kilkenny, their dramatic castles along the river valleys of the Nore and the Barrow, the splendid remains of Jerpoint Abbey and, above all, the old city of Kilkenny itself make an exploration of the county a fascinating and rewarding occupation.

Apart from the ancient and stately buildings of Kilkenny, its wooded and well-tended countryside offers fishing, golf, horse-racing and riding. In Kilkenny City itself there is an arts festival, and good design and craft shops. The county's prowess also extends to hurling, a very ancient game recorded in Irish sagas: Nowlan Park, the hurling stadium in Kilkenny City, has great matches.

Today Kilkenny is a thriving agricultural county, with many craftsmen working in Kilkenny City and in small studios in the heart of the countryside, like the Nicholas Mosse pottery at Bennettsbridge. Here there is a small pottery museum, and you can buy good value seconds of lovely spongeware decorated with farmyard animals and flowers.

History

A brief survey of the history of Kilkenny inevitably centres on the Anglo-Normans, but before they arrived, the county formed part of the old Gaelic kingdom of Ossory, an independent buffer state which sometimes joined with Leinster and sometimes with Munster. The old kingdom is remembered still in the diocese of Ossory, which stretches from near Waterford City in the south to the Slieve Bloom Mountains in the north. Its ruling family was called MacGiolla Phadruig, anglicized as Fitzpatrick. The kingdom of Ossory is said to date back to the 2nd century AD and it was such a stable force in the 11th century that the king of the time decided to try for the kingship of Leinster. The arrival of the Anglo-Normans, and the ease with which they triumphed over the ill-prepared Irish, eclipsed the Fitzpatricks. Soon the new name of Butler became all-powerful, and continued so for centuries. Theobald Fitzwalter was the first to carry the name. He came with Henry II on his great expedition in 1171, and in 1177 he was appointed Chief Butler in Ireland. Thenceforth his descendants were known as Butler, and by 1328 the head of the family was made Earl of Ormonde by

Getting There and Around

By Rail

Kilkenny City is on the main line from Dublin to Waterford, with about four trains a day in both directions.
MacDonagh Station, Kilkenny City,
t (056) 22024.

By Bus

Bus Eireann has at least six buses a day to Dublin and Cork (via Clonmel), less frequently to Waterford. Other Dublin–Waterford buses go through Thomastown instead. There's also one daily to Galway, in summer only. Contact McDonough Station in Kilkenny for details, as above.
Bus Eireann, t (056) 64933, *www.buseireann.ie*.
Kavanagh's, t (056) 31106. Private line with services between Kilkenny (from the bus stop on The Parade), Cashel and Thurles in Tipperary, as well as Carlow.

By Bike

J. J. Wall, 86 Maudlin Street, Kilkenny, t (056) 21236.

Festivals

May

The Cat Laughs. Comedy festival in Kilkenny City, held late May/early June, t (056) 51254.

June

Murphy's Irish Open Golf Championship, Mount Juliet, Thomastown. Ireland's premier international golf event.

August

Kilkenny Arts Festival. One of the most important arts festivals in Ireland – opera, art exhibitions and music of all sorts. Held in the last week of the month, t (056) 52175, f (056) 51704, *www.kilkennyarts.ie*.

Edward III. (Confusingly, in many of the places you will visit, the names Butler and Ormonde are interchangeable.) By 1391 the Butler family seat was in Kilkenny Castle, and many other castles in County Tipperary and Kilkenny became theirs as their clan grew in strength and numbers.

The Norman adventurers who first came to Ireland were brought to acknowledge the authority of the English crown by military expeditions staged by the monarch. But they frequently chafed at the restraint, and as time wore on they intermarried with the native Irish and became thoroughly Irish themselves. During the 14th century the colony went into a decline: there was the devastation of the Black Death, the native Irish began to reassert themselves, and the Norman families identified more and more with Gaelic Ireland. The effect of this was that royal authority was confined, apart from in a few walled towns, to an enclave on the east coast around Dublin – the Pale. In 1366 London reacted by calling a parliament in Kilkenny City which passed the Statutes of Kilkenny. These laws made it high treason for a Norman to marry an Irish woman, or for an Irish man to live in Kilkenny City. Normans were not allowed to wear Irish dress (the long cloak), or to adopt the customs, legal arrangements or language of the Irish. (If you go to Cahir Castle in County Tipperary, close to Kilkenny, there is an excellent permanent exhibition on the Brehon, or Gaelic, laws and customs.) The statutes were rigidly enforced for a while, but they came too late and soon fell into decline.

A mutual antagonism between the Butlers and the Fitzgeralds, another powerful Norman family, caused many a betrayal and pitched battle in the following two centuries. The Fitzgeralds in Leinster were the Earls of Kildare, and the Fitzgeralds in Munster were the Earls of Desmond. Both branches are often referred to as the

Geraldines. The ramifications of the Butler dynasty and their feud with the Fitzgeralds spread far and wide. Anne Boleyn, the second wife of Henry VIII, was the granddaughter of Thomas Butler, the seventh earl. Elizabeth I's cousin, Black Tom Butler, put down the late 16th-century revolt by the Earl of Desmond on behalf of the crown. The Bishop of Cloyne, a brave man, said at a requiem Mass for the wife of the fourth Earl of Desmond in 1391: 'Eternal God, there are two in Munster who destroy us and our property, namely the Earl of Ormonde and the Earl of Desmond with their followers, who at length the Lord will destroy, through Christ our Lord, Amen.' This prayer so incensed Butler and Geraldine that the bishop was compelled to pay Ormonde damages, and was deprived of his see. The feud was finally healed by the marriage of James Butler, first Duke of Ormonde, to his cousin Elizabeth Preston, heiress of the Earl of Desmond in 1629.

Kilkenny City played a very important part in the Great Rebellion of 1641, which broke out in Ulster. The Norman and Gaelic families made an alliance, united in resentment against the new settlers – the Protestants 'planted' by James I – and the decades of economic, political and religious oppression. In May 1642 the city became the seat of the Confederate Parliament of the Catholics, with representatives from all the counties and main towns. Government was taken into their hands, taxes levied, armies raised, weapons and powder manufactured. Owen Roe O'Neill commanded for Ulster, Preston for Leinster; Munster was under Barry, and Connacht under Burke. The Confederation lasted until 1648.

But the alliance between the 'Old Foreigners' and the 'Old Irish' was complicated by their different loyalties as the Civil War in England between Charles I and Parliament spilled over into Ireland. The Butlers of Kilkenny were loyal to the Stuart crown; the old Gaelic families felt nothing for him and turned to France and Spain, the traditional enemies of England. But this split was overshadowed in its turn by the rise of Cromwell, who began a ruthless campaign in Ireland. In March 1650, after five days' defence, Kilkenny City capitulated to him and his forces. James, Duke of Ormonde, was at this time deeply involved in the internal hostilities between the Confederates. He had supported Charles I and, after his execution, proclaimed Charles II king. The successes of Cromwell forced him to retreat to France, but he was later restored to his estates and given an English dukedom and peerage by Charles II. The Butler family was in any case probably destined to survive, for, as with many of the aristocratic families in Ireland, there were Protestant Butlers and Catholic Butlers, so they managed to keep a foot in each camp. In the more recent history of Ireland, the Butlers have ceased to play any part.

Northern and Eastern Kilkenny

Urlingford to Castlecomer

Places to visit, from west to east, include **Urlingford** on the border with Tipperary. There is a ruined 16th-century castle and the remains of a pre-Reformation church. The town itself dates only from 1755; the site was established after the bog had been

Tourist Information

Kilkenny: Shee Alms House, Rose Inn Street, t (056) 51500, f (056) 63955; *open all year.*

Sports and Activities

Fishing
There's good fishing at Graignamanagh, and also along the Lower River Barrow.
Hook, Line & Sinker, 31 Rose Inn Street, Kilkenny, **t** (056) 71699. For all fishing needs.
Town and County Sports Shop, 82 High Street, Kilkenny, **t** (056) 21517.

Golf
Mount Juliet, near Thomastown, **t** (056) 73000, *info@mountjuliet.ie.* Jack Nicklaus-designed course amidst woodland, used for top-notch international competitions.

Horse-racing
At Gowran Park throughout the year. Check the local newspapers and at the back of Tourism Ireland's *Calender of Events,* or call the following for information:
Irish Horse Racing Authority, t (01) 289 2888.

Internet Access
Compustore, Arcade James Street, off High Street, Kilkenny, **t** (056) 71200. *Open all year, Mon–Wed and Sat 10–6, Thurs–Fri 10–8.*
Webtalk, Rose Inn Street, Kilkenny, **t** (056) 50066. *Open all year Mon–Sat 10–9, Sun 2–8.*

Pleasure Cruises
Valley Boats, Barrow Lane, Graignamanagh, **t** (0503) 24945. Cruises on the river Barrow.

Pony-trekking
Mount Juliet Equestrian Centre, Thomastown, **t** (056) 24455, **f** (056) 24522.
Wallslough Equestrian Village, Sheestown, **t** (056) 23838. Located 5km south of Kilkenny, towards Thomastown.

Walking
For details of guided walking tours in Inistioge, call **t** (056) 58995.

Shopping

Crafts
Cushendale Woollen Mills, Graignamanagh. For tweed and woollen goods.
Toner's Bag Company, Thomastown, **t** (056) 24055. See leather goods being made in their workshop.

Glass
Duiske Glass, Graiguenamanagh, **t** (0503) 24174.
Jerpoint Glass Studios, Stoneyford, **t** (056) 24350. Thickly blown glass.

Where to Stay

Avalon Inn, The Square, Castlecomer, **t** (056) 41302 *(inexpensive).* B&B in an ivy-covered Georgian building.

cut away. **Ballyragget** on the River Nore has more to recommend it to historians, besides being a pretty little place. It was the scene of a dramatic trial of strength between Black Tom, Earl of Ormonde and Lord Lieutenant of Ireland in Elizabeth I's time, and Owen MacRory O'More, head of the ruling Laois family. The battle ended in the capture of the Earl in April 1600. Further east, about 7 miles (11km) north of Kilkenny, just off the N78 near Ballyfoyle, is the dramatic **Dunmore Cave** (*open mid June–mid Sept, daily 10–7, mid Mar–mid June and mid Sept–Oct, daily 10–5, rest of the year weekends only 10–5; guided tours; adm;* **t** *(056) 67726*). During the Viking raids people took refuge here, but they were found and nearly a thousand were killed. Even so, the cave continued to be used afterwards as a refuge by local people. It is a fantasy world of coloured caverns, and you can spend a good hour down there. The Office of Public Works runs the cave, which is notable for its huge chambers and

Mount Juliet Estate Hotel, Thomastown,
t (056) 73000, f (056) 73019, *www.
mountjuliet.com, info@mountjuliet.ie*
(*luxury*). This is a lovely stately house,
recently converted into a swish hotel
and country club, with beautiful
grounds, friendly staff and good
sporting facilities such as golf, riding
and fishing.

Kilrush House, Freshford, t (056) 32236
(*moderate*). Pretty 18th-century country
house north of Kilkenny. Comfortable
rooms, good simple cooking; and there's
a tennis court. Contact Sally and Richard
St George. *Families with children
over 7 welcome.*

Waterside House, The Quay,
Graiguenamanagh, t (0503) 24246
(*moderate*). Modern rooms in a restored
19th-century granary on the riverfront.

Cullintra House, The Rower, Inistioge,
t (051) 423614, *http://indigo.ie/~cullhse/,
cullhse@indigo.ie* (*moderate*). Set in
beautiful grounds with traditional
furnishings and bohemian influences
from its lively proprietress, Patricia
Cantlon. This farmhouse is a paradise for
cat-lovers, children and eccentrics who
long for the timeless qualities of the old
Ireland. The superb dinners are served
by candlelight.

Garranavabby House, The Rower,
Inistioge, t (051) 423613 (*moderate–
inexpensive*). Old farmhouse in a lovely
setting near Graignamanagh and charming
Inistioge. Contact Mrs J. Prendergast.

Eating Out

Waterside, The Quay, Graiguenamanagh,
t (0503) 24246 (*expensive–moderate*).
Refined cooking and especially good seafood
dishes, in an atmospheric stone building
overlooking the water.

Mount Juliet, Thomastown, t (056) 73000
(*expensive*). A grand setting for any meal,
this lofty restaurant is grandly decorated in
white and Wedgwood blue, and the lovely
food makes use of local produce. You might
also spot celebrity golfers.

The Hunters Yard, Mount Juliet,
Thomastown, t (056) 24455 (*moderate*).
Traditional Irish food.

Silks Restaurant, Marshes Street,
Thomastown, t (056) 54400 (*moderate*).
Excellent Mediterranean fare, with a mouth-
watering array of choices.

Thomastown Water Garden and Cafe, t (056)
24690 (*inexpensive*). Teas served on the
terrace of a lovely little water garden (*adm*)
in Thomastown. It is beautifully planted
with aquatic plants.

The Motte, Main Street, Inistioge, t (056)
58655 (*moderate–expensive*). A charming
little restaurant in this most picturesque of
villages, with adventurous food and a cosy
atmosphere that's just right.

Circle of Friends, The Bank House,
High Street, Inistioge, t (056) 58800
(*moderate–inexpensive*). Café and
evening restaurant in a converted house;
excellent cakes and snacks downstairs,
and fine meals upstairs.

'market cross' stalagmite column. Nearby **Castlecomer** was laid out in the style of an
Italian village by Sir Christopher Wandersforde in 1635. The area was once prosperous
because of the coal field in this region, which skilled Welshmen were imported to
mine. The coalmines closed in the 1970s.

Gowran to Sheastown

Gowran deserves your attention if you love horse-racing, for it has an
excellent course. The town was an important fortress of the kings of Ossory until
Theobald Fitzwalter, the first Butler and ancestor of the Dukes of Ormonde, was
granted it by Strongbow. Sadly, nothing remains of the castle he built, as
Cromwell's troops burned it down in 1650. However, the Church of Ireland **church**
has some interesting monuments, and is a mixture of 12th- and 13th-century

architectural details. There is an effigy in armour of the first Earl of Ormonde (1327). On one of the gravestones is rather a witty couplet erected to a man and his two wives:

Both wives at once alive he could not have
Both to enjoy at once he made this grave.

Goresbridge is another attractive river village that joins County Carlow to County Kilkenny across the River Barrow. Many people come and fish for brown trout and a variety of coarse fish here. At Goresbridge you can also buy ornaments and other objects made out of a speciality of the county – the highly polished black limestone which has been used as paving in Kilkenny City itself. This 'marble' is no longer mined, although you may find Kilkenny marble chimneys pointed out to you in many big houses. Off the N9, just over a mile (2km) from Kilfane, is **Kilfane Glen** (*open May–mid Sept, daily exc Mon 2–6; adm; t (056) 24558*), with a waterfall adorned by a romantic garden laid out in the 18th century, and a thatched 'cottage ornée'.

Going south you reach lovely **Thomastown** (on the Waterford road), with its mellowed grey-stone buildings. Near here, on an unmarked road to the south of the town is the ruin of **Dysart Castle**, the home of the famous idealist-philosopher George Berkeley (1685–1753), who gave his name to the city and university of Berkeley, California. The castle is not open to the public, but can be viewed from the road. To the west of Thomastown, near Stonyford, is one of the best-kept estates in Ireland, **Mount Juliet** (*t (056) 73000, f (056) 73019*). The house is an hotel, and the gardens are beautiful, especially the delphiniums in the walled garden. Part of the grounds have become a Jack Nicklaus-designed champion golf course.

But the jewel of the area must be the fine monastic ruin of **Jerpoint Abbey**, just off the N9 (*open mid Mar–May and mid Sept–Oct, daily exc Tues 10–5, June–mid Sept, 9.30–6.30; adm; t (056) 24623*), which dates from the late 12th century. It follows a typical Cistercian plan with two chapels in each transept. The ancient parts of the chancel and the transepts are in Irish Romanesque style, and appear to have been built by the same masons who raised Baltinglass in Wicklow. The abbey was founded in 1158 by Donal MacGiolla Phadruig, King of Ossory, and suppressed in 1540. Restoration work has been sympathetic and it is an impressive ruin. Take a look at the sculptured lords and ladies in the cloisters.

Due east rises the hill of Brandon, which gives you a clear view of this well-worked countryside, with the Blackstairs Mountains to the east on the Carlow-Wexford border. On your way here you will pass the charming town of **Inistioge**, home of the Tighes. This family was connected with a pair of remarkable ladies who exercised a great influence on taste in the 18th century. The 'Ladies of Llangollen', Lady Eleanor Butler and Sarah Ponsonby, exemplified the Romantic and the Gothick by running away together to live in a Welsh cottage. Inistioge square is planted with lime trees, and there are wooded stretches surrounding the town, through which the River Nore runs. A Norman **motte** overlooks the river and there are the fine ruins of an Augustinian **priory**, founded in 1210.

North of Inistioge is **Graignamanagh**, right on the Carlow border. It is picturesquely sited on a mountainous ravine and has the splendid early Cistercian **Duiske Abbey**, which survived the suppression of the monasteries in the 16th century, as did the Catholic **church**, which has some 9th-century crosses in the graveyard. Both are always accessible to the public. Notice the effigy of a knight in the church, lying crosslegged in 13th-century armour – this was medieval artists' way of expressing that the deceased had been a crusader. Before leaving the Graignamanagh district, take the opportunity to investigate the woolcrafts.

At **Ullard**, 3 miles (4.8km) north on the R705, there are remains of another foundation: a high cross and the remains of an old church, with granite carvings on the Romanesque doorway. St Fiachre set off for France from Ullard. He is one of the saints that chose the isolation of a foreign land in preference to a lonely island hermitage. He is the patron saint of Parisian taxi-drivers, because the first carriage conveyances in Paris used to congregate round the Hôtel de St Fiachre. About 3 miles (4.8km) southeast of Kilkenny City at **Sheastown**, on the way to Bennettsbridge, is a well dedicated to St Fiachre. *Patterns* are held here in late August around the time of the Arts Festival in Kilkenny.

Western and Central Kilkenny

Callan and Kells

West of Kilkenny City is the ancient town of **Callan** which seems to have nourished a fair number of Ireland's great men. One of them, Edmund Ignatius Rice (1762–1844), a candidate for canonization, founded the influential teaching order of the Christian Brothers, who now not only educate most of Ireland's politicians, but also some of the Third World's. He was born in a thatched cottage (marked by a plaque) at **Westcourt**, just outside Callan. Robert Fulton (b.1765), who designed the world's first steamship, and James Hoban (1762–1831), architect of the White House, came from near here.

Nearby on the Kings River is the complete, fortified, turreted and walled enclosure of **Kells** (*always accessible*). Since the early history of the Kingdom of Ossory, Kells has heard the murmur of prayer and the clash of warfare. Now it is a supremely peaceful place, and the impressive collection of early ecclesiastical buildings must make it a highlight of any Kilkenny tour. It was founded in the late 12th century by Geoffrey Fitzrobert de Marisco, who built a stong castle and an Augustinian priory. But it had been a centre of importance in the early history of Ossory, and most probably a mystical pagan site. St Kieran of Seer founded a monastery here in the 5th century, but it is the remains of the 12th-century **priory** which still impress. Its ruins cover 5 acres (2ha) and are divided into two courts by a moat and a wall. The north court is surrounded by a tall wall, and fortified with towers, and contains the church, cloisters and other monastic buildings. The south court is fortified, turreted and walled, but contains no buildings and was an enclosure for cattle in times of trouble.

Tourist Information

Kilkenny: Shee Alms House, Rose Inn Street,
t (056) 51500; *open all year.*

Shopping

Crafts

The Kilkenny Design Centre, Castle Yard,
Kilkenny, t (056) 22118. An excellent selection
of crafts from all over Ireland. *Open Jan–Mar
Mon–Sat 9–6, April–Dec Mon–Sun 10–6.*
Chesneau Leather, Bennettsbridge, t (056)
27456. Mostly handbags and knapsacks.

Delicacies

Shortis-Wong, 74 John Street, Kilkenny, t (056)
61305. Excellent deli.
Mileeven Ltd, Owning Hill, Piltown, t (051)
643368. Honey, cider, beeswax polish.

Crystal

Kilkenny Irish Crystal, Canal Square, Kilkenny,
t (056) 61377. The factory is at Callan and can
be visited during the summer.

Health Foods

The Good Earth, 43 Kieran Street, Kilkenny,
t (056) 52664.

Jewellery

Liam Costigan, Collierslane, off High Street,
Kilkenny, t (056) 62408.
Rudolf Heltzel, 10 Patrick Street, Kilkenny,
t (056) 21497.

Pottery

The Bridge Pottery, Chapel Street,
Bennettsbridge, t (056) 27077.

Nicholas Mosse Pottery, Bennettsbridge,
t (056) 27505, *www.nicholasmosse.com.*
Possibly the nicest pottery in Ireland;
spongeware decorated with farmyard
animals and flowers. Slight seconds are
available here, and there is an exhibition of
pottery through the ages.
Stoneware Jackson Pottery, Ballyreddin,
Bennettsbridge, t (056) 27175. Lots of swirly
bright patterns.

Sports and Activities

Golf

Kilkenny City Course, Lacken, t (056) 24725.

Pleasure Cruises

Valley Boats, Barrow Lane, Graignamanagh,
t (0503) 24945. Cruises on the river Barrow.

Pony-trekking

Warrington Top Flight Equestrian Centre,
Bennettsbridge Road, Kilkenny, t (056)
22682, *tfwarrington@eircom.net.*

Walking

Guided walks are available in **Kilkenny**;
contact the tourist office, t (056) 70241.

Where to Stay

Butler House, 16 Patrick Street, Kilkenny,
t (056) 22828/65707, f (056) 65626
(*expensive–moderate*). Smart guest house in
a restored Georgian building. Central and
comfortable.
The Club House Hotel, Patrick Street, Kilkenny,
t (056) 21994, f (056) 71920, *clubhse@iol.ie*

Kilkenny City

Kilkenny City (*Cill Chainnigh*: 'St Canice's Church') was the focal point of the Anglo-
Norman and Irish resistance to the Cromwellians in 1642, and was where they formed
their Confederate Parliament. Before that it was the seat of power for the 'old English',
the first foreign war-lords. The city (pop. 17,700), takes its name from St Canice, who
established a monastery here in the 6th century. The Church of Ireland **cathedral**
called St Canice's now occupies its site off Vicar Street, a fine Gothic work completed
in 1285, with an interior of beautiful Kilkenny stone. This is the second-largest
medieval church in Ireland, and it contains an exceptional collection of medieval

(*moderate*). Originally the headquarters of the Foxhounds Club, this old hotel has many gracious features of another age. It is very central for all the sights of Kilkenny City.

Lacken House, Dublin Road, Kilkenny, **t** (056) 61085, **f** (056) 62435 (*moderate*). A family-run guest house in attractive grounds, with well-cooked food elegantly produced by the chef-owner.

Newpark Hotel, Castlecomer Road, Kilkenny, **t** (056) 22122, **f** (056) 61111, *info@newparkhotel.com* (*moderate*). Country house-style, with sporting facilities.

Hillgrove, Bennettsbridge Road, Kilkenny, **t** (056) 51453, *hillgrove@esatclear.ie* (*moderate–inexpensive*). Comfortable B&B with many amenities, and Margaret Drennan's quite exceptional breakfasts.

Self-catering

Kilcoran House, Cuffesgrange, **t** (056) 28253, or **t** 0862 545618 (*moderate*). Attractive gate lodge and 2-bedroom apartment on Marion Woodcock's farm, 10km from Kilkenny.

Anne Murphy, Dreelingstown, Rathmoyle, **t** (056) 69281 (*moderate*). 2-bedroom thatched cottage in a quiet location.

Eating Out

Lacken House, Dublin Road, Kilkenny, **t** (056) 61085 (*expensive*). Popular, family-run restaurant serving imaginative, perfectly-cooked food.

Newpark Hotel, Castlecomer Road, Kilkenny, **t** (056) 22122 (*expensive*). Plush restaurant serving Irish and continental food.

Edward Langton's, 69 John Street, Kilkenny, **t** (056) 65133 (*expensive–moderate*). Award

winning, with good pub lunches and dinners, including vegetarian dishes.

Parliament House Restaurant, 22–24 Parliament Street, Kilkenny, **t** (056) 63666 (*expensive–moderate*). Pleasant food in one of Kilkenny's finest houses.

The Club House Hotel, Patrick Street, Kilkenny, **t** (056) 21994 (*moderate*). Good for steaks.

Lantrec's, Kieran's Street, Kilkenny, **t** (056) 62720 (*moderate*). A busy city centre brasserie.

Rinuccini Restaurant, 1 The Parade, Kilkenny, **t** (056) 61575 (*moderate–inexpensive*). Home-made pasta and seafood; Irish and Italian dishes.

Kilkenny Castle, **t** (056) 21450 (*inexpensive*). This restaurant, in the old castle kitchen, serves delicious lunches and teas. *Summer only*.

Kilkenny Design Centre, Coffee Shop, Castle Yard, Kilkenny, **t** (056) 22118 (*inexpensive*). Good soups, cooked meats and salads for lunch. *Open daily 9–5*.

Tynan's Bridge House Bar, St John's Bridge, Kilkenny, **t** (056) 21291 (*inexpensive*). Unspoilt Victorian pub, with all the original fittings.

Entertainment and Nightlife

Live Music

In Kilkenny there are several places that have music at least one night a week.

John Cleere's, Parliament Street, Kilkenny, **t** (056) 62573. Also does cabaret, comedy, plays and even poetry readings at times.

The Pumphouse, Parliament Street, Kilkenny, **t** (056) 63924.

sepulchral monuments. The 100ft (30m) **round tower** beside the church also dates from this earlier time; ask in the church if you want to climb it (*adm*). The cathedral was much restored in the 19th century, and the nearby **library** houses some 3,000 books dating from the 16th and 17th century. This grouping of ecclesiastical buildings with the Church of Ireland vicarage is curious but charming, and represents the strength of the anglicizing influence in its best aspects. On the edge of the town centre, the great fortress of the Ormondes, **Kilkenny Castle**, remains a dominant feature (*open April–May, daily 10.30–5, June–Sept, daily 10–7, Oct–Mar, Tues–Sat 10.30–12.45 Sun 11–12.45 and 2–5; guided tours only; adm; t (056) 21450*). William the

Marshall, a Norman commander who married Strongbow's daughter, built the castle between 1195 and 1207. The building today is a mixture of Gothic, Classical and Tudor styles and is very dramatic, set as it is above the River Nore. The skylit **Long Gallery**, an elegant example of the sort of space wealthy aristocrats of the 18th century built to display their paintings, is hung with superb Butler portraits, some of them going back to the 14th century. The sixth Marquess of Ormonde presented the castle and a portion of its grounds to the people of Kilkenny in 1967. Until 1935 it was the principal residence of the Butlers. Now you can go round it and enjoy the lovely gardens sheltered behind the castle walls. It has an art gallery with temporary exhibitions. The castle acts as an exhibition centre during the Arts Festival, and there is a good restaurant for snacks in the old kitchen.

Opposite the castle, on the parade, is the Castle Yard and the **Kilkenny Design Centre** *(open Mon–Sat 9–6, Sun 10–6, closed Sun in winter; t (056) 22118, www.kilkenny-design.com)*, which promotes Irish goods; its label is almost a guarantee of good taste and quality workmanship. In the shop you will find china, glass, hand-knitted jerseys, tweed coats and jackets, kitchen ware, ornaments, linen and jewellery. The National Crafts Council (**t** *(056) 61804)*, based in the Yard, aims to develop and encourage designers through travelling scholarships. Their workshops are behind the Design Centre, in the converted stables of the castle.

Architecturally the city is one of Ireland's most interesting, because it is so old. You should try to visit **Rothe House** *(open April–Oct, Mon–Sat 10.30–5, Sun 3–5, Nov–Mar, Mon–Sat 1–5, Sun 3–5; adm; t (056) 22893)*, on Parliament Street, a unique example of an Irish Tudor merchant's house, built in 1594. It has an arcaded shop-front and consists of three buildings, parallel to each other but separated by two inner court-yards and joined on one side by a linking passageway. Inside is a collection of period costumes and a genealogical centre. The Kilkenny Archaeological Society, a pioneer of its kind in Ireland and forerunner of the Royal Society of Antiquities in Ireland, also houses its collection there.

Further into the town, in the High Street, you can see the **Tholsel**, formerly the Toll House or Exchange and now the City Hall, which was built in 1761. It is built of black Kilkenny marble, and extends over the pavement to form an arcade made up of Tuscan pillars. It is possible to look inside if you ask. The **Shee Alms House** on Rose Inn Street *(open all year but hours may vary, April–Oct, daily exc Sun 9–5.30, Nov–Mar, 9–4.30, also open May–Sept, Sun 11–12.30 and 2–4.30; adm; contact the Tourist Office t (056) 51500)*, dates from 1594 and contains an interesting 'Cityscope' exhibition *(every half-hour during opening hours)* with a model of the medieval city. Nearby in Abbey Street is the **Black Abbey** that gives the street its name. Wrecked by Cromwell, it was restored in the 19th century and is once more an active place of prayer. The **Black Abbey Gate**, known also as the Black Freyre (Friar's) Gate, is the only gate remaining from the former town walls.

Across the River Nore, in Lower John Street, is **Kilkenny College**, a handsome Georgian building where some of Ireland's greatest writers were educated, including the satirist Dean Swift, the philosopher Berkeley, and the dramatist Congreve. The building is now used as seat of the Kilkenny County Council.

The city acts as host to one of the finest cultural festivals in Ireland, the Kilkenny Festival. It takes place at the end of August and includes all the arts: visual, performing and gustatory (if you go by the number of people in the smarter pubs drinking the homebrew, Smithwick's, a beer which is as popular as Guinness). The castle and many other historic buildings are used as venues. For a quiet jar after all this sightseeing try Tynan's Bridge House Bar, close to John's Bridge, and with views of the castle. Incidentally, many of the pubs in Kilkenny have hand-painted signs, which makes them much more attractive to look at.

Language

The Irish language is the purest of all the Celtic languages; and Ireland is one of the last homes of the prehistoric and medieval European oral tradition. The language was preserved by isolated farming communities, along with many expressions from the dialects of early English settlers. Irish was spoken by the Norman aristocracy, who patronized the Gaelic poets and bards. But with the establishment of an English system of land tenure and an English-speaking nobility, Gaelic became scarce, except in the poorer farming areas. The Famine in the 1840s hit those who lived here very hard; thousands died or emigrated, and spoken Gaelic was severely curtailed. The Gaelic League, founded in 1870, initiated a new interest and pride in the language and became identified with rising nationalism. In 1921 its survival became part of the new State's policy. It was decided that the only way to preserve Gaelic was to protect and stimulate it in the places where it was still a living language.

It is spoken today mostly in the west and around the mountainous coast and islands. These areas form 'the Gaeltacht'. Here, every-thing is done to promote Irish-speaking, in industry and at home. Centres have been set up for students to learn among the native speakers. There are special grants for people living in Irish-speaking areas, but the boundaries are a little arbitrary. In Galway there's a boundary line through a built-up area, so there's a certain amount of animosity between the two sides of the line, Irish speakers or no. There is also the problem of standardizing Irish, for the different dialects are quite distinct. The modern media tend to iron these out with the adoption of one region's form of words in preference to others. County Donegal seems to get the worst deal, being so much further from the centre of administration, although it has the largest number of native speakers.

One can appreciate all the reasons for promoting Irish, but it is only in the last few generations that the language has become popular. Before, it was left to Douglas Hyde and Lady Gregory to demonstrate the richness of Irish language and myth, and they had the advantage of being far away from the grim realities of hunger and poverty that the Irish speakers knew. Gaelic, like certain foods (usually vegetables), had associations with hunger and poverty, and belonged to a hard past. The cultural coercion of the 1930s had a negative effect on most Irish people. It was only in Ulster that Gaelic speaking and culture kept its appeal in the face of Protestant and official antipathy. Even now, people prefer to use English rather than stay in the Gaeltacht, existing on grants and other government hand-outs. Gaelic is a compulsory subject in schools in the Republic, and there is a certain amount in the newspapers, on TV, radio, sign-posts and street names (with English translations). The use of Gaelic amongst the more intellectual of the middle classes is now on the increase, and this is being reinforced by the establishment of Gaelic-speaking primary schools throughout the country. Irish Gaelic is one of the official languages of the European Union.

The carrying over of Irish idiom into English is very attractive and expressive. J.M. Synge captured this in his play *Riders to the Sea*. In fact, English as spoken by the Irish is in a class of its own. Joyce talked of 'the sacred eloquence of Ireland', and it is true that you could hardly find a more articulate people. Their poetry and prose is superb, and the emotions that their ballads can release is legendary. Great hardship and poverty have not killed the instinctive desire within to explain life with words. The monk who scribbled in the margin of his psalter wrote with oriental simplicity the following poem entitled 'Winter':

My tiding for you: The stag bells
Winter snows, summer is gone.
Wind is high and cold, low the sun,
Short his course, sea running high.
Deep red the bracken, its shape all gone,
The wild goose has raised his wonted cry.
Cold has caught the wings of birds;
season of ice – these are my tidings.
                9th century, translation by Kuno Meyer

That hardship brings forth great poetry is a theory strengthened by the school of contemporary northern Irish poets who have become known all over the world: Seamus Heaney, James Simmons, Derek Mahon, Medbh McGuckian. The cutting criticisms of Brian O'Nolan (known as Flann O'Brien), the gentle irony of Frank O'Connor and the furious passion of Sean O'Casey, Patrick Kavanagh, Liam O'Flaherty and John McGahern, to name only a few, have become part of our perception of the Irish spirit since Independence. The list of recent writers could go on and on. One can only urge you to read them. There is a particularly good anthology of short stories edited by Benedict Kiely (Penguin) and an anthology of Irish verse, edited by John Montague (Faber).

Even though the disciplined cadences of the Gaelic bardic order was broken by the imposition of an English nobility in the 17th and 18th centuries, the Irish skill with words has survived, and is as strong as ever. As a visitor to Ireland you will notice this way with words when you have a conversation in a pub, ask the way at a crossroads, or simply chat to the owners of the farmhouse where you spend the night.

The Meaning of Irish Place Names

The original Gaelic place names have been complicated by attempts to give them an English spelling. In the following examples, the Gaelic versions of the prefixes come first, followed by the English meaning.

agh, augh, achadh a field
aglish, eaglais a church
ah, atha, áth a ford
all, ail, aill a cliff
anna, canna, éanarch a marsh

ard, ar, ard a height
as, ess, eas a waterfall
aw, ow, atha a river
bal, bel, béal the mouth (of a river or valley)
bal, balli, bally, baile a town
ballagh, balla, bealach a way or path
bawn, bane, bán white
barn, bearna a gap
beg, beag small
boola, booley, buaile, booleying the movement of cattle from lowland to high pastures (transhumance)
boy, buidhe yellow
bun the foot (of a valley) or mouth (of a river)
caher, cahir, cathair, carraig a rock
cashel, caiseal, caislean a castle
clogh, cloich, cloch a stone
clon, clun, cluain a meadow
derg, dearg red
doo, du, duv, duf, dubh black
dun, dún a fort
dysert, disert hermitage
glas, glen, gleann a valley
illaun, oileán an island
knock, cnoc a hill
ken, kin, can, ceann a headland
kil, kill, cill a church
lis, liss, lios a fort
lough, loch a lake or sea inlet
ma, may, moy, magh a plain
mone, mona, móna turf or bog
monaster, mainistir a monastery
more, mór, mor big or great
owen, avon, abhainn a river
rath a ring-fort
rinn, reen a point
roe, ruadh red
ross, ros a peninsula, a wood
see, suidhe a seat, e.g. Ossian's seat
shan, shane, sean old
slieve, sliabh a mountain
tir, tyr, tír country
tubber, tobrid, tubbrid, tobar a well
tra, traw, tráigh, trá a strand or beach

Some Ulster and Other Expressions

an oul sceach crosspatch
assay attention, as in Hi!
auld flutter guts fussy person
balls of malt whiskey

ballyhooley a telling off (in Cork)
blow-in stranger to the area
boreen country lane
brave commendable, worthy, e.g. a brave wee sort of a girl
bravely could be worse, e.g. business is doing bravely
caution (as in 'He's a caution'), a devil-may-care-type
chawing the rag bickering couple
chick child
cleg horsefly
clever neat, tight-fitting, usually refers to a garment
coul wintry, cold
craic fun, lively chat
cranky bad-tempered
craw thumper a 'holy Mary' or hypocrite
cut insulted, hurt
dead on exactly right
deed passed away, dead
destroyed exhausted
dingle dent, mark with an impression
dip bread fried in a pan
dither slow
doley little fella he's lovely
dulse edible seaweed
eejit fool
fairly excellent, e.g. that wee lad can fairly sing
feed meal
fern foreign
in fiddler's green you're in a big mess
fierce unacceptable, extreme, e.g. it's fierce dear (expensive)
figuresome good at sums
fog feed lavish meal
foostering around fiddling about
guff impertinence, cheek
half sir landlord's son
harp six tumble
he hasn't a titter of wit no sense at all
jar a couple of drinks
lashins plenty
mended improved in health
mizzlin raining gently
mullarkey man
neb nose
nettle drive someone barmy
ni now, this moment
not the full shilling half-witted
oul or auld not young, but can be used about something useful, e.g. my oul car

owlip verbal abuse
palsie walsie great friends
paralytic intoxicated
plamas sweet words
playboy conceited fellow
poless police
put the caibosh on it mess things up
quare memorable, unusual
qurrier or cowboy bad type, rogue
rare to bring up, educate
rightly prospering, e.g. he's doing rightly now
scalded bothered, vexed, badly burned
she's like a corncrake chatterbox
skedaddled ran quickly
skiff slight shower or rain
slainte drinking toast
soft rainy, e.g. it's a grand soft day
spalpeen agricultural labourer
spittin' starting to rain
terrible same use as 'fierce'
themins those persons
thick as a ditch stupid
thundergub loud-voiced person
wean pronounced wain, child
wee little; also in the north means with, e.g. did I see you *wee* that man?
you could trot a mouse on it strong tea

Proverbs and Sayings

Wise, and beautifully expressed with a delightful wry humour, these sayings and proverbs have passed into the English language. They highlight the usual Irish preoccupations with land, God, love, words and drinking, as well as every other subject under the sun. These are just a few examples; for a comprehensive collection read *Gems of Irish Wisdom*, by Padraic O'Farrell.

On God
It's a blessing to be in the Lord's hand as long as he doesn't close his fist.
Fear of God is the beginning of wisdom.
God never closes the door without opening another.
Man proposes, God disposes.

On the Irish Character
The wrath of God has nothing on the wrath of an Irishman outbid for land, horse or woman.

The best way to get an Irishman to refuse to do something is by ordering it.

The Irish forgive their great men when they are safely buried.

It is not that the Ulsterman lives in the past... it is rather that the past lives in him.

Advice

No property – no friends, no rearing – no manners, no health – no hope!

Never give cherries to pigs, nor advice to a fool.

Bigots and begrudgers will never bid the past farewell.

When everybody else is running, that's the time for you to walk.

You won't be stepped on if you're a live wire.

If you get the name of an early riser you can sleep till dinner time.

There are finer fish in the sea than have ever been caught.

You'll never plough a field by turning it over in your mind.

Don't make a bid till you walk the land.

A man with humour will keep ten men working.

Do not visit too often or too long.

If you don't own a mount, don't hunt with the gentry.

You can take a man out of the bog but you cannot take the bog out of the man.

What is got badly, goes badly.

A watched pot never boils.

Enough is as good as plenty.

Beware of the horse's hoof, the bull's horn and the Saxon's smile.

Time is the best story-teller.

On Marriage and Love

Play with a woman that has looks, talk marriage with a woman that has property.

After the settlement comes love.

A lad's best friend is his mother until he's the best friend of a lassie.

A pot was never boiled by beauty.

There is no love sincerer than the love of food. (G. B. Shaw)

It's a great thing to turn up laughing having been turned down crying.

Though the marriage bed be rusty, the death bed is still colder.

On Argument and Fighting

Argument is the worst sort of conversation. (Dean Swift)

There is no war as bitter as a war amongst friends.

Whisper into the glass when ill is spoken.

If we fought temptation the way we fight each other we'd be a nation of saints again.

We fought every nation's battles, and the only ones we did not win were our own.

On Women

It takes a woman to outwit the Devil.

A cranky woman, an infant, or a grievance, should never be nursed.

A woman in the house is a treasure, a woman with humour in the house is a blessing.

She who kisses in public often kicks in private.

If she is mean at the table, she will be mean in bed.

On Drinking

If Holy Water was porter he'd be at Mass every morning.

It's the first drop that destroys you; there's no harm at all in the last.

Thirst is a shameless disease, so here's to a shameless cure.

On the Family

Greed in a family is worse than need.

Poets write about their mothers, undertakers about their fathers.

A son's stool in his father's home is as steady as a gable; a father's in his son's, bad luck, is shaky and unstable.

On Old Age

The older the fiddle, the sweeter the tune.

There is no fool like an old fool.

On Loneliness

The loneliest man is the man who is lonely in a crowd.

On Bravery

A man who is not afraid of the sea will soon be drowned. (J. M. Synge)

On Flattery

Soft words butter no turnips, but they won't harden the heart of a cabbage, either.

Glossary

Anglo-Norman: the name commonly given to the 12th-century invaders of Ireland, who came in the main from southwest Britain, and also their descendants, because they were of Norman origin.

Bailey: the space enclosed by the walls of a castle, or the outer defences of a motte (*see* Motte-and-bailey).

Barrel-vaulting: simple vaulting of semi-circular form, such as in the nave of Cormac's Chapel, Cashel, Co. Tipperary, where the vault is strengthened with transverse arches.

Bastion: a projecting feature of the outer parts of a fortification, designed to command the approaches to the main wall.

Battlement: a parapet pierced with gaps to enable the defenders to discharge missiles at the enemy.

Bawn: a walled enclosure forming the outer defences of a castle or tower-house. As well as being an outer defence it also provided a safe enclosure for cattle. There is a good example at Dungory Castle, Kinvara, Co. Galway.

Beehive hut: a prehistoric circular building, of wood or stone, with a dome-shaped roof, called a *clochan.*

Bronze Age: the earliest metal-using period from the end of the Stone Age until the coming of the Iron Age in Ireland, 2500 BC.

Caher: a stone fort.

Cairn: a mound of stones over a prehistoric grave; they frequently cover chambered tombs.

Cashel: a stone fort, surrounded by a rampart of dry stone walling, usually of late Iron Age date (*see* ring-fort).

Chancel or choir: the east end of a church, reserved for the clergy and choir, and containing the high altar.

Chapter house: the chamber in which the chapter or governing body of a cathedral or monastery met. One of the finest Irish examples is the 14th-century chapter house at Mellifont, Co. Louth.

Chevaux-de-frise: a stone or stake defence work set upright and spaced. It occurs at Dun Aengus, Inishmore, Aran Islands, Co. Galway.

Cist: A box-like grave of stone slabs to contain an inhumed or cremated burial, often accompanied by pottery. Usually Bronze Age or Iron Age in date.

Clochans (I): little groups of cottages, too small to be villages, grouped in straggly clusters according to land tenure and the ties of kinship between families. The land around the *clochan* forms the district known as a townland. A familiar sight is deserted or ruined *clochans* in mountain and moorland areas where huge numbers of people left with the land-clearances and the potato famine during the 19th century.

Clochan (clochaun) (II): a small stone building, circular in plan, with its roof corbelled inwards in the form of a beehive. There are many examples in the west, especially in Co. Kerry. The word *clochan* is from the Irish *cloch,* a stone. The structures were early monks' cells and nowadays they are used for storage.

Cloisters: a square or rectangular open space, surrounded by a covered passage, which gives access to the various parts of a monastery. Many medieval cloisters survive in Ireland, e.g. at Quin, Co. Clare.

Columbarium: a dovecote, as seen at Kilcooly Abbey, Co. Tipperary.

Corbel: a projecting stone in a building, usually intended to carry a beam or other structural member.

Corbelled vault: a 'false dome', constructed by laying horizontal rings of stones that overlap on each course until finally a single stone can close the gap at the centre. It is a feature of prehistoric tombs.

Corinthian: the third order of Greek and Roman architecture, a development of the Ionic. The capital has acanthus-leaf ornamentation.

Court cairn: a variety of megalithic tomb consisting of a covered gallery for burials and one or more open courts or forecourts for ritual purposes. Very common in the North of Ireland.

Crannóg: an artificial island constructed in a lake or marsh to provide a dwelling-place in an easily defended position for isolated farming families. Large numbers of *crannógs* (from *crann*, a tree) have been discovered as a result of drainage operations at Lough Gara, near Boyle, Co. Roscommon. These dwelling-places would have been in use until the 17th century.

Curragh or *currach*: a light canoe consisting of skins or, in more recent times, tarred canvas, stretched over a wickerwork frame.

Curtain wall: the high wall constructed around a castle and its bailey, usually provided at intervals with towers.

Demesne: land/estate surrounding a house which the owner has chosen to retain for his own use.

Dolmen: the simplest form of megalithic tomb, consisting of a large capstone and three or more supporting uprights. Some appear to have had forecourts.

Doric: the first order of Greek and Roman architecture, simple and robust in style. The column had no base and the capital was quite plain.

Dun: a fort, usually of stone and often with formidable defences, e.g. Dun Aengus, Inishmore on the Aran Islands, Co. Galway.

Early English: the earliest Gothic architecture of England and Ireland, where it flourished in the 13th century. It is characterized by narrow lancet windows, high pointed arches and the use of rib-vaulting.

Esker: a bank or ridge of gravel and sand, formed by sub-glacial streams. The most notable esker in Ireland stretches from the neighbourhood of Dublin to Galway Bay: Clonmacnoise and Athlone stand on offshoots of it.

Folly: a structure set up by a landlord to provide work for poor tenants in the 19th century.

Fosse: a defensive ditch or moat around a castle or fort.

Gallaun: *see* standing stone.

Gallowglass: Scottish mercenary soldier hired by Irish clan leaders to fight their enemies.

Hill-fort: a large fort whose defences follow a contour round a hill to enclose the hilltop. Hill-forts are usually early Iron Age.

Hospital: in medieval times, an almshouse or house of hospitality with provision for spiritual as well as bodily welfare, usually established to cater for a specific class of people. The foundation of the Royal Hospital, Kilmainham, at Dublin for aged soldiers, was in the medieval tradition.

Ionic: the second order of Greek and Roman architecture. The fluted column was tall and graceful in proportion and the capital had volutes (spiral scrolls in stone) at the top.

Irish-Romanesque: the Irish variety of the Romanesque style in architecture (*see* Romanesque). Cormac's Chapel, Cashel, Co. Tipperary; and Clonfert, Co. Galway, provide examples.

Iron Age: the early Iron Age is the term applied to the earliest iron-using period; in Ireland, from the end of the Bronze Age, *c.* 500 BC, to the coming of Christianity in the 5th century.

Jamb: the side of a doorway, window or fireplace. Early Irish churches have characteristic jambs inclined inwards towards the top. The incline is called the batter.

Keep: the main tower of a castle, serving as the innermost stronghold. There is a fine rectangular one at Carrickfergus, Co. Antrim, and at Trim, Co. Meath. Round keeps are rare in Ireland, but occur at Nenagh, Co. Tipperary. Castles with keeps date from the late 12th century until about 1260.

Kerne: an Irish foot-soldier of Tudor times.

Kitchen midden: a prehistoric refuse-heap, in which many articles of bronze, iron, flint and stone have been discovered; also shellfish debris, which indicates what our ancestors ate.

Lancet: a tall, narrow window ending in a pointed arch, characteristic of early English style. Often occur in groups of three, five or seven, e.g. Cashel Cathedral, Co. Tipperary.

La Tène: a pre-Christian Irish classic ornamental style, which is linked to ornamental designs found in France.

Lunula: a crescent-shaped, thin, beaten gold ornament, of early Bronze Age date; it is an Irish speciality.

Megalithic tomb: a tomb built of large stones for collective burial, neolithic or early Bronze Age in date.

Misericord or **miserere:** a carved projection on the underside of a hinged folding seat which, when the seat was raised, gave support to the infirm during the parts of a church service when they had to stand. Good examples can be found in St Mary's Cathedral, Limerick.

Motte-and-bailey: the first Norman fortresses, which were made of earth. The motte was a flat-topped mound, shaped like a truncated cone, surrounded by a fosse and surmounted by a wooden keep. An enclosure, the bailey, bounded by ditch, bank and palisade, adjoined it. The bailey served as a refuge for cattle and in it were the sheds and huts of the retainers. This type of stronghold continued to be built until the early 13th century.

Nave: the main body of the church, sometimes separated from the choir by a screen.

Neolithic: applied to objects from the New Stone Age, which was characterized by the practice of agriculture; in Ireland, between 3000 and 2000 BC.

Ogham stones: early Irish writing, usually cut on stone. The characters consist of strokes above, below or across a stem-line. The key to the alphabet may be seen in the *Book of Ballymote*, now in the library of the Royal Irish Academy, Dublin. Ogham inscriptions occur mainly on standing stones. The inscription is usually commemorative in character. They probably date from c. AD 300.

Pale: the district around Dublin, of varying extent at different periods, where English rule was effective for some four centuries after the Norman invasion of 1169.

Passage grave: a type of megalithic tomb consisting of a burial chamber approached by a long passage and covered by a round mound or cairn.

Pattern: the festival of a saint, held on the traditional day of his death.

Plantation castles: a name given to defensive buildings erected by English and Scottish settlers under the plantation scheme between 1610 and 1620, which were very common in Ulster.

Portcullis: a heavy grating in a gateway, sliding up and down in slots in the jambs, which could be used to close the entrance quickly. There is a good example at Cahir Castle, Co. Tipperary.

Rath: the rampart of an earthen ring-fort. The name is often used for the whole structure.

Rib-vaulting: roofing or ceiling in which the weight of the superstructure is carried on comparatively slender intersecting 'ribs' or arches of stone, the spaces between the ribs being a light stone filling without structural function.

Ring-fort, rath or **lis:** one or more banks and ditches enclosing an area, usually circular, within which were dwellings. It was the typical homestead of early Christian Ireland, but examples are known from c. 1000 BC– AD 1000. The bank sometimes had a timber palisade. Some elaborate examples were defensive in purpose.

Romanesque: the style of architecture, based on late classical forms, with round arches and vaulting, which prevailed in Europe until the emergence of Gothic in the 12th century. *See* Irish-Romanesque.

Round towers: stone belfries, also used as refuges and built between the 9th and 12th centuries. They are a uniquely Irish form of architecture, tall and slender, with a conical top. The door is usually about 12ft (3.5m) from the ground.

Rundale: a system of holding land in strips or detached portions. The system has survived in parts of Co. Donegal.

Sedilia: seats recessed in the south wall of the chancel, near the altar, for the use of the clergy. A richly carved example may be seen in Holycross Abbey, Co. Tipperary.

Sept: in the old Irish system, those ruling families who traced their descent from a common ancestor.

Sheila-na-Gig: a cult symbol or female fertility figure, carved in stone on churches or castles. No one is sure of its origin.

Souterrain: artificial underground chambers of wood, stone or earth, or cut into rock. They served as refuges or stores and in some cases as dwellings. They occur commonly in ring-forts and, like these, date

from the Bronze Age to at least early
Christian times.

Standing stone: an upright stone set in the
ground. These stones may be of various
dates and served various purposes, marking
burial places or boundaries, or serving as
cult objects.

Stone fort: a ring-fort built of dry-stone walling.

Sweat houses: an ancient form of
sauna. Sometimes the mentally ill were
incarcerated in them for a while in an
attempt to cure them.

Teampull: a church.

Torc: an ornament from the middle to late
Bronze Age, made of a ribbon or bar of gold
twisted like a rope and bent around to form
a complete loop. Two very large examples
were found at Tara, Co. Meath.

Tracery: the open-work pattern formed by the
stone in the upper part of middle or late
Gothic windows.

Transepts: the 'arms' of a church, extending at
right-angles to the north and south from
the junction of nave and choir.

Tumulus: a mound of earth over a grave;
usually the mound over an earth-covered
passage grave, e.g. Tara, Co. Meath.

Undertaker: one of the English or Scottish
planters given confiscated land in Ireland
in the 16th century. They 'undertook'
certain obligations designed to prevent
the dispossessed owners from reacquiring
their land.

Vaulting: a roof or ceiling formed by arching
over a space. Among the many methods,
three main types were used: barrel-vaulting,
groin-vaulting and rib-vaulting. Rib-vaulting
lent itself to great elaboration of ornament.

Zoomorphic: describing decoration based on
the forms of animals.

Chronology

BC

c. 8000 BC Humans arrive in Ireland, travelling across the land bridge with Scotland.

c. 3000 BC New Stone Age race build Newgrange in Co. Meath.

c. 2000 BC Arrival of Beaker people.

c. 100 BC Arrival of one wave of Gaelic (Celtic) peoples.

AD

200 The Kingdom of Meath is founded, and the high kingship at Tara, Co. Meath begins.

432 St Patrick starts his Mission.

700–800 Gaelic Christian Golden Age.

795 Viking raids begin.

1014 Battle of Clontarf and death of Brian Boru, the high king who won this decisive battle over the Vikings.

1170 The Anglo-Norman conquest begins with the arrival of Richard, Earl of Pembroke, called 'Strongbow'.

1171 Henry II visits Ireland, and secures the submission of many Irish leaders and that of his own Norman barons.

1314 The Bruce Invasion, which failed, under Edward Bruce.

1366 Statutes of Kilkenny, which forbade the English settler to speak the Gaelic language, adopt an Irish name, wear Irish apparel, or marry an Irishwoman.

1394–99 Irish leaders war with Richard II.

1534–35 Rebellion of Silken Thomas, known as the 'Kildare Rebellion'.

1541 Irish Parliament accepts Henry VIII as King of Ireland.

1558 Accession of Elizabeth I. The Reformation does not succeed in Ireland.

1562 on Elizabethan Conquest and settlement of various counties.

1569–73 The first Desmond Revolt.

1579–83 Final Desmond Revolt and suppression.

1592–1603 Rebellion of the Northern Lords, known as the Tyrone War.

1601 Battle of Kinsale – a defeat for Hugh O'Neill, Earl of Tyrone, and his Ulster chiefs.

1607 Flight of the Earls of Tyrone and Tyrconnell to the Continent.

1608 Plantation of Ulster with Scots begins in Derry and Down.

1641 Irish Rising begins. At this time, 59% of land in Ireland is held by Catholics.

1642–49 Catholic Confederation of Kilkenny.

1649 Cromwell arrives in Ireland.

1650 Catholic landowners exiled to Connacht.

1652 Cromwellian Act of Settlement.

1660 Restoration of Charles II.

1680 Accession of James II.

1689 April to July, Siege of Derry.

1690 July, The Battle of the Boyne. A great victory for William of Orange.

1691 September to October, Siege of Limerick.

1691 October, Treaty of Limerick.

1695 Beginning of Penal Laws. Catholics now own 14% of land.

1699 Irish woollen industry destroyed by English trade laws.

1704 Protestant nonconformists excluded from public office by Test Act.

1714 Catholics own 7% of land.

1772 Rise of the Patriot Party in parliament, known as Grattan's Parliament.

1778 Organization of Irish Volunteers.

1778 Gardiner's Relief Act for Catholics eases the Penal Laws.

1779 English concessions on trade and the repeal of most of the restrictive laws.

1782 Establishment of Irish Parliamentary independence.

1791 The Society of United Irishmen founded.

1795 Orange Order founded.

1798 Rebellion of '98.

1801 Act of Union.

1829 Catholic Emancipation Bill passed.

1842–48 The Young Ireland Movement.

1845–49 The Great Famine which began with the blight of the potato harvest.

1840s Emigration of thousands to New World.

1848 Abortive rising led by Smith O'Brien.

1867 Fenian Rising.

1869 Disestablishment of the Church of Ireland.

1875 Charles Stewart Parnell elected Member of Parliament for Co. Meath.

1877 Parnell becomes Chairman of the Home Rule Confederation.

1879–82 Land war.

1886 Gladstone's first Home Rule Bill for Ireland defeated.

1890 Parnell cited in divorce case; he loses leadership of the Irish Party in the House of Commons.

1892 Gladstone's second Home Rule Bill defeated.

1893 Gaelic League founded.

1899 Beginning of the Sinn Féin movement.

1903 Wyndham's Land Act.

1912 Third Home Rule Bill introduced.

1913 Ulster Volunteer Force founded.

1914 Outbreak of the First World War. The third Home Rule Bill receives Royal assent, but is deferred until the end of the war.

1916 The Easter Uprising.

1918–21 The Anglo-Irish War.

1920 Amendment Act to Home Rule Bill, allowing Six Counties in Ulster to vote themselves out and remain with rest of Britain.

1920–21 Heavy fighting between the Auxiliaries (known as the Black and Tans) and the Irish Nationalist forces.

1921 July, King George V officially opens the Stormont Parliament in the Six Counties.

1921 December, the Anglo-Irish treaty signed.

1922 January, the treaty is ratified in Dáil Eireann. Start of the Irish Civil War between pro-treaty majority and anti-treaty forces.

1922 November, executions of anti-treaty leaders by Free State in Dublin.

1923 End of Civil War.

1926 De Valera founds Fianna Fáil.

1932 General Election. Fianna Fáil win.

1937 Constitution of Eire.

1938 Agreement with Britain; economic disputes are ended. Britain gives up tributary and naval rights in 'Treaty' ports.

1939 IRA bombing campaign in Britain. Outbreak of Second World War; Eire neutral.

1945 End of Second World War.

1948 General Election in Ireland. Defeat of Fianna Fáil, and De Valera out of office for first time in 16 years.

1952 Republic of Ireland declared and accepted by Britain, with a qualifying guarantee of support to the Six Counties.

1956–62 IRA campaign in the North.

1968 First Civil Rights march.

1969 January, people's democracy march from Belfast to Derry. Marchers attacked at Burntollet Bridge.

1969 August, British troops sent to Derry.

1971 February, first British soldier killed by IRA. August, internment of IRA suspects. Reforms to the RUC, and electoral system.

1972 'Bloody Sunday' (Jan), when British troops kill 13 demonstrators in Derry. Direct Rule is imposed from Westminster: the Stormont Government and Irish Parliament are suspended.

1973 The Sunningdale Agreement. An Assembly established with power-sharing between different political leaders.

1974 Ulster Workers' Strike brings down Assembly. Direct Rule reimposed.

1981 Bobby Sands dies after 60-day hunger strike.

1985 Anglo-Irish Agreement.

1993 Downing Street Initiative.

1994 August, IRA ceasefire.

1996 Canary Wharf bombing in London. IRA declares ceasefire over.

1997 IRA ceasefire renewed.

1998 Good Friday Agreement.
May, Referendum Agreement.
June, New Assembly elections by Proportional Representation. Unionist Party win most seats by a small margin. Sinn Féin and SDLP do very well.
August, IRA dissidents bomb centre of Omagh, killing 28 people.
October, John Hume and David Trimble are awarded Nobel peace prize for their work in ending the conflict.

1999 Patten Commission Report on RUC reform.

2000 Orange men protest at the banning of their traditional march through Drumcree for the seventh year running.

2001 June, Irish people vote against EU's Nice Treaty. In the British general elections, the Democratic Unionists and Sinn Féin are the main winners in NI, moderate parties lose ground. David Trimble resigns as First Minister of the Northern Ireland Assembly in protest against IRA's refusal to decommission their arms, but is reinstated.

Further Reading

Archaeology, Architecture and Art

Brennan, M., *Boyne Valley Vision* (Dolmen).

Craig, Maurice, *Dublin 1660–1860* (Allen Figgis), *Classical Irish Houses of the Middle Size: Lost Demesnes* (Architectural Press).

Crookshank, Anne and the Knight of Glin, *Painters of Ireland c. 1660–1920* (Barrie & Jenkins).

Day, Angélique and McWilliams, Patrick (ed.), *Ordnance Survey Memoirs of Ireland* (Institute of Irish Studies, Belfast).

de Breffny and Folliott, *Houses of Ireland* (Thames & Hudson), *Castles of Ireland* (Thames & Hudson), *Churches and Abbeys of Ireland* (Thames & Hudson).

Estyn Evans, E., *Prehistoric Ireland* (Batsford).

Guinness, Desmond, *Georgian Dublin* (Batsford), *Great Irish Houses and Castles* (Weidenfeld & Nicolson), *Palladio* (Weidenfeld & Nicolson).

Harbison, P., Potterton, H. and Sheehy, J., *Irish Art and Architecture* (Thames & Hudson).

Henry, Françoise, *Early Christian Irish Art* (Mercier).

Kennedy, Gerald Conan, *Ancient Ireland: The User's Guide* (Morrigan Books)

Maire de Paor, *Early Irish Art* (Aspects of Ireland Series).

O'Brien, Jacqueline and Guinness, Desmond, *A Grand Tour* (Weidenfeld & Nicolson).

O'Brien and Harbison, *Ancient Ireland* (Weidenfeld & Nicolson).

O'Riordain, S. P. O., *Antiquities of the Irish Countryside* (Methuen).

Sheehy, J., *Discovery of Ireland's Past* (Thames & Hudson).

White, *John Butler Yeats and the Irish Renaissance* (Dolmen).

Burkes Guide to Country Houses: Ireland (Burkes).

Historic Monuments of Northern Ireland (HMSO 1983).

Biography and Memoirs

Bence Jones, Mark, *Twilight of the Ascendancy* (Constable).

Chambers, Anne, *Granuaile: The Life and Times of Grace O'Malley* (Wolfhound).

Davis-Gough, Annabel, *Walled Gardens* (Eland).

du Maurier, Daphne, *Hungry Hill* (Penguin).

Hunt, Hugh, *The Abbey, Ireland's National Theatre 1904–79* (Gill & Macmillan).

Joyce, James, *Portrait of an Artist as a Young Man* (Longman).

Kelly, A. A. (ed.), *Letters of Liam O'Flaherty* (Wolfhound Press).

Kenny, Mary, *Goodbye to Catholic Ireland* (Sinclair Stevenson).

Krause, David, *A Self Portrait of the Artist as a Man* (Sean O'Casey through his letters) (Dolmen).

Lyons, J. S., *Oliver St John Gogarty, A Biography* (Blackwater Press).

Moore, George, *Hail and Farewell* (Smythe).

Murphy, William, *The Yeats Family and the Pollexfens of Sligo* (Dolmen).

O'Crohan, Thomas, *The Islandman* (OUP).

O'Sullivan, Maurice, *Twenty Years a-Growing* (OUP).

Parker, Tony, *May the Lord in His Mercy Be Kind to Belfast* (Collins).

Shuilleabhain, E. H., *Letters from the Great Blasket* (Mercier).

Somerville-Large, P., *Irish Eccentrics* (Lilliput Press).

Taylor, Alice, *To School through the Fields* (Brandon).

Thomson, David, *Woodbrook* (Penguin).

Yeats, J. B., *Early Memories* (Irish Academic Press).

Yeats, W. B., *Synge and the Ireland of his Time* (Irish Academic Press).

All the Irish Heritage Series (Eason).

Cooking, Crafts, Flora, Fauna and Fishing

Allen, Myrtle, *Ballymaloe Cook Book* (Gill & Macmillan).

Davis-Goff, Annabel, *Walled Gardens* (Barrie and Jenkins).

Fitzgibbon, Theodora, *Cook Book*.

Heron, Marianne, *The Hidden Gardens of Ireland* (Gill & Macmillan).

Lewis, C. A., *Hunting in Ireland* (J. A. Allen).

O'Brien, Louise, *Crafts of Ireland* (Gilbert Dillon).

O'Reilly, Peter, *Trout & Salmon Loughs of Ireland* (Harper Collins).

O'Reilly, Peter, *Trout & Salmon Rivers of Ireland* (Merlin Unwin Books).

Reeves-Smyth, Terence, *Irish Gardens* (Appletree Press).

Webb, D. A., *An Irish Flora* (Dundalgan).

Bridgestones Guides, Where to Stay and Eat in Ireland (Estragon Press).

Traditional Irish Recipes (Appletree Press).

Gill & Macmillan do a series of fishing guides on Game, Coarse and Sea Angling.

Fiction, Poetry, Plays

Banville, John, *The Untouchable* (Pan Books).

Berry, James (ed. Horgan, M. and Gertrude), *Tales of the West of Ireland* (Dolmen).

Bowen, Elizabeth, *Elizabeth Bowen's Irish Stories* and *Bowen's Court* (Poolbeg).

Carleton, William, *The Black Prophet* (Irish University Press).

Carpenter and Fallon (ed.), *The Writers, A Sense of Ireland* (O'Brien Press).

Crone, Anne, *Bridie Steen* (Blackstaff).

Durcan, Paul, Yeats, W. B., Heaney, Seamus, Simmons, James and Clarke, Austin, *The Faber Book of Irish Verse* (Faber and Faber).

Edgeworth, Maria, *The Absentee* (OUP).

Farrell, J. G., *Troubles* (Penguin).

Kickham, C., *Knocknagow, Or the Homes of Tipperary* (Mercier).

O'Connor, Frank, *Guests of the Nation* (Poolbeg).

McGahern, John, *The Barracks* (Faber and Faber). Any other novels by him as well.

The Penguin Book of Irish Verse and *The Penguin Book of Irish Short Stories* (Penguin).

Novels by Edith Somerville and Martin Ross, especially *The Great House at Inver* (Zodiac Press) and *The Real Charlotte* (Arrow Books).

Poetry by Michael Siadhail (bilingual)

All the plays by J. M. Synge.

Any stories by Mary Lavin (Penguin).

Any novels by George Birmingham (Blackstaff, BBC and others).

Any novels by Sam Hanna Bell (Blackstaff, BBC and others).

Any novels by Roddy Doyle.

Any novels by Kate O'Brien (Blackstaff, BBC and others).

Any novels by Colm Tóibín.

Any novels by William Trevor (Penguin).

Stories and plays by Brian Friel (Penguin and others).

Folklore, Music and Tradition

Cross, E., *The Tailor and Ansty* (Mercier).

Danaher, *Folktales of the Irish Countryside* (Mercier).

Estyn Evans, E., *Irish Folk Ways* (Routledge).

Feldman, Allan and O'Doherty, *The Northern Fiddler: Music and Musicians of Donegal and Tyrone* (Blackstaff).

Flower, R., *The Irish Tradition* (Clarendon Press).

Gaffney, S. and Cashman, S., *Proverbs and Sayings of Ireland* (Wolfhound).

Gregory, Lady Isabella Augusta, *Gods and Fighting Men* (Smythe).

Healy, J. N., *Love Songs of the Irish* (Mercier).

Healy, J. N., *Percy French and his Songs* (Mercier).

Henry, S., *Tales from the West of Ireland* (Mercier).

Hyde, Douglas, *Beside the Fire* (Irish Academic Press).

Hyde, Douglas, *The Stone of Truth and other Irish Folktales* (Irish Academic Press).

O'Boyle, Sean, *The Irish Song Tradition* (Gilbert Dalton).

O'Connell, James, *The Meaning of the Irish Coast* (Blackstaff).

O'Faolain, S., *Short Stories* (Mercier).

O'Farrell, P., *Folktales of the Irish Coast* (Mercier).

O'Flaherty, Gerald, *A Book of Slang, Idiom and Wit* (O'Brien).
O'Keeffe, D. and Healy, J. N., *Book of Irish Ballads* (Mercier).
O'Sullivan, Sean, *Folklore of Ireland* (Batsford).
O'Sullivan, Patrick, *A Country Diary* (Anvil).
Wilde, William, *Irish Popular Superstitions* (Irish Academic Press).

History and Literary History

Beckett, J. C., *The Making of Modern Ireland* (Faber and Faber).
Boylan, Henry (ed.), *A Dictionary of Irish Biography* (Gill & Macmillan).
Connolly, S. J. (ed.), *The Oxford Companion to Irish History* (Oxford University Press).
Corkery, Daniel, *Hidden Ireland* (Gill & Macmillan).
Cruise O'Brien, M. and C., *Concise History of Ireland* (Thames & Hudson).
Cruise O'Brien, Conor, *States of Ireland* (Hutchinson).
Edwards, R. Dudley, *A New History of Ireland* (Gill & Macmillan).
Edwards, R. Dudley, *An Atlas of Irish History* (Methuen).
Fitzgerald, Mairéad, *World of Colmcille* (O'Brien Press).
Foster, R. F. (ed.), *The Oxford History of Ireland* (OUP).
Foster, R. F., *Modern Ireland 1600–1972* (OUP).
Kavanagh, P., *The Irish Theatre* (The Kerryman).
Kee, Robert, *The Green Flag* (Sphere).
Lyons, F. S. L., *Ireland Since the Famine* (Fontana).
MacLysaght, E., *Surnames of Ireland* (Irish Academic Press).
MacLysaght, E., *Irish Families: Their Names and Origins* (Figgins).
Maxwell, Constancia, *Country and Town under the Georges* (Dundalgan Press).
O'Farrell, P., *How the Irish Speak English* (Mercier).
O'Grada, Cormac (ed.), *Famine 150 – Commemorative Lecture Series* (Teagasc).
Pakenham, Thomas, *The Year of Liberty: The Great Irish Rebellion of 1798* (Weidenfeld & Nicolson).
Stephens, James, *Insurrection in Dublin* (Colin Smythe Ltd).

Stewart, A. T. Q., *The Narrow Ground* (Faber and Faber).
Wallace, M., *A Short History of Ireland* (David & Charles).
Woodham Smith, Cecil, *The Great Hunger* (Penguin).
Burkes Irish Family Records (Burkes).
Burkes Landed Gentry (Burkes).

Maps

Historical Map (Bartholomew).
Ireland Map, by Bord Fáilte (Ordnance Survey).
Ireland Touring Map (Bartholomew).
Irish Family Names Map (Johnson & Bacon) – divided into North, East, South and West.
Ordnance Survey Holiday Map (1:250,000) for the south is useful for Cork and Kerry.
For greater detail, 89 Ordnance Survey maps cover the whole island with a 1:50,000 scale (2cm to 1km).

Photography

Daly, Leo, *The Aran Islands* (Albertine Kennedy).
Estyn Evans, E. and Turner, B. S., *Ireland's Eye: The Photographs of Robert John Welch* (Blackstaff).
Johnstone and Kirk, *Images of Belfast* (Blackstaff).
Walker, B. M., O'Brien, A. and McMahon, S., *Faces of Ireland* (Appletree Press).

Travelogues

Donegan, Lawrence, *No News at Throat Lake* (Penguin).
Duff, Chris, *On Celtic Tides: One Man's Journey Around Ireland by Sea Kayak* (St Martin's Press).
Hawkes, Tony, *Round Ireland With a Fridge* (Ebury).
McCarthy, Pete, *McCarthy's Bar* (Hodder & Stoughton).
McCrum, Mark, *The Craic* (Orion).
McKenzie, Richard, *Turn Left at the Black Cow* (Roberts Rinehart).
Moorhouse, Geoffrey, *Sun Dancing* (Orion).
Morton, H. V., *In Search of Ireland* (Methuen).
Murphy, Dervla, *A Place Apart* (Penguin).
O'Crohan, Tomas, *Island Cross-Talk* (Oxford Paperbacks).

Praeger, R., *The Way That I Went* (Figgins).
Robinson, Tim, *The Aran Islands* (The Author).
Synge, J. M., *The Aran Islands* (Blackstaff).

Guides and Topography

Allen, F. H. A. (ed.), *Atlas of the Irish Rural Landscape* (Cork University Press).
Craig, Maurice and the Knight of Glin, *Ireland Observed* (Mercier).
Harbison, Peter, *Guide to the National Monuments of Ireland* (Gill & Macmillan).
Mason, T. H., *The Islands of Ireland* (Mercier).
A Literary Map of Ireland (Wolfhound).

Walking Guides

Fewer, Michael, *Irish Long Distance Walks* (Gill & Macmillan).
Lynam, Joss, *Best Irish Walks* (Gill & Macmillan).
O'Suilleabhain, Sean, *No. 1 South West* (Gill & Macmillan).
Whilde, Tony, *No. 2 West* (Gill & Macmillan).
Simon, Patrick and Foley, Gerard, *No. 3 North West* (Gill & Macmillan).
Boidell, Jean, Casey, M. and Kennedy, Eithne, *No. 5 East* (Gill & Macmillan).
Martindale, *No. 6 South East* (Gill & Macmillan).

Index

Main page references are in **bold**; Page references to maps are in *italics*.

Acknowledgements

Numerous people have helped me compile this book, and to them I wish to say many thanks. It would take many pages to mention all but a few by name, for through my researches on the guide I have met many delightful people who have given me an insight into their locality. In particular I would like to thank Tourism Ireland, who have always been extremely generous with information, advice and goodwill. My family have over the years been very supportive and a great help. My mother has been an enthusiastic gatherer of information and her wide general knowledge has been invaluable. My sister Angelique has been a great help, especially with Ulster, as has my sister Georgina with Co. Laois and Co. Offaly. My husband Simon has helped me in countless ways, acting as my agent and trying out hotels and restaurants on his business trips to Dublin. I am indebted to the late Araminta Swiney who advised me on what to leave out, Brian Walker for help with the historical background, Flora Armstrong for her initial help with South Ulster and Co. Armagh and John Colclough who recommended places to stay and eat. Special thanks to Amy Corzine, who updated this fifth edition, and Joss Waterfall, who edited it. A big thank-you to all Cadogan readers who have written in with their recommendations. Finally, thanks to Paula Levy, who first gave me the opportunity to explore and write about this lovely country.

Ireland touring atlas

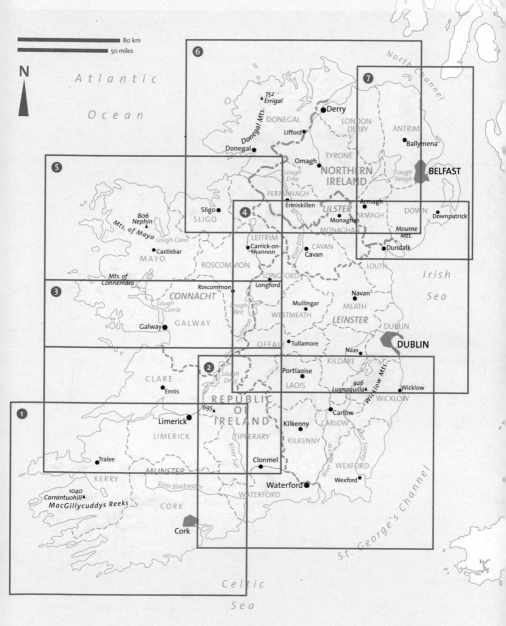

80 km
50 miles

N

Atlantic

Ocean

752 ▲ Errigal

DONEGAL

Derry

Lifford

LONDON-
DERRY

ANTRIM

Donegal

Ballymena

Omagh

TYRONE

NORTHERN
IRELAND

*Lough
Erne*

*Lough
Neagh*

BELFAST

806
Nephin
Mts. of Mayo

Lough Conn

Sligo

SLIGO

FERMANAGH

Enniskillen

ULSTER

Armagh

ARMAGH

DOWN

Downpatrick

*Mourne
Mts.*

Castlebar

MAYO

*Mts. of
Connemara*

CONNACHT

Carrick-on-
Shannon

LEITRIM

ROSCOMMON

CAVAN

Cavan

MONAGHAN

Monaghan

River Erne

*Lough
Corrib*

Roscommon

LONGFORD

Longford

LOUTH

Dundalk

*Irish
Sea*

Galway

GALWAY

*Lough
Ree*

WESTMEATH

Mullingar

MEATH

Navan

LEINSTER

DUBLIN

CLARE

Ennis

OFFALY

Tullamore

Naas

KILDARE

DUBLIN

695 ▲

REPUBLIC
OF
IRELAND

*Lough
Derg*

Portlaoise

LAOIS

926
Lugnaquilla ▲

Wicklow Mts.

Wicklow

WICKLOW

Limerick

LIMERICK

TIPPERARY

Kilkenny

KILKENNY

Carlow

CARLOW

River Barrow

River Slaney

Tralee

KERRY

MUNSTER

River Suir

Clonmel

WEXFORD

Wexford

St. George's Channel

1040
Carrantuohill ▲
MacGillycuddys Reeks

CORK

Waterford

WATERFORD

Cork

*Celtic
Sea*

North Channel

Land 0–100 metres
Land 0–200 metres
Land 200–500 metres
Land 500–1000 metres
Land over 1000 metres

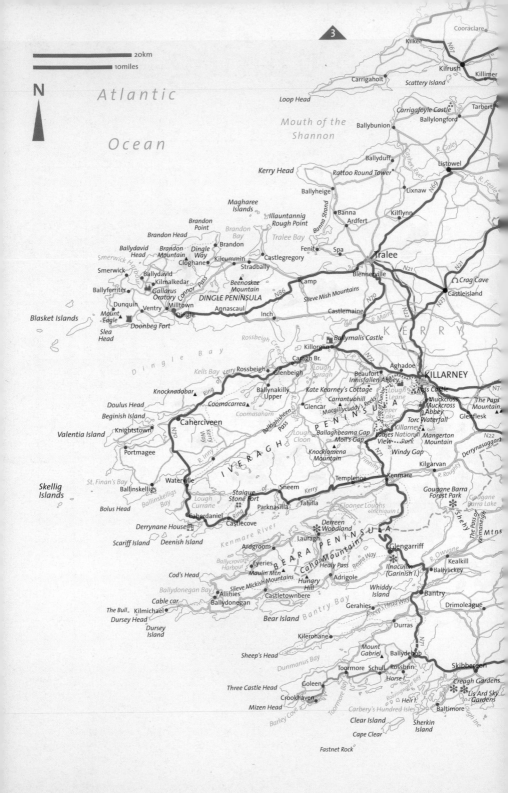

Atlantic

Ocean

Scale
20km
10miles

N

Cooraclare
Kilkee
Kilrush
Killimer
Carrigaholt
Scattery Island
Loop Head
Carrigafoyle Castle
Tarbert
Mouth of the
Shannon
Ballybunion
Ballylongford
Ballyduff
R. Galey
Listowel
Kerry Head
Rattoo Round Tower
Lixnaw
R. Feale
N69
Ballyheige
Kilflynn
Ardfert
Maghatee Islands
Illauntannig
Rough Point
Banna Strand
Banna
Brandon
Point
Brandon Head
Brandon
Bay
Tralee Bay
Fenit
Spa
Tralee
Ballydavid
Head
Brandon
Mountain
Dingle
Way
Brandon
N21
Smerwick Harbour
Cloghane
Kilcummin
Castlegregory
Blennerville
N21
Smerwick
Ballydavid
Kilmalkedar
Stradbally
Crag Cave
Ballyferriter
Gallarus
Oratory
Connor Pass
Beenoskee
Mountain
Camp
Castleisland
N33
Dunquin
Ventry
Milltown
DINGLE PENINSULA
N86
Slieve Mish Mountains
N70
Mount
Eagle
Dingle
Annascaul
Inch
Castlemaine
KERRY
Doonbeg Fort
Slea
Head
Rossbeigh Creek
Ballymalis Castle
R. Maine
Blasket Islands
Killorglin
Aghadoe
Dingle Bay
Caragh Br.
N72
Beaufort
Innisfallen Abbey
KILLARNEY
Kells Bay
Kerry Rossbeigh
Glenbeigh
Lough
Caragh
Kate Kearney's Cottage
Ross Castle
N7
Knocknadobar
Ballynakilly
Upper
Carrantuohill
Muckross
Muckross
Abbey
The Paps
Mountain
Doulus Head
Coomacarrea
Coomasaharn
Glencar
Macgillycuddy's Reeks
Torc Waterfall
Glenflesk
Beginish Island
Caherciveen
Ballaghbeama Gap
Killarney
National
Mangerton
Mountain
N22
Valentia Island
Knightstown
Kerry
Way
Ballaghisheen
Pass
Lough
Cloon
Moll's Gap
View
Park
Derrynasaggart
Portmagee
R. Inny
Knocklomena
Mountain
Windy Gap
Kilgarvan
Skellig
Islands
St. Finan's Bay
Waterville
Sneem
Kerry
Templenoe
Kenmare
R. Roughty
Gougane Barra
Forest Park
Gougane
Barra Lake
Ballinskelligs
Lough
Currane
Staigue
Stone Fort
Parknasilla
Tahilla
Cloonee Loughs
Inchiquin L.
Bolus Head
Ballinskelligs
Bay
Ring of
Kerry
The Pass of
Keimaneigh
Caherdaniel
Castlecove
Derreen
Woodland
Glengarriff
Shehy
Mtns
Derrynane House
Kenmare River
Laurach
BEARA PENINSULA
Caha Mountains
Scariff Island
Deenish Island
Ardgroom
Ilnaculin
(Garinish I.)
R. Owvane
Kealkill
Eyeries
Healy Pass
Beara Way
Ballylickey
Ballycrovane
Harbour
Maulin Mtn
Adrigole
Whiddy
Island
Bantry
Cod's Head
Slieve Mickish Mountains
Hungry
Hill
Gerahies
Drimoleague
Ballydonegan Bay
Ballydonegan
Castletownbere
Sheep's Head Way
The Bull
Kilmichael
Cable car
Bear Island
Bantry Bay
Durras
N71
Dursey Head
Dursey
Island
Kilcrohane
Mount
Gabriel
Ballydehob
Sheep's Head
Toormore
Schull
Rossbrin
Skibbereen
Dunmanus Bay
Goleen
Horse I.
Creagh Gardens
Three Castle Head
Crookhaven
Heir I.
Lis Ard Sky
Gardens
Mizen Head
Barley Cove
Carbery's Hundred Isles
Baltimore
Clear Island
Sherkin
Island
Cape Clear
Lough Ine
Fastnet Rock

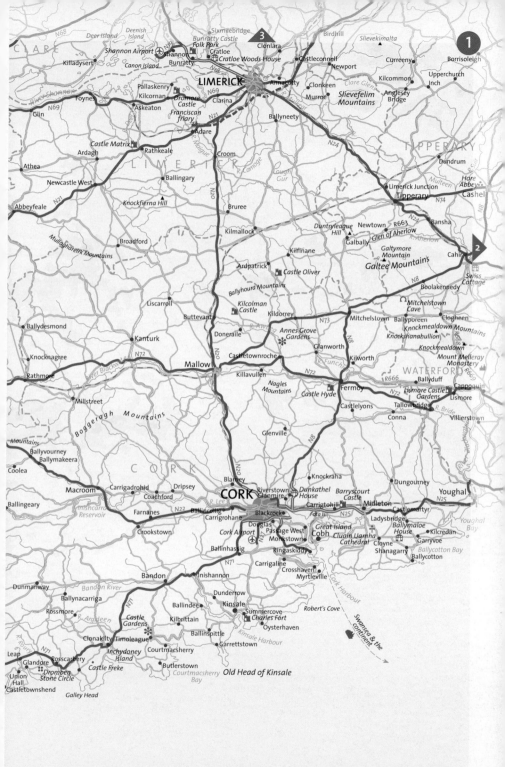

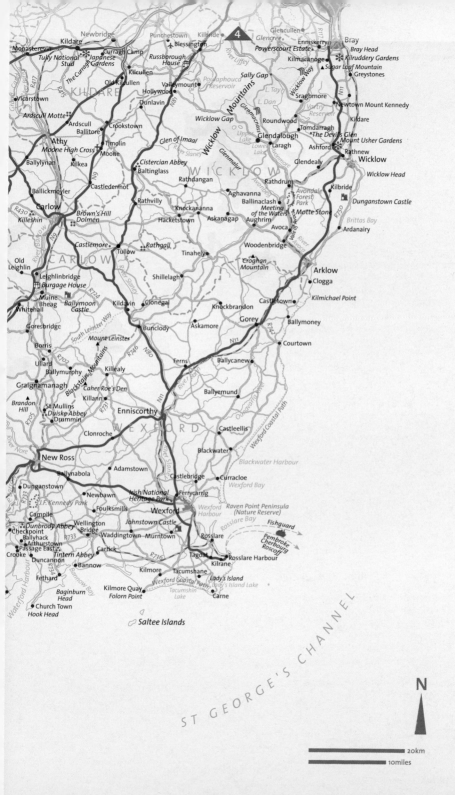

4

Newbridge
Kildare
Monasterevin
Tully National Stud
Curragh Camp
Japanese Gardens
The Curragh
KILDARE
Vicarstown
Old Kilcullen
Kilcullen
Ardscull Motte
Ardscull
Ballitore
Crookstown
Athy
Moone High Cross
Timolin
Moone
Ballylynan
Kilkea
Cistercian Abbey
Baltinglass
Ballickmoyler
Castledermot
Rathdangan
Carlow
Killeshin
Brown's Hill Dolmen
Rathvilly
Knockananna
Hacketstown
Castlemore
Tullow
Rathgall
Tinahely
Old Leighlin
Leighlinbridge
Burgage House
Shillelagh
Muine Bheag
Whitehall
Ballymoon Castle
Kildavin
Clonegal
Goresbridge
South Leinster Way
Bunclody
Askamore
Borris
Mount Leinster
Ullard
Ballymurphy
Killealy
Ferns
Graiguenamanagh
Blackstairs Mountains
Caher Roe's Den
Killann
Brandon Hill
St Mullins
Duiske Abbey
Drummin
Enniscorthy
Clonroche
WEXFORD
Castleellis
New Ross
Blackwater
Ballynabola
Adamstown
Castlebridge
Dunganstown
J.F. Kennedy Park
Newbawn
Ferrycarrig
Campile
Foulksmills
Irish National Heritage Park
Wexford
Dunbrody Abbey
Checkpoint
Wellington Bridge
Johnstown Castle
Ballyhack
Arthurstown
Waddingtown
Murntown
Passage East
Carrick
Crooke
Tintern Abbey
Duncannon
Bannow
Kilmore
Tacumshane
Fethard
Kilmore Quay
Lady's Island
Baginburn Head
Folorn Point
Carne
Church Town
Hook Head

Saltee Islands

Glencullen
Glencree
Enniskerry
Bray
Powerscourt Estate
Bray Head
Kilmacanoge
Kilruddery Gardens
Wicklow Way
Sugar Loaf Mountain
Greystones
Sally Gap
Sraghmore
L. Tay
Newtown Mount Kennedy
L. Dan
Glenmacnass
Roundwood
Kildare
Wicklow Gap
Upp. Lake
Glendalough
Tomdarragh
The Devil's Glen
Glen of Imaal
Lower Lake
Laragh
Mount Usher Gardens
Ashford
Glenmalur
Glendealy
Rathnew
WICKLOW
Wicklow
Rathdrum
Wicklow Head
Aghavanna
Rathdrum
Avondale Forest Park
Kilbride
Ballinaclash
Meeting of the Waters
Dunganstown Castle
Askanagap
Aughrim
Motte Stone
Brittas Bay
Avoca
Ardanairy
Woodenbridge
Croghan Mountain
Arklow
Clogga
Castletown
Kilmichael Point
Knockbrandon
Gorey
Ballymoney
Askamore
Courtown
Ballycanew
Ballyemund
Castleellis

St Mullins

ST GEORGE'S CHANNEL

Fishguard
Pembroke
Cherbourg
Roscoff

N

20km
10miles

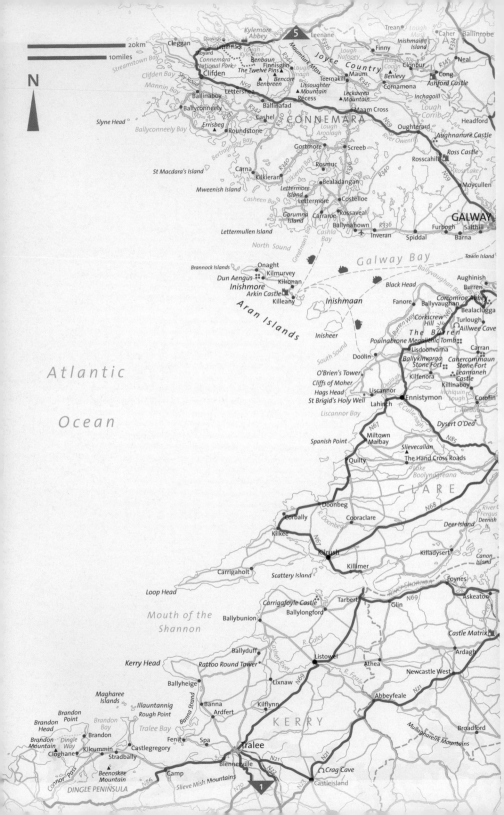